531.95

P9-DYE-040

Regulations
  (Securities and Markets) 40
REITs 599
Retirement Planning 244
Retirement Programs 250
Return Measures 119
Rights 466
Risk Analysis 134
Savings Accounts 232
Securities Markets 30
Security Analysis 308
Short Sales 166

Short-Term Securities 224
Stamps 702
Stock-Index Futures 538
Stock-Index Options 503
Strategic Metals 699
Tangible Investments 684
Taxes and Tax Planning 638
Tax-Sheltered Investments 646
Technical Analysis 359
Time Value of Money 125
Timing Transactions 766
Warrants 468

TO THE STUDENT

A Study Guide for this textbook is available in your college bookstore.
Its title is

Study Guide to accompany Gitman/Joehnk: Fundamentals of Investing, Second Edition,
by J. Markham Collins.

It has been written to help you review and study the course material.
Ask the bookstore manager to order a copy for you
if it is not in stock.

FUNDAMENTALS OF INVESTING

SECOND EDITION

LAWRENCE J. GITMAN
Wright State University

MICHAEL D. JOEHNK
Arizona State University

HARPER & ROW, PUBLISHERS, New York
Cambridge, Philadelphia, San Francisco,
London, Mexico City, São Paulo, Sydney

1817

Acknowledgments

A continuation of the copyright page with complete credit information for reprinting previously published materials appears after the Glossary at the end of the book.

Sponsoring Editor: **John Greenman**
Project Editor: **Dorothy Cappel**
Text and Cover Design: **Michel Craig**
Cover Photo: **Michel Craig**
Text Art: **Vantage Art, Inc.**
Production: **Jeanie Berke**
Compositor: **Waldman Graphics, Inc.**
Printer and Binder: **R. R. Donnelley & Sons Company**

Affectionately dedicated to
Robin
and
Charlene

FUNDAMENTALS OF INVESTING, Second Edition
Copyright © 1984 by Lawrence J. Gitman and Michael D. Joehnk

Library of Congress Cataloging in Publication Data

Gitman, Lawrence J.
　Fundamentals of investing.

　Includes bibliographies.
　1. Investments.　I. Joehnk, Michael D.　II. Title.
HG4521.G547　1984　　　332.6′78　　　84-3792
ISBN 0-06-042355-2

85 86 87　　9 8 7 6 5 4 3

CONTENTS

Preface   xiii
ON INVESTING IN THE 1980s
George L. Ball, President and Chief Executive
Prudential-Bache Securities   xx

ONE   THE INVESTMENT ENVIRONMENT   1

1   The Role and Scope of Investments   3
The Role of Investments   4
Investments Defined 5   The Structure of the Investment
Process 8   Participants in the Investment Process 8
The Rewards for Investing 10
The Personal Investment Process   10
The Importance of the Personal Investment Process 10   Steps in
the Personal Investment Process 11   Current Innovations in the
Personal Investment Process 14
Investment Vehicles   15
Short-Term Vehicles 16   Common Stock 17   Fixed Income
Securities 17   Options 18   Other Popular Investment
Vehicles 19
An Overview of the Text   22
Part One: The Investment Environment 22   Part Two: Investment
Fundamentals 22   Part Three: Investment Planning 22
Part Four: Investing in Equities 23   Part Five: Investing in Fixed
Income Securities 24   Part Six: Speculative Investment
Vehicles 24   Part Seven: Other Popular Investment Vehicles 24
Part Eight: Investment Administration 24

Summary 24
Key Terms 25
Review Questions 26
Case Problems 26
Selected Readings 27

2 Investment Markets and Transactions 29
Securities Markets 30
Types of Markets 30 Organized Securities Exchanges 33
The Over-the-Counter Market 36 NASDAQ 37 Regulation of
Securities Markets 39 General Market Conditions: Bull
or Bear 42
Making Security Transactions 42
Stockbrokers 43 Basic Types of Orders 49 Basic Types of
Transactions 50 Transaction Costs 52
Summary 57
Key Terms 59
Review Questions 59
Case Problems 61
Selected Readings 63

3 Sources of Investment Information and Advice 65
Staying in Touch with the Investment World 66
Benefits and Costs of Information 66 Types and Uses of
Information 68 Sources of Information 69
Market Averages and Indexes 87
Stock Market Averages and Indexes 87
Bond Market Indicators 93
Investment Advisors 94
The Advisor's Product 94 Regulation of Advisors 94 Types of
Advisors 95 The Cost of Investment Advice 96 Effective Use
of Investment Advice 96 Investment Clubs 97
Role of the Personal Computer 97
Hardware 98 Software 99 News Retrieval and Data
Bases 101 Annual Cost of Using a PC 103
Summary 104
Key Terms 105
Review Questions 105
Case Problems 108
Selected Readings 109

TWO INVESTMENT FUNDAMENTALS 111

4 Measuring Investment Return and Risk 113
The Concept of Return 114
Components of Return 114 Why Return Is Important 117
Level of Return 119

Measuring Return   119
Interest: The Basic Return to Savers 120   Holding Period
Return 122   The Time Value of Money 125
Risk: The Other Side of the Coin   134
The Risk-Return Tradeoff 134   Sources of Risk 134
Beta: A Modern Measure of Risk 137   Evaluating Risk 140
Summary   144
Key Terms   145
Review Questions   146
Case Problems   148
Selected Readings   151

5   Margin Trading and Short Selling   153
Margin Trading   154
The Essentials of Margin Trading 154   Margin Requirements 158
The Arithmetic of Margin Trading 159   Uses of Margin
Trading 163
Short Selling   166
The Essentials of Short Selling 166   Lending Securities 169
Uses of Short Selling 173
Summary   178
Key Terms   179
Review Questions   179
Case Problems   180
Selected Readings   182

THREE   INVESTMENT PLANNING   183

6   Establishing an Investment Program   185
Personal Financial Planning   186
Assessing Current Financial Condition 186   Establishing
Financial Goals 191   Budgeting for Goal Achievement 191
Insurance   193
Fundamentals of Insurance 193   Life Insurance 194   Other
Forms of Insurance 199   Retirement Plans 200
Personal Taxes   201
Basic Sources of Taxation 202   Type of Income and Tax
Rates 202   Determining Taxable Income 205   Investments
and Taxes 206
Investment Goals and Plans   208
Key Factors 208   Providing Needed Liquidity 210   Quantifying
Investment Goals 211   The Investment Program 212
Summary   214
Key Terms   216
Review Questions   216
Case Problems   219
Selected Readings   222

7 Meeting Liquidity and Retirement Needs   223

Meeting Liquidity Needs: Investing in Short-Term Securities   224
Some Basic Considerations 224   Alternative Short-Term
Investment Vehicles 230   Investment Suitability 242

Meeting Retirement Needs: Planning for the Long Haul   243
Retirement Planning 244   Retirement Programs 250   Funding
Keoghs and IRAs 255   Self-Directed Plans: A Summary 257

Summary   259
Key Terms   261
Review Questions   261
Case Problems   263
Selected Readings   265

FOUR   INVESTING IN EQUITIES   267

8 Common Stock Investments   269

Basic Characteristics of Common Stock   271
Common Stock as a Corporate Security 271   Voting Rights and
Procedures 277   Common Stock Values 280   An Inflation
Hedge? 282

Common Stock Dividends   283
The Dividend Decision 284   Types of Dividends 285
Dividend Policies 289

Types and Uses of Common Stock   290
Kinds of Stock 291   Alternative Investment Strategies 296

Summary   300
Key Terms   302
Review Questions   302
Case Problems   303
Selected Readings   305

9 Common Stock Analysis   307

Principles of Security Analysis   308

Economic Analysis   309
Economic Analysis and the Business Cycle 310   Developing an
Economic Outlook 313

Industry Analysis   317
Key Issues 317   Developing an Industry Outlook 318

Fundamental Analysis   319
The Concept 319   Financial Statements 322   Key Financial
Ratios 327   Interpreting Financial Ratios 337

Summary   339
Key Terms   340
Review Questions   340
Case Problems   342
Selected Readings   344

10 Common Stock Valuation, Technical Analysis, and Efficient Markets   345
Valuation: Obtaining a Standard of Performance   346
  The Company and Its Future 346   Developing an Estimate of Future Behavior 349
A Stock Valuation Framework   352
  The Valuation Model 354   Using Stock Valuation Measures in the Investment Decision 357
Technical Analysis   359
  Principles of Market Analysis 359   Measuring the Market 360   Charting 366
Random Walks and Efficient Markets   373
  A Brief Historical Overview 373   Possible Implications 376   So Who Is Right? 376
Summary   377
Key Terms   378
Review Questions   378
Case Problems   379
Selected Readings   381

FIVE INVESTING IN FIXED INCOME SECURITIES   383

11 Bond Investments   385
Why Invest in Bonds?   386
  Essential Features of a Bond Issue 386   Types of Issues 390
The Bond Market   395
  Available Vehicles 395   Bond Ratings 403   Market Interest Rates 405   Investing in the Bond Market 409
Bond Valuation and Trading   414
  Bond Yields and Prices 415   Investment Strategies 419
Summary   423
Key Terms   424
Review Questions   425
Case Problems   425
Selected Readings   427
THE FUNDAMENTAL ROLE OF FIXED-INCOME SECURITIES   428
Martin L. Leibowitz, Managing Director
Salomon Brothers, Inc.

12 Preferred Stock and Convertible Securities   431
Preferred Stocks   432
  Preferred Stocks as Investment Vehicles 432   Issue Characteristics 437   Evaluating Preferreds 440   Investment Strategies 443
Convertible Securities   446
  Convertibles as Investment Outlets 446   Important Measures of Value 452   Investment Strategies 455

Summary   459
Key Terms   460
Review Questions   460
Case Problems   461
Selected Readings   462

SIX   SPECULATIVE INVESTMENT VEHICLES   463

13   Options: Rights, Warrants, Puts and Calls   465
Rights   466
  Characteristics 466   Investment Merits 467
Warrants   468
  What Is a Warrant? 468   Characteristics of Warrants 469
  Trading Strategies 472
Puts and Calls   477
  Definitions and Characteristics 478   Options Markets 482
  Stock Options 483   Trading Strategies 489   Interest Rate and
  Currency Options 495   Stock Index Options 503
Summary   506
Key Terms   507
Review Questions   507
Case Problems   508
Selected Readings   510
WHY USE OPTIONS?   512
Gary L. Gastineau, Manager, Options Portfolio Service
Webster Management Corporation,
a subsidiary of Kidder, Peabody & Co.

14   Commodities and Financial Futures   515
The Futures Market   516
  Structure 516   Trading 520
Commodities   526
  Basic Characteristics 526   Trading Commodities 530
  Commodities and the Individual Investor 533
Financial Futures   534
  The Market 534   Trading Techniques 541   Options on
  Futures 545
Summary   547
Key Terms   548
Review Questions   548
Case Problems   550
Selected Readings   552
FINANCIAL FUTURES AS A RISK MANAGEMENT TOOL   554
Arthur L. Rebell, General Partner
Wertheim and Co., Inc.

SEVEN   OTHER POPULAR INVESTMENT VEHICLES   557

15   Mutual Funds: An Indirect Route to the Market   559
The Mutual Fund Phenomenon   560
   An Overview of Mutual Funds 560   Essential Characteristics 563
Types of Funds and Services   569
   Types of Mutual Funds 573   Special Services 577
Investing in Mutual Funds   581
   Investor Uses of Mutual Funds 582   The Selection Process 583
   Measuring Performance 588
Summary   591
Key Terms   593
Review Questions   593
Case Problems   594
Selected Readings   595

16   Real Estate Investments   597
Setting Real Estate Investment Objectives   598
   Investment Characteristics 598   Constraints and Goals 601
Scope of Analysis   601
   The Physical Property 602   Property Rights 602   Time
   Horizon 602   Geographic Area 602
Determinants of Value   603
   Demand 603   Supply 605   The Property 608   The Property
   Transfer Process 611
Estimating Market Value   613
   The Cost Approach 613   The Comparative Sales Approach 613
   The Income Approach 614   Using an Expert 616
Forecasting Investment Returns   616
   Market Value versus Investment Analysis 616   Calculating
   Discounted Cash Flows 619   Calculating Approximate Yield 620
The Campus Oaks Apartments   621
   Investor Objectives 621   Scope of Analysis 621   Determinants
   of Value 621   Calculating Investment Returns 626   Synthesis
   and Interpretation 630
Summary   630
Key Terms   631
Review Questions   632
Case Problems   633
Selected Readings   635

17   Tax-Sheltered Investments   637
Tax Fundamentals and Shelters   638
   Taxable Income 638   Determining Taxable Income 640   Tax
   Avoidance and Tax Deferral 644   Tax Shelters 646

Tax-Favored Income   646

Income Excluded from Taxation 646   Strategies That Defer Tax
Liabilities to the Next Year 649   Strategies That Pay-Off in Long-
Term Capital Gains 654   Tax Swaps: A Strategy That Reduces or
Eliminates a Tax Liability 657

Deferred Annuities   657

Annuities: An Overview 658   Characteristics of Deferred
Annuities 658   The Deferred Annuity: An Example 661
Deferred Annuities and Retirement Plans 661   Annuities as
Investment Vehicles 662

Tax Write-Offs Using Limited Partnerships   663

Pooling of Capital and Sharing of Risks 663   How Limited
Partnerships Work 664   Popular Forms of Limited
Partnerships 666   Partnership Structure: Private or Public 671
Essential Investment Considerations 674

Summary   675

Key Terms   677

Review Questions   678

Case Problems   679

Selected Readings   681

18   Gold and Other Tangible Investments   683

Investing in Tangible Assets   684

Why Were Tangibles So Popular in the 1970s? 684
Price Patterns 684   Tangibles as Investment Vehicles 685
When to Invest in Tangibles 687

Investing in Gold   687

Growth in Popularity 687   Investment Forms 691   Gold as an
Investment Vehicle 693

Other Tangible Investments   697

Precious Metals and Gemstones 697   Strategic Metals 699
Collectibles 701

Summary   705

Key Terms   706

Review Questions   706

Case Problems   707

Selected Readings   708

EIGHT   INVESTMENT ADMINISTRATION   709

19   Portfolio Management   711

Principles of Portfolio Management   712

Portfolio Objectives 712   A Complete Investment Portfolio 715

**Traditional Portfolio Management versus Modern Portfolio
Theory   716**

The Traditional Approach 716   Modern Portfolio Theory

(MPT) 718   The Traditional Approach and MPT: A
Reconciliation 721
Building a Portfolio   722
Investor Characteristics 723   Specifying Investor Objectives 724
Portfolio Objectives and Policies 724
Portfolio Management in Action   726
Carol Nakamura: Woman Wonder 727   Martin and Nancy Jacob:
Lottery Winners 728   Art and Helen Brandt: Retirees 730
Elizabeth Beckett: Widow 734
Summary   736
Key Terms   737
Review Questions   737
Case Problems   738
Selected Readings   740

20   Monitoring Your Investment Portfolio   743
Evaluating the Performance of Individual Investments   744
Obtaining Needed Data 744   Indexes of Investment
Performance 745   Measuring Investment Performance 747
Comparing Performance to Investment Goals 755   A Risk-
Adjusted, Market-Adjusted Return Measure (RAR) 756
Assessing Portfolio Performance   760
Measuring Portfolio Return 760   Comparison of Return with
Overall Market Measures 764   Portfolio Revision 765
The Role of Personal Computers 766
Timing Transactions   766
Formula Plans 767   Using Limit and Stop Orders 773
Warehousing Liquidity 774   Timing Investment Sales 775
Summary   776
Key Terms   778
Review Questions   778
Case Problems   779
Selected Readings   782

**Appendix A   Financial Information and Computer
               Software   A–1**
Sources of Financial Information   A–2
Economic and Current Event Information A–2   Institutional
Publications A–6   Professional and Academic Publications A–8
Subscription Services A–11   Mutual Fund Directories A–13
Investment Advisories and Newsletters A–15   Directories and
Source Finders for Financial Publications, Newsletters, and
Investment Advisories A–21   Major Brokerage Firms A–22
No-Load Mutual Funds A–22
Sources of Computer Software   A–32

Appendix B   Financial Tables   A–35
Table B.1 Compound-Value Interest Factors for One Dollar   A–36
Table B.2 Compound-Value Interest Factors for a One-Dollar
    Annuity   A–40
Table B.3 Present-Value Interest Factors for One Dollar   A–44
Table B.4 Present-Value Interest Factors for a One-Dollar
    Annuity   A–48

Glossary of Terms   G–1
Credits   C–1
Index   I–1

PREFACE

In recent years, exciting changes have occurred both in the process of investing and in the range of vehicles available to individual investors. New exchanges, such as the Chicago Board Options Exchange, have opened, and new mechanisms for making transactions, such as discount brokerages and electronic telequote machines, have come into widespread use. And new vehicles such as stock index options, interest rate futures, and zero-coupon bonds have been introduced. Additionally, a variety of regulatory and tax reforms has stimulated the growth of Super NOW accounts and money market mutual funds, as vehicles for maintaining liquidity, and retirement plans such as Keogh plans and Individual Retirement Accounts (IRAs), as tax-saving mechanisms. Finally, the economic recovery that began in 1982 and which is still progressing has spurred investment activity in the securities markets. This second edition of what has already proved to be an effective teaching and learning vehicle was prepared to take account of these and many other exciting changes in the investments field. In its second edition, *Fundamentals of Investing* continues to reflect the state of the art of individual investing by providing up-to-date coverage of modern investment practice in easy-to-read language.

Our principal aim in writing this book is to satisfy the needs of the individual investor who is actively developing and monitoring an investments portfolio. The book is designed for use in first courses in investments offered in colleges and universities, junior and community colleges, trade and technical schools, professional certification programs, and continuing education courses. It describes techniques, vehicles, and strategies for implementing investment goals in a portfolio context and in light of risk-return tradeoffs. Key factors in determining the makeup of a well-diversified individual portfolio are emphasized throughout.

Several features of this text help to distinguish it from other texts currently on the market:

1. The text is organized around a structural model that interrelates investment principles and practices.
2. The concepts of risk and return and of portfolio diversification lie at the heart of the book and are integrated throughout the discussion of all investment vehicles.
3. Emphasis is placed on assessing one's financial position, establishing personal financial goals, considering insurance and retirement needs, and recognizing important tax factors as they relate to investment plans.
4. A wide variety of new investment vehicles is covered in detail without slighting the traditional forms of common stocks and bonds.
5. The treatment of portfolio management has been made as practical and realistic as possible.
6. All references to structural and legal changes in the investments environment and procedures are as up-to-date as possible.
7. Each chapter contains two or more boxed essays that describe real-world situations, problems, or controversies, and underscore practical aspects of investment.
8. New commentaries by investment professionals that describe important aspects of investment practice are included as an additional learning aid.

We feel that the instructional prose for investment courses need not be stiff and colorless. In *Fundamentals of Investing, Second Edition,* we continue to use an informal, conversational tone wherever possible. Since the subject of investments is inherently interesting and dynamic, it surely does not deserve to be cloaked in "banker's gray" rhetoric. A variety of headings and visual devices enhances the presentation, and care has been taken to ensure a consistent reading level throughout the book.

CHANGES IN THE SECOND EDITION

The second edition has been thoroughly updated to reflect investing today; at the same time, it has been refined and reorganized to meet user, reviewer, and student requests. All pedagogical features, including learning objectives, boxed items, key terms, end-of-chapter review questions and case problems, and selected readings have been revised. Major changes in emphasis, organization, appendixes and content coverage have been made to enrich students' understanding of the process of investing.

Emphasis

The text's overall emphasis on the development and management of an investment portfolio consistent with one's risk-return tradeoffs has been preserved. The role of the *personal computer* in the investment process, deregulation, and the evolution of the *financial supermarket* receive increased attention in this edition.

The *investment planning* process—with specific attention to *liquidity and retirement planning,* and the need to consider *taxes* and the role of *tax-sheltered investments*—is stressed throughout.

Organizational Changes
1. "Margin Trading and Short Selling" is now Chapter 5, instead of Chapter 13, in order to provide earlier exposure to these fundamental techniques.
2. Chapter 6 (formerly Chapter 5), "Establishing an Investment Program," has been revised and now appears as the first of two chapters in a new Part Three, "Investment Planning."
3. Chapter 7, the second investment planning chapter in Part Three, is a completely new chapter: "Meeting Liquidity and Retirement Needs." It presents investment alternatives and strategies for meeting liquidity needs and planning for retirement.
4. Chapter 16 (formerly Chapter 15), "Real Estate Investments," has been completely restructured and rewritten to place greater emphasis on non-owner occupied real estate and on the process of isolating, analyzing, and estimating potential returns from alternative real estate investments.
5. A completely new Chapter 17, "Tax-Sheltered Investments," has been added to Part Seven. It reviews basic tax laws and describes strategies for minimizing taxes in order to maximize after-tax returns for given levels of risk. To maintain continuity, Chapter 6 retains its basic discussion of tax fundamentals.

Appendixes
Appendix A, "Financial Information and Computer Software," has been updated to include: (1) a list of costs, addresses, and brief descriptions of investment advisories and newsletters; (2) a list of directories and source finders for financial publications, newsletters, and investment advisories; (3) a list of no-load mutual funds, by type, with addresses and toll-free numbers; and (4) a list (with addresses and brief descriptions) of major computer software programs available to individual investors.

Appendix B, "Financial Tables," has been expanded to include "Compound-Value Interest Factors for a One-Dollar Annuity." These tables are especially useful in the retirement planning process described in Chapter 7.

Specific Content Changes
The major changes in coverage are outlined here:

1. Discussions of the use of the personal computer in investing and the concept of the financial supermarket have been added to Chapter 1, and the coverage of short-term vehicles has been streamlined.
2. A section on computer-based investment management now appears in Chapter 3. Detailed discussions of investment hardware, software, data bases, and the costs of using a personal computer (PC) system are included.

3. Discussion and illustration of the approximate yield formula have been added to the material on the time value of money in Chapter 4.

4. Coverage of insurance in Chapter 6 has been expanded to include basic features of universal life insurance and the role of the professional financial planner in the investment process.

5. Chapter 7, a new chapter, addresses the growing fields of liquidity management and retirement planning. The first part looks at a variety of short-term savings and investment vehicles (like NOW accounts, money funds, Treasury bills, and Series EE bonds); the second part deals with retirement planning, establishing future needs, funding requirements, and supplementary individual retirement programs (such as Keogh plans, IRAs, and 401(k) plans).

6. Chapter 11, on bonds, covers many new products available in this market, including zero-coupon bonds, put bonds, extendable notes, and the new role of registered bonds.

7. Chapters 13 and 14, dealing with options and futures, have been updated to include several new types of securities that are rapidly gaining in popularity, including stock-index options and futures, puts and calls on bonds and foreign currencies, and options on futures.

8. Chapter 16, "Real Estate Investments," has been restructured to encompass a detailed example of the real estate investment analysis process, including calculation of investment returns using both the discounted cash flow and approximate yield methods.

9. Chapter 17, "Tax-Sheltered Investments," describes tax shelters and strategies for realizing tax-favored income. In addition, the effects of annuities and limited partnerships on a tax-minimizing strategy are discussed.

10. Chapter 18, "Gold and Other Tangible Investments" (formerly part of Chapter 16), now covers strategic metals and includes an expanded discussion of collectibles.

11. The detailed portfolios presented in Chapters 19, "Portfolio Management," and 20, "Monitoring Your Investment Portfolio," have been revised and updated to include a brief discussion of the role of personal computers in portfolio administration.

PEDAGOGICAL FEATURES

Each part of the book opens with a brief content overview, and each chapter begins with a list of objectives that sets forth key points to be covered. Up-to-date tables and figures with full descriptive captions, boxes, and commentaries further facilitate learning. Each chapter ends with a list of key terms, 15 or more review questions and problems, and succinct case problems. A list of selected readings for each chapter directs the individual investor to recent articles from such publications as *Barron's, Changing Times, FACT, Financial World, Forbes, Fortune, Money,* and *The Wall Street Journal.*

SUPPLEMENTARY MATERIALS

In addition to an instructor's manual and a test bank that are available to the instructor, a study guide, prepared by J. Markham Collins of The University of Tulsa, is available to students. For each text chapter, this completely new supplement contains a chapter summary, a chapter outline, a programmed self-test, true-false and multiple-choice questions, and problems with detailed solutions.

ACKNOWLEDGMENTS

Many people gave us their generous assistance during the development and revision of *Fundamentals of Investing*. The expertise, classroom experience, and general advice of many colleagues and practitioners were invaluable. Reactions and suggestions from students throughout the country sustained our belief in the need for a fresh, informative, and teachable investments text.

In particular, we wish to thank seven people who provided significant subject matter knowledge, and in so doing made substantial contributions to the formation and revision of this text. They are: (1) Robert J. Doyle, Jr., of The American College, (2) Gary W. Eldred of Palo Alto, California, (3) Samuel C. Hadaway of the Texas Public Utility Commission, (4) Sheri Kole of the College for Financial Planning, (5) Terry S. Maness of Baylor University, (6) Arthur L. Schwartz, Jr., of University of South Florida at St. Petersburg, and (7) Bernard J. Winger of the University of Dayton.

We also wish to offer a special word of thanks to the following reviewers of the first two editions of this book for their excellent contributions to the manuscript.

Gary Baker, Washburn University
Harisha Batra, University of Wisconsin—Whitewater
Cecil C. Bigelow, Mankato State University
Richard B. Bellinfante, Tucson, Arizona
A. David Brummett, New York Institute of Finance
David M. Cordell, Louisiana State University
Timothy Cowling, Dean Witter Reynolds
Clifford A. Diebold, Miami-Dade Community College
James Dunn, Lansing Community College and Merrill Lynch, Pierce, Fenner & Smith
Betty Marie Dyatt, Colorado College
Robert A. Ford, Norman, Oklahoma
Harry P. Guenther, Georgetown University
Robert D. Hollinger, Kansas State University
Roland Hudson, Jr., College for Financial Planning
David S. Kidwell, University of Tennessee
Sheri Kole, College for Financial Planning
Robert T. LeClair, The American College

Weston A. McCormac, California Polytechnic State University
    at San Luis Obispo
Keith Manko, DeKalb Community College
Linda J. Martin, Arizona State University
Warren E. Moeller, Midwestern State University
Joseph Newhouse, West Virginia University
Joseph F. Ollivier, Foster & Marshall/American Express
John Park, Frostburg State College
William A. Rini, New York Institute of Finance
Dick Runyon, California State University—Long Beach
Gary G. Schlarbaum, Purdue University
Harold W. Stevenson, Arizona State University
Nancy E. Strickler, Life Management Institute
Glenn T. Sweeny, Oregon State University
Allan J. Twark, Kent State University

Because of the wide variety of topics covered in this edition, we called upon many experts for advice. We would like to thank them and their firms for allowing us to draw on their insights and awareness of recent developments in order to ensure that the text is as current as possible. In particular, we want to mention James P. Friar of Robert W. Baird & Co., Rick Hinton of Dean Witter Reynolds, N. Arthur Hulick of Investment Planning & Management (Scottsdale, Arizona), B. Paul Jones of the Valley National Bank, James H. Kerley of First Southwest Co., D. Ladd Pattillo of Paine Webber, John H. Rauscher III of Rauscher, Pierce, Refsnes, Inc., Frederick Penn Weaver of Southwest Savings and Loan (Arizona), Fred Emerson of The Greyhound Corporation, Flora Weston of Coldwell Banker (Scottsdale, Arizona), John D. Wilt of Shearson/American Express and R. Daniel Sadler of Bank One, Dayton, NA. In addition, we want to express our special thanks to George L. Ball, Prudential-Bache Securities, Inc.; Gary L. Gastineau, Webster Management Corporation; Martin L. Leibowitz, Salomon Brothers, Inc.; and Arthur L. Rebell, Wertheim and Co., Inc., for writing the commentaries appearing at various points in the text.

A number of colleagues have lent us their expertise, encouragement, and support. They include Peter W. Bacon, Russell H. Hereth, Nancy K. Mohan, John C. Talbott, and Richard E. Williams of Wright State University, and James R. Booth, A. James Ifflander, and Glenn A. Wilt of Arizona State University.

We would also like to thank J. Markham Collins of the University of Tulsa for his useful feedback, as well as for authoring the study guide. Thanks are also due to Richard E. Krebs and Dennis T. Officer for their assistance in preparing the instructor's manual and the computer-based test bank.

We are grateful for the research assistance provided by Allen D. Anthony and David Austin, and the outstanding work and clerical assistance of Tammy Johns and Cathie Dinnen Scott. John Greenman, Jim Brennan, Dorothy Cappel, and the entire staff of Harper & Row also deserve special thanks for their professional input and continuing commitment to the text.

Finally, our wives, Robin and Charlene, and our children, Jessica and Zachary, and Chris and Terry, have played important parts by providing support and understanding during the book's development, revision, and production. We are forever grateful to them and hope that this edition will help to justify the sacrifices required during the many hours we were away from them working on this book.

Lawrence J. Gitman
Michael D. Joehnk

On Investing in the 1980s

Today's investment climate is perhaps the most exciting in our nation's history—one in which the challenges and rewards to investors are greater than ever before. Some will succeed in this environment by luck; but most of those who do well will do so because they have learned to recognize opportunity, avoid pitfalls, and understand the market mechanism.

The rising demand for capital throughout the world will be a prevailing theme during the decade. And the finite supply of financial resources means that investors will be called upon to supply capital to more and more companies and governments. The laws of supply and demand suggest that the rewards for the risks offered must rise accordingly.

The emergence of a new financial services industry is a major recent phenomenon that is greatly affecting investment alternatives, information, and transactions. The headlong rush by companies into all sectors of the financial services industry is often credited to, or blamed on, deregulation. That's not really the case—unless you want to blame a bear market on lower stock prices; a disease and its causes are not the same. The loss of low-cost sources of funds has been the primary force behind the dramatic changes in the banking, brokerage, and insurance industries. As interest rates began to reflect the marketplace rather than certificate limits set by rule, these financial institutions moved into one another's territory.

GEORGE L. BALL

Equally important to the individual investor is the emergence of total financial planning and collective capitalism. Today investors want and need professional assistance to cope with the sea of financial products and the volatility of the stock and bond market. Computers are no substitute for knowledgeable decisions. Total financial planning seeks to meet the need for skilled advice, not just access to price and earnings data or a connection to a trading floor.

Collective capitalism, the other new development, refers to financial advisors' participation as partners in the investments they recommend. Rather than acting solely as intermediaries, advisors now co-invest with their clients. Such a partnership will not mark every routine 100-share order or an everyday life insurance purchase. But it will increasingly be part of transactions involving large amounts of capital. After all, it is logical to expect an advisor to participate in the risk if he or she really believes in the investment's reward potential.

Total financial planning and collective capitalism should renew and improve the trust between investors and those in the financial services industry. They should also lead to better and more stable modes of financing, as well as greater rewards to investors. The prospects for knowledgeable investors are better than ever.

GEORGE L. BALL
**President and Chief Executive
Prudential-Bache Securities**

ONE
THE INVESTMENT ENVIRONMENT

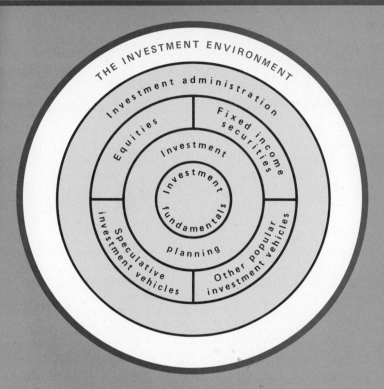

THE INVESTMENT ENVIRONMENT

Investment administration

Equities

Fixed income securities

Investment

Investment fundamentals

Speculative investment vehicles

Other popular investment vehicles

planning

A clear understanding of the investment environment is essential for developing a successful investment program. Accordingly, the purpose of Part One is to describe the investment environment and to set the stage for discussing the various aspects of investing. This part of the book contains three chapters. Chapter 1 describes the role and scope of investments, with attention to the nature and importance of the investments process and to a number of popular investment vehicles. Chapter 2 discusses key aspects of the investment markets and transactions, including procedures for making security transactions. Finally, Chapter 3 describes the major uses and sources of investment information and advice.

1
The Role and Scope of Investments

How would you like to make a million? Or own an expensive house or car, and travel the world in your own private jet? Sounds good, doesn't it? Well, the odds are probably against your achieving such financial success. Unless you inherit a large sum of money, win a lottery, or find yourself "in the right place at the right time," you will probably never make a million. But would you be upset with half that amount? Your success in achieving financial goals will depend on many factors, such as education, personality, career path, family status, and investment plans and practices. The objective of this text is to help you achieve your financial goals by creating an awareness and understanding of the exciting world of investments. Although it may not make you rich, using the information in this book should give you a better chance for personal financial success. In this introductory chapter, we will look at:

1. The meaning of the term *investment* and the implications it has for individual investors.
2. The basic structure of and key participants in the investment process, and the associated rewards for investing.
3. The importance of basic steps involved in, and current innovations in, the personal investment process.
4. Popular types of investment vehicles, including short-term securities, common stocks, and fixed income securities such as bonds, preferred stock, and convertibles.
5. Other lesser-known vehicles, including various types of options and outlets, such as commodities and financial futures, mutual funds, real estate, tax-sheltered investments, and gold and other tangible investments.
6. The content and organizational model around which this text is structured.

"What should I do with my money?" is a question for almost everyone. Once you have taken care of the basic necessities, choosing a place to put extra funds is often difficult. The process of identifying, evaluating, selecting, and monitoring the placement of funds in some medium with the expectation of preserving value and earning a positive return is called *investing*. In a more general sense, an investment is any outlet—tangible or intangible—into which funds can be placed in order to preserve and possibly increase their value and/or earn a positive return. Recognizing that money properly placed not only can preserve value but also can earn income is a prerequisite for making the most out of your financial resources.

A broad range of investment vehicles, such as savings deposits, stocks, bonds, options, commodities, mutual funds, real estate, tax shelters, and gold, is available. Because there are significant differences in the returns and risks provided by these vehicles, you need to choose not only the type of vehicle, but also the specific company or item in which to invest. For example, if you decide to buy common stock, should you buy IBM, NCR, General Motors, or Texaco? Since each type of investment reacts differently to changes in uncontrollable factors such as labor strikes, inflation, and war, you may be better off with a *portfolio* containing a variety of investment vehicles. Such an approach should allow you to get the best return for a given level of risk or to minimize risk for a given return. Because all investment vehicles tend to be traded in a marketplace that provides higher returns for higher risks, you need to be able to assess the risk-return characteristics of alternative vehicles in order to create the best portfolio for your purposes.

Our objective in this text is to provide the understanding needed to establish and fulfill investment goals by creating a portfolio that provides an acceptable return for an acceptable level of risk. Familiarity with the organizations, vehicles, procedures, costs, characteristics, and strengths and weaknesses of various investment alternatives, plus a set of well-developed investment plans, should greatly increase your chance of achieving a reasonable degree of financial success. This chapter sets the stage for an in-depth look at the essential concepts, tools, and techniques of investing presented throughout the text.

THE ROLE OF INVESTMENTS

The word *investments* may be used in a variety of ways. It can mean a stock or bond purchased to fulfill certain financial goals; it can also mean a physical asset such as a tool acquired to produce and sell a product. In the broadest sense, investments provide the mechanism needed to finance the growth and development of our economy. Although primary attention in this text is given to the individual investor, an understanding of the role of investments in a variety of other arenas is useful. To give you a general idea of the scope of the personal investment process, we will look first at the key steps involved in establishing and managing an investment program. We begin with key definitions, the structure of the investment process, the participants, and the rewards of investing.

Investments Defined

Simply stated, an *investment* is any vehicle into which funds can be placed with the expectation that they will be preserved or increase in value and/or generate positive returns. Idle cash is not an investment, since its value is likely to be eroded by inflation and it fails to provide any type of return. The same cash placed in a bank savings account would be considered an investment, since the account provides a positive return. The various types of investments can be differentiated on the basis of a number of factors, such as whether the investment is a security or property; direct or indirect; debt, equity, or options; low or high risk; and short or long term.

Securities or property

Investments that represent evidence of debt, ownership of a business, or the legal right to acquire or sell an ownership interest in a business are called *securities.* The most common types of securities are bonds, stocks, and options. *Property,* on the other hand, is investments in real property or tangible personal property. *Real property* is land, buildings, and that which is permanently affixed to the land; *tangible personal property* includes items such as gold, antiques, and art. Although security investments are likely to be more common among individual investors, many people prefer property investments because they feel more comfortable owning something they can see and touch. But because of the existence of organized mechanisms for buying and selling securities and their widespread popularity, we will focus primary attention on securities rather than property investments.

Direct or indirect

A *direct investment* is one in which an investor directly acquires a claim on a security or property. For example, when a person buys a stock, a bond, a parcel of real estate, or a rare coin in order to preserve value or earn income, that individual has made a direct investment. An *indirect investment* is an investment made in a portfolio or group of securities or properties. For example, an investor may purchase a share of a *mutual fund,* which is a portfolio of securities issued by a variety of firms. By doing so, she will own a claim on a fraction of the entire portfolio, rather than on the security of a single firm. It is also possible to invest indirectly in property— for example, by buying an interest in a limited partnership that deals in real estate, oil wells, etc. Although direct investments are preferred by most individual investors, indirect investments have certain attributes that make them attractive to individuals.

Debt, equity, or options

Usually, an investment will represent a debt or an equity interest. *Debt*—an intangible investment—represents funds loaned in exchange for the receipt of interest income and the promised repayment of the loan at a given future date. When investors buy a debt instrument like a *bond,* they are lending money to the issuer, who agrees to pay a stated rate of interest over a specified period of time, at the end of which the original sum will be returned. *Equity* represents an ownership interest in a specific business or property. An equity investment may be shown by a security or

BOX 1.1 PROFILE OF A SUCCESSFUL INVESTOR: THE FUERTGES

Penne Fuertges keeps *en pointe* these days teaching a weekly ballet class, working as a fledgling financial planner and running her family's investment portfolio. She's successful at all three, but she's proudest of her shrewd portfolio strategy. In three years Mrs. Fuertges, 39, parlayed a $10,000 Treasury bill into $57,000 worth of income-producing limited partnerships in oil and gas and real estate, common stocks and mutual funds. Although she manages the money, she shares the decision-making with her husband Don, 40, who boasts that "Penne's the one who comes up with the ideas and the initiatives."

About 15% of the Fuertges portfolio is in common stocks, and that's the portion with the biggest winners. Penne's most successful purchase was Auxton Computer Enterprises, a data-processing and consulting firm. She bought the stock in February 1982 at $13.50 a share; it split in October and her 50 shares became 75. A month later the price had soared to $37 a share, and her $675 investment grew to $2,775, a gain of more than 311%. So far she's had only one loss, and that's still on paper. In 1981 she bought 50 shares of Cutco, a beauty-salon company that was trading at $15.50. The stock soon lost its curl and fell to $5.50, but Penne held on and rightly so. The shares have started to bounce back and are now at $11.

Three years ago when the Fuertges moved to Hays, Kans. from New Mexico, the couple's investment consciousness began to be raised. That's when Penne Fuertges got her first full-time job teaching management and consumer finance at Fort Hays State University. Don is chairman of the physical-education department there. "We used to spend, spend, spend," she says with a laugh. "But once I had a good income we didn't want to piddle it away, so we decided to invest as much of my salary as possible." They consulted a local financial planner, David King, who was so impressed with Penne he asked her to join his firm. She is now a full-time financial planner at David M. King & Associates. Penne estimates that her income this year, based on fees and commissions, could be as much as $25,000. Last year she brought home $20,000 from part-time planning and full-time teaching; Don earned $38,000. The couple have two children: Kathy, 18, a freshman at Texas Tech University, where she is on a golf scholarship, and Brian, 10, who is in the fourth grade.

Penne's biggest challenge is to balance the family's immediate material needs with its longer-term ones. "It's a constant tug of war," she says. "I want to invest, invest, invest. I'm like a kid in a candy store—there are so many investments I want to get into. Yet I realize that we must live a little too. Mother can't sock everything away." This year the Fuertges hope to invest a third of their combined salaries, and Penne Fuertges has some new strategies up her sleeve. She's planning to de-emphasize income and invest in an equipment-leasing limited partnership. It will give her an investment tax credit this year and write-offs for the next four. After that, the shelter produces only taxable income. She intends to turn that over to Brian, who will presumably still be in a lower bracket, for his college education. Basically a conservative investor, she's nonetheless going to expand their growth-stock holdings. Don Fuertges wants to retire at 55, and Penne's trying to accommodate him. Says he: "She treats me like a preferred customer."

Source: Candace E. Trunzo, "Planning Your Portfolio: Four Investors' Winning Ways." *Money,* January 1983, pp. 66–67.

by title to the property. The individual investor typically obtains an equity interest in a business by purchasing securities known as *stock. Options* are neither debt nor equity; rather, they are securities that provide the investor with an opportunity to purchase another security or property at a specified price over a stated period of time. An investor may, for example, pay $500 for an option to purchase a 2 percent interest in the Alex Company for $30,000 until December 31, 1987. If a 2 percent interest is currently valued at $24,000, the person will not exercise this option. Option investments are not as common among individual investors as various types of debt and equity investments, but as we will see, they are growing rapidly in popularity.

Low or high risk

Investments are sometimes differentiated on the basis of risk. As used in finance, *risk* refers to the chance that the value or return on an investment will differ from its expected value—it is the chance of something undesirable occurring. The broader the range of possible values or returns associated with an investment, the greater its risk, and vice versa. The individual investor is confronted with a continuum ranging from low-risk government securities to high-risk commodities. Although each type of investment vehicle has a basic risk characteristic, the actual level of risk depends on the specific vehicle. For example, even though stocks are generally believed to be more risky than bonds, it is not difficult to discover high-risk bonds that are in fact more risky than the stock of a financially sound firm such as IBM.

Low-risk investments are those that are considered safe with regard to the return of the funds invested and the receipt of a positive return. High-risk investments are often considered speculative. The terms *investment* and *speculation* are used to refer to different approaches to the investment process. *Investment* is viewed as the process of purchasing securities or property for which stability of value and level of expected return are somewhat predictable. *Speculation* is the process of buying similar media in which the future value and level of expected earnings are highly uncertain. Simply stated, speculation is on the high-risk end of the investment process. Of course, because of the greater risk, the returns associated with speculation are expected to be greater. In this book we will use the term "investment" for both processes, and we will look more closely at the issue of investment return and risk in Chapter 4.

Short or long term

The life of an investment can be described as either short or long term. *Short-term* investments typically are those with lives of one year or less; *long-term* investments are those with longer maturities—or perhaps, like common stock, with no maturity at all. For example, a six-month certificate of deposit would be a short-term investment, whereas a 20-year bond would be a long-term investment. Of course, by purchasing a long-term investment and selling it after a short period of time, say six months, an individual can use a long-term vehicle to meet a short-term goal. As will become clear later in the text, it is not unusual to find investors matching the life of an investment to the period of time over which they wish to invest their funds. For instance, an investor with funds that will not be needed for six months is likely to purchse a six-month certificate of deposit, whereas the investor wishing to build a retirement fund is likely to purchase a 20-year corporate bond. The breakdown of short-term and long-term is also useful for tax purposes, since certain tax breaks are received on gains in the value of long-term investments (those owned for longer than one year). The tax considerations as well as the motives for making short-term versus long-term investments will be discussed in Chapter 6 and various types of tax-sheltered investments will be described in Chapter 17.

The Structure of the Investment Process

The activity of the individual investor is only a small part of the overall *investment process,* which is a mechanism for bringing together suppliers (those having extra funds) with demanders (those who need funds). Suppliers and demanders are most often brought together through a financial institution or a financial market. Occasionally—especially in property transactions such as real estate—buyers and sellers deal directly with one another. Financial institutions like banks and savings and loan associations typically accept deposits and then lend them out or invest them. Financial markets are forums in which suppliers and demanders of funds are brought together through intermediaries. There are a number of financial markets, such as stock markets, bond markets, and options markets. Their common feature is that the price of the investment vehicle at any point in time results from an equilibrium between the forces of supply and demand. And as new information about returns, risk, inflation, world events, and so on, becomes available, the changes in the forces of supply and/or demand may result in a new equilibrium or *market price.*

Figure 1.1 shows the investment process. Note that the suppliers of funds may transfer their resources to demanders through a financial institution, through a financial market, or directly. As the illustration shows, financial institutions are likely to participate in financial markets as either suppliers or demanders of funds. The short-term financial market is called the *money market;* the long-term sector is the *capital market,* which is dominated by various securities exchanges. The characteristics of these markets will be discussed in greater detail in Chapter 2.

Participants in the Investment Process

Government, business, and individuals are the three key participants in the investment process, and each may act as a supplier or demander of funds.

Government

Each level of government—federal, state, and local—requires vast sums of money to meet its operating needs. These needs center around capital expenditures, which are long-term projects related to the construction of schools, hospitals, roads, and highways. Usually, the financing for such projects is obtained through the issuance of various types of long-term debt securities. Another source of demand for funds results from operating needs. The federal government, for example, may spend more than it receives in taxes. A city might face a need for operating funds when the tax money it will collect is not due for some time. Usually governments finance these operating needs with short-term debt securities.

Governments are also sometimes suppliers of funds. If a city has temporarily idle cash, rather than hold these funds in a checking account, it may make a short-term investment to earn a positive return. The financial activities of governments both as demanders and suppliers of funds significantly affect the behavior of financial

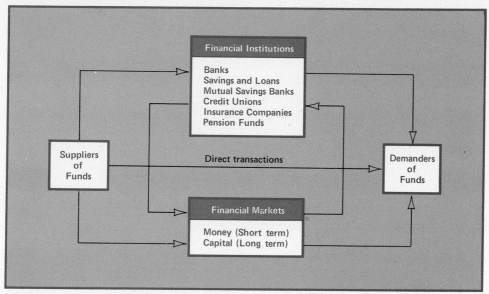

Figure 1.1 The Investment Process.
Note that financial institutions participate in the financial markets as well as transfer funds between suppliers and demanders. And although the arrows go only from suppliers to demanders, for some investment transactions, such as the sale of a bond, the principal amount borrowed by the demander from the supplier (the lender) will eventually be returned.

institutions and financial markets. In general, government is a *net demander* of funds, which means that it demands more funds than it supplies.

Business

Most business firms, no matter what the type, require large sums of money to support operations. Like government, the financial needs of business are both short and long term. On the long-term side, businesses seek funds to build plants, acquire equipment and facilities, and develop products. Short-term needs tend to revolve around the need to finance inventory, accounts receivable, and other operating costs. Business firms issue a wide variety of debt and equity securities in order to finance these long- and short-term needs. They also supply funds when they have a temporary excess amount of cash. In fact, many large business firms have active and sophisticated cash management operations and are major purchasers of short-term securities. But like government, business firms in general are *net demanders* of funds.

Individuals

Individuals supply funds through the investment process in a variety of ways. They may place funds in savings accounts, buy debt or equity instruments, buy options, or purchase various types of property. Depending upon personal investment goals and objectives, the choice of vehicles in which to place funds is often a difficult one. The key source of demand for funds by individuals typically comes in the form of loans needed to finance the acquisition of property, usually automobiles and homes. Although the demand for such funds seems great, as a group individuals are *net suppliers* of funds: they put more funds into the investment process than they take out. Since both government and business are net demanders of funds, the important role of the individual investor in providing the funds needed to finance economic growth and development should be clear.

The Rewards for Investing

The rewards, or returns, for placing funds in the investment process may be received in either of two basic forms—current income or increased value. For example, money placed in a bank savings account would provide current income in the form of periodic interest payments, whereas a raw land investment would offer returns in the form of an increase in value between the time of purchase and the time it is sold. In order for those needing funds to attract funds from those having an excess, a reward or return adequate to compensate the suppliers for the risks involved must be provided. At the same time, those in need cannot reasonably expect to obtain funds without paying for them. Simply stated, funds suppliers must be rewarded and funds demanders must provide these rewards for the investment process to function smoothly. The magnitude and form of such rewards depends on factors such as the type of security or property transaction, the length of time involved, and the risks embedded in the transaction.

THE PERSONAL INVESTMENT PROCESS

The emphasis in this text is on the personal investment process, which is concerned with the investment activities of individuals, rather than institutional investors. Because institutional investors, such as banks, savings and loan associations, insurance companies, and pension funds, tend to have large sums to invest, they can afford to employ professionals who can use sophisticated tools and techniques to create their portfolios. In this book we will present many of the theories, tools, and techniques of these professionals in a form that can be used by individual investors to create portfolios that meet their personal investment goals.

The Importance of the Personal Investment Process

The effectiveness of the economic growth process is dependent on the ready availability of funds to finance the increased needs of not only government and business, but also individuals. For example, without the ready availability of mortgage loans, very few homes would be purchased. Such a lack of mortgage money would result in fewer persons being employed to build homes as well as to manufacture the needed components (lumber, nails, glass, etc.). The net effect of decreased mortgage financing would probably contribute to a slowdown in economic activity—

a generally undesirable result since the availability of funds to qualified individuals (as well as government and business) is needed to allow the economy to grow and prosper. Because individuals as a group are net suppliers of funds while government and business are net demanders, the personal investment process has a profound economic impact.

Steps in the Personal Investment Process

The personal investment process can be conducted in various ways. One approach is to rely on plans developed to achieve specific goals. The other extreme is a haphazard "seat-of-the-pants" approach, in which actions are taken on a strictly intuitive basis. Evidence suggests that the more logical approach usually results in better returns. The serious individual investor should try to plan, develop, and execute an investment program consistent with the achievement of overall financial goals. Such a program should result in an investment portfolio that possesses the return and risk behavior he or she seeks. A brief overview of the steps in the personal investment process should help to set the stage for the more detailed discussion of the concepts, tools, and techniques presented throughout the text.

Meeting investment prerequisites

Before investing, an individual must make certain that the necessities of life are adequately provided for. Investments are not an alternative to such needs, but rather are the mechanism for using current funds to satisfy future needs. In addition, a minimum savings account (or some form of liquid short-term investment vehicle) should be established to meet emergency cash needs. Another prerequisite would be adequate protection against the losses that could result from loss of life, illness or disability, damage to property, or a negligent act. Protection against such risks is typically acquired through life, health, property, and liability insurance. Although some types of insurance possess certain investment attributes, provision for adequate insurance protection is a necessary prerequisite to investing. Provision for adequate retirement income may be viewed as an investment prerequisite, and achievement of which may depend on the success of the investment program. At a minimum, the individual needs to establish certain retirement goals prior to the establishment of specific investment goals. The process and considerations involved in establishing and satisfying investment prerequisites will be discussed in greater detail in Chapter 6.

Establishing investment goals

Once the individual has satisfied the prerequisites and has clearly defined personal financial goals, she must establish *investment goals,* specific statements of the timing, magnitude, form, and risks associated with a desired return. For example, an investment goal might be to accumulate $15,000 for the down payment on a summer home to be purchased in 1989, or to accumulate $250,000 for use at retirement in 2001. These goals must not only be consistent with overall financial goals, but they must be realistic. Adequate funds must be available for investment, and an attainable rate of return must be used to achieve them. The development of investment goals as part of the overall personal financial planning process is discussed in Chapter 6.

Evaluating investment vehicles

Before selecting investment vehicles, it is important to evaluate them in terms of investment goals. The evaluation process involves assessing the potential returns and risks offered by each vehicle. This process typically involves *valuation,* which is a procedure for estimating the true worth of an investment vehicle. The output of the valuation process includes measures of return, risk, and value for that vehicle. A general discussion of the procedures for measuring these key dimensions of potential investments is included in Chapter 4.

Selecting suitable investments

The best investments may not be those that just maximize return; other requirements, such as risk and tax considerations, may also be important. Investments must be selected to fulfill individual goals, the specification of which is a vital part of overall personal financial planning. The selection process is important because it determines a course of action and can significantly affect one's success in achieving long-term goals. For example, a person wishing to accumulate $20,000 at the end of three years may choose to invest in a particular common stock. If the firm whose stock was purchased goes bankrupt, the individual could lose the money instead. Careful analysis and selection of vehicles having acceptable levels of return, risk, and value in terms of one's goals is paramount for successful management of investments.

Constructing a diversified portfolio

An investment portfolio is a group of investments owned by an individual. Joan Smith's investment portfolio might contain 20 shares of IBM common stock, $20,000 in government bonds, and 10 shares of Putnam Equities mutual fund. Using a variety of available tools and techniques, the individual investor can combine vehicles in such a way that investment goals can be achieved, and return, risk, and investment values are optimized. *Diversification,* which involves inclusion of a number of different investment vehicles, is fundamental to constructing an effective portfolio. By diversifying, investors are able, on balance, to earn higher returns or be exposed to less risk than if they limit their investments to a few vehicles. A portfolio has the surprising quality of possessing a different risk-return characteristic from those of the individual investment vehicles that comprise it. For example, gold and other precious metals are by themselves extremely risky investments—their prices fluctuate constantly and often dramatically in commodity markets. Yet when they are held with securities such as common stock in a diversified portfolio, over time the portfolio exhibits lower risk or a higher return than if only metals or only common stock were held.

Buy low, sell high.

There are two types of diversification techniques—random and purposive. *Random diversification* takes place when investment vehicles are selected at random, such as by drawing names from a hat. This may hardly seem like a sound investment strategy, but it can work. Portfolios constructed this way have sometimes performed better than those designed by professionals. *Purposive diversification* is the process of selecting vehicles to achieve a stated portfolio objective. For example, an investor might observe that whenever the new car industry is depressed and its sales and profits are low, the car replacement parts industry is in just the reverse situation. By diversifying between firms in each industry, it might be possible to reduce risk exposure while maintaining a return equal to what could be earned by investing in only one of the two industries. Purposive diversification is usually done with more technically efficient methods than the one in the example here. We will examine these other approaches in Chapter 19.

Managing the portfolio

Once a portfolio has been constructed, the individual investor must measure and evaluate its actual behavior in relation to expected performance. If, for example, the investment return, risk, or value is not consistent with that person's objectives or expectations, corrective action may be required. Such action usually involves selling certain investments and using the proceeds to acquire other vehicles for the portfolio. Portfolio management therefore involves not only the selection of a compatible group of investments that meet the individual's goals, but also monitoring and restructuring the portfolio as dictated by the actual behavior of the investments. Chapter 20 is devoted to monitoring the investment portfolio.

Current Innovations in the Personal Investment Process

Several innovations are taking place in the personal investment process that are likely to have a profound impact on individual investors. The first of these is the widespread use of the *personal computer (PC)*—a relatively inexpensive but powerful home computer—and the second is the growing trend toward servicing investors' total financial needs through one company—the *financial supermarket.* Over the past several years, PC sales have been growing at an annual compound rate of over 30 percent, and by the end of the decade, it is estimated that dollar sales of PCs will exceed all other computer sales. This means that by 1990 the computer's use will be within the reach of almost everyone.

The personal computer (PC)

The process of evaluating and selecting securities, and then managing the resulting investment portfolio, requires considerable time and research. Historically, the investor's solution to this problem was to shift it to a stockbroker or someone else and then follow his or her advice. Many investors still operate this way and will continue to do so in the future. But a growing number are choosing instead to do their own research and make their own decisions. They are aided considerably in this effort by the personal computer (PC). Rapidly expanding PC technology has made available both very sophisticated *hardware*—the physical parts of a computer system, such as a console, a processor, and a printer—and *software,* programs designed to tell the computer what functions to perform.

Equally important, investors now have computer access to a variety of *data bases* that are needed for research. For example, Dow-Jones (the publisher of *The Wall Street Journal* and *Barron's* newspapers) offers a variety of news retrieval services ranging from current price quotations on stocks, bonds, options, and most other securities to detailed financial statistics on over 3,200 companies. It even offers transcripts from a popular TV show on investments, *Wall Street Week.* Along with news retrieval, Dow-Jones (and others) has software programs that perform analytical functions on the data available through news retrieval. An investor can thus do fundamental or technical analyses (these two basic approaches to security evaluation will be explained in Chapters 9 and 10) of the market as a whole or of specific securities with the aid of a PC.

Despite falling prices, PC systems are still too expensive for many individual investors, both in acquisition and maintenance costs and in charges for data retrieval. But these costs must be tempered by (1) the possible savings in commissions if the investor uses a discount, rather than a full-service, broker; and (2) the fact that the costs of purchasing and operating the PC are tax-deductible to the extent that it is used for investment or other income-producing activities. In addition, one would typically not limit use of a PC solely to investment activities, since it can do so much more. At minimum, the PC can be used to play video games, which for many people is not a trivial use. Whole families have been introduced to the computer's capabilities through this activity.

Some observers believe PCs will cause important changes in the investments area. Since it will be relatively simple for either individuals and/or professionals to have access to data and analytical models, less emphasis will be placed on specific security selection and more on integrating the investment process into a person's or family's total financial plan. This plan includes not only investing, but also other activities such as cash management, insurance, estate planning, credit management, tax shelters, and tax strategies.

Financial supermarkets

Within the last six years or so, important changes have taken place in the structure of financial institutions. The first of these was an innovation introduced by Merrill Lynch that combined an investor's banking and stockbrokerage activities into one account called a Cash Management Account, or CMA. It was enormously successful, attracting billions of dollars in deposits for Merrill Lynch and prompting most other major brokerage firms to follow suit. But the CMA was only the beginning; its success indicated the presence of a new, sophisticated investor—one who wants all of his or her financial needs serviced in one shop. To meet the challenge, there have been some interesting mergers. Prudential Insurance, for example, acquired Bache, and Bank of America acquired Charles Schwab and Company, both brokerage firms; even Sears got into the picture by purchasing Dean Witter Reynolds, a major brokerage house. The thrust of these mergers has been to create a marketing system and a mix of products for comprehensive financial servicing. If an agent is meeting with a client to discuss insurance needs, he or she can at the same time offer an investments package integrated within the insurance plan to create a total savings-investments-insurance plan. Illustrative of this total approach is Prudential-Bache's Total Financial Planning Program, which includes over 65 financial alternatives. It seems clear that in years to come, investors will be likely to choose a single financial service center rather than a stockbroker, an insurer, a bank, and so forth.

INVESTMENT VEHICLES

A broad range of investment vehicles is available to individual investors. Some are securities; others are not. And there are many different types of securities, each type offering vehicles having differing lives, costs, return and risk characteristics, and tax considerations. The same is true of property investments. We will devote the bulk of this book—Chapters 8 through 18—to describing the characteristics, special features, returns and risks, and possible investment strategies that can be used with vehicles available to the individual investor. Here we will introduce the various vehicles and give a brief description of each. The introduction is broken down by general types: short-term vehicles, common stock, fixed income securities, options, and other popular investment vehicles.

BOX 1.2 KROGERS: LITERALLY A "FINANCIAL SUPERMARKET!"

Shoppers used to bringing home their bacon from Kroger Co. supermarkets now can invest their dough there as well.

Kroger, taking the term "financial supermarket" literally, said it will offer life insurance, money-market and other mutual funds and other consumer financial services at its food stores.

The company said it will introduce the services at its Grove City, Ohio, store today and at other selected stores during the next several months.

The centers will be managed by Capital Holding Corp., a Louisville, Ky.-based insurance concern that is a joint venture partner with Kroger in the new enterprise, Kroger said.

Kroger announced earlier this year that it was studying the idea of offering financial services at its food stores. Kroger operates about 1,200 food stores.

Kroger said the insurance offered at the stores will include automobile, homeowners, renters, and condominium insurance and three kinds of life insurance.

Capital Holding has subcontracted with the Vanguard Group of Investment Cos. to provide two money-market funds with check-writing privileges, three bond mutual funds and two common stock mutual funds, Kroger said.

The financial services center would extend Kroger's strategy of offering one-stop shopping in its stores. Many of its supermarkets currently feature specialty shops for cosmetics, plants and flowers, cheese and other items. The company recently added "nutrition centers" that sell whole grains, vitamins and other products.

Many supermarkets have installed banking outlets or check-cashing services. Kroger's financial centers would take those services several steps farther, and the move has competitors sitting up and taking notice.

A spokesman for Fisher Foods Inc. in Bedford Heights, Ohio, said the company would study Kroger's new service, and "if it made sense, to us, we'd be interested."

Sears, Roebuck & Co., which has started to put financial service centers in its department stores, said its customers have been quick to accept such services in the new setting, an indication that supermarket shoppers might also welcome the service.

"We don't find that a different setting than people are used to is a barrier. Quite the contrary, the public welcomes the opportunity to have a comfortable and convenient location," said a Sears spokesman.

Source: "Kroger to Introduce Financial Service in Its Supermarkets." *The Wall Street Journal,* September 15, 1982, p. 12.

Short-Term Vehicles

Short-term vehicles include savings instruments that usually have lives of less than one year. The most important of these are money market certificates and deposits, money market accounts and mutual funds, Treasury bills, commercial paper, savings and NOW accounts, and even U.S. Series EE savings bonds. Often such instruments are used to "warehouse" idle funds and earn some return while suitable long-term vehicles are being evaluated; that is, they serve as a liquid reserve. Because these vehicles typically carry little or no risk of loss, they tend to be popular among those wishing to earn something on temporarily idle funds, and also with conservative investors who may use short-term vehicles as a primary investment outlet. Reliance on short-term vehicles stems from the safety and convenience investors feel such instruments offer.

In addition to the "warehousing" function served by short-term vehicles, they are also important in their own right because they round out an investor's portfolio by meeting liquidity needs, which are an important part of any total financial plan. As a rule of thumb, financial planners often argue that anywhere from three to six months of after-tax income should be held in short-term vehicles to meet unexpected needs. A serious illness or loss of a job could create a need for immediate cash, and it might come at a time when longer-term security prices are low. Being forced to sell the long-term securities at such a time can result in substantial losses and possible financial embarrassment. A closer look at meeting liquidity needs is provided in Chapter 7.

Common Stock

Common stock is an equity investment that represents ownership in a corporate form of business. Each share of common stock represents a fractional ownership interest in the firm. For example, one share of common stock in a corporation that has 10,000 shares outstanding would represent 1/10,000 ownership interest in the firm. The return on common stock investment comes from either of two sources—the periodic receipt of *dividends,* which are payments made by the firm to its shareholders, and increases in value or *capital gains,* which result from selling the stock at a price above that originally paid. For example, imagine you purchased a single share of A and L Industries common stock for $40 per share. During the first year you owned it you received $2.50 in cash dividends, and at the end of the year you sold the stock for $44 per share. If we ignore the costs associated with buying and selling the stock, you would have earned $2.50 in dividends and $4 in capital gains ($44 sale price − $40 purchase price). Next to short-term vehicles and home ownership, common stock, which offers a broad range of return-risk combinations, is the most popular form of investment vehicle. Because of the widespread popularity of common stock, three chapters—8, 9, and 10—are devoted to the study of this investment vehicle.

Fixed Income Securities

Fixed income securities are a group of investment vehicles that offer a fixed periodic return. Some forms offer contractually guaranteed returns; others have specified but not guaranteed returns. As a result of the trend toward rising interest rates that began in the late 1960s, the popularity of fixed income security investments has also increased. The key forms of fixed income securities are bonds, preferred stock, and convertible securities.

Bonds

Bonds are the IOUs of corporations and governments. A bondholder receives a known interest return, typically paid semi-annually, plus the return of the face value (say $1,000) at maturity (typically 20 to 40 years). If you purchased a $1,000 bond paying 11 percent interest in semi-annual installments, you would expect to be paid

$55 (that is, ½ yr × 11% × $1,000) every six months, and at maturity you would receive the $1,000 face value of the bond. Of course, an investor may be able to buy or sell a bond prior to maturity at a price different from its face value. As for common stock, a wide range of return-risk combinations is available to the bond investor. We will examine bond investments in detail in Chapter 11.

Preferred stock

Like common stock, *preferred stock* represents an ownership interest in a corporation. But unlike common stock, preferred has a stated dividend rate, payment of which is given preference over dividends to holders of common stock. Preferred stock has no maturity date. Investors typically purchase it for the dividends, but it may also provide capital gains. The key aspects of preferred stock are described in Chapter 12.

Convertible securities

A *convertible security* is a special type of fixed income obligation (bond or preferred stock) that possesses a conversion feature which permits the investor to convert it into a specified number of shares of common stock. Convertible bonds and convertible preferreds are attractive investment vehicles because they provide the fixed income benefit of a bond (interest) or preferred stock (dividends), while offering the price appreciation (capital gain) potential of common stock. A detailed discussion of this behavior of convertibles, along with other important characteristics of the vehicle, appears in Chapter 12.

Options

Securities that provide the investor with an opportunity to purchase another security or property at a specified price over a given period of time are called *options*. They are acquired and used by investors in a variety of ways and for a variety of reasons. Most often options are purchased in order to capitalize on an expected increase or decrease in the price of common stock. The purchaser of an option is not guaranteed any return and could lose the entire amount invested, either because the option never becomes attractive enough to use, or the life of the option termi- nates. Aside from their use in attempts to profit from the price movement of certain underlying securities, options are sometimes used to protect existing investment positions against losses. The three basic types of options are rights, warrants, and puts and calls (these are discussed in detail in Chapter 13).

Rights

A *right* is an option to buy a fraction of a share of common stock at a stated price over a specified period of time. For example, one might obtain rights which entitle the holder to buy one share of stock at $50 per share for each 10 rights held (i.e., each right is good for one-tenth of a share of common stock). A person having 1,000 rights could therefore buy 100 shares (¹/₁₀ share per right × 1,000 rights) at $50 per share. The life of a right is at most two to three months, and rights obtain their value from the fact that the price at which the underlying stock can be purchased is below the market price of the stock.

Warrants

Like a right, a *warrant* provides the holder with an opportunity to purchase a specified number of shares of common stock at a stated price (per share) over a given period of time. Warrants differ from rights in three basic ways: (1) the exercise price (at time of issue) is *above* the market price of the underlying stock; (2) each warrant typically provides for the purchase of one or more shares of stock; and (3) the life of a warrant is typically 2 to 10 years and in some cases infinite. For example, a General Manufacturing warrant might allow its holder to purchase three shares of its stock at $80 per share anytime prior to December 31, 1989. If and when the market price of General Manufacturing's stock rises above $80, the warrants have value, since at such time they permit the purchase of shares at a price below the market price.

Puts and calls

Puts and calls are types of options that have gained great popularity over the past dozen years. A *put* is an option to sell 100 shares of common stock on or before some future date at a specified price. A *call* is an option to buy 100 shares on or before some future date at a specified price. Most puts and calls have lives of 1 to 9 months and occasionally a year. The exercise or striking price of both puts and calls is set close to the market price at the time they are issued. Investors tend to purchase puts when they anticipate price declines and calls when they expect prices to rise. An example of a call option might be a six-month call to buy 100 shares of Wince Industries at $30 per share. The holder of such an option could, anytime before its expiration, buy 100 shares of Wince Industries at $30 per share, regardless of the actual market price of the stock. In addition to common stock, it is possible today to trade puts and calls on stock market indices, stock portfolios, government bonds, foreign currencies, and even options on commodity futures. As we will see in Chapter 13, although put and call options appear to be rather risky investments, they can often be used to protect an investor's position in a given stock.

Other Popular Investment Vehicles

A few other investment vehicles are also popular with individual investors. The most common ones are commodities and financial futures; mutual funds; real estate; tax-sheltered investments; and gold and other tangible investments.

Commodities and financial futures

Investors who are willing to accept a higher level of risk purchase *commodity and financial futures contracts,* which are guarantees by a seller that he or she will deliver a specified commodity, foreign currency, or financial instrument at a given price by a certain date. Commodity futures contracts exist on a wide range of commodities such as soybeans, frozen pork bellies, and cocoa; financial futures contracts are written against a foreign currency or a financial instrument such as a bond or a stock index. Trading in commodities and financial futures is generally a highly specialized, high-risk proposition, since the opportunity to make a profit depends on a variety of uncontrollable factors tied to world events and economic activity. An expanded discussion of these vehicles is presented in Chapter 14.

BOX 1.3 TWELVE MISTAKES INVESTORS COMMONLY MAKE

There are many rules and strategies for successful investing. But one of the surest is to keep mistakes to a minimum. Bernard Baruch, who made a fortune in the market and was a trusted adviser to Presidents Roosevelt and Truman, said of his early career: "I began a habit I was never to forsake—of analyzing my losses to determine where I had made my mistakes."

According to successful investors and experienced advisers, here are 12 of the most common mistakes that investors make—

- *Thinking that investing is easier than it is.* Cheap and even free financial advice is offered in advertisements for market letters, by brokerage firms and perhaps by your own broker. The message, stated or implied, is that you could have made a quick profit in this or that stock or bond and that similar opportunities are still available. In truth, if there were such an easy method to make money, it would not be for sale at any price.
- *Plunging in without a long-range plan.* Thomas W. Phelps, author of *100 to 1 in the Stock Market,* says, "Most people try to make a few points quickly . . . but not 1 in 1,000 seriously plans and acts as one must to make a fortune." The mistake, according to David L. Babson, retired president of a large family of mutual funds, involves treating stocks as pieces of paper bought and sold rather than evidence of ownership in a company to be kept as long as it makes progress. It is a mistake not to decide in advance whether your primary object is income or growth of principal and how much emphasis you want to put on safety.
- *Not doing homework.* A wealth of data and projections is available on thousands of firms. Yet many investors spend less time selecting and caring for their investments than for their autos. It would be foolish, for example, not to research any stock or bond you contemplate owning or already do own by studying the latest annual report, by using material such as Standard & Poor's stock and bond reports and by reading regularly a good financial publication.
- *Not sticking to high quality.* In the long run, securities of the best-managed companies in the fastest-growing industries tend to show the best results.

Mutual funds

A company that invests in a diversified portfolio of securities is called a *mutual fund.* The fund sells shares to investors, who thus obtain an interest in the portfolio of securities owned by the fund. Most mutual funds issue and repurchase shares as demanded at a price reflecting the proportionate value of the portfolio at the time the transaction is made. Chapter 15 is devoted to the study of this popular investment vehicle.

Real estate

The term *real estate* includes investment in such things as owner-occupied homes, raw land, and a variety of forms of income property, such as apartments. As a result of widespread inflation and its generally favorable impact on these types of investments, real estate has over the last decade or so become a popular vehicle. Its appeal also stems from the fact that real estate investments can provide income from rents, capital gains, and a variety of tax benefits that are not available from

BOX 1.3 *Continued*

- *Being ashamed to invest small amounts.* Lew G. Coit, a highly successful investment counselor, recalls that one of his largest accounts started with $300 in what is now Exxon and $350 in General Electric. By investing a fixed dollar amount regularly—so-called dollar-cost averaging—you obtain more shares at lower, and fewer at higher, prices with a resulting favorable average cost.
- *Investing money you may soon need for something else.* This could force you to cash in during a temporary dip in the market.
- *Thinking low-priced stocks are more likely to double or triple than higher-priced stocks are.* Perhaps so, but they are also more likely to drop out of sight.
- *Trying to catch the short swings in the market or a stock.* Professionals with instant market information and computerized analysis can't. It is risky, also, to buy or sell on the basis of most spot news—a new product, a strike or a change in one quarter's earnings. Such news usually has been discounted by the market.
- *Buying, selling or holding for the wrong reasons.* Selling a good and promising stock merely to nail down a profit entails a capital-gains tax, brokerage commissions and a search for another company that may be no better. Many an investor clings to a loser in the vain hope that it will come back or for sentimental reasons, such as, "It was my mother's favorite stock."
- *Being a sheep.* The big Wall Street institutional investors flock in and out of the market. Even with all of their instant knowledge, the record of most is only mediocre.
- *Not starting early enough in life.* Many retirees can't live on fixed incomes, which decline in buying power at the inflation rate. They failed to build an investment in stocks whose dividends stand to rise faster than inflation.
- *Frittering away cash dividends or interest.* Unless you need it, such income is best reinvested.

Source: John W. Hazard, "12 Mistakes Investors Make." *U.S. News & World Report,* January 10, 1983, p. 69.

alternative investment vehicles. A detailed look at the role real estate can play in a personal investment portfolio is presented in Chapter 16.

Tax-sheltered investments

Because of provisions in the federal income tax law, some investments offer certain tax advantages over others. As an example, interest received on a municipal bond is not taxed at all, and only 40 percent of a long-term capital gain is taxed. Since the income tax rate can be as high as 50 percent, many investors find that their after-tax rates of return can be far higher from *tax-sheltered investments*—investments structured to take advantage of existing tax laws in order to provide high returns to investors in high tax brackets—than from conventional investments. A comprehensive review of the more common tax shelters is presented in Chapter 17.

Gold and other tangible investments

Although not nearly as popular as the vehicles described above, gold and other tangible investments such as antiques and art can be included in the portfolio of the individual investor. In the case of these items, the underlying investment strategies are similar to those employed when using the more traditional vehicles. And items such as antiques, art, and stamp collections also enable the individual investor to gain psychic enjoyment from merely holding them. Chapter 18 presents a detailed discussion of how to make and manage these types of investments.

AN OVERVIEW OF THE TEXT

To provide the understanding needed to establish and fulfill personal investment goals by creating a portfolio that provides an acceptable return for an acceptable level of risk, we have divided the book into eight parts. Each part, which is introduced with a brief description of its contents as well as its relationship to the overall investment process, explains an important aspect of individual investing.

Part One: The Investment Environment
Part Two: Investment Fundamentals
Part Three: Investment Planning
Part Four: Investing in Equities
Part Five: Investing in Fixed Income Securities
Part Six: Speculative Investment Vehicles
Part Seven: Other Popular Investment Vehicles
Part Eight: Investment Administration

Each of the parts can be related using the model shown in Figure 1.2. The understanding of the investment process provided by this text should help you to develop, implement, and administer a program consistent with your personal financial goals.

Part One: The Investment Environment

Before investing takes place, the investor should be familiar with the way security markets operate and how transactions are made in them. Equally important is the choice of a brokerage firm to aid in executing transactions. In addition, the investor must become acquainted with the available sources of investment information and advice.

Part Two: Investment Fundamentals

At the heart of the investment process is a firm understanding of investment fundamentals. The second part of the text therefore introduces the key fundamentals and sets the stage for a discussion of the various aspects of investment planning. Specific attention is given to measuring investment return and risk, and to the use of margin trading and short selling.

Part Three: Investment Planning

Investments must be selected to create portfolios tailored to individual goals and objectives. Certain prerequisites to this process include the development of financial plans, adequate insurance coverage, tax planning, adequate liquidity, and

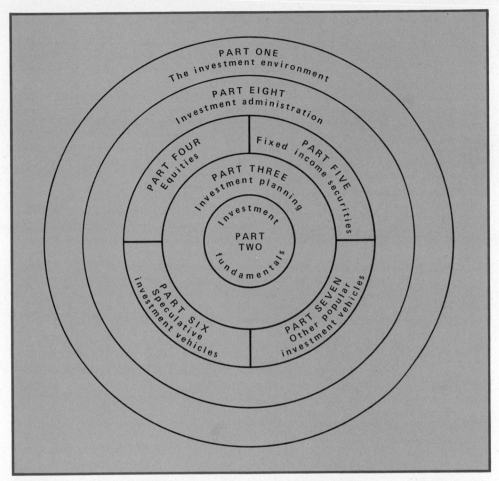

Figure 1.2   An Overview of the Major Parts of the Text.
The text approaches the individual investment process in a logical fashion beginning with an overview of the investment environment (Part One), following with a discussion of investment fundamentals (Part Two), and then covering investment planning (Part Three). This is followed with a description of the key aspects of the most popular investment vehicles (Parts Four through Seven). The text concludes with a discussion of investment administration (Part Eight).

provision for retirement needs. The variety of new techniques and vehicles now available is overwhelming, and each must be evaluated in light of the investors' risk-return goals. Investment planning, discussed in Part Three, helps the investor to place goals and objectives in proper perspective.

Part Four: Investing in Equities

One of the most popular forms of investing—common stock—is discussed in great detail in Part Four. The fundamental characteristics of common stock and the procedures available for analyzing potential investments are presented, along with some of the technical aspects of common stock, such as valuation, technical analysis, and efficient markets.

Part Five: Investing in
Fixed Income Securities

Another popular type of investment vehicle is fixed income securities, which include bonds, preferred stock, and convertibles. Part Five covers the key characteristics, types, and suitability of each of these forms of fixed income securities, with special emphasis on the role each can play in the individual's investment portfolio.

Part Six: Speculative
Investment Vehicles

For those investors willing to accept the increased risks, speculative investments provide opportunities to earn high returns. Part Six discusses several kinds of speculative securities—rights, warrants, puts and calls, commodities, and financial futures—that are readily available to the individual investor.

Part Seven: Other
Popular Investment Vehicles

This part of the text looks at a variety of less standard, but readily available, forms of investments. Specific attention is given to mutual funds; real estate; tax shelters; and gold and other tangible investments such as antiques and art. The discussion of tax shelters specifically emphasizes the use of various types of annuities and limited partnerships. The key characteristics and suitability of each of these vehicles are evaluated in light of potential inclusion in the individual's portfolio.

Part Eight: Investment Administration

The final part of the text is concerned with the administration process, which provides a basis for linking the many concepts, tools, and techniques presented in the earlier parts of the text. This link is provided by the development of the technical and applied aspects of portfolio management. In addition, this final part of the text presents a discussion of the ongoing process of monitoring an investment portfolio.

SUMMARY

For an individual, investments must be part of an overall personal financial planning process. Goals must be consistent with these plans and realistic in view of available resources. In creating a portfolio consistent with these personal investment goals, the individual must choose from among a wide range of investment vehicles. Some vehicles are tangible forms of property; others take the form of a security. Some are direct; others are indirect. An investment can represent a debt, an equity, or an option. It may possess risk ranging from very low to extremely high. And an individual may invest in short-term or long-term vehicles.

In the investment process, financial institutions and financial markets bring together suppliers and demanders of funds. Government, business, and individuals act as both suppliers and demanders of funds. Government and business demand more funds than they supply; individuals supply more funds than they demand. The factor that motivates suppliers to invest funds is an opportunity to earn current income or to experience an increase in the value of invested funds. By providing for the transfers of funds from suppliers to demanders, the investment process provides the mechanism for financing economic growth. Since individuals as a group are net suppliers, their activities are of key importance in this process.

The personal investment process involves a number of basic steps. Once investment prerequisites have been satisfied, goals must be established. Next, potential vehicles must be thoroughly evaluated in order to assess their true worth. Then the investor chooses suitable investments in view of stated goals and combines them into a portfolio using the principles of diversification. The final step is managing the portfolio. Recent innovations in the personal investment process include the use of the personal computer and the development of the financial supermarket.

A broad range of potential investment vehicles is available for consideration. Short-term vehicles usually have lives less than one year and carry little or no risk of loss. They tend to be popular among those wishing to earn a return on temporarily idle funds, and also among conservative investors who use short-term vehicles as a primary investment. Common stock is a popular investment vehicle that offers the potential for dividends and capital gains. Fixed income securities are investment vehicles offering fixed periodic returns, with some potential for gain in value. They include bonds, preferred stock, and convertible securities. The more common options are rights, warrants, and puts and calls. Other vehicles available to the individual investor are commodities and financial futures; mutual funds; real estate; tax shelters; and gold and other tangible investments, such as antiques and art.

KEY TERMS

bond	long term
call	maturity (of debt)
capital gain	money market
capital market	mutual fund
commodities (futures)	option
common stock	personal computer (PC)
convertible security	portfolio
currency future	preferred stock
debt	property
direct investment	purposive diversification
diversification	put
dividend	random diversification
equity	real estate
financial future	real property
financial institution	right
financial market	risk
financial supermarket	security
fixed income securities	short term
indirect investment	short-term vehicles
investment	speculation
investment goals	valuation
investment process	warrant

REVIEW QUESTIONS

1. Define the term *investment* and explain why individuals invest. What alternatives exist for investing idle funds?

2. Differentiate between security and property investments. Which form of investment is most popular among individual investors?

3. What is the difference between direct and indirect investments? Cite an example of each.

4. Differentiate among debt, equity, and option investments and give an example of each.

5. Describe how the term *risk* is used to depict the behavior of certain investments. Differentiate between high-risk and low-risk investments.

6. Describe the structure of the overall investment process. Define and explain the role played by financial institutions and financial markets.

7. Classify the role of: (a) government, (b) business, and (c) individuals as net suppliers or net demanders of funds. Discuss the impact of each on the investment process.

8. Briefly discuss the rewards available to those placing funds in the investment process and explain the economic importance attached to investment activity.

9. List and discuss the six steps involved in the personal investment process.

10. Describe a personal computer (PC) and the role it can play in the personal investment process.

11. What is a financial supermarket? Do you feel your investment needs could be served by one? Explain.

12. Discuss the role of short-term investment vehicles in an individual's investment plans and portfolio.

13. How much would an investor earn on a stock purchased one year ago for $63 if it paid an annual cash dividend of $3.75 and had just been sold for $67.50? Did the investor experience a capital gain? Explain.

14. Briefly define and differentiate the following fixed income securities:

a. Bonds.
b. Preferred stocks.
c. Convertible securities.

15. Explain the nature of an option and describe the opportunity for profit offered by this type of investment vehicle.

16. Describe the similarities and differences between rights and warrants.

17. What is the difference between a put and a call? If you did not own shares of a company's stock but felt that its price would decline significantly in the near future, would you be likely to buy a put or a call? Explain.

18. Briefly describe each of the following types of futures investments and indicate what factors are likely to affect the returns on each:

a. Commodity futures.
b. Financial futures.

19. What is a mutual fund, and why might such a vehicle appeal to an individual investor? Explain.

CASE PROBLEMS

1.1 INVESTMENTS OR RACQUETBALL?

Charles Owens and Mary Haxton are senior accounting majors at a large midwestern university. They have been good friends since high school and look forward to their graduation at the end of next semester. Each has already found a job, which will begin upon graduation. Charles has accepted a position as an internal auditor in a medium-sized manufacturing firm; Mary will be working for one of the major public accounting firms. Each is looking forward to the challenge of a new career and to the prospect of achieving success both professionally and financially.

Charles and Mary are preparing to register for their final semester. Each has one free elective to select. Charles is considering taking a racquetball course offered by the physical education department, while Mary is planning to take a basic investments course. Mary has been trying to convince Charles to take investments instead of racquetball. Charles believes he doesn't need to take investments, since he already knows what common stock is. He believes that whenever he has accumulated excess funds, he can invest in the stock of a company that is doing well. Mary argues that there is much more to it than simply choosing common stock. She feels an exposure to the field of investments would certainly be more beneficial than learning how to play racquetball.

Questions

1. Explain to Charles the importance and scope of the investment process.

2. Describe the personal investment process to Charles and emphasize its importance to his overall financial success.

3. List and discuss the other types of investment vehicles with which Charles is apparently unfamiliar.

4. Assuming Charles is in good physical condition, what arguments would you give to convince Charles to take investments rather than racquetball?

1.2 EVALUATING AMY POTTER'S INVESTMENT PLAN

Amy Potter's husband Orville was recently killed in an airplane crash. Fortunately, he had a sizable amount of life insurance, the proceeds of which should provide Amy with adequate income for a number of years. Amy is 33 years old and has two children, James and Becky, who are 6 and 7 years old, respectively. Although Amy does not rule out the possibility of marrying again, she feels it is best not to consider this when making her financial plans. In order to provide adequate funds to finance her children's college education as well as for her own retirement, Amy has estimated that she needs to accumulate $180,000 within the next 15 years. If she continues to teach school, she believes sufficient excess funds will be available each year (salary plus insurance proceeds minus expenses) to permit achievement of this goal. She plans to make annual deposits of these excess funds into her money market mutual fund, which currently pays 8 percent interest.

Questions

1. In view of Amy's long-term investment goals, assess her choice of a money market mutual fund as the appropriate investment vehicle.

2. What alternative investment vehicles might you recommend that Amy consider prior to committing her money to the money market fund?

3. If you were Amy, given your limited knowledge of investments, in what vehicles would you invest the excess funds? Explain.

SELECTED READINGS

Blotnick, Srully. *Winning: The Psychology of Successful Investing.* New York: McGraw-Hill, 1978.

Blume, Marshall E., and Jack P. Friedman. *Encyclopedia of Investments.* Boston: Warren, Gorham and Lamont, 1982.

Casey, Douglas R. *Crisis Investing.* New York: Harper & Row, 1981.

Gup, Benton E. *The Management of Financial Institutions.* Boston: Houghton Mifflin, 1984.

Hardy, C. Colburn. *Dun and Bradstreet Guide to Your Investments, 1982.* New York: Harper/ Colophon Books, 1982.

"How Invest-by-Phone-Rackets Hook Their Victims." *Changing Times,* January 1981, pp. 41–44.

"How to Manage All That Money," *Changing Times,* March 1981, pp. 29–33.

Kidwell, David S., and Richard L. Peterson. *Financial Institutions, Markets, and Money,* 2d ed. Hinsdale, IL: Dryden Press, 1984.

"Money: Where to Invest Now?" *U.S. News & World Report,* December 27, 1982/January 3, 1983, pp. 73–76.

"A Shoppers Guide to Investing." *Money,* September 1979, pp. 60–61.

"Stock Market Basics for Beginners." *Changing Times,* June 1981, pp. 41–46.

"Taking the Leap: How to Shop for a Home Computer." *Business Week,* December 20, 1982, pp. 86–89.

"The 1980's Will Be the Decade of Common Stocks." *Money,* September 1980, pp. 56–62.

Tobias, Andrew. *The Only Investment Guide You'll Ever Need.* New York: Harcourt Brace Jovanovich, 1978.

Trunzo, Candace. "How to Handle a Windfall." *Money,* October 1982, pp. 173–178.

2
Investment Markets and Transactions

To understand investments, an investor must be aware of the environment in which most transactions are made. In this chapter, therefore, we will look at:

1. The types of securities markets in which transactions are made.
2. The operations, functions, and nature of organized securities exchanges as well as the over-the-counter market.
3. The regulation of securities markets and the general market conditions that have prevailed over the past 60 years.
4. The role of the stockbroker in making transactions and the types of brokerage services available.
5. The basic types of orders—market, limit, and stop-loss—and their use in making security purchases and sales.
6. The key types of transactions—long, short, and margin—and the transaction costs associated with the purchase and sale of various kinds of investment vehicles.

Early in your childhood, you found out that it is difficult to play a game without fully understanding the rules. In spite of the fact that you possessed great potential and skill for playing a game, without adequate knowledge you were unable to play well. The same type of logic applies to playing the investment game. For although investing is far more than a game you play, it does have a number of important rules you need to know. Regardless of how well prepared you might be to select the best vehicle for achieving your investment goals, you would not be able to make that selection if you did not understand the workings of the market in which it is bought and sold, and if you did not know how to find and enter that market. In this chapter we will look at key aspects of the investment environment so that you will know what market to enter for your purposes, how to enter it, and what are the most efficient ways of doing so.

SECURITIES MARKETS

Securities markets are the mechanism that allows suppliers and demanders of funds to make transactions. These markets play a key role in the purchase and sales activities of individual investors. Not only do they provide a mechanism through which purchasers and sellers can make transactions, but they permit such transactions to be made *quickly* and at a fair price. Before describing the methods used to enter these markets, let us look at the various types of markets, their organization, their regulation, and their general behavior.

Types of Markets

The securities markets may be classified as money or capital markets. The *money market* is where short-term securities are bought and sold. The *capital market* is where transactions are made in longer-term securities such as stocks and bonds. Because the money market is concerned with short-term securities and because the size of these transactions is generally outside the scope of the individual investor's resources (usually $100,000 or more), we will devote most of our attention to the capital market, which is made up of a variety of types of securities exchanges through which the individual investor can make stock, bond, and options investments. These capital markets can be classified as primary or secondary.

Primary markets

The market in which new issues of securities are brought to the public is the *primary market.* When a company offers a new security, a number of institutions are likely to be involved in the selling process. The corporation issuing the security will probably use the services of an *investment banking firm,* which is a firm that specializes in selling new security issues. The investment banker's activities are often described as *underwriting,* or guaranteeing to the issuer that it will receive at least a specified minimum amount for the issue. Not only does the investment banking firm sell new security issues on behalf of issuers, it also provides the issuing corporation with advice about pricing and other important aspects of the issue. In the case of very large security issues, the banking firm will bring in other firms as partners and form an *underwriting syndicate* in order to spread the risk associated with selling the new securities. Each member of the syndicate then forms its own *selling group,* which is responsible for distributing its portion of the new issue to the investing public.

The selling group is normally made up of a large number of brokerage firms, each of which accepts the responsibility for selling a certain portion of the issue. The selling process for a new security issue is depicted in Figure 2.1. The relationships among the participants in this process can also be seen in the announcement of the offering of a new security issue shown in Figure 2.2. The role of the various firms

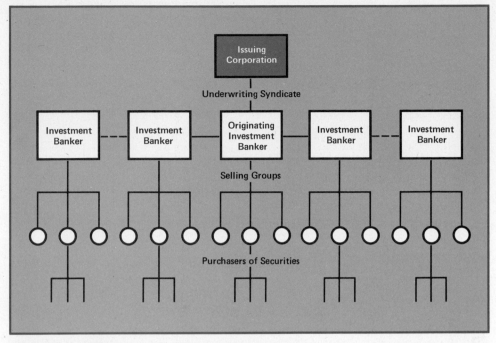

Figure 2.1   The New Security Selling Process.
The investment banker hired by the issuing corporation may form an underwriting syndicate, which then establishes selling groups to sell the new security issue in the primary market.

participating in the selling process can be differentiated on the basis of the layout of the announcement. Isolated firm names (or in many cases a larger typeface) reflect the importance of the firm in the sale process (the key participants in the offering are labeled in the margin at the right).

Compensation for underwriting and selling services typically comes in the form of a discount on the sale price of the securities. For example, an investment banker may pay the issuer $24 per share for stock to be sold for $25 per share. The investment banker may then sell the shares to members of the selling group for $24.75 per share. In this case, the original investment banker makes $0.75 per share ($24.75 sale price less $24 purchase price), and the members of the selling group make $0.25 for each share they sell ($25 sale price less $24.75 purchase price). Although some primary security offerings are sold directly by the issuer, the majority of new issues are sold through the mechanism we have described here.

Secondary markets

The market in which securities are traded after they have been issued is the *secondary market* or the aftermarket. The secondary market exists because after a security has been issued, some purchasers may wish to sell shares, and others may wish to buy them. Included among secondary markets are the various organized securities exchanges and the over-the-counter market. *Organized securities ex-*

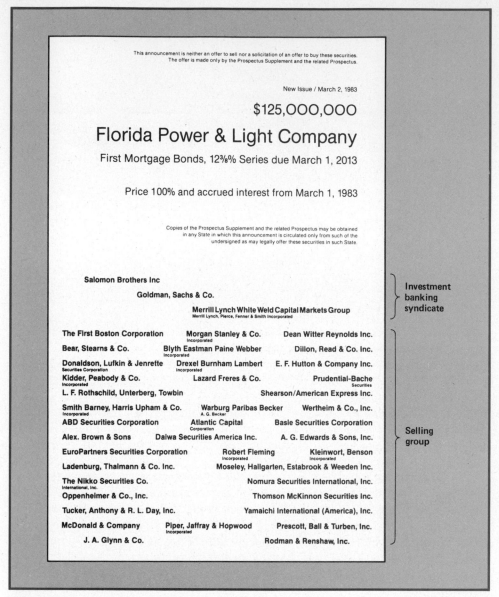

Figure 2.2   An Offering Announcement.
This form of an offering announcement is commonly referred to as a "tombstone," apparently because of its close resemblance to such markings. The participants in both the investment banking and the selling group established to sell the Florida Power & Light Company bonds are clearly noted in the tombstone. (*Source: The Wall Street Journal,* March 2, 1983, p. 31.)

changes are centralized institutions in which the forces of supply and demand for certain securities are brought together. The *over-the-counter market,* on the other hand, is a widely scattered telecommunications network through which buyers and sellers of certain securities can be brought together. Because so many different kinds of popular investment vehicles are traded on both the organized securities exchanges and over-the-counter markets, the individual investor will probably make transactions in each of these markets.

Organized Securities Exchanges

"Listed" securities are traded on organized securities exchanges and account for over 65 percent of *total* share volume traded. All trading is carried out in one place (such as the New York Stock Exchange on Wall Street) and under a broad set of rules by persons who are members of the exchange. The key exchanges on which stock and bond transactions are made are the New York Stock Exchange (NYSE) and the American Stock Exchange (AMEX), both located in New York City and accounting for approximately 81 and 9 percent, respectively, of the total annual volume of shares traded on organized exchanges. Other exchanges include the Midwest Stock Exchange, the Pacific Stock Exchange, and the Boston Stock Exchange; these are known as regional exchanges, and they account for only about 10 percent of the annual share volume on organized exchanges. There are 14 regional exchanges and each deals primarily in securities with local or regional appeal. Separate exchanges exist for options trading and trading in commodities and financial futures. Let us look now at the basic structure, rules, and operations of each of these organized securities exchanges.

The New York Stock Exchange

Since most organized securities exchanges are modeled after the New York Stock Exchange (NYSE), a description of its membership, listing policies, and trading activity will provide a basis for discussing other exchanges.

Membership.   Membership in the New York Stock Exchange is expensive. In order to become a member, an individual or firm must own a seat on the exchange. The word "seat" is used only figuratively, since members trade securities standing up. There are a total of 1,366 seats on the NYSE. Seats on the exchange have sold for as much as $515,000 (in 1968 and 1969) and as little as $4,000 (in 1876 and 1878), although most recently they have gone for about $285,000. Seats are owned by members of the exchange, the majority of which are brokerage firms owning more than one seat. The largest brokerage firm, Merrill Lynch, Pierce, Fenner & Smith, owns over 20 seats. Firms such as Merrill Lynch designate officers to occupy seats, and only such designated people are permitted to make transactions on the floor of the exchange. Membership is often divided into broad classes based on the members' activities. Although the majority of members make purchase and sale transactions on behalf of their customers, some members make transactions for other members or for their own account. Table 2.1 classifies and briefly describes member activities. It should be clear that commission brokers and specialists perform the majority of the activities on the exchange.

Listing policies.   To become listed on an organized stock exchange, a firm must file an application. Some firms are listed on more than one exchange; when this occurs, the shares are said to have *dual listing*. The New York Stock Exchange

TABLE 2.1   NYSE MEMBER ACTIVITIES

Type of member	Approximate % total membership*	Primary activities
A. MAKE TRANSACTIONS FOR CUSTOMERS		
Commission broker	52%	Make stock and bond purchase and sale transactions as requested by customers.
Bond broker	2	Commission broker who only makes bond transactions for its customers.
B. MAKE TRANSACTIONS FOR OTHER MEMBERS		
Independent broker (Two-dollar broker)	10	Executes orders for other brokers who are unable to do so due to excessive market activity.
Specialists	29	Make a continuous, fair, and orderly market in the 6 to 15 issues assigned to them. They also make odd-lot purchase and sale transactions for members of the exchange.
C. MAKE TRANSACTIONS FOR THEIR OWN ACCOUNT		
Registered traders	4	Purchase and sell securities for their own account. Must abide by certain regulations established to protect the public.

*Because approximately 3 percent of the members are inactive, the percentages given total 97 percent.

has the most stringent listing requirements. Currently over 1,500 firms, accounting for over 2,200 stocks and over 3,100 bonds, are listed on the NYSE. In order to be eligible for listing on the NYSE, a firm must have at least 2,000 stockholders owning 100 or more shares. It must have a minimum of 1 million shares of publicly held stock, a demonstrated earning power of $2.5 million before taxes at the time of the listing and $2 million before taxes for each of the preceding two years, a total of $16 million in market value of publicly traded shares, and it must pay a listing fee. Once a firm's securities have been accepted for listing, it must meet the requirements of the federal Securities and Exchange Commission (SEC), which regulates certain aspects of listed securities. If listed firms do not continue to meet specified requirements, they may be *de-listed* from the exchange.

Trading activity.   Trading is carried out on the floor of an exchange. The floor of the NYSE is an area about the size of a football field. On the floor are 18 trading posts, and around the perimeter are telephones and telegraph equipment, which are used to transmit buy and sell orders from brokers' offices to the exchange floor and back again once an order has been executed. Certain stocks are traded at each of the trading posts. Bonds and less active stocks are traded in an annex. All trades are made on the floor of the exchange by members of the exchange. Trades are made in *round lots* (usually lots of 100 shares), and not in *odd lots* (less than 100 shares). The *specialists,* members who specialize in one or more stocks, make odd-lot transactions for members desiring this service.

All transactions on the floor of the exchange are made through an auction process. The goal is to fill all buy orders at the lowest price and to fill all sell orders at the highest price, thereby giving both purchasers and sellers the best possible deal. The actual auction takes place at a post on the floor of the exchange where the particular security is traded. Members interested in purchasing a given security publicly negotiate a transaction with members interested in selling that security. The specialist's job in such a transaction is to provide for a continuous and orderly market in the security. The specialist performs this job by offering to buy or sell (at specified prices) whenever there is a lack of continuity or order in the market for the security.

The American Stock Exchange

The American Stock Exchange (AMEX) is the second largest organized security exchange. Its organization and procedures are quite similar to those of the New York Stock Exchange, except that its listing requirements are not as stringent as those of the NYSE. There are approximately 660 seats on the AMEX and over 950 listed stocks and 240 listed bonds.

Regional and Canadian stock exchanges

The number of securities listed on each of the regional exchanges is typically in the range of 100 to 500. As a group, they handle about 10 percent of all shares traded on organized exchanges. Ten of the 14 American regional exchanges are registered with an agency of the federal government; the other 4 are not large enough to require registration. Table 2.2 lists the regional stock exchanges. Of these, the Midwest, Pacific, and Philadelphia are the dominant ones. Most regional exchanges are modeled after the NYSE, but membership and listing requirements are considerably more lenient. It is not uncommon for the regional exchanges to list securities that are also listed on the NYSE or AMEX. This dual listing is often done to enhance a security's trading activity.

In addition to the regional stock exchanges, there are a few Canadian stock exchanges. The Montreal Stock Exchange, the Toronto Stock Exchange, and the Canadian Stock Exchange create a marketplace in which the securities of Canadian companies, many of which are foreign subsidiaries of American companies, can be traded. The Toronto Stock Exchange, which has over 1,100 listed securities, is the largest of the Canadian exchanges.

Options exchanges

Options, which allow the holder to purchase or sell a financial asset at a specified price over a stated period of time, are listed and traded on the Chicago Board

**TABLE 2.2   REGIONAL STOCK EXCHANGES—
REGISTERED (R), UNREGISTERED (U)**

Boston Stock Exchange (R)	Pacific Stock Exchange (R)
Cincinnati Stock Exchange (R)	Philadelphia Stock Exchange (R)
Colorado Stock Exchange (U)	Pittsburgh Stock Exchange (R)
Detroit Stock Exchange (U)	Richmond Stock Exchange (U)
Honolulu Stock Exchange (R)	Salt Lake City Stock Exchange (R)
Midwest Stock Exchange (R)	Spokane Stock Exchange (R)
National Stock Exchange (R)	Wheeling Stock Exchange (U)

Options Exchange (CBOE), as well as on the American Stock Exchange, the Pacific Stock Exchange, and the Philadelphia Stock Exchange. The dominant options exchange is the CBOE, which was established in 1973. The CBOE, like other exchanges, has membership, listing, and trading requirements. Usually an option for the purchase (a call) or sale (a put) of a given financial asset is listed on only one of the options exchanges, although dual listing does sometimes occur. Options exchanges deal only in security options; options to purchase or sell property are not traded in this marketplace.

Futures exchanges

Futures, which are contracts guaranteeing future delivery of some commodity, foreign currency, or financial instrument at a specified price at a given future date, are purchased and sold on a variety of exchanges. The dominant exchange on which commodity and financial futures are traded is the Chicago Board of Trade (CBT). It provides an organized forum in which members can make transactions in any of the listed commodity and financial futures contracts. There are a number of other futures exchanges, some of which specialize in certain commodities rather than the broad spectrum listed on the CBT. The larger of these exchanges include the Kansas City Board of Trade, the Minneapolis Grain Exchange, the Winnipeg Grain Exchange, the Chicago Mercantile Exchange, the New York Coffee, Sugar, and Cocoa Exchange, the New York Cotton Exchange, and the Commodities Exchange, Inc., in New York. The major currency futures exchange, on which financial futures are also traded, is the International Monetary Market (IMM), which is actually part of the Chicago Mercantile Exchange. The newest of these exchanges, the New York Futures Exchange (NYFE), is a subsidiary of the NYSE and deals only in financial futures.

The Over-the-Counter Market

The over-the-counter market is not a specific institution; rather, it is another way of trading securities. It accounts for about 33 percent of *all* shares traded. Securities traded in this market are sometimes called *unlisted* securities. The over-the-counter (OTC) market is the result of an intangible relationship among purchasers and sellers of securities. The active traders in this market are linked by a sophisticated telecommunications network, and the prices at which securities are traded are determined by both competitive bids and negotiation. The actual process depends on the general activity of the security. A numerical majority of stocks are traded over the counter, as are most government and corporate bonds. Of the 30,000 issues traded over the counter, approximately 5,000 have an active market in which frequent transactions take place. Over 90 percent of all corporate bonds, some of which are also listed on the NYSE, are traded in the OTC market.

New issues and secondary distributions

In order to create a continuous market for unlisted securities, the OTC market also provides a forum in which new public issues, both listed and unlisted, are sold. If they are listed, subsequent transactions will be made on the appropriate organized securities exchange; unlisted securities will continue to trade in the OTC market. *Secondary distributions* involve the sale of a large block of securities by a major shareholder and are also often made in the OTC market rather than on the appropriate organized exchange. This is done to minimize the potentially negative effects of such a transaction on the price of listed securities.

The role of dealers

The market price of OTC securities results from a matchng of the forces of supply and demand for the security by traders known as *dealers*. Each makes markets in certain securities by offering to buy or sell at stated prices. Thus, unlike the organized exchanges (where the buyer and seller of a security are brought together by a broker), these dealers are always the second party to a transaction. For example, a dealer making a market in Lomax Enterprises might offer to buy shares from investors at $29.50 and sell shares to other investors at $31. The *bid price* is the highest price offered by the dealer to purchase a given security; the *ask price* is the lowest price at which the dealer is willing to sell the security. As an investor, a person could *sell* stock in Lomax Enterprises at the (lower) bid price of $29.50 and *buy* it at the (higher) ask price of $31. The dealer makes a profit from the spread between the bid and the ask price.

NASDAQ

OTC dealers are linked with the purchasers and sellers of securities through the *National Association of Securities Dealers Automated Quotation (NASDAQ)* system, an automated system that provides up-to-date bid and ask prices on thousands of selected, highly active OTC securities. NASDAQ has provided a great deal of continuity in the OTC market because it allows buyers and sellers to locate one another easily. To trade in securities not quoted on NASDAQ, purchasers and sellers must find each other through references or through known market makers in the securities.

Third and fourth markets

The *third market* is the name given to over-the-counter transactions made in securities listed on the NYSE, AMEX, or one of the other organized exchanges. It exists to serve the needs of large institutional investors, such as mutual funds and

BOX 2.1 A PROFILE OF SHAREOWNERS IN PUBLIC CORPORATIONS

The NYSE's 1981 Shareownership Survey revealed a continuing resurgence of shareownership in the United States. After a nearly 20% increase in individual shareowners between 1975 and 1980, the number of shareowners rose by another 2.1 million (or 6.8%) between mid-1980 and mid-1981. The incidence of shareownership among adults is one-in-five in the latest survey.

NYSE-listed stocks continued to show the largest numerical increase in ownership— nearly 2.3 million. Over three-in-four of all shareowners owned at least one NYSE-listed issue in 1981 compared with 71% in 1975. This represented nearly a 10% increase in NYSE-listed shareownership.

Adult male shareowners slightly outnumbered female owners in 1981 (15.8 million to 14.2 million) as they did in 1980. In the last several surveys, the number of male vs. female shareowners has tended to seesaw around the 50-50 mark. The median age of shareowners has stabilized at a relatively youthful 46—as contrasted with $52\frac{1}{2}$ years in 1975. Even more striking, the new wave of shareowners is increasingly younger. The 9 million new shareowners who entered the market between January 1975 and June 1981 have a median age of 34.

Portfolio values, which decreased substantially between 1975 and 1980, rose from a median of $4,000 in 1980 to $5,450 in 1981. Nearly 60% of individual shareowners' portfolios were valued at under $10,000 and about one-in-four valued at $25,000 and over.

Median shareowner income increased from $27,750 to $29,200 in the period covered by the latest survey, a result which roughly parallels the percentage increase for the general population over the same period. Fewer than one-fifth of adult shareowners (18.2%) have an income of $50,000 and over.

HIGHLIGHTS OF SEVEN NYSE SHAREOWNER SURVEYS

	1959	1962	1965	1970	1975	1980	1981
Number of individual shareowners (thousands)	12,490	17,010	20,120	30,850	25,270	30,200	32,260
Number owning shares listed on NYSE (thousands)	8,510	11,020	12,430	18,290	17,950	23,804	26,084

life insurance companies, by allowing them to make large transactions at a reduced cost. These transactions are typically handled by firms or dealers that are not members of an organized securities exchange. For bringing together large buyers and sellers, these firms charge commissions below those charged for making similar transactions on the associated securities exchange. Institutional investors are thus often able to realize sizable savings in brokerage commissions as well as to have minimal impact on the price of the transaction. In recent years, the introduction of negotiated commissions on the organized exchanges has somewhat reduced the importance of this market.

BOX 2.1 *Continued*

	1959	1962	1965	1970	1975	1980	1981
Adult shareowner incidence in population	1 in 8	1 in 6	1 in 6	1 in 4	1 in 6	1 in 5	1 in 5
Median household income (prior year)	$7,000	$8,600	$9,500	$13,500	$19,000	$27,750	$29,200
Number of adult shareowners with household income:							
under $10,000 (thousands)	9,340	10,340	10,080	8,170	3,420	1,742	2,164
$10,000 & over (thousands)	2,740	5,920	8,410	20,130	19,970	25,715	26,912
$15,000 & over (thousands)	1,019	2,823	3,796	12,709	15,420	22,535	24,375
$25,000 & over (thousands)	319	780	1,073	4,114	6,642	15,605	17,547
$50,000 & over (thousands)	N/A	N/A	N/A	N/A	1,216	3,982	5,457
Number of adult female shareowners (thousands)	6,350	8,290	9,430	14,290	11,750	13,696	14,154
Number of adult male shareowners (thousands)	5,740	7,970	9,060	14,340	11,630	14,196	15,785
Median age	49	48	49	48	53	46	46

Note: Characteristics are for *all* individual shareowners, except where "adult" is designated.
ʳRevised to reflect 1980 U.S. Census data. N/A = Not available.
Source: The New York Stock Exchange 1982 Fact Book. New York: The New York Stock Exchange, 1982, p. 47.

The *fourth market* is the name given to transactions made directly between large institutional buyers and sellers. Unlike the third market, fourth-market transactions bypass the dealer. But in order to find a suitable seller or buyer, an institution may hire a firm to facilitate the transaction.

Regulation of Securities Markets

As a result of various abuses and misrepresentations, a number of state and federal laws have been enacted to provide for adequate and accurate disclosure of information to potential and existing investors. Such laws also regulate the activities of various participants in the securities markets. State laws, which regulate the sale of securities within state borders, are commonly called "blue sky laws" because they are intended to prevent investors from being sold nothing but "blue sky." These laws typically establish procedures for regulating both security issues and sellers of securities doing business within the state. As part of the process, most states have a regulatory body, such as a state securities commission, that is charged with the enforcement of the related state statutes. But the most important securities laws are those enacted by the federal government.

Securities Act of 1933

This act was passed by Congress to ensure full disclosure of information with respect to new security issues and prevent a stock market collapse similar to that which occurred in 1929–1932. It requires the issuer of a new security to file a registration statement containing information with respect to the new issue with the Securities and Exchange Commission (SEC). The firm cannot sell the security until the SEC approves the registration statement; this usually takes about 20 days.

One portion of the registration statement, called the *prospectus,* summarizes the registration data. During the waiting period between filing the statement and its approval, a *red herring,* which is a statement indicating the tentative nature of the offer, is printed in red on the prospectus. Once the statement has been approved, the new security issue can be offered for sale if the prospectus is made available to all interested parties. If the registration statement is found to be fraudulent, the SEC will reject the issue and may also sue the directors and others responsible for the misrepresentation. *Approval of the registration statement by the SEC does not mean the security is a good investment; it only indicates that the facts presented in the statement appear to reflect the firm's true position.*

Securities Exchange Act of 1934

This act expanded the scope of federal regulation and formally established the SEC as the agency in charge of the administration of federal securities laws. The act established the SEC's power to regulate the organized securities exchanges and over-the-counter markets by extending disclosure requirements to outstanding securities. It required the stock exchanges as well as the stocks traded on them to be registered with the SEC.

As a result of this act, the regulatory power of the SEC became all-encompassing: it covered exchanges, their members, brokers in the over-the-counter market, and the securities traded in these markets. Each of these participants is required to file registration statements and additional financial data with the SEC and must periodically update such data. The act has been instrumental in providing adequate disclosure of facts on both new issues and outstanding issues that are traded in the secondary markets. The 1934 act, which has been amended a few times over the years, along with the Securities Act of 1933, remain the key pieces of legislation that protect participants in the securities markets.

Maloney Act of 1938

This act, which was in fact an amendment to the Securities Exchange Act of 1934, provided for the establishment of trade associations for the purpose of self-regulation within the securities industry. The act required such associations to register with the SEC. Since its passage, only one such trade association, The National Association of Securities Dealers (NASD), has been formed. NASD members include more than 90 percent of the nation's securities firms. Membership in NASD is a must for most firms, since it allows member firms to make transactions with other member firms at rates below those charged to nonmembers. Today all securities firms that are not members of NASD must agree to be supervised directly by the SEC. Because the SEC has the power to revoke NASD's registration, its power over this organization is the same as over the exchanges. In addition to its self-regulatory role, NASD has greatly streamlined the functioning of the over-the-counter market by creating NASDAQ. From the viewpoint of the individual investor, the establishment of the NASD has created a convenient mechanism that makes transactions as well as price quotations in OTC securities readily available.

Investment Company Act of 1940

This act was passed to protect those purchasing investment company shares. An investment company is one that obtains funds by selling its shares to numerous investors and uses the proceeds to purchase securities. By buying investment company shares, an investor is indirectly investing in a wide variety of securities. There are two types of investment companies: *closed-end companies,* in which the number of shares sold is limited, and *open-end companies,* in which there is no limit on the number of shares outstanding. The dominant type of investment company, the open-end or mutual fund, is discussed in detail in Chapter 15.

The Investment Company Act of 1940 established rules and regulations for investment companies and formally authorized the SEC to regulate their practices and procedures. It required the investment companies to register with the SEC and to fulfill certain disclosure requirements. The act was amended in 1970 to prohibit investment companies from paying excessive fees to their advisors as well as from charging excessive commissions to purchasers of company shares. From the point of view of the individual investor, this act provides protection against inadequate or inaccurate disclosure of information, and against being charged excessive fees indirectly by the fund's advisors, and directly through commissions paid to purchase company shares.

Investment Advisors Act of 1940

This act was passed to protect investors against potential abuses by investment advisors, who are persons hired by investors to advise them about security investments. It was passed to make sure that advisors disclose all relevant information about their backgrounds, conflicts of interest, and so on, as well as about any investments they recommend. The act requires advisors to register and file periodic reports with the SEC. A 1960 amendment extended the SEC's powers to permit inspection of the records of investment advisors and revocation of the registration of advisors who violate the act's provisions. *This act does not provide any guarantee of competence on the part of advisors; it only helps to protect the investor against fraudulent and unethical practices by the advisor.*

TABLE 2.3   BEAR MARKETS SINCE 1919

Year	Year
1977–1982	1957
1973–1974	1948–1949
1971	1946
1968–1970	1939–1942
1966	1937–1938
1961–1962	1929–1932
1960	1919–1921

Source: Adapted from Ben Branch, *Fundamentals of Investing* (Santa Barbara, Calif.: Wiley, 1976), p. 160.

General Market Conditions: Bull or Bear

Conditions in the securities markets are commonly classified as bull or bear, depending on whether the general level of prices is rising (a bull market) or falling (a bear market). Changing market conditions generally stem from changes in investor attitudes, changes in economic activity, and government actions aimed at stimulating or slowing down the level of economic activity. *Bull markets* are favorable markets normally associated with investor optimism, economic recovery, and governmental stimulus; *bear markets* are unfavorable markets normally associated with investor pessimism, economic slowdowns, and government restraint. Over the past 60 or so years, the behavior of the stock market has been generally bullish, reflecting the growth and prosperity of the economy. However, it had been somewhat bearish in recent years until the remarkable stock market recovery that started in August of 1982—a record-breaking bull market that lifted the price of an average share of stock nearly 70 percent in a little over a year. Table 2.3 lists the 14 bear markets experienced since 1919. In general, the small investor experiences lower (or negative) returns on common stock investments during a bear market. Of course, during bear markets many investors will invest in alternative vehicles to obtain higher and less risky returns. It is not unusual to find securities that are bullish in a bear market or bearish in a bull market. Market conditions are difficult to predict and usually can be identified only after they exist. The actual assessment of market conditions and the use of this information by the individual investor will be described in greater detail in Chapter 3.

MAKING SECURITY TRANSACTIONS

Understanding the structure and functioning of the securities markets is just the first step in developing a sound investment program; an investor must also be able to enter these markets to make transactions. The individual investor must understand the procedures required to make transactions, as well as the various types of orders that can be placed. It is also important to have an appreciation of the basic types of transactions and their associated costs.

Stockbrokers

Stockbrokers, or account executives, or financial consultants as they are some-times called, enable investors to purchase and sell securities. They must be licensed by the exchanges on which they place orders and abide by the ethical guidelines of the exchanges and the SEC. Stockbrokers work for the brokerage firms that own seats on the organized securities exchanges. Members of the securities exchange actually execute orders transmitted to them by the brokers in the various sales offices. For example, the largest brokerage firm, Merrill Lynch, Pierce, Fenner & Smith, has offices in most major cities in the United States. Orders from these offices are transmitted to the main office of Merrill Lynch and then to the floor of the stock exchange (NYSE, AMEX), where they are executed. Confirmation of the order is sent back to the broker placing the order, who then relays it to the customer. This process, which can be carried out in a matter of minutes with the use of sophisticated tele-communications networks, is illustrated in Figure 2.3.

Orders for over-the-counter securities must be executed through market makers, who are dealers specializing in that security. The NASDAQ system, along with the available information on who makes markets in certain securities, allows the brokers to execute orders in OTC securities. Normally, OTC transactions can be executed rapidly, since most market makers maintain inventories of the securities in which they deal. Although the procedure for executing orders on organized exchanges differs from that in the OTC market, an investor always places orders with a broker in the same manner, regardless of the market in which the security is traded.

Brokerage services

The primary activity of stockbrokers involves making purchase and sale trans-actions as requested by clients. Account executives do not actually buy or sell se-curities; they only execute their clients' transactions at the best possible price. In addition, stockbrokers offer clients a variety of other services. For example, the stock-brokerage firm normally provides a wide variety of free information ranging from stock and bond guides that summarize the activity of securities to research reports on specific securities or industries. Quite often the firm will have a research staff that periodically issues analyses of economic, market, industry, or company behavior and relates these reports to recommendations it makes to buy or sell certain securities. It is the job of the stockbroker to provide the client with the type of information most relevant to the client's investment goals. As a client of a large brokerage firm, you can expect to receive bulletins discussing market activity and possibly including a recommended investment list. Also, you will receive a statement describing all your transactions for the month and showing commission charges, interest charges, div-idends received, interest received, and your account balance.

Today, most brokerage firms will invest idle cash left in a customer's account in a money market fund, allowing the customer to earn a reasonable rate of interest on these balances. Such arrangements help the investor to manage cash effectively and earn as much as possible on temporarily idle funds. Most brokerage offices also have electronic equipment of some sort that provides up-to-the-minute stock price quotations and world news. Price information can be obtained from the quotation

1. The account executive discusses a customer's order and will convey it to the stock exchange via a telecommunications terminal.

2. The firm's floor broker executes the sale.

3. The confirmation is teletyped back to the broker.

4. The account executive notifies the customer that the transaction has been made.

Figure 2.3 **How Stocks Are Bought and Sold on the New York Stock Exchange.**
(*Sources:* Photos 1, 3, and 4 courtesy of Prudential-Bache, Inc.; photo 2 courtesy of The New York Stock Exchange.)

board (a large screen that electronically displays all NYSE and AMEX security transactions within minutes after they take place) or by keying into the telequote system, which relies on a computer terminal to provide a capsule description of almost all securities and their prices. World news, which can significantly affect the stock market, is obtained from a wire service subscribed to by the brokerage office. Moreover, most offices have a reference library available for use by the firm's clients.

Brokerage firms will also hold your certificates for safekeeping. The stocks kept by the firm in this manner are said to be held in "street name," since the broker can liquidate them for you without having to obtain your signature. You are protected against the loss of the securities or cash held by your broker by the Securities Investor Protection Corporation (SIPC), an agency of the federal government established by the Securities Investor Protection Act of 1970. SIPC was established to protect customer accounts against the consequences of financial failure of the brokerage firm. It insures each customer's account for up to $500,000 of securities held by the brokerage firm and up to $100,000 in cash balances. Note, however, that SIPC insurance does *not* guarantee that the dollar value of the securities will be recovered; it only guarantees that the securities themselves will be returned. Some brokerage firms insure certain customer accounts for amounts in excess of the required $500,000 of SIPC insurance. Certainly, in light of the diversity and quality of services available among brokerage houses, careful consideration should be given not only to the selection of an individual broker (the *person* you deal with), but also to the choice of a *firm*.

Selecting a stockbroker

You should select a stockbroker who understands your investment goals and who can effectively assist you in pursuing these goals. If you choose a broker whose own disposition toward investing is quite similar to yours, you should be able to avoid conflict and establish a solid working relationship. It is probably best to ask friends or business associates to recommend a broker. It is not important—and often not even advisable—to know your stockbroker personally! A strict business relationship eliminates the possibility that social concerns will interfere with achievement of your investment goals. This does not mean, of course, that your broker's sole interest should be commissions. Responsible brokers make a concerted effort to establish a long-term broker-client relationship with their clients; they do not "churn accounts"—that is, attempt to have their clients make many transactions simply in order to generate numerous and sizable commissions. In addition, consideration should be given to the cost and types of services available from the firm with which the broker is affiliated. Often, significant differences can be found. The broker you select should be the person you believe best understands your investment goals and will provide the best service at the lowest possible cost to you.

Investors who wish merely to make transactions and are not interested in obtaining the full array of brokerage services mentioned above should probably consider using a *discount broker*. These brokers merely make transactions for customers—they provide little or no research information or investment advice. Transactions are initiated by calling a toll-free number; the discount broker then confirms the transaction by return mail. The rapidly growing volume of business done by discount brokers attests to their success, which has served as an incentive for other financial institutions, such as banks and insurance companies, to enter the brokerage business. The largest of the discounters—Charles Schwab and Company—was acquired by Bank of America for just that purpose. Many other banks and savings institutions are making discount brokerage services available and, as noted in Chapter 1, the financial markets appear to be heading toward the supermarket style, in which an investor's total financial needs are met in one place.

Opening an account

To open an account, the broker will ask the customer to fill out various documents that establish a legal relationship between the customer and the broker. By filling out and signing a signature card and a personal data card, the client gives the broker the information needed to identify the customer's account. The stockbroker must also have a reasonable understanding of a client's personal financial situation in order to assess his or her investment goals and also to be sure that the client can pay for what he or she orders. In addition to personal information, instructions relating to the transfer and custody of securities must also be given to the broker. If the customer wishes to borrow money in order to make transactions, a *margin account* will be established (the mechanics of margin accounts are described in a later section of this chapter). If the customer is acting as a trustee, an executor, or is a corporation, additional documents will be necessary to establish the account. No laws or rules prohibit an investor from establishing accounts with more than one stockbroker. Many investors establish accounts at different firms in order to obtain the benefit and opinions of a more diverse group of brokers.

Types of accounts

A number of different types of accounts can be established with a stockbroker. We will now look briefly at several of the more popular types.

Single or joint.   A brokerage account may be either single or joint. Joint accounts are most common between husband and wife or parent and child. The account of a minor (a person less than 18 years of age) is a custodial account in which a parent or guardian must be part of all transactions. Sometimes a married couple will have two or more accounts—each spouse will have a single account and together they will have a joint account. Regardless of which form of account is maintained, the name(s) of the account holder(s) is used to identify the account.

Cash or margin.   A *cash account* is one in which the customer can make only cash transactions; this is the most common type of account. Customers can initiate transactions via the phone, even though they may not have sufficient cash in their account to cover the cost of the transaction. They are given five business days in which to get the cash to the brokerage firm; the firm is likewise given five business days in which to deposit the proceeds from the sale of securities in the customer's account. A *margin account* is an account in which the customer has been extended

Don't tell me it was all your stockbroker's fault.
Remember I was your stockbroker.

borrowing power by the brokerage firm. By leaving securities with the firm to be held as collateral, the customer is permitted to borrow a prespecified proportion of the purchase price. Prior to opening a margin account, the brokerage firm will assess the creditworthiness of the customer, and it will of course charge the customer a specified rate of interest on borrowings. A discussion of margin transactions is included in Chapter 5.

Discretionary. Occasionally a customer will establish a discretionary account with a broker. A *discretionary account* is one in which the broker can use his discretion to make purchase and sale transactions on behalf of the customer. The organized exchanges are generally against this practice; they permit it only when an officer of the brokerage firm is involved in the supervision of such an account. A more limited type of discretionary account permits a broker to buy or sell a stated amount of a given security (as specified by the customer) at a time or price the broker believes to be in the customer's best interest. The decision to extend discretionary privileges to the broker depends on a customer's confidence in the broker, as well as the amount of time the customer has to devote to trading. Such accounts are usually established by wealthy investors rather than by the individual investor of moderate means.

Odd-lot or round-lot transactions

Security transactions can be made in either odd or round lots. An odd lot consists of less than 100 shares of a security, while a round lot is a 100-share unit

BOX 2.2 AND NOW, THE ALL-NIGHT BROKER

Eureka! The answer to your money worries hits you in a dream, and you know you'll never be able to get back to sleep until you do something about it. But it's 2:30 a.m.! You sigh in resignation. Surely there's no chance to act on the hot flash at that uncivilized hour. Or is there?

Fear not, night people, the age of the 24-hour broker may be upon us. Some of those same folks who brought you no-frills brokering in a big way are pioneering stock, commodity and other financial trading services that never close.

The firm that broke ground in this area, Eastern Capital Corporation, seems to believe that all-night brokering is an idea whose time has definitely come. The Boston-based discount broker launched its insomniac service to a sleepy start about a year ago, but an Eastern spokesman says the idea is now catching on, with business growing by leaps and bounds. Charles Schwab & Co. Inc., the country's largest discount brokerage outfit, also has a 24-hour service that has been picking up steam.

Eastern's contribution to the late-late show of the investment scene is playing to increasingly large audiences of clients who, for one reason or another, can't or won't conduct their business during "normal" trading hours. These people, says Leland Bohl, an Eastern Capital vice president, include professional people such as pilots, surgeons, or night-shift plant managers who sleep during the day. Late night service also appeals to investors who want to make their decisions based on closing prices.

People in the Pacific time zone who want orders to go through at the opening of business on the East Coast the next day are also using the late night phone lines.

And then there are those people who simply do it for the novelty of planning investment moves in the midnight hours. According to Eastern's Mr. Bohl, the cadre of people using the 24-hour service regularly has been growing. But there are lively nights, and there are dead ones. The amount of activity depends in part on what's going on in the world. When there is an international crisis of some sort going on, Eastern's night-shift traders may receive more calls than they can handle. Lots of investors, for example, will be looking to see how their gold is doing, or may want to buy or sell depending on what is happening.

During the day, Mr. Bohl says, Eastern Capital may receive 10,000 calls. The night shift, from 5:00 to midnight, may log another 2,000 or so. The graveyard shift, from midnight to 8:00 a.m. could dig up another few hundred to 1,000 calls.

With four people working the night shift, and three in the graveyard, investors may find telephone lines busy more often at night. Nonetheless, the 24-hour idea seems to be working out well for investors, and for Eastern which says the experiment is now a permanent part of its business.

Both Charles Schwab & Co. and Eastern Capital say that from the investor's standpoint, doing business in the wee hours works the same as other times. There are no added charges, they say, and all customers are able to use the service.

If you were out of touch during the day, but you're dying to know what investment fortunes befell you, the all-night brokers can fill you in. Now the urge to act on your finances that comes to you in the night need no longer be ignored.

Source: Daniel M. Kehrer, "And Now, The All-Night Broker." *FACT,* January 1983, p. 64.

or multiple thereof. Thus, you would be dealing in an odd lot if you bought, say, 25 shares of stock, but a round lot if you bought 200 shares; a trade of 225 shares would be a combination of an odd and a round lot. Since all transactions made on the floor of the major stock exchanges are made in round lots, the purchase or sale of odd lots usually requires the assistance of the specialist dealing in the given security on the floor of the exchange. Usually, an additional fee is charged for the specialist's services in making these transactions. Small investors in the early stages of their investment programs are primarily responsible for odd-lot transactions.

Basic Types of Orders

Different types of orders are used to make security transactions. The type placed normally depends on the investor's goals and expectations with respect to the given transaction. The three basic types of orders are the market order, the limit order, and the stop-loss order.

Market order

An order to buy or sell stock at the best price available at the time the order is placed is a *market order.* It is usually the quickest way to have orders filled, since market orders are usually executed as soon as they reach the exchange floor or are received by the market maker. The process by which these orders are transacted was described earlier and shown in Figure 2.3. Because of the speed with which market orders are executed, the buyer or seller of a security can be sure that the price at which the order is transacted will be very close to the market price prevailing at the time the order was placed.

Limit order

An order to buy at a specified price or lower, or sell at or above a specified price, is known as a *limit order.* When a limit order is placed, the broker transmits it to a specialist dealing in the security on the floor of the exchange. The specialist makes a notation in his or her book indicating the number of shares and price of the limit order. The order is executed as soon as the specified market price (or better) exists and all other orders with precedence (similar orders received earlier, or buy orders at a higher specified price or sell orders at a lower specified price) have been satisfied. The order can be placed to remain in effect until a certain date or until canceled; the latter type is called a *GTC* or *good 'til canceled* order. Specialists may periodically clear their books, thereby eliminating all unexecuted limit orders.

Assume, by way of example, that you place a limit order to buy 100 shares of a stock currently selling at 30½ (security market terminology for $30.50) at a limit price of $30. Once the specialist has cleared all similar orders received before yours, and once the market price of the stock has fallen to $30 or less, the order is executed. It is possible, of course, that your order might expire (if it is not a GTC order) before the stock price drops to $30. Although a limit order can be quite effective, it can also keep you from making a transaction. If, for instance, you wish to buy at $30 or less and the stock price moves from its current $30.50 price to $42 while you are waiting, your limit order has caused you to forgo the opportunity to make a profit of $11.50 per share ($42 − $30.50). Had you placed a market order, this profit of $11.50 would have been yours. Limit orders for the sale of a stock are also disadvantageous when the stock price closely approaches but does not attain the minimum sale limit before dropping substantially. Generally speaking, limit orders are most effective when the price of a stock is known to fluctuate greatly, since there is then a better chance that the order will be executed.

Stop-loss order

An order to sell a stock when its market price reaches or drops below a specified level is called a *stop-loss* or *stop order*. Stop-loss orders are *suspended orders* that are placed on stocks that are already owned. Since it is a suspended order, the order to sell the stock will not be executed until the stock drops to a certain prespecified price. The stop-loss order is placed on the specialist's book and becomes active once the stop price has been reached. When activated, the stop order becomes a market order to sell the security at the best price available. Because of this, it is possible that the actual price at which the sale is made could be well below the price at which the stop was initiated. These orders are used to protect the investor against the adverse effects of a rapid decline in share price. For example, assume you own 100 shares of Willard Industries, which is currently selling for $35 per share. Because you believe the stock price could decline rapidly at any time, you place a stop order to sell at $30. If the stock price does in fact drop to $30, the specialist will sell the 100 shares of Willard Industries at the best price available at that time. But if the market price declines to $28 prior to the sale, you will receive less than $30 per share. Of course, if the market price stays above $30 per share you will have lost nothing as a result of placing the order, as the stop order will never be initiated. Often investors will raise the level of the stop as the price of the stock rises; such action will help to lock in a higher profit when the price is increasing. Stop orders can be placed to *buy* a stock, though they are far less common than sell orders. For example, an investor may place a stop order to buy 100 shares of MJ Enterprises, currently selling for $70 per share, once its price drops to, say, $65—the stop price.

Basic Types of Transactions

In addition to a variety of orders, a number of basic types of security transactions can be made. Each type of transaction is available to investors who meet certain requirements established by various government agencies as well as by brokerage firms. Although the various types of transactions can be used in a number of ways to meet investment objectives, only the most popular use of each transaction is described here. The three most common types of transactions are the long purchase, the short sale, and the margin purchase.

Long purchase

The *long purchase* refers to the most common type of transaction, in which investors buy securities in the hope that they will increase in value and can be sold at a later date at a profit. The object is to buy low and sell high. Each of the basic types of orders described above can be used with long transactions. Because investors generally expect the price of the security to rise over the period of time they plan to hold it, their return comes from any dividends or interest received during the ownership period, plus the difference between the price at which they sell the security and the price paid to purchase it (capital gains). This return, of course, would have to be reduced by the brokerage fees paid to purchase and sell the securities.

Ignoring any dividends (or interest) and brokerage fees, the long purchase can be illustrated by using a simple example. After studying various aspects of Magnum Manufacturing, Inc., Ron Johnson is convinced that its common stock, which is currently selling for $20 per share, will increase in value over the next few years. Based on his analysis, Ron expects the stock price to rise to $30 per share within two years. He places a limit order and buys a round lot (100 shares) of Magnum for $20. If the stock price rises to, say, $40 per share, Ron will profit from his long purchase; if it drops below $20 per share, he will experience a loss on the transaction. It should be clear that one of the major motivating factors in making a long trans-action is an expected rise in the price of the security. Of course, the impact of dividends or interest on these transactions is also an important consideration; this effect will be discussed in greater detail in Chapter 4.

Short sale

Although the long purchase is most common, some investors engage in *short selling,* which can be thought of as selling high and buying low. Long transactions are made in anticipation of price increases; short transactions are made in antici-pation of price decreases. When an investor sells a security short, the broker borrows the security from someone else and then sells it on the investor's behalf. The bor-rowed shares, of course, must be replaced by the short seller when the transaction is closed. If the investor can repurchase the shares at a lower price in the future, profit will be earned and can be measured by the difference between the proceeds of the initial sale and the repurchase price. If the short seller ends up repurchasing the shares at a higher price than he sold them for, he sustains a loss.

The basic short-sale transaction can be illustrated using a simple example. Imagine that Mary Alexander, after investigating various factors, is convinced that the market price of Trenton, Inc., will decline over the next several months. In order to earn a profit from this situation, Mary decides to sell short 100 shares of the stock, which is currently selling for $40 per share. After fulfilling certain requirements, Mary's broker, Rusty Griffin, borrows the shares and sells them, receiving proceeds of $4,000. Mary does not receive the proceeds from this sale; instead, they are held by the brokerage firm as a condition of the short sale. If the price of the stock drops as Mary expects and she repurchases it later at a lower price than she sold it for, she will earn a profit. If she can buy it back at $25, she stands to make $15 per share, since she sold it at a price of $40 per share. On the other hand, if the price of the stock were to rise above $40 per share prior to her repurchase, she would sustain a loss on the transaction. When Mary, or any person, sells short, she is betting on a price decline; if the guess is wrong, the person suffers a loss. Mary, of course, will have to pay brokerage fees on the short-sale transaction (short sales will be explored more fully in Chapter 5).

Margin purchase

Security purchases do not have to be made on a cash basis; borrowed funds can be used. This is called a *margin purchase.* The Federal Reserve Board, which governs our banking system, sets the requirements that specify how much of the dollar price of a security must be the purchaser's own funds. By raising or lowering margin requirements, the Fed can depress or stimulate activity in the securities markets. Margin purchases must be approved by a broker. The brokerage firm then loans the purchaser the needed funds and retains the securities purchased as collateral. Some brokerage firms have in-house margin requirements that are stricter than those of the Fed. Margin requirements have most recently been around 50 percent. Before we illustrate the basics of margin purchases, we need to highlight two points: (1) Margin is used to make both long- and short-sale transactions; and (2) margin purchasers must pay interest at a specified rate on what they borrow.

A simple example will help to clarify the basic margin transaction. Jeffrey Lawrence wishes to purchase 70 shares of Universal Fiber common stock, which is currently selling for $63.50 per share. Since the prevailing margin requirement is 50 percent, Jeffrey will have to put up only 50 percent of the total purchase price of $4,445 ($63.50 per share × 70 shares), or $2,222.50 in cash. The remaining $2,222.50 will be lent to Jeffrey by his brokerage firm. Jeffrey will, of course, have to pay interest to his broker on the $2,222.50 he borrows, along with the applicable brokerage fees. It should be clear that with the use of margin, an investor can purchase more securities than he or she could afford on a strict cash basis and therefore can magnify his or her returns.

Transaction Costs

There are normally certain costs associated with making investment transactions. These costs are usually levied on both the purchase and the sale of securities. Transactions costs must be paid by the investor to compensate the broker for executing the transaction. It is difficult, if not impossible, for an investor wishing to buy or sell a given investment vehicle to find a suitable counterpart, on his own, with which to negotiate a transaction. Rather than going through the trouble of direct negotiation, investors make transactions through brokers or dealers. The structure and magnitude of transaction costs need to be considered when making investment decisions, since they affect returns.

Before describing specific costs, we need to look at the commissions charged by stockbrokers. With the passage of the Securities Acts Amendments of 1975, brokers have been permitted to charge whatever commission they deem appropriate. Most firms have established *fixed commission schedules* that are applicable to small transactions, which are the ones most often made by individual investors. On large institutional transactions, *negotiated commissions* are usually used. Brokerage firms can thus compete not only on the basis of services offered, but also on a cost basis. Negotiated commissions are also available to individual investors who maintain sizable accounts—typically in the range of $25,000 or more.

Stocks

The commissions charged on stock transactions are usually based on a schedule such as the one given in Table 2.4. Although not shown in the table, commissions on multiple round lots are lower (on a per share basis) than commissions on a single round-lot transaction. It should be clear from an analysis of Table 2.4 that because of the fixed cost component, the per share brokerage commission on an odd-lot

TABLE 2.4   TYPICAL BROKERAGE FEES ON A STOCK TRANSACTION (MARCH 1983)

Value of Transaction	Fees for an Odd Lot or 100 Shares
Under $800	$ 8.43 + 2.70% of the value of the transaction
$800–$2,500	$16.85 + 1.70% of the value of the transaction
$2,500–$5,000	$29.50 + 1.30% of the value of the transaction
Above $5,000	$94.50

Source: A major brokerage house.

transaction would be higher than on a similarly valued round-lot transaction. In addition, on odd-lot transactions an odd-lot differential of 12.5 cents per share on shares costing less than $40 each and 25 cents per share on shares costing more than $40 is sometimes levied. Using the fee schedule given in Table 2.4, along with the odd-lot differential, the brokerage fees on the purchase of 60 shares of Jaxto, Inc., at $30 per share, a total transaction value of $1,800, would be

Basic fee:
$16.85 + 1.7% ($1,800) = $16.85 + $30.60 = $47.45
Odd-lot differential:
12.5¢ per share × 60 shares   7.50
    Total commission   = $54.95

A common rule of thumb suggests that the brokerage fee on a round-lot stock transaction equals between 1.5 and 3 percent of the value of the transaction. The brokerage fees described here apply to both the purchase and the sale transaction. On sale transactions, certain transfer taxes are charged by the state in which the transaction takes place, and a small federal registration fee is levied by the SEC.

A discount broker would charge substantially less for the same transaction. Most discounters charge a minimum fee to discourage small orders. For example, Rose and Company of Chicago charges a flat fee of $25 for any 100-share transaction. Figure 2.4 shows an ad placed by Charles Schwab and Company, a discounter, showing commission savings on three different transactions. Depending on the size and the type of transaction, the discount broker can typically save investors between 30 and 70 percent of the commission charged by the full-service broker. The savings from the discounter are substantial, and investors must weigh the added commissions they pay a full-service broker against the value of the advice they receive, since that is the only major difference between the discount and the full-service broker.

Bonds

Brokerage commissions on bond transactions range from $2.50 to $30 per bond for $1,000 corporate bonds. Brokerage firms typically charge a minimum fee

BOX 2.3 SHOULD YOU USE A DISCOUNT BROKER?

You can save up to 50 percent or more on commissions if you buy and sell securities through a discount broker. But these bargain-rate firms aren't for everyone. Here's what you should know.

Until a few years ago, most stock brokers charged about the same fees for securities transactions, taking their cue from minimum rate schedules set by the New York Stock Exchange. But on May 1, 1975, the Securities and Exchange Commission (SEC) abolished minimum schedules in order to make all rates negotiable.

The big winners from the SEC ruling were institutional investors—banks, pension funds, and insurance and mutual fund companies who could deal from strength because of their large volume of trading. Small investors didn't fare so well. In fact, their average commissions have increased about 10 percent from the old minimum schedules, while institutional rates have dropped considerably.

How can small investors save?

One way is to use the services of discount brokers—the "no frills" traders of the securities industry. Their prime purpose is simply to execute your "buy" and "sell" orders. Most deal strictly with stocks and bonds traded on the major exchanges and over the counter. Some discounters also handle products such as options.

By holding their services to the basics, discounters minimize their overhead expenses and pass those savings on to their customers in the form of reduced commissions. Discounters generally offer no investment advice or research services. Many do not even assign a personal broker to your account (though some do pride themselves on establishing a personal rapport with customers). Their offices may be small and sparsely decorated, but many companies operate in more elaborate settings. Just remember—it's the trade, not the trimmings, that counts.

How much will you save?

You could save more than 50 percent, according to a recent phone survey we made. Comparing discounters' commissions with those of regular brokers such as Merrill Lynch and E.F. Hutton, for example, we found the big brokers would charge about $82 for a trade of 100 shares of a $40 stock (a total of $4,000). Two discount houses quoted a commission of about $34.50; a third quoted $31.90. For 200 shares of that same stock (an $8,000 transaction), two regular houses quoted about $152, a third $148. All three discounters quoted about $65.80.

Most discount brokers and regular brokerage companies will handle "odd lots" (trades of less than 100 shares), but charge a minimum commission of $25 or $30. On small trades, therefore, you may do just as well with a regular house.

Who should use a discount broker?

Discount houses are really for self-starters who want to decide their investing actions on their own. If you're a first-timer, or someone who wants investment advice, you're

of $25 to $30 regardless of the number of bonds in the transaction. Beyond this minimum, the brokerage cost typically ranges between $5 and $10 per bond. It should be quite clear that the transaction costs for bonds are considerably lower than the commissions charged on stock transactions. A discount broker would generally charge $2 to $5 a bond, with a $25 minimum.

BOX 2.3 *Continued*

---

probably better off with your own account person at a regular brokerage firm. You may find a wider choice of possible investments, and you'll also gain personal consultation, research materials, and other services. But if all you're looking for is someone to handle a securities trade, check out the discount houses.

Where do you find them?
Discount brokers operate in most major cities. Look for their ads in the newspapers and on TV or radio, or consult the Yellow Pages under "Stock and Bond Brokers" or "Investment Securities."

Is your money safe?
All legitimate brokerage houses carry Securities Investor Protection Corporation (SIPC) insurance that protects accounts up to one-half million dollars. To confirm that a company is officially registered to do business and is a member of SIPC, contact the securities department at your state capital or the Securities and Exchange Commission, Office of Consumer Affairs, 500 N. Capitol St., Washington, DC 20549.

How does an account work?
It's a simple matter to open an account. Just call the broker (most have toll-free 800-line numbers or will accept collect calls). They'll fill out an application for you by phone or send one to be returned to them. You'll be asked for basic information such as name, address, and place of business. They also may want some financial information, like where you have a bank account.

To execute a trade, simply call the broker's trading desk and they'll handle the transaction immediately. Most brokers will accept a "stop" or "limit" order stipulating a certain price that you name. The trade will be confirmed by mail.

As with all brokers, "settlement day" comes five business days after the transaction. By then you must either send them a check for what you bought or deliver the certificates you sold. Similarly, they'll send you a check within five days or register the securities you bought in your name and mail them as soon as possible. Some discounters will "safekeep" your securities in their offices if you ask them to. There's generally no fee for that service, but it can take a few days or weeks to get the certificates when you want them.

Be sure to check out the company's policies about cash and other requirements. A few discounters may require you to advance some cash or deliver the securities you're selling before they'll execute the deal. To weed out people who aren't likely to be very active traders, some firms may require a new customer to put down an advance deposit—say $250—to be applied against future commissions.

Source: Margaret Daly, "Investing: Should You Use a Discount Broker?" *Better Homes and Gardens,* May 1982, p. 176.

Options

Brokerage fees on rights and warrants are subject to the same schedule as for stocks. Fees are based on the market price of the instrument when the transaction is made. Brokerage fees on put and call options, however, are a function of the number and value of the options contact. On a contract having a value between

Figure 2.4   An Advertisement for a Discount Broker.
It should be clear from this advertisement that the key appeal of a discount broker is the low
transaction costs. (*Source: The Wall Street Journal,* February 25, 1983, p. 41.)

$100 and $800, a $25 fee is charged. The fee on a $2,000 contract would be $44.
Not only does the fee vary depending on the value of the contract, it also varies with
the number of contracts purchased. For example, the fee on the purchase of 10
options contracts, each with a value of $800, would be $185.40. On a per contract
basis this would be $18.54—less than the single contract commission of $25. Discount brokers can be used to make options transactions at much lower commissions
than those charged by the full-service broker.

Commodities and other futures contracts

The transaction costs associated with commodities and other types of futures
contracts vary with the value of the contract. This value is a function of contract size

and the price of the underlying commodity, currency, or financial instrument. For example, a live cattle contract for 40,000 pounds at a current price of 67 cents per pound has a value of $26,800, whereas a currency contract for 25,000 British pounds at a current price of $1.50 per pound has a value of $37,500. The brokerage commissions charged on commodities and other futures contracts cover both the purchase and the sale transaction, so commissions are paid only once. The "round trip" commission on one cattle contract is approximately $50; the commission on a British pound contract is approximately $80. Discount commodity brokers usually charge about half as much as the full-service commodity broker; in some instances, the charge is even less.

Mutual funds

Transaction costs for mutual funds typically vary between zero and 8.5 percent of the price of the shares. Shares of some mutual funds (known as no load funds) can be purchased directly and carry no brokerage fees. Although there is a developing trend toward no loads, currently most fund shares are not purchased directly; instead, a 3 to 8.5 percent commission must be paid on the purchase transaction. These funds are known as load funds, and the fee covers both the purchase and sale cost, so the commission is paid only once. In the case of some no load funds, it is possible to have a back-end load, or a commission of 1 to 2 percent, tacked on orders to sell the shares.

Real estate

On direct purchases of real estate, the buyer normally does not pay any commission. When real estate is sold through a real estate broker (a licensed real estate agent), the seller must pay a quoted rate of anywhere from 6 to 10 percent of the sale price. In many instances, the actual commission paid is negotiated below the stated rate when the sale is being transacted. When an investor purchases a limited interest in a specific piece of property or in a group of properties, a sales charge equal to approximately 8 percent is reflected in the purchase price. Although limited interests typically are not readily marketable, by establishing a sale price below its true market value one can sometimes sell such an interest. In such a case, the discount from market value can be viewed as a type of sales commission.

SUMMARY

An understanding of the organization of the securities markets and the procedures for assessing them is necessary in order to evaluate and select potential investment vehicles. Short-term investment vehicles are traded in the money market, while longer-term securities such as stocks and bonds are traded in the capital market. New securities are sold in the primary market by investment bankers and/ or selling groups established by them to sell the new issue. Outstanding securities are traded in the secondary market, which is made up of organized securities exchanges and the over-the-counter market. The key organized exchanges are the New York Stock Exchange (NYSE) and the American Stock Exchange (AMEX). Both are in New York City and have specific membership, listing, and trading policies. In addition to the NYSE and AMEX, there are 14 regional stock exchanges and a few Canadian exchanges. Special-purpose exchanges that specialize in certain types of investment vehicles also exist; the options exchanges and futures exchanges are examples.

The over-the-counter market (OTC) is not a specific institution like the organized stock exchanges; rather, it is an intangible relationship between purchasers and sellers of securities. It is linked together by the NASDAQ system, which is a sophisticated telecommunications network. In addition to transactions in unlisted securities, new issue and secondary distributions are made in the OTC market. Dealers make markets in OTC securities by establishing bid and ask prices. Third- and fourth-market transactions are also made in the OTC market.

The securities markets are regulated by a variety of state and federal laws, the enforcement of which is typically vested in a securities commission. The federal commission, the Securities and Exchange Commission (SEC), is responsible for the enforcement of the federal laws. The key federal laws regulating the securities industry are the Securities Act of 1933, Securities Exchange Act of 1934, Maloney Act of 1938, Investment Company Act of 1940, and Investment Advisors Act of 1940. The conditions of the securities markets are usually called "bull" or "bear"; over the past 60 or so years, the markets have been generally bullish.

Stockbrokers (full-service or discount), by executing clients' purchase and sale transactions, provide the key link between the individual investor and the markets. They execute orders for customers through a member on the floor of an organized exchange or through a market maker in the over-the-counter market. In addition, stockbrokers offer a variety of services to customers. The Securities Investor Protection Corporation (SIPC), an agency of the federal government established in 1970, insures customers' brokerage accounts for up to $500,000 of securities held by the brokerage firm and up to $100,000 in cash balances held by the firm.

The procedures for opening an account once an acceptable stockbroker has been selected are quite simple. A variety of types of accounts, such as single, joint, custodial, cash, margin, and discretionary, may be established. Once an account is opened, an investor can make odd-lot or round-lot transactions. The primary types of orders are the market order, the limit order, and the stop-loss order. The market order is executed immediately after it is placed; limit and stop-loss orders are typically executed (if at all) some time after they are placed. When making investments, the individual can make any (or some combination) of three basic transactions—the long purchase, the short sale, and the margin purchase. Most individual investors make long purchases in expectation of price increases. Short-sale transactions are much less common, although they do provide opportunities for gain when a decline in share price is anticipated. Many investors establish margin accounts in order to use borrowed funds to enhance their buying power. Margin requirements are regulated by the Federal Reserve System.

The costs associated with making investment transactions vary, depending on the method and type of investment vehicle being acquired. As a result of the passage of the Securities Acts Amendments of 1975, stockbrokers are permitted to charge whatever commission they wish. On small transactions most brokers have fixed commission schedules; on larger transactions they will negotiate commissions. Discount brokers, who usually provide most of the services offered by other brokers except research and investment advice, execute transactions at rates 30 to 70 percent below those charged by full-service brokers. The transaction cost on bonds is generally quoted on a per bond basis once a minimum-sized transaction has been achieved. Brokerage fees on rights and warrants are similar to those on stocks, while put and call options transaction costs are quoted on a per contract basis. Commodities and other futures transaction costs are quoted on a per contract basis for the combined purchase and sale transaction. Mutual funds may or may not have brokerage costs attached to their purchase and/or sale. Brokerage costs on real estate transactions also vary.

KEY TERMS

ask price
bear market
bid price
bull market
call option
capital market
cash account
closed-end investment company
dealer
de-listed securities
discount broker
discretionary account
dual listing
fixed commission schedule
fourth market
good til canceled (GTC) order
investment banking firm
limit order
long purchase
margin account
margin purchase
market order
money market

NASDAQ
negotiated commission
odd lot
open-end investment company
over-the-counter market
primary market
prospectus
put option
red herring
round lot
secondary distributions
secondary market
Securities Investor Protection Corporation
  (SIPC)
securities markets
selling group
short sale
specialists
stockbroker
stop-loss order
third market
underwriting
underwriting syndicate

REVIEW QUESTIONS

1. Define and differentiate between each of the following pairs of words.

a. Money market and capital market.
b. Primary market and secondary market.
c. Organized securities exchanges and over-the-counter market.

2. Describe the role of the investment banker in helping corporations raise money. Explain how new security issues are sold.

3. Briefly describe the following aspects of the New York Stock Exchange (NYSE).

a. Membership.
b. Listing policies.
c. Trading activity.

4. Briefly note the primary activities of each of the following types of NYSE members.

a. Commission broker.
b. Bond broker.
c. Independent broker.
d. Specialist.
e. Registered trader.

5. For each of the items in the left-hand column, match the most appropriate item in the right-hand column. Explain the relationship between the items matched.

a. AMEX.   1. Unlisted securities are traded.
b. CBT.   2. Futures exchange.
c. Boston Stock Exchange.   3. Options exchange.
d. CBOE.   4. Second largest security exchange.
e. OTC.   5. Regional stock exchange.

6. Describe the over-the-counter market and explain how it works. Be sure to mention dealers, bid and ask prices, and NASDAQ. What role do new issues and secondary distributions play in this market?

7. What are the third and fourth markets? Describe the role they play in the overall investment process.

8. Briefly describe the key rules and regulations resulting from each of the following securities acts.

a. Securities Act of 1933.
b. Securities Exchange Act of 1934.
c. Maloney Act of 1938.
d. Investment Company Act of 1940.
e. Investment Advisors Act of 1940.

9. What role does the stockbroker play in the overall investment process? Describe the types of services offered by brokerage firms and discuss the criteria for selecting a suitable stockbroker.

10. Describe the role of the Securities Investor Protection Corporation in protecting customers' accounts against the consequences of brokerage firm failure.

11. What must one do in order to open a brokerage account? Briefly differentiate among the following types of brokerage accounts:

a. Single or joint.
b. Custodial.
c. Cash.
d. Margin.
e. Discretionary.

12. Albert Cromwell places a market order to buy a round lot of Thomas, Inc., common stock, which is traded on the NYSE and currently quoted at $50 per share. Ignoring brokerage commissions, how much money would he likely have to pay? If he had placed a market order to sell, how much money would he receive? Explain.

13. Imagine that you have placed a limit order to buy 100 shares of Sallisaw Tool, which is current selling for $41, at a price of $38. Discuss the consequences, if any, of each of the following:

a. The stock price drops to $39 per share two months prior to cancellation of the limit order.
b. The stock price drops to $38 per share.
c. The minimum stock price achieved prior to cancellation of the limit order was $38.50, and when canceled the stock was selling for $47.50 per share.

14. Explain the rationale for using a stop-loss order. If you place a stop-loss order to sell at $23 on a stock currently selling for $26.50 per share, what is likely to be the minimum loss you will experience on your 50 shares if the stock price rapidly declines to $20.50 per share? Explain.

15. Define what is meant by a long purchase and a short sale and explain the expectations that generally underlie each type of transaction.

16. Elmo Inc.'s stock is currently selling at $60 per share. For each of the following situations (ignoring brokerage fees), calculate the gain or loss realized by Maureen Katz if she makes a round-lot transaction.

a. She sells short and repurchases the borrowed shares at $70 per share.
b. She takes a long position and sells the stock at $75 per share.
c. She sells short and repurchases the borrowed shares at $45 per share.
d. She takes a long position and sells the stock at $60 per share.

17. Discuss what is meant by a margin purchase. Who establishes margin requirements? Explain.

18. Ignoring any transaction costs, how much money would Hank Grimmer need in order to purchase two round lots of Anderson Industries, which is currently selling for $42.50 per share, if:

a. He made a cash purchase.
b. He made a margin purchase and the margin requirement is (1) 20 percent, (2) 80 percent.

19. Using the brokerage fee schedule given in Table 2.4, along with the odd-lot differential (if applicable), calculate the brokerage fees on the following common stock transactions:

a. Purchase 70 shares of ABC for $60 per share.
b. Sell 100 shares of DEF for $7.50 per share.

20. Describe and contrast the services offered and fees levied by full-service stockbrokers and discount brokers.

CASE PROBLEMS

2.1 THE HUMBARDS' CHOICE OF A STOCKBROKER

Alan and Pam Humbard were married three years ago upon their graduation from Southeastern State University. Since that time they each have been working for Finn International—a major computer manufacturer. Alan is a production engineer and Pam is on the firm's internal auditing staff. The Humbards are both from a small farming community in Northwest Iowa, where they were raised in a rather conservative fashion. Alan's family was involved in the pig farming business; Pam's father was a minister and her mother taught at the local elementary school. Over the past few years the Humbards have been able to save nearly $5,000, while acquiring the material items necessary for them to live comfortably. They currently maintain their savings in a joint money market account at a nearby savings and loan. The account pays them 8.5 percent interest per year. Based upon their current family and financial plans, the Humbards expect to continue to accumulate savings of $1,000 to $1,500 per year during the next five years.

Over the Christmas holidays a few weeks ago, Alan and Pam returned to their hometown to visit their parents. During the visit they ran into a high school classmate, Rex Morgan, who also had returned to visit his family. After talking with Rex for a while, Alan and Pam discovered Rex was a highly successful stockbroker in Kansas City. As a result of their conversations, it became clear to the Humbards that they might be able to earn more on their savings by making security investments. Rex strongly urged the Humbards to move their savings into the stock market. Based upon Rex's recommendations, when they returned home Alan and Pam began to look for an acceptable stockbroker with whom to do business. After talking with their friends and business acquaintances, they had narrowed the list of brokers down to three; a brief description of each is given below.

Broker 1 A 24-year-old broker who has been in the business for nearly two years. He has been reasonably successful in making speculative investments for his clients. In his conversations with Alan and Pam, he tended to emphasize the "fantastic opportunities to make a killing in the commodities markets." He suggested that since they are young and don't have children, "now is the time for them to take a risk." Even if they lost all their money, broker 1 told the Humbards, "they can always start over." He advised the Humbards to "open a discretionary account with him and before they know it they'll have tripled their money."

Broker 2 A highly successful broker who has been in the business for over 10 years. She has a large number of clients, mostly wealthy individuals or representatives of large institutional investors. Broker 2 indicated that she did not normally handle small customers like the Humbards, but if they wanted to do business with her, she would "be glad to open an account for them." Broker 2 suggested that they invest in "whatever stocks they feel comfortable with." She indicated that most of her customers "were getting into Melton Industries, due to the proposed takeover of it by Equity International." Broker 2 indicated to the Humbards that "due to her sizable workload, she would not be able to counsel them on the appropriate investments, but she could put them into the same stocks as were favored by her wealthy clients."

Broker 3 A moderately successful broker whose philosophy was to grow with her customers. She, at age 25, had been in the business for nearly four years. The majority of her clients were in their mid-to-late twenties and were interested in slowly accumulating wealth. She tended to be somewhat conservative in her advice; many of her customers held sizable portfolios of high-quality bonds, which were yielding 9 to 9.5 percent. Broker 3's philosophy was to help her clients to accumulate wealth slowly and surely rather than by investing in "high-risk, all-or-nothing" types of vehicles. She tended to provide her clients with a great deal of information on potential security investments and to make sure her clients felt comfortable with their investments.

Questions
1. Evaluate each of the three brokers and make a recommendation to the Humbards as to which one they should choose.
2. Describe the procedures the Humbards should follow to open an account with their broker of choice.
3. Should they open a single or a joint account? Cash or margin account? How about a discretionary account? Explain.
4. If the Humbards could save 40 percent in commissions by making transactions through a discount broker, what recommendation would you make? Why?

2.2 SARAH'S DILEMMA: HOLD, SELL, OR?
As a result of her recent divorce, Sarah Brown—a 40-year-old mother of two teenage children—received 400 shares of Casinos International common stock. The stock is currently selling for $54 per share. After a long discussion with a friend of hers, who is an economist with a major commercial bank, Sarah believes that the economy is turning down and a bear market is likely. She has researched, with the aid of her stockbroker, Casinos International's current financial situation and found that the future success of the company may hinge on the outcome of pending court proceedings relative to the firm's application to open a new

gambling casino in Pacific City. If the permit is granted, it seems likely that the firm's stock will experience a rapid increase in value, regardless of economic conditions. On the other hand, if the permit is not granted, the stock value is likely to be adversely affected.

Sarah felt that, based upon the available information, the price of Casinos was likely to fluctuate a great deal over the near future. Her first reaction was to sell the stock and invest the money in a safer security, such as a high-rated corporate bond. At the same time, she felt that she might be overly pessimistic due to her semi-depressed emotional state resulting from the recent divorce. She realized that if Casinos had their Pacific City application granted, she would make a killing on the stock. As a final check before making any decision, Sarah talked with her accountant, who suggested that for tax purposes it would be best to delay the sale of the stock for an additional four months. After making a variety of calculations, the accountant indicated that the consequences of selling the stock now at $54 per share would be approximately equivalent to receiving $48 per share anytime after the four-month period had elapsed.

Sarah felt the following four alternatives were open to her:

Alternative 1. Sell now at $54 per share and use the proceeds to buy high-rated corporate bonds.

Alternative 2. Keep the stock and place a limit order to sell the stock at $60 per share.

Alternative 3. Keep the stock and place a stop-loss order to sell at $45 per share.

Alternative 4. Hold the stock for an additional four months prior to making any decision.

Questions

1. Evaluate each of these alternatives, and based on the limited information presented, recommend what you feel is the best one.

2. If the stock price rises to $60, what will happen under alternatives 2 and 3? Evaluate the pros and cons of these outcomes.

3. If the stock price drops to $45, what will happen under alternatives 2 and 3? Evaluate the pros and cons of these outcomes.

4. In light of the rapid fluctuations anticipated in the price of Casinos' stock, how might the combination of a limit order to sell and a stop-loss order to sell be used by Sarah to reduce the risk associated with the stock? What is the cost of such a strategy? Explain.

SELECTED READINGS

"Banking at a Brokerage Firm." *Consumer Reports,* October 1982, pp. 528–531.

Commager, Steele. "Watch Your Language." *Forbes,* October 27, 1980, pp. 113–116.

Dougall, Herbert E., and Jack E. Gaumnitz. *Capital Markets and Institutions,* 4th ed. Englewood Cliffs, N.J.: Prentice-Hall, 1980.

Engel, Louis, and Peter Wyckoff. *How to Buy Stocks,* 6th ed. Boston: Little, Brown, 1981.

Hayes, Linda Snyder. "Boom Time for Brokers." *Fortune,* February 9, 1981, pp. 82–85.

New York Stock Exchange Fact Book, 1982. New York: New York Stock Exchange, 1982.

Putka, Gary. "Small Investors Surge Back into Market: Many Buy New Issues." *The Wall Street Journal,* March 24, 1983, pp. 1, 20.

Runde, Robert H. "What to Do When It's Time to Invest." *Money,* October 1982, pp. 82–86.

Skousen, K. Fred. *An Introduction to the SEC,* 3d ed. Cincinnati: Southwestern, 1983.

"Stock Market Basics for Beginners." *Changing Times,* June 1981, pp. 41–46.

"Wall Street's Billion-Dollar High Rollers." *U.S. News & World Report,* February 7, 1983, pp. 66–67.

"Whatever Happened to No-Frills Brokers?" *Changing Times,* February 1983, pp. 61–63.

"What If Your Broker Goes Broke?" *Changing Times,* September 1982, pp. 25–26.

Williams, Jonathan. "When Brokers Go Broke." *Money,* January 1982, pp. 57–58.

3

Sources of Investment Information and Advice

In order for individuals to make sound investment decisions, it is important that they become familiar with the workings of the economy, the market, specific investment vehicles, and other factors that might have a bearing on an investment transaction. The overview of key sources of investment information and advice provided in this chapter emphasizes the following aspects:

1. The benefits and costs, types, and uses of investment information in the decision-making process.
2. Some of the major sources of information about economic and current events.
3. Sources of information for assessing the performance of specific industries and/or companies.
4. Sources of information about both current and recent price behavior of the more popular forms of security investments.
5. The most commonly cited market averages and indexes, their interpretation, and their use in assessing market conditions.
6. The products offered, regulation of, types, cost, and effective use of the services provided by investment advisors, and features of investment clubs.
7. The role of the personal computer (PC), both as a tool in evaluating investments and as a source of data bases.

An understanding of where to find useful investment information and sound investment advice is paramount in becoming an intelligent investor. Although there are people who have made a lot of money by investing without such understanding, generally the investor who understands the state of the economy, the market, and the specific company will be more effective than those operating on the basis of pure intuition. Some individuals will buy stock like McDonald's because they like the product and have noticed large crowds at their local retail establishment. Such observations would certainly positively affect one's investment decision, but it's clearly insufficient for decision-making purposes because it leaves unanswered numerous relevant questions, such as: How will the economy change? What behavior is the stock market expected to exhibit over the near term? Is McDonald's a profitable company and will it continue so? Many of these questions can be answered by knowing where to find and how to interpret appropriate information.

Some individuals tend to shy away from certain investments because they feel unsure about the future behavior of the economy, the stock market, and therefore security investments in general. These investors usually keep their money in various types of savings instruments and government bonds. Because they are unable to assess the risks and potential returns of alternate investments, they end up receiving less return than they desire. By gaining familiarity with the key sources of investment information and advice, the individual investor should be able to expand the scope of acceptable investments. The ultimate payoff is not only an improved chance of gain, but also a reduced chance of loss from poor investments. In any case, the informed investor will probably earn better and safer returns than the uninformed investor, regardless of whether the uninformed investor makes decisions solely on the basis of intuition or merely avoids risky investments. In addition, with the increasing availability of personal computers and compatible investor-oriented software and data bases, it is important that the individual investor understand the role these new technologies can play in developing and managing a portfolio.

STAYING IN TOUCH WITH THE INVESTMENT WORLD

Investment information and advice can be considered either descriptive or analytical. *Descriptive information* presents factual data on the past behavior of the economy, the market, or a given investment vehicle; *analytical information* presents available current data, and includes projections and recommendations about potential investments. The sample page from *Value Line* included in Figure 3.1 provides both descriptive and analytical information on GTE Corporation. Items that are primarily descriptive are keyed with a *D*; analytical items are noted with an *A*. Some forms of investment information are free, others must be purchased individually or by annual subscription. Although it is difficult to assess the quality and accuracy of investment information, there are certain benefits, costs, and economic considerations involved in the choice process.

Benefits and Costs of Information

One important benefit of the use of investment information is that it provides a basis for allowing the investor to formulate expectations of the risk-return behavior of potential investments. With better estimates of risk and return, investors should be able to select vehicles exhibiting behaviors consistent with their goals. Although

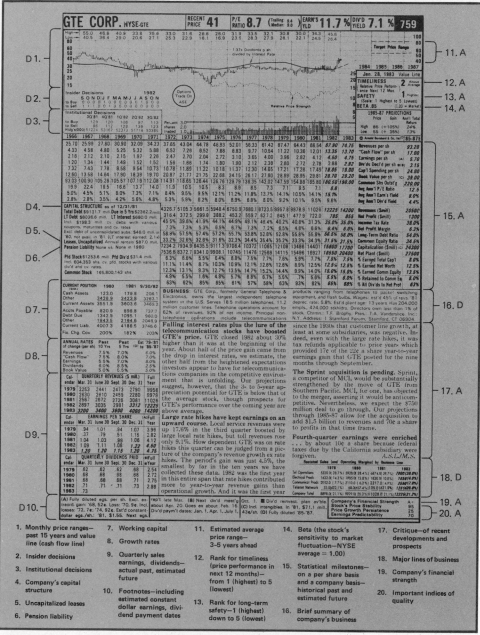

Figure 3.1 A Report Containing Both Descriptive and Analytical Information: Value Line Full-Page Report (GTE Corporation—January 28, 1983).
This report contains both descriptive (noted D) and analytical (noted A) information. Examples of descriptive information are "monthly price ranges—past 15 years" and "company's capital structure"; examples of analytical information are "estimated average price range—3–5 years ahead" and "rank for timeliness." (*Source:* Adapted from Arnold Bernhard and Co., *The Value Line Investment Survey, Ratings and Reports,* Edition 5, January 28, 1983, p. 759.)

the use of investment information to formulate risk-return expectations does not ensure success, it should help in making more informed and intelligent judgments. A second benefit of the use of investment information is that it may help the investor avoid the undesirable consequences that could result from a misrepresentation of facts by the issuer and/or seller of a vehicle. In spite of accepted accounting practices as well as a variety of federal and state laws, factual misrepresentations do occur. To avoid the potentially devastating consequences of such misrepresentations, it is often helpful to obtain and evaluate information provided by an independent source prior to making a decision.

Free information can be obtained from newspapers, magazines, and brokerage firms, and more can be found in public, university, and brokerage firm libraries. Alternatively, an investor can subscribe to services that provide clients with periodic reports summarizing the investment outlook and recommending certain actions. The services will cost the investor money, but obtaining, reading, and analyzing free information costs time. So it is necessary to calculate the worth of potential information in terms of one's investment program. For example, spending 15 hours locating or paying $40 for information or advice that increases one's return by $27 would not be economically sound; had the cost been 3 hours or $10, such action would have made economic sense. The larger an individual's investment portfolio, the easier it is to justify information purchases, since their benefit can be shared by a number of investments.

In addition to quantity, there is also the question of the quality of investment information. As is true for most products and services, some investment information and advice is good, and some is not. Often cost and quality of investment information and advice are not consistent.

Types and Uses of Information

Investment information can be conveniently broken into five types, each concerned with an important aspect of the personal investment process. (1) Economic and current event information provides background as well as forecast data related to economic, political, and social trends on a domestic as well as worldwide basis. Such information is useful to all investors, since it provides a basis for assessing the environment in which decisions are made. (2) Industry and company information provides background as well as forecast data on specific industries and companies. This type of information is used by investors to assess the outlook in a given industry and/or specific company. Because of its company orientation, it is most relevant to stock, bond, or options investments. (3) Information on alternative investment vehicles provides background and predictive data for securities other than stocks, bonds, and options, as well as for various forms of property investment. (4) Price information contains current price quotations on certain investment vehicles, particularly securities. These quotations are commonly accompanied by statistics on the recent price behavior of the vehicle. (5) Information on personal investment strategies provides recommendations on investment strategies and/or specific purchase or sale actions. In general, this information tends to be analytical or educational rather than descriptive.

Sources of Information

A complete listing of the sources of each type of investment information is beyond the scope of this book; we will look at only the basic forms of investment information here. For those desiring expanded source information, Appendix A provides an annotated listing. Detailed descriptions of relevant information sources as well as demonstrations of their use are included in the discussions of specific investment vehicles and strategies presented in Chapters 8 through 18. The discussion here is concerned with the most common sources of information on economic and current events, industries and companies, and prices.

Economic and current event information

It is clearly important for all investors to stay abreast of major economic and current events. An awareness of such events, coupled with the ability to relate them to the behavior of various investment vehicles, should translate into better decisions. The more popular sources of economic and current event information among individual investors are the financial news, business periodicals, and special subscription services.

The financial news.   *The Wall Street Journal* is the most popular source of financial news. It is published daily and has a circulation of over 1.9 million. In order to provide regionally based articles and timely distribution, it is published in a number of locations around the country. In addition to giving daily price quotations on thousands of different types of investment vehicles, it reports world, national, regional, and corporate news. The back page of the *Journal* always contains a feature story. On Mondays, part of this page, called "Your Money Matters," addresses topics that deal directly with individuals and their finances. A second popular source of financial news is *Barron's,* which is published weekly by Dow Jones, the same company that publishes *The Wall Street Journal.* Articles in *Barron's* tend to be directed more at strictly financial types of issues than those of the *Journal. Barron's* generally offers more lengthy articles on a variety of topics of interest to individual investors. Probably the most popular column in *Barron's* is Alan Abelson's "Up and Down Wall Street," which provides a critical and often humorous assessment of major developments affecting the stock market as well as specific industries and companies. In addition, current price quotations as well as a summary of statistics on a wide range of investment vehicles are included in each issue.

Another convenient source of financial news is the local newspaper. In most cities having a population in excess of 200,000, the daily newspaper will devote two or more pages to financial and business news. Major metropolitan newspapers such as *The New York Times* and the *Los Angeles Times* provide investors with a wealth of financial news. Most major newspapers contain stock price quotations for major exchanges, price quotations on stocks of local interest, and a summary of the major stock averages. Reading the financial page(s) of the local newspaper is an inexpensive way of staying abreast of key financial developments. Other sources of financial news are the *Commercial and Financial Chronicle,* the *M/G (Medial General) Financial Weekly,* and the *Journal of Commerce.* The monthly economic letters of the nation's

I don't give a damn what a Chinese fortune cookie said.
I'm not buying a thousand shares of Dewlap Consolidated.

leading banks, such as First National City Bank's (New York) *Monthly Letter,* provide useful economic information. To keep customers abreast of important news developments, most brokerage firms subscribe to a number of wire services such as the Dow Jones, AP, and UPI.

Business periodicals.   Business periodicals range in scope from those presenting general business and economic articles, to those devoted to securities markets and related topics, to those devoted solely to specific industries or property investments. Regardless of the subject matter, most financial periodicals present descriptive information, although some also include analytical information. But they rarely offer recommendations.

General business and economic articles are found in periodicals such as *Newsweek* ("Business and Finance" section), *Time* ("Business" or "Economy and Business" section), and *U.S. News and World Report.* A number of strictly business and finance-oriented periodicals are also available. These include *Business Week, Fortune, Dun's Review,* and *Nation's Business.* Other sources of general business and economic articles are government publications such as the *Federal Reserve Bulletin* and the *Survey of Current Business.*

Securities and marketplace articles can be found in a number of financial periodicals. The most basic, commonsense articles are found in *Forbes, Changing Times, Money Magazine,* and *FACT. Forbes,* which is published every two weeks, is the most investment-oriented. Each January it publishes an "Annual Report on American Industry," which compares the growth and performance of key industries over the past five years. In August of each year *Forbes* also publishes a comparative evaluation of mutual funds. Both *Changing Times* and *Money Magazine* are published monthly and contain a variety of articles concerned with managing personal finances. Each issue contains articles aimed at the individual investor. One of the newest entries to this group is a publication called *FACT.* It includes articles on a wide variety of investment vehicles—from stocks and bonds to limited partnerships and gems.

Popular periodicals aimed at the more sophisticated investor include *Financial World* and *The Magazine of Wall Street. Financial World* is published weekly and presents articles on the market and specific industries and companies. Subscribers periodically receive statistical data on listed stocks, both common and preferred, and on mutual funds. An annual reference book to leading stocks is also provided. *The Magazine of Wall Street* is similar to *Financial World* in that it also provides both investment information and advice. Even more professionally oriented are the *Financial Analysts Journal, The Money Manager, The Wall Street Transcript, The Institutional Investor,* and *AAII Journal.* Each of these periodicals offers technical analyses and information that would be useful to the professional investor.

Special subscription services.   In addition to the broad range of financial news and business periodicals, special subscription services are available for those who want additional insights into business and economic conditions. These reports tend to include business and economic forecasts and give notice of new government policies, union plans and tactics, taxes, prices, wages, and so on. One of the more popular services is the *Kiplinger Washington Letter,* a weekly publication that costs about $50 per year. It provides a wealth of economic information and analyses. Other special subscription services that concentrate on the economy in general are McGraw-Hill's *Personal Finance Letter, Babson's Reports,* and the *Wellington Financial Letter.*

Industry and company information
Of special interest to security investors is information on industries and companies. Often, after choosing an industry in which to invest, the investor will proceed to analyze specific companies in order to select a suitable investment. General articles related to the activities of specific industries can be found in trade publications such as *Steel, Oil and Gas Journal, Public Utilities Fortnightly,* and *Brewers Digest.* Those interested in a specific industry may find regular reading of these types of publications useful. More specific popular sources of industry and company information include stockholder's reports, subscription services, brokerage reports, and investment letters.

Stockholder's reports.   An excellent source of recent operating data on an individual business firm is its *stockholder's* or *annual report,* published annually by publicly held corporations. These contain a wide range of information, including financial statements for the most recent period of operation, along with summarized statements for several prior years. A sample page from the Mobil Corporation's 1981 Stockholder's Report is shown in Figure 3.2. These reports are free and useful sources of investment information on a publicly held company. In addition to the stockholder's report, many serious investors will review *Form 10-K,* which is a statement that firms having securities listed on an organized exchange or traded in the OTC market must file with the SEC.

Subscription services.   A variety of subscription services provide information on specific industries and companies. Generally, a subscriber pays a basic fee that entitles him or her to certain information published and periodically updated by the service. In addition to the basic service, a subscriber can purchase other services that provide more in-depth information or an expanded range of information. The major subscription services provide both descriptive and analytical information; but they generally do not make recommendations. Subscribers to these services include corporations, banks, insurance companies, brokerage firms, libraries, and individuals. Most individual investors, rather than subscribing to these services, gain access to them through their stockbroker or at a large public or university library. The dominant subscription services are those offered by Standard & Poor's Corporation, Moody's Investor Services, Inc., and the *Value Line Investment Survey.*

Standard & Poor's Corporation (S&P) offers over fifteen different financial reports and services. One major service, *Corporation Records,* provides detailed descriptions of issues of publicly traded securities. A second major service, *Stock Reports,* contains up-to-date reports on firms. Each report presents a concise summary of the firm's financial history, its current finances, and its future prospects (for NYSE companies only). A sample report (dated November 19, 1982) for Mobil Corporation is presented in Figure 3.3. Standard & Poor's Trade and Securities Service provides background information on business in general, as well as past, present, and future assessments of specific industries. The *Stock and Bond Guides* are another of S&P's major services. These guides, published monthly, contain statistical information on the major stocks and bonds, and include descriptive data along with an analytical ranking of investment desirability. Figure 3.4 shows a sample two-page spread from the January 1983 S&P *Stock Guide.* Mobil Corporation has an A+ rating, indicating that it is in the highest-rated group. One other S&P publication worthy of note is its weekly magazine, *Outlook,* which includes analytical articles providing investment advice about the market and about specific industries and/or securities.

Moody's Investor Services publishes a variety of useful materials. The key publications are reference manuals (*Moody's Manuals*), which are quite similar to S&P's *Corporation Records.* Each of the six reference manuals contains a wealth of historical and current financial, organizational, and operational data on all major firms within certain business groupings. In order to keep these manuals up to date, frequent supplements are made available to subscribers. Other publications are the *Hand-*

1981: A YEAR OF CHALLENGE

Mobil's strengths were evident in 1981 despite the worldwide oil surplus and weak economic conditions. Some notable achievements:

● Important hydrocarbon discoveries in the United States, Nigeria, Cameroon, and Germany.

● Third Mobil-operated production platform towed out to North Sea; construction continues on two others.

● Major expansion under way to increase liquefied natural gas production in Indonesia.

● First liftings of incentive crude oil in Saudi Arabia.

● New units completed in Singapore and under construction in Paulsboro, New Jersey, will further upgrade refining capabilities.

● Progress made in alternative energy, with construction under way on our first coal mine, engineering beginning for a major shale oil project, and a plant to make gasoline from natural gas soon to be built in New Zealand.

● Mobil Chemical expands position in plastic film and foam markets.

MOBIL CORPORATION

Financial Highlights	1981	1980[1]	1979[1]
Revenues (millions)	$68,587	$63,726	$48,292
Income before extraordinary item (millions)	2,433	2,813	2,007
Per share (based on average shares outstanding)	5.72	6.62	4.73
Net income (millions)	2,433	3,272	2,007
Per share (based on average shares outstanding)	5.72	7.70	4.73
Return on average shareholders' equity[2]	17.6%	23.9%	20.5%
Return on average capital employed[2]	14.6%	18.8%	16.0%
Income per dollar of revenue[2]	3.5¢	4.4¢	4.2¢
Energy earnings per gallon sold[2]	6.3¢	6.7¢	4.4¢
Total assets, year-end (millions)	$34,776	$32,705	$27,506
Capital expenditures, exploration, and other outlays (millions)	4,469	4,815	3,812
Shareholders' equity, year-end (millions)	14,657	13,069	10,513
Per share (based on shares outstanding at year-end)	34.45	30.74	24.77
Number of shares outstanding (thousands)	425,444	425,192	424,459

(1) Per-share amounts and shares outstanding have been adjusted for the two-for-one stock split.
(2) Excludes 1980 extraordinary item of $459 million.

The Annual Meeting of shareholders will be held on Thursday, May 6, at 10 a.m. in the Tupperware Convention Center Auditorium, Orange Blossom Trail, Orlando, Florida 32802

Figure 3.2   A Page from a Stockholder's Report (Mobil Corporation, 1981).
The first page of the Mobil Corporation's report can quickly acquaint the investor with the key aspects of the firm's operations over the past year. (*Source:* Mobil Corporation, 1981 Stockholder's Report. New York: Mobil Corporation, 1981, p. 1.)

Mobil Corp.   1529

NYSE Symbol MOB   Options on CBOE (Feb-May-Aug-Nov)

Price	Range	P-E Ratio	Dividend	Yield	S&P Ranking
Nov. 12'82	1982				
25	28⅝ - 19½	7	2.00	8.0%	A +

Summary

Operating on a worldwide scale, Mobil derives almost all of its earnings from petroleum operations, although it produces chemicals and owns Montgomery Ward and Container Corp. Mobil's stepped-up worldwide drilling programs appear to be meeting with exceptionally good results; it is also picking up domestic reserves through acquisitions, is building a position in alternate energy sources and technology, and is upgrading the value of refinery output.

Current Outlook

Earnings for 1983 are projected to rise to about $4 a share from the depressed $3.25 estimated for 1982.

Dividends are expected to continue at $0.50 quarterly.

Revenues and profits for 1983 are projected to gain. Supporting prospects include less of a negative impact from the purchase of high-cost crude supplies from Saudi Arabia, new foreign petroleum production coming on stream, and the boost to retail operations from a better economy and the lower cost of money. Partial offsets include a continuing world oversupply of oil and about flat worldwide demand for petroleum products.

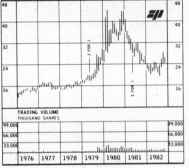

Sales (Billion $)

Quarter:	1982	1981	1980	1979
Mar.	16.13	16.86	15.09	10.18
Jun.	15.47	16.30	15.16	10.49
Sep.	---	16.60	15.41	12.22
Dec.		17.86	17.16	14.60
		67.62	62.82	47.49

Revenues for the first nine months of 1982 slipped 5.5%, year to year. Net income fell 48%, to $2.29 a share from $4.34.

Common Share Earnings ($)

Quarter:	1983	1982	1981	1980
Mar.	E1.00	0.77	1.51	1.99
Jun.	E1.00	0.74	1.65	1.62
Sep.	E1.00	0.78	1.19	1.70
Dec.	E1.00	E0.96	1.38	1.33
	E4.00	E3.25	5.72	6.62

Important Developments

Sep. '82—Mobil announced it had filed a "shelf" registration statement covering up to $500 million of debt securities. In November, $200 million of notes were sold under this shelf registration.

Aug. '82—Mobil said it had purchased part of the giant East Anschutz Ranch oil field in Utah for $500 million.

Jul. '82—Mobil said that it had held initial discussions with the U.S. Synthetic Fuels Corp. about a possible joint industry effort with government involvement to develop U.S. shale oil reserves and that a number of concerns had indicated their willingness to attend a preliminary meeting to explore the concept of a joint venture.

Next earnings report due in late January.

Per Share Data ($)

Yr. End Dec. 31	1982	1981	1980	¹1979	1978	1977	1976	1975	1974	1973
Book Value	NA	34.45	30.74	24.77	21.02	19.47	18.08	16.79	15.80	14.03
Earnings²	NA	5.72	6.62	4.73	2.66	2.38	2.27	1.99	2.57	2.09
Dividends	2.00	2.00	1.72½	1.27½	1.07½	0.97½	0.87½	0.85	0.80	0.70
Payout Ratio	NA	35%	26%	27%	40%	41%	39%	43%	31%	34%
Prices—High	28⅝	41⅛	44⅞	30¼	18⅛	17⅞	16¾	12¼	14¼	18⅞
Low	19½	24⅛	24⅞	17	14⅝	14⅝	11⅞	8⅝	7¾	10⅝
P/E Ratio—	NA	7-4	7-4	6-4	7-5	7-6	7-5	6-4	5-3	9-5

Data as orig. reptd. Adj. for stk. div(s). of 100% Jun. 1981, 100% Jun. 1979. 1. Reflects merger or acquisition. 2. Bef. spec. item(s) of +1.08 in 1980. NA-Not Available. E-Estimated.

Standard NYSE Stock Reports   **November 19, 1982**   Standard & Poor's Corp.
Vol. 49/No. 224/Sec. 17   Copyright © 1982 Standard & Poor's Corp. All Rights Reserved   25 Broadway, NY, NY 10004

Figure 3.3   Standard & Poor's Standard NYSE Stock Report for Mobil Corporation (November 19, 1982).

Standard & Poor's Stock Reports present in a concise fashion both descriptive and analytical

1529

Mobil Corporation

Income Data (Million $)

Year Ended Dec. 31	Revs.	Oper. Inc.	% Oper. Inc. of Revs.	Cap. Exp.	Depr.	Int. Exp.	Net Bef. Taxes	Eff. Tax Rate	*Net Inc.	% Net Inc. of Revs.
1981	64,488	6,623	10.3%	3,571	1,586	608	¹5,399	54.9%	2,433	3.8%
¹1980	59,510	7,651	12.9%	3,525	1,399	479	¹6,676	57.9%	2,813	4.7%
²1979	44,721	7,645	17.1%	3,433	1,086	459	¹6,856	70.7%	³2,007	4.5%
1978	34,736	4,768	13.7%	1,761	890	420	¹4,105	72.6%	1,126	3.2%
1977	32,126	4,904	15.3%	1,285	749	364	¹4,415	77.2%	1,005	3.1%
1976	26,063	4,317	16.6%	2,886	633	295	¹3,814	75.3%	943	3.6%
1975	20,620	3,936	19.1%	1,206	769	216	¹3,173	74.5%	810	3.9%
1974	18,929	4,288	22.7%	1,450	570	150	¹3,775	72.2%	1,047	5.5%
1973	11,390	2,498	21.9%	1,186	493	97	¹2,043	58.4%	849	7.5%
1972	9,166	1,802	19.7%	1,030	444	86	¹1,377	58.3%	574	6.3%

Balance Sheet Data (Million $)

Dec. 31	Cash	Assets	Current Liab.	Ratio	Total Assets	Ret. on Assets	Long Term Debt	Common Equity	Total Cap.	% LT Debt of Cap.	Ret. on Equity
1981	2,044	13,964	12,688	1.1	34,776	7.2%	3,604	14,657	20,800	17.3%	17.5%
1980	1,918	14,099	12,703	1.1	32,705	9.3%	3,571	13,069	18,821	19.0%	23.8%
1979	1,878	11,889	11,170	1.1	27,506	8.0%	3,304	10,513	15,510	21.3%	20.7%
1978	1,483	9,768	8,702	1.1	22,612	5.2%	3,409	8,910	13,319	25.6%	13.1%
1977	1,465	9,159	7,542	1.2	20,576	5.1%	3,077	8,249	12,196	25.2%	12.6%
1976	1,280	8,157	6,846	1.2	18,768	5.5%	2,882	7,652	11,143	25.9%	12.8%
1975	1,135	6,156	5,234	1.2	15,050	5.6%	1,834	6,841	9,170	20.0%	12.2%
1974	999	5,827	5,206	1.1	14,074	8.5%	1,729	6,436	8,592	20.1%	17.2%
1973	843	3,939	3,375	1.2	10,690	8.5%	1,087	5,715	7,062	15.4%	15.6%
1972	599	3,188	2,549	1.3	9,217	6.5%	1,083	5,145	6,438	16.8%	11.5%

Data as orig. reptd. 1. Incl. equity in earns. of nonconsol. subs. 2. Reflects merger or acquisition. 3. Reflects accounting change. 4. Bef. spec. item(s) in 1980.

Business Summary

Mobil is one of the major integrated international oil companies. Interests outside petroleum include chemicals, Montgomery Ward (one of the nation's largest retailers), and Container Corp. of America (a leading manufacturer of paperboard packaging).

Op. Profits	1981	1980
U.S. Expl. & Prod.	33%	24%
U.S. Ref. & Mkt.	10%	8%
Foreign Expl. & Prod.	32%	26%
Foreign Ref. & Mkt.	25%	41%
Chemicals	4%	4%
Retail Merchandising	-6%	-5%
Paperboard Packaging	2%	2%

The company's worldwide gross crude and natural gas liquids production (including substantial amounts acquired under participation agreements with countries like Saudi Arabia) averaged 1,844,000 barrels a day in 1981 (20% U.S. and 80% foreign). Natural gas sales averaged 3.3 billion cubic feet a day (64% U.S. and 36% foreign). Worldwide refinery runs were 1,773,000 b/d, while worldwide product sales averaged 2,138,000 b/d.

Net proved reserves at the 1981 year end stood at 2,887 million barrels of crude oil and natural gas liquids (31% U.S. and 69% foreign) and 17,644 billion cubic feet of natural gas (36% U.S. and 64% foreign).

Dividend Data

Dividends have been paid since 1902. A dividend reinvestment plan is available.

Amt. of Divd. $	Date Decl.	Ex-divd. Date	Stock of Record	Payment Date
0.50	Jan. 29	Feb. 2	Feb. 8	Mar. 10'82
0.50	Apr. 30	May 4	May 10	Jun. 10'82
0.50	Jul. 30	Aug. 3	Aug. 9	Sep. 10'82
0.50	Oct. 29	Nov. 1	Nov. 8	Dec. 10'82

Next dividend meeting: late Jan. '83.

Capitalization

Long Term Debt: $4,722,000,000.

Minority Interest: $108,000,000.

Common Stock: 415,593,205 shs. ($2 par).
Institutions hold about 36%.
Shareholders: 292,422.

Office—150 E. 42nd St., NYC 10017. Tel—(212) 883-4242. Chrmn & CEO—R. Warner, Jr. Pres—W. P. Tavoulareas. Secy—D. T. Bartlett. Treas—R. H. Gardner. Investor Contact—F. Halpern. Dirs—G. H. Birrell, L. M. Branscomb, H. L. Clark, A. Greenspan, S. C. Johnson, W. J. Kennedy, III, J. S. Lafontant, W. E. MacDonald, A. H. Massad, L. L. Morgan, A. E. Murray, S. S. Olayan, A. J. F. O'Reilly, J. Q. Riordan, H. Schmertz, W. W. Scranton, E. B. Sheldon, W. P. Tavoulareas, R. F. Tucker, R. Warner, Jr., P. J. Wolfe, L. M. Woods. Transfer Agent & Registrar—Chase Manhattan Bank, NYC. Incorporated in New York in 1882; reincorporated in Delaware in 1976.

Information has been obtained from sources believed to be reliable, but its accuracy and completeness are not guaranteed. E. Lester, C.F.A.

information on thousands of companies whose shares are traded on the NYAW, AMEX, or OTC. (*Source:* Standard & Poor's Corp., *Standard NYSE Stock Reports.* New York: Standard & Poor's Corporation, November 19, 1982.)

Figure 3.4 A Two-Page Spread from Standard & Poor's Stock Guide (January 1983).

In S&P's *Stock Guide,* common stocks are ranked relative to earnings and dividends, while preferred stocks are ranked relative to the issuer's capacity and willingness to make scheduled dividend payments. From the data on line 38 one can see that Mobil Corporation, having an A+ rating, falls in the highest-rated group of common stocks. (*Source:* Standard & Poor's Corporation, *Stock Guide.* New York: Standard & Poor's Corporation, January 1983, pp. 146–147.)

book of Common Stocks, which provides much financial information on over 1,000 stocks; Dividend Record, which provides recent dividend announcements and payments of thousands of companies; Bond Survey, a weekly publication that assesses market conditions and new offerings; and Bond Record, a monthly publication reporting the price and interest rate behavior of thousands of bonds.

The Value Line Investment Survey is one of the most popular subscription services used by individual investors. It is published weekly and covers more than 1,700 stocks and their industries (which account for about 96 percent of total trading in U.S. equity markets). A rating of "financial strength" and "safety" is included for each company. In exchange for an annual subscription fee of around $365, three basic services are provided Value Line subscribers. The "Summary and Index" is a weekly update showing the current ratings for each stock. "Ratings and Reports" is updated weekly and contains a full-page analysis for each of about 130 stocks. One example of such a report for GTE Corporation was included earlier in Figure 3.1. The third service, "Selection and Opinion," is a weekly section that contains a detailed analysis of an especially recommended stock.

Brokerage reports.   Another popular source of investment information is brokerage firms. In addition to making available reports from various subscription services, brokerage firms provide clients with prospectuses for new security issues and back-office research reports. A prospectus is a document describing in detail the key aspects of the issuer, its management and financial position, and the security to be issued. It contains a wealth of information that should be useful in evaluating the investment suitability of a new issue. The cover of the 28-page prospectus describing the 1983 stock issue of the Hechinger Company is shown in Figure 3.5. Back-office research reports are published by and made available to clients of brokerage firms. They include analyses of and recommendations on current and future prospects for the securities markets, specific industries, and/or specific securities. Usually a brokerage firm will publish lists of securities classified as either "buy" or "sell," depending upon the research staff's analysis of their anticipated price behavior. Brokerage research reports are available at no cost to existing as well as potential customers.

Investment letters.   Investment letters provide, on a subscription basis, the analyses, conclusions, and recommendations of various experts in different aspects of securities investment. The cost as well as general thrust of these letters vary. Some concentrate on specific types of securities, others are concerned solely with assessing the economy and/or security markets. Among the more popular investment letters are Dines Letter, Granville Market Letter, Holt Investment Advisory, Wellington Letter, and Zweig Forecast. The cost of the more popular ones, which are generally issued weekly or monthly, is usually in the range of $75 to $300 a year. Advertisements for many of these investment letters can be found in Barron's.

Price information

Price information about various types of securities is contained in their quotations, which include current price data along with statistics on recent price behavior.

PROSPECTUS

1,400,000 Shares

HECHINGER

COMPANY
Common Stock

Of the shares offered hereby. 600,000 will be sold by the Company and 800,000 will be sold by shareholders of the Company. See "Selling Shareholders." The Company will not receive any proceeds from the sale of shares by the Selling Shareholders.

The Common Stock is traded in the over-the-counter market. The highest closing bid price and lowest closing asked price on February 14, 1983, as reported by the National Association of Securities Dealers Automated Quotations System, were $23.25 and $23.75, respectively. See "Price Range of Common Stock."

THESE SECURITIES HAVE NOT BEEN APPROVED OR DISAPPROVED BY THE SECURITIES AND EXCHANGE COMMISSION NOR HAS THE COMMISSION PASSED UPON THE ACCURACY OR ADEQUACY OF THIS PROSPECTUS. ANY REPRESENTATION TO THE CONTRARY IS A CRIMINAL OFFENSE.

	Price to Public	Underwriting Discount	Proceeds to the Company(1)	Proceeds to the Selling Shareholders(1)
Per Share	$23.50	$.92	$22.58	$22.58
Total(2)	$32,900,000	$1,288,000	$13,548,000	$18,064,000

(1) Before deducting expenses estimated at $140,000, of which the Selling Shareholders will pay $35,000.

(2) The Selling Shareholders have granted the Underwriter an option to purchase up to an additional 140,000 shares at $22.58 per share to cover over-allotments. If all of such shares are purchased the total Price to Public, Underwriting Discount and Proceeds to the Selling Shareholders will be increased by $3,290,000, $128,800 and $3,161,200 respectively.

The shares of Common Stock are offered by the Underwriter when, as and if delivered to and accepted by the Underwriter, and subject to certain other conditions. It is expected that delivery of certificates will be made in New York, New York, on or about February 22, 1983.

Merrill Lynch White Weld Capital Markets Group
Merrill Lynch, Pierce, Fenner & Smith Incorporated

February 15, 1983

Figure 3.5   Cover of a Prospectus for a Stock Issue.
Some of the key factors relative to the 1983 stock issue by Hechinger Company are summarized on the cover of its 28-page prospectus. (*Source:* Hechinger Company, February 15, 1983, p. 1.)

Price quotations are readily available for actively traded securities and provide a picture of the securities' behavior in the marketplace. The most up-to-date quotations can be obtained from a stockbroker. Some brokerage offices have equipment that allows customers to key into a computer terminal and obtain quotations. Another automated quotation device found in most brokerage offices is the *ticker,* a lighted

TABLE 3.1 TICKER SYMBOLS FOR SOME WELL-KNOWN COMPANIES

Company	Symbol
American Motors	AMO
American Telephone and Telegraph	T
Coca-Cola Company	KO
Ford Motor Company	F
General Electric	GE
General Foods	GF
General Motors	GM
International Business Machines	IBM
International Harvester	HR
Minnesota Mining and Manufacturing	MMM
Occidental Petroleum	OXY
Pan American World Airways	PN
Polaroid Corporation	PRD
Procter and Gamble	PG
Safeway Stores	SA
Sears, Roebuck and Company	S
Shell Oil Company	SUO
Texas Instruments	TXN
U.S. Steel	X
Xerox Corporation	XRX

screen on which stock transactions made on the floor of the exchange are reported immediately after they occur. The ticker symbols for some well-known companies are included in Table 3.1. Today more sophisticated computer terminals are rapidly displacing the ticker as the major source of up-to-the-minute stock price information. These terminals are now available on a fee basis for home use by professional and active individual investors.

The individual investor can easily find security price quotations in the published news media, both nonfinancial and financial. Most big city newspapers report daily activity on the major exchanges, but such quotations are typically limited to stocks. Local newspaper quotations often highlight certain stocks of local interest, in addition to reporting major exchange transactions. The major source of security price quotations is *The Wall Street Journal,* which is published daily and presents quotations on the previous day's activities in all major markets. It contains quotations on stocks, bonds, listed options, commodities and financial futures, mutual funds, and other popular forms of investment.

Stock quotations. Figure 3.6 presents an example of some NYSE stock quotations and an explanation of the notes often used in these quotes. To see exactly what stock price information is reported, suppose we take a closer look at the data on the Mobil stock traded on Friday, February 25, 1983, and reported in the next

BOX 3.1 BRIEF DESCRIPTIONS OF 15 POPULAR INVESTMENT LETTERS

15 INVESTMENT LETTERS . . .
In this sampling of the better-known newsletters, **general letters** *give advice on stocks, bonds, and other securities and investment strategy.* **Mutual fund letters** *concentrate their analyses on mutual funds and strategies involving their use.*

GENERAL LETTERS

Dines Letter
P.O. Box 22, Belvedore, Cal. 94920

Dines is considered the original goldbug and a proponent of the "gloom and doom school," who believes that "the world is headed first for an economic crash and then for a gold standard at far higher prices." But for the short run, Dines is no longer bullish on gold. His letter covers a broad investment spectrum, emphasizing technical analysis and trading techniques for sophisticated high-risk, short-term traders. In addition, Dines recommends six distinct portfolios of varying degrees of risk for long-term investors.

$150 per year (12 issues). Trial: $20 for one issue.

Dow Theory Letter
P.O. Box 1759, La Jolla, Cal. 90238

Based principally on the Dow Theory of technical analysis, which relies on past movements of the market averages to forecast future trends. Covers stocks, bonds, gold and T-bills for traders and investors.

$185 per year (26 issues). Trial: $5 for three issues.

Granville Market Letter
Drawer O, Holly Hill, Fla. 32017

Highly personal, colorful comments on political and economic developments. Relies exclusively on technical analysis for market timing and stock selection for the aggressive investor. Uses unique market indicators, which are explained in a brochure included in the subscription. Granville has made some controversial market calls, the most famous of which was reversing a "buy" recommendation given in his letter with a subsequent "sell" recommendation made to those who pay an additional fee to subscribe to his telephone Early Warning Service.

$250 per year (46 issues). Trial $15 for four issues.

Helm Investment Letter
729 S.W. Alder, Suite 420, Portland, Ore. 97205

Clearly written, with unambiguous forecasts based principally on technical analysis but also taking fundamentals into account. Recommendations include market timing, stock and bond selection, gold and silver, long and short sales. Provides separate portfolios for conservative and aggressive investors who are sufficiently sophisticated to engage in short sales.

$150 per year (24 issues). Trial: $10 for two issues.

Holt Investment Advisory
290 Post Rd. West, Westport, Conn. 06880

Clear discussion of economic, fundamental and technical considerations underlying its market timing advice and stock picks. Advises on stocks, bonds, options, short sales and T-bills for long-term investors.

$180 per year (24 issues). Trial $25 for six issues.

Merrill Lynch Market Letter
P.O. Box 60, Church Street Station, New York, N.Y. 10008

Draws on Merrill Lynch's research and analytical capabilities to provide comments on stock market behavior and direction and advice on individual stocks, including ML's ratings for near- and long-term performance, quality, and dividend potential.

$44 for 24 issues. Trial: $12 for six issues.

Outlook (Standard and Poor's)
25 Broadway, New York, N.Y. 10004

Weekly commentary on principal factors, primarily fundamental but also technical, affecting stock market outlook and suggested investment strategy. Drawing on large S&P analytical staff, evaluates and recommends stocks, including four portfolios of five to ten stocks each to meet different investor objectives.

$160 per year (51 issues). Trial: $15 for six weeks.

Howard Ruff's Financial Survival Report (formerly Ruff Times)
P.O. Box 2000, San Ramon, Cal. 94583

Offers a readable, highly personal commentary on political and economic issues. Offers advice on "survival investments"—precious metals and stones, stamps and coins, gold stocks and real estate, money-market funds and U.S. Treasury bonds. Not registered with the SEC, Ruff will not give outright buy or sell signals on stocks. Provides hot lines for updated price quotes, commentary and personal investment advice.

$69 per year (48 issues); refund for new subscribers within 45 days. Trial: free copy available upon request.

United Business & Investment Report
210 Newbury St., Boston, Mass. 02116

Forecasts gross national product, interest rates, commodity prices and other economic trends, and provides recommendations on stock market timing and stock and bond selection based on fundamental analysis and economic and political factors. Reports economic and stock market views of selected other advisers. Recommended portfolios: long-term growth, cyclical and income.

$150 per year (52 issues); includes consultation privileges. Trial: $5 for four issues.

Value Line Investment Survey
711 Third Ave., New York, N.Y. 10017

Comprehensive information on 1,700 stocks and their industries, updated quarterly. Ranks all stocks weekly for timeliness of purchase (based on probable price performance relative to the market for the next 12 months) and for safety. Weekly analysis covers the economy, stock market, and investment strategy.

$330 per year (52 issues). Trial: $33 for ten issues.

Wellington Letter
Hawaii Bldg., Suite 1814, 745 Fort St., Honolulu, Hi. 96813

For speculators, traders and sophisticated investors interested in foreign currencies, interest rate futures and metals as well as stocks and bonds Recommendations based on technical and fundamental analysis and consideration of economic trends. (*Hulbert* rates only stock picks.)

$252 per year (12 issues). Trial: $75 for three issues.

Zweig Forecast
747 Third Ave., New York, N.Y. 10017

Tempers reliance on technical analysis for market timing, including several Zweig-developed indicators, with concern for basic economic trends. Stock picks derived from computer ranking based on fundamentals and market performance. Recommendations cover stocks, stock index futures and, on occasion, hard money plays. Trading is active and sophisticated, using stop-loss orders and, for traders but not investors, short sales. (Only the traders' portfolio is monitored by *Hulbert*.) Subscribers receive a telephone number to hear taped action recommendations, which are updated twice a week. Recommendations usually clear and concise.

$195 per year (18 issues). Trial: $35 for three months.

BOX 3.1 *Continued*

MUTUAL FUND LETTERS

NoLoad Fund X
DAL Investment Co., 235 Montgomery St., San Francisco, Cal. 94104

Rates performance of no-load mutual funds for the investor interested in shifting capital to the best-performing fund that meets his or her objectives. Shows total return (dividends and capital gain) for each of the roughly 240 funds covered, for past bull and bear markets and for recent periods.

$77 per year (12 issues). Trial: $27 for three issues.

Switch Fund Advisory
Schabacker Investment Management, 8943 Shady Grove Ct., Gaithersburg, Md. 20877

Identifies best-performing equity funds and recommends timing for switching between equity and money-market, fixed income and gold funds in order to outperform the market averages.

Emphasizes no-load funds and families of funds that allow switching at no or nominal cost. Also publishes *Retirement Fund Advisory* ($45 per year, 12 issues; $20 for three issues), an abbreviated report, to help investors use mutual funds for IRAs and Keogh accounts.

$105 per year (12 issues). Trial: $40 for three issues.

United Mutual Fund Selector
United Business Service Co., 210 Newbury St., Boston, Mass. 02116

One of the leading mutual fund advisory letters, with more than 10,000 subscribers, compares performance of many funds, including load, no-load, stock, municipal, corporate and convertible, and bond and gold. Broad statistical coverage of entire mutual field. Provides periodic reports and buy-sell recommendations on 40 to 50 funds on a supervised list.

$65 per year (24 issues). Trial: $5 for two issues.

. . . AND HOW THEY'RE DOING

Among the earliest of the newsletters created specifically to monitor the performance of others was the *Hulbert Financial Digest* (409 First St., S.E., Washington, D.C. 20003; $33.75 for a five-issue trial). Its editor, Mark Hulbert, invests a hypothetical $10,000 according to the instructions of each of 31 letters, changes those investments when the letters instruct subscribers to do so, and tracks the results. This table shows the investment performance, according to Hulbert's interpretations of the instructions given in the general letters described on these two pages, during the period of January 1981 through September 1982. The clarity scores represent Hulbert's judgment of how clearly each letter stated its investment instructions to subscribers.

	Gain or Loss 1/81–9/82	Clarity Score
Dines Letter		
Short-term trading	−12.8%	A
Supervised long-term lists		
Good grade	−27.1	A
Speculative	+13.0	A
Income	+28.7	A
Growth	+16.6	A
Precious metals	−63.1	A
Long-term short sales	+35.3	A
Dow Theory Letters	+21.7	D
Granville Market Letter	+ 5.7	A
Helm Investment Letter	+15.3	A
Holt Investment Advisory	+14.3	B
Merrill Lynch Market Letter	not rated	
Outlook (Standard & Poor's)		
Foundation	+13.5	B
Growth	+27.4	B
Speculative	+13.1	B
Income	+17.1	B
Howard Ruff's Financial Survival Report		
(formerly Ruff Times)	− 1.4	D
United Business and Investment Report		
Growth	−10.3	C
Cyclical	− 8.4	C
Income	+ 6.2	C
Value Line Investment Survey	not rated	
Wellington Financial Letter	+ 5.7	D
Zweig Forecast	+65.6	A

Source: "15 Investment Letters" from "Investment Advice You Get in Your Mailbox," *Changing Times,* December 1982, pp. 40–41.

A. Stock Quotations

52 Weeks High	Low	Stock	Div.	Yld %	P-E Ratio	Sales 100s	High	Low	Close	Net Chg.
365	162¾	Metrm	7	1.9	24	20	365	360	360	− 3
30	22	MtE	pfC3.90	14.	..	z130	29	28½	28½	− 1½
58⅞	41½	MtE	pf18.12	14.	..	z70	58	58	58	.....
5⅞	2¼	MexFd	.71e	21.	..	486	3½	3¼	3⅜	.....
15⅝	11¼	MchER	1.34	9.7	9	34	14	13¾	13⅞	+ ⅛
23¾	16½	MdCTel	1.80	7.8	8	85	23¾	23⅛	23⅛	− ½
29½	19	MdCT	pf2.06	7.2	..	2	28¾	28¾	28¾	− ¼
28	19⅜	Midcon	2.16	8.5	6	226	25¾	24⅞	25½	+ ¾
15⅞	12¼	MidSUt	1.70	11.	7	4182	15⅞	15¼	15⅝	− ⅛
18¾	11¾	MidRos	1.40	8.21	70	78	17¼	17	17	.....
30⅛	19¾	MilerW	1.50	5.1	13	64	29¼	28½	29¼	+ ¾
40⅛	14½	MiltBrd	1.20	3.3	14	198	37	36⅜	36⅞	.....
25⅜	12	MiltR	$ .52	2.4	13	84	22	21⅜	21⅝	− ¼
81	48¾	MMM	3.30	4.2	15	1542	80⅝	78¾	78⅞	− 1⅛
25¼	18⅜	MinPL	2.40	10.	7	90	23⅞	23⅝	23⅝	− ⅛
16¼	8⅞	MiroCp	.40	2.7	37	x10	15⅛	14⅝	14⅞	.....
38¼	16⅛	Misnin	$ 1	2.7	10	424	38	37½	37⅝	+ ⅜
16¼	10⅜	MoPSv	1.12b	7.6	5	57	14¾	14½	14¾	.....
21⅞	16¼	MoPS	pr2.61	13.	..	3	20¼	20	20	.....
32¾	26½	MoPS	pf4.13	13.	..	3	32¼	31½	31½	− ¾
30¾	12½	Mitel				3009	23¾	22⅝	22⅝	− ½
29	19½	Mobil	2	7.4	8	6396	28	27⅛	27⅛	.....
7	1⅞	MobilH		..	..	302	6½	6¼	6⅜	.....
14¾	6⅛	ModCpt		..	27	308	14⅛	13⅞	13⅞	− ⅛
17⅞	9¾	Mohasc		..	..	159	16¾	15⅝	16⅝	+1
19	9½	MohkDt		..	16	430	17⅛	16⅛	16⅜	− ⅝

B. Explanatory Notes

EXPLANATORY NOTES
(for New York and American Exchange listed issues)

Sales figures are unofficial.

The 52-Week High and Low columns show the highest and the lowest price of the stock in consolidated trading during the preceding 52 weeks plus the current week, but not the current trading day.

u—Indicates a new 52-week high. d—Indicates a new 52-week low.

g—Dividend or earnings in Canadian money. Stock trades in U.S. dollars. No yield or PE shown unless stated in U.S. money. n—New issue in the past 52 weeks. The high-low range begins with the start of trading and does not cover the entire 52 week period. s—Split or stock dividend of 25 per cent or more in the past 52 weeks. The high-low range is adjusted from the old stock. Dividend begins with the date of split or stock dividend. v—Trading halted on primary market.

Unless otherwise noted, rates of dividends in the foregoing table are annual disbursements based on the last quarterly or semi-annual declaration. Special or extra dividends or payments not designated as regular are identified in the following footnotes.

a—Also extra or extras. b—Annual rate plus stock dividend. c—Liquidating dividend. e—Declared or paid in preceding 12 months. i—Declared or paid after stock dividend or split up. l—Paid this year, dividend omitted, deferred or no action take at last dividend meeting. k—Declared or paid this year, an accumulative issue with dividends in arrears. r—Declared or paid in preceding 12 months plus stock dividend. t—Paid in stock in preceding 12 months, estimated cash value on ex-dividend or ex-distribution date.

x—Ex-dividend or ex-rights. v—Ex-dividend and sales in full. z—Sales in full.

wd—When distributed. wi—When issued. WW—With warrants. xw—Without warrants.

vi—In bankruptcy or receivership or being reorganized under the Bankruptcy Act, or securities assumed by such companies.

Figure 3.6 New York Stock Exchange Quotations and Explanatory Notes. Stock quotations provide a wealth of current information about a stock. Of greatest interest to an individual investor is probably the "High," "Low," and "Close" prices that summarize the most recent market price behavior of the stock. (*Source: The Wall Street Journal,* February 28, 1983, pp. 37–38.)

published paper (Monday, February 28, 1983). The first two columns, labeled "High" and "Low," contain the highest and lowest price at which the stock sold during the latest 52-week period. Next is the company name, which is often abbreviated. The figure immediately following the company name is the cash dividend expected to be paid in 1983—that is, $2, based on the latest quarterly or semi-annual declaration. The "yld %" figure immediately follows the dividend and is the *dividend yield,* the ratio of the level of current income from dividends to the most recent share price. The 7.4 percent yield for Mobil was calculated by dividing the expected dividend ($2) by the closing price (27 1/8) and rounding the answer to the nearest tenth of a percent. The next entry is the price/earnings (P/E) ratio, the current market price divided by the previous year's per share earnings. The P/E ratio (Mobil's was 8.0), which is discussed in detail in Chapter 9, is believed to reflect investor expectations concerning a firm's future activities. In general, the higher the ratio, the more confident investors are about the future, and vice versa. The daily volume follows the P/E ratio; for common stocks, sales are reported in lots of 100 shares. The 6,396 lots of Mobil traded on February 25, 1983, translates into 639,600 shares (6,396 $\times$ 100).

The "High," "Low," and "Close" columns contain the highest, lowest, and last (closing) prices, respectively, at which the stock sold on February 25. Unless the price of the issue is unusually low, stocks are quoted and traded in eighths of a dollar—in other words, in fractions of 12½ cents. The fractions are rounded off whenever possible; two-eighths, four-eighths, and six-eighths are expressed as one-fourth, one-half, and three-fourths, respectively. Thus, Mobil's close of 27⅛ equals $27.125; had it been 27⅞, however, the dollar price would have amounted to $27.875. The final column shows the net change between the current day's closing price and the closing price on the preceding day. Mobil Corporation closed at 27⅛, unchanged from its closing price on February 24, 1983, which means that it must have closed at 27⅛ on the preceding day.

Stock quotations for over-the-counter stocks are presented slightly differently. Although a recent change in the form of quotation has taken place for a small group of active OTC stocks that are now traded in the NASDAQ National Market, the majority of OTC stock quotations begin with the company name, which is immediately followed by its annual dividend. Next comes the sales in 100s, followed by the "Bid" and "Asked" prices, which are the highest price the stock can be sold for and the lowest price one can buy it for, respectively, at the close of the given day's trading. The final column is "Net Chg.," which is the change in the asked price from the previous day's trading. The following quotation for AEC, Inc., appeared on Monday, February 28, 1983:

Stock & Div.	Sales 100's	*Sell* Bid	*Buy* Asked	Net Chg.
AEC, Inc. .40	4	8	8½	+ ⅛

On Friday, February 25, 1983, AEC, Inc., which pays an annual dividend of 40 cents per share, had 400 shares (4 $\times$ 100) traded. At the close of the day, the stock could be sold for $8 per share and could be purchased for $8.50 per share, which was 12½ cents (⅛) more than the best purchase ("Asked") price of the preceding day.

Bond quotations. Figure 3.7 presents an example of some NYSE bond quotations and an explanation of the notes often used with bond quotes; to see the price information reported, look at the data for Mobil Corporation's bond. The column of numbers immediately following the company name gives the bond coupon and maturity date. The "8½01" means this particular bond carries an 8.5 percent interest rate and matures in 2001. Such information is important, because it allows an investor to differentiate between bonds issued by the same corporation. Notice, for example, the various Montgomery Ward Credit Company bonds ("MntWC"). The next column, labeled "Cur Yld," provides the *current yield* and is calculated by dividing the annual interest income (8.5 percent) by the current market price of the bond (a closing price of 77¾). The current yield for the Mobil Corporation bond is 11.0 percent (8.5 ÷ 77¾). This figure measures the rate of return on the current market price represented by the bond's interest earnings. The "Vol" column indicates the number of bonds traded on the given day; the trading volume for Mobil's 8½ of 01 on February 25, 1983, was 141 bonds. The next three columns, labeled "High," "Low," and "Close," refer to the highest, lowest, and last price (stated as a percentage of face value) at which the bond sold on February 25, 1983. Corporate bonds are also traded in fractions of ⅛, but each fraction is worth 1.25 *dollars,* since corporate bonds have $1,000 face values. Thus Mobil's close of 77¾ equals a dollar price of $777.50 (take the quoted price in decimal form and multiply it by 1000; .7775 × $1,000 = $777.50). The final column ("Net Chg") refers to the net change between the current day's closing price and the closing price on the preceding day. Mobil's bond closed at 77¾, up ¾ on February 25, 1983, which means that it must have closed at 77 on February 24, 1983.

Listed options quotations.   Listed options refer to put and call options that are traded on one of the major exchanges. Figure 3.8 presents some Chicago Board Options Exchange (CBOE) quotes from the February 28, 1983, financial news. From the column headings it can be seen that data for both call and put options expiring in May, August, and November are included in the quotation. In the first three columns are *call* options and in the last three columns are *put* options, all with the same expiration dates. Three Mobil call options exist for each expiration month; they are differentiated by their exercise prices ("strike price") of $20, $25, and $30 per share. If we look at the $25 option, we can see the May option traded at a price of $3 for each of the 100 shares covered in the call (price of the option = $3 × 100 = $300); August options were traded at 3⅝ (or $362.50 per call option); and November options changed hands at 3⅞ ($387.50). The closing price of the underlying common stock on the given day is shown under the name of the company. Mobil common stock closed at 27⅛ per share on February 25, 1983.

The interpretation of the options quotation may be a bit confusing. Take the May (call) option for Mobil Corporation that has an exercise price of $20 per share. Holders of this option can purchase 100 shares of Mobil common stock at $20 per share any time before the May expiration date. Since the underlying common stock is currently selling at 27⅛ per share, the option is valuable because its holders can buy stock currently worth 27⅛ per share for $20 per share. The price of $8 a share is explained in two ways: First, the difference in price between the exercise price ($20) and the current market price of the stock ($27⅛) is an intrinsic value of the

A. Bond Quotations

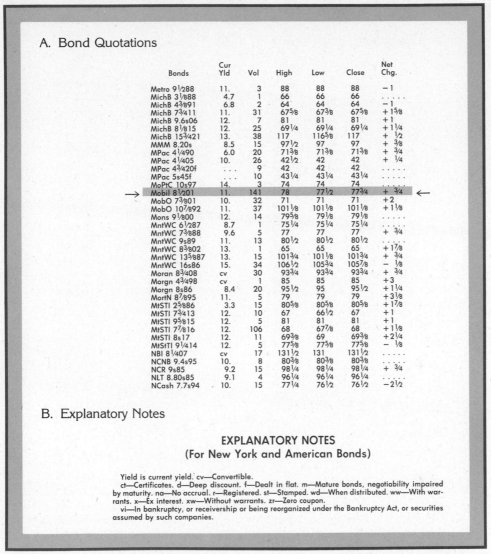

Bonds	Cur Yld	Vol	High	Low	Close	Net Chg.
Metro 9½88	11.	3	88	88	88	−1
MichB 3⅛88	4.7	1	66	66	66	.....
MichB 4⅜91	6.8	2	64	64	64	−1
MichB 7¾11	11.	31	67⅝	67⅜	67⅝	+1⅝
MichB 9.6s06	12.	7	81	81	81	+1
MichB 8⅛15	12.	25	69¼	69¼	69¼	+1¼
MichB 15¾21	13.	38	117	116⅝	117	+ ½
MMM 8.20s	8.5	15	97½	97	97	+ ⅜
MPac 4¼90	6.0	20	71⅜	71⅜	71⅜	+ ¾
MPac 4¼05	10.	26	42½	42	42	+ ¼
MPac 4¾20f	...	9	42	42	42	.....
MPac 5s45f	...	10	43¼	43¼	43¼	.....
MoPtC 10s97	14.	3	74	74	74	.....
→ Mobil 8½01	11.	141	78	77½	77¾	+ ¾ ←
MobO 7⅜01	10.	32	71	71	71	+2
MobO 10⅞92	11.	37	101⅛	101⅛	101⅛	+1⅛
Mons 9⅛00	12.	14	79⅝	79⅛	79⅛	.....
MntWC 6½87	8.7	1	75¼	75¼	75¼	.....
MntWC 7⅜88	9.6	5	77	77	77	+ ¾
MntWC 9s89	11.	13	80½	80½	80½	.....
MntWC 8⅜02	13.	1	65	65	65	+1⅞
MntWC 13⅝87	13.	15	101¾	101⅛	101¾	+ ¾
MntWC 16s86	15.	34	106½	105¾	105⅞	− ⅛
Moran 8¾08	cv	30	93¾	93¾	93¾	+ ¾
Morgn 4¾98	cv	1	85	85	85	+3
Morgn 8s86	8.4	20	95½	95	95½	+1¼
MortN 8⅞95	11.	5	79	79	79	+3⅛
MtSTI 2⅝86	3.3	15	80⅝	80⅝	80⅝	+1⅞
MtSTI 7¾13	12.	10	67	66½	67	+1
MtSTI 9⅝15	12.	5	81	81	81	+1
MtSTI 7⅞16	12.	106	68	67⅞	68	+1⅛
MtSTI 8s17	12.	11	69⅜	69	69⅜	+2¼
MtStTI 9¼14	12.	5	77⅝	77⅝	77⅝	− ⅛
NBI 8¼07	cv	17	131½	131	131½	.....
NCNB 9.4s95	10.	8	80⅜	80⅜	80⅜	.....
NCR 9s85	9.2	15	98¼	98¼	98¼	+ ¾
NLT 8.80s85	9.1	4	96¼	96¼	96¼	.....
NCash 7.7s94	10.	15	77¼	76½	76½	−2½

B. Explanatory Notes

EXPLANATORY NOTES
(For New York and American Bonds)

Yield is current yield. cv—Convertible.
ct—Certificates. d—Deep discount. f—Dealt in flat. m—Mature bonds, negotiability impaired by maturity. na—No accrual. r—Registered. st—Stamped. wd—When distributed. ww—With warrants. x—Ex interest. xw—Without warrants. zr—Zero coupon.
vi—In bankruptcy, or receivership or being reorganized under the Bankruptcy Act, or securities assumed by such companies.

Figure 3.7 New York Exchange Bond Quotation and Explanatory Notes. Bond quotations present, in a compact form, the key data relative to bond prices. Unlike stock quotations, bond price data is quoted as a percentage of face value rather than in terms of dollars. (*Source: The Wall Street Journal,* February 28, 1983, p. 38.)

option. It should never sell for a price less than this, or it would pay someone to buy and exercise the option and immediately sell the stock. The Mobil May 20 should have sold for at least 7⅛. The other difference, the ⅞, is called the option premium; it is an amount someone is willing to pay to have an option on Mobil. (These aspects of options will be discussed in detail in Chapter 13.) At this point the key thing to

A. Listed Options Quotations

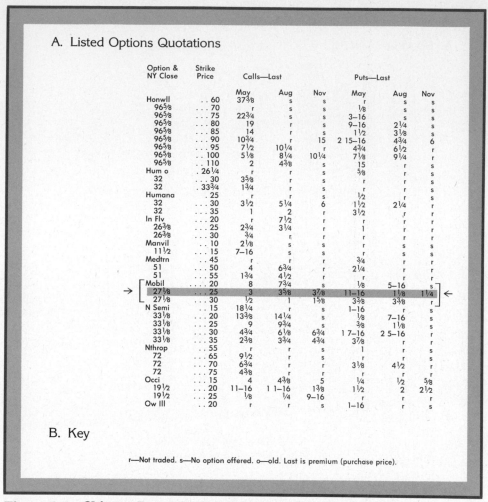

Option & NY Close	Strike Price	Calls—Last			Puts—Last		
		May	Aug	Nov	May	Aug	Nov
Honwll	.. 60	37⅜	s	s	r	s	s
96⅝	... 70	r	s	s	⅛	s	s
96⅝	... 75	22¾	s	s	3–16	s	s
96⅝	... 80	19	r	s	9–16	2¼	s
96⅝	... 85	14	r	s	1½	3⅛	s
96⅝	... 90	10¾	r	15	2 15–16	4¾	6
96⅝	... 95	7½	10¼	r	4¾	6½	r
96⅝	.. 100	5⅛	8¼	10¼	7⅛	9¼	r
96⅝	.. 110	2	4⅜	s	15	r	s
Hum o	. 26¼	r	r	s	⅝	r	s
32	... 30	3⅝	r	s	r	r	s
32	. 33¾	1¾	r	s	r	r	s
Humana	. 25	r	r	s	½	r	s
32	... 30	3½	5¼	6	1½	2¼	r
32	... 35	1	2	r	3½	r	r
In Flv	... 20	r	7½	r	r	r	r
26⅜	... 25	2¾	3¼	r	1	r	r
26⅜	... 30	¾	r	r	r	r	r
Manvil	.. 10	2⅛	s	s	r	s	s
11½	... 15	7–16	s	s	r	s	s
Medtrn	.. 45	r	r	r	¾	r	r
51	... 50	4	6¾	r	2¼	r	r
51	... 55	1¾	4½	r	r	r	r
Mobil	 20	8	7¾	s	⅛	5–16	s
→ 27⅛	... 25	3	3⅝	3⅞	11–16	1⅛	1¼ ←
27⅛	... 30	½	1	1⅝	3⅜	3⅜	r
N Semi	. 15	18¼	s	s	1–16	r	s
33⅛	... 20	13⅜	14¼	s	⅛	7–16	s
33⅛	... 25	9	9¾	s	⅜	1⅛	s
33⅛	... 30	4¾	6⅛	6¾	1 7–16	2 5–16	r
33⅛	... 35	2⅜	3¾	4¾	3⅞	r	r
Nthrop	. 55	r	r	s	1	r	s
72	.. 65	9½	r	r	r	r	s
72	.. 70	6¾	r	r	3⅛	4½	r
72	.. 75	4⅜	r	r	r	r	r
Occi	... 15	4	4⅜	5	¼	½	⅝
19½	... 20	11–16	1 1–16	1⅜	1½	2	2½
19½	... 25	⅛	¼	9–16	r	r	r
Ow III	.. 20	r	r	s	1–16	r	s

B. Key

r—Not traded. s—No option offered. o—old. Last is premium (purchase price).

Figure 3.8 Chicago Board Options Exchange (CBOE) Quotation.
The CBOE options quotations show both the per share price at which the option can be exercised and the closing price of the underlying common stock, in addition to the last price for each option (May, August, and November). (*Source: The Wall Street Journal,* February 28, 1983, p. 34.)

remember is to multiply a quoted option price by 100 to arrive at the actual cost of the option contract; thus, a May call 30 contract would cost $50 (100 × $½.)

Mutual fund quotations. Quotations for mutual funds are straightforward—quotes are in standard dollars and cents. For example, take the John Hancock Growth Fund quotation published in the financial news on Monday, February 28, 1983:

	Bid NAV	ASK Offer Price	Prior Day NAV Chg.
John Hancock: Growth	12.99	14.12	−.06

The quotation indicates that on Friday, February 25, 1983, a share in the fund could be sold for $12.99—the "NAV" or "net asset value." On the same date, a share could be purchased for $14.12. The rather large difference of $1.13 between sale and purchase prices is attributable to the commission charged on the purchase transaction. The "NAV Chg." value of −.06 indicates that the sale price (NAV) declined by 6 cents per share from the preceding day (Thursday, February 24, 1983).

Commodities and other quotations. In general, quotations for commodities and other vehicles include price data similar to that provided for the investment vehicles described above. Because commodities and other popular vehicles are more complicated, we will defer discussion of them until Chapters 14, 16, 17, and 18.

MARKET AVERAGES AND INDEXES

Investors also need to monitor and keep abreast of the behavior of securities *markets*. The ability to interpret various market measures should help an investor to select and *time* investment actions. Just as it is important to understand when the economy is moving up (expansion) or down (recession), it is also important to know whether market behavior is favorable or unfavorable. Market behavior is, of course, affected by the economy, and as a result it is difficult to view each independently. Yet it is in a given security—rather than the economy—that an investor places money, and therefore it is important that the investor understand how to measure the general behavior of the market. A popular and widely used way to assess the behavior of securities markets is to study the performance of market averages and indexes. Key measures of stock and bond market activity are discussed here; discussion of averages and indexes associated with other forms of investments is deferred to the chapters devoted to each vehicle.

Stock Market Averages and Indexes

Stock market averages and indexes are used to measure the general behavior of stock prices. Although the terms "average" and "index" tend to be used interchangeably when discussing market behavior, technically they are different types of measures. *Averages* reflect the arithmetic average price behavior of a representative group of stocks at a given point in time; *indexes* measure the current price behavior of a representative group of stocks in relation to a base value set at an earlier point in time. Many investors compare averages (or indexes) at differing points in time in order to assess the relative strength or weakness of the market. When the averages (or indexes) reflect an upward trend in prices, a bull market is said to exist; in contrast, a downward trend is reflective of a bear market. Because they provide a convenient method for capturing the general mood of the market, an understanding of the major

**TABLE 3.2   THE 30 STOCKS IN THE
DOW JONES INDUSTRIAL AVERAGE**

Allied Corporation	International Business Machines
Aluminum Company (American)	International Harvester
American Brands	International Paper
American Can	Merck & Company
American Express	Minnesota Mining and Manufacturing
American Telephone and Telegraph	Owens-Illinois
Bethlehem Steel	Procter and Gamble
DuPont	Sears Roebuck
Eastman Kodak	Standard Oil of California
Exxon	Texaco
General Electric	Union Carbide
General Foods	United Technologies
General Motors	U.S. Steel
Goodyear	Westinghouse Electric
Inco	Woolworth

averages is important. Current and recent values of the key averages are quoted daily in the financial news; most local newspapers and many radio and television news programs also quote the prevailing value of such averages. Let us take a brief look at the key averages (or indexes).

The Dow Jones averages

Dow Jones, publisher of *The Wall Street Journal,* prepares four stock averages. The most popular is the *Dow Jones Industrial Average (DJIA),* which is made up of 30 stocks selected for total market value and broad public ownership. The group consists of high-quality industrial stocks whose activities are believed to reflect overall market activity. Table 3.2 lists the stocks currently included in the DJIA. Occasionally a merger, a bankruptcy, or extreme lack of activity causes a particular stock to be dropped from the average; this happened recently with Johns Manville. Then a new stock is added—American Express replaced Johns Manville—and the average is readjusted, so that it continues to behave in a way consistent with the immediate past. The actual value of the DJIA is meaningful only when compared to earlier values. For example, the DJIA for the week ended February 25, 1983, was 1,120.94; this value in and of itself only becomes meaningful when compared to the day-earlier value of 1,121.81. Note that one DJIA "point" does not equal $1 in the value of an average share; rather, it can be translated into about 10 cents in share value. Figure 3.9 shows the DJIA over the period November 26, 1982, to February 25, 1983. Over this period the DJIA showed a rising trend, although there were ups and downs. The DJIA is the most commonly cited stock market average, and is quoted daily in the news media.

The three other Dow Jones averages are the transportation, the public utility, and the composite. The Dow Jones transportation average is based on 20 stocks,

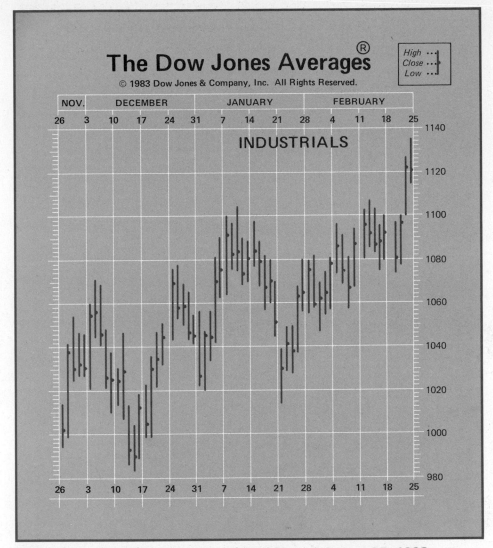

Figure 3.9   The DJIA, November 26, 1982 to February 25, 1983.
One can see that the Dow Jones Industrial Average (DJIA) over this period exhibited an
increasing trend, although up and down cycles did occur. The behavior over this period can
be called "bullish." (*Source: The Wall Street Journal,* February 28, 1983, p. 41.)

including railroads, airlines, freight forwarders, and mixed transportation companies.
The Dow Jones public utility average is computed using 15 public utility stocks. The
Dow Jones 65-stock average is a composite average made up of the 30 industrials,
the 20 transportations, and the 15 public utilities. Like the DJIA, each of the other
Dow Jones averages is calculated in a fashion that allows for continuity of the average
over time. The transportation, public utility, and 65-stock average are typically cited
alongside the DJIA in the financial news.

**BOX 3.2 THE AAII: AN ASSOCIATION FOR
SERIOUS STUDENTS OF INVESTING**

The American Association of Individual Investors, a non-profit, educational organization, is mainly for serious students of some pretty high-brow stuff.

Don't bother paying the $39 to join up, for instance, if the idea of reading a lengthy treatise on common-stock betas (a measure of a stock's price volatility relative to the market) leaves you cold. Or if you doubt that you could sit through a day-long seminar partly devoted to topics such as "the effects of diversification, portfolio-revision strategies and investment timing."

On the other hand, if you have made some investment mistakes, you might be interested. "A lot of our members have been burned once or twice," says James B. Cloonan, president of the AAII, who started the organization with $5,000 of his own money "for stamps and stationery" three years ago.

Then a partner in a local brokerage firm, Heinhold Securities Inc., Mr. Cloonan says he felt there was "a need among intelligent, conscientious investors" for objective information that would help them make their own investment decisions. "I was told I was searching for a small audience," he says with a smile.

A RELATIVE NEWCOMER

With 33,000 members, the AAII is only about half the size of the granddaddy of investor groups, the National Association of Investment Clubs, founded in 1951.

But while investment clubs are formed by investors who pool their funds to learn by doing, the AAII is oriented toward "higher-income investors (typically $60,000 and up), who either manage their own investments or simply want to become better aware of what their advisers are doing," Mr. Cloonan says.

The $39 annual membership dues include a subscription to the *AAII Journal,* published 10 times a year, and study materials, such as workbooks. A separate newsletter surveys new software for home-computer users, and investors can also get several free programs, including one for evaluating some stock-option strategies.

The organization also conducts frequent seminars in major cities on investing and financial planning, real estate and "security analysis and portfolio management." The one-day workshops, $85 for members, $110 for non-members, are taught by college professors and investment professionals.

Several investment professionals also sit on the AAII's 14-member advisory board, including a vice president of the Chicago Board Options Exchange, an institutional-portfolio manager, the head of a large real-estate firm and a precious-metals dealer.

Standard & Poor's (S&P's) indexes

Standard & Poor's Corporation, another major financial publisher, publishes five common stock indexes. Unlike the Dow Jones averages, Standard & Poor's are true indexes. They relate the current price of a group of stocks to a base established for the 1941–1943 period, which has an index value of 10. In other words, if an S&P index is currently 100, this means that the average share price of stock in the index has increased by the factor of 10 (100 ÷ 10) since the 1941–1943 period. A second way in which the S&P indexes differ from the Dow Jones averages is that whereas the Dow Jones averages are calculated so that each stock has equal impact on the average, the S&P indexes consider the relative importance of each share in the

---

BOX 3.2 *Continued*

NO SALES PITCHES

According to Mr. Cloonan, however, sales pitches aren't allowed. "If anything, we've bent over backwards to keep selling out of this," he says.

Some investors have dropped out of the organization after a few months, saying they felt that the magazine, in particular, was too technical. The same sort of sophisticated investment analysis is available from many other publications, including *Financial Analysts Journal,* for instance, or the *Journal of Portfolio Management,* which are widely used by institutional investment managers.

Says Zar A. Reader, a Farmington Hills, Mich., dentist, who quit AAII after trying the magazine for a year, "It was way over my head. I couldn't understand 90% of what they were talking about. This group isn't for small investors like me."

Still, other kinds of articles the *AAII Journal* carries would seem useful to many investors. Recent examples include tips on choosing a money-market fund and buying a home computer as an investment aid.

Local-chapter organizers are, not surprisingly, enthusiastic about the organization. They tend to be investors like Edward Graves, a compensation analyst for Sterling Drug Inc. in New York. The Manhattan-based group has sponsored three seminars in the past year and Mr. Graves says about 500 investors have expressed interest in formally organizing the chapter.

"I'm happier making my own investment decisions" (rather than relying on a broker), he explains, adding that while he appreciates the chance at AAII meetings to share experiences with other investors, "I'm selfish. I think I can do better than a group, say, an investment club."

Adds Eileen Mawn, a foreign-language teacher who helped start the 75-member Boston chapter, "Most of us joined to learn. Personally, I'm learning a lot."

The AAII's national headquarters are located at 612 North Michigan Ave., Chicago, Ill. 60611.

Source: Jill Bettner, "Non-Profit, Educational Group for Investors Attracts the Cautious Who Have Been Burned." *The Wall Street Journal,* July 26, 1982, p. 36.

---

marketplace. S&P accomplishes this by weighting each company in its idex by the number of shares outstanding. Although the Dow Jones averages are the most popular, many professional investors prefer S&P's indexes, since they are felt to reflect more accurately the price behavior of the market overall.

The five common stock indexes published by Standard & Poor's are the industrial, transportation, public utility, financial, and composite. In addition to the five major indexes, S&P also calculates indexes for capital goods companies, consumer goods, high-grade common stocks, and low-grade common stocks. The industrial index is made up of the common stock of 400 industrial firms; the transportation index includes the stock of 20 transportation companies; the public utility index is made up of 40 public utility stocks; the financial index contains 40 financial stocks; and the composite index contains the total of 500 stocks included in the industrial, transportation, public utility, and financial stock indexes. Like the Dow, the S&P indexes are normally quoted in the financial news.

Although the Dow Jones averages and S&P's indexes tend to behave in a similar fashion over time, their day-to-day magnitude, and even direction (up or down) can differ significantly, since the Dows are averages and the S&Ps are indexes. Take the industrials: on February 24, 1983, the DJIA was 1,121.81 and the S&P 400 was 168.27. Although the DJIA declined 0.87 points the following day, the S&P 400 increased 0.07 points. The magnitude of these changes is most meaningful when viewed in relation to the absolute size of the average or index. For example, on February 25, 1983, the DJIA declined by 0.08 percent (0.87 ÷ 1,121.81), and the S&P 400 increased by 0.04 percent (0.07 ÷ 168.27).

NYSE, AMEX, and NASDAQ indexes

Three exchange-based indexes are the New York Stock Exchange (NYSE), the American Stock Exchange (AMEX), and the National Association of Securities Dealers Automated Quotation (NASDAQ). The *NYSE index* includes all the approximately 2,200 stocks listed on the "big board." It is calculated in a way similar to that used for the S&P indexes. The base of 50 reflects the December 31, 1965, value of stocks listed on the NYSE. In addition to the composite index, the NYSE also publishes indexes for industrials, utilities, transportation, and finance subgroups. The behavior of the NYSE industrial index will normally be quite similar to that of the DJIA and the S&P 400 index.

The *AMEX index* reflects the price of shares on the exchange relative to a base of 100, which is set at August 31, 1973. The index reflects price changes in such a way that if the price change in the AMEX stocks (one share of each) from one day to the next is +3 percent, the AMEX index would increase by 3 percent over the previous day's value. The AMEX index tends to behave in a fashion similar to those mentioned earlier. Like the NYSE indexes, the AMEX index is often cited in the financial news.

The *NASDAQ indexes,* which reflect over-the-counter market activity, are calculated like the S&P and NYSE indexes. They are based on a value of 100 set February 5, 1971. The most comprehensive of the NASDAQ indexes is the composite index, which is calculated using more than 3,000 domestic common stocks traded on the NASDAQ system. The other six NASDAQ indexes are the industrial, the insurance, the bank, the other finance, the transportation, and the utility. Although their degrees of responsiveness may vary, the NASDAQ indexes tend to move in the same direction at the same time as the other major indexes.

Other averages and indexes

In addition to the major indexes described above, a number of others are available. Barron's publishes a 50-Stock Average, the average price of the 20 Most Active Stocks, and an index of 20 Low-Price Stocks. *The New York Times* publishes its own average, which is quite similar to the Dow Jones averages. Moody's Investors Service prepares market indicators for a variety of groupings of common stock. Value Line publishes an index that contains 1,700 stocks traded on a broad cross section of exchanges, as well as in the over-the-counter market. Each of these averages and indexes, like the major ones, reflects the general behavior of all the securities markets or a specific segment of them.

Bond Market Indicators

A number of bond market indicators are available for assessing the general behavior of these markets. Because the individual investor is less likely to trade bonds in the same way as stocks, there are not nearly as many indicators of overall bond market behavior. The key measures are bond yields, the Dow Jones bond averages, and the New York Stock Exchange bond statistics.

Bond yields

Bond yields capture the behavior of market interest rates and represent a type of summary measure of the return an investor would receive on a bond if it were held to maturity. They are reported as an annual rate of return; for example, a bond with a yield of 11.50 percent will provide its owner with a return in the form of periodic interest *and* capital gain or loss that would be equivalent to an 11.50 percent annual rate of earnings on the amount invested, if held to maturity. Typically, bond yields are quoted for a group of bonds that are similar with respect to type and quality of issuer, bond maturity, and so on. For example, *Barron's* quotes the average yields for the Dow Jones 10 utilities, 10 industrials, 20 bond composites, as well as for a group of 20 municipal bonds. The yields quoted by *Barron's* for the week ended February 25, 1983, were 12.39 percent for utilities, 11.31 percent for industrials, 11.85 percent for the composite, and 9.34 percent for the municipals. Similar bond yield data are also available from S&P, Moody's, and the Federal Reserve. Like stock market averages and indexes, bond yield data are especially useful when viewed over time; studying the trend in bond yields can help the investor time purchases and sales.

Dow Jones bond averages

The *Dow Jones bond averages* include a utility, an industrial, and a composite bond average. Each average reflects the simple mathematical average of the closing prices, rather than yields, for each group of bonds included. The utility bond average is based on the closing prices of 10 utility bonds, the industrial bond average is based on the closing prices of 10 industrial bonds, and the composite bond average is based on the closing prices of 10 utility and 10 industrial bonds. Like bond price quotations, the bond averages are presented in terms of the percentage of face value at which the bond sells. For example, the February 25, 1983, Dow Jones composite bond average of 72.49 indicates that on average bonds are (on the day reported) selling for 72.49 percent of their face or maturity value; for a $1,000 bond that means the average price of an issue would equal about $724.90. In addition to the three bond averages, Dow Jones also publishes a U.S. government bond average, which is calculated the same way. The Dow Jones bond averages are published daily in *The Wall Street Journal* and are summarized on a weekly basis in *Barron's*.

New York Stock Exchange bond statistics

The New York Stock Exchange is the dominant organized exchange on which bonds are traded, so certain summary statistics on daily bond-trading activity on the NYSE provide useful insight into the behavior of the bond markets in general. These are the number of issues traded; the number that advanced, declined, or remained unchanged; the number of new highs and new lows; and total sales volume in dollars. For example, on February 25, 1983, 1,235 issues were traded: 844 advanced, 192 declined, and 199 remained unchanged. Of the issues traded, 231 achieved new price highs for the year and none fell to new price lows. Total sales volume was $45,790,000. NYSE bond statistics are published daily in *The Wall Street Journal,* and a weekly summary can be found in *Barron's.*

INVESTMENT ADVISORS

In spite of the fact that numerous sources of financial information are available, many investors have neither the time nor the expertise to analyze this information and make decisions on their own. Instead, they use some type of investment advisor. *Investment advisors* are individuals or firms that provide investment advice—typically for a fee—to clients. They provide services ranging from recommendations on investment vehicles and strategies to complete money management, which might include tax and financial planning, tax shelters, and so on.

The Advisor's Product

The "product" provided by investment advisors ranges from broad general advice to specific detailed analyses and recommendations. The most general form of advice is a newsletter published by the advisor and provided to clients. These letters provide general advice on the economy, current events, market behavior, and specific securities. Investment advisors also provide complete investment evaluation, recommendation, and management services. For a fee, they will evaluate an investor's objectives, financial resources, and current investment portfolio, and suggest a recommended course of action. In some cases, the advisor is given total discretion over the client's portfolio.

Regulation of Advisors

As we pointed out in Chapter 2, the Investment Advisors Act of 1940 was passed in order to make sure that investment advisors make full disclosure of information about their backgrounds, conflicts of interest, and so on. The act requires professional advisors to register and file periodic reports with the SEC. A 1960 amendment extended the SEC's powers to permit it to inspect the records of investment advisors and to revoke the registration of those who violate the act's provisions. Persons such as stockbrokers, accountants, and bankers, who provide investment advice in addition to their main professional activity, are not regulated by the act.

In order to provide additional protection, many states have passed similar legislation requiring investment advisors to register and abide by the guidelines established by the state law. The federal and state laws regulating the activities of professional investment advisors do *not* guarantee competence; rather, they are intended to protect the investor against fraudulent and unethical practices. It is important to recognize that, at present, *no* law or regulatory body regulates entrance into the field. Therefore, investment advisors range from the highly informed professional to the totally incompetent amateur. Advisors possessing a professional designation such as CFA (Chartered Financial Analyst), CFP (Certified Financial Planner), ChFC (Chartered Financial Consultant), CLU (Chartered Life Underwriter), or CPA (Certified Public Accountant) are usually preferred because they have completed coursework in areas directly or peripherally related to the individual investment process.

Types of Advisors

Investment advisors are commonly stockbrokers, bankers, subscription services, or individual advisors and advisory firms. Often these advisors are recommended by or work in conjunction with a financial planner.

Financial planners

A *financial planner* is a person who works with an individual or corporate client to (1) evaluate the present financial situation, (2) identify financial goals, and (3) present a written course of action to achieve those goals. The financial planner collects and assesses all relevant data, identifies financial problems, provides written recommendations and alternative solutions, coordinates the implementation of recommendations, and provides periodic review and update. For these services the financial planner receives fees for services rendered and/or a commission for products such as insurance, investments, and legal services provided by or through them. Today, most professional financial planners possess either the CFP or ChFC designation, or both.

Stockbrokers

The primary role of the stockbroker is to make purchase and sale transactions on behalf of clients. In exchange for this service, brokers are paid a commission that is their primary source of income. Stockbrokers also provide clients with information and advice. Many firms will analyze a client's portfolio and make recommendations as to how the portfolio might be changed to better conform with the investor's goals. Although information provided to clients is generally free, portfolio analysis and advice is often provided on a fee basis.

Bankers

Bankers, like stockbrokers, commonly provide investment advice to their customers. Such advice typically comes from trust officers whose activities involve investing funds held in trust for customers. The degree of involvement of the bank may range from strict bookkeeping, in which the bank may act as custodian for the investor's securities, to managing (often as part of a trust agreement) an individual's investments.

Typically, if the bank is to become involved in keeping records, advising, or actually managing an individual's investments, a minimum portfolio of $40,000 to $50,000 is required. Because banks tend to recommend higher-quality investments, their advice and management activities tend to be rather conservative. Over the past few years, more and more banks seem to have established investment advisory departments, which for a fee will manage the investment portfolio of the small investor. A similar trend seems to be occurring in brokerage firms as well.

Subscription services

Publishers of subscription services and investment letters offer advisory service to subscribers ranging from general advice on the economy, markets, or specific securities to periodic portfolio reviews and even active management of a subscriber's portfolio. For active management, an additional fee is charged. The amount of personal advice available as part of a subscription service or investment letter is clearly stated in advance, as are services available on a fee basis.

Individual advisors and advisory firms

For a fee, individuals will manage the investment portfolios of other individuals. These people are paid to stay abreast of tax laws and market developments and to use this knowledge to fulfill their clients' investment goals. Individual advisors typically do not accept many clients and are therefore quite selective when accepting new business. They will sometimes agree to manage a portfolio only on a *discretionary basis,* which means that they are given complete control of the client's portfolio; more often, however, they will provide advice and recommendations directly to clients as developments unfold or opportunities arise.

On a larger scale, investment advisory firms deal primarily in the sale of advisory services. These operations have staffs of researchers and advisors, each specializing in certain types of portfolios. Some advisors may be specialists in managing large growth-oriented portfolios; others may concentrate on more conservative income-oriented portfolios. Often, these firms will specialize in tax-sheltered investments and other sophisticated investment strategies. Clients are assigned to staff members on the basis of the size and objectives of their portfolios. Although these firms prefer to manage portfolios on a discretionary basis, clients can arrange to have final approval over any changes. These advisory firms, like individual advisors, tend to accept accounts with total funds of $100,000 or more.

The Cost of Investment Advice

Professional investment advice typically costs between ¼ of 1 percent and 2 percent annually of the amount of money being managed. For large portfolios, the fee is typically in the range of ¼ to ¾ percent. For small portfolios (less than $50,000) an annual fee ranging from 1 to 2 percent of the amount of funds managed would not be unusual. These fees generally cover complete management of a client's money, excluding, of course, any purchase or sale commissions; the cost of periodic investment advice not provided as part of a subscription service could be based on a fixed-fee schedule or quoted as an hourly charge for consultation.

Effective Use of Investment Advice

Like most services available, some investment advisory services are better than others. In many cases the less expensive service may provide better advice than a more expensive service. It is best to study carefully the track record and overall reputation of an investment advisor prior to purchasing its services. Not only should the advisor have a good performance record, but it is important that it be responsive to the investor's personal goals. A careful assessment of the costs and potential benefits of professional investment advice should be made and, if it appears to be economically justified, the investor should purchase the best quality advice available per dollar of cost.

Investment Clubs

In order to gain both investment advice and experience in constructing and managing a portfolio, many investors—especially those of moderate means—join an investment club. The *investment club* is a legal partnership binding a group of investors (partners) to a specified organizational structure, operating procedures, and purpose. The goal of most clubs is making investments in vehicles of moderate risk to earn favorable long-run returns; only rarely are investment clubs formed to make speculative investments.

Investment clubs are typically formed by a group of people having similar goals and wishing to pool their knowledge and money to create a jointly owned portfolio. The clubs are typically structured so that certain members are responsible for obtaining and analyzing data relative to a specific investment vehicle or strategy. At periodic meetings the members present their findings and recommendations, which are discussed and further analyzed by the membership which, as a group, will decide whether or not the proposed vehicle or strategy should be pursued. Most clubs require members to make scheduled contributions to the club's treasury, thereby providing for periodic increases in the pool of investable funds. Although most clubs concentrate on security investments, they are occasionally formed to invest in options, commodities, and real estate.

Membership in an investment club provides an excellent way for the new investor to learn the key aspects of portfolio construction and investment management, while (one hopes) earning a favorable return on funds. The National Association of Investment Clubs publishes a variety of useful materials and also sponsors regional and national meetings providing information on club organization and activities, as well as emerging investment techniques and strategies. Most stockbrokers can provide information and assistance to those wishing to form or join an investment club. Moreover, with more investors turning to personal computers (our next topic) to assist them in making decisions, the investment club is an excellent arrangement for sharing common costs. A $700 software program may be too expensive for a single investor, but shared by 10 or more members of an investment club, the reduced cost per user makes it affordable.

ROLE OF THE PERSONAL COMPUTER

The increasing availability of personal computers (PCs) and their use in the investment process was noted in Chapter 1. In this section, we present detailed information about hardware, software, data bases, and the costs of using a PC system. A PC offers an individual many personal, financial, and entertainment applications in addition to investing. It can be used in family budgeting, insurance planning, paying bills and monitoring a checking account, storing data, playing video games, and more. Thus, in deciding whether or not a PC is a worthwhile investment, one must also consider the value of these other functions.

BOX 3.3 USING PC'S IN INVESTMENT MANAGEMENT

Ed Neilsen, a TV producer in New York City, used to devote 15 hours a week to managing his investments. Sometimes he would spend up to 12 hours studying a single stock before deciding whether to buy or sell. Then, in 1977, Neilsen bought an Apple I computer to help. Now he devotes five hours a week to his investments and follows 70 stocks instead of 20. Moreover, he can reach buy-or-sell decisions within minutes. Says he: "When the time is right, I know it almost immediately."

That's because with nary a shrug nor sigh, a personal computer can analyze enormous amounts of statistics. Within seconds, it can project the results on a screen as charts, tables or graphs, enabling an investor to size up a buying opportunity—or must-sell situation—quickly and probably more accurately than if he did all the calculations by hand. Says Neilsen, echoing the experience of many other small investors: "My computer has improved my investing incredibly."

Neilsen usually has eight to 10 stocks in his portfolio, which recently was worth about $75,000. He uses his computer to keep close watch on his stocks' price fluctuations and trading volume. Also, he follows moving averages—which smooth out daily ripples and reveal trends—and the revenues, earnings and other vital signs of companies whose shares he owns. He keeps similarly close tabs on about 60 other companies waiting for the right moment to buy. For example, last summer when the stock of Commodore International, a manufacturer of personal computers, reached $38.50, which Neilsen's analysis indicated was a probable peak, he sold 1,000 shares. He then invested in Great Western Financial, a large California savings and loan association that he had followed for a year. Sure enough, within a month Commodore had dropped to $26 and Great Western had risen 33% to $17.50.

As Ed Neilsen would be the first to acknowledge, a home computer is not a magic investing machine that will make you rich. However, notes Charles Gallo of Yonkers, N.Y., a computer consultant who specializes in investment programs, "a computer can make your life as an investor a lot easier."

If you're interested in buying a computer to aid in your investing, your first step, as this special report has already made clear, should not be to rush out and buy one. Instead, you should find investment programs—which enable a computer to do the analysis you need—that suit you best. Says Gallo: "I've had phone calls from people who were literally crying because they'd spent $6,000 on a computer system only to find that they can't get software to do the job they want." So far, the vast majority of investment programs have been designed for Apple computers. A few are available for

Hardware

Hardware refers to the physical components of a PC system. A critical question about hardware is the amount of memory the unit has—it must be enough to permit the investment applications the user has in mind. Smaller and less expensive units typically lack sufficient memory and would therefore not be suitable. Before purchasing any system, one must determine how it will be used, both immediately and in the more distant future. One firm specializing in this area suggests the hardware and retail costs noted in Table 3.3 as appropriate to a complete and reasonably sophisticated system that will do investment applications adequately. These costs were based on competitive prices as of September 1983. This system would be capable of utilizing most of the software available at that time, and it could be used

---

BOX 3.3 *Continued*

Radio Shack's TRS-80. It probably will be six months to a year before many have been developed for the newer IBM personal computer. Even less software is on the market for other brands.

Unfortunately, not all of the several hundred investment programs available were created equal. Only a few dozen are really useful. They range in price from $50 for one that's little more than an electronic filing folder to $2,000 for a specialized stock-analysis system. But don't forget: the cost of an investing program can be depreciated for taxes, as can part or all of what you pay for your computer; the amount depends on what proportion of its use is for investing.

There are three basic types of software for investors:

- *Management programs that keep track of your portfolio's gains and losses. These vary from $50 for a simple program to $595 for one designed for professional money managers. In addition, to make maximum use of such a program, you'll have to plug into an information service through your phone line to get current stock prices, dividends, price/earnings ratios and the volume of shares traded. The cost: from 10¢ to $1.20 a minute, which can easily add up to $500 or more a year for an active investor. Generally, investors prefer Dow Jones News/Retrieval because of its broad range of business and financial information, including five years of stock quotes.*
- *Technical analysis programs that within seconds can reduce staggering amounts of data about a stock's price and trading volume to graphs and charts.*
- *Fundamental analysis programs that will keep you abreast of companies' revenues, earnings and other signs of health.*

While computer programs—some of the best are profiled below—may improve your analysis, only you can take the investment plunge. In August, for example, Ed Neilsen's computer indicated that American Express was an especially timely buy. So he purchased 500 shares at $38.25. Within a month, the price had shot up to $48.75 and Neilsen's computer analysis persuaded him to sell. Best of all, the machine, unlike a human investment adviser, didn't expect to be taken to dinner afterward. But Neilsen did give its case a comradely pat.

Source: Augustin Hedberg, "Choosing the Best Computer for You." *Money,* November 1982, pp. 92–93.

---

to obtain securities price quotes and other information from the Dow Jones News/Retrieval Service and other systems, such as Mead's LEXIS, and to communicate with computer networks or on-line data bases.

Software

Software consists of the programs that instruct the computer about the functions it is to perform. Without adequate software, the computer is useless. As more investors purchase PCs, more software programs will be written that cater to the specialized approaches used to evaluate individual securities and the market in general. Moreover, as PCs become more "user friendly" (this means the user communicates more easily with the computer and is thus able to utilize it more fully),

**TABLE 3.3   RETAIL HARDWARE COSTS FOR A COMPLETE
AND REASONABLY SOPHISTICATED PC SYSTEM
FOR USE IN INVESTMENTS (SEPTEMBER 1983)**

Hardware	Retail Cost
Apple IIe computer, single disk with monitor	$1,500
High-quality printer with color graphics option	750
Modem (allows connection to a telephone line)	380
Second disk drive	525
Kendell's System Saver (prevents heat buildup)	90
Box of 10 disks	30
Total retail cost	$3,275

investors will be able to design their own programs, which can perfectly match their evaluation models.

As of this writing, Dow Jones has three software programs that deal with common investment problems. Other companies also offer software, but these three are illustrative of the kinds of functions PCs perform. They are explained below and, although all the terms used may not be familiar to you yet, they indicate the very impressive capabilities of PCs. (You may wish to return to this discussion later in the course.) With PCs, the boring and monotonous work in securities evaluation is eliminated, and the investor's time is freed for the more important analytical work. For example, the PC does a remarkable job of screening a large number of potential investments to arrive at a final list that meets all the investor's requirements. Starting with hundreds of possible securities, you may wind up with only a dozen or so—and these can receive a much more intensive evaluation analysis.

Dow Jones Market Analyzer™

Dow Jones in its advertising describes this program as follows: "A powerful technical analysis tool for the serious or professional investor who uses charts and graphs for decision making. The Market Analyzer automatically collects historical and daily market quotes from Dow Jones, and stores the information for later viewing. Then you can construct relative strength and analysis charts or individual price and volume charts with moving averages, straight line constructions, price/volume indicators, oscillator charts and more." The program has some special features:

Automatic entry of one year of daily historical data on stocks, automatic updating of daily data on stocks, bonds, mutual funds and options.
Allows for intput of special indicators.
Stores data on 104 stocks for 128 days or 52 stocks for 256 days on one data disk.
Easy access to all News/Retrieval services.

The suggested retail price of this program is $350.

Dow Jones Market Microscope™

In contrast to the Market Analyzer, which deals with *technical* analysis, the Market Microscope is designed for *fundamental* analysis. Dow Jones advertisements describe it this way: "A fundamental analysis tool for professional money managers, institutional investors, bank trust officers, pension fund managers and private investors. The Market Microscope collects, stores and updates information on extensive lists of companies and industry groups. You can then print out data on individual companies, rank lists with respect to indicators followed, specify screens for buying and selling, and set support and resistance levels for automatic notification when stocks reach critical points." Here are the special features:

Automatic entry of fundamental data, price and volume information on 3,150 companies and 170 industries.

Select from 68 indicators, and set support and resistance levels.

Store 50 lists, each with up to 20 stocks or industry groups, on one data disk.

Easy access to all News/Retrieval services.

The suggested retail price of this program is $700.

Dow Jones Market Manager™

This program, which has a suggested retail price of $300, is described as follows: "A portfolio management program for private and professional investors who need an accounting and control system. The Market Manager maintains one or more security portfolios. You have access to up-to-date prices and financial information, and can track stocks, bonds, options, mutual funds and treasury issues. In addition to automatic valuation of positions, you can get printed reports for individual accounts and an overall securities holding report." Here are the special features:

Easy-to-use data entry for buys, sells, and cash transactions.

Complete year-to-date transaction audit trail.

Complete year-to-date realized gains/losses tax record.

Automatic cash entry system for buys and sells.

Easy access to all News/Retrieval services.

Judging from the description, this program would be particularly helpful in monitoring a portfolio, both for investment decisions and for preparing the year-end tax return.

News Retrieval and Data Bases

Just as hardware is useless without software, the whole PC system is useless without news-retrieval capabilities and *data bases*—organized collections of historical as well as current information. Investment analyses, as will be demonstrated in Chapters 9 and 10, require considerable amounts of economic and financial information, and the more current it is, the better. As you will notice when you become involved in the investment process, securities prices react quickly to unexpected news. Professional investors are in constant contact with many news sources, and

October, 1982

Summary of Services

Intro
- Free online information on News/Retrieval
- Includes new data base announcements and other information of interest to subscribers
- How-to-guides, ideas and applications for News/Retrieval

Dow Jones Business and Economic News

Dow Jones News
- From The Wall Street Journal, Barron's, and the Dow Jones News Service
- Search through headlines and retrieve stories as recent as 90 seconds, as far back as 90 days

Wall Street Journal Highlights Online
- Provides online headlines and summaries of major stories as early as 6 a.m. (Eastern Time)
- Includes front page news items, front and back page features, market pages, and editorial columns and commentary

Free Text Search
- Search the news data base using any combination of words, dates or numbers back to June, 1979.
- A powerful way to find specific data on any subject

Weekly Economic Update
- A review of the week's top economic events and a glimpse of the month ahead
- A single source for economic news

Financial and Investment Services

Corporate Earnings Estimator
- Timely earnings forecasts for 2,400 of the most widely-followed companies
- Compiled by Zacks Investment Research, Inc. from the research of top analysts at 45 major brokerage firms

DISCLOSURE II
- 10-K extracts, company profile, and other detailed data on over 6,000 publicly-held companies
- Information filed with the U.S. Securities and Exchange Commission

Media General Financial Services
- Detailed corporate financial information on 3,150 companies and 170 industries
- Major categories include: revenue, earnings, dividends, volume, ratio, shareholdings, price changes and dividends

Money Market Services
- Weekly economic survey from 40–50 of the nation's top financial institutions
- Includes median forecasts of monetary and economic indicators

Dow Jones Quotes

Current Quotes
(Minimum 15-minute delay during market hours)
- Common and preferred stocks and bonds
- Mutual funds, U.S. Treasury issues, options

Historical Quotes
- Daily volume, high, low and close (now covers a full year)
- Monthly summaries back to 1979; Quarterly summaries back to 1978

Historical Dow Jones Averages
- Available for industrials, transportation, utilities and 65 stock composites
- Daily historical quotes accessible by specific date; composites for monthly and quarterly requests

General News and Information Services

Master Menu
- A complete online listing of the information contained in the service, along with detailed instructions on how to access each data base

Encyclopedia
- Contains more than 28,000 carefully researched and concisely written articles
- Revised and electronically updated twice a year

News/Retrieval World Report
- Features foreign and national news in an easy-to-use electronic package
- Continuously updated throughout the day

News/Retrieval Sports Report
- Scores, stats, standings, stories and schedules for most major sports
- Professional, major college, top amateur

News/Retrieval Weather Report
- Weather tables for over 50 major cities
- National weather summary & forecast by geographic region

Cineman Movie Reviews
- Provides up-to-date movie reviews that are interesting, informative and concise
- New releases, current movies and coming attractions

Wall $treet Week Online
- Online transcripts from the popular PBS television program, Wall $treet Week
- Four most recent programs available at any one time

Dow Jones & Company, Inc. • PO Box 300 • Princeton, New Jersey 08540 • 1-800-257-5114 • in New Jersey 609-452-1511

Figure 3.10 Summary of Services Provided by Dow Jones News Retrieval®.
Dow Jones News Retrieval Services offer a wide variety of business and economic news, financial and investment services, price quotations, and general news and information services that would prove useful to individual investors who can access this information using a PC. (*Source:* Dow Jones News Retrieval® Advertising Brochure, October 1982.)

they buy or sell securities almost automatically when important events take place. In addition to having access to current news, the PC user can also use this same news to update his or her data base. Notice in the description of the Dow Jones Market Analyzer that it automatically collects market quotes and uses them to update technical graphs and charts. As hardware and software become more available, so will news-retrieval systems. Currently, Dow Jones is the unquestioned leader. Figure 3.10 illustrates the considerable news coverage now available. The costs of these services depend on whether news is retrieved during prime or nonprime time. For instance, the Dow Jones Quotes cost $0.90 a minute in prime time and $0.15 a minute in nonprime time; the Financial and Investment Services is $1.20 and $0.90, respectively. In addition, there is a monthly service charge of $50. Finally, Dow Jones makes special rates available to academic customers, and these should be looked into if you are a student.

Annual Cost of Using a PC

If we take the cost estimate for hardware given in Table 3.3 and assume all three Dow Jones software programs are purchased, a user's total investment would be $3,275 + $1,350 = $4,625. As a rough estimate of the annual cost, we might assume the hardware would last five years and maybe be worth $1,000 at the end of that period. Annual depreciation can then be estimated at about $455 ($2,275 ÷ 5). Assuming software has a perpetual life (this might be unrealistic if better programs become available), and allowing an interest rate of, say, 15 percent would add an annual opportunity cost (what could be earned on the money in a similar-risk alternative investment) of $694 (0.15 × $4,625). Finally, assuming news retrieval costs are $200 a year, the estimated annual cost before taxes for the system would be as follows:

Item	Annual Cost
Depreciation	$ 455
Opportunity cost	694
News retrieval	200
Total annual cost	$1,349

Is the system worth this annual cost? That depends, of course, on whether or not the investor could increase his or her annual dollar return by an amount greater than this cost. This, in turn, depends on the size of the investor's portfolio. If the total amount invested is relatively small—for example, $5,000—it would seem almost impossible to justify an annual cost of $1,349. On the other hand, if the portfolio has, say, $50,000 to $100,000 of securities, the PC system may be worthwhile. However, remember that services of a professional manager could be purchased for an annual fee of 1 to 2 percent of the portfolio. Assuming a 2 percent fee, at about $67,450 ($1,349 ÷ .02), the investor would incur an equal annual cost with the PC or the professional manager—*as long as* he or she can do as well as the professional.

If his or her performance is below the professional's, then that must be considered an added cost of using the PC. Of course, it is also possible to do better than the professional; and if the hardware has other uses, this should also be considered in the decision. In addition, certain tax benefits accruing to the investor from ownership of a PC for use in managing investments may significantly lower the annual cost.

SUMMARY

Investment information can be descriptive or analytical, and regardless of which it is, is likely to vary in quality. The types of investment information can be classified as economic and current event; industry and company; alternative investment vehicles; price information; and personal investment strategies.

The key source of economic and current event information is the financial news. Business periodicals also provide general business and economic information plus specific securities and market-related articles. Other sources of economic and current event information are special subscription services such as the *Kiplinger Washington Letter.* Industry and company information can be found in trade publications such as *Steel,* and in stockholder's reports and Form 10-Ks.

Subscription services provide a wide range of investment information on specific industries and companies. Costs vary depending upon the service; many of the services can be used at no charge through a brokerage firm or a public or university library. The major publishers of such services are Standard & Poor's Corporation, Moody's Investor Services, and the *Value Line Investment Survey.* Brokerage firms provide prospectuses as well as back-office research reports at no cost to clients. Investment letters, which provide analytical data along with the conclusions and recommendations of experts, are also available on a subscription basis.

Information on specific security prices and returns can be obtained from a variety of sources. Price quotations can be obtained from a stockbroker or from the financial news. The most comprehensive and up-to-date quotations are published in *The Wall Street Journal.*

Investors commonly rely on stock market averages and indexes to stay abreast of market behavior. The most cited averages are the Dow Jones, which consist of four separate averages—30 industrials, 20 transportation, 15 utilities, and the 65-stock composite. Other popular averages and indexes are Standard & Poor's, the New York Stock Exchange index, the American Stock Exchange index, and the NASDAQ index. Each includes different groups of representative stocks and relies on one of a variety of different computational schemes. Bond market statistics are most often reported in terms of average bond yields and average prices. The Dow Jones bond averages, which include a utility bond average, an industrial bond average, and a composite bond average, are among the more popular. Both stock and bond market statistics are published daily in *The Wall Street Journal* and summarized weekly in *Barron's.*

Investment advice varies from the general information provided in a newsletter to specific detailed analyses and recommendations. Investment advisors typically provide advice for a fee. Those who provide advice as a profession are regulated by the Investment Advisors Act of 1940, as well as by certain state laws. Investment advisors are usually stockbrokers, bankers, subscription services, or individual advisors or advisory firms. They often are recommended by or work in conjunction with a financial planner, who possesses a CFP or ChFC designation, or both. Although some basic services offered to clients may be free, the fees for advisory services range from ¼ of 1 percent to 2 percent annually of the amount being managed. Investment clubs are a popular method used by individual investors to obtain advice and experience in constructing and managing an investment portfolio.

Personal computers (PCs) are increasing in popularity, and more investors are using them to make investment decisions. The important component parts of PC systems are hardware, software, and data bases. The last item is often part of a news-retrieval system. The use of a PC may permit the individual investor to perform the functions of an investment advisor at a lower cost.

KEY TERMS

American Stock Exchange (AMEX) index
annual report
average (stock market)
back-office research report
Barron's
bond yield
current yield
data base
dividend yield
Dow Jones averages
Dow Jones bond averages
Dow Jones Industrial Average (DJIA)
Dow Jones News/Retrieval
financial planner
Form 10-K
hardware
index (stock market)

investment advisor
investment club
investment letter
Moody's Investor Services
NASDAQ indexes
New York Stock Exchange (NYSE) indexes
personal computer (PC)
price/earnings (P/E) ratio
prospectus
quotations (security)
software
Standard & Poor's Corporation
Standard & Poor's (S&P's) indexes
stockholder's report
subscription service
The Wall Street Journal
ticker
Value Line Investment Survey

REVIEW QUESTIONS

1. Define and differentiate between the following types of information.

a. Descriptive.
b. Analytical.

2. Explain how one might logically assess whether or not the acquisition of investment information or advice is economically justified. Be sure to discuss the following as part of your answer.

a. Benefits.
b. Costs.
c. Quality of information.

3. List and briefly discuss a few of the more popular financial business periodicals providing

a. Financial news.
b. General business and economic news.

4. Describe the role played by special subscription services in providing insight into general business and economic conditions.

5. Briefly describe the following sources of company information. Indicate the types of information available from each source.

a. Stockholder's report.
b. Form 10-K.
c. Standard & Poor's *Stock Reports.*
d. Moody's *Handbook of Common Stocks.*

6. List and briefly describe the subscription services available from:

a. Standard & Poor's Corporation.
b. Moody's Investor Services.
c. *Value Line Investment Survey.*

7. Describe the type of information and associated cost available from:

a. Prospectuses.
b. Back-office brokerage research.
c. Investment letters.

8. What are security quotations? Describe the various sources of security quotations available to the individual investor.

9. Given the following stock quotation for ABC (a NYSE stock) from the Thursday, April 10, *The Wall Street Journal,* answer the following questions.

254   150½   ABC   6.00   3.2   15   755   194¼   189   189⅛   −3⅞

a. On what day did the trading activity occur?
b. At what price did the stock sell at the end of the day on Wednesday, April 9?
c. What are the highest and lowest prices at which the stock sold on the day quoted?
d. What is the firm's price/earnings ratio? What does it indicate?
e. What is the last price at which the stock traded on the day quoted?
f. How large a dividend is expected in the current year?
g. What is the highest and lowest price at which the stock was traded during the latest 52-week period?
h. How many shares of stock were traded on the day quoted?
i. How much, if any, of a change in stock price took place between the day quoted and the immediately preceding day?

10. Given the following stock quotation for DEF (traded in the OTC market) for a given day, answer the following questions.

DEF   1.10   86   41⅝   42⅛   + ¼

a. At what price could the stock be purchased at the end of the given day? What is this price called?
b. What is the annual dividend per share on DEF's stock?
c. How many shares of DEF were traded on the day reported above?
d. At what price could one have purchased a share of DEF on the day preceding that quoted above? Explain.
e. At what price could the stock be sold at the end of the given day? What is this price called?

11. Given the quotation for the GHI Company bond below, answer the following questions.

GHI   9½09   10.6   225   91⅛   89¾   89⅝   +⅜

a. When does the bond mature?
b. If the bond has a $500 face value, what is the last price at which it sold on the day quoted above?
c. How large is the current yield on the bond? Explain how this value is determined.
d. What is the bond's coupon rate? How many dollars of interest would the bondholder get each year?

12. For each of the JKL call options cited below, answer the following questions.

Calls—Last

JKL		Jan.	Apr.	July
35⅛	. . . 40	⅝	1½	2¼

a. What is the per share price of the underlying common stock at the close of the day quoted?
b. What price would one have had to pay in order to buy a single option contract on the day quoted for each option?
c. At what price per share of underlying stock is the call option exercisable in each case?

13. Describe the basic philosophy and use of stock market averages and indexes. Explain how the behavior of an average or index can be used to classify general market conditions as bull or bear.
14. List each of the major averages or indexes prepared by (1) Dow Jones and Company and (2) Standard & Poor's Corporation. Indicate the number and source of the securities used in calculating each average or index. Where are these averages and indexes most easily found? Explain.
15. Briefly describe the composition and general thrust of each of the following indexes.

a. New York Stock Exchange indexes.
b. American Stock Exchange index.
c. NASDAQ indexes.
d. Value Line index.

16. Discuss each of the following as they relate to assessing bond market conditions.

a. Bond yields.
b. Dow Jones bond averages.
c. New York Stock Exchange bond statistics.

17. What is a financial planner? What role might he or she play in providing investment advice? Discuss the role of each of the following in providing investment advice.

a. Stockbrokers.
b. Bankers.
c. Subscription services.
d. Individual advisors and advisory firms.

18. What is the range of cost for investment advice, and what type of minimum portfolio sizes do professional investment advisors require? How should the decision to purchase investment advice be made? Explain.

19. What is an investment club? What benefits does it offer the small investor?

20. Explain how hardware, software, and news retrieval are used in personal computer systems. What factors need to be considered before you invest in a PC system? Would you advise the purchase of a PC for an investor with $5,000 to invest? Discuss.

CASE PROBLEMS

3.1 A READING PROGRAM FOR HARRIET

Harriet Starkovich recently graduated from a large West Coast university with a degree in communications and accepted a job with Allen Brothers, a large San Francisco advertising agency. During her senior year, at the advice of a close friend, Harriet took an elective course called "Basic Investments." She found the course, which was taught by Alex Krok, a multi-millionaire who only 20 years earlier had come to the United States as a poor Russian immigrant, most enlightening. Harriet hoped that like Professor Krok, she too could some day make a great fortune in the securities markets.

Now that she has settled into her new job, Harriet wishes to gain practical experience in monitoring economic and current events as well as following the general behavior of the securities markets. She plans to spend the next two to three years gaining general familiarity with economic and market activity prior to attempting to choose the best securities in which to invest. Harriet feels that such familiarity will help her to choose securities when she has accumulated sufficient funds actually to make investments. Although Harriet knows that the odds are against her achieving great wealth through security investments, she strongly believes that by gaining economic and market familiarity over the next few years, she will enhance her chances of success. Harriet's plans center around reading economic and business articles and following various indicators of market activity. The only constraints facing Harriet are a budget of $200 per year and about 12 hours per week of reading time.

Questions

1. List and describe the major sources of financial news available to Harriet.

2. List and describe the key periodicals Harriet may wish to consider, assuming she is interested only in stock and bond investments.

3. Explain to Harriet how each of the following might be used to stay abreast of the stock and bond markets. Recommend specific averages and indexes she might want to watch. Explain.

a. Stock market averages and indexes.
b. Bond market indicators.

4. In light of Harriet's objective, and given her budget and time constraints, recommend a regular reading program. Mention specific publications and point out the parts of them Harriet should read. Be sure to explain why you are making such recommendations.

3.2 A RICH UNCLE—THE PEREZES' GOOD FORTUNE

Tony and Marie Perez own a small pool hall located in southern New Jersey. They enjoy running the business, which they have owned for nearly three years. Tony, a retired professional pool shooter, saved for nearly 10 years to buy this business, which he and his wife own free and clear. The income from the pool hall is adequate to allow Tony, Marie, and their two children, Mary (age 10) and José (age 4), to live comfortably. Although lacking any formal education beyond the tenth grade, Tony has become an avid reader. He enjoys reading about current events and consumer affairs. He especially likes *Consumer Reports,* from which he has gained numerous insights for making various purchase transactions. Because of the long hours required to run the business, Tony can devote three to four hours a day (on the job) to reading.

Recently Tony and Marie were notified that Marie's uncle had died and left them a portfolio of stocks and bonds having a current market value of $200,000. They were elated to learn of their good fortune, but decided it would be best not to change their life style as a result of this inheritance. Instead, they wanted their new-found wealth to provide for their children's college education as well as their own retirement. They decided that like their uncle, they would keep these funds invested in stocks and bonds. Tony felt that in view of this, he needed to acquaint himself with the securities currently in the portfolio. He knew that if he were to manage the portfolio himself, he would have to stay abreast of the securities markets as well as the economy in general. He also realized he would need to follow each security in the portfolio and continuously evaluate possible alternative securities which could be substituted as conditions warranted. Because Tony had plenty of time in which to follow the market, he strongly believed that with proper information, he could manage the portfolio. Because of the amount of money involved, Tony was not too concerned with the information costs; rather, he wanted the best information he could get at a reasonable price.

Questions

1. Explain what role *The Wall Street Journal* and/or *Barron's* might play in fulfilling Tony's needs. What other general sources of economic and current event information might you recommend to Tony? Explain.

2. How might Tony be able to use the services of Standard & Poor's Corporation, Moody's Investor Services, and/or *Value Line Investment Survey* in order to acquaint himself with securities in the portfolio? Indicate which, if any, of these services you would recommend, and why.

3. Explain to Tony the need to find a good stockbroker and the role the stockbroker could play in providing information and advice.

4. Describe the services and sources of investment advice available to Tony. Would you recommend that he hire an advisor to manage the portfolio for him? Explain the potential costs and benefits of such an alternative.

5. Give Tony a summary prescription for obtaining information and advice that will help to assure the preservation and growth of Marie's and his new-found wealth.

SELECTED READINGS

Asinof, Lynn. "Data Retrieval Services Are Used Increasingly by Brokers and Investors for News and Prices." *The Wall Street Journal,* September 27, 1982, p. 34.

Barnfather, Maurice. "Cottage Money Men." *Forbes,* August 30, 1982, pp. 158–160.

"Be Your Own Investment Advisor." *Changing Times,* February 1980, pp. 7–10.

Connelly, Julie. "Seven Forecasters with Foresight." *Money,* June 1982, pp. 54–58.

Edgerton, Jerry. "A Starter Kit for Investors." *Money,* June 1981, pp. 54–56.

Farrell, Maurice C. *Dow Jones Investor's Handbook.* Homewood, IL: Dow Jones-Irwin, 1980.

Harris, Marlys. "How a High Flier Crashed." *Money,* October 1982, pp. 199–206.

Hedberg, Augustin. "Computers for Finance & Business." *Money,* November 1982, pp. 92–94.

"How to Get Started in Stocks." *Business Week,* August 4, 1980, pp. 78–81.

Kadzis, Peter. "First-Class Market-Timing Letters." *Money,* June 1982, p. 63.

Levine, Sumner N. *Financial Analysts Handbook.* Homewood, IL: Dow Jones-Irwin, 1980.

Mamis, Justin. *How to Buy: An Insider's Guide to Making Money in the Stock Market.* New York: Farrar, Straus, and Giroux, 1982.

Redding, William. "The Clubs Come Back." *Money,* September 1981, pp. 123–128.

Rolo, Charles J. "An Inside Guide to Stock Market Guides." *Money,* April 1981, pp. 55–62.

"Three Ways to Profit from an Annual Report," *Changing Times,* March 1980, p. 8.

TWO
INVESTMENT
FUNDAMENTALS

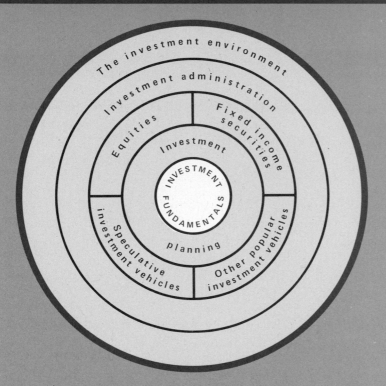

The investment environment

Investment administration

Equities

Fixed income securities

Investment

INVESTMENT FUNDAMENTALS

Speculative investment vehicles

Other popular investment vehicles

planning

Once the individual understands the investment environment, he or she must obtain a firm grasp of investment fundamentals. At the heart of just about every successful investment program is a basic understanding of return and risk, and a fundamental knowledge of what margin trading and short selling are all about. This part of the book contains two chapters. Chapter 4 examines return and risk, concepts underlying all investment decisions regardless of the specific vehicle or technique involved. Chapter 5 introduces two ways in which the risk-return behaviors of certain investment vehicles can be altered—margin trading and short selling.

4
Measuring Investment Return and Risk

The question of value is an important one in the investment process, and answering the question "How much is an investment worth?" is a vital part of making intelligent decisions. In fact, a necessary prerequisite to the effective evaluation and selection of alternative investment vehicles is an understanding of return and risk. The development of risk-return concepts and their use in investment decision-making are the topics of this chapter. More specifically, we will look at:

1. The concept of return, its component parts, and the forces that affect the level of return realized by an investor.
2. Interest income and the use of holding period return in the valuation process.
3. The concept of time value, its underlying computations, its use in the decision process, and the role yield can play in investment decision-making.
4. The concept of risk, its relationship to return, and the major sources of risk.
5. The two types of risk and the use of beta to measure the relevant risk in order to assess potential investments.
6. The basic steps involved in evaluating the risk-return characteristics of alternative investment vehicles.

When buying goods and services, most people have preconceived notions of value which they use to decide whether or not to acquire an item. For relatively inexpensive goods and services, individuals will pay the "marked" or "quoted" price; in the purchase of more expensive items, considerations of value and price will become more important. The value of a good or service to individuals largely depends on the satisfaction they expect to receive from it. Because price and value are not necessarily the same, an economically rational individual would never pay a price in excess of value.

When making investment decisions, the same logic should apply in an even stricter sense. Purchases of goods and services are a necessary activity, but the process of investing tends to center on the achievement of long-term financial goals. An investment can be viewed as a financial commodity, the price of which results from the interaction of supply and demand. But while the lack of real physical qualities tends to complicate the valuation process, keep in mind that just as a physical commodity such as an automobile has certain characteristics (age, mileage, condition), so does an investment vehicle. The key characteristics of investment vehicles are return and risk. An understanding of these dimensions and their measurement is a necessary prerequisite to making wise decisions. Let us look first at the concept of return.

THE CONCEPT OF RETURN

Although a return on an investment is not necessarily guaranteed, it is expected return that motivates people to invest in a given vehicle. The *return* can be seen as the reward for investing. Suppose, for example, you have $1,000 in a savings account paying 5 percent annual interest, and a business associate has asked you to lend her that much money. If you lend her the money for one year, at the end of which time she pays you back, your return would depend on the amount of interest you charged. If you made an interest-free loan, your return would be zero. If you charged 5 percent interest, your return would be $50 (.05 × $1,000). Since prior to making the loan you were earning a safe 5 percent on the $1,000, it seems clear that you should charge a minimum of 5 percent interest. Such a strategy would allow you to receive the same reward you would have received had you not made the loan.

Because investment vehicles differ, every one does not guarantee a return. For example, the $1,000 deposited in a savings account at a large bank would be viewed as a certain return, whereas the $1,000 loan might be less so. In other words, what is your return in the event that the person to whom you lent the $1,000 runs into financial difficulty? Assume that at the end of one year you are able to recover only $950. In this case, your return would be minus $50 ($950 − $1000) or minus 5 percent ($50 ÷ $1,000). The size of the expected return from an investment in a given vehicle is one important factor in choosing suitable investments.

Components of Return

The return on an investment may be made up of more than one source of income. The most common source is periodic payments such as interest or dividends. The other source of return results from appreciation in value—the ability to sell an investment vehicle for more than its original purchase price. We will call these sources of return current income and capital gains (or losses).

TABLE 4.1 PROFILES OF TWO INVESTMENTS

	INVESTMENT	
	A	B
Purchase price (beginning of year)	$1,000	$1,000
Cash received		
1st quarter	$ 10	$ 0
2nd quarter	20	0
3rd quarter	20	0
4th quarter	30	120
Total (for year)	$ 80	$ 120
Sale price (end of year)	$1,100	$ 960

Current income

Current income, which is received periodically, may take the form of interest, dividends, rent, and so on. To be considered income, it must be received in the form of cash or be readily convertible into cash. Interest received on a bond, dividends received from a stock, or rent received from real estate are current income. For our purposes, *current income* will be defined as cash or near-cash that is periodically received as a result of owning an investment.

Using the data given in Table 4.1, we can calculate the current income from investments A and B over a one-year period of ownership. By investing in A, a person would have received current income of $80; investment B would have provided a $120 return. On the basis of the current income received over the one-year period, it appears that investment B would be preferred. Of course, because the total return on each of these investments must include some consideration of what happened to the invested funds, it would be premature to draw conclusions as to which investment is best.

Capital gains (or losses)

The second dimension of return is concerned with the change, if any, in the market value of an investment. Investors pay a certain amount for an investment from which they expect to receive not only current income, but also the return of the invested funds sometime in the future. In the case of a bond, the return of invested funds will occur at maturity, or the investor can sell the bond prior to maturity. Since stocks and other investment vehicles may not have a specific maturity date, the amount of invested funds that will be returned in the future is generally not known with certainty. The amount by which the proceeds from the sale of an investment exceed the original purchase price is called a *capital gain*. If an investment is sold for less than its original purchase price, a *capital loss* results.

The calculation of a capital gain or loss can again be illustrated by Table 4.1.

BOX 4.1 A LOOK AT PAST INVESTMENT RETURNS

Each summer, for the last six years, the investment banking firm of Salomon Brothers Inc. has ranked a selection of tangible assets (commodities & collectibles) along with conventional financial assets. Each item scores on the basis of its compound annual rate of return, as calculated by Salomon Brothers.

With financial-type instruments (bonds, stocks, etc.) competing with commodities and collectibles for position in an investor's portfolio, the rankings provide a convenient bird's eye view of how the competition is going. It includes this year's lineup, last year's, and how the items compare on a five and ten-year time span. The consumer price index (CPI) is included so you can see which outpaced inflation, and which did not.

From mid-1981 to mid-1982, only one investment category licked the CPI—bonds. ... Last year (1981), Chinese ceramics were riding the crest. The five-year winner is U.S. stamps, and the ten-year champion is oil. ... Second-best over ten years, and third-best over five is U.S. coins. ...

Here are Salomon Brothers' rankings ... judge for yourself.

LAST TEN YEARS	Return*	LAST FIVE YEARS	Return*
1) Oil	22.9%	1) U.S. Stamps	26.6%
2) U.S. Coins	22.5%	2) Chinese Ceramics	23.7%
3) U.S. Stamps	21.9%	3) U.S. Coins	21.4%
4) Oriental Rugs	19.1%	4) Oil	21.2%
5) Gold	18.6%	5) Gold	17.3%
6) Chinese Ceramics	15.3%	6) Oriental Rugs	17.1%
7) Farmland	13.7%	7) Diamonds	13.7%
8) Silver	13.6%	8) Old Masters	13.7%
9) Diamonds	13.3%	9) Farmland	10.7%
10) Housing	9.9%	10) Housing	10.0%
11) Old Masters	9.0%	11) CPI	9.6%
12) CPI	8.6%	12) Stocks	7.7%
13) Stocks	3.9%	13) Silver	5.5%
14) Foreign Exchange	3.6%	14) Foreign Exchange	1.6%
15) Bonds	3.6%	15) Bonds	0.6%

For investment A, a capital gain of $100 ($1,100 sale price − $1,000 purchase price) is realized over the one-year period. In the case of investment B, a $40 capital loss ($960 sale price − $1,000 purchase price) results. Combining the capital gains with the current income calculated in the preceding section gives the *total return* on each investment:

	INVESTMENT	
Return	A	B
Current income	$ 80	$120
Capital gain (loss)	100	(40)
Total return	$180	$ 80

BOX 4.1 *Continued*

LAST YEAR**	Return*	THIS YEAR***	Return*
1) Chinese Ceramics	36.5%	1) Bonds	11.4%
2) Stocks	25.3%	2) CPI	6.6%
3) Old Masters	22.9%	3) Oil	6.3%
4) U.S. Stamps	18.0%	4) Housing	3.4%
5) Oil	14.3%	5) Diamonds	0.0
6) CPI	10.0%	6) Chinese Ceramics	−0.5%
7) Farmland	9.7%	7) Farmland	−0.9%
8) Housing	8.1%	8) Foreign Exchange	−1.9%
9) Diamonds	0.0	9) U.S. Stamps	−3.0%
10) Oriental Rugs	−0.2%	10) Stocks	−10.5%
11) U.S. Coins	−8.0%	11) Oriental Rugs	−16.2%
12) Bonds	−9.6%	12) Old Masters	−22.0%
13) Gold	;13.9%	13) U.S. Coins	−27.8%
14) Foreign Exchange	−17.3%	14) Gold	−34.0%
15) Silver	−26.6%	15) Silver	−44.5%

*Compound annual rate of return
**6/80–6/81
***6/81–6/82
Source: Salomon Brothers Inc.

Source: "Battle of the Investments." *FACT,* September 1982, p. 64.

It should be clear that in terms of the total return earned on the $1,000 investment over the one-year period, investment A is superior to investment B. Stated as a percentage of the initial investment, an 18 percent return ($180 ÷ $1,000) was earned on investment A, whereas B yielded only an 8 percent return ($80 ÷ $1,000). Although at this point investment A appears preferable, consideration of differences in risk as well as certain tax factors might cause some investors to prefer B (we will see why later in the chapter).

Why Return Is Important

Return is a key variable in the investment decision because this measure allows us to compare the amount of actual or expected gain provided by various investments. Return can be measured in a historical sense and used to formulate future expectations. By using historical data in combination with other environmental factors, expected returns can be estimated and utilized in making the investment decision.

Historical performance

Although most people recognize that the future is not necessarily a reflection of the past, they would agree that past data often provide a meaningful basis for formulating future expectations. A common practice in the world of investing is to

**TABLE 4.2   HISTORICAL INVESTMENT DATA
            FOR A HYPOTHETICAL INVESTMENT**

		MARKET VALUE (PRICE)			TOTAL RETURN	
Year	(1) Income	(2) Beginning of the Year	(3) End of the Year	(4) (3) − (2) Capital Gain	(5) (1) + (4) ($)	(6) (5) ÷ (2) (%)*
1975	$4.00	$100	$ 95	− $ 5.00	− $ 1.00	− 1.00%
1976	3.00	95	99	4.00	7.00	7.37
1977	4.00	99	105	6.00	10.00	10.10
1978	5.00	105	115	10.00	15.00	14.29
1979	5.00	115	125	10.00	15.00	12.00
1980	3.00	125	120	− 5.00	− 2.00	− 1.60
1981	3.00	120	122	2.00	5.00	4.17
1982	4.00	122	130	8.00	12.00	9.84
1983	5.00	130	140	10.00	15.00	11.54
1984	5.00	140	155	15.00	20.00	14.29
Average	$4.10			$ 5.50	$ 9.60	8.10%

*Percent return on beginning-of-year market value of investment.

look closely at the historical performance of a given vehicle when formulating expectations about its future performance. Because interest rates and other financial return measures are most often cited on an annual basis, evaluation of past investment returns is typically done on the same basis. Consider the data presented in Table 4.2. Two aspects of this historical return data are important: First, we can get a feel for the average level of return generated by this investment over the past 10 years; second, the trend in this return can be analyzed. As a percentage, the average total return (column 6) over the past 10 years was 8.10 percent. Looking at the yearly returns, we can see that after the negative return in 1975, four years of positive and generally increasing returns occurred before the negative return in 1980. From 1981 through 1984, positive and increasing returns were again realized.

Expected return

The return measure can be more directly used in the decision process in terms of expected rather than historical behavior. Looking at the historical return data in Table 4.2, an investor might note the increasing trend in returns from 1981 through 1984. But to project returns for 1985, 1986, and so on, insight into the prospects for the investment are needed. If continuation of the trend in returns seems likely, an expected future return in the range of 12 to 15 percent would seem reasonable. On the other hand, if future prospects seem poor or the investment is found to exhibit a cyclical behavior pattern, an expected return of 8 to 9 percent may be a more reasonable estimate. Because over the past 10 years the returns have cycled from one poor year (1975 and 1980) to four years of increasing return (1976–1979 and 1981–1984), we might expect low returns in 1985 to be followed by increasing returns in the 1986–1989 period.

Level of Return

The level of return achieved or expected from an investment will depend on a variety of factors. The key forces are internal characteristics, external forces, and inflation.

Internal characteristics

Certain characteristics such as the type of investment vehicle, the way the investment is financed, the customer base of the issuer, the management, and so on, all affect the level of return. The common stock of a large, well-managed, completely equity-financed steel manufacturer whose major customer is General Motors would be expected to provide a level of return different from that of a small, poorly managed, largely debt-financed, clothing manufacturer whose customers are small specialty stores. As we will see in later chapters, an assessment of internal factors and their impact on the return offered by a specific investment vehicle is an important step in the process of analyzing potential investments.

External forces

External forces such as war, shortages, price controls, Federal Reserve actions, and political events, which are not under the control of the issuer of the investment vehicle, may also affect the level of return. Because investment vehicles are affected differently by these forces, it is not unusual to find two vehicles with similar internal characteristics offering significantly different returns. As a result of the same external force, the expected return from one vehicle may increase while that of another may be reduced.

Inflation

Inflation, which has been relatively common in the U.S. economy for many years, tends to have a favorable impact on certain types of investment vehicles, like real estate, and a negative one on others, like stocks and fixed income securities. Rising interest rates, which normally accompany increasing rates of inflation, can significantly affect returns. Depending upon what, if any, actions are taken by the federal government to control inflation, its presence can increase, decrease, or have no effect on investment returns. The return on each *type* of investment vehicle exhibits its own unique response to inflation.

MEASURING RETURN

The preceding discussion oversimplified the computations usually involved in determining historical or expected return. In order to compare returns from different investment vehicles, we need to apply a consistent measure. Such a measure must consider differences in the timing of investment income and/or capital gains (or losses), and allow us to place a current value on future benefits. Here we will look

TABLE 4.3   SAVINGS ACCOUNT BALANCE DATA (5% INTEREST COMPOUNDED ANNUALLY)

Date	(1) Deposit or (Withdrawal)	(2) Beginning Account Balance	(3) 0.05 × (2) Interest for Year	(4) (2) + (3) Ending Account Balance
1/1/83	$1,000	$1,000.00	$50.00	$1,050.00
1/1/84	(300)	750.00	37.50	787.50
1/1/85	1,000	1,787.50	89.38	1,876.88

first at the role of interest as a basic return to savers, and then at the concepts of holding period return and the time value of money.

Interest: The Basic Return to Savers

A savings account at a financial institution is one of the most basic forms of investing. The saver receives interest in exchange for placing idle funds in an account. The interest received is clearly current income; but the saver will not experience a capital gain or loss, since the value of the investment (the initial deposit) will change only by the amount of interest earned. For the saver, the interest earned over a given period of time is that period's current income. In other words, to the saver, total return comes from the current income provided through interest.

Simple interest

The interest paid on such vehicles as certificates of deposit (CDs), bonds, and other forms of investment that pay interest is most often calculated using the *simple interest* method. Interest is paid only on the actual balance for the actual amount of time it is on deposit. If you have $100 on deposit in an account paying 6 percent interest for $1\frac{1}{2}$ years, you would earn $9 in interest ($1\frac{1}{2}$ × .06 × $100) over this period. Had you withdrawn $50 at the end of half a year, the total interest earned over the $1\frac{1}{2}$ years would be $6, since you would earn $3 interest on $100 for the first half year ($\frac{1}{2}$ × .06 × $100) and $3 interest on $50 for the next full year (1 × .06 × $50).

Using the simple interest method, the stated rate of interest is equal to the *true rate of return (interest)*—the rate of return earned on the actual balance for the actual amount of time it is on deposit. In the example above the true rate of return would be 6 percent. Because the interest rate reflects the rate at which current income is earned regardless of the size of the deposit, it is a useful measure of current income.

Compound interest

Compound interest is interest paid not only on the initial deposit, but also on any interest accumulated from one period to the next. It is the method usually used

	(1)	(2) Beginning	(3) 0.05 × ½ × (2)	(4) (2) + (3)
Date	Deposit or (Withdrawal)	Account Balance	Interest for Period (6 mo.)	Ending Account Balance
1/1/83	$1,000	$1,000.00	$25.00	$1,025.00
7/1/83		1,025.00	25.63	1,050.63
1/1/84	(300)	750.63	18.77	769.40
7/1/84		769.40	19.24	788.64
1/1/85	1,000	1,788.64	44.72	1,833.36
7/1/85		1,833.36	45.83	1,879.19

TABLE 4.4 SAVINGS ACCOUNT BALANCE DATA (5% INTEREST COMPOUNDED SEMI-ANNUALLY)

by savings institutions. When interest is compounded annually, compound and simple interest calculations would provide similar results; in this case, the stated interest rate and the true interest rate would be equal. The data presented in Table 4.3 can be used to illustrate compound interest. In this case, the interest earned each year is left on deposit rather than withdrawn. The $50 of interest earned on the $1,000 on deposit during 1983 becomes part of the balance on which interest is paid in 1984, and so on. *Note that the simple interest method is used in the compounding process;* that is, interest is earned only on the actual balance for the actual amount of time it is on deposit.

When compound interest is used, the stated and true interest rates are equal *only* when interest is compounded annually. In general, *the more frequently interest is compounded at a stated rate, the higher will be the true rate of interest.* The interest calculations for the deposit data presented in Table 4.3, assuming that interest is compounded semi-annually (twice a year), are included in Table 4.4. The interest for each six-month period is found by multiplying the balance for the six months by half of the stated 5 percent interest rate (see column 3 of Table 4.4). Comparing the end of 1985 account balance of $1,876.88 calculated in Table 4.3 at 5 percent compounded annually with the end of 1985 account balance of $1,879.19 calculated in Table 4.4 at 5 percent compounded semi-annually, we can see that larger returns are associated with more frequent compounding. Clearly, with semi-annual compounding the true rate of interest is greater than the 5 percent rate associated with annual compounding. Using techniques beyond the scope of this text, the true interest rate for the deposit shown in Table 4.4 is 5.063 percent. A summary of the true rate of interest associated with a 5 percent stated rate and various compounding periods is given in Table 4.5.

Continuous compounding, which is compounding over the smallest interval of time possible, reflects the maximum rate of interest that can be achieved with a stated rate of interest. It should be clear from the data in Table 4.5 that the more frequently interest is compounded, the higher the true rate of interest. Because of differences in compounding periods, a saver should evaluate the true rate of interest

TABLE 4.5   TRUE RATE OF INTEREST FOR VARIOUS COMPOUNDING PERIODS (5% STATED RATE OF INTEREST)

Compounding Period	True Rate of Interest
Annually	5.000%
Semi-annually	5.063
Quarterly	5.094
Monthly	5.120
Weekly	5.125
Continuously	5.127

associated with various savings account alternatives prior to making a deposit. Simply stated, the return earned by the saver is best measured by the true rate of return or interest.

Holding Period Return

From the preceding discussion, it should be clear that the returns to a saver are a function of the amount of current income (interest) earned. But the amount on deposit in a savings account is not subject to change in value, as it is for investments such as stocks, bonds, and real estate. Because we are concerned with a broad range of investment vehicles, most of which have some degree of marketability, we need a measure of return that captures *both* periodic benefits and changes in value. This measure is called holding period return. The *holding period* is the relevant period of time over which one wishes to measure the return on an investment vehicle. When making return comparisons, the use of holding periods covering the same period in time adds further objectivity to the analysis. For example, comparison of the return on a stock over a six-month holding period ended December 31, 1983, with the return on a bond over a one-year holding period ended June 30, 1983, could result in a poor investment decision. To avoid this type of situation, the holding period should be defined and consistently applied or annualized to create a standard holding period; similar periods *in* time should be used when comparing the returns from alternative investment vehicles.

Understanding return components

Earlier in this chapter, we isolated the two components of investment return, current income and capital gains (or losses). The portion of return considered current income is a *realized return,* since it is generally received by the investor during the period. Returns in the form of capital gains may not be realized; they may merely be *paper returns.* Capital gain returns are realized only when the investment vehicle is actually sold at the end of the holding period. For example, the capital gain return on an investment that experiences an increase in market value from $50 to $70 during a year is $20. To be realized, the investor would have had to have purchased the investment at the beginning of the year for $50 and sold it for $70 at the end of the year. The investor who purchased the investment three years earlier and plans to hold it for another three years would also have experienced the $20 capital gain return during the year, although he or she would not have realized the gain in terms of cash flow. In spite of the fact that the capital gain return may not be realized during the period over which the total return is measured, it must be included in the return calculation.

A second point to recognize about returns is that *both* the current income and the capital gain component could have a negative value. Occasionally an investment may have negative current income, which means that the investor may be required to pay out cash in order to meet certain obligations. This situation is most likely to occur in various types of property investments. For example, an investor may purchase an apartment complex, and because of poor occupancy, the rental income may be inadequate to meet the payments associated with its operation. In such a case, the investor would have to pay the deficit in operating costs, and such a payment would represent negative current income. A capital loss can be experienced by most investment vehicles. Stocks, bonds, options, commodities, mutual funds, real estate, and gold all behave in such a way that their market value can decline over a given holding period.

Computing the holding period return (HPR)

The *holding period return (HPR)* is the total return earned from holding an investment for a specified period of time (the holding period). It represents the sum of current income and capital gains (or losses) achieved over the holding period, divided by the beginning investment value; it is customarily used with holding periods of one year or less. The equation for HPR is as follows:

$$HPR = \frac{\text{current income } + \text{ capital gain (or loss)}}{\text{beginning investment value}}$$

where

$$\begin{array}{l} \text{ending investment value} \\ - \ \underline{\text{beginning investment value}} \\ = \ \text{capital gain (or loss)} \end{array}$$

HPR provides a convenient method for measuring the total return realized or expected on a given investment. Table 4.6 summarizes the key financial variables for four investment vehicles over the past year. The total current income and capital gain or loss for each during the one-year holding period is given in the lines labeled (1) and (3), respectively. By adding these two sources of return, the total return over the year is calculated, as shown in line (4). Dividing the total return value [line (4)] by the beginning-of-year investment value [line (2)], the holding period return, given in line (5), is calculated. Over the one-year holding period, the common stock had

**TABLE 4.6   KEY FINANCIAL VARIABLES
FOR FOUR INVESTMENT VEHICLES**

	INVESTMENT VEHICLE			
	Savings Account	Common Stock	Bond	Real Estate
Cash received				
1st quarter	$15	$ 10	$ 0	$ 0
2nd quarter	15	10	50	0
3rd quarter	15	10	0	0
4th quarter	15	15	50	0
(1) Total current income	$60	$ 45	$100	$ 0
Investment value				
End-of-year	$1,000	$2,100	$ 970	$3,200
(2) Beginning-of-year	1,000	2,000	1,000	3,000
(3) Capital gain (loss)	$ 0	$ 100	($ 30)	$ 200
(4) Total return [(1) + (3)]	$ 60	$ 145	$ 70	$ 200
(5) Holding period return [(4) ÷ (2)]	6.00%	7.25%	7.00%	6.67%

the highest HPR, 7.25 percent, and the savings account had the lowest, 6 percent. It should be clear from these calculations that in order to find the HPR, all that is needed are beginning- and end-of-period investment values, along with the value of current income paid to investors during the period. Note that the HPR values calculated in line (5) of Table 4.6 would be the *same* regardless of whether the holding period were less or greater than one year. Had the same data been drawn from a six-month period rather than a one-year period, the resulting HPRs would still be valid.

Using the HPR in investment decisions

The holding period return provides a convenient and easy-to-calculate mechanism for use in making investment decisions. Because it considers both current income and capital gains relative to the beginning-of-period investment value, it tends to overcome any problems that might be associated with comparing investments of different size. If we look at the total returns [line (4)] calculated for each of the four investments presented in Table 4.6, it would appear that the real estate investment is best, since it has the highest total return. But upon further investigation, it should be clear that the real estate investment would require the largest dollar outlay ($3,000). By dividing the total return by the amount of the investment (beginning-of-year investment value), a relative comparison can be made. In order to choose the investment alternative providing the highest total return, a simple comparison of HPRs should provide the needed information; in line(5) of Table 4.6, the common stock's

HPR of 7.25% is the highest. Since the return per invested dollar tends to reflect the efficiency of the investment, the HPR provides a logical method for evaluating and comparing the investment returns.

The HPR can take on negative as well as positive values. The presence of negative returns should not cause any problem when using the HPR to assess alternative investments. HPRs can be calculated using either historical (as in the preceding example) or forecast data. Regardless of whether historical or forecast data are used to calculate the HPR, the formula presented earlier would still be applicable.

The Time Value of Money

One problem associated with the use of HPR is its failure to consider the *time value of money*. In general, the sooner one receives a given investment return the better, since an opportunity to invest it and earn additional returns nearly always exists. Two investments each requiring $1,000 outlays and expected to return $100 over a two-year holding period, at the end of which time their values are both expected to remain $1,000, are *not* necessarily equally desirable. If the first investment returns the $100 at the end of one year while the second investment returns the $100 at the end of two years, the first investment would be preferred. *In general, it is best to receive a given return sooner as opposed to later.* So time becomes another factor in the evaluation and decision process.

Future value: An extension of compounding

Future value is the amount to which a current deposit will grow over a period of time when it is placed in an account paying compound interest. Take a deposit of $1,000 that is earning 8 percent compounded annually. In order to find the future value of this deposit at the end of one year, the following calculation would be made:

$$\text{amount of money at end of year } 1 = \$1,000 (1 + .08)$$
$$= \$1,080$$

If the money were left on deposit for another year, 8 percent interest would be paid on the account balance of $1,080. At the end of the second year, there would be $1,166.40 in the account. This $1,166.40 would represent the beginning-of-year balance of $1,080 plus 8 percent of the $1,080 ($86.40) in interest. The future value at the end of the second year is calculated below.

$$\text{amount of money at end of year } 2 = \$1,080 (1 + .08)$$
$$= \$1,166.40$$

In order to find the future value of the $1,000 at the end of year n, the procedures illustrated above would have to be repeated n times. Because this process can be quite tedious, tables of compound interest factors are available. A complete set of compound interest tables is included in Appendix B, Table B.1. A sample of

TABLE 4.7   COMPOUND-VALUE INTEREST FACTORS FOR ONE DOLLAR

	INTEREST RATE					
Year	5%	6%	7%	8% ↓	9%	10%
1	1.050	1.060	1.070	1.080	1.090	1.100
→2	1.102	1.124	1.145	1.166	1.188	1.210
3	1.158	1.191	1.225	1.260	1.295	1.331
4	1.216	1.262	1.311	1.360	1.412	1.464
5	1.276	1.338	1.403	1.469	1.539	1.611
6	1.340	1.419	1.501	1.587	1.677	1.772
7	1.407	1.504	1.606	1.714	1.828	1.949
8	1.477	1.594	1.718	1.851	1.993	2.144
9	1.551	1.689	1.838	1.999	2.172	2.358
10	1.629	1.791	1.967	2.159	2.367	2.594

Note: All table values have been rounded to the nearest one-thousandth; thus calculated values may differ slightly from the table values.

Table B.1 is shown in Table 4.7. The factors in the table represent the amount to which an initial $1 deposit would grow for various combinations of years and interest rates. For example, a dollar deposited in an account paying 8 percent interest and left there for two years would accumulate to $1.166. Using the compound-value interest factor for 8 percent and 2 years (1.166), the future value of an investment (deposit) that can earn 8 percent over 2 years is found by multiplying the amount invested (or deposited) by the appropriate interest factor. In the case of $1,000 left on deposit for 2 years at 8 percent, the resulting future value is $1,166 (1.166 × $1,000), which agrees (except for a slight rounding error) with the value calculated earlier.

A few points with respect to the compound value table should be highlighted. First, values in the table represent factors for determining the future value of one dollar at the end of the given year. Second, as the interest rate increases for any given year, the compound-value interest factor also increases. Thus, the higher the interest rate, the greater the future value. Finally, note that for a given interest rate, the future value of a dollar increases with the passage of time. It is also important to recognize that the compound-value interest factor is always greater than 1; only if the interest rate were zero would this factor equal 1.000, and therefore the future value equal the initial deposit.

Present value: An extension of future value

Present value is the inverse of future value. That is, rather than measuring the value of a present amount at some future date, *present value* is concerned with finding the current value of a future sum. By applying present value techniques, the value today of a sum to be received at some future date can be calculated.

**BOX 4.2 DON'T FORGET TO CONSIDER
THE TIME VALUE OF MONEY!**

On February 17, 1978, Larry—a corporate executive who "dabbles" in the market—bought 300 shares of Itek Corp., traded on the NYSE, at $26 per share. The total cost, including commissions, was $7,712. "I think I'll get a good bounce out of it," he said at the time. On Feb. 1, 1980 he sold the 300 shares at $30, which brought him $8,950. "It's topping out," he said, "It looks to me like it's gone as far as it's going to go." The stock doesn't pay a dividend, so Larry's gain (if there were to be any) would have to come from capital appreciation. The stock's increase in price was the only source of potential profit.

How well did Larry do? In his own estimation, the answer is "very." What was his reason for that judgment? "Well," he said, "I spent about $7,700. And I got back $8,950. That's a $1,250 gain on a $7,700 investment. Not bad."

Is he right? Suppose he had invested the $7,700 in a one-year money market instrument that earned him 10% per annum, the interest to be paid in a lump sum at maturity. Ignoring tax considerations for a moment, suppose he then repeated the process. Investing the $7,700 + $770 = $8,470 at 10% would have brought him $847. At the second maturity date, Larry would have had $9,317.

He held his Itek stock for approximately two years. Even taking into consideration the more favorable tax treatment accorded capital gains than interest earned, he in fact did no better than he'd have done had his $7,700 remained in a money market fund. Actually, the picture was far worse than it seems, because during the period he owned it, the stock suffered a dramatic sinking spell, falling ten points from the price at which he bought it. At that point, he had a $3,000 loss on a $7,700 investment.

In essence he wasn't rewarded for the added risk he took in buying stocks instead of CDs or T-bills. Nor, of course, did he expect a guarantee that his profit would be greater merely because he was taking more of a chance. He simply hoped he'd do well, and in the end, he concluded that he definitely had.

Larry's view of stock market profits is entirely typical. What he omits from his calculations, the majority of investors I survey also overlook. Namely, the time value of money. A dollar you own today differs from the one you owned yesterday, and a dollar you receive tomorrow is not the same as one you receive today. There is a date attached to every investment you make, and the longer your money is invested, the more it has to earn just for you to break even.

That seemingly simple fact has a profound impact on the way seasoned investors calculate their stock market profits and make their investment decisions.

Gaining a sense of the time value of money is essential for two reasons: It will prevent you from thinking you've made a profit, when in fact you've barely broken even, and it will bring you into closer contact with the investment climate that now prevails. That doesn't mean you'll automatically make a killing in the market. . . . However, it will allow you to better understand the atmosphere of mild panic, which is an integral part of every period of high inflation, especially this one.

When determining the present value of a future sum, the basic question being answered is this: "How much would have to be deposited today into an account paying *Y* percent interest in order to equal a specified sum to be received so many years in the future?" The applicable interest rate when finding present value is commonly called the *opportunity cost* or the *discount rate*. It represents the annual rate of return that could be earned currently on a similar investment. The basic present value calculation is best illustrated using a simple example. Imagine that you are offered an opportunity that will provide you with exactly $1,000 one year from today. If you could earn 8 percent on similar types of investments, how much is the most you would pay for this opportunity? In other words, what is the present value of $1,000 to be received one year from now discounted at 8 percent? Letting X equal the present value, the following equation can be used to describe this situation:

$$X(1 + .08) = \$1,000$$

Solving the equation for X, we get:

$$X = \frac{\$1,000}{(1 + .08)} = \$925.93$$

It should be clear from this result that the present value of $1,000 to be received one year from now, discounted at 8 percent, is $925.93. In other words, $925.93 deposited today into an account paying 8 percent interest will accumulate to $1,000. To check this conclusion, *multiply* the compound-value interest factor for 8 percent and one year, or 1.080 (from Table 4.7) by $925.93. This yields a future value of $1,000 (1.080 × $925.93).

Because the calculations involved in finding the present value of sums to be received in the distant future are more complex than for the one-year case, the use of present value tables can greatly simplify them. A complete set of present value tables is included in Appendix B of this text, and a sample portion of Table B.3 is given in Table 4.8. The factors in the table represent the present value of $1 associated with various combinations of years and discount rates. For example, the present value of $1 to be received one year from now discounted at 8 percent is $0.926. Using this factor (.926), the present value of $1,000 to be received one year from now at an 8 percent discount rate can be found by *multiplying* it by $1,000. The resulting present value of $926 (.926 × $1,000) agrees (except for a slight rounding error) with the value calculated earlier.

Another example may help clarify the use of present value tables. The present value of $500 to be received seven years from now, discounted at 6 percent, would be calculated as follows:

$$\text{present value} = .665\ (\$500) = \$332.50$$

The .665 represents the present-value interest factor for seven years discounted at 6 percent.

A few points with respect to present value tables should be highlighted. First, the present-value interest factor for a single sum is always less than 1; only if the discount rate were zero would this factor equal 1. Second, the higher the discount

TABLE 4.8 **PRESENT-VALUE INTEREST FACTORS FOR ONE DOLLAR**

	DISCOUNT (INTEREST) RATE					
Year	5%	6% ↓	7%	8% ↓	9%	10%
→1	0.952	0.943	0.935	0.926	0.917	0.909
2	0.907	0.890	0.873	0.857	0.842	0.826
3	0.864	0.840	0.816	0.794	0.772	0.751
4	0.823	0.792	0.763	0.735	0.708	0.683
5	0.784	0.747	0.713	0.681	0.650	0.621
6	0.746	0.705	0.666	0.630	0.596	0.564
→7	0.711	0.665	0.623	0.583	0.547	0.513
8	0.677	0.627	0.582	0.540	0.502	0.467
9	0.645	0.592	0.544	0.500	0.460	0.424
10	0.614	0.558	0.508	0.463	0.422	0.386

rate for a given year, the smaller the present-value interest factor. In other words, the greater an individual's opportunity cost, the less an amount to be received in a certain future year is worth today. Finally, the further in the future a sum is to be received, the less it is worth presently. It is also important to note that given a discount rate of 0 percent, the present-value interest factor always equals 1, and therefore in such a case the future value of a sum equals its present value.

The present value of a stream of income

In the preceding section, we illustrated the technique for finding the present value of a single sum to be received at some future date. Because the returns from a given investment are likely to be received at various future dates rather than as a single lump sum, the ability to find the present value of a stream of returns is needed. A stream of returns can be viewed as a package of single-sum returns and may be classified as a mixed stream or an annuity. A *mixed stream* of returns is one that exhibits no special pattern; an *annuity* is a pattern of equal annual returns. Table 4.9 illustrates each of these types of return patterns. In order to find the present value of each of these streams (measured at the beginning of 1984), the present value of each component return must be calculated and totaled. Because certain shortcuts can be used in the case of an annuity, the calculation of the present value of each return stream will be illustrated separately.

Mixed stream. In order to find the present value of the mixed stream of returns given in Table 4.9, the present value of each of the returns must be found and totaled. Assuming a 9 percent discount rate, the calculation of the present value of the mixed stream is illustrated in Table 4.10. The resulting present value of $187.77 represents the amount today (beginning of 1984) invested at 9 percent that would

TABLE 4.9   MIXED AND ANNUITY RETURN STREAMS

	RETURNS	
Year	Mixed Stream	Annuity
1984	$30	$50
1985	40	50
1986	50	50
1987	60	50
1988	70	50

be equivalent to the stream of returns given in column 1 of Table 4.10. Once the present value of each return is found, the values can be added, since each is measured at the same point in time.

Annuity.   The present value of an annuity can be found in the same way used to find the present value of a mixed stream. But fortunately, a simpler approach exists. Financial tables of present-value interest factors for annuities are available. A complete set of present-value interest factors for an annuity is included in Appendix B, Table B.4; a sample portion is given in Table 4.11. (*Note:* A similar table of interest factors is provided for the *compound value of an annuity*; this is found in Appendix B, Table B.2 and will be used later in the text.) The factors in the table represent the present value of a one-dollar annuity associated with various combinations of years and discount rates. For example, the present value of $1 to be received each year for the next five years discounted at 9 percent is $3.890. Using this factor, the present

TABLE 4.10   MIXED-STREAM PRESENT VALUE CALCULATION

Year	(1) Return	(2) 9% Present-Value Interest Factor	(3) (1) ×· (2) Present Value
1984	$30	0.917	$ 27.51
1985	40	0.842	33.68
1986	50	0.772	38.60
1987	60	0.708	42.48
1988	70	0.650	45.50
		Present value of stream	$187.77

Note: Column (1) values are from Table 4.9. Column (2) values are from Table 4.8 for 9 percent discount rate and 1 through 5 years.

TABLE 4.11	**PRESENT-VALUE INTEREST FACTORS FOR A ONE-DOLLAR ANNUITY**					

	DISCOUNT (INTEREST) RATE					
Year	5%	6%	7%	8%	9% ↓	10%
1	0.952	0.943	0.935	0.926	0.917	0.909
2	1.859	1.833	1.808	1.783	1.759	1.736
3	2.723	2.673	2.624	2.577	2.531	2.487
4	3.546	3.465	3.387	3.312	3.240	3.170
→5	4.329	4.212	4.100	3.993	3.890	3.791
6	5.076	4.917	4.767	4.623	4.486	4.355
7	5.786	5.582	5.389	5.206	5.033	4.868
8	6.463	6.210	5.971	5.747	5.535	5.335
9	7.108	6.802	6.515	6.247	5.995	5.759
10	7.722	7.360	7.024	6.710	6.418	6.145

value of the $50, five-year annuity (given in Table 4.9) at a 9 percent discount rate can be found. The resulting present value of $194.50 is calculated as follows:

present value of annuity = 3.890 ($50) = $194.50.

Defining a satisfactory investment

The present value concept can be used to define an acceptable investment. Ignoring risk at this point, a satisfactory investment would be one for which the present value of benefits (discounted at the appropriate rate) equals or exceeds the present value of costs. Since the cost (or purchase price) of the investment would be incurred initially (at time zero), the cost and its present value are viewed as one and the same. If the present value of the benefits just equals the cost, an investor would earn a rate of return equal to the discount rate. If the present value of benefits exceeds the cost, the investor would earn more than the discount rate; and if the present value of benefits were less than the cost, the investor would earn less than the discount rate. It should be clear that an investor would therefore prefer only those investments for which the present value of benefits equals or exceeds cost; in these cases, the return would be equal to or in excess of the discount rate.

The information in Table 4.12 can be used to illustrate the application of present value to investment decision-making. Assuming an 8 percent discount rate to be appropriate, we can see that the present value of the benefits over the assumed seven-year holding period (1984–1990) is $1,175.28. If the cost of the investment were any amount less than or equal to $1,175.28, it would be acceptable; at a cost above $1,175.28, the investment would not be acceptable. At a cost of less than or equal to the $1,175.28 present value of benefits, a return at least equal to 8 percent

TABLE 4.12 PRESENT VALUE APPLIED TO AN INVESTMENT

Year	(1) Benefits	(2) 8% Present-Value Interest Factor	(3) (1) × (2) Present Value
1984	$ 90	0.926	$ 83.34
1985	100	0.857	85.70
1986	110	0.794	87.34
1987	120	0.735	88.20
1988	100	0.681	68.10
1989	100	0.630	63.00
1990	1,200	0.583	699.60
		Present value of benefits	$1,175.28

would be earned; at a cost greater than $1,175.28, the return would be less than 8 percent.

Yield: An alternative present value measure

An alternative way to define a satisfactory investment would be in terms of the annual rate of return it earns. The actual rate of return earned by a long-term investment is often referred to as its *yield.* While holding period return (HPR) is useful with investments that will be held for a period of one year or less, it is generally inappropriate for longer holding periods. Because HPR fails to consider the time value of money, a present-value-based measure of yield is used to determine the (annual) rate of return on investments held for two years or more. As such, the yield on an investment can be defined as the discount rate that produces a present value of benefits which is just equal to its cost. The yield approach answers this question: "What is the true rate of return earned on a given investment?" Once the yield has been determined, acceptability can be decided. As long as the yield on an investment is greater than or equal to the appropriate discount rate, the investment would be acceptable. Investments having yields below the appropriate discount rate would not be.

In most cases, the yield on a given investment is difficult to calculate. The most accurate approach is based on searching for the discount rate that produces a present value of benefits just equal to the cost of the investment. If we use the investment given in Table 4.12 and assume that its cost is $1,100, it should be clear that the yield must be greater than 8 percent, since at an 8 percent discount rate, the present value of benefits is greater than the cost ($1,175.28 vs. $1,100, respectively). The present values at both 9 percent and 10 percent discount rates are calculated in Table 4.13. If we look at the present value of benefits calculated at the 9 and 10 percent rates ($1,117.61 and $1,063.08, respectively), it is seen that the yield on the investment is somewhere between 9 and 10 percent. The discount rate

TABLE 4.13 YIELD CALCULATION FOR A $1,100 INVESTMENT

Year	(1) Benefits	(2) 9% Present-Value Interest Factor	(3) (1) × (2) Present Value at 9%	(4) 10% Present-Value Interest Factor	(5) (1) × (4) Present Value at 10%
1984	$ 90	0.917	$ 82.53	0.909	$ 81.81
1985	100	0.842	84.20	0.826	82.60
1986	110	0.772	84.92	0.751	82.61
1987	120	0.708	84.96	0.683	81.96
1988	100	0.650	65.00	0.621	62.10
1989	100	0.596	59.60	0.564	56.40
1990	1,200	0.547	656.40	0.513	615.60
	Present value of benefits		$1,117.61		$1,063.08

that causes the present value of benefits to be closest to the $1,100 cost is 9 percent, since it is only $17.61 away from $1,100 ($1,117.61 − $1,100). At the 10 percent rate, the present value of benefits is $36.92 away from $1,100 ($1,100 − $1,063.08). If the investor requires an 8 percent return on this investment it is clearly acceptable, since the yield of approximately 9 percent is greater than this minimum.

For a given investment, the *present value and yield will provide the same conclusion with respect to acceptability.* It is clearly simpler to calculate present value as opposed to the yield, although many calculators provide the capability to find yields quickly. Even without a calculator, it is possible to estimate the yield on an investment if the annual benefits are not radically different on a year-to-year basis. This estimate is made using the *approximate yield formula* shown below:

$$\text{approximate yield} = \frac{\text{average annual benefit} + \dfrac{\begin{array}{c}\text{future price} \\ \text{of investment}\end{array} - \begin{array}{c}\text{current price} \\ \text{of investment}\end{array}}{\text{number of years in investment horizon}}}{\dfrac{\begin{array}{c}\text{future price} \\ \text{of investment}\end{array} + \begin{array}{c}\text{current price} \\ \text{of investment}\end{array}}{2}}$$

We can use the data in Table 4.12 to illustrate the application of the approximate yield formula. Suppose that in the year 1990 the investment is sold for the future price of $1,200 shown in the table, and that it is the only benefit in that year. Further, assume the current price of the investment is $1,175.28. (*Note:* Setting the investment up this way should lead to an exact 8 percent yield, since that is the present-value interest factor used to discount the benefits to obtain the $1,175.28 value.) The average annual benefit is calculated by dividing the total annual benefits from years 1984 through 1989 of $620 ($90 + $100 + $110 + $120 + $100 + $100) by 7—the number of years in the 1984 through 1990 investment horizon. An average annual benefit of $88.57 ($620 ÷ 7) results. Substituting into the equation on the preceding page results in the following calculations:

$$\text{approximate yield} = \frac{\$88.57 + \dfrac{\$1,200 - \$1,175.28}{7}}{\dfrac{\$1,200 + \$1,175.28}{2}}$$

$$= \frac{\$88.57 + \$3.53}{\$1,187.64} = \frac{\$92.10}{\$1,187.64}$$

$$= 0.0776, \text{ or } 7.76\%$$

The approximate yield of 7.76 percent is reasonably close to the true yield of 8 percent. The approximate yield formula will be used at several points throughout the text to simplify what would otherwise be tedious yield calculations.

RISK: THE OTHER SIDE OF THE COIN

Thus far the primary concern of this chapter has been return. Unfortunately, this important investment dimension cannot be looked at without also looking at *risk,* the chance that the actual return from an investment may differ from its expected value. In general, the more variable, or broader, the range of possible return values associated with a given investment, the greater its risk, and vice versa. In this part of the chapter we will examine the risk-return tradeoff; sources of risk; and beta, a modern measure of risk. Then we will discuss how to evaluate the risk associated with a potential investment.

The Risk-Return Tradeoff

The risk associated with a given investment is directly related to its expected return. Investors therefore require higher levels of return for increased levels of risk. In general, an investor will attempt to minimize risk for a given level of return or maximize return for a given level of risk.

The inverse relationship between risk and return is depicted in Figure 4.1. It results from the fact that increasing risk is a negative factor, whereas increasing return is a positive factor. The point labeled R_F in Figure 4.1 is there because it is possible to receive a positive return for zero risk; the return associated with such an investment is commonly referred to as the *risk-free rate of interest, R_F.* In practice the risk-free rate is about equal to the return on a U.S. government security and represents the return to investors for giving up current-period consumption in order to invest.

Sources of Risk

The total risk associated with a given investment vehicle may result from a combination of any of a variety of possible sources. Because a number of these sources are interrelated, it would be virtually impossible to measure the risk resulting

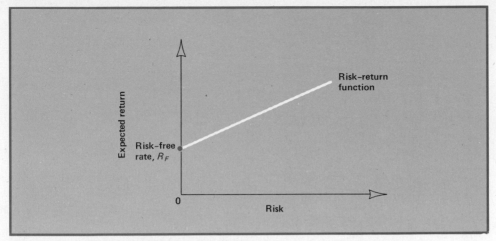

Figure 4.1   The Risk-Return Tradeoff.
The tradeoff between risk and return operates in a way such that higher returns are associated with higher risk, and vice versa. At zero risk, investors can earn the risk-free rate of interest, R_F, which is equal to the return on a U.S. government security.

from each one. The major sources of risk include business risk, financial risk, purchasing power risk, interest rate risk, liquidity risk, and market risk.

Business risk

It is possible for a business firm or property to experience poor earnings and fail as a result. In this case, business and/or property owners could receive no return when earnings are not adequate to meet obligations. Debtholders, on the other hand, are likely to receive some—but not necessarily all—of the amount owned them because of the preferential treatment they are legally afforded. Although bankruptcy is the most severe outcome, in general *business risk* is concerned with the degree of uncertainty associated with an investment's earnings and ability to pay investors interest, dividends, and any other returns owed them.

Much of the business risk associated with a given investment vehicle is related to the kind of business. For example, the business risk associated with investment in the common stock of a public utility differs from the business risk associated with a high-fashion clothing manufacturer or a parcel of commercial real estate. It is generally believed that investments in similar types of firms or properties have similar business risk, although differences in management, costs, and location can cause similar businesses or properties to have considerably different levels of risk.

Financial risk

The risk associated with the mix of debt and equity financing used to finance a firm or property is called *financial risk*. The larger the proportion of debt used to finance a firm or property, the greater its financial risk. The increased risk results from the fact that debt financing means obligations to make interest payments as well as to repay the debts. These fixed payment obligations must be met prior to

What I really want is a stock with no risks, which will quadruple in four weeks.

distributing any earnings to the owners of such firms or properties. Inability to meet obligations associated with the use of debt could result in failure, and in losses for bondholders as well as stockholders and owners.

Purchasing power risk

The possibility of changes in price levels within the economy also results in risk. In periods of rising prices, known as *inflation,* the *purchasing power* of the dollar will decline. This means that a smaller quantity of some commodity can be purchased with a given number of dollars than could have been purchased in the past. For example, if a dollar one year ago would buy five candy bars, an increase in the price of a candy bar to 25 cents would mean that only four candy bars could be bought with the same dollar today. In periods of declining price levels, the purchasing power of the dollar will increase. In general, investments whose values move with general price levels are most profitable during periods of rising prices, whereas those providing fixed returns are preferred during periods of declining price levels. The returns on common stocks and property investment values tend to move with the general price level, whereas returns from savings accounts, bonds, and preferred stock investments do not.

Interest rate risk

Securities that offer purchasers a fixed periodic return are especially affected by *interest rate risk.* As interest rates change, the prices of these securities fluctuate, decreasing with increasing interest rates and increasing with decreasing interest rates. As we will see in greater detail in Chapters 11 and 12, the prices of fixed income securities drop when interest rates rise in order to provide purchasers with the same rate of return that would be available at prevailing rates. Increases in price due to declining interest rates result from the fact that the return on a fixed income security is adjusted downward to a competitive level by upward adjustment in its market price. The actual interest rate changes causing the market price adjustments result from changes in the general relationship between the supply and demand for money. All investment vehicles are actually subject to interest rate risk. Although fixed income securities are most directly affected by interest rate movements, other vehicles such as common stock and property are also influenced by them. Generally, the higher the interest rate the lower the value, and vice versa.

Liquidity risk

The risk of not being able to liquidate an investment conveniently and at a reasonable price is called *liquidity risk*. The liquidity of a given investment vehicle is an important consideration for an investor who wishes to maintain flexibility in an investment portfolio. In general, investment vehicles traded in *thin markets*, where demand and supply are small, tend to be less liquid than those traded in *broad markets*. However, to be liquid an investment must be easily sold at a reasonable price. One can generally enhance the liquidity of an investment merely by cutting its price. For example, a security recently purchased for $1,000 would not be viewed as highly liquid if it can be sold only at a significantly reduced price such as $500. Vehicles such as bonds and stocks of major companies listed on the New York Stock Exchange are generally highly liquid, whereas others, such as an isolated parcel of raw land located in rural Georgia, are not.

Market risk

Changes in the level of returns on investment vehicles often result from *market risk*. The risk tends to be caused by factors independent of the given security or property investment vehicle, such as political, economic, and social events, or changes in investor tastes and preferences. For example, in spite of the fact that a real estate investment is well managed, a major shift in consumer housing preferences could adversely affect its market value and therefore the actual return realized. The impact of these market factors on investment returns is not uniform; the degree as well as the direction of change in return resulting from a change in some market factor differs among investment vehicles. A threat of war in the oil-rich Middle East may result in a significant increase in the value (and therefore return) of a military aircraft manufacturer's stock, whereas the stock value and return of an oil company might significantly decline.

Beta: A Modern Measure of Risk

Over the past 15 years or so, much theoretical work has been done on the measurement of risk and its use in assessing returns. The two key components of this theory are *beta*, which is a measure of risk, and the *capital asset pricing model*

(CAPM), which relates the risk measured by beta to the level of expected or required return. In this text, we will look only at measuring risk with beta; a discussion of the use of the capital asset pricing model to link risk and return is left to more advanced texts. Beta is used to measure the risk of securities, but an understanding of this measure will give us further insight into the general concept of risk.

Basic types of risk

The total risk of an investment consists of two components: diversifiable and nondiversifiable risk. *Diversifiable risk,* which is sometimes called *unsystematic risk,* represents the portion of an investment's risk that can be eliminated through diversification. It results from uncontrollable or random events, such as labor strikes, lawsuits, and regulatory actions, and affects various investment vehicles differently. *Nondiversifiable risk,* which is also called *systematic risk,* is attributed to forces that affect all investments and are therefore not unique to a given vehicle, such as war, inflation, international events, and political events. The relationship between total risk, diversifiable risk, and nondiversifiable risk is given by the equation below.

total risk = diversifiable risk + nondiversifiable risk

Because any intelligent investor can eliminate diversifiable risk by holding a diversified portfolio of securities, *the only relevant risk is the nondiversifiable risk.* Studies have shown that by carefully selecting eight to fifteen securities to be included in a portfolio, diversifiable risk can be eliminated, or almost completely so. Nondiversifiable risk, which is like the market risk discussed earlier, is inescapable. Each security possesses its own unique level of this risk, which we can measure with beta.

Calculating beta

Beta is a market measure of risk; it shows how the price of a security responds to market forces, and is found by relating the historical returns on a security with the historical returns for the market. The *market return* is typically measured by the average return on all (or a large sample of) securities. The Standard & Poor's 500-stock composite index or some other stock index is commonly used to measure market return. The beta for the market is equal to 1; all other betas are viewed in relation to this value. Betas may be positive or negative. The majority of betas are positive and fall between 0.2 and 2. Table 4.14 gives some selected beta values and their associated interpretations.

Many of the large brokerage firms as well as subscription services publish betas for a broad range of securities. The ready availability of security betas has enhanced their use in assessing investment risks. In general, the higher the absolute value (ignoring the positive or negative sign) of the beta, the riskier the investment. The positive or negative sign merely indicates whether the risk behaves in a fashion similar to the general market (positive beta) or in an opposite fashion (negative beta). The importance of beta in developing and monitoring portfolios of securities will be discussed in greater detail in Chapter 19.

TABLE 4.14	SELECTED BETAS AND ASSOCIATED INTERPRETATIONS	
Beta	Comment	Interpretation*
2.0	Move in same direction as market.	Twice as responsive as the market.
1.0		Same response or risk as the market.
0.5		Only half as responsive as the market.
0		Unaffected by market movement.
−0.5	Move in opposite direction to market.	Only half as responsive as the market.
−1.0		Same response or risk as the market.
−2.0		Twice as responsive as the market.

*A stock that is twice as responsive as the market will experience a 2 percent change in its return for each 1 percent change in the return of the market portfolio; the return of a stock that is half as responsive as the market will change by ½ of 1 percent for each 1 percent change in the return of the market portfolio.

Using beta

The individual investor will find beta useful in assessing market risk and understanding the impact the market can have on the return expected from a share of stock. Beta measures a security's market risk by revealing the type of response a security has to market forces. For example, if the market is expected to experience a 10 percent increase in its rate of return over the next period, then a stock having a beta of 1.50 would be expected to experience an increase in return of approximately 15 percent (1.50 × 10%) over the same period of time. Because the beta of this particular stock is greater than 1, it is more volatile than the market as a whole.

For stocks having positive betas, increases in market returns result in increases in security returns. Unfortunately, decreases in market returns are likewise translated into decreasing security returns—and this is where the risk lies. Take the preceding example: If the market is expected to experience a 10 percent decline in its return, then the stock with a beta of 1.50 should experience a 15 percent decrease in its return. Because the stock has a beta of greater than 1, it is more responsive than the market, experiencing a 15 percent decline in its return as compared to the 10 percent decline in the market return. Stocks having positive betas of less than 1 will, of course, be less responsive to changing returns in the market and therefore are considered to be less risky. For example, a stock having a beta of 0.50 will experience an increase or decrease in its return of about half that in the market as a whole; thus, as the market goes down by 8 percent, such a stock will probably experience only about a 4 percent decline.

Here are some important points to remember about beta:

1. Beta measures the nondiversifiable, or market, risk of a security.
2. The beta for the market is 1.

BOX 4.3 USING BETA TO MEASURE RISK

A reader asks, "What are 'betas,' and what good are they?" The short answer is that betas are a measure of risk, and using them might help you pick winners or avoid losses.

Modern investment theory teaches that an investor faces two sorts of risk in any purchase of stock. The first risk is that a company will do poorly even in the best of times. There's always a chance of something going wrong. You can minimize that risk by diversifying your holdings among varied industries and corporations so that mistakes or bad luck suffered by some firms will be offset by the successes of others.

That does not take care of the second kind of risk—that the stock market as a whole may decline, pulling down the shares of even the most successful enterprises.

That's where betas come in.

Some stocks tend to have comparatively stable prices, while others tend to fluctuate more sharply when the broad market moves up or down. Betas are a measure of these relative price patterns. A stock that, over the years, moves just about in line with broad market indexes is assigned a beta of 1.00. But a stock that drops twice as fast as the index in a sell-off and gains twice as fast in a rising market gets a beta of 2.00, and one that moves only half as fast as the index gets a beta of 0.5.

Calculating betas is beyond the average investor. One company that computes these figures quarterly for hundreds of stocks is Value Line. Its reports are available in many public libraries and brokerage houses. The accompanying table gives Value Line's latest computation for 31 firms, based on weekly data for the past five years.

How should you use this information? Roy Brady, Value Line statistician, like most experts, counsels against using the beta to decide whether to buy a particular stock. In any year, the price of a stock may for many reasons trace a pattern at odds with past performance. Betas, Brady advises, are much more consistent when applied to 10 or more issues as a way of assessing your exposure to market trends.

To compute the beta for your portfolio, multiply the beta for each stock you own by the current dollar value of your holding, add those products and divide by the total value of the portfolio. It's something many big investment managers do.

If you find your portfolio has a high beta and you want to reduce risk, you can weed out some volatile stocks and substitute steadier ones.

3. Stocks may have positive or negative betas; most are positive.
4. Stocks with betas of greater than 1 are more responsive to changes in market return—and therefore more risky—than the market; stocks with betas less than 1 are less risky than the market.
5. Because of its greater risk, the higher a stock's beta, the greater should be its level of expected return, and vice versa.

Evaluating Risk

Although a variety of techniques is available for quantifying the risk of a given investment vehicle, investors must somehow relate the risk perceived in a given vehicle not only to the expected return, but also to their own dispositions toward risk. Thus the evaluation process is not one in which a calculated value of risk is compared to a maximum risk level associated with an investment offering a given return. Rather the individual investor typically tends to seek answers to these questions: "Is the

BOX 4.3 *Continued*

But note: Studies show that, over the long run, investors who accept more risk— that is, higher betas— reap the greatest returns, as measured by dividends plus capital gains. . . . Burton Malkiel, one-time member of the Council of Economic Advisers, puts it this way:

"The beta of a portfolio does seem to be not only a useful risk measure but also a good predictor of the long-run rate of return to be expected from that portfolio."

"BETAS" OF LEADING COMPANIES*

Alcoa	1.05	General Motors	.90
Allied Stores	.85	Gulf Oil	1.15
American Brands	.70	Ingersoll-Rand	.90
AT&T	.65	IBM	.95
Bethlehem Steel	1.25	Johnson & Johnson	.95
Burroughs	.95	McDonald's	1.05
Campbell Soup	.65	J. C. Penney	1.00
Caterpillar Tractor	.95	Philip Morris	.90
Coca-Cola	.85	Polaroid	1.20
Dow Chemical	1.25	Safeway Stores	.80
Du Pont	1.10	Sears, Roebuck	.90
Eastman Kodak	1.00	J. P. Stevens	.75
Exxon	.90	Texaco	.95
Ford Motor	.85	U.S. Steel	1.00
General Electric	.95	Winn-Dixie Stores	.55
General Foods	.75		

*A figure of 1.00 means price of stock usually changes about as much as the Value Line index. A stock above 1.00 is more volatile than the index.

Source: William C. Bryant, "One Way to Reduce Risk." *U.S. News & World Report,* April 19, 1982, p. 105.

amount of risk perceived worth taking in order to get the expected return?" "Can I get a higher return for the same level of risk or a lower risk for the same level of return?" A look at the general risk-return characteristics of alternative investment vehicles, the question of an acceptable level of risk, and the decision process may help shed light on the nature of risk evaluations.

Risk-return characteristics
of alternative investment vehicles

A wide variety of risk-return behaviors is associated with each type of investment vehicle. Some common stocks offer low returns and low risk; others exhibit high returns and high risks. In general, the risk-return characteristics of each of the major investment vehicles can be depicted on a set of risk-return axes, as shown in Figure 4.2. Although the locations on the risk-return axes are only approximate, it should be clear that an investor can select from a wide variety of vehicles, each having

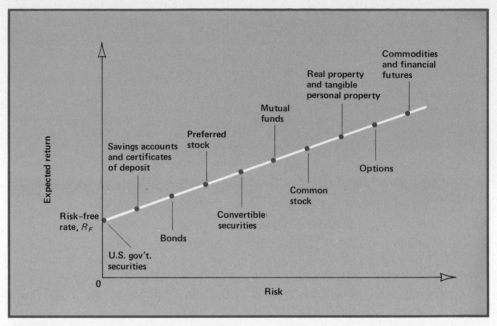

Figure 4.2   Risk-Return Tradeoffs for Various Investment Vehicles.
A risk-return tradeoff exists such that for higher risk one expects a higher return, and vice versa. Low-risk–low-return investment vehicles are U.S. government securities, savings accounts, and so on; high-risk–high-return vehicles include real property and tangible personal property, options, and commodities and financial futures.

certain characteristic risk-return behaviors. Of course, for each type of investment vehicle, a broad range of risk-return behaviors exists for specific investments. In other words, once the appropriate type of vehicle is selected, the decision as to which specific security or property to acquire must still be made.

An acceptable level of risk

Because of differing investor preferences, it is impossible to specify a general acceptable level of risk. The three basic risk preference behaviors—risk-averse, risk-indifferent, and risk-taker—are depicted graphically in Figure 4.3. From the graph it can be seen that as risk goes from X_1 to X_2, for the risk-indifferent investor the required return increases proportionally from Y_1 to Y_2; in essence, the increase in return closely corresponds to the increase in risk. In the case of the risk-averse investor, the required return increases more than proportionally; for the risk-taker, it exhibits a less than proportional increase. *Most investors are risk-averse, since for a given increase in risk they require a greater than proportional increase in return.* Of course, the amount of more than proportional return required by each investor for a given increase in risk will differ depending upon the investor's degree of risk aversion. Although in theory the risk disposition of each investor could be measured, in practice individual investors tend to accept only the risks with which they feel

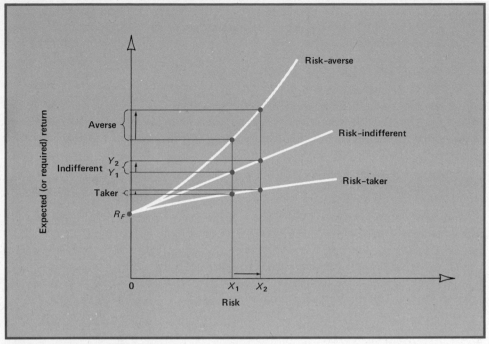

Figure 4.3   Risk Preference Functions.
The risk-indifferent investor requires proportional increases in return for given increases in
risk, while the risk-averse investor requires greater than proportional increases in return for a
given risk increase, and the risk-taker requires less than proportional increases in return for a
given increase in risk. The majority of investors are risk-averse.

comfortable. And they generally tend to be conservative rather than aggressive when
accepting risk.

The decision process

In the decision process, investors should take the following steps when selecting
from among alternative investments:

1. Using historical or projected return data, estimate the expected return over
   a given holding period. Use present value or yield techniques to make sure
   that the time value of money is given adequate consideration.
2. Using historical or projected return data, assess the risk associated with the
   investment. The use of subjective risk assessment of past returns and beta
   (for securities) are the primary approaches available to the individual investor.
3. Evaluate the risk-return behavior of each alternative investment to make
   sure that the return expected is "reasonable" given its level of risk. If other
   vehicles with equal or lower levels of risk provide equal or greater returns,
   the investment would not be deemed acceptable.

4. Select the investment vehicles that offer the highest returns associated with the level of risk the investor is willing to take. Since most investors are risk-averse, they will acquire lower-risk vehicles, thereby receiving lower investment returns. As long as they get the highest return for the acceptable level of risk, they have made a "good investment."

Probably the most difficult step in this process is assessing risk. Aside from risk and return considerations, other factors such as taxes, liquidity, and portfolio considerations will affect the investment decision. We will look at these in later chapters.

SUMMARY

Returns can be viewed as the reward for investing. The returns provided by an investment may come in the form of current income, such as interest and dividends, or capital gains (or losses). Current income occurs periodically over the time an investment is owned; capital gains (or losses) result from selling an investment vehicle at a price above (or below) its original purchase price. Total return, which includes current income and capital gains (or losses) over a given period of time, is commonly calculated on a historical basis and then used to project expected returns.

The level of return provided by a given investment vehicle depends on a variety of factors. Internal characteristics such as the type of investment vehicle, the way the investment is financed, the customer base of the issuer, the management, and so on, will affect the level of return. External forces such as war, shortages, Federal Reserve actions, and so on also affect the level of return. In addition, the impact of inflation on interest rates can significantly affect investment returns.

Interest, which is the basic return to savers, can provide a meaningful basis for measuring other investment returns. Interest on a savings account represents current income to the saver and is typically calculated using the simple interest method, which applies the stated interest rate to the actual balance on deposit for the period of deposit. The stated interest rate will thus equal the true interest rate. With compound interest, simple interest is paid not only on the initial deposit, but also on any interest accumulated from period to period. When interest is compounded annually, the stated interest rate and true interest are equal. When interest is compounded more frequently, the true interest rate will be greater than the stated rate.

The holding period is the relevant period of time over which one measures an investment's past or expected return. Equal-length holding periods measured over the same period in time should be used to compare returns from alternative investments. The holding period return (HPR) is the return earned over the holding period.

The timing as well as the magnitude of returns should be considered as part of the decision process. The future value of a current sum can be found using compound interest concepts. Of greater importance in the decision process is the use of present value. The present value of a future sum is the amount deposited today into an account earning at a given rate that would accumulate to the future sum. The present value of streams of future returns can be found by adding the individual return present values. A satisfactory investment is one for which the present value of benefits discounted at the appropriate rate equals or exceeds the present value of costs. An alternative approach would be to compare the yield, which is the discount rate that causes the present value of benefits to equal cost, to the appropriate discount rate. If the yield is greater than or equal to the appropriate discount rate, the investment would be accepted. The yield on an investment can be estimated using the approximate yield formula.

Risk, the chance that the actual investment return will differ from its expected value, is of key importance in the evaluation process. There is a tradeoff between risk and return: for accepting greater risk, an investor must receive an increased return. Total risk derives from a variety of sources such as business risk, financial risk, purchasing power risk, interest rate risk, liquidity risk, and market risk. Total risk can be divided into diversifiable and nondiversifiable risk. Beta can be used to measure the relevant, or nondiversifiable, risk associated with a security investment. Beta is an index that measures the relative responsiveness of a security's return to the market return.

In general, each type of investment vehicle displays certain risk-return characteristics. For a given vehicle, a broad range of risk-return behaviors will be available. Each investor has a unique and nonquantifiable disposition toward risk. Most are risk-averse, which means that in exchange for a given increase in risk, they require a greater than proportional increase in return. Other investors may be risk-indifferent or risk-takers. The investment decision will ultimately be made by combining the investors' risk preferences with the expected return and risk data for a given investment.

KEY TERMS

annuity
approximate yield formula
beta
broad market
business risk
capital asset pricing model (CAPM)
capital gain
capital loss
compound interest
continuous compounding
current income
discount rate
diversifiable (unsystematic) risk
expected return
financial risk
future value
holding period
holding period return (HPR)
interest rate risk
liquidity risk
market return
market risk
mixed stream of returns

nondiversifiable (systematic) risk
opportunity cost
paper returns
present value
purchasing power risk
realized return
required return
return
risk
risk-averse
risk-free rate of interest, R_F
risk-indifferent
risk-return tradeoff
risk-taker
simple interest
stated interest rate
stream of returns
thin market
time value of money
total return
true rate of return (interest)
yield

REVIEW QUESTIONS

1. Define what is meant by the return on an investment. Explain why a person wishing to invest should be able to earn a positive return.

2. Define and differentiate between current income and capital gains (or losses). If you purchased a share of stock for $50 one year ago and sold it today for $60, and during the year received three dividend payments totaling $2.70, calculate:

a. Current income.
b. Capital gain (or loss).
c. Total return.

3. Given the historical data below:

a. Calculate the total return (in dollars) for each year.
b. Indicate the level of return you would expect in 1985 and 1986.
c. Comment on your forecast.

		MARKET VALUE (PRICE)	
Year	Income	Beginning	Ending
1980	$1.00	$30.00	$32.50
1981	1.20	32.50	35.00
1982	1.30	35.00	33.00
1983	1.60	33.00	40.00
1984	1.75	40.00	45.00

4. Define, discuss, and contrast the following terms:

a. Interest.
b. Simple interest.
c. Compound interest.

5. For the following savings account transactions, calculate:

a. End-of-year account balance (assume that the account balance at December 31, 1983, is zero).
b. Annual interest, using 6 percent simple interest and assuming all interest is withdrawn from the account as it is earned.
c. True rate of interest, and compare it to the stated rate of interest. Discuss your finding.

Date	Deposit or (Withdrawal)
1/1/84	$5,000
1/1/85	(4,000)
1/1/86	2,000
1/1/87	3,000

6. Using the deposit-withdrawal data given in problem 6 and using 6 percent compound interest, determine the account balance at the end of 1987 if interest is compounded:

a. Annually.
b. Semi-annually.
c. Quarterly.

Explain the impact more frequent compounding has on the future value (end-of-1987 account balance) and on the true rate of interest.

7. Define what is meant by the holding period and explain why it is advisable to use equal-length holding periods covering the same period in time when comparing alternative investment vehicles.

8. Calculate the holding period return (HPR) for the following two investment alternatives. Which, if any, of the return components is likely *not* to be realized if you continue to hold each of the investments beyond one year? Which vehicle would you prefer, assuming they are of equal risk? Explain.

	INVESTMENT VEHICLE	
	X	Y
Cash received		
1st quarter	$1.00	$ 0
2nd quarter	1.20	0
3rd quarter	0	0
4th quarter	2.30	2.00
Investment value		
End of year	$29.00	$56.00
Beginning of year	30.00	50.00

9. Describe, compare, and contrast the concepts of future value and present value. Explain the role of the opportunity cost or discount rate in the present value calculation.

10. Using the appropriate table of interest factors found in Appendix B, calculate:

a. The future value of a $300 deposit left in an account paying 7 percent annual interest for 12 years.
b. The present value of $500 to be received four years from now using an 11 percent discount rate.
c. The present value of the following end-of-year benefit streams using a 9 percent discount rate and assuming it is now the beginning of 1985.

Year	Stream A	Stream B
1985	$80	$140
1986	80	120
1987	80	100
1988	80	80
1989	80	60
1990	80	40
1991	80	20

11. Assume the investment generating benefit stream B in question 10 can be purchased at the beginning of 1985 for $1,000 and sold at the end of 1991 for $1,200. Calculate the approximate yield for this investment. If the appropriate discount rate is 9 percent, would you (ignoring risk) recommend this investment? Explain.

12. Explain how either the present value or the yield measure can be used to find a satisfactory investment. Given the following data, indicate which, if any, of the following investments is acceptable. Explain your findings.

	INVESTMENT		
	A	B	C
Cost	$200	$160	$500
Appropriate discount rate	7%	10%	9%
Present value of returns	—	$150	—
Yield	8%	—	8%

13.   Explain what is meant by the risk-return tradeoff. Graphically depict this behavior. What is the risk-free rate? What happens to the required return as risk increases? Explain.

14.   Define and briefly discuss each of the following sources of risk:

a. Business risk.   d. Interest rate risk.
b. Financial risk.   e. Liquidity risk.
c. Purchasing power risk.   f. Market risk.

15.   Define and give examples of diversifiable risk (unsystematic risk) and nondiversifiable risk (systematic risk) and explain how they relate to total risk.

16.   Explain what is meant by beta. What is the relevant risk measured by beta? To which of the sources of risk listed in question 14 is it most often likened? Explain.

17.   Explain what is meant by the market return. Where is it obtained? What range of values does beta typically exhibit? Are positive or negative betas most common? Explain.

18.   Assume the betas for securities A, B, and C are as given below.

Security	Beta
A	1.40
B	.80
C	− .90

a. Calculate the change in return for each security if the market experiences an increase in its rate of return of 13.2 percent over the next period.
b. Calculate the change in returns for each security if the market experiences a decrease of 10.8 percent.
c. Rank and discuss the relative risk of each security based on your findings. Which security might perform best during an economic downturn? Explain.

19.   Differentiate among risk-indifference, risk-aversion, and risk-taking. Which of these behaviors best describes that of most investors? Explain. How does investor preference typically enter the decision process?

20.   Describe the basic steps involved in the investment decision process. Be sure to mention how returns and risks can be measured and used to determine the group of acceptable or "reasonable" investments from which the final selection can be made.

CASE PROBLEMS

4.1 (ED) SOLOMON SAYS: A OR B?

Ed Solomon, a 23-year-old mathematics teacher at Xavier High School, recently received a tax refund of exactly $1,100. Because Ed doesn't currently have any need for this money, he decided to make a long-term investment. After surveying a large number of alternative investments costing no more than $1,100, Ed isolated two that seemed most suitable to his needs. Each of the investments cost $1,050 and was expected to provide benefits over a 10-year period. Investment A provided a relatively certain stream of benefits, while Ed was a little less certain of the benefits provided by investment B. From his search for suitable alternatives, Ed found that his opportunity cost for a relatively certain investment was 12 percent. Because he felt a bit uncomfortable with an investment such as B, he estimated that such an investment would have to provide a return at least 4 percent *higher* than for investment A. Although Ed planned to spend the funds returned from the investments, he wished to keep the extra $50 ($1,100 − $1,050) invested for the full 10 years in a savings account paying 8 percent interest compounded annually. In order to make his investment decision, Ed has asked for your help in answering the questions which follow the expected return data for each investment.

	EXPECTED RETURNS	
Year	A	B
1985	$ 150	$100
1986	150	150
1987	150	200
1988	150	250
1989	150	300
1990	150	350
1991	150	300
1992	150	250
1993	150	200
1994	1,150	150

Questions

1. Assuming investments A and B are equally risky, using the 12 percent opportunity cost apply the present value technique to assess the acceptability of each investment as well as the preferred investment. Explain your findings.

2. Recognizing the fact that investment B is more risky than investment A, reassess the two alternatives applying a 16 percent opportunity cost to investment B. Compare your findings relative to acceptability and preference to those found for question 1.

3. From your findings in questions 1 and 2, indicate whether the yield for investment A is above or below 12 percent and for investment B above or below 16 percent. Approximately what is the yield for investment B? Explain.

4. From the information given, which if either of the two investments would you recommend Ed make? Explain your answer.

5. Indicate to Ed how much money the extra $50 will have grown to equal by the end of 1994, given that he makes no withdrawals from the savings account.

4.2 THE RISK-RETURN TRADEOFF: MOLLY O'ROURKE'S STOCK PURCHASE DECISION

Over the past 10 years, Molly O'Rourke has slowly built a diversified portfolio of common stock. Currently her portfolio includes 20 different common stock issues and has a total market value of $82,500. Molly is presently considering the addition of 50 shares of either of two common stock issues—X or Y. In order to assess the return and risk of each of these issues, she has gathered dividend income and share price data for both over each of the last 10 years (1975 through 1984). Molly's investigation of the outlook for these issues suggests that each will, on average, tend to behave in the future just as it has in the past. She therefore believes that the expected return can be estimated by finding the average holding period return (HPR) over the past 10 years for each of the stocks.

Molly plans to use the betas to assess the risk of each stock. Her broker, Jim McDaniel, indicated that the betas for stocks X and Y are 1.90 and 1.10, respectively. Armed with this data, Molly prepared to assess the return and risk of each stock in order to determine which, if either, should be purchased. The historical dividend income and stock price data collected by Molly are given below.

| | | STOCK X | | | | STOCK Y | |
| | | SHARE PRICE | | | | SHARE PRICE | |
Year	Dividend Income	Beginning	Ending	Dividend Income	Beginning	Ending
1975	$1.00	$20.00	$22.00	$1.50	$20.00	$20.00
1976	1.50	22.00	21.00	1.60	20.00	20.00
1977	1.40	21.00	24.00	1.70	20.00	21.00
1978	1.70	24.00	22.00	1.80	21.00	21.00
1979	1.90	22.00	23.00	1.90	21.00	22.00
1980	1.60	23.00	26.00	2.00	22.00	23.00
1981	1.70	26.00	25.00	2.10	23.00	23.00
1982	2.00	25.00	24.00	2.20	23.00	24.00
1983	2.10	24.00	27.00	2.30	24.00	25.00
1984	2.20	27.00	30.00	2.40	25.00	25.00

Questions

1. Determine the holding period return (HPR) for each stock in each of the preceding ten years. Find the expected return for each stock using the approach specified by Molly.

2. Subjectively evaluate and discuss the return and risk associated with stocks X and Y. Which stock seems preferable? Explain.

3. Using the expected return and beta as measures of return and risk, respectively, determine which if either investment would be acceptable to Molly, given her risk preference function as plotted below. Explain you findings.

4. Compare and contrast your findings in questions 2 and 3. What recommendation would you give Molly in light of the investment decision currently under consideration? Explain why Molly would be better off using beta rather than a strictly subjective approach to assess investment risk.

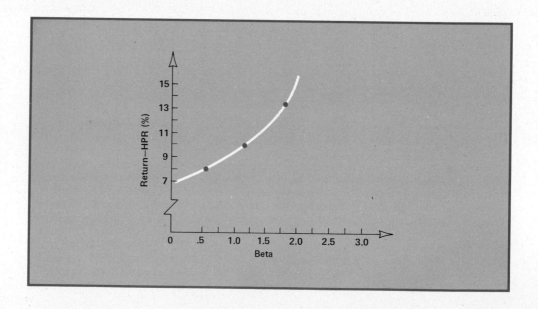

SELECTED READINGS

Angrist, Stanley W. "Risk versus Reward." *Forbes,* April 12, 1982, pp. 226–227.

Blotnick, Srully. "The Time Value of Money." *Forbes,* March 3, 1980, pp. 114–115.

Cissell, Robert, Helen Cissell, and David C. Flaspohler. *Mathematics of Finance,* 5th ed. Boston: Houghton Mifflin, 1978.

Clayton, Gary E., and Christopher B. Spivey. *The Time Value of Money.* Philadelphia: Saunders, 1978.

Connelly, Julie. "A Guide to the Real Risks of Investing In . . . ." *Money,* January 1982, pp. 46–50.

Gitman, Lawrence J. *Principles of Managerial Finance,* 3d ed. New York: Harper & Row, 1982.

Haller, Ellis. "Dealing with Investment Risk." *U.S. News and World Report,* August 3, 1979, p. 89.

Heinlein, Carston. "Beta to Omega: Here's a Simple Way to Figure a Stock's Volatility." *Barron's,* May 30, 1977, pp. 9, 18.

"How to Figure Risk When You Invest." *Changing Times,* August 1978, pp. 6–10.

Moffitt, Donald. "Volatility, Beta for the Individual Investor." *The Wall Street Journal,* June 20, 1977.

Rob, Charles J. "Anticipating Major Ups and Downs." *Money,* June 1982, pp. 44–50.

————. "A Strategy for All Seasons." *Money,* January 1982, pp. 38–44.

Siverd, Bonnie. "Risk-Taking Equals Self-Worth plus Networth." *Working Woman,* March 1982, pp. 85–89.

5
Margin Trading and Short Selling

The individual investor has a wide variety of investment outlets to choose from, including such vehicles as stocks, bonds, puts and calls, convertibles, and so on. In most cases, an investor will simply buy the securities at full price (i.e., pay cash) and then turn around some time later and sell them, hoping to make a profit. Although this is the most common type of investment transaction, two other *trading strategies* are popular with some investors because of the unusual return opportunities they provide; they are margin trading and short selling. In order to develop a better understanding of these investment techniques, we will now look at:

1. The basic concepts and mechanics of margin trading and short selling.
2. How investors make money in these transactions, as well as the types of risk to which they are exposed.
3. The various types of margin requirements and the restrictions they impose on trading.
4. The investment merits of margin trading and the various ways it can be used by investors.
5. The parties to a short sale and how they benefit from these transactions.
6. The speculative as well as conservative ways short selling can be used in individual investment programs.

Margin trading and short selling represent different ways investment securities can be used. Margin trading, for example, is used when the price of an issue is expected to rise; short selling, on the other hand, is used when prices are expected to fall. In simple terms, *margin trading* is nothing more than buying securities in part with borrowed money. It is like buying a home: you put up some of the money and the rest is obtained through a mortgage. Investors use margin to reduce their equity in an investment and therefore to magnify the returns from invested capital. *Short selling,* in contrast, involves the practice of selling borrowed securities. A short sale transaction begins with the sale of borrowed securities and ends when the securities are bought back (presumably at a price lower than what they were sold for) and returned to the lender. The investment principle of short selling is exactly like any other: buy low and sell high. The only difference is that the investment process is reversed.

Both margin trading and short-selling are fairly simple in concept, yet they both require special skills and know how. Both are speculative by nature, although short selling can, under the proper circumstances, be used in a highly conservative manner. Knowing when and how to use these techniques is, of course, at the heart of the problem. Properly used, they can be very rewarding; misused, they can have devastating effects. We begin our review by looking at margin trading.

MARGIN TRADING

Margin trading is used for one basic reason: to magnify returns. This is possible because securities acquired on margin are partly financed with borrowed money, which reduces the amount of capital that must be put up by the investor. As peculiar as it may sound, although margin trading means investing with borrowed funds, the term "margin" itself refers to the amount of *equity* in an investment, or to the amount that is not borrowed. If an investor uses 75 percent margin, for example, it means that 75 percent of the investment position is being financed with the person's own capital, and the balance (25 percent) with borrowed money.

The Essentials of Margin Trading

Margin trading can be used with most kinds of securities; it is regularly used, for example, with common and preferred stocks, corporate and Treasury bonds, convertible debentures, warrants, commodities, financial futures, and mutual funds. It is not widely used with municipal bonds, since the interest paid on such margin loans is not deductible for income tax purposes. For simplicity, we will use common stock as the trading vehicle in our discussion of margin trading, and assume that the stock selection process has been completed (i.e., that the securities have already been analyzed along the lines to be discussed in Chapters 9 and 10). In essence, we are assuming that the investor has uncovered a security which promises to go up in the near future, so the major concern at this point is whether or not to use margin in the investment transaction. Although margin trading normally leads to increased returns, there are also some substantial risks to be considered. One of the biggest is that the issue will not perform as expected. If this occurs, then no amount of margin trading is going to correct matters. For margin trading can only magnify returns—it cannot *produce* them. Because the security being margined is always the ultimate source of return, *the security selection process is critical to this trading strategy.*

TABLE 5.1   THE EFFECTS OF MARGIN TRADING ON SECURITY RETURNS

	Without Margin (100% Equity)	WITH MARGINS OF		
		80%	65%	50%
Number of $50 shares purchased	100	100	100	100
Cost of investment	$5,000	$5,000	$5,000	$5,000
Less: borrowed money	0	1,000	1,750	2,500
Equity in investment	$5,000	$4,000	$3,250	$2,500
A. INVESTOR'S POSITION IF PRICE RISES TO $80/SHARE				
Value of stock	$8,000	$8,000	$8,000	$8,000
Less: cost of investment	5,000	5,000	5,000	5,000
Capital gain	$3,000	$3,000	$3,000	$3,000
Return on investor's equity (capital gain/equity in investment)	60%	75%	92.3%	120%
B. INVESTOR'S POSITION IF PRICE FALLS TO $20/SHARE				
Value of stock	$2,000	$2,000	$2,000	$2,000
Less: cost of investment	5,000	5,000	5,000	5,000
Capital *loss*	$3,000	$3,000	$3,000	$3,000
Return on investor's equity (capital loss/equity in investment)*	(60%)	(75%)	(92.3%)	(120%)

*With a capital loss, return on investor's equity is *negative*.

Magnified profits and losses

Using an investor's equity as a base, the idea of margin trading is to employ financial leverage to magnify returns. Here is how it works. Suppose you have $5,000 to invest and are considering the purchase of 100 shares of stock (at $50 per share) because you feel the stock in question will go up in price. Now if you do not margin, you can buy 100 shares of the stock. If you margin the transaction—for example, at 50 percent—you could acquire the same $5,000 position with only $2,500 of your own money. This would leave you with $2,500 to use for other investments, or to buy another 100 shares of the same stock. Either way, you will reap greater benefits from the stock's price appreciation if you margin the transaction.

The concept of margin trading is more fully illustrated in Table 5.1. An unmargined (100 percent equity) transaction is depicted along with the same transaction using various margins. Remember that the margin rates (such as 65 percent) indicate the equity in the investment, or the amount of capital the investor must come up with. When the investment is unmargined and the price of the stock goes

TABLE 5.2   THE RETURN POTENTIAL OF MARGIN TRADING

PERCENTAGE CHANGE IN PRICE OF SECURITY	PERCENTAGE CHANGE IN RETURN ON INVESTOR'S MONEY WITH MARGINS OF				
	90%	75%	50%	25%	10%
20%	22.2%	26.6%	40%	80%	200%
50	55.6	66.7	100	200	500
75	83.3	100.0	150	300	750
100	111.1	133.3	200	400	1,000
200	222.2	266.6	400	800	2,000

up by $30 per share, the investor enjoys a very respectable 60 percent rate of return. However, observe what happens when margin is used: The rate of return shoots up to as high as 120 percent, depending on the amount of equity in the investment. This is so because the gain is the same ($3,000) *regardless of how the transaction is financed.* Clearly, as the investor's equity in the investment *declines* (with lower margins), rate of return *increases* accordingly.

Three facets of margin trading become obvious from the table: (1) The price of the stock will move in one way or another regardless of how the position is financed; (2) the lower the amount of the investor's equity in the position, the greater the rate of return the investor will enjoy when the price of the security rises; and (3) the risk of loss is also magnified (by the same rate) when the price of the security falls.

Advantages and disadvantages

A magnified return is the major advantage of margin trading. Table 5.2 shows the return potential of margin trading and reveals how important this benefit can be. The table demonstrates that the size of the magnified return will depend on both the price behavior of the security being margined and the amount of margin being used. For example, with a 90 percent margin, a 50 percent change in the price of the security results in an investor return of 55.6 percent; with a 50 percent margin, the 50 percent change in the security price results in a 100 percent return to the investor. Another, more modest benefit of margin trading is that it allows for greater diversification of security holdings, since investors can spread their capital over a greater number of investments.

The major disadvantage of this trading strategy, of course, is that the security being margined may not behave in the desired fashion, resulting in magnified losses rather than gains. Another disadvantage is the cost of the margin loans themselves. A *margin loan* is the official vehicle through which the borrowed funds are made available in a margin transaction; they are used with all types of margin transactions except commodities, financial futures, and short sales. All margin loans are made at

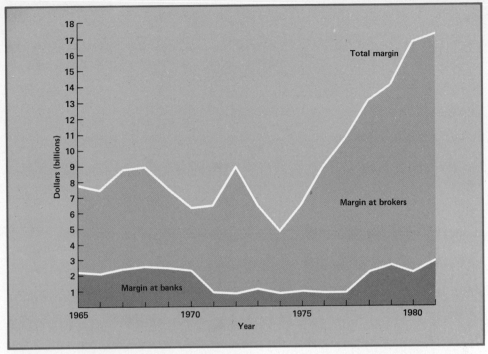

Figure 5.1 Margin Credit Outstanding.
The terms and conditions for margin credit are much the same at brokers and banks, though brokers have a decided edge when it comes to convenience. (*Source: Federal Reserve Bulletin, 1966–1982.*)

a stated interest rate, the amount of which depends on prevailing market rates and the amount of money being borrowed. This cost, which must be absorbed by the investor, will mount daily and reduce the level of profits (or magnify losses) accordingly.

Margin transactions

To execute a margin transaction, it is necessary to set up a *margin account*. This is a special type of account set up at a broker's office to handle all types of margin transactions, regardless of the type of security being margined. It is opened with a minimum of $2,000 in equity, either in the form of cash or by depositing securities. Margin transactions are executed like any others; they can be used with any type of order and are subject to normal commissions and transfer taxes. Of course, once margin transactions have been made, interest begins to accumulate on any margin loans taken out, and the broker will retain any securities purchased on margin as collateral for the loan. Margin credit can be obtained from a broker or a banker. But as Figure 5.1 shows, nearly all margin trading is done through brokers, primarily because it is so convenient.

**TABLE 5.3   INITIAL MARGIN REQUIREMENTS FOR
VARIOUS TYPES OF SECURITIES (DECEMBER 1982)**

Security	Minimum Initial Margin (Equity) Required
Listed common and preferred stock	50%
Regulated OTC stock	50
Convertible bonds	50
Warrants	25
Investment-grade corporate bonds	25
Treasury and agency bonds	5% of principal

Margin Requirements

Margin requirements are established by the Federal Reserve Board, the same organization that regulates our national banks. These requirements establish the minimum amount of equity for margin transactions. This does not mean, of course, that investors must execute all margin transactions by using exactly the minimum amount of margin; they can use more than the minimum if they wish. For example, if the minimum margin requirement on stock were 50 percent, an investor could buy the shares by using a 75 percent margin instead. Moreover, it is not unusual for brokerage houses and the major exchanges to establish their own margin requirements, which are more restrictive than those of the Federal Reserve. This is done to curb trading excesses and to provide added credit protection for the brokers. There are basically two types of margin requirements: initial margin and maintenance margin.

Initial margin

Initial margin is used to prevent overtrading and excessive speculation; it stipulates the minimum amount of money (or equity) that must be provided by the investor *at the time of purchase.* Generally, it is this margin requirement investors refer to in discussing margin trading. Any security that can be margined has a specific initial requirement, although these can be changed by the authorities from time to time. As Table 5.3 shows, initial margin requirements vary by type of security. The more stable investment vehicles, such as Treasury bonds, generally enjoy substantially lower margin requirements and therefore offer greater leverage opportunities. Note also that the OTC securities denoted in Table 5.3 are "regulated" stocks that can be margined like listed securities; over 1,400 OTC common and preferred stocks have been so designated—including most of the "major" firms traded over-the-counter (issues of banks, insurance companies, industrial and retail firms, etc.). All other OTC stocks are considered to have *no* collateral value and therefore *cannot* be margined.

Initial margin requirements also provide a check on the current status of an investor's margin account. As long as the margin in the account remains at a level equal to or greater than prevailing initial requirements, the investor is free to use the account in any way he or she sees fit. Should the value of the investor's holdings decline, the margin in his or her account will also drop, and can lead to what is known as a *restricted account.* A restricted account is one that carries a margin level less than prevailing initial margin requirements. For example, if initial margin requirements are, say, 50 percent, an account would become restricted when its margin falls to 49 percent or less. A restricted account does not mean that the investor has to put up additional cash or equity. However, one of the important restrictions placed on the account is that should the investor sell securities while the account is restricted, the amount that can be withdrawn is limited until the account is brought back up to initial margin levels.

Maintenance margin

Maintenance margin is used to protect the creditors in margin transactions— the brokerage houses and banks doing the lending. It specifies a minimum amount of equity that investors must carry in their margin accounts at all times. It is the absolute minimum amount of margin an account must carry before the broker is authorized to sell enough of the investor's securities to bring the account back up to standard. As we will see below, when an insufficient amount of margin exists, an investor will receive a margin call to remedy the situation. In this way, brokers avoid having to absorb excessive investor losses, and investors avoid being wiped out. The maintenance margin on equity securities is currently at 25 percent and rarely changes, although it is often set slightly higher by brokerage houses for the added protection of both brokers and their customers. For straight debt securities like Treasury bonds, there is no real maintenance margin except that set by the brokerage houses themselves.

A margin account is considered restricted as long as its equity remains below the initial margin requirement; it will stay restricted until it finally falls to the maintenance level. At that point, the account will become undermargined. An *undermargined account* is serious because the investor has only one course of action: to bring the equity all the way back up to the prevailing initial margin level (which could involve substantial sums of money). When an account becomes undermargined, an investor receives what is known as a *margin call.* This call gives the investor a short period of time (perhaps 72 hours) to find some way to bring the equity up to the prevailing initial margin. Should the investor fail to do so, the broker has no alternative but to sell enough of the margined holdings to bring the equity in the account up to the required level.

The Arithmetic of Margin Trading

Margin trading is an exciting investment strategy that offers the potential for generating handsome returns. Here we will briefly review some basic mathematics of margin trading. We will look at two measures: the basic margin formula and return on invested capital. Neither is particularly difficult, but both are vital to the margin trading concept.

BOX 5.1 A RATIONALE FOR LEVERAGING IN STOCKS

"Incredible," exclaimed Donald Regan, chief executive of Merrill Lynch, referring to the news that the margin debt of Big Board member firms had jumped again during February [1980] to $12.46 billion (see chart). What made this so hard to believe, Regan remarked, was that it happened while interest rates were reaching heights unscaled in modern American history. As the chart shows, the rates brokers charge to margin customers moved from around 16 percent to well over 20 percent during the first quarter of [1980]. ... [Ed. note: And while interest rates moved even higher in 1980 and 1981, so too did the amount of margin borrowing which peaked on the NYSE at nearly $15 billion in July 1981.]

Why, in the face of such high interest rates, would customers be borrowing so enthusiastically? Some observers have suggested that the borrowers are buying things besides stocks. Customers have been known to apply the borrowed funds to purchases of houses, co-op apartments, cars, and other big-ticket items. ... The exchange does not keep statistics on these extracurricular loans, but people on Wall Street say they are only a small fraction of the total.

The rise in borrowing probably has a straightforward explanation: investors expect a rise in stock values that will justify the historically high interest costs. Leonard Haynes, executive vice president of Shearson Loeb Rhoades, believes that most customers are "emotionally locked in" by a feeling that their stocks are undervalued. These investors are meeting margin calls and making still more investments on margin.

The behavior may not be as outlandish as it appears. Even now, when customers are being charged 21 percent and more to maintain their margin accounts, it would not require unheard-of gains in stock prices to make the borrowing worth while. That is because the interest is tax-deductible, which takes a lot of the sting out.

Consider a hypothetical example. An investor buys $10,000 worth of stock yielding 8 percent. He puts down $5,000, or 50 percent, as margin (the current minimum). His goal is to sell the stock in a year at a price that will keep him even, after taxes, with the rate of inflation. If the investor is in the 49 percent tax bracket (for married taxpayers, $45,000 to $60,000 in taxable income), his $1,050 in interest payments during the year will cost only $535.50 after taxes. And he will receive $800 in dividends, or $408 after taxes. That leaves him $127.50 in the hole. (Commissions aren't included in the calculations.)

If he assumes inflation over the year will be 18 percent, his goal will be to emerge with an after-tax gain of $900—i.e., 18 percent of his $5,000 outlay. The stock must therefore move up enough to leave him at least $1,027.50 after taxes. For someone in his bracket, the gain is taxed at 19.6 percent, so the pretax gain in the market value would have to be $1,278—or 12.8 percent on the $10,000 investment. If the investor

The basic margin formula

The amount of margin in a transaction (or account) is always measured in terms of its relative amount of equity. A simple formula can be used with all types of long transactions to determine the amount of margin in a transaction (or account) at any given point in time. (As we will see below, a different formula is used for margins in short sale transactions.) Basically, only two pieces of information are required: (1) the prevailing market value of the securities being margined, and (2) the amount of money being borrowed, or the size of the margin loan, which is known as the *debit balance*. Given this information, we can compute margin according to the following equation:

BOX 5.1 *Continued*

envisions only a 12 percent inflation rate, he would be gambling on a rise in the stock of only 9 percent.

The N.Y.S.E. composite index has risen at least 9 percent in seven of the last fourteen calendar years, and by 13 percent or more in five of them. Viewed in this light, the borrowing binge doesn't seem quite so "incredible."

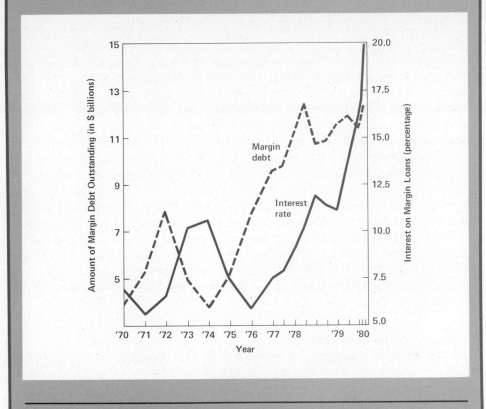

Source: Fortune, May 5, 1980, p. 306. Reprinted by permission, © 1980, Time, Inc.

$$\text{margin (\%)} = \frac{\text{value of securities} - \text{debit balance}}{\text{value of securities}}$$

$$= \frac{V - D}{V}$$

To illustrate its use, consider the following example: Assume an investor wants to purchase 100 shares of stock at $40 per share, using a 70 percent margin. The first thing we must determine is how this $4,000 transaction will be financed. Since we know that 70 percent of this transaction (the stated prevailing initial margin requirement) must be financed with equity, the balance (30 percent) can be financed with a margin loan. Therefore, the investor will borrow $1,200 ($4,000 × .30 = $1,200); this, of course, is the debit balance. The remainder ($2,800) represents the investor's equity in the transaction, and is measured as the difference between the value of the securities being margined ($4,000) and the amount being borrowed ($1,200). In other words, *equity* is represented by the numerator $(V - D)$ in the margin formula. If over time the price of the stock moves to $65, the margin would then be:

$$\text{margin (\%)} = \frac{V - D}{V} = \frac{\$6,500 - \$1,200}{\$6,500} = 81.5\%$$

Notice that while the "value of securities" in the equation changes with the market price of the stock $(V = \$65 \times 100 = \$6,500)$, the size of the debit balance does not change—and it will not *unless* the investor pays off or takes out more margin loans. Also note that the margin (equity) in this investment position has now risen to 81.5 percent. Such behavior results from the fact that when the price of the stock goes up, the investor's margin also increases. When the price of the security goes down, so does the amount of margin. For instance, if the price of the stock in our illustration should drop to $30 per share, the new margin would equal only 60 percent—in which case we would be dealing with a restricted account, since the margin level has dropped below the prevailing initial margin. Finally, note that although our discussion has been couched mostly in terms of individual transactions, the same margin formula is used with *margin accounts*. The only difference is that we would be dealing with input that applies to the account as a whole. To find the prevailing margin in an account, simply determine the value of all securities held in the account and the total amount of margin loans, and use this information in the basic margin formula.

Return on invested capital

Most investors who trade on margin do so by using fairly short investment periods; the lengths of such transactions are usually measured in months and seldom exceed a year. Because of these short holding periods, investment yield is usually measured in terms of holding period return. With margin transactions, however, it is necessary to take into account the fact that the individual puts up only part of the funds, the balance being provided by borrowed money. Therefore, in assessing return, we are concerned with the rate of profit earned on only that portion of the funds provided by the investor. Using both total current income received from dividends or interest and total interest paid on the margin loan, we can determine return on invested capital in a margin transaction as follows:

$$\text{return on invested capital} = \frac{\begin{array}{c}\text{total current}\\\text{income}\\\text{received}\end{array} - \begin{array}{c}\text{total interest}\\\text{paid on}\\\text{margin loan}\end{array} + \begin{array}{c}\text{market value}\\\text{of securities}\\\text{at sale}\end{array} - \begin{array}{c}\text{market value}\\\text{of securities}\\\text{at purchase}\end{array}}{\text{amount of equity invested}}$$

This form of the equation can be used to compute the expected or actual holding period return from a margin transaction. To illustrate: consider an investor who wants to buy 100 shares of stock at $50 per share because he or she feels it will rise to $75 within six months. The stock pays $2 per share in annual dividends (though with the six-month holding period, the investor will only receive half of that amount, or $1 per share); in addition, the investor is going to buy the stock with 50 percent margin and pay 10 percent interest on the margin loan. Thus, our investor is going to put up $2,500 equity to buy $5,000 worth of stock that he or she hopes will increase to $7,500 in six months. Since the investor will have a $2,500 margin loan outstanding at 10 percent for six months, he or she will pay $125 in total interest costs ($2,500 $\times$ .10 $\times$ $^6/_{12}$ = $125). Using this information, we can compute the expected return on invested capital for this transaction as follows:

$$\frac{\text{return on}}{\text{invested capital}} = \frac{\$100 - \$125 + \$7,500 - \$5,000}{\$2,500} = \frac{\$2,475}{\$2,500} = 99\%$$

Keep in mind that the 99 percent figure calculated above represents the rate of return earned over a six-month holding period. If we wanted to compare this rate of return to other investment opportunities, we could determine the transaction's *annualized* rate of return by multiplying by 2—the number of six-month periods in a year. This would amount to 198 percent (.99 $\times$ 2 = 198%).

Uses of Margin Trading

Margin trading can be used in several ways. As we have seen, it can be used to magnify transaction returns. Pyramiding is another margin tactic; this is the most powerful and extensive use of margin trading and takes the concept of magnified returns to its limits. Finally, the tactic can sometimes be used to increase the level of current income. Margin trading is simple, but it is also risky; as a result, it should be used only by investors who fully understand the strategy and appreciate its risks.

Increasing transaction returns

This strategy is relatively straightforward and is perhaps the most basic use of margin trading. The investor seeking to increase capital gains from a specific transaction finds a security that offers promising price appreciation and then margins it at (or above) the prevailing initial margin level in order to stretch his or her investment resources as far as they will go. For example, assume an investor has $4,000 of available capital and the prevailing initial margin requirement for common stock is 50 percent. She has uncovered a stock that presently trades at $20 per share, though she is convinced it will move to $30 within six months. Because she feels so strongly about the appreciation potential of this stock, she decides to margin it at the limit— the prevailing initial margin. Her capital is limited to $4,000, but she can borrow another $4,000 on margin and increase the size of her investment to $8,000.

Ignoring dividends, Table 5.4 summarizes what happens in this transaction if, in fact, the price of the stock does go to $30 within a six-month time frame. Note that the $12,000 received at sale was divided three ways: (1) The investor recovered

**TABLE 5.4 MARGIN TRADING
TO INCREASE TRANSACTION RETURNS**

Invested capital (equity)	$4,000
Borrowed funds (margin loan)	4,000
Total investment (to purchase 400 shares)	$8,000
Cost to *buy* 400 shares (at $20/share)	$8,000
6 months later—stock *sold* at $30/share: proceeds at sale	12,000
Gross profit from transaction	$4,000
Less: interest cost* on borrowed funds	200
Net profit	$3,800
Return on invested capital	
(net profit/invested capital = $3,800/$4,000)	95%
Annualized rate of return (95% × $^{12}\!/_6$)	190%

*The investor is assumed to pay 10% interest on borrowed funds; thus her interest cost for 6 months = .10 × 4,000 × $^{6}\!/_{12}$ = $200.

her initial capital ($4,000); (2) the margin loan ($4,000) and interest costs ($200) were paid off; and (3) the investor took her net profit ($3,800). Compared to the 50 percent holding period return she would have earned had she not used margin, the 95 percent return on invested capital is indeed an improvement.

Pyramiding profits

The whole idea of pyramiding is to use the margin account to build up investment holdings. When investors hold securities that go up in value, they earn what are known as *paper profits:* the investor has made money on the transactions but has not sold the securities, so any profit is still only on paper. *Pyramiding* uses the paper profits in margin accounts to partly or fully finance the acquisition of additional securities. This allows such transactions to be made at margins below prevailing initial margin levels, and sometimes substantially so. In fact, with this technique, it is even possible to buy securities with no new cash at all; rather, they can all be financed entirely with margin loans. This is because the paper profits in the account lead to *excess margin,* which means there is more equity in the account than necessary. For instance, if a margin account held $60,000 worth of securities and had a debit balance of $20,000, it would be at a margin level of 66⅔ percent. This account would hold a substantial amount of excess margin if the prevailing margin requirement were only 50 percent. The principle of pyramiding is to use the excess margin in the account to purchase additional securities. The only constraint, and the key to pyramiding, is that after the additional securities are purchased, the investor's margin account must remain at or above the prevailing required initial margin level. For it is the account, and not the individual transactions, that must meet the minimum standards. If the account has excess margin, the investor is free to use it to build up security holdings.

TABLE 5.5 BUILDING A MARGIN PYRAMID

Step A:
THE ORIGINAL MARGIN TRANSACTION

400 shares purchased at $20/share using	Value of securities	$8,000
50% margin (first transaction)	Debit balance	4,000
	Equity	4,000

Step B:
SOME TIME LATER

Price of the 400 shares rises to $30 per share	Value of securities	$12,000
	Debit balance	4,000
	Equity	8,000

$$\text{New margin} = \frac{V - D}{V} = \frac{\$12,000 - \$4,000}{\$12,000} = \underline{\underline{66\frac{2}{3}\%}}$$

Step C:
THE INVESTOR PYRAMIDS HER MARGIN ACCOUNT

400 shares of *another* stock purchased at	Value of securities	$4,000
$10/share (second transaction)	Debit balance	4,000
	New capital (equity)	0

Step D:
THE NEW MARGIN ACCOUNT

Total of the two transactions *after* the	Value of securities	$16,000*
pyramiding	Debit balance	8,000**
	Equity	8,000

$$\text{New margin} = \frac{\$16,000 - \$8,000}{\$16,000} = \underline{\underline{50\%}}$$

---

*400 shares at $30/share (first transaction) *plus* another 400 shares at $10/share (second transaction) = $12,000 + $4,000 = $16,000.

**Debit balance from first transaction *plus* debit balance from second transaction = $4,000 + $4,000 = $8,000.

Here is an example of how pyramiding works. Let us continue the illustration we began above (ignoring any dividends received or interest paid) and suppose that the stock actually does rise to $30 per share. Our investor wants to continue to ride with this stock but has just recently uncovered another issue she feels is also ready to take off. Naturally, she would like to buy some, but unfortunately, she has just about exhausted her investment capital. She is in luck, however, since she can use the excess margin that now exists in her account to purchase shares of the new stock—in effect, she can start pyramiding her paper profits. Assume that while the old stock is trading at $30, the second issue is trading at $10. Table 5.5 summarizes what happens when the investor uses pyramiding to buy the additional shares of stock. Notice that at step B, because of paper profits, the account held excess margin—66⅔ percent versus the prevailing initial margin requirement of only 50 percent. And even after the second transaction was completely financed with margin loans (see step C which shows that *no* new capital was used), the margin account still carried the required level of 50 percent (as shown in step D). This type of pyramiding can continue as long as there are additional paper profits in the margin account and as long as the margin level exceeds the prevailing initial requirement. The tactic is somewhat complex but it is also profitable, especially in light of the fact that it minimizes the amount of new capital required in the account.

Increasing current income

This is the least common use of margin trading and can be done only when the interest cost for margin loans is relatively low. The technique also requires securities with *high* levels of current income (in the form of dividends or coupon interest payments). For example, a stock with a dividend yield of 8 percent would be a possible candidate when interest rates on margin loans are, say, 6 percent. To illustrate the simplicity of this strategy, consider an investor with $2,000 who can use 50 percent margin to borrow another $2,000 in order to purchase 100 shares of stock at $40 per share. Assume the investor can obtain margin money at 6 percent. Because annual dividends on the stock amount to $3.20 per share, it has an 8 percent current yield ($3.20 ÷ $40.00 = .08), which exceeds the cost of margin funds. In the course of a year, the investor would realize $320 in dividends and pay only $120 in interest ($2,000 × .06); this would provide net dividend income of $200 per year (for a dividend yield of 10 percent on the $2,000 of invested capital). Had he not margined, the investor would have realized the 8 percent dividend yield, or $160 in dividend income.

By using margin, the investor can realize a slight improvement in dividend income and current yield. However, note that this tactic has one major drawback: That is, because it is a margin transaction, it is subject to magnified losses should the market move against the investor. Thus, we have to question whether the small amount of additional return (the added dividends) is worth the fairly substantial increase in risk exposure.

SHORT SELLING

Short selling is used when a decline in security prices is anticipated. The technique enables investors to profit from falling security prices; however, as we shall see, it can also be used to *protect* investors from falling security prices. Almost any type of security can be shorted—common stocks, preferred stocks, corporate bonds, government and agency bonds, municipal bonds, convertible securities, puts and calls, warrants, and listed mutual funds can all be sold short. Although the list is fairly extensive, the short selling activities of most individual investors are limited almost exclusively to common stocks and puts and calls. The material that follows will review the short selling tactic and discuss some of the essential ingredients of this trading technique; we will then look at the practice of lending securities, and examine some of the popular uses of short selling.

The Essentials of Short Selling

Short selling has been defined as the practice of selling borrowed property. And that is exactly what is is. For short sales start when securities that have been

---

TABLE 5.6 THE MECHANICS OF A SHORT SALE

1. 100 shares of stock are *sold* at $50/share;
   Proceeds from sale to investor $5,000
2. Later, 100 shares of the stock are *purchased* at $25/share;
   Cost to investor 2,500
   Net profit $2,500

---

borrowed from a broker are sold in the marketplace. Later, when the price of the issue goes down, the short seller buys back the securities, which are then returned to the lender. Of foremost concern in a short sale transaction is that the lenders of the securities being shorted be provided total and constant protection.

Making money when prices fall

Although the idea may seem un-American, making money when security prices fall is what short selling is all about. Like their colleagues in the rest of the investment world, short sellers are also trying to make money by buying low and selling high. The only difference is that they reverse the investment process by starting the transaction with a sale and ending it with a purchase. An investor becomes a short seller when, working through a broker, he or she sells *borrowed* securities. Some time later, the investor covers the short sale by buying back the necessary shares and closing out (ending) the transaction. At this point the borrowed securities are returned to their original owners. Table 5.6 shows how a short sale works and how investors can profit from such transactions. In the illustration, we assume the investor has found a stock he feels will drop from its present level of $50 per share to about $25. As a result, it has all the ingredients of a profitable short sale. It is evident from the table that the amount of profit or loss generated in a short sale is dependent on the price at which the short seller can buy back the stock. Short sellers make money only so long as the proceeds from the sale of the stock are greater than the cost of buying the stock back. There is an unusual tax angle to short selling, however, that should be understood by all investors: The profits from such transactions are always taxed as regular short-term income. Put another way, no matter how long a security is shorted, the profit from the transaction is never considered long-term capital gains for tax purposes.

High risk, limited return

A fact of many short sale transactions is that the investor must settle for high risk exposure in the face of limited return opportunities. This is so since the price of a security can fall only so far (to a value of or near zero), yet there is really no limit to how far such securities can rise in price (remember, when a security goes up in price, a short seller loses). For example, notice in Table 5.6 that the stock in question cannot possibly fall by more than 50 points, yet who is to say how high it can go in price?

Another, less serious, disadvantage is that short sellers never earn dividends

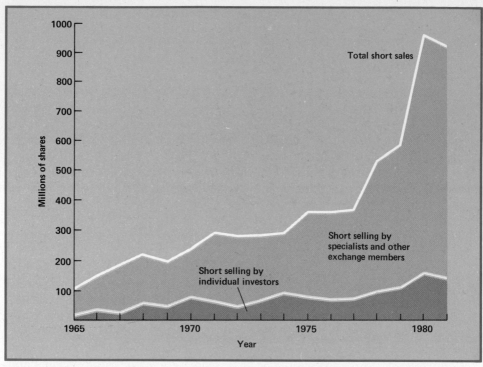

Figure 5.2   Short Selling on the New York Stock Exchange, 1965–1981.
The number of shares of common stock sold short on the NYSE has risen dramatically over
the past 15 years, as both floor members and individual investors step up their use of this
trading tool. (*Source: New York Stock Exchange Fact Book,* 1982.)

(or interest income). In fact, short sellers are actually responsible for making up
dividends (or interest) that are paid while the transaction is outstanding. That is, if a
dividend is paid during the course of a short sale transaction, the *short seller* must
pay an equal amount to the lender of the stock (the mechanics of which are taken
care of automatically by the short seller's broker). The major *advantage* of selling
short is, of course, the chance to convert a price decline into a profit-making situation.
In addition, the technique can be used by investors to protect profits that have already
been earned and to defer the taxes on such profits. And as we will see, when used
in this manner, it becomes a highly conservative investment strategy.

Short sale transactions

Almost a billion shares of stock were sold short on the NYSE in 1981, accounting for about 8 percent of total share volume. As Figure 5.2 shows, this is up
considerably from the level that existed in 1965. Although most short selling is done
by exchange specialists and other floor members, short sales by individual investors
did amount to nearly 150,000,000 shares in 1981—and this was just on the New
York Stock Exchange. In addition to NYSE stock, just about any type of (listed or

OTC) security can be shorted, and such transactions can be executed in odd or round lots. Moreover, they are subject to the same commissions and transaction costs as any other type of transaction. In fact, about the only difference is that a short sale transaction must be identified as such on the broker's order execution form. The reason for this is that these transactions are stringently regulated by the SEC, and can be executed only when the price of a stock has gone up.

Extensive regulation of short-selling was required in order to curb the many abuses and misuses of this tactic that occurred prior to the great crash of 1929. Today, a short sale can be executed only when the price of a security rises. This is known as an *uptick,* and indicates that the price of an issue has gone up since its last transaction. For example, a stock can be sold short at 51⅛ if the transaction just before was at 51; but it cannot be shorted at a price of 50⅞, since this would be less than the preceding price of 51. The latter situation is known as a *downtick* and indicates that the price of the security is off from its last transaction. As an investor, you can place a short sell order at any time, but your broker will not be able to execute it until the issue undergoes an uptick.

One point that is often the cause of much misunderstanding on the part of uninitiated short sellers concerns the amount of investment capital required to make such transactions. Many people seem to think that since the transactions start with a sale, there is no need for the investor to put up any money. This is simply not true. For certain (minimal) amounts of equity, capital must be put up by the short seller in order to initiate a short sale transaction. The amount of investment required is defined according to a special margin requirement for short sale transactions. Specifically, there is an initial margin requirement which designates the minimum amount of cash (or equity) the investor must deposit with a broker in order to execute a short sale. This requirement is currently 50 percent for equity securities like common stock. Thus, if an investor wished to short $5,000 worth of stock at a time when the prevailing short sale margin requirement was 50 percent, he or she would have to deposit $2,500 with a broker.

Lending Securities

Because selling short *always* involves the use of borrowed securities, it follows that someone or some institution has to agree to lend the securities. Obviously, there has to be an incentive for these parties to agree to such loans, and safeguards must exist in order to assure the lenders that they are always fully protected. We have looked at the seller's side of a short sale; let us now take a brief look at the lender's to see why people would let their security holdings be used in such a way.

Who lends the securities?

Acting through their brokers, short sellers obtain securities from brokerage houses or from other individual investors. Of the two, brokers are the principal source of borrowed securities. They lend securities they hold in their own portfolios, or in what are known as *street name* accounts. Street name securities are those held by brokers for their customers; the stock certificates are issued in the brokerage house's name but held in trust for the account of their clients. It is actually a common way

BOX 5.2 MARGIN ACCOUNTS: QUICK, LOW-COST CREDIT

You've decided on a family purchase that will cost $5,000, but you don't have ready access to the cash. One possible solution: You call your broker and ask that a check for $5,000 be sent immediately. A few days later, the money arrives in the mail.

Sound simple? Millions of people are borrowing billions of dollars through margin accounts with brokerage firms because it is just about that quick and easy. Once the account is established, there's no paper work, no personal questions, no stringent payback schedules. And compared to other avenues of borrowing (except perhaps for the six- to eight-percent loan on an old life insurance policy), it might be one of the lowest cost sources of quick money available to you.

How a Margin Account Works

You open a margin account with a broker by agreeing to leave securities you own in your account and to let the brokerage firm use them as collateral. Completing this agreement form is the only paper work involved. Most brokers require a minimum of $2,000 in marketable securities and/or cash to set up an account, but once it's open, you can borrow against the securities.

If you deposit fully paid-for stock in your margin account, you'll be able to borrow up to 50 percent of its current value. If you have U.S. Government bonds, you'll be able to borrow as much as 90 percent of the value. Although those percentages are subject to change, they have not moved since the early 1970s.

Interest on money borrowed through a margin account is charged daily at the prevailing rate and is added to the amount of the loan. You can keep the borrowed funds indefinitely or pay back the loan in any amount at any time. Most people repay the loan when they sell some of their securities. The rate of interest on margin is based on a lending rate set by the Federal Reserve Board— which also regulates margin accounts. The rate can and does change and in recent years has been lower than 10 percent and higher than 20 percent.

The New York Stock Exchange requires that the equity in your account be at least 25 percent of the current market value of the stocks or bonds. If the value of your securities declines so that equity in the account falls below 25 percent, you will be subject to a margin call or "maintenance call." This points up one of the major risks of a margin account. If the value of your securities does decline below the minimum level, the broker does call, and you must deposit additional cash or securities. If you can't provide either, the broker is forced to sell enough securities from your account to bring the borrowing up to the required level. This may occur in the same declining market that caused your margin call in the first place. The result is that a paper loss becomes a real loss.

The utmost in borrowing convenience through a margin-type account may be the central assets accounts that most of the major brokerage firms have set up in the last few years. These include the Merrill Lynch Cash Management Account; the Financial Management Account at Shearson/American Express; and, Paine Webber's Resource Management Account, among others. These accounts allow you immediate access to the borrowing power in your securities through a special debit card such as VISA, or through bank checks.

of buying securities, since many investors do not want to be bothered with handling and safeguarding stock certificates. In such cases, the certificates are issued in the street name of the broker, who then records the details of the transaction and keeps track of these investments through a series of bookkeeping entries. When dividends, notices, proxies, and so on, are received by the broker, they are automatically forwarded to the proper owner of the securities.

BOX 5.2 *Continued*

Comparing Lending Rates

Interest rates on margin loans have been looking very attractive. They are generally based on the "broker call" rate, which is the interest rate that banks charge brokers for overnight or very short-term money. Brokers then tack on an additional percentage when lending to customers. This add-on varies with the size of the debit balance.

For example, in December 1982, the broker call rate was 10 percent and the prime rate was 11½ percent. Margin interest rates at full service brokerage firms ranged from 10¾ to 12¼ percent, with the lowest rate for amounts of $50,000 or more and the highest rate for amounts under $10,000. These rates might be even lower at some discount firms.

These interest rates contrast sharply with current personal loan rates still in the 17 to 19 percent range at banks, and conventional mortgage rates of 13½ to 14½ percent plus "points" (an extra, loan-origination fee paid up-front).

Using Margin to Enhance Income

The main use for margin is investment. It can be used effectively to increase income or to increase opportunities for capital gains. With the bond yields recently available, it was possible to earn more on borrowed money than what the money cost.

Assume that you have $30,000 to invest and you can buy A-rated corporate bonds yielding 13¾ percent. If you buy the bonds outright for cash, the income from the bonds would be $4,125 per year.

But look at the same bonds purchased on margin with a 30-percent cash payment. You could buy $100,000 of the bonds, which would pay annual income of $13,750. Your borrowing at 10¾ percent would cost $7,525, so your net income would be $6,225, or an extra $2,100, a 20.7-percent yield on your $30,000 investment.

If you're a stock investor, margin can give you greater leverage than outright purchase for cash. Suppose IBM is selling at 60 and you are convinced it will rise to 100. With $6,000 to invest, you can buy 100 shares for cash or up to 200 shares on margin. If your expectations prove correct, which position would you prefer? The cash position generates a return of 66 percent while the margin position creates a gain of 133 percent. *If, however, your judgment on IBM proves wrong, your loss will also be doubled.* But IBM stock would have to decline below $43 per share, a 29-percent drop, before you received a margin call.

Other Uses For Margin

In addition to its use in investing, margin can also be utilized to take advantage of buying opportunities or as a "bridge loan." You might have a chance to make a major purchase at a bargain price, if you could pay cash. Or you may need money for paying taxes, until your dividends or commission payments come in. Margin provides the needed bridge loan for a few weeks.

Margin may be less expensive than using a credit card. Even allowing for the card's "grace period" of a month before payment is due, a margin loan at 12 percent can be cheaper than a 19-percent credit card interest rate after the third month.

Source: William H. Arlen. "Margin Accounts: Quick, Low-Cost Credit." *FACT*, February 1983, pp. 23–24.

Brokers lend securities for short sale transactions as a service to their customers. In contrast, individuals lend securities for one simple reason: because of the *interest-free loans* they receive. All an individual investor need do is notify his or her broker that he or she is willing to lend securities to investors who want to sell short.

The only condition is that the lender must hold a stock certificate issued in his or her name; as such, investors who own securities in street names can *not* lend securities and therefore are not eligible to receive interest-free loans. Normally, individuals will lend securities they are holding for the long haul and which they have no intention of liquidating in the near future.

When the occasion arises, the broker, and not the individual investor, will actually arrange for the securities to be used in a short sale. When the short sale transaction is executed, the lender then becomes eligible to receive an interest-free loan equal to the collateral value of the securities being used in the short sale. *Collateral value* represents the amount of money that can be borrowed in a margin transaction: For example, when the margin requirement equals 60 percent, collateral value will amount to 40 percent since that is the maximum margin loan that can be made on the transaction. Thus, if an individual lends $10,000 worth of securities and the prevailing margin requirement is 60 percent, he or she can receive an interest-free loan of $4,000 (40 percent of $10,000).

As we will see below, the lender still retains virtually all benefits of ownership, yet now has an added $4,000 to invest. Such money, however, is normally used as conservatively as possible, since there is no telling when the short seller will want to cover his or her position and recover the money that has been loaned out (the "loan" has to be repaid when the short sale transaction is terminated). Most investors will use this windfall for investments like savings accounts, Treasury bills, and money market funds. These are all liquid securities which offer at least a modest rate of return. For example, if the short sale in our illustration above remained outstanding for a period of, say, nine months, the investor would be able to generate an additional $240 in income by committing the $4,000 interest-free loan to some type of liquid investment that pays 8 percent per year ($.08 \times \frac{9}{12} \times \$4,000 = \$240$).

Who receives the benefits of ownership?

Except for voting rights, the individual investor who lends the securities in a short sale transaction retains virtually all other benefits and rights of ownership. He is entitled to the full and prompt payment of dividends, even though he does not legally own the securities; the only catch is that rather than receiving quarterly dividends from the corporation that issued the stock, the lender receives his dividends from the short seller. If preemptive stock rights are issued, the lender is entitled to them and again will receive them, or their equivalent value in cash, from the short seller. Likewise, if stock splits or stock dividends are declared while the short is outstanding, the lender's position is adjusted accordingly. In effect, one of the conditions of obtaining the required borrowed securities is that the short seller agrees to become the surrogate firm and as such, is responsible for dividends, stock rights, and the like (stock dividends, stock splits, and stock rights are discussed in Chapters 8 and 13). The broker, of course, is always there to make sure that the short seller lives up to these responsibilities. In fact, this is the major reason a margin deposit is required in short sale transactions; it is held (by the broker) not for the benefit of the short seller, but for the benefit and protection of the lender.

Full protection

When a security is sold short, the net proceeds from the sale of the issue, along with the short seller's margin deposit, are held by the broker for safekeeping. *None of the funds is turned over to the short seller.* Instead, the broker establishes two accounts: one for the short seller, and one for the party lending the securities. Such accounts are held for one major purpose: to provide full protection to the lender. This is done by a process known as *mark-to-the-market.* It works like this: When the price of the stock being shorted goes up, the short seller's account is reduced and funds are transferred to the lender's account. If the price of the stock goes down, the opposite occurs. In this way, the lender enjoys 100 percent protection at all times—and the short seller is fully covered as well, since there are always funds in that account to see to it that he or she receives the rewards of shorting. These accounts also serve other purposes. The lenders of securities receive their interest-free loans from this source, and dividends are paid to the lender by simply charging the short seller's account and crediting the lender's. When the transaction is finally terminated, the funds held in the account of the lender are used to purchase the stock (at which time the lender will be notified to repay immediately any interest-free loans outstanding on the account). The short sale position is considered covered when the stocks are returned to the lender. Any funds left after commissions and transaction costs are then turned over to the short seller; presumably, this will include the investor's initial margin deposit, plus some profit earned on the transaction.

Uses of Short Selling

Investors short sell for one of two reasons: to seek speculative profits when the price of a security is expected to drop, or to protect a profit and defer taxes by hedging their position. The first use is more common and represents the standard short sale transaction. The hedge tactic, in contrast, is a conservative use of short selling and is employed to lock in a given profit level. All shorts are executed on margin, so it seems appropriate to begin our discussion of investor uses of short selling by looking at how margin fits into a short sale and affects returns.

Shorting on margin

There is an old saying on Wall Street: "Bulls pay interest, bears do not." This has to do with margin trading and the fact that margins are used with both long and short transactions. However, there are no borrowed funds with margined short sales. With short selling, the term "margin" simply indicates the size of the equity deposit the investor must make in order to initiate the transaction. The absence of borrowing means there will be no interest. Margined short sales are executed in the same margin account as margined long transactions. They are subject to initial margin require-ments; have maintenance margin levels; and if the price of the security being shorted goes *up* too much, the account can become restricted or even subject to a margin call. In fact, the only thing that we do not have to be concerned about with a margined short sale is the account's debit balance. Margining a short sale, then, is much like margining a long transaction; many of the investment principles, margin features, and behavioral characteristics we discussed previously apply equally well here.

A $2 stock sounds WONDERFUL. After all, how far down can it possibly go?

The margin on a short sale, however, is figured with a different formula than that used with long transactions. Specifically, the margin position of a short sale account is determined as follows:

$$\text{margin (\%)} = \left(\frac{\text{sales proceeds} + \text{equity deposit}}{\text{value of securities}} \right) - 1$$

$$= \left(\frac{SP + ED}{V} \right) - 1$$

The sales proceeds (*SP*) represent the net amount realized from the sale of the securities when the short transaction was established; the equity deposit (*ED*) denotes the required initial margin that was deposited by the short seller at the time of the transaction; and the value of securities (*V*) represents the prevailing market value (price) of the securities being shorted. Note that the values for "sales proceeds" and "equity deposit" never change for a given margin transaction; instead, as with long transactions, the only item that is subject to change in the equation is *V* (value of securities), and that changes only as the market price of the securities being shorted changes.

To see how this margin formula works, consider the following hypothetical investment situation: Assume an investor wants to short 100 shares of stock at $60 per share by using the prevailing 70 percent margin. In this instance, the value of the securities (V) amounts to $6,000 (100 × $60), and so too do the sales proceeds (SP), as this is the amount of money that would be realized by selling 100 shares of stock at $60 per share. The size of the equity deposit (ED) is $4,200 and is easily found by taking the amount of the transaction relative to the prevailing initial margin requirement ($6,000 × .70). Now let us see what happens when the price of the stock rises 10 points to $70 per share. Using our short sale margin formula, we discover that the margin amounts to only 46 percent:

$$\text{margin (\%)} = \left(\frac{SP + ED}{V}\right) - 1 = \left(\frac{\$6,000 + \$4,200}{\$7,000}\right) - 1 = 46\%$$

The sales proceeds and equity deposit remain unchanged at $6,000 and $4,200, respectively; only the value of the collateral changes (and this has gone up to $7,000). But notice what is happening: As the price of the stock goes up, the amount of margin in the position drops. This is so because the investor loses money in a short position when the price of the stock goes up, and as a result the amount of equity deteriorates accordingly. Because (at 46 percent) the amount of margin has dropped below the initial margin requirement (70 percent), the investor would be faced with a restricted account. The reverse would happen if, instead of rising, the price of the stock falls 10 points to $50 per share. In this case, the amount of margin would rise to 104 percent ([($6,000 + $4,200)/$5,000] − 1), and we would have excess equity which could then be used for pyramiding.

Return on invested capital

Because short sales are executed on margin, the amount of invested capital is limited to the investor's equity deposit. This is all the investor puts up in the transaction and therefore is the basis for figuring the rate of return. Moreover, since these are usually short-term transactions, return is generally measured on a holding period basis. The only complication in this yield measure is that any dividends paid by the short seller to the lender of the securities must be netted out of the profit. Other than that, no dividends are received by the short seller and no interest is paid, so this return formula is fairly straightforward:

$$\frac{\text{return on}}{\text{invested capital}} = \frac{\text{proceeds from sale} - \begin{array}{c}\text{cost to purchase} \\ \text{securities}\end{array} - \begin{array}{c}\text{dividends paid} \\ \text{by short seller}\end{array}}{\text{equity deposit}}$$
from a
short sale

To illustrate, assume an investor wants to use 70 percent margin to short a stock at $60 per share he feels is going to drop to $40 within a six-month period. Because the company pays annual dividends of $2 per share, the short seller estimates he will probably be liable for about $1 per share over the expected six-month holding period. Computing the return on a per share basis (this figure will be the

TABLE 5.7   SPECULATING WITH A SHORT SALE

Short sale initiated: 300 shares of the stock sold at $50/share	$15,000
Short sale covered: 300 shares of the stock bought back at $30/share	$ 9,000
Net profit	$ 6,000
Equity deposit (.50 × $15,000)	$ 7,500

$$\text{Return on invested capital*} = \frac{\$15,000 - \$9,000}{\$7,500} = \frac{\$6,000}{\$7,500} = 80\%$$

*Assume the stock pays no dividends and therefore the short seller has no dividend liability.

same regardless of how many shares are actually involved in the transaction), we see that the expected return on invested capital for this short sale will equal 45 percent:

$$\text{return on invested capital from a short sale} = \frac{\$60 - \$40 - \$1}{\$42} = \frac{\$19}{\$42} = 45\%$$

This hefty profit rate is made possible not only because of the profit earned when the price of the stock drops, but also because of the limited amount of capital put up by the investor (the equity deposit equaled only 70 percent of the transaction amount).

Speculating with short sales

Selling short for speculative purposes is perhaps the most basic use of this technique. Because the short seller is betting against the market, the technique is highly speculative and subject to a considerable amount of risk exposure. It works like this: Assume an investor has uncovered a stock that she feels is about to tumble over the next eight months from its present level of $50 per share to somewhere around $30. She therefore decides to short sell 300 shares of the stock at $50 by using 50 percent margin (the prevailing initial margin requirement). Table 5.7 shows the highlights of this hypothetical transaction. Note that the transaction generates a profit of $6,000 to the investor (ignoring commissions and other transaction costs) and, provided it can be executed with an equity deposit of only $7,500, should yield a return on invested capital of 80 percent. Understandably, if the market moves against the short seller, all or most of her $7,500 investment could be lost.

Shorting-against-the-box

This exotic-sounding name describes a conservative hedging technique used to protect existing security profits. Like insurance, the purpose of a hedge is to minimize or eliminate exposure to loss. *Shorting-against-the-box* is a hedging program set up *after* the investor has already generated a profit in an earlier transaction. The short sale, in effect, provides the hedge by giving complete protection to earned

TABLE 5.8 SHORTING-AGAINST-THE-BOX (HEDGING WITH A SHORT SALE)

Transaction 1: Purchase 100 shares of stock at $20		$2,000
PRICE OF STOCK RISES TO $50/SHARE		
Current profit in transaction:		
Current value of stock		$5,000
Cost of transaction		<2,000>
Net profit		$3,000
Transaction 2: Short sell 100 shares at $50		
A. NOW PRICE OF STOCK RISES TO $80/SHARE		
Current profit in *both* transactions:		
Value of stocks owned (trans. 1)		$8,000
Cost of transaction		<2,000>
Profit		$6,000
Less loss on short sale:		
Short sale initiated	$5,000	
Short sale covered	<8,000>	<3,000>
Net profit		$3,000
B. PRICE OF STOCK FALLS TO $30/SHARE		
Current profit in *both* transactions:		
Value of stock owned (trans. 1)		$3,000
Cost of transaction		<2,000>
Profit		$1,000
Plus profit from short sale:		
Short sale initiated	$5,000	
Short sale covered	<3,000>	2,000
Net profit		$3,000

profits. Shorting-against-the-box is done by combining a short sale with a profitable long transaction. An investor who already owns 100 shares of stock (the long transaction) would short an equal number of shares of stock in the same company. By doing this, he or she is able to protect the profit already made in the long transaction, and, as an added by-product, can defer the taxes on this profit until the next taxable year.

Here is how it works. Suppose that early last year you bought 100 shares of Rose Colored Glasses, Inc., at $20 per share, and have since watched the price of RCG rise to $50. You presently have a $3,000 capital gain. Although you do not want to sell the stock right now, you do not want to lose any of your profit either. In essence, you would like to ride things out for a while and still protect the profit you have earned up to now. A simple short sale against the box will allow you to do this—just short 100 shares of RCG at $50 per share, and you have "locked in" your profit of $3,000. For no matter what happens to the price of the stock, you are guaranteed $3,000. You now have two positions—one long and one short—but both involve an equal number of RCG shares. Table 5.8 summarizes this tactic and demonstrates how the profit becomes locked in. Note, however, that while this short sale transaction is executed with borrowed securities, it is not necessary to put up an equity deposit because your current holdings of the stock serve this purpose. Thus, the cost of shorting-against-the-box is reasonably low and involves only the commission and transaction costs of initiating and covering the short sale. One precaution is in order: That is, while shorting-against-the-box does lock in a specific profit level, this tactic can *not* be used to convert a short-term profit to a long-term capital gain. Thus, if an investor held the stock for less than a year before he shorted-against-the-box, that short-term profit will remain subject to ordinary income tax rates no matter how long the short hedge stays in effect; in contrast, if the investor had a long term capital gain to begin with (held the stock for more than a year before he shorted), it remains eligible for the preferential tax treatment accorded such profits. And, of course, regardless of the type of profit on the long transaction, any gains from the short sale are always taxed as ordinary income.

SUMMARY

Margin trading and short selling are two widely used investment strategies. They are generally considered to be speculative forms of investing, but in some cases can be used as highly conservative investment techniques. Buying on margin is simply using borrowed money to pay for part of the securities being purchased. Short selling is more complicated, but it basically involves the practice of selling borrowed securities. The purpose of margin is to use financial leverage to magnify the rate of return on investments. In a short sale, the purpose is to sell borrowed securities in order to profit from a decline in the market price.

When stock is bought on margin, the investor puts up equity in the form of cash or securities equal to a portion of the purchase price; this equity deposit is called the investor's margin. The remainder of the purchase price is provided (loaned) by a brokerage house or commercial bank. Financial leverage magnifies both the gains and the losses from an investment. When a margin purchase is made, the investor deposits a portion of the cost and takes out a loan for the balance. The brokerage house (or commercial bank) making the loan holds the stock as collateral and charges interest on the borrowed amount. If the stock increases in price, the investor's profit is the gain on the entire purchase, less interest costs. Since the investor's funds are only a part of the total purchase price, the rate of return on these funds is larger than it would have been on a straight cash purchase. If the stock declines, however, just the reverse is true. For investors with limited resources, a margin account may provide the opportunity to diversify among more issues than would otherwise be the case, thus reducing the risk from a share price decline in any one issue.

The Federal Reserve Board sets the minimum down payment (initial margin) required to purchase securities. By requiring a sizable amount of initial margin, the Fed provides some measure of protection for both the investor and the lender, as well as for the market as a whole. After a margin purchase is made, the lender (brokerage house) will carefully monitor price movements. If the security declines in price, reducing its collateral value below the minimum initial margin, the account becomes restricted. Should prices continue to decline, the maintenance margin requirement may come into play; for when account equity drops below the maintenance level, the investor receives a margin call and must deposit additional equity with the lender.

Executing a short sale also requires a margin account. In this case, however, securities, rather than money, are borrowed (the short seller agrees to return the securities at a later date). If the price declines after the sale is executed, the seller can repurchase and return the securities at a lower price, thus extracting a profit. To execute a short sale, the investor borrows the necessary shares through a broker. The original owner of the shares loses voting rights but retains all other important benefits of ownership, like quarterly dividends. In addition, under certain circumstances, the lender of securities in a short sale is entitled to an interest-free loan equal to the collateral value of the securities being shorted. Because no funds are borrowed in a short sale, no interest is charged to the seller, but the seller must pay any dividends declared on the stock during the short sale period.

The short seller must be willing to accept the possibility that the price of the securities being shorted may increase rather than decline. If that occurs, then the short seller may be required to deposit additional margin, or may even incur an outright loss if the shares are eventually repurchased at a higher price. Since there is no limit to the amount a stock may increase in price, a short seller is exposed to potentially unlimited losses, while gains are limited to the amount of the short sale price. In special situations, however, short sales can be used by conservative investors as a way to reduce risk. The most common use is shorting-against-the-box, usually employed to protect earned profits and to defer the associated taxes.

KEY TERMS

collateral value	margin trading
covering a short sale	mark-to-the-market
debit balance	paper profits
downtick	pyramiding profits
excess margin	restricted account
initial margin	shorting-against-the-box
maintenance margin	short selling
margin account	street name securities
margin call	undermargined account
margin loan	uptick

REVIEW QUESTIONS

1. Describe margin trading; note how leverage is created with this trading strategy.
2. Explain how profits (and losses) are magnified with margin trading.
3. What is the difference between initial margin and maintenance margin; when does an account become undermargined and what are the ramifications of an undermargined account?
4. Assume an investor buys 100 shares of stock at $50 per share, putting up a 70 percent margin:

a. What would be the debit balance in this transaction?

b. How much equity capital would the investor have to come up with in order to make this margin transaction?

c. If the stock rises to $80 per share, what would be the investor's new margin position?

5. Identify the two basic sources of margin loans, and indicate whether or not there are costs associated with such loans.

6. Miss Jerri Kingston bought 100 shares of stock at $80 per share using an initial margin of 60 percent. Given a maintenance margin of 25 percent, how far does the stock have to drop before Miss Kingston faces a margin call (assume there are no other securities in the margin account)?

7. What advantages and disadvantages does margin trading hold for the individual investor?

8. What is pyramiding? Note and discuss other investor uses of margin trading.

9. An investor buys 200 shares of stock selling for $80 per share, using a margin of 60 percent; if the stock pays annual dividends of $1 per share and a margin loan can be obtained at an annual interest cost of 8 percent, determine the return on invested capital the investor would realize if the price of the stock increased to $104 within six months. What is the annualized rate of return of this transaction?

10. Not long ago, Dave Edwards bought 200 shares of Almost Anything, Inc., at $45 per share; he bought the stock on margin of 60 percent. The stock is now trading at $60 per share and the Federal Reserve has recently lowered initial margin requirements to 50 percent. Dave now wants to do a little pyramiding and buy another 300 shares of the stock; what's the minimum amount of equity he'll have to put up in this transaction?

11. Describe the process of short selling; note how profits are made in such transactions.

12. Explain how margin is used in a short sale transaction. What is meant by the saying "Bulls pay interest, bears do not"?

13. Assume an investor short sells 100 shares of stock at $50 per share, putting up a 70 percent margin:

a. How much cash would the investor have to deposit in order to execute this short sale transaction?

b. What is the new margin for this transaction if the price of the stock falls to $20 per share?

14. If short selling is always done with borrowed securities, who lends the securities in such transactions? Why would an individual agree to lend securities in short sale transactions?

15. What is shorting-against-the-box, and how does it differ from a normal short sale?

16. What are the advantages and disadvantages of short selling?

17. A well-heeled investor, Mr. Oliver Stanley, recently purchased 1,000 shares of stock at $48 per share. They have since risen to $55 per share, and while Mr. Stanley wants to sell out, he hesitates to do so because it is so near the end of the year—he wants to defer the tax liability until next year. As a result, Oliver decides to short-against-the-box; he does this by shorting 1,000 shares of the stock at its current price of $55. What total profit will Mr. Stanley make if the price of the stock continues to rise to $60 per share? How much of this will come from the long transaction and how much from the short sale?

CASE PROBLEMS

5.1 JIM FRIAR'S HIGH-FLYING MARGIN ACCOUNT

Jim Friar is a stockbroker who lives with his lovely wife Pat and their five children in Milwaukee, Wisconsin. Jim likes to practice what he preaches; specifically, he firmly believes that the only way to make money in the market is to follow an aggressive investment posture—for example, to use margin trading. In fact, Jim himself has built a substantial margin account over the years. He presently holds some $75,000 worth of stock in his margin account, though the debit balance in the account amounts to only $30,000. Recently Jim uncovered a stock which, based on extensive analysis, he feels is about to take off—in a big way. The stock, Amalgamated Fertilizer, currently trades at $20 per share. Jim feels it should soar to at least $50 within a year. AF pays no dividends, the prevailing initial margin requirement is 50 percent, and margin loans are now carrying an interest charge of 10 percent. Because Jim feels so strongly about AF, he wants to do some pyramiding by using his margin account to purchase 1,000 shares of the stock.

Questions
1. Discuss the concept of pyramiding as it applies to this investment situation.
2. What is the present margin (%) position of Jim's account?
3. Jim buys the 1,000 shares of AF through his margin account (bear in mind that this is a $20,000 transaction). Now:

   a. What would the margin position of the account be *after* the AF transaction if Jim followed the prevailing (50 percent) initial margin and used $10,000 of his money to buy the stock?
   b. What if he uses only $2,500 equity and obtains a margin loan for the balance ($17,500)?
   c. How do you explain the fact that the stock can be purchased with only 12.5 percent margin when the prevailing initial margin requirement equals 50 percent?

4. Assume that Jim buys 1,000 shares of the AF stock at $20 per share with a minimum cash investment of $2,500, and that the stock does take off by moving to $40 per share in a year:

   a. What is the return on invested capital for this transaction?
   b. What return would Jim have earned had he bought the stock without margin—if he had used all of his own money?

5. What do you think of Jim's idea to pyramid? What are the risks and rewards of this strategy?

5.2 THE BARLOES CONSIDER SHORT SELLING

General Bob Barloe is a career officer with some 24 years in the U.S. Air Force. He lives with his wife Maggie and their three children in the Washington, D.C., area, where he is a high-ranking staff officer at Andrews Air Force Base. In his late forties, General Bob (as his men call him) plans to retire soon and enter civilian life. The general has a modest five-figure portfolio which he personally manages; he has a balanced holding of stocks and bonds, and usually follows a fairly conservative approach to investing. Although General Bob prefers current income, he has on occasion been known to go after capital gains, if the opportunity is right. As a matter of fact, it just so happens that the general feels the situation may once more be right; but this time he is considering doing some short selling as the way to earn capital gains. In particular, General Barloe has heard about International Ballistics and Nuclear, which is expected to tumble in price because of some earnings problems. Word has it that IBN should drop from its present $72 per share to somewhere around $35 to $40. Bob's never done any short selling before, but he feels with this kind of info he can't go wrong. He originally intended to short 100 shares of IBN, but when he learned from his broker that he could short by using 50 percent margin, he decided to double the size of the transaction.

Questions
1. Are there any flaws in General Barloe's decision to short sell 200 shares of IBN? Explain.

2. If 200 shares of IBN are shorted at $72, using 50 percent margin:

a. Determine the size of the initial margin deposit the general would have to make to execute the transaction.

b. What would the new margin (%) be if the stock does, in fact, drop to $50 per share?

c. What kind of ($) profit and return on invested capital would Bob make if he covered at $50 per share?

3. Assume that instead of dropping, the price of the stock rises to $86.50 per share:

a. What would the new margin (%) position be under this circumstance?

b. If the account is restricted to a 25 percent maintenance margin, would it be subject to a margin call? Explain.

4. If you were Bob's stockbroker, would you recommend he short sell IBN? Defend your position.

SELECTED READINGS

Angrist, Stanley W. "The Fast Buck: Selling Short." *Forbes,* December 21, 1981, p. 147.

Arlen, William H. "Margin Accounts: Quick, Low-Cost Credit." *FACT,* February 1983, pp. 23–24.

"Eager Advocate of Short Selling." *Business Week,* October 4, 1976, p. 74.

Elia, Charles J. "Here's a Short Story of a Short Gamble That Didn't Pay Off." *The Wall Street Journal,* October 6, 1978, pp. 1, 32.

Harris, Diane. "Making Sense Out of Buying on Margin." *Money,* November 1983, pp. 175–179.

"How to Get Started in Short Selling." *Business Week,* October 26, 1981, pp. 230–234.

"Longs and the Shorts." *Money,* December 1976, p. 49.

Marcial, Gene G. "Margin Calls Rise as Share Prices Drop." *The Wall Street Journal,* October 31, 1978, p. 13.

Mayer, Martin. "Merrill Lynch Quacks Like a Bank." *Fortune,* October 20, 1980, pp. 134–144.

Moffitt, Donald. "Borrowing from Your Broker: How Margin Works to Inflate Investors Gains— And Losses." *The Wall Street Journal,* October 15, 1979, p. 40.

"Short Sales." *Financial World,* March 15, 1978, p. 62.

THREE
INVESTMENT
PLANNING

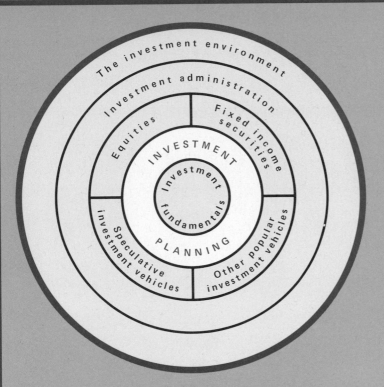

The investment environment

Investment administration

Equities

Fixed income securities

INVESTMENT

Investment fundamentals

Speculative investment vehicles

Other popular investment vehicles

PLANNING

Before an investor proceeds with the evaluation and selection of investment vehicles, investment plans should be prepared. Planning requires the investor to give adequate attention to maintaining needed insurance coverage, reducing and meeting taxes, maintaining sufficient liquidity, and providing for retirement needs. The two chapters in this part address these and other issues related to the planning process. Chapter 6 focuses on establishing an investment program, which involves personal financial planning, insurance, taxation, and investment planning. Chapter 7 develops the procedures for meeting liquidity and retirement needs—two important aspects of investment planning.

6

Establishing an Investment Program

Prior to developing an investment program, an individual investor needs to develop personal financial plans that take into account not only current income and expenditures, but also insurance and personal taxes. In order to provide such knowledge, in this chapter we will look at:

1. The types, roles, and interrelationships among the personal financial statements used in assessing one's financial position.
2. The process of establishing both short-run and long-run financial goals and developing budgets consistent with their achievement.
3. The need for and types of insurance, and the role it plays in the financial plans of the individual investor.
4. The basic sources of taxation, the types of taxable income, and the potential impact of each on the individual investor.
5. The key factors to consider in the process of establishing investment goals and plans.
6. Methods of establishing an investment program to fulfill investment goals, provide for contingencies, and permit monitoring of the investment plan.

How would you like to be left aboard a drifting ship, not knowing where you are within the vast expanse of the ocean? Although most people probably wouldn't find that situation very enjoyable, it is precisely the way many individuals handle their personal finances. Regardless of a ship's destination, the first thing one must determine is current location. Once that is known, the ship can be directed toward a desired destination. The same is true of an individual's finances. Before establishing financial goals, one must assess one's financial position by preparing and analyzing key personal financial statements: the balance sheet and the income statement. Once available resources are known, an investor can develop financial goals and then prepare plans and budgets that will guide him from his current position toward the achievement of these goals. As in the case of navigating a ship toward a destination, the individual establishes short-run goals against which the progress toward long-run goals can be assessed, and takes into account environmental forces such as the various taxes and their potential impact on finances.

PERSONAL FINANCIAL PLANNING

Common sense would suggest that by carefully developing financial plans, an individual should be better able to achieve his or her goals. Because investment goals must be consistent with overall goals, an understanding of the total financial planning process is an important prerequisite to the development of an investment program. The personal financial planning process is made up of three major activities: (1) assessing current financial condition; (2) establishing financial goals; and (3) budgeting for goal achievement. The first of these activities shows us where we are, financially, at present, the second indicates where we would like to be, and the third provides a path for getting there. Each of these aspects of the personal financial planning process is discussed below.

Assessing Current Financial Condition

The measures used to assess current financial condition must be standardized so that meaningful comparisons can be made consistently over time. The basic financial reporting techniques used for similar purposes by business firms can also be employed by individuals. The two key financial statements are the balance sheet and the income statement. The balance sheet can be used to measure financial position, which can be viewed as one's wealth at a specified point in time; an income statement can be used to measure financial performance or the relationship between income and expenses over a given period of time.

The personal balance sheet

The *balance sheet* or statement of financial position reflects an individual's wealth position at a given point in time. The key categories of accounts found on the balance sheet are assets, liabilities, and net worth. The basic relationship between these accounts is reflected in the balance sheet equation:

total assets = total liabilities + net worth

On the left side of the equation, *assets* represent what is owned; on the right side, *liabilities* represent debts currently outstanding; and *net worth* is the ownership position or amount of wealth, or equity, in the assets owned. The equation basically indicates that what is owned must be financed either by borrowing (liabilities) or by investment of the individual's own wealth (net worth). Let us look at each of these components.

Assets.   The assets held by an individual can be classified as either financial or nonfinancial. Financial assets are items that can be readily converted into cash. They include cash, savings deposits, security investments, and money loaned out. Nonfinancial assets typically include property purchased for the service it provides. They include items such as real estate, automobiles, boats, recreational equipment, personal property, collections, and business ownership interests. Regardless of how they are purchased (for cash or by borrowing), all items owned by an individual would be classified as personal assets. Items that have been borrowed or leased by the individual do not represent assets included on a personal balance sheet.

Liabilities.   The liabilities, or debts, of an individual can be derived from any of a number of sources. They include bills outstanding for various credit card, charge account, and deferred-payment transactions; instalment loan balances; mortgage loans; and other loans. Since the balance sheet reflects an individual's financial position at a given point in time, liabilities represent only the actual loan balance outstanding. For example, if the current amount owed on an original loan of $10,000 is $6,500, the liability would be only the $6,500 currently outstanding—which represents the *principal* amount still owed.

Net worth.   Net worth represents an individual's actual wealth, or equity, in his or her assets. Rearranging the first equation, it can be seen that:

net worth = total assets − total liabilities

In other words, net worth is the amount that would remain after selling all assets and paying all outstanding liabilities. Because net worth reflects wealth, it acts as an important gauge of financial success that can be used in the financial planning process.

The statement.   Like the balance sheet equation, the balance sheet is presented with all assets on the left and liabilities followed by net worth on the right. The statement is preceded by a date reflecting the point in time at which the data included in the statement were measured. A sample balance sheet dated December 31, 1984, for Mary and Mark Adair is presented in Table 6.1. It can be seen that the Adairs have total assets of $96,500, consisting of $8,500 in financial assets and $88,000 in nonfinancial assets. Their liabilities total $57,000, which leaves them with a net worth of $39,500.

The personal income statement

The *income statement* describes the financial activities that have taken place during a specified period of time, which is typically one year. It contains three basic components: income, expenses, and contribution to savings or investment. The basic format of the statement begins with a listing and total of all income received during the period covered by the statement. A listing and total of all items of expense paid during the statement period follows. Subtracting total expenses from total income

TABLE 6.1   BALANCE SHEET FOR MARY AND MARK ADAIR (DECEMBER 31, 1984)

Assets		Liabilities and Net Worth	
Financial assets:		**Liabilities:**	
Cash	$ 200	Bills outstanding	$ 350
Savings deposits	1,800	Instalment loan bal.	4,650
Security investments	6,500	Mortgage loan	51,000
Total financial assets	$ 8,500	Personal loan	1,000
		(2) Total liabilities	$57,000
Nonfinancial assets:			
Real estate	$65,000		
Automobiles	9,500		
Boat	2,000	Net worth [(1) − (2)]	$39,500
Recreational equip.	400		
Personal property	9,600		
Stamp collection	1,500		
Total nonfinancial assets	$88,000	Total liabilities	
(1) Total assets	$96,500	and net worth	$96,500

results in the contribution to savings or investment, which may be positive or negative, depending on whether total income is greater than or less than total expenses, respectively.

contribution to savings or investment = total income − total expenses

Because the income statement describes activities that took place over a specified period of time, this period is noted at the beginning of the statement.

Income.   *Income* items represent cash received during the period and include wages, salaries, bonuses, commissions, dividends, rent, and interest received. Also included are gains (or losses) on the sale of securities, proceeds from the sale of assets, as well as any other money received during the period.

Expenses.   *Expense* items include cash payments made during the period. The key categories of expense for an individual would include housing, utilities, food, automobile, medical, clothing and shoes, insurance, taxes, household goods, health and hygiene, and recreation and entertainment.

Contribution to savings or investment.   The *contribution to savings or investment* represents the difference between total income and total expenses during the given period of time. If positive, it can be viewed as a profit that can be used to increase savings or investment or to repay debt; a negative value reflects a loss that must be covered by reducing savings or investment or by borrowing.

TABLE 6.2   INCOME STATEMENT FOR MARY AND MARK ADAIR
(FOR YEAR ENDED DECEMBER 31, 1984)

Income:
Wages and salaries	$24,500
Bonuses and commissions	1,500
Dividends	300
Interest	450
Gains (or losses) on security sales	(250)
Proceeds from sale of assets	50
Other income	150
(1) Total income	$26,700

Less: Expenses
Housing	$ 5,700
Utilities	1,100
Food	2,500
Automobiles	5,200
Medical	900
Clothing and shoes	2,000
Insurance	600
Taxes	2,950
Household goods	1,100
Health and hygiene	400
Recreation and entertainment	1,500
Other expenses	450
(2) Total expenses	$24,400
Contribution to savings or investment [(1) − (2)]	$ 2,300

The statement.   The income statement for the year ended December 31, 1984, for Mary and Mark Adair is presented in Table 6.2. It shows that their total income for the year was $26,700 and their total expenses were $24,400. The resulting contribution to savings or investment was, therefore, $2,300. The $2,300 excess of income over expense could be used to increase savings or investment or to repay debts.

The relationship between the balance sheet and income statement

The key accounts linking the balance sheet and the income statement are net worth (on the balance sheet) and contribution to savings or investment (on the income statement). In general, regardless of how it is used (to increase savings or investment or repay a debt), a positive contribution to savings or investment will increase net worth; and a negative contribution to savings or investment, regardless of what it is used for, will decrease net worth.

Assessing current position

Once they are prepared, personal financial statements must be reviewed. A review of the balance sheet should allow investors to evaluate both the current value

BOX 6.1 THE REAGANS' 1982 PERSONAL FINANCIAL STATEMENTS

The 1982 financial statements—balance sheet and income statement—drawn from the Reagans' 1982 financial disclosure statement are given below. Because the disclosure statements allow listing of income, assets, and liabilities in broad ranges, not in exact dollar amounts, the declared values are minimums only. Residences and government salaries need not be reported, nor do investments placed in blind trusts. Clearly, the Reagans' financial picture appears rosy!

	MINIMUM AMOUNTS
Assets	**$1,394,000**
California ranch	$ 653,000
Trusts	$ 500,000
Installment payment due from house sale	$ 100,000
Bank savings and checking accounts	$ 70,000
Life insurance	$ 61,000
Ranch equipment	$ 5,000
Ranch savings account	$ 5,000
Liabilities	**$ 310,000**
Loan on California ranch	$ 250,000
Life-insurance loans	$ 60,000
Net worth	**$1,084,000**

	EXACT AMOUNTS
Income	**$ 741,253**
Taxable capital gains (home sale trust)	$ 256,978
Interest	$ 247,061
Presidential salary	$ 200,000
Pensions from California governorship	$ 24,769
Dividends	$ 4,910
Other income including $3,015 from Mrs. Reagan's autobiography	$ 3,935
Rent from radio-repeater station on ranch	$ 3,600

Note: Figures are for 1982. Reagan's income is drawn from his 1982 tax return.
Source: Robert A. Kittle, Joseph P. Shapiro, and Robert F. Black, "When Washington Bigwigs Open Their Books," *U.S. News & World Report,* May 30, 1983, pp. 32–34.

and the mix of their assets. The values of the assets can be compared to those in earlier periods to evaluate the benefit of retaining such assets. A review of liabilities should allow individuals to determine whether or not they are using debt effectively. The value of the net worth is especially meaningful when compared to earlier periods. Clearly, positive and increasing net worth is desired. If we look at the balance sheet presented in Table 6.1, we can see that the Adairs' dominant assets are real estate, personal property, and automobiles—all likely to be necessities. Their security investments, savings deposits, and stamp collection are the dominant assets held solely as investment. Their key liabilities are the mortgage loan on their home and the instalment loan balance that probably resulted from financing their automobile and/

or personal property. In view of their assets, the $57,000 of total debt owed by the Adairs does not seem excessive. The Adairs' net worth of $39,500 represents their wealth on December 31, 1984.

From the income statement, individuals can see whether or not they are living within their means. Clearly, the preferred situation is one in which total income exceeds total expenses; this provides a positive contribution to savings or investment and thereby increases net worth. Reviewing the Adair's income statement presented in Table 6.2, we can see that this is their situation. Their total income of $26,700 exceeded total expenses of $24,400 by $2,300, thereby adding this amount to net worth. It appears that the Adairs are in good shape: their indebtedness is not excessive, their net worth is positive, and they have added to their net worth in the current year.

Establishing Financial Goals

Once current financial condition has been assessed, goals must be established. The goals must be reasonable in the sense that, with proper budgeting, they can actually be achieved. Goal-setting involves preparing long-run financial goals to be achieved five or more years ahead and then setting short-run goals consistent with them. Long-run goals are difficult to specify, but in general they can be viewed as an individual's wants and desires over the next 30 to 40 years. These goals are most meaningful when they are accompanied by dates—for example, to retire at age 55 with $400,000 of net worth; to purchase a summer home for $80,000 in 2000; or to send a child through four years of college in the period 1994–1998 at a cost of $8,000 per year. Short-run goals can be more clearly specified than the long-run goals. They are generally set for a period of only one to two years and must be consistent with the long-run goals. Examples of short-run financial goals are these: to accumulate net worth of $60,000 at the end of the coming year; to buy $800 worth of shop equipment during the next two years; and to take a $2,000 tour of Europe next summer. These goals act as a key input into the budgeting process.

Short-run goals must contribute toward the achievement of the long-run goals. If the short-run goals are not attained, the likelihood that longer-run goals will be achieved is reduced. Consistent underachievement of short-run goals calls for a reevaluation of long-run goals; they could be unrealistic. On the other hand, an ability to achieve short-run goals easily might suggest that the short-run as well as the long-run goals are not sufficiently optimistic. Periodic reassessment of long-run goals in view of short-run financial outcomes is needed to monitor the effectiveness of the personal financial planning process.

Budgeting for Goal Achievement

The actual process of directing personal financial activities toward short-run goals can be guided by a *budget,* which is a schedule of income and expenditure commonly broken into monthly intervals covering a one-year period. The monthly interval is used because it is consistent with the billing cycle of most organizations. The budget provides a mechanism for enhancing the possibilities that the short-run goals will be achieved, thereby contributing toward the achievement of long-run goals. The three key aspects of a budget are estimating income, estimating expenses, and providing for surpluses and deficits.

Total monthly income is estimated by adding monthly income estimates from a variety of sources, such as wages, salaries, bonuses, commissions, dividends, interest, gains (or losses) on security sales, and proceeds from the sale of assets. Each source is estimated on a cash basis. In other words, the income source is recorded in the month that the cash is expected to be received.

Total monthly expense estimates are made using past expense data in combination with data on new expenditures needed to achieve short-run goals. The potential impact of inflation on the level of future expenditures should be incorporated into expenditure estimates, and any scheduled contributions to savings or investment should be treated as expenditures. Like estimated income, estimated expenditures should be recorded in the month during which the actual cash outlay is scheduled to occur.

By subtracting the total monthly expense estimates from the total monthly income estimates, we can determine whether a surplus or deficit exists. A *surplus* is the amount by which total income exceeds total expenses; a *deficit* is the amount by which total expenses exceed total income. An analysis of monthly surpluses or deficits as well as the annual surplus or deficit must be made next to determine whether adjustments are needed. Adjustment in short-run goals may have to be made in order to bring the budget into balance for the year. Monthly surpluses and deficits can be handled by investing excesses and borrowing or using savings, respectively. As long as the annual budget is in balance, any monthly deficits can be met through borrowing or using savings.

The format of the actual budget typically begins with a listing of income items followed by their totals for each month. Itemized expenses and their monthly totals are next. Finally, total monthly expenses are subtracted from total income for each month in order to get the monthly surplus or deficit. A summary of the total monthly income and expense estimates and the associated monthly surpluses or deficits as well as the cumulative surpluses or deficits for the 1985 budget of Mary and Mark Adair is presented in Table 6.3. A few points should be noted. First of all, although deficits occur in five months of the year, the annual budget is in balance. It reflects a $100 surplus (total annual income of $28,000 minus total annual expenses of $27,900). Second, on a monthly basis, the data in column 3 indicate that deficits will occur in April, May, June, October, and November. More important are the cumulative deficits shown in column 4. They will occur in the May–August and October–November periods. In order to meet these deficits, the Adairs could borrow or use savings. If we refer back to the Adairs' December 31, 1984, balance sheet (see Table 6.1), it seems clear that the $1,800 in savings deposits should allow them to meet the $900 peak cumulative deficit occurring in June. In order to manage this process efficiently, the Adairs should plan to place the monthly surpluses into an interest-earning medium that will earn a positive return on these temporarily idle funds. A final point to remember is that *a budget merely reflects estimates.* As new information is obtained, the budget may have to be reassessed, and corresponding adjustments in short-run goals may be required.

**TABLE 6.3   BUDGET SUMMARY FOR
MARY AND MARK ADAIR
(FOR YEAR ENDED DECEMBER 31, 1985)**

Month	(1) Total Estimated Income	(2) Total Estimated Expenses	(3) (1) − (2) Surplus (Deficit)	(4) Cumulative Surplus (Deficit)
Jan.	$ 2,000	$ 1,800	$ 200	$ 200
Feb.	2,000	1,900	100	300
Mar.	2,500	2,400	100	400
Apr.	2,700	3,000	(300)	100
May	2,100	3,000	(900)	(800)
June	2,400	2,500	(100)	(900)
July	2,100	1,900	200	(700)
Aug.	2,100	1,900	200	(500)
Sept.	2,500	1,900	600	100
Oct.	2,200	2,400	(200)	(100)
Nov.	2,200	2,600	(400)	(500)
Dec.	3,200	2,600	600	100
Total	$28,000	$27,900	$ 100	

INSURANCE

Insurance is an important element of personal financial planning. It is important for two reasons: It can provide protection against the consequences of events that can adversly affect finances, and it may provide certain long-run cash benefits. Insurance generally requires a current payment in exchange for potential as well as future benefit. Decisions regarding insurance purchases may affect the amount of funds available for investment. It is important that you select insurance carefully, because costs and benefits can vary widely among insurance companies. Although insurance is a necessary expenditure, its cost can consume funds that might otherwise be directly invested in any of a wide variety of alternative investment vehicles.

Fundamentals of Insurance

The many different types of insurance available to the public can be broken down into three basic forms: life insurance, health insurance, and property and liability insurance. Although each form provides a different type of protection, they all have certain characteristics in common; these include risk, the mechanism through which insurance coverage is provided, and the characteristics of an insurable risk.

Risk in insurance

Risk as used in discussing insurance is defined as the uncertainty related to economic loss. Because the consequences of economic loss are not favorable, one way to avoid such a loss is to purchase insurance.

The insurance mechanism

Insurance is a mechanism that allows people to reduce financial risk by sharing in the losses associated with the occurrence of uncertain events. Insurers combine the experience of a large group of people and apply certain statistics in order to predict the losses that might occur. Using these predictions, they establish ratings as well as an associated fee structure. Each insured pays a small premium (relative to the amount of coverage) to the insurance company in exchange for the promise that he or she will be reimbursed for losses up to a specified limit. Because of its reliance on the "law of large numbers," the insurer can predict reasonably well the amount of losses it will have to pay over a given period. The insured benefits from the ability to transfer risk to the insurer. The insurer, if it accurately predicts actual loss experience, gains from the profit that has been built into the premiums charged the insured.

Characteristics of an insurable risk

For a risk to be insurable, it must display certain characteristics: (1) There must be a large group of persons with similar loss exposure; (2) the loss exposure must be one that results from unintentional and unexpected causes; (3) the cost of insurance must be relatively low; and (4) the risk should not have the potential for widespread catastrophe such as would result from war or nuclear explosion. Let us look at some of the more common forms of insurance, all of which meet these criteria.

Life Insurance

Life insurance provides a mechanism that can be used to provide financial protection to a family in the event that the primary breadwinner or any other family member dies prematurely. Some types of life insurance provide only death benefits; others also allow for the accumulation of savings. We will look at four basic types of life insurance: term, whole life, endowment, and universal life.

Term insurance

A *term life insurance* policy is one in which the insurance company is obligated to pay a specified amount if the insured dies within the policy period. *Term is the least expensive form of life insurance protection.* It provides life insurance protection but does not contain the savings features of the three other types of life insurance. Many types of term insurance are available. These include straight term, renewable term, and convertible term.

A *straight term policy* is written for a fixed number of years. A *renewable term policy* guarantees that it may be renewed at the option of the insured for another term of equal length. *Convertible term* provides that the policy may be converted to a whole life or endowment policy at the insured's option. Usually, straight term is the least expensive of all types of life insurance. Its cost, however, will rise with the insured's age, and it can be very expensive for persons 60 years of age or older. Renewable term costs slightly more but it does assure the continued insurability of the insured. Despite its slightly higher cost, renewable term may be a good choice for those needing life insurance protection.

Term life insurance can also be designed to meet an insured's debt obligations should he or she die. *Mortgage life insurance,* for example, will pay off the outstanding principal balance of the insured's home loan should he or she die. This type of term insurance has a fixed monthly payment, but the amount of insurance protection declines each month as the home loan's principal balance is paid off. *Credit life insurance,* a similar form of term insurance, will pay off the insured's instalment loan balances upon his or her demise. Term life insurance of this type should be selected very carefully, because some life insurance companies charge relatively high premiums for it. Occasionally, mortgage life and credit life are sold via high pressure tactics and by unscrupulous insurance agents. It is probably best to avoid this type of insurance altogether. If you believe you need term life insurance protection to meet a debt, a straight term policy may be a much better buy.

Many employers offer free and/or low-cost *group term insurance* protection for their employees. Very frequently, this benefit is the lowest-cost way to obtain life insurance. If you need term life insurance, you may be able to purchase additional amounts at low cost through group insurance. Keep in mind that many of these plans are not transportable, however. That means that you can't take your term protection with you if you quit or leave your job for some reason or another.

Whole life

As the name implies, *whole life insurance* provides insurance coverage over the entire life of an insured. In addition, it also offers a savings benefit that is commonly called the *cash value.* The cash value is the amount of money set aside by the insurer to provide for the payment of the death benefit. Since the insurer's earnings and premium receipts increase over time, the cash value increases as the age of the insured increases. From the insurer's view, increased cash values are necessary since as the insured gets older the probability of death increases. Either the beneficiaries of the insured will receive the amount of the death benefit upon the death of the insured, or the policyholder can terminate the policy and receive its cash value. Like term insurance, whole life policies may contain a variety of options and features.

Compared to term insurance, whole life insurance is advantageous in the sense that the premium payments contribute toward the accumulation of value regardless of whether the insured lives or dies. It also provides insurance protection at a given premium rate over the whole life of the insured. On the other hand, more death protection per premium dollar can be obtained by purchasing term insurance, and the actual cash value accumulation of a whole life policy reflects an annual earnings rate of approximately 5 to 8 percent, *far below* what could be earned on alternative investments. Some financial advisors recommend purchasing the cheaper term insurance and investing the premium savings.

Endowment

An *endowment insurance* policy offers life insurance protection for a specified period of time, at the end of which it may be redeemed for its face value. The policy provides for the payment of face value upon the death of the insured or at the end of the policy period, which is commonly twenty years or until age 65. Like whole life, it provides for cash value accumulation; but unlike whole life, an endowment policy provides coverage for only a limited period of time, and the premiums are higher. The appeal of an endowment policy is the fact that it acts as a form of forced savings. In terms of death protection, its cost is quite high. And like whole life insurance, the actual return on the savings accumulation is lower than that obtainable through investing directly in low-risk vehicles.

Universal life

Universal life insurance is a recent innovation in the life insurance field. It has many new features that distinguish it from whole life or endowment life insurance. In particular, it retains the savings features of whole life but provides a higher return on the cash value portion of the policy than most whole life policies. Universal life has many progressive features, which include: full disclosure of all buyer-paid costs; higher yields on cash value than whole life or endowment life; flexibility in level of coverage and premium costs; and greater policyholder flexibility.

Most whole life policies do not explicitly provide information about such items as sales commissions, the true cost of insurance, and other policy costs. Usually, whole life sellers quote the premium amount and little else. In contrast, sellers of universal life provide a detailed breakdown of policy costs as well as benefits. All charges for costs such as sales commissions, insurance company service fees, and actual insurance protection are explicitly listed. Table 6.4 contains an excerpt from a universal life sales guide and is a fairly typical disclosure listing. As you can see, the policy's sales commissions, rate of return on cash value, service charge, and insurance cost are explicitly listed. Thus, one notable advantage of universal life over whole life is that the purchaser is more aware of what he or she is buying.

When a universal life policy is purchased, premiums are deposited in a fund that is called the policy's cash value to conform with insurance terminology. Then, the insurance company that issues the policy will deduct from this cash value the cost of insurance as well as commissions and service charges. After these costs are deducted, the balance earns interest. Most issuers of universal life pay higher interest rates on these cash values than on whole life policies. In early 1983, for example, universal life policyholders were earning 9 to 13 percent annual returns on their cash values at various insurance companies. These returns were well in excess of those being paid on the traditional whole life policies.

The cash value buildup in a universal life policy can be partially withdrawn or borrowed against at the policyholder's option, though there may be penalties for withdrawals. In contrast, whole life policies generally have no withdrawal provisions. The policyholder can also borrow from the insurance company an amount up to the policy's cash value. This is similar to whole life policy provisions. The interest rate charged on these borrowings is usually fairly low, often around 8 percent.

Another feature of universal life is that many policies allow a buyer to skip or reduce a premium payment if the policy's cash value is sufficient to pay the monthly cost of insurance protection. The universal life policy itself will not lapse unless the cash value has been exhausted. Most whole life policies, in contrast, have a more rigid premium payment schedule. Another plus factor for universal life is that the

TABLE 6.4 SAMPLE DISCLOSURE STATEMENT: UNIVERSAL LIFE

Disclosures	Charges
Ongoing expense charges	1. Every premium paid during the first 10 years is subject to a 7.5% sales charge. Premiums paid thereafter are subject to a 5.5% sales charge. Policy loan repayments are not subject to the sales charge.
	2. A policy fee of $3.50 per month is deducted from the cash value.
First-year-only expense charges	3. A first year only charge of $21.00 per month—$252.00 for the year—is deducted from the cash value.
	4. A first year only charge of .09 per month for each $1,000 of initial specified amount of insurance on the insured and spouse (if covered) is deducted from the cash value. This totals $1.08 per thousand for the year. This charge also applies to elective increases.

Issue Ages

Completelife may be issued from ages 0 through 80 on an age last birthday basis.

Policy Minimums

The minimum premium payment is $25.00
The minimum specified amount on the insured is as follows:

Issue Ages	Specified Amount
0–54	$25,000
55–59	20,000
60–64	15,000
65–80	10,000

Source: Completelife Sales Guide, Hutton Life, E. F. Hutton Life Insurance Company, pp. 5–6.

buyer pays only for actual insurance protection—the difference between the face amount and the cash value. Whole life premiums are usually based on the policy's face amount.

Table 6.5 presents a summary comparison of some key features of term insurance, whole life insurance, and universal life. Overall, universal life appears to be a competitive alternative to whole life insurance. It retains the general investment features of whole life while providing a higher return on cash value. Universal life is not as inexpensive as term life insurance; however, term insurance has no savings feature. If you want life insurance that has a savings feature, universal life merits consideration.

**TABLE 6.5   A COMPARISON: UNIVERSAL LIFE
VS. TRADITIONAL LIFE INSURANCE**

Feature	Term Insurance	Whole Life	Universal Life
Premium	Increases on preset schedule	Constant	Flexible
Company-fee portion of premium	Undisclosed	Undisclosed	Disclosed
Protection	Fixed	Fixed	Flexible
Cash value (savings)	None usually	Increases on preset schedule	Variable

Source: Consumer Reports, January 1982, p. 43.

Fulfilling life insurance needs

Using any of a number of possible techniques, a person's life insurance needs can be estimated. This process is most often based on assessing the individual's financial situation to determine how much protection is required to leave his or her dependents (or beneficiaries) in a desired financial position or by looking at the individual's projected earnings and converting them into a present value that would represent the amount of needed insurance protection. Another approach is to use a multiple of earnings. For example, assume the appropriate multiple for a 25-year-old wishing to obtain enough insurance to replace 75 percent of his or her income, which is currently $23,500 per year, is 6.5. Multiplying the $23,500 by 6.5 indicates that this person needs $152,750 of life insurance coverage. Regardless of which technique is used, logical bases for determining the appropriate amount of life insurance coverage are available.

Once the desired amount of life insurance coverage is estimated, the form(s) of insurance used to meet this need must be determined. The form selected will depend on the age of the family (or individual), their financial position, and their ability and/or desire to save or invest. Generally, young families need large amounts of death protection while older individuals and maturing families tend to need more moderate amounts of protection. For the young family with a limited budget, term insurance would probably best fulfill its needs; more mature families might prefer whole life policies. Families (or individuals) more concerned with accumulation of savings than the acquisition of death protection might find an endowment insurance policy best suited to their needs. Those who feel comfortable with their ability to save and invest and who do not need the forced savings of whole life or universal life probably are best off with term insurance. If you wish life insurance with a savings feature, universal life could be the best alternative. When evaluating life insurance, the choice seems to be term insurance or universal life. If you want inexpensive life insurance with no savings feature, look for a term policy. If you want life insurance with a competitive savings feature, then consider universal life. An individual should acquire an amount of life insurance protection that adequately protects his or her financial position and that provides a death benefit and savings accumulation mix with which he or she feels comfortable.

Other Forms of Insurance

Although adequate life insurance is needed to protect against the financial consequences of a premature death, it does not fulfill all of an individual's insurance needs. Other risks include illness, accident, property loss, and lawsuits. Because the consequences of these risks can result in sizable financial costs, insurance can play an important role in reducing the potential losses associated with them.

Health insurance

Health insurance is designed to pay the expenses associated with an illness or accident. The major types include *disability insurance,* which provides periodic payments to replace income when the insured is unable to work due to a covered illness, disease, or injury; *hospital insurance,* which covers hospital room and board; *surgical expense insurance,* which covers the cost of surgery; *physician's expense insurance,* which provides coverage for nonsurgical physician's charges; *major medical,* which covers all types of medical expenses resulting from sickness or accident; and *comprehensive major medical,* which is similar in scope but provides higher dollar coverage than major medical. Most of these forms of health insurance have certain deductibles as well as coverage limits. Coverage can be obtained from a variety of sources, such as social security, worker's compensation, Blue Cross/Blue Shield, group insurance, and individual policies. The cost of health insurance varies depending on the coverage, and many employers provide health insurance coverage as part of an employee benefit plan.

Property and liability insurance

Property and liability insurance is used to protect against the risks associated with the physical loss of property and loss from liability resulting from negligent acts. In the case of *property insurance,* certain perils, which are causes of loss, such as damage from weather, riots, vandalism, fire, and so on, can be insured against. The most common types of property insurance are homeowner's insurance and automobile insurance. Because these two nonfinancial assets often represent a significant portion of most people's assets, they should be protected. Other assets having relatively high value, such as a collection of rare books or a recreational vehicle, should also be adequately insured. The cost of property insurance depends not only on the specific coverage purchased, but on the value of the asset, its age, its use, and its characteristics.

Liability insurance, which is commonly included as part of homeowner's and automobile insurance policies, provides protection against the risk that the insured might as the result of negligence cause property damage or bodily injury to someone else. For legal purposes, a person is considered to have been negligent if he or she fails to act in a "reasonable manner." Examples of negligent acts would include

BOX 6.2 ESTIMATING YOUR LIFE INSURANCE NEEDS

Every year or two, people who need life insurance should recalculate whether they have enough. This worksheet eases the task and takes you through it with a real family, the Fulcos. ... The reason they need more than minimal insurance is the usual one: children. They have a son, 2, and another child on the way.

You can work out all the entries for yourself except Social Security payments. Those amounts are based on a parent's age at death—you should assume that it occurs this year—and on his earnings history. Your nearest Social Security office can find out for you what your survivors would get. Ask for your maximum monthly benefit per survivor and your maximum family benefit. Multiply these amounts by 12 to get annual income and enter the results on lines 14a and 14b of the worksheet.

To determine the years of eligibility for various levels of survivors' benefits, start with line 14c, 14f, or 14i, depending on your family size, and fill in each subsequent blank. Keep in mind that children are eligible until they're 18, and that while any child is still under 16 a parent who earns less than $4,440 a year [in 1982] is also eligible. (Benefits start to diminish above that earnings level.)

The Fulcos counted Mrs. Fulco as a Social Security beneficiary for only six years because after that she would go back to work. But while she stayed home, three survivors would be eligible, so the Fulcos started computing Social Security on line 14c. Both children would remain eligible for 10 more years (line 14g). The younger child, then 16, would collect for a final two years (line 14j).

	MICHAEL FULCO	YOU
Funds Needed		
1. Annual contribution to household	$ 16,000	$
2. Remaining years of child rearing	× 18	×
3. Multiply line 1 by line 2	$ 288,000	$
4. College contribution per child	$ 40,000	$
5. Number of children	× 2	×
6. Multiply line 4 by line 5	$ 80,000	$
7. Funeral and estate costs and debts (excluding mortgage)	$ 20,000	$
8. Total needed now: add lines 3, 6, and 7	$ 388,000	$

failure to keep a sidewalk in proper repair and reckless driving. Most states require motor vehicle owners to carry specified minimum levels of liability coverage (or show that level of financial responsibility) to operate a motor vehicle within state boundaries. Professionals whose business activity exposes them to above-average liability can purchase professional liability insurance to cover this risk; medical malpractice insurance is an example of this type of coverage.

Retirement Plans

Another important aspect of the personal financial planning process is retirement planning. Not only must the individual provide for the possibility of premature death and disability by purchasing life and health insurance, he or she must also prepare for the reduction in earnings that accompanies retirement. Without retire-

---

BOX 6.2 *Continued*

Existing Resources

9. Life insurance	$	85,000	$
10. Savings and investments	$	2,000	$
11. Wife's earning power per year	$	12,000	$
12. Years she'd work during child rearing	×	10	×
13. Multiply line 11 by line 12	$	120,000	$
14. Social Security (per year):			
14a. Benefit for each survivor	$	3,912	$
14b. Maximum family benefit	$	9,720	$
14c. Benefit for three or more survivors: enter amount on line 14b	$	9,720	$
14d. Years of eligibility	×	6	×
14e. Multiply line 14c by line 14d	$	58,320	$
14f. Benefit for two survivors: multiply line 14a by 2	$	7,824	$
14g. Years of eligibility	×	10	×
14h. Multiply line 14f by line 14g	$	78,240	$
14i. Benefit for one survivor: enter amount on line 14a	$	3,912	$
14j. Years of eligibility	×	2	×
14k. Multiply line 14i by line 14j	$	7,824	$
15. Total resources: add lines 9, 10, 13, 14e, 14h, and 14k	$	351,384	$

Insurance Needed

16. Subtract line 15 from line 8	$	36,616	$

Source: Malcolm N. Carter, "How Much Do You Really Need?" *Money,* April 1982, p. 134.

ment plans, a person may find it necessary to make extreme cuts in his or her standard of living. To avoid this, a person should begin the retirement planning process at an early age. First, he or she should establish a desired retirement age, financial position, and goals. Based upon these goals, the person can estimate the needed level of retirement income and plan for various sources of such income. The major sources of retirement income include social security, employer-sponsored retirement programs, and individual self-directed retirement plans. These programs as well as the key aspects of planning for retirement needs are discussed in detail in Chapter 7.

PERSONAL TAXES

In addition to return and risk, the tax consequences associated with various investment vehicles and strategies must be considered in establishing an investment program. As a matter of fact, tax considerations affect nearly all personal financial decisions. So knowledge of the tax laws should help an individual to employ strategies that result in the reduction of taxes, thereby increasing the amount of after-tax dollars available for achieving financial goals. Because tax laws are complicated and subject to frequent revision, here we will present only basic concepts and their application to basic investment transactions.

Basic Sources of Taxation

The two major types of personal taxes are those levied by the federal government and by state and local governments. The major federal tax is the income tax, which is also the major source of personal taxation. It is levied on a "pay-as-you-go" basis, since employers withhold a portion of each employee's wages each pay period and send these withheld taxes on to the federal government. Self-employed persons as well as individuals who are not employees (consultants, attorneys) are required to make estimated tax payments, generally on a quarterly basis. At the end of the year, each taxpayer files a return that reconciles the payments made with what is owed. Unlike federal taxes, state and local taxes vary from area to area. Some states have income taxes that may range as high as 15 percent or more of income. Some cities, especially large East Coast cities, also have local income taxes that may amount to as much as 1 to 4 percent of income. Most state and local income taxes are also on a pay-as-you-go basis. In addition to income taxes, state and local governments rely heavily on sales and property taxes as a source of revenue. Sales taxes are typically in the range of 3 to 8 percent. Property taxes, which are levied on real estate and personal property, such as furniture and automobiles, are the primary source of revenue for local communities and school districts. These taxes vary from community to community; in some states a portion of this tax goes to the state.

State and local taxes, especially income and property taxes, are important in the overall personal financial planning process. Income taxes have the greatest impact on security investments, while property taxes could have a sizable impact on real estate and other forms of property investment. Although primary emphasis here is given to the federal income tax, individuals should acquaint themselves with the potential impact state and local taxes may have on alternative investment vehicles and strategies.

Types of Income and Tax Rates

The income of individuals can be classified as either ordinary or capital gain (or loss) income. A clear distinction between these forms of income and the tax consequences of each are important considerations in the investment process.

Ordinary income

Income from all sources such as salaries, dividends, interest, and earnings from unincorporated businesses (sole proprietorships or partnerships) is treated as *ordinary income*. After certain computations, which will be described in this chapter, this income is taxed at progressive rates, which means that tax rates become higher as the amount of taxable income increases. Although the applicable tax rates depend on an individual's filing status (single, married filing jointly, married filing separately,

TABLE 6.6   1982 TAX RATES FOR SINGLE TAXPAYERS (SCHEDULE X)

Over	But Not Over	Tax	Of the Amount Over	Average Tax Rate on Upper Limit
$ 0	$ 2,300	0%	$ 0	0%
2,300	3,400	12%	2,300	3.9
3,400	4,400	$ 132 + 14%	3,400	6.2
4,400	6,500	272 + 16%	4,400	9.4
6,500	8,500	608 + 17%	6,500	11.1
8,500	10,800	948 + 19%	8,500	12.8
10,800	12,900	1,385 + 22%	10,800	14.3
12,900	15,000	1,847 + 23%	12,900	15.5
15,000	18,200	2,330 + 27%	15,000	17.5
18,200	23,500	3,194 + 31%	18,200	20.6
23,500	28,800	4,837 + 35%	23,500	23.2
28,800	34,100	6,692 + 40%	28,800	25.8
34,100	41,500	8,812 + 44%	34,100	29.1
41,500	—	12,068 + 50%	41,500	—

Source: Adapted from U.S. Department of the Treasury, Internal Revenue Service, *1982 Federal Income Tax Forms* (Washington, D.C.: U.S. Government Printing Office, 1982), p. 29.

or unmarried head of household), Table 6.6 (which is for single taxpayers) clearly illustrates the progressive nature of individual income taxes.

Consider, for example, the Ellis sisters, Joni and Charlyn. They are single, and Joni's taxable income is $18,000. Charlyn's is $36,000. Using Table 6.6, their taxes are calculated as follows:

Joni: $2,330 + .27($18,000 − $15,000) = $2,330 + $810 = $3,140
Charlyn: $8,812 + .44($36,000 − $34,100) = $8,812 + $836 = $9,648

The average tax rate is calculated by dividing tax liability by amount of taxable income; for Joni it is 17.4 percent ($3,140 in taxes ÷ $18,000 taxable income), and for Charlyn it is 26.8 percent ($9,648 in taxes ÷ $36,000 taxable income). The progressive nature of the federal income tax structure can be seen by the fact that although Charlyn's taxable income is twice that of Joni ($36,000 versus $18,000), her income tax is over three times Joni's ($9,648 versus $3,140).

The Economic Recovery Tax Act of 1981, as amended, provided for income tax rate cuts in 1981, 1982, and 1983. Additionally, the law reduced the maximum tax bracket from 70 to 50 percent. In 1985 and beyond, further tax bracket adjustments could occur because of the law's indexing provisions. These indexing features basically require tax-rate adjustments to reflect inflation. In early 1983, there were discussions in Congress aimed at repealing the indexing provision. At present it appears likely this feature will be repealed.

Capital gains and losses

The other major form of income that an individual may receive is capital gains, gains that result from the sale of capital assets at prices above their original purchase price. A *capital asset* is property owned and used by the taxpayer for personal reasons, pleasure, or investment. The most common types are securities and real estate, including one's home. A *capital gain* represents the amount by which the proceeds from the sale of a capital asset exceed its original purchase price. Capital gains can be classified as either short- or long-term, depending upon the length of time they are owned. *Long-term* capital gains result from assets held for more than one year; gains on assets held for one year or less are considered *short term.* Short-term gains are taxed as ordinary income. Long-term capital gains, however, receive preferential treatment. *Sixty percent of long-term capital gains is totally exempt from taxes;* the remaining 40 percent is taxed at the ordinary rate. This results in a maximum tax rate on long-term gains of 20 percent (40% of gain taxable at the maximum rate of 50%).

The taxation of capital gains can be illustrated with a simple example. Imagine that James McFail, who is in the 30 percent tax bracket, recently sold 100 shares of two stocks, A and B, for $10 and $14 per share, respectively. Stock A was originally purchased for $8 per share and held for nine months; stock B was purchased fifteen months earlier for $12 per share. The total capital gain on stock A, therefore, amounted to $200, and the total capital gain on stock B also amounted to $200. Since stock A was held less than one year, the $200 gain on it will be taxed as ordinary income. Since McFail is in the 30 percent bracket, the tax on the short-term capital gain would amount to $60. The tax on the $200 long-term capital gain on stock B, which was held for more than a year, would amount to only $24 (note that only 40 percent of the gain is taxable so the taxes are determined as: $200 \times .40 \times .30 = $24). Although McFail's gain on each of the transactions was the same ($200), the taxes differ because the long-term gain on stock B receives more favorable tax treatment than stock A's short-term capital gain.

Capital losses result when a capital asset is sold for less than its original purchase price. These losses may also be either short- or long-term, depending upon whether or not the asset was held for longer than one year. Before taxes are calculated, all gains and losses must be netted out. Up to $3,000 of *net short-term losses* can be applied against ordinary income, while half of *net long-term losses* up to an annual maximum of $3,000 (or $6,000 of net long-term losses) can be applied against ordinary income. Losses that cannot be applied in the current year may be carried forward and used to offset future income, subject to certain conditions.

Because capital losses can be used to reduce taxable income, the IRS has established certain regulations to prevent the abuse of the capital loss deduction. The regulations prohibit what are commonly called *wash sales,* selling securities on which capital losses can be realized and then immediately buying them back. The IRS requires that any loss on the sale of a security that is offset by a purchase of the same security within thirty days before or after the sale cannot be claimed as a loss for tax purposes. Instead, the purchase and sale are washed out, and for tax purposes the sale is considered not to have occurred. A way around this law is to use a *tax swap,* which involves replacing the security sold at a loss with a *similar* security issued by a *similar* firm in the same industry. In this case the rule has not been violated, but the desired result has been obtained. Many brokerage firms provide lists of securities and suitable replacements for use in tax swaps. As one might expect, these swaps are most prevalent at year-end. The IRS also has regulations governing transactions made between relatives to capitalize on certain tax benefits that might be achieved from realizing a capital gain or loss.

Determining Taxable Income

An individual's taxable income is determined by applying certain procedures outlined by the Internal Revenue Service (IRS), and the tax is computed using a variety of tax forms and schedules. The first step in this process involves the calculation of gross income, which is all income subject to federal taxes. Some types of income are exempt from inclusion in gross income. One exemption is the first $100 in dividends received on investments in domestic corporations. Married persons filing joint returns and jointly owning securities are eligible for an exclusion of $100 each, or a total $200 exemption.

Starting in 1982, shareholders of qualified public utilities such as electric companies, telephone companies, and natural gas distributors gained a new tax break if they participated in the utility's dividend reinvestment program. A *dividend reinvestment plan* allows shareholders to have cash dividends automatically reinvested in the company's common stock. Utility dividend reinvestment plans can provide an investor with a helpful tax break. This is because up to $750 in reinvested dividends ($1,500 for married taxpayers filing a joint return) may be excluded from current income taxes. Normally, cash dividends are taxed as ordinary income (except for the $100 to $200 dividend exclusion). The existence of such a qualified dividend reinvestment program may enhance the securities' appeal for inclusion in one's portfolio.

A number of deductions can be made from gross income; these include a variety of trade and business expenses. Included among these expenses is depreciation which, as will be explained in Chapter 16, can provide important tax benefits to investors in real estate and other forms of property. After deducting all allowable deductions from gross income, the resulting balance is called adjusted gross income. From adjusted gross income, a variety of personal deductions, or itemized nonbusiness expenses, can be taken. Actually, the taxpayer may itemize these expenses, which include interest expense, medical expenses, property taxes, and so forth, or take the zero-bracket amount, which is a type of blanket deduction. The choice between itemizing and taking the zero-bracket depends, of course, upon the level of eligible expenses available.

Those itemizing must adjust for any excess itemized deductions. In addition, personal exemptions provide a $1,000 deduction for the taxpayer and each dependent. Computing taxable income and using the tax tables provided by the IRS, the taxpayer can determine his or her tax liability. From this tax liability, the taxpayer can deduct any tax credits, such as the one allowed for child care. The amount resulting after deduction of credits represents total taxes due. The difference between

TABLE 6.7 DETERMINING CARL AND PATTI HARTLEY'S TOTAL TAX LIABILITY FOR 1982

Salary and wages:		
Carl		$22,000
Patti		26,000
Interest and dividends received ($600 + $600) =	$ 1,200	
Less: Dividend exclusion	200	1,000
Capital gains:		
Short term	$ 500	
Plus: Taxable long-term .40($1,250)	500	1,000
Gross income		$50,000
Less: Carl's business expenses		4,000
Adjusted gross income		$46,000
Total itemized deductions:	$11,600	
Less: Zero-bracket amount	3,400	
Less: Excess itemized deductions		8,200
Less: Personal exemptions (2 × $1,000)		2,000
Taxable income		$35,800
Tax (from tax table, not shown)*		$ 7,567

*"1982 Tax Table for Persons with Taxable Incomes of Less than $50,000," *1982 Instructions for Preparing Form 1040* (Washington, D.C.: U.S. Department of the Treasury, Internal Revenue Service, 1982), p. 38.

this value and the amount paid in through withholding and estimated tax payments represents either a refund (if more has been paid in than the total taxes owed) or an amount due (if less has been paid in than is owed). An individual's federal income tax return must be filed by April 15 each year.

A general idea of the process used to calculate an individual's federal income taxes can be provided through an example. Carl and Patti Hartley are a married couple with grown children. They both work, Carl as a real estate agent and Patti as an attorney. During 1982, Carl earned $22,000 and Patti earned $26,000. In addition to their salaries, they received $600 in interest from their joint savings account, $600 in cash dividends from stock they jointly own, and $1,750 in capital gains. Of the $1,750 in capital gains, $500 was short term and $1,250 was long term. During 1982, Carl incurred $4,000 in business expenses. Their itemized nonbusiness expenses (home mortgage interest, property taxes, state income taxes, state sales taxes, charitable contributions, and so on) totaled $11,600, while their zero-bracket amount was $3,400. They claimed two personal exemptions. Carl and Patti have calculated their tax liability as shown in Table 6.7. Based on their calculations, the Hartley's total tax liability for 1982 is $7,567.

Investments and Taxes

From an individual investor's point of view, the key tax dimensions are current income, capital gains, tax shelters, and tax planning. Persons investing in vehicles

His last request is to call up the Internal Revenue Service and tell them to go to hell!

providing current income tend to be those in low tax brackets, where the marginal tax rate is less than, say, 30 percent. The predominant form of current investment income is interest and dividends. As pointed out above, with the exception of a small dividend exclusion, these forms of income are taxed as ordinary income. Another item of current income is rental income, which may be received from some type of real estate investment. From a strict tax point of view, a capital gain resulting from appreciation in the value or price of an investment vehicle is very appealing to many investors. The fact that only 40 percent of gains earned on an investment held longer than one year is taxable provides tax advantages on long-term capital gains. Of course, short-term capital gains are taxed as ordinary income and do not provide any tax advantage. Because of the generally higher risk associated with capital gain income versus current investment income, the choice of investment vehicles cannot be made solely on the basis of taxation. The levels of return and risk need to be viewed in light of their tax effects. Clearly, *it is the after-tax return and associated risk* that should be considered.

Tax shelters

Especially popular among individuals in high tax brackets are *tax shelters,* certain forms of investment that capitalize on available "tax writeoffs." Some forms of real estate and natural resource investments provide these desirable deductions. The writeoffs come in the form of deductions from (gross) income that are permitted by the IRS, but in fact do not involve any current outlay on the part of the investor. Since an investor can reduce taxable income by the amount of such noncash expenditures, these deductions can be used to lower tax liability. For example, an individual could invest in an apartment complex that in a given year provides actual annual cash flow of $4,000 and a depreciation writeoff (deduction from gross income) of $14,000. What this means is that the $4,000 of cash flow is completely "sheltered," and an additional $10,000 ($14,000 − $4,000) can be deducted from other sources of income. In other words, $10,000 of income from other sources such as wages, salaries, dividends, interest, and capital gains will be "sheltered." No taxes will be due on this sheltered income. Chapter 17 presents a detailed discussion and illustrations of the basic mechanics of tax-sheltered investments.

Tax planning

Because of the differing tax treatments to which ordinary as well as investment income is subjected, tax planning is important in the investment process. *Tax planning* involves looking at an individual's current and projected earnings and developing strategies that will defer and minimize the level of taxes. The tax plan should guide the investors' activities in such a way that over the long run they will achieve maximum after-tax returns for an acceptable level of risk.

Tax plans should reflect the desired form in which returns are to be received—current income, short- or long-term capital gains, or tax-sheltered income. These plans might also specify certain investment strategies; one common one is to claim losses as soon as they occur and to delay profit taking. Such a strategy allows one to benefit from the tax deductibility of a loss and to delay having to claim income from gains. Although the use of tax planning, which is commonly done in cooperation with an accountant, tax expert, or tax attorney, is most common among individuals in high tax brackets (40 percent and above), sizable savings could result for individual investors in lower tax brackets as well.

INVESTMENT GOALS AND PLANS

Establishing investment objectives consistent with overall personal financial goals is an important aspect of the personal financial management process. After establishing short- and long-run financial goals, plans must be developed in a manner that provides both for protection of assets through the use of insurance and for an adequate level of retirement income. As an aid in achieving long-run personal financial and retirement goals, investment goals and associated plans should be developed. Such plans should provide the mechanism whereby funds currently set aside for fulfillment of long-run goals can provide the returns needed for their achievement.

Key Factors

When developing investment goals and plans, a number of factors must be considered. Although numerous classifications of these factors could be developed, for purposes of this text they can be classified into three groups—return factors, risk factors, and tax factors. A general discussion of return and risk was included in Chapter 4, while taxes were discussed in the preceding part of this chapter. A brief look at the key aspects of each of these areas as they relate to investment goals and plans follows.

Return

Returns reflect how well an investment has earned on behalf of its owner. Not only are return measures useful for assessing past investment performance, but they also provide a reasonable mechanism for use in establishing investment goals and plans. The two types of return—current income and capital gains—can each be specified as part of one's investment goals and plans. For example, an investment goal might be to generate annual income of $10,000 per year until 1990 or to accumulate a lump sum of $75,000 for use in purchasing a yacht in 1989. The first investment goal might best be met using a vehicle providing current income, while the second goal might best be met with a vehicle providing capital appreciation that would result in a capital gain. Of course, by reinvesting the current income provided from an income-oriented investment vehicle one could accumulate a lump sum; and by investing a lump sum in certain vehicles, one could likewise create a stream of current income. Although the use of income-oriented vehicles such as government bonds to meet current income needs and the use of capital gain-oriented vehicles such as raw land to meet future requirements seems most logical, such an approach is not necessarily the best one. Clearly, other factors bear upon this decision.

Risk

Risk reflects the certainty of return. The more risk associated with an expected return, the less certain one can be of actually realizing it. In general, investors are risk-averse, which means that given the choice, they will take less as opposed to more risk. Investment goals and plans should be consistent with the investor's own risk disposition. Although investment goals will generally center on achievement of a given level of return, they should also include some indication of what levels of risk are acceptable. Since risk is difficult to quantify, the level might be indicated as "low," "average," or "high." In the case of rated securities such as bonds, the risk level could be specified as "BBB-rated or higher"; for common stock, one could indicate that "stocks with betas in the range .5 to 1.2" are acceptable. The investment plan should be developed so that it provides for achievement of the goals (assuming they are reasonable) while remaining consistent with the decision-maker's risk disposition. Since risk is as important as return, it must be addressed in one's investment goals and plans.

An investor may choose to be more specific in defining risk. Investment goals and plans may specifically address risk components. Although the certainty of return is perhaps the most important aspect of risk, the return could be broken into its current income and capital gain components, and specific risk statements relative to each could be made. For example, one could desire a certain stream of current income and reasonable *safety of principal,* which refers to the stability of the market value of the investment. One could also specify a desired level of inflation protection. Concern over the liquidity of investment vehicles may also be specified in the investment goals and plans. By investing in marketable vehicles, one can reduce the risk of running out of cash, since in the event of a severe shortage, one could quickly liquidate the vehicle in order to obtain the needed funds. If liquidity plays an important role in one's goals and plans, the desired level of marketability might be specified. In summary, it is important that the key aspects of risk be specified as part of one's investment goals and plans; such specification should act as a constraint on the choice of investment vehicles used to fulfill return goals and plans.

Taxes

Because taxes can significantly affect investment returns, it is important to consider their impact when setting goals and plans. The key factor to consider about taxes is the type of taxable income generated by alternative investment vehicles. The discussion of personal taxation presented earlier differentiated between ordinary income and capital gain income. The returns expected from a given investment vehicle should be viewed in light of these components, as well as any tax shelter it might provide. Investors in high tax brackets will probably have investment goals and plans that center on the achievement of long-term capital gains. The impact of taxes on investment returns can be significant. Some investors may choose to defer the receipt of income from investment until they retire; at that time their income (from employment) would drop, placing them in a lower tax bracket and thereby reducing the tax impact associated with investment income. Certain tax-sheltered investments (described in Chapter 17), some of which may be part of a retirement plan (discussed in Chapter 7), may appeal to those in high tax brackets.

The important point to recognize is that taxes can significantly affect the amount of "spendable" investment returns. Investment goals and plans should reflect this fact by considering the after-tax returns from investment. For example, one might have as a goal the achievement of annual after-tax income of $10,000 over the next 20 years. In order to achieve this goal, the investment plan could include investment in tax-exempt securities providing a total of $10,000 annual income, or the plan might provide for investment in taxable corporate bonds providing total income of $15,000 per year. If the investor is in the 33 percent tax bracket, the corporate bonds would provide $10,000 of after-tax income similar to the tax-exempt security. At this point, it should be clear that investment goals and plans should consider the individual's tax bracket, current and future, in terms of the differences in treatment of ordinary, capital gain, and tax-sheltered income provided by prevailing tax laws. The after-tax investment returns should, of course, be viewed in light of the associated investment risks.

Providing Needed Liquidity

Investment goals and plans should be developed in a fashion that provides the individual with adequate liquidity. *Liquidity* as used here refers to the ability to convert an investment into cash quickly and without loss. Certain investment vehicles may be acquired because they possess a desired degree of liquidity. There are three basic reasons for the acquisition of liquid investments. The most common motive is to maintain an ability to meet unexpected needs while earning a return. A second motive for holding liquid investments is anticipation of spending the money or fear of investing because of soaring inflation rates or an anticipated opportunity for a better investment. A third motive is as a desired, and sometimes permanent, investment outlet; when short-term interest rates are high, as in 1981–1982, the returns provided by these vehicles make them quite attractive. The first motive can be met by investing in all but such illiquid vehicles as business ventures and individually owned real estate. The second and third motives are more exclusive, eliminating all but short-term investment vehicles.

Liquidity is most often introduced into one's portfolio, regardless of motive, by holding short-term investments such as savings accounts, certificates of deposit, money market certificates, money market funds, treasury bills, and U.S. savings bonds. Such vehicles are an important part of an investment portfolio, since they can bring needed liquidity without sacrificing a great deal of return. Because the primary motive for incorporating short-term investment vehicles into one's investment plans is to provide a warehouse of liquidity for use in meeting unexpected needs, the following comments focus on this motive.

The amount of liquidity built into any investment plan will depend on the investor's disposition toward risk; the more risk-averse the individual, the greater the desired liquidity, and vice versa. Of course, with added liquidity one can expect to reduce the returns on these investable balances. The returns available on longer-term vehicles such as stocks and bonds are typically greater than those available on liquid short-term investments. There is a tradeoff between the amount of liquidity maintained and the level of return. In other words, the less risk (the more liquidity), the lower the return, and vice versa. This risk-return tradeoff is consistent with that described in Chapter 4. Each investor must recognize the importance as well as the risk-return tradeoff associated with providing adequate liquidity in investment goals and plans. Care should be taken to avoid excessive liquidity, since its consequence is reduced returns. A detailed discussion of the role and methods of meeting liquidity needs with any of a variety of short-term investments is presented in Chapter 7.

Quantifying Investment Goals

The procedures for quantifying investment goals begin with the established long-run personal financial goals, which include retirement goals. Generally, any long-run financial goal specifying the creation of an annual cash flow stream or the accumulation of a lump sum at some future date must be viewed as an investment goal, since it is through some type of investment that such a goal can be achieved. In spite of the fact that individuals may receive certain benefits from the government and/or employers contribute toward achievement of the goal, the goal must be stated and therefore established as a target toward which financial activities will be directed.

A series of supporting investment goals can be developed for each long-run goal. For example, if one long-run goal is to accumulate $80,000 in cash at the end of 10 years, it clearly can be treated as an investment goal. In this case, one must specify the desired return, acceptable risk, and relevant tax considerations associated with this goal. The preceding example could be more precisely stated as an investment goal to accumulate $80,000 in cash by investing in a portfolio evenly divided between blue-chip and speculative stocks providing a total return of 8 percent per year split between 20 percent current income and 80 percent long-term capital appreciation. By stating an investment goal in this fashion, return (8 percent per

---

BOX 6.3 THE PERSONAL FINANCIAL PLANNER: A PROFILE

Essentially a personalized money-management service, the business of financial planning takes an overview of a person's money affairs based on his total objectives. Planners, who are generalists rather than specialists, are expected to have the training and skill to assess and analyze a family's financial situation—net worth, income, insurance, cash flow and other elements—and make specific recommendations to help them meet their goals.

Some planners go beyond the preparation of a comprehensive strategy and provide assistance in maintaining and updating it, through specific programs in such areas as budgeting and retirement planning. And many, particularly the larger financial-planning concerns that serve high-income individuals, also coordinate such plans and put them into effect.

The thousands of these planners in the United States are professionals in selecting from among a myriad of financial products on the market, like certificates of deposit, asset-management accounts, tax-sheltered investments, annuities, trusts, individual retirement accounts, real estate, limited partnerships and financial futures.

"The public is demanding financial planning, partly because of inflation and partly because of tax-bracket creep," said Vernon D. Gwynne, executive director of the International Association for Financial Planning, a professional group with more than 10,000 members.

"In these economic times," added Dianna Rampy, executive director of the Institute of Certified Financial Planners, another professional association with almost 7,000 members, "middle-income people need to know how to cut their taxes, how to make their money go further. Many people don't want to go to five separate individuals to get their advice. They want to go to one person who has expertise in all these areas."

Many planners can be found among the ranks of investment advisers, stockbrokers, insurance agents, lawyers, mutual-fund representatives, bank-trust officers, real-estate brokers and accountants. Most of them are paid through commissions from the financial products sold—such as insurance policies, mutual-fund shares and tax shelters—or a combination of commissions and fees. Others, a much smaller group, do nothing but financial planning and earn their compensation on a fee-only basis, either at an hourly rate or based on the value of their client's assets or income.

"It's harder to make a living on a fee basis," asserted Terry Gill, a principal in the Professional Financial Group of Fort Worth, Tex., and a past president of the Society

---

year), risk (half blue-chip and half speculative stock), and taxes (20 percent current income and 80 percent long-term capital gains) have all been specified. The more specific one can be in the statement of investment goals, the easier it will be to establish an investment plan consistent with these goals.

When quantifying investment goals and looking at ways to meet them, personal computers can help. A well-programmed personal computer can aid in the evaluation of investment alternatives and in analyzing your tax situation. The personal computer can provide alternative ideas based on the data you input. Of course, as pointed out in Chapter 3, the cost of the PC must be justified by the benefits it provides its user.

The Investment Program

Once goals have been specified, a program must be developed. The backbone of the program is the investment plan, which makes the investment goals operational. The plans indicate the general strategy that will be used to achieve each goal. Since

> **BOX 6.3** *Continued*
>
> of Independent Financial Advisers, an association restricted to fee-only planners with just a handful of members. "But it is a lot easier to be more objective."
>
> Since there are no state licensing requirements for planners as there are for such professionals as lawyers or accountants, anyone can use that title. "A lot of people in it do not have the proper credentials and you're not going to teach it to yourself," observed Herbert Paul, a partner in the accounting firm of Touche Ross & Company, who does financial planning from his New York headquarters.
>
> One way that some financial planners attempt to differentiate themselves is by obtaining a professional designation. Two institutions—the College for Financial Planning in Denver and the American College in Bryn Mawr, Pa.—offer courses leading to such a designation, primarily by self-study, but also through classes in different parts of the country. Many of their students are already life-insurance agents, brokers and others in financial services who want to expand their capabilities.
>
> The College for Financial Planning gives a Certified Financial Planner designation to those who successfully complete five [six] courses over a period that for most students is 18 to 24 months. Since its founding in 1971, the institution has issued more than 3,500 of these designations to students who have passed examinations in such subjects as tax planning and estate planning.
>
> The American College recently issued the designation of Chartered Financial Consultant to about 2,000 students, the first to graduate from its program. This designation follows the completion of a 10-course program, which typically takes about four years and includes topics like economics, financial statement analysis and wealth accumulation planning. The college even started a program recently leading to a master of financial services degree.
>
> "We're looking for people with a good understanding of taxation, investments, cash flow, estate planning and the ability to integrate that into financial planning," said Gary D. Tuckman, president of Thompson Tuckman Anderson, a West Coast concern. "For those people, the opportunities are tremendous."
>
> *Source:* Leonard Sloane, "Financial Planners on a Rise." *The New York Times,* October 17, 1982, section 12, p. 26.

some portion of the goals may be achieved through government and/or employer pension programs outside the individual's control, any contribution of such plans toward goal achievement must be recognized. For example, in the case of achieving the $80,000 goal mentioned in the preceding section, assume the individual will have a fully vested $30,000 in a retirement plan at the end of the 10-year period. If the retirement plan permits a cash lump-sum withdrawal upon vesting, a portion of the individual's investment plan would already be provided. Primary emphasis would therefore center on the accumulation of the additional $50,000.

One overriding consideration that should be incorporated in the plan to accumulate $50,000 is diversification. This concept emphasizes the need to hold a variety of investment vehicles to minimize the possibility that one bad investment will hinder the achievement of the goal of accumulating a specified amount of wealth. In general, when developing an investment portfolio, it is best to include a number of vehicles in it. As noted in Chapter 4, a well-balanced portfolio lessens the risk that one bad apple will spoil the entire barrel.

Considering available resources and projected budget surpluses, a plan that will provide for the accumulation of $50,000 by investing in an equal mix of blue-chip and speculative stocks providing a total return of 8 percent per year, of which 20 percent is current income and 80 percent is long-term capital gains, must be developed. If we assume the individual feels she can earn an 8 percent total return in the desired form by investing in the specified mix of common stock, we must isolate the source of investment capital that will provide for the $50,000 accumulation. The source can be current investable balances not committed to achievement of an investment goal and/or an allocation of income earned over future years. Let's assume that the individual currently has available $10,000 that can be used in achieving this goal. By investing this money in the desired types of vehicles earning an 8 percent return over the 10-year period, a future sum of $21,590 ($10,000 × 2.159, which is the compound-value interest factor for 10 years and 8 percent found in Appendix B, Table B.1) would be accumulated. Subtracting this amount from the $50,000 leaves $28,410 that must be obtained from the investment of current income over the period. At an 8 percent rate, an individual would have to invest approximately $2,000 per year at the end of each of the next 10 years in order to accumulate this sum. This was found by dividing the desired future value, $28,410, by the compound-value interest factor for a one-dollar annuity for 10 years and 8 percent obtained from Appendix B, Table B.2 ($28,410 ÷ 14.487 = $1,961). If the investor believes that $2,000 of each of the next 10 years' income can be allocated to this activity, specific securities can be selected for investment. On the other hand, if an allocation of $2,000 annually does not seem feasible, the goals must be revised to reflect this situation.

It should be clear from the example that once goals have been established, one must develop plans to provide for their achievement. The process of developing a plan means first adjusting for knowns, which in the example were an existing retirement plan and a currently available $10,000 investable balance, and then determining how much, if any, current income will have to be allocated in order to achieve the goal ($2,000 per year in the example). Since it is based on forecasts of both the return that will be earned and the size of investable balances available, an investment plan must be closely and constantly monitored. Checkpoints should be established at various time intervals to allow for assessment of progress. Adjustments in both goals and plans may be required as new information is received; goals may be too lax or too restrictive, or plans may be unrealistic. By monitoring actual outcomes and making needed adjustments, an investor should be better able to establish and achieve realistic financial goals over the long run.

SUMMARY

An understanding of personal financial plans—current income and expenditure, as well as insurance and taxes—is needed to develop a realistic investment program. The personal financial planning process involves first assessing current financial condition, then establishing financial goals, and finally preparing plans that will carry one from the current position toward these goals. Current financial position can be assessed using the two key personal financial statements, the balance sheet and the income statement. The balance sheet or statement of financial position reflects an individual's wealth position at a given point in time. The income statement describes the financial activities that have occurred over a given period of time. The balance sheet and income statement are linked together through the contribution to savings or investment; if it is positive, net worth should increase, and vice versa.

Establishing financial goals begins with setting long-run financial goals with associated goal dates. Short-run goals, which are set one to two years into the future, must be established to be consistent with the achievement of the long-run goals. Using the short-run goals as a basis, a budget is prepared. The surplus or deficit resulting after subtracting budgeted expense from income will determine investment plans.

Provision for adequate insurance to protect one's financial position should be included in personal financial management. In order for a risk to be insurable: (1) There must be a large group of persons with similar loss exposure; (2) the loss exposure must be one that results from unintentional and unexpected causes; (3) the cost of insurance must be relatively low; and (4) the risk should not have the potential for widespread catastrophe. Life insurance, which provides financial protection in the event of premature death, may be bought in any of four basic forms: term, whole life, endowment, and universal life insurance. A variety of techniques is available for determining life insurance needs and choosing the best form of coverage. Term and universal life insurance tend to be the most attractive forms currently available. Health insurance, designed to pay the expenses associated with illness or accident, is another necessary protection. Property and liability insurance is necessary to protect against the risk of physical loss of property and loss from liability resulting from negligent acts. Retirement planning is a related and important aspect of the personal financial planning process aimed at providing for adequate income during retirement.

In addition to return and risk, personal taxes can affect the choice of investment vehicles and strategies used in the personal financial management process. At the federal level, income taxes are a major source of revenue; state and local governments tend to rely primarily on sales and property taxes, although some also levy income taxes. An individual's income can be classified as ordinary, which is subject to a progressive tax schedule, or capital gains, which if long-term result in only 40 percent of the gain being treated as ordinary income. Tax-free utility dividend reinvestment plans allow investors to convert dividend income into capital gains that will be taxed at a lower rate. From an individual investor's point of view, the key tax dimensions to consider are current income, capital gains, and tax shelters. Tax planning is an important prerequisite for the investment process.

Investment goals should be consistent with long-run personal financial and retirement goals. They should take into account return, risk, and tax factors. Investment goals and plans must also be developed in a fashion that provides for adequate liquidity. Once goals are quantified, the investment program, or the plan for achieving these goals, must be established. Such a plan should first consider any known benefits as well as available funds to determine the level of annual investment required to meet each goal.

KEY TERMS

assets
balance sheet
budget
capital asset
capital gain (or loss)
cash value (insurance)
contribution to savings or investment
convertible term
credit life insurance
deficit (budget)
disability insurance
dividend reinvestment plan
endowment (life) insurance
expenses
group term insurance
health insurance
income
income statement
insurance
liabilities
liability insurance

liquidity
long-term capital gain
mortgage life insurance
net worth
ordinary income
property insurance
renewable term policy
safety of principal
short-term capital gain
straight term policy
surplus (budget)
tax credit
tax planning
tax shelter
tax swap
term (life) insurance
universal life insurance
wash sale
whole life insurance

REVIEW QUESTIONS

1. Briefly describe the three major activities involved in the personal financial planning process and discuss the importance of this process.

2. Describe and differentiate between the two key personal financial statements:

a. Personal balance sheet.
b. Personal income statement.

3. Determine the net worth for Joan Thomas, given the following assets and liabilities at the end of 1984. Arrange these values in the proper balance sheet format and discuss her year-end 1984 wealth position.

Mortgage loan	$30,000
Cash	1,200
Automobiles	11,000
Bills outstanding	700
Instalment loan balance	6,500
Security investments	2,300
Real estate	49,500
Bank note payable	3,000
Personal property	4,500

4. Given the following items of income and expense, prepare the year-end 1984 personal income statement for the Erker family. Evaluate their contribution to savings or investment and discuss their financial performance during the year.

Interest (earned)	$ 2,000
Housing	7,500
Insurance	700
Gain on sale of stock	450
Wages and salaries	27,500
Dividends	1,200
Automobile	6,700
Bonus and commissions	2,150
Clothing and shoes	2,300
Taxes	4,300
Proceeds from sale of asset	300
Health and hygiene	700
Food	3,600
Recreation, entertainment, and other	4,000

5. Given the following simplified balance sheet, illustrate how each of the following values for the contribution to savings or investment for the current year can be used to adjust the statement. Indicate the amount of net worth that would result after adjustment in each case.

   a. Contribution to savings or investment: $4,000.
   b. Contribution to savings or investment: − $2,000.

Balance Sheet

Assets	$40,000	Liabilities	$32,000
		Net worth	8,000
Total	$40,000	Total	$40,000

6. Describe the financial goal-setting process and explain the role of long-run and short-run goals and the associated reconciliation process.

7. Describe the role of the budget in the personal financial planning process. Explain its relationship to long- and short-run financial goals.

8. Given the following estimated total income and expense data for the first six months of 1985 for the Lee family, determine:

   a. Monthly budget surpluses and deficits.
   b. Cumulative surpluses and deficits.
   c. Six-month budget position.
   d. The action that should be taken on both a monthly basis and for the six months in order to manage the budget. Explain.

Month	ESTIMATED TOTAL	
(1985)	Income	Expense
Jan.	$3,000	$3,500
Feb.	3,100	2,900
Mar.	3,100	2,700
Apr.	3,200	4,000
May	3,200	2,500
June	3,000	2,600

9. Explain the general role insurance should play in one's personal financial plans. Briefly describe and explain the specific role of the following types of insurance.

a. Life.
b. Health.
c. Property and liability.

10. Define insurance and discuss the basic characteristics of an insurable exposure.

11. Briefly define and differentiate among the following types of life insurance. Describe the basic motives that should underlie the use of each of these forms.

a. Term insurance.
b. Whole life insurance.
c. Endowment insurance.
d. Universal life insurance.

12. Explain why term insurance and universal life insurance would most likely be the best forms of insurance for use in fulfilling life insurance needs.

13. Briefly describe the role and importance of retirement plans in the personal financial planning process.

14. For each of the following items in the left-hand column, match the most appropriate item in the right-hand column. Explain the relationship between the items matched.

a. Withheld and estimated taxes.   1. 40 percent taxable.
b. Income tax.   2. Local government.
c. Sales tax.   3. Federal government.
d. Property tax.   4. "Pay-as-you-go basis."
e. Long-term capital gain.   5. State government.

15. Define, differentiate, and explain federal income taxes as they relate to the following forms of income:

a. Ordinary (current) income.
b. Capital gains
   1. Short-term.
   2. Long-term.
c. Capital loss
   1. On a wash sale.
   2. On a tax swap.
d. Tax shelters.

16. Briefly describe the features of tax-free utility dividend reinvestment plans and explain why they might be an attractive inclusion in a portfolio.

17. For each of the following items in the left-hand column, match the most appropriate item in the right-hand column. Explain the relationship between the items matched.

a. Deductions from gross income.   1. $1,000 per dependent.
b. Zero-bracket amount.   2. Trade and business expenses.
c. Itemized nonbusiness expenses.   3. Deduct from tax liability.
d. Exemptions.   4. Personal deductions.
e. Tax credit.   5. Taxable income.
f. Gross income.   6. Blanket deduction.

18. Briefly describe the importance of each of the following factors as they relate to the process of setting investment goals and developing associated investment plans.

a. Return.
b. Risk.
c. Taxes.
d. Liquidity.

19. Explain how one should go about preparing an investment plan that provides for achievement of a given investment goal. Be sure to explain how existing investments or retirement benefits and current investable balances can be important factors to consider when estimating the amount of annual income that must be invested to achieve the goal. Also comment on the role monitoring an investment plan plays in the total investment program.

20. Use Appendix B, Tables B.1 and B.2 to answer each of the following questions.

a. If Charles Harper currently has $12,000 he wishes to invest at a 7 percent annual rate of interest, how much will he have available when he retires at the end of 15 years?

b. Beth Kluett wishes to accumulate $40,000 needed for retirement in exactly 20 years by making annual deposits into an account currently paying 11 percent annual interest. How much must Beth deposit at the end of each of the next 20 years in order to meet her goal?

CASE PROBLEMS

6.1 THE WASHINGTONS' LESSON: BUDGET FOR TAXES!

At the end of last year, Leroy and Pearl Washington, a married couple with two young children, found themselves in the undesirable position of having to liquidate U.S. savings bonds in order to pay their federal income taxes. During the year they had felt their expenses were in line with income, but at year-end they found they had failed to recognize that their tax liability could be in excess of their withholding. Fortunately, they were able to liquidate $1,200 in U.S. savings bonds to meet their tax bill. In order to avoid a recurrence of this situation, Leroy and Pearl agreed to learn how better to manage their personal finances. They enrolled in and recently completed a two-month seminar on personal financial planning sponsored by a local bank. Based upon the seminar, Leroy and Pearl are in the process of preparing their 1985 budget.

In preparing that budget, they estimate that total cash income and cash expenses for the year will be $26,750 and $25,400, respectively. They feel fairly certain about these estimates, which do not include any provision for savings or investment. Two things about the budget are of concern to the Washingtons. First, they realize that the total taxes withheld during the year will amount to $2,300, which may not be adequate to meet the actual tax liability incurred. Although any additional taxes wouldn't have to be paid until the following year, they feel it would be unfair to penalize next year's budget by not providing for taxes this year. Second, the Washingtons had hoped to be able to set aside $2,000 per year for each of the next three years in order to accumulate funds needed to meet a long-run goal related to the purchase of a new home.

In order to relieve the budget pressure, Pearl, who currently is a housewife, has contemplated operating a typing service out of their home. Based upon discussions with a friend who operates such a service, Pearl believes that the business could generate income of $3,500 per year and add business expense of approximately $1,000. She and Leroy are not sure if it is necessary or worthwhile for her to work, because of the additional taxes that would have to be paid. Wishing to resolve the two issues raised, Leroy and Pearl have gathered the following tax information, along with the relevant portion of the applicable tax table. (Note: The information refers to their existing situation—Pearl *not* working as proposed.)

Salary and wages	$27,000
Total itemized deductions	7,700
Leroy's business expense	1,300
Interest received (jointly owned)	500
Dividends (jointly owned)	500
Capital gains	
Short-term	200
Long-term	1,000

Questions

1. Using the tax table data presented on the following page, calculate the Washingtons' tax liability for the budget year.

2. Compare your finding in question 1 to the amount of withheld taxes, and in view of the Washington's budget, comment on their situation. Will they actually be living within their means? Explain.

3. Determine the Washingtons' tax liability in the event that Pearl undertakes the proposed establishment of the typing service. How much will they net after taxes from the typing service?

4. In view of your findings in the preceding questions, make recommendations to the Washingtons on the two key issues: (a) paying taxes and (b) meeting their long-run home-purchase goal.

6.2 PREPARING MARILYN THOMAS'S INVESTMENT PLAN

Marilyn Thomas, who just turned 55, is a widow currently employed as a receptionist for the Xcon Corporation, where she has worked for the past 20 years. She is in good health, lives alone, and has two grown children. A few months ago her husband, who was an alcoholic, died of liver disease. Although at one time a highly successful automobile dealer, Marilyn's husband has left her with only their home and the proceeds from a $30,000 life insurance policy. After paying medical and funeral expenses, $20,000 of the life insurance proceeds remained. In addition to the life insurance proceeds, Marilyn has $15,000 in a savings account, which she had secretly built over the past 10 years. Recognizing that she is within 10 years of retirement, Marilyn wishes to use her limited resources to develop an investment program that will allow her to live comfortably once she retires.

Marilyn is quite superstitious. After consulting with a number of psychics and studying her family tree, she feels certain she will not live past 80. She plans to retire at either 62 or 65, whichever will best allow her to meet her long-run financial goals. After talking with a number of knowledgable individuals—including, of course, the psychics—Marilyn estimates that to live comfortably, she will need $20,000 per year before taxes once she retires. This amount will be required annually for each of 18 years if she retires at 62 or for each of 15 years if she retires at 65. As part of her financial plans, Marilyn intends to sell her home at retirement and rent an apartment. She has estimated that after taxes, she will net $37,000 if she sells the house at 62 and $41,000 if she sells it at 65. Marilyn has no financial dependents and is not concerned about leaving a sizable estate to her heirs.

If Marilyn retires at age 62, she will receive from social security and an employer pension-sponsored plan a total of $604 per month ($7,248 annually); if she waits until age 65 to retire, her total retirement income would be $750 per month ($9,000 annually). For convenience, Marilyn has already decided that in order to convert all her assets at the time of retirement into a stream of annual income, she will at that time purchase an annuity by paying a single premium. The annuity will have a life just equal to the number of years remaining until her eightieth birthday. Because Marilyn is uncertain as to the actual age at which she will retire,

TAX TABLE

If line 37 (taxable income) is—		And you are—			
At least	But less than	Single	Married filing jointly *	Married filing separately	Head of a household
		Your tax is—			
16,250	16,300	2,674	2,074	3,224	2,515
16,300	16,350	2,688	2,085	3,241	2,527
16,350	16,400	2,701	2,096	3,257	2,538
16,400	16,450	2,715	2,107	3,274	2,550
16,450	16,500	2,728	2,118	3,290	2,561
16,500	16,550	2,742	2,129	3,307	2,573
16,550	16,600	2,755	2,140	3,323	2,584
16,600	16,650	2,769	2,151	3,340	2,596
16,650	16,700	2,782	2,162	3,356	2,607
16,700	16,750	2,796	2,173	3,373	2,619
16,750	16,800	2,809	2,184	3,389	2,630
16,800	16,850	2,823	2,195	3,406	2,642
16,850	16,900	2,836	2,206	3,422	2,653
16,900	16,950	2,850	2,217	3,439	2,665
16,950	17,000	2,863	2,228	3,455	2,676
17,000					
17,000	17,050	2,877	2,239	3,472	2,688
17,050	17,100	2,890	2,250	3,488	2,699
17,100	17,150	2,904	2,261	3,505	2,711
17,150	17,200	2,917	2,272	3,521	2,722
17,200	17,250	2,931	2,283	3,538	2,734
17,250	17,300	2,944	2,294	3,554	2,745
17,300	17,350	2,958	2,305	3,571	2,757
17,350	17,400	2,971	2,316	3,587	2,768
17,400	17,450	2,985	2,327	3,604	2,780
17,450	17,500	2,998	2,338	3,620	2,791
17,500	17,550	3,012	2,349	3,637	2,803
17,550	17,600	3,025	2,360	3,653	2,814
17,600	17,650	3,039	2,371	3,671	2,826
17,650	17,700	3,052	2,382	3,691	2,837
17,700	17,750	3,066	2,393	3,710	2,849
17,750	17,800	3,079	2,404	3,730	2,860
17,800	17,850	3,093	2,415	3,749	2,872
17,850	17,900	3,106	2,426	3,769	2,883
17,900	17,950	3,120	2,437	3,788	2,895
17,950	18,000	3,133	2,448	3,808	2,906
18,000					
18,000	18,050	3,147	2,459	3,827	2,918
18,050	18,100	3,160	2,470	3,847	2,929
18,100	18,150	3,174	2,481	3,866	2,941
18,150	18,200	3,187	2,492	3,886	2,952
18,200	18,250	3,202	2,503	3,905	2,965
18,250	18,300	3,217	2,514	3,925	2,979
18,300	18,350	3,233	2,525	3,944	2,993
18,350	18,400	3,248	2,536	3,964	3,007
18,400	18,450	3,264	2,547	3,983	3,021
18,450	18,500	3,279	2,558	4,003	3,035
18,500	18,550	3,295	2,569	4,022	3,049
18,550	18,600	3,310	2,580	4,042	3,063
18,600	18,650	3,326	2,591	4,061	3,077
18,650	18,700	3,341	2,602	4,081	3,091
18,700	18,750	3,357	2,613	4,100	3,105
18,750	18,800	3,372	2,624	4,120	3,119
18,800	18,850	3,388	2,635	4,139	3,133
18,850	18,900	3,403	2,646	4,159	3,147
18,900	18,950	3,419	2,657	4,178	3,161
18,950	19,000	3,434	2,668	4,198	3,175

If line 37 (taxable income) is—		And you are—			
At least	But less than	Single	Married filing jointly *	Married filing separately	Head of a household
		Your tax is—			
19,000					
19,000	19,050	3,450	2,679	4,217	3,189
19,050	19,100	3,465	2,690	4,237	3,203
19,100	19,150	3,481	2,701	4,256	3,217
19,150	19,200	3,496	2,712	4,276	3,231
19,200	19,250	3,512	2,723	4,295	3,245
19,250	19,300	3,527	2,734	4,315	3,259
19,300	19,350	3,543	2,745	4,334	3,273
19,350	19,400	3,558	2,756	4,354	3,287
19,400	19,450	3,574	2,767	4,373	3,301
19,450	19,500	3,589	2,778	4,393	3,315
19,500	19,550	3,605	2,789	4,412	3,329
19,550	19,600	3,620	2,800	4,432	3,343
19,600	19,650	3,636	2,811	4,451	3,357
19,650	19,700	3,651	2,822	4,471	3,371
19,700	19,750	3,667	2,833	4,490	3,385
19,750	19,800	3,682	2,844	4,510	3,399
19,800	19,850	3,698	2,855	4,529	3,413
19,850	19,900	3,713	2,866	4,549	3,427
19,900	19,950	3,729	2,877	4,568	3,441
19,950	20,000	3,744	2,888	4,588	3,455
20,000					
20,000	20,050	3,760	2,899	4,607	3,469
20,050	20,100	3,775	2,910	4,627	3,483
20,100	20,150	3,791	2,921	4,646	3,497
20,150	20,200	3,806	2,932	4,666	3,511
20,200	20,250	3,822	2,943	4,685	3,525
20,250	20,300	3,837	2,956	4,705	3,539
20,300	20,350	3,853	2,968	4,724	3,553
20,350	20,400	3,868	2,981	4,744	3,567
20,400	20,450	3,884	2,993	4,763	3,581
20,450	20,500	3,899	3,006	4,783	3,595
20,500	20,550	3,915	3,018	4,802	3,609
20,550	20,600	3,930	3,031	4,822	3,623
20,600	20,650	3,946	3,043	4,841	3,637
20,650	20,700	3,961	3,056	4,861	3,651
20,700	20,750	3,977	3,068	4,880	3,665
20,750	20,800	3,992	3,081	4,900	3,679
20,800	20,850	4,008	3,093	4,919	3,693
20,850	20,900	4,023	3,106	4,939	3,707
20,900	20,950	4,039	3,118	4,958	3,721
20,950	21,000	4,054	3,131	4,978	3,735
21,000					
21,000	21,050	4,070	3,143	4,997	3,749
21,050	21,100	4,085	3,156	5,017	3,763
21,100	21,150	4,101	3,168	5,036	3,777
21,150	21,200	4,116	3,181	5,056	3,791
21,200	21,250	4,132	3,193	5,075	3,805
21,250	21,300	4,147	3,206	5,095	3,819
21,300	21,350	4,163	3,218	5,114	3,833
21,350	21,400	4,178	3,231	5,134	3,847
21,400	21,450	4,194	3,243	5,153	3,861
21,450	21,500	4,209	3,256	5,173	3,875
21,500	21,550	4,225	3,268	5,192	3,889
21,550	21,600	4,240	3,281	5,212	3,903
21,600	21,650	4,256	3,293	5,231	3,917
21,650	21,700	4,271	3,306	5,251	3,931
21,700	21,750	4,287	3,318	5,270	3,945

If line 37 (taxable income) is—		And you are—			
At least	But less than	Single	Married filing jointly *	Married filing separately	Head of a household
		Your tax is—			
21,750	21,800	4,302	3,331	5,290	3,959
21,800	21,850	4,318	3,343	5,309	3,973
21,850	21,900	4,333	3,356	5,329	3,987
21,900	21,950	4,349	3,368	5,348	4,001
21,950	22,000	4,364	3,381	5,368	4,015
22,000					
22,000	22,050	4,380	3,393	5,387	4,029
22,050	22,100	4,395	3,406	5,407	4,043
22,100	22,150	4,411	3,418	5,426	4,057
22,150	22,200	4,426	3,431	5,446	4,071
22,200	22,250	4,442	3,443	5,465	4,085
22,250	22,300	4,457	3,456	5,485	4,099
22,300	22,350	4,473	3,468	5,504	4,113
22,350	22,400	4,488	3,481	5,524	4,127
22,400	22,450	4,504	3,493	5,543	4,141
22,450	22,500	4,519	3,506	5,563	4,155
22,500	22,550	4,535	3,518	5,582	4,169
22,550	22,600	4,550	3,531	5,602	4,183
22,600	22,650	4,566	3,543	5,621	4,197
22,650	22,700	4,581	3,556	5,641	4,211
22,700	22,750	4,597	3,568	5,660	4,225
22,750	22,800	4,612	3,581	5,680	4,239
22,800	22,850	4,628	3,593	5,699	4,253
22,850	22,900	4,643	3,606	5,719	4,267
22,900	22,950	4,659	3,618	5,740	4,281
22,950	23,000	4,674	3,631	5,762	4,295
23,000					
23,000	23,050	4,690	3,643	5,784	4,309
23,050	23,100	4,705	3,656	5,806	4,323
23,100	23,150	4,721	3,668	5,828	4,337
23,150	23,200	4,736	3,681	5,850	4,351
23,200	23,250	4,752	3,693	5,872	4,365
23,250	23,300	4,767	3,706	5,894	4,379
23,300	23,350	4,783	3,718	5,916	4,393
23,350	23,400	4,798	3,731	5,938	4,407
23,400	23,450	4,814	3,743	5,960	4,421
23,450	23,500	4,829	3,756	5,982	4,435
23,500	23,550	4,846	3,768	6,004	4,450
23,550	23,600	4,863	3,781	6,026	4,466
23,600	23,650	4,881	3,793	6,048	4,482
23,650	23,700	4,898	3,806	6,070	4,498
23,700	23,750	4,916	3,818	6,092	4,514
23,750	23,800	4,933	3,831	6,114	4,530
23,800	23,850	4,951	3,843	6,136	4,546
23,850	23,900	4,968	3,856	6,158	4,562
23,900	23,950	4,986	3,868	6,180	4,578
23,950	24,000	5,003	3,881	6,202	4,594
24,000					
24,000	24,050	5,021	3,893	6,224	4,610
24,050	24,100	5,038	3,906	6,246	4,626
24,100	24,150	5,056	3,918	6,268	4,642
24,150	24,200	5,073	3,931	6,290	4,658
24,200	24,250	5,091	3,943	6,312	4,674
24,250	24,300	5,108	3,956	6,334	4,690
24,300	24,350	5,126	3,968	6,356	4,706
24,350	24,400	5,143	3,981	6,378	4,722
24,400	24,450	5,161	3,993	6,400	4,738
24,450	24,500	5,178	4,006	6,422	4,754

*This column must also be used by a qualifying widow(er).

she obtained the following interest factors from her insurance agent in order to estimate the annual annuity benefit provided for a given purchase price:

Life of Annuity	Interest Factor
15 years	11.118
18 years	12.659

By dividing the factors into the purchase price, the annual annuity benefit can be calculated. Marilyn plans to place any funds currently available into a savings account paying 6 percent compounded annually until retirement. She does not expect to be able to save or invest any additional funds between now and her retirement.

Questions

1. By placing currently available funds in the savings account, determine the amount of money Marilyn will have available at retirement once she sells her house if she retires at (a) age 62, and (b) age 65. (*Note:* You will need to use Appendix B, Table B.1 to make this calculation.)

2. Using the results from question 1 and the interest factors given above, determine the level of annual income that will be provided to Marilyn through purchase of an annuity at (a) age 62, and (b) age 65.

3. With the results found in the preceding questions, determine the total annual retirement income Marilyn will have if she retires at (a) age 62, and (b) age 65.

4. From your findings, do you think Marilyn will be able to achieve her long-run financial goal by retiring at (a) age 62? or (b) age 65? Explain.

5. Evaluate Marilyn's investment plan in terms of her use of a savings account and an annuity rather than some other investment vehicles. Comment on the return and risk characteristics of her plan. What recommendations might you offer Marilyn? Be specific.

SELECTED READINGS

"The Bewildering Facts of Life Insurance for First-Time Buyers." *Changing Times,* April 1980, pp. 45–48.

Carter, Malcolm. "There's Help Out There." *Money,* October 1982, pp. 91–94.

Eisenberg, Richard. "Protecting Yourself from the Tax Bite." *Money,* February 1983, pp. 52–56.

Gitman, Lawrence J. *Personal Finance,* 3d ed. Hinsdale, IL: Dryden Press, 1984.

Hazard, John W. "Term or Whole Life Insurance?" *U.S. News & World Report,* October 31, 1983, p. 84.

Hedberg, Augustin. "Should You Do It Yourself?" *Money,* April 1982, pp. 64–66.

J.K. Lasser's Your Income Tax. New York: Simon and Schuster, annual.

"The Latest in Life Insurance with an Inflation Twist." *Changing Times,* August 1981, pp. 45–47.

Lewis, Stephen W. "Seven Serious Mistakes with Your Money." *Money,* November 1981, pp. 101–104.

Malkiel, Burton. *Winning Investment Strategies.* New York: Norton, 1982.

Phillips, Lawrence C., and William H. Hoffman, eds. *West's Federal Taxation: Individual Income Taxes.* St. Paul, MN: West Publishing, annual.

Sivy, Michael. "How Computers Can Help You Manage Money." *Money,* June 1981, pp. 111–116.

Trunzo, Candace E. "Choosing a Financial Planner." *Money,* April 1982, pp. 46–50.

Tuhy, Carrie. "Knowing What You're Really Worth." *Money,* October 1982, pp. 70–71.

———. "Winning the Budget Battle." *Money,* October 1982, pp. 74–78.

"Universal Life Insurance." *Consumer Reports,* January 1982, pp. 42–44.

7

Meeting Liquidity and Retirement Needs

Maintaining an adequate level of liquidity and planning for retirement are both important to the development of a successful investment program. Investors need some liquidity to keep their options open and to meet unforeseen emergencies; at the same time, some part of the portfolio should be set aside to provide income for retirement. Fortunately, there are a number of convenient and attractive ways of meeting liquidity and retirement needs. This chapter will examine these requirements and see how such portfolio objectives can be met; specifically, we will consider:

1. The concept of liquidity and the role that short-term securities play in meeting liquidity needs.
2. The various types of liquid investments and how they earn interest.
3. The investment merits and suitability of alternative short-term investments, including their availability, yield, safety, and liquidity.
4. Retirement planning and procedures for determining income needs.
5. The retirement coverage provided by social security and basic employer-sponsored retirement plans.
6. The availability and nature of self-directed retirement plans—Keogh accounts and IRAs—and how they compare to employer-sponsored supplemental retirement plans.

Prior to the early 1970s, most individual investors had very few alternatives when it came to savings and short-term investment vehicles. For the most part, they could put their money in low-paying passbook savings accounts or Series E bonds. The other alternatives (which usually offered the best returns) were simply too expensive for most individuals. The situation began to change dramatically with the advent of the money market mutual fund so that today individual investors have a whole menu of attractive short-term investments from which to choose. Some people use these securities as temporary investment outlets; others view them as permanent investments and, for one reason or another, may never invest in any other kind of security. In a similar fashion, it was found that as inflation took its toll of individuals living on fixed incomes, the importance of making retirement planning an integral part of one's investment portfolio began to come home to many more people. The staying power of the social security system became suspect, and new retirement programs—like Individual Retirement Accounts (IRAs)—were introduced. The net result was that people began taking more responsibility for meeting their own retirement needs via their investment programs. Liquidity and retirement needs took on new roles in the investment process. Though meeting these objectives may seem straightforward enough, these are not simple tasks. They require a knowledge not only of investment vehicles, but also of tax laws and financial planning. We will look now at the liquidity and retirement needs of individuals to see what they are, as well as how they can be met. We begin by examining the question of liquidity.

MEETING LIQUIDITY NEEDS: INVESTING IN SHORT-TERM SECURITIES

An asset has high *liquidity* when it can be converted to cash easily and with little or no loss in value. A checking account is almost perfectly liquid, whereas stocks and bonds are not, because there is little assurance of being able to sell the securities at a price equal to or greater than their purchase price. Within the past decade, but particularly since the Depository Institutions Deregulation and Monetary Control Act of 1980, the number and variety of investment vehicles serving liquidity needs has increased significantly. Although all these vehicles meet the same basic needs to one degree or another, they are different in terms of how they pay interest and the relative ease with which they can be converted to cash. It is important to recognize these differences and to understand why liquid assets are held in the first place.

Some Basic Considerations

Short-term securities are an important part of most savings and investments programs. While they do generate income—which can be quite high during periods of high interest rates—their primary savings function is to provide a pool of reserves that can be used for emergencies, or simply to accumulate funds for some specific purpose, such as buying a home or a car. When viewed as part of an investment portfolio, short-term securities are usually held as a temporary, highly liquid investment outlet until something better comes along, or as a more permanent form of investment by individuals who like the yields they offer and/or are more comfortable with these kinds of investment vehicles. Whatever the reasons for holding them, short-term securities should be evaluated within a general risk-return framework.

Role of short-term securities

Careful financial planning dictates that a portion of your investments should be suitable for meeting liquidity needs. Opinions differ on how much to hold as liquid reserves, but the general consensus is that three to six months of after-tax income is best for most families. This means that if you clear $1,500 a month, you should have between $4,500 and $9,000 in liquid reserves. If your employer has a strong salary continuation program that is available during extended illnesses and/or you have a line of credit available through a local financial institution (such as a credit card or a check reserve/overdraft account), the lower figure is probably suitable; if you lack one or both of these, however, the higher amount is probably appropriate. A specific savings plan is needed to accumulate funds. In this regard, saving should be viewed as important as any other item in a budget—not as a pleasant, chance event that occurs whenever income happens to exceed expenditures. Some people do this by arranging savings withholding directly from their paychecks. This has been a common practice for many years with U.S. savings bonds and credit union shares; today it is also possible to have funds transferred to other financial institutions, such as commercial banks, savings and loans, and even money market mutual funds. Not only do direct deposit arrangements help the savings effort, they also enable your funds to earn interest sooner.

After sufficient liquid reserves have been accumulated, consideration can be given to going beyond this minimum level. This kind of saving is done for two reasons. First, while an investor might prefer long-term securities, prices might be considered too high (yields too low) so that short-term securities will be held as a temporary "parking place" for funds until the long-term markets become more attractive. Many professional portfolio managers design strategies aimed at determining an appropriate balance of funds to be invested in long- and short-term securities. The second reason for holding short-term securities is that they are viewed as a better investment outlet than long-term securities. This is usually done by investors who lack the knowledge or expertise to invest in other securities, or who simply like the returns they can obtain from such securities. In fact, this approach has considerable merit during periods of economic (and investment) instability, much like those we experienced during the 1970s and early 1980s. For as we will see later in the chapter, the realized rates of return on many long-term securities were often *below* those of short-term securities during much of this period.

Determining interest on short-term securities and deposits

Short-term investments earn interest in one of two ways. First, some are sold on a *discount basis.* This means that the security is sold for a price that is less than its redemption value, the difference being the interest earned. Treasury bills, for example, are issued on a discount basis. This return can be expressed as an annual rate, using the following equation:

$$\text{annual rate of return on a discount security} = \left[\frac{360}{\text{number of days to maturity}}\right] \times \left[\frac{\text{redemption value} - \text{purchase price}}{\text{purchase price}}\right]$$

$$= [360/n] \times \left[\frac{R - P}{P}\right]$$

To illustrate, suppose you buy a T-bill for $9,700 that can be redeemed for $10,000 at the end of 90 days. The total interest on this security is $300 (redemption value − purchase price), and its annual rate of return is:

$$\text{annual rate of return} = (360/90) \left(\frac{\$10,000 - \$9,700}{\$9,700} \right)$$

$$= (4.000)(.03093) = .12372, \text{ or } 12.372\%$$

Another way interest is earned on short-term investments is by direct payment, such as when interest is credited to a passbook savings account. Although this is a simple process, determining the actual rate of return can involve several complications. The first of these relates to the compounding method used to arrive at the amount, and rate, of interest earned annually. You have probably read or seen advertisements by banks or savings and loans touting the fact they pay daily, rather than simple, interest. To show what this means, consider the following example: Assume you invest $1,000 in a savings account that advertises an annual interest rate of 10 percent simple. This means that if the $1,000 is left on deposit for one year, you will earn $100 in interest and the account will be worth $1,100 at the end of the year. Note in this case that the *nominal* (or stated) rate of interest is the same as the *effective* rate—or the annual rate of return actually earned on the investment. That is, since $100 was earned over the year on an investment of $1,000, the effective rate is found by dividing annual interest income by the amount invested; or: $100/$1,000 = 10%, which is the same as the stated or advertised rate of interest. But suppose you could have invested your funds elsewhere at a 10 percent rate *compounded semiannually*. Since interest is added to your account at midyear, this means you will earn *interest on the interest* for the last six months of the year, thereby increasing the total interest for the year. The actual dollar earnings are determined as follows:

$$\text{first six-months' interest} = \$1,000 \times 0.10 \times 6/12 = \$\ 50.00$$
$$\text{second six-months' interest} = \$1,050 \times 0.10 \times 6/12 = \underline{\quad 52.50}$$
$$\text{total interest} = \$102.50$$

Interest is being generated on a larger investment in the second half of the year, since the amount of invested capital went up by the amount of interest earned in the first half ($50). Although the nominal rate on this account is still 10 percent, the effective rate is 10.25 percent ($102.50/$1,000). As you might have guessed, the more frequently interest is compounded, the greater the effective rate for any given nominal rate. These relationships are shown for a sample of interest rates and compounding periods in Table 7.1. Notice that with a 10 percent nominal rate, daily compounding adds 0.52 percent (52 basis points) to the size of the total return—not a trivial amount.

Not only are there differences among financial institutions in the way interest is compounded, but there may also be differences with respect to how balances

TABLE 7.1	NOMINAL AND EFFECTIVE INTEREST RATES WITH DIFFERENT COMPOUNDING PERIODS				
Nominal Rate	EFFECTIVE RATE				
	Annually	Semiannually	Quarterly	Monthly	Daily
7%	7.00%	7.12%	7.19%	7.23%	7.25%
8	8.00	8.16	8.24	8.30	8.33
9	9.00	9.20	9.31	9.38	9.42
10	10.00	10.25	10.38	10.47	10.52
11	11.00	11.30	11.46	11.57	11.62
12	12.00	12.36	12.55	12.68	12.74

qualify to earn interest—that is, how the size of the account balance is determined. There are four methods in wide use: (1) the minimum balance method, (2) the FIFO method, (3) the LIFO method, and (4) the day of deposit to day of withdrawal method. The differences in these methods is illustrated best with an example, such as the one given in Table 7.2. Here, the depositor is assumed to have $10,000 at the beginning of the quarter and adds $2,000 to this balance 30 days after the quarter starts; then, on the 60th day, a withdrawal of $6,000 takes place, leaving an ending balance of $6,000. Either simple or compound interest could be used, but we will assume, for computational simplicity, that the account pays *simple* interest of 10 percent. In all illustrations, interest earned is computed in the following manner:

$$\text{interest earned} = \text{amount invested (or on deposit)} \times \text{annual interest rate} \times \frac{n}{360}$$

where

$$n = \text{number of days funds are on deposit}$$

Notice that a 360-day year is assumed, which is common for many money market calculations. To see how this equation works, consider the sum of $1,000 left on deposit for 30 days at an annual rate of $7\frac{1}{2}$ percent; the depositor in this case would earn interest of:

$$\$1,000 \times .075 \times 30/360 = \$6.25$$

Minimum balance method.   With this method, interest is paid on the *lowest* balance in the account during the quarter. Since this figure is $6,000 in our illustration, the interest earned amounts to only $150. This method places a heavy penalty on withdrawals made late in the period, and such an account is not recommended if substantial withdrawals are anticipated.

**TABLE 7.2   FOUR METHODS FOR DETERMINING INTEREST:
NOMINAL ANNUAL RATE = 10%**

I.   QUARTERLY ACTIVITY

Day	Transaction	Account Balance
1	Opening balance	$10,000
30	Deposit $2,000	12,000
60	Withdrawal $6,000	6,000
90	Ending balance	6,000

II. INTEREST CALCULATIONS

1. *Minimum balance method:*

$$\$6,000 \times 0.10 \times 90/360 = \underline{\underline{\$150.00}}$$

2. *FIFO method:*

$$\$4,000 \times 0.10 \times 90/360 = \$100.00$$
$$2,000 \times 0.10 \times 60/360 = \underline{33.33}$$
$$\text{Total} = \underline{\underline{\$133.33}}$$

3. *LIFO method:*

$$\$6,000 \times 0.10 \times 90/360 = \underline{\underline{\$150.00}}$$

4. *Day of deposit to day of withdrawal method:*

$$\$10,000 \times 0.10 \times 30/360 = \$83.33$$
$$12,000 \times 0.10 \times 30/360 = 100.00$$
$$6,000 \times 0.10 \times 30/360 = \underline{50.00}$$
$$\text{Total} = \underline{\underline{\$233.33}}$$

FIFO method.   FIFO means *first-in, first-out.* It is an assumption the financial institution makes with respect to when withdrawals are charged; specifically, it assumes withdrawals are charged against the earlier or opening balances of an account. Thus, the $6,000 withdrawal on the 60th day is assumed to reduce the opening balance of $10,000, leaving a balance of $4,000. Table 7.2 shows how the interest income of $133.33 is determined. Note that because the $6,000 withdrawal is charged against the opening balance, it is only the remaining amount ($4,000) that earns interest over the full quarter (90 days), whereas the deposit ($2,000) earns interest only over the 60 days it was on deposit. For the data given in this illustration, the depositor earns even less with this method than with the minimum balance method, although this is not always the case.

LIFO method.   LIFO means *last-in, first-out,* and with this method, the bank or S&L assumes withdrawals are charged to the most recent deposits or balances. This is to the depositor's advantage, since it means earlier deposits are left untouched and thereby earn interest for the entire period. Thus, the $6,000 withdrawal on day 60 is assumed to first reduce the $2,000 deposit made on day 30, with the remaining $4,000 then going back to offset the opening balance of $10,000. This leaves $6,000 ($10,000 − $4,000) against which interest is earned. As it works out in this illustration, the interest earned of $150 is the same as with the minimum balance method. Although this method is somewhat fairer to the depositor than the FIFO method, it still does not provide interest for the full period over which the money is on deposit.

Day of deposit to day of withdrawal method. This method is the most accurate and gives depositors the most interest for the period; it is also considered the fairest procedure, as it gives depositors full credit for all funds on deposit. This procedure is sometimes called "daily interest," but it should not be confused with the daily compounding of interest, which is an entirely different concept. Daily interest does not necessarily mean daily compounding, although competition among financial institutions is moving most of them in that direction. Before opening a deposit account, a depositor should ask two questions: How often does compounding take place and what method is used to determine which balances earn interest? Table 7.2 indicates how the interest of $233.33 is calculated for our example using the day of deposit to day of withdrawal method; as can be seen, more is earned under this method than with any of the other methods.

Risk characteristics

In Chapter 4 we pointed out the different sources of investment risk; they included business and financial risk, purchasing power risk, interest rate risk, liquidity risk, and market risk. Short-term investments are generally considered low in all these risks, with the possible exception of purchasing power risk, which can result if the earnings on these investments fall short of the inflation rate. Unfortunately, this has been the case with deposits having regulated maximum rates, such as passbook savings accounts; most other short-term investments have averaged, over long periods of time, rates of return that are about equal to, or maybe even slightly higher than, the average inflation rate.

Risk of default (accruing from business and/or financial risk) is virtually nonexistent with short-term investment outlets. The principal reason for this is that the primary issuers of most money market securities are highly reputable institutions, such as the U.S. Treasury, large money center banks, and major corporations. What's more, deposits in federally regulated commercial banks, savings banks, S&Ls, and credit unions are insured by the government for up to $100,000. Commercial banks and mutual savings banks are insured by the Federal Deposit Insurance Corporation (FDIC), and savings and loan associations and national credit unions are insured by the Federal Savings and Loan Insurance Corporation (FSLIC) and the National Credit Union Administration (NCUA), respectively. Most savings institutions that do not have federal insurance have other deposit insurance arrangements, but whether these have the strength of federal insurance in a major financial crisis is an untested question. Finally, short-term investments are also very low in interest rate risk. In other words, exposure to wide savings in security prices either does not exist (as with passbook savings accounts) or is *very* low with these investments. So exposure to capital loss is correspondingly low. This is so because these securities have such short maturities (often measured in days and never exceeding a year), and the shorter the maturity of an issue, the less volatile the market price. This is perhaps most evident with six-month Treasury bills; their yields may vary over a wide range, but their prices change relatively little.

Advantages and disadvantages of short-term investments

Among the major advantages of short-term investments is the fact that they are convenient and highly liquid. Most are available from local financial institutions and can be readily converted to cash with minimal inconvenience. What is more, they are a safe investment outlet, almost totally free from risk of default or exposure to capital loss. Finally, the returns on most short-term investments vary with inflation and market interest rates so that investors can readily capture the higher returns as rates move up. For example, although investors who buy long-term bonds will suffer income and capital losses as market rates rise, investors who buy short-term securities (like T-bills or money funds) will see their returns increase along with interest rates. Of course, there is a negative side to this, which occurs when interest rates go down—and returns to short-term investors drop as well.

Although a decline in market rates has undesirable effects on most short-term investment vehicles, perhaps the biggest disadvantage of these securities and deposits is their relatively low yield. Because these securities are generally so low in risk, and because low risk is usually translated into low return, you can expect the returns on short-term investments to average less than the returns on long-term investments. This can be seen in Table 7.3, which compares the rate of return on 90-day T-bills with the rate of return on long-term Aaa-rated corporate bonds. Observe that the bond rate exceeded the bill rate in every year except one, 1979; notice further that the difference was *less than one percentage point* in 10 of the 23 years, and the average difference for the entire period was only 1.4 percentage points. As an investor, you must decide whether or not this difference in yield is sufficient compensation for holding the riskier corporate bonds. If it is, then you should hold only a minimum amount of short-term securities and place your extra investment funds in long-term securities. If the extra return is not adequate, you should increase your holdings of short-term investments.

Alternative Short-Term Investment Vehicles

Over the past decade or so, there has been a tremendous proliferation of savings and short-term investment vehicles, particularly for the individual investor of modest means. Saving and investing in short-term securities is no longer the easy task it once was, when the decision for most people boiled down to whether funds should be placed in a passbook savings account or in Series E bonds. Today, even checking accounts can be set up in interest-bearing deposits. The variety of savings and short-term investment vehicles from which investors can choose includes passbook savings accounts, NOW and Super NOW accounts, money market deposit accounts and mutual funds, certificates of deposit, repurchase agreements, Treasury bills, sweep accounts, and Series EE bonds. Along with the dramatic increase in the

TABLE 7.3	NOMINAL INTEREST RATES ON BILLS AND BONDS, 1960–1982		
Year	90-Day T-Bill Rate	Aaa Corporate Bond Rate	Bond Rate Less the Bill Rate
1960	2.9%	4.4%	1.5%
1961	2.4	4.4	2.0
1962	2.8	4.3	1.5
1963	3.2	4.3	1.1
1964	3.6	4.4	0.8
1965	4.0	4.5	0.5
1966	4.9	5.1	0.2
1967	4.3	5.5	1.2
1968	5.3	6.2	0.9
1969	6.7	7.0	0.3
1970	6.5	8.0	1.5
1971	4.4	7.4	3.0
1972	4.1	7.2	3.1
1973	7.0	7.4	0.4
1974	7.9	8.6	0.7
1975	5.8	8.8	3.0
1976	5.0	8.4	3.4
1977	5.3	8.0	2.7
1978	7.2	8.7	1.5
1979	10.0	9.6	−0.4
1980	11.5	11.9	0.4
1981	14.1	14.2	0.1
1982	11.7	14.9	3.2
Averages	6.1%	7.5%	1.4%

Source: Federal Reserve Bank of St. Louis, *Review*, December 1982, p. 9.

number of investment alternatives has come increased sophistication in short-term investment management. Short-term vehicles can be used as safe, secure investment outlets for the long haul, or as a place to hold cash until the market becomes stronger and a more permanent outlet for the funds can be found. To gain the most from short-term investment funds, you must fully understand what the alternatives are. In the material that follows we will examine each of the major savings and short-term investment vehicles and deposits; later we will look at several ways in which these securities/deposits can be used in an investment portfolio. (Note that all the *deposit* accounts discussed below are issued by commercial banks, S&Ls, mutual savings banks, and credit unions; very often we will simply use the term "bank" to refer to any one or all of these financial institutions and not necessarily to commercial banks alone.)

Passbook savings account

The *passbook savings account* has been the traditional savings vehicle for many Americans. The name "passbook" arises from the fact that activity in the account is often recorded in a passbook, although bank statement report forms are replacing the old passbooks. Generally, there are no minimum balances on these accounts and you can make as many withdrawals from them as you choose, though there may be a slight fee for some of the withdrawals (for example, there often is a charge if withdrawals exceed a predetermined number in a month or quarter). These accounts are offered by banks and other thrift institutions—but, as noted earlier, it is a good idea to determine how interest will be figured on your account, since it can make a difference. Interest paid on passbook accounts is regulated by law and is kept fairly low; for example, the current maximum rate for commercial banks is 5¼ percent, with other thrift institutions allowed to pay ¼ percent more; and credit unions are allowed to pay up to 7 percent. These relatively low maximum rates make passbook accounts unattractive during periods of high interest rates, and as long as such rates exist, passbook accounts will probably continue to decline in popularity. They are used primarily by depositors who like the convenience of maintaining a savings account at their local bank, who lack sufficient resources for the higher minimum deposit requirement on other accounts, or who are simply unaware that higher-yielding and equally safe accounts are available. Passbook accounts are generally viewed as a convenient savings vehicle (appropriate perhaps for the accumulation of emergency funds), but have little or no role in an investment program.

NOW and Super NOW accounts

A *NOW (Negotiated Order of Withdrawal) account* is simply a checking account that pays interest at the maximum allowable rate on passbook savings—5¼ or 5½ percent; a *Super NOW account* (introduced in January 1983) is a variation of the NOW checking account that allows the financial institution to pay interest at any rate it chooses. When they were first introduced, the interest rates offered on Super NOWs were extremely high relative to rates offered on competitive deposits, such as money market mutual funds. However, these rates came down quickly and have remained at, or slightly below, competitive rates. The minimum balance requirement for a Super NOW is $2,500; there is no legal minimum for a regular NOW, but many banks impose their own requirement, which is often between $500 and $1,000. (Some banks have no minimum and pay interest on any balance in the account.) Many banks offer combination NOW and Super NOW accounts that pay interest at a higher rate for all balances over $2,500; at the 5¼ or 5½ percent rate on balances between, say, $1,000 and $2,500, and zero if the balance is under $1,000. Usually interest is calculated on the average daily balance within these brackets.

Both NOW and Super NOW accounts should be viewed primarily as checking accounts that can also serve as potentially attractive savings vehicles. Since they serve as checking accounts, investors are able to earn interest on balances that must be kept for transactions purposes anyway; thus, an individual can earn interest on

That's our new penalty for early withdrawal!

what would otherwise be idle balances. In most cases service charges on NOWs and Super NOWs—if there are any—are no greater than what would be levied on a regular checking account. However, despite their apparent appeal, alternatives should be examined closely before one of these accounts is opened. The key is how the rates on these accounts stack up to the rates you might earn by investing in alternative short-term vehicles. If alternative rates are much higher than the NOW or Super NOW rates, it may be to your advantage to maintain a conventional checking account while investing the excess funds in one of the alternative outlets. Of course, in reaching this decision, other factors have to be considered as well—like the inconvenience of maintaining a "side" account along with a regular checking account, and the fact that you do not earn interest while your funds are in transit from one account to the other.

Money market deposit accounts

Money market deposit accounts (MMDAs) were introduced in December 1982 and were extremely popular with depositors almost at once. They were created as a way to give banks and thrift institutions a vehicle to compete with money market mutual funds (discussed below). Banks and thrifts were losing large sums in deposits to money funds, and they needed something to fight back with. That the MMDAs were successful is evident in the fact that within eight weeks of their introduction, a whopping $254 *billion* poured into these accounts, a good chunk of which came from money funds. As with Super NOWs, banks introduced MMDAs with great fanfare and temporarily high rates; a bank in Atlanta, for example, offered 20 percent interest on its MMDAs—but only for a very short period. MMDAs also have a minimum balance requirement of $2,500, but the deposit institutions are free to pay any interest rate they wish. Most banks have lowered their high introductory rates to levels that approximate those being offered by money market mutual funds. MMDAs are popular with savers and investors because they offer highly competitive short-term rates; the deposits (unlike those in money funds) are federally insured, and they are convenient.

Depositors have access to their MMDAs through checkwriting privileges or through automated teller machines; a total of six transfers (only three by checks) is allowed each month, after which a penalty is charged for excessive withdrawals. This feature reduces the flexibility of these accounts and makes them less attractive than Super NOWs. However, most banks offer higher rates on MMDAs, which enhances their appeal. And since most depositors apparently look upon MMDAs as a savings outlet, rather than as a convenience account, the limited access feature has not been a serious obstacle to investing in them.

Money market mutual funds

A *money market mutual fund* (MMMF) is simply a mutual fund that pools the capital of a great number of investors and uses it to invest exclusively in high-yielding, short-term securities, such as Treasury bills, corporate commercial paper, jumbo certificates of deposit issued by commercial banks, and the like. Since these securities are sold in denominations of $10,000 to $1 million (or more), they are outside the reach of most small investors, yet they very often offer the highest short-term yields. The MMMF makes these rates available to even small investors. MMMFs can be purchased (through brokers, investment dealers, and so on) with initial investments as low as $500 to $1,000 (although $1,000 to $5,000 is a more typical number). Just about every major brokerage firm has a money fund of its own, and there are another 150 or so that are unaffiliated with a specific brokerage house and are sold primarily as no-load funds (see Chapter 15).

The returns on money funds equal what fund managers are able to earn from their investment activity in various short-term securities; as such, the returns rise and fall with money market interest rates. As Figure 7.1 shows, these are *highly volatile rates* that cause investor yields to vary accordingly. The returns on MMMFs are closely followed in the financial media and, in fact, the current yields on over 100 of the largest funds are regularly reported in *The Wall Street Journal* and other major newspapers (see Figure 7.2). Note in this case that not only are yields reported, but so are average maturities. MMMFs provide convenient and easy access to funds through checkwriting privileges, though the checks often have to be written for a stipulated minimum amount (usually $500); the nice feature of this privilege is that you continue to earn interest while the check is being cleared through the banking system. In addition, the larger funds often allow investors to transfer money from their MMMF to other funds they manage.

We describe mutual funds more thoroughly in Chapter 15, which is devoted exclusively to such securities; but several characteristics of money funds should be noted here. One concern of many investors revolves around the question of safety. Since they are not federally insured, one could argue that MMMFs will always be less secure than deposits in federally insured institutions; banks underscored this theme when they introduced their Super NOWs and MMDAs. But the fact is that the history of MMMFs has been virtually free of even the threat of failure. Default risk is almost zero, since the securities the funds purchase are very low in risk, and diversification by the funds lowers the risk even more. On several occasions, however, there have been problems in meeting shareholder redemptions, but in each instance the prob-

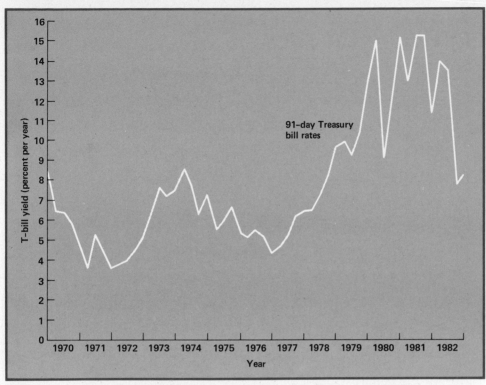

Figure 7.1 The Behavior of Short-Term Market Rates over Time.
The yields on marketable short-term securities (like those on Treasury bills) are highly unstable and as such, have a dramatic effect on returns to investors in money funds and other short-term vehicles (like MMDAs).

lem arose because the fund had invested in securities with relatively long maturities and there was an unexpected increase in the redemption rate. To avoid future situations of this sort, all funds now use a 60-day maturity provision; one of the problem funds mentioned above had a 300-day maturity. Despite this remarkable record of safety, it is impossible to say with certainty that MMMFs are as risk-free as federally insured deposits—and in the event of a massive financial crisis, they probably are not. On the other hand, the amount of extra risk might be viewed as so small that it is easily offset by a slightly higher yield. This is a choice individual investors must make within their own risk-return frameworks.

Actually, there are several different kinds of money market mutual funds. In addition to the standard fund, there are tax-exempt money funds and government securities money funds. The *tax-exempt money fund* limits its investments to tax-exempt municipal securities with very short (30 to 90 days) maturities. Except for this feature, they are like the standard money market funds; they are highly liquid, they offer checkwriting privileges, and so on. Since their income is free from federal (and some state) income tax, they yield less than standard, fully taxable money funds.

Money funds

NEW YORK (AP) — The following quotations, collected by the NASD Inc., are the average of annualized yields and dollar-weighted portfolio maturities for the seven-day period ended Monday, June 27. Yield based upon actual dividends paid (total return) to shareholders.

YHi	YLw	Name	Avg Mat	Avg Yld	Chg
7.22	6.67	AAA US	29	7.25	+ .03
7.99	7.68	AARPUS	36	7.99	
7.86	7.24	ActAsGvt	42	7.62	+ .03
8.14	3.93	ActAsMny	45	8.14	+ .03
8.26	8.00	AlexBrwn	28	8.29	+ .03
8.76	8.00	ABrwnGvt	31	8.22	− .02
7.94	7.64	AlliaCpRs f	49	7.96	+ .03
8.69	7.39	AlliaGvRs f	36	7.68	− .05
8.26	7.71	AmGnMM a	19	8.29	+ .03
8.67	7.41	AmGnRsv a	16	8.12	+ .11
8.52	8.07	AmNatl	77	8.24	
8.18	7.97	Babson	31	8.23	+ .05
8.78	7.81	BirrWil	22	8.44	− .10
8.75	8.04	BostonCo	28	1.31	− 6.96
8.43	7.62	BullBDir	18	7.71	
9.38	6.38	CMA Gvt a	42	7.53	− .19
10.08	6.64	CMA Mny a	43	7.42	− .27
NA	NA	CMA Tax		NA	
8.74	8.01	CalvPrm	20	8.30	+ .01
8.07	7.56	CalvUS	44	7.78	
9.11	8.28	CalvSoc af	21	8.51	+ .02
6.20	5.72	CalvTerm	602	6.18	
8.24	4.03	CalvMMkt	85	4.84	− .01
8.40	7.97	CapCash	19	8.50	+ .10
7.64	7.38	CapPresrv	28	7.67	+. 03
8.23	7.52	CapPresv II	3	8.19	+ .03
8.48	7.93	CardinGvt	19	8.51	+ .03
8.15	7.78	Carnegie	15	8.16	+ .01
8.38	8.27	CashEqM	31	8.40	+ .05
8.23	7.96	CashEqGv	41	8.26	+ .03
8.77	8.00	CshMgtA a	22	8.42	− .20
8.60	8.23	CashRsM a	34	8.56	− .01
8.01	7.67	Centen	28	8.08	+ .12
4.59	4.26	CentenTx	90	4.52	+ .01
8.06	7.65	Colonial	30	7.98	+ .05
7.92	7.75	ColDin af	30	7.87	
8.09	7.90	Comand a	32	8.12	+ .03
8.07	7.33	CmpCs af	26	8.13	+ .06
7.86	7.36	CAM Fd	19	7.68	− .03
7.98	7.75	CurrentIntr	33	7.96	+ .03
7.87	7.54	CurntIUS	41	7.91	+ .04
8.36	8.07	DBL Port	49	8.37	+ .03
8.21	7.67	DBL Gvt	44	8.04	− .02
8.08	7.88	DailCsh 1	25	8.13	+ .05
8.29	7.13	DailCshGvt	1	8.22	− .06
4.59	4.29	DlyCshTx c	109	4.49	− .01
8.20	7.92	DailyInco	32	8.01	− .19
7.83	7.73	DailPasprt f	32	7.83	+ .01
9.87	4.79	DailTx c	50	4.81	
8.13	7.93	DWitrLqd	42	8.14	+ .02
8.17	7.34	DWitrUS	41	7.70	+ .08
8.20	7.91	DelaCR f	40	8.24	+ .04
4.82	4.54	DelaTax	96	4.81	+ .04
7.84	7.58	DelaTr	28	7.94	+ .10
8.43	8.18	DryInst	71	8.43	
8.30	8.13	DryfLA	56	8.29	− .01
8.20	8.10	DryGvt	71	8.19	+ .01
8.24	8.03	DryinG	73	8.20	− .01
8.40	8.02	DryMM	64	8.41	+ .01
4.79	4.61	DreyTxEx c	80	4.67	
7.93	7.68	EGT f	30	7.94	+ .01
8.12	7.84	EalVCsh		NA	
7.84	7.54	MonMinst	32	7.77	+ .04
7.93	7.71	MonMMgt f	31	7.94	+ .01
8.38	8.12	MonMk Trst	29	8.41	+ .03
8.38	8.23	MonMtA	25	8.39	+ .01
7.63	7.37	MorganK f	18	7.65	+ .02
8.05	4.69	MunCshR c	84	5.06	+ .02
4.59	4.42	MuniTinv c	59	4.60	+ .01
8.22	7.49	MultiOmah	34	7.92	+ .07
7.91	7.41	MtlOmahC	32	7.67	+ .02
8.21	8.02	NEL Csh b	35	7.83	− .19
7.96	7.66	NEL USGvt	47	7.98	+ .02
8.12	7.94	NatlCash	41	8.14	+ .02
8.25	8.09	NatLiqRes	34	8.16	
7.38	7.11	NatnUS	39	7.43	+ .06
5.23	4.81	NuveenTx c	41	4.86	+ .01
5.58	4.54	NuvenTFr	67	4.54	
8.05	7.43	Offerman	24	7.92	+ .04
8.36	8.00	OppMoney	24	8.43	+ .11
8.25	7.95	Oxfrd	16	8.25	
8.29	8.05	PaineWCs f	31	8.34	+ .05
8.05	7.57	ParkCsh	28	8.09	+ .07
8.20	7.72	Phonix	26	8.18	− .02
7.90	7.70	Plimoney	29	7.93	+ .03
8.41	7.94	PrimeCsh	22	8.40	− .01
8.20	7.55	PrudBGvt	39	8.20	
4.53	4.27	PrudBchTx	94	4.52	− .01
8.09	7.75	PutDDiv a	28	8.09	+ .03
9.16	8.14	RsveCsh	1	9.04	− .01
8.19	7.44	ReserveFd	29	8.22	+ .03
8.10	7.60	ResrveFd Gvt	1	8.15	+ .05
8.23	8.02	Rothscd	31	8.12	
8.31	8.04	RowePrice f	43	8.31	
5.02	4.86	RowePr cf		NA	
7.71	7.30	RowePr f	22	7.70	− .01
8.40	8.03	Safeco f	21	8.48	+ .08
8.00	7.54	StPaulMFd	21	8.48	+ .55
8.07	7.11	ScudCshin	34	7.84	
7.96	7.45	ScudGovt	34	7.86	+ .02
4.44	4.04	ScudTxF cf	89	4.31	+ .01
7.87	7.44	SelectedMM	27	7.89	+ .02
8.25	7.41	SecurityCsh	12	8.34	+ .09
7.92	7.57	SeligCsh pr	27	7.92	
7.86	7.72	SentCsh b	37	7.89	+ .03
7.94	7.64	Sentry	28	7.93	+ .08
8.24	8.05	ShearDDv f	40	8.21	− .02
8.10	7.89	ShrFMACsh	36	8.04	− .01
8.02	7.64	ShrFMAGvt	33	8.06	+ .04
4.40	4.13	ShrFMAMu	58	4.34	− .04
8.19	7.85	ShearsonGv	41	8.19	
8.17	7.89	ShrtTrmInc	32	7.89	+ .01
7.86	7.37	ShrtTrY a	11	7.73	+ .01
8.89	6.11	Sigma	9	8.15	+ .10
8.04	7.27	SouFarm	22	7.99	+ .02
8.24	8.03	Standby	31	8.21	− .02
8.20	7.84	SteinroeCRs	27	8.19	+ .07
7.93	7.68	Sutro f	29	7.93	
7.55	4.39	TxExmp c	99	4.46	− .07
4.58	4.36	TxFreeM c	68	4.52	− .01
8.62	8.33	TemporInv	41	8.68	+ .06
8.57	8.20	TransamCs	34	8.61	+ .04
8.48	8.14	Trinity	18	8.49	+ .01
8.32	7.53	TrustCshR f	33	7.75	+ .01
8.40	8.02	TrstfdTr	38	8.44	+ .04
8.27	8.08	TrstfdUS	28	8.30	+ .03
8.37	8.20	TrstfdPrme	30	8.38	+ .01
8.50	8.23	TrstfdCmcl	26	8.50	
8.49	8.21	TrustShTrm	36	8.52	+ .03
8.49	8.13	TrstShrtFdl	35	8.50	+ .01
8.71	8.00	TrstShtGv	41	8.34	+ .02
8.26	7.92	TrstUSTrOb	36	8.29	+ .03

Figure 7.2 Published Yield Information on Major Money Market Mutual Funds.

Data on money funds is widely quoted in the financial press; here we see that the information includes the high and low yields for the year, the portfolio's average maturity (in days), a seven-day average of the yield currently available, and the change in that yield. (*Source: Phoenix Gazette,* June 28, 1983.)

TABLE 7.4 CERTIFICATES OF DEPOSIT (CDs): POPULAR TYPES AND KEY CHARACTERISTICS

Characteristic	Money Market Certificate	Small Saver Certificate	Wild Card Certificate	91-Day Certificate	7–31 Day Certificate	Jumbo Certificate
Term*	6 mo.	30 mo.	3½ yr or longer	91 days	7–31 days	14 days to 1 yr
Minimum investment*	$2,500	$500	$500	$2,500	$2,500	$100,000
Maximum yield	None	None	None	None	None	None
Rate of compounding	Simple interest	Can be compounded	Can be compounded	Simple interest	Can be compounded	Simple interest
Penalty for early withdrawal	Loss of 1 mo. interest	Loss of 3 mo. interest	Loss of 3 mo. interest	Loss of 1 mo. earned	Loss of all interest but not less than the interest for half original period	All interest for CDs under 3 mo.; minimum 3 mo. on longer maturities

*These are the most common terms and minimum investment amounts; technically, banks and S&Ls are free to offer *any* maturity and to accept *any* deposit they wish on these CDs.

They appeal predominantly to investors in the high tax brackets, for whom the lower tax-free yield is better than the *after-tax* return they could earn on standard money funds. *Government securities money funds* were established as a way to meet investor concerns for safety. In essence, these funds effectively eliminate any risk of default by confining their investments to Treasury bills and other short-term securities of the U.S. government or its agencies (like the Federal National Mortgage Association). They are like standard MMMFs in all other respects, except for the slightly lower yields they offer (which is the price you pay for the higher quality). As one might suspect, the closest competitor today for the MMMF (in terms of yield and liquidity) is the money market deposit account offered by banks and other financial institutions.

Certificates of deposit

Certificates of deposit (CDs) differ from the savings instruments discussed above in that funds must remain on deposit for a specified period of time, which can range from seven days to a year or more. Although it is possible to withdraw funds prior to maturity, an interest penalty (of 31–90 days of interest, depending upon the original maturity of the CD) usually makes withdrawal somewhat costly. In the fall of 1983, all maturity and yield restrictions on these securities were removed, and as such the banks and S&Ls today are free to offer any rate and maturity they wish. Some institutions will even let you specify the maturity date (for example, on a birthday or anniversary). A wide variety of CDs is offered by most banks and thrift institutions, and they go by an equally wide variety of names. Table 7.4 highlights characteristics of some of the more popular CDs available in late 1983 and indicates the assortment of choices available to investors. CDs are convenient to buy and hold, and all offer attractive and highly competitive returns, plus federal insurance protection. The critical factor in deciding whether to invest in one of these, or in, say, MMDAs or MMMFs, is the willingness to tie up funds for a certain time period. If you think interest rates will be falling and that the return on your MMDA or MMMF might go much below what is now available on CDs, you should choose CDs; if you believe interest rates will rise, the MMDA or MMMF may be the better choice.

Repurchase agreements

An innovative and high-yielding investment being offered by some financial institutions is the *repurchase agreement,* usually called a *repo.* With a repo, you buy a share in a portfolio of government securities from a bank or S&L *and,* at the time of purchase, receive a commitment from the financial institution that it agrees to buy back your share *at a specified price* at the end of a specified period of time. In effect, you loan money to the bank and have your loan collateralized by the government securities. Two things must be understood: First, you do not buy the government securities, so the interest you earn is not what they yield, but rather what the bank agrees to pay on your loan. Second, your investment is not federally insured, nor is it clear that you have an uncontestable legal claim against the government securities serving as collateral. Thus, your investment is only as safe as the bank selling the repos. The minimum investment in a repo is set by the bank and varies, usually from $1,000 to $10,000. Since the bank is free to set any interest rate it chooses, these have ranged from about ½ to as much as 2 percentage points above the underlying T-bill rate. Repo maturities vary from a few days to many weeks, but most tend to have repurchase dates of around 84 days (or 12 weeks). In contrast to CDs, there is no early redemption penalty on the repo, although the bank charges a transaction fee, usually between $10 and $25.

U.S. Treasury bills

Prior to the many changes that have taken place in the financial markets in recent years, *U.S. Treasury bills* were the key short-term investment for most people who had sufficient funds to meet their rather high minimum investment requirement. T-bills are obligations of the U.S. Treasury, issued as part of its ongoing process of funding the national debt. T-bills are sold on a discount basis in minimum denominations of $10,000, with $5,000 increments above that. Treasury bills are issued with 3-month (13-week), 6-month (26-week), and 1-year maturities. The 3- and 6-month bills are auctioned off every Monday, and there is an auction for 1-year bills roughly every four weeks. An individual investor may purchase T-bills directly (through participation in the weekly Treasury auctions) or indirectly through local commercial banks or security dealers who buy bills for investors on a commission basis. Outstanding Treasury bills can also be purchased in the secondary market through banks or brokers—the biggest advantage of this approach is that the investor has a much wider selection of maturities to choose from, ranging from less than a week to as long as a year. It is actually relatively simple to buy T-bills directly. All one need do is submit a tender to the nearest Federal Reserve Bank, or branch, specifying both the amount and maturity desired (tender forms are short and are available from commercial banks). The Treasury tries to accommodate individual investors through its noncompetitive bidding system, which most individual investors use because of its simplicity. In essence, all noncompetitive tender offers are awarded T-bills at a price equal to the average of all the accepted competitive bids. Thus, the investor is assured of buying bills in the quantity desired, while obtaining the benefits of an open auction system—all without going through the hassle of a competitive bid.

Treasury bills are quoted daily in *The Wall Street Journal* and other major financial media. A particularly attractive feature of T-bills is that they are exempt from state and local income taxes, which in some areas can be as high as 20 percent. Because they are issued by the U.S. Treasury, T-bills are regarded as the safest of all investments, even safer than federally insured deposits, since their insurers are not actually the Treasury, but separate federal agencies. In the event of a financial collapse, it is questionable if the resources of the FDIC, FSLIC, and NCUA would be sufficient to cover the deposits of failing institutions unless they received support from Congress and the Treasury. There is a highly active secondary market for Treasury bills, so they can easily be sold if the investor needs the cash.

Universal and sweep accounts

A *universal account*—such as Merrill Lynch's cash management account, or CMA—or a *sweep account*, offered by many financial institutions, are not separate investment vehicles, but rather comprehensive accounts that service a wide range of checking, investing, and borrowing activities. Their distinguishing feature is that they automatically place ("sweep") excess funds into short-term investments. For example, a bank sweep account might be set up to combine a Super NOW and a repo. At the end of each day, if the balance exceeds $2,500, the excess is automatically swept into the higher-yielding repo. Merrill Lynch's CMA automatically sweeps the accountholder's funds into its MMMF, and if securities are purchased for an amount greater than the current balance, the needed funds are automatically supplied through a margin loan. Along with one-stop financial supermarkets, universal and sweep accounts are exceptionally popular with investors. However, they do have minimum balance requirements—the CMA, for example, requires an initial balance of $20,000 in cash or securities—that limit their availability.

Series EE savings bonds

Series EE bonds are the well-known savings bonds that have been around for decades—they were first issued in 1941 and used to be called Series E bonds. They are often purchased through payroll deduction plans. Though issued by the U.S. Treasury, they are quite different from T-bills; in fact, perhaps their only similarity is that they are sold on a discount basis and are also free of state and local income taxes. These bonds are *accrual-type securities*, which means that interest is paid when the bond is cashed, on or before maturity, rather than periodically over the life of the bond. (The government does make Series HH bonds available to those who want savings bonds that pay interest regularly. HH bonds are sold in denominations

BOX 7.1 YOU, TOO, CAN BUY TREASURY BILLS

In periods of uncertain times for investors, the ultimate safe haven for funds earmarked for future purchase of stocks or bonds is the U.S. Treasury bill, or T-bill. These short-term securities, maturing in 3, 6 or 12 months, are backed by the full faith and credit of the government. They pay an attractive yield that is not subject to state and local taxes. And they are almost as liquid as cash, since they may be sold at any time without interest penalty. But should you sell before maturity, you may lose money if interest rates have risen, and you'll have to pay a broker's fee.

If you have $10,000 or more to invest and learn the buying procedures, you can purchase T-bills yourself and keep rolling them over without paying any commission or redemption fee. Or your bank or broker will buy them for you for fees of $20 to $50.

T-bills are unique in that they do not pay interest after the lender has had the use of your money, as do certificates of deposit, savings accounts or most bonds. Instead, the T-bill gives you your yield shortly after you buy it. This comes about because you buy the bills at a discount from face value. For example, you send the Treasury $10,000, which is the minimum, to buy a bill at auction. At the recent [1981] interest-rate level, the actual cost of a 91-day, or three-month, bill would be around $9,640. Thus you would shortly receive a check for $360. At the end of 91 days, you would either receive the full $10,000, or you could roll it over into a new bill and again get a discount. Since you receive the discount well in advance of the maturity of the bill, the true yield on an annual basis works out to be higher than the discount. The difference could be a percentage point or more.

There are several ways to buy Treasury bills. You may buy them in person at any Federal Reserve Bank or branch. Or you can buy by mail by obtaining a form from a Federal Reserve Bank or branch or by writing the Bureau of the Public Debt, Securities Transaction Branch, Main Treasury Building, Room 2134, Washington, D.C. 20226.

The form requires only name, address, Social Security number, signature, whether

of $500 to $10,000; but unlike EE bonds, they are sold at their full face value and pay interest, at the current fixed rate of 7½ percent, semiannually. Series HH bonds are far less popular than the EEs, although as we will see, they do offer nice tax shelter features when used in conjunction with maturing EE bonds.) Series EE bonds are backed by the full faith and credit of the U.S. government, and can be replaced without charge in case of loss, theft, or destruction. They can be purchased at banks or other thrift institutions, or through payroll deduction plans. They are issued in denominations of $50 through $10,000, with the purchase price of all denominations being 50 percent of the face amount (thus, a $100 bond will cost $50 and be worth $100 at maturity).

The actual maturity date on EE bonds is unspecified, since the issues pay a variable rate of interest. The higher the rate of interest being earned, the shorter the period of time it takes for the bond to accrue from its discounted purchase price to its maturity value. In an effort to make these securities more attractive to investors, all EE bonds held five years or longer receive interest at 85 percent of the average return on five-year Treasury securities, as calculated every six months. The yield, therefore, changes every six months in accordance with prevailing Treasury note

---

BOX 7.1 *Continued*

---

you are submitting a competitive or noncompetitive bid and whether you want to reinvest at maturity at whatever rate then prevails. Automatic reinvestment can be done only once. But when you receive your money back at a bill's maturity, you will again receive a form to buy a new bill if you wish. Generally speaking, purchasers in amounts under 1 million dollars buy on a noncompetitive basis. This means the buyer will receive a price, or discount, equal to the average bid of all the big-money bidders.

To buy a $10,000 bill, you need to send with the form a bank cashier's check or a certified personal check. Above $10,000, you buy in $5,000 increments. What you get as evidence of ownership is a receipt. Engraved certificates are no longer given, which is an advantage since they could be stolen or counterfeited.

Three and six-month T-bills are sold by the Treasury at weekly auctions, generally on Mondays. If you buy by mail, the envelope containing the form and check must be postmarked no later than midnight of the day preceding the auction. If it is late, it will automatically be held until the next week's auction unless you cancel. If you buy in person, you must hand in the form and money not later than 1:30 p.m. of the day of the auction.

The yield on Treasury bills is subject only to federal income tax—as ordinary income—and the tax is payable in the year the bill matures, not necessarily the year in which you receive the income or discount.

Whether to buy the short or relatively long-term bills depends on individual situations and a guess as to the future course of interest rates. In a period of declining rates, it would be prudent to nail down current yields by buying the longer-term bills. In fact, every four weeks the Treasury sells 52-week bills in the same manner as the others. But in periods of uncertainty, many investors prudently stick to the short-term bills.

Source: John W. Hazard, "You, Too, Can Buy Treasury Bills." *U.S. News & World Report,* September 28, 1981, p. 79.

---

yields, though it can never drop below a minimum guaranteed rate of 7½ percent. EEs held for less than five years (they can be redeemed any time after the first six months) earn interest at a fixed graduated scale that increases with the length of time the bonds are held.

In addition to being exempt from state and local taxes, Series EE bonds provide their holders with an appealing tax twist: That is, investors need not report interest earned on federal tax returns until the bonds are redeemed. Although interest can be reported annually (this might be done, for example, if the bonds are held in the name of a child who has no other reportable income), most investors choose to defer it. In effect, this means the funds are being reinvested at an after-tax rate of no less than the guaranteed minimum of 7½ percent. What's more, it is even possible to defer the tax shelter *beyond* the redemption date of your Series EE bond. For you can extend your tax shelter if, instead of cashing in the bonds, you exchange them for Series HH bonds. The accumulated interest on the Series EE bonds remains free of federal income tax for a while longer, since you will not have to pay the tax on those interest earnings until the HH bonds reach maturity, or you cash *them* in. Thus, in contrast to their predecessors, not only do today's Series EE bonds represent a safe and secure form of investment, but they also provide highly competitive yields and offer attractive tax incentives.

Investment Suitability

The accounts and securities discussed above are widely used by individuals as both savings and investment vehicles. They are used to build up or maintain a desired level of *savings* to meet unforeseen emergencies (like the loss of a job or serious injury to a family member) and/or for major expenditures that will or are likely to occur in the future (such as furnishing a new home or meeting the expenses of a child's education); some people may also use their savings to take advantage of the unexpected opportunities that sometimes materialize. Whatever the reason, savings are viewed chiefly as a way to accumulate funds that will be readily available when and if the need arises—in essence, to provide the family with a safety net or cushion. In this case yield or return is less important than safety, liquidity, and convenience. Passbook savings accounts and Series EE savings bonds are popular savings vehicles and, to a lesser extent, so are money market deposit accounts, money funds, and some CDs (like money market certificates of deposit or small saver certificates).

When used for *investment* purposes, yield is often just as important as these vehicles' liquidity characteristics. Because the objective is different, the securities tend to be used much more aggressively than in savings programs. Most investors will hold at least a part of their portfolio in short-term, highly liquid securities, if for no other reason than to be able to act on unanticipated investment opportunities. Some investors, in fact, may as a matter of practice devote all or most of their portfolios to such securities in the belief that these investments provide attractive risk-adjusted rates of return, because they are unfamiliar with other investment vehicles, or simply because they do not wish to devote the time necessary to managing their portfolios. One of the most common uses of short-term securities as investment vehicles is to employ them as temporary investment outlets. This is done for two reasons: either until an attractive permanent investment can be found, or as a temporary holding place in times of unsettled or undesirable market conditions. For example, an investor who has just sold some stock from his portfolio and does not have a suitable long-term investment alternative might place the proceeds in a money fund until he finds a more permanent use for them. Or, an investor who feels that interest rates are about to rise sharply sells her long-term bonds and uses the proceeds to buy T-bills. The high-yielding securities—like money funds, MMDAs, T-bills, and CDs—are generally preferred for use as part of an investment program, as are the universal/sweep accounts at major brokerage houses.

Deciding which securities are most appropriate for a particular situation requires consideration of such issue characteristics as availability, safety, liquidity, and yield. Although all the investments satisfy the basic liquidity demand, they do so to varying degrees. A NOW or Super NOW account is unquestionably the most liquid of all, since you can write as many checks as you wish and for any amount. A certificate of deposit, on the other hand, is not as liquid, since early redemption involves an interest penalty. Table 7.5 summarizes the key characteristics for most of the short-term investments discussed here. The letter grade assigned the invest-

TABLE 7.5 A SCORECARD FOR SHORT-TERM ACCOUNTS AND SECURITIES

Savings or Investment Vehicle	Availability	Safety	Liquidity	Yield (Average Rate)*
Passbook savings account	A+	A+	A	D (5.5%)
NOW account	A+	A+	A+	D (5.25%)
Super NOW account	B	A+	A+	B− (8.0%)
Money market deposit account (MMDA)	B	A+	A−	B (8.8%)
Money market mutual fund (MMMF): Standard and government security funds	B	A/A+	B+	B− (7.9%)
Certificate of deposit: 6-month money market certificate	B	A+	C	A (9.4%)
Repurchase agreement	B−	B−	B	A (9.5%)
91-day U.S. Treasury bill	B−	A++	A−	A− (9.1%)
U.S. Series EE bond	A+	A++	C−	B (8.6%)

*The average rates reflect representative or typical rates that existed at midyear 1983.

ments for each characteristic reflects an estimate of the investment's quality in that area. For example, MMMFs received only a B+ on liquidity, since withdrawals usually require a minimum of $500; MMDAs, on the other hand, are judged somewhat better in this respect, since a withdrawal can be for any amount and is also available through automated teller machines. Yields are in the main self-explanatory, although you should note that as an investment scores lower on availability, safety, or liquidity, it will generally offer a higher yield.

MEETING RETIREMENT NEEDS: PLANNING FOR THE LONG HAUL

When we are young, retirement is often viewed as far away; it is a bit difficult to get excited about an event that may not take place for another 40 or 45 years. In some respects this is unfortunate, because the sooner one plans for retirement, the better the chances are that he or she will be able to put together a successful program. This is so for several reasons. First, retirement requires careful planning, both in terms of having the financial resources to sustain us when we no longer produce income, and also with respect to determining what our needs will be during the retirement years. Second, the sooner you invest to accumulate a retirement nest egg, the more productive your funds will be. This is a simple matter of the power of compound interest, or of how money grows over time. For example, if you invest $1,000 today for, say, 30 years, you will amass $17,449, assuming you can achieve a 10 percent rate of return during the entire 30-year period. But if you can invest the same $1,000 for 10 years longer, your investment would grow to a whopping $45,258—over 2.5 times more! (As described in Chapter 4, to find the future value of an investment, simply find the appropriate interest factor, CVIF, from Table B.1 and multiply it by the amount invested. In the examples above, we see in Table B.1 that the compound interest factor for a 10 percent, 30-year investment is 17.449; thus, the future value of $1,000 invested for 30 years at 10 percent would be: 17.449 × $1,000 = $17,449. Likewise, for the 40-year, 10 percent investment: 45.258 × $1,000 = $45,258.) Of course, you may not realize a 10 percent rate of return over the full life of the investment; and even if you do, inflation will probably account for a good part of it. Nevertheless, the crucial point is that the sooner you invest for retirement, the *progressively* greater amount you will accumulate, regardless of the reinvestment rate.

After you draw up your retirement plans, you need to consider how much you can logically expect from the principal sources of retirement income—social security and employer-sponsored programs. If these fall short of your income requirements, you will have to supplement them with your own self-directed program. In addition to developing such a self-directed program, you will need to determine how it will be funded. These are all topics we consider now.

Retirement Planning

Planning begins by considering retirement as one part of your overall investment program. Then you must consider your needs, usually by viewing them within your entire life cycle of needs. Finally, you must determine whether your retirement income will match your retirement needs.

Role in an investment program

As we have noted throughout this text, investment activity is usually best undertaken to accomplish specific goals. In the first part of this chapter, we examined investments appropriate for meeting the goal of liquidity. This same matching of investments to objectives is necessary for retirement planning. This is true even if the investing is done for you; that is, if most of your retirement income (other than social security) will be derived from an employer-sponsored program. To illustrate this point, consider the diagram in Figure 7.3. Here, total investment needs are divided into three areas—liquidity, retirement, and other needs, each of which is represented by an equal slice of the circle (remember this is just an illustration; we are not suggesting these needs are equal). Now, suppose you believe that a portion of your retirement assets should be in common stock, say, the amount designated A; if your employer-sponsored program does not provide for common stock investments, the only way you can meet your goal is to do it yourself, by investing amount A in stocks. On the other hand, if your employer-sponsored program is heavily invested in stocks, you may want to put less of your own retirement portfolio in stocks and more in other securities, like bonds or other fixed income securities. The important point is that meeting retirement needs should be an integral part of every investment program, and the assets or investments held for retirement purposes should be just as actively managed as all other parts of the portfolio. The ultimate target is to derive a final portfolio that meets all of one's needs within a level of risk considered appropriate for the expected return.

BOX 7.2 EARLY PLANNING FOR RETIREMENT

It was midmorning coffee time at the neighborhood restaurant, and talk among the half-dozen businessmen at the table turned to plans for retirement.

One man in his early 60s, just back from the golf course, commented: "I took early retirement three years ago. Thought I could live comfortably on my pension, some investments and Social Security. But if I'd known how hard inflation was going to hit, I'd have stayed on the job a while longer. And I'd certainly have tried to set aside more in savings."

While circumstances vary widely, the golfer's words sound a warning for everyone who hopes to maintain even a modest standard of living when working days are over. No longer is it possible to wait until a year or two before retirement to chart a financial course. Planning is more important than ever, and constantly rising prices must enter into every calculation. . . .

Guidelines offered by financial authorities can help families who are planning for retirement in an inflationary environment:

1. Be realistic in calculating future living costs. Some expenses will go down: The tab for business lunches, new clothes, commuting, and probably housing costs, if a home mortgage is paid off. But there will be more time for travel and leisure pursuits. A budget should include sums for such spending, and probably for increased health-care and medical bills.

2. Don't count on Social Security alone to provide enough income for a comfortable lifestyle. Other resources will be needed. Social Security, as one economist notes, "was intended to keep people from living in abject poverty. It was never intended to be more than a supplement to personal savings."

3. Try to accumulate as substantial an investment fund as possible between now and retirement, even if that means doing without some luxuries it would be nice to enjoy today. The reason: Unearned income does not reduce Social Security benefits in the same way as earnings from wages or salary.

4. To help build up a retirement nest egg, try to shelter from taxes as much current income as possible. A home, rental property, U.S. savings bonds, municipal bonds and mutual funds that are invested in tax-exempt securities all offer tax-shelter possibilities. If you aren't covered by a corporate pension plan, consider setting up an individual retirement account or, if you're self-employed, a Keogh Plan.

5. Don't be afraid to draw on capital if your retirement income is skimpy. An old Yankee precept holds that it's a sin to dip into principal, but there are ways to do just that if careful plans are set up, taking life expectancy into account. One way is to invest in a mutual fund that offers a cash-withdrawal program. Such a fund will pay the investor a regular sum every month, drawing partly on invested assets and partly on the earnings from those assets.

6. Diversify your retirement investments. If you own substantial amounts of growth-type common stock, you may want to move some of that money into securities that offer a higher and more dependable yield. But remember that the fixed return on bonds is also a drawback, because there's no protection against loss of purchasing power of the interest. Stocks that have increased earnings and dividends steadily in past years can help offset, to some degree at least, the toll of inflation in years ahead.

Source: Ellis Haller, "Early Planning for Retirement." *U.S. News & World Report,* October 22, 1979, p. 102.

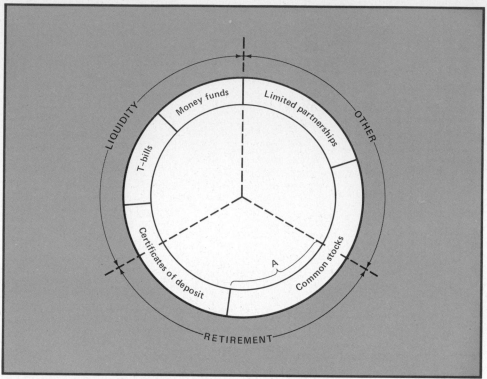

Figure 7.3 Retirement Planning within an Overall Investment Program.
There are many parts to an investment portfolio, and meeting retirement needs is certainly
one of them; in fact, the securities held for retirement should be viewed as an integral part of
the total portfolio, and actively managed as such.

Life cycle of needs

Our needs change in tune with the changing seasons of our lives. In youth, we
are concerned with family formation and career planning. Although income and
assets are hardly in bountiful supply, still, if we have no dependents and few responsibilities, we are in a better position to invest in high-risk securities than when we
approach retirement. As we approach retirement, our concern logically shifts to
investments that are exceptionally low in risk and high in current dividend or interest
return. Along with a changing risk-return investment profile over time, our living
needs also change as we age. If you purchase a home when you are young, you
probably will have paid off your mortgage by retirement. So your housing costs are
usually lower, as are many other expenses, such as education and those for household appliances and furniture. But other expenses might increase. Many elderly people begin to travel, or they pursue a favorite—and maybe expensive—hobby now
that they have the time available for it. Obviously, the importance of budgeting does
not diminish in retirement. What you must do prior to actual retirement is estimate
what you believe your expenditure needs will be. This is a difficult task, particularly
if retirement is many years away. Not only is it hard to know what activities will be

TABLE 7.6   A RETIREMENT PLAN FOR BOB AND SHIRLEY MASON

	Current Dollars	Inflation Factor	Future Needs
ESTIMATED EXPENDITURES			
Housing and utilities	$ 5,600		
Food—at home and dining out	6,000		
Transportation	2,200		
Travel and entertainment	5,200		
Medical	2,000		
All other	7,000		
Total expenditures	$28,000 ×	4.322* =	$121,016
ESTIMATED INCOME			
Social security	$12,000 ×	4.322* =	$ 51,864
Employer retirement plan	7,000 ×	5.743** =	40,201
Subtotal	$19,000		$ 92,065
Additional required income	9,000		28,951
Total income	$28,000		$121,016
ASSET REQUIREMENT			
Anticipated return on assets held during retirement			0.10
Assets required ($28,951/.10)			$289,510

*Inflation rate (or growth rate) of 5% per year, CVIF, for 5% and 30 years, from Table B.1.
**Growth rate of 6% per year, CVIF, for 6% and 30 years, from Table B.1.

important then, but the prospect of estimating their cost in an environment of changing inflation rates is an even more challenging task. But it must be done.

Determining future needs and income

To illustrate the process of coordinating future needs and income, let us consider the Bob and Shirley Mason family. The Masons are in their mid-thirties. They have two children and an annual income of about $45,000 before taxes. They have given little thought to retirement, but now believe that even though it is still some 30 years away, they should review their situation to see if they will be able to pursue a life-style in retirement that appeals to them. Table 7.6 shows how the Masons have estimated their retirement income and how they must accumulate investment assets of roughly $289,510 to meet their retirement objectives. Let's see how they did this.

Bob and Shirley began their calculations by determining their expenditures on the assumption that retirement would take place *immediately;* this allowed them to think in terms of today's dollar. They determined that it would take $28,000 a year to attain their retirement life-style. The next step was to see how much their retirement income would be, given retirement today. The Masons believe social security will provide $12,000, and Bob's retirement plan would add another $7,000; unfortunately, the total of $19,000 was $9,000 short of their estimated expenditures. But this short-fall is in today's dollars and not in the dollars that will exist when retirement will actually take place. The Masons face the difficult task of estimating future values. Bob and Shirley believe that inflation will average 5 percent over the next 30 years (when their retirement will begin). This means the $28,000 of expenditures will grow to $121,016; this number is calculated by referring to Appendix B, Table B.1, and finding the CVIF for 5 percent and 30 years. It is 4.322; multiplying the $28,000 by this number equals $121,016. Bob and Shirley also believe that social security in-creases will match the inflation rate, and based on past performance, they think the retirement plan should do a little better and grow by 6 percent (this CVIF is 5.743). Given these assumptions about future income growth, the Masons should have a total annual income of some $92,000, which means their annual shortfall in future dollars is $28,951.

The next step is to estimate the rate of return the Masons think they will be able to earn on their investments *after* they retire. This will tell them how big their nest egg will have to be *by retirement* in order to eliminate the expected annual shortfall of $28,951. Let's assume this return is estimated to be 10 percent, in which case the Masons must accumulate $289,510 by retirement. That figure is found by capitalizing the estimated shortfall of $28,951 at a 10 percent rate of return: $28,951/.10 = $289,510. Such a nest egg will yield $28,951 a year, given that a 10 percent rate of return can be earned ($289,510 × .10 = $28,951). And so long as the capital ($289,510) remains untouched, it will generate the same annual amount for as long as the Masons live and can eventually become a part of their estate.

Now that they know how big their nest egg has to be, the final question is how are they going to accumulate such an amount by the time they retire? For most people, that means setting up a *systematic savings plan* that involves putting away a certain amount *each* year. To find out how much must be saved each year to achieve a targeted sum in the future, we can use the compound interest factors for an annuity (CVIFA), from Table B.2 in the appendix. The appropriate CVIFA is a function of the rate of return one can (or expects to) generate and the length of the investment period. In the case of the Masons, they have 30 years to go to retirement, so the length of their investment period is 30 years; now if they feel they will be able to earn an average rate of return of 10 percent on their investments over this 30-year period, then they will want to use a 10 percent, 30-year CVIFA—from Table B.2, we see this equals 164.491. Given the Masons need to accumulate $289,510 by the time they retire, the amount that they will have to *save each year* can be found by *dividing* the amount they need to accumulate by the appropriate CVIFA; that is: $289,510/164.491 = $1760. This is the amount ($1760) that the Masons will have to put away each year, for the next 30 years, in order to accumulate $289,510 by retirement. But there's more. For our calculations also assume that the Masons will, in fact, be able to achieve a 10 percent rate of return on their investments! Failure to do so will mean they won't achieve their targeted nest egg—e.g., if they can earn only 8 percent on their investments, they will have only $199,376 by retirement (to find the future value of an annuity, simply multiply the annuity by the appropriate CVIFA: $1,760 × CVIFA for 8 percent, 30 years = $1,760 × 113.282 = $199,376). While it is true the Masons will have accumulated an investment pool of nearly

TABLE 7.7 **FINANCING THE MASONS'**
           FIRST THREE YEARS OF RETIREMENT

	YEARS		
	1	2	3
Expenditures*	$121,016	$127,067	$133,420
Income			
Social security*	$51,864	$ 54,457	$ 57,180
Employer retirement plan	40,201	40,201	40,201
Supplemental income	28,951	28,951	28,605
Total income	$121,016	$123,609	$125,986
Budget deficit	$ 0	$ 3,458	$ 7,434
Retirement assets at end of year	$289,510	$286,052	$278,618

*Assumes a rate of growth of 5% for years 2 and 3.

$200,000 (certainly not a paltry sum), the fact remains that they will be about $90,000 short of their target by retirement, and hence will either have to reduce their standard of living in retirement or start tapping their capital earlier than expected. Similar results will occur if they fail to put aside the needed amount each year—for example, if the best they can do is save $1,200 per year (but still achieve a 10 percent rate of return on their investments), the Masons' nest egg will grow to only $197,389 ($1,200 × 164.491).

Actually, we have simplified the Masons' retirement plan a bit, for there are other complications to consider. First, inflation will probably continue after their retirement. Although social security income will continue to grow at the annual rate of inflation, the benefits from Bob's retirement plan will not, and neither will the income from their investment assets. This means that each retirement year would require a drawing down of these assets to sustain their life-style. Table 7.7 illustrates this process for the first three years. The question now is how long these assets will last if they are constantly being depleted. Naturally, one cannot answer that unless an assumption is made about how long Bob and Shirley live beyond the onset of retirement. Planning retirement income, then, is no easy task. In the Masons' case, $289,510 probably should be sufficient for their retirement years, but their estate will decrease as time goes on. To provide a hedge against this type of uncertainty, the Masons might want to increase the size of their annual retirement contribution (to $2,000 or $2,500) to build up a bigger nest egg. A second simplification in the Mason example is that we have ignored the impact of federal income taxes. Under recent changes in the social security law (discussed below), a portion of their social security income may be taxable. Depending on how Bob's retirement plan is structured, a portion or all of their retirement income may also be taxable. And in all likelihood, all their investment income will be taxable. Holding everything else the same but adding in taxes means the additional required income would have to be greater than $9,000 a year, and the required retirement assets would need to be more than $289,510.

Retirement Programs

There are three basic sources of retirement income: (1) social security; (2) employer-sponsored retirement programs, both basic and supplemental; and (3) individual self-directed retirement plans, specifically Keoghs and IRAs. Although most people still rely on social security and employer-sponsored programs to supply the bulk of their retirement income, recent changes in the federal income tax law have heightened the popularity of self-directed plans. These plans are the most important to students of investments, since they must be established and managed by the individual. We will examine all three retirement programs below, but our emphasis will be on the self-directed plans.

Social security

Virtually no American is untouched by *social security*. With recent congressional changes in the law, if your income is $20,000 in 1984, the social security tax withheld from your wage will be $1,400; at the maximum, you would pay $2,625. Someone who retires in 1985 at age 65, and who had earned the maximum amount of earnings used to determine benefits, would receive about $850 *monthly* from social security. If this person is a man who is married, his wife would also be eligible to receive social security benefits, the exact amount of which would depend on whether or not she was also employed and had paid into social security. At the minimum, she would be eligible to receive half of her husband's benefits, so their combined social security benefits would amount to about $1,250 per month. Of course, the actual amount of benefit received depends on a formula used by the Social Security Administration. This formula is so complex that the SSA no longer publishes tables that fit all situations. Moreover, the 1983 changes in the law also modified the cost-of-living adjustments (COLAs), which will affect future benefits, and some observers believe additional changes may be coming in the future. If an individual is currently in the process of planning retirement income, he or she should contact the Social Security Administration and obtain current benefit information for his or her particular situation. If actual retirement is far in the future, however, current benefits may be altered substantially by the time retirement age is reached—which, by the way, was also lengthened from 65 years of age to 66 (by 2009) and 67 (by 2020).

Starting for the first time in 1984, social security benefits may be subject to income tax. A retiree must add half of his or her benefits to adjusted gross income, and if this total exceeds $25,000 for an individual and $32,000 for a couple filing a joint return, up to half of the benefits are subject to tax, based on a graduated scale. Moreover, the retiree must include tax-free income in determining the base amount. To illustrate the impact of this new tax, consider that a retired married couple with an adjusted gross income of $35,000 in 1984 will pay $1,783 more in taxes under the new law. Prior to the 1983 changes in the law, a rough rule of thumb was that an average wage earner could expect social security benefits to be between 40 to 60 percent of his or her wages in the year before retirement. (If your income was much above the average—as was the case for the Mason family—the percentage is less.) Although this rule is probably still valid for the average wage earner, those with higher incomes will have to rely less on social security—particularly when potential additional income taxes are considered—and more on other sources of retirement income.

Employer-sponsored programs—basic plans

Many employers provide retirement programs as part of the total compensation package offered employees. These programs are popular for several reasons: First, most retirees find that social security benefits are inadequate to sustain their retirement life-styles. Second, having contributions provided by an employer in many cases means they escape federal income taxation, both when they are withheld and initially invested, and as their earnings are subsequently reinvested. If you had to provide your own retirement funds and no individual tax relief were available, you could do so only with after-tax dollars. If you are in the 30 percent tax bracket, this means for every $70 you put into retirement on your own, you could have $100 invested through an employer plan. A difference this large compounded over many years leads to an incredibly large difference in total dollars at retirement.

Employer plans are *noncontributory* if the employer bears all the cost, or *contributory* if you share in the cost, which usually amounts to 3 to 8 percent of your total wages. Benefits accumulated under a pension plan at some point in time become your nonforfeitable rights; they are then described as *vested*. Prior to the Employee Retirement Income Security Act (ERISA) of 1974, there was considerable variation, and occasional abuse, of vesting. ERISA established minimum vesting requirements so that full vesting must take place after 15 years of service—but this minimum is often shortened by many employers.

Every retirement program must explain how your retirement benefits will be determined. Two basic methods are used to make such determinations. A *defined benefit plan* indicates exactly what your benefits will be by linking them to a formula that generally includes factors for level of earnings and length of service with the employer. A typical plan might pay 1 percent of your average annual salary for the last three years of employment for each year of your employment. For example, if you averaged $35,000 a year over the last three years of service and had 20 years of employment, your annual retirement income would be $7,000 (0.01 × $35,000 × 20). A *defined contribution plan* does not spell out your retirement income, but defines precisely the amounts you and your employer contribute to the plan. Your actual retirement income then depends on how much is accumulated for you at retirement. Obviously, this amount cannot be known with certainty until the retirement date. A defined contribution plan requires more effort in planning your retirement income and managing your overall investment portfolio than does the defined benefit plan. (As explained earlier in the chapter, these retirement assets should be considered a part of your portfolio.)

Employer-sponsored programs—supplemental plans

In addition to a basic retirement plan, many employers offer supplemental plans. As a result of a 1978 amendment to the income tax code [entered as section 401(k)], there is a strong tax incentive for employers to provide—and employees to participate in—such plans. Many large companies have adopted so-called *401(k) deferred compensation plans* and many more, large and small, are planning to do so in the future. Early reluctance to move on these plans was due to uncertainty about IRS guidelines for determining their tax status, but with this uncertainty apparently resolved, the road is now clear for widespread adoption. There is a good chance your employer will have a 401(k), and you will have to decide whether or not to participate, and to what extent.

Basically, a 401(k) plan gives you, as an employee, the option to divert a portion of your salary to a company-sponsored tax-sheltered savings account. In this way, the earnings diverted to the savings plan accumulate tax-free. Taxes will have to be paid eventually, but not until you start drawing down the account at retirement, presumably when you are in a lower tax bracket. An individual can put as much as 25% of his or her annual pay (up to a maximum of $30,000 per year) into a tax-deferred 401(k) plan. The exact limits, however, are set by the sponsoring firm, and most companies set *lower* limits—the maximum generally ranges from 4 to 16 percent of an employee's base pay. To encourage savings for retirement, such contributions are locked up until the employee turns 59½, or leaves the company; a major exception to this rule lets employees tap their accounts, without penalties, in the event of "financial hardships." Best of all, an individual can contribute to a 401(k) plan and still be eligible to set up an IRA and possibly even a Keogh account as well (both IRAs and Keoghs are explained in the following sections).

To see how such tax-deferred plans work, consider an individual who earns $35,000 per year and has the opportunity to contribute up to 16 percent of her pay to a 401(k) plan. Under these conditions, she can contribute $5,600 (per year) to the company savings plan (i.e., $35,000 × .16). This would reduce her taxable income to $29,400 and in so doing enable her to lower her federal tax bill by some $1,500. Such tax savings will offset a good portion of her contribution to the 401(k) savings plan—specifically, it will fund about 27 percent of her contribution. In effect, she has added $5,600 to her retirement program with only $4,100 of her own money; the rest came from the IRS, via a reduced tax bill! What's more, all the *earnings* on her savings account will accumulate tax-free as well. But there's more. For a special attraction of most 401(k) plans is that the firms offering them often sweeten the pot by matching all or a part of the employee's contribution. The most commonly followed program is one in which the company kicks in 50 cents for each dollar contributed by the employee. Such matching programs provide both tax and savings incentives to individuals and clearly enhance the appeal of 401(k) plans. This also explains why employers often have limits on the amount of allowable employee deferred compensation.

Self-directed retirement programs—
Keogh plans

Keogh plans go back to 1962, when they were introduced as part of the Self-Employment Individuals Retirement Act—HR10, or simply the Keogh Act. They allow self-employed individuals to establish tax-deferred retirement plans for themselves and their employees. Like contributions to 401(k) plans, payments to Keogh accounts may be taken as deductions from taxable income. As a result, they reduce the tax bill of self-employed individuals. The maximum contribution to this tax-deferred retirement plan is $30,000 per year or 20 percent of earned income, whichever is less. Any individual who is self-employed, either full- or part-time, is eligible to set up a Keogh account. Not only can the self-employed businessman or professional use Keoghs, they can also be used by individuals who hold full-time jobs *and* who "moon-light" on a part-time basis—for example, the engineer who has a small consulting business on the side, or the accountant who does tax returns in the evenings and on weekends. Take the engineer for example; if he earns $10,000 a year from his part-time consulting business, he can contribute 20% of that income ($2,000) to his Keogh account and in so doing reduce both his taxable income and the amount he pays in taxes. And he is still eligible to receive full retirement benefits from his full-time job, as well as having his own IRA. The only catch to Keogh accounts is that the individual has to be self-employed—that is, the income must be derived from the net earnings (after all expenses except taxes and retirement contributions) of a self-employed business.

Keogh accounts can be opened at banks, insurance companies, brokerage houses, mutual funds, and other financial institutions. Annual contributions must be made at the time the respective tax return is filed, or by April 15th of the following calendar year (e.g., you have until April 15, 1985, to make the contribution to your Keogh for 1984). While a designated financial institution acts as custodian of all the funds held in a Keogh account, the actual investments held in the account are under the complete direction of the individual contributor. For unlike 401(k) plans, these are self-directed retirement programs and as such, the *individual* decides which investments to buy and sell (subject to just a few restrictions). The income earned from the investments must be plowed back to the account and it, too, accrues tax-free. All Keogh contributions and investment earnings must remain in the account until the individual turns 59½, unless the individual becomes seriously ill or disabled. However, you are *not required* to start withdrawing the funds at age 59½; rather, they can stay in the account (and continue to earn tax-free income) until you turn 70½, at which time you have 10 years to clean out the account. In fact, so long as the self-employment income continues, an individual can continue to make tax-deferred contributions to a Keogh account until reaching the maximum age of 70½. Of course, once an individual starts withdrawing funds from a Keogh account (on or after he or she is 59½), all such withdrawals are treated as ordinary income and subject to the payment of normal income taxes, which presumably should be *lower* when an individual is retired. Thus, the taxes on all contributions to and earnings from a Keogh account are eventually going to have to be paid, a characteristic of any tax-*deferred* (as opposed to tax-*free*) program.

Self-directed retirement programs—
Individual Retirement Accounts (IRAs)

Some people mistakenly believe that an IRA is a specialized type of investment. It is not. Actually, an *Individual Retirement Account (IRA)* is virtually the same as any other investment account you open with a bank, savings and loan, credit union, stockbroker, mutual fund, or insurance company. The form you complete designates the account as an IRA and makes the institution its trustee. That is all there is to setting up an IRA account. The next step is to take the amount you invest in the account as a tax deduction. For an IRA is another form of a tax-deferred retirement program. The annual limits are $2,000 for an individual and $2,250 for an individual and a nonworking spouse. If both spouses work, each can deduct up to $2,000 from his or her earned income, and it makes no difference if they already participate in other retirement programs. Like Keoghs and 401(k) programs, payments to individual retirement accounts are deductible from taxable income, and the earnings on invested funds are tax-deferred as well. You can deposit as much or as little as you want (up to the ceilings), and there are no percentage of income limitations; if your earned income is only, say, $1,800, you can contribute *all* of it to your IRA. IRAs are *self-directed accounts* (i.e., you are free, within limits, to make whatever investment decisions you want with the capital held in your IRA). Of course, your investment options are limited by the types of products offered by competing financial institutions—banks and thrifts push their savings vehicles, insurance companies have their annuities, and brokerage houses offer everything from mutual funds to stocks, bonds, and annuities. IRAs are the simplest and most flexible of all self-directed retirement plans to start and maintain. There are, however, restrictions on withdrawing funds. For except for serious illness, any funds withdrawn from an IRA prior to age 59½ are subject to a 10 percent penalty, on top of the regular tax you pay on the withdrawal.

Bear in mind that IRAs, along with all other retirement plans permitting contributions on a pretax basis, only *defer*—they do not eliminate—taxes. When you receive the income (contributions and investment earnings) in retirement it is then taxed, but usually at a lower rate than when the contribution was made. Even so, the impact of tax deferral is substantial. As Table 7.8 indicates, accumulated funds under an IRA are about twice as great as the non-IRA after only 10 years—and the difference increases as time goes on; after 45 years, they are nearly 4.4 times as great ($417,417 versus $94,925). This example assumes that you have $1,000 of earned income each year that is also available for investment. If you choose an IRA, you shelter from taxes both the $1,000 initial investment and its subsequent earnings, so that at the end of the first year, for example, you accumulate $1,080. If you select the same investment vehicle but do not make it an IRA, you must first pay $400 in taxes (assuming a 40 percent tax rate), leaving only $600 to invest; the subsequent earnings of $48 ($600 × 0.08) are also taxed at 40 percent, leaving after-tax income of only $29 ($48 − 0.4($48) = $48 − $19 = $29). Thus, the first-year accumulation is just $629.

Many other regulations for IRAs should be understood before you open one. Some of the more important are these:

- You do not have to stay with the same IRA every year—in fact, you may have as many different IRAs as you wish.
- You can switch from one IRA account to another—either by having the trustee make the transfer or by withdrawing the funds yourself and depositing them in the new account; the latter can be done only once a year, and you have

TABLE 7.8 ACCUMULATED FUNDS FROM A $1,000 A YEAR INVESTMENT IN AN IRA AND FROM A FULLY TAXABLE (NON-IRA) ACCOUNT*

Years Held	IRA	Non-IRA
1	$ 1,080	$ 629
5	6,335	3,461
10	15,645	7,835
15	29,323	13,366
20	49,421	20,356
25	78,951	29,195
30	122,341	40,369
35	186,097	54,494
40	279,774	72,351
45	417,417	94,925

*Contributions and earnings are taxed at 40% in the non-IRA account, but are tax-free in the IRA; a rate of return of 8% is assumed in both cases.
Source: Beth Brophy, "Saving the Tax-Deferred Penny." *Forbes,* April 27, 1981, pp. 68–70.

only 60 days to complete the switch without incurring a penalty. (Notice, though, that you can use the funds for 60 days, which really makes them a source of short-term liquidity for that period.)

- After age 59½, you can withdraw funds as you see fit, including in a lump sum, although this may not be practical from a tax point of view. You cannot use the 10-year averaging rule, which in effect allows a pensioner to average benefits over 10 years, thereby reducing taxes in the year of the lump-sum distribution.
- You *must* begin withdrawing by age 70½.
- You cannot borrow on your IRA account.

The popularity of IRAs increased considerably toward the end of 1982 and into early 1983 (the deadline for making contributions to an IRA is April 15 of the year following the year for which the deduction is claimed) as taxpayers realized it was either an IRA or the IRS. This surge in popularity has prompted some people to believe Congress will expand IRA coverage by allowing greater maximum deductions.

Funding Keoghs and IRAs

As with investments in general, an individual can be conservative or aggressive in choosing investment vehicles for a Keogh or IRA. However, the nature of these investment programs generally favors a more conservative approach. This does not mean, of course, that it would be altogether inappropriate to place a good-quality growth stock or mutual fund in a Keogh or IRA. In fact, such an investment may pay off handsomely since it can appreciate totally free of taxes. However, such high-return investments also involve high risks, and that is the problem, particularly for

BOX 7.3 NEW "TIGERS" SCORING WELL WITH INVESTORS

Merrill Lynch will put a tiger not in your tank but in your safe-deposit box.

Merrill Lynch's tiger is technically called a Treasury Investment Growth Receipt (TIGR), less formally a tiger. It's a new fixed-income instrument, backed by U.S. Treasury bonds. The receipt pays no current interest. Instead, it's sold at a discount from the amount of either the interest or the principal repayment that secures it. When the interest or principal payment comes due, the holder of the receipt gets his money.

The appeal to an investor is simple: Buying a discounted, non-interest-bearing security eliminates his reinvestment risk. The total return to an investor in conventional interest-bearing securities depends on the yields he can obtain when he reinvests his periodic interest payments, and the return will fall if interest rates fall.

The U.S. Treasury likes the broadening of the market for the bonds the government must sell to finance its budget deficit.

THE FIRST LITTER

Merrill Lynch White Weld Capital Markets Group introduced its first litter of tigers [in August 1982]. It sold receipts representing claims on the $500 million of principal on 14% U.S. Treasury bonds maturing in 2011, and on the $2.065 billion in interest that will be paid over the life of the bonds. W. Joseph Wilson, a managing director of Merrill Lynch, says the receipts were "virtually all sold"—within days. "The issue has gone very well. . . ."

Other securities firms have already grabbed the tiger by the tail. "There's a sizable market for these new issues out there," says Timothy Howard, chief economist for the Federal National Mortgage Association. Francois de St. Phalle, a managing director of Lehman Brothers Kuhn Loeb Inc., figures the market "to be huge, in the billions of dollars."

Pension funds and other tax-exempt institutional investors who need to avoid reinvestment risk in order to fund, or finance, their obligations may create most of the demand for tigerlike instruments. James J. O'Leary, economic consultant to U.S. Trust Co., estimates that in 1982 alone private and governmental pension funds will invest $37.5 billion of new pension-fund contributions and billions of dollars more in interest and dividends on existing investments.

With an eye on that market, Lehman Brothers and two other firms have offered receipts, or certificates, for Treasury bond principal and interest payments, and many other firms are trying to package their own issues. . . .

The Treasury prefers not to talk specifically of Merrill Lynch's tigers. But, says Mark Salnecker, deputy assistant secretary for federal financing, "Anything that increases the underlying demand for Treasury issues is something we would welcome."

He says the Treasury itself has no plans to issue its own zero-coupon securities—which, effectively stripped of their interest coupons, tiger bonds amount to. "It's premature to say how successful a zero"—offered directly by the Treasury—"might be," he says. Also, he says, "We feel there's no way we can compete for the retail customer. We'll let the Street do the marketing." Presumably, Treasury Secretary Donald Regan, who used to run Merrill Lynch, doesn't violently object to that idea.

Source: E. P. Foldessy, "New 'Tigers' Scoring Well with Investors." *The Wall Street Journal,* August 23, 1982, p. 21.

something as important as one's retirement program. As a rule, the most attractive funding vehicles are low-default-risk investments offering high, fully taxed dividends or interest. However, this statement needs to be qualified by assuming you have sufficient funds to invest in an IRA or Keogh and for other nonretirement purposes. If that is not the case, and if retirement investing is more important than other investing, then you have a broader choice of investment vehicles, since the maximum deduction is worth having even if you invest in securities that are not ideal IRA or Keogh candidates. In short, if you feel strongly about an emerging growth company and if you have only $2,000 to invest, it may be better to make the investment a part of your IRA than not to invest in it at all.

Investors can select from a wide variety of vehicles to fund IRA and Keogh accounts. Very few vehicles are prohibited outright (for example, certain collectibles or endowment plans involving a life insurance contract), though there are some that should be avoided simply because they are inappropriate for such accounts (like municipal securities: the tax shelter from an IRA or Keogh would be redundant since their income is tax exempt anyway). Table 7.9 lists some of the more popular funding vehicles and provides an indication of the diversity of investment options open to individual investors. In addition to the long-term securities listed in Table 7.9, money market accounts—both bank deposits (MMDAs) and mutual funds (MMMFs)—also appeal to IRA and Keogh investors, especially to those who view short-term securities as one way to capture volatile market rates. Not surprisingly, as the size of an account begins to build up, investors will often use more than one kind of security, which makes sense from a portfolio diversification point of view. For remember, although IRAs and Keoghs offer attractive tax shelter incentives, they in no way affect the underlying risks of the securities held in these accounts.

Most IRA accounts were set up initially with banks and other thrifts. Later, investors began looking more toward brokerage firms, insurance companies, and mutual funds as a source of IRA investments. You can expect wide variations in the charges each of these levies to open and administer your account. Brokerage firms appear to be the most expensive, with initial fees of $50 to $80 not uncommon, and maintenance fees about the same. Banks and thrifts are much lower, while mutual funds have charged about the same as banks and thrifts. By all means, ask what these costs will be before you open an account.

Self-Directed Plans: A Summary

Choosing the correct supplemental retirement plan is not a simple decision. We have discussed a number of topics that are summarized in Table 7.10. At the outset, it is very likely that anyone would choose to participate in a wage reduction [401(k)] plan *so long as the employer offers a contribution-matching arrangement.* To turn this down in favor of a Keogh or IRA would, in most cases, not seem sensible. The only possible disadvantage is if the funding is exclusively with stock of the employer company, since this offers poor diversification. In addition, remember that with *any* of these tax-sheltered programs—401(k) plans, Keoghs, and IRAs— *part of your contributions are being funded by the IRS.* For whatever you save in taxes means less money that you have to come up with when making your annual contributions to these programs.

Relative to IRAs, there are two main advantages to voluntary wage reduction [401(k)] plans and Keoghs: First, and perhaps most important, you can shelter

---

**TABLE 7.9 INVESTMENT VEHICLES FOR
FUNDING IRA AND KEOGH ACCOUNTS**

I. THESE INVESTMENTS REQUIRE LITTLE OR NO MANAGEMENT. THEY FEATURE
FIXED, PREDICTABLE RETURNS, RELATIVELY LONG MATURITY, AND NO
REQUIREMENT TO REINVEST PERIODIC INCOME DISTRIBUTIONS

- *Zero-coupon bonds.* Pay all interest and principal at maturity. Issued by corporations with maturities anywhere from 5 to 20 years. Will yield about 11% annually if held to maturity.

- *Zero-coupon certificates of deposit.* Similar to zero bonds, but issued by major banks. Maturities 10 years and up. Yield slightly less than corporate zero issues, since they are federally insured deposits.

- *Stripped Treasury obligations.* An artificial equivalent of zero-coupon bonds, featuring Treasury issues, with the safety of government debt. Represents a call on interest payments of U.S. government obligations, with maturities from three months to 29 years. Yields range from 9% at the short end, through 11.8% at about 10 years, to 10.2% to 15 years.

- *Fixed insurance annuities.* Variable premiums pay either a lump sum, or a guaranteed minimum monthly income at retirement. Yield varies. First-year guarantee for each annual contribution usually competitive with bank certificates of deposit, or about 11½% recently. Reinvested funds in account tend to earn somewhat less.

- *Bank certificates of deposit.* Most popular is the 42-month CD, which some banks will extend to as long as 10 years at current rates. Earnings reinvested and compounded, often daily. Effective annual yield, including compounded earnings, is more than 12%.

---

considerably more income with them. Second, withdrawing from them at retirement is somewhat more flexible, since each allows use of the 10-year averaging rule for a lump-sum distribution. This rule allows you to treat the distribution as though it were your only income for tax purposes and being received in equal amounts over 10 years. The difference in taxes between reporting income this way versus the conventional way, where it is included in total in the year the lump sum is received, is considerable. The main disadvantage to Keoghs and 401(k) plans—which proves to be the main advantage of an IRA—is their lack of flexibility. With a 401(k) you are tied to the retirement plan your employer provides, whether or not it suits your investment objectives. With a Keogh, you are forced to make the retirement plan available to all your employees—if you have any—and contribute to their retirement at the same rate that you contribute to your own; thus, if you put 20 percent of your earnings into a Keogh, you must contribute 20 percent of the compensation of qualified employees. As a last point, we should mention that an IRA can be established along with any other plan, so it may not be a matter of one or the other, but of whether or not you should have more than one.

TABLE 7.9 *Continued*

II. THESE INVESTMENTS REQUIRE PERIODIC DECISIONS ON REINVESTMENT OF
PRINCIPAL AND INCOME

- *GNMA certificate unit trusts.* Backed by government-guaranteed mortgages. Maturities of 12 years or less. Big brokerage houses sweep monthly checks for interest and returned principal from mortgage amortization into market-rate money fund. Requires periodic reinvestment decision. Yield, about 12.5%.

- *Corporate-bond unit trusts.* Similar to GNMA trust units, but without monthly return of principal. Yield is close to a point less.

- *Oil and gas royalty trusts.* Maturity varies with life of the underlying wells. Yields about 10% currently, and reinvestment problem is similar to that of unit trusts.

- *Real estate income partnerships.* Maturity 8 to 12 years, yields 7% to 8%, plus chance of high additional profit when properties are sold. Problem of reinvestment of cash distributions similar to that of unit trusts.

- *Stock and bond mutual funds, self-directed stock portfolios.* Income easily reinvested, but constant decisions on investment required.

- *High coupon bonds with long maturities.* The high rates are appealing but continual inflation exposes them to sustained interest-rate risk, which is less of a problem if the bonds are purchased on a regular, annual basis, since you should average a higher rate than with short-term securities.

Note: The indicated yields represent rates of return available at year-end 1982.
Source: Adapted from *Business Week,* December 6, 1982, p. 121.

SUMMARY

Liquidity needs can be met by holding a variety of short-term investments. In addition to providing liquidity, these vehicles earn interest, which occasionally is higher than that available on long-term securities. Because of this feature, some depositors choose to hold more short-term securities than what would be required to meet liquidity needs. Short-term investments earn interest in one of two ways: They are sold on a discount basis, or interest is paid as a separate item. For accounts that pay interest, the effective rate depends on the compounding period and the method used to define the account balance. Four methods are in wide use—minimum balance, FIFO, LIFO, and day of deposit to day of withdrawal. Short-term investments usually are free of default risk, and also have almost no interest-rate risk. But because they are low in risk, they also tend to have lower rates of return than long-term securities over long periods of time. Most saving or short-term investing is done in the following accounts and securities: passbook savings accounts, NOW and Super NOW accounts, money market deposit accounts, money market mutual funds, certificates of deposit, repurchase agreements, U.S. Treasury bills, universal

**TABLE 7.10 A COMPARISON OF
SELF-DIRECTED RETIREMENT PLANS**

Characteristic	Voluntary Wage Reduction [401(k)] Plans	Keogh	IRA
Ease of opening and maintaining	Easy—employer does all work	Some difficulty if there are employees who must also be covered	Easy—fill out simple application form
Maximum contributions	20% of compensation, up to a maximum of $30,000	25% of earned compensation, up to a maximum of $30,000	$2,000 for an individual
Access to funds before retirement	Only in case of hardship	Similar to 401(k)	Yes, but with penalty; except in disability or death
Borrowing from the account	Possibly, depends on the plan	Yes, usually	No
Vesting	Yes, immediately (though the vesting of the company matching portion is usually deferred)	Yes, for your employees	Not an issue
Withdrawal of funds at retirement	Easy, with 10-year averaging rule for lump-sum distribution	Same as 401(k)	Easy, but 10-year averaging rule is disallowed

or sweep accounts, and Series EE savings bonds. The suitability of any of these for the individual investor depends on his or her attitude toward availability, return, risk, and liquidity.

Retirement planning is most effective when it is started early in life. It should be part of an overall investment program and should be evaluated as such. Planning for retirement begins by reviewing needs for the retirement years. After this is done, an estimate is made of how much retirement income will be necessary to support those needs. This in turn tells us how much must be accumulated in investment assets to produce the supplemental income if income from social security and employer-sponsored plans is not adequate. Social security has been the cornerstone of most retirement plans, but it is changing and many people are relying less on it. Employer-sponsored retirement programs are of two types: basic plans provided by most employers, and supplemental plans that often allow employees the choice of reducing their wages in favor of additional retirement contributions. Changes in the tax law have created so-called 401(k) plans that offer attractive supplemental retirement options. Basic employer-sponsored programs are either defined benefit plans that define clearly what a retiree can expect in benefits, or defined contribution plans that indicate exactly how much the employee and employer will contribute to the plan.

A Keogh plan is a self-directed retirement plan available to self-employed individuals. An individual retirement account (IRA), in contrast, is a self-directed retirement plan available to everyone. IRAs are easy to open and administer and are usually funded with low-risk and high-yielding investments, such as certificates of deposit. The accumulation of funds over time from an IRA versus a non-IRA shows an enormous advantage for the IRA. However, the final selection of an IRA, voluntary wage reduction program, or a Keogh plan is determined by the investor's attitude toward the key factors of each: (1) ease of opening and maintaining an account; (2) maximum contribution; (3) access to funds; (4) ability to borrow from the account; (5) vesting; and (6) retirement withdrawal provisions.

KEY TERMS

accrual-type securities
certificate of deposit (CD)
day of deposit to day of withdrawal
    method
defined benefit plan
defined contribution plan
discount securities
effective rate of interest
employer-sponsored retirement
    program—basic plan
employer-sponsored retirement
    program—supplemental plan
FIFO method
401(k) deferred compensation plan
government securities money fund
individual retirement account (IRA)
Keogh plan

LIFO method
liquidity
minimum balance method
money market deposit account
money market mutual fund
nominal rate of interest
NOW account
passbook savings account
repurchase agreement (repo)
social security
Super NOW account
sweep account
Series EE savings bonds
tax-exempt money fund
U.S. Treasury bills
universal account
vesting

REVIEW QUESTIONS

1. What makes an asset liquid? Would 100 shares of IBM stock be considered a liquid investment? Explain.

2. Why would you want to hold liquid assets, and how much would be considered adequate for this purpose?

3. Suppose you can purchase a 90-day T-bill, with a $10,000 face value, for $9,500; calculate the annual rate of return on this investment, assuming you hold the bill to maturity.

4. Sue Enright has read ads in the paper encouraging her to deposit funds in different types of accounts. Account A, for example, advertises an 11 percent simple interest rate; account B offers 10 percent, but is compounded quarterly. She isn't sure which is the better account and has asked you for an answer.

5. Burton Brody's activity in his savings account last quarter looked like this:

Opening balance	$1,000
Day 30—deposit	$1,000
Day 60—withdrawal	$ 900
Day 90—closing balance	$1,100
Interest rate, 10%	

Determine the interest Burton would earn during the quarter with each of the following methods: (1) minimum balance, (2) FIFO, (3) LIFO, (4) day of deposit to day of withdrawal.

6. Explain the characteristics of short-term investments with respect to both default risk and interest-rate risk.

7. Should short-term investments show a better or poorer return than long-term investments? Does the history of these two rates confirm that expectation?

8. Complete the following table for the short-term investments listed. You will have to make assumptions about their yields.

Investment	Insured	Yield	Minimum Balance	Method and Ease of Withdrawing Funds
1. Passbook account	Yes	5.5%	None	In person or through teller machines; very easy
2. NOW account				
3. Super NOW account				Unlimited checkwriting privileges
4. Money market deposit account				
5. Money market mutual fund				
6. 3½ year certificate of deposit				
7. Repurchase agreement				
8. U.S. Treasury bills		8.0%		
9. U.S. Series EE bonds			Virtually none	

9. Find the effective rate of interest on a $2,000 deposit in an account that pays 12 percent interest, compounded quarterly (assume the funds are left on deposit for one year).

a. How large would the account be after 2 years?

b. What effective rate of interest would an investor earn if he bought a 1-year, $10,000 T-bill for $8,950?

10. Explain why it is important to begin planning for retirement early in your career. Use Table B.1 in Appendix B to support your answer.

11. Is retirement planning a part of—or distinct from—an overall investment program? Explain.

12. Explain the impact of inflation on a retirement plan; be sure to cover retirement income as well as retirement expenditures.

13. Assume an individual has 35 years to go to retirement; he has been working with a financial planner who advises him that his annual income from social security and company-sponsored retirement programs will be about $45,000 short of what he would like his retirement income to be. How big will his nest egg have to be and how much will he have to save yearly (for the next 35 years) if he feels he can earn an 8 percent rate of return on his investments both before and after he retires?

  a. What rate of return would he have to obtain if he wanted to end up with the same size nest egg (as above), but he could only afford to save $2,000 per year (for the next 35 years)?
  b. How big will his nest egg have to be and how much will he have to save each year if he can earn 12 percent on his investments both before and after he retires?

14. Distinguish between a defined benefit plan and a defined contribution plan; also, indicate how retirement benefits might be determined under a typical defined benefit plan.

15. What is a 401(k) plan? In what way(s) might it serve your supplemental retirement program?

16. Briefly explain Keoghs and IRAs, and compare their relative advantages and disadvantages.

17. Explain what investment vehicles might be suitable for funding a Keogh or IRA; indicate several investments that might not be appropriate and explain why they are not.

CASE PROBLEMS

7.1 THE YOUNGS' DILEMMA OVER HOW TO SAVE

Allen and Linda Young are a recently married couple. Each has a professional career and earns about $25,000 a year before taxes (with a combined income of $50,000 per year, they're in the 40 percent tax bracket). Although their incomes are fairly high, Al and Linda have not yet accumulated many investment assets. Their net worth is about $15,000, and most of it is the difference between the market values of their two cars—$12,000—and the instalment loan balances still due on them—$3,000. They have about $1,100 in a passbook savings account, and the average balance in their checking account (a regular account, not a NOW) is about $800. Other than the instalment loans on their cars, the Youngs have virtually no liabilities except $100 in unpaid charge accounts. Both Al and Linda have very good retirement plans where they work, but only very average loss-of-income protection and medical insurance.

Not long ago, Al and Linda set a goal for themselves of trying to save $7,000 a year for the next five to eight years, and they now need to decide how to invest the savings they are starting to accumulate. Al is of the opinion that most of the money—if not all of it—should go into speculative growth common stocks. He reasons that now is the time to take risks, and you might as well "make it or break it." Linda is not in complete agreement with this view. For one thing, she is disturbed by how low their liquid reserves are; an accident or a layoff could play havoc with their budget, not to mention that it might force them to sell one of the cars to pay off their loans. Besides, Linda doesn't think they are currently managing their liquid assets very well. They very often let the checking account get too high before they transfer funds to the savings account. Because they are kept busy with their careers, they really don't have the time to get to the bank as often as they should. Linda thinks all their extra savings should go into 3½ year CDs; she would even withdraw the $1,100 from the passbook account and put it in CDs as well. Al believes Linda worries too much about catastrophes that probably will never happen. He agrees that they manage their cash poorly, but if he has his way, their checking account will never get too high because he will systematically buy shares in a mutual fund investing in high-technology, small-sized firms.

Questions
1. Do you think the Youngs have sufficient liquid assets? Explain your position.
2. Provide details for a liquid asset plan for the Youngs, pinpointing how much you

think should be invested in short-term accounts or securities and the specific accounts they should use.

3. The Youngs are in a fairly high tax bracket (40%); do you think it would be advantageous for them to make IRAs a part of their savings plan?

7.2 THE HAGANS START PLANNING FOR RETIREMENT

Bill and Mary Hagan are a couple in their early fifties who are starting to think about retirement in 15 years. Bill has been talking to a friend of his at the office, Bob Grimm, who will retire next year. Bob has a lot of information about retirement that he is sharing with Bill. Based on this information, it appears that if Bill retired today, he would receive a monthly income of $800 from his employer's basic retirement plan. On top of that, he guesses that social security would provide him and Mary with about $1,000 a month. The Hagans want to enjoy their retirement years and they see no reason why their budget should be any different than it is now; excluding savings and taxes, that would be about $35,000 a year.

The Hagans have saved and invested over the years, but not specifically for retirement. Since they have no children, they have always lived in rented apartments, but they very much want to buy a vacation home when Bill retires. The kind they like costs about $60,000 today; of course, it will cost more in the years ahead, but how much more is unclear. Past trends suggest the house will increase in price at the same rate as the overall cost of living, which the Hagans think will average 5 percent a year between now and retirement. Bill and Mary currently have about $75,000 in a variety of savings and investment vehicles. Looking at the past performance of their portfolio, they have been able to average, before taxes, about five percentage points better each year than cost of living increases, and they expect this performance to continue in the future.

A quick glance at their budget shows that the Hagans would be in trouble if Bill retired today; their annual income would be as follows:

Social security	$12,000
Employer plan	9,600
Investments (0.08 × $75,000)	6,000
Total	$27,600

Their estimated expenses of $35,000 would clearly leave a deficiency of $7,400 a year. As a result, Bill and Mary think they should start additional savings and investing if they are to achieve their retirement goals. Bill's employer has a supplemental retirement plan that allows Bill voluntarily to deduct up to $5,000 of his income each year, before taxes, to be invested in a mix of guaranteed annuities and securities that has beaten the cost of living by only one percentage point a year in the past, and will probably continue at this pace in the future. The same rate of return is also earned on the company's basic retirement plan. In addition to this supplemental plan, the Hagans could invest up to $2,250 a year in IRAs. If they did, these would be funded by the same portfolio investments they now have.

Questions

1. Assuming for simplicity that the Hagans will be in a zero tax bracket in their first retirement year and that their portfolio can earn 10 percent in that year, calculate what the accumulated value of their portfolio assets must be if they are to achieve their retirement goals, which includes purchasing the vacation home.

2. By how much will the $75,000 they now have on hand increase over the next 15 years if they are able to earn a 10 percent rate of return on their investments and they are in the 40 percent tax bracket?

3. Determine how much the Hagans can accumulate if they invest the maximum amounts in both the supplemental retirement plan and the IRAs. Combine this value with your answers to questions 1 and 2 and discuss the Hagans' retirement situation.

4. Apart from the numbers you calculated in question 3, discuss other aspects of the two supplemental retirement plans that might be important to the Hagans.

SELECTED READINGS

Allen, Anthony. "The Explosion in CDs." *FACT*, November 1982, pp. 32–35.

Asinoff, Lynn. "Retirement Planning Involves Many Decisions About Home and Nest Egg—and Your Needs." *The Wall Street Journal*, April 18, 1983, p. 48.

Brophy, Beth. "Saving the Tax-deferred Penny." *Forbes*, April 27, 1981, pp. 68–70.

Daly, Margaret. "Individual Retirement Accounts—A Tax-Sheltered Nest Egg for You." *Better Homes and Gardens*, February 1982, pp. 60–65.

"Defer Part of Your Pay and Get a Tax Break." *Changing Times*, August 1983, pp. 66–68.

"Getting a Hunk of Cash from a Retirement Fund?" *Changing Times*, October 1981, pp. 48–55.

Goodman, Jordan E. "Pumping Up Earnings in Your Checking Account." *Money*, January 1982, pp. 105–112.

"Instant-Everything Accounts for Investors." *Changing Times*, January 1982, pp. 55–56.

"IRAs: Your Complete New Money Guide." The Editors of *Money*, 1983, 104 pages.

"Know the Pension Plan *Before* You Start the Job." *Changing Times*, January 1981, pp. 47–50.

"Savings Bonds—Do They Make Sense Now?" *Changing Times*, April 1980, pp. 35–38.

"Social Security Rescue—What It Means to You." *U.S. News & World Report*, April 4, 1983, pp. 23–25.

Straus, Irving L. "Money Market Funds: What's the Risk?" *FACT*, May 1982, pp. 49–50.

Trunzo, Candace E. "Do-It-Yourself Pensions." *Money*, March 1981, pp. 64–68.

Tyson, David Otto. "How Safe Is Your Money-Market Fund?" *Money*, March 1981, pp. 137–140.

"What You Need to Know About Social Security." *U.S. News & World Report*, June 8, 1981, pp. 73–76.

"Where to Put Your Savings Now." *U.S. News & World Report*, August 16, 1982, pp. 60–62.

"Where to Stash Your IRA Cash." *Changing Times*, February 1982, pp. 34–38ff.

"Your IRA: When It's Time to Take the Money *Out*." *Changing Times*, November 1982, pp. 68–72.

FOUR
INVESTING
IN EQUITIES

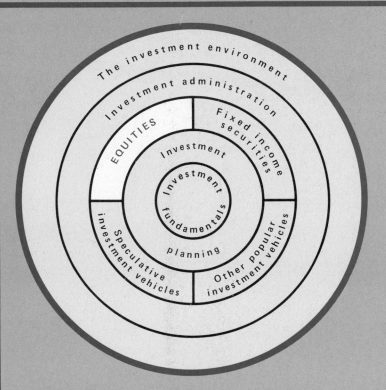

The investment environment

Investment administration

EQUITIES

Fixed income securities

Investment

Investment fundamentals

Speculative investment vehicles

Other popular investment vehicles

planning

Next to savings accounts and home ownership, more people put their money into common stocks than any other type of investment vehicle. This part takes a closer look at common stocks as investment vehicles. Chapter 8 examines some of the basic investment attributes of common stock. Chapter 9 continues the discussion of common stocks by introducing the concept of fundamental analysis as a way to appraise the investment suitability of these securities. Chapter 10 addresses the matter of stock valuation and the procedures that can be used to assess whether or not a particular stock will make a good investment. Chapter 10 also looks at technical analysis and the challenges to investors in an efficient market.

8
Common Stock Investments

Common stocks appeal to investors for a variety of reasons. To some, investing in stocks is a way to hit it big if the issue shoots up in price; to others, it is the level of current income they offer. In fact, given the size and diversity of the stock market, it's safe to say that no matter what the investment objective, there are common stocks that fit the bill. Not surprisingly, as investment vehicles, stocks are virtually unsurpassed in popularity—they are used by literally millions of individuals and by a variety of financial institutions. To learn more about common stocks and to see how they can be used by individual investors, we will devote our attention in this chapter to the following:

1. The basic issue characteristics of common stock, and the advantages and disadvantages of ownership.
2. The different kinds of common stock values and the ability of common stocks to serve as a hedge against inflation.
3. Common stock dividends, including how dividend decisions are made, types of dividends, and dividend policies.
4. The kinds of common stocks and their investment merits.
5. The uses of common stocks as investment vehicles, and the strategies that can be used to meet various investment goals.

The basic investment attribute of a common stock is that it enables investors to participate in the profits of the firm. This is how stocks derive their value. Every shareholder is in effect a part owner of the firm and as such is entitled to a piece of the firm's profit. But this claim on income is not without its limitations, for common stockholders are really the residual owners of the company. That is, they are entitled

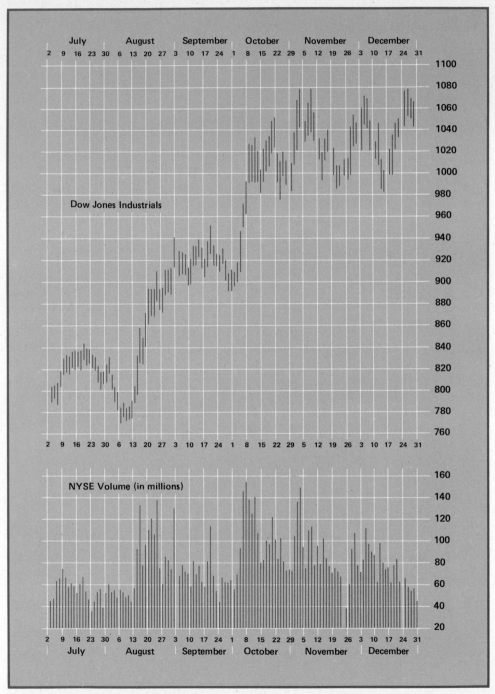

Figure 8.1   The Dow Jones Industrial Averages and Share Volume on the NYSE, June–December 1982.
The stock market chalked up one of its best performances on record in the second half of 1982 as stock prices and share volume set new levels of achievement; the period from mid-August to early-November was especially good. (*Source: The Wall Street Journal.*)

to dividend income and a prorated share of the company's earnings only after all the other obligations of the firm have been met. Equally important, as residual owners, holders of common stock have *no* guarantee that they will ever receive any return on their investment.

The stock market can perform beautifully, or it can behave like a real dog. An extraordinary example of the former occurred just recently, in the second half of 1982. As Figure 8.1 shows, stock prices literally went wild as the market repeatedly scored record-breaking or near-record-breaking days in terms of both share volume and price behavior. In fact, in the month of August alone, there were 1.7 *billion* shares traded just on the NYSE as the DJIA went from a low of 776.92 (on August 12) to a high of 901.31 at month end. The focal point of this explosion came on August 17 when, with the shares of many corporations selling at their lowest prices in years, investors went on an unprecedented buying spree that saw the Dow Jones industrial average soar 38.81 points and the market value of NYSE issues increase by some $43 *billion* in a single day. The market closed the year with the Dow above 1000, and went on to become one of the biggest market rallies in 50 years, as the DJIA soared to nearly 1300 by late fall 1983. Although such behavior is, of course, the exception to the rule, it does demonstrate the return potential offered by common stocks.

The problem is there are so many stocks to choose from. For counting all stocks traded on organized exchanges and over-the-counter (OTC) markets, it's estimated that there are 30 to 40 thousand publicly traded stocks; many of these are, of course, closely held companies with very thin (or even nonexistent) secondary markets. But with this many stocks available, how do you select the one or two that will provide the kind of investment performance you seek? This is a problem investors have to grapple with every day. Unfortunately, because investing is not an exact science, there is no hard and fast answer to this question. But in this chapter we will try to point you in the right direction. This is the first of three chapters on common stock investing. Here, we will be concerned with some of the basic principles of investing in common stock; the next two chapters will look at how stocks can be valued and how to judge whether or not an issue might make an acceptable investment vehicle.

BASIC CHARACTERISTICS OF COMMON STOCK

Common stocks represent ownership in a corporation. Each share of common stock represents an equal part ownership of the firm; for example, if a company has 1,000 shares outstanding, every share symbolizes an identical 1/1000 ownership position. Each share entitles the holder to equal participation in the corporation's earnings and dividends, an equal vote, and an equal voice in management. A typical share of common stock is illustrated in Figure 8.2.

Common Stock as a Corporate Security

Common stocks are a form of *equity capital,* such shares being evidence of an ownership position in a firm. The shares of many corporations, however, are never

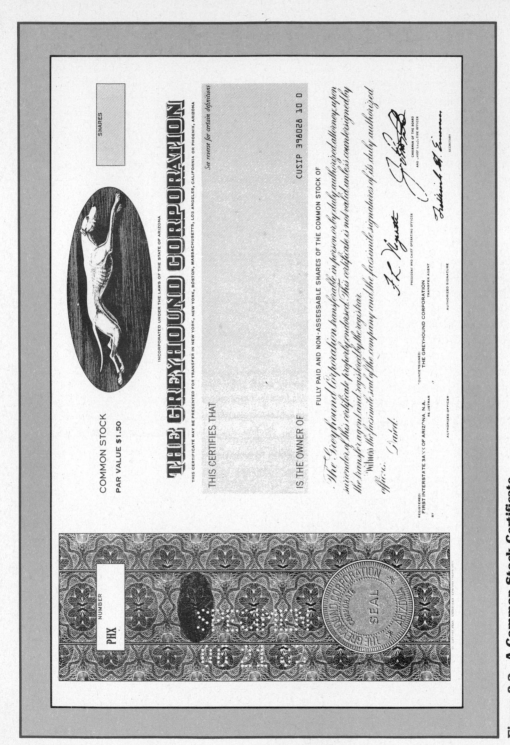

Figure 8.2 A Common Stock Certificate.
This certificate is evidence that the shareholder owns shares of the stock and is entitled to all the rights and privileges of ownership. Note the stock carries a par value of $1.50 per share. (*Courtesy:* The Greyhound Corp.)

traded because the firms are either too small or are strictly family controlled and run. The stocks of interest to us in this book are the so-called *publicly traded issues*— the shares that are readily available to the general public and that are bought and sold in the open market. The firms range from giants like American Telephone and IBM to the much smaller regional or local firms, traded either over-the-counter or on one of the regional exchanges. The dimensions of the market for publicly traded stocks are immense; for example, the market value of all stocks listed on U.S. exchanges at the end of 1982 amounted to more than $1.6 *trillion* (and this did *not* include the OTC segment of the market). Let us now look more closely at common stocks—at the basic nature and investment merits of this popular security.

Kinds of issues

Just about every facet of American industry is represented in the stock market. You can buy shares in public utility firms, airlines, mining concerns, and retail organizations, or in financial institutions like banks and insurance companies. The number of shares issued by a firm depends on the size of the corporation and its financial needs. Common stock has no maturity date and, as a result, remains outstanding indefinitely.

Shares of common stock can be issued in one of several ways. One popular method is a *public offering*. The corporation, working with its underwriter, simply offers the investing public a certain number of shares of its stock, at a certain price. Figure 8.3 depicts an announcement for such a public offering—note that Gulf States Utilities is issuing 5 million shares of common at a price of 12⅝ a share. When issued, the new shares of stock will be co-mingled with the outstanding shares (since they're all the same class of stock), and the net result will be an increase in the number of shares outstanding. A *rights offering* is another popular way of issuing common stock. Such offerings are compulsory in states which require that existing stockholders be given first crack at the new issue and be allowed to purchase new shares in proportion to their current ownership position in the firm. For instance, if a stockholder currently owns 1 percent of a firm's stock and the firm issues 10,000 additional shares, that stockholder will be given the opportunity (via a rights offering) to purchase 1 percent (or 100 shares) of the new issue. (We will learn more about stock rights as an investment vehicle in Chapter 13.)

Still another way to issue common stock is through the use of *deferred equity securities*. Warrants and convertible securities are issued to enable holders to buy a stipulated number of shares of common stock at a stipulated price within a certain time period (as in the case of warrants), or to exchange them for a certain number of shares of common stock (as in the case of convertibles). Either way, the securities are initially issued in one form and then later redeemed or converted into shares of common stock. The net result is the same as with a public offering or a rights offering: The firm ends up with more equity in its capital structure and the number of shares outstanding increases.

Stock splits

Companies can also increase the number of shares outstanding by executing what is known as a *stock split*. A firm merely announces its intention to increase the

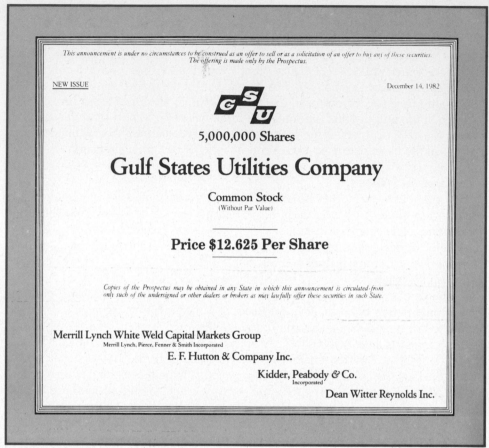

Figure 8.3   An Announcement of a New Common Stock Issue.
The company is issuing 5.0 million shares of common at a price of 12⅝ per share; for Gulf States Utilities, that means more than $60 million of fresh new capital. (*Source: The Wall Street Journal,* December 14, 1982.)

number of shares outstanding by exchanging a specified number of new shares for each outstanding share of stock. For example, in a 2 for 1 stock split, two new shares of stock are exchanged for each old share; in a 3 for 2 split, three new shares are exchanged for every two shares outstanding. A stockholder who owned 200 shares of stock before a 2 for 1 split will automatically become the owner of 400 shares, while that same investor would hold 300 shares if there had been a 3 for 2 split.

Stock splits are used whenever a firm, believing the price of its stock is too high, wants to enhance the stock's trading appeal and activity by lowering its market price. In fact, it is normal market behavior for the price of a stock to fall in relation to the terms of its stock split. Using the ratio of the number of old shares to new, we can expect a $100 stock, for example, to trade at $50 after a 2 for 1 split. That same $100 stock would trade at about $66 with a 3 for 2 split. Most stock splits are executed in order to increase the number of shares outstanding. Sometimes, however, a *reverse stock split* is declared; such splits serve to reduce the number of shares outstanding and increase the share price of the stock by exchanging less than one share of new stock for each outstanding share. For example, in a 1 for 2 split, one new share of stock is exchanged for two old shares. Reverse stock splits are also used to enhance the trading appeal of the stock, but this time by boosting the price of a stock to a more respectable range. (A popular variation of the stock split, known as a *stock dividend,* will be discussed later in this chapter.)

Treasury stock

Corporations sometimes find it desirable to reduce the number of shares in the hands of the investing public, and they do this by buying back their own stock. Generally, firms repurchase stock when they view it as a worthwhile or attractive investment; when, for example, the price of the stock is unusually low. In essence, the company acquires the stock in the open market by becoming an investor like any other individual or institution. When these shares are acquired, they become known as *treasury stock.* Technically, treasury stocks are simply shares of stock that have been issued and subsequently repurchased by the issuing firm. Treasury stocks are retained by the corporation and can be used by it for purposes of mergers and acquisitions, to meet employee stock option plans, or as a way to pay stock dividends. In fact, most treasury stock usually is reissued by the firm. From the investor's point of view, unless the stock repurchase plan is a substantial one, the impact of this activity is fairly limited. Stockholders' equity in the firm is increased slightly, and there may be a modest upward effect on market price.

Transaction costs

Common stock can be bought in round or odd lots. A *round lot* is 100 shares of stock; an *odd lot* denotes transactions that involve less than 100 shares. The sale of 400 shares of stock would be considered a round lot transaction, but the purchase of 75 shares would be an odd lot transaction; trading 250 shares of stock would involve a combination of two round lots and an odd lot. The cost of executing common stock transactions has risen dramatically since the introduction of negotiated commissions. Negotiated commissions are fine for large institutional investors and individuals of substantial means, but they have not proved so beneficial for the individual investor of more modest means.

Basically, an investor incurs two types of transaction costs when buying or selling stock. The major component is, of course, the brokerage fee paid at the time of transaction. As a rule, brokerage fees will equal between 1 and 3 percent of most transactions. Table 8.1 shows a commission schedule used by one major brokerage house. Not surprisingly, the amount of commission paid increases as the number and price of the shares traded increases. Thus, the cost of selling 50 shares of stock trading at $35 per share amounts to $45.79, whereas the cost of trading 200 shares of a $75 stock is $175.97. Although the dollar cost obviously increases with the size of the transaction, on a relative basis it actually declines. For instance, in the examples above, the brokerage fees for the 50-share transaction are equal to 2.6 percent of

TABLE 8.1   A SCHEDULE OF BROKERAGE COMMISSIONS PAID IN COMMON STOCK TRANSACTIONS

Share Price	NUMBER OF SHARES						
	5	10	25	50	100	200	500
$ 1	$ 1.66	$ 2.24	$ 4.00	$ 6.94	$12.82	$ 24.57	$ 59.81
5	3.79	6.52	12.65	16.09	22.98	44.90	101.13
10	6.46	11.86	15.83	22.45	33.92	66.77	129.73
25	12.43	15.66	25.36	37.52	58.71	103.63	225.03
35	13.71	18.21	31.06	45.79	70.15	132.11	284.83
50	15.61	22.02	37.26	58.18	84.77	168.00	354.60
75	18.79	28.38	47.58	72.48	88.52	175.97	434.33
100	21.97	32.96	57.91	84.23	88.52	175.97	438.33
125	25.15	37.10	65.06	87.99	88.52	175.97	438.33
150	28.32	41.22	72.21	87.99	88.52	175.97	438.33

Source: A major brokerage house.

the transaction, whereas those for the 200-share trade represent a cost of only 1.1 percent. The other component of the transaction cost is the transfer fees and taxes levied on the *seller* of the securities. Fortunately, these fees and taxes are modest when compared with the brokerage commission.

Advantages and disadvantages of stock ownership

One of the major reasons common stocks are so appealing to individual investors is the substantial return opportunities they offer. Although there is no guarantee of success, the potential for profit, particularly from capital gains, can be enormous. This kind of investment return is possible simply because common stocks, as equity securities, are entitled to participate fully in the residual profits of the firm. The market price of a share of stock generally reflects the profit potential of the firm; increasing corporate profits, therefore, translate into rising share prices (capital gains) and are the first step in earning attractive investment returns.

But stocks offer other benefits. Another important advantage is the current income from the annual dividends paid. Because of the uncertain investment environment during the past decade or so, many investors placed higher values on dividends and in effect forced firms to increase their dividend payout. Still another advantage is that these investments are highly liquid and easily transferable. Common stock is easy to buy and sell, and the transaction costs are modest; moreover, price and market information is widely disseminated in the news and financial media. A final advantage of common stock ownership is that the unit cost of a share of common stock is usually fairly low and well within the reach of most individual savers and investors. Unlike bonds, which carry minimum denominations of at least $1,000, and some mutual funds that have fairly hefty minimum requirements, common stocks present no such investment hurdles. Instead, most stocks today are priced at less than $50 per share—and any number of shares, no matter how few, can be bought or sold.

There are also disadvantages to investing in common stock. The risky nature of the security is perhaps the most significant disadvantage. Stocks are subject to a number of different types of risks, including business and financial risk, purchasing power risk, and market risk, all of which can adversely affect a stock's earnings and dividends, its price appreciation, and, of course, the rate of return earned by the investor. Even the best of stocks possess elements of risk that are difficult to overcome. A major reason for this is that common stock represents residual ownership of a company whose earnings are at the mercy of many factors, including government control and regulation, foreign competition, and the state of the economy. Because such factors can affect sales and profits, they can also affect the price behavior of the stock and possibly even dividends. This leads to another disadvantage: Since the earnings and general performance of stocks are subject to such wide swings, it is extremely difficult to value common stock and consistently select top performers. The selection process is difficult and complex because so many elements go into formulating expectations of how the price of the stock should perform in the future. In other words, not only is the future outcome of the company and its stock uncertain, but the evaluation and selection process itself is far from perfect. A final disadvantage is the sacrifice in current income. Several types of investments—bonds for instance—not only pay higher levels of return, but also do so with much greater certainty. Figure 8.4, which compares the dividend yield of common stocks with the current yield of bonds, shows how the spread in current income has widened over time, and reveals the kind of sacrifice common stock investors make. Although dividend payoffs have improved, they still have a long way to go before they catch up with the current income levels available from alternative investment vehicles.

Voting Rights and Procedures

As a rule, the holders of common stock receive voting rights enabling them to vote on matters affecting general corporate operations. The principle at work here is that since stockholders are owners, they should have some input on important issues that have a bearing on earnings and dividends. Of course, stockholders do not vote on every minor company decision; instead, selected major items are placed on an agenda, and voting takes place at the *annual stockholders' meeting*. These meetings are generally held at or near the headquarters of the corporation and all stockholders are welcome, regardless of the number of shares owned. At this meeting, company executives present and discuss the annual report and future prospects, members of the board of directors are elected, and other special issues are voted on. Each stockholder is entitled to cast one vote for each share of stock held. If a stockholder cannot or chooses not to attend the meeting, he or she may cast votes in absentia by means of a *proxy*. A proxy is a signed form that assigns the stockholder's voting rights to another party, usually a member of the board of directors,

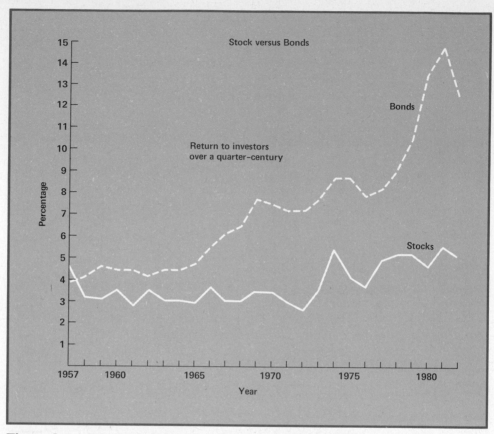

Figure 8.4   The Current Income of Stocks versus Bonds.
Clearly, current income (dividends) to stockholders has failed to keep pace with the amount of income paid to bondholders.

who is then bound to cast the vote as indicated for the stockholder. Figure 8.5 depicts a typical proxy statement. In order for it to be valid, it must be signed by the stockholder and returned prior to the date of the annual meeting.

Majority or cumulative voting

There are two ways in which the stockholders can cast votes when electing members of the board of directors. The most common system is known as *majority voting*. Each stockholder is entitled to one vote per share of stock owned, and he or she may cast that number of votes for each position on the board. If you hold 100 shares of stock and three directors are being elected, you can cast 100 votes for *each* of your three candidates. (Those receiving the majority of votes are elected.) Under this system, it is impossible for minority interests to elect board members by themselves. An alternative system that has been devised to overcome or at least

PROXY THE GREYHOUND CORPORATION
P.O. Box 21688, Phoenix, Arizona 85036

The undersigned hereby appoints John W. Teets or Robert Minge Brown or John M. Martin, each of them, to have all the powers hereunder, including full power of substitution, as Proxies for the undersigned to vote as indicated below at the Annual Meeting of the shareholders of The Greyhound Corporation to be held on Tuesday, May 10, 1983, and at any adjournment thereof, all shares of stock which the undersigned is entitled to vote, with all voting rights the undersigned would have if personally present.

1. ☐FOR ☐AGAINST ☐ABSTAIN Approval of amendment to articles to provide for classes of directors
2. ☐FOR ☐AGAINST ☐ABSTAIN Approval of amendment to articles to provide for a two-thirds shareholder vote for approval of certain business combinations
3. ☐FOR ☐AGAINST ☐ABSTAIN Approval of 1983 Stock Option and Incentive Plan
4. Election of directors
   ☐FOR all nominees listed below (except as indicated to the contrary below) ☐WITHHOLD AUTHORITY to vote for all nominees listed below

Class I		Class II		Class III	
	R. Batastini		F. Holland		S. Casey
	R. Brown		J. Martin		J. Hay
	M. Griffiths		H. Stuart		J. Johnson
	F. Nageotte		D. Tatum		D. Stanfill
			G. Trautman		J. Teets

or if Proposal 1 above is not approved, then the above nominees without regard to class
(INSTRUCTIONS: To withhold authority to vote for any of the above nominees write that nominee's name in the space below.)

5. ☐FOR ☐AGAINST ☐ABSTAIN Approval of Touche Ross & Co. as auditors

The Board of Directors recommends a vote FOR all the above Proposals
PLEASE SIGN AND DATE ON REVERSE SIDE AND RETURN PROMPTLY IN THE ENCLOSED ENVELOPE

111703

6. In their discretion, the Proxies are authorized to vote upon such other business as may properly come before the meeting. This proxy when properly executed will be voted in the manner directed herein by the undersigned shareholder. If no direction is given, this proxy will be voted FOR Proposals 1, 2, 3, 4 and 5.

Dated________________, 1983

Signature

Signature if held jointly

(Please sign exactly as name appears hereon. Executors, Administrators, Trustees, etc., should so indicate when signing. For joint accounts, each joint owner should sign.)

THIS PROXY IS SOLICITED ON BEHALF OF THE BOARD OF DIRECTORS

Figure 8.5 A Typical Proxy Statement.
This proxy statement, not valid until signed by the shareholder, enables stockholders to vote without actually being present at the meeting—in this case, to cast their votes for members of the board, to approve a CPA firm as auditors, and to vote on other matters that require stockholders' approval. (*Courtesy:* The Greyhound Corp.)

minimize this problem is *cumulative voting.* (A handful of states require cumulative voting, and all others permit its use.) This system allows shareholders to cast all their combined votes in any manner they wish. In the example above, in which an investor held 100 shares of stock and was voting on the election of three directors, all 300 votes could be cast for *one* director. The advantage of this system is that it provides minority shareholders with the opportunity to elect at least one or two directors and thereby have at least some voice on the board.

Classified common stock

For the most part, all the stockholders in a corporation enjoy the same benefits of ownership. Occasionally, however, a company will issue different classes of common stock, each of which entitles the holder to different privileges and benefits. These are known as *classified common stock*. Even though issued by the same company, each class of common stock is different and each has its own value. Classified common stock is customarily used to denote either different voting rights and/or different dividend obligations. For instance, class A could be used to designate nonvoting shares, while class B would carry normal voting rights; or the class A stock could receive *no* dividends, whereas class B receives regular cash dividends. A variation of this concept, used by some public utility firms, is to automatically reinvest the dividend income into additional company shares for the class A stock, and pay out dividends (in cash) for the class B stock. Finally, a few firms *combine* voting rights and dividend privileges in their classification systems. Class A stock may have no voting rights but receive extra-large dividends; class B may have extra voting rights but receive lower than normal dividends; and class C stock may have normal voting rights and dividend privileges. The best example of this type of arrangement is the Ford Motor Company, which divides stockholders into the Ford Foundation, the Ford Family, and the general public. For the most part, only one class of common stock is ever publicly traded (the other one or two classes are held by the owners or their designated beneficiaries). Even so, whenever there are two or more classes of common stock outstanding, the potential investor should be sure to check the privileges, benefits, and limitations of each.

Common Stock Values

The worth of a share of common stock can be described in a number of ways. Terms such as par value, book value, liquidation value, market value, and investment value are all found in the financial media and each designates some accounting, investment, or monetary attribute of the stock in question.

Par value

The term *par value* is used to denote the stated or face value of a stock. It is not really a measure of anything, so except for accounting purposes, is relatively useless. In many ways, it is a throwback to the early days of corporate law, when par value was used as a basis for assessing the extent of a stockholder's legal liability; today, however, it holds little or no significance for investors. As a result, many stocks today are issued as no par stock, like the Gulf States issue in Figure 8.3. And even when stocks are issued with par values, these values are often very small and may amount to less than $1 per share.

Book value

Book value represents the amount of stockholders' equity in a firm. It is an accounting measure which, as we will see in the next chapter, is widely used in security analysis and stock valuation. Book value is determined by subtracting the firm's liabilities and preferred stock from the amount of assets it holds. It indicates

BOX 8.1 "UNDERVALUED" COMPANIES

By one test, stocks of large American corporations have rarely been cheaper than they were in mid-1982.

According to Standard & Poor's, the shares of the 400 firms represented in its index of industrial companies were selling, on average, at only about 10 percent over book value—the amount of assets shown on corporate balance sheets after deducting all debts. Book value is one measure of what the shareholders actually own. S&P statistician Elliott Shurgin says that in March (1982), prices relative to book value were the lowest they have been for at least 30 years. In many cases, the shares were even selling for *less* than book value—and this included some very well known companies like AT&T, Bendix, Firestone Tire, Martin Marietta, and Sherwin-Williams.

Many firms are in a sense worth even more than the book-value figures. Properties typically are listed on the company balance sheets at original cost, with little or no allowance for the effects of years of inflation. The understatement can be especially great for outfits with large tracts of land, timber or deposits of oil, gas and other natural resources.

Factories, offices and other facilities are valued on the books at cost less depreciation, usually far less than current replacement cost.

Why were the nation's industrial assets being sold in the stock market so cheaply? For two reasons—

- *Investors are mainly interested in what a company can earn on its assets, not what the assets will bring if the firm is liquidated. That's why stocks of companies that are growing rapidly and have shown an ability to earn a high rate of return on their investments frequently sell for far more than book value.*
- *Financial health also is important. People don't buy stock with the idea of picking up the pieces if the company goes on the block. Firms struggling to stay afloat with heavy loads of debt are avoided by most investment managers no matter how valuable their assets look on paper.*

Does book value have any significance for investors? Many advisers think its does for several reasons.

For one thing, a price below book value provides a certain amount of protection. A stock of this type often attracts bargain hunters—including other companies that may decide to make a takeover offer at a somewhat higher price. Alternatively, firms with shares selling below book value may decide to buy back some stock and thus raise the earnings per share for investors who hang on.

Book value, in short, is one of a number of factors the canny investor takes into account.

Source: William C. Bryant, " 'Underpriced' Companies." *U.S. News & World Report,* May 5, 1982, p. 81.

the amount of stockholder funds used to finance the firm. Let's assume that a firm has $10 million in assets, owes $5 million in various forms of short- and long-term debt, and has $1 million worth of preferred stock outstanding. The book value of this firm would be $4 million. This amount can be converted to a per share basis—book value per share—by simply dividing it by the number of shares outstanding. For example, if this firm has 100,000 shares of common stock outstanding, then its book value per share would amount to $40. As a rule, most stocks have market prices above their book values.

Liquidation value

Liquidation value is an indication of what the firm would bring on the auction block, were it to close its doors and cease operations. After the assets are sold or auctioned off at the best possible price, and liabilities and preferred stockholders paid off, what is left is known as the liquidation value of the firm. Obviously, if and until liquidation actually occurs, this measure is no more than an estimate of what the firm would be worth under such circumstances. Because investors usually assess stocks on the assumption that the firm will continue to operate as a "going concern," liquidation value means little to most investors.

Market value

This is one of the easiest of all values to determine, since *market value* is simply the prevailing market price of an issue. In essence, market value is an indication of how the market participants as a whole have assessed the worth of a share of stock. By multiplying the market price of the stock by the number of shares outstanding, we can also obtain the market value of the firm. For example, if a firm had 1 million shares outstanding and its stock was trading at $50 per share, the firm would have a market value of $50 million. Because investors are always interested in an issue's market price, the market value of a share of stock is generally of considerable importance to most stockholders; it is obviously something an investor wants to know when formulating investment policies and programs.

Investment value

Investment value is probably the most important measure for a stockholder, for it is an indication of the worth investors place on the stock—in effect, it is what they think the stock should be trading for. Determining a security's investment worth is a fairly complex process, but in essence it is based on expectations of the return and risk behavior of a stock. Any stock has two potential sources of return: annual dividend payments and the capital gains that arise from appreciation in market price. In establishing investment value, investors try to determine how much money they will make from these two sources, and then use such estimated information as the basis for formulating the return potential of the stock. At the same time, they try to assess the amount of risk to which they will be exposed by holding the stock. Together, such return and risk information helps them place an investment value on the stock. This is represented by a *maximum* price they would be willing to pay for the issue.

An Inflation Hedge?

For a long time, many people were convinced that common stocks were the ideal inflation hedge. This line of reasoning followed from the belief that common stocks, on average, could provide rates of return that were large enough to cover the annual rate of inflation and still leave additional profits for the stockholder—or,

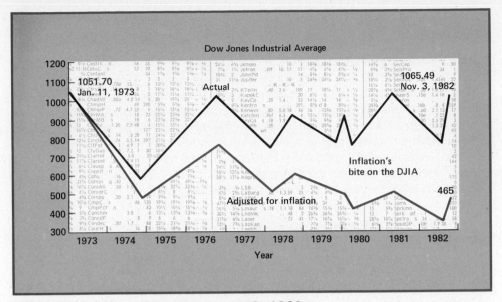

Figure 8.6 Stocks and Inflation, 1973–1982.
It was a long time between highs, but look what inflation did to the "real" value of the DJIA over the interim. (*Source: U.S. News & World Report,* November 1, 1982, p. 7.)

put another way, that stocks could be counted on to provide rates of return that consistently exceeded the annual inflation rate. Through the mid-1960s, stocks did indeed perform as inflationary hedges. For example, over the long haul, they generated rates of return of about 9 percent. That was usually well above the prevailing inflation rate. But in the late 1960s, inflation in this country rose alarmingly, and most stocks simply could not keep up. Instead, many other investment vehicles, such as fixed income securities and even short-term Treasury bills, actually began to outperform common stocks. With the quality of earnings declining in an inflationary economy, stock prices reacted predictably: They began to stagnate. The net result was a stock market that also stagnated—a market, as Figure 8.6 shows, that took almost a decade to match the all-time DJIA record set in January 1973. Even more alarming is the effect inflation has had on the "real" value of stocks. Note that two lines appear in Figure 8.6; one is for the actual reported behavior of the DJIA, and the other shows what happens when the DJIA is adjusted for inflation. Interestingly, the Dow in 1982 would have had to hit 2,400 just to equal its "real" value in 1973.

COMMON STOCK DIVIDENDS

In 1981, corporations paid out some $65 billion in dividends. That is up almost $25 billion from the level that existed only five years earlier, in 1977. Dividend income is one of the two basic sources of return to investors and has become increasingly important in recent times. In fact, for some issues, dividends represent the major, or only, source of return to investors. We will now look more closely at this important source of current income and examine several procedural aspects of the corporate dividend decision.

The Dividend Decision

Most companies pay dividends on a fairly regular basis, generally quarterly. The question of how much to pay in dividends is decided by the firm's board of directors. The directors evaluate the firm's operating results and financial condition to determine whether or not, and in what amount, dividends should be paid. Should it be decided that the payment of dividends is in order, several important payment dates are also established by the board. Investors should have some understanding of those factors that go into determining whether or not companies pay dividends, since such insight is helpful in assessing the dividend potential of a stock.

Corporate versus market factors

When the board of directors assembles for a regular dividend meeting, it will weigh a variety of factors in determining the size of forthcoming dividend payments. First, the board will look at the firm's earnings. Obviously, profits are vital to the dividend decision, as a bright profit picture enhances the outlook for dividends. But a company does *not* have to show a profit to pay dividends (though it certainly does help). With stocks, the annual earnings of a firm are usually measured and reported in terms of *earnings per share* (*EPS*). Basically, EPS translates total corporate profits into profits on a per share basis, and provides a convenient measure of the amount of earnings available to stockholders. Earnings per share is found by using the following simple formula:

$$EPS = \frac{\text{net profit after taxes} - \text{preferred dividends paid}}{\text{number of shares of common stock outstanding}}$$

For example, if a firm reports a net profit of $1.25 million, pays $250,000 in dividends to preferred stockholders, and has 500,000 shares of common outstanding, it would have an EPS of $2 [($1,250,000 − $250,000)/500,000]. Note that preferred dividends are *subtracted* from profits, since they have to be paid before any monies can be made available to common stockholders.

Dividends are actually charged against the firm's *retained earnings*, which represents the amount of past and current earnings not paid out as dividends and left to accumulate in the firm to finance the operations of the company. Of course, any cash that has to be paid will come from the firm's cash resources, since retained earnings is only a bookkeeping entry and does *not* represent a pool of cash. While profit and retained earnings are being assessed, the board will also look at the firm's growth prospects. Very likely, some of the firm's present earnings will be needed for investment purposes and to partly finance expected growth. Then the firm's cash position will be examined to make sure there is sufficient liquidity to meet a cash dividend of a given size. Finally, the board will want to assure itself that it is meeting all legal and contractual constraints—for example, the firm may be subject to a loan agreement that legally limits the amount of dividends it can pay.

After having looked at internal matters, the board will consider certain market effects and responses. Frankly, the market likes dividends and generally places a high value on them. Moreover, most investors feel that if a company is going to retain earnings rather than pay them out in dividends, it should exhibit extraordinary growth and profit levels. The market's message is clear: If the firm is investing the money wisely and at a high rate of return, fine; otherwise, pay a larger portion of earnings out in the form of dividends. Moreover, to the extent that different types of investors tend to be attracted to certain types of firms, the board must make every effort to meet the dividend expectations of its shareholders. For example, income-oriented investors are attracted to firms that generally pay high dividends; failure to meet these expectations can lead to disastrous results in the marketplace.

Some important dates

When the directors declare a dividend, they also indicate the payment times and other important dates associated with the dividend. Normally, the directors issue a statement to the press indicating their dividend decision, along with the pertinent dividend payment dates. These statements are widely quoted in the financial media; typical of these releases are the dividend news captions depicted in Figure 8.7. Three dates are particularly important to the stockholder: date of record, ex-dividend date, and payment date. The *date of record* is the date on which the investor must be a registered shareholder of the firm to be entitled to receive a dividend. These stock-holders are often referred to as *holders of record*. When the board specifies the date of record, it means that all investors who are official stockholders of the firm as of the close of business on that date will receive the dividends that have just been declared.

Because of the time needed to make bookkeeping entries when a stock is traded, the stock will sell on an ex-dividend basis for four business days prior to the date of record. Thus, the *ex-dividend date* will dictate whether or not you were an official shareholder and therefore eligible to receive the declared dividend. If you sell a stock after the ex-dividend date, you receive the dividend; if you sell before, the new shareholder will receive the recently declared dividend. The *payment date* is also set by the board of directors and generally follows the date of record by a few weeks. It is the actual date on which the company will mail dividend checks to holders of record.

Types of Dividends

Normally corporations pay dividends in the form of cash, and sometimes by issuing additional stock to shareholders. The first type is known as *cash dividend;* the latter is called a *stock dividend*. Occasionally, dividends will be paid in still other forms. For example, the firm might pay what is known as a *spinoff dividend*. A spinoff dividend is like a stock dividend, except that the company pays its stock-

Corporate Dividend News

Higher Payout, Split Are Set at National Service Industries Inc.

By a WALL STREET JOURNAL *Staff Reporter*

ATLANTA—National Service Industries Inc. declared a four-for-three stock split and raised its dividend 8.1%.

The linen service, industrial-chemicals and lighting-equipment concern said the split will be paid Jan. 15 to stock of record Dec. 27.

It said a quarterly dividend of 30 cents a share will be paid on the new shares Jan. 11 to stock of record Dec. 27. The company said the new rate is equivalent to 40 cents a share on the pre-split shares, on which it was paying 37 cents quarterly.

National Service also reported increases of 1% in earnings and 3.3% in sales for its fiscal first quarter ended Nov. 30. Net income rose to about $12.3 million, or $1 a share on the pre-split shares, from about $12.1 million, or 97 cents a share, a year earlier. Sales increased to $227.5 million from $220.3 million a year earlier.

Erwin Zaban, chairman and chief executive officer, said that although the economy "appears to be treading water between recession and recovery," he is becoming "increasingly optimistic that fiscal 1983 will be another record year for the company."

For the year ended Aug. 31, the company earned a record $50.6 million, or $4.08 a share, on record sales of $884.9 million.

In other action yesterday, directors authorized the repurchase of as many as one million of the company's common shares in the open market and through negotiated transactions in the next 12 months. The company had about 12.3 million shares outstanding before the split.

* * *

West Point-Pepperell Lifts Payout 11%; Net Rose 11% in Quarter

WEST POINT, Ga. – West Point-Pepperell Inc. showed yesterday that it is still outrunning the hard times that have overtaken most of the textile industry.

Directors raised the quarterly dividend 11% after management reported an 11% increase in fiscal first-quarter profit and predicted an increase in the current quarter and possibly record earnings for all of fiscal 1983.

The dividend was increased to 50 cents a share from 45 cents, payable Feb. 15 to stock of record Jan. 25.

The company said that earnings in its first quarter ended Nov. 27 increased to $11.7 million, or $1.15 a share, from $10.6 million, or $1.05 a share, a year earlier. Tha[t] was despite a 2.5% sales decline to ... million from $294.6 millio[n] ...

The compan[y] ...

about 687,000 shares outstanding, would proceed with the split "as soon as possible" following the meeting, if the proposal passes. In addition, management seeks an increase in authorized shares to five million from 1.2 million, and to start an employee incentive stock option plan. Bayly is an apparel manufacturer.

Bralorne Resources Ltd. is omitting the semiannual dividend normally paid in January. The oil field systems and petroleum company said it needs to conserve working capital during the current industry downturn. The company has been paying 7½ cents (Canadian) a share semiannually.

Southwest Airlines Co. declared a two-for-one stock split payable Jan. 21 to stock of record Dec. 29. Southwest, which currently has 11,171,562 common shares outstanding, also said it intends to maintain its current quarterly rate of eight cents a share in future, post-split cash dividends by paying four cents a share. Herbert D. Kelleher, chairman and president, said, "Our stock split-up was declared in recognition of the profitable growth which Southwest has enjoyed."

First Boston Inc. declared an extra dividend of $3 each on capital shares and Class A shares as well as the 25-cent quarterly payout. Both are payable by the securities firm Jan. 17 to stock of record Dec. 27.

Lynch Corp., a glass machinery and quartz test equipment company, cut its quarterly to five cents a share from 10 cents, payable Jan. 28 to stock of record Jan. 7.

Stone & Webster Inc. declared an extra payout of 40 cents a share in addition to the 40-cent quarterly dividend, both payable Feb. 15 to stock of record Jan. 3. The engineering and construction concern last paid an extra, of 25 cents a share, last February.

Woodstream Corp. reduced its quarterly dividend to 10 cents a share from 15 cents. The sporting goods concern made it payable Feb. 15 to stock of record Jan. 21.

* * *

Dividends Reported December 15

Company	Period	Amt.	Payable date	Record date
REGULAR				
American Natural Res	Q	.75	2– 1–83	1–
Automatic Switch Co	Q	.23	2– 8–83	1
Bank of Commerce NY	Q	.40	1–14–83	1
Bank of Virginia	Q	.33	1–26–83	
Barnwell Indus Inc	Q	.05	1–26–83	
Barry Wright Corp	Q	.10	2–11–	
Carolina Pwr & Light	Q	.60	2– 1–	
Centran Corp	Q	.10	1–14	
Ducommun Inc	Q	.17½	2–	
Duplex Products Inc	Q	.17	1–	
Duplex Prods $1.45pf	Q	.36¼	12	
First Boston Inc	Q	.25		
Fluorocarbon Co	Q	.04		
Friedman Indus	Q	.06		
Hartford Natl Corp	Q	.50		
Hoover Universal Inc	Q			
Keystone Intl Inc	Q			
Kinder-Care LearningsCtr	Q			
Natl Convenience Stores				
Natl Medical Care				
Realex Corp				
Reliable Life In				
Sealed Pow				
Stone & W				
Super				
W				

Company	Period	Amt.		Payable date	Record date
Ziegler Co	Q	.11	.10	1–27–83	1–14
REDUCED					
		--Amounts--			
		New	Old		
Automotive Hdw ClA	Q	b.10	b.15	1–14–83	12–31
Lynch Corp	Q	.05	.10	1–28–83	1– 7
National Steel	Q	.06¼	.25	1–31–83	1– 3
Woodstream Corp	Q	.10	.15	2–15–83	1–21
INITIAL					
Dunkin' Donuts new	Q	.06		3–18–83	2–11
Natl Service Indus new	Q	tt.30		1–11–83	12–27
tt-An effective increase following a 4-for-3 stock split.					
Southland Corp new	Q	t.21		3–22–83	3– 1
t-An effective increase following a 3-for-2 stock split.					
FOREIGN					
Anglovaal Ltd ADR	G	w		2–14–83	12–20
w-Approximately $.686 per Depositary share.					
HartebeestfonteinGoldADR	G	y		2–14–83	12–20
y-Approximately $2.310 per Depositary share.					
OMITTED					
Bralorne Resources Ltd					
Resource Services Gr					

A-Annual; Ac-Accumulation; b-Payable in Canadian funds; F-Final; G-Interim; h-From income; k-From capital gains; M-Monthly; Q-Quarterly; S-Semi-annual.

* * *

Dividends Reported December 14

Company	Period	Amt.	Payable date	Record date
REGULAR				
Fluor Corp	Q	.20	1–17–83	12–27
Neutrogena Corp	A	.25	1–17–83	12–15
Warner Communications	Q	.25	2–15–83	1–14
STOCKS				
Neutrogena Corp		10%	1–17–83	12–15

A-Annual; Ac-Accumulation; b-Payable in Canadian funds; F-Final; G-Interim; h-From income; k-From capital gains; M-Monthly; Q-Quarterly; S-Semi-annual.

* * *

Stocks Ex-Dividend December 17

Company	Amount	Company	Amount
Canal-Randolph	.16	PhilaElec7.80%pf	1.95
ConroyInc	.10	PhilaElec7.85%pf	1.96¼
CountrywideCredit	.06	PhilaElec7.75%pf	1.93¾
EdisonBrosStrs	.36	PhilaElec7%pf	1.75
Everest&Jennings clA	.05	PhilaElec4.68%pf	1.17
Everest&Jen clB	.02½	PhilaElec4.4%pf	1.10
FinclCrpAmer new	.17	PhilaElec4.3%pf	1.07½
FisherFoods	.10	PhilaElec3.8%pf	.95
Greyhound$4.75pf	1.18¾	PhilaEl17.125%pf	4.28⅛
GuardianIndus	.09	PiedmontNatGas	.47
Hi-ShearIndus	.12½	PremierIndustrl	.10½
HubbardRealEstInv	.50	RansburgCorp	.18
INTERCO	.72	RavenIndus	.15
INTERCO$7.75	1.93¾	RavenIndus	n
IntercoleInc	k	n-5% stk	
k-10% stk		RibletPrdts	.03
JameswayCorp	.03	StPaulSecurs	.097
PayLessDrugStrsNW	.11	SandersAssocs	.18
PhilaElec15.25%pf	3.81¼	TootsieRollIndus	.10
PhilaElec9.52%pf	2.38	Tri-ContinentalCrp	.28
PhilaElec9.50%pf	2.37½	Tri-Continentalpf	.62½
PhilaElec8.75%pf	2.18¾		

Figure 8.7 Important Dates and Data about Dividends. The dividend actions of corporations are big news in the financial community. (*Source: The Wall Street Journal,* December 16, 1982.)

holders in shares of stock *other than its own.* Generally, these are shares in subsidiary companies that the corporation owns and in which, for one reason or another, it is reducing (or eliminating) its investment. Some public utility firms use what are known as *return of capital dividends.* These are cash dividends, but because they are not charged to retained earnings, they are considered different from normal cash dividends. As such, they are highly valued by knowledgeable income-oriented investors because they are *not* subject to income tax. But dividends in the form of either cash or stock remain by far the most popular, so let us take a closer look at these.

Cash or stock

More firms use cash dividends than any other type of dividend payment procedure. It is also the most popular with investors because it comes in such a convenient form. If the directors declared a quarterly cash dividend of 50 cents per share, and if you owned 200 shares of stock, you would receive a check for $100. A popular way of assessing the amount of dividends paid by a firm is to measure the stock's *dividend yield.* Basically, dividend yield is a measure of common stock dividends on a relative (%), rather than absolute ($), basis; that is, the dollar amount of dividends received is related to the market price of the stock. As such, it is an indication of the rate of current income earned on the investment dollar. It is computed as follows:

$$\text{dividend yield} = \frac{\text{annual dividends paid per share}}{\text{market price per share of stock}}$$

Thus, a company that annually pays $2 per share in dividends to its stockholders, and whose stock is trading at $25, would have a dividend yield of 8 percent.

Occasionally, a firm may declare a stock dividend instead of a cash dividend. A stock dividend simply means that the dividend is paid in additional shares of stock. For instance, if the board declares a 10 percent stock dividend, each shareholder will receive 1 new share of stock for each 10 shares currently owned. If you own 200 shares of stock, you will receive 20 new shares under such an arrangement. Although they seem to satisfy the needs of investors, stock dividends really have no value because they represent the receipt of something already owned. This is so since the market will respond to stock dividends by adjusting share prices accordingly. Thus, in the example above, we would normally find that a 10 percent stock dividend will lead to a 10 percent decline in the per share price of a stock. As a result, if the market value of your shareholdings amounted to, say, $10,000 before a stock dividend, it is likely that the same total market value will prevail after the stock dividend (you may have more shares, but each will carry a lower market price). Often, a firm will combine a modest stock dividend with a cash dividend.

Tax considerations

One important tax provision that has a bearing on the after-tax dividend income of stockholders is known as the *dividend exclusion feature.* This provision is found in the federal and many state income tax laws, and exempts the first $100 of common stock dividends from taxation (or $200 for a couple filing a joint return). In essence,

BOX 8.2 MORE MILEAGE FROM DIVIDENDS

If you are a stockholder, or plan to become one, you should be aware of dividend-reinvestment plans—also known as DRP's or DIP's—offered by some 1,300 companies.

By use of such plans, your dividends can be automatically reinvested in additional stock at little or no cost and in many cases at an actual discount from market value. This provides the magic of compounding of dividends, which, if received in cash, often are frittered away or left in low-yielding savings accounts until enough accumulates to buy additional shares. Also, almost all of the companies offering DRP's will accept new money in addition to dividends to be invested in company shares on favorable terms.

In order to join such a plan, you must, of course, first own shares in the company. The next step is to obtain from the company a DRP authorization form, fill it in and mail it to the plan administrator, usually a bank. From then on, you will receive periodic statements showing the number of whole and fractional shares to your credit.

As an example, if you had put 100 shares of American Telephone & Telegraph common in the dividend-reinvestment plan when it started in 1973, you would now have 206 shares. If you had started five years ago, the 100 shares would have grown to 157. Since 1975, dividends have been reinvested at 95 percent of average market price.

There are several versions of these plans. Most of them permit purchase of additional shares up to a limit, typically $3,000 a quarter, in the same way that shares are purchased through dividend reinvestment. According to Robert D. Ferris of Georgeson & Company, a New York stockholder-relations firm, in about 75 percent of all plans the sponsor picks up the participant's share of any brokerage commission and transaction or service charges.

The Georgeson survey also found that some 160 companies offer a 5 percent discount on reinvested dividends, and about 20 percent of these extend the discount to additional cash purchases.

Income taxes are payable on dividends even though they are reinvested. However, the tax act of 1981 allows shareholders in qualified utilities to defer taxes on reinvested dividends up to $750 on an individual return and $1,500 on a joint return. More than 100 electric, gas and water utilities offer such plans.

Several market services keep track of companies that offer variations of DRP's. *United Business and Investment Report,* for example, shows on its supervised stock list the companies that offer DRP's.

Also, Standard & Poor's has a list of some 750 companies traded on the New York and American stock exchanges with such plans.

Source: John W. Hazard, "More Mileage from Dividends." *U.S. News & World Report,* July 12, 1982, p. 72.

this means that a certain portion of an investor's dividend income is tax free. The provision is particularly important to small investors and especially to those who seek high levels of current income. Another tax consideration of interest here has to do with the sale of stock dividends. Any profits earned on such transactions are eligible for preferential long-term capital gains treatment so long as the *original shares* were held for more than 12 months. Note that it is not necessary to hold the shares received as dividends for 12 months, but only the original shares. For example, if you bought some stock 18 months ago (which qualifies the transaction for preferential capital gains treatment) and recently received a stock dividend you decided to sell, any profit from such a sale is considered long-term capital gains and therefore subject to the lower tax rate.

Finally, there is a special provision of the tax laws, which will remain effective through 1985, that pertains to the dividend reinvestment plans of public utilities. In a *dividend reinvestment plan,* a stockholder agrees to receive cash dividends in the form of additional shares of the company's common stock. There are over a thousand dividend reinvestment plans in existence (most major corporations have them), but only the plans of *qualifying public utilities* are eligible for the special tax treatment. More specifically, shareholders who participate in such qualifying plans can exclude annually up to $750 of reinvested dividends ($1,500 in the case of joint returns) from taxable income—normally, the value of stocks received through a dividend reinvestment plan is subject to ordinary income tax even though no cash is received. Dividend reinvestment plans are attractive since they provide investors with a convenient and inexpensive way to accumulate capital, but in the case of qualifying public utilities, they're even more attractive since all or a portion of the dividends received in this manner are free from taxes (so long as the stock is held). As an added feature, if the stock received through a qualified dividend reinvestment plan is held for more than a year, it is taxed at the preferential long-term capital gains rate when sold.

Dividend Policies

Most firms have a stated or implied policy that sets the dividend payment practices followed by that firm. The policy is usually established with an eye toward the financing requirements of the firm and the needs of its stockholders. Because they can affect the level and consistency of dividend payoffs, these policies are of concern to all investors. We will look here at three of the most widely used dividend policies.

Regular dividends

Perhaps the most common type of dividend policy, the *regular dividend* approach, is based on the payment of a fixed dollar dividend in each quarter. The idea is to keep the level of dividends as regular and consistent as possible. Firms that follow this policy go to almost any extent to avoid missing or decreasing the level of dividends. On the other hand, the amount of per share dividends paid over time usually increases as the firm's profit level increases, but only after a proved increase in earnings has taken place. A firm may therefore have an annual dividend rate of, say, $2 per share and hold that level for several years or more until earnings have moved to a new and higher plateau. Only then will the level of dividends be increased to, say, $2.50 per share. The object of this policy is to minimize the uncertainty of the dividend flows to stockholders, whose faith in regular dividends is severely tried when a firm fails to maintain payments.

Regular-extra dividends

Some firms will periodically declare *extra dividends* whenever the level of earnings is higher than normal and the firm has an extra-large pool of funds from which

TABLE 8.2   A REGULAR-EXTRA DIVIDEND POLICY IN ACTION

Year	Earnings per Share	Regular Dividend per Share	Extra Dividend per Share	Total Dividend per Share
1973	$2.50	$1.00		$1.00
1974	2.63	1.00		1.00
1975	2.98	1.00		1.00
1976	3.02	1.00	$ .75	1.75
1977	2.01	1.00		1.00
1978	2.18	1.00		1.00
1979	3.12	1.00	.90	1.90
1980	4.68	1.00	1.00	2.00
1981	5.01	2.00		2.00
1982	4.85	2.00		2.00
1983	5.11	2.00		2.00
1984	5.26	2.00	.65	2.65

to pay dividends. Extra dividends are usually, but not always, paid in the final quarter of the year and are designated as "extra" in order to avoid giving stockholders the impression that a new level of regular dividends is about to be established. Table 8.2 shows how extra dividends are combined with a regular dividend policy. Note that the level of regular dividends is kept fairly stable and extra dividends are used only when corporate earnings are extra good.

Fixed payout ratio

The dividend policy that gives most attention to the firm, and that some would argue gives too little weight to the needs of stockholders, is the *fixed payout ratio*. It is used by a number of firms, particularly newer ones or those experiencing high growth rates. By definition, a payout ratio describes the percentage of each dollar earned that is distributed to the owners in the form of cash dividends. Little attention is given to the dollar level of dividends, as the thrust of this policy is to keep the ratio of the amount paid out as constant as possible. As a result, if earnings fluctuate, then so (obviously) do dividends; Table 8.3 illustrates this policy in action. In this example, we assume that the firm uses a constant 25 percent payout ratio. The amount of dividends paid per share is determined by multiplying the earnings per share by the payout ratio (e.g., for 1970: $2.50 × .25 = $.62½). Note that the biggest drawback of this policy is that the instability of dividends often leads to erratic and sometimes depressed market prices for the common stock.

TYPES AND USES OF COMMON STOCK

Common stocks appeal to individual investors because they are simple, relatively straightforward investment vehicles. Their sources of return are relatively easy to identify, and they offer the potential for everything from current income and stability

TABLE 8.3 A FIXED PAYOUT RATIO DIVIDEND POLICY IN ACTION

Year	Earnings per Share	Payout Ratio	Annual Dividends Paid per Share
1973	$2.50	25%	$ .62½
1974	2.63	25	.66
1975	2.98	25	.74½
1976	3.02	25	.75½
1977	2.01	25	.50¼
1978	2.18	25	.54½
1979	3.12	25	.78
1980	4.68	25	1.17
1981	5.01	25	1.25
1982	4.85	25	1.21
1983	5.11	25	1.28
1984	5.26	25	1.31½

of capital to attractive capital gains. The market contains a wide range of different types of stock, from the most conservative to the highly speculative. Generally, the kinds of stock sought by investors will depend on their investment objectives and their investment program. We will examine several of the more popular kinds of common stock, as well as the various ways such securities can be used in different types of investment programs.

Kinds of Stock

It is helpful to understand the market system for classifying common stock because a stock's general classification denotes not only its fundamental source of return, but also the quality of the company's earnings, the issue's susceptibility to market risks, the nature and stability of its earning per share and dividends, and even the susceptibility of the stock to adverse market and economic conditions. Such insight is useful in selecting stocks that best fit the overall investment objectives of the investor. Among the many different types of stock, blue chips, income stocks, growth stocks, speculative stocks, cyclical stocks, and defensive stocks are the most common. We will now look at each of these types of stocks not only to see what they are, but also to see how they might be used.

Blue chips

These are the cream of the crop; *blue chips* are stocks that are unsurpassed in quality and have a long and stable record of earnings and dividends. They are issued by the strongest companies and include AT&T (shown here) and many other public utilities, as well as the industrial shares of IBM, GE, Procter & Gamble, and Standard Oil of Indiana, to name just a few. All blue chip companies are not alike. Some, like many of the public utilities, provide consistently high dividend yields, whereas others are more growth-oriented. Good examples of blue chip growth firms include IBM, Eastman Kodak, and American Home Products. Blue chips are particularly attractive to investors who seek quality investment outlets offering respectable dividend yields and modest growth potential. Many use them for long-term investment purposes (they are seldom viewed as trading vehicles), and because of their relatively low risk exposure, as a way of obtaining modest but dependable rates of return on their investment dollars. They are popular with a large segment of the investing public and as a result are often relatively high in price, especially when the market is unsettled and investors become more quality-conscious.

American Tel. & Tel.

NYSE Symbol T   Options on CBOE

Price Nov. 8'82	Range 1982	P-E Ratio	Dividend	Yield	S&P Ranking
62	63¼–49⅞	7	5.40	8.7%	A+

SUMMARY: AT&T is undergoing a major reorganization pursuant to an antitrust settlement of January, 1982 with the Justice Department, as modified by Judge Harold Green in August, 1982. By early 1984 AT&T will spin off to shareholders its 22 local Bell operating subsidiaries. AT&T will retain the intercity facilities of the operating companies, the Long Lines Department, Western Electric and Bell Labs, and will have greater freedom to engage in unregulated activities.

Source: Standard & Poor's *NYSE Stock Reports,* November 15, 1982.

Income stocks

Some stocks are appealing simply because they pay out attractive dividend yields. This is the case with *income stocks,* issues that have a long and sustained record of regularly paying higher than average dividends. Income shares are ideally suited for individuals who seek a relatively safe and high level of current income from their investment capital. Unlike holders of bonds and preferred stocks, holders of income stocks can expect the amount of dividends paid to increase over time. The major disadvantage of these securities is that some of the firms may be paying high dividends because their growth potential is fairly limited. Therefore, income shares generally exhibit only low or modest rates of growth in earnings.

This does not mean that such firms are unprofitable or lack future prospects; quite the contrary, most firms whose stocks qualify as income shares are highly profitable organizations and have excellent future prospects. A number of income stocks are among the giants of American industry, and many are also classified as quality blue chip stocks. Most public utility shares are considered income stocks, such as Pacific Gas and Electric (shown here), as well as selected industrial and financial issues like Avon Products, Beneficial Finance, Champion Spark Plug, and Scovill Mfg. By their nature, income stocks are not exposed to extensive business and market risks, but instead are subject to a fair amount of interest rate risk.

Pacific Gas & Electric

NYSE Symbol PCG

Price Aug. 26'82	Range 1982	P-E Ratio	Dividend	Yield	S&P Ranking
27	27¼–20¼	6	3.00	11.1%	A

SUMMARY: This electric-gas utility, which is one of the largest in the U.S., serves a major part of northern and central California. It now appears that many of the problems surrounding its Diablo Canyon nuclear plant are being solved and that the first unit should become commercially operative in the first half of 1983. Short-term earnings prospects are bolstered by a company-wide program to control costs.

Source: Standard & Poor's *NYSE Stock Reports,* September 2, 1982.

Growth stocks

Shares that have experienced, and are expected to continue to experience, consistently high rates of growth in operations and earnings are known as *growth stocks.* A good growth stock might exhibit a sustained rate of growth in earnings of 12 to 15 percent over a period when common stocks, on average, are experiencing growth rates of only 5 to 6 percent. Litton Industries, Schlumberger, Wendy's (shown here), Honeywell, and Digital Equipment are all prime examples of growth stock. As this list suggests, some growth stocks also rate as blue chips and provide quality growth, whereas others possess higher levels of speculation. Growth stocks normally pay little or no dividends, and their payout ratio seldom exceeds 25 percent of earnings because all or most of the profits are reinvested in the company and used to at least partially finance its rapid growth. Thus the major source of return to investors is price appreciation. Growth shares generally appeal to investors who are looking for attractive capital gains rather than dividends, and who are willing to assume a higher element of risk (which is an outgrowth of the uncertain nature of the investment payoff). Most growth stock investors, however, view this added risk exposure as completely acceptable in light of the relatively high potential return these securities offer.

Wendy's International

NYSE Symbol WEN   Put & Call Options on Pac

Price Sep. 7'82	Range 1982	P-E Ratio	Dividend	Yield	S&P Ranking
19⅜	20–12¼	12	0.28	1.4%	B+

SUMMARY: This company operates, and licenses others to operate, Wendy's Old Fashioned Hamburgers fast-food restaurants. Earnings for 1982 should benefit from the larger number of units in operation, more stable labor costs and commodity prices, and gradually improving margins at formerly franchised units acquired during 1981.

Source: Standard & Poor's *NYSE Stock Reports,* September 14, 1982.

Speculative stocks

Shares that offer little more than the hope that their prices will go up are known as *speculative stocks.* They are a special breed of stock and enjoy a wide following, particularly when the market is bullish. Speculative stocks lack proved records of success; their earnings are uncertain and highly unstable; they are subject to wide swings in price; and they usually pay little or nothing in dividends. On the plus side, speculative stocks like Apple Computer, shown here, offer the prospects for growth and the chance to hit it big in the market. The idea is that some new information, discovery, or production technique will come along, favorably affect the growth prospects of the firm, and inflate the price of the stock. But to be successful, an investor has to identify the big-money winners before the rest of the market does, and before the price of the stock is driven up. Speculative stocks, then, are obviously highly risky and require not only a strong stomach, but considerable knowledge and expertise as well. They are used to seek capital gains, and most investors who buy speculative stocks do so on a fairly short-term basis and will often aggressively trade in and out of these securities as the situation demands.

Apple Computer

NASDAQ Symbol **AAPL**   (Incl. in Nat'l Market; marginable)

Price Oct. 28'82	Range 1982	P-E Ratio	Dividend	Yield	S&P Ranking
25⅛	26¾–10¾	24	None	None	NR

SUMMARY: This company is a leading manufacturer of microprocessor-based personal computer systems. The Apple II and Apple III are its major systems. New products are expected to be introduced in 1983. While the substantial earnings gains of recent years are likely to moderate as sales and earnings bases expand, commitments to new product and market development enhance longer-term prospects.

Source: Standard & Poor's *OTC Stock Reports,* November 5, 1982.

Cyclical stocks

Cyclical stocks are those issued by companies whose earnings are closely linked to the general level of business activity. They tend to reflect the general state of the economy, and move up and down as the business cycle moves through its peaks and troughs. Companies that serve markets tied to capital equipment spending on the part of business, or consumer spending for big-ticket durable items like houses and cars typically head the list of cyclical stocks. These would include machine tool manufacturers like Chicago Pneumatic Tools (shown here), or those in the auto, chemical, or copper industries, such as Ford, Union Carbide, and Phelps Dodge. For obvious reasons, these stocks have the most appeal when the economic outlook is strong, and are perhaps best avoided when the economy begins to weaken. Because their prices have a tendency to move with the level of economic activity, they are probably more suitable for investors who are willing to trade in and out of these issues (as the economic outlook dictates), and who can tolerate the accompanying exposure to risk.

Chicago Pneumatic Tool

NYSE Symbol CGG

Price Oct. 21'82	Range 1982	P-E Ratio	Dividend	Yield	S&P Ranking
14⅛	19⅞–10⅞	NM	—	—	B

SUMMARY: The principal markets of this prominent manufacturer of pneumatic machinery and tools are auto and truck servicing, construction and industrial assembly. European operations, which have produced losses in the past few years, are being restructured. With demand from capital goods markets at a depressed level, CGG is expected to incur a net loss in 1982, and little improvement is likely in 1983. The quarterly dividend has been omitted.

Source: Standard & Poor's *NYSE Stock Reports,* October 28, 1982.

Defensive stocks

Sometimes it is possible to find stocks whose prices will remain stable, or even prosper, when economic activity is tapering off. These securities are known as *defensive stocks* and tend to be less affected by downswings in the business cycle than the average issue. Examples of defensive stocks include the shares of many public utilities, as well as industrial and consumer goods companies that produce or market such staples as beverages, drugs, and foods (as is the case with Safeway Stores, shown here). Perhaps the best known of all defensive stocks, particularly in inflationary periods, are gold mining shares; these stocks literally flourish when inflation becomes a serious problem. Defensive shares are commonly used by the more aggressive investors. For the most part, such investors tend to "park" their funds temporarily in defensive stocks while the market and/or economy is off (and until the investment atmosphere improves).

Safeway Stores

NYSE Symbol SA   Put & Call Options on CBOE

Price Oct. 15'82	Range 1982	P-E Ratio	Dividend	Yield	S&P Ranking
44⅛	45¾–26¼	8	2.80	6.3%	B +

SUMMARY: Safeway, with stores primarily west of the Mississippi, is the largest supermarket chain in the U.S., and has significant foreign operations. Earnings in 1982 have been aided by efforts to streamline operations and strengthen the firm's competitive position in key markets. The outlook for 1983 is favorable. Over the longer term, growth prospects hinge on SA's ability to improve its share in existing markets on a sustained basis by generating continued real growth in same-store sales.

Source: Standard & Poor's *NYSE Stock Reports,* October 22, 1982.

*I know it has great potential, it's in a growth industry,
and it's a leader in its field—but a 12¢ dividend check?*

Alternative Investment Strategies

Basically, common stocks can be used in three ways: (1) as a warehouse of value, (2) to accumulate capital, and/or (3) as a source of income. Storage of value is important to all investors, since nobody likes to lose money. However, some investors are more concerned about it than others and therefore put safety of principal first in their stock selection process. These investors are more quality-conscious and tend to gravitate toward blue chips and other nonspeculative shares. Accumulation of capital is generally an important goal to individuals with long-term investment horizons. They use the capital gains and/or dividends that stocks provide to build up their wealth. Some use growth stocks for such purposes; others do it with income shares; still others use a little of both. Finally, some people use stocks as a source of income; to them, a dependable flow of dividends is essential. High-yield, good-quality income shares are usually the preferred investment vehicle for these individuals.

Individuals can use a number of different *investment strategies* to reach one or more of these investment goals; these include buy-and-hold, high income, quality long-term growth, aggressive stock management, and speculation and short-term trading. The first three strategies would probably appeal to investors who consider storage of value important. Depending on the temperament of the investor and the time he or she has to devote to an investment program, any one of the five strategies might be used to accumulate capital; the high-income strategy is the most logical choice for those using stocks as a source of income.

Buy-and-hold

This is the most basic and certainly one of the most conservative of all investment strategies; the objective is to place money in a secure investment outlet (safety of principal is vital) and watch it grow over time. High-quality stocks that offer attractive current income and/or capital gains are selected and held for extended periods—perhaps as long as 15 or 20 years. This type of strategy is often used to finance future retirement plans, to meet educational requirements, or simply as a convenient way of accumulating capital over the long haul. Generally, investors will pick out a few stocks and invest in them on a regular basis for extended periods of time; they will stick with these securities until either the investment climate or corporate results change dramatically. Not only do investors regularly add fresh capital to their portfolios (many treat it like a savings plan), but most of the income from annual dividends is also plowed back into the portfolio and reinvested in additional shares. In fact, the investor might even participate in a dividend reinvestment plan. The buy-and-hold strategy minimizes the amount of time an investor must devote to portfolio management. Risk is also kept low; most buy-and-hold investors are conservative, quality-conscious individuals who are satisfied with more modest rates of return over the long haul.

High income

Often investors use common stocks to seek high levels of current income. Common stocks are viewed as desirable outlets for such purposes not only because of their current yields, but also because their *dividend levels tend to increase over time.* Safety of principal and stability of income are vital; capital gains are of secondary importance. Quality income shares are the popular investment medium for this kind of strategy. Because of the high yields available from many income shares today, more investors are adopting this strategy simply as a way of earning high (and relatively safe) returns on their investment capital. More often than not, however, high-income strategies are used by those trying to supplement their income and who plan to use the added income for consumption purposes, such as a retired couple supplementing their social security benefits with income from stocks.

Quality long-term growth

This is a less conservative strategy that seeks capital gains as the primary source of return. There is a fair amount of trading with this approach, although most of it is confined to quality growth stocks offering good growth prospects and the chance for robust price appreciation. In essence, the strategy simply capitalizes on a fundamental source of common stock returns: capital gains. The approach is somewhat risky, and so substantial diversification is often used. When the market becomes depressed, many of these investors will retreat to the sidelines by selling their stocks and converting to cash or some other type of defensive security. Long-

BOX 8.3 THE TOP 20 STOCKS OF THE DECADE, 1971–1981

Very likely nobody had the wit or the temerity in 1971 to snap up all or even most of the 20 stocks on the Fortune 500 list that have yielded the purest gold to investors over the past decade. The gold is best weighed by a stock's total return, which measures both a share's appreciation in price and its dividends—in this case from the end of 1971 to the end of 1981. The calculations assume that investors used all dividends and payments for stock fractions from splits to buy more stock, and that the accumulated investment was liquidated at the close of last year (1981).

The list below would have defeated most investors' powers of foresight. It is a jumble of conglomerates and one-product companies, of famous names and inconspicuous ones. Not surprisingly, it tilts toward companies that did poorly in 1971. Storage Technology, now a $922-million-a-year maker of computer memory systems, and Marion Corp., an independent oil and gas producer, were then drenched in red ink. Moore McCormack Resources, at the time a cargo shipper, was suffering organizational problems, having lost a thumping $17 million in 1970. Storage Technology, Marion, and eight others were also probably too small to have riveted investors' attention ten years ago. All ten posted under $3 million in net profits then, and all had sales below the $176 million it took to make the Fortune 500 in 1971.

THE DECADE'S TOP 20

Rank	Company	Total Return, 1971–81 Average	Growth in Earnings per Share, 1971–81 Average	Dividend Payout,[1] 1981	Price-earnings Ratio, Early April[2]
1	Teledyne	31.9%	41.7%	0%	5.6
2	Intel	30.3%	35.2%	0%	29.5
3	NVF	30.1%	0.1%	80.4%	5.1
4	Oak Industries	29.7%	26.1%	10.8%	9.3
5	Nucor	29.6%	26.5%	9.6%	7.1
6	Moore McCormack	29.5%	40.5%	15.5%	3.5
7	Cooper Industries	27.8%	45.2%	21.8%	6.6
8	Northrop	27.2%	12.9%	54.4%	9.5
9	Trinity Industries	26.8%	31.6%	12.7%	3.7

term accumulation of capital is the most common reason for using this approach; but in contrast to the buy-and-hold tactic, the investor aggressively seeks a bigger payoff by doing considerably more trading and assuming more market risk.

Aggressive stock management

This type of investment program is also based on the principle of using quality issues, but this time to seek attractive rates of return through a fully managed portfolio, one in which the investor aggressively trades in and out of various stocks in order to achieve handsome yields from both current income (dividends) and capital gains. Blue chips, income shares, growth stocks, and cyclical issues are the primary

BOX 8.3 Continued

Rank	Company	Total Return, 1971–81 Average	Growth in Earnings per Share, 1971–81 Average	Dividend Payout,[1] 1981	Price-earnings Ratio, Early April[2]
10	Dorchester Gas	26.3%	34.3%	8.4%	8.6
11	Handy & Harman	26.2%	31.6%	30.7%	7.4
12	Marion	26.0%	*	7.7%	11.2
13	Storage Tech.	25.8%	*	0%	7.9
14	NL Industries	25.3%	52.3%	17.9%	4.7
15	Consol. Papers	25.2%	26.5%	39.6%	5.1
16	Dean Foods	24.2%	22.2%	21.3%	6.9
17	Wang Labs	23.3%	23.6%	8.8%	16.4
18	Colt Industries	23.3%	25.3%	38.3%	6.9
19	Carpenter Tech.	23.3%	27.2%	38.5%	7.2
20	Freeport-McMoRan	23.1%	27.9%	19.6%	6.0
	Top 20 (median)	29.3%	27.1%	20.8%[3]	7.0
	Benchmark	8.5%	13.4%	42.7%	7.3

*Loss in 1971. N.A., Not available.
[1]As percent of earnings.
[2]Based on 1982 earnings estimates compiled by Institutional Brokers Estimate System.
[3]Average.

Of all the stocks in the Fortune 500, investors reaped the highest returns from 1971–81 in these 20. A benchmark of average performance of stocks in the S&P 500 is provided for comparison purposes. Not surprisingly, note that all but a few of the companies in the Top 20 were above the benchmarks in earnings per share growth, and below average in dividend payout; a big surprise was that only 8 of the companies were selling at price-earnings multiples higher than the market's.

Source: Gwen Kinkead, "The Top 20 Stocks of the Decade." *Fortune,* May 3, 1982, pp. 299–300.

investment vehicles. Income, cyclical, and/or growth stocks would probably be the major investments during bull markets, and defensive securities, cash, or some short-term debt instrument would likely be used when the market is off. This approach is somewhat similar to the quality long-term growth strategy, but it involves considerably more trading, and the investment horizon is generally much shorter. For example, rather than waiting two or three years for a stock to move, an aggressive stock trader would go after the same investment payoff in six months to a year. Timing security transactions and turning investment capital over more rapidly are both key elements of this strategy. It has obvious and substantial risks, and also places real demands on the individual's time and investment skills. But the rewards of success can be equally substantial.

Speculation and short-term trading

This is the least conservative of all investment strategies and carries the idea of speculation and short-term trading to its extreme. The sole investment objective is capital gains; and if it can be achieved in two weeks, all the better. Although such investors confine most of their attention to speculative common stocks, they are not averse to using other forms of common stock if they offer attractive short-term capital gains opportunities. Many speculators find that information about the industry or company itself is much less important in this kind of strategy than market psychology or the general tone of the market itself. Getting out as quickly as possible with substantial capital gains is what this strategy is all about. It is a process of constantly switching from one position to another as new investment opportunities unfold. Because the strategy involves so much risk, many transactions end with little or no profit, or even substantial losses. The hope is, of course, that when one does hit it big, returns will be more than sufficient to offset losses; that is, that the net result will lead to a hefty rate of return commensurate with the risk involved. Investing this way obviously requires considerable knowledge, time, and—perhaps most important—the psychological and financial fortitude to withstand the shock of financial losses.

SUMMARY

Common stocks have traditionally been popular with investors. They provide an almost unlimited opportunity to tailor an investment program to individual needs and preferences. For many investors, stocks offer a speculative appeal because of their potential for generating especially attractive returns. For retired people and others living on accumulated wealth, stocks provide an excellent opportunity to preserve capital and gain current income. For still others, common stocks are the basis for long-run wealth-accumulation programs, and are used very much like a savings account. During much of the past, various buy-and-hold programs have been quite successful, producing substantially higher returns than bonds or other conservative investment media. Within the past 15 years or so, however, fits of inflation and general economic uncertainty have taken a heavy toll on common stock returns. There have been exceptions, of course, but too often even the soundest of common stocks has failed to provide sufficiently attractive yields—at least in real terms.

Shares of common stock represent ownership in a business. As owners, shareholders are entitled to the profits left over after all expenses and creditor claims are paid. This "residual" feature provides the potential for exceptional returns on investment, and for exceptional losses. If profits remain after all expenses are paid, they are paid out in the form of dividends, or reinvested for the owners' future benefit. If revenues do not cover expenses and debt costs, however, it is the owners who stand to lose.

There are several ways to calculate the value of a stock. Book value is determined by subtracting total liabilities from total assets. Liquidation value is another measure of an owner's position that may be viewed as a conservative estimate of worth under the most adverse conditions—failure of the company. Market value represents the market price of a share of stock; and investment value is the price an investor should be willing to pay for a share of stock. Only if investment value equals or exceeds market value would a stock be considered a worthwhile investment.

Cash dividends are one form of return to investors, and they are paid out by companies according to certain policies. Normally, the board of directors specifies the level of dividends to be paid by considering the tradeoff between the reinvestment of profits in the business and higher current income to the shareholders. Some firms select a target level, or dollar amount, of dividends, with the target changing every few years as profits change. Others choose a modest regular dividend, but pay year-end extras when the profits are there to justify them. Still others select a target payout ratio and attempt to pay a set percentage of profits to shareholders. The dividend decision has several important dates associated with it. The day of the board of directors' decision is called the declaration date; at that time, the board also sets the date of record and payment dates. To receive a dividend, a shareholder's name must appear on the shareholder list on the date of record. To facilitate the payment process, the brokerage industry has established an ex-dividend date four days prior to the date of record. This date provides time for transferring shares bought and sold near the date of record. To be eligible to receive the dividend, an investor must purchase a stock before the ex-dividend date.

The type of stock selected depends on an investor's particular needs and preferences. Those of the largest, most stable companies are called blue chips; these stocks normally produce rates of return commensurate with the general level of growth in the economy, and as such often form the foundation for many long-term portfolios. Other conservative stocks that pay high dividends are called income stocks. They are often held by individuals in lower tax brackets and by those who need the dividends for current income and consumption. Growth stocks offer increases in earnings consistently above the average level of growth in the economy. Speculative stocks offer the potential for exceptional growth, but they are highly risky; the investor, in effect, takes the risk that such companies may fail or that their profits may be extremely erratic. Cyclical stocks tend to move closely with general economic conditions. Defensive stocks, in contrast, are those of companies that do relatively well during periods of economic uncertainty; their products are related to basic consumer needs, and thus provide consistent profits regardless of economic conditions. A special category of defensive stocks are those that actually prosper during periods of uncertainty—notably, gold stocks.

Generally speaking, common stocks can be used as a storage of value, to accumulate capital, and/or as a source of income. Determining which of these objectives is being sought will, of course, influence the type of stock that the individual invests in. Depending on the type of stock being used and the particular investment objectives being sought, different investment strategies can be followed: buy-and-hold techniques, high income, quality long-term growth, aggressive stock management, or speculative and short-term trading.

KEY TERMS

annual stockholders' meeting	income stocks
blue chip stock	investment value
book value	liquidation value
cash dividend	majority voting
classified common stock	market value
cumulative voting	par value
cyclical stock	payment date (dividend)
date of record	proxy
defensive stock	publicly traded stock
deferred equity	public offering
dividend exclusion feature	regular dividend
dividend reinvestment plan	retained earnings
dividend yield	reverse stock split
earnings per share (EPS)	rights offering
equity capital	speculative stock
ex-dividend date	spinoff dividend
extra dividend	stock dividend
fixed payout ratio	stock split
growth stock	treasury stock
holder of record	voting rights

REVIEW QUESTIONS

1. What is a common stock? What is meant by the statement that holders of common stock are the residual owners of the firm?

2. Explain the difference between a stock split and a stock dividend.

   a. Assume that Davy Jones holds 250 shares of Consolidated Everything, Inc.; how many shares of stock would he hold after the firm declared a 2 for 1 stock split?
   b. What would happen if the firm declared a 200 percent stock dividend?

3. Why do firms issue treasury stock? Are they like classified stock? Are some types of classified stock particularly appealing to certain types of investors?

4. Define and differentiate among each of the following pairs of terms:

   a. Par value and liquidation value.
   b. Cash dividends and stock dividends.
   c. Date of record and payment date.
   d. Growth stock and speculative stock.

5. The Porter Pottery Company has total assets of $2.5 million, total short- and long-term debt of $1.8 million, and $200,000 worth of 8 percent preferred stock outstanding. What is the firm's total book value? What would its book value per share amount to if it had 50,000 shares of common stock outstanding?

6. Are stocks a good inflation hedge? Explain.

7. What are the major types of risk to which stockholders are exposed?

8. What are the advantages and disadvantages of owning common stock?

9. The W. C. Fields Beverage Company recently reported net profits after taxes of $15.8 million; it has 2.5 milion shares of common stock outstanding, and pays preferred dividends of $1 million per year.

   a. Compute the firm's earnings per share (EPS).
   b. What would the firm's dividend yield be if it paid $2 per share to common stockholders (assume the stock currently trades at $60 per share)?

10. What is the dividend exclusion provision and how does this tax statute benefit "small" stockholders? Are there any special tax provisions that apply to stock dividends? Explain.

11. Judy Thompson holds 400 shares of the Fourth National Bank and Trust Company; there are three vacancies on the board of directors that will be voted on at the next stockholders' meeting, which Judy plans to attend. One candidate is Mrs. Lucille Sharp, a woman who would bring excellent credentials to the board; Judy feels that the time is long overdue for a woman to be represented on Fourth National's board. How many votes could Judy cast for Mrs. Sharp if the bank used a majority voting system? If it used a cumulative voting system?

a. Explain the basic difference between these two voting procedures.
b. Which one is designed to help minority stockholders?

12. Discuss the investment merits of each of the following:

a. Blue chips.
b. Income stocks.
c. Defensive stocks.

13. Why do most income stocks offer only limited capital gains potential? Does this mean the outlook for continued profitability is also limited? Explain.

14. What is the difference between a fixed dollar level of dividends and a fixed dividend payout policy? Assume that the Southwest Hamburger Company has the following five-year record of earnings per share:

Year	EPS
1980	$1.40
1981	2.10
1982	1.00
1983	3.25
1984	0.80

Which procedure would provide the greatest amount of dividends to stockholders over this five-year period?

a. Paying out dividends at a fixed payout ratio of 40 percent.
b. Paying out dividends at the fixed regular dividend level of $1 per share.

15. Why is the ex-dividend date so important to stockholders?

16. Briefly explain each of the following types of investment programs, and note the kinds of common stock (blue chip, speculative stocks, and so on) that would best fit with each:

a. A buy-and-hold strategy.
b. A high income portfolio.
c. Aggressive stock management.

CASE PROBLEMS

8.1 JEANNIE CONSIDERS THE STOCK MARKET

Jeannie Kidswell holds a Ph.D. in child psychology and has built up a thriving practice in her hometown of Nashville, Tennessee. Her practice has been so lucrative, in fact, that over the past several years she has been able to accumulate a substantial sum of money, held in several savings accounts, and still have plenty left to live very comfortably. She has worked long and hard to be successful but never imagined anything like this. Fortunately, success has not spoiled Jeannie; still single, she keeps to her old circle of friends. One of her closest friends is Dave Brisco, who happens to be a stockbroker (and a fairly successful one at that). Jeannie sees a lot of Dave, who, among other things, has acted as her financial advisor of sorts.

Not long ago, the two attended a cocktail party where the subject of the stock market and investing seemed to be the major topic of conversation. Like a lot of other folks, Jeannie was beginning to feel that holding all her money in savings accounts was a serious mistake. On the way home, Jeannie started talking about investing and confided to Dave that she had been doing some reading lately about the stock market and had found several stocks she thought looked "sort of interesting." She describes them as follows:

1. *North Atlantic Swimsuit Company:* It's a highly speculative stock and pays no dividends. While the earnings of NASS have been a bit erratic, Jeannie feels that its growth prospects have never been brighter—"what with more people than ever going to the beaches the way they are these days."
2. *Town and Country Oil Company:* This is a long-established oil firm that pays a modest dividend yield (of about 3 to 5 percent). It's considered a quality growth stock and from one of the stock reports she'd read, Jeannie understands that it offers excellent long-term growth and capital gains potential.
3. *Southeastern Public Utility Company:* An income stock, it pays a nice dividend yield of around 8 percent. While it's a solid company, it has limited growth prospects because of its location.
4. *International Gold Mines, Inc.:* This stock has really been doing well, and Jeannie feels that if it can do so well in inflationary times, it will do even better when the economy gets better. Unfortunately, the stock has experienced wide price swings in the past and pays almost no dividends.

Questions

1. What do you think of the idea of Jeannie keeping "substantial sums" of money in savings accounts? Would common stocks make better inflation hedges than savings accounts?

2. What is your opinion of the four stocks Jeannie has described; do you think they are suitable for her investment needs?

3. What kind of common stock investment program would you recommend for Jeannie? What investment objectives do you think she should set for herself, and how can common stocks help her achieve her goals?

8.2 BUTCH GOES AFTER DIVIDEND YIELD

Butch Peterson is a commercial artist who owns and operates a prosperous design studio in the Seattle area. He does layout and illustration work primarily for local ad agencies and for major institutional clients like large department stores. Butch has been investing in the stock market for some time, buying mostly high-quality growth stocks. He has been seeking long-term growth and capital appreciation, and feels that with the limited time he has to devote to his security holdings, high-quality issues are his best bet. He has been a bit perplexed lately with the market, disturbed that some of his growth stocks aren't even doing as well as many good-grade income shares. He therefore decides to have a chat with his broker, Al Fried.

During the course of their conversation, it becomes clear that both Al and Butch are thinking along the same lines. Al points out that dividend yields on income shares are, indeed, way up and, because of the state of the economy, the outlook for growth stocks is not particularly bright. He suggests that Butch seriously consider putting some of his money into income shares to capture some of the high dividend yields that are available—after all, as Al points out, "the bottom line is not so much where the payoff comes from, as how much it amounts to!" They then talk about a high-yield public utility stock, Hydro-Electric Light and Power. Al digs up some forecast information about Hydro-Electric and presents it to Butch for his consideration:

Year	Expected EPS	Expected Dividend Payout Ratio
1985	$3.25	40%
1986	3.40	40
1987	3.90	45
1988	4.40	45
1989	5.00	45

The stock presently trades at $60 per share, and Al thinks that within five years it should be trading at a level of $75 to $80. Butch realizes that in order to buy the Hydro-Electric stock, he will have to sell his holdings of Amalgamated Oil—a highly regarded growth stock with which Butch has become disenchanted because of recent substandard performance.

Questions

1. How would you best describe Butch's present investment program? How do you think it fits him and his investment objectives?
2. Looking at the Hydro-Electric stock:

   a. Determine the amount of annual dividends Hydro-Electric is expected to pay over the years 1985 to 1989.
   b. Compute the total dollar return Butch would make from Hydro-Electric if he invests $6,000 in the stock and all the dividend and price expectations are realized.

3. Would Butch be going to a different investment strategy if he decided to buy shares in Hydro-Electric? If the switch is made, how would you describe his new investment program? What do you think of this new approach, and is it likely to lead to more trading on Butch's behalf? If so, how do you think that stacks up with the limited amount of time he has to devote to his portfolio?

SELECTED READINGS

"The Boom in Foreign Stocks: How to Get a Piece of It." *Changing Times,* August 1981, pp. 21–24.

Bryant, William C. "Time to Look at Cyclicals." *U.S. News and World Report,* August 18, 1980, p. 76.

Buffett, Warren E. "How Inflation Swindles the Equity Investor." *Fortune,* May 1977, pp. 76–82.

"Bull Market—It's Not Over Yet." *U.S. News & World Report,* August 15, 1983, pp. 27–31.

Connelly, Julie. "Picking Up Those Mining Stocks." *Money,* May 1981, pp. 117–118.

"The Death of Equities: How Inflation Is Destroying the Stockmarket." *Business Week,* August 13, 1979, pp. 54–59.

Ehrbar, A. F. "The Trouble with Stocks." *Fortune,* August 1977, pp. 89–93.

———. "Giant Payoffs from Midget Stocks." *Fortune,* June 30, 1980, pp. 111–114.

Edgerton, Jerry. "Doubts about Dividends." *Money,* December 1981, pp. 143–146.

———. "Investing in New Industries." *Money,* March 1982, pp. 44–47.

Greenebaum, Mary. "The Rewards of Investing in Foreign Stocks." *Fortune,* April 9, 1979, pp. 129–130.

———. "Profiting from Investments in Corporate Failures." *Fortune,* May 7, 1979, pp. 317–320.

Haller, Ellis. "The Boom in Reinvestment." *U.S. News and World Report,* May 5, 1980, p. 86.

Hayes, Linda Snyder. "Fresh Evidence That Dividends Don't Matter." *Fortune,* May 4, 1981, pp. 351–354.

Malkiel, Burton. "Common Stocks—The Best Inflation Hedge for the 1980's." *Forbes,* February 18, 1980, pp. 118–128.

Massey, Jay R. "For the Long Haul: Stocks Invariably Out Perform Both Bills and Bonds." *Barron's,* January 31, 1977, p. 5–16.

Merjos, Anna. "Roller Coaster Ride: Low Price Shares Move Faster (Up and Down) Than the Averages." *Barron's,* December 4, 1978, pp. 11–16.

Rolo, Charles J. "Homing In on New Issues." *Money,* November 1980, pp. 101–107.

Schulz, John W. "Who Needs the Blue Chips?" *Barron's,* April 2, 1979, pp. 11–14.

"Should You Turn on to Utility Stocks?" *Changing Times,* January 1982, pp. 30–34.

Sivy, Michael. "Making Big Money on 'Little' Stocks." *Money,* July 1981, pp. 42–48.

"When 'Quality' Is What You Want in a Stock." *Changing Times,* December 1981, pp. 35–38.

Winthrop, Grant F. "Buying Discount Stocks with Dividends." *Fortune,* October 9, 1978, pp. 193–196.

9
Common Stock Analysis

To many individuals, common stocks are synonymous with investments. Stories recounting shrewd market plays seem to fascinate people from all walks of life. The prospect of seeing a small sum grow to a vast fortune has the same attraction for the homemaker, the service station attendant, or the college professor as it does for the Wall Street tycoon. Careful security selection and market timing are key ingredients of success in the stock market and lie at the heart of security analysis. In this, the first of two chapters dealing with security analysis, we will introduce some of the principles and techniques used in evaluating the investment suitability of common stocks; specifically, our presentation centers on the following key areas:

1. An overview of the security analysis process, including its goals and the functions it performs for the individual investor.
2. The role and importance of economic and industry analysis in the stock valuation process.
3. The concept of fundamental analysis and how it is used to assess a company's financial position and operating results.
4. The various types of accounting statements and financial ratios used in evaluating the historical performance of a company.
5. An overview of fundamental analysis at work, and how such insight forms the basic input to the valuation process.

In December 1938, an investor could have purchased 100 shares of Xerox for $850. Adjusting for stock splits, that investment by July 1981 would have grown to 18,000 shares, worth some $938,000! Unfortunately, for every story of great success in the market, there are dozens more that do not end nearly so well. Most of the disasters can be traced not only to bad timing, but to greed, poor planning, and failure to use simple common sense in making decisions. Although these next two chapters cannot offer the keys to sudden wealth, they do provide sound principles for formulating a successful long-range investment program. The techniques described are quite traditional; they are the same methods that have been used by millions of investors to achieve satisfactory rates of return on their capital.

PRINCIPLES OF SECURITY ANALYSIS

Security analysis consists of gathering information, organizing it into a logical format, and using the information to determine the intrinsic value of a common stock. That is, given a desired rate of return and an assessment of the amount of risk involved in a proposed transaction, *intrinsic value* provides a measure of the underlying worth of a stock. It provides a standard for helping an investor judge whether a particular stock is undervalued, fairly priced, or overvalued. As with any investment vehicle, it is not the past but the future that counts. The investment, however, must not only promise to be profitable, it must be *sufficiently* profitable. More specifically, a satisfactory investment candidate is one that offers a level of expected return commensurate with perceived exposure to risk.

The whole concept of security analysis is based on the assumption that investors are capable of formulating reliable estimates of a stock's future behavior. This, of course, is a pretty strong assumption, and there are many who, for one reason or another, just do not buy it. These are the "efficient market" advocates who argue that it is virtually impossible to outperform the market consistently. We will study the idea and implications of efficient markets in some detail in Chapter 10; for now, however, we will assume that traditional stock analysis is useful in identifying attractive investments.

If you had $10,000 to invest, you would probably want a vehicle that offered preservation of capital along with a satisfactory level of current income and/or capital gains. The problem, of course, is finding such a security. One approach is to buy whatever strikes your fancy; a more rational approach is to use security analysis to seek out promising investment candidates. Security analysis addresses the question of *what to buy* by determining what a stock *ought to be worth*. Presumably, an investor would consider buying a stock only so long as its prevailing market price does not exceed its worth (its computed intrinsic value). Ultimately, intrinsic value will depend on: (1) estimates of the stock's future cash flows (the amount of dividends the investor can expect to receive over the holding period and the estimated price of the stock at time of sale); (2) the discount rate used to translate these future cash flows into a present value; and (3) the amount of risk imbedded in achieving the forecasted level of performance. (All these elements of return were introduced and reviewed in Chapter 4.)

Traditional security analysis usually takes a "top-down" approach that begins with economic analysis, then moves to industry analysis, and finally to fundamental analysis. *Economic analysis* is concerned with assessing the general state of the economy and its potential effects on security returns; *industry analysis* deals with

TABLE 9.1 REACTION OF STOCK PRICES TO CHANGES IN ECONOMIC ACTIVITY

Economic Period	Change in Standard & Poor's Stock Index	Change in Economic Activity (Index of Industrial Production)
Strong economy: March 1961–November 1969	+49.8%	+71.8%
Recession: December 1969–November 1970	− 7.5	− 4.0
Strong economy: December 1970–November 1973	+13.2	+30.3
Recession: December 1973–March 1975	−11.6	−11.8
Strong economy: April 1975–December 1979	+23.6	+35.4
Recession: January 1980–July 1980	+ 6.5	− 7.9
Strong economy: August 1980–July 1981	+ 8.5	+ 9.6
Recession: August 1981–June 1982	−10.7	− 9.9

Source: Standard & Poor's *Statistical Service;* and U.S. Department of Commerce, Bureau of Economic Analysis, *Survey of Current Business.*

the industry within which a particular company operates and the outlook for that industry; *fundamental analysis* looks in depth at the financial condition of a specific company and the underlying behavior of its common stock.

ECONOMIC ANALYSIS

Security analysis begins with a study of general economic conditions. It is important that an investor not only have a grasp of the *underlying nature of the economic environment,* but that he or she be able to assess the *current state* of the economy and formulate expectations about its *future course.* Economic analysis may include a detailed examination of each sector of the economy, or it may be done on a very informal basis. Regardless of how it is performed, the purpose is always the same: to establish a sound foundation for the valuation of common stock. Let us examine the economic analysis process and see how it can be carried out by an individual investor.

If we lived in a world where economic activity had absolutely no effect on the stock market or security prices, we could avoid studying the economy altogether. The fact is, of course, that we do not live in such a world and that stock prices are indeed influenced by the state of the economy. More specifically, as Table 9.1 shows, stock prices generally do tend to move up when the economy is strong and retreat when the economy softens. Such behavior can be traced to the fact that the overall performance of the economy has a significant bearing on the performance and

Gross National Product

(in billions of dollars; quarterly data are at seasonally adjusted annual rates)

Account	1979	1980	1981	1981			1982	
				Q2	Q3	Q4	Q1	Q2^r
GROSS NATIONAL PRODUCT								
→ 1 Total	**2,417.8**	**2,633.1**	**2,937.7**	**2,901.8**	**2,980.9**	**3,003.2**	**2,995.5**	**3,045.2**
By source								
2 Personal consumption expenditures	1,507.2	1,667.2	1,843.2	1,819.4	1,868.8	1,884.5	1,919.4	1,947.8
3 Durable goods	213.4	214.3	234.6	230.4	241.2	229.6	237.9	240.7
4 Nondurable goods	600.0	670.4	734.5	729.6	741.3	746.5	749.1	755.0
5 Services	693.7	782.5	874.1	859.4	886.3	908.3	932.4	952.1
6 Gross private domestic investment	423.0	402.4	471.5	475.5	486.0	468.9	414.8	431.5
7 Fixed investment.	408.8	412.4	451.1	450.9	454.2	455.7	450.4	447.7
8 Nonresidential	290.2	309.2	346.1	341.3	353.0	360.2	357.0	352.2
9 Structures	98.3	110.5	129.7	127.0	132.7	139.6	141.4	143.6
10 Producers' durable equipment	191.9	198.6	216.4	214.3	220.2	220.6	215.6	208.6
11 Residential structures	118.6	103.2	105.0	109.5	101.2	95.5	93.4	95.5
12 Nonfarm.	114.0	98.3	99.7	104.7	95.6	89.4	87.9	89.6
13 Change in business inventories	14.3	−10.0	20.5	24.6	31.8	13.2	−35.6	−16.2
14 Nonfarm	8.6	−5.7	15.0	19.3	24.6	6.0	−36.0	−15.0
15 Net exports of goods and services.	13.2	25.2	26.1	23.7	25.9	23.5	31.3	34.9
16 Exports	281.4	339.2	367.3	368.9	367.2	367.9	359.9	365.8
17 Imports	268.1	314.0	341.3	345.1	341.3	344.4	328.6	330.9
18 Government purchases of goods and services . . .	474.4	538.4	596.9	583.2	600.2	626.3	630.1	630.9
19 Federal.	168.3	197.2	229.0	218.2	230.0	250.5	249.7	244.3
20 State and local	306.0	341.2	368.0	365.0	370.1	375.7	380.4	386.6
By major type of product								
21 Final sales, total	2,403.5	2,643.1	2,917.3	2,877.2	2,949.1	2,989.9	3,031.1	3,061.4
22 Goods	1,065.6	1,141.9	1,289.2	1,276.0	1,317.0	1,298.5	1,269.4	1,283.1
23 Durable	464.8	477.3	528.1	538.2	547.3	504.9	482.4	505.9
24 Nondurable	600.8	664.6	761.1	737.8	769.7	793.6	787.0	777.2
25 Services	1,089.7	1,225.6	1,364.3	1,340.2	1,382.1	1,421.5	1,444.4	1,476.7
26 Structures	262.5	265.7	284.2	285.6	281.9	283.3	281.7	285.3
27 Change in business inventories.	14.3	−10.0	20.5	24.6	31.8	13.2	−35.6	−16.2
28 Durable goods	10.5	−5.2	8.7	18.5	19.8	−5.6	−30.9	−6.6
29 Nondurable goods	3.8	−4.8	11.8	6.1	12.0	18.9	−4.8	−9.6
30 MEMO: **Total GNP in 1972 dollars**	**1,479.4**	**1,474.0**	**1,502.6**	**1,502.2**	**1,510.4**	**1,490.1**	**1,470.7**	**1,478.4**

Figure 9.1 Measures of Economic Activity.
GNP and the index of industrial production, shown on the next page, are two measures that capture the behavior of the business cycle. (*Source:* Board of Governors of the Federal Reserve System, *Federal Reserve Bulletin;* and Council of Economic Advisers, *Economic Indicators.*)

profitability of the companies that issue common stock. As the fortunes of the issuing firms change with economic conditions, so will the prices of their stocks. But not all stocks are affected in the same way and to the same extent. Some sectors of the economy may be only mildly affected; others, like the construction and auto industries, are often hard hit when times get rough.

Economic Analysis and the Business Cycle

Economic analysis sets the tone for security analysis. If the future looks bleak, then you can probably expect most stock returns to be equally dismal; if the economy looks strong, stocks should do well. The behavior of the economy is captured in the *business cycle,* which is an indication of the change in total economic activity over

Index of Industrial Production
(Data are seasonally adjusted)

Period	Total industrial production		Industry production indexes. 1967 = 100					Manufacturing		Materials (Federal Reserve series)
	Index, 1967 = 100	Percent change from year earlier	Manufacturing			Mining	Utilities	Federal Reserve series	Commerce series	
			Total	Durable	Non-durable					
1967 proportion	100.00	. . . . . .	87.95	51.98	35.97	6.36	5.69	. . . . . .	77	73.4
1975	117.8	−8.9	116.3	109.3	126.4	112.8	146.0	72.9	77	73.4
1976	130.5	10.8	130.3	122.3	141.8	114.2	151.7	79.5	81	81.1
1977	138.2	5.9	138.4	130.0	150.5	118.2	156.5	81.9	83	82.7
1978	146.1	5.7	146.8	139.7	156.9	124.0	161.4	84.4	84	85.6
1979	152.5	4.4	153.6	146.4	164.0	125.5	166.0	85.7	83	87.4
1980	147.0	−3.6	146.7	136.7	161.2	132.7	168.3	79.1	78	80.0
1981	151.0	2.7	150.4	140.5	164.8	142.2	169.1	78.5	76	79.9
1981: Oct.	149.1	1.7	148.0	137.8	162.8	145.3	168.1	76.6	. . . . .	77.7
Nov	146.3	−1.9	145.0	134.4	160.3	143.3	168.9	74.8	. . . . .	75.5
Dec	143.4	−4.7	142.0	131.3	157.4	142.6	168.2	73.1	72	72.4
1982: Jan	140.7	−7.1	138.5	127.1	155.1	144.5	171.8	71.1	. . . . .	71.4
Feb.	142.9	−5.9	140.9	129.3	157.8	142.4	170.4	72.2	. . . . .	72.9
Mar	141.7	−6.8	140.1	128.2	157.3	138.1	170.0	71.6	72	71.8
Apr	140.2	−7.7	138.7	126.7	156.1	134.1	171.0	70.8	. . . . .	70.5
May	139.2	−8.8	137.9	126.1	155.0	128.9	170.9	70.2	. . . . .	69.4
June	138.7	−9.3	137.7	125.5	155.3	123.5	169.4	70.0	71	68.8
July ʳ	138.8	−9.8	138.1	125.9	155.7	120.1	167.7	70.0	. . . . .	68.5
Aug ʳ	138.4	−9.9	138.0	124.9	156.8	118.1	168.2	69.8	. . . . .	68.4
Sept ʳ	137.4	−9.4	137.2	123.5	156.8	114.9	168.7	69.2	. . . . .	67.7
Oct ᵖ	136.3	−8.6	135.8	121.5	156.5	115.7	169.1	68.4	. . . . .	67.2

Figure 9.1 Continued

time. Two widely followed measures of the business cycle are gross national product and industrial production; each of these measures, along with their component parts, is shown in Figure 9.1. *Gross national product* (or GNP as it is more commonly known) represents the market value of all goods and services produced by a country over the period of a year. *Industrial production* is a measure (actually it's an index) of the activity/output in the industrial or productive segment of the economy. Normally, GNP and/or the index of industrial production move up and down with the business cycle; the nature of this relationship is illustrated in Figure 9.2. Note especially how the index tends to fall when the economy slips into a recession (the shaded area in the graph).

Key economic factors

Several parts of the economy are especially important because of the impact they normally have on total economic activity; they include:

Government fiscal policy
   Taxes
   Government spending
   Debt management
Monetary policy (actions of the Federal Reserve Board)
   Money supply
   Interest rates
Other factors
   Consumer spending
   Business investments
   The cost and availability of energy

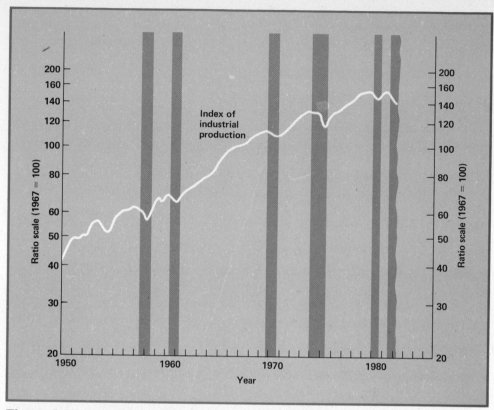

Figure 9.2 The Behavior of the Index of Industrial Production over Time.
The unshaded areas represent periods of prosperity; the shaded areas are recessions. The index of industrial production is a reflection of the prevailing economic climate. (*Source: Federal Reserve Chart Book, 1982.*)

Fiscal policy tends to be *expansive* when it encourages spending—when the government reduces taxes and/or increases the size of the budget; in a similar fashion, monetary policy is said to be expansive when money is readily available and interest rates are relatively low. An expansive economy also depends on a generous level of spending by consumers and business concerns, as well as an abundant supply of energy that is reasonably priced. Of course, these variables can also have a recessionary impact on the economy—for example, when taxes, interest rates, and/ or the cost of energy increase, or when spending by consumers and businesses falls off.

The impact of these major forces filters through the system and affects several key dimensions of the economy, the most important of which are industrial production, corporate profits, retail sales, personal income, the unemployment rate, and inflation. For example, a strong economy exists when industrial production, corporate profits, retail sales, and personal income are moving up and unemployment is down. Thus, when conducting economic analysis, an investor will want to keep an eye on fiscal and monetary policies, consumer and business spending, and the cost of energy *for the potential impact they have on the economy,* and at the same time, stay abreast of the level of industrial production, corporate profits, retail sales, personal income, unemployment, and inflation *in order to assess the state of the business cycle.*

Finally, as we noted in Chapter 8, inflation has had devastating effects on common stocks (and many other investment vehicles as well). In fact, inflation has been a special cause for concern in this country since the early 1970s, because of the serious implications sustained high rates of inflation hold for the economy. The alleged causes of inflation include continued deficit spending by government, excessive government regulation, declining worker productivity, an antiquated tax system that discourages capital accumulation, and unreasonable growth in the money supply. In such an environment many companies may report higher profits, but the quality of these earnings actually declines as profit margins are "squeezed" and the purchasing power of the dollar deteriorates. What is more, the high interest rates that accompany inflation not only contribute to rising costs, but also reduce the competitive edge of common stocks. That is, as interest rates rise, the returns to bonds and preferred stocks improve and make the investment merits of stocks look less attractive. Because of the pervasive nature of inflation and the serious consequences it holds for stock prices, investors should devote special attention to this factor as they analyze the economy and its prospects.

Developing an Economic Outlook

Conducting an economic analysis involves studying fiscal and monetary policy, inflationary expectations, consumer and business spending, and the state of the business cycle. Usually, individual investors do this on a fairly informal basis; many rely on one or more of the popular published sources (like the *Wall Street Journal, Fortune,* or *Business Week*), as well as periodic reports from major brokerage houses to form their economic judgments. As Figure 9.3 shows, such sources provide a convenient summary of economic activity, and enable investors to develop a general feel for the condition of the economy.

Consider, for example, an investor with an interest in apparel stocks. Because of the nature of the business (durable fashion goods), these stocks are susceptible to changing economic conditions. Especially important is the level of discretionary consumer spending; normally, such spending tends to pick up when the economy is strong and slacken when the economy slows down. In this instance, our imaginary investor would first want to assess the current state of the business cycle and then, using this insight, formulate some expectations about the future.

Let's assume that the economy has just recently entered the recovery stage of the business cycle. Employment is starting to pick up, inflation and interest rates are at "modest" levels, and Congress is putting the finishing touches on a major tax cut. More important, because the economy now seems to be in the early stages of a

DEAN WITTER REYNOLDS

RESEARCH

ECONOMIC MEMORANDUM
November 24, 1982   RR 2730/17
Arnold X. Moskowitz, First Vice President
and Economist

ECONOMIC MODEL UPDATE
The Economy's Path — Irreversibly Upward in 1983

In our report "The Economic Outlook — A Coiled Spring for 1983" (RI 2117), dated September 27, 1982, we likened the economy to a compressed spring waiting for the latch to be pulled, the latch being high interest rates. What has happened in the interim? Has the spring sprung or just unwound?

In the normal course of a business expansion from a recession trough, interest rates provide the driving force and impact the economy in a number of ways. Lower interest rates propel the stock and bond markets upward, raising consumer wealth as well as confidence. The lower rates then allow housing to improve as mortgage money becomes available and affordable, and auto sales improve as consumer wealth, income, reasonable financing costs, combined with increased confidence, and finally, the upward momentum in profits from productivity improvement set the stage for general business activity to expand. In this simplistic three-stage analogy, the first and second stages (stock and bond market, housing recovery) have occurred, and the last stage (autos, profit expansion) is in the process of developing. But, as it unfolds over the next six months, real activity will pick up smartly, just as housing starts are now outpacing the industry's forecast made just two months ago. Housing is important as it is the most consistent leading indicator of economic activity. Historically, housing starts have bottomed, on average, three to four months before the trough in the business cycle. This barometer is more reliable than the stock market in defining the turning points of the business cycle. Housing starts bottomed about a year ago, but for the first six months of 1982 they only inched upward from depressed levels. However, housing starts continue to show improvement, and the number of building permits and existing home sales has increased at a quickened pace over the past three months.

This recovery, though, will be short-lived and stunted if interest rates stabilize at present levels. However, our view remains that interest rates have much further to fall — 3-4% for bonds, as the inflation rates drop to the 3% zone over the next two years. Obviously, the road to lower rates will be bumpy, but the pattern is set; the forces of disinflation are in place as a result of financial deregulation. Therefore, the economics path is irreversibly upward in 1983 as interest rates continue to move downward.

The Data

Real GNP output was unchanged from the second to the third quarter, as a result of significant weakness in the international accounts, with deteriorating economic conditions in Mexico and Canada lowering net exports in the third quarter to $2.7 billion from $30 billion in the second quarter. This $27 billion decline in the international accounts was offset by a $39.7 billion increase in consumer spending, a $1.7 billion increase in housing, and a $12.1 billion gain in federal spending. Capital spending continued to weaken, as expected, and state and local spending remained flat, continuing the pattern of the last eight quarters. Therefore, most of the economic··

Figure 9.3 An Economic Overview.
Reports such as this one, and the one on the next page, provide the individual investor with a convenient overview of the current state of the economy . . .

recovery, it should be getting even stronger in the future. The Fed has been cautious about pumping money into the economy, so inflation should not be a problem; and personal income is expected to pick up. This should be good for apparel companies,

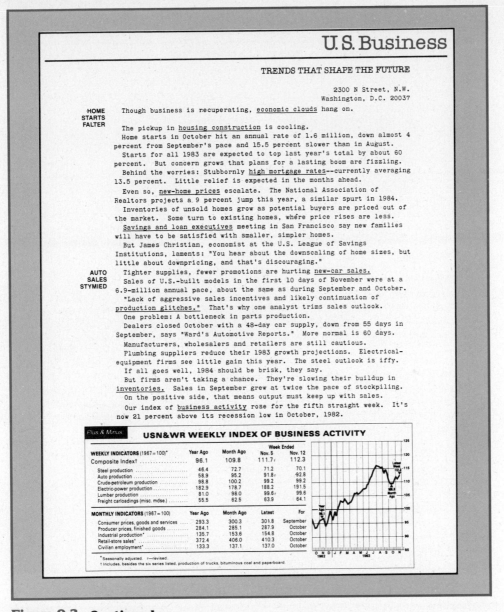

Figure 9.3 Continued

... and some observations on where it may be heading. (*Source:* Dean Witter Reynolds *Economic Memorandum,* November 24, 1982; and *U.S. News & World Report,* November 28, 1983.)

since a good deal of their sales and an even larger portion of their profits depend on the level of discretionary disposable income. In short, our investor sees an economy that appears to be in good shape and set to become even stronger, the consequences of which are all favorable for apparel stocks. Note that these conclusions

BOX 9.1 HOW TO TRACK THE U.S. ECONOMY

Is the economy nearing the bottom of a recession? Or will the upturn be delayed a little longer? Economists and other professional forecasters follow dozens of indicators in search of the answers. But by keeping an eye on only a few key statistics compiled by government agencies, you can make your own educated guesses as to where the economy is heading. To sort out the confusing array of figures that flow almost daily from Washington, here are some of the most important reports to watch. . . . Note that all figures are seasonally adjusted except those for prices.

Gross national product—This is the broadest measure of the economy's performance. Issued every three months by the Commerce Department, it is the best estimate of the total dollar value of the nation's output of goods and services. Movements in many areas of the economy are closely related to changes in GNP, making it a good analytic tool. In particular, watch the annual rate of growth or decline in "real" or "constant" dollars. This eliminates the effects of inflation, so that the actual volume of production is measured. Remember, though, that frequent revisions of GNP figures sometimes change the picture of the economy.

Industrial production—Issued monthly by the Federal Reserve Board, this index shows changes in the physical output of America's factories, mines and electric and gas utilities. The index tends to move in the same direction as the economy, making it a good guide to business conditions between reports on GNP. Detailed breakdowns of the index give a reading on how individual industries are faring.

Leading indicators—This boils down to one number, the movement of a dozen statistics that tend to predict—or "lead"—changes in the GNP. The monthly index issued by the Commerce Department includes such things as layoffs of workers, new orders placed by manufacturers, changes in the money supply and the prices of raw materials. If the index moves in the same direction for several months, it's a fair sign that total output will move the same way in the near future.

Personal income—A monthly report from the Commerce Department, this shows the before-tax income received by people in the form of wages and salaries, interest and dividends, rents, and other payments such as Social Security, unemployment and pensions. As a measure of individuals' spending power, the report helps explain trends in consumer buying habits, a major part of total GNP. When personal income rises, it often means that people will increase their buying. But note a big loophole: Excluded are the bilions of dollars that change hands in the so-called underground economy—cash transactions that are never reported to tax or other officials.

were arrived at by relying on sources no more sophisticated than *Barron's* and *Business Week;* in fact, about the only special thing the investor did was to pay careful attention to those economic forces especially important to the apparel industry (like personal income). The economics portion of the analysis, in effect, has set the stage for further evaluation by indicating the type of economic environment to expect for the near future. The next step is to narrow the focus a bit and conduct the industry phase of the analysis.

BOX 9.1 *Continued*

Retail sales—The Commerce Department's monthly estimate of total sales at the retail level includes everything from cars to a bag of groceries. Based on a sample of retail establishments, the figure gives a rough clue to consumer attitudes. It can also indicate future conditions: A long slowdown in sales can lead to cuts in production.

Consumer prices—Issued monthly by the Labor Department, this index shows changes in prices for a fixed market basket of about 360 goods and services. The most widely publicized figure is for all urban consumers. A second, used in labor contracts and some government programs, covers urban wage earners and clerical workers. Both are watched as a measure of inflation, but many economists believe that flaws cause them to be wide of the mark.

Producer prices—This is a monthly indicator from the Labor Department showing price changes of goods at various stages of production, from crude materials such as raw cotton, to finished goods like clothing and furniture. An upward surge may mean higher consumer prices later. The index, however, can miss discounts and may exaggerate rising price trends. Watch particularly changes in the prices of finished goods. These do not fluctuate as widely as crude materials and thus are a better measure of inflationary pressures.

Employment—The percentage of the work force that is involuntarily out of work is a broad indicator of economic health. But another monthly figure issued by the Labor Department—the number of payroll jobs—may be better for spotting changes in business. A decreasing number of jobs is a sign that firms are cutting production.

Housing starts—A pickup in the pace of housing starts usually follows an easing of credit conditions—the availability and cost of money—and is an indicator of improvement in economic health. This monthly report from the Commerce Department also includes the number of new building permits issued across the country, an even earlier indicator of the pace of future construction.

Source: "How to Track the U.S. Economy." *U.S. News & World Report,* December 14, 1981, p. 61.

INDUSTRY ANALYSIS

An industry is made up of similar firms involved in producing similar goods and services—the oil industry, for example, is made up of firms that produce gasoline and other oil-related products. Companies in an industry may be different in size, manner of operation, and product lines, but they have similar operating characteristics and are subject to similar socioeconomic forces.

Key Issues

Have you ever thought about buying oil stocks, or autos, or chemicals? How about conglomerates or electric utility stocks? Looking at securities in terms of industry groupings is a popular way of viewing stocks, and is widely used by both individual and professional investors. They do this because stock prices are influenced, at least in part, by industry conditions. The level of demand in an industry and other industry forces set the tone for individual companies; clearly, if the outlook is good for an industry, then the prospects are likely to be strong for the companies that make up that industry. Industry analysis can be used to establish the competitive position of a particular industry and to identify companies within the industry that hold particular promise. It sets the stage for a more thorough analysis of individual companies and securities.

Analyzing an industry means looking at such things as the makeup and basic characteristics of the industry, key economic and operating variables that are important in defining industry performance, and the outlook for the industry. The investor will also want to keep an eye out for specific companies that appear well situated to take advantage of industry conditions. Normally, an investor can gain valuable insight about an industry by seeking answers to these questions:

1. *What is the nature of the industry?* Is it monopolistic or are there many competitors; do a few set the trend for the rest?
2. *To what extent is the industry regulated?* Is it regulated (like public utilities and railroads) and if so, how "friendly" are the regulatory bodies?
3. *What is the role of "big labor" in the industry?* How important is "big labor"; are there good labor relations within the industry, and when is the next round of contract talks?
4. *How important are technological developments?* Are there any taking place, and what is the likely impact of potential breakthroughs?
5. *What economic forces are especially important to the industry?* Is demand for the industry's goods and services related to key economic variables and if so, what is the outlook for those variables? How important is foreign competition to the health of the industry?
6. *What are the important financial and operating considerations?* Is there an adequate supply of labor, material, and capital; what are the capital spending plans and needs of the industry?

Developing an Industry Outlook

Industry analysis can be conducted from scratch by individual investors, or, as is more often the case, it can be done with the help of published industry reports, such as the popular S&P *Industry Surveys*. These surveys cover all the important economic, market, and financial aspects of an industry, with commentary as well as vital statistics being provided. Other widely used sources of industry information include brokerage house reports and various writeups in the popular financial media; an example of each of these is provided in Figure 9.4.

Let us continue with the example of the hypothetical investor who is interested in apparel stocks. Recall that his economic analysis suggested a strong economy for the foreseeable future and one in which the level of personal disposable income would be expanding. Now he is ready to shift his attention to the apparel industry. A logical starting point is to assess the expected industry response to forecasted economic developments. Demand for the product and industry sales would be especially important. The industry is made up of many large and small competitors, and although it is an unregulated industry, it is labor-intensive and big labor is an important force. Thus our investor may want to look closely at these factors and especially at their potential effect on the industry's cost structure. Also important would be the outlook for imported fashion goods and foreign competition.

Industry analysis provides an understanding of the nature and operating characteristics of an industry that can then be used to form judgments about the prospects for industry growth. Let us assume that our investor, by using various types of published reports, has examined the key elements of the apparel industry and has concluded that it is indeed well placed to take advantage of the improving economy. Apparel demand should be up, and although profit margins may tighten a bit, the level of profits should move up smartly. Several companies within this industry stand out, but one looks particularly attractive: Palm Springs Industries, a moderately sized but rapidly growing producer of medium- to high-priced apparel for men and women. Everything about the economy and the industry looks favorable, so our hypothetical investor has decided to study Palm Springs Industries more closely.

FUNDAMENTAL ANALYSIS

Fundamental analysis is the study of the financial affairs of a business and enables investors to better understand the nature and operating characteristics of companies that issue common stocks. In this part of the chapter we will deal with several aspects of fundamental analysis: We will examine the general concept of fundamental analysis, introduce and discuss the several types of financial statements that provide the raw material for this phase of the analytical process, describe the types and explain the rationale for some of the key financial ratios widely used in fundamental analysis, and end with a look at the interpretation of financial ratios.

The Concept

Fundamental analysis rests on the belief that *the value of a stock is influenced by the performance of the company that issued the stock.* If company prospects look strong, we would expect the market price of the stock to reflect that and be bid up. However, the value of a security depends not only on the return it promises, but also on the amount of its risk exposure. Fundamental analysis captures these dimensions and conveniently incorporates them into the valuation process.

Fundamental analysis begins with a historical analysis of the financial strength of a firm. Using the insights obtained, along with economic and industry figures, an investor can then formulate expectations about the future growth and profitability of a company. In the historical phase of the analysis (which is of primary interest to us at present), attention is centered on the financial statements of the firm for the purpose of learning the strengths and weaknesses of the company, identifying any underlying trends and developments, evaluating operating efficiency, and generally

Why Apparel Stocks Are in Style

by Aimée L. Morner

Apparel stocks are coming back into fashion. Since the end of 1980, shares of three major manufacturers of men's and women's clothing are way up: Hart Schaffner & Marx, Palm Beach, and Warnaco have risen by more than 50%. Among the jeans makers, VF Corp. (Lee jeans) has moved up 32%, and Blue Bell (Wrangler) 11%. But shares of Levi Strauss, the world's largest apparel company, have shrunk by 18% in value—a lot more than the S&P 400, which is down 5%.

Still, the price-earnings ratios of the apparel stocks are at bargain-basement levels, ranging from six times estimated 1981 earnings (for Warnaco, Palm Beach, and VF) to 7.7 times (Hart Schaffner). The S&P 400, by comparison, is selling at eight times this year's estimated earnings. Many analysts think apparel makers should sell at least in line with the market when investors catch on to the idea that the rag trade can offer growth.

Clothing manufacturers have traditionally been regarded as the weakest link in the soft-goods chain. They get squeezed whenever textile mills raise fabric prices because merchants respond by trying to keep the lid on prices paid for finished goods. And sudden changes in fashion have been treacherous. But according to analyst Brenda Gall, a vice president of Merrill Lynch, all that is changing. Says she: "The apparel group is no longer the consumer industry's stepchild."

A cyclical rebound

Short term, the case for apparel rests on the assumption that earnings for some companies will rise dramatically over the next 18 months. For two years, retailers have kept their inventories unusually low, owing to the high cost of credit. No one expects the merchants to return to their old ways, ordering goods far in advance and keeping inventories high. But recently retailers have begun to replenish their stocks at a faster rate.

Research associate: John J. Curran

A cyclical rebound could give the biggest lift to companies like Oxford Industries, which makes a lot of low-priced, private-label apparel for mass merchandisers such as Sears Roebuck, whose sales are showing strength. Even though Oxford's stock sells for less than seven times estimated 1981 earnings, many analysts are wary of it because competition in the private-label business is fierce, and the customers—notably Sears and J.C. Pen-

ney—drive a hard bargain. Yet Oxford has won some fans on Wall Street because it has been diversifying and is now less dependent on mass merchandisers.

Fundamental changes have brightened the longer-term prospects of some large companies that sell mostly to department and specialty stores. Many of them now make all sorts of apparel, so it matters less when one item falls out of fashion. And they have found ways out of the cost

Where There Were Riches in Rags

Since the end of 1973, shares of the top jeans makers—Levi, Blue Bell, and VF—and three other major apparel manufacturers have outperformed the market nicely. The best of the group, Palm Beach, and the worst, Hart Schaffner, have a big stake in men's suits. Suit sales sagged in

the Seventies, but Palm Beach's Evan-Picone women's line brought it button-popping growth. Now suits are back and Hart Schaffner's stock is up 60% this year, the best showing in this group. (This chart displays equal percentage increases as lines of equal height.)

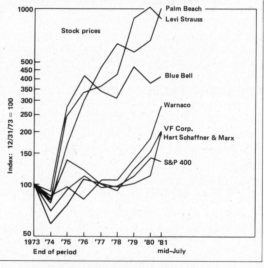

Figure 9.4   Two Popular Sources of Industry Information.
Brokerage house reports, like the one shown on the next page, and articles that appear in the popular financial media are just two sources of industry information; they provide easy-to-digest overviews of an industry, its outlook, and vital industry statistics. (*Source: Fortune,* August 24, 1981; and Dean Witter Reynolds, September 1982.)

trying to understand the nature and operating characteristics of the firm. The following points are of particular interest:

1. The competitive position of the company
2. Its composition and trend in sales
3. Profit margins and company earnings
4. The composition and liquidity of corporate resources (the company's asset mix)
5. The company's capital structure (its financing mix)

 *DEAN WITTER REYNOLDS INC.*

APPAREL INDUSTRY

Overview

The poor sell-through of spring merchandise and slow start for the fall heightened the concern of the already cautious retailers. Store inventories have been difficult to maintain under control. Store buyers, who had been conservative, continue to cut back more. Most orders have been for near-term delivery, while forward orders exist primarily within areas that require a long lead time or where supply is limited. In some cases, the lead time was shortened further. The resultant impact upon the apparel industry has been quite significant in many cases. Cancellations and returns have been on the rise, with production correspondingly curtailed. It would appear as if retailer inventories, plus their on-order positions, are quite a bit below last year. Thus stocks could become pretty lean over the next few months if sales improve only slightly.

Most merchandise categories have been affected. Sportswear and accessories are doing relatively better, in many cases an addition to existing wardrobes. The better-quality and fashion merchandise are still outselling the lower-priced goods, although at a slower pace than earlier in the year. In this period of trying to minimize inventory exposure, retailers continue their programs of merchandise intensification. The goal is to eliminate some of the fringe items and potential markdowns. Commitments remain with the larger, branded sources of supply, provided the sell-through remains high.

Women's wear maintains its lead over men's wear in terms of strength at retail. That is typical of most recessions, but also reflective of a greater percentage of working women. The junior sector remains the weakest, barely showing any signs of life. Men's tailored clothing has probably hit bottom, with fall 1982 shipments up slightly for many manufacturers. Prospects for spring 1983 appear flat for now. This sector appears headed for a long-awaited recovery. The women's dress business, on the other hand, still remains in the doldrums. Only selected manufacturers are doing well in this area.

We are forecasting that apparel shipments will generally track in line with our consumption forecast, on the basis that we expect retailers to maintain low stocks. This translates into a decent cyclical increase for 1982, possibly 2.8%, versus a 6.1% increase in 1981. A further gain of 3.5% is likely in 1983. Imports are increasing from the very low levels of last year. At the same time, the larger, branded producers continue to increase market share.

Investment Posture

The shares of Levi Strauss, Blue Bell, and Palm Beach had been under pressure because of temporary problems, but they offer good value over the longer term. While they have bounced off their lows, we would prefer to remain on the sidelines for now. We remain more positive toward Hart Schaffner & Marx, Jonathan Logan, Liz Claiborne, Oxford Industries, V.F. Corp., and Warnaco, as they should continue to outperform the market.

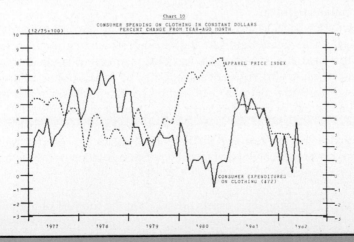

Chart 10
CONSUMER SPENDING ON CLOTHING IN CONSTANT DOLLARS
PERCENT CHANGE FROM YEAR-AGO MONTH

The historical phase of fundamental analysis is, in many respects, the most demanding and the most time-consuming. Most investors have neither the time nor the inclination to conduct such an extensive study; they rely on published reports for the needed background material. The investor has many sources to choose from, including the reports and recommendations of major brokerage houses, the popular financial media, and/or various financial subscription services. These are all valuable sources of information, and the paragraphs that follow are not intended to replace them. Yet to be an intelligent investor, it is important to understand fully the content and implications of such financial reports, and to be able to use the information provided to make one's own judgments about the company and its stock.

Financial Statements

Financial statements are a vital part of fundamental analysis to the extent that they enable investors to grasp an awareness of the operating results and financial condition of a firm. A complete set of financial statements is made up of four parts: (1) a balance sheet, (2) an income statement, (3) a statement of changes in stockholders' equity, and (4) a flow of funds statement. The first two are essential for carrying out fundamental analysis. Company statements are prepared on a quarterly basis (these are *abbreviated* statements compiled for each three-month period of operation) and again at the end of each calendar or *fiscal year* (a 12-month period the company has defined as its operating year, which may or may not end on December 31). Annual financial statements must be fully verified by independent certified public accountants (CPAs), filed with the U.S. Securities and Exchange Commission, and distributed on a timely basis to all stockholders in the form of annual reports. By themselves, corporate financial statements are a most important source of information to the investor; when used with financial ratios and in fundamental analysis, they become even more powerful. Because of their importance, we will now examine each of the four major accounting statements.

The balance sheet

The *balance sheet* is a statement of the company's assets, liabilities, and shareholders' equity. The *assets* represent the resources of the company (the things that belong to the firm), the *liabilities* are its debts, and *equity* is the amount of stockholders' capital in the firm. A balance sheet may be thought of as a summary of the firm's assets balanced against its debt and ownership positions *at a single point in time* (on the last day of the calendar or fiscal year, or at the end of the quarter). In order to balance, the total assets must equal the total amount of liabilities and equity. A typical balance sheet is illustrated in Table 9.2. It shows the comparative 1982–1983 figures for our hypothetical apparel firm, Palm Springs Industries (note that the fiscal year ends on November 30).

Assets.   The company's assets are listed in the top half of the balance sheet and are broken into two parts: current and long-term assets. Current assets are made up of cash and other assets that will be converted into cash (or in the case of "prepaid

TABLE 9.2 A CORPORATE BALANCE SHEET, PALM SPRINGS INDUSTRIES ($ IN THOUSANDS, NOVEMBER 30)

	1983	1982	
Current assets	$ 7,846	$ 14,459	Cash and short-term investments
	105,400	102,889	Accounts receivable
	164,356	159,238	Inventories
	1,778	2,111	Prepaid expenses
	$279,380	$278,697	Total current assets
Long-term assets	$ 1,366	$ 1,317	Land
	13,873	13,889	Buildings
	75,717	73,199	Furniture, fixtures, and equipment
	49,412	50,209	Leasehold improvements
	$140,368	$138,614	Gross long-term assets
	(85,203)	(80,865)	Accumulated depreciation
	$ 55,165	$ 57,749	Net long-term assets
	$ 4,075	$ 4,108	Other assets
Total assets	$338,620	$340,554	
Current liabilities	$ 2,000	$ 11,500	Notes payable
	4,831	1,090	Current maturities
	68,849	69,696	Accounts payable and accrued expenses
	3,806	3,119	Taxes on earnings
	5,460	4,550	Accrued taxes
	$84,946	$89,955	Total current liabilities
Long-term debt	$53,723	$61,807	Long-term debt, less current maturities
Stockholders' equity	$ 21,787	$ 21,777	Common shares, $2.50 par value
	20,068	20,028	Capital surplus
	158,096	146,987	Retained earnings
	$199,951	$188,792	Stockholders' equity
Total liabilities and stockholders' equity	$338,620	$340,554	

expenses," consumed) in one year or less. The four most common current assets are listed: cash and short-term investments, accounts receivable, inventory, and prepaid expenses. The cash account is self-explanatory; accounts receivable represents the amount due the company from customers who purchased goods on credit; inventories are the raw materials used in the production process, work-in-process, and the finished goods ready for shipment to customers; and prepaid expenses

Happy days are here again ...

represent payments made in advance for such services as utilities and insurance. These assets are the firm's working capital and provide the funds for day-to-day operations. Other than the cash account, such assets represent allocations of corporate funds to the resource in question; for example, Palm Springs Industries had invested more than $105 million in accounts receivable as of November 30, 1983.

The long-term assets of PSI are represented mostly by land and facilities, which is typical of most companies. These assets have extended lives (more than one year) and are resources not intended for sale, but for use over and over again in the manufacture, display, warehousing, and transportation of the company's product. The most common long-term assets are land, buildings, plant and equipment, office furnishings, and leasehold improvements (capital improvements made on property leased by the company). The net amount of long-term assets shown on the balance sheet changes each year because depreciation is charged against these assets. (Depreciation is an accounting entry used to account systematically for the wear and tear of an asset over time.) The "accumulated depreciation" entry reflects the total of past depreciation charged against property still on the books; it is strictly an accounting entry and does *not* represent cash.

Liabilities.   The firm's financial structure appears in the lower half of Table 9.2, where the liabilities and stockholders' position are listed. This portion of the balance sheet is divided into three parts: (1) current liabilities, (2) long-term debt, and (3) equity. Current liabilities are the debts owed to lenders (notes payable and current maturities), suppliers (trade and accounts payable), employees (accrued expenses), and the government (accrued taxes). Like their counterparts on the asset side of the balance sheet, they are due and payable within a period of one year or less. The current liabilities listed for PSI are typical of those found on most corporate balance sheets. Long-term debts have maturities that extend beyond one year. If the firm leases any of its assets, the capitalized value of such obligations would appear at this point. Note that only the principal amount of current and long-term debt is recorded on the balance sheet; the interest portion appears only on the income statement, as an expense. Long-term liabilities are normally broken into the term portion of the debt and that portion due in one year or less, which is known as current maturities. Current maturities are like the next 12 monthly payments on a four-year instalment loan. The amount due in the next year would be listed as current maturities, whereas the amount due in years 2 through 4 would be listed as long-term debt.

Equity. In addition to money the company owes, another type of claim against assets is that of the firm's owners (its stockholders). This is represented by the equity (or net worth) accounts on the balance sheet and is a *residual* position—that is, the claims of all short- and long-term lenders take precedence over those of the owners. The major components of stockholders' equity are the common stock account, capital surplus, and retained earnings. The first two represent paid-in capital and are equal to the proceeds realized by the company from the sale of its stock to the investing public (the common stock account equals the par or stated value of the stock times the number of shares issued, and capital surplus equals the excess of the net proceeds from the sale of the stock above the stock's par value). Retained earnings, in contrast, are an accumulation of prior earnings that have been retained in the company; they are the earnings left after dividends have been paid. Retained earnings are used to pay off debt, acquire facilities, and invest in receivables, inventories, and the like. They do *not* represent cash or a pool of untapped financing, but instead are resources that have been previously allocated to various areas of the firm.

The income statement

The *income statement* provides a financial summary of the operating results of the firm. Unlike the balance sheet, the income statement covers activities that have occurred over the course of time, or for a given operating period. Typically, this extends no longer than a fiscal or calendar year; Table 9.3 shows Palm Springs Industries' income statements for the years 1982 and 1983. Note that these annual statements cover operations over a 12-month (fiscal) period ending on November 30, which corresponds to the date of the balance sheet. The income statement indicates how successful the firm has been in using the assets listed on the balance sheet; that is, the amount of success management has in operating the firm is reflected in the profit or loss the company generates during the year.

The income statement is simply a summary of the amount of revenues (sales

**TABLE 9.3   A CORPORATE INCOME STATEMENT,
PALM SPRINGS INDUSTRIES
($ IN THOUSANDS, YEAR ENDED NOVEMBER 30)**

1983	1982	
$606,610	$567,986	Net sales
6,792	6,220	Other income
1,504	895	Interest income
$614,906	$575,101	Total revenues
$377,322	$354,424	Cost of goods sold
195,864	184,419	Selling, administrative, and occupancy expenses
5,765	5,523	Interest expense
$578,951	$544,366	Total costs and expenses
$ 35,955	$ 30,735	Earnings before taxes
$ 17,950	$ 15,230	Taxes on earnings
$ 18,005	$ 15,505	Net earnings (profit)
$ 2.09	$ 1.80	Earnings per share
8,601	8,601	Number of common shares outstanding (in thousands)

and income) generated over the period, the cost and expenses incurred over the same period, and the company's profits (which, of course, are obtained by subtracting all costs and expenses, including taxes, from revenues). Note in Table 9.3 that there are four basic types of expenses: *cost of goods sold,* which is often the largest cost item and represents labor, material, and factory overhead expenses; *selling, administrative, and occupancy expenses,* representing salaries, advertising and promotion costs, travel and entertainment, office expenses, utilities and insurance, and other costs of operating the firm; *interest expense,* which reflects the cost of borrowing; and *taxes* on earnings, which is the share of profits that goes to various levels of government. The net earnings of the firm are the "bottom line" of the income statement. If not used to pay common and/or preferred dividends, they go to retained earnings, where they are used to finance growth or repay debt.

Other statements

Other statements are also made available to investors. One is the *statement of changes in stockholders' equity,* which recaps the amount of profits reinvested in the business, the amount of dividends paid out to investors, and other changes in the firm's equity position. The company's balance sheet and its income statement are linked in a number of ways, one of which is the tie between net profits and retained earnings. A statement of changes in stockholders' equity shows this relationship and records how profits, dividends, and other transactions affected the stockholders' position. Table 9.4 depicts the 1982–1983 statement for PSI. Corresponding to the operating period covered in the income statement, it shows how and why retained earnings changed over the 12-month period ending November 30, and what accounted for other changes in this important source of financing.

TABLE 9.4 STATEMENT OF CHANGES IN STOCKHOLDERS' EQUITY, PALM SPRINGS INDUSTRIES ($ IN THOUSANDS, YEAR ENDED NOVEMBER 30)		
	1983	1982
Stockholders' equity—beginning of the fiscal year	$188,792	$179,047
Plus: Net earnings for the year	$ 18,005	$ 15,505
Less: Dividends paid during the year	(6,896)	(6,220)
Additions to retained earnings	$ 11,109	$ 9,285
Plus: Proceeds from stock issued	10	300
Plus: Excess above par value realized from sale of stock	40	160
Stockholders' equity—end of the year	$199,951	$188,792

Because working capital management is crucial to meeting day-to-day expenses, a *statement of changes in financial position,* or "flow of funds," is also included in a complete set of financial statements. Table 9.5 presents the 1982–1983 report for Palm Springs Industries. Notice that the flow of funds statement brings together items from *both* the balance sheet and income statement to show where the company obtained working capital and what these funds were used for during the year. Observe that in 1983, Palm Springs generated almost $27.4 million in working capital from the operations of the firm; a good portion of this (almost $21.7 million) was used to pay off debt, pay dividends, and acquire new property. The balance ($5.7 million) accounted for the firm's increase in working capital. The layout shown in Table 9.5 is typical of the format found in most corporate reports. The top part shows the sources and uses of working capital; the bottom half ("changes in components of working capital") reconciles the increase or decrease in working capital.

Key Financial Ratios

Ratios lie at the very heart of company analysis; indeed, fundamental analysis as a system of information would be incomplete without this key ingredient. *Ratio analysis* is the study of the relationships among and between various financial statement accounts. Ratios provide a different perspective of the operating results and financial condition of the firm and, as a result, expand the information content of financial statements. Each measure relates one item on the balance sheet (or income statement) with another; or as is more often the case, a balance sheet account is related to an operating (or income statement) element. In this way, attention is centered not on the absolute size of the financial statement accounts, but on the liquidity, activity, and profitability of the resources, financial structure, and operating results of the firm.

The most significant contribution of financial ratios is that they enable an investor to assess the firm's past and present financial condition and operating results. The mechanics are actually quite simple: Selected information is obtained from

**TABLE 9.5   A FLOW OF FUNDS STATEMENT,
PALM SPRINGS INDUSTRIES
($ IN THOUSANDS, YEAR ENDED NOVEMBER 30)**

	1983	1982	
Working capital provided by:	$18,005	$15,505	Net earnings for the year
	8,792	8,300	Depreciation and amortization
	560	(44)	Other
	$27,357	$23,761	Working capital provided by operations
	—	7,950	Proceeds from long-term borrowing
	$27,357	$31,711	
Working capital used for:	8,084	1,090	Reduction of long-term debt
	6,896	6,220	Payment of dividends
	6,685	10,686	Property additions—net
	$21,665	$17,996	
Increase in working capital:	$5,692	$13,715	
Changes in components of working capital:	$(6,613)	$(1,789)	Cash and short-term investments
	2,511	6,549	Accounts receivable
	5,118	15,101	Inventories
	(333)	45	Prepaid expenses
	9,500	2,500	Notes payable to banks
	(3,741)	(150)	Current maturities and early retirements of long-term debt
	(153)	(8,712)	Accounts payable and accrued expenses
	(687)	2,481	Taxes on earnings
	90	(2,310)	Deferred taxes on earnings
Increase in working capital:	$ 5,692	$13,715	

annual financial statements and used to compute a set of ratios, which are then compared to historical and/or industry standards to evaluate the financial condition of a company. When historical standards are used, the company's ratios are compared and studied from one year to the next; industry standards, in contrast, involve a comparison of a particular company's ratios to the average performance of other companies in the same line of business.

Financial ratios can be divided into five groups: (1) liquidity, (2) activity, (3) leverage, (4) profitability, and (5) common stock, or market measures. Using the 1983 figures from the Palm Springs financial statements (Tables 9.2 and 9.3), we will now identify and briefly discuss some of the more popular and widely used measures in each of these five categories.

Measures of liquidity

Liquidity is concerned with the ability of the firm to meet its day-to-day operating expenses and satisfy its short-term obligations as they come due. Of major concern is whether or not a company has adequate cash and other liquid assets on hand to service its debt and operating needs in a prompt and timely fashion. A general overview of a company's liquidity position can often be obtained with two simple measures: current ratio and net working capital.

Current ratio. The current ratio is perhaps the most commonly cited of all financial ratios; it is computed as follows:

$$\text{current ratio} = \frac{\text{current assets}}{\text{current liabilities}}$$

In 1983, Palm Springs Industries had a current ratio of

$$\text{current ratio for PSI} = \frac{\$279,380}{\$84,946} = \underline{\underline{3.29}}$$

This figure indicates that PSI had $3.29 in short-term resources to service every dollar of current debt; by most standards, such a current ratio would be considered generous.

Net working capital. An absolute measure of a company's liquidity, net working capital indicates the dollar amount of equity in the working capital position of the firm. It is the difference between current assets and current liabilities, and for 1983, the net working capital figure for PSI equaled:

$$\text{net working capital} = \text{current assets} - \text{current liabilities}$$
$$= \$279,380 - \$84,946 = \underline{\$194,434}$$

A net working capital figure that approaches the $200 million mark is substantial indeed and suggests that the liquidity position of PSI is good—so long as it is not made up of slow-moving and obsolete inventories and/or past due accounts receivable.

Activity ratios

Measuring general liquidity is only the beginning of the analysis, for we must also assess the composition and underlying liquidity of key current assets and evaluate how effectively the company is managing its assets. Activity ratios capture the way the company is utilizing its assets by comparing company sales to various asset categories. Three of the most widely used activity ratios deal with accounts receivable, inventory, and total assets.

Accounts receivable turnover. A glance at most financial statements will reveal that the asset side of the balance sheet is dominated by just a few accounts which make up 80 to 90 percent, or even more, of total resources. Certainly this is the case with PSI where, as can be seen in Table 9.2, three entries (accounts receivable, inventory, and net long-term assets) accounted for about 95 percent of assets in 1983. Most firms invest a significant amount of capital in accounts receivable, and for this reason they are viewed as a crucial corporate resource. Accounts receivable turnover is a measure of how these resources are being managed and is computed as follows:

$$\text{accounts receivable turnover} = \frac{\text{annual sales}}{\text{accounts receivable}}$$

$$\text{for PSI} = \frac{\$606,610}{\$105,400} = \underline{\underline{5.76}}$$

In essence, this turnover figure is an indication of the kind of return the company is getting from its investment in accounts receivable. Other things being equal, the higher the turnover figure, the more favorable it is. Observe that in 1983, PSI turned its receivables over about 5.8 times; put another way, each dollar invested in receivables supported $5.76 in sales.

Inventory turnover. Another important corporate resource, and one that requires a considerable amount of management attention, is inventory. Control of inventory is important to the well-being of a company and is commonly assessed with the following turnover measure:

$$\text{inventory turnover} = \frac{\text{sales}}{\text{inventory}}$$

$$\text{for PSI} = \frac{\$606,610}{\$164,356} = \underline{\underline{3.69}}$$

Again, the more mileage (sales) the company can get out of its inventory, the better the return on this vital resource. A figure of 3.69 for PSI reveals the goods were bought and sold out of inventory about 3.7 times a year. Generally, the higher the turnover figure, the less time an item spends in inventory and the better the return the company is able to earn from funds tied up in inventory.

Total asset turnover. Total asset turnover indicates how efficiently assets are being used to support sales; it is calculated as follows:

$$\text{total asset turnover} = \frac{\text{sales}}{\text{total assets}}$$

$$\text{for PSI} = \frac{\$606,610}{\$338,620} = \underline{\underline{1.79}}$$

The arrival of spring brings a flood tide of annual reports from the country's corporations. As many as 100 million of these informative and generally colorful booklets come off the presses each year at a total cost estimated at 120 million dollars. American Telephone & Telegraph Company alone prints 4.5 million. General Motors turns out more than 1.8 million and International Business Machines about 1 million.

A typical company prints many more reports than it has shareholders; extras go to investment analysts, employees, customers, public-affairs offices and corporate-sales divisions.

Some shareholders are so bewildered by the array of financial tables and footnotes in the reports that they only leaf through the booklet's opening pages, then toss it away. That can be a mistake, say investment experts.

"Investors owe it to themselves to study the annual reports of companies in which they already have financial interests or in which they are contemplating making investments," according to a study by Drexel Burnham Lambert, Inc. And Standard & Poor's Corporation notes: "The reports are not as complicated as they may seem. Though some effort is required to dig beneath the surface, they can be extremely valuable investment aids."

[The] reports. . . . [provide information on] how inflation has affected operations and discuss in . . . detail plans for capital spending, adequacy of working capital and the availability of bank credit.

What should a reader look for in an annual report? [One recent] study advises being alert to these things:

- *The forthrightness of management in evaluating its past successes and its disappointments.*
- *Targets for growth of earnings and return on investment and steps toward achieving these goals. The latter would include plans for new products, marketing programs and capital additions.*
- *An assessment of how rapidly markets are expanding and whether the company must gain a larger market share to meet growth aims.*
- *The changing character of the enterprise. Is the company maturing? Are its once exclusive products being marketed by competitors?*
- *Capital needs. Can internal cash flow provide for both growth objectives and higher dividends?*
- *How does management's team stack up? Is this a one-man show or is there management in depth?*
- *What is the likely trend in profits? Is the growth rate in earnings on the rise or slowing?*

Details such as these are only one guideline an individual should follow in charting investment strategy. But careful reading of an annual report can provide valuable insights into a company's current financial position and its prospects.

Source: Ellis Haller, "It's Annual Report Time," *U.S. News & World Report,* March 30, 1981, p. 78.

Like receivables and inventory, a high (or increasing) total asset turnover figure is viewed as positive because it has a beneficial effect on profitability and return on investment. The principle at work here is much like the return to an individual investor: Earning $100 from a $1,000 investment is far more desirable than earning the same $100 from a $2,000 investment. A high total asset turnover figure suggests that corporate resources are being managed efficiently and that the firm is able to realize a high level of sales (and ultimately, profits) from its asset investments.

Leverage measures

Leverage deals with different types of financing and indicates the amount of debt being used to support the resources and operations of the company. The amount of indebtedness within the financial structure and the ability of the firm to service its debt are major concerns in leverage analysis. There are two widely used leverage ratios: The first, the debt-equity ratio, measures the amount of debt being used by the company; the second, times interest earned, assesses how well the company can service its debt load.

Debt-equity ratio.   A measure of the relative amount of funds provided by lenders and owners, the debt-equity ratio is computed as follows:

$$\text{debt-equity ratio} = \frac{\text{long-term debt}}{\text{stockholders' equity}}$$

$$\text{for PSI} = \frac{\$53,723}{\$199,951} = \underline{\underline{.27}}$$

The debt-equity ratio measures the amount of financial leverage being used by a company. Since highly leveraged firms (those using large amounts of debt) run an increased risk of bankruptcy, this ratio is particularly helpful in assessing a stock's risk exposure. The 1983 debt-equity ratio for PSI is a *low* 27 percent and discloses that most of the company's capital comes from its owners—put another way, this figure means there was only 27 cents of debt in the capital structure for every dollar of equity.

Times interest earned.   This so-called coverage ratio measures the ability of the firm to meet its fixed interest payments, and is calculated as follows:

$$\text{times interest earned} = \frac{\text{earnings before interest and taxes}}{\text{interest expense}}$$

$$\text{for PSI} = \frac{\$35,955 + \$5,765}{\$5,765} = \underline{\underline{7.24}}$$

The ability of the company to meet its interest payments (which, with bonds, are fixed contractual obligations) in a timely and orderly fashion is also an important consideration in evaluating risk exposure. In the case of PSI, there is about $7.24 available to cover every dollar of interest expense. Usually, there is little concern until the measure drops to something less than two or three times earnings.

Measures of profitability

Profitability is a relative measure of success. Each of the various profitability measures relates the returns (profits) of a company to its sales, assets, or equity.

There are four widely used profitability measures: operating ratio, net profit margin, return on total assets, and return on investment.

Operating ratio. The major components of a company's cost structure are captured in its operating ratio, a measure that relates total operating expenses to sales:

$$\text{operating ratio} = \frac{\text{cost of goods sold } + \text{ selling,}}{\text{net sales}}$$

$$\text{for PSI} = \frac{\$377,322 + \$195,864}{\$606,610} = \underline{94.5\%}$$

Note that the operating ratio ignores interest, taxes, and other "nonoperating" income and expenses, and deals only with internally generated operating costs incurred in the normal course of business. In essence, this ratio indicates the relative amount of operating expenses used to generate the current level of sales; it provides a measure of the firm's operating efficiency. For Palm Springs Industries, operating expenses, consisting primarily of cost of goods sold, absorbed about 94.5 percent of sales.

Net profit margin. This is the "bottom line" of operations; it indicates the rate of profit from sales and other revenues. The net profit margin is computed as follows:

$$\text{net profit margin} = \frac{\text{net profit after taxes}}{\text{total revenues}}$$

$$\text{for PSI} = \frac{\$18,005}{\$614,906} = \underline{2.9\%}$$

The net profit margin presents profits as a percentage of sales, and because it moves with costs, also reveals the type of control management has over the cost structure of the firm. Note that PSI had a net profit margin of 2.9 percent in 1983—that is, the company's return on sales was roughly 3 cents on the dollar.

Return on total assets. This profitability measure looks at the amount of resources needed by the firm to support its operations. Return on total assets (ROTA) reveals management effectiveness in generating profits from the assets it has available, and is perhaps the single most important measure of return; it is computed as follows:

$$\text{ROTA} = \frac{\text{net profit after taxes}}{\text{total assets}}$$

$$\text{for PSI} = \frac{\$18,005}{\$338,620} = \underline{5.3\%}$$

Because both return on sales (net profit margin) and asset productivity (total asset turnover) are embedded in ROTA, it provides a clear picture of a company's managerial effectiveness, and the overall profitability of its resource allocation and investment decisions. In the case of PSI, the company earned 5.3 percent on its asset investments in 1983.

Return on investment.   This ratio measures the return to stockholders by relating profits to stockholders' equity:

$$\text{return on investment (ROI)} = \frac{\text{net profit after taxes}}{\text{stockholders' equity}}$$

$$\text{for PSI} = \frac{\$18,005}{\$199,951} = \underline{\underline{9.0\%}}$$

Essentially, ROI is an extension of ROTA and introduces the company's financing decisions into the assessment of profitability; that is, it denotes the extent to which leverage can increase return to stockholders. ROI shows the annual payoff to investors, which in the case of PSI amounts to about 9 cents for every dollar of equity.

Common stock ratios

A number of common stock, or so-called market, ratios convert key bits of information about the company to a per share basis and are used to assess the performance of a company for stock valuation purposes. These ratios tell the investor exactly what portion of total profits, dividends, and equity is allocated to each share of stock. Popular common stock ratios include earnings per share, the price/earnings ratio, dividends per share, dividend yield, payout ratio, and book value per share. We have already examined two of these measures in Chapter 8 (earnings per share and dividend yield); let's look now at the other four.

Price/earnings ratio.   This measure is an extension of the earnings per share ratio, and is used to determine how the market is pricing the company's common stock. The price/earnings (P/E) ratio relates the company's earnings per share (EPS) to the market price of its stock:

$$\text{P/E} = \frac{\text{market price of common stock}}{\text{EPS}}$$

To compute the P/E ratio, it is necessary first to calculate the stock's EPS; using the earnings-per-share equation from the previous chapter, we see that EPS for Palm Springs Industries in 1983 was:

$$\text{EPS} = \frac{\text{net profit after taxes} - \text{preferred dividends}}{\text{number of common shares outstanding}}$$

$$\text{for PSI} = \frac{\$18,005 - \$0}{8,601} = \underline{\underline{\$2.09}}$$

BOX 9.3 RATING A FIRM'S FINANCIAL VIGOR

[In 1981, the] financial strength—or weakness—of American corporations [was] being questioned by [many] economists. . . . [And there were] reasons aplenty for worry. Some old and famous companies are struggling to avoid insolvency. International Harvester is pleading with creditors to reschedule debts, give it more time to pay. Several major airlines are selling assets to raise cash, delaying purchases of planes, pressing unions to take pay cuts. Scores of savings and loans are flirting with disaster.

These crises reflect a general letdown in financial standards. In recent years, corporations have piled on more debt, especially short-term loans. They've drawn down their bank accounts, sold off assets readily converted into cash. It's a strategy that is encouraged by inflation.

In view of all this, it is remarkable that many studies issued by brokers make no reference to the finances of the companies they recommend. It's as if investors were to assume that any business analyzed and touted by the experts could be assumed to have respectable balance sheets. . . .

Under any . . . market condition . . . it is prudent to check on a company's debts and assets before buying its shares. But many people are uncertain how to do that. What should they look for? What standards should they apply?

Wright Investors' Service, an investment adviser whose clients include many banks, applies a set of tests that are fairly clear-cut and might be applied by almost any investor with access (through a public library or broker's office) to data published by Standard & Poor's Corporation. Wright uses 32 "quality standards," including the following "preferred" financial conditions—

1. Current assets at least double current liabilities. Less is acceptable if the company has an unusually light burden of long-term debt.
2. Long-term debt not more than 40 percent of total capital, measured by stockholder equity plus long-term debt. Utilities are allowed 60 percent debt; banks and insurance companies, 70 percent; transportation companies, 35 to 50 percent.
3. Not more than 10 percent of total capital in preferred stock.
4. Income before taxes 3½ times "fixed charges" payable on debt, leases and preferred stock. Utilities are allowed 2 to 1.
5. No risk that the number of common shares will be raised more than 30 percent by tenders of warrants or convertible securities.
6. Earnings unlikely to be "diluted" by more than 15 percent if all warrants and convertibles are tendered for common stock.
7. Stockholder equity totaling at least 50 million dollars. Smaller concerns tend to have thin markets, making it difficult to sell big blocks of their stock without sharp price reductions. Investors who are likely to hold only 100 or so shares have less cause to worry on that score.

Wright applies its standards with some flexibility. A company may be allowed a lower current ratio and more debt if it's no worse than average for others in the same industry.

These rules disqualify more than 90 of the companies in Standard & Poor's 500-stock index, and some analysts consider them a bit old-fashioned. But the average investor would do well to remember the old adage: Better safe than sorry.

Source: William C. Bryant, "Rating a Firm's Financial Vigor," *U.S. News & World Report,* September 7, 1981, p. 73.

In this case, the company's profits of $18 million translated into earnings of $2.09 for *each share* of outstanding common stock. Given this EPS figure and the stock's current market price (assume it is currently trading at 31½), we can now determine the P/E ratio for Palm Springs Industries:

$$P/E = \frac{\$31.50}{\$2.09} = \underline{15.1}$$

In effect, the stock is currently selling at a multiple of about 15 times its 1983 earnings. Price/earnings multiples are widely quoted in the financial press and are an essential part of many stock valuation models.

Dividends per share.   The principle here is the same as EPS; to translate total aggregate (dollar) dividends paid by the company into a per share figure. Dividends per share is measured as follows:

$$\text{dividends per share} = \frac{\text{annual dividends paid}}{\text{number of common shares outstanding}}$$

$$\text{for PSI} = \frac{\$6,896}{8,601} = \underline{\$.80}$$

For fiscal 1983, PSI paid out dividends of 80 cents per share—or at a quarterly rate of 20 cents per share. As we saw in the preceding chapter, we can relate dividends per share to the market price of the stock to determine its present dividend yield: $0.80/$31.50 = 2.5\%$.

Payout ratio.   Another important dividend measure is the payout ratio; it provides an indication of the amount of earnings paid out to stockholders in the form of dividends. The payout ratio is calculated according to the following equation:

$$\text{payout ratio} = \frac{\text{dividends per share}}{\text{earnings per share}}$$

$$\text{for PSI} = \frac{\$.80}{\$2.09} = \underline{.38}$$

For PSI in 1983, dividends accounted for about 38 percent of earnings. This is fairly typical; for most companies that pay dividends tend to pay out somewhere between 40 and 60 percent of earnings.

Book value per share.   The last common stock ratio is book value per share, a measure that deals with stockholders' equity. Actually, book value is simply another word for equity (or net worth); it represents the difference between total assets and total liabilities. Book value per share is computed as follows:

$$\text{book value per share} = \frac{\text{stockholders' equity}}{\text{number of common shares outstanding}}$$

$$\text{for PSI} = \frac{\$199,951}{8,601} = \underline{\underline{\$23.25}}$$

Presumably, a stock should sell for *more* than its book value (note that PSI does). Otherwise, it could be an indication that something is seriously wrong with the outlook and profitability of the company.

Interpreting Financial Ratios

Rather than compute all the financial ratios themselves, most individual investors rely on published reports for such information. Many large brokerage houses and a variety of financial services publish such reports, an example of which is given in Figure 9.5. These reports provide much vital information in a convenient and easy-to-read format and relieve the investor of the drudgery of computing the financial ratios. But investors still need to be able to evaluate this information. To see how this is done, consider the case of Palm Springs Industries, and take a look at Table 9.6, which provides a summary of historical and industry figures for most of the ratios discussed above. To begin with, we can see a modest improvement in an already strong liquidity position, as the current ratio remains well above the industry standard. A look at the activity measures shows that although receivables and inventory turnover are improving, they still remain below industry standards. Accounts receivable turnover appears to be especially out of line and is almost 40 percent below normal. Unless there is an operating or economic explanation for this, it would appear that a lot of excess (nonproductive) resources are being tied up in accounts receivable, which is costing the firm millions of dollars a year in profits. The inventory position, in contrast, has improved, and though it is still a bit below average, it certainly does not appear to be much of a problem. Finally, note that total asset turnover is up from last year and well above average.

The leverage position of PSI seems well controlled; the company tends to use a lot less debt in its financial structure than the average firm in the apparel industry. The payoff for this judicious use of debt comes in the form of a coverage ratio that is well above average. The profitability picture for PSI is equally attractive; profit rate, return on total assets, and ROI are all improving and remain well above the industry norm. In summary, our analysis suggests that Palm Springs Industries is, with the possible exception of accounts receivable, a fairly well managed and highly profitable business. The results of this show up in common stock ratios that are consistently equal or superior to industry figures. Certainly, the company has done well in the past and appears to be a well-managed firm today. Our major concern at this point (and the topic of the first part of Chapter 10) is whether or not Palm Springs Industries will continue to be an industry leader and provide above-average returns to investors.

Liz Claiborne, Inc.

Income Data (Million $)

Year Ended Dec. 31	Revs.	Oper. Inc.	% Oper. Inc. of Revs.	Cap. Exp.	Depr.	Int. Exp.	Net Bef. Taxes	Eff. Tax Rate	Net Inc.	% Net Inc. of Revs.
1981	117	22.9	19.6%	2.19	0.43	1.75	20.7	50.8%	10.2	8.7%
1980	80	14.0	17.6%	1.48	0.22	1.17	12.6	50.7%	6.2	7.8%
1979	48	8.0	16.8%	0.20	0.18	0.86	7.0	49.8%	3.5	7.3%
1978	23	3.1	12.9%	0.39	0.09	0.59	2.3	48.8%	1.2	5.1%
1977	7	NA	NA	NA	NA	NA	NA	NA	0.3	4.6%
¹1976	2	NA	NA	NA	NA	NA	NA	NA	0.1	2.4%

Balance Sheet Data (Million $)

Dec. 31	Cash	Current Assets	Current Liab.	Ratio	Total Assets	Ret. on Assets	Long Term Debt	Common Equity	Total Cap.	% LT Debt of Cap.	Ret. on Equity
1981	0.49	41.6	18.1	2.3	44.9	31.7%	Nil	26.8	26.8	Nil	54.0%
1980	0.21	17.7	8.4	2.1	19.3	41.3%	0.02	10.9	10.9	0.2%	78.4%
1979	0.09	10.2	5.8	1.8	10.8	44.1%	0.08	4.9	5.0	1.5%	108.1%
1978	NA	NA	NA	NA	5.1	33.8%	0.12	1.6	1.7	6.9%	117.5%

Data prior to 1981 as reptd. in prospectus dated 5-1-81. **1.** From 1-19-76 (date of incorp.) through 12-31-76. NA-Not Available.

Net Sales (Million $)

13 Weeks:	1982	1981	1980	1979
Mar.	41.1	26.5	20.7	10.7
Jun.	32.2	22.7	13.2	7.9
Sep.		35.5	25.4	15.0
Dec.		32.1	20.1	14.0
		116.8	79.4	47.6

Net sales for the 26 weeks ended June 26, 1982, rose 49% from those of the comparable year-earlier period. Cost of sales increased at a slightly faster rate, paring the gain in pretax income to 45%. After taxes at 50.7%, against 50.9%, net income was up 46%, to $6,199,980, from $4,254,686. Share profits were up less than proportionately, to $1.78 from $1.34, reflecting a 9.7% increase in weighted average shares outstanding.

Sales have a seasonal pattern, peaking in response to shipments of the Spring (December–March) and Fall (June–September) collections.

Common Share Earnings ($)

13 Weeks:	1982	1981	1980	1979
Mar.	1.13	0.86	0.62	0.25
Jun.	0.65	0.49	0.20	0.17
Sep.		1.10	0.74	0.40
Dec.		0.60	0.42	0.30
		3.06	1.98	1.12

Dividend Data

Although the company has paid dividends in the past, it has no present plan to pay any in the foreseeable future.

Finances

The initial public offering of Liz Claiborne, Inc., stock took place June 9, 1981, when underwriters led by Merrill Lynch White Weld Capital Markets Group sold 1,150,000 common shares at $19 each. Of the total, 805,000 shares were sold for certain stockholders and 345,000 represented new financing for Liz Claiborne. Proceeds to the company were earmarked to repay short-term debt incurred to finance inventories and accounts receivable and for plant expansion, equipment purchases and general corporate purposes.

During 1981, the company obtained a $25 million line of bank credit that may be used to cover letters of credit issued by the bank at the company's request, direct borrowings and borrowings under bankers' acceptances. Interest charged on direct borrowings is at ³/₄ of 1% over the bank's prime rate and 1¼% over the bank's discounted buying rate for bankers' acceptances.

Anticipated capital expenditures of $1.2 million for equipment and leasehold improvements during 1982 is expected to be financed through available capital and earnings.

Capitalization

Long Term Debt: None.

Common Stock: 3,480,935 shs. ($1 par). Arthur and Elisabeth C. Ortenberg own about 21%, Leonard Boxer 11% and Jerome A. Chasen 11%.
Institutions hold about 28%.
Shareholders: 621 of record (3/82).

Office—1441 Broadway, NYC 10018. **Tel**—(212) 354-4900. **Pres**—Elisabeth C. Ortenberg. **Secy & Treas**—A. Ortenberg. **VP-Fin & Investor Contact**—Harvey L. Falk. **Dirs**—L. Boxer, J. A. Chazen, J. J. Gordon, A. Ortenberg, E. C. Ortenberg. **Registrar & Transfer Agent**—Chase Manhattan Bank, NYC. **Incorporated** in Delaware in 1981; predecessor incorporated in New York in 1976.

Information has been obtained from sources believed to be reliable, but its accuracy and completeness are not guaranteed.   H. Saftlas

Figure 9.5 An Example of a Published Analytical Report with Financial Statistics.

These and similar reports are widely available to investors and play an important part in the security analysis process. (*Source:* Standard & Poor's *Standard NYSE Stock Reports.*)

TABLE 9.6 COMPARATIVE HISTORICAL AND INDUSTRY RATIOS

	HISTORICAL FIGURES FOR PALM SPRINGS INDUSTRIES		1983 Industry Averages for the Apparel Industry
	1982	1983	
Liquidity measures			
Current ratio	3.10	3.29	2.87
Activity measures			
Receivables turnover	5.52	5.76	8.00
Inventory turnover	3.57	3.69	3.75
Total asset turnover	1.67	1.79	1.42
Leverage measures			
Debt equity ratio	.33	.27	.49
Times interest earned	6.56	7.24	4.70
Profitability measures			
Operating ratio	94.9%	94.5%	94.5%
Net profit margin	2.7%	2.9%	2.7%
Return on total assets	4.6%	5.3%	3.9%
Return on investment	8.2%	9.0%	7.9%
Common stock measures			
Earnings per share	$1.80	$2.09	$1.45
Price/earnings ratio	16.20	15.10	14.00
Dividends per share	$0.70	$0.80	$0.40
Dividend yield	2.4%	2.5%	1.9%
Payout ratio	39.0%	38.0%	28.0%
Book value per share	$21.95	$23.25	$16.00

SUMMARY

Common stocks are popular investment vehicles, but success in this market is largely a function of careful security selection and investment timing. The desire to know something about the stock being purchased is at the heart of security analysis. Security analysis helps the investor make the crucial selection decision by determining the intrinsic value of a stock—its underlying worth.

Security analysis consists of an economic study, industry analysis, and fundamental (company) analysis. The idea is to work down from the broad view of the economy to the specific details concerning the financial condition of a company and the future prospects for its stock. Economic analysis deals with an evaluation of the general state of the economy and its potential effects on security returns. In addition to basic economic conditions, international developments and domestic politics are also important because of the potential effect they can have on the state of the economy. In essence, economic analysis attempts to identify the kind of future economic environment the investor will be facing and tends to set the tone for the security analysis process. Such economic forces as the business cycle, fiscal and monetary policies, corporate profits, unemployment rates, and inflation are all studied for clues about the future of the economy. The next step is to narrow the focus to a study of one or more industries. Again, it is the outlook for an industry that is important, and toward this end, the investor evaluates such aspects as the nature of the industry, its operating characteristics, important technological developments, and key economic variables.

The next stage in the process is fundamental analysis, or the in-depth study of the financial condition and operating results of a specific company. This deals first with a historical look at the firm. Then future expectations are formulated about the company and its stock. All of this provides the basis for establishing the value (or intrinsic worth) of the stock. Fundamental analysis is conducted on the premise that the value of a stock is influenced, in part, by the performance of the company issuing the stock. It is done by studying the competitive position of the company, its sales and profit margins, asset mix, and capital structure. Corporate financial statements are an essential part of company analysis and form the raw material of this analytical process. They include the balance sheet, the income statement, the statement of changes in stockholders' equity, and the flow of funds statement.

Financial ratios expand the perspective and information content of financial statements, and are an essential part of fundamental analysis. Ratio analysis involves the study of relationships among and between various financial accounts. The process is helpful in assessing the strengths, weaknesses, and developing trends of a company. Depending upon which dimension of the balance sheet and/or income statement is being emphasized, financial ratios can be divided into five groups: liquidity, activity, leverage, profitability, and common stock ratios.

KEY TERMS

accounts receivable turnover
activity ratio
balance sheet
book value per share
business cycle
common stock (or market) ratio
current ratio
debt-equity ratio
dividends per share
economic analysis
financial ratios
flow of funds statement
fiscal year
fundamental analysis
gross national product (GNP)
income statement
index of industrial production
industry analysis

intrinsic value
inventory turnover
leverage ratio
liquidity ratio
net profit margin
net working capital
operating ratio
payout ratio
price/earnings (P/E) ratio
profitability ratio
ratio analysis
return on investment (ROI)
return on total assets (ROTA)
security analysis
statement of changes in stockholders' equity
times interest earned
total asset turnover

REVIEW QUESTIONS

1. Identify the three major parts of security analysis and discuss why security analysis is so important to the stock selection process. What is intrinsic value, and how does it fit into security analysis?

2. What is a satisfactory investment vehicle? How does security analysis help in identifying such investment candidates?

3. Discuss the general concept of economic analysis. Is this type of analysis really necessary, and can it help the investor make a decision about a stock? Explain.

4. Why is the business cycle important to economic analysis? Identify each of the following and note how each would probably behave in a strong economy:

a. Fiscal policy.
b. Interest rates.
c. Industrial production.
d. Retail sales.

5. What is industry analysis and why is it important? Explain.
6. Identify and briefly discuss several aspects of an industry that are important to its behavior and operating characteristics; note especially how economic issues fit into industry analysis.
7. The Amherst Company has net profits of $10 million and 2.5 million shares of common stock outstanding; it pays $1 per share in common dividends and trades at $20 per share. Given this information, determine:

a. Amherst's earnings per share (EPS).
b. The firm's price/earnings (P/E) ratio.
c. Its dividend payout ratio.

8. Describe fundamental analysis. Does the performance of a company have any bearing on the value of its stock? Explain.
9. Why do investors bother to look at the historical performance of a company when future behavior is what really counts?
10. Identify and briefly discuss four different types of financial statements companies regularly make available to stockholders.
11. Southwest Solar Products produces $2 million in profits from $28 million in sales and has total assets of $15 million; calculate SSP's total asset turnover and compute its net profit margin; also find the company's ROTA, ROI, and book value per share, given SSP has a total net worth of $6 million and 500,000 shares of common stock outstanding.
12. What is ratio analysis? Describe the role and contribution of ratio analysis to the study of a company's financial condition and operating results.
13. Match the specific ratios from the left-hand column with the ratio categories listed in the right-hand column:

a. Inventory turnover.
b. Debt-equity ratio.
c. Current ratio.
d. Net profit margin.
e. Return on total assets.
f. Net working capital.
g. Price/earnings ratio.
h. Times interest earned.
i. Total asset turnover.
j. Payout ratio.

1. Profitability ratios.
2. Activity ratios.
3. Liquidity ratios.
4. Leverage ratios.
5. Common stock ratios.

14. The Shasta Flower Firm has total assets of $10 million, an asset turnover of 2.0 times, and a net profit margin of 15 percent; what is Shasta's return on total assets?
15. Contrast historical standards of performance with industry standards. Briefly note the role of such standards when analyzing the financial condition and operating results of a company.
16. Find the P/E ratio and dividend yield of a company that has 5 million shares of common stock outstanding (the shares trade in the market at $25), earns 10 percent after taxes on annual sales of $150 million, and has a dividend payout ratio of 35 percent.

CASE PROBLEMS

9.1 SOME FINANCIAL RATIOS ARE REAL EYE-OPENERS

Sammy Joe Hataway is a resident of Turkey, Texas, where he is a prosperous rancher and businessman; he has also built up a sizable portfolio of common stocks which, he believes, is due to the fact that he thoroughly evaluates each stock he invests in. As Sammy Joe says, "Y'all can't be too careful about these things! Anytime I'm fixing to invest in a stock, you can bet I'm gonna learn as much as I can about the company." Sammy Joe prefers to compute his own ratios even though he could easily afford to purchase professionally prepared analytical reports or obtain similar types of reports from his broker at no cost (in fact, Billy Bob Smith, his broker, has been volunteering such services for years).

Recently, Sammy Joe has been keeping an eye on a small chemical issue. This firm, South Plains Chemical Company, is big in the fertilizer business—which, not by coincidence, is something that Sammy Joe knows a lot about. Not long ago, he received a copy of the company's latest financial statements (summarized below) and decided to take a closer look at the company.

BALANCE SHEET
(DOLLARS IN THOUSANDS)

Cash	$ 1,250		
Accounts receivable	8,000	Current liabilities	$10,000
Inventory	12,000	Long-term debt	8,000
Current assets	$21,250	Stockholders' equity	12,000
Fixed and other assets	8,750		
Total	$30,000	Total	$30,000

INCOME STATEMENT
(DOLLARS IN THOUSANDS)

Sales	$50,000
Cost of goods sold	25,000
Operating expenses	15,000
Operating profit	$10,000
Interest expense	2,500
Taxes	2,500
Net profit	$ 5,000

Notes: Dividends paid (dollars in thousands)	$1,250
Number of common shares outstanding	5 million
Recent market price of the common stock	$25

Questions
1. Compute the following ratios, using the South Plains Chemical Company figures:

	Latest Industry Averages
LIQUIDITY	
a. Net working capital	N.A.
b. Current ratio	1.95

	Latest Industry Averages
ACTIVITY	
c. Receivables turnover	5.95
d. Inventory turnover	4.50
e. Total asset turnover	2.65
LEVERAGE	
f. Debt-equity ratio	0.45
g. Times interest earned	6.75
PROFITABILITY	
h. Operating ratio	85.0%
i. Net profit margin	8.5%
j. Return on total assets	22.5%
k. ROI	32.2%
COMMON STOCK RATIOS	
l. Earnings per share	$2.00
m. Price/earnings ratio	20.0
n. Dividends per share	$1.00
o. Dividend yield	2.5%
p. Payout ratio	50.0%
q. Book value per share	$6.25

2. Compare the company ratios you prepared to the industry figures. What are the company's strengths? What are its weaknesses?

3. What is your overall assessment of South Plains Chemical? Do you think Sammy Joe should continue with his evaluation of South Plains Chemical? Explain.

9.2 KATHLEEN MARIE LOOKS AT AN AUTO ISSUE

Kathleen Marie is a young career woman; she lives in Chicago, where she owns and operates a highly successful modeling agency. Kathy manages her modest but rapidly growing investment portfolio, made up primarily of high-grade common stocks. Because she's young and single, and has no pressing family requirements, Kathy has invested primarily in stocks that offer attractive capital gains potential. Kathy's broker recently recommended one of the auto issues, and sent her some literature and analytical reports to study. Among the reports was one prepared by the brokerage house she deals with; it provided an up-to-date look at the economy, an extensive study of the auto industry, and an equally extensive review of several auto companies (including the one her broker recommended). She feels very strongly about the merits of security analysis and feels it is important to spend some time studying a stock before making an investment decision.

Questions

1. Kathy Marie tries to stay abreast of the economy on a regular basis; at the present time, most economists agree that the economy, now well into the third year of a recovery, is robust, with industrial activity remaining strong. What other information about the economy do you think Kathy would find helpful in evaluating an auto stock? Prepare a list—be specific. Which three items of economic information (from your list) are especially important? Explain.

2. In relation to a study of the auto industry, briefly note the importance of each of the following:

a. Auto imports.
b. The United Auto Workers union.
c. Interest rates.
d. The price of a gallon of gas.

3. A variety of financial ratios and measures is provided about one of the auto companies and its stock; however, these are a bit incomplete, so some additional information will have to be computed. Specifically, we know that:

Net profit rate is	15%
Total assets are	$250 million
Earnings per share are	$3.00
Total asset turnover is	1.5
Net working capital is	$75 million
Payout ratio is	40%
Current liabilities are	$75 million
Price/earnings ratio is	12.5

Given this information, calculate the following:

a. Sales.
b. Net profits after taxes.
c. Current ratio.
d. Market price of the stock.
e. Dividend yield.

SELECTED READINGS

Anreder, Steven S. "Those Bottom Lines: Annual Reports Make Increasingly Valuable Reading." *Barron's,* April 10, 1978, pp. 4–5.

"Bargains in Bankrupt Firms." *Money,* October 1982, pp. 105–106.

Bernstein, Aaron. "Reading Between the Lines." *Forbes,* May 10, 1982, p. 78.

Biel, Heinz H. "Growth Versus P/E." *Forbes,* August 17, 1981, p. 126.

Bryant, William C. "Don't Overlook the Book Value." *U.S. News and World Report,* February 9, 1981, p. 79.

Curran, John J. "Making Economic Sense of Foreign Earnings." *Fortune,* November 2, 1981, pp. 157–160.

Dreman, David N. "For Widows and Orphans—Low Multiple Stocks Consistently Outperform the Rest." *Barron's,* December 3, 1979, pp. 11, 22–27.

Ehrbar, A. F. "An Unconventional View: Inflation Doesn't Matter." *Fortune,* November 17, 1980, pp. 129–132.

Eisenberg, Richard. "Who Cares About the Deficit?" *Money,* August 1982, pp. 68–70.

Gardner, Judith B. "Why Those Crystal Balls Are Often Cloudy." *U.S. News and World Report,* August 2, 1982, p. 102.

Hayes, Linda Snyder. "The Myth of the Stock Split." *Fortune,* February 26, 1979, pp. 101–102.

"How to Pick Stocks the Smart Way." *Changing Times,* March 1980, pp. 39–43.

Levenson, Mark. "The CPI: Six Decades of Controversy—With No End in Sight." *Dun's Review,* May 1980, p. 111–112.

Merjos, Anna. "Well-Timed Repurchases: For Some Companies, the Grass Is Greener in Their Own Back Yards." *Barron's,* January 8, 1979, pp. 11–14.

———. "Clear Crystal Ball? Many Stocks Show Handsome Gains in Advance of Takeovers." *Barron's,* February 2, 1981, pp. 11, 23–24.

Merrill Lynch, Pierce, Fenner & Smith, Inc. *How to Read a Financial Report,* 4th ed. New York, May 1979.

"The Profit Illusion." *Business Week,* March 19, 1979, pp. 108–112.

"Red Doesn't Mean Dead." *Forbes,* September 29, 1980, pp. 121–122.

Rolo, Charles J. "Judging What a Stock Is Worth." *Money,* May 1977, pp. 45–47.

Sivy, Michael. "A Fed Watcher's Guide." *Money,* December 1981, pp. 77–82.

"Tomorrow's Big Growth Stocks: How to Spot Them Today." *Changing Times,* June 1982, pp. 22–25.

"When a Company Is Better Dead." *Business Week,* March 26, 1979, p. 88.

10
Common Stock Valuation, Technical Analysis, and Efficient Markets

How much would you be willing to pay for a share of stock? That's a tough question and one that investors have been wrestling with for about as long as common stocks have been traded. The answer, of course, depends on the kind of return you expect to receive and the amount of risk involved in the transaction. In this chapter we will look at the question of a stock's worth in considerable detail as we continue the examination of the valuation process; in particular, we will focus on the following key areas:

1. The role a company's future prospects plays in the stock valuation process and a framework for developing such forecasts.
2. The concept of intrinsic value as a standard of performance, and its use in judging the investment suitability of a share of common stock.
3. A popular and widely used stock valuation model that takes into account both expected return and potential risk.
4. Technical analysis, its role in the security analysis and stock selection process, and the various measures of market performance that make up technical analysis.
5. The idea of random walks and efficient markets, including their implications and the serious challenges these theories hold for the whole analytical process.

In Chapter 9 we dealt with several preliminary aspects of security analysis: economic analysis, industry analysis, and the historical phase of fundamental company analysis. Now we need to develop estimates for the future prospects of the company and the expected returns from the stock. Then we can complete the valuation process and arrive at a judgment concerning whether a particular stock will make a potentially attractive investment vehicle. This chapter will also examine one of the most serious challenges traditional security analysis has ever faced: That is, as professed by the "efficient market" advocates, that security analysis and all its trappings are largely an exercise in futility.

VALUATION: OBTAINING A STANDARD OF PERFORMANCE

Obtaining a standard of performance that can be used to judge the investment merits of a share of stock is the underlying purpose of stock valuation. A stock's intrinsic value furnishes such a standard since it provides an indication of the future (return and risk) performance of a security. The question of whether, and to what extent, a stock is under- or overvalued is resolved by comparing its current market price to its intrinsic value. At any given point in time, the price of a share of common stock depends on investor expectations about the behavior of the security. If the outlook for the company and its stock is good, the price will probably be bid up; if, however, conditions deteriorate, the price of the stock can be expected to go down. Let us now look at the single most important issue in the stock valuation process: *the future.*

The Company and Its Future

Thus far, we have examined the historical performance of the company and its stock. It should be clear, however, that it's *not the past* per se that is important, *but the future.* We look at past performance to gain a better understanding of the security, and to obtain some insights about the future direction of the company and its stock. This will help us to value the stock. Because such value is a function of future returns, the investor's task is to project key financial variables into the future. Thus, our major concern at this point is to determine the future outlook for the company and the benefits that might be derived by investing in the stock. We are especially interested in dividends and price behavior. For the purposes of our discussion, we will assume that dividends and capital gains are equally important.

Forecasted sales and profits

The key to our forecast is, of course, the future behavior of the *company,* and the most important aspects to consider in this regard are the outlook for sales and the trend in the net profit margin. One way to develop a sales forecast is to assume that the company will continue to perform as it has in the past, and simply extend the historical trend. For example, if sales have been growing at a rate of 10 percent per year, then assume they will continue that rate of growth. Of course, if there is some evidence about the economy, industry, and/or company that suggests a faster (or slower) rate of growth, the forecast should be adjusted accordingly. Chances are, more often than not, this "naive" approach will be just about as effective as some other, more complex, technique.

The sales estimate is the crucial dimension of the forecast. Normally, we would expect such forecasts to cover a period of one to five years. Extending it further introduces too many uncertainties and subjects the validity of the forecasts to serious question. Once the sales forecast has been generated, we can shift our attention to the net profit margin. We want to know what kind of return on sales we can expect from the company. A naive estimate can be obtained simply by using the average profit margin that has prevailed for the last few years; again, it should be adjusted to account for any unusual industry or company developments. For the individual investor, valuable insight about future revenues and earnings can be obtained from industry and/or company reports put out by brokerage houses, advisory services (like Value Line), and the financial media (such as *Forbes*).

Given a satisfactory sales forecast and estimate of the future net profit margin, we can combine these two pieces of information to arrive at future earnings:

$$\begin{matrix} \text{future after tax} \\ \text{earnings in year } t \end{matrix} = \begin{matrix} \text{estimated sales} \\ \text{for year } t \end{matrix} \times \begin{matrix} \text{net profit margin} \\ \text{expected in year } t \end{matrix}$$

The "year t" notation simply denotes a given calendar or fiscal year in the future—it can be next year, the year after that, or any other year in which we happen to be working. Let us say that in the year just completed, a company reported sales of $100 million, and it is estimated that revenues will grow at an 8 percent annual rate, while the net profit margin should amount to about 6 percent. Thus, estimated sales next year will equal $108 million, and with a 6 percent profit margin, we should see earnings next year of:

$$\begin{matrix} \text{future after-tax} \\ \text{earnings next year} \end{matrix} = \$108 \text{ million} \times .06 = \underline{\$6.5 \text{ million}}$$

Using this same process, we would then estimate sales and earnings for all other years in our forecast period.

Forecasted dividends and prices

At this point we have an idea of the future earnings performance of the company—assuming, of course, that our expectations and assumptions hold up. We are now ready to evaluate the effects of this performance on returns to common stock investors. Given a corporate earnings forecast, we need three additional pieces of information:

1. An estimate of future payout ratios
2. The number of common shares that will be outstanding over the forecast period
3. A future price/earnings (P/E) ratio

For the first two variables, unless we have evidence to the contrary, we can simply project recent historical experience into the future and assume that these estimates will hold for the forecast period. Payout ratios are usually fairly stable, so there is little risk in using a recent average figure (or, if a company follows a fixed dividend policy, we could use the latest dividend rate in our forecast); at the same time, it is generally

While diversifying into North Sea oil exploration, new TV channels and the U.S. property market, your Board will endeavor to maintain our high reputation in canned peas.

safe to assume that the number of common shares outstanding will hold at the latest level.

The only really thorny issue is defining the future P/E ratio. This is an important figure, since it has considerable bearing on the future price of the stock. The P/E ratio is a function of several variables: (1) the growth rate in earnings, (2) the general state of market psychology, (3) the level of dividends, and (4) the amount of debt in a company's capital structure. As a rule, higher ratios can be expected with higher growth rates in earnings, an optimistic market outlook, greater dividends, and lower debt levels (because less debt means less financial risk). An estimated price/earnings ratio can be obtained by assessing the general outlook for each of these variables. For example, using the existing P/E multiple as a base, an *increase* (to a higher P/E ratio in the future) might be justified if you believe the market will become more bullish, and both dividends and the rate of growth in earnings will be up. Given an estimate for the payout ratio, the number of shares outstanding, and the price/earnings multiple, we can now forecast earnings per share:

$$\text{estimated EPS in year } t = \frac{\text{future after-tax earnings in year } t}{\text{number of shares of common stock outstanding in year } t}$$

From here, we can estimate dividends per share, as follows:

$$\frac{\text{estimated dividends}}{\text{per share in year } t} = \frac{\text{estimated EPS}}{\text{in year } t} \times \frac{\text{estimated}}{\text{payout ratio}}$$

The last item is the future price of the stock, which can be determined as:

$$\text{estimated share price at the end of year } t = \text{estimated EPS in year } t \times \text{estimated P/E ratio}$$

For example, if the company had 2 million shares outstanding, and that number was expected to hold in the future, then given the estimated earnings of $6.5 million we computed above, the firm should generate earnings per share (EPS) next year of:

$$\text{estimated EPS next year} = \frac{\$6.5 \text{ million}}{2 \text{ million}} = \underline{\underline{\$3.25}}$$

Using this EPS of $3.25, along with an estimated payout ratio of 40 percent, we see that dividends per share next year should equal:

$$\text{estimated dividends per share next year} = \$3.25 \times .40 = \underline{\underline{\$1.30}}$$

Of course, if the firm adheres to a *fixed dividend policy,* this estimate may have to be adjusted to reflect the level of dividends being paid. For example, if the company has been paying annual dividends at the rate of $1.25 per share, *and is expected to continue doing so for the near future,* then estimated dividends should be adjusted accordingly—i.e., use $1.25/share. Finally, if it has been estimated that the stock should sell at 17.5 times earnings, then a share of stock in this company should be trading at a price of about 56⅞ by the *end* of next year:

$$\text{estimated share price at the end of next year} = \$3.25 \times 17.5 = \underline{\underline{\$56.88}}$$

Actually, we are interested in the price of the stock at the end of our anticipated *investment horizon*—the period of time over which we expect to hold the stock. Thus, if we had a one-year horizon, the 56⅞ figure would be appropriate. However, if we had a three-year holding period, we would have to extend the EPS figure for two more years and repeat our calculations with the new data. As we will see, estimated share price is important because it has imbedded in it the capital gains portion of the stock's total return.

Developing an Estimate of Future Behavior

Before illustrating the forecast procedure with a concrete example, let us look again at the steps in summary form.

1. Estimate future sales.
2. Estimate a future net profit margin.

BOX 10.1 DON'T OVERLOOK LOCAL FIRMS

Investors seeking stocks for the long pull should not overlook relatively small but capable companies in their own back yards. Most big corporations had such beginnings.

Marriott Corporation, one of the largest hotel and restaurant chains, began as a root-beer stand in Washington, D.C., and now has revenues nearing 2 billion dollars a year.

Spotting good companies early is a major route to investment success. William B. Astrop, chairman of Atlanta Capital Management Company, a counseling firm, explains that successful enterprises normally go through four phases. In their early years, earnings rise at an accelerating rate, often 20 to 30 percent a year, with occasional setbacks. In the second phase, management consolidates gains and maintains consistent growth, still fast. Then comes maturing with declining growth rates and finally sedate old age.

The initial period can produce a sharp increase in market price for a stock. Astrop notes that, if investors value two firms earning $1 per share at 10 times earnings and one reports a rise in profits from $1 to $1.61 in five years—a 10 percent annual growth rate—while the other grows from $1 to $3.71—a 30 percent rate—the market at the period's end will be $16.10 for the slower firm and $37.10 for the faster, assuming no change in price-earnings ratios. Actually, the market will tend to accord a higher PE ratio to the second stock, boosting it even more.

The investor takes a risk that setbacks in the early stages may cause a stock to fall dramatically. But the rewards for patience can be substantial. Astrop points to Scientific-Atlanta, an electronics firm that first sold stock to the public in 1967, was listed on the American Stock Exchange in 1968 and moved to the New York Stock Exchange in 1979. Its shares recently sold for about $29 each, were higher than $34 earlier this year [1981] and could have been bought as recently as 1979 for the equivalent of $5.38, taking account of stock splits.

William G. Staton, senior vice president and research director at Interstate Securities, a regional broker headquartered in Charlotte, N.C., suggests that a person who invests in a local firm may know someone who works there and gets a feel for the business beyond what appears in official reports. If it's a retail company, the investor can visit its shops to see how well they are run and how well they are patronized.

Another reason for not ignoring local companies is suggested by Richard McFarland, president of Dain Bosworth, a broker with offices from Milwaukee to Boise. Brokers, McFarland says, may give better advice on nearby firms because they can visit with management more often. He says that from his office in Minneapolis he can drive within 30 minutes to the headquarters of 50 companies that Dain Bosworth watches.

Just about every regional broker points to local companies that have blossomed. Staton cites Nucor Corporation, now on the Big Board, which developed a network of small steel mills from Darlington, S.C., to Plymouth, Utah. Its stock sold for the equivalent of $3.35 to $5.75 in 1971, taking account of stock splits. It traded recently at $57 after a peak of $82.25 earlier this year.

Those who do invest in local firms should not allow hometown loyalties to outweigh cold facts. Knowing a company's president or liking the food in its restaurants is no substitute for careful study of financial statements. Keep in mind that an emerging local firm may not have as ready recourse to credit as a big national concern—a good reason to insist on strong balance sheets. Many smaller companies have them.

Source: William C. Bryant, "Don't Overlook Local Firms." *U.S. News & World Report,* November 2, 1981, p. 93.

3. Derive future after-tax earnings (per first equation).
4. Estimate a future payout ratio (for fixed dividend rate).
5. Estimate the number of common shares outstanding in the future.
6. Estimate a future price/earnings (P/E) ratio.
7. Derive a future EPS figure (per second equation).
8. Derive future dividends per share (per third equation).
9. Derive a future share price (per fourth equation).
10. Repeat the process for each year in the forecast period.

Much of the required forecast data can be obtained from published sources or the analytical reports prepared by major brokerage firms. But investors still have to interject their own judgments and opinions about the future course of a company and its stock, and as a result *cannot* rely solely on published reports. We either agree or disagree with the published reports. If we agree, then we are inferring that our expectations are in conformity with those imbedded in the published reports; if we disagree, then we must adjust the forecasts to come up with our own figures.

Now, using the hypothetical firm of Palm Springs Industries, we can illustrate this forecasting process. Recall from Chapter 9 that an assessment of the economy and the apparel industry was positive, and that the company's operating results and financial condition looked strong, both historically and relative to industry standards. Because everything looks favorable for PSI, we decide to take a look at the future of the company and its stock. Assume we have chosen a three-year investment horizon as a result of our belief (formulated from earlier studies of economic and industry factors) that the economy and the market for apparel stocks should start running out of steam sometime near the end of 1986 or early 1987.

Selected historical financial data are provided in Table 10.1; they cover an eight-year period (ending with the latest 1983 fiscal year) and will provide the basis for much of our forecast. An assessment of Table 10.1 reveals that except for 1977 and 1978 (which were off years for PSI), the company has performed at a fairly stable pace and been able to maintain a respectable rate of growth. Our economic analysis suggests that things are beginning to pick up. And based on earlier studies, we feel the industry and company are well situated to take advantage of the upswing. Therefore, we conclude that the rate of growth in sales should pick up in 1984 to about 9.5 percent; then, once a modest amount of pent-up demand is worked off, the rate of growth in sales should drop to about 9 percent in 1985 and stay there through 1986.

Since various published industry and company reports suggest a comfortable improvement in earnings, we decide to use a profit margin of 3.0 percent in 1984, followed by an even better 3.2 percent in 1985; finally, because of some capacity problems prominently mentioned in one of the reports, we show a drop in the margin in 1986 back to 3.0 percent. Assume also that our assessment indicates the company will be able to handle the growth in assets and meet financing needs without issuing any additional equity (new common stock). What is more, assume the dividend payout ratio will hold at about 40 percent of earnings, as it has for most of the recent

TABLE 10.1 SELECTED HISTORICAL FINANCIAL DATA, PALM SPRINGS INDUSTRIES (FOR FISCAL YEARS ENDING NOVEMBER 30)

	1976	1977	1978	1979	1980	1981	1982	1983
Total assets (millions)	$262.8	$254.2	$220.9	$240.7	$274.3	$318.2	$340.5	$338.6
Debt-equity ratio	31%	37%	31%	29%	30%	33%	33%	27%
Total asset turnover (times)	1.73×	1.66×	1.72×	1.81×	1.75×	1.65×	1.67×	1.79×
Net sales (millions)	$454.7	$422.0	$397.9	$435.6	$480.0	$525.0	$568.0	$606.6
Annual rate of growth in sales*	—	−7.2%	−5.7%	9.5%	10.2%	9.4%	8.2%	6.8%
Interest and other income (millions)	$ 6.8	$ 6.5	$ 6.3	$ 6.0	$ 6.8	$ 7.7	$ 7.1	$ 8.3
Net profit margin	2.6%	0.6%	1.1%	2.0%	3.6%	3.0%	2.7%	2.9%
Payout ratio	36.0%	83.0%	97.0%	38.0%	40.0%	40.0%	39.0%	38.0%
Price earnings ratio (times)	14.5×	6.2×	8.3×	12.8×	9.5×	13.6×	16.2×	15.1×
Number of common shares outstanding (millions)	7.0	7.0	7.1	7.1	8.5	8.6	8.6	8.6

*Annual rate of growth in sales = change in sales from one year to the next divided by the level of sales in the base (or earliest) year; for 1979, the annual rate of growth in sales equaled 9.5% = (1979 sales − 1978 sales)/1978 sales = ($435.6 − $397.9)/$397.9 = .095.

past, with the notable exceptions of 1974 and 1975. The last element is the forecasted P/E ratio. Based primarily on an outlook for a strong market, coupled with the expectations of improved growth in revenues and earnings, we are projecting a multiple that will rise (from its present 15.1) to 17 times earnings by 1986.

The essential elements of the financial forecast for 1984, 1985, and 1986 are provided in Table 10.2. Also included is the sequence involved in arriving at forecasted dividends and price behavior. Note that the company dimensions of the forecast are handled first and that after-tax earnings are derived according to the first equation given earlier; then per share data are estimated following the procedures established in the second, third, and fourth equations. The bottom line of these forecasts is, of course, the dividend and capital gains returns the investor can expect from a share of Palm Springs stock, given that assumptions about net sales, profit margins, earnings per share, and so forth, hold up. We see in Table 10.2 that dividends should go up by about 30 cents per share over the next three years and that the price of a share of stock should undergo a better than 50 percent appreciation in value, rising from its latest price of $31.50 to $47.60 per share. We now have the needed figures on expected shareholder return and are in a position to establish an intrinsic value for Palm Springs Industries stock.

A STOCK VALUATION FRAMEWORK

At any point in time, a stock is worth just what investors are willing to pay for it: To some, the prevailing market price may seem too high; to others, it may appear to be a bargain. Here we will look at a popular stock valuation model and examine the mechanics of the valuation process more closely, using Palm Springs Industries (and the forecast data in Table 10.2) as a basis of illustration.

TABLE 10.2 SUMMARY FORECAST STATISTICS, PALM SPRINGS INDUSTRIES

	Latest Actual Figures (fiscal 1983)	Average for the Last 5 Years (1979–1983)	FORECASTED FIGURES		
			1984	1985	1986
Annual rate of growth in sales	6.8%	8.8%	9.5%	9.0%	9.0%
Net sales (millions)	$606.6	N.A.*	$664.2**	$724.0**	$789.2**
+ Interest and other income (millions)	$ 8.3	$ 7.2	$ 7.2	$ 7.2	$ 7.2
= Total revenue (millions)	$614.9	N.A.	$671.4	$731.2	$796.4
× Net profit margin	2.9%	2.8%	3.0%	3.2%	3.0%
= Net after-tax earnings (millions)	$ 18.0	N.A.	$ 20.1	$ 23.4	$ 24.0
÷ Common shares outstanding (millions)	8.6	8.3	8.6	8.6	8.6
= Earnings per share	$ 2.09	N.A.	$ 2.34	$ 2.72	$ 2.80
× Payout ratio	38.0%	39.0%	40.0%	40.0%	40.0%
= Dividends per share	$ 0.80	$ 0.71	$ 0.95	$ 1.10	$ 1.12
Earnings per share	$ 2.09	N.A.	$ 2.34	$ 2.72	$ 2.80
× P/E ratio	15.10	13.45	15.50	16.00	17.00
= Share price at year end	$ 31.50	N.A.	$ 36.25	$ 43.50	$ 47.60

*N.A. = Not applicable.
**Forecasted sales figures = Sales from *preceding* year × growth rate in sales = growth in sales. Growth in sales + sales from *preceding* year = forecast sales in following year. For example, for 1985: $664.2 × .09 = $59.8 + $664.2 = $724.0 million.

The essence of stock valuation is to determine what the stock *ought to be worth* given estimated returns to stockholders (future dividends and price behavior) and the amount of potential risk exposure. Stock valuation models determine either an expected rate of return or the intrinsic worth of a share of stock, which in effect represents the stock's "justified price." In this way, we can obtain a standard of performance based on *future* stock behavior that can be used to judge the investment merits of a particular stock. Clearly, if the computed rate of return exceeds the yield the investor feels is warranted, or if the justified price (intrinsic worth) is in excess of the current market price, the stock under consideration should be considered a worthwhile investment candidate.

The Valuation Model

Some valuation models, such as the so-called Graham and Dodd model, emphasize appropriate price/earnings multiples as the key element; others are based on culling out the bad investments from the good and then using the principles of portfolio diversification (which we will examine in more detail in Chapters 19 and 20) as a basis for selecting stock; still others use such variables as dividend yield, book value per share, abnormally low P/E ratios, and so on, as key elements in the decision-making process. Our discussion will center on a model that is not only popular with a large segment of the investing public, but is also a theoretically sound procedure. It is derived from a valuation procedure known as *the dividend model*.

Basically, the dividend model assumes that the value of a share of stock is equal to the present value of all its future dividends. In its purest form, the dividend model uses an infinite holding period and assumes that dividends grow at a constant (fixed) rate forever. Although the essential features of the model have considerable theoretical merit, there are some obvious problems in applying it in practice—notably, the heroic task of forecasting dividends to perpetuity. The valuation model we employ is not only based on the present value of future dividends and other cash flows, but is relatively easy to use, primarily because it has a *finite* holding period that seldom exceeds three to five years. There are four main elements to this model: the stock's present market price, its future price, the level of future dividends, and the required yield on the investment. As we will see, the model gains much of its strength from the fact that it considers both risk and return in a convenient format, and recognizes the time value of money.

Holding period return

Holding period return (HPR) was first introduced in Chapter 4 and shown to be useful whenever the holding period is one year or less. It is computed as follows:

$$HPR = \frac{\substack{\text{future dividend} \\ \text{receipts}} + \substack{\text{future sale} \\ \text{price of the stock}} - \substack{\text{current purchase} \\ \text{price of the stock}}}{\text{current purchase price of the stock}}$$

Holding period return provides a measure of the yield that will be realized *if* the actual performance of the stock lives up to its expectations. The holding period return for Palm Springs Industries, assuming that the stock can be purchased at its current market price of $31.50 and sold one year later at a price of $36.25, would be as follows:

$$HPR = \frac{\$.95 + \$36.25 - \$31.50}{\$31.50} = \frac{\$.95 + \$4.75}{\$31.50} = \underline{18.1\%}$$

Note that although we do not use capital gains specifically in the valuation model, it is imbedded in the formula and appears as the difference between the future selling price of the stock and its current purchase price; as it turns out, PSI should provide a capital gain of around $4.75 a share in the first year.

Desired rate of return

In the preceding example, we saw that if an investor had a one-year investment horizon, the holding period return on Palm Springs Industries would be 18.1 percent. That expected yield is, in effect, our standard of performance. To decide whether that is acceptable or not, it is necessary to formulate a *desired rate of return*. Generally speaking, the amount of return that should be earned by an investor is related to the level of risk exposure that must be assumed in order to generate that return. The higher the amount of perceived risk, the greater the return potential that should be offered by the investment.

If our assessment of the historical performance of the company had uncovered wide swings in sales and earnings, we could conclude that the stock is probably subject to a high degree of intrinsic risk. Assessments of the economy, industry, and/or company tell a lot about the risk exposure of a stock, and as a rule, the higher the intrinsic risk, the greater the return the stock should offer. Another important source of risk is market risk. Generally speaking, high betas (for example, a beta of 1.5; see Chapter 4) suggest the stock has high market risk. Although beta is difficult to compute, it is widely available from brokerage houses and a variety of investor subscription services.

A valuable reference point in arriving at a measure of risk is the rate of return available on less risky but competitive investment vehicles. For example, if the rate of return on Treasury bonds or high-grade corporate issues is at a certain level, we can use that benchmark as a starting point in defining our desired rate of return. That is, starting with yields on long-term, low-risk bonds, we can adjust such figures accordingly for the level of intrinsic and market risks to which we believe the common stock is exposed.

To see how these elements make up the desired rate of return, consider the case of Palm Springs Industries; assume it is now early 1984, and rates on high-grade corporate bonds are hovering around the 12 to 13 percent mark. Given that our analysis thus far has indicated that the apparel industry and Palm Springs Industries in particular are subject to a fair amount of intrinsic risk, we would want to adjust that figure upward. In addition, given its beta of 1.55, we can conclude that the stock carries a good deal of market risk that should also result in increasing our base rate of return. Given our base (high-grade corporate bond) rate, along with our assessment of the stock's intrinsic and market risks, we conclude that an appropriate (desired) rate of return should be around 20 percent for an investment in Palm Springs Industries common stock. Using this desired rate of return, it is clear that a holding period return of 18.1 percent (as computed in the preceding section) is an *insufficient* yield. Although something close to 18 percent may not seem like a bad return, and indeed for many securities it may be more than sufficient, because of the perceived risk exposure, such a level of return is simply an inadequate reward in this case.

Deriving the justified price

Although holding period return is effective for assessing the investment merits of securities held for a period of one year or less, HPR should not be used with investment horizons that extend for longer periods. Lengthy holding periods mean that we have to introduce the time value of money and deal in terms of present value (see Chapter 4). A stock valuation model has been developed that conveniently captures the essential elements of expected risk and return, and does so in a present value context. The model is as follows:

$$\frac{\text{present value of}}{\text{a share of stock}} = \frac{\text{present value of}}{\text{future dividends}} + \frac{\text{present value of the price of the}}{\text{stock at date of sale}}$$

$$= (D_1 \times IF_1) + (D_2 \times IF_2) + \cdots + (D_N \times IF_N) + (SP_N \times IF_N)$$

where:

D_i = future annual dividend in year i
IF_i = present-value interest factor, specified as the desired rate of return for the given year i (use the appropriate interest factor from the "single cash flow" table, Appendix B, Table B.3)
SP_N = estimated share price of the stock at date of sale, year N
N = number of years in the investment horizon

When used in this form, the present-value-based stock valuation model generates a *justified price* based on estimated returns to stockholders (future dividends and share price behavior). What is more, in this version of the model, the desired rate of return (and therefore the aspect of risk) is built right into the valuation process because it is included in the present value interest factor. The equation above produces the present value of the stock, which represents the elusive intrinsic value we have been seeking. This intrinsic value represents the price we should be willing to pay for the stock given its expected dividend and price behavior, and assuming we want to realize a return that is equal to or greater than our desired rate of return.

To see how this procedure works, consider once again the case of Palm Springs Industries. Let us return to our original three-year investment horizon. Given the forecasted annual dividends and share price from Table 10.2, along with a 20 percent desired rate of return, we can see from the computations below that the present worth of PSI is:

$$\frac{\text{present value of a}}{\text{share of PSI stock}} = \frac{(\$0.95 \times .833) + (\$1.10 \times .694) + (\$1.12 \times .579)}{+ (\$47.60 \times .579)}$$

$$= \$0.79 + \$0.76 + \$0.65 + \$27.56$$

$$= \underline{\$29.76}$$

In this case, a present value of $29.76 means that, with the projected dividend and share price behavior, we would realize our desired rate of return *only* if we were able to buy the stock at around $29.75. Because PSI is currently trading at $31.50, we would have to conclude that Palm Springs Industries is *not* (at the present time at least) an attractive investment vehicle. For if we pay $31.50 for the stock—and our dividend and price expectations hold up—we would fail to generate our desired rate of return. Palm Springs Industries might look relatively appealing, but it simply does not provide sufficient returns to enable us to realize a yield commensurate with our perceived risk exposure.

Determining approximate yield

Sometimes investors find it more convenient to deal in terms of expected yield rather than present worth or justified price. Fortunately this is no problem, nor is it necessary to sacrifice the present value dimension of the stock valuation model to achieve such an end. For the approximate yield measure enables investors to find a present-value-based rate of return from long-term transactions. This version of the stock valuation model uses forecasted dividend and price behavior, along with the *current market price* of the stock, to arrive at an approximate yield. This measure of return, first introduced in Chapter 4, is determined as follows:

$$\frac{\text{approximate}}{\text{yield}} = \frac{\text{average} \atop \text{annual dividend} + \dfrac{\genfrac{}{}{0pt}{}{\text{future sale}}{\text{price of the stock}} - \genfrac{}{}{0pt}{}{\text{current purchase}}{\text{price of the stock}}}{\text{number of years in investment horizon}}}{\dfrac{\text{sales price of the stock} + \text{purchase price of the stock}}{2}}$$

The approximate yield formula is an indication of the fully compounded rate of return available from a long-term investment. To see how it works, look at the case of Palm Springs Industries:

$$\text{approximate yield} = \frac{\$1.06 + \dfrac{\$47.60 - \$31.50}{3}}{\dfrac{\$47.60 + \$31.50}{2}}$$

$$= \frac{\$1.06 + \$5.37}{\$39.55} = \underline{\underline{16.3\%}}$$

We see that PSI will yield a return of around 16.3 percent, assuming that the stock can be bought at $31.50, held for three years (during which time annual dividends will average out at about $1.06 per share), and then sold for $47.60 per share. Note that in this version of the stock valuation model it is the average annual dividend that is used, rather than the specific dividend. For PSI, dividends will average $1.06 per share over each of the next three years: ($0.95 + $1.10 + $1.12)/3 = $1.06. When compared to the 20 percent desired rate of return, the 16.3 percent yield this investment offers is clearly inadequate!

Using Stock Valuation Measures in the Investment Decision

The security analysis process begins with economic and industry analysis and culminates in the determination of a stock's value according to one of the valuation models reviewed above. We can deal in expected yield, as in the case of holding period return and approximate yield measures, or in justified price, as in the case of

BOX 10.2 AN INVESTMENT STRATEGY BASED ON INSIDER TRADING FIGURES

Over the past dozen years, a stock portfolio recommended by Perry Wysong has out-performed the Dow Jones industrial average by about 4½ to one. So when out-of-town corporate executives run into Mr. Wysong at analysts' meetings here, they often ask for his secret.

His reply: "It's easy—we watch to see whether *you* buy or sell."

Mr. Wysong, a 62-year-old former statistician works on the premise that whatever is done by corporate insiders—officers, directors and persons holding 10% or more of a company's stock—ought to be imitated by outsiders. He doesn't try to guess why insiders act, he simply believes they know better than anyone else how a company is likely to do in the next six to twelve months.

"It's as if we're walking in people's footprints in the snow," says Larry Unterbrink, 46, a former builder of bowling alleys, who is Mr. Wysong's business partner and friend. "We don't know where they're going or why, but we stay right behind them."

Each week, aided by two elderly sisters who work at card tables in their home, the team sifts through insiders' reports to the Securities and Exchange Commission of their stock purchases, sales, and exercises of options to buy shares from their company.

Trying to imitate insiders isn't new, of course, but what distinguishes Mr. Wysong's approach is his insistence that only the number of insiders who trade in a stock is important, rather than who they are, or the amounts of shares they trade. "We count noses, not names," he says. "If Henry Ford had liquidated 200,000 Ford Motor Co. shares while he was chairman, and 20 other officers had each bought 500, we would have said, 'buy.' Regardless of how much clout they have, every one has equal feelings of greed."

Insider buys of a company's stock are a better guide to its future than sales, Mr. Unterbrink says, because people sometimes sell stock for a reason irrelevant to a company's prospects, such as a child about to enter college. "There's only one reason to buy," he says—"to make money."

Source: Susan Harrigan, "Insider Trading Figures Provide Basis for a Florida Analyst's Market Advice." *The Wall Street Journal,* October 10, 1980, p. 6.

the present worth of the stock. In any case, the standard of performance obtained can be used in the decision-making process to determine the merits of a particular stock.

If yield is used as the standard, it is compared to a desired rate of return to determine investment suitability; so long as the approximate yield (or HPR) is *equal to or greater than* the desired rate of return, the stock should be considered worthwhile. This is so because the particular security promises to meet or exceed the minimum rate that has been stipulated, and in so doing will provide adequate compensation for the risk exposure imbedded in the investment. Note especially that a security is considered acceptable even if its yield simply *equals* the desired rate of return; this is rational to the extent that the security has met the minimum standards established.

If we determine the present worth of a stock, we will compare the computed justified price with its actual market price. So long as the actual market price of the issue is *equal to or less than* the justified price, it would be considered a worthwhile investment. Again, this is so because only under these conditions would we be able to realize the desired rate of return we have stipulated for this particular security. But remember that although valuation models play an important part in the investment process, there is *absolutely no assurance* that the actual outcome will be remotely similar to the forecasted behavior. The stock is still subject to economic, industry, company, and market risks that could well negate all assumptions about the future. Security analysis and stock valuation models are used not to guarantee success, but to help investors better understand the return and risk dimensions of transactions.

TECHNICAL ANALYSIS

How many times have you turned on the TV and in the course of the day's news heard a reporter say: "The market was up 7½ points today"; or "The market remained sluggish in a fairly light day of trading." Such comments reflect the importance of the stock market itself. And rightly so; for as we will see, the market is indeed important because of the role it plays in determining the price behavior of common stocks. In fact, some experts believe the market is so important that studying it should be the major, if not the only, ingredient in the stock selection process. These experts argue that much of what is done in security analysis is largely useless because it is the market that matters, and not individual companies. Others would argue that studying the stock market is only one element in the security analysis process and is useful in helping the investor time decisions. Analyzing the stock market is known as *technical analysis,* and it involves a study of the various forces at work in the marketplace. Here we will examine the principles of market analysis and the various elements of technical analysis, as well as some of the techniques used to assess market behavior.

Principles of Market Analysis

Analyzing market behavior dates back to the 1800s, when there was no such thing as industry or company analysis. Detailed financial information simply was not made available to stockholders, let alone the general public. There were no industry figures, balance sheets, or income statements to study, no sales forecasts to make, and no earnings per share data or price/earnings multiples. About the only thing investors could study was the market itself. Some analysts used detailed charts in an attempt to monitor what large market operators were doing. These charts were intended to show when major buyers were moving into or out of particular stocks and to provide information that could be used to make profitable buy and sell decisions. The charts centered on stock price movements, because it was believed that these movements produced certain "formations" that indicated when the time was right to buy or sell a particular stock. The same principle is still applied today: Technical analysts argue that internal market factors, such as trading volume and price movements, often reveal the market's future direction before the cause is evident in financial statistics.

If the behavior of stock prices was completely independent of movements in the market, market studies and technical analysis would be useless. But we have ample evidence that this is simply not the case; in fact, stock prices do tend to move with the market. Studies of stock betas have shown that, as a rule, anywhere from 20 to 50 percent of the price behavior of a stock can be traced to market forces. When the market is bullish, stock prices, in general, can be expected to behave accordingly; in contrast, when market participants turn bearish, most issues will feel the brunt to one extent or another. Stock prices, in essence, react to various supply and demand forces that are at work in the market: after all, it's the *demand* for securities and the *supply* of funds in the market that determines a bull or a bear market. So long as a given supply and demand relationship holds, the market will remain strong (or weak); when the balance begins to shift, however, future prices can be expected to change as the market itself changes. More than anything, technical analysis is intended to monitor the pulse of the supply and demand forces in the market, and to detect any shifts in this important relationship.

Measuring the Market

If assessing the market is a worthwhile endeavor, it follows that some sort of tool or measure is needed to do it. Charts are popular with some investors because they provide a convenient visual summary of the behavior of the market and the price movements of individual stocks. An alternative approach involves the use of various types of market statistics. We will now examine some of the tools of technical analysis; we will first consider some basic approaches to technical analysis, including technical indicators and the use of technical analysis, and then address the concept of charting.

Approaches to technical analysis

Technical analysis addresses those factors in the marketplace that operate in such a way as to have an effect on the price movements of stocks in general. Investment services, major brokerage houses, and popular financial media (like *Barron's*) provide technical information at little or no cost. Of the many approaches to technical analysis, several are particularly noteworthy: (1) the Dow theory, (2) trading action, (3) bellwether stocks, and (4) the technical condition of the market. Let us look at each in turn.

The Dow theory.   This approach is based on the idea that it is the price trend in the overall market as a whole that is important. Named after Charles H. Dow, one of the founders of Dow Jones, the Dow theory is supposed to signal the end of both bull and bear markets. Note that the theory does not indicate when a reversal will occur; rather, it is strictly an after-the-fact verification of what has already happened. It concentrates on the long-term trend in market behavior (known as the primary trend) and largely ignores day-to-day fluctuations or secondary movements. The Dow Jones industrial and transportation averages are used to assess the position of the market. Once a primary trend in the Dow Jones industrial average has been established, the market tends to move in that direction until the trend is canceled out by both the industrial and transportation averages. Known as *confirmation,* this crucial part of the Dow theory occurs when the secondary movements in the industrial average are confirmed by the secondary movements in the transportation average. When confirmation occurs, the market has changed from bull to bear, or vice versa.

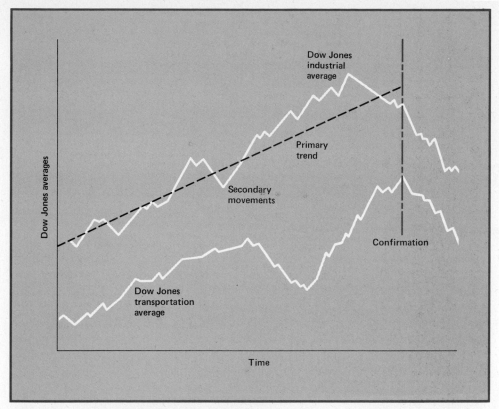

Figure 10.1   The Dow Theory in Operation.
Secondary movements are largely unimportant with the Dow theory; however, the primary trend in the DJIA, which is seen to remain on the upswing until a reversal is confirmed by the transportation average, is of key importance.

and a new primary trend is established. The key elements of the Dow theory are captured in Figure 10.1. Observe that in this case, the bull market comes to an end at the point of confirmation. The biggest drawbacks of the Dow theory are that it is an after-the-fact measure with *no* predictive power, and that the investor really does not know at any given point whether an existing primary trend has a long way to go or is just about to end.

   Trading action.   This approach to technical analysis concentrates on minor trading characteristics in the market. Daily trading activity over long periods of time (sometimes extending back a quarter century or more) is examined in detail to determine whether or not certain characteristics occur with a high degree of frequency. The results of this statistical analysis are a series of trading rules, some of which are a bit bizarre. For example, did you know that Monday is the worst day to buy stocks, and Friday is the best? Other trading rules suggest that if the year starts out strong (that is, if January is a good month for the market), the chances are that it is going to be a good year as well; that if the party in power wins the presidential election, it is also going to be a good year for the market; and that it is best to buy air conditioning stocks in October and sell the following March (this buy-and-sell strategy was found to be significantly more profitable over the long haul than buy-and-hold). Clearly, the trading action approach is based on the simple assumption that the market moves in cycles that have a tendency to repeat themselves. As a result, the contention is that what has happened in the past (on Mondays or Fridays or in January) will probably happen again and again in the future.

Bellwether stocks.   There is a saying that holds, "as GM goes, so goes the nation." Whether or not this is true today remains debatable, but to advocates of bellwether stocks, it's a fact of life. This is so because the stock of General Motors is considered a key bellwether stock, as are IBM, DuPont, AT&T, Exxon, and Merrill Lynch. The idea behind the bellwether approach is that a few major stocks in the market are consistently highly accurate in reflecting the current state of the market. Although the prices of bellwether stocks tend to move in close unison with the Dow Jones industrial average, the bellwether procedure itself is much more than a simple reflection of the current state of affairs in the market. For it is believed that it can also be used to determine shifts in market behavior. In particular, bellwether advocates hold that in a bull market, when a bellwether stock fails to hit a new yearly high for three or four months in a row, a market top is at hand; in a bear market, when the selected stock fails to hit a new low for three or four months, a market bottom is coming. Although there are many skeptics on Wall Street, the bellwether approach does seem to have some merit with respect to appraising the current state of the market.

Technical condition of the market.   This approach is based on assessing several key elements of market behavior. For example, market prices are affected by such things as the volume of trading, the amount of short selling, the buying and selling patterns of small investors (known as odd-lot transactions), and similar market forces. Normally, several of these indicators would be used together to assess the technical condition of the market. This is one of the more popular approaches to technical analysis and is often used with some other approach like trading action and/or bellwether stocks. We will examine several of the more popular technical indicators below.

Technical indicators

Technical indicators are used to assess the current state of the market, as well as the possibility of changes in direction. The idea is to stay abreast of those aspects that reflect supply and demand conditions, underlying price pressures, and the general state of the market. In essence, the premise is that the forces of supply and demand will be reflected in various price and volume patterns. Although there are many technical indicators, we will look only at several of the more popular and closely followed measures: (1) market volume, (2) breadth of the market, (3) short interest, (4) odd-lot trading, and (5) the confidence index.

Market volume. Market volume is an obvious indicator of the amount of investor interest. Volume is a function of the supply of and demand for stocks, and is indicative of underlying market strengths and weaknesses. The market is considered to be strong when volume goes up in a rising market or drops during market declines; in contrast, it is considered weak when volume rises during a decline or drops off during rallies. For instance, it would be considered strong if the Dow Jones industrial average went up by, say, 8 points while market volume was very heavy. Investor eagerness to buy or sell is felt to be captured by market volume figures. The financial press regularly publishes volume data, so investors can conveniently stay abreast of this important technical indicator; an example of this and other vital market information is given in Figure 10.2.

Breadth of the market. Each trading day, some stocks go up in price and others go down; in market terminology, some stocks *advance* and others *decline.* The breadth of the market indicator deals with these advances and declines. The idea behind it is actually quite simple: so long as the number of stocks that advance in price on the day exceeds the number that decline, the market is considered strong. Of course, the extent of that strength depends on the spread between the number of advances and declines—for example, if the spread narrows (such that the number of declines starts to approach the number of advances)—market strength is said to be deteriorating. In a similar fashion, the market is considered weak when the number of declines exceeds the number of advances. The principle behind this indicator is that the number of advances and declines reflects the underlying sentiment of investors—when the mood is optimistic, for example, look for advances to outnumber declines. Again, information on advances and declines is published daily in the financial press.

Short interest. Investors will sometimes sell a stock short—that is, they will sell borrowed stock in anticipation of a market decline. The number of stocks sold short in the market at any given point in time is known as the *short interest*; the more stocks that are sold short, the higher the short interest. Since all short sales must eventually be "covered" (the borrowed shares must be returned), a short sale, in effect, assures future demand for the stock. Thus, when the level of short interest reaches relatively high levels by historical standards, the situation is viewed optimistically. The logic is that as shares are bought back to cover outstanding short sales, the additional demand will push prices up. The amount of short interest on the NYSE and AMEX is published twice a month in *Barron's*. Keeping track of the level of short interest can indicate future market demand, but it can also reveal *present* market optimism or pessimism. Short selling is usually done by knowledgeable investors, and it is felt that a significant buildup or decline in the level of short interest may reveal the sentiment of supposedly sophisticated investors about the current state of the market. For example, a significant shift upward in short interest has pessimistic overtones concerning the current state of the market, even though it may be an optimistic signal with regard to future levels of demand.

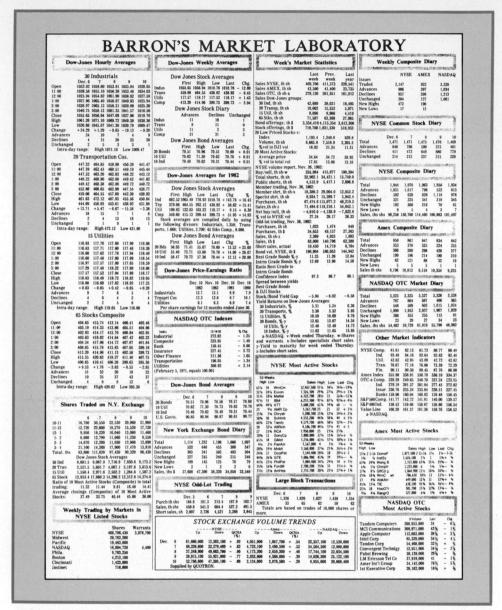

Figure 10.2 Some Market Statistics.
A variety of information is available about market volume, odd-lot trading, price/earning ratios, the confidence index, and market averages. (*Source: Barron's*, December 13, 1982, p. 116.)

Odd-lot trading. There is a rather cynical saying on Wall Street that suggests that the best thing to do is just the opposite of what the small investor is doing. The reasoning behind this is that the small investor is notoriously wrong and does a horrible job of timing investment decisions: The investing public usually does not come into the market in force until after a bull market has pretty much run its course, and does not get out until late in a bear market. Whether or not this view is valid is debatable, but it is the premise behind a widely followed technical indicator and is the basis for the *theory of contrary opinion.* This theory uses the amount and type of odd-lot trading as an indicator of the current state of the market and pending changes. Because many individual investors deal in small transactions of less than 100 shares, the combined sentiments of this type of investor are supposedly captured in the odd-lot figures. The idea is to see what odd-lot investors are doing "on balance." So long as there is little or no difference in the spread between the volume of odd-lot purchases and sales, we can conclude that the market will probably continue pretty much along its current line (either up or down). But when the balance of odd-lot purchases and sales begins to change dramatically, it may be a signal that a bull or bear market is about to end. For example, if the amount of odd-lot purchases starts to exceed odd-lot sales by an ever-widening margin, it may suggest that speculation on the part of small investors is beginning to get out of control— an ominous signal that the final stages of a bull market may be at hand.

Confidence index. Another measure that attempts to capture the sentiment of market participants is the *confidence index,* which, unlike other technical measures of the stock market, deals with *bond* returns. Computed and published weekly in *Barron's,* the confidence index is a ratio of the average yield on high-grade corporate bonds to the average yield on low-grade corporate bonds. The theory is that the trend of "smart money" is usually revealed in the bond market before it shows up in the stock market. Although low-rated bonds provide higher yields than high-grade issues, the logic is that the spread in yields between these two types of obligations will change over time as the amount of optimism or pessimism in the market outlook changes. Thus, a sustained rise in the confidence index suggests an increase in investor confidence and a stronger stock market; a drop in the index portends a softer market.

Using technical analysis

Individual investors have a wide range of choices with respect to technical analysis. They can use the charts and complex ratios of the technical analysts or follow a more informal approach and use technical analysis just to get a general sense of the market. Presumably, in the latter case, it's not market behavior per se that is important as much as the implications such market behavior can have on the price performance of a particular common stock. It would be used in conjunction with fundamental analysis to determine whether or not it is the proper time to add a particular investment candidate to one's portfolio. Most individual investors will rely on published sources, such as that depicted in Figure 10.3, to obtain necessary technical insights. Many find it helpful to use several different approaches. For example, an investor might follow a favorite stock, such as IBM or GM, and at the same time keep track of information on market volume and breadth of the market. This is information that is readily available to every investor, and is a low-cost way of keeping track of the market.

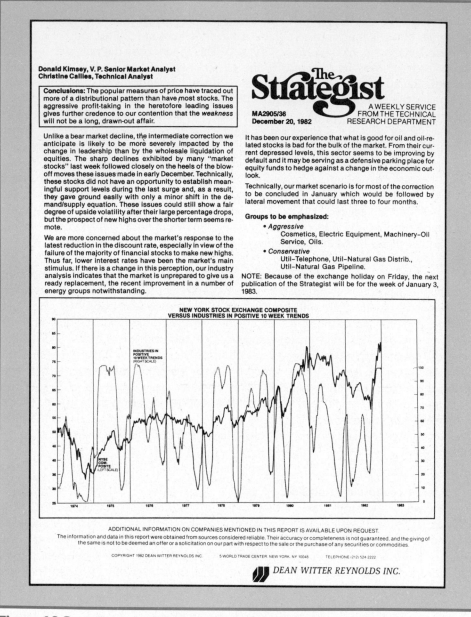

Donald Kimsey, V. P. Senior Market Analyst
Christine Callies, Technical Analyst

Conclusions: The popular measures of price have traced out more of a distributional pattern than have most stocks. The aggressive profit-taking in the heretofore leading issues gives further credence to our contention that the *weakness* will not be a long, drawn-out affair.

Unlike a bear market decline, the intermediate correction we anticipate is likely to be more severely impacted by the change in leadership than by the wholesale liquidation of equities. The sharp declines exhibited by many "market stocks" last week followed closely on the heels of the blow-off moves these issues made in early December. Technically, these stocks did not have an opportunity to establish meaningful support levels during the last surge and, as a result, they gave ground easily with only a minor shift in the demand/supply equation. These issues could still show a fair degree of upside volatility after their large percentage drops, but the prospect of new highs over the shorter term seems remote.

We are more concerned about the market's response to the latest reduction in the discount rate, especially in view of the failure of the majority of financial stocks to make new highs. Thus far, lower interest rates have been the market's main stimulus. If there is a change in this perception, our industry analysis indicates that the market is unprepared to give us a ready replacement, the recent improvement in a number of energy groups notwithstanding.

The **Strategist**

MA2905/36
December 20, 1982

A WEEKLY SERVICE
FROM THE TECHNICAL
RESEARCH DEPARTMENT

It has been our experience that what is good for oil and oil-related stocks is bad for the bulk of the market. From their current depressed levels, this sector seems to be improving by default and it may be serving as a defensive parking place for equity funds to hedge against a change in the economic outlook.

Technically, our market scenario is for most of the correction to be concluded in January which would be followed by lateral movement that could last three to four months.

Groups to be emphasized:

- *Aggressive*
  Cosmetics, Electric Equipment, Machinery–Oil Service, Oils.
- *Conservative*
  Util–Telephone, Util–Natural Gas Distrib., Util–Natural Gas Pipeline.

NOTE: Because of the exchange holiday on Friday, the next publication of the Strategist will be for the week of January 3, 1983.

NEW YORK STOCK EXCHANGE COMPOSITE
VERSUS INDUSTRIES IN POSITIVE 10 WEEK TRENDS

ADDITIONAL INFORMATION ON COMPANIES MENTIONED IN THIS REPORT IS AVAILABLE UPON REQUEST.
The information and data in this report were obtained from sources considered reliable. Their accuracy or completeness is not guaranteed, and the giving of the same is not to be deemed an offer or a solicitation on our part with respect to the sale or the purchase of any securities or commodities.

COPYRIGHT 1982 DEAN WITTER REYNOLDS INC.   5 WORLD TRADE CENTER, NEW YORK, NY 10048   TELEPHONE (212) 524-2222

DEAN WITTER REYNOLDS INC.

Figure 10.3   A Technical Report about the Market.
This technical report is prepared weekly and contains valuable information about the market in general . . .

Charting

Charting is perhaps the best-known activity of the technical analyst. Technicians—analysts who believe supply-and-demand forces establish stock prices—use various types of charts to plot the behavior of everything from the Dow Jones in-

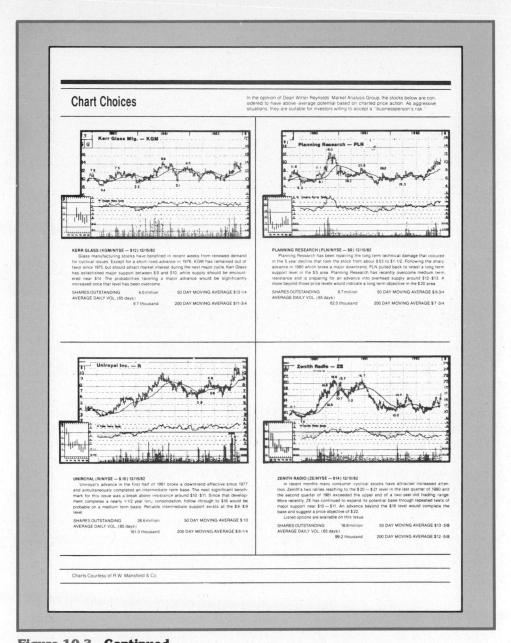

Figure 10.3   Continued

... and several promising stocks in particular. (*Source:* Dean Witter Reynolds.)

dustrial average to the share price movements of individual listed and OTC stocks. Also, just about every kind of technical indicator is charted in one form or another. Figure 10.4 shows a typical stock chart; in this case, the price behavior of Hart Schaffner & Marx has been plotted, along with a variety of supplementary information. Charts are popular because they provide a visual summary of activity over time, and

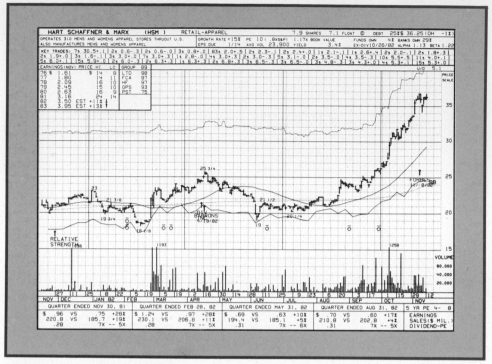

Figure 10.4 A Stock Chart.
This chart for Hart Schaffner & Marx contains information about the daily price behavior of the stock, a popular technical measure (the 200-day moving average) that shows the long-range trend in price, the stock's relative strength, its trading volume, and several other pieces of supplementary data. (*Source:* William O'Neil & Co., Inc., *NYSE/OTC Daily Graphs.*)

perhaps more important, because in the eyes of technicians at least, they contain valuable information about developing trends and the future behavior of the market and/or individual stocks. Chartists believe price patterns evolve into *chart formations* that provide signals about the future course of the market or a stock. We will now briefly review the practice of charting, including popular types of charts, chart formations, and investor uses of charts.

Bar charts

The simplest and probably most widely used type of chart is the *bar chart.* Market or share prices are plotted on the vertical axis, and time on the horizontal axis. This type of chart derives its name from the fact that prices are recorded as vertical bars that depict high, low, and closing prices. A typical bar chart is illustrated in Figure 10.5; note that on 12/31, this particular stock had a high price of 31, a low of 27, and closed at 27½. Because they contain a time element, technicians will frequently plot a variety of other pertinent information on these charts; for example, volume is often put at the base of most bar charts (see the Hart Schaffner & Marx chart in Figure 10.4).

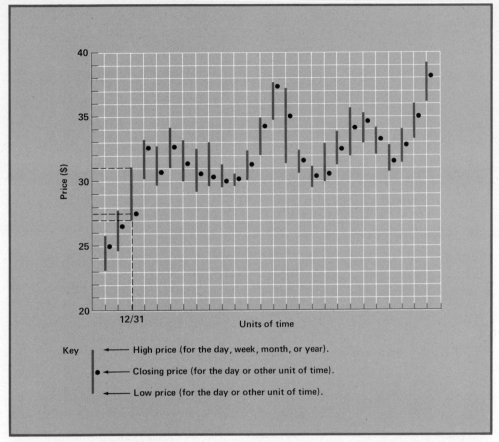

Figure 10.5 A Bar Chart.
Bar charts are widely used to track stock prices, market averages, and all sorts of technical measures.

Point-and-figure charts

These charts are used strictly to keep track of emerging price patterns. Because there is no time dimension on point-and-figure charts, they are *not* used for plotting technical measures. In addition to the time feature, point-and-figure charts are unique in two other ways: first, only *significant* price changes are recorded on these charts (i.e., prices have to move by a certain minimum amount—usually at least a point or two—before a new price level is recognized); and second, price reversals show up only after a predetermined change in direction occurs. Usually, only closing prices are charted. An *X* is used to denote an increase in price, and an *O* for a decrease. Figure 10.6 shows a common point-and-figure chart; in this case, the chart employs a 2-point box, which means that the stock must move by a minimum of 2 points before any changes are recorded. The chart could cover a span of one year or less (if the stock is highly active), or it could cover a number of years (if the stock is not very active, the chart could reflect price movements over, say, the past three to five

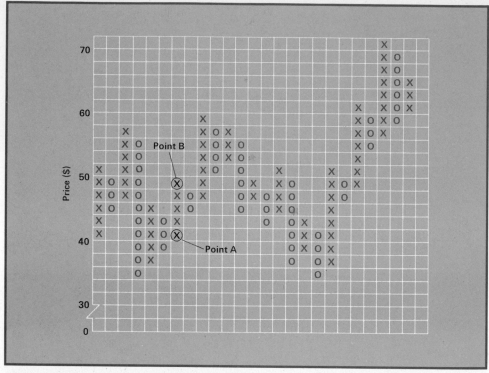

Figure 10.6   A Point-and-Figure Chart.
Point-and-figure charts are unusual because they have no time dimension; rather, a column of Xs is used to reflect a general upward drift in prices and a column of Os is used when prices are drifting downward.

years). As a rule, low-priced stocks will be charted with 1-point boxes, moderately priced shares will use increments of 2 to 3 points, and high-priced securities will appear on charts with 3- to 5-point boxes.

Here is how they work. Suppose we are at point A on the chart in Figure 10.6, where the stock has been hovering around the $40–$41 mark for some time. Assume, however, that it just closed at 42⅛; because the minimum 2-point movement has been met, the chartist would place an X in the box immediately *above* point A. The chartist would remain with this new box as long as the price moved (up or down) within the 2-point range of 42 to 43⅞. Thus, although the chartist follows *daily* closing prices, a new entry is made on the chart only after the price has changed by a certain minimum amount and moved into a new 2-point box. We see that from point A, the price generally moved up over time to nearly $50 a share. At that point (indicated as point B on the chart), things began to change as a reversal set in. That is, the price of the stock began to drift downward and in time moved out of the 48–50 box. This reversal prompts the chartist to change columns and symbols: He moves one column to the right and records the new price level with an O in the 46–48 box. And the chartist will continue to use the Os as long as the stock continues to close on a generally lower note.

Chart formations

The information charts supposedly contain about the future course of the market or a stock is revealed in *chart formations*. That is, in response to certain supply and demand forces, chartists believe that emerging price patterns will result in various types of formations which historically have indicated that certain types of behavior are imminent. If you know how to interpret charts (which, by the way, is no easy task), you can see formations building and will know how to recognize buy and sell signals. Some popular formations have such exotic names as these:

Head-and-shoulders	Broadening top
Double top	Dormant bottom
Triple bottom	Ascending triangle
Diamond	Exhaustion gap
Falling wedge	Island reversal
Pennant	Trend channel
Scallop and saucer	Complex top

Figure 10.7 shows six popular formations. The patterns form "support levels" and "resistance lines" which, when combined with the basic formations, yield buy and sell signals. Panel A is an example of a *buy* signal, which occurs when prices break out above a resistance line after a particular pattern has been formed; in contrast, when prices break out below a support level, as they do at the end of the formation in panel B, a *sell* signal is said to occur. Supposedly, a sell signal means everything is in place for a major drop in the market (or in the price of a share of stock), and a buy signal indicates that the opposite is about to occur. Unfortunately, one of the major problems of charting is that the formations rarely appear as neatly and cleanly as those in Figure 10.7; rather, their identification and interpretation often require considerable imagination on the part of the chartist.

Investor uses

Charts are nothing more than tools used by market analysts and technicians to assess conditions in the market and/or the price behavior of individual stocks. Unlike other types of technical measures, charting is seldom done on an informal basis—you either chart because you believe in its value, or you don't use it at all. A chart by itself tells you little more than where the market or a stock has been. But to a chartist, those price patterns yield formations which, along with things like resistance lines, support levels, and breakouts, tell him or her what to expect in the future. Chartists believe that history repeats itself, so they study the historical reactions of stocks (or the market) to various formations and devise trading rules based on these observations. It does not make any difference to chartists whether they are following the market or an individual stock, because it is the formation that matters, not the issue being plotted. The value of charts lies in knowing how to "read" them and how to respond to the signals they supposedly give off about the future. There is a long-standing debate on Wall Street (some would call it a "feud") regarding the merits of charting; while it may be scoffed at by a large segment of those following the market, to avid chartists, charting is no laughing matter.

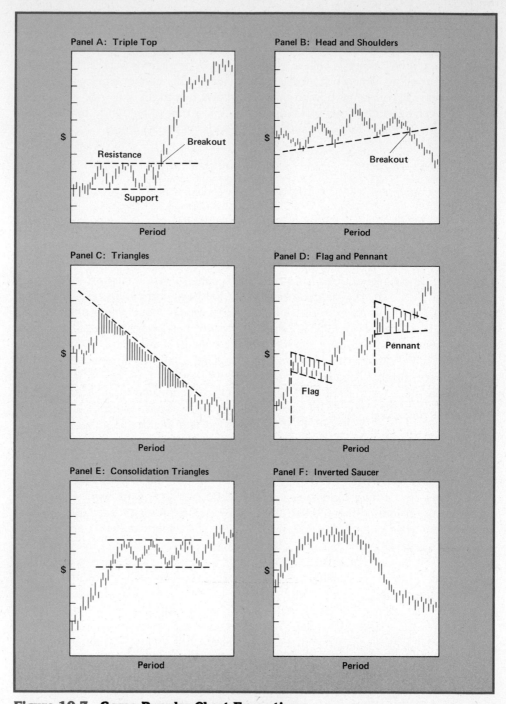

Figure 10.7 Some Popular Chart Formations.
To chartists, each of these formations has meaning about the future course of events.

RANDOM WALKS
AND EFFICIENT MARKETS

If a drunk were abandoned in an open field at night, where would one begin to search for him the next morning? The answer, of course, is the spot where the drunk was left the night before. To some analysts, stock prices seem to wander about in a similar fashion. Observations of such erratic movements have led to a body of evidence called the *random walk hypothesis.* Its followers believe that price movements are unpredictable and that, as a result, security analysis will not help to predict future behavior. This obviously has serious implications for much of what we have discussed in the last two chapters.

A Brief Historical Overview

To describe stock prices as a random walk suggests that price movements cannot be expected to follow any type of pattern; that is, that price movements are independent of one another. In order to find a theory for such behavior, researchers developed the concept of *efficient markets.* Basically, the idea behind an efficient market is that the market price of securities always fully reflects available information and therefore it is difficult, if not impossible, to outperform the market consistently by picking "undervalued" stocks.

Random walk

The first evidence about random price movements dates back to the early 1900s. During that period, statisticians interested in random processes noted that commodity prices seemed to follow a "fair game" pattern; that is, prices seemed to move up and down randomly, giving no advantage to any particular trading strategy. Although a few studies appeared in the 1930s, thorough examination of the randomness in stock prices did not begin in earnest until 1959. From that point on, particularly through the decade of the 1960s, the random walk issue has become one of the most keenly debated topics in stock market literature. Some rather ingenious tests, aided by the development of high-speed computers, have compiled convincing evidence that stock prices do come very close to a random walk.

Efficient markets

Given the extensive random walk evidence, market researchers were faced with another question: What sort of market would produce prices that seem to fluctuate randomly? Such behavior could be the result of investors who are irrational and make investment decisions on whim. But it has been argued, much more convincingly, that investors are not irrational at all; rather, random price movements simply reflect a highly competitive market. Investors, searching for stock market profits, compete vigorously for new information and do extremely thorough analysis. This very competition holds security prices close to their correct level. It is not random behavior on the part of investors, but *random events,* such as labor strikes, shifts in the economy, and changes in product demand, that cause stock prices to change

BOX 10.3 THE FORBES DART BOARD FUND SCORES AGAIN

In June of 1967, Chairman Malcolm S. Forbes, Publisher James J. Dunn and Editor James Michaels flung ten darts each at the stock market page of that day's *Wall Street Journal*. Thus was created a portfolio that has probably driven more than one money manager to drink. Over the period, the fund has increased by 239%, while the S&P's 500 is up a mere 35%. . . .

It wasn't that Forbes, Dunn and Michaels had nothing better to do that morning. At that time some people were saying that a monkey throwing darts could pick stocks as well as most of the experts could. There were no monkeys handy, so Forbes roped Dunn and Michaels into testing the hypothesis.

What's the secret of our fund's success? One of Malcolm Forbes' darts speared Texas Oil & Gas, which dutifully took off. . . . That single holding now accounts for nearly half (44%) of our portfolio.

[The 1982] Dart Board Fund contains several new names, because six companies were taken over since our last update, in February 1980. We followed our standing rule of converting the takeover proceeds into stock in the acquiring company, and the 1981 rash of acquisitions made our portfolio excel. MacAndrews & Forbes, for example, was taken over by Cohen-Hatfield, and shares in the renamed company, MacAndrews & Forbes Group, have appreciated by 115% since December 1980. We also lost a component when Aguirre was liquidated. We decided to redistribute the $646 cash proceeds over the rest of our holdings.

Over the years, gains of 300% or more have also come from our holdings in Baker International, Cooper Industries, Florida Steel, Pittston and Standard Oil of Indiana. The biggest loser was Singer common and preferred stock, which came into the portfolio when General Precision was acquired in 1968. The value of this holding is down some 74%.

After a decade and a half the Dart Board has an average return of just over 18% a year, excluding dividends. The S&P's 500 over that same time span had an average return of only 2.5% and the DJIA not even 1%. But don't try to prove anything by this, and, above all, don't use the method for managing your own investments. Supposing Malcolm Forbes' dart had landed on Chrysler Corp? Or International Harvester? If there is a moral in all this, it has nothing to do with the Random Walk theory or with technical analysis versus fundamental analysis. It's simply one more reminder that there is a large element of luck in all success, the stock market included.

THE DART BOARD FUND

	VALUE OF PORTFOLIO		CHANGE IN VALUE SINCE	
Present Portfolio	2/5/80	12/31/81	2/5/80	6/30/67
Allegheny Intl—$11.25 pfd	$ 600.80	$ 791.29	+32%	−21%
Allied Corp—$6.74 pfd	1,213.40	2,176.74	+79	+118
Arvin Industries	1,181.44	1,361.21	+15	+36
Baker International	3,957.72	4,695.66	+19	+370
Carolina P&L	439.09	522.86	+19	−48
Chase Manhattan	1,003.03	1,339.33	+34	+34
Checker Motors	2,191.78	1,846.08	−16	+85
Cooper Industries	2,836.60	5,515.65	+94	+452

BOX 10.3 *Continued*

Present Portfolio	VALUE OF PORTFOLIO		CHANGE IN VALUE SINCE	
	2/5/80	12/31/81	2/5/80	6/30/67
Federal Paper Board—common	940.30	795.69 ⎫		+115
—$1.20 pfd	775.52	618.66 ⎬ −9		
Rexham*	652.43	736.80 ⎭		
Firestone Tire & Rubber	404.46	571.28	+41	−43
Florida Steel	2,830.71	4,560.71	+61	+356
General Dynamics	2,666.41	1,683.64 ⎫		+87
Houston Natural Gas†	184.50	183.79 ⎬ −34		
Helene Curtis	504.17	798.96	+58	−20
INCO Ltd	762.47	387.32	−49	−61
INCO (originally ESB)	1,807.72	918.13	−49	−8
International Paper	1,303.49	1,347.07	+3	+35
Interpace	1,508.96	1,222.64	−19	+22
MacAndrews & Forbes Group	2,765.95	5,937.37	+115	+494
Pacific Tin Consol	2,000.05	1,549.98	−23	+55
JC Penney	779.63	907.99	+16	−9
Pittston	4,172.44	4,021.26	−4	+302
Singer—common	75.74	124.46 ⎫		−74
—$3.50 pfd	169.26	140.52 ⎬ +8		
Standard Oil Indiana	4,873.50	5,372.12	+10	+437
Texas Oil & Gas	20,036.98	41,986.37	+110	+4,099
Textron	772.30	723.40	−6	−28
Thorn-EMI Ltd—ordinary	685.71	563.85 ⎫ +26		−14
—pfd		300.33 ⎭		
Tyco Labs	547.73	1,197.90	+119	+20
Total	65,400.99	94,899.06	+45	+239
S&P's 500	114.66	122.55	+7	+35
DJIA	876.62	875.00	0	+2

*Shareholders of Riegel Paper received both Federal Paper Board common and preferred shares and Rexham common.

†General Dynamics divested Liquid Carbonic, which was subsequently acquired by Houston Natural Gas.

Source: "The Forbes Dart Board Fund Scores Again." *Forbes,* February 1, 1982, p. 99.

in response to the new information. Swift reaction by investors to this new information causes prices to adjust quickly, and in a manner that reflects the randomness of the arrival of new information. It is, in fact, the keen competition among investors and rapid evaluation of new information that causes stock prices to shift to new levels.

Possible Implications

The concept of an efficient market holds serious implications for investors. In particular, it could have considerable bearing on traditional security analysis and stock valuation procedures and on the way stocks are selected for investment. There are, in fact, some who contend that rather than trying to beat the market, investors should spend less time analyzing securities and more time on such matters as the reduction of taxes and transaction costs, the elimination of unnecessary risk, and the construction of a widely diversified portfolio that is compatible with the investor's risk temperament. Make no mistake about it, even in an efficient market, there are all sorts of return opportunities available. But to proponents of efficient markets, the only way to increase returns is to invest in a portfolio of higher-risk securities.

For technical analysis

The most serious challenge the random walk evidence presents is to technical analysis. If price fluctuations are purely random, charts of past prices are not likely to produce significant trading profits. In a highly efficient market, shifts in supply and demand occur so rapidly that technical indicators simply measure after-the-fact events, with no implications for the future. If markets are less than perfectly efficient, however, information may be absorbed slowly, producing gradual shifts in supply and demand conditions and therefore profit opportunities for those who recognize the shifts early. Although the great bulk of evidence supports a random walk, many investors follow a technical approach because they believe it improves their investment results.

For fundamental analysis

Many strict fundamental analysts were at first pleased by the random walk attack on technical analysis. The further development of the efficient markets concept, however, has not been so well received. For, in an efficient market, prices react so quickly to new information that not even security analysis will enable investors to realize consistently superior returns on their investments. Because of the extreme competition among investors, security prices are seldom far above or below their justified levels, and fundamental analysis thus loses much of its value. The challenge is not that fundamental analysis is poorly done; to the contrary, it is done all too well! As a result, so many investors, competing so vigorously for profit opportunities, simply eliminate the opportunities before investors can capitalize upon them.

So Who Is Right?

Some type of fundamental analysis probably has a role in the stock selection process. Even in an efficient market, there is no question about the fact that stock prices reflect a company's profit performance. Some companies are fundamentally strong and others are fundamentally weak, and investors must be able to distinguish between the two. Thus, some time can profitably be spent on evaluating a company and its stock to determine not if it is undervalued, but whether or not it is fundamentally strong.

The level of investor return, however, is more than a function of the fundamental condition of the company; the level of risk exposure is also important. We saw earlier that fundamental analysis can be helpful in assessing potential risk exposure and in identifying securities that possess risk commensurate with the return they offer. Whether or not the markets are efficient is still subject to considerable debate. But in the final analysis, it is the individual investor who must decide on the merits of fundamental and technical analysis. Certainly, a large segment of the investing public believes in security analysis, even in a market that may be efficient. What is more, the principles of stock valuation (that an investment should be considered acceptable only so long as its promised return is commensurate with the amount of risk exposure) are valid in any type of market setting.

SUMMARY

Fundamental analysis is the phase of security analysis that deals with assessing the investment merits of a specific company and its stock, and is ultimately aimed at formulating expectations about the company's future prospects and the potential return and risk behavior of its stock. Such information as projected sales, forecasted earnings, and estimated dividends are all important in establishing the intrinsic worth of a stock. This is what the investor feels the stock *ought* to be worth, based on expected return and risk performance. Such a value, when compared to prevailing market prices, enables the investor to determine whether the stock is undervalued, fairly priced, or overvalued.

There are a number of stock valuation models in use today, but one that enjoys wide application is a present value approach. Given expected security returns (dividends and future share price behavior), an investor can determine the justified price of a security or the fully compounded yield it offers at today's prices. Both techniques provide the same accept or reject signals: The stock is considered a worthwhile investment so long as its computed justified price is equal to or greater than the current market price, or the computed yield is equal to or greater than the desired rate of return.

Technical analysis is another phase of the analytical process. It deals with the behavior of the market and the various economic dimensions at work in the marketplace. Many investors use technical analysis as a way to help them with market timing—to determine whether or not the time is right to buy or sell. There are a number of approaches to technical analysis, including the use of bellwether stocks and/or following several key elements of market behavior, such as market volume, breadth of the market, short interest positions, odd-lot trading, and confidence index.

Probably the best-known tool of the technical analyst is *charting*. Charts are popular because they provide, in a convenient format, a visual summary of activity over time. Chartists believe price patterns evolve into chart formations that provide signals about what to expect for the market or a stock. Technical analysts use bar charts or point-and-figure charts to keep track of the market and individual stocks.

In recent years, both technical and fundamental analysis have been challenged by the random walk and efficient market hypotheses. Considerable evidence indicates that stock prices do, indeed, follow a random pattern. The efficient market hypothesis is an attempt to explain why prices behave in a random fashion. The idea behind an efficient market is that available information is always fully reflected in the price of securities, and therefore investors should not expect to outperform the market consistently.

KEY TERMS

bar charts

bellwether stocks

breadth of the market

chart formations

charting

confidence index

confirmation

desired rate of return

the dividend model

Dow theory

efficient market

justified price

point-and-figure charts

random walk hypothesis

short interest

stock valuation

technical analysis

theory of contrary opinion

trading action approach

REVIEW QUESTIONS

1. Are the expected future earnings of the firm important in determining a stock's investment suitability? Explain. Discuss how these and other future estimates fit into the stock valuation framework.

2. An investor estimates that next year's sales for Carpenter Products, Inc., should amount to about $75 million; the company has 2.5 million shares outstanding, generates a net profit margin of about 5 percent, and has a payout ratio of 50 percent—all figures are expected to hold for next year. Given this information, compute:

   a. Estimated net earnings for next year.
   b. Next year's dividends per share.
   c. The expected price of the stock (assuming the P/E ratio is 12.5 times earnings).

3. Briefly discuss procedures that might be used by individual investors to forecast the following types of information about a company and its stock:

   a. Sales.
   b. Net profit rate.
   c. Price/earnings ratio.

4. Can the growth prospects of a company affect its price/earnings multiple? Explain. How about the amount of debt that a firm uses? Are there other variables that affect the level of a firm's P/E ratio?

5. Identify and briefly discuss three different ways of determining (or assessing) a stock's investment value. Note how such information is used in the investment decision-making process.

6. Charlene Lewis is thinking about buying some shares of Education, Inc., at $50 per share; she expects them to rise to $75 over the next three years, during which time she also expects to receive annual dividends of $5 per share.

   a. What is the intrinsic worth of this stock, given a 10 percent desired rate of return?
   b. What is its approximate yield?

7. The price of Consolidated Everything is now $75; the company pays no dividends, and Mr. Bruce expects the price three years from now to be $100 per share. Should Mr. B. buy Consolidated E. if he desires a 10 percent rate of return? Explain.

8. Discuss the concept of a desired rate of return; explain its role in the valuation process.

9. Explain how risk fits into the stock valuation process (note especially its relationship to the investment return of a security).

   a. Note and briefly discuss several different types of risk a stock investor should be aware of.
   b. How can market risk be evaluated? How about the business (or intrinsic) risk of a company?

  10. Able Company's stock sells at a P/E ratio of 14 times earnings; it is expected to pay dividends of $2 per share in each of the next five years and generate an EPS of $5 per share in year 5. Using the present value model and a 12 percent discount rate, compute the stock's justified price.
  11. What is the purpose of technical analysis? Explain how and why it is used by technicians; note how it can be helpful in timing investment decisions.
  12. Can the market really have a measurable effect on the price behavior of individual securities? Explain.
  13. Briefly define each of the following and note the conditions which would suggest that the market is strong:

   a. Breadth of the market.
   b. Dow theory.
   c. Bellwether stocks.
   d. Theory of contrary opinion.
   e. Head-and-shoulders.

  14. What is a chart? What kind of information can be put on charts and what is the purpose of charting?

   a. What is the difference between a bar chart and a point-and-figure chart?
   b. What are chart formations and why are they important?

  15. What is the random walk hypothesis and how does it apply to stocks? What is an efficient market; how can a market be efficient if its prices behave in a random fashion?
  16. Explain why in an efficient market it is difficult or impossible to consistently outperform the market.

   a. Does that mean that high rates of return are not available in the stock market?
   b. Explain how an investor can earn a high rate of return in an efficient market.

  17. What are the implications of random walks and efficient markets for technical analysis? for fundamental analysis? Do random walks and efficient markets mean that technical and fundamental analysis are useless? Explain.
  18. A particular company has sales of $250 million; these are expected to grow by 20 percent next year (year 1). For the year after next (year 2), the growth rate in sales is expected to equal 10 percent. Over each of the next two years, the company is expected to have a net profit margin of 8 percent, a payout ratio of 50 percent, and to maintain the number of shares of common stock outstanding at 15 million shares; the stock always trades at a P/E ratio of 15 times earnings and the investor has a desired rate of return of 20 percent. Given this information:

   a. Find the stock's intrinsic value (its justified price).
   b. Determine its approximate yield, given the stock is presently trading at $15 per share.
   c. Find the holding period returns for year 1 and for year 2.

CASE PROBLEMS

10.1 CHRIS LOOKS FOR A WAY TO INVEST HIS NEW WEALTH

  Chris Norton is a young Hollywood writer who is well on his way to television superstardom. After writing several successful television specials, he was recently named the head writer for the top rated TV sitcom "No Breakfast for Bozos." Chris fully realizes that his business is a fickle one, and on the advice of his dad and manager, has decided to set up an investment program. Chris will earn about half a million dollars this year, and because of his age, income level, and desire to get as big a bang as possible from his investment dollars, he has decided to invest in speculative, high-growth stocks.

He's presently working with a respected and highly regarded Beverly Hills broker, and is in the process of building up a diversified portfolio of speculative stocks. His broker recently sent him information on this hot new stock and suggested Chris study the numbers and if he likes them, to buy as many as 1,000 shares of the stock. In particular, the broker forecasts corporate sales for the next three years at:

Year	Sales
1	$22.5 million
2	35.0
3	50.0

The firm has 1.2 million shares of common outstanding (they are currently being traded at 62½ and pay no dividends), has been running a phenomenal net profit rate of 20 percent, and its stock has been trading at a P/E ratio of 25 times (which is definitely on the high side). All these operating characteristics are expected to hold in the future.

Questions

1. Looking first at the stock:

a. Compute the company's net profits and EPS for each of the next three years.
b. Compute the price of the stock three years from now.
c. Assuming all expectations hold up and that Chris buys the stock at 62½, determine the approximate yield he can expect from this investment.
d. What risks is he facing by buying this stock? Be specific.
e. Should he consider the stock a worthwhile investment candidate? Explain.

2. Now, looking at his investment program in general:

a. What do you think of his investment program; what do you see as its strengths and weaknesses?
b. Are there any suggestions you would make?

10.2 AN ANALYSIS OF A HIGH-FLYING STOCK

Glenn Wilt is a recent university graduate, and a security analyst with the Kansas City brokerage firm of Lippman, Brickbats, and Shaft. Wilt has been following one of the hottest issues on Wall Street, C&I Construction Supplies, a company which has turned in outstanding performance lately and, even more important, has exhibited excellent growth potential. It has 5 million shares outstanding and pays a nominal annual dividend of 25 cents per share. Wilt has decided to take a close look at C&I to see whether or not it still has any investment play left. Assume the company's sales for the *last* five years have been:

Year	Sales
1979	$10.0 million
1980	12.5
1981	16.2
1982	22.0
1983	28.5

Wilt is concerned with the future prospects of the company, not its past; as a result, he pores over the numbers laboriously and generates the following estimates of future performance:

Expected net profit margin	12½%
Estimated annual dividend per share	25¢
Number of common shares outstanding	No change
P/E ratio at the end of 1984	35
P/E ratio at the end of 1985	50

Questions

1. Determine the average annual rate of growth in sales over the last five years.

a. Use this average growth rate figure to forecast revenues for next year (1984) and the year after that (1985).

b. Now determine the company's net earnings and EPS for each of the next two years (1984 and 1985).

c. Finally, determine the expected future price of the stock at the end of this two-year period.

2. Because of several intrinsic and market factors, Wilt feels that 20 percent is a viable figure to use for a desired rate of return. Using this rate and the forecasted figures you came up with above, compute the stock's justified price.

a. If C&I is presently trading at $25 per share, should Wilt consider the stock a worthwhile investment candidate? Explain.

3. The stock is actively traded on the AMEX and enjoys considerable market interest. Recent closing prices are listed in the table below.

a. Prepare a point-and-figure chart of these prices (use a 1-point system—i.e., make each box worth $1).

b. Discuss how these and similar charts are used by technical analysts.

c. Cite several other types of technical indicators and note how they might be used in the analysis of this stock.

RECENT PRICE BEHAVIOR: C&I CONSTRUCTION SUPPLIES

14 ← (8/15/83)	18½	20	17½
14¼	17½	20¼	18½
14⅞	17½	20¼	19¾
15½	17¼	20⅛	19½
16	17	20	19¼
16	16¾	20¼	20
16½	16½	20½	20⅞
17	16½	20¾	21
17¼	16⅛	20½	21¾
17½	16¾	20	22½
18	17⅛	20¼	23¼
18 ← (9/30/83)	17¼	20	24
18½	17¼	19½	24¼
18½	17¼ ← (10/31/83)	19¼	24⅛
18¾	17¾	18¼ ← (11/30/83)	24¾
19	18¼	17½	25
19⅛	19¼	16¾	25½
18⅞	20½	17	25½ ← (12/31/83)

SELECTED READINGS

"Are Seat Prices a Good Market Indicator?" *Financial World,* February 15, 1979, p. 46.

Barnfather, Maurice. "Small Isn't Beautiful." *Forbes,* February 1, 1982, pp. 95–98.

Bryant, William C. "Diagnosing the Bull Market." *U.S. News and World Report,* November 22, 1982, p. 92.

————. "When Henry Kaufman Talks—." *U.S. News and World Report,* August 30, 1982, p. 66.

————. "Copying Big Buyers—The Pitfalls." *U.S. News and World Report,* August 2, 1982, p. 71.

"Corporate Takeovers: How Shareholders Can Avoid the Tender Traps." *Changing Times,* August 1982, pp. 29–31.

Dreman, David. "The Myth of Market Timing." *Forbes,* January 4, 1982, pp. 298–299.

————. "Why High P/Es Are Dangerous." *Forbes,* August 3, 1981, pp. 104–105.

Elia, Charles J. "Swinging Stocks: Market's Volatility Has Grown in Decade." *The Wall Street Journal,* March 30, 1979, pp. 1, 33.

Farrell, Robert J. "Seers' Comeback?" *Barron's,* March 10, 1980, p. 9.

Haller, Ellis. "A Question of Timing." *U.S. News and World Report,* March 2, 1981, p. 78.

"How to Pick Your Stocks by Computer." *Business Week,* September 12, 1983, pp. 121–122.

Morner, Aimee L. "Takeovers Are Not Just a Tapewatcher's Game." *Fortune,* July 16, 1979, pp. 173–176.

————. "Speculations on the Stock Market Rally." *Fortune,* November 1, 1982, pp. 169–172.

Scharff, Edward E. "How Outsiders Cash In on Stocks Insiders Trade." *Money,* June 1980, pp. 99–106.

Schulz, John W. "Back to Graham and Dodd—Investors Have Embraced the Total Return Approach." *Barron's,* March 14, 1977, pp. 11–17.

————. "Messing Up the Tea Leaves: Where Technical Analysis Went Wrong." *Barron's,* September 13, 1982, pp. 15, 18–19.

"Second Thoughts about the Efficient Market." *Fortune,* February 26, 1979, pp. 105–107.

"Sign of the Times: They're Talking about the Hemline Theory Again—and Perhaps Not Entirely in Jest." *Financial World,* March 1, 1979, pp. 36–37.

"Taking Stock—Those Who Think Stocks Are Over-the-Hill Should Look Again." *Financial World,* February 15, 1980, pp. 68–69.

Train, John. "The Use and Abuse of Technical Analysis." *Forbes,* January 4, 1982, p. 303.

"Why Some Experts Say You Can't Beat the Stock Averages." *Changing Times,* May 1980, pp. 27–29.

Zucker, Seymour. "How the Market Leads the Way to Recovery." *Business Week,* October 11, 1982, p. 30.

FIVE
INVESTING IN FIXED INCOME SECURITIES

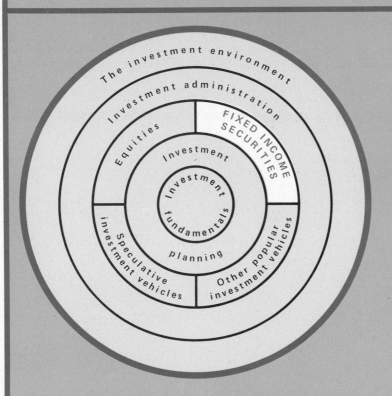

The investment environment

Investment administration

Equities

FIXED INCOME SECURITIES

Investment

Investment fundamentals

Speculative investment vehicles

planning

Other popular investment vehicles

Ever since interest rates began to climb in the late 1960s, the appeal of various types of fixed income securities has increased in a similar fashion. Today, securities such as bonds, preferred stocks, and convertible issues are found in an increasing number of investment portfolios and are being actively used to fulfill a variety of investor objectives. Chapter 11 looks at bonds—basic issue characteristics as well as a host of different types of bond vehicles are reviewed with an eye toward the various ways these issues can be used by individual investors. Chapter 12 provides a similar review of the issue characteristics and investment merits of preferred stock and convertible securities.

11
Bond Investments

For many years, bonds were viewed as unexciting investment vehicles that offered current income and little else. No more. The high interest rates that have existed since the late 1960s have changed all that. In particular, two things occurred: (1) Interest rates moved to levels that were highly competitive with other securities, and (2) at the same time, these market rates began to fluctuate widely and provide investors with attractive capital gains opportunities. Bonds have thus become highly sought after as investment vehicles and have begun to appear in a growing number of individual investment portfolios. In order to gain a more thorough understanding of bonds and an appreciation of their investment merits, this chapter will review:

1. The basic features of bonds and the principles of bond price behavior.
2. The advantages and disadvantages of investing in bonds, including the types of risks to which investors are exposed.
3. The many types of bond vehicles currently available and the wide array of investment objectives they can fulfill.
4. Fundamentals of the bond valuation process, including basic measures of return and investment behavior.
5. Various types of investment programs and the ways these issues can be used by individual investors.

Bonds are publicly traded long-term debt securities; they are issued in convenient denominations and by a variety of borrowing organizations, including the U.S. Treasury, various agencies of the U.S. government, state and municipal governments, and corporations, as well as institutions like private nonprofit hospitals and church-related schools. This is the first of two chapters dealing with various types of fixed income securities; in this chapter we will examine bonds, and in the next, preferred stocks and convertible securities. As with any investment program, successful bond investing requires a knowledge of issue characteristics and the special kinds of trading strategies used with these investment vehicles. Let's begin by reviewing some important issue characteristics, such as the sources of return to investors, different types of bond features, and types of issues.

WHY INVEST IN BONDS?

Most people would not buy an expensive piece of property sight unseen, as there are too many obvious and costly pitfalls to such a course of action. Similarly, we would not expect rational investors to spend money on securities they know nothing about. Bonds are no exception; in fact, it is especially important to know what you are getting into with bonds since, as we will see below, many seemingly insignificant features can have dramatic effects on the behavior of an issue and its investment return.

Like any other type of investment vehicle, bonds provide investors with two kinds of income: (1) They provide a generous amount of current income; and (2) they can often be used to generate substantial amounts of capital gains. The current income, of course, is derived from the interest payments received over the life of the issue. Capital gains, in contrast, are earned whenever market interest rates fall. A basic trading rule in the bond market is that interest rates and bond prices move in opposite directions. When interest rates rise, prices fall; and when rates drop, bond prices move up. So it is possible to buy bonds at one price and, if interest rate conditions are right, to sell them some time later at a higher price. Of course, it is also possible to incur a capital loss, should market rates move against the investor. Taken together, the current income and capital gains earned from bonds can lead to attractive and highly competitive investor yields.

In addition to their yields, bonds are a versatile investment outlet. They can be used conservatively by those who primarily (or exclusively) seek high current income as a way to supplement other income sources. Or they can be used aggressively for trading purposes by those who actively go after capital gains. Bonds have long been considered excellent vehicles for those seeking current income, but it has only been since the advent of high and volatile interest rates that bonds have also become recognized as excellent trading vehicles. This is so because, given the relation of bond prices to interest rates, investors found that the number of profitable trading opportunities increased substantially as wider and more frequent swings in interest rates began to occur. Finally, because of the general high quality of many bond issues, they can also be used for the preservation and long-term accumulation of capital. Many individuals, in fact, regularly and over the long haul commit all or a major portion of their investment funds to bonds because of this investment attribute. Some may never use any other type of investment vehicle.

Essential Features of a Bond Issue

A *bond* is a negotiable, long-term debt instrument that carries certain obligations on the part of the issuer. Unlike the holders of common stock, bondholders have no ownership or equity position in the firm or organization that issues the bond. This is so because bonds are debt and because, in a roundabout way, bondholders are only lending money to the issuer, and therefore are not entitled to an ownership position or any of the rights and privileges that go along with it.

Bond interest and principal

Bond issues are considered to be fixed income securities because the debt service obligations of the issuer are fixed. The issuing organization agrees to pay a fixed amount of periodic interest to the bondholder and to repay a fixed amount of principal at or before maturity. Put another way, in the absence of trading, a bond-holder's return is limited to these fixed interest and principal payments; bonds thus involve a fixed claim on the issuer's income (as defined by the size of the periodic interest payments) and a fixed claim on the assets of the issuer (equal to the repayment of principal).

As a rule, bonds pay interest every six months. There are exceptions, however; some issues carry interest payment intervals as short as a month and a few as long as a year. The amount of interest due is a function of the *coupon,* which defines the annual interest income that will be paid by the issuer to the bondholder. For instance, a $1,000 bond with an 8 percent coupon would pay $80 in interest annually— generally in the form of two $40 semi-annual payments. The principal amount of a bond, also known as an issue's *par value,* specifies the amount of capital that must be repaid at maturity. For example, there is $1,000 of principal in a $1,000 bond. To facilitate the marketing of bonds, the issues are broken into standard principal amounts, known as *denominations.* Of course, debt securities regularly trade at market prices that differ from their principal (or par) values. This occurs whenever an issue's coupon differs from the prevailing market rate of interest. The price of the issue will change inversely with interest rates until its yield is compatible with the prevailing market yield. Such behavior explains why a 7 percent issue will carry a market price of only $825 in a 9 percent market; the drop in price is necessary to raise the yield on this bond from 7 to 9 percent. Issues with market values lower than par are known as *discount bonds* and carry coupons that are less than those on new issues. In contrast, issues with market values in excess of par are called *premium bonds* and have coupons greater than those currently being offered on new issues.

Maturity date

Unlike common stock, all debt securities have limited lives and expire on a given date, the issue's *maturity date.* Although a bond carries a series of specific interest payment dates, the principal is repaid only once: on or before maturity. Because the maturity date is fixed (and never changes), it not only defines the lives of new issues, but denotes the amount of time remaining for older, outstanding bonds as well. Such life spans are known as an issue's *term to maturity.* A new issue may come out as a 25-year bond and five years later have twenty years remaining to maturity. Two types of bonds can be distinguished on the basis of maturity: term and serial. A *term bond* has a single, fairly lengthy, maturity date and is the most common type of issue. A *serial bond,* in contrast, has a series of different maturity

BOX 11.1 BONDHOLDERS STRIKE IT RICH OFF THE ERIE

When the Erie Lackawanna Railway prospered a century ago, it made Jay Gould rich. Now it's in bankruptcy and liquidation—and still making speculators rich.

Erie bonds bought dirt cheap after the railroad entered bankruptcy proceedings in 1972 will produce staggering returns when trustees begin divvying up the assets later this year. Much of the cash is coming from the federal government, which in February handed over $360 million it owed for Erie assets that it transferred to Consolidated Rail Corp. (Conrail) in 1976.

The Erie settlement is about to produce cash payouts to holders of 10 of 16 bond issues. Holders of other issues will get cash and stock in a new concern.

C. A. Botzum Jr., a Los Angeles stock broker, bought Erie bonds in 1973 for $117 each. Now each bond will yield him $1,361 in principal and accumulated interest. Nick Schmit, a marketing manager for Minnesota Mining & Manufacturing Co.'s medical products division in Minneapolis, bought Erie bonds in November 1980 for $5,900. They're now worth about $26,500, and they may bring more. Carl Burg, a retired Minneapolis businessman, put nearly $99,000 into five Erie bond issues in late 1980. He will get $278,700. "I don't believe in Santa Claus," he says, "but this is too good to be true."

The Minneapolis bondholders are clients of Bruce Hendry, a junk-bond specialist at the Minneapolis investment firm of Craig-Hallum Inc. Mr. Hendry was one of the first to foresee a windfall in Erie bonds, and he bought heavily. One issue he bought in 1980 at $90 a bond. He'll cash in for $1,735 a bond. "I'm pleased beyond words," he says.

Jay Gould had grabbed control of the Erie in 1860 and began manipulating the market in its stock. He panicked speculators into dumping the stock, then bought it up himself cheaply, and took enormous gains. In the 1893 depression the Erie went into bankruptcy and reorganized. Two years later, it emerged again as an operating railroad. To finance rebuilding its deteriorating track, the railroad sold construction bonds with maturities as long as 100 years. Tangible property, such as rail, locomotives and real estate, secured the bonds. They shrank in value when the Erie again entered bankruptcy proceedings in 1972.

At the time, the value of the Erie's assets was undeterminable, and conservative investors dumped their bonds. John Hancock Mutual Life Insurance Co., for example, which held bonds for $7.5 million, sold them all at a loss in 1974. Speculators, meanwhile, set about trying to anticipate what the bonds ultimately would be worth.

One of those was Mr. Botzum, of Los Angeles. Digging into Erie records, he discovered that one series of bonds he already owned was secured by rail, warehouses,

dates, perhaps as many as fifteen or twenty, within a single issue. For example, a 20-year term bond issued in 1983 would have a maturity date of 2003, but that same issue as a serial bond might have twenty annual maturity dates that extend from 1984 through 2003. At each of these annual maturity dates, a certain portion of the issue would come due and be paid off.

Call feature

Every bond is issued with a *call feature,* which specifies whether or not the issuer will be allowed to retire the bond prematurely. There are three types of call provisions: (1) a bond can be *freely callable,* which means that the issuer can retire the bond at any time; (2) it can be *noncallable,* in which case the issuer would be

BOX 11.1 *Continued*

wharves and even an small commuter rail line in Hoboken, N.J., just across the Hudson River from New York. The properties had been valued at $32 million in 1900, when the bonds were issued. Mr. Botzum figured the value had easily doubled since then, leaving more than enough to satisfy incumbrances. And he figured that even a payout of 30 cents on the dollar—or $300 a bond—made the bonds, then selling for only $117, an attractive speculative plunge. "I started buying more," he says.

Mr. Hendry searched the records, too. He also recruited Barney Donahue, of St. Paul, Minn., to help him evaluate the Erie's condition. Mr. Donahue was a friend—and a train buff. He spent two weeks driving along the entire length of the Erie from Chicago to New York, inspecting the track and facilities and talking to trainmen along the way.

"It was an investigative exercise," Mr. Donahue says. "I talked with section foremen, engineers, anybody that would talk, and asked them about the volume of traffic on the line and anything else I could think of. I was pleasantly surprised that it was a well-maintained railroad. It was better maintained than the Penn Central."

Mr. Hendry, meanwhile, was working on an estimate of how much the government might pay for the 80% of the Erie's assets it turned over to Conrail in 1976. He looked into the market for scrap rail, used box cars and locomotives. He guessed that the government might allow 8% interest a year from 1976 until the bondholders were paid, and he weighed his findings against the government's handling of its payment for property taken from the Reading Railroad.

His estimate, a government payout between $303 million and $392 million, turned out right on target. Last October, the government said it would pay $360 million.

The proceedings aren't entirely completed. Holders of some bonds will get part payment in the stock of a new concern that will own the 20% of the Erie's assets that Conrail didn't get. Probably that concern will merely liquidate, or sell, those assets, and parcel out the cash proceeds. But stockholders won't know until then how much they will get.

To Mr. Hendry, there's a lesson in the tale: What you know does count. He says some clients would ask about the bonds: " 'If these are so good, why didn't someone else buy them?' They always assumed that someone else is smarter than them. But in this case, I guess I knew more than the others."

Source: Catherine L. Kissling, "Bondholders Strike It Rich Off the Erie." *The Wall Street Journal,* August 3, 1982, p. 33.

prohibited from retiring the bond prior to maturity; or (3) the bond could carry a *deferred call feature,* which stipulates that the obligation cannot be called until after a certain length of time has passed (generally five to ten years). Call features are used most often to replace an issue with one that carries a lower coupon; the issuer benefits by being able to realize a reduction in annual interest cost. In a half-hearted attempt to compensate investors who find their bonds called out from under them, a *call premium* is tacked onto the par value of a bond and paid to investors, along with the issue's par value, at the time the bond is called.

The sum of these two (par value and call premium) is known as the issue's *call price* and represents the price the issuer must pay to retire the bond prematurely. As a general rule, such call premiums usually equal about one year's interest at the earliest date of call, and become systematically smaller as the issue nears maturity. Using this rule, the initial call price of a 9 percent bond would be $1,090, with $90 representing the call premium. Some bonds contain a specific *refunding* provision which is exactly like a call feature except that it prohibits one thing: the premature retirement of an issue from the proceeds of a lower coupon refunding bond. The distinction is important, since it means that a "nonrefunding" or "deferred refunding" issue can still be called and prematurely retired for any reason other than refunding. Thus, an investor may have a high-yield issue called out from under him or her if the issuer has the cash to do so!

Sinking fund

Another provision important to investors is the *sinking fund,* which specifies how a bond will be paid off over time; this provision, of course, applies only to term bonds, since serial issues already have a predetermined method of repayment. Some bonds have sinking funds, others do not. For those that do, a sinking fund simply specifies the annual repayment schedule that will be used to pay off the issue; it indicates how much principal will be retired each year. Sinking fund requirements generally begin one to five years after the date of issue, and continue annually thereafter until all or most of the issue is paid off. Any amount not repaid by maturity (this might equal 10 to 25 percent of the issue) would then be retired with a single balloon payment. Like a call provision, the sinking fund feature also carries a call premium, although it is generally nominal and amounts to perhaps 1 percent or less of the principal being retired.

Types of Issues

A single issuer may have many different bonds outstanding at a single point in time. In addition to coupon and maturity, one bond can be differentiated from another by the type of collateral behind the issue. Issues can be either junior or senior. *Senior bonds* are secured obligations, since they are backed by a legal claim on some specific property of the issuer. Such issues would include *mortgage bonds,* which are secured by real estate, and *equipment trust certificates,* which are backed by equipment and are popular with railroads and airlines. *Junior bonds,* on the other hand, are backed only by a promise of the issuer to pay interest and principal on a timely basis. There are several classes of unsecured bonds. The most popular is known as a *debenture.* In addition, *subordinated debentures* are also used; these issues have a claim on income secondary to other debenture bonds. *Income bonds,* probably the most junior of all, are unsecured debts which require that interest be paid only after a certain amount of income is earned; there is no legally binding requirement to meet interest payments on a timely or regular basis so long as a specified amount of income has not been earned. In the municipal market, these issues are called *revenue bonds.*

Specialty issues

In recent years, Wall Street has brought out a number of new products to meet the ever-changing needs of fixed income investors. For the most part, these are debt

BOX 11.2 ZEROING IN ON ZERO-COUPON BONDS

One of the newest ways to invest your money is to put it into zero-coupon bonds. The idea behind this kind of investment actually is old, but its current revival is enjoying a surprisingly strong run.

With a conventional bond you clip a coupon and receive an interest payment, typically every six months. "Zeros," on the other hand, eliminate both the coupon and the interest. Instead, they operate like a U.S. savings bond: You buy the bond at a substantial discount from its face value, then collect the full value when it matures years later.

The idea sounds simple enough to attract lots of investors. Until recently, however, there's been one big hitch. Even though you receive no annual interest, the IRS requires that you report it as if you had. The difference between what you paid for the bond and what you'll receive when it matures is taxable annually on a prorated basis.

That rule was largely outmaneuvered [in 1982] when tax-sheltered Individual Retirement Accounts were made available to most working people. If you qualify, you can buy a zero-coupon bond, sock it away in an IRA and forget about taxes until you actually withdraw the money. Zeros are also an attractive way to give financial gifts to minors, who are likely to be taxed at a low rate, if at all.

The bonds have proven popular for a couple of other reasons as well. For one thing, you don't have to worry about where to reinvest your interest payments because you don't receive any. For another, you don't need a hunk of cash to buy a zero. They usually come in denominations as low as $1,000 and are sold at discounts from face value of 50% to 75%, depending on the maturity. . . .

[Some] zeros . . . come due in ten years or less, but . . . firms have issued bonds with maturities of 30 years. Depending on the maturity, issuers promise to double, triple, or quadruple your money if you hold the bond to its full term. A few firms have christened their zeros "money multiplier notes."

But before you get carried away by visions of retiring a millionaire, keep in mind one of the main risks associated with zeros: Because they carry a fixed yield, the value of your holdings would decline if interest rates rose. And you wouldn't be receiving any interest payments that you could reinvest at the new, higher rates, as you would with conventional bonds. If rates rise, conventional bonds lose less of their value than zeros.

If, on the other hand, you expect rates to fall, you can lock in a fixed return with a zero. A conventional bond serves the same purpose, but there's a catch.

Take the case of a ten-year conventional bond and a zero, each paying 15%. Because of the way interest is figured on the zero, in order to earn as much on the conventional bond you'd have to reinvest every interest payment at 15%. At a lower rate you'd earn less than with the zero.

Suppose the zero were priced instead to yield 13.5% (zeros often carry a lower rate than comparable coupon bonds). M.D. Sass Investors Services, Inc., estimates you'd have to reinvest at between 11% and 12% to earn a comparable return on a 15% conventional bond. If you're deciding between a zero and a traditional bond, your broker can quote you a "break-even" reinvestment rate.

So whether you buy a zero or a conventional bond depends to a great extent on whether you think interest rates will fall and how far.

The company issuing your zero-coupon bond could default without having paid you any interest. But there are ways to hedge your bets. A number of brokers have zero-coupon "unit trusts" that invest in a portfolio of bonds. At least one firm, Merrill Lynch, offers a federally insured zero-coupon certificate of deposit.

Source: "Zeroing in on Zero Coupon Bonds." *Changing Times,* July 1982, p. 8.

securities with unusual coupon or repayment provisions; most are issued by corporations, though they are being used increasingly by municipal issuers as well. Variable-rate notes, zero-coupon bonds, put bonds, and extendable notes are all examples of specialty issues. One of the oldest is the *variable-rate note*; first issued in this country in 1974, it has two unique features: (1) After the first 6 to 18 months of an issue's life, the coupon "floats" so that every six months it is pegged at a certain amount above prevailing Treasury bill or Treasury note rates; and (2) after the first year or two, the notes are redeemable (at par and at the holder's option) every six months. Thus, variable-rate notes represent long-term commitments on the part of borrowers (they're usually issued with 15- to 25-year maturities), yet they provide investors with all the advantages (especially price stability) of short-term obligations.

The specialty issue most popular with investors is the *zero-coupon bond.* As the name implies, such issues have no coupons; rather, much like a Treasury bill, the bonds are sold at a discount from their par value and then pay *nothing* to investors until they mature, at which time the investor receives the full par or stated value of the bond. For example, an investor might pay $250 for a bond, which in 10 years will pay four times the amount of the investment, or $1,000. The difference between the cost of the bond and its value at maturity represents the amount of income earned by the investor. Unfortunately for the individual investor, the IRS has ruled that bondholders must report interest earned on an accrual basis, even though no interest is actually received—for example, in the illustration above, because the investor stands to make $750 over 10 years, he or she would have to report $75 per year on tax returns. Not a very good deal! For this reason, most fully taxable zero coupons should be used only in tax-sheltered investments, like IRAs or Keogh plans.

On the plus side, zero coupons are very attractive because they enable the individual investor to lock in a high return without the risk of reinvesting periodic interest payments. There are several popular variations of the zero-coupon concept, including compound interest bonds (issued by municipalities, the attractive feature of these securities is that the interest accrues tax-free), strip bonds (a practice of separating the coupons from the bond itself and marketing the various coupon and principal receipts separately, which is all Merrill Lynch does with its Tiger bonds) and the predecessor of zero coupons, original-issue deep discount bonds, which are nothing more than new issues coming out with coupons that are much below current market rates (a bond with a 6 percent coupon in a 14 percent market). Figure 11.1 shows an announcement of a recent zero-coupon bond issue, and illustrates how the spread between purchase price and par value widens as maturity lengthens (a necessary condition to maintain a desired yield to the investor).

Another specialty issue is the *put bond.* Such an issue gives the holder the right to redeem bonds before they mature—usually, this can be done five years after the date of issue, and then every one to five years thereafter. In return for the right to periodically "put the bond" for redemption, the investor receives a lower yield (but it is fixed for the life of the issue). Finally, there are *extendable notes,* which are actually short-term securities, typically with one- to five-year maturities, which can be redeemed or renewed for the same period at a new interest rate. For example, an issue might come out as a series of 3-year renewable notes, over a period of 15

A registration statement relating to these securities has been filed with the Securities and Exchange Commission but has not yet become effective. These securities may not be sold nor may offers to buy be accepted prior to the time the registration statement becomes effective. This advertisement shall not constitute an offer to sell or the solicitation of an offer to buy nor shall there be any sale of these securities in any State in which such offer, solicitation or sale would be unlawful prior to registration or qualification under the securities laws of any such State.

$400,000,000

Money Multiplier Notes*
(Zero Coupon)

Price to the Public per Note	Amount Payable at Maturity per Note	Approximate Maturity
$500.00	$1,000	June 1987
$250.00	$1,000	July 1992
$166.67	$1,000	November 1995
$125.00	$1,000	August 1998
$100.00	$1,000	July 2000

In lieu of interest, a purchaser of Money Multiplier Notes will receive 2, 4, 6, 8 or 10 times the original investment if the Notes are held to maturity. Money Multiplier Notes will be offered at the prices shown above and will be payable at maturity at $1,000 per Note. The actual maturities of the Notes will be established on the offering date expected in mid April 1982 and will reflect general market conditions and demand for the Notes.

This proposed new issue of securities is designed primarily for IRAs, Keogh plans, IRA rollovers, pension plans and other investors not subject to federal income taxes.

Allied Corporation reports its operations under five business segments: chemicals; fibers and plastics; oil and gas; electrical and electronic; and other operations, which includes health and scientific products, industrial products and automotive safety restraints.

A Preliminary Prospectus, which gives details of the offering, is available now. To obtain a copy, please contact your broker, dealer or investment advisor, or

Copies of the Preliminary Prospectus may be obtained in any State from securities dealers who may legally offer these securities in compliance with the securities laws of such State.

Salomon Brothers Inc

Blyth Eastman Paine Webber
Incorporated

Goldman, Sachs & Co.

E. F. Hutton & Company Inc.

Dean Witter Reynolds Inc.

*Trademark of Salomon Brothers Inc

Figure 11.1   An Announcement of a Zero-Coupon Bond.
This $400 million zero-coupon issue (called "Money Multiplier Notes" by the investment bankers) was issued in 1982 and gave the investor the option of selecting any one of five maturity dates, each with a different purchase price. (*Source: The Wall Street Journal,* April 6, 1982.)

$150,000,000

Three-Year Extendable Notes

Interest on the Notes is payable semiannually on July 15 and January 15 each year, commencing January 15, 1983. The annual interest rate on the Notes until July 15, 1985 is 14.75%. The Notes are repayable at the option of noteholders on July 15, 1985, 1988, 1991 or 1994 at their principal amount together with interest payable to the date of repayment. Any Notes outstanding on July 15, 1997 will mature on that date. The annual interest rate on the Notes will be adjusted on July 15, 1985, 1988, 1991 and 1994, to a rate not less than 102% of the effective three-year Treasury rate.

Price 100%

plus accrued interest from July 15, 1982

Upon request, a copy of the Prospectus describing these securities and the business of the Company may be obtained within any State from any Underwriter who may legally distribute it within such State. The securities are offered only by means of the Prospectus, and this announcement is neither an offer to sell nor a solicitation of any offer to buy.

Goldman, Sachs & Co.

Lehman Brothers Kuhn Loeb
Incorporated

Merrill Lynch White Weld Capital Markets Group
Merrill Lynch, Pierce, Fenner & Smith Incorporated

The First Boston Corporation   Salomon Brothers Inc

Bache Halsey Stuart Shields   Bear, Stearns & Co.   Blyth Eastman Paine Webber   Dillon, Read & Co. Inc.
          Incorporated   Incorporated

Donaldson, Lufkin & Jenrette   Drexel Burnham Lambert   E. F. Hutton & Company Inc.
    Securities Corporation   Incorporated

Kidder, Peabody & Co.   Lazard Frères & Co.   L. F. Rothschild, Unterberg, Towbin
        Incorporated

Shearson/American Express Inc.   Smith Barney, Harris Upham & Co.   Warburg Paribas Becker
                                                    Incorporated   A. G. Becker

Wertheim & Co., Inc.   Dean Witter Reynolds Inc.

William Blair & Company   J. C. Bradford & Co.   Alex. Brown & Sons   A. G. Edwards & Sons, Inc.

Interstate Securities Corporation   Ladenburg, Thalmann & Co. Inc.

Moseley, Hallgarten, Estabrook & Weeden Inc.   Oppenheimer & Co., Inc.   Piper, Jaffray & Hopwood
                                                                                        Incorporated

Rauscher Pierce Refsnes, Inc.   Rotan Mosle Inc.   Thomson McKinnon Securities Inc.

Tucker, Anthony & R. L. Day, Inc.   Wheat, First Securities, Inc.

July 21, 1982

Figure 11.2   A New Three-Year Extendable Note Issue.
Although this $150,000,000 issue has a final maturity some 15 years out, the obligation actually consists of notes that are subject to renewal every three years. (*Source: The Wall Street Journal,* July 22, 1982.)

years; every three years, the notes are extendable for another three years, but at a new yield (coupon) comparable to the market interest rates that prevail at the time of renewal. Figure 11.2 shows an announcement of a $150 million, three-year extendable note issue.

Registered or bearer bonds

Regardless of the type of collateral or kind of issue, a bond may be registered or issued in bearer form. *Registered bonds* are issued to specific owners, and the names of all bondholders are formally registered with the issuer, who keeps a running account of ownership and automatically pays interest to the owners of record by check. In contrast, with *bearer bonds,* the holders of such bonds are considered to be the owners, as the issuing organization keeps no record of ownership; interest is received by "clipping coupons" and sending them in for payment. Bearer bonds were the most prevalent type of issue, but they are destined to become a thing of the past, as Congress has mandated that effective July 1983, all bonds be issued as registered bonds. A typical bond certificate is depicted in Figure 11.3; in this case it is a registered bond.

THE BOND MARKET

Thus far, our discussion has dealt primarily with basic bond features; now we shift our attention to a review of the market in which these securities are traded. The bond market is chiefly over-the-counter in nature, since listed bonds represent only a small portion of total outstanding obligations. In comparison to the stock market, the bond market is more price stable. Granted, interest rates (and therefore bond prices) do move up and down and have become a bit volatile in recent times, but when bond price activity is measured on a daily basis, it is remarkably stable. Table 11.1 lists the value of bonds outstanding at selected yearly intervals. A glance at the table reveals not only the rapid growth of the market, but also its enormous size. We will examine this important and increasingly popular segment of the capital market by looking at available investment vehicles, the market's widespread use of bond ratings, the structure and behavior of interest rates, and several important bond investment considerations.

Available Vehicles

There are issues available in today's bond market to meet almost any type of investment objective and to suit just about any investor (no matter how conservative or aggressive). As a matter of convenience, the bond market is usually divided into five segments, according to type of issuer: Treasury, agency, municipal, corporate, and institutional. As we will see below, each sector has developed its own issue and operating features, as well as trading characteristics.

Treasury bonds

"Treasuries" (or "governments" as they are sometimes called) are a dominant force in the fixed income market, and if not the most popular, are certainly the best

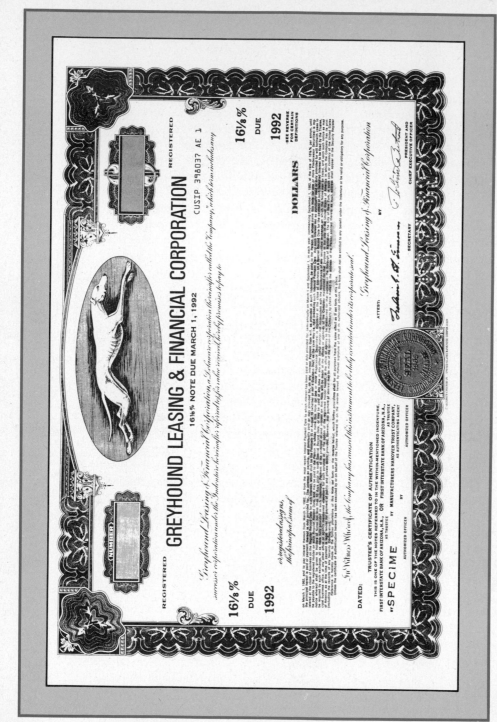

Figure 11.3 A Registered Bond.
This obligation was originally issued as a 10-year note at a time when interest rates were at record highs which accounts for the very high coupon of 16⅛%. It provides the bondholder with annual income of $161.25 for every $1000 bond held, and will mature on March 1, 1992, at which time the bondholder will recover the original investment. (*Courtesy:* The Greyhound Corp.)

TABLE 11.1 ECONOMIC DIMENSIONS OF THE BOND MARKET

Type of Issuer*	YEAR-END AMOUNTS OUTSTANDING (IN BILLIONS)				
	1950	1960	1970	1980	1982
U.S. Treasury	$138.7	$149.5	$159.8	$407.0	$533.6
U.S. agencies	1.1	8.8	17.6	280.7	359.0
States and municipalities	24.0	66.5	144.4	431.8	514.0
Corporations	93.8	105.4	181.0	476.9	542.3
Total	$257.6	$330.2	$502.8	$1596.4	$1948.9

*Excludes institutional issues as such data are not available.
Source: *Federal Reserve Bulletin, U.S. Treasury Bulletin,* and *Survey of Current Business.*

known. The U.S. Treasury issues bonds, notes, and other types of debt securities (such as Treasury bills) as a means of meeting the ever-increasing needs of our federal government. All Treasury obligations are of the highest quality (they are backed by the full faith and credit of the U.S. government) and this feature, along with their liquidity, makes them extremely popular with individuals and institutions. Treasury notes carry maturities of 10 years or less, whereas Treasury bonds have maturities as long as 25 years or more. Except for a few of the older issues, Treasury bonds and notes come in denominations of $1,000 and $10,000, and are issued in registered form. Interest income is subject to normal federal income tax but is exempt from state and local taxes.

Government bonds are either noncallable or issued with very lengthy deferred call features that are measured in relation to the maturity date of the obligation, rather than the date of issue. Deferment features that expire five years before final maturity seem to be most common. Moreover, these deferred call features are a specific part of the bond listing system; for example, the 4¼ percent issue of 1987–92 signifies that this Treasury bond has a maturity date of 1992 and a deferred call feature that extends through 1987. Another unique feature is the unusual capital gains opportunity they offer. That is, many older government bonds can be used, at par, to pay federal estate taxes. It is possible, in effect, to purchase a Treasury issue at a discount and shortly thereafter use it at par to pay estate taxes. Of course, the initial (purchase) transaction has to take place prior to death and the provision is beneficial only to the heirs (and only to the extent that there is a federal estate tax liability). Such bonds have been nicknamed *flower bonds.* Although the Treasury can no longer issue new flower bonds, there are still approximately a half-dozen such issues available in the market, most of which carry 2¾ to 4½ percent coupons and have maturities that range as far out as 1999. This is advantageous to investors, since the lower coupons provide deeper price discounts and therefore more assurance of price appreciation at "the time of departure."

Agency bonds

Agency bonds are the fastest growing segment of the U.S. bond market. These issuers are actually political subdivisions of the U.S. government, although their securities are not direct obligations of the Treasury. An important feature of agencies is that they customarily provide yields comfortably above the market rates for Treasuries; as such, they offer investors a way to increase returns with little or no real difference in risk. There are two types of agency issues—government sponsored and federal agencies. Although there are only six government-sponsored organizations, the number of federal agencies exceeds two dozen. To overcome some of the problems that exist in the marketing of many relatively small federal agency securities, Congress established a Federal Financing Bank in 1974 to consolidate the financing activities of all federal agencies and as a way to realize substantial cost savings. As a rule, the generic term "agency" is used to denote both government-sponsored and federal agency obligations. Table 11.2 provides selected characteristics of some of the more popular government-sponsored and federal agency bonds.

Although these issues are not the direct obligations of the U.S. government, a number of them actually do carry government guarantees and therefore effectively represent the full faith and credit of the U.S. Treasury. Moreover, some have unusual interest payment provisions (interest is paid monthly in a few instances and yearly in one case), and many are exempt from state and local taxes. Except for these provisions, there is really nothing unique about most agency issues. There *is* one issue worth noting, however: *mortgage-backed pass through certificates.* These obligations are issued by the Government National Mortgage Association (GNMA), the Federal National Mortgage Association (FNMA), and other federal agencies involved in home mortgages, and represent an undivided interest in a pool of federally insured mortgages. As a result, they carry coupons related to the interest rate charged in the mortgage market. Bondholders receive monthly payments from the issuer, such payments being made up of both principal and interest. Since the principal part of the monthly cash flow represents return of capital, it is considered tax-free. Not so with interest income, however; it is subject to ordinary federal, state, and local taxes. The issues carry minimum denominations of $25,000 and come with maturities of 20 to 25 years—thought they generally have average lives of about 12 years because so many of the pooled mortgages are paid off early.

Municipal bonds

These bonds are the issues of states, counties, cities, and other political subdivisions such as school districts and water and sewer districts. They are unlike other bonds because their interest income is immune from federal income tax (which is why these issues are known as tax-free bonds). Any capital gains that might be earned from municipals, however, are subject to the usual federal taxes. Normally, the obligations are also exempt from state and local taxes in the state in which they were issued. For example, a California issue would be free of California tax if the bondholder lived in California, but its interest income would be subject to state tax if the investor resided in Connecticut. Municipalities issue two types of bonds: general obligation and revenue bonds. *General obligation bonds* are backed by the full faith

TABLE 11.2 CHARACTERISTICS OF POPULAR AGENCY ISSUES

	Minimum Denomination	Initial Maturity	TAX STATUS*		
			Federal	State	Local
GOVERNMENT SPONSORED					
Federal Intermediate Credit Banks	$ 5,000	9 months to 4 years	T	E	E
Federal Home Loan Bank	10,000	1 to 20 years	T	E	E
Federal Land Banks	1,000	1 to 10 years	T	E	E
FEDERAL AGENCIES					
Farmers Home Administration	25,000	1 to 25 years	T	T	T
Federal Housing Administration	50,000	1 to 40 years	T	T	T
Government National Mortgage Association (GNMA) pass throughs	25,000	1 to 25 years	T	T	T
Tennessee Valley Authority (TVA)	1,000	3 to 25 years	T	E	E
U.S. Postal Service	10,000	25 years	T	E	E
FEDERAL FINANCING BANK	1,000	1 to 20 years	T	E	E

*T = taxable; E = tax exempt.

and credit (and taxing power) of the issuer; *revenue bonds* are serviced from the income generated from specific income-producing projects—for example, toll roads. Although general obligations dominated the municipal market prior to the mid-1970s, the new issue volume of revenue bonds is today far greater than general obligations (for example, in 1982, approximately 72 percent of the new issues were revenue bonds). General obligation bonds are almost universally issued as serial bonds; revenues tend to be mainly term issues. Regardless of the type, municipal bonds are almost always issued in $5,000 denominations.

The tax-free yield is probably the most important feature of municipal bonds and is certainly a major reason why individuals invest in them. Table 11.3 shows what a taxable bond would have to yield to equal the take-home yield of a tax-free bond. It reveals the effects of income brackets on after-tax yield and demonstrates how the yield attractiveness of municipals varies with an investor's income level; clearly, the higher the individual's tax bracket, the more attractive municipal bonds become. A rough rule of thumb suggests that an investor must be in the 30 to 35 percent tax bracket before a municipal bond offers yields that are competitive with fully taxable issues. This is so because municipal yields are substantially lower than

**TABLE 11.3   TAXABLE EQUIVALENT YIELDS
FOR VARIOUS TAX-EXEMPT RETURNS**

Taxable Income, Joint Return ($000)	Tax Bracket (%)	TAX-FREE YIELD*									
		5%	6%	7%	8%	9%	10%	11%	12%	13%	14%
$ 20.2–24.6	22%	6.41	7.69	8.97	10.26	11.54	12.82	14.10	15.38	16.67	17.95
$ 24.6–29.9	25	6.67	8.00	9.33	10.67	12.00	13.33	14.67	16.00	17.33	18.67
$ 29.9–35.2	28	6.94	8.33	9.72	11.11	12.50	13.89	15.28	16.67	18.06	19.44
$ 35.2–45.8	33	7.46	8.96	10.45	11.94	13.43	14.93	16.42	17.91	19.40	20.90
$ 45.8–60.0	38	8.06	9.68	11.29	12.90	14.52	16.13	17.74	19.35	20.97	22.58
$ 60.0–85.6	42	8.62	10.34	12.07	13.79	15.52	17.24	18.97	20.69	22.41	24.14
$ 85.6–109.4	45	9.09	10.91	12.73	14.55	16.36	18.18	20.00	21.82	23.64	25.45
$109.4–162.4	49	9.80	11.76	13.73	15.69	17.65	19.61	21.57	23.53	25.49	27.45
Over $162.4	50	10.00	12.00	14.00	16.00	18.00	20.00	22.00	24.00	26.00	28.00

*Calculations are based on tax tables effective January 1, 1984.

the returns available from fully taxable issues (such as corporates), and unless the tax effect is sufficient to raise the yield on a municipal to a figure that equals or surpasses taxable rates, it is obviously not wise to buy municipal bonds.

We can find out what return a fully taxable bond would have to provide in order to match the after-tax return of a lower yielding tax-free issue by computing what is known as a municipal's *fully taxable equivalent yield*. This measure is simply an adjustment to a municipal bond's yield, and can readily be determined according to the following simple formula:

$$\text{fully taxable equivalent yield} = \frac{\text{yield of municipal bond}}{1 - \text{tax rate}}$$

For example, if a certain municipal offered a yield of 5.75 percent, then an individual in the 40 percent tax bracket would have to find a fully taxable bond with a yield of nearly 9.6 percent—5.75 percent/.6 = 9.583 percent—in order to reap the same after-tax returns as the municipal.

One facet of municipal bonds that is somewhat unusual is the widespread use of *municipal bond guarantees*. These guarantees provide the bondholder with the assurance of a party other than the issuer that principal and interest payments will be made in a prompt and timely manner. As a result, bond quality is improved. The third party, in essence, provides an additional source of collateral in the form of insurance placed on the bond, at the date of issue, which is nonrevocable over the life of the obligation. Four states and two private organizations provide municipal bond guarantees; the two private insurers are the Municipal Bond Insurance Association (MBIA), and the American Municipal Bond Assurance Corporation (AMBAC). Figure 11.4 shows a typical municipal bond issue and illustrates many of the characteristics customarily associated with such obligations.

In the opinion of Bond Counsel, under existing statutes and court decisions, interest on the Series 1982 Bonds is exempt from Federal income taxes. Under the laws of the State of Tennessee, the Series 1982 Bonds and the income therefrom are exempt from state, county and municipal taxation except inheritance, transfer and estate taxes.

New Issue / December 2, 1982

$420,165,000

The Metropolitan Government of Nashville and Davidson County (Tennessee)

Water and Sewer Revenue Bonds, Series 1982

Dated: December 1, 1982 for Serial Bonds, Term Bonds and Term Discount Bonds
Date of Delivery for Zero Percent Discount Bonds
Due: December 1, as shown below

Interest on the Series 1982 Bonds is payable semi-annually on June 1 and December 1 of each year, commencing June 1, 1983. Principal and interest on the Series 1982 Bonds are payable at the principal office of First American Bank of Nashville, N.A., Nashville, Tennessee, paying agent. Commerce Union Bank, Nashville, Tennessee is the trustee for the Series 1982 Bonds. The Series 1982 Bonds will be issued in coupon form, in the denomination of $5,000 each, registrable as to principal at the option of the holder, or in registered form, in the denominations of $5,000 or any whole multiple thereof.

The Series 1982 Bonds will be subject to redemption prior to maturity as more fully described in the Official Statement.

AMOUNTS, MATURITIES, RATES AND YIELDS OR PRICES

$44,865,000 Serial Bonds

Principal Amount	Maturity	Interest Rate	Price	Principal Amount	Maturity	Interest Rate	Price	Principal Amount	Maturity	Interest Rate	Price
$1,835,000	1984	6¼%	100%	$6,270,000	1989	8½%	100%	$1,850,000	1994	9.70%	100%
2,915,000	1985	6¾	100	1,600,000	1990	8¾	100	1,930,000	1995	9.90	100
5,010,000	1986	7¼	100	1,650,000	1991	9	100	2,025,000	1996	10.10	100
5,375,000	1987	7¾	100	1,710,000	1992	9¼	100	2,130,000	1997	10.20	100
5,790,000	1988	8¼	100	1,775,000	1993	9½	100	3,000,000	1998	10.30	100

$44,215,000 Zero Percent Serial Discount Bonds (MBIA Insured)

Principal Amount	Maturity	Interest Rate	Price	Principal Amount	Maturity	Interest Rate	Price	Principal Amount	Maturity	Interest Rate	Price
$5,205,000	1990	0%	$53.00	$5,475,000	1993	0%	$38.50	$5,665,000	1995	0%	$30.50
5,290,000	1991	0	48.00	5,570,000	1994	0	34.50	5,765,000	1996	0	27.00
5,380,000	1992	0	43.00					5,865,000	1997	0	24.00

$47,600,000 10½% Term Bonds Due December 1, 2002 NR*
$20,000,000 10⅝% Term Bonds Due December 1, 2007 NR*
$27,175,000 10¾% Term Bonds Due December 1, 2012, Price 100%
$37,800,000 10½% Term Bonds (MBIA Insured) Due December 1, 2013, Price 100%
$175,975,000 Zero Percent Term Discount Bonds Due December 1, 2013, To Yield 10.685%
$22,535,000 6½% Term Bonds Due December 1, 2014, To Yield 10.475%
(Plus Accrued Interest, if any)   *Not Reoffered

Bonds of particular maturities may or may not be available from the undersigned or others at the above prices on and after the date of this announcement.

The Series 1982 Bonds are being offered for delivery when, as and if issued and received by the Underwriters and subject to the approval of legality by Webster & Sheffield, New York, New York, Bond Counsel. Certain legal matters will be passed upon for the Underwriters by their counsel, Kutak Rock & Huie, Atlanta, Georgia. Certain other legal matters will be passed upon for the Metropolitan Government by Donald W. Jones, Director of Law.

The offering of these Bonds is made only by the Official Statement, copies of which may be obtained in any state from such of the undersigned as may lawfully offer these securities in such State.

E. F. Hutton & Company Inc.   The Cherokee Securities Company

Shearson/American Express Inc.

J. C. Bradford & Co.

Equitable Securities Corporation

Figure 11.4   An Announcement of a New Municipal Bond Issue.
This $420 million issue has serial maturities, though most of the obligation (nearly 80 percent) is due on five rather lengthy terminal dates; note also that part of the issue consists of zero coupons insured by MBIA. (*Source: Business Week,* December 27, 1982.)

Corporate bonds

The major nongovernmental issuers of bonds are corporations. The market for "corporates" is customarily subdivided into several segments, which include industrials (the most diverse of the groups); public utilities (the dominant group in terms of volume of new issues); rail and transportation bonds; and financial issues (banks, finance companies, and so forth). Not only is there a full range of bond quality available in the corporate market, but it also has the widest range of different types of issues. There are first mortgage bonds, convertible bonds (which we will discuss in the next chapter), debentures, subordinated debenture bonds, income bonds, and collateral trust bonds (which are backed by financial assets that can be sold in order to pay off the bonds in case of default). Interest on corporate bonds is paid semi-annually, and sinking funds are popular. The bonds usually come in $1,000 denominations, and are issued on a term basis, with a single maturity date. Maturities usually range from 25 to 40 years, and nearly all corporates carry deferred call provisions that prohibit prepayment for the first 5 to 10 years. Corporate issues are popular with individuals because of their relatively attractive yields.

There are several unusual types of corporate bonds. One is the *equipment trust certificate,* which is issued by railroads (the biggest users of these obligations), airlines, and other transportation concerns. The proceeds from equipment trust certificates are used to purchase equipment, like freight cars and railroad engines, which in turn serve as the collateral for the issue. They are usually issued in serial form and carry uniform annual installments throughout. These bonds normally carry maturities that range from 1 year to a maximum that seldom exceeds 15 to 17 years. An attractive feature of equipment trust certificates is that in spite of a near-perfect payment record that dates back to predepression days, they offer yields to investors that are well above average. *Mortgage-backed bonds* are also used in the corporate sector and were first issued as corporate obligations in September 1977. These securities are issued by banks, savings and loans, and mortgage lenders, and are exactly like GNMA and FNMA pass throughs. In fact, the only real difference is that they are obligations of private corporations and as a result do not enjoy the full faith and credit of the United States government. These bonds are backed by a pool of mortgages, are issued in large denominations ($25,000), and enjoy fairly active secondary markets; they too offer attractive yields and a monthly cash flow to investors, part of which is tax-exempt, since it represents a return of principal.

Institutional bonds

By far the smallest segment of the bond market, these obligations are marketed (usually in $1,000 denominations) by a variety of private, nonprofit institutions like schools, hospitals, and churches. Many of the issuers are affiliated with religious orders, and hospitals have been dominant. The bonds are sometimes called *heart bonds* because of their emotional appeal—some investors actually view investing in these bonds as a charitable activity. Even though these obligations have a virtually spotless default record, institutional bonds regularly provide returns that are 1 to 1½ percentage points above comparable corporates. They do so because the secondary market for these issues is almost nonexistent. However, because these bonds are issued on a serial basis, with relatively short maximum maturities (seldom exceeding 15 to 18 years), an investor can often overcome this deficiency by purchasing maturities that are in line with portfolio needs—thereby reducing (or even eliminating) the need for subsequent trading.

Bond Ratings

Bond ratings are like grades; a letter grade is assigned to a bond issue on the basis of extensive, professionally conducted, financial analysis that designates its investment quality. Ratings are widely used and are an important part of the municipal, corporate, and institutional markets; where such issues are regularly evaluated and rated by one or more of the rating agencies. Even some agency issues, like the Tennessee Valley Authority (TVA), are rated, although they always receive ratings that confirm the obvious—that the issues are prime grade. The two largest and best-known rating agencies are Moody's and Standard & Poor's.

How ratings work

Every time a large new issue comes to the market, it is analyzed by a staff of professional bond analysts to determine default risk exposure and investment quality. The financial records of the issuing organization are thoroughly worked over and its future prospects assessed. Although the specifics of the actual credit analysis conducted by the rating agencies change with each issue, several major factors enter into most bond ratings; for example, with corporate issuers, these include an analysis of the issue's indenture provisions, an in-depth study of the firm's earning power (including the stability of its earnings), a look at the company's liquidity and how it is managed, a study of the company's relative debt burden, and an in-depth exploration of its coverage ratios to determine how well it can service both existing debt and any new bonds that are being contemplated or proposed. (A fee that usually ranges from $500 to $15,000 is charged for rating each corporate bond, and is paid by the issuer or the underwriter of the securities being rated.) The product of all this is a bond rating assigned at the time of issue which indicates the ability of the issuing organization to service its debt in a prompt and timely fashion. Table 11.4 lists the various ratings assigned to bonds by each of the two major services. In addition to the standard rating categories as denoted in Table 11.4, Moody's uses numerical modifiers (1, 2, or 3) on bonds rated double A to B, while S&P uses plus (+) or minus (−) signs on the same rating classes to show relative standing within a major rating category—for example, an A+ (or A1) means a strong, high A rating, but an A− (or A3) indicates the issue is on the low end of the scale. Except for slight variations in designations (Aaa vs. AAA), the meaning and interpretation is basically the same. Most of the time, Moody's and S&P assign identical ratings. Sometimes, however, an issue will carry two different ratings; these are known as *split ratings* and are viewed simply as "shading" the quality of an issue one way or another. For example, an issue might be Aa rated by Moody's, but A or A+ by S&P. Older, outstanding issues are also regularly reviewed to ensure that the assigned rating is still valid. Most issues will carry a single rating to maturity, but it is not uncommon for some to undergo revisions. Finally, although it may appear that the firm is re-

TABLE 11.4 BOND RATINGS

Moody's	S&P	Definition
Aaa	AAA	*High-grade investment bonds.* The highest rating assigned, denoting extremely strong capacity to pay principal and interest. Often called "gilt edge" securities.
Aa	AA	*High-grade investment bonds.* High quality by all standards, but rated lower primarily because the margins of protection are not quite as strong.
A	A	*Medium-grade investment bonds.* Many favorable investment attributes, but elements may be present which suggest susceptibility to adverse economic changes.
Baa	BBB	*Medium-grade investment bonds.* Adequate capacity to pay principal and interest but possibly lacking certain protective elements against adverse economic conditions.
Ba	BB	*Speculative issues.* Only moderate protection of principal and interest in varied economic times.
B	B	*Speculative issues.* Generally lacking desirable characteristics of investment bonds. Assurance of principal and interest may be small.
Caa	CCC	*Default.* Poor-quality issues that may be in default or in danger of default.
Ca	CC	*Default.* Highly speculative issues, often in default or possessing other market shortcomings.
C		*Default.* These issues may be regarded as extremely poor in investment quality.
	C	*Default.* Rating given to income bonds on which no interest is paid.
	D	*Default.* Issues actually in default, with principal or interest in arrears.

Source: Moody's *Bond Record* and Standard & Poor's *Bond Guide.*

ceiving the rating, it is actually the issue. As a result, a firm can have different ratings assigned to its issues; the senior securities, for example, might carry one rating, and the junior issues another, lower rating.

What ratings mean

Most bond investors pay careful attention to ratings since they can affect not only potential market behavior, but comparative market yield as well. Specifically, the higher the rating, the lower the yield of an obligation, other things being equal. Thus, whereas an A-rated bond might offer an 10 percent yield, a comparable triple-A issue would probably yield something like 9½ to 9¾ percent. What is more, investment-grade securities (those that receive one of the top four ratings) are more interest-sensitive and tend to exhibit more uniform price behavior than lower rated (speculative-grade) issues. Most important, bond ratings serve to relieve individual investors from the drudgery of evaluating the investment quality of an issue on their own. Large institutional investors often have their own staff of credit analysts who independently assess the creditworthiness of various corporate and municipal issuers; individual investors, in contrast, have very little (if anything) to gain from conducting their own credit analysis. After all, the credit analysis process is time-consuming and costly, and involves a good deal more expertise than the average individual investor possesses. Most important, the ratings have historically proved to be valid, and they are closely adhered to by a large segment of the bond investment community. Thus, individual investors normally rely on assigned agency ratings as a measure of the creditworthiness of the issuer and an issue's risk of default. A word of caution is in order, however: Bear in mind that bond ratings are intended as a measure of an issue's default risk only, all of which has no bearing on an issue's exposure to market risk. Thus, if interest rates increase, then even the highest-quality issues can (and will) go down in price and subject investors to capital loss and market risk.

Market Interest Rates

The subject of market interest rates is important to every bond investor, and for good reason! For as shown in Figure 11.5, interest rates have risen to new levels in the past decade or so and since the late 1960s, have become increasingly unstable. In fact, look at what's happened to interest rates just since the summer of 1980: From a level of around 10 percent, corporate Aaa rates rose to nearly 16 percent by October 1981, before beginning a retreat that saw Aaa corporate yields fall to less than 11½ percent by year-end 1982. Such behavior, not surprisingly, has significance for both conservative and aggressive bond investors. It is important to conservative investors, since one of their major objectives is to lock in high yields. Aggressive traders also have a stake in interest rates because their programs are built on the capital gains opportunities that accompany major swings in rates. Just as there is no single bond market, but a series of different market sectors, so too there is no single interest rate applicable to all segments of the market. Rather, each segment has its own, somewhat unique, level of interest rates. Granted, the various rates tend to drift in the same direction and to follow the same general pattern of behavior, as shown in Figure 11.5. But the figure also illustrates the kind of rate differentials (or *yield spreads*) that have existed in the various market sectors over time. We can summarize some of the more important market yields and yield spreads as follows:

1. Municipal bonds carry the lowest market rates because of the tax-exempt feature of the obligations; as a rule, their market yields are about two-thirds that of corporates. In the taxable sector, governments have the lowest yields (because they have the least risk), followed by agencies, corporates, and finally, institutional obligations, which provide the highest returns.
2. Those issues that normally carry agency ratings (such as municipals or

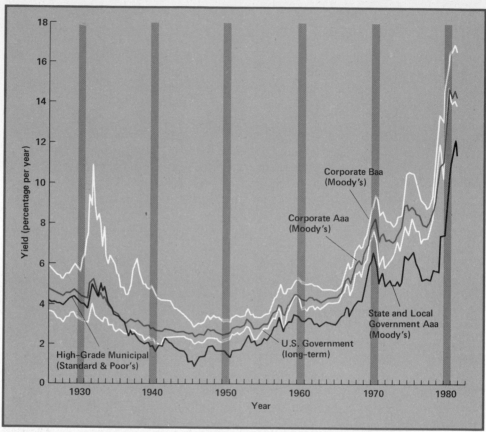

Figure 11.5   Historical Behavior of Selected Market Interest Rates.
Although rates in various sectors of the market are different, they usually tend to drift in the same general direction over time. (*Source: Historical Chart Book, 1982,* Board of Governors of the Federal Reserve System.)

corporates) generally display the same behavior: the lower the agency rating, the higher the yield.

3. There is generally a direct relationship between the coupon an issue carries and its yield—discount (low-coupon) bonds yield the least, and premium (high-coupon) bonds the most.

4. In the corporate sector, industrials generally provide the lowest yields, followed by utilities and rails.

5. In the municipal sector, revenues yield more than general obligations.

6. Bonds that are freely callable provide higher returns, at least at date of issue, than deferred call obligations, with noncallable bonds yielding the least.

7. As a rule, bonds with long maturities tend to yield more than short issues; however, this rule does not hold all the time, since there are periods, such as in 1980–1981, for example, when short-term yields exceeded the yields on long-term bonds.

The preceding list can be used as a general guide to the higher-yielding segments of the bond market. For example, income-oriented municipal bond investors might do well to consider revenue bonds as a way to increase yields; and utilities, rather than industrials, might be selected for the same reason by corporate bond investors.

Investors should pay close attention to interest rates and yield spreads, and try to stay abreast not only of the current state of the market, but also the future direction in market rates. If a conservative (income-oriented) bond investor thinks, for example, that rates have just about peaked out, that should be a clue to try to lock in the prevailing high yields with some form of call protection (such as buying high-yield bonds—like A- or Baa-rated utilities—that still have lengthy call deferments). In contrast, if an aggressive bond trader thinks rates have peaked (and are about to drop), that should be a signal to buy bonds which offer maximum price appreciation potential—like low-coupon bonds that still have a long time to go before they mature. Clearly, in either case, *the future direction of interest rates is important!*

But how does an individual investor formulate such expectations? Unless the investor has considerable training in economics, he or she will have to rely on various published sources. Fortunately, there is a wealth of such information available. One's broker is an excellent source for such reports, as are investor services like Moody's or Standard & Poor's; finally, there are widely circulated business and financial publications—like *The Wall Street Journal, Forbes, Business Week,* and *Fortune*—that regularly address the current state and future direction of market interest rates (one of the best is illustrated in Figure 11.6). Make no mistake, it's not an easy task! And even worse, it's next to impossible to consistently predict the future direction of interest rates with a high degree of precision. But by taking the time to regularly and carefully read some of the publications and reports, the individual investor can readily keep track of the behavior of interest rates and at least get a handle on what is likely to occur in the near future (say over the next 6 to 12 months, maybe more). Such information is vital to serious bond investors, whether they are aggressive or conservative, since it is probably the single most important element in determining the amount of return realized from an investment in bonds.

What causes interest rates to move?

Although the subject of interest rates is a complex economic issue, we do know that certain forces are especially important in influencing the general behavior of market rates. As individual bond investors, it's in our best interests to become familiar with the major determinants of interest rates and to try to monitor these variables—at least in an informal fashion. Perhaps no variable is more important in this regard than inflation. Changes in the inflation rate (or even expectations about the future course of inflation) have had a direct and pronounced affect on market interest rates, and have been a leading cause of the wide swings in interest rates. Clearly, if expectations are for inflation to slow down (enter a period of "disinflation"), then market interest rates should fall as well. Other important determinants (some of which are closely linked with inflation) include: (1) changes in the money supply, (2) the amount of red ink in the federal budget (the size of the federal deficit), and (3) the demand for loanable funds. An increase or big jump in any one of these will put upward pressure on interest rates. Finally, there are the actions of the Federal Reserve—

Bond Prices Drop; U.S. Financing Needs And Uncertainty About Fed Policy Cited

By LYNN ASINOF and EDWARD P. FOLDESSY
Staff Reporters of THE WALL STREET JOURNAL

NEW YORK—Worries about the government's heavy financing needs and uncertainty over the course of Federal Reserve System policy pushed bond prices lower yesterday.

Dealers and investors became especially jittery after the Fed moved to drain reserves from the banking network. Analysts said the action was designed to mop up an unexpected surplus of reserves that had sharply depressed the closely followed interest rate on federal funds in recent days.

Many traders had been hoping the drop in the rate on federal funds, which are reserves banks lend each other, was a sign the central bank would soon cut its discount rate from the current 9% level. Yesterday's move by the Fed "undermined hopes for an imminent discount-rate cut," said Jeffrey R. Leeds, a vice president of Chemical Bank. By draining reserves the Fed indicated that the decline in the funds rates "was technical" and wasn't a product of central-bank policy.

Mr. Leeds and most other economists contend that a cut in the discount rate—the fee charged by the Fed on loans to banks and savings institutions—still is in the cards because of the weak state of the economy. But they say the timing is uncertain.

Albert Wojnilower, chief economist for First Boston Corp., believes the discount rate will be cut to 8½% after the Dec. 21 meeting of the Federal Open Market Committee, the Fed's policy-making arm. It will be "a sort of Christmas present" to the economy, he told a gathering of the First Boston clients.

Although the "economic downturn seems to be bottoming," there isn't "much prospect of any strong economic upturn," Mr. Wojnilower said. "There is virtually no danger of any material rebound in interest rates," he added.

Mr. Wojnilower predicted that short-term interest rates would decline as much as two percentage points by mid-1983. Interest rates on long-term corporate and Treasury issues aren't likely to drop further in coming months and probably will rise a bit by the end of next year, he said.

Traders have been worried that a large supply of new Treasury securities to be auctioned in coming weeks could put some mediate upward pressure on long-t... terest rates. The Treasury today nounce details of an auction notes expected next wee... say this issue could tot... tion, the Treasury... disclose plans fo... funding pack... total abo... In... ha...

Credit Markets

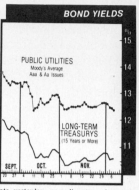

late yesterday, according to underwriters led by Prudential-Bache Securities Inc. The 30-year bonds, priced after auction at 99.64 to yield 12.17%, are rated double-A-3 by Moody's Investors Service Inc. and double-A-minus by Standard & Poor's Corp.

Jewel Cos. Notes

Also offered was a $50 million issue of 11½% Jewel Cos. notes priced at par. Underwriters led by Morgan Stanley & Co. declined to comment on sales of the 10-year notes, which are rated single-A-2 by Moody's and single-A by S&P.

On the tax-exempt front, a $124.4 million offering of general-obligation bonds by Broward County, Fla., got a warm investor reception. About $26 million of the bonds, rated single-A-1 by Moody's and single-A-plus by S&P, remained unsold late yesterday, underwriters said. The bonds were priced to yield from 6.25% in 1984 to 10.4% in 2012.

A $40 million offering of bonds by the Maryland Department of Transportation was off to a somewhat slower sales start. Underwriters said about $15.6 million of the bonds remained unsold late yesterday. Rated single-A-1 by Moody's and double-A by S&P, the bonds were priced to yield from 8.2% in 1991 to 9.2% in 1997.

Figure 11.6   A Popular Source of Information about Interest Rates and Credit Markets.
The "Credit Markets" column appears everyday in *The Wall Street Journal* and provides a capsule view on current conditions and future prospects in the bond market. (*Source: The Wall Street Journal.*)

notably, the level at which it set its discount rate. Figure 11.7 shows the considerable impact inflation and the demand for loanable funds have had on movements in interest rates.

Bond yield curves

Although many factors affect the behavior of market interest rates, one of the most popular and widely studied is bond maturity. As noted above, we would normally expect yields to increase as bond maturities are lengthened. The relationship between yield and maturity is often captured in a *yield curve*, which graphically relates term to maturity to a bond's yield at a given point in time. An example of a yield curve is illustrated below:

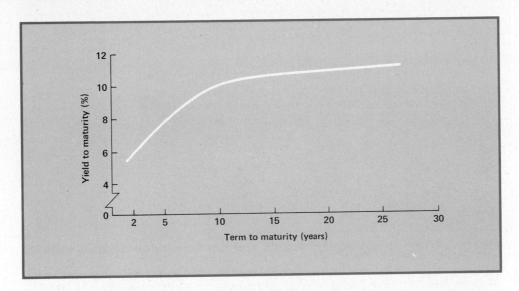

Yield curves are constructed by plotting the yields for a group of bonds that are similar in all respects but maturity; treasury bonds, for example, are homogeneous with respect to quality and issue characteristics, and their yield curves enjoy widespread publicity in the financial media. A yield curve, in effect, depicts how yields respond to changes in maturity. Note in our illustration that bond returns increase with longer maturities. A particular yield curve exists for only a short period of time; as market conditions change, so does its shape and location. It can shift upward, or rather than an ascending curve (as depicted in the illustration), its shape can become flat or even descending. Information about changes in the shape and location of yield curves is helpful in formulating ideas about what interest rates should do in the future, and how they can affect price behavior and comparative returns.

Investing in the Bond Market

In many respects, dealing in bonds is unlike investing in any other type of security. For one thing, the size of the minimum denominations of these issues is much larger than most. Before we examine in detail the various ways that bonds

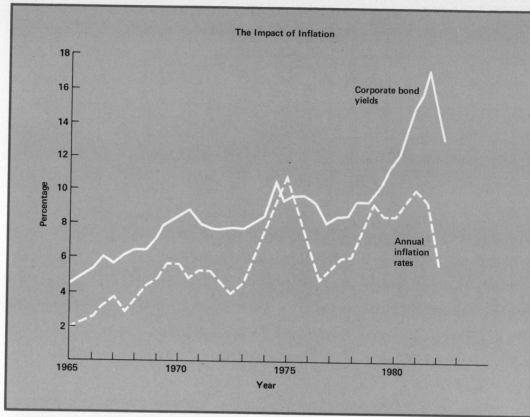

Figure 11.7 The Impact of Inflation and the Demand for Loanable Funds on Interest Rates.
Both inflation and the demand for funds have contributed to the rise in interest rates and to the lofty yields that have existed over the past decade or so in the bond markets. (*Source: Federal Reserve Bulletin* and *Barron's.*)

can be used, we need to look first at the principles of bond price behavior, bond quotes and basic transaction costs, and the advantages and disadvantages of bond ownership.

Principles of bond price behavior

The price of a bond is a function of its coupon, maturity, and movement of market interest rates. When interest rates go down, bond prices go up, and vice versa. However, the extent to which bond prices move in one direction or another depends upon the magnitude of interest rate movements, for the greater the moves in interest rates, the greater the swings in bond prices. But bond prices are more complex than this: for bond price volatility will also vary according to the coupon and maturity of an issue. That is, bonds with lower coupons and/or longer maturities will respond more vigorously to changes in market rates and therefore undergo

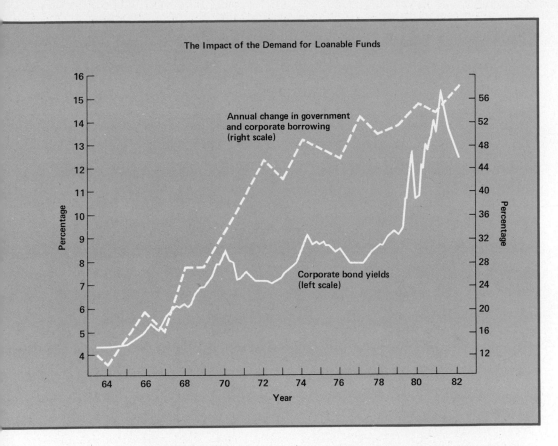

The Impact of the Demand for Loanable Funds

Annual change in government and corporate borrowing (right scale)

Corporate bond yields (left scale)

Year

greater price swings. It should be obvious, therefore, that if a *decline* in interest rates is anticipated, an investor should seek lower coupons and longer maturities (since this would produce maximum amounts of capital gains). When interest rates move *up,* the investor should do just the opposite by seeking high coupons with short maturities; this will cause minimal price variation and act to preserve as much capital as possible.

Reading the quotes

One thing you learn quickly in the bond market is that transactions are not always as easy to conduct as they may seem. In the first place, many bonds have relatively thin markets; some issues may trade only five or ten bonds a week, and many may have no secondary market at all. There are, of course, numerous high-volume issues, but even so, particularly close attention should be paid to an issue's trading volume—especially if an investor is looking for lots of price action and needs prompt order executions. In addition, there is the problem of the lack of market information. For except for Treasury, agency, and some corporate bonds, it is very difficult to readily and conveniently obtain current information on bond prices and other market developments. Finally, investors often have to look to both brokers and

CORPORATES

Bonds	Cur Yld	Vol	High	Low	Close	Net Chg
Pugt 10³/₄83	11.	2	99 7-16	99 7-16	99 7-16	....
Pugt 10.45s85	11.	8	97⅛	97	97	− 2
Puritn 16s97	17.	1	96	96	96	+ 1
QuaStO 9s95	12.	10	78⅛	78⅛	78⅛	....
RCA 4½s92	cv	48	62½	62	62	− ½
RalsP 5¾s00	cv	5	116	116	116	
Ramln 10s00	cv	40	92	92	92	+ ¼
Ramln 10s93	15.	15	67	65⅞	65⅞	− 1⅛
RapA72 7s94	13.	62	55⅜	55⅛	55⅛	− ⅛
RapA69 7s94	13.	57	55⅜	55	55⅜	+ ¼
RapA 6s88	9.2	10	65⅜	65⅜	65⅜	+ ⅝
RapA 10³/₄03	15.	83	72	71⅜	72	+ ⅛
RapA 10³/₄04	15.	4	70⅛	70⅛	70⅛	− 1⅞
RecogE 11s06	cv	4	84	84	84	....
RepStl 8.9s95	14.	12	65	65	65	+ 1
ReshCtr 10½06	cv	10	112	112	112	+ 1⅞
→ RevrG 5½292f	cv	22	41⅛	41⅛	41⅛	....
Revl 8.45s85	8.8	5	95¾	95¾	95¾	+ ½
Rexn 10½285	11.	15	96	96	96	− 1½
Rexn 9¼05	cv	25	85	84½	85	+ ¼
Reyln 7³/₈s01	11.	5	70⅛	70⅛	70⅛	− ⅛
Reyn 10.4590	11.	20	98¼	98¼	98¼	+ ¾
ReyM 4½291	cv	20	58⅛	58⅛	58⅛	....
Ryder 10s94	12.	5	83½	83½	83½	+ 3⅜
SCM 5½s88	cv	10	77¼	77¼	77¼	....
SCM 9¼s90	11.	10	83½	83	83½	+ 1¼
SfgdS d12s96	16.	14	77	77	77	....
StLSaF 4s97	9.1	6	43¾	43½	43¾	+ ¼
StRegP 10s90	11.	15	91½	91½	91½	+ ¾
SanD 10s06	13.	10	79	77½	77½	− 2½
SanD 8³/₄07	13.	15	70	67	67	− 3
Sandrs 5s92	cv	56	100	98¾	100	+ 2
SaveEl 9.8s86	11.	3	89	89	89	+ ½
Savin 11³/₈898	16.	19	74⅝	73⅛	73⅛	+ 1¼
Savin 14s00	16.	10	85⅜	85⅜	85⅜	− 2⅛
Schltz 9½299	14.	3	69⅜	69⅜	69⅜	− ½
Scot 8⅞82000	12.	1	74	74	74	− 1

GOVERNMENTS
U.S. Treasury Issues

Rate	Mat.	Date	Bid	Asked	Bid Chg.	Yld.
9³/₈s,	1982	Dec n..........	100.1	100.5	....	6.48
15⅛s,	1982	Dec n..........	100.14	100.18	+.1	5.33
13⅝s,	1983	Jan n..........	100.24	100.28	−.1	7.14
8s,	1983	Feb n..........	99.29	100.1	+.1	7.64
13⅞s,	1983	Feb n..........	101.7	101.11	....	7.48
9¼s,	1983	Mar n..........	100.7	100.11	+.2	7.97
12⅝s,	1983	Mar n..........	101.7	101.11	+.2	7.96
14½s,	1983	Apr n..........	102.7	102.11	+.1	8.20
7⅞s,	1983	May n..........	99.21	99.25	+.1	8.36
11⅝s,	1983	May n..........	101.6	101.10	+.1	8.42
15⅝s,	1983	May n..........	103.5	103.9	−.1	8.42
3¼s,	1978–83	Jun	97.14	97.30	+.2	7.39
8⅞s,	1983	Jun n..........	100.1	100.5	....	8.58
14⅝s,	1983	Jun n..........	103.5	103.9	....	8.51
15⅞s,	1983	Jul n..........	104.8	104.12	+.1	8.77
9¼s,	1983	Aug n..........	100.4	100.8	....	8.87
11⅞s,	1983	Aug n..........	101.26	101.30	....	8.91
16¼s,	1983	Aug n..........	104.30	108.2	+.1	8.90
9¾s,	1983	Sep n..........	100.16	100.20	−.1	8.93
16s,	1983	Sep n..........	105.7	105.17	....	8.86
15½s,	1983	Oct n..........	105.9	105.17	−.1	8.93
→ 7s,	1983	Nov n..........	98.19	98.23	+.5	8.46
6³/₈s,	1984	Aug	95.9	96.9	+.3	8.79
7¼s,	1984	Aug n..........	96.31	97.7	+.3	9.06
11⅝s,	1984	Aug n..........	102.25	102.29	+.1	9.76
13¼s,	1984	Aug n..........	105.4	105.12	+.3	9.72
12⅛s,	1984	Sep n..........	103.23	103.31	+.2	9.76
9¾s,	1984	Oct	100.2	100.10	+.2	9.57
9⅞s,	1984	Nov n..........	100.9	100.13	+.1	9.64
14³/₈s,	1984	Nov n..........	107.21	107.25	+.1	9.85
16s,	1984	Nov n..........	110.17	110.25	+.2	9.75
14s,	1984	Dec n..........	107.16	107.24	+.2	9.76
8s,	1985	Feb n..........	96.26	97.2	....	9.52
14⅝s,	1985	Feb n..........	108.26	109.2	+.1	9.91
13⅜s,	1985	Mar n..........	106.26	107.2	+.1	9.88
3¼s,	1985	May..........	88	89	....	8.34
4¼s,	1975–85	May..........	89.19	90.19	+.1	8.62
10³/₈s,	1985	May n...........	101.4	101.12	+.2	9.73

Source: The Wall Street Journal.

bankers to complete transactions. This is so because most brokerage houses tend to confine their activities to new issues and to secondary market transactions of listed Treasury obligations, agency issues, and corporate bonds; commercial banks, in contrast, are still the major dealers in municipal bonds and are fairly active in government securities as well.

Except for municipal issues (which are usually quoted in terms of the yield they offer), all other bonds are quoted on the basis of their dollar prices. Such quotes are always interpreted as a percent of par; thus, a quote of 97½ does not equal $97.50, but instead means that the issue is trading at 97.5 percent of the par value of the obligation. If a bond has a par value of $1,000, then a quote of 97½ translates into a dollar price of $975; a par value of $5,000, in contrast, means a dollar price of $4,875. As shown on the facing page, price quotations follow one system for corporate bonds and another for governments.

Corporates are usually quoted in fractions of one-eighths of a point (97⅛), though they will occasionally appear in sixteenths (99⁷⁄₁₆); in contrast, government bonds (Treasuries and agencies) are listed in thirty-seconds of a point. With governments, the figures to the right of the decimal indicate the number of thirty-seconds in the fractional bid or ask. For example, look at the bid price of the 7 percent issue of November 1983; this note (the letter n behind the month of maturity means this is a Treasury Note) has a listed bid price of 98.19. Such a quote translates into a price of 98¹⁹⁄₃₂, or 98.5938 percent of par. Thus, an investor who wants to buy $15,000 of this issue can expect to pay a price of $14,789.07 (.985938 × $15,000). The fractional price of a corporate, in contrast, is included directly in the quote, which need only be converted to a percentage of par to be used. Note the small letter f in the quote for the *RevrC 5½92* issue; the f means that the issue is trading *flat* because the issuer is not presently meeting interest payments on the bond.

Transaction costs

Aside from transfer and sales taxes, which are fairly minimal, the major expense in bond transactions is the brokerage fee paid when bonds are bought and sold. The advent of negotiated commissions has done away with standard commission tables, but we can indicate representative transaction costs that are likely to be incurred when individuals buy bonds (see Table 11.5). The cost of executing small transactions is fairly expensive, but as the size of the transaction increases, the relative cost declines quickly. Consider the cost of acquiring 40 corporate bonds:

For the first 5 bonds	5 × $10.00 =	$ 50.00
For the next 20 bonds	20 × $ 7.50 =	$150.00
For the next 15 bonds	15 × $ 5.00 =	$ 75.00
Total commissions		$275.00

In relation to the $40,000 worth of bonds being purchased, commission costs amount to less than 1 percent. In fact, compared to most other types of securities, bond transaction costs are on the low side.

TABLE 11.5 REPRESENTATIVE BOND TRANSACTION COSTS—BROKERAGE FEES

CORPORATES AND AGENCIES

	Brokerage Fee
First 5 bonds, or $5,000 par value	$10 each bond, or per $1,000 of par value
Next 20 bonds, or $20,000 par value	$7.50 each bond, or per $1,000 of par value
For everything above 25 bonds, or $25,000 par value	$5 each bond, or per $1,000 of par value

TREASURIES

For transactions involving par value of $50,000 or less	Net bid or ask price* plus $20 oddlot charge (per trade)
For transactions involving par value of $50,000 or more	Net bid or ask price*

*The "net" bid or ask price differs from the bid or ask price quotations by the amount of the brokerage fee charged on the transaction.
Source: A major brokerage house.

Advantages and disadvantages of bond ownership

One of the advantages of investing in bonds is the high and competitive rates of return that are available, even with nominal amounts of trading and minimal risk exposure. Another advantage is the occasional opportunity to realize substantial capital gains. Also attractive to some are the tax shields that can be obtained with certain types of issues; municipal obligations are perhaps the best known in this regard, but there are also some unusual advantages to Treasury and agency issues as well.

On the other side, there are disadvantages to investing in bonds. For the individual investor, one of the biggest is the relatively large denominations of the issues. Another is that the coupons are usually fixed for the life of the issue and therefore cannot move up over time in response to the ravages of inflation: 5 percent coupons may have looked good in the early 1960s, but they are not very competitive today. In fact, inflation is probably the biggest worry for bond investors today. Not only does it erode the purchasing power of the principal portion of a bond, but it also has a strong influence on the behavior of interest rates. And as we noted earlier, violent swings in interest rates will lead to violent swings in bond prices, all of which can cause substantial capital losses. A final disadvantage is the often inactive secondary market, which tends to limit the amount of aggressive bond trading and speculation that can take place.

BOND VALUATION AND TRADING

Thus far, most of our discussion has dealt with the technical side of bonds— what they are and how they operate. Now we shift our attention to the bond valuation process and bond trading strategies, where we try to establish what the various bonds are actually worth and how they can be used. Bond investors are basically concerned with two measures of performance: bond yields and bond prices. When evaluated along with interest rate expectations and an issue's technical dimensions (such as call feature and sinking fund), these measures provide important information for making intelligent decisions and formulating sound investment strategies.

Bond Yields and Prices

Yield is the single most important bond market measure and is used in a variety of ways. It serves to track the behavior of the market in general, as well as to measure the return of a single issue. There are basically three types of yield: current yield, promised yield, and realized yield.

Current and promised yields

Current yield is the simplest of all return measures and has the most limited application. It indicates the amount of current income a bond provides relative to its prevailing market price:

$$\text{current yield} = \frac{\text{annual interest income}}{\text{current market price of the bond}}$$

For example, an 8 percent bond would pay $80 per year in interest (for every $1,000 of principal); however, if the bond were currently priced at $800, it would have a current yield of 10 percent ($80/$800 = .10). Current yield is a measure of a bond's annual coupon income and as such would be of interest to investors seeking current income.

Promised yield, the most important and widely used bond valuation measure, evaluates both interest income and price appreciation, and considers total cash flow received over the life of an issue. Also known as "yield to maturity," it indicates the fully compounded rate of return available to an investor, assuming the bond is held to maturity. Promised yield provides valuable insight about an issue's investment merit and is used to determine the competitive attractiveness of alternative vehicles. Other things being equal, the higher the promised yield of an issue, the more attractive it is. Although there are several ways to compute promised yield, the simplest is to use a procedure first introduced in Chapter 4, known as the approximate yield method:

$$\text{promised yield} = \frac{\text{annual coupon income} + \dfrac{\$1,000 - \text{current market price}}{\text{years remaining till maturity}}}{\dfrac{\$1,000 + \text{current market price}}{2}}$$

$$= \frac{C + \dfrac{\$1,000 - P}{N}}{\dfrac{\$1,000 + P}{2}}$$

As an example, consider the following hypothetical situation: Assume a 7½ percent bond (with a par value of $1,000) has 18 years remaining to maturity and is currently priced at $825. Using this information, we see that the promised yield of this bond is:

$$\text{promised yield} = \frac{\$75 + \dfrac{\$1{,}000 - \$825}{18}}{\dfrac{\$1{,}000 + \$825}{2}} = \frac{\$75 + \$9.72}{\$912.50} = \underline{9.28\%}$$

This same approximate yield formula can also be used to find the promised yield to maturity of a zero-coupon bond—the only variation is that the coupon income portion of the equation can be ignored since it will, of course, equal zero. To illustrate, consider a zero-coupon issue that can be purchased for $200, but which will be worth $1,000 at maturity in 15 years. This bond would have a promised yield of:

$$\text{promised yield} = \frac{0 + \dfrac{\$1000 - \$200}{15}}{\dfrac{\$1000 + \$200}{2}} = \frac{0 + \$53.33}{\$600} = \underline{8.89\%}$$

This is only an *approximate* promised yield and, as will be the case with any zero-coupon bond, the precise yield to maturity will always be a bit higher.

Our promised yield figure, although approximate, is nonetheless based on the concept of present value; as a result, it has important reinvestment implications. In particular, the promised yield figure itself is the minimum *required reinvestment rate* the investor must subsequently earn on each of the interim coupon receipts to realize a return equal to or greater than promised yield. The calculated yield-to-maturity figure is only the return "promised" so long as the issuer meets all interest and principal obligations on a timely basis, *and* the investor reinvests all coupon income (from the date of receipt to maturity) at an average rate equal to or greater than the computed promised yield. In our first example above, the investor would have to reinvest (to maturity) each of the coupons received over the next 18 years at a rate of about 9¼ percent. Failure to do so would result in a realized yield less than the 9.28 percent promised. In fact, if the worst did occur and the investor made no attempt to reinvest any of the coupons, he or she would earn a realized yield over the 18-year investment horizon of only 6 percent. Thus, unless it's a zero-coupon bond, a significant portion of a bond's total return over time is derived from the reinvestment of coupons.

Realized yield

Rather than buying an issue and holding it to maturity (as presumed in the promised yield formula), many investors will trade in and out of a bond long before it matures. These investors obviously need a measure of return to assess the in-

Interest rates are peaking ... interest rates are peaking ...

vestment appeal of any bonds they intend to trade. If the anticipated investment horizon is one year or less, it would be appropriate to use the simple holding period return measure described in Chapter 4. When the holding period extends much beyond a year, as many do, *realized yield* should be used to compare the expected payoff of bonds with alternative investment vehicles. It is computed as follows:

$$\text{realized yield} = \frac{\text{annual coupon} + \dfrac{\text{expected future selling price} - \text{current market price}}{\text{years in holding period}}}{\dfrac{\text{expected future selling price} + \text{current market price}}{2}}$$

$$= \frac{C + \dfrac{FP - P}{n}}{\dfrac{FP + P}{2}}$$

This measure is simply a variation of promised yield, as only two variables are changed in the promised yield formula to provide realized yield. Future price is used in place of par value ($1,000), and the length of the holding price is used in place of term to maturity. The future price of a bond has to be determined when computing expected realized yield; this is done by using the standard bond price formula explained below. The most difficult part of coming up with a reliable future price, however, is the estimation of future market interest rates that are expected to exist when the bond is sold. Based on an informal analysis of market interest rates (per the discussion above), the investor estimates a promised yield that the issue is expected to carry at the date of sale, and then uses this yield figure to compute future price.

To illustrate, consider our 7½ percent, 18-year bond again. Assume this time that we anticipate holding the bond for only three years and that we have estimated interest rates will change in the future so that the bond's price will move to about $950 from its present level of $825. (Actually, we did this by assuming interest rates would fall to 8 percent in three years and then used the standard bond price formula to find the value of a 7½ percent, 15-year obligation, which is how many years to maturity an 18-year bond would have at the end of a three-year holding period.) Thus, we are assuming that an investor will buy the bond today at a market price of $825 and sell the issue three years later—after interest rates have declined to about 8 percent—at a price of $950. Given these assumptions, the expected realized yield of this bond would be:

$$\text{realized yield} = \frac{\$75 + \dfrac{\$950 - \$825}{3}}{\dfrac{\$950 + \$825}{2}} = \underline{13.15\%}$$

The better than 13 percent this investment offers is a fairly substantial figure, but keep in mind that this is a measure of *expected* realized yield only. It is, of course, subject to variation if things do no pan out as anticipated, particularly with regard to the market yield expected to prevail at the end of the holding period.

Bond prices

Although yield is an important measure of return, it is occasionally necessary to deal in bond prices. For example, as we saw above, the determination of a bond's future price is an essential ingredient in measuring expected realized yield. Also, some issues (municipals, for example) are regularly quoted on a yield basis and have to be converted to dollar prices. Unlike comparative yield measures, price data cannot be used alone as a basis for making investment decisions, since they are not an indication of return. A basic present value model is used to compute bond price. Along with a table of present value interest factors (see Appendix B, Tables B.3 and B.4), the following information is needed to determine the price of a bond: (1) the annual coupon payment, (2) par value, and (3) the number of years remaining to maturity. The prevailing market yield (or an estimate of future market rates) is then used to compute bond price:

bond price = present value of the annuity of annual interest
payments + present value of the bond's par value

= $(C \times IFA) + (PV + IFS)$

where:

C = Size of annual coupon income
IFA = Present value interest factor for an annuity (Appendix B, Table B.4)
PV = Par value
IFS = Present value interest factor for a single cash flow (Appendix B, Table B.3)

Information on the prevailing (or forecasted) market interest rate is obtained or estimated by the bond investor, and represents the issue's current or expected promised yield. Such yield data, along with the bond's remaining years to maturity, are used in specifying *the appropriate present-value interest factor*. To illustrate the bond price formula in action, let us return to the realized yield problem above and compute the future price of the bond used in that illustration. Recall we were considering the purchase of an 18-year, 7½ percent obligation priced at $825. We expect the market rate to drop in three years to 8 percent and therefore the price of the bond to increase by the anticipated date of sale. Our task at hand is to find the price of this bond three years hence, when it will be a 15-year issue trading at a yield of 8 percent. Using this maturity and interest rate information, we can find the appropriate present value interest factors (in Appendix B, Tables B.3 and B.4) and compute the expected bond price as follows:

bond price = ($75 × present-value interest factor for an annuity of
8% for 15 years) + ($1,000 × present-value interest factor
for a single cash flow of 8% received after 15 years)

= ($75 × 8.560) + ($1,000 × .315) = $957.00

We now have a price that can be used in the realized yield measure. The important thing to remember is that it is the issue's current (or expected) promised yield which is used to determine its price.

Investment Strategies

Generally, bond investors tend to follow one of three kinds of investment programs. First, we have the individual who lives off the income—the conservative, quality-conscious, income-oriented investor who seeks to maximize current income. In contrast, the speculator or bond trader has a considerably different investment objective: to maximize capital gains, often within a very short time span. This highly speculative investment approach requires considerable expertise, as it is based almost entirely on estimates of the future course of interest rates. Finally, there is the serious long-term investor, whose objectives are to maximize total income—to maximize both current income and capital gains over fairly long holding periods.

In order to achieve the objectives of any one of these three programs, an investor needs to adopt a strategy compatible with his or her goals. Professional money managers use a variety of techniques to manage the multimillion-dollar bond portfolios under their direction. They vary from passive approaches, to semi-active strategies (that employ elaborate procedures with equally exotic names like "bond duration," "immunization," and "dedicated portfolios"), to active/fully managed strategies using interest-rate forecasting and yield-spread analysis. Most of these strate-

BOX 11.3 LOCK IN THAT YIELD

Interest rates have fallen so far from the August [1982] peaks that there can scarcely be an issuer of long-term taxable and tax-free bonds who isn't thinking about calling in his higher-cost debt for redemption before maturity. For that reason, it is imperative that holders of such issues be familiar with their call provisions.

Most U.S. Treasury debt is not callable. In theory, at least, the Treasury has the right to redeem some longer-maturity U.S. issues five years before their final due dates. But in fact it's not likely.

But look closely at corporate bonds. Generally, these have covenants prohibiting redemption only for the first five or ten years, particularly when the funds used for refunding would come from the sale of issues carrying lower interest rates. In other words, even though they mature in 25 or 30 years, most corporate debt can be paid off after 5 or 10 years.

Given the sharp decline in interest rates, the Pacific Gas & Electric 16¼s of 2014, which came to market April 1981, look especially attractive right now [November 1982]. Selling at 109, they carry a current return of 15%. How wonderful it would be to get back 15 cents on every dollar of cost for the next 32 years. But here's the hitch: The issue is callable starting Nov. 30, 1985 at a price of $113.69. So if interest rates continue to drop, that 32-year investment could turn out to be a 3-year investment.

Still this high-coupon A-rated bond has its uses—namely, as an *intermediate term* investment carrying high yield. The yield is about 4% greater than on U.S. Treasury notes due in 1985. Moreover, if the bond is not redeemed before final maturity, an investor would continue to receive a juicy 16.25%.

But if you are determined to pin down today's rates for the next 20 to 30 years, then you will have to accept a somewhat lower yield now in exchange for insurance against early call. This can be done through purchase of an older issue, one that came to market bearing coupons substantially lower than those now prevailing. These are termed discount coupon bonds and generally sell substantially below the face amount.

Take the Pacific Gas & Electric 8½s of 2009. These came to market in 1977, when 8.5% was the prevailing rate of return. . . . A $10,000 bond in that issue trades around $6,800. That gives it a current return of 12.5% and a yield to maturity (including appreciation from $6,800 to $10,000) of 12.85%.

In return for that sacrifice of 2% to 3% of current yield, the investor picks up a security that would not be refunded until interest rates are well below the 8.5% coupon.

gies are fairly complex and require considerable computer support. Not surprisingly, the individual investor has considerably different needs and resources than the large institutional investors. As a general rule, the following bond investment strategies are popular with individuals: the buy-and-hold strategy, bond trading based on forecasted interest rate behavior, and bond swaps.

The buy-and-hold technique

This is the simplest strategy and is obviously not a technique unique to bonds. The approach is based on finding an issue with desired quality, coupon, maturity, and indenture provisions (such as call feature), and then holding it for an extended period—often to maturity. The buy-and-hold strategy involves little trading; rather, it seeks modest returns and minimal risk exposure. It is a highly conservative strategy that often involves little more than clipping coupons and collecting income. Many investors who like the basic philosophy of this approach often prefer a modified

BOX 11.3 *Continued*

And if the bonds are called over the next few years, they would be redeemed at a price of 107 or so, bringing a gain of 37 points over today's cost.

The same tradeoff applies to tax-frees. Most issues have provisions permitting the issuer to refund the bonds prior to maturity if interest rates drop. Investors are protected against such redemption for the first five to ten years. After that, the bonds are callable.

If you are considering a tradeoff in taxables, avoid bonds that carry an "original issue discount." The reason is that as the OIDs rise from issue price to par at maturity, the annual gain is subject to income tax each year—even though no cash is received.

A few mutual funds offer an investor an opportunity to buy into a portfolio of discount-priced bonds. Among these are Keystone Discount Bond Fund B-4 and Merrill Lynch Equi-Bond I Fund.

Both funds seek total return rather than just yield. Discount bond prices move faster than current coupon bond prices when interest rates are changing. The Keystone B-4, for example, had a total return of 106% in the past ten years when the Salomon Brothers' high-grade bond index was expanding only 34% and Dow Jones industrial stocks had a total return of 62%. For 1981, Keystone's total return was 10.3% against a decline of 1% for the Salomon bond index and 3.8% for DJI. Charles Morgan, a Keystone portfolio manager, says that he has been swapping out of higher-coupon bonds, and taking profit, and buying lower-coupon issues. At $8.27 a share, the current yield is 11.12%.

The Merrill Lynch Equi-Bond fund, like Keystone, is a load fund. Merrill's up-front charge is 4%, while Keystone starts out with an 8.5% charge. Its portfolio is selected to minimize loss of principal. It does this by investing in discount bonds and a portfolio of common stock designed to match the performance of the S&P's 500 index.

The Salomon Brothers' computation of total rate of return—interest plus appreciation—shows that the bond market posted enormous gains in September [1982], the third consecutive month of improvement. The monthly gains ranged from a low of 3.8% (not annualized) on medium-term Treasury notes to a high of 7.05% on long-term Treasuries. Corporate bonds returned about 6% over the month. During the last 12 months, the total return on bonds as a whole was in the 30%-to-45% range. That's why it is so necessary to take advantage of today's yields. They are considerably lower than the year-ago peaks, but the betting here is that they will go lower still.

Source: Ben Weberman, "Lock in That Yield." *Forbes,* November 8, 1982, p. 263.

version of the tactic. That is, an investment is made with the full intent that, like any buy-and-hold position, it will be held to the end of a fairly lengthy investment horizon; but subsequent trading is endorsed and used as a means of improving portfolio return. The key ingredient for any buy-and-hold strategy is investment vehicles that possess attractive features, maturities, and yields.

Trading on forecasted interest rate behavior

This approach is highly risky, as it relies heavily on the imperfect forecast of future interest rates. It seeks attractive capital gains when interest rates are expected to decline, and the preservation of capital when an increase in interest rates is anticipated. An unusual feature of this tactic is that most of the trading is done with high-grade investment securities, since a high degree of interest sensitivity is required to capture the maximum amount of price behavior. Once interest rate expectations have been specified, this strategy rests largely on technical matters. For example, when a decline in rates is anticipated, aggressive bond investors will often seek long-maturity and low-coupon (discount) issues because this is the best and quickest way of earning capital gains during such periods. These interest swings are usually short-lived, so bond traders try to earn as much as possible in as short a time as possible. Margin trading (or the use of borrowed money to buy bonds) is also used as a way of magnifying returns. When rates start to level off and move up, these investors begin to shift their money out of long, discounted bonds and into high-yielding issues with short maturities; in other words, they do a complete reversal. During these periods, when bond prices are dropping, investors try to preserve their capital position by protecting their money from capital losses and at the same time obtaining a high yield. Thus, such high-yield, short-term obligations as Treasury bills, marketable certificates of deposit, money funds, or even variable rate notes are used.

Bond swaps

In a bond swap, an investor simply liquidates one position and simultaneously buys a different issue in its place; in essence, it is nothing more than the replacement of one bond with another. Swaps can be executed to increase current yield or yield to maturity, to take advantage of shifts in interest rates, to improve the quality of a portfolio, or for tax purposes. Although some are highly sophisticated, most are fairly simple transactions. They go by a variety of colorful names, such as "profit take-out," "substitution swap," and "tax swap," but they are all used for one basic reason: to seek portfolio improvement. We will briefly review two types that are fairly simple and have considerable appeal for individual investors: the yield pickup swap and the tax swap.

In a yield pickup swap, an investor switches out of a low-coupon bond into a comparable higher-coupon issue in order to realize an automatic and instantaneous pickup of current yield and yield to maturity. For example, you would be executing a yield pickup swap if you sold the 20-year, A-rated 6½ percent bonds you held (which were yielding 8 percent at the time) and replaced them with an equal amount of 20-year, A-rated, 7 percent bonds that were priced to yield 8½ percent. By executing the swap, you would be able to improve your current yield (by moving from coupon income of $65 a year to $70 a year), as well as your yield to maturity (which would rise from 8 to 8½ percent). The mechanics are fairly simple, and any investor can execute such swaps by simply watching for swap candidates and/or by asking your broker to do so. In fact, the only thing one has to be careful of is that commissions and transaction costs do not eat up all the profits.

The other type of swap popular with many individual investors is the tax swap; it is also relatively simple and involves few risks. The technique would be used whenever an investor has a substantial capital gains tax liability as a result of selling some security holdings at a profit; the objective is to execute a bond swap in such a way that the (long-term) capital gains tax liability can be eliminated or substantially reduced. This is done by selling an issue which has undergone a capital *loss* and replacing it with a comparable obligation. For example, assume that an investor held $10,000 worth of corporate bonds for a period of three years and sold the securities (in the current year) for $15,000, resulting in a long-term capital gain of $5,000. The investor can eliminate the tax liability that accompanies the capital gain by selling securities that have long-term capital losses of $5,000. Let's assume the investor finds he holds a 20-year, 4¾ percent municipal bond which, strictly by coincidence of course, has undergone the needed $5,000 drop in value. The investor has the needed tax shield in his portfolio, so now all he has to do is find a viable swap candidate. Suppose he finds a comparable 20-year, 5 percent municipal issue currently trading at about the same price as the issue being sold. By selling the 4¾s and simultaneously buying a comparable amount of the 5s, the investor will not only increase his tax-free current yield (from 4¾ to 5 percent), but also eliminate the capital gains tax liability. The only caution that should be kept in mind is that identical issues cannot be used in such swap transactions, since the IRS would consider this a wash sale (see Chapter 6) and therefore disallow the loss. Moreover, it should be clear that the capital loss must occur in the same taxable year as the capital gain. These are the only limitations and explain why this technique is so popular with individual investors, particularly at year end, when tax loss sales (and tax swaps) multiply as investors hurry to establish capital losses.

SUMMARY

Interest in bonds has increased substantially in recent years as higher and more volatile interest rates have attracted both income- and capital-gains-oriented investors to the bond market. A bond is basically a debt security representing a loan between the issuer and an investor; the bondholder receives periodic interest payments and repayment of principal at a specified date in the future. Although traditionally the domain of large institutions such as banks, retirement funds, and insurance companies, the bond market has in the past decade or so become attractive to individual investors as well. The high interest rates that have been available for the past 15 years offer investors bond yields that are competitive with and in many cases superior to the total returns historically available from the stock market. Dramatic shifts in interest rates have offered excellent opportunities for capital gains as well. And tax-free municipals have become attractive as inflation has pushed more and more individuals into higher tax brackets.

Bonds offer a number of features that make them attractive to investors. Promised coupon payments, for example, provide fixed income for those who require current returns for living expenses. Because of their senior position, bonds are relatively secure and usually are viewed as relatively default-free vehicles. There is price risk, however, as even the highest-grade bonds will fall in price when interest rates begin to move up. In effect, since the provisions of a bond are fixed at the time of issue, changes in market conditions will cause the price of the bond to change.

Although the vast majority of bond trading is done in the over-the-counter market, many corporate and most government issues are also traded on various bond exchanges and are regularly quoted in the financial media in a manner similar to that for common stocks. Individual investors may purchase bonds through a brokerage house or commercial bank at commission rates that are competitive with, and often lower than, common stocks. Basically, the bond market is divided into five segments: Treasuries, agencies, municipals, corporates, and institutional issues. Treasury obligations are issues of the U.S. Treasury and have maturities that extend for more than 25 years; they are a dominant force in the bond market and are considered to be virtually default-free. Agency bonds are issued by various political subdivisions of the U.S. government and are the fastest-growing segment of the bond market. The municipal market deals in the issues of state and local governments. Municipal bonds are tax-exempt and come in two types: general obligations, which are backed by the full taxing powers of the issuer, and revenue bonds, which rely on the receipts from specified projects for their payment. In the corporate market, the bonds are backed by the assets and profitability of the issuing company. Municipal and corporate issues are regularly rated for their level of safety by independent rating agencies. A rating of Aaa indicates an impeccable record; lower ratings, such as A or Baa, indicate less protection for the investor. As with all financial investments, the returns required of lower-quality instruments are higher than those required of high quality bonds.

The value of a bond depends on certain issue characteristics and the behavior of interest rates. Several measures of return are important to investors. Promised yield, or yield to maturity, is one of them; it captures both current yield and capital gains. In making a bond investment decision, the investor should use yield to maturity or expected realized yield as the measures of return. By estimating the yield expected to prevail at the end of the investment horizon, the bondholder can project the total return from interest receipts and the expected selling price of the bond. Such estimates are the basis for several trading strategies, including buy-and-hold and more aggressive strategies like those based on forecasted interest rate behavior; even many bond swaps are based on these types of yield evaluations.

KEY TERMS

agency bond	municipal bond
bearer bond	municipal bond guarantee
bond ratings	noncallable bond
bond swap	par value
call feature	premium bond
call premium	principal
call price	promised yield
corporate bond	put bond
coupon	realized yield
current yield	refunding provision
debenture	registered bond
deferred call feature	required reinvestment rate
denomination	revenue bond
discount bond	serial bond
equipment trust certificate	sinking fund
extendable notes	split ratings
flower bond	subordinated debenture
freely callable bond	term bond
fully taxable equivalent yield	term to maturity
general obligation bond	Treasury bond
heart bond	variable rate note
income bond	yield curve
institutional bond	yield spread
maturity date	yield to maturity
mortgage-backed bond	zero-coupon bond
mortgage bond	

REVIEW QUESTIONS

1. Note some of the major advantages and disadvantages of investing in: (a) Treasury bonds, (b) agency issues, (c) municipal issues, (d) corporate bonds, and (e) institutional obligations.

2. Do issue characteristics (such as coupon and call features) affect the yield and price behavior of bonds? Explain.

3. A 6 percent, 15-year bond has 3 years remaining on a deferred call feature (call premium is equal to 1 year's interest); the bond is currently priced in the market at $650. What is the issue's current yield and promised yield?

4. Is there a single market rate of interest applicable to all segments of the bond market, or does a series of market yields exist? Explain and note the investment implications of such a market environment.

5. Why is the reinvestment of interest income so important to bond investors?

6. An investor is in the 35 percent tax bracket. He is trying to decide which of two bonds to purchase: one is a 7½ percent corporate bond which is selling at par; the other is a municipal bond with a 5¼ percent coupon, which is also selling at par. If all other features of these two bonds are comparable, which should the investor select? Explain why.

7. Why is interest sensitivity so important to bond speculators? Does the need for interest sensitivity explain why active bond traders tend to use high-grade issues? Explain.

8. Two bonds have par values of $1,000; one is a 5 percent, 15-year bond priced to yield 8 percent and the other is a 7½ percent, 20-year bond priced to yield 6 percent. Which of these two has the lower price?

9. Treasury securities are guaranteed by the U.S. government; therefore, there is no risk in ownership of such bonds. Briefly discuss the wisdom (or folly) of this statement.

10. Is risk of default important in the bond evaluation and selection process? Explain.

11. Why should an investor be concerned with the trading volume of a particular issue?

12. Compute the current yield of a 10 percent, 25-year bond that is currently priced in the market at $1,200.

13. What are the unusual tax features of: (1) Treasury issues; (2) agency obligations; and (3) municipal bonds?

14. What three attributes are most important in determining an issue's price volatility? Explain.

15. Assume that an investor pays $800 for a long-term bond that carries an 8 percent coupon; in three years she hopes to sell the issue for $850. If her hopes come true, what realized yield would this investor earn? What would her holding period return be if she is able to sell the bond (at $850) after only six months?

16. Explain why interest rates are important to both conservative and aggressive bond investors. What causes interest rates to move, and how can individual investors monitor such movements?

17. What is a tax swap, and why are such transactions so popular with individual investors?

18. An investor is considering the purchase of a 7 percent, 20-year bond that is presently priced to yield 12 percent. Based on extensive analysis of market interest rates, he thinks rates will fall so that over the course of the next two years the market yield of this issue will drop to 9 percent. If his expectations are correct, what kind of realized yield will the investor earn on this bond? What is the major risk of this investment?

CASE PROBLEMS

11.1 MIKE AND JAY LUTZ DEVELOP A BOND INVESTMENT PROGRAM

Mike and Jay Lutz, along with their two teenage sons, Lou and Lamar, live in Jenks, Oklahoma. Mike is in his late thirties and works as an electronics salesman, while Jay is a personnel officer at a local bank; together, they earn an annual income of around $40,000. Mike has just learned that his recently departed rich uncle has named him in his will to the tune of some $150,000, after taxes. Needless to say, Mike, Jay, Lou, and Lamar are elated. Mike intends to spend $50,000 of his inheritance on a number of long-overdue family items (like some badly needed remodeling of their kitchen and family room, a new Porsche 944, and braces to correct Lamar's overbite); he wants to invest the remaining $100,000 in various types of fixed income securities. Mike and Jay have no unusual income requirements, health problems, or the like. Their only investment objectives are that they want to achieve some capital appreciation, and they want to keep their funds invested for a period of at least 20 years; they do not intend to rely on their investments as a source of additional current income.

Questions

1. What type of bond investment program do you think would be best suited to the needs of Mike and Jay? Explain.

2. Would you recommend they follow a "buy-and-hold" investment strategy, or that they use some other approach? Explain.

3. List several different types of issues you would recommend, and briefly indicate why you selected each.

4. How big would their investment account be after five years if they were lucky enough to consistently earn an average (after tax) rate of return of 10 percent? How big would it be if they earned 10 percent, but regularly withdrew $10,000 a year for living purposes?

11.2 THE BOND INVESTMENT DECISIONS OF GEORGE JOCK

George and Penelope Jock live in the Boston area, where he has a successful orthodontics practice. The Jocks have built up a sizable investment portfolio and have always had a major portion of their investments in fixed income securities. They adhere to a fairly aggressive investment posture and actively go after both attractive current income and substantial capital gains. Assume that it is now 1984 and George is currently evaluating two investment decisions: one involves an addition to their portfolio, and the other a revision to it.

The Jocks' first investment decision involves a short-term trading opportunity. In particular, George has a chance to buy a 7½ percent, 25-year bond that is currently priced at $852 to yield 9 percent; he feels that in two years the promised yield of the issue should drop to 8 percent.

The second is a bond swap; the Jocks hold some Beta Corporation 7 percent, 2002 bonds that are currently priced at $785. They want to improve both current income and yield to maturity, and are considering one of three issues as a possible swap candidate: (a) Dental Floss, Inc., 7¼ percent, 2002, currently priced at $780; (b) Root Canal Products of America, 6½ percent, 2000, selling at $885; and (c) Kansas City Dental Insurance, 8 percent 2004, priced at $950. All of the swap candidates are of comparable quality and have comparable issue characteristics.

Questions

1. Regarding the short-term trading opportunity:

a. What basic trading principle is involved in this situation?
b. If George's expectations are correct, what will be the price of this bond in two years?
c. What is the expected realized yield of this investment?
d. Should this investment be made? Why?

2. Regarding the bond swap opportunity:

a. Compute the current and promised yields of the bond the Jocks currently hold and each of the three swap candidates.
b. Do any of the three swap candidates provide better current income and/or current yield than the Beta Corporation bond the Jocks currently hold? Which one(s)?

   c. Do you see any reason why George should switch from his present bond holding into one of the other three issues? If so, which swap candidate would be the best choice? Why?

SELECTED READINGS

Arlen, William H. "A Beginner's Guide to Bond Basics." *Fact,* November 1982, pp. 43—45.

Benston, George J. "Interest Rates Are a Random Walk Too." *Fortune,* August 1976, pp. 105—113.

Bettner, Jill. "Projected Yields on Ginnie Maes Lure Savers, But the Mortgage Pools' True Yields are Elusive." *The Wall Street Journal,* October 20, 1980, p. 44.

Bladen, Ashby. "Bonds as a Trading Vehicle." *Forbes,* August 3, 1981, p. 109.

"Bonds: Playing for Capital Gains and Yield." *Business Week,* February 16, 1981, pp. 110—113.

Daly, Margaret. "Investing ABC's: Bonds." *Better Homes and Gardens,* November 1978, pp. 258—263.

"Discount Bonds; Income Now, Capital Gains Later." *Changing Times,* November 1977, pp. 17—18.

"Flat Bonds—Sometimes There's More Fizz Than Fizzle." *Financial World,* December 15, 1978, p. 41.

Hazard, John W. "Locking In Higher Yields." *U.S. News and World Report,* November 1, 1982, p. 89.

Hertzberg, Daniel. "Some Gimmicks Used to Sell Bonds Sour as Rates Fall, Inflation Slows." *The Wall Street Journal,* December 4, 1982, p. 29.

"How to Invest as Rates Fall." *Business Week,* November 23, 1981, pp. 144—147.

"How to Plot an Interest Rate Strategy." *Business Week,* November 12, 1979, pp. 140—144.

"Investing in Tax Exempts." *Business Week,* July 25, 1977, pp. 127—134.

Moffitt, Donald. "Ginnie Mae Pass-Through Certificates Offer High Yields Plus Safety for Cautious Savers." *The Wall Street Journal,* September 18, 1978, p. 38.

Sivy, Michael. "Bonds Unbound." *Money,* August 1981, pp. 55—59.

Sloan, Allan. "Buying Bonds for Riskier Times." *Money,* April 1982, pp. 86—94.

Weberman, Ben. "When BBBs Become AAAs." *Forbes,* April 27, 1981, p. 175.

———. "A Swinger's Guide to Bonds." *Forbes,* June 22, 1981, p. 147.

———. "Good-Bye Safety, Hello Appreciation." *Forbes,* November 10, 1980, p. 260.

"What Those Bond Ratings Mean." *Changing Times,* March 1980, pp. 20—21.

White, Shelby. "Not for Widows, Orphans: But Speculative Opportunities Abound in Junk Bonds." *Barron's,* March 8, 1976, pp. 9, 18.

———. "Many Happy Returns: Savvy Investors Are Beginning to Buy Long-Term Bonds." *Barron's,* July 26, 1982, p. 18.

"Why Investors Bet on Junk Bonds." *Changing Times,* May 1981, pp. 31—33.

The Fundamental Role of Fixed-Income Securities

At the heart of all fixed-income investments lies the general concept of the loan, a form of economic "time exchange" that enables one party to obtain purchasing power in return for a commitment to provide a schedule of future payments. The time exchange concept is almost as basic an act of economic faith as that of money itself. It is no accident that one form of a loan contract is called a "bond," with its implication of the serious commitment undertaken by the debtor. It is also no coincidence that the idea of a loan is tied to a structure of other concepts, such as the stream of interest payments, the rate of interest, and present and future value. This structure of ideas and measurement is fundamental to the analysis of all investments.

There are many interesting parallels between the investment process in the fixed-income securities market and in the equity market. However, fixed-income securities have two distinctive features derived from their basic contractual nature. First, they are readily classified into clear-cut groups of securities. Second, there exists a generally accepted yardstick for measuring the value of a given fixed-income security for at least one class of investor: those who hold their bonds to maturity. This yardstick is, of course, the conventional yield to maturity (and its variants). The level of the overall market is stated in terms of yield to maturity. The relationship between market sectors is expressed in terms of differences, or "spreads," in yields to maturity. The bid and offering market prices of individual securities are quoted as yields to maturity. The relationship between individual securities is also stated as a yield spread.

This general acceptance of yield, together with the clear-cut categories of securities, enables relationships within the bond market to be described in precise terms. In the equity market, however, one does not generally try to measure relationships so closely. This fine resolution of relationships is a unique characteristic of the fixed-income securities market.

Most of the options available to the bond portfolio manager are relationship trades. In practice, the analysis and decision making associated with these trades are almost invariably expressed in terms of yield spreads. The dependence on yield spreads as a relationship measure can

MARTIN L. LEIBOWITZ

perhaps be seen most dramatically in substitution swaps, where trades are often initiated by changes of a few basis points (a few 1/100ths of 1 percent!).

The pervasiveness of conventional yield and yield spread measures in the bond market lays a dual burden on anyone who wishes to analyze or trade in bonds. First, he or she must learn the different manifestations of yield to maturity and yield to call, and then must delve into the more fundamental questions of total prospective return offered by a given debt instrument. He or she must also examine how this prospective return is affected by changing market levels, changing (conventional) yield curves, tax effects, price volatilities, and other factors—all over both fixed and sliding time horizons.

The past decade has witnessed a revolution in the practice of bond portfolio management, brought about partly by the recent heightened level of volatility in interest rates. This, combined with the general trend toward "performance results," has shifted many institutional investors from the traditional "buy-and-hold" approach to a more active and intensive management style. Also, there has been an explosion in the variety of fixed-income securities (e.g., original issue discounts; zero-coupon bonds; mortgage securities; financial futures that relate to fixed-income benchmarks; options on fixed-income securities; floating rate instruments; bonds with puts, calls, and warrants attached; extendables; and retractables). Moreover, developments in new portfolio management techniques—such as various forms of "immunization," hedging, and scenario analysis—can be broadly characterized as methods for attaining better defined patterns of return over time. The combined effect of these events has been to make the bond market into a more exciting and more challenging sector for both institutional and individual investors.

MARTIN L. LEIBOWITZ
Managing Director
Salomon Brothers Inc.

12
Preferred Stock and Convertible Securities

Preferred stocks and convertible securities are corporate issues that hold a senior position to common stock. Although preferreds are actually a form of equity ownership, they, along with convertibles, are considered fixed income securities because their level of current income is fixed. In order to provide a basic appreciation of the investment merits and behavioral characteristics of preferred stock and convertible issues, in this chapter we will examine:

1. The fundamental aspects of preferred stock, including sources of value and risk.
2. Basic rights and claims of preferred stockholders, and some of the popular issue characteristics often found with these securities.
3. Various measures of investment suitability and several preferred stock investment strategies.
4. General characteristics of convertible securities and the nature of the conversion privilege.
5. The evaluation of convertible security returns and the investment techniques that can be used with these obligations.

Convertible securities, initially issued as bonds or preferred stocks, are subsequently convertible into shares of the issuing firm's common stock. Preferred stocks, in contrast, are issued and remain as equity, and derive their name in part from the preferential claim on income they command: That is, all preferred dividends must be paid before any payments can be made to holders of common stock. In many respects, these two issues represent types of *hybrid securities*—there is a bit of equity and debt in both of them. The investment merits of convertibles are based principally on the *equity kicker* they provide; that is, the tendency for the market price of these issues to behave much like the common stock into which they can be converted. Preferred stocks, in contrast, derive their investment value principally from their high current yields. Let us look at the characteristics of each.

PREFERRED STOCKS

Preferred stocks carry a fixed dividend that is paid quarterly and stated either in dollar terms, or as a percentage of the stock's par (or stated) value. By year-end 1982, there were over 875 OTC and listed preferred stocks outstanding, with a market value of some $40 billion. Most preferreds are issued by public utilities, although the number of industrial, financial, and insurance issues is increasing. Preferreds are available in a wide range of quality ratings—from high-grade investment issues to highly speculative stocks. A sample preferred stock is shown in Figure 12.1.

For many years, the preferred stock market was dominated by institutional and corporate investors. But things changed dramatically in the early 1970s, when preferred stocks became increasingly popular with individual investors. Corporate issuers responded by making preferreds more attractive to individuals, principally by reducing the par value on new issues to the $10 to $25 range and by pushing annual dividend levels to new heights. Fixed income investments were thus finally available to individual investors at both reasonable unit prices and attractive current yields.

Preferred Stocks as Investment Vehicles

Preferred stocks are considered hybrid securities because they possess features of both common stocks and corporate bonds. They are like common stocks in that they pay dividends, which may be passed when corporate earnings fall below certain levels. Moreover, preferreds are equity ownership and are issued without stated maturity dates. Preferreds are also like bonds in that they provide investors with prior claims on income and assets, and the level of current income is usually fixed for the life of the issue. Too, preferred stocks can carry call features and sinking fund provisions, and a firm can have more than one issue of preferred outstanding at any point in time. Most important, because these securities usually trade on the basis of the yield they offer to investors, they are in fact viewed in the marketplace as fixed income obligations and, as a result, are competitive with bonds.

Advantages and disadvantages

Investors are attracted to preferred stocks because of their high current income. Moreover, such dividend income is highly predictable, even though it lacks legal backing and can be passed. Figure 12.2 illustrates the yield levels available from preferred stocks and shows how they compare with high-grade bond returns. Note the tendency of preferreds to yield returns that are slightly *less* than those on high-grade bonds. This is due to the fact that 85 percent of preferred dividends received by corporations are tax exempt. Safety is another desirable feature of preferreds. For despite a few well-publicized incidents (such as the passing of preferred dividends by Consolidated Edison in 1974), high-grade preferred stocks have an excellent

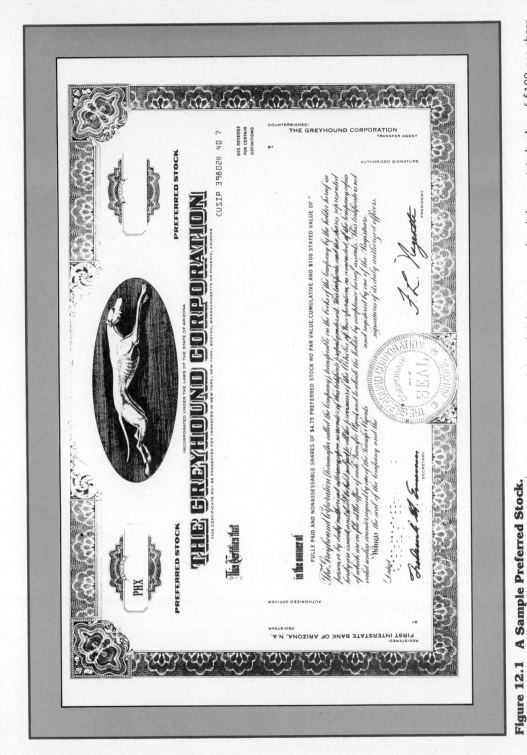

Figure 12.1 A Sample Preferred Stock.
This preferred stock pays an annual dividend of $4.75 per share, and though it has no par value, it has a stated value of $100 per share. The stock is also cumulative, which means that any preferred dividends that are in arrears must be made up in full before dividends can be paid to common stockholders. (*Courtesy:* The Greyhound Corp.)

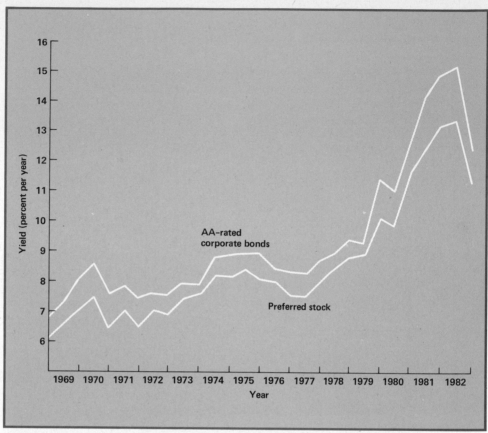

Figure 12.2 Average High-Grade Preferred Stock Yields versus Average Market Yields on AA-Rated Corporate Bonds.
Note how preferred stock yields tend to move in concert with the market behavior of bond returns. (*Source:* Standard & Poor's *Trade and Securities Statistics,* 1982.)

record of meeting dividend payments in a prompt and timely manner. A final advantage of preferred stocks is the low unit cost ($10 to $25 per share) of the issues themselves, which enables even small investors to participate actively in preferreds.

The major disadvantage of preferred stocks is, of course, their susceptibility to the ravages of inflation and high interest rates. Like many financial assets, preferred stocks simply have not proved to be satisfactory long-term hedges against inflation. Another disadvantage is that most preferreds lack substantial capital gains potential. Although it is possible to enjoy fairly attractive capital gains from preferred stocks when interest rates decline dramatically, these amounts generally do not match the price performances of common stocks.

Sources of value

With the exception of convertible preferreds, the value of high-grade preferred stocks is a function of the dividend yield they provide to investors. More specifically, the value (or market price) of a preferred stock is closely related to prevailing market rates. As the general level of interest rates moves upward, so do the yields of preferreds, and their prices decline accordingly; when interest rates drift downward, so will the yields on preferreds, as their prices rise. The price behavior of a preferred stock, therefore, is inversely related to market interest rates. Moreover, its price is directly linked to the issue's level of income—that is, other things being equal, the higher the dividend payout, the higher the market price of an issue. As such, the price of a preferred stock can be defined as follows:

$$\text{price} = \frac{\text{annual dividend income}}{\text{prevailing market yield}}$$

This equation is simply a variation of the dividend yield formula; it is used to price preferred stocks and to compute the future price of a preferred, given an estimate of expected market interest rates. For example, a $2.50 preferred stock (which implies that the stock pays a dividend of $2.50 per year) would be priced at $20.83 if the prevailing market yield were 12 percent.

$$\text{price} = \frac{\$2.50}{.12} = \underline{\underline{\$20.83}}$$

Note that higher prices are obtained with this formula by increasing the dividend level and/or decreasing market yield.

In addition to yield, the value of a preferred stock is also a function of the issue's quality—that is, the lower the quality of a preferred, the higher its yield. Such behavior is, of course, compatible with the risk-return tradeoffs that usually exist in the marketplace. Fortunately, the quality of preferred stocks is also rated, much like bonds, by Moody's and Standard & Poor's. Finally, the value of a preferred is affected by issue characteristics such as call features and sinking fund provisions. For example, freely callable preferreds will normally provide higher yields to investors than noncallable issues because of the greater call risk inherent in the former type of security. Quality and issue features, however, have only slight effects on price behavior over time, and certainly do not compare in importance to the movement of market yields.

Risk exposure

Preferred stock investors are exposed to business risk and interest rate risk. Business risk is important with preferreds, since they are a form of equity ownership and lack many of the legal protections available with bonds. Annual operating costs and corporate financial strength, therefore, are of concern to preferred stockholders. Moody's and S&P preferred stock ratings can be used to assess the amount of business risk embedded in an issue—i.e., higher quality/higher rated issues are believed to possess less business risk. Interest rate risk is important because of the fixed income nature of preferred stocks. In fact, because of the effect of interest rates on the price of investment-quality preferreds, this is generally the most important type of risk. Certainly it can be the most damaging, should interest rates move against the investor.

Transaction costs

Preferred stocks are subject to the same transaction costs as shares of common stock: Brokerage fees and transfer taxes are identical. In addition, preferred investors use the same types of orders (market, limit, or stop-loss) and operate under the same margin requirements. Even the quotes of preferred stock are intermingled with those of common. Fortunately, preferreds are easy to pick out in the financial pages; simply look for the two letters *pf*:

52 Weeks High	Low	Stock	Div.	Yld %	P-E Ratio	Sales 100s	High	Low	Close	Net Chg.
29³⁄₈	17¹⁄₈	BelcoPt	.70	3.6	5	314	19³⁄₄	18	19¹⁄₂	+ 1⁵⁄₈
10¹⁄₈	5³⁄₈	BeldnH	.36	3.8	13	72	9⁷⁄₈	9¹⁄₂	9¹⁄₂	− ³⁄₈
33¹⁄₂	17³⁄₄	BelHow	.96	2.9	11	485	33³⁄₈	32⁷⁄₈	32⁷⁄₈	. . . .
24¹⁄₂	13⁷⁄₈	BellInd	.24	1.0	15	152	24³⁄₈	24	24¹⁄₄	+ ¹⁄₈
18³⁄₄	13¹⁄₄	BelCd	g 2.08	. . .	. . . .	60	u19	18⁷⁄₈	19	+ ¹⁄₄
35¹⁄₂	23¹⁄₂	Bemis	1.60	4.6	11	37	35¹⁄₄	34³⁄₄	34³⁄₄	− ¹⁄₂
82¹⁄₄	45	Bendix	3.32	4.2	14	285	79	78	79	+ ³⁄₈
62¹⁄₂	38¹⁄₄	Bendx	pf4.04	6.7	. . . .	54	60¹⁄₄	60¹⁄₄	60¹⁄₄	. . . .
27¹⁄₈	14⁵⁄₈	BenfCp	2	8.7	13	161	23¹⁄₂	23	23	− ¹⁄₈
33¹⁄₂	24¹⁄₈	Benef	pf4.30	13.	. . . .	4	32¹⁄₈	32¹⁄₈	32¹⁄₈	− ³⁄₈
36¹⁄₂	20	Benef	pf4.50	14.	. . . .	z370	33	32¹⁄₂	33	. . . .
20¹⁄₂	14³⁄₄	Benef	pf2.50	14.	. . . .	z80	18¹⁄₂	18¹⁄₄	18¹⁄₄	− ⁵⁄₈
7¹⁄₈	2¹⁄₄	BengtB	.10e	1.5	15	693	6⁷⁄₈	6¹⁄₂	6¹⁄₂	− ³⁄₈
6⁵⁄₈	2¹⁄₂	Berkey		. . .	44	124	6¹⁄₈	6	6¹⁄₈	+ ¹⁄₈
29¹⁄₄	13³⁄₄	BestPd	.32	1.2	19	309	26¹⁄₄	25³⁄₄	25³⁄₄	− ¹⁄₂
23⁷⁄₈	14¹⁄₂	BethStl	1	5.7	. . . .	832	17⁵⁄₈	17¹⁄₈	17⁵⁄₈	+ ³⁄₈
41³⁄₈	18¹⁄₄	Beverly	.40	1.0	21	330	u42¹⁄₄	40³⁄₈	41¹⁄₄	+ ³⁄₈
30¹⁄₂	15¹⁄₈	BigThr	.72	3.3	9	1206	21³⁄₄	21	21⁵⁄₈	+ ⁵⁄₈
36¹⁄₄	23³⁄₄	Binney	1.20	3.6	11	296	33¹⁄₈	32¹⁄₂	33	− ¹⁄₈
12	2¹⁄₂	BisFSL		. . .	. . . .	288	8³⁄₈	7⁷⁄₈	8	+ ¹⁄₄
19¹⁄₂	12	BlackD	.52	2.9	. . . .	1162	18	17¹⁄₂	17³⁄₄	− ¹⁄₈
32	21⁵⁄₈	BlkHPw	2.40	7.8	6	18	30⁷⁄₈	30³⁄₈	30⁷⁄₈	+ ³⁄₄
45¹⁄₂	21³⁄₄	BlairJn	1	2.2	10	85	45	44	44¹⁄₂	− ¹⁄₄
43	25¹⁄₄	BlckHR	1.92	4.5	13	897	u43³⁄₄	42¹⁄₄	42¹⁄₄	− ³⁄₄
34¹⁄₂	20¹⁄₂	BlueB	1.80	6.0	10	121	29⁷⁄₈	29¹⁄₈	29⁷⁄₈	+ ³⁄₈
35	15	Boeing	1.40	4.3	11	3017	33⁷⁄₈	32³⁄₄	32³⁄₄	− 1¹⁄₈
40¹⁄₄	19³⁄₄	BoiseC	1.90	5.2	27	160	37¹⁄₄	36¹⁄₈	36⁵⁄₈	+ ⁵⁄₈
52¹⁄₂	26⁷⁄₈	Borden	2.22	4.3	9	1387	52¹⁄₄	51	51³⁄₄	+ ³⁄₈
40³⁄₄	22	BorgWa	1.52	4.1	9	458	37³⁄₄	37¹⁄₄	37³⁄₈	− ⁵⁄₈
10	2	Bormns		1.4	5	382	u10³⁄₄	9⁷⁄₈	10³⁄₄	+ ⁷⁄₈
24³⁄₄	20	BosEd	2.80	12.	8	106	24¹⁄₂	24¹⁄₄	24¹⁄₄	. . . .
70	57¹⁄₂	BosE	pf8.88	13.	. . . .	z360	69¹⁄₂	69	69	. . . .
10	7⁷⁄₈	BosE	pf1.17	12.	. . . .	16	9⁵⁄₈	9¹⁄₂	9⁵⁄₈	− ¹⁄₈
12¹⁄₈	9³⁄₈	BosE	pf1.46	13.	. . . .	47	11¹⁄₂	11¹⁄₈	11³⁄₈	− ¹⁄₈
35¹⁄₂	22⁷⁄₈	BrigSt	1.36a	4.1	12	99	33¹⁄₂	33	33¹⁄₄	. . . .
74	50³⁄₄	BristM	2.10	3.0	14	912	71¹⁄₄	69	69	− 1
77	54	BrstM	pf 2	2.7	. . . .	3	74¹⁄₂	74¹⁄₂	74¹⁄₂	+ 1
26	17¹⁄₂	BritPt	1.71e	8.9	4	48	19⁵⁄₈	19¹⁄₄	19¹⁄₄	− ¹⁄₄
17¹⁄₂	8	Brock	.10	.9	14	1178	11¹⁄₄	10³⁄₄	11¹⁄₄	+ ¹⁄₂
17⁷⁄₈	12⁵⁄₈	Brckwy	1.32	7.7	8	1079	17³⁄₄	17¹⁄₄	17¹⁄₄	− ¹⁄₄
31¹⁄₈	22³⁄₈	BkyUG	2.70	9.6	6	59	28¹⁄₄	27⁵⁄₈	28	+ ¹⁄₄
33¹⁄₄	25	BkUG	pf3.95	12.	. . . .	1	32³⁄₄	32³⁄₄	32³⁄₄	− ¹⁄₄
19⁵⁄₈	10³⁄₄	BwnSh	.20	1.8	. . . .	15	11¹⁄₂	11¹⁄₄	11³⁄₈	+ ¹⁄₈
61	26¹⁄₄	BwnGp	1.96	3.2	11	468	u61¹⁄₂	58³⁄₄	61¹⁄₂	+ 1
55¹⁄₄	24¹⁄₂	BwnFer	1.20	2.2	18	181	55¹⁄₄	53³⁄₄	55¹⁄₈	+ ³⁄₈

Source: The Wall Street Journal

The quotes are interpreted exactly like those for common stock, except that the price/earnings ratio is not listed. Note also that the preferreds are always listed after the common stock of the firm. Here we see that Boston Edison (*BosEd*) has three issues of preferred stocks outstanding; they pay annual dividends of $8.88 per share, $1.17 per share, and $1.46 per share, respectively, and at current market prices provide current yields of 12 to 13 percent. Observe also the relatively low unit cost of the stock, as two of the preferreds are priced at less than $12 per share and the third is moderately priced at $69 per share. As an aside, note the small letter *z* in the volume (or sales) column of the $8.88 preferred; this symbol has important meaning to serious preferred stock traders since it signifies *the actual number of shares traded,* rather than the round lot volume—that is, in this instance, there was a total of only 360 shares traded.

Issue Characteristics

Preferred stocks possess features that not only distinguish them from other types of securities, but also help differentiate one preferred from another. For example, preferred stocks may be issued as convertible or nonconvertible, although the majority fall into the nonconvertible category. A conversion feature allows the holder to convert preferred stock into a specified number of shares of the issuing company's common stock. Because convertible preferreds are, for all intents and purposes, very much like convertible bonds, a thorough examination of this vehicle will be deferred to later in the chapter; at this point, we'll concentrate on nonconvertible issues, though many of the features and measures of investment merit we are about to discuss are equally applicable to convertible preferreds.

In addition to convertibility, several key features of preferred stocks should be understood by investors, including the rights of such stockholders, the provisions for cumulative and participating dividends, call features, and sinking fund provisions.

Right of preferred stockholders

The contractual agreement of a preferred stock specifies the rights and privileges of a preferred stockholder. The most important of these deal with the level of annual dividends, the claim on income, voting rights, and the claim on assets. The issuing company agrees that it will pay stockholders a (minimum) fixed level of quarterly dividends, and that such payments will take priority over common stock dividends. The only condition is that the firm generate income sufficient to meet the preferred dividend requirements. The firm, however, is not legally bound to honor the dividend obligation. Of course, the company cannot pass dividends on preferred stocks and then turn around and pay dividends on common stock, as this would clearly violate the preferreds' prior claim on income. Although most preferred stocks are issued with dividend rates that remain fixed for the life of the issue, in the early 1980s some began to appear with floating dividend rates. Known as *adjustable (or floating) rate preferreds,* the dividends on these issues are adjusted quarterly in line with yields on specific Treasury issues. Figure 12.3 shows an announcement of a $200 million floating rate preferred stock. Note that while the quarterly dividend rate will be tied to the returns on Treasury obligations, in no case can the (annual) dividend rate fall below 7.50 percent or rise above 15.25 percent.

Although they hold an ownership position in the firm, preferred stockholders normally have no voting rights. If, however, conditions are bad and the firm needs to pass one or more consecutive quarterly dividends, preferred shareholders are usually given the right to elect a certain number of corporate directors so that their views may be represented. If liquidation becomes necessary, the holders of preferreds are given a prior claim on assets. These preferred claims, limited to the par or stated value of the stock, must be satisfied before those of the common stockholders. Of course, this does not always mean that the full par or stated value of the preferred will be recovered, since the claims of senior securities, like bonds, must be met first.

Cumulative provisions

Most preferred stocks are issued on a *cumulative* basis. This means that any preferred dividends passed must be made up in full, and this obligation must be met

This advertisement is neither an offer to sell nor a solicitation of an offer to buy any of these securities.
The offering is made only by the Prospectus.

July 29, 1982

4,000,000 Shares

Ætna

Aetna Life and Casualty Company

Cumulative Floating Rate Preferred Stock

(Stated Value $50 Per Share)

The dividend rate through September 30, 1982 will be 13.20% per annum. For each quarter thereafter, dividends will be at the rate of .90% below the highest of the three-month U.S. Treasury bill rate, U.S. Treasury ten-year constant maturity rate and U.S. Treasury twenty-year constant maturity rate, determined in advance. However, the dividend rate for any quarter will in no event be less than 7.50% or greater than 15.25% per annum.

Price $50 Per Share

and accrued dividends from date of issue

Copies of the Prospectus may be obtained in any State in which this announcement is circulated from only such of
the underwriters, including the undersigned, as may lawfully offer these securities in such State.

WARBURG PARIBAS BECKER
A.G.BECKER

THE FIRST BOSTON CORPORATION

SALOMON BROTHERS INC

MORGAN STANLEY & CO.
Incorporated

GOLDMAN, SACHS & CO.

MERRILL LYNCH WHITE WELD CAPITAL MARKETS GROUP
Merrill Lynch, Pierce, Fenner & Smith Incorporated

BACHE HALSEY STUART SHIELDS
Incorporated

BEAR, STEARNS & CO.   BLYTH EASTMAN PAINE WEBBER
Incorporated

DILLON, READ & CO. INC.

DONALDSON, LUFKIN & JENRETTE   DREXEL BURNHAM LAMBERT   E. F. HUTTON & COMPANY INC.
Securities Corporation   Incorporated

KIDDER, PEABODY & CO.   LAZARD FRERES & CO.   LEHMAN BROTHERS KUHN LOEB
Incorporated   Incorporated

L. F. ROTHSCHILD, UNTERBERG, TOWBIN   SHEARSON/AMERICAN EXPRESS INC.

SMITH BARNEY, HARRIS UPHAM & CO.   WERTHEIM & CO., INC.   DEAN WITTER REYNOLDS INC.
Incorporated

Figure 12.3   A New Floating Rate Preferred Stock Issue.
The quarterly dividend on this preferred stock varies with U.S. Treasury yields; note, however, that it does have a minimum (7.50%) and maximum (15.25%) dividend rate. (*Source: Investment Dealer's Digest*, August 3, 1982.)

before dividends can be restored to common stockholders. Thus, as long as the dividends on preferred stocks remain in *arrears* (which denotes that there are outstanding unfulfilled preferred dividend obligations), a corporation will not be able to make dividend payments on common shares. Assume, for example, that a firm normally pays a $1 quarterly dividend on its preferred stock, but has missed paying the dividend for three quarterly payments. In this case, the firm has preferred dividends in arrears of $3 a share, which it is obligated to meet along with the next quarterly dividend payment. It could fulfill this obligation by paying, say, $2 per share to the preferred stockholders at the next quarterly dividend date, and $3 per share at the following one (the $3 would cover the remaining $2 arrears and the current

---

BOX 12.1 HOW TO USE USABLE BONDS

"Usable bonds" are a little-known variety of subordinated debentures that benefit from rising stock prices but, unlike convertibles, do not require the bondholder to play the equities markets. So far, they have been issued by a relatively small number of companies, usually to sweeten a debt financing.

Here's how usables work: The issuer sells units, each made up of a debenture and a detachable stock purchase warrant. Through exercise of the warrants, the debentures can be used at face value in lieu of cash to pay for the company's stock at the price specified on the warrant. That's why they're called usable bonds. The debentures carry maturities of 10 to 20 years, while the warrants usually expire in about 5 years. The two split apart after issue and trade separately in the secondary market.

What happens when investors who bought the warrants decide to exercise them? They could, of course, ignore the bonds and simply pay cash for the stock. But most warrant holders don't do this; they go looking for debentures to match up with warrants. Why? Because many usable bonds sell at a discount; many, in fact, were issued below par. So for the warrant holders, buying the debentures at 75 cents or 80 cents on the dollar and exchanging them at face value for stock beats paying cash. The result is that as the warrants' expiration date draws near, demand for the debentures forces their price up.

So what's the best way to play all this? Buy the debentures and ignore the warrants, says Larry Post, fixed-income-analyst with the Los Angeles high-yield bond department of Drexel Burnham Lambert. Holding both is the equivalent of a convertible; to an extent, you're playing the market. If you buy the warrants only, it's a straight stock market play. But if you buy only the debenture—and buy carefully—you have a standard fixed-income investment, often with a generous yield, which may ultimately benefit as well from upward movement in the stock.

Source: Forbes, July 18, 1983, p. 163.

$1 quarterly payment). Only at this point could the firm resume dividend payments to common stock. If the preferred stock had carried a *noncumulative* provision— and some do—the issuing company would have no obligation to make up any of the passed dividends. Of course, the firm could not make dividend payments on common stock either; but all it would have to do to resume such payments would be to meet the next quarterly preferred dividend. Other things being equal, a cumulative preferred stock should be more highly valued than an issue without such a provision—that is, it should increase the price (and in so doing lower the yield) of these issues.

Participating preferreds

Most preferred stocks do not carry participating provisions. Occasionally, however, a preferred is issued on a *participating* basis, which means that the preferred stockholder can enjoy additional dividends if payments to common stockholders exceed a certain amount. This type of preferred stock not only specifies the annual dividend, but also sets a maximum common stock dividend. Once that maximum has been met, any additional dividends to common stockholders must be shared on a specified basis (perhaps 50–50) with preferred stockholders. For example, assume the maximum common stock dividend is $2 per share and the participation provision calls for equal participation. Under these conditions, if the firm wanted to pay another $1 per share to common stockholders, it would have to also pay an equal amount ($1 per share) to the participating preferred stockholders. And unless the provision is subsequently amended, the company would have to continue to pay participating dividends to preferred stockholders for as long as the amount of dividends to common shareholders exceeded the maximum. Obviously, with the tendency for common stock dividends to increase over time, the participating provision has considerable appeal to preferred stockholders and, other things being equal, increases the value of these issues.

Call features

Beginning in the early 1970s, it became increasingly popular to issue preferred stocks with call features. Today many preferreds carry this provision, which gives the firm the right to call the preferred for retirement. Usually, preferreds are issued on a deferred-call basis, meaning that they cannot be called for a certain number of years after the date of issue. After the deferral period, which often extends for five to seven years, the preferreds become freely callable. Of course, such issues are then susceptible to call if the market rate for preferreds declines dramatically, which explains why the yields on freely callable preferreds should be higher than those on noncallable issues. As with bonds, the call price of a preferred is made up of the par value of the issue and a call premium that generally amounts to approximately one year's dividends.

Sinking fund provisions

Another preferred stock feature that became popular in the 1970s was the sinking fund provision, which denotes how (all or a part of) an issue will be amortized, or paid off, over time. Such sinking fund preferreds actually have implied maturity dates. They are used by firms to reduce the cost of financing (sinking fund issues yield less). A typical sinking fund preferred might require the firm to retire half the issue over a 10-year period by retiring, say, 5 percent of the issue per year. Unfortunately, the investor has no control over which shares are called for sinking fund purposes.

Evaluating Preferreds

Evaluating the investment suitability of preferreds involves an assessment of comparative return opportunities. Let us look now at some of the return measures that are important in this regard, as well as the role of agency ratings in the evaluation process.

Dividend yield: A critical measure

Dividend yield is the key in determining the price and return behavior of most preferred stocks. It is computed according to the following simple formula:

$$\text{dividend yield} = \frac{\text{annual dividend income}}{\text{preferred stock price}}$$

The *dividend yield* is a reflection of an issue's current yield, and is the basis on which comparative preferred investment opportunities are evaluated. Here is how it works: Suppose an 8 percent preferred stock has a par value of $25 and is currently trading at a price of $20 per share. The annual dividend of this stock is $2. For preferreds whose dividends are denoted as a percent of par (or stated) value, the dollar value of the annual dividend is found by multiplying the dividend rate (of 8 percent) by the par value (of $25). The dividend yield in this example is:

$$\text{dividend yield} = \frac{\$2}{\$20} = \underline{\underline{10\%}}$$

The 10 percent figure represents the "promised" yield of this particular preferred issue. In practice, we would expect investors to compute, or have available, a current dividend yield measure for each preferred under consideration, and then to make a decision by assessing the yields offered with alternative preferreds—relative, of course, to the risk and issue characteristics of each.

A variation of this dividend yield formula was shown earlier as the way to determine preferred stock price (preferred stock price = annual dividend income divided by dividend yield). Long-term investors consider promised dividend yield critical in their investment decisions; short-term traders, in contrast, generally center their attention on anticipated price behavior and the expected return from buying and selling the issue over a short period of time. Thus, the expected future price of a preferred is important to short-term traders. It is found by first forecasting future market interest rates, and then using this information to determine expected future price. To illustrate, suppose a preferred stock pays $3 in dividends and its yield is expected to decline to 6 percent within the next two years. If such market rates prevail, then two years from now, the issue would have a market price of $50 (annual dividend ÷ yield = $3 ÷ .06 = $50). This forecasted price, along with the current market price and level of annual dividends, would be used to compute the expected realized yield from the transaction.

To continue the example, if the stock were currently priced at $28 per share, the expected realized yield of this issue (over the two-year investment horizon) would be a very attractive 35.9 percent:

$$\text{realized yield} = \frac{\text{annual dividend} + \dfrac{\text{expected future selling price} - \text{current market price}}{\text{years in holding period}}}{\dfrac{\text{expected future selling price} + \text{current market price}}{2}}$$

$$= \frac{\$3 + \dfrac{\$50 - \$28}{2}}{\dfrac{\$50 + \$28}{2}} = \frac{\$3 + \$11}{\$39} = \underline{\underline{35.9\%}}$$

Such information is used to judge the relative attractiveness of preferred stock. Other things being equal, the higher the expected realized yield figure, the more appealing the investment.

Book value

The *book value* (or *net asset value*) of a preferred stock is simply a measure of the amount of debt-free assets supporting each share of preferred stock. Book value is found by subtracting all the liabilities of the firm from its total assets and dividing the difference by the number of preferred shares outstanding. It reflects the quality of an issue with regard to the preferred's claim on assets. Obviously, a preferred with a book (or net asset) value of $150 per share enjoys generous asset support, and more than adequately secures a par value of, say, $25 a share. Net asset value is most relevant when it is used relative to an issue's par or stated value; other things being equal, the quality of an issue improves as the margin by which book value exceeds par or stated value increases.

Fixed charge coverage

This is a measure of how well a firm covers its preferred dividends; attention is on the firm's ability to service its preferred stock and live up to the preferred's preferential claim on income. As such, it is an important ingredient in determining the quality of a preferred issue. Fixed charge coverage is computed as follows:

$$\text{fixed charge coverage} = \frac{\text{earnings before interest and taxes (or EBIT)}}{\text{interest expense} + \dfrac{\text{preferred dividends}}{.5}}$$

The preferred dividends are adjusted by a factor of .5 (which is equivalent to multiplying dividends by 2) to take account of corporate taxes and to place preferred dividends on the same base as interest paid on bonds (recall that bond interest is tax deductible, whereas preferred dividends are not). Other things being equal, the higher the fixed charge coverage, the greater the margin of safety (a ratio of 1.0 means the company is generating just enough earnings to meet its preferred dividend payments—certainly not a very healthy situation). A coverage ratio of 0.5 would suggest the potential for some real problems, whereas a coverage of, say, 5.0 would indicate that the preferred dividends are rather secure.

Agency ratings

Standard & Poor's has long rated the investment quality of preferred stocks, and since 1973, so has Moody's. S&P uses basically the same rating system as with bonds; Moody's uses a slightly different system. Figure 12.4 shows Moody's system and indicates why the various ratings are assigned. These agencies evaluate and assign ratings largely on the basis of their judgment regarding the relative safety of dividends. Although preferreds come with a full range of agency ratings, most tend to fall in the medium-grade categories (a and baa); generally speaking, higher agency ratings reduce the market yield of an issue and increase its interest sensitivity. Agency ratings are important to serious, long-term investors, as well as to those who use preferreds for short-term trading. Not only do they eliminate much of the need for fundamental analysis, but they also reveal the yield and potential price behavior of an issue.

Rating Symbol	Definition
aaa	Indicates a "top quality" issue which provides good asset protection and the least risk of dividend impairment.
aa	A "high grade" issue with reasonable assurance that earnings will be relatively well-protected in the near future.
a	"Upper medium grade." Somewhat greater risk than aa and aaa, but dividends are still considered adequately protected.
baa	"Lower medium grade." Earnings protection adequate at present, but may be questionable in the future.
ba	A "speculative" type issue, its future earnings may be moderate and not well safeguarded. Uncertainty of position is common for this class.
b	Generally lacking in desirable investment quality, this class may have little assurance of future dividends.
caa–c	Likely to already be in arrears on dividend payments. These categories are reserved for securities that offer little or no likelihood of eventual payment.

Note: Preferred stock ratings should not be compared with bond ratings as they are not equivalent; preferreds occupy a position junior to the bonds.

Figure 12.4 Moody's Preferred Stock Rating System.
These agency ratings are intended to provide an indication of the quality of the issue and are based largely on an assessment of the firm's ability to pay preferred dividends in a prompt and timely fashion. (*Source:* Moody's Investor's Service, Inc.)

Investment Strategies

Several investment strategies can be followed by preferred stockholders. As we will learn, these are useful in meeting different investment objectives and offer different levels of return and risk.

Using preferreds to obtain attractive yields

This strategy is perhaps the most popular use of preferred stocks and is ideally suited for serious long-term investors. High current income is the objective here, and the procedure basically involves seeking out those preferreds with the most attractive yields. Of course, consideration must also be given to such features as the quality of the issue, the cumulative/participating nature of dividends, and its call feature. Certainty of income and safety are important in this strategy, since yields are attractive only as long as dividends are paid. Some investors may never buy anything but the highest-quality preferreds. Others may sacrifice quality in return for higher yields when the economy is strong, and use higher-quality issues only during periods of economic distress. But whenever the investor leaves one of the top four agency ratings, he or she must recognize the speculative position he or she is assuming and the implications it holds for an investment portfolio. This is especially so with preferreds, since their dividends lack legal enforcement. Individual investors should keep in mind, however, that this investment strategy generally involves a *yield give-up* relative to what could be obtained from comparably rated corporate bonds. For as we saw in Figure 12.2, preferreds usually generate somewhat lower yields than bonds, even though they are less secure and may be subject to a bit more risk.

Trading on interest rate behavior

Rather than assuming a "safe" buy-and-hold position, the investor who trades on interest rates adopts an aggressive short-term investment posture. This is done for one major reason: capital gains. Of course, although a high level of return may be possible with this approach, it is not without the cost of higher risk exposure. Because preferreds are fixed income securities, the market behavior of investment-grade issues is closely linked to the movements in interest rates. If market interest rates are expected to decline substantially, attractive capital gains opportunities may be realized from preferred stocks. As is probably clear by now, this strategy is identical to that used by bond investors; in fact, many of the same principles used with bonds apply equally well to preferred stocks. For example, it is important to select high-grade preferred stocks, since interest sensitivity is an essential ingredient of this investment configuration. Moreover, margin trading is often used as a way of magnifying short-term holding period returns. A basic difference is that the very high leverage rates of bonds are not available with preferreds, since they fall under the same (less generous) margin requirements as common stocks. The investment selection process is simplified somewhat, since neither maturity nor the size of the annual preferred dividend (which is comparable to a bond's coupon) have an effect on the *rate of price volatility;* that is, a $2 preferred will appreciate just as much (percentagewise) as an $8 preferred for a given change in market yields.

Speculating on turnarounds

This speculative investment strategy can prove profitable, but it can be followed only rarely. The idea is to find preferred stocks whose dividends have gone into arrears and whose rating has tumbled to one of the speculative categories. The price of the issue, of course, would be depressed to reflect the corporate problems of the issuer. There is more to this strategy, however, than simply finding a speculative-grade preferred stock: The hard part is to uncover a speculative issue whose fortunes, for one reason or another, are about to undergo a substantial turnaround. This requires sound fundamental analysis of the corporate issuer, and the ability to predict such situations before they are widely recognized in the marketplace. The tactic is obviously highly risky and is in many respects akin to investing in speculative common stock. In essence, the investor is banking that the firm will undergo a turnaround, and will once again be able easily to service its preferred dividend obligations. Un-

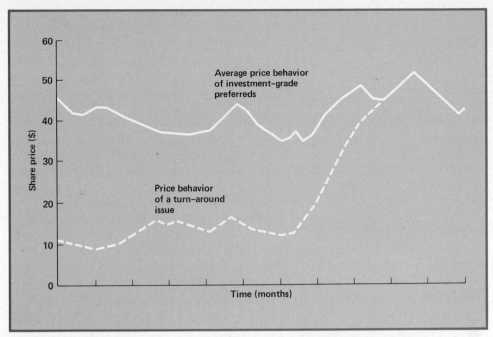

Figure 12.5 Illustrative Price Pattern of a Hypothetical Preferred "Turn-around" Candidate.
Although the turnaround issue will seek the price level of other preferreds of comparable quality and dividend payout, this level also acts as a type of price cap and clearly limits capital appreciation.

fortunately, although rewards can be substantial, they are somewhat limited. For example, if the turnaround candidate is expected to recover to a single-a rating, we would expect its capital gains potential to be limited by the price level of other a-rated preferreds. This condition is depicted in Figure 12.5. As can be seen, while price performance may be somewhat limited, it is still substantial and can readily amount to holding period returns of 100 percent or more. But in view of the substantial risks involved, these returns are certainly not out of line.

Using convertible and participating preferreds

The investor following this strategy uses certain preferred stock features to go after speculative opportunities and the chance for attractive returns. The use of convertible preferreds is based on the equity kicker of the issue and the belief that it will provide generous price appreciation. Convertibles will be reviewed in detail below; at this point suffice it to say that as the price of the underlying common stock appreciates in value, so will the market price of a convertible preferred. This strategy can offer handsome returns, but remember that such investors are actually speculating on the common stock dimension of the convertible preferred, and therefore it is the equity position of the issue that should be subjected to scrutiny. In essence, the investor seeks equity situations that hold considerable promise for appreciation and then, rather than buying the common stock of the firm, purchases its convertible preferred instead.

Participating preferreds are fairly rare, but the use of such issues can sometimes prove rewarding so long as the issuing firm is enjoying prosperity and is likely to be in a position to declare participating dividends to preferred stockholders. It works like this: If the investor believes strongly that the fortunes of the firm are such that the likelihood of a declared participating dividend is fairly high, the purchase of that preferred may be appropriate. Of course, the investor would want to see to it that the market has not already discounted such a possibility; this can be done by making sure that the issue is not trading at a yield well below comparable preferreds (which would happen if the price of the preferred were forced up by the likelihood of a participating dividend). Assuming this is not the case, given the manner in which preferred stocks are priced, a participating dividend very likely would lead to an increase in the price of the stock. For example, consider a $4 preferred stock that is priced to yield 6 percent; this issue would be trading at about $67. If the firm declared a participating dividend of, say, $1 per share, the price of the stock should jump to about $83, so long as it continues to yield 6 percent. The catch, of course, is to identify a participating preferred before it actually begins to participate, and that there is some assurance that the firm will continue to pay this level of participating dividend for the foreseeable future.

CONVERTIBLE SECURITIES

Convertible issues, more popularly known simply as "convertibles," represent still another type of fixed income security. They are also hybrid and, although possessing the features and performance characteristics of both a fixed income security and equity, should be viewed primarily as a form of equity. Most investors commit their capital to such obligations not because of the attractive yields they provide, but rather because of the potential price performance the stock side of the issue offers. In fact, it is always wise to determine whether a corporation has convertible issues outstanding whenever you are considering a common stock investment, for there may well be circumstances in which the convertible will be a better investment than the firm's common stock.

Convertibles as Investment Outlets

Convertible securities are popular with individual investors because of the *equity kicker* they provide. They are issued by all types of corporations, and in 1982 there were over 750 convertible bonds and several hundred convertible preferreds available to investors. They are usually viewed as a form of *deferred equity* because they are intended to be converted eventually into shares of the company's common stock. Not surprisingly, whenever the stock market is strong, convertibles tend to be strong; when the market softens, so does interest in convertibles. Convertible bonds and convertible preferreds are both equally linked to the equity position of the firm, and are therefore usually considered interchangeable for investment purposes. Except for a few peculiarities, such as the fact that preferreds pay dividends rather than interest, and do so on a quarterly basis rather than semi-annually, convertible bonds and convertible preferreds are evaluated similarly. Our discussion will be mostly in terms of bonds, but the information and implications apply equally well to both.

Convertible bonds

Convertible bonds are issued as debentures (long-term, unsecured corporate debt), but carry the provision that within a stipulated time period, the bond may be converted into a certain number of shares of the issuing corporation's common stock. Generally, there is little or no cash involved at the time of conversion, since the investor merely trades in the convertible bond for a stipulated number of shares of common stock. Figure 12.6 depicts a new convertible bond issue announcement. The bondholder is the one who has the right to convert the bond at any time, but more commonly the issuing firm will initiate conversion by calling the bonds—a practice known as *forced conversion*. Convertibles are issued as freely callable bonds to provide the corporation with the flexibility to retire the debt and force conversion. To force conversion, the corporation would call for the retirement of the bond and give the bondholder one of two options: to convert the bond into common stock, or to redeem the bond for cash at the stipulated call price (which, in the case of convertibles, contains very little call premium). So long as the convertible is called when the market value of the stock exceeds the call price of the issue, seasoned investors would never choose the second option. Instead, they would opt to convert the bond, as the firm wants them to. After the conversion is complete, the bonds no longer exist; instead, there is additional common stock in their place.

Conversion privilege

The key element of any convertible issue is its *conversion privilege,* which stipulates the conditions and specific nature of the conversion feature. To begin with, it states exactly when the debenture can be converted. Generally, there will be an initial waiting period of six months to perhaps two years after the date of issue, during which time the debenture cannot be converted. The *conversion period* then begins, after which the issue can be converted at any time. Although the conversion period typically extends for the rest of the life of the debenture, it may exist for only a certain number of years. This is done to provide the issuing firm with more control over its capital structure, and means that if the issue has not been converted at the end of its conversion period, it then reverts to a straight debt issue with *no* conversion privilege.

From the investor's point of view, the most important item of information is the conversion price, or conversion ratio. These terms are used interchangeably and specify the number of shares into which the bond can be converted. *Conversion ratio* denotes the number of common shares into which the bond can be converted; *conversion price* indicates the stated value per share at which the common stock will be delivered to the investor in exchange for the bond. For example, a $1,000 convertible bond might stipulate a conversion ratio of 20, or that the bond can be converted into 20 shares of common stock. This same privilege could be stated in

This announcement is neither an offer to sell nor a solicitation of an offer to buy any of these securities.
The offer is made only by the Prospectus.

May 19, 1982

MCI

$250,000,000

MCI Communications Corporation

10% Convertible Subordinated Debentures due May 15, 2002
Interest Payable May 15 and November 15

The Debentures are convertible into shares of MCI Common Stock at $45 per
share (equivalent to a conversion rate of approximately 22.22 shares of Common Stock
for each $1,000 principal amount of Debentures), subject to certain adjustments.

Price 100%
(Plus accrued interest from May 15, 1982)

*Copies of the Prospectus may be obtained in any State only from such of the undersigned
and the other several underwriters as may lawfully offer the securities in such State.*

Shearson/American Express Inc.		**Drexel Burnham Lambert** Incorporated
Bache Halsey Stuart Shields Incorporated	**Bear, Stearns & Co.**	**Dillon, Read & Co. Inc.**
Kidder, Peabody & Co. Incorporated	**Lazard Frères & Co.**	**Lehman Brothers Kuhn Loeb** Incorporated
L. F. Rothschild, Unterberg, Towbin	**Salomon Brothers Inc**	**Warburg Paribas Becker** A. G. Becker
Sanford C. Bernstein & Co., Inc.	**Alex. Brown & Sons**	**Hambrecht & Quist**

Figure 12.6   A New Convertible Bond Issue Announcement.
Observe that each bond in this $250 million debenture is convertible (at a conversion price
of $45 per share) into 22.22 shares of common stock ($1,000 par value divided by $45
conversion price) any time prior to maturity. (*Source: Institutional Investor,* June 1982.)

terms of a conversion price—that the $1,000 bond may be used to acquire stock in the corporation at a "price" of $50 per share. (One basic difference between a convertible debenture and a convertible preferred is that while the conversion ratio of a debenture generally deals with large multiples of common stock, such as 15, 20, or 30 shares, the conversion ratio of a preferred is generally very small, often less than 1 share of common and seldom exceeding more than 2 or 3 shares.)

The conversion ratio is generally fixed over the conversion period, although some convertibles are issued with variable ratios/prices. In such cases, the conversion ratio decreases (while the conversion price increases) over the life of the conversion period to reflect the supposedly higher value of the equity. The conversion ratio is also normally adjusted for stock splits and significant stock dividends to maintain the conversion rights of the investor. As a result, if a firm declares, say, a 2-for-1 stock split, the conversion ratio of any of its outstanding convertible issues would also double. When the ratio includes a fraction, such as $33\frac{1}{3}$ shares of common, the conversion privilege will specify how any fractional shares are to be handled: either the investor can put up the additional funds necessary to purchase another full share of stock at the conversion price, or the investor can receive the cash equivalent of the fractional share (at the conversion price). Table 12.1 lists some basic features of a number of actively traded convertible bonds and preferreds, and reveals a variety of conversion privileges.

Sources of value

Because convertibles are fixed income securities linked to the equity position of the firm, they are normally valued in terms of both the bond and the stock dimensions of the issue. In fact, it is ultimately the stock and the bond dimensions of the convertible which give the security its value. This, of course, explains why it is so important to analyze the underlying common stock *and* formulate interest rate expectations when considering convertibles as an investment outlet. Let's look first at the stock dimension.

Convertible securities will trade much like common stock—in effect, they derive their value from the common stock—whenever the market price of the stock is equal to or greater than the stated conversion price. Assume, for example, that a convertible carries a conversion ratio of 20 and that the market price of the common is greater than the conversion price ($50) of the convertible. For every point the common stock goes up (or down), the convertible will move in the same direction by a multiple of 20. In essence, whenever a convertible trades as a stock, its market price will approximate a multiple of the share price of the common, with the size of the multiple being defined by the conversion ratio.

When the price of the common is depressed, so that its trading price is well below the conversion price, the convertible will loose its ties to the underlying common stock and begin to trade as a bond. The issue should then trade according to prevailing bond yields, which would prompt an investor to focus major concern on market rates of interest. However, because of the equity kicker and their relatively low agency ratings, convertibles generally do not possess high interest rate sensitivity. Gaining more than a rough idea of what the prevailing yield of the convertible obli-

TABLE 12.1   FEATURES OF SOME ACTIVELY TRADED CONVERTIBLE ISSUES

Issue	S&P Rating	Amount Outstanding (millions)	Conversion Ratio
CONVERTIBLE BONDS			
Amfac 5¼ (1994)	BB+	$ 31.1	22.90
Bank of NY 6¼ (1994)	NR	24.7	26.67
Computer Sciences 6 (1994)	B+	39.7	37.04
Eastern Air Lines 11¾ (2005)	CCC	35.0	76.92
Ford Motor Credit 4⅞ (1998)	A−	87.4	18.04
Georgia-Pacific 5¼ (1996)	BBB+	119.0	32.39
Gulf States Utilities 7¼ (1992)	BBB−	20.5	75.47
Mapco 10 (2005)	BBB−	140.0	21.86
Northwest Bancorp 6¾ (2003)	AA	50.0	33.33
U.S. Steel 5¾ (2001)	A−	353.0	15.94
CONVERTIBLE PREFERREDS*			
American Tel & Tel $4 pfd	AA	6.5	1.05
Atlantic Richfield $2.80 pfd	AA	3.1	2.40
Beatrice Foods $3.38 pfd	AA	5.0	1.86
Champion International $4.60 pfd	BBB	3.0	1.67
GAF Corp. $1.20 pfd	CCC	2.5	1.25
Gulf & Western $2.50 pfd	BB	2.0	2.50
Ingersol-Rand $2.35 pfd	BBB+	2.8	.60
Libby-Owens-Ford $4.75 pfd	BBB	1.0	1.50
Pitney-Bowes $2.12 pfd	NR	2.8	1.00
Weyerhaeuser $2.80 pfd	A+	4.0	1.21

NR = nonrated issue; not rated by this particular rating agency.
*The amount outstanding for preferreds is measured in millions of shares.
Source: Standard & Poor's Bond Guide and Stock Guide, November 1982.

gation ought to be is often difficult. For example, if the issue is rated Baa by Moody's, and if the market rate for this quality range is 9 percent, the convertible should be priced to yield something around 9 percent, plus or minus perhaps as much as half a percentage point. The bond feature will also tend to establish a price floor for the convertible. This price floor tends to parallel interest rates, and exists independently of the depressed behavior of the common share prices.

Risk exposure

The risk exposure of a convertible is a function of the issue's fixed income and equity characteristics. Because of the vital role equity plays in defining the stock value of a convertible, the investor should evaluate the business, financial, and market risks to which the underlying common stock is exposed. Likewise, because of the fixed

I'm afraid we can't play bridge tonight, Cynthia.
Lawrence did some profit taking today and he'd like to savor it.

income nature of convertibles, and because this aspect defines its price floor, purchasing power (inflation) risk and interest rate risk are also important.

Advantages and disadvantages

The major advantage of a convertible issue is that it reduces downward risk (via the issue's bond value or price floor) and at the same time provides an upward price potential comparable to that of the firm's common stock. This two-sided feature is critical with convertibles and is impossible to match with straight common or straight debt. Another benefit is that the current income from bond interest payments normally exceeds the income from dividends that would be paid with a comparable investment in the underlying common stock. For example, a $1,000 convertible with an 8 percent coupon would yield $80 per year to the holder; if the convertible carried a conversion ratio of 20 and if each share of stock paid $2.50 in dividends, an investment in 20 shares of the firm's stock would provide only $50 in dividend income per year. Thus, it is possible with convertibles to reap the advantages of common stock (in the form of potential upward price appreciation) and yet generate improved current income.

On the negative side, there is the *conversion premium,* or as it is sometimes called, "water." Unless the market price of the stock is very high and exceeds the conversion price by a wide margin, a convertible will almost always trade at a price above its true value. This conversion premium has an unfortunate side effect to the extent that it will dilute the price appreciation potential of a convertible. What is more, an investor who truly wants to hold bonds can almost certainly find better current and promised yields from straight debt obligations, and because of conversion premiums, he or she can probably realize greater capital gains by investing directly in the common stock. So if improved returns are normally available from the direct investment in either straight debt and/or straight equity, why buy a convertible? The answer is simple: Convertibles provide a sound way to achieve attractive risk-return tradeoffs. In particular, convertibles offer some risk protection and at the same time considerable, although perhaps not maximum, upward price potential. Thus, although the return may not be the most in absolute terms, neither is the risk.

Transaction costs

Convertible bonds are subject to the same brokerage fees and transfer taxes as straight corporate debt; convertible preferreds trade at the same costs as straight preferreds and common stock. Any type of market or limit order that can be used with bonds or stocks can also be used with convertibles. Convertible debentures are listed along with corporate bonds; they are distinguished from straight debt issues by the "cv" in the "Cur Yld" column of the quote:

Bonds	Cur Yld	Vol	High	Low	Close	Net Chg
UCarb 10s06	cv	140	$101\frac{3}{4}$	101	$101\frac{3}{4}$	$+ \frac{1}{4}$
UnCp 6s88	cv	4	62	62	62	. . . . . .
UnCp 7s89	cv	10	$70\frac{1}{2}$	$70\frac{1}{2}$	$70\frac{1}{2}$	. . . . . .
UnEl $8\frac{7}{8}$06	13.	4	$70\frac{3}{8}$	$70\frac{3}{8}$	$70\frac{3}{8}$	$+ 1\frac{3}{8}$
UPac 8.6s83	8.7	25	$99\frac{1}{4}$	$99\frac{1}{4}$	$99\frac{1}{4}$	$- 1\text{-}32$
UPac 8.4s01	11.	2	76	76	76	$+3$
Uniryl $5\frac{1}{2}$96	cv	35	$61\frac{3}{4}$	$61\frac{3}{4}$	$61\frac{3}{4}$	$+ \frac{1}{4}$
UnAL 5s91	9.3	21	$54\frac{1}{2}$	$53\frac{3}{4}$	$53\frac{3}{4}$	$+ \frac{1}{4}$
UnAL $4\frac{1}{4}$92	8.6	10	$51\frac{1}{2}$	$49\frac{1}{2}$	$49\frac{1}{2}$	-2
UBrnd $5\frac{1}{2}$94	cv	86	$44\frac{1}{4}$	$44\frac{1}{8}$	$44\frac{1}{8}$	$- \frac{1}{8}$
UBrnd $9\frac{1}{8}$98	15.	54	62	$59\frac{5}{8}$	62	$+ \frac{1}{8}$
UGsP $9\frac{1}{2}$84	9.6	15	$98\frac{3}{4}$	$98\frac{3}{4}$	$98\frac{3}{4}$	$- \frac{1}{8}$
UJer $7\frac{3}{4}$97	12.	5	65	65	65	. . . . . .
USAir $9\frac{1}{4}$07	cv	44	130	130	130	-2
USHo 10s87	12.	10	$85\frac{1}{8}$	$85\frac{1}{8}$	$85\frac{1}{8}$	$- 1\frac{5}{8}$
USBO $7\frac{3}{4}$02	12.	5	$64\frac{7}{8}$	$64\frac{7}{8}$	$64\frac{7}{8}$	$+ \frac{1}{4}$
USPIC 8s96	12.	5	69	69	69	$- 1\frac{7}{8}$

Source: The Wall Street Journal.

Note the tendency for some convertibles (the USAir $9\frac{1}{4}$ percent issue, for example) to trade at very high prices. These situations are justified by the correspondingly high values attained by the underlying common stock. Convertible preferreds, in contrast, are not isolated from other preferreds. They are listed with the "pf" markings, but they carry no other distinguishing symbols. As a result, the investor must find out from some other source whether or not a preferred is convertible.

Important Measures of Value

Evaluating the investment merits of convertible securities must include consideration of both the bond and stock dimensions of the issue. Fundamental security analysis of the equity position is, of course, especially important in light of the key role the equity kicker plays in defining the price behavior of a convertible. Agency ratings are helpful and widely used in evaluating the bond side of the issue. In addition to analyzing the bond and stock dimensions of the issue, it is essential to evaluate the conversion feature itself. The two critical areas in this regard are conversion value and investment value. These measures have a vital bearing on a convertible's price behavior and can therefore affect realized holding period return.

Conversion value

In essence, *conversion value* is an indication of what a convertible issue should trade for if it were priced to sell on the basis of its stock value. Conversion value is easy to find: simply multiply the conversion ratio of the issue by the current market price of the underlying common stock. For example, a convertible that carries a conversion ratio of 20 would have a conversion value of $1,200 if the firm's stock traded at a current market price of $60 per share (20 × $60 = $1,200). Sometimes an alternative measure is used and the *conversion equivalent,* or what is also known as *conversion parity,* may be computed. The conversion equivalent indicates the price at which the common stock would have to sell in order to make the convertible security worth its present market price. To find conversion equivalent, simply divide the current market price of the convertible by its conversion ratio. If, for example, a convertible were trading at $1,400 and it had a conversion ratio of 20, then the conversion equivalent of the common stock would equal $70 per share ($1,400 ÷ 20 = $70). In effect, we would expect the current market price of the common stock in this example to be at or near $70 per share in order to support a convertible trading at $1,400.

Unfortunately, convertible issues seldom trade precisely at their conversion values; rather, they invariably trade at a conversion premium. The absolute size of an issue's premium is determined by taking the difference between the convertible's market price and its conversion value. To place the premiums on a relative basis, simply divide the dollar amount of the conversion premium by the issue's conversion value. For example, if a convertible trades at $1,400 and its conversion value equals $1,200, it would have a conversion premium of $200 ($1,400 − $1,200 = $200); in relation to what the convertible should be trading at, this differential would amount to 16.7 percent (the dollar amount of the conversion premium divided by the issue's conversion value, or $200 ÷ $1,200).

Investors are willing to pay a conversion premium because of the added current income over common stock, and so long as the issue possesses promising price potential. An investor can recover the conversion premium only by subsequently selling the issue at a premium equal to or greater than that which existed at the time of purchase. Unfortunately, conversion premiums generally diminish as the price of the issue increases. Therefore, if a convertible is bought for its potential price appreciation, all or a major portion of this price premium will have to be absorbed by the investor as the convertible appreciates and moves closer to its true conversion value. As a result, investors should not be particularly anxious to absorb high levels of conversion premium unless the chances of achieving rather substantial price appreciation are also high.

Investment value

The price floor of a convertible is defined by its bond value and is the object of the investment value measure; it is the only point within the evaluation process where attention is centered on current and expected market interest rates. *Investment value* is the price at which the bond would trade if it were nonconvertible and if it were priced at (or near) the prevailing market yields of comparable issues. The same

BOX 12.2 CONVERTIBLE BONDS MAY BE RIGHT FOR YOU, BUT DO SOME FIGURING BEFORE YOU BUY

Rising stocks and falling interest rates are a winning combination for convertibles—bonds that can be swapped for common stock....

But picking convertibles is tricky business for newcomers. You have to warm up your calculator and do some figuring to spot good buys.

A few months ago [in late 1982] brokers were telling their customers that buying convertibles was a heads-you-win, tails-you-win proposition. For the most part, it was. ... Many bonds that were selling at discounts before the late-summer [1982] stock rally took off [and] now are trading above par.

When interest rates are declining and prospects are good for stocks, convertibles offer high current yield compared with other investments plus the chance to participate in the appreciation on the underlying stock. There is also protection: if the stock goes down, the price of the convertible won't fall below what it would fetch if it were simply an ordinary bond.

Because convertibles frequently have an income edge over the underlying stock, however, they often sell at premiums over their conversion value. In picking them, the big question is whether the premium on a particular bond is justified.

HIGHER YIELD, DIFFERENT RISKS

[Seasoned investors] use several guidelines. The first is, don't buy a convertible unless you would be happy owning the stock. The company may call the bonds, giving you the choice of exchanging them for the underlying common or accepting the call price—which may be below the bond's current market value or the value of the stock it could be converted into. Some convertibles that look to be the most attractive at first blush because of their high current yields pose the most risk of an early call. ...

A decline in interest rates generally increases the risk of a call, as companies seek to refinance their outstanding debt more cheaply. In recent months, the surge in stocks has pushed the prices of many convertibles above their call prices.

As a rule of thumb, most professional money managers advise against paying a premium of more than a half year's interest for a convertible that is selling near or above its call price. That means you should expect to recover the premium in about six months, limiting the risk that the bond will be called before you have at least made up in interest what you paid extra to get in the first place.

In any case, you should expect to recover the premium in less than four years.... Otherwise, you would probably be better off owning the stock.

bond price formula given in Chapter 11 is used to compute investment value. Since the coupon and maturity are known, the only additional piece of information needed is the market yield to maturity of comparably rated issues. For example, if nonconvertible bonds are trading at 9 percent yields, and if a particular 20-year convertible carries a 6 percent coupon, its investment value would be $725. (Note: This value was calculated using techniques discussed in Chapter 11.) This figure indicates how far the convertible will have to fall before it hits its price floor and begins trading as a straight debt instrument. Other things being equal, the greater the distance between the current market price of a convertible and its investment value, the farther the issue can fall in price before it hits its bond floor, and as a result, the greater the downside risk exposure.

BOX 12.2 *Continued*

A CLOSER LOOK

In a rising stock market, a company's common will generally appreciate faster than any convertible it offers because of the premium. So, you have to figure how much you are paying to get the difference in income.

For instance, last summer [1982] Storer Broadcasting Co.'s common stock fell to a low of 19, while the company's 8½% convertible, due in 2005, sold as low as 73.75. The bonds, which are exchangeable for 25 shares, had a conversion value, based on that price, of 475.

An investor who bought the convertible got an 11.53% current yield. Storer common, on the other hand, pays quarterly dividends of 18 cents a share, for a 3.8% current yield on an annual basis. The bond investor, then, paid a 55% premium to get the additional yield. But he will have to hang on to it for almost four years to make it up.

What has happened to the appreciation on both securities? Storer common was trading last week at around $30 a share, for almost a 59% gain. The 8½% convertible was being offered at 97, for about a 31% gain. While the bond investor gave up the appreciation he could have had on the stock, he enjoyed the extra income and took less risk than the stock buyer. . . .

PRIME EXAMPLE

While examining premiums takes some number crunching, it can prevent you from making bad choices. Take the case of Prime Computer's 10% convertibles, due in 2000. At a low of 94 last summer, they also looked like a good buy when the company's common shares were selling at about $16.

At the time, the bonds were yielding 10.99%, while the common has never paid a dividend. The bonds are exchangeable for 31.58 shares. But at a price of 94, they were selling at an 86% premium over their conversion value. And because the bonds were trading close to their call price, the payback until an investor would recover that premium was more than four years, or eight times the six-month rule the pros stick to.

Since then, Prime Computer's stock has more than doubled, but when the bonds recently surged over their 107 call price, the company decided to redeem them. Investors who bought the bonds last summer were foolish to pay so much of a premium over conversion value for convertibles trading that close to their call price. . . .

As a final caveat, . . . check for special provisions in a convertible-bond offering, such as a sinking fund that permits the company to redeem a certain number of the bonds each year. And look to see if the terms change some time down the road. It isn't unusual for the number of shares a convertible can be exchanged for to vary at different times over the bond's life. . . .

Source: The Wall Street Journal, December 13, 1982.

Investment Strategies

Convertible securities offer some unusual, though rewarding, investment opportunities; some people invest in them because of the underlying stock, others because of the attractive yields they offer as fixed-income securities. But before we examine some of the investment strategies used to capture the benefits of these securities, we need to review the general price and investment behavior of convertibles.

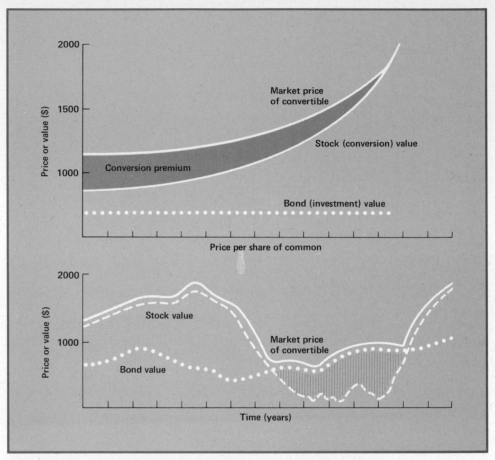

Figure 12.7   Typical Price Behavior of a Convertible Issue.
The price behavior of a convertible security is tied to the stock or the bond dimension of the
issue—when the price of the underlying stock is up, the convertible will trade much like the
stock, whereas the bond value will act as a price floor for the convertible.

An overview of price
and investment behavior

The price behavior of a convertible security is influenced by the equity and the
fixed income elements of the obligation. The variables that play key roles in defining
the market value of a typical convertible therefore include: (1) the potential price
behavior of the underlying stock; and (2) expectations regarding the pattern of future
market yields and interest rates. The typical price behavior of a convertible issue is
depicted in Figure 12.7. In the top panel are the three market elements of a convertible bond: the bond value, or price floor, the stock (conversion) value of the issue,
and the actual market price. The figure reveals the customary relationship between
these three important elements. Note especially that the conversion premium tends

to diminish as the price of the stock increases. The top panel of Figure 12.7 is somewhat simplified, however, because of the steady price floor (which unrealistically assumes no variation in interest rates) and the steady upswing in the stock's value. The lower panel of Figure 12.7 relaxes these conditions, although for simplicity we will ignore conversion premium. The figure illustrates how the market value of a convertible will approximate the price behavior of the underlying stock, so long as stock value is greater than bond value. When the stock value drops below the bond value floor, as it does in the shaded area of the illustration, the market value of the convertible becomes linked to the bond value of the obligation, and it continues to move as a debt security until the price of the underlying stock picks up and approaches, or equals, this price floor.

Convertibles as deferred equity investments

The usual reason for buying a convertible is because of its attractive equity attributes. It represents an alternative to common stock, since an investor may be able to generate a better return by investing in a firm's convertibles rather than directly into its common stock; also, relative to stocks, convertibles offer a chance to improve current income. Convertibles can be profitably used as alternative equity investments whenever it is felt that the underlying stock offers desired capital gains opportunities. In order to achieve maximum price appreciation under such circumstances, the investor would want assurance that the convertible is trading in concert with its stock value, and that it does not have an inordinate amount of conversion premium. If these necessary conditions do in fact exist, investor attention should logically center on the potential market behavior of the underlying stock. To assess such behavior, it is necessary to evaluate current and expected conversion value.

For example, assume a 7 percent convertible bond carries a conversion ratio of 25, and is presently trading in the market at $900; in addition, assume the stock (which pays no dividends) is currently trading at $32, and the convertible is trading at a conversion premium of $100, or 12.5 percent. The formulation of future interest rates also comes into play with this trading strategy as the investor will want to assess the bond price floor and the extent of downward risk exposure; using the same technique developed in Chapter 11, future interest rates would be forecast and used to determine the possible bond price behavior of the issue. Generally speaking, a *drop* in interest rates would be viewed positively by convertible bond investors, since such behavior would signal a rise in the price floor of the convertible issue and therefore a reduction in downside risk exposure. That is, should the common stock not perform as expected, the price of the convertible could still go up as the (bond) price floor rises—or at the least, it would reduce any drop in the price of the convertible issue. But most of the attention is centered not on the bond price floor; rather, it is directed toward the anticipated behavior of the common stock and the conversion premium. To continue our example, assume the investor expects the price of the stock to rise to $60 per share within the next two years. A conversion ratio of 25 would then yield a future conversion value of $1,500. If an expected conversion premium of 6 to 7 percent (or about $100) is added, it follows that the market price of the convertible should rise to about $1,600 by the end of the two-year investment horizon. This expected future price of the convertible, along with its annual coupon payment and current market price, would then be used in the approximate realized yield equation to determine the issue's expected realized yield. For example,

$$\text{expected realized yield} = \frac{\$70 + \dfrac{\$1,600 - \$900}{2}}{\dfrac{\$1,600 + \$900}{2}} = \frac{\$70 + \$350}{\$1,250} = \underline{33.6\%}$$

The realized yield equation above is identical to the one used with straight bonds and preferred stocks. Although this 33.6 percent rate of return may indeed appear attractive, the investor should be sure of several points before committing capital to this security—in particular, that this approach is, in fact, superior to a direct investment in the issuer's common stock (at least from a risk-return tradeoff point of view), and that there is no better rate of return (with commensurate risk exposure) available from some other investment vehicle. To the extent that these conditions are met, investing in a convertible may be a suitable course of action, especially if: (1) The price of the underlying common stock is under strong upward pressure; (2) bond interest rates are falling off sharply; and (3) there is little or no conversion premium in the price of the convertible. The first attribute means conversion value should move up, leading to appreciation in the price of the convertible; the second that the bond value (price floor) should also move up, and thereby reduce exposure to risk; and the third feature means the investor should be able to capture all or most of the price appreciation of the underlying common stock, rather than lose a chunk of it to the inevitable drop in conversion premium.

Convertibles as high-yield fixed income investments

Another common use of convertibles is to buy such issues for the attractive fixed income returns they offer. The key element in this strategy is the issue's bond dimension. Many convertible securities provide current yields and yields to maturity that are safe and highly competitive with straight debt obligations. Care must be taken, however, to make certain that the high yields are not a function of low (speculative) ratings. Normally, such investors would seek discount issues, particularly those that are trading close to their bond price floor—otherwise, the issue would be trading at a premium price, which would certainly involve a yield give up, perhaps a substantial one. Most of these investors view convertibles as ideal for locking in high rates of return. Convertibles are not widely used for speculating on interest rates, however, because even investment-grade convertibles often lack the needed interest sensitivity (due to the equity kicker of the issue). Yet for those who use convertibles to seek high, safe yields, the equity kicker can provide an added source of return if the underlying stock does indeed take off. The investor then has a bond that offers a handsome rate of return and an equity kicker to boot.

SUMMARY

Preferred stocks and convertible securities play an important role in a sound, well-balanced investment program. Preferred stocks provide excellent dividend yields and, when interest rates decline, may produce capital gains as well. Preferreds are normally low-risk investments because their shareholders enjoy a senior position with regard to dividend payments and asset claims. Convertible securities enjoy a similar senior position, and more; they offer the opportunity for equity participation and the potential for excellent capital gains. The combination of a generous fixed income and an equity kicker makes convertible securities highly attractive. The one drawback is that these excellent risk-return features do not come cheaply. Their prices are often bid up to premium levels in the market, and the investor must be careful that the premium paid is not excessive relative to the benefits received.

Preferred stocks are considered hybrid securities since they offer some features of debt and some features of common stock. Preferreds pay cash dividends, which are eligible for an 85 percent tax exclusion if received by a corporation. This feature provides corporations with a distinct advantage over individuals in holding preferreds. Except for floating rate and participating issues, preferreds are fixed income securities that hold a senior position to common stocks in the firm's capital structure. Although failure to pay preferred dividends does not carry with it the same serious consequences as missing interest payments, no common stock dividends can be paid until all preferred obligations are satisfied. If bankruptcy does occur, holders of preferreds have a claim on assets senior to that of the holders of common. Because preferreds are often issued with par or stated values of under $50, they offer the small investor an inexpensive way to participate in fixed income securities.

Preferreds are bought and sold on the various exchanges and in the over-the-counter market in exactly the same manner as common stocks: Commissions are the same; price quotations are the same; and quotations are presented along with common stock prices in the financial press and daily newspapers. The principal purpose for holding preferreds is their attractive yield; in addition, preferreds can be held for capital gains purposes by investors willing to trade on interest rate behavior or on turnaround situations.

Convertible securities (either preferreds or debentures) offer the attraction of equity participation not available in ordinary fixed income issues. Since such securities are convertible into common stock, their value depends largely on the price fluctuations of the underlying common. The conversion value represents the worth of a convertible if it were to be converted into common stock; that is, the conversion ratio times the price of the common. The conversion value rises in direct proportion to increases in share prices. Should the price of common decline, the conversion value will also decline, but the fixed income feature of the convertible will tend to serve as a floor for its market price. The convertible's price will not fall below the straight debt value of the issue, regardless of the decline in the price of the underlying common stock. Convertibles, therefore, provide good upside potential from the equity feature, and good downside protection through their fixed income characteristics. This combination, plus the fact that they can be used for current income and/or capital gains, makes convertibles potentially very attractive.

KEY TERMS

adjustable rate preferreds   dividend arrears
book value   dividend yield
conversion equivalent   equity kicker
conversion parity   fixed charge coverage
conversion period   forced conversion
conversion premium   hybrid securities
conversion price   investment value
conversion privilege   net asset value
conversion ratio   nonconvertible security
conversion value   participating dividends
convertible security   preferred (agency) ratings
cumulative dividends   preferred stock
deferred equity   turnarounds

REVIEW QUESTIONS

1. Define a preferred stock. What types of prior claims do preferred stockholders enjoy?

2. In what ways is a preferred stock like equity? like a bond?

3. Distinguish a cumulative preferred from a participating preferred. Do cumulative and participating provisions affect the investment merits of preferred issues?

4. Describe some of the advantages and disadvantages of investing in preferreds.

5. Assume an $8 preferred stock is currently selling at a current dividend yield of 10 percent. The company then pays a $2 participating dividend, which is expected to hold in the future. What would be the new current yield of this issue if its market price does not change?

6. Discuss why dividend yield is critical in evaluating the investment merits of high-grade preferred stocks during periods when market yields are expected to decline.

7. Briefly discuss several investment uses of preferred stocks. Would preferreds be suitable for both conservative and aggressive investors? Explain.

8. The Beta Company has 500,000 shares of $2 preferred stock outstanding; it generates an EBIT of $40,000,000 and has annual interest payment requirements of $2,000,000. Given the above information, determine the fixed charge coverage of the preferred stock.

9. Is it possible for a firm to pass dividends on preferred stocks, even if it earns enough to pay them? Explain. Does this apply to adjustable rate preferreds as well?

10. Charlene Weaver likes to speculate with preferred stock by trading on movements in market interest rates. Right now, she thinks the market is poised for a big drop in rates; accordingly, she is seriously thinking about investing in a certain preferred stock that pays $8 in annual dividends and is presently trading at $65 per share. What rate of return would she realize on this investment if the market yield on the preferred drops to 8 percent within two years?

11. What is a convertible debenture? How does a convertible bond differ from a convertible preferred?

12. Identify the equity kicker of a convertible security and explain how it affects the value and price behavior of convertibles.

13. Explain why it is necessary to examine both the bond and stock dimensions of a convertible debenture when determining its investment appeal.

14. What are the investment attributes of convertible debentures? What are the disadvantages of such vehicles?

15. A certain 6 percent convertible bond (maturing in 20 years) is convertible at the holder's option into 20 shares of common stock; the bond is currently trading at $800 and the stock at $35 per share:

a. What is the current yield of the convertible bond?
b. What is the conversion price?

c. What is the conversion ratio?
d. What is the conversion value of this issue?
e. What is the conversion premium, in dollars and as a percentage?
f. What is the approximate yield to maturity of the convertible bond?
g. If comparably rated nonconvertible bonds sell to yield 8 percent, what is the investment value of the convertible?

16. What is the difference between conversion parity and conversion value? What is the bond investment value of a convertible and what does it reveal?

17. An 8 percent convertible bond carries a par value of $1,000 and a conversion ratio of 20. Assume that an investor has $5,000 to invest and that the convertible sells at a price of $1,000 (which includes a 25 percent conversion premium). How much total income (coupon plus capital gains) would this investment offer if, over the course of the next 12 months, the price of the stock moves to $75 per share and the convertible trades at a price which includes a conversion premium of 10 percent? What is the holding period return on this investment? Finally, given the information in the problem, what is the underlying common stock currently selling for?

18. Discuss the various uses of convertible debentures. What are the three major attributes that make for an ideal investment outlet and that investors should look for when using convertibles as deferred equity investments?

CASE PROBLEMS

12.1 JUNE VIALPANDO SHOWS A PREFERENCE FOR PREFERREDS

Ms. June Vialpando is a young career woman who has built a substantial investment portfolio. Most of her holdings are preferreds stocks—a situation she does not want to change. Ms. Vialpando is now considering the purchase of $4,000 worth of LaRamie Gold Mine's $5 preferred, which is currently trading at $40 per share. June's stockbroker, Mr. Mike, has told her that he feels the market yield on preferreds like LaRamie should drop to 10 percent within the next two years, and that these preferreds would now make a sound investment. Instead of buying the LaRamie preferred, June has an alternate investment (with comparable risk exposure) which she is confident can produce earnings of about 12 percent over each of the next two years.

Questions
1. If preferred yields behave like June's stockbroker thinks they will, what will be the price of the LaRamie $5 preferred in two years?
2. What realized yield would this investment offer over the two-year holding period if all the expectations about it come true (particularly with regard to the price it is supposed to reach)? How much profit (in dollars) will June make from her investment?
3. Would you recommend that Ms. Vialpando buy the LaRamie preferred? Why?
4. What are the investment merits of this transaction? What are its risks?

12.2 DAVE AND MILLIE CONSIDER CONVERTIBLES

Dave and Millie Normington live in Irvine, California, where she is an elementary school reading specialist and he runs a small construction firm. Depending on the number of jobs Dave can get, their annual income is usually in the mid to upper twenties; they have no children and maintain a modest life style. Recently, they came into a bit of money and are anxious to invest it in some high-yielding fixed income security. Although not aggressive investors, they like to maximize the return on every investment dollar they have. For this reason, they like the high yields and added equity kicker of convertible bonds, and are presently looking at such an issue as a way to invest their recent windfall. In particular, they have their eyes on the convertible debentures of Maria Pottery, Inc. They have heard that the price of the stock is on the way up, and after some in-depth analysis of their own, feel the company's prospects are indeed bright. They've also looked at market interest rates, and based on economic reports obtained from their broker, expect interest rates to decline sharply.

The details on the convertible they're looking at are as follows: It's a 20-year, $1,000 par value issue that carries an 11 percent coupon and is presently trading at $825; the issue is convertible into 15 shares of stock and the stock, which pays no dividends, was recently quoted at $49.50 per share.

Questions

1. Ignoring conversion premium, find the price of the convertible if the stock goes up to $66.67 per share; what if it goes up to $75 per share, or $100 per share? Repeat the computations, assuming the convertible will trade at a 5 percent conversion premium.

2. Find the approximate promised yield of the convertible (*Hint:* Use the same approach as we did with straight bonds in Chapter 11.)

   a. Now find the bond value of the convertible if, within two years, interest rates drop to 11 percent (remember: in two years, the security will have only 18 years remaining to maturity); what if they drop to 9 percent?

   b. What implication does the drop in interest rates hold as far as the investment appeal of the convertible is concerned?

3. Given expected future stock prices and interest rate levels (per above), find the minimum and maximum realized yield this investment offers over the two-year holding period.

   a. What is the worst return (realized yield) Dave and Millie can expect over their two-year holding period if the price of the stock drops to $40 per share and interest rates drop to only 12 percent? What if the price of the stock drops (to $40) and interest rates rise to 15 percent?

4. Should the Normingtons invest in the Maria convertibles? Discuss the pros and cons of the investment.

SELECTED READINGS

Bettner, Jill. "Convertible Bonds May be Right for the Times, But Do Some Figuring Before You Buy Them." *The Wall Street Journal,* December 13, 1982, p. 50.

"Convertibles: Stocks and Bonds in One Package." *Changing Times,* March 1982, pp. 64–66.

"Convertibles: Time for a Break?" *Financial World,* June 1, 1980, pp. 36–37.

Geczi, Michael L. "Convertible Buyers Are Alive and Well." *The Wall Street Journal,* March 29, 1976, p. 17.

Greenebaum, Mary. "The Climate Is Right for Convertibles." *Fortune,* October 6, 1980, pp. 107–108.

"Is This the Time for Convertibles?" *Financial World,* October 29, 1975, pp. 38–39.

Merjos, Anna. "Investor's Choice: Preferred Stocks Have Suddenly Returned to Favor." *Barron's,* November 3, 1975, pp. 5–6, 15.

Metz, Tim. "Risk Cutting Investors Snap Up Convertibles, But Professionals Fret over Price, Liquidity." *The Wall Street Journal,* April 16, 1979, p. 32.

"Predatory Preferreds." *Forbes,* February 15, 1976, pp. 86–87.

"Preferred Stocks Are Not What They Seem." *Business Week,* July 21, 1976, pp. 52–53.

"The Profits in Collecting Preferred Dividends." *Business Week,* October 17, 1977, pp. 118–120.

Rolo, Charles J. "Investing for Income (Not If-come)." *Money,* November 1978, pp. 77–82.

"Wall Street's Latest—Hybrid Convertibles." *Forbes,* August 18, 1980, pp. 104–106.

Weberman, Ben. "The Case for Convertibles." *Forbes,* April 16, 1979, p. 152.

———. "The Convertible Bond Scam." *Forbes,* January 19, 1981, p. 92.

———. "Busted Converts." *Forbes,* June 20, 1983, p. 167.

"Why Convertibles Are In." *Forbes,* October 1, 1979, pp. 75–78.

SIX
SPECULATIVE INVESTMENT VEHICLES

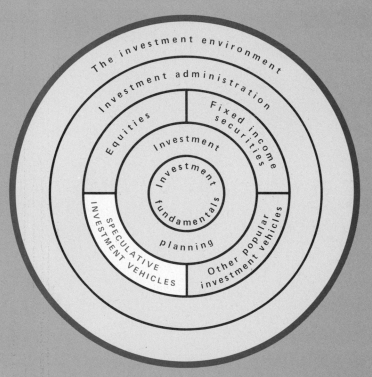

The investment environment

Investment administration

Equities

Fixed income securities

Investment planning

Investment fundamentals

SPECULATIVE INVESTMENT VEHICLES

Other popular investment vehicles

Many individuals like to use various forms of speculation as a way to increase returns from their investment capital. This part of the book will consider several popular ways of speculating. Chapter 13 looks at options: rights, warrants, and puts and calls. It examines the basic features and investment merits of these vehicles and focuses on the risk-return behavior of several options-based investment strategies. Chapter 14 reviews the fast-paced world of commodities and financial futures; these intriguing instruments are explained and then several basic trading strategies are outlined.

13
Options: Rights, Warrants, Puts and Calls

When investors buy shares of common or preferred stock, they become the registered owners of the securities and are entitled to all the privileges of ownership. Investors who acquire bonds or convertible issues are also entitled to the benefits of ownership. But options are another matter. For investors who buy options acquire the right to subsequently buy or sell other securities. In discussing options and the investment attributes of these unusual securities, we will look at:

1. The basic features and investment merits of stock rights.
2. General attributes and behavioral characteristics of warrants.
3. The effects of leverage on the speculative appeal of warrants, and the trading strategies that can be used to gain maximum benefits from this investment vehicle.
4. The exciting world of puts and calls, and their growing popularity in the investment community.
5. The increasing number of different kinds of listed options, including options on stocks, debt securities, foreign currencies, and stock indexes.
6. The risk and return behavior of various put and call investment strategies.

Today options are available on a wide variety of financial assets, including options on various common stocks (which account for most of the trading volume in options), on certain government securities, foreign currencies, stock indexes, and even on a small (but growing) number of commodities and financial futures contracts. Basically, an *option* gives the holder the right to buy or sell certain amounts of an underlying security at a specified price over a specified period of time. Regardless of the type of option or the underlying security, the price behavior of the option itself is directly linked to the price movement of the underlying security in much the same way as convertible securities. Options have their own value, and many are actively traded in the secondary markets. The three basic kinds of options are (1) rights, (2) warrants, and (3) puts and calls. The first type has little investment appeal to the average individual investor, but the latter two enjoy considerable popularity today as attractive trading vehicles, especially among individual investors of limited resources. This is the first of two chapters dealing with unusual investment vehicles; the common denominator is that they cover vehicles or techniques that are somewhat speculative. This does not mean, however, that all these securities are highly risky; rather, as we will learn, they can also be used in very conservative investment situations. For it is the underlying nature of these securities that is speculative, and *not* the ways in which they can be used. But they are unusual, and their use requires special investor knowhow. Thus, the thrust of the present chapter is to learn what we can about the essential characteristics and investment merits of these options, and to see how they can be used by individuals in various types of investment programs.

RIGHTS

A *right* is a special type of option that has a short market life; it usually exists for no more than several weeks. Essentially, rights originate when corporations wish to raise money by issuing more shares of common stock. From an investor's perspective, a right enables a stockholder to buy shares of the new issue at a specified price, over a specified (fairly short) time period. Although not specifically designed for speculation or for use as trading vehicles, they do have value and as a result should never be lightly discarded; instead, unwanted rights should always be sold in the open market.

Characteristics

Let's say a firm has 1 million shares of common stock outstanding and has decided to issue another 250,000 shares. This might well be done through a *rights offering* whereby the firm, rather than directly issuing the new shares of common, would issue stock rights instead. These rights would then be used by the holders to purchase the new issue of stock. This procedure would be followed when existing stockholders are given the right to maintain their proportionate share of ownership in a firm, a privilege known as a *preemptive right.* Since each stockholder would receive, without charge by the issuing firm, one right for each share of stock currently owned, it would take, in our example, four rights to buy one new share of common.

Rights and privileges

Because most stock rights allow their holders to purchase only a fractional share of the new common stock, two or more rights are usually needed to buy a single share. The price of the new stock is spelled out in the right. This is known as the *exercise* (or *subscription*) *price,* and it is always set below the prevailing market price of the stock. For each new share of common stock purchased, the investor would be expected to redeem a specified number of rights and pay the stipulated subscription price in cash. Rights not used by their expiration date lose all value and simply cease to exist. Unfortunately, many investors allow their rights to expire and in so doing, lose money.

The value of a right

Technically, the precise measure of a right's value depends on whether the security is trading rights-on or rights-off. *Rights-on* indicates that the common stock is trading with the right attached to it; an investor who buys a share of stock during such a period also receives the attached stock right. Issues trading *rights-off,* or "ex-rights", means the company's stock and its rights are trading in separate markets and distinct from one another. Regardless of how these securities are trading, we can use the following approximation formula to measure the value of a right:

$$\text{value of a right} = \frac{\text{market price of old stock} - \text{subscription price of new stock}}{\text{number of rights needed to buy one new share}}$$

As an example of how the formula works, we will continue the illustration above. Assume the prevailing market price of the old stock is $50 and the new shares carry a subscription price of $40 per share. Remember that it takes four rights and $40 to buy one new share of stock. We thus find the approximate value of a right as follows:

$$\text{value of a right} = \frac{\$50 - \$40}{4} = \frac{\$10}{4} = \$2.50$$

Each right in our hypothetical example will have a market value of about $2.50 (as long as the price of the stock remains at $50).

Investment Merits

The major investment attribute of a stock right is that it allows the holder to acquire stock at a reduced price. It also enables the holder to acquire additional shares of stock without paying the customary commission fees. Although the savings may not be enormous, the opportunity to execute commission-free transactions should not be overlooked. But except for the commission savings, the cost of buying the stock will be the same regardless of whether the shares are bought outright or through the use of rights—that is, the cost of the rights plus the subscription price of the stock should just about equal the market price of the common. Unfortunately, stock rights hold little opportunity for profitable trading. The life of these securities is simply too short and the range of price activity too narrow to allow for any significant trading profits. Thus, the role of stock rights is limited in most individual investor portfolios to selling unwanted rights or to buying them to reduce the commissions on subsequent stock transactions.

WARRANTS

A *warrant* is also an option enabling the holder to acquire common stock and, like rights, is found only in the corporate sector of the market. Occasionally warrants can be used to purchase preferred stock or even bonds, but common stock is the leading redemption vehicle.

What Is a Warrant?

A warrant is a long-lived option. In fact, of the various types of options, warrants have the longest lives, with maturities that regularly extend to 5, 10, or even 20 years. Occasionally, they have no maturity date at all. They have no voting rights, pay no dividends, and have no claim on the assets of the company. All the warrant offers is the chance to participate indirectly in the market behavior of the issuing firm's common stock and generate some capital gains. (Price behavior and capital appreciation are the only dimensions of return with warrants.)

General attributes

Warrants come into existence as "sweeteners" to bond issues. As a way to make the bond more attractive, the issuing corporation will sometimes attach war-

52 Weeks High	Low	Stock	Div.	Yld %	P-E Ratio	Sales 100s	High	Low	Close	Net Chg.
4	1¼	Marcde		. . .	. . . .	306	3¼	3	3	− ¼
26¼	13⅜	MarMid	1.40	5.5	5	203	25⅞	25½	25⅝	− ¼
70¼	28½	Marion	.64	.9	63	261	u74½	69⅞	74½	+4¾
15¾	6⅞	MarkC	.32	2.2	46	95	14¾	14⅜	14⅝	. . .
21¾	11¾	Mark	pf1.20	5.9	. . . .	4	20½	20½	20½	− ½
65⅝	32	Marriot	.36	.5	19	961	u68½	67⅞	68⅛	+2½
45	29⅝	MrshM	2.20	5.0	13	1877	43⅝	43	43⅝	+ ⅛
53¼	22¼	MartM	1.92	3.7	18	207	52⅜	51⅝	52⅛	+ ¼
61½	48½	MartM	pf4.88	7.9	. . . .	183	u61¼	61¼	61¾	+ ¼
44⅞	12	MaryK	s			1471	44	41½	42⅞	− ⅞
33⅞	21½	Md Cup	s .64	2.0	10	42	32⅛	31½	32	+ ¼
34½	14⅞	Masco	s .44	1.3	19	766	33¾	33	33½	. . . .
59	17¾	Masnit	n1.32	2.4	. . . .	25	55	54¾	55	. . . .
19½	11½	MasM	1.76e	9.0	14	455	u19⅞	19⅜	19½	+ ¼
4⅜	1⅝	MaseyF		. . . .	. . . .	2102	3⅝	3¼	3⅝	+ ⅜
23¼	17⅜	MasCp	2.56	11.	. . . .	47	23	22¾	23	+ ⅛
12	9⅛	MasInc	1.32	11.	. . . .	82	11⅞	11⅝	11⅝	− ⅛
62½	36	MatsuE	.34e	.6	14	372	59	58	58¾	+ ⅝
31½	10⅝	Mattel	.30	2.4	7	3345	12½	11⅜	12⅜	+ ¾
27⅜	7⅛	Matel	wt	. . . .	. . . .	538	9¼	8⅝	9¼	+ ¾
66¼	26¼	Mattl	pf2.50	8.5	. . . .	393	29⅝	28	29½	+1½
55¼	24⅛	MayDS	2	3.6	11	529	u55⅞	54¾	55½	+1
50½	26½	Maytg	2a	4.1	18	91	48¾	47¾	48¾	+ ¾
27¼	17½	McDr	pf2.20	9.6	. . . .	549	23¼	22¾	22⅞	+ ⅜
24⅜	17½	McDr	pf2.60	11.	. . . .	22	22¾	22¾	22¾	. . . .
21¼	16⅜	McDrl	n1.80	9.5	. . . .	852	19	18⅝	18⅞	+ ⅛
71½	43	McDnl	s .88	1.2	14	1961	u71¾	69¾	71¾	+2⅞
56⅝	33¼	McDnD	1.42	2.5	10	602	56¼	55½	56	− ⅛
48½	24⅛	McGEd	2	4.4	14	117	45⅛	44¾	45	. . . .
96½	45¼	McGrH	2.16	2.3	21	79	95	94½	94½	−1
28½	17¼	McInt	g	. . .	. . . .	29	22½	22⅛	22½	− ⅛
19⅜	12¼	McNeil	.90	4.8	. . . .	21	18¾	18¾	18¾	. . . .
24⅞	13½	Mead	1	4.1	. . . .	657	24½	24⅛	24⅜	. . . .
62½	35	Mea	pfB2.80	4.6	. . . .	2	61	61	61	−1½
23	13	Measrx		. . .	443	578	22⅜	22	22⅛	. . . .
56¼	34⅛	Medtrn	.64	1.5	13	1165	44	41½	41⅞	−1⅞
52¼	27½	Mellon	2.44	4.7	7	421	52	51¼	51⅝	− ⅜
50½	49½	Melln	wi	. . .	. . . .	1	50	50	50	− ½
27¾	27	Mellon	pf2.80	10.	. . . .	28	u28	27¾	27¾	. . . .
82½	45	Melville	2.18	2.7	15	451	81	80	80⅛	− ⅜

Source: The Wall Street Journal.

rants, which give the holder the right to purchase a stipulated number of stocks at a stipulated price any time within a stipulated period of time. A single warrant usually enables the holder to buy one full share of stock, although some involve more than one share per warrant and an even fewer number involve fractional shares. The life of a warrant is specified by its *expiration date*, and the stock purchase price stipulated on the warrant is known as the *exercise price*. A typical warrant is shown in Figure 13.1.

Warrants are issued by all types of firms, and by prime-grade as well as highly speculative companies; because warrants are a type of equity issue, they can be margined at the same rate as common stock. They are purchased through brokers and are subject to commission and transaction costs similar to those for common stock. Warrants are usually listed with the common and preferred stock of the issuer, and their quotes are easy to pick out, since the letters *wt* appear in the dividend column. See the bottom of page 468.

Advantages and disadvantages

Warrants offer several advantages to investors, not the least of which is their tendency to exhibit price behavior much like the common stock to which they are linked. This tendency to behave like stock provides the individual investor with an alternative way of achieving capital gains from an equity issue. That is, rather than buy the stock, the investor can purchase warrants on the stock instead; and such a tactic may be even more rewarding than investing in the stock. Another advantage is the relatively low unit cost of warrants and the attractive leverage potential that accompanies this low unit cost. The concept of *leverage* rests on the principle of reducing the level of required capital in a given investment position without affecting the payoff or capital appreciation of that investment. That is, an investor can use warrants to obtain a given equity position at a substantially reduced capital invest-ment, and in so doing magnify returns, since the warrant provides basically the same capital appreciation as the more costly common stock. Finally, the low unit cost of warrants also leads to reduced downside risk exposure. In essence, the lower unit cost simply means there is less to lose if the investment goes sour. For example, a $50 stock can drop to $25 if the market becomes depressed, but there is obviously no way the same company's $10 warrant can drop by a comparable amount.

There are, however, some disadvantages. For one, warrants are somewhat unusual and therefore require specialized investment knowhow. Another disadvan-tage is that warrants pay no dividends; as such, investors sacrifice current income. And because these issues carry an expiration date, there is only a certain period of time during which an investor can capture the type of price behavior sought. Although this may not be much of a problem with long-term warrants, it can prove to be an obstacle for those with fairly short remaining lives (perhaps one or two years).

Characteristics of Warrants

Three aspects of warrants are particularly important: (1) the issue's exercise price; (2) the value of a warrant; and (3) the amount of premium. These features not

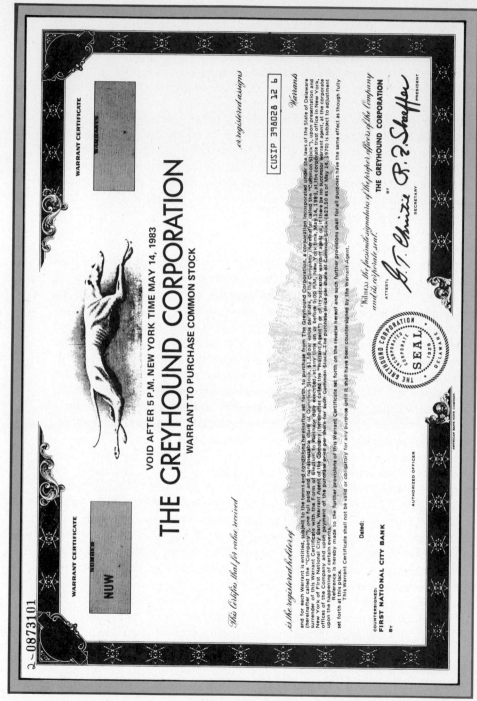

Figure 13.1 A Typical Stock Warrant.
With this particular warrant, an investor can buy one share of stock in the company, at an exercise price of $23.50 per share, any time up to the warrant's expiration date of May 14, 1983. (*Courtesy:* The Greyhound Corp.)

TABLE 13.1 SELECTED FEATURES OF A SAMPLE OF WARRANTS

Issuer	Market Where Traded	Shares of Common Purchased with One Warrant	Exercise Price	Expiration Date
Allegheny Corp.	American	1	$ 3.75	None
American Express	American	1.333	55.00*	2/28/87
Atlas Corp.	American	1	31.25	None
Eastern Air Lines	New York	1	10.00	6/1/87
Grant Industries	American	1	11.36	7/28/86
Mattel, Inc.	New York	1	4.00	4/5/86
Towner Petroleum	American	1	14.75	1/22/86
U.S. Air	American	1.04	17.31	4/1/87
Warner Communications	American	1	55.00	4/30/86

*Exercise price drops to $40 on 3/1/84.

only affect the price and return behavior of warrants, but also have a bearing on formulating an appropriate investment strategy.

Exercise price

The exercise price is the stated price the warrant holder will have to pay to acquire a share of the underlying common stock. It is the share price paid to the firm when the warrant is used to buy the stock—that is, when the option is "exercised." Usually the exercise price remains fixed for the issue's full life, but some warrants may provide for an increase or decrease in the exercise price as the instrument nears its expiration date. In addition, the exercise price of a warrant will automatically be adjusted for stock splits or major stock dividends. Table 13.1 illustrates selected features of a sample of warrants.

Value

Warrants possess value whenever the market price of the underlying common equals or exceeds the exercise price stated on the warrant. This value is determined as follows:

$$\text{value of a warrant} = (M - E) \times N$$

where

M = prevailing market price of the common stock
E = exercise price
N = number of shares of stock that can be acquired with one warrant (if one warrant entitles the holder to buy one share of stock, $N = 1$; if, however, two warrants are required to buy one share of stock, $N = .5$, etc.)

The equation indicates what the market value of a warrant *should be* given the market and exercise price of the common and the number of shares of stock that can be acquired with one warrant. As an example, consider a warrant that carries an exercise price of $40 per share and enables the holder to purchase one share of stock per warrant; if the common stock has a current market price of $50 a share, then the warrants would be valued at $10 each:

$$\text{value of a warrant} = (\$50 - \$40) \times 1 = (\$10) \times 1 = \$10$$

Obviously, the greater the spread in the market and exercise prices, the greater the market value of a warrant. And so long as the market price of the stock equals or exceeds the exercise price and the redemption provision carries a 1 to 1 ratio (one share of common can be bought with each warrant), the value of a warrant will be directly linked to the price behavior of the common stock. Thus, other things being equal, if the stock goes up (or down) by $2, the warrant should do likewise.

Premium

Our formula indicates what the value of warrants should be, but they are seldom priced exactly that way in the marketplace; instead, the market price of a warrant invariably exceeds its computed value. This happens when warrants with negative values trade at prices greater than zero. It also occurs when warrants with positive values trade at even higher market prices; for example, when a $10 warrant trades at $15. This discrepancy is known as *premium,* and it exists because warrants possess speculative value. As a rule, the amount of premium embedded in the market price of a warrant is directly related to the option's time to expiration and the volatility of the underlying common stock—that is, the longer the time to expiration date and the more volatile the stock, the greater the size of the premium. On the other hand, the amount of premium does tend to diminish as the value of a warrant increases. This can be clearly seen in Figure 13.2, which shows the typical price behavior of warrant premiums. Premium is easy to measure: Just take the difference between the value of a warrant (as computed according to the formula above) and its market price. For instance, a warrant has $5 in premium if it has a value of $10 but is trading at $15. We can also put the amount of premium on a relative basis by dividing the dollar premium by the warrant's true (computed) value. For example, there is a 50 percent premium embedded in the price of our $15 warrant above; the dollar premium ÷ value of the warrant = $5 ÷ $10 = .50.

Trading Strategies

Warrants are used by individuals chiefly as alternatives to common stock investments; their attraction is based on the capital gains opportunities they provide. Let us look now at warrant trading strategies and the basic ways in which these securities can be profitably used by individual investors.

The basic price behavior of warrants

Assume an investor has uncovered a company he or she feels will experience strong performance in the foreseeable future. The investor would like to invest in this company and has the ready capital. Being an astute investor, always on the lookout for alternative investment vehicles, this person discovers that the firm also

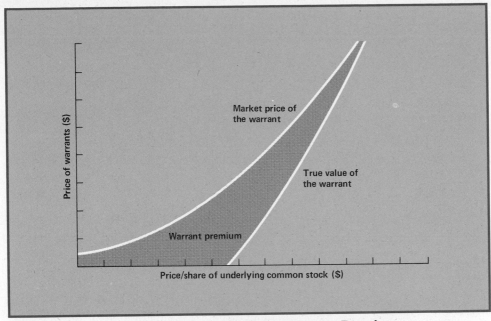

Figure 13.2   The Normal Price Behavior of Warrant Premiums.
Observe that as the price of the underlying common stock increases, the amount of premium in the market price of the warrant tends to decrease—though it never totally disappears.

has warrants outstanding. Under such conditions, *both* the stock and the warrants should be evaluated before a decision is made. This scenario highlights several important investment ground rules: (1) Investors should always determine whether alternative vehicles exist before a decision is made; and (2) the basic investment use of a warrant, at least by the nonprofessional individual investor, is as a substitute for common stock.

Because warrants carry relatively low unit costs, they possess much greater price volatility and the potential for generating substantially higher rates of return than a direct investment in the underlying common stock. Consider the following illustration, which involves the common shares and warrants of the same company. Say the price of the common is now $50 per share and the warrant, which carries a one-to-one redemption provision, has a $40 exercise price (we will ignore premium in this illustration). Observe below what happens when the price of the stock increases by $10:

	Common Stock	Warrant
Issue price *before* increase	$50	$10
Increase in price of common	$10	—
Issue price *after* increase	$60	$20
Increase in market value	$10	$10
Holding period return (increase in value/beginning issue price)	20%	100%

BOX 13.1 BEHIND THE BOOM IN WARRANTS

A warrant is a piece of paper that entitles the holder to buy shares of the issuing company at a predetermined price, in most cases for a period of years. People usually buy warrants when they feel sure that the company is going to do well and that the price of its stock will rise.

Warrants enable the buyers to get bigger bangs for the bucks they risk—providing they are smart or lucky. In this year's [1979] rising market, some people have been aggressive purchasers with enviable results. Through September 19, more than 49 million warrants had changed hands on the New York Stock Exchange, about 2½ times as many as a year ago. Trading has been heavy in warrants of American Airlines, Mattel, Greyhound and, at times, Chrysler Corporation. But Charter Company has seen the most action and provides a good example of why people buy warrants and what's involved in buying them.

CASE HISTORY

Charter Company is a conglomerate with interests in petroleum, insurance and publishing. Its warrants were issued in conjunction with a sale of debentures, as often happens. In effect, the company gave its creditors a chance to profit from any rise in the company's stock in return for a somewhat lower rate of interest on its debt.

The Charter warrants let holders buy common at $10 a share through Sept. 1, 1988, with a proviso that the date may be advanced to Sept. 1, 1983, under certain conditions.

Charter currently is involved in operations that could yield great—but not sure-fire—rewards. It has taken over the Carey Energy Corporation, a financially troubled firm that is the largest independent marketer of fuel oil on the East Coast. One aim of the merger is to get a half interest in the world's fifth-largest refinery, which is in the Bahamas. Success hinges partly on arrangements with Carey's creditors, the National Iranian Oil Company and Bahamian courts. A Venezuelan group also is vying for the refinery.

An investor who thinks Charter will win out has a choice of buying its common or its warrants. Earlier this year, the warrants traded at $1 each and the stock at $4 a share. At that point, anyone who bought warrants and converted them would have been out $11 for stock worth only $4. But see what happened—

As Charter cleared some of the hurdles in its paths, its stock on September 19 hit $47.75 a share and the warrants rose to nearly $42.38. A person who had bought 1,000 warrants at $1 each could have resold them for $42,375. However, $1,000 spent on Charter stock at the year's low would have bought only 250 shares worth about $11,938. So the gain from the warrants was over 3½ times as great.

Note that warrants also can be a quick way to lose money if share prices slide. What's more, warrants pay no dividends.

Warrants are not for the casual investor. To succeed with them requires careful study of the terms on which they were issued, close attention to the company's activities and a sharp pencil.

Source: William C. Bryant, "Behind the Boom in Warrants," reprinted from *U.S. News & World Report,* October 1, 1979, p. 69. Copyright 1979 U.S. News & World Report, Inc.

The fact that the warrants provide a rate of return five times greater than that available from the common is due to the fact that the two issues move parallel to one another, even though the warrant carries a lower unit cost.

As in our illustration above, holding period return would normally be used to assess the payoff when the investment horizon equals one year or less, whereas approximate yield would be used when the investment horizon amounts to two years or more. More specifically, we would measure holding period return (HPR) for warrants as:

$$HPR = \frac{\text{sale price of warrant} - \text{purchase price of warrant}}{\text{purchase price of warrant}}$$

The holding period return for the warrants in our illustration would be:

$$HPR = \frac{\$20 - \$10}{\$10} = \frac{\$10}{\$10} = 100\%$$

In contrast, if we assumed a three-year investment horizon, the approximate yield on the transaction would amount to:

$$\text{approximate yield} = \frac{\dfrac{\text{sale price of warrant} - \text{purchase price of warrant}}{\text{years in investment horizon}}}{\dfrac{\text{sale price} + \text{purchase price}}{2}}$$

$$= \frac{\dfrac{\$20 - \$10}{3}}{\dfrac{\$20 + \$10}{2}} = \frac{\dfrac{\$10}{3}}{\dfrac{\$30}{2}} = \frac{\$3.33}{\$15} = 22.2\%$$

Note that with both HPR and approximate yield we have ignored dividends, as they are not paid to warrant holders.

Trading with warrants

Warrant trading generally follows one of two approaches: (1) The leverage embedded in warrants is used to magnify dollar returns; or (2) their low unit cost is used to reduce the amount of invested capital and limit losses. The first approach is obviously the more aggressive, whereas the second has considerable merit as a potentially conservative strategy. Our comparative illustration above can be used to demonstrate the first technique, which seeks to magnify returns. Obviously, if an investor wishes to make a $5,000 equity investment and if price appreciation is the main objective, he or she would be better off by committing such a sum to the warrants. This is so since a $5,000 investment in the common will buy 100 shares of stock ($5,000 ÷ $50 = 100 shares) which will generate only $1,000 in capital gains ($10 profits per share × 100 shares), whereas that same $5,000 invested in the lower-priced warrants will buy 500 of these securities ($5,000 ÷ $10 = 500 warrants) and will result in $5,000 in profits ($10 in profits per warrant × 500 warrants). The common stock thus provides a 20 percent HPR, whereas the warrants yield 100 percent.

The major drawbacks to this approach are that the investor receives no dividends, and that price appreciation has to occur before the warrant expires. The biggest risk in this investment is the potential loss exposure; observe that if the price of the stock in our example decreases by $10, the warrant holder (without a warrant premium) is virtually wiped out. In contrast, the price of the stock would drop "only" to $40, and the investor would still have $4,000 in capital left.

One way to limit this exposure to loss is to assume a more conservative investment posture (and to follow the second trading approach). This can be done by buying only enough warrants to realize the same level of capital gains as is available from the common stock. Referring again to our illustration, since we are dealing with options that carry one-to-one redemption provisions, the investor would need to acquire only 100 warrants to obtain the same price behavior as 100 shares of stock. Thus, rather than buying $5,000 worth of stock, the investor need purchase only $1,000 worth of the warrants to realize the same capital gains. If the stock does perform as expected, the warrant investor will realize a 100 percent holding period return (as computed above) by generating the same amount of capital gains as the stock—$1,000. But since this will be done with substantially less capital, there will be not only greater yield with the warrants, but also less loss exposure. In this case, if the price of the stock does drop by 10 points, the most the warrant holder can lose is $1,000, although this is unlikely because premium will probably keep the price above zero.

Security selection: A critical dimension

Regardless of how warrants are used by individual investors, security selection is a critical dimension of the investment process. So long as the price behavior of the underlying common stock is a key element in defining the price behavior of a warrant, it is important that the investor be satisfied that the common stock does indeed have the type of price potential desired. As a technical matter, in order to obtain maximum price behavior, it is also important that the market price of the common be equal to or greater than the exercise price of the warrant. Given that the price potential of the common stock and the exercise price of the warrant have been fully assessed, the question of stock versus warrant reduces to one of comparative returns, risk exposure, and investor preferences.

Leverage and the importance of timing

Thus far, we have assumed that the price behavior of a warrant is unaffected by outside variables. This assumption, while convenient, is not altogether true, for both leverage and downside risk protection are functions of the market price of the warrant. To realize maximum price appreciation, it is generally recommended that lower-priced issues be used. Other things being equal, the lower the price of the warrant, the greater its leverage potential. Not only does the amount of magnified return potential become less and less as the price of the warrant increases, but the risk exposure of a subsequent drop in price also becomes greater. For example, consider a $40 stock and a $5 warrant (the warrant in this case would have an exercise price of $35). If the stock price increases by $40, it will generate a 100 percent rate of return as it moves to its new $80 level; conversely, the warrant will move to $45 and provide an 800 percent rate of return. Note, however, that when

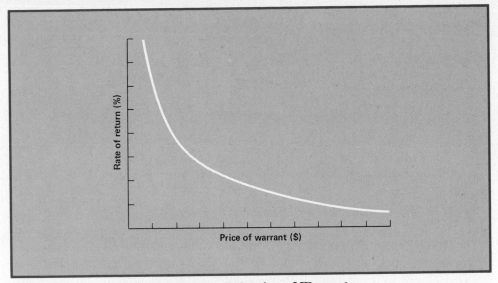

Figure 13.3   The Normal Return Behavior of Warrants.
As a rule, higher-priced warrants provide lower rates of return because they offer less leverage than lower-priced warrants.

the stock is at $160 and then undergoes that same $40 price appreciation (to $200 per share), this performance yields only a 25 percent rate of return. Under such circumstances, our warrant would now have a price of $125 and should move to $165, generating a yield of some 32 percent.

Clearly, as its price increases, the warrant begins to behave more like its underlying common stock. With our warrant at $125, it no longer has a low unit cost, its leverage and rate of return are not much different from the underlying common stock, and the risk exposure of a drop in price may now be substantial. Figure 13.3 illustrates how the return behavior of a warrant is related to its price level. The shape of the curve clearly indicates that a warrant's rate of return potential drops dramatically with increases in its market price. Certainly, a low warrant price alone will not guarantee success, but it is obvious that, other things being equal, a low warrant price is more desirable than a higher one since the low unit price allows the investor to capture both increased price volatility and reduced downside risk.

PUTS AND CALLS

Puts and calls generally have longer maturities than rights, though they are considerably shorter than those on warrants; their life span ranges from thirty days to nine months in duration, and occasionally to one year. They are much like warrants to the extent that they provide attractive speculative outlets, offer appealing leverage potential, and can act as a nice alternative to the direct investment in common stock. Although for years puts and calls were written almost exclusively on common stocks, dramatic changes occurred in this market in the autumn of 1981, when trading began in other kinds of options. Today, investors can trade puts and calls on:

- Common stock
- Debt instruments
- Foreign currencies
- Stock indexes
- Commodities and financial futures

As we will see, although the underlying financial assets may vary, the basic features and behavioral characteristics of these securities are much the same.

Definitions and Characteristics

One of the phenomena of the market of the 1970s was the remarkable performance and investment popularity of stock options—puts and calls on common stock. By the early 1980s, the interest in options spilled over to other kinds of financial assets and was a major factor behind the development of interest rate, currency, index, and futures options. Not surprisingly, much of the popularity of the options market derived from the fact that individual investors can buy a lot of price action with a limited amount of capital, and yet nearly always enjoy limited risk exposure with puts and calls. For example, an investor can buy an option on $200,000 worth of Treasury bills for as little as $600.

A negotiable instrument

Puts and calls are negotiable instruments issued in bearer form that allow the holder to buy or sell a specified amount of a specified security at a specified price (as an example, puts and calls on common stocks cover 100 shares of stock in a specific company). A *put* enables the holder to sell the underlying security at a specified price over a set period of time; a *call,* in contrast, gives the holder the right to buy the securities at a stated price within a certain time period. Puts and calls possess value to the extent that they allow the holder to participate in the price behavior of the underlying financial asset. As with any option, there is no interest or dividend income, no voting rights, and no privileges of ownership.

Puts and calls are traded on listed exchanges and, on a much smaller scale, in the over-the-counter market. They provide attractive leverage opportunities because they carry relatively low prices—at least relative to the market price of the underlying financial assets. To illustrate, consider a call on a common stock that gives the holder the right to buy 100 shares of a $50 stock at a price of, say, $45 a share. The stock would be priced at $50, but the call would trade at an effective price of only $5 a share (or the difference between the market price of the common and the price it can be purchased at, as specified on the call). However, since a single stock option always involves 100 shares of stock, the actual market price of our $5 call would be $500—$5 × 100 shares = $500.

Maker versus purchaser

Puts and calls are a unique type of security since they are not issued by the corporations that issue the underlying stocks and bonds. Instead, puts and calls *are created by investors*. It works like this: Suppose one individual wants to sell to another the right to buy 100 shares of common stock. This individual would *write* a call; the individual or institution writing the option is known as the *option maker* or *writer*. The maker who writes (and sells) an option is entitled to receive the price paid for the put or call (less modest commissions and other transaction costs). The put or call option is now a full-fledged financial asset and trades in the open market much like any other security. Puts and calls are both written and purchased through security brokers and dealers, and they can be actively bought and sold in the secondary market. The writer stands behind the option at all times, regardless of how many times the security has been traded or who the current owners are, for it is the *writer* who must buy or deliver the stock or other financial asset according to the terms of the option.

Puts and calls are written for a variety of reasons, most of which we will explore below. At this point, however, suffice it to say that writing options can be a viable investment strategy and can be a profitable course of action since, more often than not, *options expire unexercised*. But when options do hit, they usually hit big. As a result, individuals are also lured to the buy side of these securities by the profits they offer and the low-cost, speculative nature of the issue. In essence, the buyers of puts and calls are willing to invest their capital in return for the right to participate in the future price performance of the underlying security, and to do so at low unit cost and limited risk exposure.

How puts and calls work

Using the buyer's point of view, let us now briefly examine how puts and calls work and how they derive their value. To understand the mechanics of puts and calls, it is best to look at their profit-making potential. For example, consider a stock currently priced at $50 a share; assume we can buy a call on the stock for $500, with the call enabling us to purchase 100 shares of the stock at a fixed price of $50 each. A rise in the price of the underlying security (in this case, common stock) is what the investor would hope for. What is the profit from this transaction if the price of the stock does indeed move up to, say, $75 by the expiration date on the call? The answer is that we will earn $25 ($75 − $50) on *each* of the 100 shares of stock in the call—or a total gross profit of some $2,500; and all from a $500 investment. This is so since we can buy 100 shares of the stock—from the option writer—at a price of $50 each and immediately turn around and sell them in the market for $75 a share. We could have made the same profit by investing directly in the common stock, but because we would have had to invest $5,000 (100 shares × $50 per share), our rate of return would have been much lower. Obviously, there is a considerable difference between the profit potential of common stocks and calls; and it is this differential which attracts investors and speculators to calls whenever the price outlook for the underlying financial asset is upward. (Note that although our illustra-

---

BOX 13.2 PLAYING THE OPTIONS GAME

One of the most dramatic changes in the stock market has been the explosive growth of trading in options. These contracts—rights to buy or sell 100 shares of a stock at a prearranged price for a limited time—are being used by more and more people. In 1980, reported the Option Clearing Corporation, 96.7 million option contracts were traded, up from 64.3 million in 1979.

The bulk of this activity is speculative. Market experts such as Macon Brewer at Dean Witter Reynolds estimate that 70 to 80 percent is done by people who are buying or selling options in the hope of being able to resell or repurchase at a profit without actually dealing in the underlying shares. It is a game for those who calculate costs and returns to a fine point, watch the markets closely and have brokers who are quick to point out any oversights.

Because all options expire within three to nine months, those who trade in them are concerned essentially with what happens in the short run. There are, however, conservative investors who use options to increase income or insure against losses on shares purchased for the long pull. An investor in North Carolina writes that he made enough on options last year to "pay for groceries."

How? By selling call options against stocks he held that were not likely to appreciate much, if any, in the near future and were no longer favorites in his portfolio. A call is an option to buy a stock at a prescribed "striking price" any time before the contract expires. In effect, the North Carolinian sold the right to call away some shares he was no longer intent on keeping. Rather than sell the shares outright, he pocketed the "premiums" paid for the calls, minus a broker's commission.

Suppose you own 100 shares of Burroughs, a stock that sold for almost $80 in 1980 but has tumbled to about $50 since the firm reported a sharp drop in profits. You know it has new management working hard to solve its problems and new products that may boost earnings, but you're not sure you should keep the shares.

On March 10, you could collect $150, minus about $25 in fees, for giving someone the right to buy your 100 shares for $60 a share until July 18. If the stock does not rise

---

tion is couched in terms of common stock, this same valuation principle is applicable to any of the other securities that may underlie call options, such as bonds, foreign currencies, or futures contracts.)

A similar situation can also be worked out for puts. Assume that for the same $50 stock we could buy a put to sell 100 shares of the stock at $50 for $500. Now we, as the buyer of a put, want the price of the stock to drop, so that we can use the put as a way to make money. Assume our expectations are correct and the price of the stock does indeed drop, to $25 a share. Here again, we would realize a profit of $25 for each of the 100 shares in the put. We can do this by going to the market and buying 100 shares of the stock at a price of $25 a share, and immediately turning around and selling them to the writer of the put at a price of $50 per share. Fortunately, put and call investors do *not* have to exercise these options and make simultaneous buy and sell transactions in order to receive their profit, since options do have value and can be traded in the secondary market. The value of both puts and calls is directly linked to the market price of the underlying financial asset. The

BOX 13.2 *Continued*

to $60 or more by that time, the striking price will be unattractive to the person who bought your option, the option will expire and you will keep the premium and the stock—and you may repeat the process. Unless Burroughs falls below 49 by July 18, you will be no worse off than if you had sold the stock at the outset instead of selling the call.

What if the market price rises to $60 and you can decide to keep the stock? You can buy back the call before it is exercised. Unless some startling development has sent the price through the roof, the cost of doing that will probably not be too much more than the $125 you cleared on the sale of the option. You'll have a short-term loss to report for tax purposes.

Maybe you do not own Burroughs but plan to buy 100 shares. An option can provide some insurance against loss. You could, for instance, buy an "October 50 call"—the right to buy the stock at $50 a share until October 17—for $6 a share, or a total of $600, plus $25 commission. If your hopes are fulfilled and the stock rises, you will be able to resell the call at a profit or buy the stock at less than market value. Meanwhile, instead of risking about $5,000, the amount it costs to buy the stock now, you risk only about 12 percent as much.

To be sure, if Burroughs drops, you are out the entire investment and still do not own the stock.

An alternative is to buy the shares and sell a call at the same time. Say you pay about $5,000, plus commission, for 100 shares and receive $600, minus commission, for the October call on the stock at $50. If the price drops, the call will expire, and the premium you got for it will help cover any loss in value of the stock. If the price rises, say, to $55 before October 17, you can buy back the call and chalk off the loss on it to insurance. Your initial premium plus the increased value of the shares will more than compensate.

Source: William C. Bryant, "Playing the Options Game," *U.S. News and World Report,* March 23, 1981, p. 79.

value of calls increases as the market price of the underlying security rises, whereas the value of puts increases as the price of the security declines.

Advantages and disadvantages

The major advantage of investing in puts and calls is their leverage feature. This feature also carries the advantage of being able to limit risk exposure, since there is only a set amount of money that can be lost (the purchase price of the option). Also appealing is the fact that puts and calls can be used profitably when the price of the underlying security goes up *or* down. Finally, some unusual tax advantages can be obtained by using puts and calls in fairly specialized investment profiles.

A major disadvantage of puts and calls is that the holder enjoys no interest or dividend income or any other ownership benefit. Moreover, because the instruments have limited lives, the investor has a limited time frame in which to capture desired price behavior. Another disadvantage is the fact that puts and calls cannot be margined. And the issues themselves are a bit unusual and many of their trading strategies are complex; because of this, investors must possess special knowledge and fully understand the subtleties of this trading vehicle.

Options Markets

Although the concept of options can be traced back to the writings of Aristotle, option trading in the United States did not begin until the late 1700s, and until the early 1970s this market remained fairly small, largely unorganized, and the almost private domain of a handful of specialists and traders. All this changed, however, on April 26, 1973, when a new securities market was created with the launching of the Chicago Board Options Exchange (the CBOE).

Conventional options

Prior to the creation of the CBOE, put and call option trading was conducted exclusively in the over-the-counter market through a handful of specialized dealers. Investors who wished to purchase puts and calls dealt with these options dealers via their own brokers, and the dealers would actually find individuals (or institutions) willing to write the options. If the buyer wished to exercise the option, he or she did so with the writer, and no one else—a system that largely prohibited any secondary trading. On the other hand, there were virtually no limits on what could be written, so long as the buyer was willing to pay the price. Put and call options were written on New York and American stocks, as well as on regional and over-the-counter securities; and they were written for as short as thirty days and as long as a year. Over-the-counter options, known today as *conventional options,* were hard hit by the CBOE and other options exchanges. The conventional market still exists today, although on a reduced scale, and it is still possible for investors to use this market, along the lines set out above, to create conventional options.

Listed options

The creation of the CBOE marked the first time in American capital market history that stock options were traded on listed exchanges. It marked the birth of so-called *listed options,* a term used to denote put and call options traded on organized exchanges, as opposed to the conventional options traded in the over-the-counter market. The CBOE created the listed options concept by launching trading in calls on 16 firms. These 16 issues quickly doubled to 32, and soon after, the American Stock Exchange also began trading listed calls. The Pacific and Philadelphia stock exchanges followed; and finally, in June 1977, all four options exchanges began trading in puts. By 1983, the number of issues listed on the options exchanges had grown from the original 16 to over 350, and most of these are written on stocks traded on the New York Stock Exchange.

The listed options concept provided not only a convenient market for the trading of puts and calls, but also standardized the expiration dates and the prices specified on the options. The exchanges created a clearinghouse organization that eliminated direct ties between buyers and writers of options, and reduced the cost of executing put and call transactions. They also developed an active secondary market, with wide distribution of price information. It is now as easy to trade a listed option as a listed stock.

Stock Options

The advent of the CBOE and other listed options exchanges had a quick and dramatic impact on the trading volume of puts and calls. As Figure 13.4 shows, the level of activity in listed stock options grew by more than a hundredfold in just eight years. Equally impressive was the fact that the 1981 volume shown in Figure 13.4 covered almost 11 *billion* shares of stock (since each contract is for 100 shares of stock)—a figure that was equivalent to 95 percent of all shares traded on the NYSE in that year. Eventually, listed options became available on other financial assets. Today, investors can trade listed options on stocks and stock indexes, debt instruments, foreign currencies, and futures contracts. The creation and continued expansion of listed options exchanges has truly given the field of investments a whole new dimension. But in order to use these instruments correctly and avoid serious (and possibly expensive) mistakes, the individual investor must fully understand the basic features of these securities. In the material that follows, we will look closely at the investment attributes and trading strategies that can be used with stock options; later we'll explore interest rate, currency, and index options, and then take up futures options in Chapter 14.

Stock option provisions

There are three major provisions of put and call options that investors should be aware of: (1) the price at which the stock can be bought or sold, (2) the amount of time remaining until expiration, and (3) the purchase price of the option itself.

Striking price.   The *striking price* represents the price contract between the buyer of the option and the writer. For a call, the striking price specifies the price at which each of the 100 shares of stock can be bought; with a put, it represents the price at which the option buyer may sell the stock to the writer. The striking price is also known as the exercise price. With conventional (OTC) options, there are no constraints on what the striking price must be (although it is usually specified at or near the market price of the stock prevailing at the time the option is written). With listed options, however, for stocks selling at less than $50 per share the striking price must be in increments of $5. For stocks selling between $50 and $100 per share, the options must be written with striking prices in $10 increments. Finally, for stocks that trade at prices in excess of $100, the striking price is in $20 increments. The striking price of both conventional and listed options is adjusted for substantial stock dividends and stock splits.

Expiration date.   The expiration date is also an important provision because it specifies the life of the option much the same way as the maturity date indicates

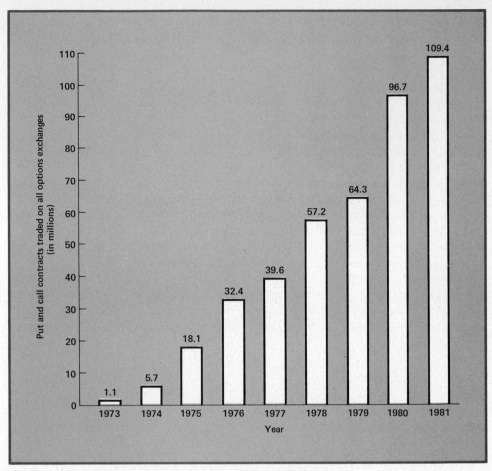

Figure 13.4 The Growth in Listed Options Trading.
Clearly, the market for listed stock options has grown rapidly every year since the concept was first introduced in the spring of 1973. (*Source:* CBOE Market Statistics—1982.)

the life of a bond. Expiration dates for options in the conventional market can fall on any working day of the month. In contrast, expiration dates are standardized in the listed options market. The exchanges have created three expiration date cycles for all listed options, and each issue is assigned to one of the three cycles. One cycle is January, April, July, and October; another is February, May, August, and November; and the third is March, June, September, and December. Prices are quoted for only three of the four maturities, with the expiration dates rolling over every three months. For example, the January, April, and July expiration dates would be quoted until the January options expire, then the April, July, and October dates would be used.

Options can be bought, sold, or written for any one of the three dates currently outstanding; since no transaction can take place in the fourth (unlisted) expiration date of a cycle, it follows that nine months is the longest option on the listed exchanges. Given the month of expiration, the actual day of expiration is always the same: the Saturday following the third Friday of each expiration month. Thus, for all practical purposes, all listed options expire the third Friday of the month of expiration.

Premium.   The purchase price of an option is known as the *premium*. With most securities, the term "premium" is used to denote that portion of the purchase price which exceeds some predetermined theoretical value. With puts and calls, "premium" represents the cost of an option and the price the buyer would have to pay to the writer (or seller) in order to acquire the put or call. The size of the option premium is obviously important to buyers, writers, and sellers. One factor that affects the size of option premiums is the current market price of the underlying stock: The greater the difference between the price of the stock and the striking price on the option, the greater the value of the put or call. Another factor is the length of time until the expiration date of the option; the longer the time until expiration, the greater the size of the premium. Still another is the volatility of the underlying security, which is important to the extent that it enhances (or detracts from) the speculative appeal of the option. Other, less important variables include the dividend yield of the underlying stock, the trading volume of the option, and the exchange on which the option is listed.

Put and call transactions

Option traders are subject to commission and transaction costs whenever they buy or sell an option, or when an option is written. The writing of puts and calls is subject to normal options transaction cost, since it effectively represents remuneration to the broker or dealer for *selling* the option. In relation to the number of shares of common stock controlled (100 shares per option), the transaction costs for executing put and call trades is relatively low. However, when the transaction costs are compared to the size of the transaction itself, we discover that option transactions are fairly costly. Table 13.2 gives a variety of commission costs on listed options and it can be used to demonstrate this principle. For example, note that the cost to buy one $5 option would involve an investment of $500 and a transaction cost of only $26.75. Although this may be low compared to what it would take to buy outright 100 shares of the underlying stock, a little simple arithmetic indicates that it involves a 5.4 percent charge ($26.75 ÷ $500 = .054). This is fairly steep, especially when we consider the fact that this commission must be paid both when the option is bought and when it is sold. As Table 13.2 shows, options have their own unique structure of commissions based on the number of options in the transaction and the size of the option premium.

Listed options also have their own market place and quotation system. Finding the price (or premium) for a listed stock option is fairly easy, as the illustration on page 486 indicates:

LISTED OPTIONS QUOTATIONS

Wednesday, April 20, 1983

Closing prices of all options. Sales unit usually is 100 shares. Security description includes exercise price. Stock close is New York or American exchange final price.

Option & NY Close	Strike Price	Calls—Last			Puts—Last		
		May	Aug	Nov	May	Aug	Nov
Amdahl	. 30	10¾	10¾	s	⅛	⅞	s
41	35	6⅛	r	r	⅝	2¼	3⅝
41	40	3¼	5½	6½	2⅛	4¼	5½
41	45	13-16	3⅛	4½	5½	7	r
A E P	...15	r	4⅝	r	r	r	r
19¾	...20	3-16	½	¾	15-16	1⅛	r
Am Hos	35	14¼	r	r	r	r	r
48¾	...40	9¼	9½	r	r	⅜	r
48¾	...45	4⅛	5¾	6½	¼	1⅛	r
48¾	...50	15-16	3	4	2	r	r
A M P	...75	12	r	r	r	r	r
86¼	...80	7	9¾	r	9-16	2⅛	r
86¼	...85	2¾	r	r	r	r	r
86¼	...90	1	r	5¾	r	r	r
Baxter	..40	r	17⅞	r	r	r	r
56½	...45	12¼	13	r	r	r	r
56½	...50	7	8	r	r	r	1⅛
56½	...55	2⅜	4½	5½	½	r	r
56½	...60	s	2½	3½	s	r	r
Blk Dk	..15	7⅛	7	r	r	r	r
22	20	2 1-16	3	3⅝	⅛	1	1¼
22	25	3-16	13-16	1 7-16	r	r	r
Boeing	..20	20¼	s	s	r	s	s
40¾	...25	15¼	14⅞	s	r	r	s
40¾	...30	11	11¼	11	1-16	r	r
40¾	...35	5⅞	6⅝	7	⅛	⅝	1⅛
40¾	...40	1 13-16	3½	4⅜	1¼	2½	3¼
40¾	...45	¼	1⅜	2½	r	r	r

Source: The Wall Street Journal.

Note that quotes are provided for calls and puts separately, and for each option, there are three expiration dates listed (in this case, May, August, and November). Along with the striking price, such information is the basis for differentiating among various options. For example, there are numerous puts and calls outstanding on Boeing stock, each with its own expiration date and striking price.

The quotes are standardized and are read as follows: the name of the company and the closing price of the underlying stocks are listed first (note Boeing's stock closed on April 20th at 40¾); the striking price is listed next; then the closing prices of the calls and puts are quoted relative to the three expiration dates. Thus, we can see that a Boeing *call* with a $30 striking price and a May expiration date is quoted at 11; in contrast, a Boeing *put* with a $40 striking price and an August expiration date is trading at 2½. Recall, however, that option premiums are listed on a per share basis, and therefore the actual price of the Boeing options is a multiple of 100: The call would cost $1,100 and the put would cost $250.

Measuring value

The value of a put and call depends on its exercise price and the prevailing market price of the underlying stock. The value of a call is determined according to the following simple formula:

TABLE 13.2 COMMISSION COSTS ON LISTED OPTIONS

Option Premium	NUMBER OF OPTIONS														
	1	2	3	4	5	6	7	8	9	10	11	12	13	14	15
1/16	3.88	4.55	5.22	5.89	6.56	7.22	7.90	8.56	9.23	9.90	10.57	11.24	11.91	12.57	13.25
1/8	4.55	5.89	7.22	8.56	9.90	11.24	12.57	13.91	14.45	14.45	15.78	17.12	18.46	19.80	21.13
3/16	5.22	7.22	9.23	11.24	13.25	14.45	15.12	17.12	19.13	21.13	23.14	25.15	27.16	29.16	31.17
1/4	5.89	8.56	11.24	13.91	14.45	17.12	19.80	22.47	25.15	27.82	30.50	33.17	35.85	38.52	41.20
5/16	6.56	9.90	13.25	14.45	17.79	21.13	24.48	27.82	31.17	34.51	37.86	41.20	44.54	47.88	51.23
3/8	7.22	11.24	14.45	17.12	'21.13	25.15	29.16	33.17	37.18	41.20	45.21	49.22	53.23	57.25	61.26
7/16	7.90	12.57	15.12	19.80	24.48	29.16	33.84	38.52	43.21	47.88	52.57	57.25	61.93	66.61	71.29
1/2	8.56	13.91	17.12	22.47	27.82	33.17	38.52	43.87	49.22	54.57	59.92	65.27	70.62	75.97	81.32
9/16	9.23	14.45	19.13	25.15	31.17	37.18	43.21	49.22	55.24	61.26	67.28	73.30	79.32	85.33	91.36
5/8	9.90	14.45	21.13	27.82	34.51	41.20	47.88	54.57	61.26	67.95	74.63	81.32	88.01	94.70	101.38
11/16	10.57	15.78	23.14	30.50	37.86	45.21	52.57	59.92	67.28	74.63	81.99	89.35	96.71	104.06	109.74
3/4	11.24	17.12	25.15	33.17	41.20	49.22	57.25	65.27	73.30	81.32	89.35	97.37	105.40	110.75	114.76
13/16	11.91	18.46	27.16	35.85	44.54	53.23	61.93	70.62	79.32	88.01	96.71	105.40	111.08	115.43	119.78
7/8	12.57	19.80	29.16	38.52	47.88	57.25	66.61	75.97	85.33	94.70	104.06	110.75	115.43	120.11	124.79
15/16	13.25	21.13	31.17	41.20	51.23	61.26	71.29	81.32	91.36	101.12	107.35	113.59	119.78	124.79	129.80
$ 1	26.75	32.38	40.97	49.56	58.15	66.75	75.34	83.93	92.52	101.12	107.35	113.59	119.83	126.07	132.31
					...										
$ 5	26.75	44.62	59.33	74.04	88.76	101.12	113.47	125.83	138.19	150.55	167.81	178.26	188.73	199.18	209.65
1/8	26.75	45.00	59.91	74.81	89.42	101.92	114.40	126.89	139.38	158.73	169.33	179.92	190.51	201.13	211.72
1/4	26.75	45.39	60.49	75.57	90.08	102.71	115.34	127.95	140.58	160.11	170.86	181.59	192.32	203.05	213.80
3/8	26.75	45.77	61.05	76.34	90.75	103.50	116.26	129.01	141.76	161.51	172.37	183.25	194.12	205.00	215.86
1/2	26.75	46.15	61.63	77.10	91.41	104.29	117.19	130.07	142.96	162.89	173.90	184.91	195.92	206.94	217.95
5/8	26.75	46.53	62.20	77.87	92.06	105.10	118.11	131.13	150.65	164.27	175.42	186.57	197.71	208.87	220.02
3/4	26.75	46.92	62.78	78.63	92.74	105.89	119.04	132.19	151.91	165.65	176.95	188.23	199.52	210.81	222.10
7/8	26.75	47.30	63.34	79.40	93.39	106.68	119.96	133.25	153.15	167.04	178.45	189.89	201.32	212.75	224.18
					...										
$ 9	28.96	56.86	76.75	93.35	109.94	132.24	149.60	166.94	184.30	201.64	216.54	231.42	246.31	261.20	276.09
1/8	29.16	57.25	77.15	93.88	110.61	113.08	150.56	168.05	185.54	203.03	218.06	233.08	348.10	263.15	278.17
1/4	29.35	57.63	77.55	94.41	111.27	113.90	151.53	169.16	186.79	204.41	219.59	234.75	249.91	265.07	280.24
3/8	29.54	58.02	77.94	94.94	111.93	134.73	152.50	170.27	188.03	205.80	221.09	236.41	251.71	267.02	282.31
1/2	29.74	58.39	78.35	95.47	112.60	135.57	153.47	171.37	189.27	207.18	222.62	238.06	253.50	268.96	284.40
5/8	29.92	58.78	78.74	96.00	113.25	136.40	154.44	172.48	190.51	208.56	224.14	239.72	255.30	270.89	286.47
3/4	30.11	59.16	79.14	96.52	113.92	137.23	155.41	173.59	191.78	209.94	225.67	241.39	257.11	272.83	288.55
7/8	30.30	59.55	79.53	97.06	114.58	138.06	156.37	174.70	193.02	211.34	227.18	243.05	258.91	274.77	290.62
$10	30.50	59.92	79.93	97.58	115.24	138.69	157.34	175.80	194.26	212.72	227.71	244.71	260.71	276.70	292.70

Source: A major brokerage firm.

$$\text{value of a call} = \left(\begin{array}{c} \text{market price of} \\ \text{underlying} \\ \text{common stock} \end{array} - \begin{array}{c} \text{striking price} \\ \text{on} \\ \text{the call} \end{array} \right) \times 100$$

$$V = (MP - SPC) \times 100$$

In other words, the value of a call is nothing more than the difference between market price and striking price; while it can be a negative number, such figures really have little or no meaning. A simple illustration will show that an option carrying a striking price of $50 on a stock presently trading at $60 has a value of $1,000 [($60 − $50) × 100 = $10 × 100]. A put, on the other hand, cannot be valued in the same way, since the two options allow the holder to do different things. To find the value of a put, simply reverse the order of the equation a bit, so that we have:

$$\text{value of a put} = \left(\begin{array}{c} \text{striking price} \\ \text{on the} \\ \text{put} \end{array} - \begin{array}{c} \text{market price of} \\ \text{underlying} \\ \text{common stock} \end{array} \right) \times 100$$

$$V = (SPP - MP) \times 100$$

Put and call values denote what the options should be valued and trading at. Unfortunately, this rarely occurs. Instead, these securities almost always trade at prices higher than their true value, especially for options that still have a long time to run. This difference is known as the *investment premium* and indicates the amount of "water" or excess value embedded in the quoted price of the put or call. Investment premium can be found as follows:

$$\text{investment premium} = \frac{\text{option premium} - \text{value of the option}}{\text{value of the option}}$$

$$IP = \frac{OP - V}{V}$$

For example, if a put has a value $2,000—found according to the valuation formula above—and carries a price (option premium) of $2,200, it would be trading at an investment premium of 10 percent ($2,200 − $2,000) ÷ $2,000 = $200 ÷ $2,000 = .10). Many of the same factors that affect option premium also affect investment premium; for example, investment premium tends to increase for longer options and for those on highly volatile stock. Unless it can be recovered when the investor sells the option, investment premium represents a form of sunk cost that is lost for good.

In-the-money/out-of-the-money

When written, options do not necessarily have to carry striking prices at the prevailing market price of the underlying common stock. And as options subsequently trade on the listed exchanges, the price of the option will move in response to moves in the price of the underlying common stock. When a call has a striking price less than the market price of the underlying common stock, it has a positive value and is known as an *in-the-money* option. A major portion of the option premium is based on (or derived from) the true value of the call. When the striking price exceeds the market price of the stock, the call has no "real" value and is known as an *out-of-the-money* option. Since the option has no value, its price is made up solely of investment premium. These terms are much more than convenient, exotic names given to options, for as we will see below, they characterize the investment behavior of options and can affect return and risk. A put option, by the way, is "in-the-money" when its striking price is greater than the market price of the stock; it is "out-of-the-money" when the market price of the stock exceeds the striking price.

I'm pleased to report, gentlemen, we're making a bundle.

Trading Strategies

For the most part, stock options can be used in three types of trading strategies: (1) buying puts and calls for speculation; (2) hedging with puts and calls; and (3) option writing and spreading.

Buying for speculation

This is the simplest and most straightforward use of puts and calls. Basically, it is just like buying stock (buy low and sell high) and, in fact, represents an alternative to investing in stock. For example, if an investor feels the market price of a particular stock is going to move up, one way of capturing that price appreciation is to buy a call on the stock. In contrast, if an investor feels the stock is about to drop in price, a put could convert the price decline to a profitable situation. In essence, investors buy options rather than stock whenever the options are likely to yield a greater return. The principle here, of course, is to get the largest return from one's investment dollar as possible—something that can often be done with puts and calls because of the desirable leverage they offer.

To illustrate the essentials of speculating with options, consider a situation where we have uncovered a stock we feel will move up in price over the next six months. What we would like to find out at this point is this: What would happen if we were to buy a call on this stock rather than investing directly in the firm's common? To find out, let us see what the numbers show. Assume the price of the stock is now $49, and we anticipate that within six months it should rise to about $65. In order to determine the relative merits of our investment alternatives, we need to determine the expected return associated with each course of action. Because call options have short lives, we will use holding period return to measure yield. Thus, if our expectations about the stock are correct, it should go up by $16 and in so doing provide stockholders with a 33 percent holding period return [($65 − $49) ÷ $49 = $16 ÷ $49 = .33]. But there are also some listed options available on this stock, so let us see how they would do. We will use as illustration two six-month calls that carry $40 and $50 striking prices, respectively. A recap of these two call alternatives, relative to the behavior of the underlying common stock, is summarized in Table 13.3. Clearly, either option alternative represents a superior investment to buying the stock. The dollar amount of profit may be a bit more with the stock, but notice that the size of the required investment ($4,900) is also *a lot* more.

Observe that one of the calls is an in-the-money option (the one with the $40 striking price); the other is out-of-the-money. The difference in returns generated by these calls is rather typical. Investors are usually able to generate better rates of return with lower-priced (out-of-the-money) options and also enjoy less exposure to loss. Of course, the major drawback of out-of-the-money options is that their price is made up wholly of investment premium—a sunk cost which would be lost if the stock does not move in price.

To see how investors can speculate in puts, consider the following situation: Assume that the price of our stock is now $51, but this time we anticipate a drop in price to about $35 within the next six months. If that occurs, then we could short sell the stock and make a profit of $16 per share (see Chapter 5 for a detailed discussion of short selling). Alternatively, an out-of-the-money put (with a striking price of $50) can be purchased for, say, $300. Again, if the price of the underlying stock does indeed drop, investors will make money with the put. The profit and rate of return on the put is summarized below, along with the comparative returns from short selling the stock:

	Buy 1 Put	Short Sell 100 Shares of Stock
Purchase price (today)	$ 300	
Selling price (6 months later)	1,500	
Short sell (today)		$5,100
Cover (6 months later)		3,500
Profit	$1,200	$1,600
Holding period return	400%	63%*

*Assumes the short sale was made with a required margin deposit of 50 percent.

Once more, in terms of holding period return, the stock option is the superior investment vehicle—by a wide margin. Of course, not all option investments end up nearly so well as the ones in our examples; clearly, success in this strategy rests on picking the right underlying common stock. Thus, *security analysis and proper stock selection are critical dimensions of this technique.* It is a highly risky investment strategy, but it may be well suited for the more speculatively inclined investor.

Hedging

A *hedge* is really nothing more than a combination of two or more securities into a single investment position for the purpose of reducing risk. This strategy might involve, for example, buying stock and simultaneously buying a put on that stock;

TABLE 13.3 SPECULATING WITH CALL OPTIONS

	100 Shares of Underlying Common Stock	SIX-MONTH CALL OPTIONS ON THE STOCK	
		$40 Striking Price	$50 Striking Price
TODAY			
Market value of stock (at $49/sh.)	$4,900		
Market price of calls*		$1,100	$ 400
SIX MONTHS LATER			
Expected value of stock (at $65/sh.)	$6,500		
Expected price of calls*		$2,500	$1,500
Profit	$1,600	$1,400	$1,100
Holding period return	33%	127%	275%

*The price of the calls was computed according to the call valuation formula and includes some investment premium in the purchase price of the calls, but *none* in the expected sales price.

or buying stock and then writing a call. There are many types of hedges, some very sophisticated, some very simple; but they all are used as a way to earn or protect profit without exposing the investor to excessive loss. An options hedge may be appropriate if you generated a profit from an earlier common stock investment and wish to protect that profit, or if you are about to enter into a common stock invest-ment and wish to protect your capital (by limiting potential capital loss). If you hold a stock that has gone up in price, the purchase of a put would provide the type of downside protection you need. The purchase of a call would provide protection to a short seller of common stock. Thus, option hedging always involves two trans-actions—one is the initial common stock position (long or short), and the other involves the simultaneous or subsequent purchase of the option.

Let us examine a simple options hedge by seeing how a put can be used to limit capital loss or protect profit. Consider an investor who wants to buy 100 shares of stock. Being a bit apprehensive about the stock's outlook, this investor decides to use an option hedge to protect his capital against loss. He therefore simultaneously buys the stock and a put on the stock (which fully covers the 100 shares owned). Preferably, the put would be a low-priced option with a striking price at or near the current market price of the stock. Suppose the investor purchases the common at $25 and pays $150 for a put with a $25 striking price. Now, no matter what happens to the price of the stock (over the life of the put), the investor can lose no more than $150; at the same time, the gains are almost unlimited. If the stock does not move, the investor will be out the cost of a put; if it drops in price, then whatever is lost on the stock will be made up with the put. However, if the price of the stock goes up (as hoped), the put becomes useless, but the investor rakes in the capital gains profit

TABLE 13.4 LIMITING CAPITAL LOSS WITH A PUT HEDGE

	Stock	Put*
TODAY		
Purchase price of the stock	$25	
Purchase price of the put		$1½
*Put is purchased simultaneously and carries a striking price of $25		
SOME TIME LATER		
A. Price of common goes *up* to:	$50	
Value of put		$0
Profit:		
100 shares of stock ($50 − $25)	$2500	
Less: Cost of put	− 150	
Profit:	$2350	
B. Price of common goes *down* to:	$10	
Value of put (see put valuation formula)		$15
Profit:		
100 shares of stock (loss)	− $1500	
Value of put (profit)	+ 1500	
Less: Cost of put	− 150	
Loss:	$ 150	

from the stock. The essentials of this option hedge are shown in Table 13.4. The $150 paid for the put is sunk cost, and that is lost no matter what happens to the price of the stock; in effect, it is the price paid for the hedge. Moreover, this hedge is good only as long as the investor holds the put. When this put expires, the investor will have to replace it with another put or forget about hedging his or her capital.

The other basic use of an option hedge involves entering into the options position after a profit has already been made on the stock. This could be done because of investment uncertainty in the foreseeable future, or for tax purposes (to carry over a profit to the next taxable year). For example, if an investor bought 100 shares of stock at $35 and it moved to $75, there would be a profit of $40 per share to protect. The profit could be protected with an option hedge by again buying a put. Assume the investor buys a three-month put with a $75 striking price at a cost of $250. Now, regardless of what happens to the stock over the life of the put, the investor would be guaranteed a minimum profit of $3,750 (the $4,000 profit in the stock made so far, less the $250 cost of the put). This can be seen in Table 13.5. Notice that if the price of the stock should fall, the worst that can happen is a guaranteed minimum profit of $3,750. And there is no limit to how much profit can be made—as long as the stock goes up, the investor will reap the benefits. (This discussion pertained to put hedges, but it should be clear that call hedges can also be set up to limit the loss or protect a profit on a short sale. For example, when a

TABLE 13.5 PROTECTING PROFITS WITH A PUT HEDGE

	Stock	Three-month Put with a $75 Striking Price
Purchase price of the stock (some time ago)	$35	
TODAY		
Market price of the stock	$75	
Market price of the put		$2½
THREE MONTHS LATER		
A. Price of common keeps going *up* to:	$100	
Value of put		$0
Profit:		
100 shares of stock ($100 − $35)	$6500	
Less: Cost of put	−250	
Profit:	$6250	
B. Price of common goes *down* to:	$50	
Value of put (see put valuation formula)		$25
Profit:		
100 shares of stock ($50 − $35)	$1500	
Value of put (profit)	2500	
Less: Cost of put	−250	
Profit:	$3750	

stock is sold short, a call can be purchased to protect the short seller against a rise in the price of the stock—with the same basic results outlined above.)

Option writing and spreading

The advent of listed options has led to many intriguing options trading strategies. In spite of the appeal of these exotic techniques, there is one important point that all the experts agree on: Such specialized trading strategies should be left to experienced investors who fully understand their subtleties. Our goal at this point is not to master these specialized strategies, but to learn in general terms what they are and how they operate. There are two types of specialized options strategies: (1) writing options, and (2) spreading options.

Writing options. Generally, investors write options because they feel the price of the underlying stock is going to move in their favor; that is, it is not going to rise as much as the buyer of a call expects, or fall as much as the buyer of a put hopes. And more often than not, the option writer is right—that is, he or she is going to make money far more often than the buyer of the put or call! Such favorable odds explain, in part, the underlying economic motivation for writing put and call options. Options writing represents an investment transaction to the writers, since they receive the full option premium (less normal transaction costs, of course) in exchange for agreeing to live up to the terms of the option.

Investors can write options in one of two ways. One is to write *naked options,* which are options on stock not owned by the writer. The investor simply writes the put or call, collects the option premium, and hopes that the price of the underlying stock does not move against him or her. If successful, naked writing can be highly profitable because of the very modest amount of capital required. One thing that should be kept in mind, however, is that the amount of return to the writer is always limited to the amount of option premium received. Yet there is really no limit to loss exposure. And that is the catch: The price of the underlying stock can rise or fall by just about any amount over the life of the option, and in so doing deal a real blow to the naked put or call writer.

Such risk exposure can be partially offset by writing *covered options,* which involves writing options against stocks the investor (writer) already owns, or has a position in. An investor, for example, could write a call against stock he or she owns, or a put against stock he or she has short sold. In this way, the investor can use the long or short position to meet the terms of the option. Such a strategy represents a fairly conservative way to generate attractive rates of return. The object is to write a slightly out-of-the-money option, pocket the option premium, and hope that the price of the underlying stock will move up or down to (but not exceed) the option striking price. In effect, what an investor is doing is adding option premium to the other usual sources of return that accompany stock ownership or short sales (dividends and/or capital gains). But there is more; for while the option premium adds to the return, it also reduces risk exposure, since it can be used to cushion a loss should the price of the stock move against the investor. There is a hitch to all this, however: The amount of return the covered option investor can realize is limited. For once the price of the underlying common stock begins to exceed the striking price on the option, the option becomes valuable. And once this happens, the option writer starts *losing* money. From this point on, for every dollar the investor makes on the stock position, he or she loses an equal amount on the option position.

Spreading options.   *Options spreading* is nothing more than combining two or more options into a single transaction. We could create an options spread by simultaneously buying and writing options on the same underlying stock. These cannot be identical options; they must differ with respect to striking price and/or expiration date. Spreads are a popular use of listed options, and account for a substantial amount of the trading activity on the listed options exchanges. These spreads go by a variety of exotic names, such as "bull spreads," "bear spreads," "money spreads," "calendar spreads," and "butterfly spreads." Each is different and constructed to meet a certain type of investment goal. For example, bull spreads are used with call options when prices are moving up as a way to capture the benefits of a rising market. Others are used to profit from a falling market, and still others to try to make money when the price of the underlying stock goes up *or* down! Whatever the objective most spreads are written to take advantage of differences in prevailing option premiums. The payoff from spreading is usually substantial, but so is the risk. In fact, some spreads that seem to involve almost no risk may end up with devastating results if the market and the "spread" (or difference) between option premiums move against the investor.

One variation of this theme involves *option straddles,* the simultaneous purchase of a put and a call on the same underlying common stock. Unlike spreads, straddles often involve the same striking price and expiration date. Here the object is to earn a profit from a modest increase or decrease in the price of the underlying stock. Otherwise, the principles of straddles are much like those for spreads: to build an investment position with combinations of options that will enable an investor to capture the benefits of certain types of stock price behavior. But keep in mind that if the price of the underlying stock and/or the option premiums do not behave in the anticipated manner, the investor loses. Spreads and straddles are extremely tricky and should not be used by novice investors.

Interest Rate and Currency Options

In addition to common stock, put and call options are also available on a select but growing list of debt instruments, foreign currencies, and commodity and financial futures. There are even stock index options that are written on the whole market (such as the S&P 500), or on certain industries (like the computer technology industry). Although the number of financial assets that underlie put and call options seems to be growing almost daily, our interest here is with debt instruments and foreign currencies (we'll look at stock index and futures options later in this chapter and in the next). Interest rate options are used for speculating on the behavior of interest rates, or as a hedge device to protect fixed income investments from capital loss. For example, an investor who wants to speculate on interest rate movements has two choices: He or she can do so with fixed income securities (as outlined in Chapter 11), or by buying put or call options on debt securities. As we'll see below, the latter choice gives the investor just as much price action, but at reduced risk. Foreign exchange options, in contrast, provide investors with a way to speculate on foreign exchange rates, or to hedge foreign currency holdings. The basic characteristics of interest rate and currency options are similar to those of stock options, but there are some significant differences in contract provisions, price behavior, and valuation concepts that should be fully understood by investors.

Contract provisions

The expansion of listed options into nonstock areas began in the autumn of 1981 when the CBOE introduced puts and calls on fixed income (debt) securities. Known as *interest rate options,* these new options, and the others that followed, work just like options on stocks. A call, for example, enables the holder to buy a certain amount of fixed income securities (or foreign currency) at a stipulated (striking) price for a specific period of time (as defined by the option's expiration date); a put, in contrast, gives the holder the right to sell these financial assets under comparable provisions. Interest rate and currency options are created by writers (just like stock options) and they expire on quarterly cycles, with the actual expiration date occurring on the Saturday following the third Friday of the expiration month.

At the present time, trading in interest rate options is conducted on the CBOE and American Exchange. There is presently available, or on the drawing board, a full menu of options on fixed income securities, including:

13- and 26-week Treasury bills
Prime-grade certificates of deposit
Intermediate-term Treasury notes
GNMA mortgage-backed securities
Long-term Treasury bonds

Specific government securities underlie the Treasury note and Treasury bond options—for example, in April 1983, Treasury note options were available on the 13¾ percent government note that matures in May 1992, the 10½ percent issue of November 1992, and the 10⅞ percent notes of February 1993. In contrast, the securities underlying the T-bill and GNMA options are determined via some fairly complex schemes (which probably explains, at least in part, the lack of popularity of these options). One noteworthy feature of the Treasury note and bond options is that, with one exception, the securities will exist for only one 9-month cycle. That is, unless the debt security is considered to be a bellwether issue (an issue closely followed in the marketplace), once the initial three-, six-, and nine-month options have expired, no additional puts and calls will be written on the securities. Rather, they will constantly be replaced with new government security issues. This is in sharp contrast to what is done with stock options, since new expiration dates are introduced every quarter to provide a continuous and ongoing market for each listed stock option.

Options on foreign currencies are available on most of the countries we have strong trading ties with. These options are traded on the Philadelphia Exchange, and in late April 1983 included the following currencies:

British pound
Swiss franc
West German mark
Canadian dollar
Japanese yen

In essence, puts and calls on these currencies give the holders the right to sell or buy large amounts of the specified foreign currency. This is a feature shared with interest rate options; unlike stock options, which are all keyed to 100-share round lots, the unit of trading in the debt and foreign exchange markets varies with the particular underlying financial asset and involves large dollar amounts. The details of the size of the contracts are spelled out in Table 13.6. Note that both large and small contracts are authorized on most of the interest rate options.

TABLE 13.6 SIZE OF INTEREST RATE AND FOREIGN CURRENCY OPTION CONTRACTS

INTEREST RATE OPTIONS

Underlying Security	Size of Contract (dollars)	
13-week T-bill	Large:	$1,000,000
	Small:	200,000
26-week T-bill	Large:	500,000
	Small:	100,000
Bank certificates of deposit		1,000,000
Treasury notes	Large:	100,000
	Small:	20,000
GNMA securities		100,000
Treasury bonds	Large:	100,000
	Small:	20,000

FOREIGN CURRENCY OPTIONS

Underlying Currency	Size of Contract
British pound	12,500 pounds
Swiss franc	62,500 francs
West German mark	62,500 marks
Canadian dollar	50,000 dollars
Japanese yen	6,250,000 yen

Price behavior

With interest rate options, the price of a call (its option premium) increases when the yield or interest rate on the underlying debt security decreases. Just the reverse occurs with puts. The quoted price of puts increases as market interest rates increase. This is so since such interest rate behavior will cause the underlying debt security to increase or decrease in value. That is, recall from Chapter 11 that a drop in interest rates results in an increase in the value of a debt security. Since an option should reflect the market behavior of the underlying security, the same valuation principle applies with options as with the securities themselves. If the market yield on Treasury notes and bonds drops, the market value of these securities and the price of calls on them will go up together, while the value of puts will decline. The puts and calls on foreign currencies will behave in a similar fashion as the exchange rate relative to our dollar goes up or down. For example, if the Canadian dollar becomes stronger relative to the American dollar, causing the exchange rate to improve, the price of a call option on the Canadian dollar will increase while the price of a put will decline. However, like stock options, puts and calls on debt securities and foreign currencies normally trade at prices that exceed the "true" intrinsic value of the options—investment premium (or "water") is present in the quoted prices of these options. Investment premium tends to increase with longer options and for securities that offer a lot of price action.

The price system used with debt and currency options is much like that used with stock options to the extent that the quoted premiums are expressed per unit of the underlying financial asset. Thus, to find the price of a put or call, we must multiply the quoted premium by the size of the contract. Listed debt and currency options are widely quoted in the financial media, an example of which is provided opposite. Note that the Treasury bill and Treasury note options in the illustration are "small" contracts, whereas the Treasury bonds are "large." Observe also that the quote system on these standardized (debt and currency) options is exactly like the one used with stock options; the underlying security is listed first, followed by the striking price on the option, and then by the premium quotes for three-, six-, and nine-month calls and puts.

For interest rate options, the premiums are expressed as a percentage of the par value of the underlying security. This is basically the same procedure used to quote fixed income securities in the bond market. Options on Treasury notes and bonds and GNMA securities are expressed in terms of 32nds, while T-bills and CDs are expressed in basis points, where 1 basis point equals $\frac{1}{100}$ of 1 percent. Thus, the June call on the 13¾ percent Treasury note (with a striking price of 116) carries a quoted premium of 1.12; since the numbers to the right of the decimal represent 32nds, this quote of 1.12 translates into a price of $1\frac{12}{32}$ percent of par. Because the size of this contract is $20,000 (as the illustration above shows, the size of the contract is stated in all debt and currency option quotes), the calls are trading at $1\frac{12}{32}$ or 1.3750 percent of par. Converting the quote to a decimal and multiplying by the par value of the contract, we have .01375 × $20,000 = $275. This interest rate option can be obtained for just $275, plus modest transaction costs. (Note that if this had been a "large" contract, involving $100,000 of the underlying Treasury note, the price would have been .01375 × $100,000 = $1,375.) Since each call covers $20,000 in the underlying security, a lot of price action can be obtained for a small amount of money. And regardless of what the underlying security does over the life of the option, $275 is the most the investor can lose.

Treasury bills and CDs follow a similar procedure, except they use $\frac{1}{100}$ of 1 percent as a price basis. The June calls on the 13-week T-bills (with the striking price of 91) are quoted at 0.82, which translates into a quote of 82 basis points. Now, rather than going through a complex procedure of relating this quote to the par value of the underlying security, we can follow a shortcut method for finding dollar premiums. That is, simply multiply the number of basis points in the quote by $5 for a small contract, or $25 for a large contract. Since our T-bill options are small contracts, the dollar price of the June call is $410—82 × $5. With foreign currency options, the quotes are stated in cents per unit of the underlying currency for all currencies except the Japanese yen, which is expressed in hundredths of a cent per unit. Thus, we see in the illustrated quotes above that the June puts on West German marks (strike price = 42) are trading at 3.26, which is read as "3.26 cents." To find the dollar premium, simply multiply this 3.26 cents by the 62,500 marks in the contract. Doing this, we find the dollar price of the put is $2,037.50 (.0326 × 62,500).

Interest Rate Options

Thursday, April 21, 1983
For Notes and Bonds, decimals in closing prices represent 32nds; 1.1 means 1 1/32. For Bills, decimals in closing prices represent basis points; $5 per .01.

American Exchange

U.S. TREASURY NOTE—$20,000 principal value

Underlying Issue	Strike Price	Calls—Last			Puts—Last		
		June	Sept	Dec	June	Sept	Dec
13¾ note due 5/15/92	112	5.0	...	...			
	116	1.12	...	...			
		June	Sept	Dec	June	Sept	Dec
10½ note due 11/15/92	96	...	...	...	0.16	...	...
		June	Sept	Dec	June	Sept	Dec
10⅞ note due 2/15/93	104	0.18	...	...	...	...	...

13-WEEK U.S. TREASURY BILL—$200,000 principal value

	Strike Price	Calls—Last			Puts—Last		
		June	Sept	Dec	June	Sept	Dec
	91	0.82	...	0.90	...	...	...
	92	0.12	...	0.36	...	...	...
	93	...	...	0.12			

Total call vol. 1107   Call open int. 5331
Total put vol. 11   Put open int. 1642

Chicago Board Options Exchange

U.S. TREASURY BOND—$100,000 PRINCIPAL VALUE

Underlying Issue	Strike Price	Calls—Last			Puts—Last		
		June	Sept	Dec	June	Sept	Dec
14% bond due 11/11	122	5.4	...	...	...	...	...
	126	2.2	...	...	1.11	...	...
	128	1.2	...	...	2.20	...	...
	130	0.12	...	...			
		June	Sept	Dec	June	Sept	Dec
10⅜% bond due 11/12	96	3.5	...	...	0.15	...	...
	100	0.22	...	...	2.0	...	...
	104	...	...	...	5.20	...	...

Total call vol. 99   Call open int. 5973
Total put vol. 64   Put open int. 1654

Foreign Currency Options

Philadelphia Exchange

Thursday, April 21, 1983
Premium expressed in cents per unit of currency.

Underlying Currency	Strike Price	Calls—Last			Puts—Last		
		Jun	Sep	Dec	Jun	Sep	Dec
12,500 British pounds	145	...	...	...	0.40	...	...
	150	6.00	...	...	...	...	...
	155	...	4.75	...	...	...	...

Pound open int. 1719   Pound spot close .5462

		Jun	Sep	Dec	Jun	Sep	Dec
62,500 Swiss francs	50	0.60	1.53	2.40	...	...	...
	52	0.18	...	...	...	...	...

Franc open int. 1661   Franc spot close .4849

		Jun	Sep	Dec	Jun	Sep	Dec
62,500 West German marks	38	...	...	...	0.11	...	...
	40	1.58	...	...	0.61	0.94	...
	42	0.64	1.12	1.60	3.26	...	...
	44	0.13	0.70	...	...	...	...

Mark open int. 1297   Mark spot close .4074

		Jun	Sep	Dec	Jun	Sep	Dec
50,000 Canada dollars	80	...	...	...	0.25	...	...
	82	...	...	...	1.10	...	...
	84	0.05	...	0.29	...	...	...

Dollar open int. 885   Dollar spot close .8138
Premium expressed in hundredths of a cent per unit of currency.

		Jun	Sep	Dec	Jun	Sep	Dec
6,250,000 Japanese yen	40	2.71	...	...	0.10	...	...
	42	1.15	...	...	...	...	...
	44	0.30	1.00	...	...	...	...

Yen open int. 445   Yen spot close .004231
Total volume 488

Source: The Wall Street Journal.

BOX 13.3 NEW OPTIONS FOR TRADERS

Investors who want to gamble on the fortunes of the computer industry or the oil and gas industry now can do so without having to choose a particular stock. Instead they can place their bet on the entire field by buying one of the newest stock market index options. And they can speculate with as little as a few hundred dollars.

The American Stock Exchange's computer technology index is a composite of 30 computer stocks weighted by their market value, with IBM making up 54% of the index. Other stocks in the index include Honeywell and Digital Equipment. The Chicago Board Options Exchange (CBOE) has an S&P computer and business equipment index based on 12 stocks—with IBM representing 73% of their value. For the oil and gas stocks, the ASE is offering an index of 30 domestic and international energy companies, while the CBOE's international oil index consists of six world giants.

You can buy call options, which give you the right to buy the underlying index at a fixed price (the strike or exercise price) for a limited time—up to six months. Or you can buy put options, which offer the right to sell the index. Call buyers make money if the index rises; put owners profit if it falls. When you trade options, you risk losing your entire investment. But you also can make money fast. In early October, Richard Donsky, head of Shearson/American Express' options department, was recommending a call in the computer technology index with a strike price of 110 and a March expiration date. The call was then quoted at 6⅛, meaning that a contract would cost $612.50 plus commission. At the time, the index itself was around 106. If it reached 120 by mid-December, an investor probably could sell the option for about $1,300.

Source: Money, November 1983, p. 8.

How profits are made

Interest rate and foreign currency options are valued like other puts or calls to the extent that it is the difference in the market price of the underlying security and the striking price stated on the option that determines fundamental value. To see how this works, consider a Treasury bond call—these options are traded on the CBOE. Let's take the 10⅜ percent issue due in November 2012. The striking prices on intermediate- and long-term securities are expressed as a percentage of par. Thus, an exercise price of 100 on a 10⅜ percent issue implies the bond will be priced at par in the marketplace and therefore be trading at a yield of 10⅜ percent. A lower strike price (say, 96) implies a yield in excess of 10⅜ percent and a higher strike price (say, 104) means a lower yield. (See Chapter 11 for a detailed discussion of how bond prices are determined and how bonds are quoted in the financial press.) Now, as the market price of the underlying security moves with interest rates, the value of the call is affected accordingly.

For example, if we bought a call with a striking price of 100 at a premium of 0.22 (or $687.50), and if the yield on the 10⅜ percent issue moved down by the expiration date so that the market price of the bond was 105, we would make a profit on the transaction. Specifically, at expiration the call would be worth 5 points (market price of 105 less striking price of 100), so our *net* profit would be:

$$5.00 - 0.22 = 4.10 = 4^{10}/_{32}$$

Multiplying by the par value of the call yields:

$$4^{10}\!/_{32} = .043125 \times \$100,000 = \$4,312.50$$

$$HPR = \$4,312.50/\$687.50 = \underline{627.3\%}$$

Not bad for a $687 investment! Market interest rates have to decline by a substantial amount in order to realize this kind of profit, but such interest rate behavior certainly does occur. Of course, the concept would be reversed for puts—investors make money in puts when interest rates rise so that the market price of the underlying security drops (to, say, 95). And the same basic pricing concept applies to options on short-term debt securities (T-bills and CDs), except that the actual computation procedures are far more complex. Clearly, the key to success with these securities is the ability to forecast future interest rate behavior correctly, which is *not* an easy task.

The situation is similar for foreign currency options. With these securities, the striking price is stated in terms of exchange rates, as expressed in cents. In essence, the exchange rate measures the value of the foreign currency relative to U.S. dollars. A strike price of 150, for example, implies each unit of the foreign currency (such as one British pound) is worth 150 cents, or $1.50, in American money. If an investor held a (150) call on this foreign currency, she would make money if the foreign currency strengthened relative to the U.S. dollar so that the exchange rate rose (to, say, 155); in contrast, if she held a (150) put, she would profit from a decline in the exchange rate (to, say, 145). Let's use a put on the British pound to illustrate what happens. Say we could buy a (150) put at a premium of 1.50; this means the put would cost us $187.50 (.0150 × 12,500). Now if the exchange rate actually does drop to 145 by expiration, the put would be worth the difference in the prevailing (spot) exchange rate and the exchange rate stipulated in the striking price; in our example, the puts would be trading at 5.00 and each one would be worth $625.00 (.05 × 12,500). For each put we held, we would make a profit of $625.00 − $187.50 = $437.50, and generate a holding period return of ($625.00 − $187.50)/$187.50 = 233.3 percent. Success in forecasting movements in foreign exchange rates is obviously essential to a profitable foreign currency options program.

Trading strategies

Interest rate and currency options are appealing to investors because of their limited exposure to loss, as well as the attractive leverage they offer—which can lead to substantial capital gains and very high rates of return. They also provide an effective yet inexpensive way to hedge a position in fixed income securities or foreign currency. But these options *and the financial assets underlying them* are far more complex than stocks and stock options. They should be used *only* by knowledgeable and experienced investors who understand the mechanics of interest rates and/or currency options, and are familiar with the debt and/or foreign exchange markets.

Interest rate and currency options can be used in just about any way that a stock option can. They can be used for speculation, as a hedging vehicle, in an options writing program, and for spreading purposes. For example, a put option on a Treasury bond might be purchased to protect an investor's bond portfolio against a decline in value. Or an investor might want to pursue the rewards of a covered writing program by writing calls against bonds or other fixed income securities he or she holds. Because debt and currency options are so much like stock options when it comes to the ways they can be used, the only trading technique we'll look at here is that of *speculation,* and we'll use speculating in interest rate options for purposes of illustration.

Consider an individual who has done a good deal of investing in fixed income securities. Assume further that she considers herself an aggressive investor who likes to speculate on interest rate movements. With the advent of interest rate options, she now has an attractive alternative to investing in debt securities as a way of capturing the capital gains that accompany a drop in market rates. To see how this works, and to gain an appreciation of the comparative returns available from these two investment vehicles, let's look at a situation in which our investor thinks interest rates are about to fall. Assume Treasury bond yields are now 12 percent. Based on extensive economic analysis, our investor feels very strongly that they will drop to 10 percent within nine months. The ability to forecast interest rates is the key to success with this trading strategy, for as we'll see, the amount of investment success or failure (profit or loss) is directly linked to how well interest rates are forecast. On the other hand, because of the limited loss exposure of interest rate options, the use of a call will at least lessen the potential impact of faulty judgment (in other words, if you are wrong, there's only so much you can lose with calls, which is not the case when you speculate directly in bonds).

Given that our investor is satisfied her interest rate projections are sound, she's ready to decide which vehicle to use for purposes of speculation: the Treasury *bond* or the Treasury bond *call.* For simplicity, let's assume she can choose either a 12 percent, 30-year Treasury bond presently trading at par (100), or a call on the same 12 percent, 30-year issue that carries a striking price of 100 and is presently trading at a premium of, say, 1 point (1.00). If market rates do fall to 10 percent by the expiration date on the call, given the investor has $10,000 to invest, then:

	Alternative 1: Buy Treasury Bonds	Alternative 2: Buy 10 Treasury Bond Calls*
I. Purchase price today, with interest rates at 12%		
Buy bonds at par	$10,000	
Buy calls at 1.00		$10,000
II. Estimated values of securities at expiration date of calls, with market interest rates at 10%:		
Value of 12%, 30-year bonds priced to yield 10% (118.8)	$11,880	
Value of Treasury bond calls, with strike price = 100(18.8)		$188,000
Net profit	$ 1,880	$178,000

*Each call contract covers $100,000 in the underlying security.

Clearly, there is a substantial comparative advantage to speculating with the call options. For whereas speculating with the bonds would yield a very respectable return of around 19 percent, the calls generate nearly 100 times that amount. The reason is simple: leverage. That is, since *each* call contract involves $100,000 in Treasury securities, the 10 calls enable the investor to participate in the price action of $1 million in securities—versus only $10,000 when alternative 1 is used (where the investor speculates by buying the bonds directly). In fact, just one call would have given our investor nearly *10 times* the return of alternative 1; that is, she could have invested just $1,000 in a call and still earned a net profit of some $17,800! And this is precisely what most speculators would do, thus freeing up $9,000 for other investment purposes. Such an approach not only provides the sought-after price action; it also limits exposure to loss to the cost of the option (in this case, $1,000). To appreciate the importance of that, consider what happens in our example if interest rates rise—to, say, 14 percent—by the expiration date of the call. The speculator who uses a call is out $1,000, since the options are now useless; in contrast, speculating with the bonds in such a situation would cost our investor $1,400, since the value of 12 percent, 30-year bonds will drop to $8,600. Thus, speculating with interest rate options does have its rewards. But in addition to not earning any interest income over the course of the investment (as bondholders do), it also has one other very significant shortcoming that simply cannot be eliminated; its *limited life.* For if nothing happens to the market price of the bond over the life of the call, the investor is out the cost of the option, whereas the bond investor at least still has a position in the securities.

Stock Index Options

Perhaps the most intriguing type of option, and one that is rapidly growing in popularity, is the *stock index option.* Such options permit investors to play the market as a whole, or to invest in a whole industry with a single transaction. As of late 1983, there were five market index options available, including the following:

S&P 100 Index
S&P 500 Index
Major Market Index
Market Value Index
NYSE Index

In addition, trading was being conducted in the following four industry index options:

International Oil Stocks
Computers & Business Equipment Stocks
Oil & Gas Stocks
Computer Technology Stocks

Because of the substantial popularity in index options, it is anticipated that there will be a big increase in the number of both market and industry options available in the near future.

Market options differ from *industry options* in that the former are written on

Index Options

Chicago Board

S&P 100 INDEX

Strike Price	Calls—Last Dec	Mar	June	Puts—Last Dec	Mar	June
150	...		...	1/16		...
155	12 7/8	...	...	1/16	...	...
160	8 1/4	11	...	3/8	1 13/16	...
165	4 1/8	7 3/4	...	1 7/16	3 3/8	...
170	1 9/16	4 7/8	...	4	5 3/4	...
175	5/16	2 7/8	...	8 1/4	9	...
180	1/16	1 1/2	...	13 1/4	...	...

Total call volume 32,344. Total call open int. 227,130.
Total put volume 31,687. Total put open int. 206,459.
The index closed at 166.71, −0.09.

S&P 500 INDEX

Strike Price	Calls—Last Dec	Mar	June	Puts—Last Dec	Mar	June
160	...	...	...	11/16	...	...
165	...	...	...	2	...	...
170	1 1/8	...	...	4 1/2	...	...
175	1/4	...	...	...	...	...

Total call volume 42. Total call open int. 489.
Total put volume 30. Total put open int. 518.
The index closed at 166.13, +0.05.

American Exchange

MAJOR MARKET INDEX

Strike Price	Calls—Last Jan	Apr	July	Puts—Last Jan	Apr	July
110	...	...	...	3/16	...	...
115	...	...	...	1/2	...	...
120	4 3/4	7	...	1 1/2	3 1/4	...
125	2	4 3/8	...	3 7/8	5 1/4	...
130	1/2	2 3/16	...	...	...	...

Total call volume 2,324 Total call open int. 30,218
Total put volume 2,054 Total put open int. 30,819
The index closed at 122.28, +0.02

AMEX MARKET VALUE INDEX

Strike Price	Calls—Last Dec	Mar	June	Puts—Last Dec	Mar	June
210	11 1/2	...	...	1/2	...	...
220	4 3/8	...	...	3 3/8	...	...
230	7/8	5	...	10 3/4	10 3/4	...
240	...	...	...	...	...	...
250	...	...	...	...	...	...
260	...	...	...	...	...	...

Total call volume 188 Total call open int. 3,426
Total put volume 160 Total put open int. 1,872
The index closed at 219.94, +.36

COMPUTER TECHNOLOGY INDEX

Strike Price	Calls—Last Dec	Mar	Puts—Last Dec	Mar
90	...	...	1/8	...
95	5 3/4	...	1/2	2
100	2 3/8	5 1/4	2 1/8	3 7/8
105	11/16	3 7/8	5 3/4	...
110	1/8	1 3/4	10	...

Total call volume 979 Total call open int. 31,195
Total put volume 1,999 Total put open int. 21,120
The index closed at 99.93, −0.17

OIL & GAS INDEX

Strike Price	Calls—Last Dec	Mar	Puts—Last Dec	Mar
95	4 1/2	...	...	...
100	1 1/2	4 1/4	2 5/8	3 7/8
105	3/8	2 1/8	6 1/4	...
110	3/16	...	...	...
115	1/16	...	...	...

Total call volume 348 Total call open int. 4,725
Total put volume 373 Total put open int. 2,773
The index closed at 99.14, −0.28

N.Y. Stock Exchange

NYSE INDEX OPTIONS

Strike Price	Calls—Last Nov	Feb	Puts—Last Nov	Feb
90	5 1/2	7 1/4	...	11/16
95	15/16	3 3/4	1/16	2
100	...	1 7/16	4 1/4	4 7/8
105	...	3/8	...	...

Total call volume 5,251 Total call open int. 42,607
Total put volume 4,165 Total put open int. 27,829
The index closed at 95.93, +0.04

Source: The Wall Street Journal, November 18, 1983.

mythical, broad-based portfolios of stocks (like the 500 stocks in the S&P Index) intended to capture the overall behavior of the stock market, whereas industry options are written on much more narrowly defined portfolios of stocks from specific industries, which are supposed to track the average price performance of stocks in specific industries. Actually, price movements in *both* market and industry options are linked to the *indexes* that underlie the respective options; thus, just as there is an index (such as the S&P 500) that supposedly reflects movements in the overall market, there is also an index that is used to determine the price of a particular industry option. For example, underlying the AMEX's computer technology option is an index that is composed of 30 computer stocks, weighted by their market value. As it moves up or down—in conjunction with the weighted average market price of the stocks that make up the index—the option premiums move accordingly.

Both puts and calls are available on index options. They are valued and have issue characteristics like any other put or call, except they are issued only with three- and six-month expiration dates (there are no nine-month index options). When the underlying market (or industry) index goes up, the value of a *call* increases; when the index goes down, the value of a *put* goes up. As seen on page 504, they even have a quotation system that is virtually identical to the other types of puts and calls.

The value of these puts and calls is a function of the difference in the striking price on the option (which is stated in terms of the underlying index) and the latest market (or industry) index. To illustrate, the AMEX Oil & Gas *Index* recently closed at 99.14; at the same time there was a *call* on this index, with an index striking price of 95, that was trading at 4½. This call had an underlying true value of: 99.14 − 95.00 = 4.14; the difference between the quoted price of 4.50 and its theoretical value of 4.14 was, of course, investment premium (or "water"). Now, if the index were to go up to 115 by the expiration date on the call, this option would be quoted at: 115 − 95 = 20; as a result, since all industry options are valued in multiples of $100, this option would be worth: 20 × $100 = $2000. If an investor had bought this security when it was quoted at 4½, the call would have cost just $450 (4½ × $100) and it would have a holding period return of a very attractive 344% [($2000 − $450)/$450]. Note that two of the *market* options are also valued in multiples of $100 (they are the S&P 100 and the Major Market Indexes), and the others (the S&P 500, the AMEX Market Value, and the NYSE Indexes) use multiples of $500.

Index options can be used for speculation or for hedging. They provide investors the opportunity to play the market or invest in a whole industry with a relatively small amount of capital. For example, if an investor thinks the market is heading up, she can capitalize on those expectations by buying a call on one of the *market* indexes; in contrast, if her analysis leads her to believe very strongly that computer stocks are about to drop off sharply, she may be able to profit from that by buying puts on one of the computer *industry* indexes. These options are equally effective as a hedging vehicle—for instance, one way to protect holdings of computer stocks against a drop in price is to buy computer industry puts. Like any other put or call, these options provide attractive leverage opportunities and, at the same time, limit the exposure to loss in any transaction to the price paid for the option. Further discussion of index securities, including more detailed illustrations of how they can be used, will be deferred to the next chapter where we examine stock index futures.

SUMMARY

Options, unlike common stocks or bonds, do not provide buyers with the privileges of ownership; rather, the owner of an option is entitled only to the right to subsequently buy or sell other securities. Stock options permit the holder to buy or sell shares of stock at a specified price over a specified period of time. There are three kinds of options: (1) rights, (2) warrants, and (3) puts and calls.

A right has a very short market life (of no more than several weeks) and enables the holder to purchase a new issue of common stock at a subscription price, set below the prevailing market price of the existing outstanding stock. Only if the shareholder exercises the right or sells it will he or she realize any financial benefit from its issue. If the rights are exercised, the investor obtains stock, commission-free; if they are sold, the investor receives the market value of the right. Trading opportunities in rights are limited due to their short life, the narrow range of their price activity, and their irregular issuance.

A warrant is similar to a right but its maturity is much longer. Attached to bond issues as "sweeteners," warrants allow the holder to purchase the corporation's common stock at a set exercise price on or before the stipulated expiration date. A warrant becomes valuable when the market price of its underlying common stock equals or exceeds the exercise price. Frequently, warrants trade at a premium price due to their speculative value. Warrants offer advantages to their owners in the form of: (1) attractive capital gains (since warrant prices move with stock prices); (2) low unit cost; and (3) the benefits of leverage (which accompanies the low unit cost). In weighing these advantages, the investor must consider the fact that warrants pay no dividends and carry an expiration date. Trading in warrants is done primarily as a substitute for common stock investing and is based on the magnified capital gains they offer. The value of a warrant changes directly with and generally by the same amount as the underlying common stock; but since a warrant's unit cost is often much lower than common stock, the same dollar change in price represents a considerably larger percentage yield. In addition to using warrants to magnify the amount of dollar return, they may also be used to limit loss exposure.

Other options that offer attractive speculative value and leverage potential are puts and calls. A put enables the holder to sell a certain amount of a specified security at a specified price over a specified time period. A call, in contrast, gives the holder the right to buy the same securities at a specified price over a specified period of time. The three basic features of puts and calls are striking price (or the contract price between the buyer and writer), the expiration date (which determines the life of the option), and the purchase price of the option itself. The value of a call is the difference in the market price of the underlying security less the striking price designated on the call. The value of a put is its striking price less the market price of the security. The major drawbacks to put and call options include their limited life, the absence of ownership rights (like the receipt of interest and dividends), and the level of specialized knowledge needed to master the trading strategies involved. Since April 26, 1973, the Chicago Board Options Exchange has made option trading easy and convenient; contracts have been standardized (with regard to striking prices and expiration dates), trading activity has increased, and options trading has become a widely used investment technique. Today, standardized listed put and call options are available on over 350 common stocks, a number of debt securities (from T-bills to Treasury bonds), about half a dozen foreign currencies, a small but growing number of stock market industry indexes, and commodities and financial futures.

Puts and calls offer a variety of trading strategies. Buying options for their speculative appeal can be used in place of speculating with the underlying securities themselves. Since these options have a lower unit cost than the underlying financial asset, they yield greater returns per investment dollar. Conservative investors may be attracted to put and call purchases because they offer limited risk in absolute dollar terms. More likely, however, conservative investors will use options to form hedge positions in combination with other securities. A put can be used to provide downside protection for securities held long; a call can be used to provide upside protection in a short sale. Writing and spreading options are two other popular uses of this investment vehicle.

KEY TERMS

calls
conventional options
covered options
currency options
exercise price
expiration date
ex-rights
hedge (option hedging)
industry options
in-the-money option
interest rate options
investment premium
leverage
listed options
market options
naked options
options

option spread
option straddle
option writer (or maker)
out-of-the-money option
preemptive right
premium (option)
premium (warrant)
puts
rights-off
rights-on
rights offering
stock index options
stock rights
striking price
subscription price
warrants

REVIEW QUESTIONS

1. Describe a stock right and its relation to the preemptive rights of investors.

2. How would a stock right be used by an investor? Why does it have such limited investment appeal?

3. Assume a company has 1 million shares of common stock outstanding and intends to issue another 200,000 shares via a rights offering; the rights will carry a subscription price of $48. If the current market price of the stock is $53, what is the value of one right?

4. What is a warrant? What is the chief attraction of a warrant?

5. Assume that one warrant gives the holder the right to buy one share of stock at an exercise price of $40; what is the value of this warrant if the current market price of the stock is $44? At what ($ and %) premium would the warrants be trading if they were quoted in the market at the price of $5?

6. Why are warrants often considered viable investment alternatives to common stock?

7. Describe the leverage feature of a warrant and note why leverage is so attractive to investors.

8. A warrant carries an exercise price of $20; assume it takes three warrants to buy one share of stock. At what price would the warrant be trading if it sold at a 20 percent premium while the market price of the stock was $35 per share?

9. Why might it be unwise to exercise warrants?

10. What factors are important in determining the investment appeal of warrants? Why is the price of the warrant itself so important in the investment decision?

11. Describe put and call options. Are they issued like other corporate securities?

12. Why are puts and calls gaining in popularity?

13. What are listed options? Contrast these with conventional options.

14. What is the difference between option premium and investment premium?

15. Assume an investor buys a six-month put on a particular stock for $600; the put has a striking price of $80, and the current market price of the underlying stock is $75. How much investment premium is there in the put?

16. What are the main investment attractions of put and call options? What are the risks?

17. Briefly discuss the differences and similarities in interest rate options and stock options; do likewise for foreign currency options (relative to stock options).

18. Use the quotations on page 499 to find the dollar price of the following interest rate and foreign currency option quotes:

a. 10½ percent U.S. Treasury Note due 11/15/92, quoted at 3.24.
b. 13-week T-bill quoted at 1.79.
c. Swiss francs quoted at 0.55.
d. Japanese yen quoted at 3.65.

19. Note the various ways puts and calls can be used by investors.

20. A six-month call on a certain common stock carries a striking price of $60; it can be purchased at a cost of $600. Assume that the underlying stock rises to $75 per share by the expiration date of the option. How much profit would this option generate over the six-month holding period, and what is its rate of return?

21. Otis Q. Hummer is a bond investor who likes to speculate on the future movements in interest rates. Since the introduction of listed interest rate options, Otis has confined most of his speculation activity to puts and calls on long-term debt securities. After extensive economic analysis, Otis feels market interest rates are now headed down; accordingly, he buys a (large contract) call on a U.S. Treasury bond, with a striking price of 98—the call was trading at a quote of 2.25 when he purchased it. What holding period return would Otis earn if the *underlying Treasury bond* trades at 110 just prior to the expiration date of the call?

22. Dorothy Cappel does a lot of investing in the stock market and is a frequent user of stock index options. She is convinced that the market is about to undergo a broad retreat and has decided to buy a put on the S&P 500 Index—the put carries a striking price of 190 and is quoted in the financial press at 4½. Although the S&P Index of 500 stocks is presently at 186.45, Dorothy thinks it will drop to 165 by the expiration date on the option. How much profit will she make, *and* what will her holding period return be if she is right?

CASE PROBLEMS

13.1 THE PABLICKS' INVESTMENT OPTIONS

Tom Pablick is a highly successful businessman in Atlanta. The box manufacturing firm he and his wife Judy founded several years ago has prospered. Because he is self-employed, he is building his own retirement fund. So far he has accumulated a substantial sum in his investment account, mostly by following an aggressive investment posture; he does this be-cause, as he puts it, "you never know when the bottom's gonna fall out in this business." Tom has been following the stock of Rembrandt Paper Products (RPP), and after conducting ex-tensive analysis, feels the stock is about ready to move. Specifically, he believes that within the next nine months, RPP could go to about $80 per share, from its current level of $57.50. The stock pays annual dividends of $2.40 per share, and Tom figures he would receive three quarterly dividend payments over his nine-month investment horizon. In studying the company, Tom has learned that it has some warrants outstanding (they mature in eight years and carry an exercise price of $45); also, it has nine-month call options (with $50 and $60 striking prices) listed on the CBOE. Each warrant is good for one share of stock, and they are currently trading at $15, while the CBOE calls are quoted at $8 for the options with $50 striking prices, and $5 for the $60 options.

Questions

1. How many alternative investment vehicles does Tom have if he wants to invest in RPP for no more than nine months? What if he has a two-year investment horizon?

2. Using a nine-month holding period and assuming the stock does indeed rise to $80 over this time frame:

a. Find the market price of the warrant at the end of the holding period, given it then trades at a premium of 10 percent.

b. Find the value of both calls, given that at the end of the holding period, neither contains any investment premium.

c. Determine the holding period rate of return for each of the four investment alter-natives open to Mr. Pablick.

3. Which course of action would you recommend if Tom simply wants to maximize profit? Would your answers change if other factors (like comparative risk exposure) were considered along with return? Explain.

13.2 FRED'S QUANDARY—TO HEDGE OR NOT TO HEDGE

A little more than ten months ago, Fred Weaver, a mortgage banker in Dallas, bought 300 shares of stock at $40 per share. Since then, the price of the stock has risen to $75 per share. It is now near the end of the year, and the market is starting to weaken; Fred feels there is still plenty of play left in the stock, but is afraid the tone of the market will be detrimental to his position. His wife Denise is taking an extension course on the stock market and has just learned about put and call hedges. She suggests that he use puts to hedge his position. Fred is intrigued with the idea, which he discusses with his broker—who advises him that, indeed, the needed puts are available on his stock. Specifically, he can buy three-month puts, with $75 striking prices, at a cost of $550 each (quoted at 5½).

Questions

1. Given the circumstances surrounding Fred's current investment position, what bene-fits could be derived from using the puts as a hedge device? What would be the major drawback?

2. What would Fred's minimum profit be if he buys three puts at the indicated option premium? How much would he make if he did not hedge, but instead sold his stock imme-diately at a price of $75 per share?

3. Assuming Fred uses three puts to hedge his position, indicate the amount of profit he would generate if the stock moves to $100 by the expiration date of the puts. What if the stock drops to $50 per share?

4. Should he use the puts as a hedge? Explain. Under what conditions would you urge him not to use the puts as a hedge?

SELECTED READINGS

Ansbacher, Max C. "The Bear Facts About Puts." *Money,* August 1977, pp. 64–65.

Bornstein, Paul. "Is Your Optimism Warranted?" *Forbes,* August 16, 1982, pp. 90–91.

Brophy, Charles. "The Lure of Bonds with Warrants." *FACT,* September 1982, pp. 49–52.

Bulkeley, William M. "As Options Trading Expands, Every Investor Should Get the Hang of Using Puts and Calls." *The Wall Street Journal,* April 28, 1980, p. 38.

"Buying and Selling Puts and Calls." *Nation's Business,* August 1977, p. 42.

"Criteria for Selecting Calls and Puts." *Financial World,* March 1, 1976, p. 86.

Edgerton, Jerry. "The Explosion in Options." *Money,* May 1981, pp. 122–128.

Greenebaum, Mary. "An Optional Way to Bet on Interest Rates." *Fortune,* August 10, 1981, pp. 235–236.

Gross, LeRoy, and Allan C. Snyder. "Covered Call Switch-Hitting." *Financial World,* December 1, 1978, p. 52.

"How to Play the Options Game." *Business Week,* December 22, 1980, pp. 88–92.

"How to Trade Options." *Business Week,* March 7, 1977, pp. 77–82.

Kichen, Steve. "Stock Options Come of Age." *Forbes,* November 24, 1980, pp. 82–84.

"New Ways to Play the Interest-Rate Markets." *Business Week,* February 8, 1982, pp. 102–106.

"Options: The Mysterious, Turbulent Market." *Business Week,* September 25, 1978, pp. 90–101.

Shepherd, W. "New Risks in Warrants." *Business Week,* August 3, 1974, p. 42.

Stabler, Charles N. "Hedging Your Bets: More Investors Using Options as Way to Cut Stock Ownership Risk." *The Wall Street Journal,* August 15, 1975, p. 1.

"Stock Warrants—A Way to Get Leverage." *Forbes,* June 9, 1980, pp. 102–104.

"Strictly for Speculators." *Money,* March 1977, pp. 68–69.

Train, John. "Selling Options: A Strategy That Doesn't Make Sense." *Forbes,* October 16, 1978, p. 204.

———. "Options: Don't be the Pigeon." *Forbes,* March 30, 1981, pp. 156–157.

Turov, Daniel. "Variety of Options—There Are Many Ways to Deal in Puts." *Barron's,* June 20, 1977, pp. 11, 25.

Why Use Options?

Popular literature perpetuates many myths about the advantages and disadvantages of trading in options. Aside from tax considerations, the only reason for using stock options in constructing a portfolio is that buying underpriced and selling overpriced options enables an investor to take more efficient common stock positions. Buying underpriced or selling overpriced options will mean a higher expected rate of return than an investor could obtain using common stocks alone. Let us see how this works.

The stock equivalence of an option is simply another way of describing the price change of the option in response to the price change of the stock. For example, if an option changes in price by one-half point when the stock changes in price by one point, that one-half point price change on an option on 100 shares of stock is a change in the option's value of $50. This $50 equals the exact change in value that a holder of 50 shares of stock would experience if the stock price changed by $1. Therefore, the option is the equivalent of 50 shares of stock. In constructing a portfolio we use the option as if it were actually 50 shares. If another option changed in price by one-quarter point in response to a one-point move in the stock price, that option would be the equivalent of 25 shares of stock.

Every option—in-the-money or out-of-the-money, put or call—can be translated into a common stock equivalent. When a portfolio containing options is viewed from the perspective of stock equivalents, conventional techniques of diversification management and risk measurement are useful. Now the obvious question is this: "Why use options if they are simply another way of creating a common stock portfolio?" The answer is that options can be a way of creating a common stock portfolio more efficiently—that is, by offering a higher expected rate of return than a conventional portfolio can provide. In the language of modern portfolio theory, more efficient portfolios will provide a risk-return combination that falls above the risk-return tradeoff line.

The intelligent investor does not buy calls just because they are undervalued; nor does he or she buy stock and sell calls just because the option premium is large. The investor is interested in the stock because it is fundamentally attractive. The options are simply part of a more

GARY L. GASTINEAU

efficient way to take a stock equivalent position. Option evaluation is a supplement to stock evaluation, not a substitute for it.

Perhaps the best way to illustrate the significance of option value for investment results is through an example. The stock in this example is priced at $48 per share. If we buy 50 shares, we pay $2,400:

50 shares $\times$ $48 per share = $2,400

At the same time, a four-month call option to buy the stock at $50 per share is selling for $2 per underlying share. Assuming the option price changes by about $0.50 for each $1 change in stock price, this option is the equivalent of 50 shares of stock. After feeding appropriate assumptions into our evaluation model, we calculate that the fair value of this option is $3 per underlying share. The valuation suggests it is more economical to take a 50-share equivalent position by buying one of these underpriced calls and putting an appropriate amount of cash in a money market fund:

One 50-share-equivalent call option at $2	$ 200
Investment in money market fund	$2,100
	$2,300

The total investment for this equivalent postion is $100 less ($2,300 vs. $2,400) when we use the option and the money market fund. Buying an underpriced option or selling an overpriced option affects the prospective return in a portfolio in essentially the same way as buying the stock at a discount from its market price. In this example we have computed the value of the call to be $300, but we are able to buy it for $200. The $100 advantage from buying the underpriced call is the equivalent of buying 50 shares of stock at $46 per share, $2 per share below market.

GARY L. GASTINEAU
Manager, Options Portfolio Service
Webster Management Corporation,
a subsidiary of Kidder, Peabody & Co.

14

Commodities and Financial Futures

Pssst, wanna buy some copper? Well how about some gold, or pork bellies, or plywood? Maybe the Japanese yen or Swiss franc strikes your fancy. Sound a bit unusual? Perhaps, but all these items have one thing in common: They represent investment vehicles that are popular with millions of individual investors. This is the more exotic side of investing—the market for commodities and financial futures. In order to learn more about these investments and how they can be used, in this chapter we will examine:

1. The origins and basic operating characteristics of the futures market.
2. The major organized exchanges that deal in commodities and financial futures, and the role of hedgers and speculators.
3. How prices in the futures market behave, and how profits are made and lost.
4. Trading in physical commodities, including the types of contracts used and how investment return can be measured.
5. Trading in financial futures—like foreign currency, interest rate, and stock index futures—as well as options on futures.
6. The different investment strategies individuals can use when dealing in commodities and financial futures.

Investing in commodities and financial futures often involves a considerable amount of speculation; in fact, the risks are enormous. But the payoffs in these markets can, at times, be nothing short of phenomenal. For example, a $1,200 investment in a live hog futures contract in July of 1980 would have brought a whopping $6,165 in profits in just six months. A little bit of luck is obviously helpful in such situations, but equally important is the need for patience and knowhow. These are specialized investment vehicles that require specialized investor skills. We will now look at these investment outlets in more detail to see not only what they are, but how they can be used in various types of investment programs. First, we will examine the futures market itself; then we will look at investing in commodities and financial futures.

THE FUTURES MARKET

The volume of futures trading in the United States has mushroomed over the past decade or so. The reason for this growth is twofold: (1) More and more people turned to futures trading as a way to beat inflation; and (2) the number of contracts available for trading grew annually—and continues to do so. In addition to the traditional so-called primary commodities, such as grains and metals, markets also exist for live animals, processed commodities, crude oil and gasoline, foreign currencies, money market securities, mortgage interest rates, U.S. Treasury notes and bonds, and common stocks (via stock market indexes). Now there are even listed put and call options available on a select but growing list of futures contracts. All these commodities and financial assets are traded in what is known as the futures market.

Structure

When a bushel of wheat is sold, the transaction takes place in the *cash market;* in other words, the bushel changes hands in exchange for a cash price paid to the seller. The transaction takes place at that point in time and for all practical purposes is completed then and there. Most traditional securities are traded in this type of market. But a bushel of wheat could also be sold in the *futures market;* under these conditions, the seller would not actually deliver the wheat until a mutually agreed upon date in the future. As a result, the transaction would not be completed for some time; the seller would receive partial payment for the bushel of wheat at the time the agreement was entered into, and the balance on delivery. The buyer, in turn, would own a highly liquid futures contract that could be held (and presented for delivery of the bushel of wheat), or traded in the futures market. No matter what the buyer does with the contract, as long as it is outstanding, the seller has a legal and binding obligation to deliver the stated quantity of wheat on a specified date. In many respects, futures contracts are closely related to the call options we studied earlier. Both involve the future delivery of an item at an agreed-upon price. But there is a significant difference between a futures contract and an options contract. A futures contract obligates the holder to buy or sell a specified amount of a given commodity at a stated price on or before a stated date (unless the contract is canceled or liquidated before it expires); an option gives the holder the right to buy or sell a specific amount of a real or financial asset at a specific price over a specified period of time. Moreover, the risk of loss with an option is limited to the price paid for it, which is *not* the case with a futures contract.

The development and growth of a futures market

Although futures contracts can be traced back to biblical times, their use on an organized basis in this country did not occur until the mid-1800s. They originated in the agricultural segment of the economy, where individuals who produced, owned, and/or processed foodstuffs sought a way to protect themselves against adverse price movements. Subsequently, these futures contracts came to be traded by individuals who wanted to make money with commodities by speculating on their price swings. The first organized commodity exchange in the United States, the Chicago Board of Trade, opened its doors in 1848. Over time, additional exchanges came into existence, and the number and variety of commodities traded grew to include not only foodstuffs, but metals, processed goods, wood, and even foreign currencies, debt instruments, and stocks. Trading activity on these exchanges expanded at a rapid rate almost from the beginning, and in the 1970s it literally began to soar. Thus, not only has the futures market become a trillion-dollar institution (as measured by the value of futures contracts traded on all U.S. exchanges), but the rate of growth in futures trading is far outracing that of all U.S. stock exchanges combined.

Inflation

Although high rates of inflation usually have devastating effects on the more traditional investments like stocks and bonds, just the reverse seems to occur with futures contracts, particularly commodities. Commodities do well in periods of abnormally high inflation because they tend to reflect the price behavior of the economy as a whole. Coffee triples in price, and futures contracts on coffee naturally shoot up; when the price of putting meat on the table starts to skyrocket, look to cattle futures to behave in much the same way. After all, the futures market deals in the commodities that are so much a part of inflation—in beef and pork, gold and copper, in coffee, sugar, and wheat. Not surprisingly, this type of behavior in periods of inflation has acted like a magnet to pull more and more individuals into this market, where a knowledgeable investor has at least a fighting chance against inflation. Figure 14.1 demonstrates how commodity futures react to the ups and downs of inflation, and how real or perceived inflation can affect the profits and losses of commodity investors.

Major exchanges

Today, futures trading in commodities and financial instruments is conducted on 12 North American exchanges—11 U.S. markets and one Canadian:

Chicago Board of Trade
Chicago Mercantile Exchange
Commodities Exchange of New York
Kansas City Board of Trade
MidAmerica Commodities Exchange
Minneapolis Grain Exchange

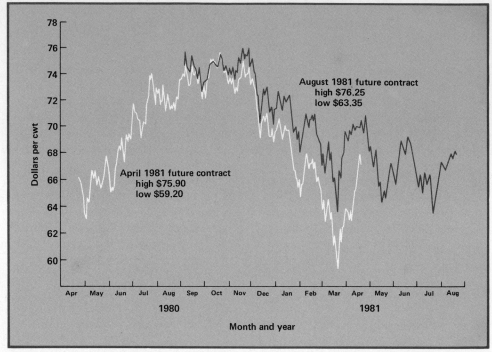

Figure 14.1 The Effects of Inflation on the Price of Cattle Futures.
The price behavior of cattle futures (here, daily settlement prices for live cattle futures traded on the Chicago Mercantile Exchange) is typical of many though certainly not all commodities during periods of inflation. Usually, futures contracts can be expected to respond in a fashion similar to the actual price behavior of the goods underlying the contract. (*Source: 1981 Chicago Mercantile Exchange Year Book,* p. 249.)

> New Orleans Commodity Exchange
> New York Coffee, Sugar and Cocoa Exchange
> New York Cotton Exchange
> New York Futures Exchange (a NYSE subsidiary)
> New York Mercantile Exchange
> Winnipeg Grain Exchange

Each exchange deals in a variety of futures contracts, although some are more limited in their activities than others. For example, in contrast to the New York Coffee, Sugar and Cocoa Exchange, which deals in only a few contracts, the Chicago Mercantile Exchange trades pork bellies, cattle, eggs, lumber, potatoes, turkeys, butter, gold, and various types of foreign currencies. Table 14.1 provides a list of where the major commodities, financial futures, and futures options are traded. Note that all but one of the exchanges deal in more than one commodity or financial asset, and

TABLE 14.1 WHERE FUTURES ARE TRADED

	Chicago Board of Trade (CBOT)	Chicago Mercantile Exchange (MERC)	Kansas City Board of Trade (KCBT)	Mid-America Commodities Exchange (MIDAM)	Minneapolis Grain Exchange	New Orleans Commodity Exchange	New York Coffee, Sugar & Cocoa Exchange (NYSCTE)	New York Cotton Exchange	New York Commodities Exchange (COMEX)	New York Futures Exchange (NYFE)	New York Mercantile Exchange (NYMERC)
Certificates of deposit		X									
Foreign currencies		X									
Eurodollar futures		X									
GNMAs	X										
Gold	X	X		X					X		
Standard & Poors Index—futures		X									
VL Composite Average Stock Index—futures			X								
NYSE Composite Index—futures										X	
Silver	X			X					X		
U.S. Treasury bills (90-day)		X		X							
10-Year Treasury notes	X										
U.S. Treasury bonds	X			X						X	
Copper									X		
Cocoa							X				
Cattle		X									
Live cattle		X		X							
Corn	X			X		X					
Cotton						X		X			
Leaded gasoline											X
Heating oil											X
Unleaded gasoline	X										
Hogs		X		X							
Lumber		X									
Oats	X			X							
Orange juice								X			
Platinum											X
Plywood	X										
Pork bellies		X									
Potatoes											X
Milled and rough rice						X					
Soybeans	X			X		X					
Soybean meal	X										
Soybean oil	X										
Sugar				X			X				
Wheat	X		X	X	X						
Broilers		X									
Eggs		X									
Value Line—options			X								
Gold Futures—option contracts									X		
U.S. T-Bonds futures—options	X										
Sugar futures—options							X				
2-Year Treasury note futures	X										

Source: Cashflow, April 1983.

many commodities and financial futures are traded on more than one exchange (for example, gold is traded on four exchanges). Although the exchanges are highly efficient and annual volume has surpassed the trillion-dollar mark, futures trading is still conducted by *open outcry auction;* in other words, as shown in Figure 14.2, actual trading on the floors of these exchanges is done through a series of shouts, body motions, and hand signals.

Futures contracts

A *futures contract* is a commitment to deliver a certain amount of some specified item at some specified date in the future. The seller of the contract agrees to make the specified future delivery, and the buyer agrees to accept it. Each exchange establishes its own contract specifications, which include not only the quantity and quality of the item, but the delivery procedure and delivery month as well. For example, the Chicago Board of Trade specifies that each of its soybean contracts will involve 5,000 bushels of USDA grade No. 2 yellow soybeans; delivery months include January, March, May, July, August, September, and November. The *delivery month* for a futures contract is much like the expiration date used on put and call options; it specifies when the commodity or item must be delivered and thus defines the life of the contract.

The maximum life of a futures contract is about one year or less, although some commodities and financial instruments (like silver and Treasury bonds) have lives as long as three years. Table 14.2 lists several popular commodities and financial futures, along with the size of their respective contracts; a brief glance at the table shows that investing in the futures market involves large quantities of the underlying commodity or financial instrument. However, although the value of a single contract is normally quite large, the amount of investor capital required to deal in these vehicles is actually rather small, because all trading in this market is done on a margin basis.

Trading

Basically, the futures market contains two types of traders: hedgers and speculators. The market simply could not exist and operate efficiently without either one. The *hedgers* are the producers and processors (which today include financial institutions and corporate money managers) who use futures contracts as a way to protect their interest in the underlying commodity or financial instrument. For example, if a rancher thinks the price of cattle will drop in the near future, he will act as a hedger and sell a futures contract on cattle in the hope of locking in as high a

---

Figure 14.2 The Auction Market at Work on the Floor of the Chicago Board of Trade.
Traders employ a system of open outcry and hand signals to indicate whether they wish to buy or sell and the price at which they wish to buy or sell. Fingers held vertically indicate the number of contracts a trader wishes to buy or sell. Fingers held horizontally indicate the fraction of a cent above or below the last traded full cent price at which the trader will buy or sell. (*Source:* Chicago Board of Trade, *Action in the Marketplace: Commodity Futures Trading,* 1978.)

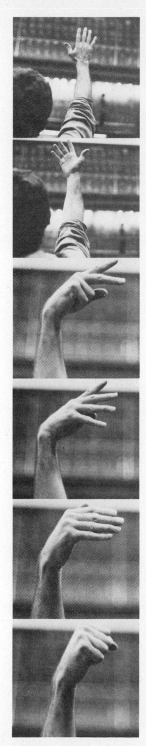

TABLE 14.2   FUTURES CONTRACT DIMENSIONS

Contract	Size of a Contract	Recent* Market Value of a Single Contract
Corn	5,000 bu	$ 17,575
Wheat	5,000 bu	16,975
Live cattle	40,000 lb	24,760
Pork bellies	38,000 lb	22,325
Coffee	37,500 lb	54,994
Cotton	50,000 lb	39,860
Gold	100 troy oz	37,720
Copper	25,000 lb	15,475
Japanese yen	12.5 million yen	53,175
Treasury bills	$1 million	977,550
S&P 500 Stock Index	500 times the index	83,550

*The contract values are representative of those that existed on November 18, 1983.

price as possible for his herd. In effect, the hedgers provide the underlying strength of the futures market and represent the very reason for its existence. *Speculators,* in contrast, give the market liquidity; they are the ones who trade futures contracts not because of a need to protect a position in the underlying commodity, but simply to earn a profit on expected swings in the price of a futures contract. They are the risk-takers, the individual investors who have no inherent interest in the commodity or financial future other than the price action and potential capital gains it can produce.

Trading mechanics

Like common stocks and other traditional investment vehicles, futures contracts are bought and sold through local brokerage offices. Most firms have at least one or two people in each office (perhaps more in some cases) who specialize in futures contracts; in addition, a number of commodity firms that deal only in futures contracts are also always ready to help individuals with their investment needs. Except for setting up a special commodity trading account, there is no real difference between trading futures and dealing in stocks or bonds. The same types of orders are used, and the use of margin is a standard way of trading futures. Any individual can buy or sell any contract, with any delivery month, so long as it is currently being traded on one of the exchanges.

Buying a contract is referred to as taking a *long position,* whereas selling one is termed taking a *short position.* It is exactly like going long or short with stocks and has the same connotation: the investor who is long wants the price to rise, and the short seller wants it to drop. Both long and short positions may be liquidated simply by executing an offsetting transaction; the short seller, for example, would cover his or her position by buying an equal amount of the contract. In general, less than 1 percent of all futures contracts are settled by delivery; the rest are offset prior to the delivery month. All trades are subject to normal transaction costs, which

TABLE 14.3   MARGIN REQUIREMENTS FOR A SAMPLE OF COMMODITIES AND FINANCIAL FUTURES*

	Initial Margin Deposit	Maintenance Margin Deposit
Corn	$1,000	$ 750
Wheat	1,500	1,200
Live cattle	1,500	1,200
Pork bellies	1,500	1,200
Coffee	3,500	2,600
Cotton	1,500	1,200
Gold	3,500	2,600
Copper	1,600	1,200
Japanese yen	1,800	1,400
Treasury bills	2,000	1,500
S&P 500 Stock Index	6,000	4,500

*Note that these are margin requirements that were specified by several full-service brokerage houses in late 1983.

include *round trip commissions* of about $50 to $80 for each contract traded (a round trip commission includes the commission costs on both ends of the transaction—to buy and sell a contract). The exact size of the commission depends on the number and type of contracts being traded.

Margin trading

Buying on margin means putting up only a fraction of the total price in cash; margin, in effect, is the amount of equity that goes into the deal. *Margin trading* plays a crucial role in futures transactions because all futures contracts are traded on a margin basis—it is the normal way of trading in this market. The margin required usually ranges from about 2 to 10 percent of the value of the contract which, compared to the margin required for stocks and most other types of securities, is very low. There is no borrowing required on the part of the investor to finance the balance of the contract, for the margin, or *deposit* as it is called with futures, exists simply as a way to guarantee fulfillment of the contract. The margin deposit is not a partial payment for the commodity or financial instrument, nor is it in any way related to the value of the product or item underlying the contract. Rather, it represents security to cover any loss in the market value of the contract that may result from adverse price movements.

The size of the required margin deposit is specified as a dollar amount and varies according to the type of contract and, in some cases, the exchange. Table 14.3 gives the margin requirements for several types of commodities and financial instruments. In sharp contrast to the size and value of futures contracts, margin requirements are kept very low.

The *initial deposit* noted in Table 14.3 specifies the amount of investor capital that must be deposited with the broker at the time of the transaction, and represents the amount of money required to make a given investment. After the investment is

BOX 14.1 LURE OF BIG PROFITS AND NEW TRADING TECHNIQUES ARE DRAWS OF THE HIGHFLYING FUTURES MARKET

Part-time amateur traders [continue to] jump into the futures market in search of speculative profits.

Many of them get clobbered.

But they keep coming back for more, though some now are seeking help in trading from a growing group of professionals who manage other people's futures-trading money.

Trading futures contracts—agreements for the future delivery of such things as wheat, pork bellies, gold and treasury bills—is risky at best.

Margin or cash requirements are tiny—usually 5% compared with 50% for stocks—so small price moves can make and erase fortunes in minutes. . . .

There isn't any way to avoid substantial risk in the highly speculative futures market. In fact, both brokers and commodity-mutual-fund managers say an investor who wants to put $5,000 in the commodity market should have about $50,000 in net liquid assets to back his stake.

Perhaps the most-cautious approach is to buy into a commodity fund. This is a pooled account—usually $5 million to $50 million in size—with a professional manager who makes all the decisions. Such funds may be publicly offered to thousands of people or privately organized by a few dozen. Either way, the funds strive for steady if slow profits rather than a quick killing.

Commodity funds have grown rapidly, with investments in the publicly offered ones quadrupling to $500 million in three years. While that's a drop in the mutual-fund bucket, the popularity of the funds is testimony that the small speculator—defined by industry experts as one with less than $20,000 to risk—isn't about to abandon futures-trading no matter how dismal his chances of making money at it. . . .

The principal advantage of a commodity fund, like any other mutual fund, is diversification and professional management. And most funds say they will self-liquidate, rather than go back to investors for a margin call. So, a speculator generally can't lose more than his original investment—even if the fund is wiped out by a negative price move.

And that happens. [In 1980, for example,] the value of the assets of two funds held by ContiCommodity Services Inc. went to zero, and investors lost everything. One fund was wiped out during the silver-price plunge in March and the other was a casualty of the December across-the-board crash in commodity prices.

Despite that, the publicly offered funds are probably one of the least risky avenues of commodities trading since they are regulated by both the Securities and Exchange Commission and the Commodity Futures Trading Commission. To offer a fund to the public, a commodities or securities concern must file a prospectus with the SEC that describes the risk involved.

The prospectus offers an insight into the fund manager's trading style, giving his win-loss record for the past three years. "You should find his worst period on record and ask yourself if you can live through that," a spokesman for one brokerage firm says.

The main drawback of the funds is the associated costs, which include management and incentive fees for the trading adviser and admission charges by the general partner—the firm that organizes and offers the fund—plus brokerage commissions. These

BOX 14.1 *Continued*

commissions often are discounted, but not by much. "Too many hands in the pot," says Leon Rose, editor and publisher of Managed Accounts Report, which tracks the performance of both public and private funds.

[In 1980,] the 17 publicly offered funds followed by the newsletter had an average 25% profit, compared with a 13.5% annual inflation rate. But the six private pools tracked by Managed Accounts had an average 96% profit. That isn't because the private pools have better trading managers, Mr. Rose points out, as three private accounts share trading managers with three public ones. Those three managers brought an average 70% profit to the private accounts and a 40% profit to the public funds.

The principal difference is lower administrative cost, Mr. Rose says. But the private funds aren't regulated by the SEC, nor are they particularly accessible to small traders, because private pools typically cater to fewer speculators with a lot more money.

Prospective traders who are more adventurous and have more money to risk can venture into a much less public domain, the managed account. A managed-account trader has to find his own professional trading adviser, who must be registered with the CFTC, and must give the adviser legal authority to trade using his money. A trader usually needs $50,000 to open a managed account and should be suspicious of advisers who ask for a lot less, experts say.

The managed-account trader theoretically gains the expertise of the trading adviser and usually gets a break on commission rates arranged by the trading adviser with his broker. Also, the trading adviser usually gets an incentive fee for successful trading but has no share in commissions and thus no incentive to overtrade or "churn" the account. A managed account differs in that way from what is usually called a "discretionary account," in which the trading adviser is an account executive or broker whose pay depends on commissions.

But unlike a participant in a commodity fund, the managed-account trader hasn't any protection from margin calls, and he can easily lose more money than he initially puts down. Unless he has a great deal of money to trade, he can't get the diversification offered by big funds.

And the managed-account trader's success depends completely on the skill of his adviser. He should seek someone "long established and well known," advises Ted Thomte, president of Thomte & Co., Boston commodity-trading advisers. Unsuccessful or dishonest advisers often try to obscure their past by "going out of business under one name and starting in business again under another," Mr. Thomte says. It's a futures-industry problem likened to crab grass by one federal prosecutor....

For traders who are less prosperous but eager to call their own shots, a conventional account with a brokerage house usually requires only a $5,000 deposit and offers trading advice from an account executive and periodic market letters. The drawbacks: The conventional trader has to spend time studying the markets, and he has little chance for diversification. He also risks margin calls and the loss of more than his initial $5,000.

A handful of discount brokerage concerns offer cheap commission rates by trimming such "frills" as account executives and market letters. Although some require only a $5,000 deposit, the streamlined nature of their operations makes them unsuitable for inexperienced traders....

Source: "Lure of Big Profits and New Trading Techniques Are Draws of the Highflying Futures Market," *The Wall Street Journal,* February 9, 1981, p. 32.

made, the market value of a contract will, of course, rise and fall as the quoted price of the underlying commodity or financial instrument goes up and down. Such market behavior will cause the amount of margin on deposit with the broker to change. To be sure that an adequate margin is always on hand, investors are required to meet a second type of margin requirement, the *maintenance deposit.* It is slightly less than the initial deposit and establishes the minimum amount of margin that must be kept in the account at all times. For instance, if the initial deposit on a commodity is $1,000 per contract, its maintenance margin might be $750. So long as the market value of the contract does not fall by more than $300 (the difference between this contract's initial and maintenance margins), the investor has no problem. But if the market moves against the investor and the value of the contract drops by more than the allowed amount, the investor will receive a *margin call,* which means he or she must immediately deposit enough cash to bring the position back to the initial margin level. An investor's margin position is checked daily via a procedure known as *mark-to-the-market.* That is, the gain or loss in a contract's value is determined at the end of each session, at which time the broker debits or credits the trader's account accordingly. In a falling market, an investor may receive a number of margin calls and be required to make additional margin payments (perhaps on a daily basis) in order to keep the position above the maintenance margin level. Failure to do so will mean that the broker has no choice but to close out the position.

COMMODITIES

Physical commodities like grains, metals, wood, and meat make up a major portion of the futures market; they have been actively traded in this country for well over a century and still account for much of the trading activity. Before looking at how to trade commodities, we need to review the basic characteristics and investment merits of these vehicles.

Basic Characteristics

Various types of physical commodities are found on nearly all of the 12 North American futures exchanges—in fact, 6 of them deal only in commodities. The market for commodity contracts is divided into five major segments: grains and oilseeds, livestock and meat, food and fiber, metals and petroleum, and wood. Such segmentation does not affect trading mechanics and procedures, but provides a convenient way of categorizing commodities into groups based on similar underlying characteristics. Certainly, they indicate the diversity of the commodities market, and as Table 14.4 shows, the variety of contracts available. The list is growing yearly, but we can see from the table that individual investors had nearly 40 different commodities to choose from in late 1983—and a number of these (like soybeans and wheat) are available in several different forms or grades.

A commodities contract

Every commodity contract has its own specifications regarding the amount and quality of the product being traded. Figure 14.3 is an excerpt from the "Futures" section of *The Wall Street Journal,* and shows the contract and quotation systems

---

TABLE 14.4   MAJOR CLASSES OF COMMODITIES

GRAINS AND OILSEEDS	METALS AND PETROLEUM
Corn	Copper
Oats	Gold
Soybeans	Platinum
Wheat	Silver
Barley	Palladium
Flaxseed	Mercury
Rapeseed	Gasoline
Sorghum	Heating oil
Rye	Crude oil
Rice	
	WOOD
LIVESTOCK AND MEAT	
	Lumber
Cattle	Plywood
Hogs and pork bellies	Stud lumber
Broilers	
Turkeys	**OTHER**
FOOD AND FIBER	Propane
	Rubber
Cocoa	Silver coins
Coffee	Gold coins
Cotton	
Orange juice	
Sugar	
Eggs	
Potatoes	
Butter	

---

used with commodities. Although some commodities (such as wheat and gold, for instance) are traded on more than one exchange, each commodity contract is made up of the same five parts, and all prices are quoted in an identical fashion. Every contract specifies: (1) the product; (2) the exchange on which the contract is traded; (3) the size of the contract (in bushels, pounds, tons, or whatever); (4) the method of valuing the contract, or pricing unit (like cents per pound, or dollars per ton); and (5) the delivery month. Using a corn contract as an illustration, we can see each of these parts in the illustration below:

① ② ③ ④
Corn (CBT)—5,000 bu.; cents per bu.

	Open	High	Low	Settle	Change	Lifetime High	Lifetime Low	Open Interest
May	253½	253¾	252¼	252½	−1¾	286½	230½	42,796
July	258	258	256½	256¾	−1¾	288	233	60,447
Sept	260	260½	259	259	−1½	263	236	7,760
Dec	263½	264	262½	263	−1¼	267¼	244	41,638
Mar 80	271¾	272	270¼	271	−1¼	276	254¾	11,098
May	277¼	278	276¼	277	−1	281	273¼	1,326

⑤ (brackets left of May–May rows)

KEY
① the product
② the exchange
③ the size of the contract
④ the pricing unit
⑤ the delivery months

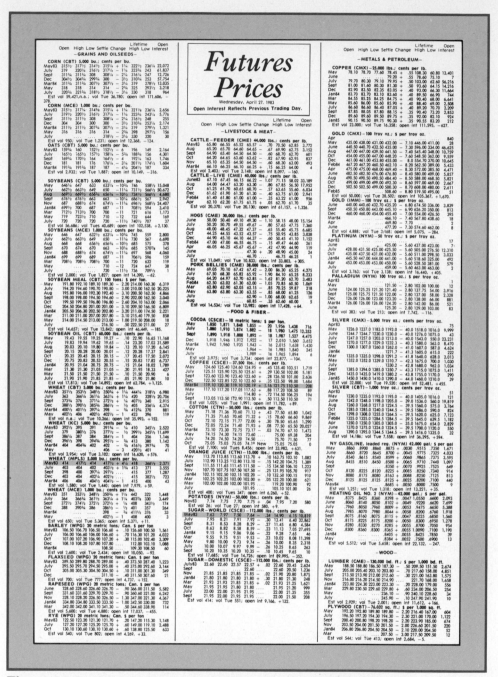

Figure 14.3   Quotations on Active Commodity Futures Contracts.
These quotes reveal at a glance key information about each commodity contract and its price activity on the various exchanges. (*Source: The Wall Street Journal.*)

The quotation system used for commodities is based on the size of the contract and the pricing unit. The financial media generally report the open, high, low, and closing prices for each delivery month (with commodities, the last price of the day, or the closing price, is known as the *settle price*). Also reported, at least by *The Wall Street Journal,* is the amount of *open interest* in each contract—that is, the number of contracts presently outstanding. Note in the illustration above that the settle price for May corn was quoted at 252½. Since the pricing system is cents per bushel, this means that the contract was being traded at $2.52½ per bushel, and that the market value of the contract was $12,625 (since each contract involves 5,000 bushels and each bushel is worth $2.52½, we have 5,000 × $2.525 = $12,625).

Price behavior

Commodity prices react to a unique set of economic, political, and international pressures—not to mention the weather. Although the explanation of why commodity prices change is beyond the scope of this book, it should be clear that they do move up and down just like any other investment vehicle—which is precisely what speculators are after. However, because we are dealing in such large trading units (like 5,000 bushels of this or 40,000 pounds of that), even a rather modest price change can have an enormous impact on the market value of a contract, and therefore on investor returns or losses. For example, if the price of corn goes up or down by just 20 cents per bushel, the value of a single contract will change by $1,000. Since a corn contract can be bought with a $1,000 initial margin deposit, it is easy to see the effect this kind of price behavior can have on investor return. But do commodity prices really move all that much? Judge for yourself. If we examine the price change columns in Figure 14.3, we can uncover some excellent examples of sizable price changes that occur from one day to the next. Note, for example, that August soybeans dropped $525, May wheat on the Minneapolis exchange rose by $212, (world) sugar for May delivery declined by some $380, and next year's March coffee went up $435. These are *daily* price movements which, relative to the size of the original investment, are clearly substantial. They occur not because the underlying prices are so volatile, but because of the sheer magnitude of the commodities contracts themselves.

Clearly, such price behavior is one of the magnets that draws investors to commodities. The exchanges recognize the volatile nature of commodities contracts and try to put lids on price fluctuations by imposing daily price limits and maximum daily price ranges (similar limits are also put on financial futures). The *daily price limit* restricts the interday change in the price of the underlying commodity—for example, the price of corn can change by no more than 10 cents per bushel from one day to the next, and the daily limit on copper is 3 cents per pound. Such limits, however, still leave plenty of room to turn a quick profit. For the daily price limits on corn and copper translate into per day changes of $500 for one corn contract and $750 for a copper contract. The *maximum daily price range,* in contrast, limits the amount the price can change *during* the day and is usually equal to twice the daily limit restrictions (for example, the daily price limit on corn can be 10 cents per bushel and its maximum daily range 20 cents per bushel).

Holding period return

Futures contracts have only one source of return: the capital gains that can be earned when prices move in a favorable fashion. There is no current income of any kind. The volatile nature of the price of futures contracts is one reason high returns are possible with commodities; the other is leverage. That is, the fact that all futures trading is done on margin means that it takes only a small amount of money to control a large investment position and to participate in the large price swings that accompany many futures contracts. Of course, the use of leverage also means that it is possible to be wiped out in just one or two bad days.

Investment return can be measured by calculating *return on invested capital*. This is simply a variation of the standard holding period return formula that bases return to investors on the amount of money actually invested in the contract, rather than the value of the contract itself; it is used because of the generous amount of leverage (margin) used in commodities trading. The return on invested capital for a commodities position can be determined according to the following simple formula:

$$\text{return on invested capital} = \frac{\substack{\text{selling price of} \\ \text{commodity contract}} - \substack{\text{purchase price of} \\ \text{commodity contract}}}{\text{amount of margin deposit}}$$

This formula can be used for both long and short transactions. To see how it works, assume you bought two September corn contracts at 245 ($2.45 per bushel) by depositing the required initial margin of $2,000 (or $1,000 for each contract). Your investment amounts to only $2,000, even though you control 10,000 bushels of corn worth $24,500 at the time they were purchased. Assume September corn has just closed at 259, so you decide to sell out and take your profit. Your return on invested capital would be as follows:

$$\text{return on invested capital} = \frac{\$25,900 - \$24,500}{\$2,000}$$

$$= \frac{\$1,400}{\$2,000} = \underline{70.0\%}$$

Clearly, this high rate of return was due not only to an increase in the price of the commodity, but also, and perhaps most important, to the fact that you were using very low margin. The initial margin in this particular transaction equaled only about 6 percent.

Trading Commodities

Investing in commodities takes one of three forms. First is *speculating*, which is popular with individual investors who use commodities as a way to seek capital gains. In essence, they try to capitalize on the wide price swings that are characteristic of so many commodities. Figure 14.4 provides an index of the behavior of commodity prices over time, and clearly reveals their volatile nature. Although such price

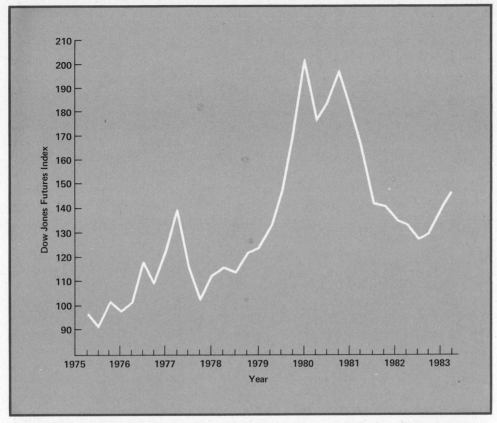

Figure 14.4 The Behavior of Commodity Prices over Time (1975 to Early 1983).
This graph shows the volatile nature of commodity prices and underscores the need for investor knowhow when dealing in commodities.

movements may be appealing to speculators, they can frighten a lot of others. Some of these more cautious investors turn to *spreading,* the second form of commodities investing; they use sophisticated trading techniques intended to capture the benefits of volatile prices, but at the same time limit exposure to loss. Finally, producers and processors use various *hedging* strategies as a way to protect their interests in the underlying commodities. We will briefly examine each of these trading tactics not only to see what they are, but to gain a better understanding of the various ways commodities can be used as an investment vehicle.

Speculating

Speculators are in the market for one reason: They expect the price of a commodity to go up or down, and they hope to capitalize on it by going long or short. To see why a speculator would go long when prices are expected to rise, consider an individual who buys a February silver contract at 533½ by depositing the required initial margin of $1,000. Since one silver contract involves 5,000 troy ounces, it has a market value of $26,675. If silver goes up, the investor makes money. Assume it does and that by January (one month before the contract expires), the price of the contract rises to 552. The speculator then liquidates and makes a profit of 18½ cents per ounce (552 − 533½). That means $925 profit from an investment of just $1,000—which translates into a return on invested capital of 92.5 percent. Of course, instead of rising, the price of silver could have dropped by 18½ cents per ounce. In this case our investor could have lost just about all his original investment ($1,000 − $925 leaves only $75, out of which would have to come a round trip commission of $50). But to the short seller, the drop in price would be just what she was after, for she could profit from such a turn of events. Here's how: She sells (shorts) the February silver at 533½ and buys it back some time later at 515. Clearly, the difference between her selling price and purchase price is the same 18½ cents, but in this case it is *profit,* since the selling price exceeds the purchase price (see Chapter 5 for a review of short selling).

Spreading
Instead of attempting to speculate on the price behavior of a futures contract, an investor might choose to follow a more conservative tactic. This could be done by using a strategy known as spreading (the principles of spreading futures contracts are much like those for stock options). The idea is to combine two or more different contracts into one investment position that offers the potential for generating a modest amount of profit, while restricting exposure to loss. One very important reason for their use in the commodities market is that, unlike the case of stock options, there is no limit to the amount of loss that can occur with a futures contract. An investor will set up a spread by buying one contract and simultaneously selling another. Although one side of the transaction will lead to a loss, the investor obviously hopes that the profit earned from the other side will be more than enough compensation, and that the net result will be at least a modest amount of profit. If the investor is wrong, the spread will serve to limit (but not eliminate) losses.

Here is a simplified version of how a spread might work: Suppose we buy contract A at 533½ and at the same time short sell contract B for 575½. Some time later we close out our interest in contract A by selling it at 542 and simultaneously cover our short position in B by purchasing a contract at 579. Although we made a profit of 8½ points on the long position, contract A (542 − 533½), we lost 3½ points on the contract that we shorted, B (575½ − 579). The net effect, however, is a profit of 5 points, which, if we were dealing in cents per pound, would mean a profit of $250 on a 5,000 pound contract. All sorts of commodity spreads can be set up for just about any type of investment situation, but most are highly sophisticated and require specialized skills.

Hedging
A hedge is a "technical" approach to commodity trading used by producers and processors to protect a position in a product or commodity. For example, a producer or grower would use a commodity hedge to obtain as high a price for the

goods as possible; the processor or manufacturer who uses the commodity, however, would employ a hedge to obtain the goods at as low a price as possible. A successful hedge, in effect, means added income to producers and lower costs to processors. An example will show how hedging works and why it is done. Suppose a manufacturer uses platinum as a basic raw material in the production of catalytic converters. It is early in the year and platinum is selling for $180 per ounce, but it is expected to shoot up in price and be much more expensive by the end of the year. To protect against future price increases, our manufacturer decides to buy a platinum futures contract, now trading at $205 per ounce. Assume that eight months later the price of platinum has indeed gone up (to $280 per ounce), but so has the price of the futures contract, which is now trading at $325 per ounce. The manufacturer has made $120 per ounce on the 50-ounce futures contract, and is $6,000 ahead on the transaction—a gain that will be used to offset the increase in the cost of platinum. As it turns out, the gain on the futures contract is $1,000 more than the increased cost of 50 ounces of platinum on the open market, for the cost of platinum rose by only $100 per ounce and the cost of 50 ounces of platinum went up by only $5,000. This was a successful hedge for the manufacturer because it kept the cost of this raw material in check, at least for the time being. (Technically, the manufacturer could take delivery of the contracted platinum—at an effective cost of $205 per ounce, the price at which the futures contract was purchased—but that is unlikely in this case, since the manufacturer would have to forego the $1,000 profit in order to do so.)

Commodities and the Individual Investor

For the most part, individual investors use commodities in one of two ways: for speculation and/or spreading. Commodities appeal to investors because of the high rates of return they offer, and because of their ability to act as inflation hedges during periods of rapidly rising consumer prices. When continued inflation becomes a problem, traditional investment outlets just do not seem to be able to provide the type of return necessary to keep investors ahead of the game. That is, it seems that more often than not, in periods of high inflation investors lose more in purchasing power than they gain from after-tax returns. Under such circumstances, investors can be expected to seek outlets that provide better protection against inflation, all of which explains the growing interest in commodities.

These vehicles can play an important role in a portfolio so long as the investor understands the risks involved and is well versed in the principles and mechanics of commodities trading. The fact is that over the long run, the average return to commodities investors is *negative*. The quickest way to lose money in commodities is to jump in without knowing what you are doing. Because there is a lot of price volatility in commodities and because commodity trading is done on very low margin, the potential for loss is enormous. Speculating with commodities involves high risk, and spreading requires substantial investor knowhow and sophistication. Commodities investing is not for amateurs.

Only a portion of an individual's investment capital should be committed to commodities—the specific amount would, of course, be a function of investor aversion to risk and the amount of resources the person has. An investor has to be prepared mentally and should be in a position financially to absorb losses, perhaps a number of them. Not only should an investor keep an adequate cash reserve on hand (to absorb losses and/or meet margin calls), but it is also probably best for him or her to maintain a diversified holding of commodities to spread the risks. Individuals can invest directly in the commodities market, or they can buy put and call *options* on certain futures contracts; alternatively, they can buy commodities mutual funds, or they can buy into limited partnerships established for the purpose of conducting commodities investment programs. (Options on futures are discussed in this chapter; mutual funds and limited partnership investments will be examined in Chapters 15 and 17, respectively.) The latter two approaches might be used by individuals who want to invest in the commodities market but who lack the time and/or expertise to manage their own investments. But remember that although these approaches offer professional management, they certainly do not guarantee a profit; instead, they can only reduce some of the more obvious risks of commodity investing.

FINANCIAL FUTURES

Another dimension of the futures market is that for *financial futures,* a segment of the market where futures contracts are traded on a variety of financial instruments. Actually, financial futures are simply an extension of the commodities concept. They were created for much the same reason as commodity futures; they are traded in the same market; their prices behave a lot like those of commodities; and they have common investment merits. Yet in spite of all these similarities, financial futures are a unique kind of investment vehicle. Let's look more closely at these instruments and how they can be used.

The Market

The financial futures market is not as large or diverse as the market for commodities, but it is still an important segment of the futures market and accounts for a considerable amount of the increased trading volume. For investors who regularly deal in bonds and other forms of fixed income securities, they offer still another way of speculating on the behavior of interest rates; in addition, they offer a convenient way to speculate in the highly specialized, and often highly profitable, foreign currency markets. There are even futures available that enable investors to speculate in the stock market.

The financial futures market was established only recently and developed in response to the economic turmoil the United States had been experiencing in the 1970s. The dollar had become unstable on the world market and was causing serious problems for multinational firms; closer to home, interest rates had begun to behave in a volatile manner, which caused severe difficulties for corporate treasurers, financial institutions, and money managers in general. All these parties needed a way to

*Gentlemen, I believe the time has come for us to join together
in singing "Nearer My God to Thee."*

protect themselves from the ravages of wide fluctuations in the value of the dollar
and interest rates, and so a market for financial futures was born. Hedging provided
the economic rationale for the market in financial futures, but speculators were quick
to respond as they found the price volatility of these instruments attractive and, at
times, highly profitable. At the present time, financial futures are traded on six exchanges: the New York Futures Exchange (NYFE), the Kansas City Board of Trade,
the MidAmerica Commodities Exchange, the Amex Commodities Exchange, the
Chicago Mercantile Exchange, and the Chicago Board of Trade. The three basic
types of financial futures include those on foreign currencies, debt securities, and
stock indexes.

Foreign currencies,
interest rates, and stocks

Trading in foreign currencies began in May 1972; known as *currency futures,*
trading is handled much like commodities, and is conducted in the following eight
foreign currencies:

British pound	Mexican peso
German mark	Japanese yen
Swiss franc	Dutch guilder
Canadian dollar	French franc

All these currencies involve countries with which the United States has strong international trade and exchange ties. A few years later, in October 1975, the first futures
contract on debt securities, or *interest rate futures* as they are more commonly
known, was established when trading started in GNMA pass-through certificates (a
special type of mortgage-backed bond issued by a branch of the U.S. government).

	Open	High	Low	Settle	Change	Lifetime High	Lifetime Low	Open Interest
				—FINANCIAL—				
BRITISH POUND (IMM)—25,000 pounds; $ per pound								
June83	1.5650	1.5740	1.5645	1.5690	+.0075	1.7550	1.4480	20,441
Sept	1.5615	1.5695	1.5605	1.5650	+.0080	1.6360	1.4460	2,581
Dec	1.5630	1.5700	1.5590	1.5625	+.0075	1.6425	1.4460	731
Mar	1.5680	1.5680	1.5665	1.5615	+.0075	1.5680	1.4470	279
Est vol 4,966; vol Fri 2,396; open int 24,032, + 51.								
CANADIAN DOLLAR (IMM)—100,000 dlrs.; $ per Can $								
June83	.8168	.8183	.8158	.8165	+.0003	.8190	.7810	10,296
Sept	.8164	.8177	.8154	.8158	+.0002	.8185	.7960	2,098
Dec	.8160	.8160	.8150	.8150	. . . . .	.8171	.8005	615
Mar84	. . . . .	. . . . .	. . . . .	.8144	. . . . .	.8128	.8040	6
Est vol 3,730; vol Fri 2,126; open int 13,015, + 346.								
JAPANESE YEN (IMM) 12.5 million yen; $ per yen (.00)								
June83	.4220	.4226	.4215	.4217	. . . . .	.4467	.3650	29,673
Sept	.4254	.4256	.4245	.4247	+.0001	.4380	.4210	1,473
Dec	.4285	.4285	.4278	.4278	. . . . .	.4395	.4250	232
Est vol 9,132; vol Fri 8,847; open int 31,378, −1,449								
SWISS FRANC (IMM)—125,000 francs-$ per franc								
June83	.4862	.4867	.4854	.4857	−.0014	.5355	.4616	29,291
Sept	.4919	.4922	.4913	.4916	−.0013	.5428	.4635	1,329
Dec	.4979	.4981	.4977	.4978	−.0011	.5450	.4815	246
Mar84	. . . . .	. . . . .	. . . . .	.5040	−.0010	.5175	.5030	11
Est vol 8,673; vol Fri 12,777; open int 30,887, +1,389.								
W. GERMAN MARK (IMM)—125,000 marks; $ per mark								
June83	.4075	.4086	.4071	.4081	. . . . .	.4450	.3915	21,224
Sept	.4117	.4126	.4114	.4123	. . . . .	.4370	.4110	1,235
Dec	.4158	.4164	.4157	.4163	−.0001	.4400	.4154	485
Est vol 4,254; vol Fri 6,225; open int 22,944 +610.								

EURODOLLAR (IMM)—$1 million; pts of 100%

	Open	High	Low	Settle	Chg	Yield Settle	Yield Chg	Open Interest
June	91.02	91.07	90.99	91.00	+.05	9.00	−.05	10,116
Sept	90.83	90.94	90.83	90.86	+.09	9.14	−.09	7,567
Dec	90.56	90.69	90.56	90.62	+.09	9.38	−.09	4,986
Mar84	90.45	90.45	90.42	90.42	+.13	9.58	−.13	251
Est vol 1,757; vol Fri 2,331; open int 22,920, −137								
GNMA 8% (CBT)—$100,000 prncpl; pts. 32nds. of 100%								
June	72–05	72–06	71–22	71–29	+2	12.728	−.013	18,860
Sept	71–08	71–11	70–29	71–01	+2	12.918	−.013	7,608
Dec	70–16	70–18	70–07	70–08	+2	13.090	−.014	4,354
Mar84	69–29	69–29	69–18	69–20	+3	13.230	−.021	4,146
June	69–07	69–08	69–01	69–02	+4	13.358	−.028	2,847
Sept	68–23	68–25	68–17	68–20	+1	13.458	−.008	1,179
Dec	68–13	68–13	68–08	68–09	+1	13.537	−.008	1,771
Mar85	. . . . .	. . . . .	. . . . .	67–30	+2	13.617	−.015	107
June	. . . . .	. . . . .	. . . . .	67–22	+2	13.676	−.015	230
Sept	. . . . .	. . . . .	. . . . .	67–15	+1	13.727	+1	12
Dec	. . . . .	. . . . .	. . . . .	67–09	. . . . .	13.772	. . . . .	219
Est vol 8,500; vol Fri 15,211; open int 41,333 −7,081.								
TREASURY BONDS (CBT)—$100,000; pts. 32nds of 100%								
June	79–06	79–10	78–21	78–27	−3	10.561	+.013	74,156
Sept	78–17	78–23	78–02	78–08	−3	10.649	+.014	19,177
Dec	78–02	78–06	77–19	77–23	−4	10.728	+.019	8,630
Mar84	77–18	77–21	77–06	77–08	−5	10.798	+.023	12,515
June	77–05	77–09	76–25	76–25	−5	10.860	+.024	11,961
Sept	76–28	76–28	76–15	76–15	−6	10.917	+.029	7,048
Dec	76–19	76–19	76–03	76–08	−4	10.951	+.020	5,651
Mar85	76–10	76–10	75–28	75–28	−9	10.009	+.039	1,901
June	76–00	76–00	75–20	75–20	−9	10.048	+.044	844
Sept	. . . . .	. . . . .	. . . . .	75–13	−10	11.082	+.049	210
Dec	. . . . .	. . . . .	. . . . .	75–07	−11	11.111	+.054	2
Est vol 70,000; vol Fri 78,671; open int 142,095, −6,764.								
TREASURY NOTES (CBT)—$100,000; pts. 32nds of 100%								
June	86–23	86–25	86–12	86–17	+1	10.178	−.005	7,429
Sept	85–29	85–29	85–19	85–25	+2	10.312	−.011	248
Dec	. . . . .	. . . . .	. . . . .	85–03	+2	10.437	−.011	100
Mar84	. . . . .	. . . . .	. . . . .	84–15	+2	10.551	−.012	215
Est vol 2,500; vol Fri 2,609; open int 7,992, + 344.								

Figure 14.5   Quotations on Selected Actively Traded Financial Futures.
The trading exchange, size of the trading unit, pricing unit, and delivery months are all vital information about a futures contract and are all part of the quotation system used with financial futures. (*Source: The Wall Street Journal.*)

TREASURY BILLS (IMM)—$1 mil.; pts. of 100%

	Open	High	Low	Settle	Chg	Discount Settle	Chg	Open Interest
June83	92.02	92.09	91.99	92.01	− .03	7.99	− .03	24,180
Sept	91.86	91.96	91.86	91.90	+ .09	8.10	− .09	12,447
Dec	91.64	91.74	91.64	91.68	+ .09	8.32	− .09	5,309
Mar84	91.50	91.54	91.46	91.50	+ .08	8.50	− .08	1,553
June	91.26	91.34	91.26	91.31	+ .08	8.69	− .08	644
Sept	91.14	91.14	91.09	91.13	+ .09	8.87	− .09	343
Dec	. . . .	. . . .		90.94	+ .08	9.06	− .08	149
Mar85	. . . .	. . . .		90.77	+ .07	9.23	− .07	13

Est vol 12,817; vol Fri 11,477; open int 44,638, −371.

BANK CDs (IMM)—$1 million; pts. of 100%

	Open	High	Low	Settle	Chg	Discount Settle	Chg	Open Interest
June83	91.59	91.65	91.53	91.57	+ .03	8.43	− .03	7,371
Sept	91.35	91.45	91.34	91.37	+ .08	8.63	− .08	3,711
Dec	91.05	91.17	91.05	91.10	+ .10	8.90	− .10	1,880
Mar84	90.79	90.95	90.79	90.89	+ .13	9.11	− .13	48

Est vol 3,611; vol Fri 2,675; open int 13,010, − 510.

S&P 500 FUTURES INDEX (CME) 500 Times Index

	Open	High	Low	Settle	Chg	Discount Settle	Chg	Open Interest
June	164.40	164.55	162.10	163.05	−1.20	164.70	102.50	22,322
Sept	165.45	165.50	163.10	164.05	−1.20	165.60	120.70	2,027
Dec	165.60	166.50	164.40	165.30	−1.10	166.70	138.00	194
Mar84	167.80	167.80	165.50	166.40	−1.20	167.80	153.00	13

Est vol 28,665; vol Fri 37,790; open int 25,556, +232.

S&P 500 STOCK INDEX (Prelim)

Open	High	Low	Settle	Chg			
163.48	164.42	161.99	162.11	−2.32	. . . . .	. . . . . .	. . . . .

NYSE COMPOSITE FUTURES (NYFE) 500 Times Index

	Open	High	Low	Settle	Chg	Discount Settle	Chg	Open Interest
June	94.40	94.50	93.15	93.55	− .90	94.65	59.25	7,401
Sept	95.15	95.20	93.80	94.10	−1.05	95.30	59.65	879
Dec	95.55	95.55	94.45	94.65	−1.10	95.90	60.88	505
Mar84	96.25	96.25	95.30	95.20	−1.15	96.25	79.25	214
June	96.75	96.75	96.00	95.75	−1.20	96.75	82.30	85
Sept	97.25	97.25	96.50	96.30	−1.25	97.25	89.25	36

Est vol 15,131; vol Fri 13,876; open int 9,120, −191.

NYSE COMPOSITE STOCK INDEX

Open	High	Low	Settle	Chg			
94.21	94.21	92.99	93.04	−1.23	. . . . .	. . . . . .	. . . . .

KC VALUE LINE FUTURES (KC) 500 Times Index

	Open	High	Low	Settle	Chg	Discount Settle	Chg	Open Interest
June	191.05	191.20	188.65	189.40	−1.20	191.20	111.00	2,261
Sept	192.00	192.10	189.90	190.40	−1.20	192.10	111.35	468
Dec	191.90	192.00	190.90	191.40	−1.20	192.80	111.40	187
Mar	192.75	193.00	192.00	192.40	−1.20	193.75	161.65	32

Est vol 2,564; vol Fri 2,055; open int 2,948, − 144.

KC VALUE LINE COMPOSITE STOCK INDEX

Open	High	Low	Settle	Chg			
190.53	190.71	188.76	188.87	−1.65	. . . . .	. . . . . .	. . . . .

Figure 14.5   Continued

In time, other types of issues were added, so that today trading is carried out in the following kinds of debt securities:

90-day Treasury bills
1-year Treasury bills
90-day bank CDs (certificates of deposit)
90-day Eurodollar deposits
GNMA pass-through certificates
U.S. Treasury notes
U.S. Treasury bonds

All these futures contracts are based on *domestic* securities except the Eurodollar time deposits, which are dollars deposited in interest-bearing accounts in banks outside the United States. Interest rate futures were immediately successful, and their popularity grew rapidly. In fact, they had become so popular that by 1982, the Chicago Board of Trade's U.S. Treasury bond futures contract was the most actively traded contract in the whole commodities and financial futures market.

In February 1982, a new trading vehicle was introduced: the stock index futures contract. *Stock index futures,* as they are called, are contracts pegged to the widely reported broad measures of stock market performance; presently, trading is done in three stock-index futures:

> The S&P 500 Stock Index
> The NYSE Composite Stock Index
> Value Line Composite Stock Index

In addition, there's a "mini" version of the S&P 500 contract that was introduced in order to attract the smaller investor. Known as the *S&P 100* (and traded on the Chicago Mercantile Exchange), this contract requires a smaller margin deposit and is valued at only 200 times the S&P Index. However, as of late 1983, this mini-contract still had not caught on, as trading volume in it was only about one-tenth that of the standard S&P 500 contract. Stock index futures—which are similar to the index options discussed in the preceding chapter—allow investors to participate in the general movements of the entire stock market (or at least in the *listed* segment of the market). Because the various stock indexes represent weighted portfolios of anywhere from 500 to 1,700 stocks (see Chapter 3 for a discussion of the various market indexes), investors in stock index futures are able to buy the market—or a reasonable proxy thereof—and thereby participate in broad market moves. Thus, for the first time, investors were able to buy and sell *the market as a whole,* rather than deal in just a handful of selected common stock issues. If an investor feels, for example, that the stock market is headed up, he or she no longer has to try to outguess the market by selecting that one issue or portfolio of issues that will fully capture the performance of the market. Instead, the investor can now deal in stock index futures as a way to capture the desired price behavior. For when an investor buys a stock index future, he or she is, in effect, buying the market to the extent that the underlying stock index itself is a reflection of the price behavior in the entire stock market.

Contract specifications

In principle, financial futures contracts are like the commodities contracts we looked at above. They control large sums of the underlying financial instrument, and are issued with a variety of delivery months. All this can be seen in Figure 14.5, which lists quotes for several foreign currency, interest rate, and stock index futures. Looking first at currency futures, we see that the contracts entitle the holders to a certain position in a specified foreign currency—in effect, the owner of a currency future holds a claim on a certain amount of foreign money. The precise amount ranges from 25,000 British pounds to 12.5 million Japanese yen. In a similar fashion, holders of interest rate futures have a claim on a certain amount of the underlying debt security. This claim is also quite large, as it amounts to $100,000 worth of

GNMA and Treasury notes and bonds, and $1 million worth of Eurodollar deposits, Treasury bills, and bank CDs. Stock index futures, however, differ slightly from other commodity and financial futures contracts because the seller of a stock index futures contract is not obligated to deliver the underlying stocks at expiration date. Instead, ultimate delivery is in the form of cash (which is fortunate, since it would indeed be a task to make delivery of the nearly 1,700 stocks that make up the Value Line Index, or the 500 issues in the S&P Index). The commodity underlying stock index futures, therefore, is *cash;* except for the S&P 100 contract, the amount of underlying cash is set at 500 times the value of the stock index. For example, if the Value Line Index stood at 185, the amount of cash underlying a single Value Line stock index futures contract would be 500 × 185 = $92,500. Again, the value is substantial. In terms of delivery months, the lives of financial futures contracts run from about 18 months or less for stock index and currency futures to about 3 years or less for interest rate instruments.

Prices and profits

All currency futures are quoted in dollars or cents per unit of the underlying foreign currency—for instance, in dollars per British pound, or cents per Japanese yen. Thus, according to the closing ("settle") prices in Figure 14.5, one June British pound contract was worth $39,225 (25,000 pounds × $1.5690), and a December Japanese yen was valued at $53,475 (since a quote of .4278 cents per yen amounts to less than half a cent, we have 12,500,000 yen × $0.004278). Except for contracts on Treasury bills and other short-term securities, which will be examined below, the quotes for interest rate futures operate in a similar fashion. In particular, the contracts are priced at a percentage of the par value of the underlying debt instrument. Since the instruments are quoted in increments of $1/32$ of 1 percent, a quote of 78-08 for the settle price on September Treasury bonds, like that in Figure 14.5, translates into $78 8/32$—which, when you divide 32 into 8, translates into 78.25 percent of par. Applying this rate to the par value of the underlying security, we see that a September Treasury bond contract is worth $78,250 ($100,000 × 0.7825). Stock index futures are quoted in terms of the actual index, but carry a face value of 500 times the index. Thus if the March S&P 500 Index closes at 166.40 (as it did in Figure 14.5), then the face value of the contract would be $83,200 (500 × 166.40). Stock index futures do not move point-for-point with the underlying indexes, but they do stay close enough to act as effective proxies for the respective indexes, and by extension, for the stock market as a whole.

The value of all interest rate contracts responds to interest rates exactly like the underlying debt instruments. That is, when interest rates go up, the value of an interest rate futures contract goes down, and vice versa. However, the quote system for all interest rate as well as currency and stock index futures is set up to correspond to the market value of the contract. Thus, when the price or quote of a financial futures contract increases, the investor who is long makes money; in contrast, when the price decreases, the short seller makes money. Price behavior is the only source of return to speculators; for even though stocks and debt securities are involved in some financial futures, such contracts have no claim on the dividend and interest income of the underlying issues. Even so, huge profits (or losses) are possible with financial futures because of the equally large size of the contracts. For instance, if the price of Swiss francs goes up by just 2 cents against the dollar, the investor is ahead $2,500, since one futures contract covers 125,000 Swiss francs; likewise, a 3-point drop in the NYSE Composite Index means a $1,500 loss to an investor (3 × 500). When related to the relatively small initial margin deposit required to make transactions in the financial futures markets, such price activity can mean very high rates of return, or very high risk of a total wipeout.

Pricing futures on Treasury bills and other short-term securities

Because Treasury bills and other short-term securities are normally traded in the money market on what is known as a "discount" basis, it was necessary to devise a special pricing system that would reflect the actual price movements of these futures contracts. To accomplish this, an *index price* system was developed whereby the yield is subtracted from an index of 100. Thus, a Treasury bill contract would be quoted at an index of 94.75 when the T-bill's yield is 5.25 percent (100.00 − 5.25). Under such a system, when someone buys a T-bill future and the index goes up, that individual has made money; when it goes down, a short seller has made money. Also, note that T-bill, CD, and Eurodollar futures contracts are quoted in *basis points*, where 1 basis point equals $1/100$ of 1 percent. Thus, a quote of 91.68 (which was the settle price of the December T-bill contract) translates into a T-bill yield of 8.32 percent (100.00 − 91.68).

But the index traces only the price behavior of the futures contract; to find the *actual price or value* of a 90-day T-bill, CD, or Eurodollar contract, we have to use the following formula:

$$\text{price of a 90-day futures contract} = \$1,000,000 - \left(\frac{\text{security's yield} \times 90 \times \$10,000}{360} \right)$$

Notice that this price formula is based not on the quoted price index, but on the yield of the security itself, which can be determined by subtracting the price index quote from 100.00. To see how it works, consider a 90-day CD futures contract quoted at 90.70; in this case, the CD would be priced to yield 9.30 percent (100.00 − 90.70). Using our formula, we find that the price of the futures contract is:

$$\text{price of 90-day (CD) futures contract} = \$1,000,000 - \left(\frac{9.30 \times 90 \times \$10,000}{360} \right)$$

$$= \$1,000,000 - \$23,250$$

$$= \underline{\$976,750}$$

A handy shortcut for tracking the price behavior of T-bill, CD, or Eurodollar futures contracts is to remember that the price behavior of a 90-day contract will change by $25 for every 1 basis point change in yield. Thus, when the yield on the underlying 90-day security moves from 9.30 to 9.45 percent, it goes up by 15 basis points and causes the price of the futures contract to drop by $375 ($25 × 15).

Trading Techniques

Financial futures can be used for purposes of hedging. Multinational companies and firms that are active in international trade might at times consider hedging with currency or Eurodollar futures, whereas various types of financial institutions and corporate money managers often use interest rate futures for hedging purposes. In either case, the objectives are the same: to lock in the best money exchange or interest rate possible. In addition, individual investors and portfolio managers might use stock index futures for hedging purposes in order to protect their security holdings against temporary market declines. Financial futures can also be used for spreading; this tactic is popular with individual investors, who often adopt elaborate strategies of simultaneously buying and selling combinations of two or more contracts to form a desired investment position. Finally, financial futures are widely used for speculation. As this brief review suggests, although the instruments may differ, the techniques used with financial futures are virtually identical to those used with commodities. Although all three techniques are widely used by individual investors, we will illustrate the use of financial futures by speculators and hedgers only (see the material in the commodities section above for more discussion of spreading). We will first examine speculating in currency and interest rate futures, and then look at hedging with stock index futures.

Speculating in financial futures

Speculators are especially interested in financial futures because of the large size of the futures contracts. For instance, in mid-1983, Canadian dollar contracts were worth almost $82,000, GNMA contracts were going for about $72,000, and Treasury bill contracts were being quoted at close to a million dollars. With contracts this big, it obviously does not take much movement in the underlying currency or debt security to produce big price swings and therefore big profits. An investor can use currency or interest rate futures for just about any speculative purpose. For example, if an investor expects the dollar to be devalued in relation to the German mark, he or she would buy mark currency futures, since the contracts should go up in value. If a speculator anticipates a rise in interest rates, then he or she might consider going short (selling) interest rate futures, since they should then go down in value. Because margin is used and financial futures have the same source of return as commodities (appreciation in the price of the futures contract), the return on invested capital formula is used to measure the profitability of speculating in financial futures.

Let us look at an example of a foreign currency contract. Suppose an individual investor feels that the Japanese yen is about to appreciate in value *relative to the dollar*. As a result, this investor decides to buy three September yen contracts at .4704. Each contract is worth $58,800 (12.5 million × .004704), so the total market value of three contracts would be $176,400. Even so, the investor has to deposit only $5,400 to acquire this position (recall from Table 14.3 that the required initial margin for Japanese yen is $1,800 per contract). If the price of the yen moves up just a fraction (from .4704 to .5200), the value of the three contracts will rise to $195,000 and the investor, in a matter of months, will make a profit of $18,600.

Using the return on invested capital formula introduced above, such a profit translates into an enormous 344 percent rate of return. Of course, an even smaller fractional change in the other direction would have wiped out this investment, so it should be clear that these high returns are not without equally high risks.

Now consider an investment in an interest rate future. Assume the investor is anticipating a sharp rise in long-term rates. Because a rise in rates means that interest rate futures will drop in value, the investor decides to short sell two December GNMA contracts at 87–22; this quote translates into a price of $87^{22}/_{32}$, or 87.6875 percent of par. The two contracts are worth $175,375 ($100,000 × .876875 × 2), but the amount of money required to make the investment is only $3,000 (initial margin deposit is $1,500 per GNMA contract). Assume interest rates do in fact move up, and as a result, the price on GNMA contracts drops to 80. Under such circumstances, the investor could cover his short position (buy back the two December GNMA contracts) and in the process make a profit of $15,375—recall he originally sold the two contracts at $175,375 and then bought them back some time later at $160,000. Like any investment, the difference between what you pay for a security and what you sell it for is profit; the only unusual thing about a short sale is the order in which these events occur. In this case, the return on invested capital amounted to a whopping 512 percent. Again, this kind of return is due in no small part to the enormous risk of loss the investor assumes.

Trading stock index futures

Most investors use stock index futures for speculation or hedging. (The same can be said of the *index options,* which were introduced in Chapter 13; in fact, much of the discussion that follows about trading stock index futures also applies to index options.) Whether speculating or hedging, the key to success is *predicting the future course of the stock market.* Because investors are buying the market with stock index futures, it is important to get a handle on the future direction of the market via technical analysis (as discussed in Chapter 10) or some other technique. Once an investor feels she has this, she can formulate a stock index futures trading or hedging strategy. For example, if she feels strongly that the market is headed up, she would want to go long (buy) stock index futures; in contrast, if her analysis of the market suggests a sharp drop in equity values is on the horizon, she could make money by going short (selling) stock index futures. Speculating in this way would prove profitable so long as our investor's expectations about the market actually materialize. And not only can the rewards be substantial, but there is a nice by-product to speculating with stock index futures: Once expectations about the future course of the market are formulated, the investor does not have to go through the drudgery of analyzing individual common stocks, only to select an issue that fails to capture the movements in the market.

Consider, for instance, an investor who believes the market is undervalued and therefore a move up is imminent. He can try to identify one or a handful of stocks that should go up with the market (and assume the stock selection risks that go along with this approach), or he can buy a NYSE stock index future presently trading at, say, 85.50. To execute such a transaction, the speculator need deposit an initial margin of only $3,500. Now, if his expectations are correct and the market does rise so that the NYSE Composite Index moves to 102.00 by the expiration of the futures contract, the investor will earn a profit of $8,250: (102.00 − 85.50) × 500 = $8,250. Given this was earned on a $3,500 investment, his return on invested capital would amount to a whopping 236 percent. Of course, keep in mind that if the market drops by only 7 points, the investment will be a *total loss*.

Stock index futures also make excellent hedging vehicles that provide investors with a highly effective way of protecting stock holdings in a declining market. Although the tactic is not perfect, it does enable investors to obtain desired protection without disturbing their equity holdings. Here's how a so-called short hedge, which is used to protect an investor's stock portfolio against a decline in the market, would work. Assume an investor holds a total of 1,000 shares of stock in 15 different companies, and that the market value of this portfolio is $55,000. If the investor thinks the market is about to undergo a temporary sharp decline, he can sell his shares, short sell all his stock holdings against the box, or buy puts on each of his stock. Clearly, these options are either cumbersome and/or costly, and therefore are undesirable ways of protecting a widely diversified portfolio. The desired results could be achieved, however, by short selling stock index futures. (Note that basically the same protection can be obtained in this hedging situation by turning to options and buying a *market index put*.)

Suppose the investor short sells one NYSE stock index future at 105.75. Such a contract would provide a close match to the current value of the investor's portfolio, as it would be valued at approximately $53,000, and yet would require an initial margin deposit of only $1,500 (margin deposits are less for hedgers than for speculators). Now if the market does drop to an NYSE Composite Index of, say, 85.00, the investor will make a profit from the short sale transaction of some $10,000 (20.75 points × 500), which can then be used to offset some or all of the loss in the value of his stock portfolio. Ignoring taxes, this profit can be added to the portfolio (additional shares of stock can be purchased at their new lower prices), with the net result being a new portfolio position that will approximate that which existed prior to the decline in the market. How well the before and after portfolio positions match will depend on how far the portfolio dropped in value. If the average price dropped about $10 per share in our example, the positions will closely match. But this does not always happen; the price of some stocks will change more than others and, as such, the amount of protection provided by this type of short hedge depends on how sensitive the stock portfolio is to movements in the market. Thus, the type of stocks held in the portfolio is an important consideration in structuring the stock index short hedge. OTC and highly volatile stocks will probably require more protection (perhaps the use of two futures contracts rather than one, or the use of a higher-priced index, like the Value Line Index rather than the NYSE Composite) than stocks which are relatively more price-stable or have betas closer to 1.0. In any event, hedging with stock index futures can be a low-cost yet effective way of obtaining protection against loss in a declining stock market.

BOX 14.2 NOW, INDEX FUTURES FOR SMALL INVESTORS

Looking for a way to age your short-term gains on the stock market instantly into long-term gains? Who isn't.

But one hedge idea that will be getting a lot of hype is worth a long double look before you leap. The new wrinkle: index futures, specifically geared to the investor with a portfolio that does *not* total six figures. They are tempting, but buyer beware. Indeed, in his *Forbes* column of July 18, [1983], David Dreman opined that financial futures are suitable only for "masochists and . . . wild-eyed dice players." He pointed out that with financial futures you can be right about the market and still take a beating because of the thin margins involved. Nevertheless, a lot of brokers are touting futures as a means of protecting short-term gains until they age into those juicy, lightly taxed, long-term capital gains.

Sniffing commissions, Wall Street has scaled futures contracts down to a size that smaller investors can afford—"mini" stock index futures, smaller versions of the contracts professional traders use to participate in broad stock market moves or to hedge against losses in their own portfolios.

The Chicago Mercantile Exchange brought out the first "mini" in mid-July. It reflects the Standard & Poor's 100-stock index, a market-weighted average of mostly blue chip issues with names like AT&T, IBM and General Motors. (Market-weighted simply means some stocks on the list are weighted more than others in coming up with the index.) The S&P's 100 is a miniversion of the S&P's 500, currently the most popular of the big index futures.

The Kansas City Board of Trade, which gave birth to the high-flying market for index futures a year and a half ago with its Value Line contract, plans to offer a "mini" version by Sept. 1. The Value Line index is an unweighted average of 1,685 common stocks. Right now, the New York Futures Exchange doesn't plan a "mini" version of its contracts.

The appeal of these mini-index futures is threefold:

- *They permit even small investors to bet on the direction of the market, with a cash outlay of as little as $1,800 in the case of the S&P's 100.*
- *They allow investors to hedge their portfolios during bear markets without the expense of liquidating.*
- *They permit short-term speculation on market movement with favorable tax treatment. (Gains realized on futures trading are taxed at a maximum rate of 32%.)*

Financial futures and the individual investor

Financial futures can play an important role in an individual's investment portfolio so long as: (1) The individual thoroughly understands these investment vehicles; (2) he or she clearly recognizes the tremendous risk exposure of such vehicles; and (3) he or she is fully prepared (financially and mentally) to absorb some losses. Financial futures are highly volatile securities that have enormous profit and loss potential. For instance, in the nine months from mid-1982 through early 1983, the Value Line stock index contract fluctuated in price from a low of 111.00 to a high of 191.20. This range of 80.20 points for a single contract translated into a profit, or loss, of $40,100—and all from an initial investment of only $6,000. Investment diversification is obviously essential as a way to reduce the potentially devastating

BOX 14.2 *Continued*

How does all this work? Index futures work like other futures contracts, except that there are no pork bellies or gold or cocoa beans involved. Four times each year, in June, September, December and March, the contracts are "settled." In other words, you can buy contracts for 3-, 6-, 9-, or 12-month periods. The price of the contract depends upon the current value of the index.

Each futures contract for the S&P's 100, for example, represents $200 multiplied by the current value of the index. If the index is at 162.35, the value of the contract is $32,470. A speculator may have to put up only 10% of the value of the contract to hold it (hedgers pay even less). If, on the settlement date, the index is higher than 162.35, you are ahead of the game by $200 for each point.

In theory, the small investor can thereby cushion his portfolio against a big market drop, for example. If his stocks drop, the theory goes, so will the S&P's 100. And if he has hedged himself by shorting the index, he will have at least partially offset the losses. There is no guarantee that this index will reflect exactly what happens to his particular portfolio. For example, if the market goes up but the stocks you own go down—it happens, you know—you will lose both on your stock position and on your short position in futures. Some hedge.

To buy or sell one of the new S&P's 100 contracts on the Chicago exchange can cost as little as $1,800 in cash or funds borrowed against the value of the securities in your portfolio. The Kansas City Exchange also plans an $1,800 minimum on the proposed "mini" Value Line futures.

By contrast, the initial ante is $6,000 for regular contracts linked to the broader S&P's 500 stock index. It's currently about $6,500 on existing Value Line contracts, $3,500 for futures on the NYSE composite. Obviously, these positions are highly leveraged—and that is why Dreman and others think they are so poisonous: If you are long in futures on 10% margin and the market drops even 3% you have to cough up more margin. Otherwise they sell you out and you have lost half or more of your money and your hedge is gone as well. So, go ahead and take the plunge if you want to and can afford it. But know you are shooting craps rather than hedging.

Source: Jill Bettner, "Now, Index Futures for Small Investors." *Forbes,* August 15, 1983, p. 98.

impact of such price volatility. Financial futures are exotic investment vehicles, but if properly used, they can provide generous returns to investors.

Options on Futures

The evolution that began with listed stock options and financial futures in time spread to interest rate options and stock index futures; eventually, this led to the merger of options and futures, and to the creation of the ultimate leverage vehicle: options on futures contracts. Known as *futures options,* they represent listed puts and calls on a select but growing number of standardized futures contracts. In essence, they give the holders the right to buy (calls) or sell (puts) a single standardized futures contract for a specified period of time at a specified striking price. They have the same standardized striking prices, expiration dates, and quotation system as other listed options (see Chapter 13 for more discussion of listed options).

Itemized below is information on the futures options available at mid-year 1983:

Option	Size of Underlying Futures Contract	Quotation System	Illustrative Quote and Its Dollar Value
Treasury bonds	$100,000	% of par, in 64ths	4–44 = $4,687.50
Gold	100 troy oz	$ per oz	19.50 = $1,950.00
S&P 500 Stock Index	500 times index	500 times premium	9.40 = $4,700.00
NYSE Composite Stock Index	500 times index	500 times premium	6.35 = $3,175.00
Sugar	112,000 lb	cents per lb	1.51 = $1,691.20

Depending on the striking price on the option and the market value of the underlying futures contract, these options can also be in-the-money and out-of-the-money. Futures options are valued like any other listed puts and calls—by the difference in the option's striking price and the market price of the underlying futures contract (see Chapter 13). And they can also be used like any other listed option—that is, for speculating or hedging, in writing programs, or for spreading.

The biggest difference between a futures option and a futures contract is that the option limits the loss exposure of the investor to the price of the option. The most the option investor can lose is the price paid for the put or call, whereas there is no real limit to the amount of loss a futures investor can incur. To see how futures options work, consider an investor who wants to trade some gold contracts. She feels very strongly that the price of gold is going to increase over the next nine months from its present level of $455 an ounce to around $500 an ounce. She can buy a futures contract at 464.50 by depositing the required initial margin of $3,500, or she can buy a futures call option with a $440 per ounce striking price that is presently being quoted at, say, 20.00 (the total cost of the option would therefore be $2,000). Note that the call is an in-the-money option (since the market price of gold exceeds the exercise price on the option), and that both the futures contract and the futures option cover 100 ounces of gold. The table below summarizes what happens to both investments if the price of gold reaches $500 per ounce by the expiration date; in addition, it shows what happens if the price of gold drops by $45 to $410 an ounce:

	FUTURES CONTRACT		FUTURES OPTION	
	Dollar Profit (or Loss)	Return on Invested Capital	Dollar Profit (or Loss)	Return on Invested Capital
If price of gold *increases* by $45 an ounce	$3,550	101.4%	$4,000	200.0%
If price of gold *decreases* by $45 an ounce	($5,450)	—	($2,000)	—

Clearly, the futures option provides a much higher rate of return, as well as a reduced exposure to loss (and note that the risk-return differences would have been even greater had the investor not used an in-the-money option). Futures options offer interesting investment opportunities, though they should be used only by knowledgeable commodities and financial futures investors.

SUMMARY

Commodities and financial futures are traded on what is known as the futures market, a market that has its roots in the agricultural segment of our economy. Today there are 12 exchanges (11 American and 1 Canadian) that conduct trading in a variety of grains, meat and other foodstuffs, processed goods, metals, wood, foreign currencies, debt instruments, and stock indexes. The exchanges deal in futures contracts, which are commitments to make (or accept) delivery of a certain amount of some specified item or commodity at a specified date in the future.

From the investor's point of view, the key thing about futures contracts is that they control large amounts of the underlying commodity or financial instrument and, as a result, can experience wide price swings and produce very attractive rates of return (or very unattractive losses). All futures contracts have fairly short lives, defined by the contract's delivery month. The futures market is made up of hedgers and speculators who provide both the supply and demand for futures contracts. They do this by buying and selling commodities and/or financial futures (that is, depending upon their outlook, they go either long or short). The hedgers are the producers, processors, and corporate money managers who use futures as a way to protect their position in the underlying commodity or financial instrument; the speculators, in contrast, are the ones who give the market liquidity by trading futures solely for the profit potential they offer.

Commodities like grains, metals, meat, and wood make up the major portion of the futures market. Recently, investors could choose from no less than 39 different types of physical commodities, and several of these were available in different forms or grades; many were traded on more than one exchange. Financial futures are the newcomers—trading in these vehicles did not begin until 1972. There are three types of financial futures: currency futures, interest rate futures, and stock index futures. The first type deals in eight different kinds of foreign currencies, and the holder of a currency futures contract actually has a claim on a certain amount of the underlying foreign currency. In contrast, interest rate futures involve various types of short- and long-term debt instruments, like GNMA bonds, Treasury bonds, Treasury bills, and bank CDs. As a rule, financial futures contracts are much larger than commodities futures because they are often worth about $100,000, and some even approach the $1 million mark (Treasury bill futures). Stock index futures are contracts pegged to broad movements in the stock market, as measured by the S&P 500, the NYSE Composite Index, or the Value Line Stock Index. They enable investors to buy the market by dealing in the widely diversified portfolios that make up these popular stock market indexes. The newest, and perhaps the most unusual, futures trading vehicle is the futures option: listed puts and calls on a select but growing number of commodities and financial futures.

The same trading strategies are used with both commodities and financial futures, and they offer the same investment objectives. Futures can be used for speculating, spreading, or hedging. Regardless of how they are used, all futures trading is done on margin. The required margin is very low (it usually equals no more than 2 to 10 percent of the market value of the contract), and acts to magnify returns to investors. Irrespective of whether investors are in a long or short position, they have only one source of return from commodities and financial futures: that is, appreciation (or depreciation) in the price of the contract. Investors use the rate of return on invested capital to assess the actual or potential profitability of a futures transaction. This measure evaluates the amount of capital gains earned in relation to the amount of margin put up in the transaction. Commodities and financial futures can play an important part in one's portfolio as long as the individual is well versed in the mechanics and pitfalls of futures trading, can afford to take losses, and appreciates the kind of risk exposure he or she is assuming. Equally important, individuals should hold a well-diversified portfolio of futures contracts to at least partially reduce the tremendous risk exposure of these speculative investment vehicles.

KEY TERMS

cash market	maintenance margin deposit
commodities	margin call
currency futures	margin trading
delivery month	mark-to-the-market
daily price limit	maximum daily price range
financial futures	open interest
futures market	open outcry auction
futures options	return on invested capital
hedgers	round trip commission
index price system	settle price
initial margin deposit	short position
interest rate futures	speculators
long position	stock index futures

REVIEW QUESTIONS

1. What is a futures contract? Briefly explain how it is used as an investment vehicle.
2. Discuss the difference between a cash market and a futures market.

a. Note some of the reasons why the futures market has become so popular.
b. What effect does inflation have on the futures market?

3. What is the major source of return to commodities speculators? How important are various types of current income like dividends and interest to these investors?
4. Using Figure 14.3, indicate the dollar value of the following changes in the price of a single contract:

a. Cattle feeders go up by 12 cents per pound.
b. Sugar drops by 3 cents per pound.
c. Lumber goes down by $2.50 per thousand board feet.
d. Gold rises by $6 per ounce.
e. Soybean meal goes up by $7.50 per ton.

5. Why are both hedgers and speculators so important to the efficient operation of a futures market?

6. Explain how margin trading is conducted in the futures market.

a. What is the difference between an initial deposit and a maintenance deposit?
b. Are investors ever required to put up additional margin? When?
c. What is the effect of margin trading on an investor's rate of return?

7. Note and briefly define the five essential parts of a commodity contract. Which parts have a direct bearing on the price behavior of the contract?

8. Briefly define each of the following:

a. Settle price.
b. Daily price limit.
c. Open interest.
d. Maximum daily price range.
e. Delivery month.

9. Len Sharpe considers himself a shrewd commodities investor. For instance, not long ago he bought one July cotton contract at 54 cents per pound and recently sold it at 58 cents per pound. How much profit did he make? What was his return on invested capital if he had to put up a $1,500 initial deposit?

10. Note several approaches to investing in commodities and explain the investment objectives of each.

11. What is the difference between physical commodities and financial futures? What are their similarities?

12. Mrs. Shirley Ledbetter is a regular commodities speculator; she is presently considering a short position in July oats, which are now trading at 148. Her analysis suggests that July oats should be trading at about 140 in a couple of months. Assuming her expectations hold up, what kind of return on invested capital would she make if she shorts three July oats contracts by depositing an initial margin of $500 per contract?

13. Describe a currency future and contrast it with an interest rate future. What is a stock index future, and how can it be used by investors?

14. Explain the index price system used with Treasury bill futures contracts; also, find the value of the following financial futures contracts:

a. September German marks quoted at .5392.
b. December GNMA bonds that settled at 87–22.
c. March 90-day T-bills quoted at 93.55.
d. June S&P 500 index that opened at 162.15.

15. Buddy Phillips is thinking about doing some speculating in interest rates; he thinks rates will fall and in so doing, the price of Treasury bond futures should move from 92–15, their present quote, to a level of about 98. Given a required margin deposit of $4,000 per contract, what would Buddy's return on invested capital be if prices behave as he expects?

16. Explain why it is so important that an individual be well versed in the behavior and investment characteristics of commodities and financial futures. Why should futures holdings be well diversified?

17. Discuss how stock index futures can be used for purposes of speculation; for purposes of hedging. What advantages are there to speculating with stock index futures rather than specific issues of common stock?

18. Denise Engle has been an avid stock market investor for years; she manages her portfolio fairly aggressively and likes to short sell whenever the opportunity presents itself. Recently, she's become fascinated with stock index futures, especially the idea of being able to play the market as a whole. At the present time, Denise thinks the market is headed down, and she decides to short sell some Value Line stock index futures. Assume she shorts three contracts at 187.95 and that she has to make a margin deposit of $3,500 for each contract.

How much profit will she make, and what will her return on invested capital be if the market does indeed drop so that Value Line contracts are trading at 165.00 by the time they expire?

19. What are futures options? Explain how they can be used by speculators. Why, for example, would an investor want to use an option on an interest rate futures contract rather than the futures contract itself? How much profit would an investor make if she or he bought a call option on gold at 7.20 when gold was trading at $482 an ounce, given the price of gold went up to $525 an ounce by the expiration date on the call? (*Note:* Assume the call carried a striking price of 480.)

CASE PROBLEMS

14.1 T. J.'S FAST TRACK INVESTMENT PROGRAM

T. J. Patrick is a successful young architect who enjoys the excitement of commodities speculation. Although only 29 years old, T. J. has been dabbling in commodities since he was a teenager. He was introduced to it by his dad, who was a grain buyer for one of the leading food processors. T. J. recognizes the enormous risks involved in commodities speculating but feels that since he's still single, now is the perfect time to take chances. And he can well afford it too; for this Honolulu resident is not only a principal in a thriving architecture firm, he also holds a substantial interest in several residential and commercial building projects. T. J.'s income ranges between $60,000 and $75,000 per year—enough to allow him to enjoy some of the finer things in life (like the slightly used Porsche 930 Turbo he recently purchased). Even so, he does follow a well-disciplined investment program, and annually adds $10,000 to $15,000 to his portfolio.

Recently, T. J. has started playing with financial futures—interest rate futures, to be exact. He admits he is no expert in interest rates, but likes the price action these investment vehicles offer. This all started several months ago when T. J. was at a party and became acquainted with Mr. Vinnie Banano, a broker who specializes in financial futures. T. J. liked what Vinnie had to say (mostly how you couldn't go wrong with interest rate futures), and set up a trading account with Vinnie's firm: Banano's of Honolulu. The other day, Vinnie called T. J. and suggested he get into T-bill futures. As Vinnie saw it, interest rates were going to continue to head up at a brisk pace, and T. J. should short sell some 90-day T-bill futures. In particular, he thinks that rates on T-bills should go up by another half-point (moving from about 8½ up to 9 percent) and recommends that T. J. short four contracts. This would be an $8,000 investment, since each contract requires an initial margin deposit of $2,000.

Questions

1. Assume 90-day T-bill futures are now being quoted at 91.35.

a. Determine the current price (underlying value) of this T-bill futures contract.

b. What would this futures contract be quoted at if Vinnie is right and the yield goes up by ½ of 1 percent?

2. Determine how much profit T. J. would make if he shorts four contracts at 91.35, and T-bill yields do go up by ½ of 1 percent—that is, that T. J. covers his short position when T-bill futures contracts are quoted at 90.85. Also, calculate the return on invested capital from this transaction.

3. What happens if rates go down; for example, how much would T. J. make if the yield on T-bill futures goes down by just ¼ of 1 percent?

4. What risks do you see in the recommended short sale transaction? What is your assessment of T. J.'s new interest in financial futures; how do you think it stacks up to his established commodities investment program?

14.2 JIM BOOTH TRIES HEDGING WITH STOCK INDEX FUTURES

Jim Booth and his wife, Wanda, live in Birmingham, Alabama; like many young couples today, the Booths are a two-income family, as both are graduates of professional schools and hold well-paying jobs. Jim has been an avid investor in the stock market for a number of years and over time has built up a portfolio that is currently worth nearly $75,000. The Booths' portfolio is well balanced: it contains quality growth stocks, some high-income utilities, and a small amount of moderately speculative stock. The Booths' reinvest all dividends and regularly add investment capital to their portfolio; up to now, they have avoided short selling and do only a modest amount of margin trading.

The portfolio has undergone a substantial amount of capital appreciation in the last 18 months or so, and Jim is anxious to protect the profit he has earned. And that's the problem! For Jim feels the market has pretty much run its course and is about to enter a period of decline. Booth has studied the market and economic news very carefully, and as a result does not believe the retreat will be of a major magnitude or cover an especially long period of time. He feels fairly certain, however, that most, if not all, of the stocks in his portfolio will be adversely affected by these market conditions—though they certainly won't all be affected to the same degree (some will drop more in price than others). Jim has been following stock index futures since they were first introduced in 1982. He's done some investing in them (with a moderate amount of success) and feels he knows the ins and outs of these securities pretty well. After careful deliberation, Jim decides to use stock index futures—in particular, the S&P 500 futures contract—as a way to protect (hedge) his portfolio of common stocks.

Questions

1. Explain why Booth would want to use stock index futures to hedge his stock portfolio and note how he would go about setting up such a hedge; be specific.

    a. What alternatives does Jim have to protect the capital value of his portfolio?

    b. What are the benefits and risks of using stock index futures for such purposes (as hedging vehicles)?

2. Presume S&P 500 futures contracts are presently being quoted at 165.60. How many contracts would Booth have to buy (or sell) to set up the hedge?

    a. If the value of the Booth portfolio dropped 12 percent over the course of the market retreat, to what price must the stock index futures contract move in order to cover that loss?

    b. Given that a $5,000 margin deposit is required to buy or sell a single S&P 500 futures contract, what would be the Booths' return on invested capital if the price of the futures contract changes by the amount computed in part 2(a)?

3. Assume the value of the Booth portfolio declined by $12,000, while the price of an S&P 500 futures contract moved from 165.60 to 147.60 (assume Jim short sold one futures contract to set up the hedge).

    a. Add the profit from the hedge transaction to the new (depreciated) value of the stock portfolio; how does this compare to the $75,000 portfolio that existed just before the market started its retreat?

    b. Why did the stock index futures hedge fail to give complete protection to the Booth portfolio? Is it possible to obtain *perfect* (dollar-for-dollar) protection from these types of hedges? Explain.

4. What if, instead of hedging with futures contracts, Booth decides to set up the hedge by using *futures options*. Suppose a put on an S&P 500 futures contract (strike price = 165) is presently quoted at 5.80, while a comparable call is being quoted at 2.35. Use the same portfolio and futures price conditions as set out in question 3 (above) to determine how well the portfolio would be protected. (*Hint:* Add the net profit from the hedge to the new depreciated value of the stock portfolio.) What are the advantages and disadvantages of using futures options to hedge a stock portfolio, rather than the stock index futures contract itself?

SELECTED READINGS

Angrist, Stanley W. "Spreading for Fun and Profit." *Forbes,* October 26, 1981, p. 230.

Bradley, Harold S. "Stock Index Futures: A Way to Buy the Entire Market." *FACT,* January 1983, pp. 43–46.

Bronson, Gail. "New Ways to Play the Futures Game." *Money,* June 1982, pp. 157–160.

"Commodities—Are They for You?" *Money,* October 1979, pp. 71–86.

"Commodity Funds: A Safer Way to Play a Hot Market." *Business Week,* April 11, 1983, pp. 134–136.

Dreyfus, Patricia A. "Commodity Futures for the Small Investor." *Money,* May 1979, pp. 90–92.

"The Fast Action in Interest-Rate Futures." *Business Week,* September 15, 1980, pp. 156–158.

Feduniak, Robert B. "Commodity Futures: Still Riding Inflation's Coattails." *Financial World,* April 15, 1979, pp. 42–45.

"Getting into the Foreign Exchange Game." *Business Week,* May 25, 1981, pp. 182–185.

Gigot, Paul A. "Uncertainty over Direction of Interest Rates Attracts Investors to Financial-Futures Market." *The Wall Street Journal,* October 19, 1981, p. 48.

Greenebaum, Mary. "Playing the Exchange Rates Is Not for the Fainthearted." *Fortune,* January 14, 1980, pp. 101–102.

———. "A New Way to Play the Market." *Fortune,* October 4, 1982, pp. 157–160.

"How to Avoid the Traps in Commodity Futures." *Business Week,* March 31, 1980, pp. 124–126.

"How to Trade the New Stock-Index Futures." *Business Week,* June 7, 1982, pp. 126–129.

Kerwin, Kathleen. "Pin-Striped Pork Bellies: Why Stock Index Futures Are Red Hot." *Barron's,* February 14, 1983, pp. 14, 32–34.

Kulkosky, Edward. "How to Play Interest Rate Futures." *Financial World,* February 1, 1980, pp. 16–21.

Mackay-Smith, Anne. "Trading in New Futures and Options Contracts Involves Tricky Decisions for Novice Investors." *The Wall Street Journal,* April 4, 1983, p. 30.

———. "Commodity-Futures Options Trading Resumes, with Exchanges Hoping to Avoid Past Pitfalls." *The Wall Street Journal,* October 4, 1982, p. 54.

O'Donnell, Thomas. "A Victim of Deflation." *Forbes,* August 16, 1982, p. 32.

Rustin, Richard E. "Big Risks and Complex Rules of Trading Commodities through a Managed Account." *The Wall Street Journal,* October 22, 1980, p. 25.

Schwarz, Edward W. "Financial Futures—The Long and the Short of It." *Financial World,* March 15, 1980, pp. 84–85.

Weberman, Ben. "Futures Follies." *Forbes,* September 29, 1980, p. 172.

Financial Futures as a Risk Management Tool

Several years ago, Wertheim and Co. became interested in the possibility of commodities being used to manage interest rate volatility. For decades, commodity futures have been important economic tools for participants in agricultural, metals, and other markets subject to unpredictable but violent price swings. As a risk-transfer mechanism, futures permitted business to operate efficiently; volatility risks were transferred to those most capable and willing to assume them—speculators. A speculator seeks a risk for profit that he or she otherwise would not have. A hedger has an existing risk and seeks to manage it at the lowest possible cost.

Until the 1970s, interest rates were fairly stable. A change in the prime rate of a quarter of a point was considered major. The combination of changes in monetary policy, government spending, and inflation have altered this picture dramatically. It is not surprising that financial futures markets arose as changes in interest rates became no more predictable than changes in agricultural commodity prices. The earnings reports of many companies in the late 1970s are testimony to the effects of interest rate volatility.

Nevertheless, the use of financial futures as a risk management tool has been very difficult for regulators and investors to accept. Those involved in financial markets always viewed the commodity markets from the standpoint of the speculator since, with rare exceptions, the hedging function was not something that applied to them. Most of their interest was in cocktail party talk about pork bellies and the amount of money lost by speculators. Regulators, of course, received the same type of impression. Existing legislation did not reflect the use of futures as an investment—all it reflected was the concept that futures are a high-risk business.

Over the past three or four years, Wertheim has worked hard to develop hedging techniques and to educate institutions in the benefits of using futures. We have had some success. For a company that has inventory to finance in nine months, the use of futures today to guarantee the cost of the money it will borrow then is a sensible tool. It is

ARTHUR L. REBELL

no different from fixing the cost of the goods to be purchased. Failure to use futures is in fact speculation—inertia speculation. Unfortunately, inertia speculation is still considered acceptable, whereas the risk of interest declining after one has "locked in a certain rate" is still considered speculation. But this is changing.

As an example, insurance companies should be major users of futures, but they generally have been thwarted by regulations. Most states do not permit insurance companies to use futures. This is beginning to change. We have clients who have created sound insurance policies of approximately $1 billion based on rate of return applications using futures. Most important, however, we and many others have begun to make regulators understand that futures can reduce risks. Within the past few months, California, Illinois, New York, Texas, and Virginia have granted insurance companies the right to use futures, although in some cases on a very limited basis.

Savings banks are another area of major potential use. Federal agencies have in fact encouraged banks that have fixed mortgage costs and variable liability deposit costs to use futures. The use of futures allows them to stabilize their liability costs. However, due to inertia and lack of knowledge, the use of futures by savings institutions is also small.

The use of futures as hedging tools is in its infancy. More analytical work is required. Managers of insurance companies, banks, corporations, pension funds, and so on have a new tool—one that really works to reduce speculative activity in the volatile interest rate world. If we as a nation are successful in reducing interest rate volatility, the use of futures will disappear. If not, they may become one of the most important tools for managing risk efficiently. Because futures reduce the cost of volatility by transferring the risk to those who see fit to assume it, society pays the lowest cost.

ARTHUR L. REBELL
General Partner
Wertheim and Co., Inc.

SEVEN
OTHER POPULAR INVESTMENT VEHICLES

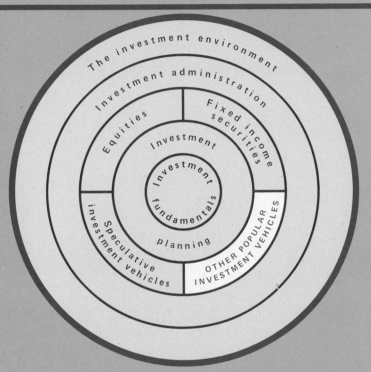

While equities, fixed-income securities, options, and futures contracts make up the bulk of the investment universe, there is another segment of the market that offers a host of interesting investment opportunities. Four chapters are devoted to these investment vehicles, beginning with Chapter 15, which examines mutual funds and shows how these securities can be used by individuals. Chapter 16 looks at various ways of investing in real estate and considers the risk-return characteristics of this investment outlet. Tax sheltered investments are discussed in Chapter 17, and Chapter 18 examines the investment merits of gold and other tangible investments.

15

Mutual Funds: An Indirect Route to the Market

Mutual funds are popular investment vehicles that not only provide a variety of interesting investment opportunities, but also offer services many investors find appealing. In order to learn more about these securities and to see how they can be used, this chapter will look at:

1. Basic characteristics of mutual funds, and how diversification and professional management are the cornerstones of the industry.
2. The advantages and disadvantages of owning mutual funds.
3. The kinds of funds available and the variety of investment objectives these funds seek to fulfill.
4. The array of special services offered by mutual funds and how these services can fit into an investment program.
5. Investor uses of mutual funds, and ways of assessing and selecting funds that are compatible with the investment needs of the individual.

Mutual funds are unlike any security we have examined so far since they really represent ownership in a professionally managed portfolio of securities. When investors buy common stock, bonds, preferreds, convertible issues, or even options, they are investing directly in the securities themselves. Mutual funds, however, handle all the investment chores, and individual investors, in turn, buy shares in the funds. The mutual fund investor thus becomes an indirect owner of a portfolio of securities. There is a mutual fund to meet almost any type of investment objective. They can be used to accumulate wealth, as a storage of value, or as a means of seeking high returns. Mutual funds are truly versatile investment vehicles that have much to offer individual investors, especially those with limited resources. We will now take a close look at the operating characteristics, sources of return, and uses and limitations of mutual funds. We begin by looking at the mutual fund concept and some of the basic characteristics of mutual funds and mutual fund ownership.

THE MUTUAL FUND PHENOMENON

In 1929, there were only 19 mutual funds, with assets of less than $200 million; by the end of 1981, that number had grown to over 850 funds, and as Figure 15.1 shows, assets had increased to nearly $250 billion. Over 15 million people in this country own shares in mutual funds and investment companies. They come from all walks of life and are at all income levels; and they all share a common view: Each has decided, for one reason or another, to turn over all or a part of their investment management activities to professionals. The widespread acceptance of the mutual fund concept has, in itself, been something of a phenomenon. From rather meager beginnings only a few decades ago, mutual funds have grown so that they are today a powerful force in the securities markets and a major financial institution in our economy.

An Overview of Mutual Funds

Questions of which stock or bond to select, when to buy, and when to sell have plagued investors for as long as we have had organized capital markets. Such concerns lie at the root of the mutual fund concept and explain, in large part, the growth mutual funds have experienced. Many investors lack the time, the knowhow, or the commitment to manage their own portfolios. As a result, they turn to others; more often than not, this means the professional portfolio management of mutual funds.

Pooled diversification

The mutual fund concept is based on a simple idea; that is, turning the problems of security selection and portfolio management over to professional money managers. In essence, a mutual fund is a company that combines the investment funds of many people with similar investment goals, and invests the funds for these people in a wide variety of securities. The individual investors receive shares of stock in the mutual fund and, through the fund, are able to enjoy much wider investment diversity than they could otherwise achieve. Each shareholder, in effect, owns a part of a diversified portfolio that has been acquired with the pooled money. As the securities held by the fund move up and down in price, the market value of the mutual fund shares moves accordingly. When dividend and interest payments are received by the fund, they are passed on to the mutual fund shareholders and distributed on the basis of prorated ownership. For example, if you owned 1,000 shares of stock in a mutual fund and that represented 10 percent of all shares outstanding, you would receive 10 percent of the dividends paid by the fund. When a security held by the fund is sold for a profit, this capital gain is also passed on to fund shareholders. The whole mutual fund idea, in fact, rests on the concept of *pooled diversification,* and it works much like the idea of insurance. Individuals pool

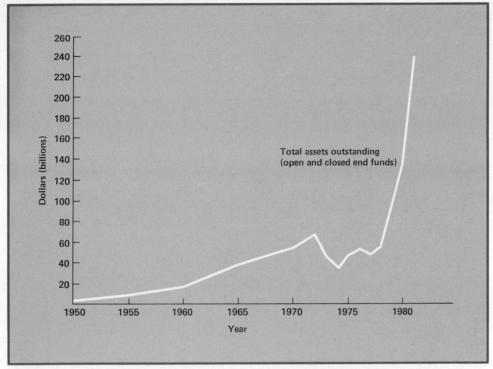

Figure 15.1   Growth in Mutual Fund and Investment Company Assets.
The mutual fund industry has mushroomed in the last two decades and has become one of
the leading financial forces in our money and capital markets. (*Source:* Wiesenberger's Investment Company Service.)

their resources for the collective benefit of the individual contributors. Table 15.1
illustrates the notion of diversification at work in mutual funds.

Attractions and drawbacks
of mutual fund ownership

The attractions of mutual fund ownership are numerous. One of the most
important is something we have touched on above: *diversification.* Diversification
has been an underlying theme of this book, and diversification is exactly what the
investor obtains with mutual funds. Diversification is beneficial since it reduces the
risk inherent in any one investment by spreading out holdings to include a wide
variety of industries and companies. Another appeal is the full-time professional
management mutual funds offer, which removes much of the day-to-day management and recordkeeping chores from the shoulders of individual investors. What's
more, it may even provide better investment talents than the investor himself has to
offer. Still another advantage is that most (but not all) mutual fund investments can
be started with a modest capital outlay. Sometimes there is no minimum investment

TABLE 15.1　DIVERSIFICATION IN THE COMMON STOCK HOLDINGS OF MUTUAL FUNDS*

	1971 Market Value (billions)		1981 Market Value (billions)	
Agricultural equipment	$ 34.7	0.12%	$ 161.7	1.02%
Aircraft mfg. and aerospace	279.6	0.97	271.5	1.71
Air transport	902.7	3.15	259.3	1.63
Auto and accessories (excl. tires)	1,068.7	3.72	175.2	1.11
Building materials and equipment	1,128.9	3.93	220.0	1.39
Chemicals	1,375.4	4.79	924.2	5.82
Communications (TV, radio, motion pictures)	402.9	1.40	394.3	2.48
Containers	155.9	0.54	98.6	0.62
Drugs and cosmetics	1,392.6	4.85	1,356.5	8.54
Elec. equip. and electronics (excl. TV and radio)	1,845.8	6.43	1,212.8	7.64
Foods and beverages	820.9	2.86	480.9	3.03
Financial (incl. banks and insurance)	2,920.4	10.18	1,486.6	9.36
Machinery	371.8	1.30	247.7	1.56
Metals and mining	588.8	2.05	245.1	1.55
Office equipment	1,952.2	6.80	1,200.8	7.56
Oil	2,507.2	8.74	1,930.8	12.16
Paper	590.1	2.06	307.0	1.93
Public utilities (incl. telephone and natural gas)	2,142.0	7.46	1,775.7	11.18
Railroad	748.6	2.61	163.7	1.03
Railroad equipment	63.5	0.22	77.7	0.49
Retail trade	1,971.2	6.87	578.4	3.64
Rubber (incl. tires)	392.0	1.37	96.7	0.61
Steel	292.8	1.03	228.2	1.44
Textiles	95.2	0.33	38.0	0.24
Tobacco	303.3	1.06	339.3	2.14
Miscellaneous	4,349.3	15.16	1,607.4	10.12
Totals	$28,696.5	100.00%	$15,878.1	100.00%

*Composite industry figures as drawn from the security holdings of the 40 largest mutual funds.
Source: 1982 Mutual Fund Fact Book.

required at all. After the initial investment has been made, additional shares can usually be purchased in small amounts. The services mutual funds offer also make them appealing to many investors; these include the automatic reinvestment of dividends, withdrawal plans, exchange privileges, checkwriting privileges, and the like. Finally, mutual funds offer convenience; they are relatively easy to acquire, the funds handle the paperwork and recordkeeping, their prices are widely quoted, and it is often possible to deal in fractional shares.

There are, of course, some major drawbacks. One of these is the lack of liquidity that characterizes many mutual funds. Most funds are fairly easy to buy, but they are not so easy to sell. That is, selling mutual funds is more often than not a do-it-yourself project that involves selling the shares back to the fund itself. Since there are usually no commissions on sales, some brokers are unenthusiastic about handling such transactions for investors. Another drawback is that mutual funds are fairly costly to acquire. Many funds carry sizable commission charges (or what are known as "load charges"). In addition, a management fee is levied annually for the professional services provided, and this is deducted off the top, regardless of whether it has been a good or bad year. Finally, in spite of all the professional management and advice, it seems that their performance over the long haul is at best just about equal to what you would expect from the market as a whole. There are always some funds which, at one time or another, have performed much above average and have indeed generated attractive rates of return. But for the most part, mutual funds are simply not the vehicle to use for consistently high or above-average rates of return. This is not to say that the long-term returns from mutual funds are substandard, or that they fail to equal what one could achieve by putting money in, say, a savings account (or some similar risk-free investment outlet). Quite the contrary: The long-term returns from mutual funds have been substantial; but a good deal of this is often due to the reinvestment of dividends and capital gains.

Essential Characteristics

Not only are there many types of mutual funds available, there are also significant differences in organization, fees charged to investors, and methods of buying and selling funds. Let us now look at some of these characteristics.

Open end investment companies

The term *mutual fund* is commonly used to denote an open end investment company. Mutual funds are the dominant type of investment company and account for well over 95 percent of the assets under management. Many of these funds are fairly large, with some having portfolios that amount to a billion dollars or more. In an *open end investment company,* investors actually buy their shares from, and sell them back to, the mutual fund itself. When the investor buys shares in an open end fund, the fund issues new shares of stock and fills the purchase order with these new shares. There is no limit on the number of shares the fund can issue; the only restraint on the number of shares issued is investor demand. Furthermore, all open end mutual funds stand behind their shares and buy them back when investors decide to sell. Thus, there is never any trading between individuals.

Both buy and sell transactions are carried out at prices based on the current value of all the securities held in the fund's portfolio. This is known as the fund's *net asset value (NAV);* it is calculated at least once a day and represents the value of a share of stock in a particular mutual fund. NAV is found by taking the total market value of all securities held by the fund, less any liabilities, and dividing this amount by the number of fund shares outstanding. For example, if on a given day the market value of all the securities held by the XYZ mutual fund equaled some $10 million, and if XYZ on that particular day had 500,000 shares outstanding, the fund's net asset value per share would amount to $20 ($10,000,000/500,000 = $20). This figure, as we will see below, would then be used to derive the price at which the fund shares are bought and sold.

Closed end investment companies

While the term *mutual fund* is supposed to be used only with open end funds, it is, as a practical matter, regularly used with closed end investment companies as well. Basically, *closed end investment companies* operate with a fixed number of shares outstanding and do not regularly issue new shares of stock. In effect, they have a capital structure like that of an ordinary corporation, except that the corporation's business happens to be investing in marketable securities. There are about 70 publicly traded closed end funds whose shares, at the end of 1981, had a combined market value of some $8 billion; Table 15.2 lists the 12 largest. Closed end company shares are actively traded in the secondary market, like any other common stock. Most are traded on the New York Stock Exchange, several are on the American Exchange, and a few are traded in the OTC market. As seen below, the shares of closed end companies are listed right along with other common stocks. In this case ASA Ltd. and Adams Express (two of the largest closed end investment companies) are quoted on the NYSE.

52 Weeks High	52 Weeks Low	Stock	Div.	Yld %	P-E Ratio	Sales 100s	High	Low	Close	Net Chg.
				—A—A—A—						
9¼	5¾	AAR	.44	4.8	25	48	9⅛	9	9⅛	+ ⅛
42	27½	ACF	2.76	8.8	6	229	31¼	31	31¼	+ ¼
28½	12¼	AMF	1.36	7.9	6	1388	17⅝	16½	17⅛	+ ⅛
25	9¼	AMR Cp		...	....	11793	24	22¾	22¾	−1¾
11⅞	3¼	AMR	wt	...	....	2383	11⅛	10¼	10¼	−1¼
16⅝	12⅜	AMR	pf2.18	13.	....	138	16⅝	16⅜	16⅝	+ ⅛
5⅛	2½	APL		...	19	42	3¾	3⅝	3⅝	− ⅛
36	23½	ARA	2	5.9	10	227	34⅜	33⅝	34⅛	+ ½
66⅞	24½	ASA	3a	4.8	....	868	64⅝	61½	62¼	−2⅝
26⅞	11¾	AVX	.32	1.4	37	80	24⅜	23¼	23⅝	− ⅜
41	25⅜	AbtLab	.84	2.2	17	2439	38½	37¾	37⅞	− ⅛
24¾	15⅝	AcmeC	1.40	8.1	7	74	17⅝	17¼	17⅜	− ¼
9¾	5¾	AcmeE	n.32b	3.9	14	14	8¼	8¼	8¼	+ ¼
10⅝	4⅛	AdmDg	.04	.4	11	57	10⅜	10	10	− ½
17	12½	AdaEx	2.25e	13.	....	54	17	16¾	17	....
9¾	4⅝	AdmMl	.20e	2.2	17	84	9¼	9	9⅛	− ⅛
26	20⅞	Advest	n 20	.8	21	45	23⅝	22⅞	23⅝	+ ½
28	10¼	AMD	s	...	45	3070	27⅛	25	25¼	− ⅛
48¼	32⅞	AetnLf	2.52	6.5	7	3439	38⅝	38	38½	+ ⅛
61¼	52⅜	AetL	pf2.49e	4.2	....	1486	u61½	59	59	−1¾
33⅛	8	Ahmns	.60	1.9	....	252	32¾	31¾	32⅛	− ⅜
3½	2¼	Aileen		...	....	117	3¼	3⅛	3⅛	....
41⅛	23⅝	AirPrd	.80	2.3	9	950	35⅛	34¾	34⅞	− ⅛
17½	7¾	AirbFrt	.60	3.7	20	91	16⅞	16⅛	16⅛	− ⅝
2⅞	2	AlMoa	n	...	3	153	2⅛	2	2	....
30¾	23¾	AlaP	pfA3.92	14.	....	53	29	28½	29	+ ⅛
7¼	5½	AlaP	dpf.87	13.	....	14	7	6⅞	6⅞	....
93	73½	AlaP	pf 11	12.	....	z1020	92	92	92	− ½
73¾	55	AlaP	pf 9.44	13.	....	z450	70⅝	69½	70⅝	+1⅛
63½	48⅜	AlaP	pf 8.16	13.	....	z30	61¼	61¼	61¼	− ¼
64	50	AlaP	pf 8.28	14.	....	z1300	63	61	61	−1½
17½	13	Alagsco	1.60	9.6	5	13	16¾	16⅝	16¾	....
33⅞	23⅛	Albany	1.40	4.8	10	27	29⅛	28⅞	29⅛	− ⅜
24⅛	10¾	Alberto	.54	2.3	14	55	23⅞	23⅜	23⅝	+ ¼
49⅜	24⅛	Albtsn	1	2.0	14	16	u49½	49⅛	49¼	+ ¼

Source: The Wall Street Journal.

The share prices of closed end companies are determined not only by their net asset value, but also by general supply and demand conditions in the stock market. As a result, closed end companies generally trade at a discount or premium to NAV. For example, if a fund has a net asset value of $10 per share and is trading

TABLE 15.2	THE TWELVE LARGEST CLOSED END INVESTMENT COMPANIES, 1981	

Fund	Exchange	1981 Total Assets (millions)
Adams Express	NYSE	$320.5
American General Convertible Securities	NYSE	99.8
American General Bond Fund	NYSE	170.0
ASA, Ltd.	NYSE	628.4
General American Investments	NYSE	211.9
John Hancock Income Securities	NYSE	104.0
Heizer	ASE	308.9
Madison Fund	NYSE	604.8
Massachusetts Mutual Income Investments	NYSE	106.9
Niagara Share Corporation	NYSE	175.0
Petroleum & Resources	NYSE	257.3
Tri-Continental Corporation	NYSE	807.3

at $9, it would be selling at a discount of $1; it would be selling at a premium of $1 if it were quoted at a price of $11. Share price discounts can at times become quite large—for example, it's not unusual for discounts to amount to as much as 25 to 30 percent of net asset value. In contrast, price premiums are rare and seldom exceed single-digit figures.

Investment trusts

An *investment trust* (or *unit investment trust,* as it is also known) represents little more than an interest in an unmanaged pool of investments. In essence, a portfolio of securities is simply held in safekeeping for investors under conditions set down in a trust agreement. The portfolios usually consist of corporate, government, or municipal bonds, though occasionally they are made up of preferred stock or money market instruments. There is *no trading* in the portfolios; as a result, the returns, or yields, are fixed and predictable. Unit trusts are like second cousins to mutual funds: Unlike conventional mutual funds whose securities are actively traded, a trust manager simply puts together a stated portfolio. After they are deposited with a trustee, no new securities are added and, with rare exceptions, none is sold.

Various sponsoring brokerage houses put these diversified pools of securities together and then sell units of the pool to investors (each unit is like a share in a mutual fund). For example, a brokerage house might put together a diversified pool of corporate bonds that amount to, say, $10 million. The sponsoring firm would then sell units in this pool to the investing public at a price of $1,000 per unit (a common price for these issues). The sponsoring organization does little more than routine recordkeeping, and services the investments by clipping coupons and distributing the income (often on a monthly basis) to the holders of the trust units. Figure 15.2 depicts a municipal bond trust announcement. Like all such trusts, this one will

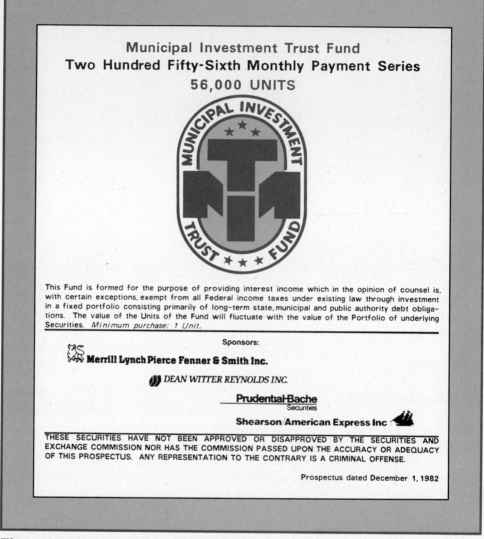

Figure 15.2 A Newly Formed Bond Trust.
This is a $56 million investment trust (it will issue 56,000 units at $1,000 each) that will invest in tax-exempt municipal bonds and pay income on a monthly basis; note that this is issue number 256 of this series—which means 255 similar trust funds have been put together and marketed by this group in the past. (*Source:* Dean Witter Reynolds.)

eventually expire when the bonds in the portfolio mature. Trusts are appealing to investors because they allow individuals with limited resources the opportunity to acquire a diversified portfolio of generally high-yielding securities, and to earn monthly (rather than semiannual) income. If an investor decides to sell the trust units before the end of the life of the trust, he or she can do so by selling them back to the sponsor at a price equal to the prevailing net asset value, less a sales commission.

Load and no load funds

The question of whether a fund is "load" or "no load" is a matter of concern only to investors in open end funds. The load charge of a fund is the commission the investor must pay when buying shares in a fund. A *load fund* means that the mutual fund charges a commission when shares are bought; a *no load fund*, in contrast, means no sales charges are levied. Load charges can be fairly substantial and often range from 7 to 8.5 percent of the purchase price of the shares. Most mutual funds, however, offer quantity discounts (which usually start with single investments of 1,000 shares or more). In 1981, over 400 funds (half of which were money funds) were of the no load type, and the number is growing as investors continue to show an appetite for such funds. The reason for the growing interest in no load funds has to do in part with the growth in money funds and in part with the fact that investors can save load charges and thereby invest more in the fund itself. Although there may be little or no difference in the performance of the investment portfolios of load and no load funds, the cost savings with no load funds tend to give investors a real head start in achieving superior rates of return.

Fortunately, it is possible to tell the players apart without a program: The quotation system used with mutual funds distinguishes the no load from the load funds. That is, all open end mutual funds are priced according to their net asset value, and this information is included in the customary mutual fund quotations, as we can see in the illustration below:

	NAV	Offer Price	NAV Chg
Devl Fd	55.96	N.L.	+ .03
Income	11.53	N.L.	− .02
Intl Fnd	16.78	N.L.	− .04
Muni Bd	7.47	N.L.	+ .03
Security Funds:			
Bond Fd	8.00	8.23	− .01
Equity	6.80	7.43	− .04
Invest	9.86	10.78	. . . . .
Ultra Fd	9.26	10.12	+ .05
Selected Funds:			
Selct Am	8.36	N.L.	− .01
Selct Spl	18.95	N.L.	− .05
Seligman Group:			
Captl Fd	12.02	12.96	+ .02
Com Stk	12.93	13.94	− .06
Growth	7.61	8.20	− .13
Income	12.31	13.27	− .01
Sentinel Group Funds:			
Bal Fund	8.88	9.70	− .07
Bond Fd	6.36	6.95	− .04
Com Stk	15.59	17.04	− .10
Growth	14.18	15.50	− .14
Sentry Fd	23.04	25.04	− .03
Sequoia	31.99	N.L.	− .01
Shearson Funds:			
Apprec	15.67	16.49	+ .03
High Yld	18.52	19.49	− .06
Income	18.80	19.79	− .08
Mg Muni	12.75	13.42	− .07
N Direct	16.06	16.91	− .15
Shrm Dean	7.27	N.L.	− .06

Source: The Wall Street Journal.

The NAV (Net Asset Value) column is the price the mutual fund will pay to buy back the fund shares (or, from the investor's point of view, it is the price at which the shares can be sold). Next to the NAV is the "offer price," the price the investor would have to pay in order to buy the shares. Note that the Sentry Fund, for example, has a higher offer price ($25.04) than net asset value ($23.04); this difference of $2 per share represents the load charge. For the Sentry Fund, the load charge amounts to 8 percent of the offer price. However, the load rate is actually *more* when the commission is related to a more appropriate base—the NAV of the fund. When stated as a percent of NAV, the load charge for the Sentry Fund becomes 8.7 percent.

Thus, whenever there is a difference between NAV and offer price, the investor knows the fund is of the load type. In contrast, note the repeated use of the letters *N.L.* in the offer price column; for example, see the Sequoia Fund. Those letters indicate that the fund is a no load and, as a result, the shares are bought and sold at the same net asset value ($31.99). Occasionally, a no load fund will have a small *back-end load,* which amounts to a 1 to 2 percent commission on the sale of shares.

Other fees and costs

Regardless of whether a fund is load or no load, or whether it is open end or closed, another cost of owning mutual funds is the *management fee,* the compensation paid to the professional managers who administer the fund's portfolio. Fees generally equal .25 to .75 percent of the average dollar amount of assets under management (although small funds sometimes have assessments in excess of 1 percent). Unlike load charges, which are one-time costs, management fees are assessed annually and are paid regardless of the performance of the portfolio. In addition, there are the administrative costs of operating the fund; these are fairly modest and represent the normal cost of doing business (like the commissions paid when the fund buys and sells securities).

A final cost is the taxes paid on security transactions. In order to avoid double taxation, nearly all mutual funds operate as "regulated investment companies." This means that all (or nearly all) of the dividend and interest income is passed on to the investor, as are any capital gains realized when securities are sold. The mutual fund thus pays no taxes, but instead passes the tax liability on to its individual shareholders. This holds true regardless of whether such distributions are reinvested in the company (in the form of additional mutual fund shares) or paid out in cash. Mutual funds will annually provide each stockholder with a convenient summary report on the amount of dividends and capital gains received, and the nature of the tax liability of such income—that is, whether it is taxed at the ordinary rate or subject to the preferential long-term capital gains rate.

Buying and selling fund shares

Buying and selling shares of closed end investment companies is no different from buying a share of common stock. The transactions are executed on listed exchanges or in the OTC market through brokers or dealers who handle the orders in the normal way. They are subject to usual transaction costs, and because they are treated like any other listed or OTC stock, the shares of closed end funds can even be margined or sold short. The situation is considerably different, however, with open end funds. There are several ways of acquiring such shares, depending on whether the fund is load or no load. However, it should first be pointed out that regardless of whether the fund is load or no load, it must provide you with a recent *prospectus* that explains in detail the operations of the fund, its investment objectives, and other key financial matters. With load funds, investors buy the stocks from a broker or through salespeople employed by the mutual fund. Most brokerage firms are authorized to sell shares in a variety of load funds, and this is the easiest and most convenient way of buying funds for investors who have established brokerage accounts. Sometimes, however, the fund may not be sold through brokerage houses, in which case the investor would deal directly with the fund's commissioned sales-people—individuals who are employed by the mutual fund for the sole purpose of selling its shares.

If you happen to be interested in a no load fund, you are strictly on your own. You must write or call the mutual fund directly to obtain information. You will then receive an order form from the fund and instructions on how to buy shares; no salesperson will ever call on you. To complete the transaction, you simply mail your check, along with the completed order form, to the mutual fund or its designated agent. Appendix A provides the names, addresses, telephone numbers, and purchase requirements for nearly 150 no load funds.

Selling shares in a fund is also a do-it-yourself affair, whether the fund is load or no load. Because commissions are not usually levied on fund sales, brokers and salespeople have little motivation to execute a sell order. Normally, redemption of shares is by direct notification to the mutual fund of your intention to sell. The fund then buys the shares back and mails the investor a check. An alternative is available with funds that offer checkwriting privileges. It is possible to redeem shares in these funds simply by writing a check on the fund large enough to clean out the balance of the account. It is as simple as writing a check on a checking account, and is obviously much easier and quicker than having to notify the fund directly. (We will examine checkwriting privileges more fully below.)

TYPES OF FUNDS AND SERVICES

Some mutual funds specialize in stocks, others in bonds; still others have maximum capital gains as an investment objective, and some seek high income. Some funds will thus appeal to speculators and others will be of interest primarily to income-oriented investors. Every fund must specify its particular investment objective; the objective must be clearly stated and outline exactly what the fund is established to achieve and how it intends to attain these stated goals. Some common investment objectives include growth, income, tax-exempt income, preservation of investment capital, or some combination thereof. Figure 15.3 shows the stated investment objective of a popular mutual fund. Such disclosure is required by the SEC, and each fund is expected to do its best to conform to its stated investment policy and objective.

Basically, there are six major types of funds: growth, performance, income, balanced, bond, and money market. Table 15.3 lists these funds by asset size and shows the significant changes that have taken place over the five years from 1976 to 1981. Note that although balanced funds and growth funds are still important, money funds have become the dominant type and account for approximately 75 percent of total mutual fund assets. Let's look at each of these funds, as well as at two other types that are popular with some investors: dual funds and specialty funds.

BOX 15.1 TAXES AND YOUR MUTUAL FUND

Mutual funds, the darlings of small investors in the 1960s but abandoned by many in the 1970s, are once again being viewed with ardor. If mutual funds look good to you, you should know how federal income tax rules apply to your investment.

In general, most mutual funds distribute all of their income (after expenses) to shareholders, exempting the funds from paying federal income tax on their earnings. Shareholders must report the income passed through to them on their personal income tax returns, even if all distributions are automatically reinvested in additional shares of the fund.

Your mutual fund will inform you of the amount and kinds of distributions you receive during the year and will spell out their differences for income tax purposes. Some funds send Form 1099-DIV in January, detailing distributions for the previous calendar year. Often, however, such information will be included as part of the regular distribution notice you receive after the last distribution for the year; it will be labeled "income tax" or "1099" information.

How you account for distributions on your tax return varies with the kinds of distributions you receive. There are three common types: ordinary dividends, capital gain distributions and exempt-interest dividends.

ORDINARY DIVIDENDS

These must be reported on your federal tax return as ordinary income. They represent your share of dividends from stocks in the fund's portfolio or interest on bonds or on money temporarily placed in back accounts or short-term bank or commercial paper until it can be used to buy portfolio securities.

Distributions of a fund's ordinary income are always characterized as dividends, even if the income was received by the fund as interest. This is the case whether the fund invests primarily in stocks, bonds or the money market.

If your fund receives dividends that do not qualify for the dividend exclusion, such as dividends from foreign corporations, these will be noted on your 1099 information as nonqualifying amounts.

CAPITAL GAIN DISTRIBUTIONS

Mutual fund managers buy and sell securities for the fund's portfolio. When these transactions result in a net loss for the year, there are no immediate tax consequences to the shareholders because losses are "carried over" by the fund to offset future capital gains. But if the portfolio trading produces a net profit for a year, a fund will generally make a once-a-year capital gain distribution to the shareholders.

The amount of any capital gain distribution will be on the 1099 the fund sends to you. You should always report such amounts as a long-term capital gain on your tax return, even if you have owned all your shares for less than a year.

EXEMPT-INTEREST DIVIDENDS

Some mutual funds, such as tax-exempt bond funds, invest in state and municipal bonds, the interest from which is exempt from federal taxation. Thus, you don't count such interest as income on your return. It may be taxable on your state income tax return, however.

A small part of the income from tax-exempt bond funds may be subject to federal tax if, for example, there is any taxable interest from interim investments or capital gain distributions from the sale of portfolio securities. Your 1099 will identify such income.

Some mutual funds invest in obligations of the federal government or its agencies. Any income from these securities is subject to federal but exempt from state tax. Again, the 1099 will identify such amounts for you.

BOX 15.1 *Continued*

GAIN OR LOSS ON REDEMPTION

When you redeem mutual fund shares, you can produce a capital gain or loss. Capital gains and losses are reportable on your tax return even if they come from a sale of shares of a tax-exempt mutual fund. (If you exchange shares within a family of funds, you have redeemed one kind and bought another, as far as the IRS is concerned.)

The profit or loss upon redemption is the difference between the adjusted basis of the shares you sold and the amount you receive on redemption (minus expenses of the transfer). In most cases the basis of your mutual fund shares is whatever they cost you.

Unlike capital gain distributions—all of which are considered long-term regardless of how long you've owned your shares in the fund—redemptions of mutual fund shares are governed by the same rules that apply to sales or exchanges of other capital assets: Sale of shares owned for a year or less creates a short-term gain or loss; sale after more than a year creates a long-term gain or loss.

There are two exceptions, however. If you have owned the shares for 30 days or less and received a capital gain distribution during that period, any loss on the sale up to the amount of the capital gain distribution is considered long-term. Also, if you have owned the shares for 30 days or less and received exempt-interest dividends during that period, then any loss on the sale up to the amount of the dividend is not allowed.

Calculating the gain or loss is relatively simple if you made a one-time purchase of shares and have taken all dividends and other distributions in cash. Assuming that there has been no return-of-capital distribution, your basis is what you paid for the shares, including any sales charge. Your gain or loss is the difference between your basis and what you get for the shares after subtracting selling expenses.

Determining gain or loss becomes more complicated if you have accumulated shares in a number of separate transactions at different prices over a period—for example, by a periodic investment program or by the reinvestment of dividends or both. When you eventually redeem all or part of your shares, you will still have to establish the adjusted cost basis for the shares redeemed in order to calculate the amount of capital gain or loss on the transaction.

THE IMPORTANCE OF TIMING

When you buy shares in a mutual fund, you pay the net asset value on the date of purchase, plus a sales fee in the case of a load fund.

Capital gains and income have generally been accumulating in the fund during the course of the year, and all amounts to date are reflected in the net asset value on any given day. But when the fund makes a distribution to shareholders, the net asset value is reduced by the amount of the per-share distribution.

This means that if you buy shares shortly before the record date of a capital gain or income distribution, the amounts that have been accumulating since the last record date are reflected in the price, even though they haven't yet been paid. When you do get the distribution a short time later, you must report—and pay tax on—the full amount.

So in effect you will be paying income tax on a return of your own money—the money you just paid for the value of the accumulated capital gains and income.

From a tax standpoint, therefore, and assuming no major market rise in the interim, you can save a little tax money by buying shares just after rather than just before the record date on a capital gain or income distribution. The prospectus or a representative of the fund should be able to tell you when gains and income will be distributed.

Source: "Taxes and Your Mutual Fund," *Changing Times,* September 1981, pp. 56–58.

Templeton Growth Fund, Ltd.

44 Victoria Street, Toronto, Ontario M5C 1Y2 / Telephone: (416) 364-4672

United States Prospectus   **August 31, 1983**

TABLE OF CONTENTS

	Page		Page
Summary	2	—No Canadian Taxes on Estates of U.S. Residents	14
Per Share Data	3	—Further Tax Information	14
Investment Policy	4	—Different Tax Effects for Shareholders of	
Risk Considerations	5	Templeton Funds, Inc.	14
Investment Restrictions	6	Description of Shares	14
Net Asset Value	7	Directors and Officers of the Fund	15
Purchase of Shares	8	Principal Shareholders	17
—Cumulative Quantity Discount	9	Investment Manager	17
—Letter of Intent	9	—Investment Management Contract	17
—Pre-Authorized Check	9	—Management Fees	18
Reinvestment of Dividends and Distributions	10	—Templeton Investment Counsel Limited	18
Cash Withdrawal Program	10	—Research Services	19
Interchange Privilege with Templeton World Fund		Illustration of an Assumed Investment	20
or Templeton Foreign Fund	10	Allocation of Portfolio Brokerage	22
Exchange Privilege with The Reserve Fund, Inc.	11	Principal Underwriter	24
Redemption and Repurchase of Shares	11	Custodians and Transfer Agents	25
Dividend Policy and Tax Information	12	Legal Counsel	26
—No U.S. Corporate Income Tax	13	Independent Accountants	26
—Canadian Income Taxes	13	Reports to Shareholders	26
—Tax Status of U.S. Shareholders	13	Additional Information	26
A. Canadian Taxes	13	Financial Statements	27
B. United States Taxes	13	Application Forms	35

SUMMARY

The Fund: Templeton Growth Fund, Ltd. was incorporated under the laws of Canada on September 1, 1954 and is subject to the Canada Business Corporations Act. Its head office and principal office is at Suite 800, 44 Victoria Street, Toronto, Ontario M5C 1Y2. The Fund is registered under the United States Investment Company Act of 1940 as an open-end, diversified investment company. The Fund's adviser is Templeton Investment Counsel Limited. (See ''Investment Manager''—page 17.) The Fund's Common Shares (see ''Description of Shares''—page 14) are offered continuously by Securities Fund Investors, Inc. (See ''Principal Underwriter''—page 24.)

Investment Objective: Long-term capital growth, through a flexible policy of investing in stocks and debt obligations of companies and governments of any nation. (See ''Investment Policy''—page 4.)

Risk Considerations: The Fund has the right to purchase securities in any foreign country, listed on a stock exchange or, to a limited extent, unlisted. Because of such wide investment discretion, Shares of the Fund involve substantial risks which should be considered carefully in advance of purchase. (See ''Risk Considerations''—page 5.)

Offering Price: Net asset value plus sales commission of 8½% of Offering Price (9.29% of net amount invested). The commission is reduced on single purchases over $10,000 on a graduated scale down to ½% of Offering Price (see page 8) on single purchases of $2,000,000 or more. For certain employee benefit plans with ten or more employee accounts the sales commission is 4% of Offering Price (4.17% of net asset value) regardless of the amount purchased.

Minimum Purchase: $500 initial purchase (other than in intended monthly plans). Subsequent purchases or purchases in monthly plans $25 minimum. (See ''Purchase of Shares''—page 8.)

Redemption: Shares are redeemed at net asset value. There is no redemption charge.

Management Fee: The Fund pays an investment management fee to Templeton Investment Counsel Limited equivalent to 0.50% of its average daily net assets during the year, reduced to 0.45% of net assets in excess of $200,000,000.

Taxes: For information as to Canadian and U.S. taxes see ''Dividend Policy and Tax Information''—page 12.

Templeton Growth Fund, Ltd. (the "Fund") has long-term capital growth for its investment objective which the Fund seeks to achieve through a flexible policy of investing in stocks and debt obligations of companies and governments of any nation.

THESE SECURITIES HAVE NOT BEEN APPROVED OR DISAPPROVED BY THE SECURITIES AND EXCHANGE COMMISSION, NOR HAS THE COMMISSION PASSED UPON THE ACCURACY OR ADEQUACY OF THIS PROSPECTUS. ANY REPRESENTATION TO THE CONTRARY IS A CRIMINAL OFFENSE.

Investors are advised to read and retain this Prospectus for future reference. All monetary figures appearing in this Prospectus are in United States currency unless otherwise indicated.

Figure 15.3   Statement of a Mutual Fund's Investment Objective as Drawn from Its Prospectus.
The fund's investment objective (in this case, long-term capital growth through a flexible policy of investing in stocks and debt obligations of companies and governments of any nation), its risk exposure, and other vital information are clearly spelled out for the investor. (*Source:* Templeton Growth Fund, Ltd.)

TABLE 15.3	AMOUNT OF ASSETS UNDER MANAGEMENT BY THE MAJOR TYPES OF FUNDS	
	FUND ASSETS (BILLIONS)	
Type of Fund	Year-End 1976	Year-End 1981
Growth	$13.9	$ 15.2
Performance	2.2	5.0
Income	4.6	4.5
Balanced	23.1	21.0
Bond	3.8	9.0
Money market	3.7	186.1

Source: Mutual Fund Fact Book, 1979 and 1982.

Types of Mutual Funds

Growth funds

The objective of a growth fund is simple: capital appreciation. Long-term growth and capital gains are the primary goals of such funds, and as a result they invest principally in common stocks that have above-average growth potential, but offer little (if anything) in the form of dividends and current income. Because of the uncertain nature of their investment income, growth funds are felt to involve a fair amount of risk exposure. They are usually viewed as long-term investment vehicles most suitable for the more aggressive investor who wants to build capital and has little interest in current income.

Performance funds

These are the so-called go-go funds that were popular during the 1960s. They are highly speculative funds that seek large profits from capital gains; in many respects, they are really an extension of the growth fund concept. Most are fairly small, and their portfolios consist mainly of high-flying common stocks. Performance funds often buy stocks of small, unseasoned companies, stocks with relatively high price/earnings multiples, and common stocks whose prices are highly volatile. Some performance funds even go so far as to use leverage in their portfolios (that is, they buy stocks on margin by borrowing part of the purchase price). All this is designed, of course, to yield big returns. But performance funds are also highly speculative and are perhaps the most volatile of all the types of funds. When the markets are good, performance funds do well; when the markets are bad, these funds typically experience substantial losses.

Income funds

The primary investment objective of an income fund is current income (interest and dividend income). Any capital gain earned is strictly coincidental and usually insignificant (although at times it may amount to a tidy sum). The portfolios of these funds are heavily invested in various combinations of high-yielding common stocks, different types of bonds, and/or attractive preferred stocks. With income funds, the type of security held is not as important as the type (and amount) of income generated. Safety of principal is also important, so most or all bonds and preferred stocks usually carry investment-grade ratings. These funds may appeal to individuals seeking high current (monthly or quarterly) income. Because of the relatively high yields paid by many income funds, they are also bought by individual investors who may not need the income, but who like the attractive returns. Income funds are usually considered to be fairly conservative investment outlets possessing only a modest amount of risk.

Balanced funds

The objective of a balanced fund is to earn both capital gains and current income. The funds usually do this by investing liberally in high-grade common stocks, while at the same time committing a substantial portion of their portfolios (25 to 40 percent) to more conservative fixed income securities, like bonds and preferred stock. The common stock is used to provide the capital gains, and the fixed income securities are there to provide the current income component of total return. Their security holdings usually involve only a modest amount of risk, and they tend to attract investors who wish to receive a reasonably good—and safe—return. Not surprisingly, although the money invested in a balanced fund is usually fairly secure, capital growth is normally not as great as that from growth funds, nor is the level of current income as great as that from income funds.

Bond funds

As the name implies, these mutual funds invest exclusively in various kinds and grades of bonds. Income is the primary investment objective, although capital gains are not ignored. There are two important advantages to buying shares in bond funds rather than investing directly in bonds. First, the bond funds are generally more liquid; and second, they offer diversification. Bond funds are usually considered to be fairly conservative investment vehicles, but they are not totally without risk, since the prices of the bonds held in the fund's portfolio will fluctuate with changing interest rates. Though many of the funds are basically conservative, a growing number are becoming increasingly aggressive. In fact, much of the growth bond funds have experienced recently can be attributed to this new investment attitude. For many years, bond funds seemed to hold little appeal as investment vehicles; in the mid-1970s, however, fund managers began assuming more aggressive postures and started managing their portfolios more fully. Also contributing to the growth of bond funds was a revision in the federal tax law. It has only been since April 1976 that investors have been able to purchase municipal bond funds that offer tax-free income. Of course, the tax-exempt feature applies only to the interest earned (and not capital gains), and in many states this income is exempt only from *federal* tax. Still, the revised tax statute did enable investment companies, for the first time, to pass along the benefits of tax-free income to investors. Certainly, for individuals seeking tax-sheltered income, municipal bond funds have proved especially attractive.

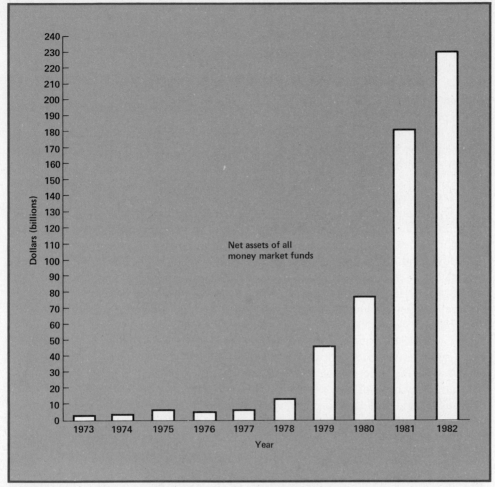

Figure 15.4   The Growth in Money Market Funds.
Money market funds have undergone truly dramatic growth in just a few short years and have
provided the mutual fund industry with a real shot in the arm.

Money market funds

The first money market fund was set up in November 1972 with only $100,000
in total assets. It was a new concept that applied the mutual fund notion to the buying
and selling of short-term money market instruments—such as bank certificates of
deposit, U.S. Treasury bills, and the like. For the first time, money funds offered
individual investors with modest means access to the high-yielding money market,
where many instruments require minimum investments of $100,000 or more (money
funds are discussed in greater detail in Chapter 7, along with other short-term investment vehicles). As Figure 15.4 shows, the idea caught on quickly; the growth in
money funds was nothing short of phenomenal. (Note, however, that the growth in
money market mutual funds did peak in 1982, as the introduction of money market
deposit accounts by banks in 1983 caused money fund assets to drop to below

$200 billion.) Money market funds usually require minimum investments of $1,000 to $10,000. Because of the nature of the investments, money funds are highly liquid vehicles and are very low in risk, since they are virtually immune to capital loss. However, the interest income produced by the funds tends to follow interest rate conditions, so the return to shareholders is subject to ups and downs as market interest rates vary. Many individual investors consider money funds to be viable alternatives to savings accounts. More often than not, the yield on money funds is much better than that available from passbook savings accounts and, with the check-writing privileges they offer, these funds are usually just as liquid as savings accounts. They are viewed by many as a convenient, safe, and profitable way to accumulate capital and temporarily store idle funds.

Dual funds

Dual purpose funds are offered only by closed end investment companies. They are confined to the closed end segment of the industry because a fixed capitalization structure is required to achieve their objectives. The investment objectives of a dual fund are large amounts of both capital gains and current income. Such objectives are achieved in a unique manner, however; for *two* types of shares are issued by the investment company. First, there are the income shares (senior securities) whose shareholders are entitled to all the interest and dividend income of the portfolio; in addition, an equal number of capital shares (junior securities) is issued, whose shareholders are entitled to all the capital gains earned by the portfolio. Because an equal amount of senior and junior securities is issued, the income shares receive twice as much current income as they normally would (since they receive the current income of not only their own shares, but of the capital shares as well). The capital shareholders, in contrast, receive twice as much capital gains, as they give up their claim to current income in return for the capital appreciation of not only their shares, but of the income shares as well. Thus, both the junior and senior shareholders receive double doses of either current income or capital gains.

Dual purpose funds are normally established with limited lives of approximately 15 years or less. When they are liquidated by the investment company, the holders of income shares receive their original investment or a stipulated minimum amount, and any remaining amount is then distributed among the capital shares. These funds are somewhat specialized investment vehicles, and as a result require special analysis and investment knowhow.

Specialty funds

A number of funds seek to achieve their objectives by concentrating their holdings within a single industry (or a group of related industries), or within a specified geographical area. These funds usually invest in the common stocks of high-quality companies that offer unique investment opportunities. Long-term capital growth is a common objective, although current dividend income is also welcome. Specialty industries like electronics, gold, chemicals, and the health field are popular candidates, and some even invest exclusively or heavily in foreign securities, such as Japanese stocks. There are also some unusual variations of this specialty fund concept, like mutual funds for options trading, commodity funds, oil drilling and cattle funds, and others. The one thing they have in common is the fact that they all strive to achieve fairly attractive (and sometimes even spectacular) rates of returns by concentrating their investments in particular industries and/or areas. They are often very risky investment vehicles, and require specialized knowledge on the part of the individual investor. This is particularly so for some foreign specialty funds, where international exchange rules and taxes are important considerations in assessing (and understanding) the true investment appeal of the fund.

Special Services

There are mutual funds available today to meet just about any type of investment need. Many people are drawn to funds because of their attractive returns; but there are other reasons to invest as well, including the savings and reinvestment plans they offer, their regular income programs, conversion and checkwriting privileges, retirement plans, and insurance programs. These are all examples of mutual fund *services,* which many investors consider valuable. In fact, some investors buy funds primarily to receive one or more of these services.

Savings and automatic reinvestment plans

These two very important services allow investors to adhere to a systematic and routine plan of savings and capital accumulation. Most funds offer both services, and it is possible to use one without the other, though the two usually do go together.

Savings plans. In a *savings plan,* an investor agrees, either formally or informally, to add a certain amount of money to the mutual fund account on a regular (monthly or quarterly) basis. For example, an investor might agree to add $250 to the account every quarter. The money is then used to buy additional shares in the fund. *Voluntary savings plans* are excellent devices for regularly adding to an investment program. In contrast, caution should be exercised when dealing with contractual savings plans that involve substantial *front-end loads.* These plans set up formal contractual agreements that supposedly (though *not* legally) compel the investor to a long-term investment program, and then stack all the commissions that will be paid over the life of the contract onto the front end. Thus, the fund will collect all the commissions that will ever come due in the first several years of the contract, and will not begin fully crediting the investor's account with share purchases until *after* these load charges have been met.

For example, if an individual agrees to invest $1,000 a year for each of the next 15 years, the total size of this contractual accumulation plan would be $15,000. If the fund uses an 8.5 percent sales commission (and most funds that offer front-end contractual plans tend to charge the maximum), the total commission that would be paid over the life of this contract would be $1,275 (that is, .085 × $15,000). The catch is that this full commission will be deducted from the first several payments, whether the investor sticks with the plan for 15 years or not. Such arrangements can be very costly, since investors who drop out sacrifice some or all of the prepaid commissions and find that the number of shares that they actually own is consid-

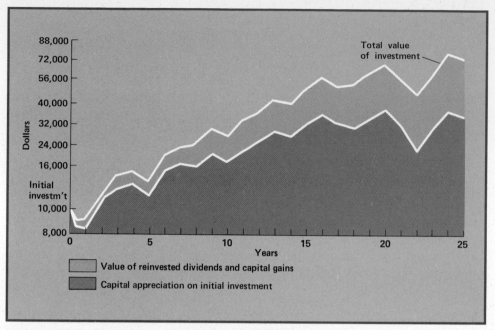

Figure 15.5   The Effects of Reinvesting Income.
Reinvesting dividends and/or capital gains can have tremendous effects on one's investment
position. Note the results of a hypothetical investor who initially invested $10,000 and for 25
years reinvested all dividends and capital gains distributions in additional fund shares. (Results
assume investor achieved an average performance of the 32 growth and income funds in
existence over the 25-year period 1953-1977.) (*Source:* Investment Company Institute.)

erably *less* than what they could have bought through regular purchases. While the
SEC requires a full refund of prepaid commissions if the investor cancels the plan
within 45 days, it requires a refund of only 85 percent of prepaid loads for persons
who cancel within 18 months of enrollment and no refund at all for those who cancel
later. These contractual arrangements have been under considerable fire for some
time, and are prohibited in some states (for example, California, Illinois, Ohio, and
Wisconsin).

   Automatic reinvestment plans.   Through this service, dividend and/or capital
gains income is used to buy additional shares in the fund. Rather than taking such
distributions in the form of cash, the shareholder reinvests the proceeds in additional
shares of the fund. Keep in mind, however, that even though an investor may reinvest
all dividends and capital gains distributions, the IRS will treat them as cash receipts
and as such, tax them as either ordinary income or capital gains in the year in which
they were paid! Most funds deal in fractional shares, and such purchases are often
commission-free. The effects of these plans on total accumulated capital over the
long haul can be substantial. Figure 15.5 shows the long-term impact of one such
plan. In the illustration, we assume the investor starts with $10,000 and, except for
the reinvestment of dividends and capital gains, adds no new capital over time. Even

so, note that the initial investment of $10,000 grew to almost $80,000 over a 25-year period (which, by the way, amounts to a compounded rate of return of about 8.7 percent). Of course, not all 25-year periods will be able to match this performance, nor will all mutual funds be able to perform as well even in strong markets. But the point is that as long as care is taken in selecting an appropriate fund, attractive benefits can be derived from the systematic accumulation of capital offered by savings and/or automatic reinvestment plans. So investors should seriously consider incorporating one or both of these plans into their mutual fund investment program.

Regular income

Many funds offer shareholders the opportunity to receive payments at regular intervals; these are known as *withdrawal plans*. The plans are set up so that the fund will automatically pay out a predetermined amount of money on a monthly or quarterly basis to the shareholder. Usually, the funds require a minimum investment of $5,000 or more in order to participate in such plans, and the size of the minimum payment must normally be $50 or more per period (though there is no limit on the maximum). Fund managers will pay out the monthly or quarterly income first from dividends and realized capital gains; should this source prove to be inadequate and should the shareholder so authorize, the fund can tap the principal or original paid-in capital in the account to meet the required periodic payments.

There are several popular variations of systematic withdrawal plans, the most common of which is for the investor to specify the withdrawal of a fixed dollar amount per period. For example, an investor might choose to receive $200 a month, every month, regardless of the source of payment. Another popular arrangement specifies a fixed number of shares to be liquidated each period. This system will result in an uneven level of income, as the price of the fund's shares will vary in the marketplace. Still another arrangement is to pay out a fixed percentage of the net asset *growth*. Since the stated percentage value is generally less than 100 percent, this plan produces a periodic, although uncertain, payout of income, and yet still allows for some reinvestment and growth in the account. In essence, so long as the fund is profitable, the shareholder will receive some monthly or quarterly income and still have something left over to plow back into the fund itself.

Conversion privileges

Sometimes investors find it necessary, for one reason or another, to switch out of one fund and into another. The investor's investment objectives may change, or the investment climate itself could change. *Conversion (or exchange) privileges* were devised to meet the needs of such investors in a convenient and economical manner. Many investment management companies offer a number of different kinds of mutual funds, and each of these "family of funds" offers a conversion privilege that enables shareholders to move money from one fund to another at little or no cost. The only limitation is that the investor must confine the switches within the same family of funds. For example, an investor can switch from a Dreyfus growth fund to a Dreyfus money fund, or its income fund, or to any other fund managed by Dreyfus.

TABLE 15.4   SOME FUND FAMILIES THAT OFFER FREE EXCHANGE PRIVILEGES

Fund Family	Number of Funds in Family	Switch Limits
Fidelity Group	19	4 times per year
Financial Programs, Inc.	6	14–16 times per year
Lehman Management Company	4	None
Lexington Management Corporation	7	Can change every 7 days
Heritage Investment Advisors	3	None
T. Rowe Price Associates	8	Once every 3 months
PRO Services, Inc.	4	None
Safeco Asset Management Company	6	Can switch every 30 days
Value Line Securities	6	8 times per year
Lincoln National Investment Management Company	4	None
Unified Management Corporation	5	None
Scudder, Stevens & Clark	9	4 times per year
The Vanguard Group	20	Telephone exchange: 6 times per year; written exchange: no limit
Stein Roe & Farnham	8	Telephone exchange: $1,000 minimum; can change every 30 days. Written exchange: no minimum; no limit

Source: FACT, September 1982.

There are more than 60 fund groups (investment management companies) that together offer more than 300 different mutual funds. They all provide low-cost exchange privileges, and although most groups contain only three or four funds, a few have as many as a dozen (or more) within which the investor can switch back and forth. Table 15.4 provides a sample of fund families that offer *free* exchange privileges—though note that most do have limits on the number of times such switches can occur. Exchange privileges are usually considered to be beneficial from the shareholder's point of view, since they allow investors to meet their ever-changing long-term investment goals. In addition, they permit investors to manage their mutual fund holdings more aggressively by allowing them to move in and out of funds as the investment environment changes. Unfortunately, there is one major drawback: For tax purposes, the exchange of shares from one fund to another is regarded as a sale transaction, followed by a subsequent purchase of a new security. As a result, if any capital gains exist at the time of the exchange, the investor is liable for the taxes on that profit even though he or she did not truly liquidate holdings.

Checkwriting privileges

This service is now available from virtually every money fund and a handful of other funds. Exactly as the name implies, shareholders are given a supply of checks that can be used to draw against the money invested in their mutual funds; note, however, that federally insured money funds (at banks and thrift institutions) impose a limit on the number of checks that can be written against the account. These checks are like any other, except they are drawn on the fund account and paid through the fund's bank. The one catch is that the checks usually have to be written in minimum amounts ($500 or more is the most common figure). A major benefit of this privilege is that the checks, once written, continue to draw income until they actually clear. For example, if an individual holds a money fund and writes a $1,000 check against that fund which takes a week to clear, the person receives the full daily interest on that $1,000 for each of the seven days the check is in "float."

Retirement plans and insurance programs

A variety of other services are also provided by mutual funds. For example, Congress recently enacted some far-reaching changes in legislation governing individual and corporate retirement plans. The mutual fund industry was quick to respond to these changes, and today nearly all funds provide a special service that enables individuals and companies to set up tax-deferred retirement programs. This can be done under Keogh plans for self-employed individuals and their employees and/or under Individual Retirement Accounts (IRAs) for any wage earner who is under the age of 70½ (these and other retirement programs are discussed in detail in Chapter 7). The funds set up the plans and handle all the administrative details in such a way that the shareholders can take full advantage of available tax savings.

Another relatively new service involves insurance programs that protect an investment in a mutual fund against long-term loss. Such insurance can be obtained to cover investments from $3,000 to almost $200,000, and for periods extending to 10 or 15 years. Normally, the premium equals about 6 percent of the total amount being insured; for example, it would cost about $1,200 to insure a $20,000 investment for a period of 10 years. It works like this: If the total value of the investment at the close of the insurance period, including the value of shares received by reinvesting dividends and capital gains, is less than the original investment, the insurance company makes up the difference. Thus, if the investor bought, say, $10,000 worth of a given fund 10 years ago and today redeemed the shares for only $7,500, the insurance company would cover the loss of $2,500. Because the chance of a loss on shares held for 10 or more years on which all income has been reinvested is quite small, the purchase of mutual fund insurance is generally not recommended.

INVESTING IN MUTUAL FUNDS

Suppose you are confronted with the following situation: You have money to invest and are trying to select the right stock in which to put it. You obviously want to pick an issue that meets your idea of acceptable risk, but also one that will generate an attractive rate of return. The problem is you have to make the selection from a list of some 800 securities. Sound like a mission impossible? Well that is basically what the individual investor is up against when faced with trying to select a suitable mutual fund. But perhaps if the problem is approached systematically, it may not turn out to be so formidable a task. As we will see, it is possible to whittle down the list of alternatives by matching one's investment needs with the investment objectives of the funds. But before we do that, it will be helpful to examine more closely the various investor uses of mutual funds; with this background, we can then look in detail at the selection process and at several measures of return that can be used to assess performance.

Investor Uses of Mutual Funds

Mutual funds can be used by individual investors in a variety of different ways. For instance, performance funds can serve as a vehicle for capital appreciation, whereas bond funds may be used to provide current income. Regardless of the kind of income a fund provides, individuals tend to use these investment vehicles for one of three reasons: (1) as a way to accumulate wealth; (2) as a speculative vehicle for achieving high rates of return; and (3) as a storehouse of value.

Accumulation of wealth

This is probably the most common reason for using mutual funds. Basically, it involves using mutual funds over the long haul for the sole purpose of building up investment capital. The money accumulated is then used at some future date for retirement, to educate the children, or for some other purpose. Depending upon the investor's personality, a modest amount of risk may be acceptable, but usually preservation of capital and capital stability are considered important. Moreover, the source of return is far less important than the amount; investors are therefore just as likely to use income or balanced funds for capital accumulation purposes as they are to use growth funds. The whole idea is to form a "partnership" with the mutual fund in building up as big a capital pool as possible: You provide the capital by systematically investing and reinvesting in the fund, and the fund provides the return by doing its best to invest the resources wisely.

Speculation and short-term trading

This is not a very common use of mutual funds; the reason, of course, is that most mutual funds are long term in nature and simply are not suitable as aggressive trading vehicles. But some funds do cater to speculators, and some investors find that mutual funds are indeed attractive outlets for speculation and short-term trading. One way to do this is to trade in and out of funds aggressively as the investment climate changes. For example, an investor might use a performance fund when the market is strong, and switch to a money fund when it begins to soften. Load charges can be avoided by dealing in "families" of funds offering low-cost conversion privileges and/or by dealing only in no load funds. Some investors might choose to invest in funds for the long run, but still seek extraordinarily high rates of return by investing in aggressive mutual funds. There are a small number of funds which follow very aggressive trading strategies and which may well appeal to the investor who is willing to accept the substantial risk exposure. These are usually the fairly specialized smaller funds; sophisticated hedge funds, leverage funds, option funds, and commodity funds are examples, not to mention performance or go-go funds. In essence, such investors are simply applying the basic mutual fund concept to their investment needs by letting professional money managers handle their accounts in a way they would like to see them handled: aggressively. There are also those who occasionally use mutual funds for short-term speculation. Some excellent examples are investors who use gold funds when the dollar weakens, or selected foreign funds when the international economy becomes unsettled.

Storehouse of value

Investors may also use mutual funds as a storehouse of value. The idea here is to find a place where investment capital can be fairly secure and relatively free from deterioration, yet still generate a relatively attractive rate of return. Income and bond funds are the logical choices for such purposes, and so are money market funds (which are rapidly becoming the most popular way of meeting this investment objective). Capital preservation and income over the long haul could be important to some investors. Still others might seek storage of value only for the short term, as a way to "sit it out" until a more attractive opportunity comes along. Money funds would be used under these circumstances by fairly aggressive investors, who would use the funds to store their money while the market is weak or until they find better outlets.

The Selection Process

In many respects, the mutual fund selection process is the critical dimension in defining the amount of investment success one will have with mutual funds. It means putting into action all one has learned about funds in order to gain as much return from the investment dollar as possible for an acceptable level of risk. The selection process begins with an assessment of one's own investment needs; this sets the tone of the investment program. Obviously, what we want to do is select from those 800 or so funds the one or two we feel will best meet our total investment needs. Let us now look more closely at how this might be done.

Objectives and motives for using funds

Selecting the right investment outlet means finding those funds which are most suitable to your total investment needs. *The place to start is with your investment objectives.* In other words, why do you want to invest in mutual funds, and what are you looking for in a fund? Obviously, an attractive rate of return would be desirable; but there is also the matter of a tolerable amount of risk exposure. Face it: Some people are more willing to take risks than others, and this is certainly an important ingredient in the selection process. More than likely, when we look at our own risk temperament in relation to the various types of mutual funds, we will discover that certain types of funds are more appealing to us than others. For instance, performance funds will probably not be particularly attractive to individuals who wish to avoid high exposure to risk.

Another important factor in the selection process is the intended use of the mutual fund. That is, do we want to invest in mutual funds as a means of accumulating wealth, to speculate for high rates of return, or as a storehouse of value? This is helpful information, since it puts into clearer focus the question of exactly

**BOX 15.2 HIGH-PERFORMING MUTUAL FUNDS—AND
SOME TIPS ON FINDING WINNERS OF YOUR OWN**

The table below lists the top 25 mutual funds for the five-year period 1977–1982.

The Top 25 Mutual Funds, 1977–1982	Five-Year Rates of Return (June 1977–June 1982)
1. Fidelity Magellan Fund	305.48%
2. Strategic Investments Fund	281.97
3. International Investors, Inc.	279.73
4. Twentieth Century Growth Investors	269.71
5. American General Pace Fund	269.23
6. United Services Gold Shares	249.46
7. Research Capital Fund	243.32
8. Lindner Fund	323.99
9. American General Venture Fund	230.26
10. Twentieth Century Select Investors	226.28
11. St. Paul Growth Fund	214.48
12. Value Line Leveraged Growth Investors	212.52
13. Lehman Capital Fund	211.13
14. Quasar Associates	202.53
15. Massachusetts Capital Development Fund	195.68
16. Growth Fund of America	192.88
17. Evergreen Fund	191.44
18. IDS Growth Fund	187.79
19. Explorer Fund	184.75
20. AMCAP Fund	181.69
21. Scudder Development Fund	181.09
22. United Vanguard Fund	179.86
23. Sigma Venture Shares	175.02
24. NEL Growth Fund	169.70
25. Over-the-Counter Securities Fund	164.27

Climbing into the top 25 requires extraordinary astuteness, or luck, or whatever else may contribute to a fund's success. Its managers have to beat out scores of competing funds, many of which would be considered good investments.

The list brings to light some curious as well as some expectable aspects of mutual fund performance.

Few funds [stay] in the top 25 for extended periods; most [fall] out after one to three appearances. Nevertheless, a fund that placed among the champions for even one five-year period amply rewarded its investors. . . .

Despite their outstanding records, many of the funds may be unfamiliar even to investors with experience in mutual funds. Many of the top scorers are not members of those giant "families" run by prominent advisory firms. . . . Some of the most successful funds are run by one or two people who make all the major buying and selling decisions. . . .

Spotting funds capable of rising to the top performance ranks is probably no easier than picking an individual stock that's going to beat the market, but these few pointers should help.

BOX 15.2 Continued

Set your objectives. By taking into account price gains and losses as well as dividends, total return figures—such as those used in the . . . rankings—provide an excellent performance measure. But they do not tell the whole story. You want a fund whose high performance comes in a form consonant with your investment objectives. For instance, if you're looking for a high, steady dividend income, you don't want a fund that emphasizes growth stocks, which typically have low dividend payouts. If you're uncomfortable with investments that tend to fluctuate sharply, avoid the aggressive funds that concentrate assets in just a few fields and that employ speculative methods.

Funds are normally classified according to investment objective. The categories are not airtight, but they at least indicate what the fund managers are trying to achieve.

Check the records. What a fund has done in the past does not guarantee future performance. Still, the past is one of the few hard facts investors have to work with. Your library and local brokerage office may carry publications of Wiesenberger Investment Companies Service, Johnson's Investment Co. Charts and other services that track mutual fund performance. The reports of Lipper Analytical Services are prepared for institutional clients, but the figures are often published in abbreviated form in periodicals that deal with investment subjects regularly.

Look for consistency. Many funds rocket to the top one year only to dive the next. The fund should show the ability to stay in or near the upper ranks for an extended period.

Be sure management hasn't changed. Try to find out whether the people who managed the fund when it produced big gains are still in control. Often it's sufficient that the same advisory firm is continuing to manage the fund because strategy may be set by the advisory company rather than any one person. Mutual fund prospectuses generally do not provide detailed histories, but some of that material is available in Wiesenberger Investment Companies Service's annual directory.

Learn the fund's policy. The customary fund prospectus tells you what its objective is and the kinds of investments it *may* make. It does not explain what it is actually doing at the moment. For that information you have to read the fund's quarterly and annual financial reports and they, too, can be irritatingly fuzzy. You might be able to deduce the manager's current approach to the market by comparing the latest portfolio with previous ones (a good reason to keep them for a while). . . .

Develop your own viewpoint. However successful the fund may have been, you had better invest elsewhere if you think the fund is on the wrong track now. A fund that made money with one type of stock or bond may slip if it fails to follow market trends.

It's a rare fund that manages to anticipate stock market preferences consistently. Also, funds don't have much flexibility. Each fund positions itself to serve a certain type of investor. The fund usually has to obtain shareholders' approval to make a fundamental change, which is only fair. After all, people who have put money into a fund that specializes in, say, utility issues may not want their money switched into gold stocks.

In practice, therefore, you are freer than the average fund to change tactics. It's up to you to pick the investment field likely to produce superior results and then to select a fund that has demonstrated skill in selecting securities in that field.

Source: Changing Times, October 1981 and November 1982.

what we are trying to do with our investment dollars. Finally, there is the matter of the types of services provided by the fund. If there are services we are particularly interested in, we should be sure to look for them in the funds we select. All these variables (expected return performance, risk exposure, desired use of the fund, and

1982 FUND RATINGS

Performance in UP markets	in DOWN markets		Average annual total return 1970–1982	Investment results Latest 12 months Return from capital growth	Return from income dividends	Total assets 6/30/82 (millions)	Total assets % change '82 vs. '81	Maximum sales charge	Annual expenses per $100
		Standard & Poor's 500 stock average	8.4%	−16.5%	6.2%				
		FORBES stock fund composite	9.6%	−15.5%	4.6%				
		FORBES balanced fund composite	8.1%	−9.1%	9.7%				
		FORBES bond and preferred stock fund composite	6.3%	−5.1%	13.9%				
				Group averages					
		STOCK FUNDS (NO LOAD)	9.4%	−16.2%	4.1%				
A	A	Janus Fund	18.4%	−9.7%	2.0%	$ 44.9	16.9%	none	$1.43
A	D	Lexington Growth Fund	10.5	−31.1	3.1	13.1	−31.1	none	1.43
C	D	Lexington Research Fund	8.9	−18.0	4.8	76.6	−20.1	none	1.04
B	C	Loomis-Sayles Capital Development Fund	12.6	−2.6	2.7	67.1	−5.1	none	0.82
C	D	Mairs & Power Growth Fund	8.7	−9.0	3.8	12.6	−11.9	none	0.94
C	F	Manhattan Fund	1.3	−11.6	3.5	51.4	−17.6	none	1.40
C	D	Horace Mann Fund	7.4	−21.2	2.2	50.6	−27.8	none	0.85
A	D	Mathers Fund	12.7	−26.4	3.9	159.5	−28.7	none	0.59
B	D	W L Morgan Growth Fund	11.1	−14.9	3.4	209.1	−16.8	none	0.90
B	B	Mutual Shares	18.6	−10.1	5.2	130.0	−2.4	none	0.75
B	A	Naess & Thomas Special Fund	13.1	−19.6	0.3	16.5	1.9	none	1.52
C	C	National Aviation & Technology	9.7	−22.9	4.7	73.1	−28.8	none	1.17
B	F	National Industries Fund	8.6	−18.4	4.2	25.5	−18.3	none	1.66
C	F	Neuwirth Fund	5.9	−18.9	0.8	15.0	−3.2	none	1.87
B	D	Newton Growth Fund	7.4	−12.7	2.7	15.6	−11.9	none	1.20
A	B	Nicholas Fund	15.4	−14.6	4.0	56.1	−11.5	none	1.03
●D	C	North Star Stock Fund	—*	−10.8	5.8	17.1	4.3	none	0.80
A	D	Omega Fund	10.6	−31.4	none	23.5	−35.6	none	1.39
D	C	The One Hundred & One Fund	6.1	−22.0	6.2	.8	−27.3	none	2.00
D	D	The One Hundred Fund	2.8	−22.3	2.3	9.4	−28.8	none	1.63

Figure 15.6   Performance Information about Mutual Funds.
There is a wealth of information available to investors about mutual funds; most of it, like the *Forbes* fund ratings depicted here, is in a format that allows for quick review of a large number of funds. (*Source: Forbes,* August 30, 1982.)

services sought) are important in defining why we use funds and are helpful in the selection process. Having assessed what we are looking for in a fund, we now want to look at what the funds have to offer us.

What funds offer

The ideal mutual fund would achieve maximum capital growth when security prices rise, provide complete protection against capital loss when prices decline, and achieve high levels of current income at all times. Unfortunately, this fund does not exist. Instead, just as each individual has a set of investment needs, each fund has its own *investment objective,* its own *manner of operation,* and its own *range of*

1982 FUND RATINGS *Continued*

Performance in UP markets	in DOWN markets		Average annual total return 1970–1982	Return from capital growth	Return from income dividends	6/30/82 (millions)	% change '82 vs. '81	Maxi- mum sales charge	Annual expenses per $100
B	D	The One William Street Fund	9.9	−11.6	5.4	252.9	−16.5	none	0.58
●C	●B	Partners Fund	—*	−2.2	7.3	74.4	21.8	none	1.32
D	C	Penn Square Mutual Fund	9.9	−18.7	7.4	126.1	−21.5	none	0.65
B	C	Pennsylvania Mutual Fund	8.0	−20.1	none	26.7	−28.2	none	1.84
D	D	Pine Street Fund	9.3	−16.2	6.0	34.5	−20.1	none	1.22
B	C	Plitrend Fund	12.7	−23.4	3.5	16.9	−28.7	none	1.24
C	F	T Rowe Price Growth Stock Fund	5.1	−22.0	5.0	802.3	−22.0	none	0.49
A	D	T Rowe Price New Era Fund	10.1	−28.9	7.3	342.1	−30.5	none	0.64
A+	F	T Rowe Price New Horizons Fund	10.8	−24.7	4.7	787.6	−19.9	none	0.53
D	F	PRO Fund	3.1	−22.9	2.9	28.8	−33.2	none	1.21
D	F	Revere Fund	0.9	−20.5	2.8	3.0	−36.2	none	2.10
C	D	SAFECO Equity Fund	10.5	−23.7	8.0	27.2	−26.7	none	0.62
B	C	SAFECO Growth Fund	11.0	−23.2	4.9	35.7	−23.2	none	0.64
D	B	SAFECO Income Fund	10.9	−14.6	9.1	14.3	−16.4	none	0.63
C	D	Schuster Fund	6.4	−20.6	none	9.7	−28.2	none	1.65
C	F	Scudder Common Stock Fund	8.4	−14.0	4.6	139.7	−11.2	none	0.73
●A	C	Scudder Development Fund	—*	−17.8	1.8	88.8	11.0	none	1.17
C	F	Scudder Special Fund	6.7	−21.2	3.8	94.7	−21.8	none	0.93
D	D	Selected American Shares	5.2	−9.2	8.1	65.1	−15.8	none	0.94
D	F	Selected Special Shares	4.2	−23.5	3.2	24.1	−29.5	none	1.10
●B	A	Sequoia Fund	—*	4.2	5.2	149.8	32.5	none	1.10
B	A	Sherman, Dean Fund	8.8	−36.1	none	4.6	−42.5	none	1.91
●B	●F	Sierra Growth Fund	—*	−22.9		3.0	−26.8	none	2.03
D	F	Steadman American Industry Fund Trust	0.2	−23.3	2.9 5.4	10.8	−29.4	none	3.61
D	D	Steadman Investment Fund	5.2	−16.7	7.0	13.3	−21.3	none	2.43
C	C	Steadman Oceanographic, Tech & Growth Fund	5.3	−23.6	2.8	7.3	−27.7	none	3.91
A+	F	Stein Roe & Farnham Capital Opportunities Fund	12.5	−17.9	2.0	110.5	−12.4	none	0.91
A	F	Stein Roe & Farnham Stock Fund	8.8	−15.0	2.7	169.9	−15.8	none	0.62

●Fund rated for two periods only; maximum allowable rating A. *Fund not in operation for full period.

Figure 15.6   Continued

services. These three parameters are useful in helping us to assess investment alternatives. But where does the investor obtain such information? Several excellent sources provide a wealth of operating and performance information in a convenient and easy-to-read format. For instance, *Forbes* rates hundreds of mutual funds each year (see Figure 15.6 for an excerpt from its 1982 report), and every quarter *Barron's* publishes an extensive mutual fund performance report. In addition, publications like *Money* and *Changing Times* will (monthly or periodically) list the top-performing funds; and of course there are services available which supply background on and assessments of a wide variety of different kinds of funds (Appendix A provides a detailed list of these mutual fund services and publications). The publications provide investors with valuable insight on what the funds seek, how they operate, and what they have to offer shareholders.

Whittling down alternatives

At this point, fund selection becomes a process of elimination as individual needs are weighed against the types of funds available. Large numbers of funds can be eliminated from serious consideration because they fail to meet these needs. Some may be too risky; others may be unsuitable as a storehouse of value. Thus, rather than trying to evaluate 800 different funds, we can use a process of elimination to narrow the list down to two or three *types* of funds that are most compatible with our investment needs. From here, we can whittle the list down a bit more by introducing other constraints—for example, because of cost considerations, we may want to deal only in no load funds, or we may be seeking certain services that are important to our investment goals. Now we introduce the final (but certainly not the least important) element in the selection process: the fund's investment performance. Useful information includes (1) how the fund has performed over time; (2) the type of return it has generated in good markets as well as bad; (3) the level of dividend and capital gains distributions; and (4) the type of investment stability the fund has enjoyed over time. By evaluating such information, it is possible to identify some of the more successful mutual funds—the ones that not only offer the investment objectives and services we seek, but which should provide the best payoffs as well.

Measuring Performance

Investment performance is a major dimension in the mutual fund selection process. The level of dividends paid by the fund, its capital gains, and growth in capital are all important aspects of return. Rate of return and investment performance are just as meaningful with mutual funds as with any other type of investment vehicle. Such information enables the investor to judge the investment behavior of the fund, and to appraise its performance in relation to other funds and investment vehicles. Here we will look at different rate of return measures that can be used by mutual fund investors to assess return; also, because risk is so important in defining the investment behavior of a fund, we will briefly review it as well.

Sources of return

An open end fund has three potential sources of return: (1) dividend income, (2) capital gains distribution, and (3) change in the price (or net asset value) of the fund. Depending on the type of fund, some mutual funds will derive more income from one source than another; for example, we would normally expect income funds to have much higher dividend income than capital gains distributions.

Dividend income is that derived from the dividend and interest income earned on the security holdings of the mutual fund. When the fund receives dividend or interest payments, it passes these on to shareholders in the form of dividend payments. The fund accumulates all the current income it has received for the quarter and then pays it out on a prorated basis. If a fund earned, say, $1 million in dividends and interest in a given quarter, and if that fund had 1 million shares outstanding, each share would receive a quarterly dividend payment of $1.

Capital gains distributions work on the same principle, except that these payments are derived from the capital gains earned by the fund. It works like this:

Finley, how come OUR mutual fund isn't on the Forbes *honor roll*
of nine investment funds that have consistently outperformed the averages
and amply protected their investors against inflation?

Suppose the fund bought some stock a year ago for $50 and sold that stock in the current quarter for $75 per share. Clearly, the fund has achieved capital gains of $25 per share. If it held 50,000 shares of this stock, it would have realized a total capital gain of $1,250,000 ($25 × 50,000 = $1,250,000). Given that the fund has 1 million shares outstanding, each share is entitled to $1.25 in the form of a capital gains distribution. Note that this capital gain distribution applies only to *realized* capital gains—that is, the security holdings were actually sold and the capital gains actually earned.

Unrealized capital gains (or paper profits) are what make up the third and final element in a mutual fund's return. For when the fund's holdings go up or down in price, the net asset value of the fund moves accordingly. Suppose an investor buys into a fund at $10 per share, and some time later it is quoted at $12.50; the difference of $2.50 per share is the unrealized capital gains contained in the fund's security holdings. It represents the profit shareholders would receive (and are entitled to) if the fund were to sell its holdings.

The return on closed end investment companies is derived from the same three sources as that of open end funds, and from a fourth source as well: Changes in price discounts or premiums. Because closed end companies are traded like any common stock, they seldom trade exactly at their net asset value. Instead, they tend to trade below (at a discount) or above (at a premium) their NAV. As these discounts or premiums change over time, the return to shareholders is affected accordingly. This is because such changes in discount or premium actually affect the market price of the fund. Because discount or premium is already embedded in the share price of a fund, it follows that for a closed end fund, the third element of return (change in share price) is made up not only of changes in the net asset value of the fund's holdings, but also of changes in price discount or premium.

An annual rate of return measure

A simple but effective measure of performance is to describe mutual fund return in terms of the three major sources noted above: dividends earned, capital gains distributions received, and change in price. These payoffs can be converted to a convenient yield figure by using the standard holding period return formula. The computations necessary to calculate such a return figure are illustrated below; we will use data from a hypothetical no load mutual fund that paid dividends of 50 cents and capital gains of distributions of 25 cents per share over the course of the year, and had a price at the beginning of the year of $9.50 that rose to $10.50 per share by the end of the year.

Price (or NAV) at *beginning* of the year		$ 9.50
Price (or NAV) at *end* of the year		10.50
Return for the year:		
Dividends received	.50	
Capital gains distributions	.25	
Change in price	$1.00	
Total return	$1.75	
Holding period return		18.4%
(Total return/beginning price = $1.75/$9.50)		

The measure is simple to calculate and follows the standard HPR format; it not only captures all the important elements of mutual fund return, but also provides a handy indication of yield. Notice we had a total dollar return of $1.75 and based on a beginning investment of $9.50 (the initial share price of the fund), were able to realize an annual rate of return of 18.4 percent.

But what happens if dividends and capital gains distributions are reinvested into the fund? In this case, rather than cash, the investor receives additional shares of stock. Holding period return can still be used to measure return, the only modification is that the investor has to keep track of the number of shares acquired through reinvestment. To illustrate, let's continue with the example above and assume that the investor initially bought 200 shares in the mutual fund. Assume also that the investor was able to acquire shares through the fund's reinvestment program at an average price of $9 per share; thus, the $150 in reinvested dividends and capital gains distributions (0.75 × 200 = $150) provided the investor with another 16.67 shares in the fund ($150/$9 = 16.67). Holding period return under these circumstances would relate the market value of the stock holdings at the beginning of the period with holdings at the end, or:

$$\text{holding period return} = \frac{\left(\begin{array}{c}\text{number of shares} \times \\ \text{ending price}\end{array}\right) - \left(\begin{array}{c}\text{number of shares} \times \\ \text{initial price}\end{array}\right)}{(\text{number of shares} \times \text{initial price})}$$

Thus, the holding period return for our hypothetical investor would be:

$$\text{holding period return} = \frac{(216.67 \times \$10.50) - (200 \times \$9.50)}{(200 \times \$9.50)}$$

$$= \frac{\$2275 - \$1900}{\$1900} = \underline{19.7\%}$$

This holding period yield, like the one on the preceding page, provides a rate of return measure that can now be used to compare the performance of this fund to that of other funds and other investment vehicles.

The matter of risk

Because most mutual funds are so diversified, their investors, for the most part, are immune to the business and financial risks normally present with individual securities. Even with extensive diversification, however, the investment behavior of most funds is still exposed to a considerable amount of *market risk*. In fact, because mutual fund portfolios are so well diversified, they often reflect the behavior of the marketplace itself and as a result tend to perform very much like the market. Thus, if the market is drifting downward, most funds that are made up heavily of stocks will also be drifting downward. A few funds, like gold funds, tend to be defensive (or countercyclical), but for the most part, market risk is an important behavioral ingredient in a large number of mutual funds, both open and closed end. Investors should be aware of the effect the general market has on the investment performance of a fund and try to use such insight when formulating a mutual fund investment program. For example, if the market is trending downward and you see a continuation of such a trend, it might be best to place any new investment capital into something like a money market fund until the market reverses itself. At that time, you can make a more permanent commitment.

Another important risk consideration revolves around the management practices of the fund itself. If the portfolio is managed conservatively, the risk of a loss in capital is likely to be much less than for aggressively managed funds. Obviously, the more speculative the investment goals of the fund, the greater the risk of instability in the net asset value. On the other hand, a conservatively managed portfolio does not necessarily eliminate all price volatility, since the securities in the portfolio are still subject to inflation, interest rate, and/or general market risks. But these risks will generally be reduced or minimized as the investment objectives and portfolio management practices of the fund become more and more conservative.

SUMMARY

Mutual fund shares represent ownership in a managed portfolio of securities. By investing in mutual funds, shareholders enjoy a level of diversification and performance they might otherwise find difficult to achieve. Several factors attract investors to mutual funds, including their diversified portfolios, professional management, and the possibility of establishing a sound investment program with a limited amount of capital. In addition, funds offer convenience and services not available elsewhere. Against these advantages must be weighed the loss of flexibility in managing one's own funds, costly commissions (with load funds), and annual management fees.

Open end funds, which have no limit on the number of shares they may issue, account for two-thirds of the number of funds. Investors buy from and sell their shares back to the fund at prices based on the current value of all the securities held in the fund's portfolio. Closed end funds, in contrast, have a fixed number of shares outstanding, which trade among individuals in secondary markets like any other common stock. An investment trust is a variation of the mutual fund concept that consists of an unmanaged pool of securities held for safekeeping by a sponsoring institution, and often paying income on a monthly basis. All open and closed end funds charge a management fee, and some may charge a commission when shares are bought. These are known as load funds.

Funds may be categorized by their objectives. Growth funds offer long-term growth and capital gains with a fair amount of risk exposure. Rapid capital appreciation from stocks of small, unseasoned companies with relatively high price/earnings multiples is the objective of performance funds. Income funds offer safety of principal and high income by investing in high-yielding common stocks, bonds, and attractive preferred stocks. For the investor who desires both current income and capital gains, balanced funds generate both by investing in high-grade common stocks and senior securities. Bond funds invest exclusively in bonds and offer liquidity and diversification not available from the direct investment in many kinds of fixed income securities. Since 1972, individuals desiring low risk, liquidity, and modest income have been turning to money funds, which provide investors of modest means access to high-yielding money market instruments. A dual fund is a special type of closed end fund that attempts to provide both large amounts of capital gains and current income by issuing equal amounts of senior securities (which receive all the interest and dividend income of the portfolio) and junior securities (which receive all the capital gains). Specialty funds typically concentrate their holdings in a specific industry or geographic area and usually provide long-term growth with some current income.

Many people invest in funds to take advantage of the special services they offer. Voluntary savings plans and automatic reinvestment plans are examples of such services. Many funds also offer their shareholders the opportunity to receive periodic payments of income through withdrawal plans. Popular variations of these plans include the withdrawal of a fixed dollar amount per period, liquidation of a fixed number of shares each period, and payment of a fixed percentage of the net asset growth. Low-cost conversion privileges are another feature offered by companies that manage a number of different kinds of funds. Other services include check-writing privileges, retirement plans, and insurance programs.

An investor will use a mutual fund to build a pool of investment capital over the long haul, to speculate in order to achieve high rates of return by trading in and out of funds, and/or as a storehouse of investment capital. Generally, funds provide returns to shareholders in the form of dividends, capital gains, and growth in capital. In addition, closed end funds yield returns from changes in price discounts or premiums. Return is important to mutual fund investors, but so is risk, and although a fund's extensive diversification may protect many investors from business and financial risks, considerable market risk remains because most funds tend to perform very much like the market as a whole.

KEY TERMS

automatic reinvestment plan
back-end load
balanced fund
bond fund
capital gains distribution
checkwriting privilege
closed end investment company
conversion privilege
dual fund
front-end load
go-go fund
growth fund
income fund
investment trust
load fund

management fee
money fund
mutual fund
net asset value (NAV)
no load fund
open end investment company
performance fund
pooled diversification
prospectus
savings plan
specialty fund
tax-free (municipal bond) fund
unit investment trust
withdrawal plan

REVIEW QUESTIONS

1. What is a mutual fund? Discuss the mutual fund concept; why are diversification and professional management so important?

2. Briefly define each of the following:

a. Closed end investment company.
b. Open end investment company.
c. Investment trust.

3. What is the difference between a load fund and no load fund? Are there some advantages to either type? How can you tell if a fund is load or no load?

4. What are the attractions and drawbacks of mutual fund ownership?

5. Contrast mutual fund ownership with the direct investment in common stocks and bonds; who should own mutual funds and why?

6. Can the shares of a mutual fund be margined or sold short? Explain.

7. Briefly discuss each of the following types of mutual funds:

a. Performance fund.
b. Income fund.
c. Balanced fund.
d. Money fund.
e. Dual fund.

8. What is so special about specialty funds? How do their investments differ from those of other types of mutual funds?

9. If growth, income, and capital preservation are the primary objectives of mutual funds, why do we bother to categorize them by type? Are such classifications helpful in the fund selection process?

10. List and briefly describe several services provided by mutual funds; how important should these services be in the mutual fund selection process?

11. Identify and discuss three investor uses of mutual funds.

12. How important is the general behavior of the market in affecting the price performance of mutual funds? Explain.

13. Identify three potential sources of income to mutual fund investors and briefly discuss how each could affect total return to shareholders; explain how the discount or premium of a closed end fund can also be treated as a return to investors.

14. A year ago, an investor bought 200 shares of a mutual fund at $8.50 per share; over the past year the fund has paid dividends of 90 cents per share and had a capital gains distribution of 75 cents per share. Find the investor's holding period return given this no load fund now has a net asset value of $9.10. Find the holding period return assuming all the dividends and capital gains distributions are reinvested into additional shares of the fund at an average price of $8.75 per share.

15. Discuss the various types of risk to which mutual fund shareholders are exposed; what is the major risk exposure of mutual funds? Are all funds subject to the same level of risk? Explain.

CASE PROBLEMS

15.1 REVEREND ROBIN PONDERS MUTUAL FUNDS

Reverend Robin is a young minister of a church in the Denver area. He is married with one young child, and needless to say earns what could best be described as a "modest income." Since religious organizations are not notorious for their generous retirement programs, the Reverend has decided it would be best for him to do a little investing on his own. He would like to set up a program that enables him to supplement the church's retirement program and at the same time provide some funds for his child's college education (which is still some 12 years away). He is not out to break any investment records, but feels that he desperately needs some backup in order to provide for the long-run needs of his family. Although his income is meager, the Reverend Robin feels that with careful planning, he could probably regularly invest about $125 a quarter (and, with luck, maybe increase this amount over time). He has about $2,500 in a passbook savings account which he would be willing to use to kick off this program. In view of his investment objectives, he is not interested in taking a lot of risk. Because his knowledge of investments extends to savings accounts, series EE bonds, and a little bit about mutual funds, he approaches you for some investment advice.

Questions

1. In view of the Reverend Robin's long-term investment goals, do you think mutual funds are an appropriate investment vehicle for him?

2. Do you think he should use his $2,500 savings to start off a mutual fund program?

3. What type of mutual fund investment program would you set up for the Reverend? Include in your answer some discussion of the types of funds you would consider, the investment objectives you would set, and any investment services (like withdrawal plans) you would seek. Would taxes be an important consideration in your investment advice? Explain.

15.2 TOM LASNICKA SEEKS THE GOOD LIFE

Tom Lasnicka is a widower who recently retired after a long and illustrious career with a major midwestern manufacturer. Beginning as a skilled craftsman, he worked his way up to the level of shop supervisor over a period of more than 30 years with the firm. Tom receives social security benefits and a generous company pension—in all, these two sources amount to over $1,500 per month (part of which is tax free, of course). The Lasnickas had no children, so he lives alone. Tom owns a two-bedroom rental house that is next to his home, with the rental income from it covering the mortgage payments for both the rental and his house. Over the years, Tom and his late wife, Camille, always tried to put a little money aside each month; the results have been nothing short of startling as the value of Tom's liquid investments (all held in passbook savings accounts) runs well into six figures. Up to now, Tom has just let his money grow and has not used any of his savings to supplement his social security, pension, and rental income. But things are about to change. Tom has decided, "What the heck, it's high time I start living the good life!" Tom wants to travel and do some exciting things with his life—in effect, he is determined to start reaping the benefits of his labors. He has therefore decided to move $75,000 from one of his savings accounts to one or two high-yielding mutual funds. He would like to receive $1,000 a month from the fund(s) for as long as possible, since he plans to be around for a long time.

Questions
1. Given Tom's financial resources and investment objectives, what kind of mutual funds do you think he should consider?
2. Are there any factors in Tom's situation that should be taken into consideration in the fund selection process and if so, how might these affect Tom's course of action?
3. What types of services do you think he should look for in a mutual fund?
4. Assume Tom invests in a mutual fund that earns about 7 percent annually from dividend income and capital gains. Given that Tom wants to receive $1,000 a month from his mutual fund, what would be the size of his investment account five years from now? How large would the account be if the fund could earn 10 percent on average and everything else remains the same? How important is the fund's rate of return to Tom's investment situation? Explain.

SELECTED READINGS
Bettner, Jill. "With Disinflation, Tax-Managed Stock Funds Offer Utility Investors Chance for Double Play." *The Wall Street Journal,* May 10, 1982, p. 38.
———. "Tax-Exempt Mutual Funds Have Advantages over Taxable Ones Even If You Aren't Rich." *The Wall Street Journal,* October 25, 1982, p. 52.
Boland, John C. "Switch in Time: Holders of Mutual Funds Try to Profit by Swapping." *Barron's,* December 18, 1978, pp. 11–18.
Daly, Margaret. "Investing ABC's: Mutual Funds." *Better Homes and Gardens,* April 1979, pp. 84–90.
"How's Your Mutual Fund *Really* Doing?" *Changing Times,* November 1983, pp. 34–35.
———. "Investing: How to Make the Most of Mutual Funds." *Better Homes and Gardens,* October 1982, pp. 72–76.
Eisenberg, Richard. "Money-Market Funds Go Tax-Free." *Money,* November 1979, pp. 101–104.
Glenn, Armon. "Reaching for Yield—Investors Snap Up Offerings of Speculative Bond Funds." *Barron's,* March 13, 1978, pp. 11–14.
Greenebaum, Mary. "Funds: The New Way to Play Commodities." *Fortune,* November 19, 1979, pp. 137–140.
———. "Closed-End Funds for Bond Bulls." *Fortune,* May 17, 1982, pp. 131–134.
Hazard, John W. "Should You Buy Mutual Funds?" *U.S. News and World Report,* July 26, 1982, p. 68.
Moffitt, Donald. "Exploiting the Float and the Junk: Managers of Mutual Funds Offer Some Offbeat Buys." *The Wall Street Journal,* January 9, 1978, p. 30.
"Mutual Funds Resurgence." *Business Week,* March 31, 1980, pp. 68–78.
Phalon, Richard. "Ugly Ducklings: Dual Purpose Funds." *Forbes,* November 23, 1981, pp. 188–190.

Quinn, Jane Bryant. "Mutual Funds to Match Your Money Goals." *Woman's Day,* November 20, 1978, pp. 118, 120, 174–176.

Runde, Robert. "Mutual Funds: The Leapfrog Route to Investment Profit." *Money,* September 1982, pp. 87–92.

"Shopping for Unit Investment Trusts." *Business Week,* August 3, 1981, pp. 88–92.

Sloan, Allan. "Buying Stocks and Bonds at Discount Prices." *Money,* July 1982, pp. 55–62.

"Taxes and Your Mutual Fund." *Changing Times,* September 1981, pp. 56–58.

"These Mutual Funds Seek Tax-Favored Gains." *Changing Times,* April 1980, pp. 33–34.

"25 High-Performance Mutual Funds and What You Can Learn From Them." *Changing Times,* July 1980, pp. 21–24.

Real Estate Investments

Real estate offers an attractive way to diversify an investment portfolio and also achieve favorable risk-return tradeoffs. Like investments in stocks, bonds, options, and other investment vehicles, you must choose real estate investments carefully and in light of your particular objectives. A property can be a good buy only when its chances for loss and gain match your needs. To help you learn how to analyze and choose your real estate investments profitably, this chapter explains:

1. How to set real estate investment objectives.
2. The scope of real estate analysis.
3. The determinants of real estate value.
4. The techniques used to estimate market value.
5. The steps necessary to forecast investment returns.
6. How to apply the real estate investment analysis process.

Real estate can be an exciting investment because you control it. When you buy most other types of investments, you accept the returns the market offers. Of course, you might be able to use judgment and foresight to beat the market, but you can do little to influence it. With real estate, managerial decisions greatly affect the returns a property earns. In real estate you must answer questions such as these: What rents should be charged? How much should be spent on maintenance and repairs? What advertising media should be selected? How should ad copy be written? What purchase, lease, or sales contract provisions should be used? Along with market forces, it is the answers to these and other questions that determine whether or not you will profit from a real estate investment. So investing in real estate means more than just buying right or selling right; it also means managing the property right!

As you read through this chapter, keep in mind that the analytical framework we present here has two purposes. First, it can help you decide what price to pay for a property; second, it can be used to guide you through the many operating decisions you will need to make. You can maximize returns only when you consider both types of decisions. Let's now move through the process of real estate investment analysis, beginning with objectives.

SETTING REAL ESTATE INVESTMENT OBJECTIVES

Setting objectives involves two steps. First, you should consider how the characteristics of real estate investments differ; second, you should establish investment constraints and goals.

Investment Characteristics

Individual real estate investments differ in their characteristics even more than individual people differ in theirs. So, just as you wouldn't marry without thinking long and hard about the type of person you'd be happy with, you shouldn't select an investment property without some feeling for whether or not it is the right one for you. To select wisely, you need to consider: (1) the available types of properties, (2) whether you want an equity or debt position, and (3) whether you want to invest individually or through a group.

Types of properties

For our purposes, we can classify real estate into three categories: personal residences, income properties, and speculative properties. *Personal residences* include single-family houses, condominiums, cooperatives, and townhouses; the *income properties* category refers to properties that are leased out, such as small apartment buildings, apartment complexes, office buildings, and shopping centers; *speculative properties* typically include land, special-purpose buildings, such as churches and gas stations, and the like.

In terms of risk and return, personal residences generally provide the safest investment. Except in certain boom-bust markets such as the one that recently prevailed in many California cities, owner-occupied housing historically has offered little downside risk for loss of capital, and reasonable potential for appreciation of 3 to 8 percent per year. With respect to income properties, the chance of loss is greater than for personal residences, but so is the chance for gain. Losses can result from tenant carelessness, excessive supply of competing rental units, or poor management. On the profit side, though, income properties can provide good tax shelter, increasing rental incomes due to a growing population, and appreciation.

As the term implies, speculative properties give their buyers a chance to make a killing, but also the chance for heavy loss. This speculative characteristic usually arises from high uncertainty. For instance, rumors may start that a new multimillion-dollar plant is going to be built on the edge of town. Land buyers would jump into the market, and prices soon would be bid up. The right buy-sell timing could yield returns of several hundred percent or more. But people who bought into the market late, or those who failed to sell before the market turned, might lose the major part of their investment. So you can see that before you invest in real estate, you should determine the risks various types of properties present, and then decide which risks you can afford to take.

Equity versus debt

In this chapter we discuss real estate investment primarily from the standpoint of equity. It is also possible for individuals to invest in instruments of real estate debt, such as mortgages and deeds of trust. Usually these instruments provide a fairly safe rate of return if the borrowers are required to maintain at least a 20 percent equity position in the mortgaged property (no more than an 80 percent loan-to-value ratio). This owner equity position gives the real estate lender a margin of safety should foreclosure have to be initiated. Often property owners are asked to take back a debt position (owner financing) when they sell a property. Their willingness to accept this type of financing arrangement can help them get their property sold more quickly and at a higher price. Yet even though owner financing can benefit sellers, they should not accept it until they determine both the buyer-borrower's ability to pay, and the loan-to-value ratio necessary to provide the desired level of investment safety.

Individual versus group investment

The most popular ways to invest in real estate are through individual ownership, limited partnerships, and real estate investment trusts. (Because of adverse tax consequences, real estate investors typically have avoided the corporate form of ownership, although recent liberalization of Subchapter S of the Internal Revenue Code may result in an increase in corporate real estate investment groups.) The strongest advantage of individual ownership is personal control, and the strongest drawback is limited capital. We emphasize real estate investment analysis for the individual, but you should also know the basics of investing in real estate through investment trusts and limited partnerships.

Real estate investment trust.   A *real estate investment trust (REIT)* is a type of closed end investment company that invests money (obtained through the sale of its shares to investors) in mortgages and various types of investment real estate. REITs must abide by the Real Estate Investment Trust Act of 1960, which governs their formation and operation. Because they must distribute their earnings to owners, REITs commonly borrow to finance the acquisition of property.

REITs have been formed by a number of large financial institutions, such as banks and insurance companies. The stocks of many REITs are traded on securities exchanges, providing investors with a marketable interest in a real estate investment portfolio. Like mutual funds, the income distributed to REIT owners is designated and taxed as either ordinary income or long-term capital gains. Although the poor performance of REITs during the 1973–1975 recession caused them to fall into disfavor among investors, subsequent restructuring of their portfolios has rekindled investor interest. Recently providing returns ranging from 5 to 15 percent, some of

When the tide comes in, I'm going to give you an object lesson in ill-advised, unsound and badly-researched real estate investment.

the larger REITs (such as General Growth Properties, ICM Realty, and Southmark Corporation) provide an attractive mechanism through which the small investor can safely invest in real estate. Information on the objectives, performance, and portfolios held by various REITs can be obtained from your stockbroker. Before investing in a REIT, however, carefully assess its investment objectives and expected risk and return in light of your own investment objectives.

Limited partnership.   The *limited partnership* is an organizational form under which certain partners are designated as limited partners—that is, their liability is limited to no more than their initial investment. Limited partners play a passive role in these partnerships; the general partner is the managing partner who accepts liability and makes most decisions. Because of the limited liability, along with the potentially high returns and/or tax shelters provided by these arrangements, they often appeal to the individual investor wishing to buy real estate. (A detailed discussion of the structure and operation of limited partnerships is presented in Chapter 17.)

By making an initial investment typically ranging from $2,500 to $10,000, you can buy an ownership interest in yet-to-be-named properties or in specific properties to be acquired by the general partner. Like REITs, partnerships often borrow to finance the purchase of properties; unlike REITs, however, partnerships typically have finite lives of 5 to 10 years, or longer. They have specific objectives in regard to income, capital gains, and tax shelter. In the past, some limited partnerships have provided annual rates of return ranging from 10 to 25 percent. Because limited partnership shares are not traded on organized exchanges, they possess an element of risk attributable to their lack of marketability. In spite of the appeal provided by professional management, you should carefully consider the investment's relative lack of liquidity—in addition to the record of the general partner and other more standard risk-return factors—when evaluating limited partnership investments. Information on real estate limited partnerships can be obtained from a variety of sources, including stockbrokers, the financial news media, and commercial real estate brokers.

Constraints and Goals

When you decide to invest in real estate, you face a number of choices. In light of these options, you need to set financial and nonfinancial constraints and goals.

Financial constraints and goals

One financial constraint pertains to the risk-return relationship you find acceptable. In addition, you must consider how much money you want to allocate to the real estate portion of your portfolio. Do you want to invest $1,000, $10,000, or $50,000? Further, you should define some quantifiable financial objective. Often this financial goal is stated in terms of net present value (also referred to as discounted cash flows) or approximate yield. Some investors also consider payback period, first-year cash on cash return, and tax shelter ratios. We will show how these constraints and goals can be applied to real estate investing in the Campus Oaks Apartments example later in the chapter.

In recent years, several popular "how to get rich" real estate books have become best sellers. Usually these books present various "rule of thumb" financial and valuation guidelines. Indeed, the popularity of these books is often directly related to the simplicity of the techniques they present. One word is in order: Beware. Successful real estate investing requires you to develop your own criteria based on your needs and the market conditions in your locality. A rule of thumb that has worked well in southern California may take a Peoria, Illinois, investor into bankruptcy.

Nonfinancial constraints and goals

Although you will probably want to invest in real estate for its financial rewards, you also need to consider how your technical skills, temperament, repair skills, and managerial talents fit a potential investment. Do you want a prestige, trouble-free property? Or would you prefer a fix-up special on which you can release your imagination and workmanship? Would you enjoy living in the same building as your tenants (as in a fourplex investment) or would you like as little contact with them as possible? Just as you wouldn't choose a career solely on the basis of money, neither should you buy a property just for the money.

SCOPE OF ANALYSIS

The framework of real estate investment analysis suggested in this chapter can aid in estimating a property's investment potential. Yet before really evaluating this potential, a scope of analysis must be established. This includes four parts: (1) identifying the physical property, (2) defining the applicable property rights, (3) deciding the time horizon for your investment, and (4) delineating a geographic area.

The Physical Property

When buying real estate, make sure you are getting both the quantity and quality of property you think you are getting. Problems can arise if you fail to obtain a site survey; an accurate square footage measurement of the buildings; or an inspection for defects such as termite infestation, dry rot, improper settling, and an inadequate electrical system. In addition, most real estate transactions do not automatically include *personal property*—which may be loosely defined as property that is not attached in a more or less permanent fashion to the real estate. So you might buy a property and think the sale includes window air conditioning units, drapes, refrigerator, and fireplace screen and equipment. Then you discover it doesn't. When signing a contract to buy a property, make sure it accurately identifies the real estate, and lists all items of personal property that you expect to receive.

Property Rights

Strange as it may seem, when buying real estate, you do not really buy the physical property. What you buy is a bundle of legal rights that not only limit the ways you can benefit from your property, but also establish certain obligations. These rights and obligations fall under concepts in law such as deeds, titles, easements, liens, and encumbrances. Too often people have bought real estate and then discovered they didn't receive good title, or they couldn't use the property the way they intended. When investing in real estate, make sure that along with termite, plumbing, structural, and electrical inspections, you also get a legal inspection from a qualified attorney. Real estate sale and lease agreements should not be the work of amateurs.

Time Horizon

Like a roller coaster, real estate prices go up and down. Sometimes market forces pull them up slowly but surely; in other periods, prices can fall so fast they take an investor's breath (and money) away. Before judging whether a prospective real estate investment will appreciate or depreciate, you must decide what time period is relevant. Investors who like to hold properties for the long term virtually ignore month to month price movements. At the other extreme are investors (speculators) who "flip" properties. As soon as they sign a sales contract, they're out looking for a quick profit. Because of these various time emphases, real estate investors weigh the specific factors that relate to demand and supply very differently. The short-term investor might count on a quick drop in mortgage interest rates and buoyant market expectations, whereas the long-term investor might look more closely at population growth potential.

Geographic Area

Real estate is a spatial commodity. Its value is directly linked to what is going on around it. With some properties, the area of greatest concern consists of a few square blocks; in other instances, an area of hundreds or even thousands of miles could serve as the relevant market area. For example, a 7-Eleven convenience store's success is determined within a geographic area of 6 to 12 blocks. A large shopping mall such as the Omni in Miami, Florida, or The Galleria in Houston, Texas, brings in customers from hundreds and even thousands of miles away. As a result of these spatial differences in the market areas that apply to properties, you must try to delineate boundaries before you can analyze real estate demand and supply in a productive manner.

DETERMINANTS OF VALUE

In real estate investment analysis, value generally serves as the central concept. Will a property increase in value? Will it produce increasing amounts of cash flows? These are questions most real estate investors need to answer. To address these questions intelligently, you should evaluate the four major determinants of real estate value: demand, supply, the property, and the property transfer process.

Demand

Demand refers to people's willingness and ability to buy or rent a given property. Generally, demand stems from a market area's economic base, the characteristics of its population, and the terms and conditions of mortgage financing.

Economic base

In most real estate markets, the source of buying power comes from jobs. Property values follow an upward path when employment is increasing, and values typically fall when employers begin to lay off people. Therefore, the first question you should ask about demand is this: "What is the outlook for jobs in the relevant market area?" Are schools, colleges, and universities gaining enrollment? Are major companies planning expansion? And are wholesalers, retailers, and financial institutions increasing their sales and services? Upward trends in these indicators often signal rising demand for real estate.

Population characteristics

All properties, though, do not benefit (or suffer) equally from changes in an area's overall growth rate. To analyze demand for a specific property, you should look at an area's population demographics and psychographics. *Demographics* refers to such things as household size, age structure, occupation, sex, and marital status. *Psychographic characteristics* are those that describe people's mental dispositions, such as personality, life style, and self-concept. By comparing demographic and psychographic trends to the features of your property, you can judge whether it is likely to gain or lose favor among potential tenants or buyers.

Mortgage financing

Tight money can choke off demand for real estate. As we saw in the early 1980s, rising interest rates and the relative unavailability of mortgages caused inventories of unsold properties to grow and prices to fall. Conversely, as mortgage

TABLE 16.1   MORTGAGE PAYMENT PLANS

Type of Payment Plan	Pros and Cons	Who Benefits
FIXED-RATE-AND-PAYMENT MORTGAGE (FRPM)		
Both the interest rate and the monthly payment are fixed over the life of the mortgage. This is the traditional form of mortgage loan.	The size of the payments being fixed over the life of the loan allow you to know with certainty your payment obligation. On the other hand, the plan does not offer any of the special-purpose benefits one might get from other payment plans.	No special group benefits from this traditional or most basic plan.
GRADUATED-PAYMENT MORTGAGE (GPM)		
Monthly payments are arranged to start out low and get bigger later, perhaps in a series of steps at specified intervals. The term of the loan and the interest rate remain unchanged.	The object is to make buying easier in the beginning. Initial payments have to be balanced by larger payments later. One disadvantage: Possible "negative amortization" in the early years, which means that for a time your debt grows instead of diminishes.	Mainly first-time buyers, who have a hard time become homeowners, but can look forward to higher earnings that will enable them to afford the bigger payments later.
ADJUSTABLE-RATE MORTGAGE (ARM)		
Instead of a fixed interest rate, this loan carries an interest rate that may change within limits—up or down—from time to time during the life of the loan, reflecting changes in market rates for money.	Because the size of the payments in the future is uncertain, this loan is a bit of a gamble. If money rates go down in the future, payments will go down. But if the rates go up, so will payments.	Helps lenders keep their flow of funds in step with changing conditions, and this in turn could make home loans easier to get when money is tight. You may get fractionally lower interest at first or other inducements to make future uncertainties more palatable.

interest rates fell during late 1982 and early 1983, sales activity in many cities throughout the United States more than doubled compared to the same period a year earlier.

Some good, though, came out of the recent topsy-turvy market for real estate financing. Lenders now offer a wide variety of mortgage instruments. This variety of mortgage payment plans helps lenders and borrowers meet their respective needs. The more popular and widely available mortgage payment plans are shown in Table 16.1.

TABLE 16.1 *Continued*

Type of Payment Plan	Pros and Cons	Who Benefits
ROLLOVER (RENEGOTIABLE) MORTGAGE (ROM)		
The rate of interest is fixed, but the whole loan—including principal, rate of interest, and term—is renegotiated, or rolled over, at stated intervals, usually every five years.	If interest rates go up, you can expect to be charged more when you renegotiate. But you also have the opportunity to adjust other aspects of the loan, such as term and principal. Or you can pay off the outstanding balance without penalty. Renegotiation is guaranteed.	Lenders benefit for the same reason that variable rate loans are good for them. Benefits to borrowers are as shown for adjustable-rate loans, with this plus: Periodic renegotiation gives you a chance to adjust the loan to suit changing needs without all the expense of refinancing.
GROWING-EQUITY MORTGAGE (GEM)		
The interest rate remains fixed, but the payments are scheduled to rise by 4 to 7½ percent a year, causing the loan to be paid off within about 15 years.	Because of the accelerated payback, most lenders are willing to give borrowers a break on the interest rate. Provides for accelerated payoff of the loan, but forces the borrower to make larger mortgage payments each year.	Both lenders and borrowers benefit, since the lender gets its money back sooner and the borrower who wishes to repay a mortgage quickly can do so at a lower and fixed interest rate.
SHARED-APPRECIATION MORTGAGE (SAM)		
The rate of interest is lower—a mortgage banker might knock 4 percent off a 12 percent rate of interest—in exchange for a partial (about one-third) share of any gain in the property's value.	The main object is to make it easier to afford today's high-priced homes. The major drawback is that the lender usually wants to claim its share after 10 years. If the borrower can't raise the cash, the home has to be sold.	Homeowners who could not otherwise afford to buy the home they desire. Benefits to lenders come in the ability to share in any anticipated appreciation in the value of the home.

Source: Adapted from "New Ideas for Home Loans," *Changing Times,* May 1978, p. 22.

Supply

An analysis of supply really means sizing up the competition. Nobody wants to pay you more for a property than the price they can pay your competitor; nor when you're buying (or renting) should you pay more than the prices asked for other similar properties. As a result, an integral part of value analysis requires that you identify sources of potential competition, and then inventory them by price and features.

BOX 16.1 FINDING A TENANT: SOME HELPFUL ADVICE

The very first tenants, of course, were Adam and Eve—and they were evicted from the Garden of Eden for violating the terms of their lease. Finding good tenants today is still a landlord's biggest headache, whether he has been renting out property for years or is among the increasing number of people who are becoming landlords for the first time. Some are leasing their vacation cottages for a season or renting their homes for a few years because they've been transferred temporarily to other cities. Thousands of other people have bought houses, condominiums or apartment buildings as investments and are now looking for tenants to fill them.

But making sure that prospective tenants will pay the rent on time and treat your property with care requires lots of legwork—and some intuition about people. If you don't trust your own judgment or don't have the time, you can hire a real estate agent or property manager to search out tenants for you. He will generally charge half or all of a month's rent; if you want him to collect the rent and be on call for repairs and emergencies, you'll have to pay him an additional 3% to 10% of the rent.

If you decide to do the renting yourself, you can start your career as a landlord by taking a property-management course at a local community college. You can join your city's apartment association, which can give you guidance on accounting and management techniques. You might also talk with your lawyer about local landlord-tenant statutes, so that you'll be well versed in your rights and obligations as a landlord. Finally, make sure that in your mortgage or condominium regulations there are no limitations on renting and that your property is adequately insured.

To determine what rent to charge, add up all your expenses—mortgage, taxes, management and maintenance. Then, investigate the local rental market by studying advertisements for comparable units. If your price is right, you'll probably have a choice of tenants. . . . Ask all serious prospects to fill in a detailed application form. It should include the applicant's name, Social Security number, monthly salary, the names of his employer and supervisor and his bank. You should get the name and phone number of his present landlord—and his previous ones, if possible. You should also require a deposit—as much as a month's rent—which you will have to give back if you turn him down.

LITTERBUGS

To begin verifying the facts on the application, first visit a local credit bureau for a report on the applicant's record of paying bills. A credit check often costs only $5 to $10. To confirm the applicant's salary, you'll have to ask him to get a letter from his supervisor if his employer won't give such personal information to strangers. To determine the applicant's reliability as a tenant, try to call his previous landlords: his present one might be so eager to have him move out that he will give a glowing report. In the end, however, you'll have to rely mostly on your own judgment. One real estate consultant recommends escorting an applicant to his car to see if the back seat is littered. If it is, chances are he will be equally sloppy with your property.

Sources of competition

In general, people in real estate think of competitors in terms of similar properties. If you are trying to sell a house, then it seems natural to see your competition as the other houses for sale in your neighborhood. For longer-term investment decisions, though, you should expand your concept of supply. You should identify

BOX 16.1 *Continued*

Once you have selected a tenant and want him to sign a lease, you can get standard forms from office-supply stores, your real estate agent or lawyer. If necessary, you can amend the lease. For example, you should specify who must pay for utilities and whether you will charge a late fee if the rent is not paid on time. If the tenant wants a sublet clause, you should retain the right of final approval on subtenants. List the names of all occupants of the property, and have each adult sign the lease. This procedure helps ensure that the rent will still be paid if a couple splits up, and gives you some protection if you rent to three students and discover that six have moved in.

Leases are often for a year, though some are renewed every month, which makes it easier to get rid of unruly tenants or raise the rent, when necessary. If you want one for longer than a year, you can write in an escalator clause specifying that the tenant will pay increases in taxes and other landlord expenses. You should also include with the lease an inventory of all furniture, fixtures and other personal property in the house or apartment; walk through it with the tenant and check on the condition of each item. Anything not in good order should be noted in writing—a spotted carpet, for instance. When the tenant is ready to move out, go over the list with him again and decide who is responsible for fixing any damage. You must pay for normal wear and tear, such as handprints on the walls or scuff marks on the floors. But the tenant must pay if he has painted the walls purple without your consent.

To cover the cost of repairs, most landlords require a security deposit to be paid along with the first month's rent. The traditional deposit is equal to a month's rent, but you probably should ask for more than that. This way, the tenant is less likely to skip out without paying the last month's rent, leaving you with nothing for damages.

VISITATION RIGHTS

While the tenant is living in your house or apartment, you will naturally want to keep an eye on it. But unless there is an emergency such as a fire, you can't just barge in—you and the tenant must agree in advance on a date and time for visits. You might include in the lease a schedule of regular visits for you to do routine maintenance, such as replacing an oil-burner filter.

No matter how closely you watch your property, the best insurance against damage is to treat tenants fairly. One experienced real estate investor doesn't charge as much rent as he could, on the assumption that a tenant who thinks he is getting a bargain is more likely to take good care of the property. Another investor asks his tenants when it's easiest for them to pay the rent: if payday is the 15th, he adjusts the lease accordingly. In the long run, say seasoned landlords, that kind of consideration minimizes the risk of having resentful tenants who will try to get even for some slight—real or imagined—by treating your property carelessly. Moreover, when a satisfied tenant moves out, he might recommend you to his friends—which may be the best way of all to find good tenants.

Source: Sarah E. Button, "How to Find a . . . Tenant." *Money,* August 1981, pp. 25–26, 28.

competitors through use of the *principle of substitution*. This principle holds that people do not really rent or buy real estate per se. Instead, they judge properties as different sets of benefits and costs. Properties fill people's needs, and it is really these needs that create demand. Thus, an analysis of supply should not limit potential competitors to geographically and physically similar properties. In some markets, for example, low-priced single-family houses might compete with condominium units, mobile homes (often called manufactured housing), and even rental apartments. So, before you invest in any property, you should decide what market that property appeals to, and then define its competitors as those properties that its buyers or tenants typically choose from.

Inventory competitors

After identifying all relevant competitors, real estate investment analysis requires that you inventory these properties in terms of features and respective prices. (Many large real estate investors hire professional market consultants to do the research that the analysis of demand and supply require.) In other words, you look for the relative pros and cons of each property. With this market information, you can develop a competitive edge for your (potential) property.

The Property

Up to now we have shown that a property's rental or sales value is influenced by demand and supply. The price that people will pay is governed by their needs and the relative prices of the properties available to meet those needs. Yet in real estate the property itself is also a key ingredient. What is the best use for a property? What benefits should be offered? These are issues potential property owners should address. To address these issues, to try to develop a property's competitive edge, an investor should consider five items: (1) restrictions on use, (2) location, (3) site characteristics, (4) improvements, and (5) property management.

Restrictions on use

In today's highly regulated society, none of us has the right to do as we please with a property. Both state and local laws and private contracts limit the rights of all property owners. Government restrictions derive from zoning laws, building and occupancy codes, and health and sanitation requirements. Private restrictions derive from deeds, leases, and condominium bylaws and operating rules. As a result of all these restrictions, then, you should not invest in a property until you (or your lawyer) determine that what you want to do with the property fits within applicable laws, rules, and contract provisions.

Location analysis

You may have heard the adage, "The three most important determinants of real estate value are location, location, and location." Of course, location is not the only factor that affects value; yet a good location does increase a property's investment potential. But with that said, you still need to learn how to tell a bad location from a good location. We can add that a good location is one that meets the needs of a defined buyer (tenant) segment better than other locations. A good location rates highly on the two dimensions: convenience and environment. The analytical framework for residential location analysis briefly discussed below is depicted in Figure 16.1.

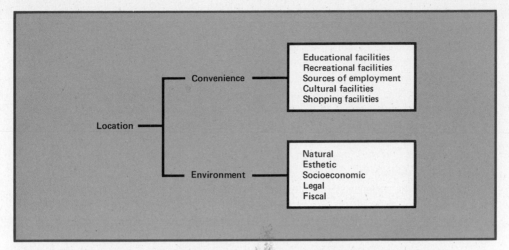

Figure 16.1   Analytical Framework for Residential Location Analyses.
This framework is useful in analyzing real estate locations; note that a good location is one
that rates highly in terms of convenience and environment—each of which involves a number
of key dimensions.

Convenience.   Convenience refers to how accessible a property is to the places
the people in a target market frequently need to go. In judging the relative convenience of a residential location, for example, most tenants and home buyers try to see
how nearby there are schools and colleges; recreational facilities such as parks,
swimming pools, and tennis courts; sources of employment; cultural facilities such
as churches, libraries, and museums; and retail stores, household services, restaurants, and places of entertainment. Any selected residential or commercial market
segment will have a set of preferred places its buyers or tenants will want to be close
to. Another element of convenience refers to the availability of bus, taxi, subway, or
commuter train services. For example, in Piedmont, California, a suburb of San
Francisco, homes close to the commuter train station and bus stops are generally
preferred to similar homes that are farther away.

Environment.   With all the attention on ecology in recent years, you probably
think of "the environment" in terms of trees, rivers, lakes, and air quality. But in the
analysis of real estate, the term environment has broader meaning. When you invest
in real estate, you should really consider not only the natural environment, but also
the esthetic, socioeconomic, legal, and fiscal environments.

Neighborhoods with an *esthetic environment* are those where buildings and
landscaping are well maintained. There is no intrusion of noise, sight, or air pollution,
and encroaching unharmonious land uses are not evident. The *socioeconomic environment* refers to the demographics and life styles of the people who live or work
in nearby properties; the *legal environment* relates to the restrictions on use that

apply to nearby properties. Remember, in the absence of zoning or deed restrictions, properties near, say, a fourplex that you buy might be developed in a way that would lower your building's value. And last, you need to consider a property's *fiscal environment.* This environment refers to the amount of property taxes and municipal assessments you will be required to pay, and the government services you will be entitled to receive (police, fire, schools, parks, water, sewers, trash collection, libraries). Property taxes are a two-sided coin. On the one side they pose a cost, but on the other they give a property's users the right to services that may be of substantial benefit.

Site analysis

One of the most important features of a site is its size. For residential properties, such as personal residences, apartments, and condominiums, some people want a large yard for kids to play in or for a garden. Others may prefer virtually no yard at all. With respect to commercial properties, such as office buildings and shopping centers, adequate parking space is necessary. Also, with respect to site size, if you are planning a later addition of space, make sure the site is large enough to accommodate it, both physically and legally. Site quality is also important, and refers to such things as soil fertility, topography, elevation, and drainage capacity. These features are important, for example, because grass may be difficult to grow in certain types of soil, and sites with relatively low elevation may be subject to flooding. Nobody likes a basement full of water after a hard rain. In examining a site, you should further note any extras such as fencing, paved driveway and parking areas, sewer and utility connections, landscaping, and sidewalks. Each of these can add to the benefits a property can produce, and to its cash flows.

Improvements

In real estate, the term *improvements* refers to the man-made additions to a site. Under site analysis we talked about improvements such as paved parking areas and sidewalks. Here, we are talking about the analysis of building size and quality and on-site amenities (swimming pools, tennis courts, golf course).

Building size and floor plan.   Typically, building size is examined in terms of square footage. For instance, with respect to residences and by American standards, a small house is one of less than, say, 1400 square feet; medium-size houses range between 1400 and 2200 square feet, and to most people a house of more than 2200 square feet would be thought of as large. Because square footage is so important in building and unit comparison, you should get accurate square footage measures on any properties you consider investing in.

Another measure of building size is room count and floor plan. For example, a well-designed 750-square-foot apartment unit might in fact be more livable than one of 850 square feet. Therefore, you should determine whether the sizes of individual rooms are in proportion to their intended use. One way to check for this feature is to take measurements of furniture that would be typical and see if rooms are too small, adequate, or excessively large. You should make sure that floor plans are logical, that traffic flows throughout a building will pose no inconveniences, that there is sufficient closet, cabinet, and other storage space, and that the right mix of rooms exists. For example, in an office building you should not have to cross through other offices to get to the building's only bathroom, or as an exclusive access to any other room; small merchants in a shopping center should not be placed in locations where they do not receive the pedestrian traffic generated by the larger (anchor) tenants.

Amenities, style, construction quality. As another item, you should determine what amenities and personal property might be included with your potential invest-ment properties. It is now common for houses, condominiums, and apartments to be furnished with items such as drapes, carpeting, garbage disposal, refrigerator, dishwasher, and compactor. In addition, when buying an existing property, items such as window air conditioners, chandeliers, fireplace equipment, and even some furniture might be included. From shopping the market and thumbing through ar-chitectural books and magazines, you should develop a sense of style, and some knowledge of construction materials and quality workmanship.

Property management
In recent years, real estate owners and investors have increasingly recognized that investment properties (apartments, office buildings, shopping centers, and so on) do not earn maximum cash flows by themselves. They need to be guided toward that objective. Indeed, skilled property management is important to property owners. Without effective property management, no real estate investment can produce max-imum benefits for its users and owners. In this context, we are not talking about someone who merely collects rents, calls the plumber, and hangs out vacancy signs. Today, property management requires you (or a hired manager) not only to perform day-to-day chores, but also to run the entire operation. You need to segment buyers, improve a property's site and structure, keep tabs on competitors, and develop a marketing campaign. Management also assumes responsibility for the maintenance and repair of buildings and their physical systems (electrical, heating, air condition-ing); and managers keep records to account for revenues and expenses. In addition, property managers decide the best ways to protect properties against loss from perils such as fire, flood, theft, storms, and negligence. In its broadest sense, property management means finding the optimal level of benefits for a property, and then providing them at the lowest costs. Of course, for speculative investments such as raw land, the managerial task is not so pronounced—the manager has less control over the profit picture.

The Property Transfer Process
In Chapter 10, we introduced the concept of efficient markets. You may recall from that discussion that an efficient market is one in which information flows so quickly among buyers and sellers that it is virtually impossible for an investor to outperform the average systematically. As soon as something good (an exciting new product) or something bad (a multimillion-dollar product liability suit) occurs, the

price of the affected company's stock adjusts to reflect its current potential for earnings or losses. Some people accept the premise that securities markets are efficient, and others do not. But one thing is sure: *No one believes real estate markets are efficient.* What this means is that real estate market research pays off. Skillfully conducted economic analysis, property type analysis (industry analysis), and property analysis (fundamental analysis) can help you beat the averages. (*Note:* In real estate markets, the tools of technical analysis are virtually undeveloped.) The reasons real estate markets differ from securities markets is that no good system exists for complete information exchange among buyers and sellers, and among tenants and lessors. In addition, real estate returns are partially controlled by the property owners themselves. As pointed out above, profits in real estate depend on how well you (or your property manager) can manage the property. In the property *transfer process* itself, the inefficiency of the market means that how you collect and disseminate information will affect your results. The cash flows a property will earn can be influenced significantly through promotion and negotiation.

Promotion

Promotion refers to the task of getting information about a property to its buyer segment. You can't sell or rent a property quickly and for top dollar unless you can reach the people you want to reach in a cost-effective way. Among the major ways to promote a property are advertising, publicity, sales gimmicks, and personal selling.

Both advertising and publicity involve media coverage for your property. In the case of advertising, you pay for this coverage; with publicity, you create a newsworthy event. For example, in Dallas, the Dondi Development Corporation used a new type of financing plan—the "Rich Uncle" program—to get good (and free) press coverage for its condominium units. A sales gimmick often relies on some type of contest or perhaps a gift of some sort. A Houston office building developer, for example, perked up demand for his project when he offered a new Mercedes to new tenants who signed a five-year lease. This sales gimmick also got the developer's project a great deal of publicity. Personal selling is often the most costly, but also the most effective way to attract buyers or tenants to a property. It places you or your sales agent in a one-on-one customer relationship.

In most instances, property owners use two or more ways to promote their property. Space does not permit us to show how such an approach should be made, nor to discuss the technical requirements necessary to create a promotion campaign. But at the least, you should now see that maximizing a real estate investment's cash flows through promotion entails more than dashing off a classified newspaper advertisement.

Negotiation

Seldom does the minimum price a seller is willing to accept just equal the maximum price a buyer is willing to pay; often some overlap occurs. Also, in real estate the asking price for a property may be anywhere from 5 to 60 percent above the price that a seller (or lessor) will accept. Therefore, the negotiating skills of each party determine the final transaction price.

ESTIMATING MARKET VALUE

In real estate, the concept of *market value* must be interpreted differently from the way it is in stocks and bonds. This difference arises for a number of reasons, among which are these: (1) Each property is unique; (2) terms and conditions of sale may vary widely; (3) market information is imperfect; (4) properties may need substantial time for market exposure, time that may not be available to any given seller; and (5) buyers too sometimes need to act quickly. All these things mean that no one can tell for sure what a property's "true" market value is, and that many properties sell for prices significantly above and below their estimated market values.

In other words, when you learn that a property has an appraised market value of, say, $150,000, interpret that value a little skeptically. Because of both technical and information shortcomings, this estimate of what a property will sell for can be subject to substantial error. Although you can tell the market values of frequently traded stocks simply by looking at current quotes, in real estate, appraisers and investors typically must use three complex techniques and then correlate results to come up with one best estimate. These three imperfect approaches to real estate market value are (1) the cost approach, (2) the comparative sales approach, and (3) the income approach. Because of the complexity of this process, it is often helpful to use an expert.

The Cost Approach

The *cost approach* is based on the notion that an investor should not pay more for a property than it would cost to rebuild it at today's prices for land, labor, and construction materials. This approach to estimating value generally works well for new or relatively new buildings. Older properties, however, often suffer from wear and tear, and outdated materials or design, so the cost approach is more difficult to apply. To value these older properties, you would have to subtract some amount for physical and functional depreciation from the replacement cost estimates. Most experts agree that the cost approach is a good method to use as a check against a price estimate, but rarely should it be used in isolation.

The Comparative Sales Approach

The *comparative sales approach* uses the sales prices of properties that are similar to a subject property as the basic input variable. This approach is based on the idea that the value of a given property is about the same as the prices for which other similar properties have recently sold. Of course, the catch here is that all properties are unique in some respect. Therefore, the price that a subject property could be expected to bring must be adjusted upward or downward to reflect its superiority or inferiority to comparable properties. Nevertheless, because the comparable sales approach is based on *selling* prices, not asking prices, it can give you a good feel for the market. As a practical matter, if you can find at least one sold property slightly better than the one you're looking at, and one slightly worse, their recent sales prices can serve to bracket an estimated market value for a subject property.

BOX 16.2 BUYING CONDOS TO RENT OUT

"For the urban investor, condominiums are one of the best alternatives to single-family houses," says Kenneth R. Harney, author of the book *Beating Inflation with Real Estate* (Random House, $10). Financing is readily available. You can borrow 80% to 90% of the purchase price; it often takes no more than $5,000 to become a landlord.

Harney also points out that condos offer investors three other advantages over houses and small apartment buildings:

- *Ease of management.* All repairs and maintenance on the building and grounds are handled by the condominium association. The owner has only the apartment's interior, windows and built-in appliances to maintain and repair.
- *High rents and low vacancy rates.* Because many new apartments are built as condominiums, and many older buildings are being converted to condominiums or co-ops, rental housing in many areas is becoming scarce and expensive—making it a landlords' market.
- *High depreciation deductions.* A condo's land is allocated to owners according to the size of the units in the condominium. The cost of the land cannot be depreciated, so its value is subtracted from the apartment's purchase price for calculating depreciation. But since land is usually a smaller part of the value of an apartment than of a house, condo owner-landlords can often depreciate 90% or more of their purchase price while investors in single-family houses rarely are able to go above 80%.

In addition to the tax deduction for depreciation, owner-landlords are entitled to write off virtually all the maintenance fees. Exception: assessments for capital improvements such as new recreational facilities, major repairs and expansions. Owner-residents aren't entitled to take any tax deductions for either depreciation or maintenance.

Despite these tax advantages, owner-landlords are much more likely to make money on appreciation of an apartment's value—generally 10% or more a year recently—than on the rental. That's particularly true when the owner makes only a minimum down payment.

Take a typical one-bedroom $50,000 condo with a $45,000 mortgage at 12 percent for 30 years. The monthly payment is $470, including mortgage insurance. Maintenance charges and taxes can add another $200 a month to the owner's cash outgo—for a total of around $670. But the condo will probably rent for something more like $450. This creates a yearly cash loss on the rental of $2,640. But then tax deductions come into play.

The Income Approach

The most popular *income approach* used to estimate market value is called direct capitalization. This approach is represented by the formula:

$$\text{market value } (V) = \frac{\text{annual net operating income (NOI)}}{\text{market capitalization rate } (R)}$$

$$V = \frac{\text{NOI}}{R}$$

BOX 16.2 *Continued*

If the apartment is depreciated by the straight line method, dividing the cost minus land for the 15-year depreciable life of the building, the owner gets a depreciation deduction of $3,000 per year during the first 15 years, assuming land accounts for 10 percent of purchase price.

The owner can also deduct roughly another $7,878—for the interest on the mortgage payments (an average of $5,194 for each of the first five years), mortgage insurance ($84), maintenance and taxes ($2,400), and rental expenses ($200). Subtracting the rental income of $5,400 from the expenses gives a tax loss of $5,478, which is deductible from the owner's taxable income for the year. For a taxpayer in the 30 percent bracket (which means a taxable income of roughly $29,900 to $35,200 on a joint return [in 1983]), that will lower his tax bill by $1,643. So he's cut the loss to about $1,000, the difference between the tax savings and the rental income deficit of around $2,640. But that $1,000 loss is handsomely offset by appreciation—$5,000 if the conservative 10 percent figure is used.

One unknown that confronts owner-landlords is the possibility that rent controls will spread beyond New York, parts of California and a few other areas. The same tight rental market that makes condos such an attractive investment is making landlords out as villains: renters are demanding limitations on rent increases. But generally owner-landlords aren't being scared off; most existing laws allow annual raises in the 7%-to-10% range.

Harney and other owner-landlords offer these tips to buyers:

- Newly constructed or converted condos are usually the best buys. They have the greatest variety of apartments, the lowest prices and the most favorable financing.
- Tenants pay the highest rents for city condos that are near business districts, shopping, schools, public transportation and entertainment centers.
- Suburban condos with swimming pools, saunas, tennis courts and other recreational facilities are expensive to maintain. A little luxury is a good investment, but too much can price your rents right out of the market.
- Restrictive clauses in a condo's bylaws can cause problems for owner-landlords. Such clauses may require that rentals be approved by the full board or management committee, or may limit the use of recreational facilities and free parking to owners only.

Source: Adapted from Patrick Flanagan, "Buying Condos to Rent Out." *Money,* June 1979, p. 78. Reprinted by special permission, © 1979, Time, Inc.

Annual net operating income is calculated by subtracting vacancy and collection losses and property operating expenses, including property taxes and property insurance, from an income property's *gross potential* rental income. An estimated *capitalization rate*—which technically means the rate used to convert an income stream to a present value—is obtained by looking at recent market sales figures and seeing what rates investors currently require. Then, by dividing the annual net operating income by the appropriate capitalization rate, you get an income property's estimated market value. An example of the application of the income approach is given in Table 16.2.

TABLE 16.2   APPLYING THE INCOME APPROACH

Comparables	(1) NOI	(2) Sales Price	(3) (1) ÷ (2) Rate
2301 Maple Ave.	$16,250	$182,500	.0890
4037 Armstrong St.	15,400	167,600	.0919
8240 Ludwell St.	19,200	198,430	.0968
7392 Grant Blvd.	17,930	189,750	.0945
Subject property	$18,480	?	?

From this market-derived information, an appraiser would work through the equation:

$$V = \frac{NOI}{R}$$

$$V = \frac{\$18,480}{R}$$

$$V = \frac{\$18,480}{.093^*}$$

$$V = \$198,710$$

*Based on an analysis of the relative similarities of the comparables and the subject, the appraiser decides the appropriate R equals .093.

Using an Expert

Real estate valuation is a complex and technical procedure that requires reliable information about the features of comparable properties, their selling prices, and applicable terms of financing. As a result, rather than rely exclusively on their own judgment, many investors hire a real estate agent or a professional real estate appraiser to advise them about the market value of a property. As a form of insurance against paying too much, the use of an expert can be well worth the cost.

FORECASTING INVESTMENT RETURNS

Estimates of market value play an integral role in real estate decision making. Yet today more and more investors supplement their market value appraisals with investment analysis. This extension of the traditional approaches to value (cost, comparative sales, and income) gives investors a better picture of whether a selected property is likely to satisfy their investment objectives.

Market Value versus
Investment Analysis

The concept of market value differs from investment analysis in four important ways: (1) retrospective versus prospective, (2) impersonal versus personal, (3) unleveraged versus leveraged, and (4) net operating income (NOI) versus after-tax cash flows.

Retrospective versus prospective

Market value appraisals look backward; they attempt to estimate the price a property will sell for by looking at the sales prices of similar properties in the recent past. Under static market conditions, such a technique can be reasonable. But if, say, interest rates, population, or buyer expectations are changing rapidly, past sales prices may not accurately indicate the current value or the future value of a subject property. In contrast, an *investment analysis* not only considers what similar properties have sold for, but also looks at the underlying determinants of value that we have discussed. An investment analysis tries to forecast such things as economic base, population demographics and psychographics, buying power, and potential sources of competition.

Impersonal versus personal

As defined by the professional appraisers, a market value estimate represents the price a property will sell for under certain specified conditions—in other words, a sort of market average. But in fact each buyer and seller has a unique set of needs, and each real estate transaction can be structured to meet those needs. So an investment analysis looks beyond what may constitute a "typical" transaction and attempts to evaluate a subject property's terms and conditions of sale (or rent) as they correspond to a given investor's constraints and goals.

For example, a market value appraisal might show that with normal financing and conditions of sale, a property is worth $180,000. Yet because of personal tax consequences, it might be better for a seller to ask a higher price for the property and offer owner financing at a below-market interest rate.

Unleveraged versus leveraged

As intimated earlier, the returns a real estate investment offers will be influenced by the amount of the purchase price that is financed. But simple income capitalization $[V = (NOI/R)]$ does not incorporate alternative financing plans that might be available. It assumes a cash or unleveraged purchase.

The use of financing or *leverage* gives differing risk-return parameters to a real estate investment. Leverage automatically increases investment risk because borrowed funds must be repaid. Failure to repay a mortgage loan results in foreclosure and possible property loss. Alternatively, leverage may also increase return. If a property can earn a return in excess of the cost of the borrowed funds, the investor's return will be increased to a level well above what could have been earned from an all-cash deal. This is known as *positive leverage*. Conversely, if return is below debt cost, the return on invested equity will be less than an all-cash deal. This is called *negative leverage*. The following example shows how leverage affects return and provides insight into the possible associated risks.

Assume an investor purchases a parcel of land for $20,000. The investor has

**TABLE 16.3   THE EFFECT OF POSITIVE
LEVERAGE ON RETURN: AN EXAMPLE***

Purchase price: $20,000
Sale price: $30,000
Holding period: one year

Item Number	Item	Choice A No Leverage	Choice B 80% Financing
1	Initial equity	$20,000	$ 4,000
2	Loan principal	0	16,000
3	Sales price	30,000	30,000
4	Capital gain [(3) − (1) − (2)]	10,000	10,000
5	Interest cost [.12 × (2)]	0	1,920
6	Net return [(4) − (5)]	10,000	8,080
	Return on investor's equity [(6) ÷ (1)]	$\frac{\$10,000}{\$20,000} = +50\%$	$\frac{\$ 8,080}{\$ 4,000} = +202\%$

*To simplify this example, all values are presented on a *before-tax* basis. To get the true return, taxes on the capital gain and the interest expense would be considered.

two financing choices. Choice A is all cash; that is, no leverage is employed. Choice B involves 80 percent financing (20 percent down payment) at 12 percent interest. With leverage (choice B), the investor signs a $16,000 note (.80 × $20,000) at 12 percent interest with the entire principal balance due and payable at the end of one year. Now suppose the land appreciates during the year to $30,000. (A comparative analysis of this occurrence is presented in Table 16.3.) Had the investor chosen the all-cash deal, the one-year return on the investor's initial equity is 50 percent. The use of leverage would have magnified that return, no matter how much the property appreciated. The leveraged alternative (choice B) involved only a $4,000 investment in personal initial equity, with the balance financed by borrowing at 12 percent interest. The property sells for $30,000, of which $16,000 goes to repay the principal balance on the debt, $4,000 represents the recovery of the initial equity investment, and another $1,920 of gain is used to pay interest ($16,000 × .12). The balance of the proceeds, $8,080, represents the investor's return. The return on the investor's initial equity is 202 percent—over four times that provided by the no-leveraged alternative, choice A.

No matter what the eventual outcome, risk is inherent in leverage; it can easily turn a bad deal into a disaster. Suppose the $20,000 property discussed above dropped in value by 25 percent during the one-year holding period. The comparative results are presented in Table 16.4. The unleveraged investment has resulted in a negative return of 25 percent. This is not large, however, when compared to the leveraged position in which the investor loses not only the entire initial investment of $4,000, but an additional $2,920 ($1,000 additional principal on the debt +

TABLE 16.4 THE EFFECT OF NEGATIVE
LEVERAGE ON RETURN: AN EXAMPLE*

Purchase price: $20,000
Sales price: $15,000
Holding period: one year

Item Number	Item	Choice A No Leverage	Choice B 80% Financing
1	Initial equity	$20,000	$ 4,000
2	Loan principal	0	16,000
3	Sales price	15,000	15,000
4	Capital loss [(3) − (1) − (2)]	5,000	5,000
5	Interest cost [.12 × (2)]	0	1,920
6	Net loss [(4) − (5)]	5,000	6,920
	Return on investor's equity [(6) ÷ (1)]	$\dfrac{\$ 5,000}{\$20,000} = -25\%$	$\dfrac{\$ 6,920}{\$ 4,000} = -173\%$

*In order to simplify this example, all values are presented on a *before-tax* basis. To get the true return, taxes on the capital loss and the interest expense would be considered.

$1,920 interest). The total loss of $6,920 on the original $4,000 of equity results in a (negative) return of − 173 percent. The loss in the leverage case is nearly seven times the loss experienced in the unleveraged situation.

NOI versus after-tax cash flows

Recall that to estimate market value, the income approach capitalizes net operating income. To most investors, though, the NOI figure holds little meaning. This is because, as discussed above, the majority of real estate investors finance their purchases. In addition, few investors today can ignore the effect of federal income tax law on their investment decisions. Investors want to know how much cash they will be required to put into a transaction, and how much cash they are likely to get out. The concept of NOI does not address these questions. Thus, in real estate the familiar finance measure of investment return—discounted cash flow—is a prime criterion for selecting real estate investments. Sometimes, approximate yield is used instead to assess the suitability of a prospective real estate investment.

Calculating Discounted Cash Flows

Calculating *discounted cash flows* involves the techniques of present value as discussed in Chapter 4; in addition, you need to learn how to calculate annual after-tax cash flows and the after-tax proceeds of sale. With this knowledge, you can discount the cash flows an investment is expected to earn over a specified holding period. This figure gives you the present value of the cash flows. Next, you find the *net present value*—the difference between the present value of the cash flows and the amount of equity required to make the investment. The resulting difference tells you whether the proposed investment looks good (a positive net present value) or bad (a negative net present value).

This process of discounting cash flows to calculate the net present value (NPV) of an investment can be shown by the following equation:

$$NPV = \left[\frac{CF_1}{(1 + r)^1} + \frac{CF_2}{(1 + r)^2} + \cdots + \frac{CF_{n-1}}{(1 + r)^{n-1}} + \frac{CF_n + CF_{R_n}}{(1 + r)^n} \right] - I_0$$

where

I_0 = the original required investment

CF_i = annual after-tax cash flow for year i

CF_{R_n} = the after-tax net proceeds of sale (reversionary after-tax cash flow) occurring in year n.

r = the discount rate and $[1/(1 + r)^t]$ is the present-value interest factor for $\$1$ received in year t using an r percent discount rate.

In this equation, the annual after-tax cash flows, CFs, may be either inflows to investors or outflows from them. Inflows would be preceded by a ($+$) sign, and outflows by a ($-$) sign.

Calculating Approximate Yield

An alternate way of assessing investment suitability would be to calculate the *approximate yield,* which was first presented in Chapter 4. Restating the formula in terms of the variables defined above we have:

$$\text{approximate yield} = \frac{\overline{CF} + \dfrac{CF_{R_n} - I_0}{n}}{\dfrac{CF_{R_n} + I_0}{2}}$$

where

$$\overline{CF} = \begin{array}{l}\text{average annual}\\ \text{after-tax cash}\\ \text{flow}\end{array} = \frac{CF_1 + CF_2 + \cdots + CF_{n-1} + CF_n}{n}$$

If the calculated approximate yield is greater than the discount rate appropriate for the given investment, the investment would be acceptable. In such an event, the net present value would be positive.

When consistently applied, the net present value and approximate yield approaches will always give the same recommendation for accepting or rejecting a proposed real estate investment. Now, to show how all of the elements discussed in the chapter can be applied to a real estate investment decision, let's look at an example.

THE CAMPUS OAKS APARTMENTS

We will assume that Jack Wilson is deciding whether or not to buy the Campus Oaks Apartments. Jack believes he can improve his real estate investment decision making if he follows a systematic procedure. He designs a schematic framework of analysis that corresponds closely to the topics we've discussed in this chapter. Following this framework (Figure 16.2), Jack (1) sets out his investment objectives, (2) defines the scope of analysis, (3) investigates the determinants of the property's value, (4) derives his forecast of investment returns, and (5) synthesizes and interprets the results of his analysis.

Investor Objectives

Jack is a tenured associate professor of management at Ivy Halls College. He's single, age 35, and earns from salary, consulting fees, stock dividends, and book royalties an income of $55,000 per year. Jack wants to further diversify his investment portfolio. He would like to add a real estate investment that has good appreciation potential, but also provides a positive yearly after-tax cash flow. For convenience, Jack requires the property to be close to his office, and he feels his talents and personality suit him for ownership of apartments. Jack has $60,000 cash to invest. On this amount, he would like to earn a 15 percent rate of return; toward this end, he has his eye on a small apartment complex, the Campus Oaks Apartments.

Scope of Analysis

The Campus Oaks building is located six blocks from the Ivy Halls College student union. The building contains eight 2-bedroom, 2-bath units of 1,100 square feet each. It was built in 1967, and all systems and building components appear to be in good condition. The present owner gave Jack an income statement reflecting the property's 1983 income and expenses. The owner has further assured Jack that no adverse easements or encumbrances affect the building's title. Of course, if Jack decides to buy Campus Oaks, he would have a lawyer verify the quality of the property rights associated with the property. For now, though, he accepts the owner's word.

In this instance, Jack thinks a five-year holding period is reasonable. At present he's happy at Ivy Halls and thinks he will stay there at least until age 40. Jack defines the market for the property as a one-mile radius from campus. He reasons that students who walk to campus (the target market) would limit their choice of apartments to those that fall within that geographic area.

Determinants of Value

Once Jack has outlined his scope of analysis, he next thinks about the factors that will determine the property's investment potential. As we have noted, these factors (the property's determinants of value) include: (1) demand, (2) the property, (3) supply, and (4) the transfer process.

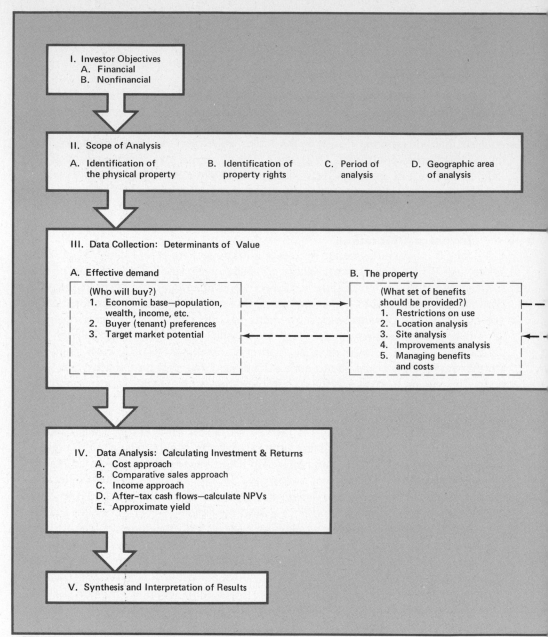

Figure 16.2 Framework for Real Estate Investment Analysis.
This framework depicts the logical approach to analyzing potential investment properties in

Demand

The major institution, indeed the lifeblood institution in the market area, is Ivy Halls College. The base of demand for the Campus Oaks Apartments will grow (or decline) with the size of the college's employment and student enrollment. On this

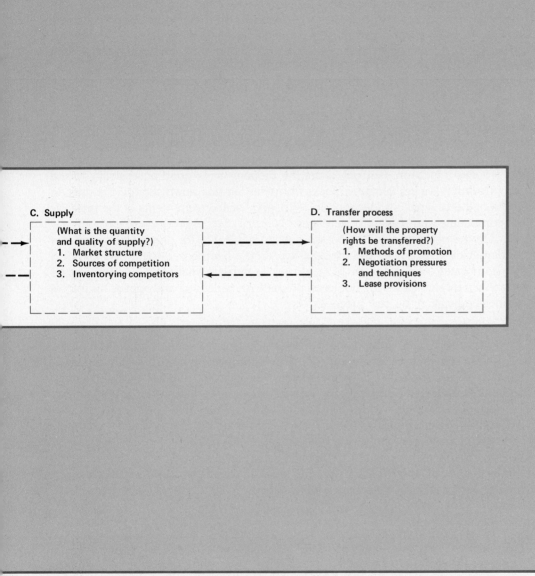

C. Supply

    (What is the quantity
    and quality of supply?)
    1. Market structure
    2. Sources of competition
    3. Inventorying competitors

D. Transfer process

    (How will the property
    rights be transferred?)
    1. Methods of promotion
    2. Negotiation pressures
       and techniques
    3. Lease provisions

order to assess whether or not they are acceptable investments that might be included in one's investment portfolio. (*Source:* © Gary W. Eldred, Palo Alto, California.)

basis, Jack judges the prospects for the area to be good to excellent. During the coming five years, major funding (due to a $25 million gift) will increase Ivy Halls' faculty by 35 percent, and expected along with faculty growth is a rise in the student population from 3,200 full-time students to 4,600 full-time students. Through further investigation, Jack learns that 70 percent of the *new* students will live away from home. In the past, Ivy Halls largely served the local market, but with its new affluence—and the resources this affluence can buy—the college will draw students from a wider geographic area. Furthermore, because Ivy Halls is a private college with relatively high tuition, the majority of students come from upper-middle-income families. Parental support can thus be expected to heighten students' ability to pay. Overall, then, Jack believes the major indicators of demand for the market area look good.

The property

Now the question becomes, will the Campus Oaks Apartments appeal to the desired market segment? On this issue, Jack concludes the answer is "yes." The property already is zoned multifamily and its present (and intended) use complies with all pertinent ordinances and housing codes. Of major importance, though, is the property's location. Not only does the property have good accessibility to the campus, but it is also just three blocks from the Campus Town shopping district. In addition, the esthetic, socioeconomic, legal, and fiscal environments of the property are compatible with student preferences.

On the negative side, the on-site parking has space for only six cars. Still, the building itself is attractive, and the relatively large 2-bedroom, 2-bath units are ideal for roommates. And although Jack has no experience managing apartments, he feels that if he studies several books on property management and applies his formal business education, he can succeed.

Supply

Jack realizes that even strong demand and a good property cannot yield profits if a market suffers from oversupply. Too much competition has pushed many property owners and real estate developers into bankruptcy. Fortunately, Jack thinks that Campus Oaks is well insulated from competing units. Most important is the fact that the designated market area is fully built up, and as much as 80 percent of the area is zoned single-family residential. Any efforts to change the zoning would be strongly opposed by neighborhood residents. The only potential problem that Jack sees is that the college might build more student housing on campus. There has been some administrative talk about it, but as yet no funds have been allocated to such a project. In sum, Jack concludes that the risk of oversupply in the Campus Oaks market area is low.

The transfer process

Real estate markets are inefficient. Thus, before a property's sales price or rental income can reach its potential, an effective means to get information to buyers or tenants must be developed. Here, of course, Jack has great advantage. Notices on campus bulletin boards and announcements to his classes should be all he needs to keep the property rented. Although he might experience some vacancy during the summer months, Jack feels he could overcome this problem by requiring students to sign 12-month leases, but then grant them the right to sublet—as long as the sublessees meet the tenant selection criteria.

BOX 16.3 OPERATING EXPENSE DATA FOR SMALL MULTIFAMILY BUILDINGS

The graph shown here suggests that many investors in small multifamily buildings (low-rise structures with 12 to 24 units) have managed to beat the inflationary rise in operating expenses since 1965. Although expenses have climbed almost continuously, the ratio of expenses to income from the properties (mostly rents) has been moving generally downward for some time. In 1965 owners paid out close to 56% of their income for operating expenses, compared with 48% in 1980. Those are median figures: Half the ratios were more, half less. The improvement reflects rent increases and the transfer of utility costs to tenants.

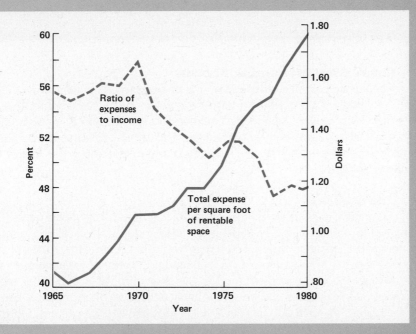

The actual situation probably isn't quite so rosy for investors. Operating expenses do not include such items as ground rents, mortgage interest payments and capital expenditures. Also, the figures, which are from the Institute of Real Estate Management, are weighted toward younger buildings, which are less expensive to run. In 1980 the median expense ratio for a building built in the 1920s was 61%, versus 42% for a building put up between 1968 and 1980. And there are marked regional differences. Expense ratios in the Northeast and Middle Atlantic States stayed nearly level or rose between 1976 and 1980.

Source: "Winning the Cost War." From "Timely Tips for Real Estate Investors," *Changing Times,* October 1982, pp. 55–60.

TABLE 16.5   INCOME STATEMENT, CAMPUS OAKS APARTMENTS, 1983

Gross rental income (8 × $335 × 12)		$32,160
Operating expenses		
Utilities	$2,830	
Trash collection	675	
Repairs and maintenance	500	
Promotion and advertising	150	
Property taxes	3,200	
Property insurance	840	
Less: Total operating expenses		8,195
Net operating income (NOI)		$23,965

Calculating Investment Returns

Real estate cash flows depend on the underlying characteristics of the property and the market. That is why we have devoted so much attention to analyzing the determinants of value. Often real estate investors lose money because they "run the numbers" without doing their homework. So, as we go through our investment calculations, remember that the numbers coming out will be no better than the numbers going in.

The numbers

At present Mrs. Bowker, the owner of Campus Oaks Apartments, is asking $260,000 for the property. To assist in the sale, though, she is willing to offer owner financing to a qualified buyer. The terms would be 20 percent down, 11.5 percent interest, and full amortization of the outstanding mortgage balance over 30 years. The owner's income statement for 1983 is shown in Table 16.5. After talking with the owner, Jack believes she would probably accept an offer that gave her $60,000 down, a price of $245,000, and a 30-year mortgage at 11 percent. On this basis, Jack prepares his investment calculations.

Cash flow analysis

As a first step in cash flow analysis, Jack reconstructs the owner's income statement (as shown in Table 16.6). This reconstruction reflects higher rent levels, higher expenses, and a lower net operating income. Jack believes that due to poor owner management and deferred maintenance, the present owner is not getting as much in rents as the market could support. In addition, her expenses understate those he is likely to incur. For one thing, a management expense should be deducted. Jack wants to separate what is rightfully a return on labor from his return on capital. Also, once the property is sold, a higher property tax assessment will be levied against it. Except for promotion and advertising, other expenses have been increased to adjust for inflation and a more extensive maintenance program. With these adjustments, the expected NOI for Campus Oaks during 1984 is estimated at $22,822.

TABLE 16.6 RECONSTRUCTED INCOME STATEMENT, CAMPUS OAKS APARTMENTS, 1984

Gross potential rental income	$37,800	
Less: Vacancy and collection losses at 4%	1,512	
Effective gross income (EGI)		$36,288
Operating expenses:		
Management at 5% of EGI	$ 1,814	
Utilities	3,100	
Trash collection	750	
Repairs and maintenance	2,400	
Promotion and advertising	150	
Property insurance	960	
Property taxes	4,292	
Less: Total operating expenses		$13,466
Net operating income (NOI)		$22,822

To move from NOI to after-tax cash flows, we need to perform the calculations shown in Table 16.7. From this table, you can see that to calculate ATCF, you must first compute the income taxes or income tax savings Jack would incur as a result of property ownership. In this case, tax savings accrue because the allowable tax deductions of interest and depreciation exceed the property's net operating income. In other words, the property ownership provides Jack a *tax shelter:* Jack uses the income tax losses sustained on the property to shelter (offset) the taxable income he receives from salary, consulting fees, stock dividends, and book royalties. Once the amount of taxes (or tax savings) is known, this amount is subtracted (or added) to the before-tax cash flow.

The "magic" of simultaneously losing and making money is caused by *depreciation.* Tax statutes incorporate this tax deduction to reflect the declining economic life of a building. However, since the deduction depends on law and not on market forces, a property can gain in market value but still be entitled to an expense for depreciation. In part, the law is purposely structured in this way to encourage people to invest in real estate.

Proceeds of sale

In this next step in his evaluation of the Campus Oaks Apartments, Jack must estimate the net proceeds he will receive when he sells the property. For purposes of this analysis, Jack has assumed a five-year holding period. Now he must forecast a selling price for the property; from that amount, he must subtract selling expenses, the outstanding balance on the mortgage, and applicable federal income taxes. The remainder equals Jack's after-tax net proceeds of sale. These calculations are shown in Table 16.8.

Jack wants to estimate his net proceeds from sale conservatively. He believes that, at a minimum, market forces will push up the selling price of the property at the rate of 5 percent per year beyond his assumed purchase price of $245,000.

TABLE 16.7 CASH FLOW ANALYSIS, CAMPUS OAKS APARTMENTS, 1984–1988

	1984	1985	1986	1987	1988
INCOME TAX COMPUTATIONS					
NOI	$22,822	$24,419	$26,128	$27,957	$29,914
− Interest*	20,350	20,259	20,146	20,022	19,877
− Depreciation**	21,600	18,000	16,200	14,400	12,600
Taxable income (loss)	($19,128)	($13,840)	($10,218)	($ 6,465)	($ 2,563)
Marginal tax rate	.40	.40	.40	.40	.40
Taxes (−) or tax savings (+)	+$7,651	+$5,536	+$4,087	+$2,586	+$1,025
AFTER-TAX CASH FLOW (ATCF) COMPUTATIONS					
NOI	$22,822	$24,419	$26,128	$27,957	$29,914
− Mortgage payment	21,280	21,280	21,280	21,280	21,280
Before-tax cash flow	$ 1,542	$ 3,139	$ 4,848	$ 6,677	$ 8,634
+ Tax savings	7,651	5,536	4,087	2,586	1,025
After-tax cash flow (ATCF)	$ 9,193	$ 8,675	$ 8,935	$ 9,263	$ 9,659

$$\text{Average annual after-tax cash flow } (\overline{CF}) = \frac{\$9,193 + \$8,675 + \$8,935 + \$9,263 + \$9,659}{5} = \underline{\$9,145}$$

*Based on $185,000 mortgage at 11%, compounded annually. Some rounding has been used.

**Based on 15-year accelerated cost recover system (ACRS) and a depreciable basis of $180,000. Land value is assumed to equal $65,000.

Thus, he estimates the selling price in 5 years to be $312,620; he does this by multiplying the $245,000 by the compound-value interest factor of 1.276 from Appendix B, Table B.1 for 5 percent and 5 years (i.e., $245,000 × 1.276 = $312,620). Making the indicated deductions from the forecasted selling price, Jack computes an after-tax net proceeds from the sale equal to $63,099.

Discounted cash flow

In this step, Jack discounts the projected cash flows to their present value. In making this calculation (see Table 16.9), Jack finds that at his required rate of return of 15 percent, the net present value of these flows equals $1,894. Looked at another way, the present value of the amounts Jack forecasts he will receive exceeds the amount of his initial investment by nearly $1,900. The investment therefore meets (and exceeds) his acceptance criterion.

Approximate yield

Alternatively, the approximate yield formula could be applied using the initial equity, I_0, of $60,000, along with the average annual after-tax cash flow, $\overline{CF}$, of $9,145

TABLE 16.8 ESTIMATED AFTER-TAX NET PROCEEDS FROM SALE, CAMPUS OAKS APARTMENTS, 1988

INCOME TAX COMPUTATION

Forecasted selling price (at 5% annual appreciation)	$312,620
− Selling expenses at 7%	21,883
− Book value (purchase price less accumulated depreciation)	97,200
Gain on sale	$193,537
× Tax rate on gain*	25%
Taxes payable	$ 48,384

COMPUTATION OF AFTER-TAX NET PROCEEDS

Forecasted selling price	$312,620
− Selling expenses	21,883
− Mortgage balance outstanding	179,254
Net proceeds before taxes	$111,483
− Taxes payable (calculated above)	48,384
After-tax net proceeds of sale ($CF_{R_{1988}}$)	$ 63,099

*Assumed at 25 percent. The actual calculation is beyond the scope of this discussion; in practice, this important matter should be taken up with a reputable tax accountant or attorney.

(calculated at the bottom of Table 16.7) and the after-tax net proceeds of sale, $CF_{R_{1988}}$, of $63,099 (calculated in Table 16.8). Substituting these values into the approximate yield formula presented earlier gives:

$$\text{approximate yield} = \frac{\overline{CF} + \dfrac{CF_{R_n} - I_0}{n}}{\dfrac{CF_{R_n} + I_0}{2}}$$

$$= \frac{\$9,145 + \dfrac{\$63,099 - \$60,000}{5}}{\dfrac{\$63,099 + \$60,000}{2}} = \frac{\$9,145 + \$620}{\$61,550}$$

$$= \frac{\$9,765}{\$61,550} = \underline{15.9\%}$$

Since the approximate yield of 15.9 percent is in excess of Jack's required rate of return of 15 percent, the investment meets (and exceeds) his acceptance criterion. Although we have merely approximated his return here, this technique, when consistently applied, should always result in the same conclusion as to acceptability as that obtained using net present value.

TABLE 16.9   NET PRESENT VALUE, CAMPUS OAKS APARTMENTS*

$$NPV = \left[\frac{CF_1}{(1 + r)^1} + \frac{CF_2}{(1 + r)^2} + \frac{CF_3}{(1 + r)^3} + \frac{CF_4}{(1 + r)^4} \right.$$
$$\left. + \frac{CF_5 + CF_{R_5}}{(1 + r)^5} \right] - I_0$$

$$NPV = \left[\frac{\$9,193}{(1 + .15)^1} + \frac{\$8,675}{(1 + .15)^2} + \frac{\$8,935}{(1 + .15)^3} + \frac{\$9,263}{(1 + .15)^4} \right.$$
$$\left. + \frac{\$72,758^{**}}{(1 + .15)^5} \right] - \$60,000$$

$$NPV^{***} = \$7,998 + \$6,558 + \$5,879 + \$5,298 + \$36,161 - \$60,000$$

$$NPV = \$61,894 - \$60,000$$

$$NPV = \underline{+\$1,894}$$

*All inflows are assumed to be end-of-period receipts.
**Includes both the 5th year annual after-tax cash flow of $9,659 and the after-tax net proceeds of sale of $63,099.
***Calculated using present-value interest factors from Appendix B, Table B.3.

Synthesis and Interpretation

Now comes the time for Jack to review his work. He evaluates his market analysis, checks all the facts and figures in the investment return calculations, and then evaluates the results in light of his stated financial and nonfinancial objectives. He must ask himself: All things considered, is the expected payoff worth the risk? In this case, he decides it is. The property looks good. Even a positive finding, though, does not necessarily mean Jack should buy this property. He might still want to shop around to see if he can locate an even better investment. Also, he might be wise to hire a real estate appraiser to confirm that the price he is willing to pay seems reasonable with respect to the recent sales prices of similar properties in the market area. Nevertheless, being an academic, Jack realizes that any problem can be studied to death; no one ever can obtain all the information that will bear on a decision. He gives himself a week to investigate other properties and talk to a professional appraiser. If nothing turns up to cause him second thoughts, he decides that he will offer to buy the Campus Oaks Apartments. On the terms presented, he is willing to pay up to a maximum price of $245,000.

SUMMARY

The purpose of this chapter has been to give you an overview of real estate investment analysis. The discussions have focused on a framework—or conceptual checklist—of the key factors that influence real estate values. By logically applying the analysis, you should be able to make better real estate investment decisions.

The starting point for real estate investment analysis is setting objectives. Real estate can be extremely safe or highly speculative; can involve an equity or debt investment; and can involve an individual or a group investment, such as a real estate investment trust or limited partnership. It can provide annual income, with apartment buildings, office complexes, and retail space; or it can result in negative annual cash flows, as with raw land. So it is imperative that you decide what route is best for you. Next, you need to fix the scope of your analysis. This means you should accurately identify the physical property you are considering and the quality of its associated legal rights and obligations. You should also determine what time period and geographic area are relevant to your analysis.

The four determinants of value—demand, supply, the property, and the transfer process—form the basis for most real estate analyses. Demand refers to those factors that contribute to people's willingness and ability to buy (or rent), and supply includes all those properties from which potential buyers or tenants can choose. To analyze a property, you need to evaluate applicable restrictions on its use; its location, site characteristics, and improvements; and how the property can best be managed. The transfer process includes getting information about a property to the market, and negotiating the transfer contracts (sales contracts and leases).

With an analysis of the four determinants of value completed, you then can use a market value appraisal or investment cash flow analysis to estimate value. Market value appraisals rely on the cost approach, the comparative sales approach, and the income approach. Some people use an expert to prepare or substantiate their market analyses. Investment returns can be assessed by forecasting cash flows and calculating either the net present value or the approximate yield. By applying these techniques to market-derived data, you can assess whether a selected real estate investment is right for you. Of course, you must consider the risk involved, which can be altered depending on the degree of leverage employed in financing a real estate investment. The quantitative analysis must then be integrated with various subjective and market considerations to make the final investment decision.

KEY TERMS

after-tax cash flow (ATCF)
approximate yield
capitalization rate
comparative sales approach
cost approach
demand
demographics
depreciation
discounted cash flow
esthetic environment
fiscal environment
improvements
income approach
income property
investment analysis
legal environment
leverage (positive or negative)

limited partnership
location
market value
natural environment
net operating income (NOI)
net present value (NPV)
personal property
personal residence
principle of substitution
psychographics
real estate investment trust (REIT)
socioeconomic environment
speculative property
substitution principle
supply
tax shelter
transfer process

REVIEW QUESTIONS

1. Why should real estate investment analysis start with a definition of objectives?

2. How can adding real estate to your investment portfolio decrease your overall risk? Explain.

3. Define and differentiate between (a) personal residences, (b) income properties, and (c) speculative properties.

4. Briefly describe and compare the following forms of group ownership of real estate: (a) real estate investment trusts (REITs) and (b) limited partnerships.

5. Which are most important when considering real estate investments, financial or nonfinancial considerations?

6. What is the difference between real estate and personal property? Discuss why this difference is important to real estate investors.

7. Demand is often shown on a graph as a downward-sloping curve. For purposes of real estate analysis, what does such a curve actually reflect?

8. Supply is often shown on a graph as an upward-sloping curve. For purposes of real estate analysis, what does such a curve actually reflect?

9. Are real estate markets efficient? Why or why not?

10. Comment on the following: Market value is always the price at which a property sells.

11. Why is property management important to a real estate investor?

12. Briefly describe each of the three approaches commonly used by real estate appraisers to estimate the market value of investment properties.

13. Real estate investments can be structured to meet a variety of investment goals. Explain various investment needs and the types of properties that best meet them.

14. Charles Cook, an investor, is considering two alternative financing plans for purchasing a parcel of real estate costing $50,000. Alternative X involves paying cash; alternative Y involves obtaining 80 percent financing at 10.5 percent interest. If the parcel of real estate appreciates in value by $7,500 in one year, calculate: (a) Charles's net return and (b) his return on equity for each alternative. If the value dropped by $7,500, what effect would this have on your answers to (a) and (b)?

15. Define tax depreciation. Explain why it is said to provide tax shelter potential. What real estate investments provide this benefit? Explain.

16. Define: (a) net operating income (NOI) and (b) after-tax cash flow (ATCF) as they apply to income from rental properties.

17. In the coming year, Nicki Gressis expects a potential rental property investment costing $120,000 to have gross potential rental income of $20,000, vacancy and collection losses equaling 5 percent of gross income, and operating expenses of $10,000. The mortgage on the property is expected to require annual payments of $8,500. The interest portion of the mortgage payments as well as depreciation is given below for each of the next three years. Nicki is in the 35-percent marginal tax bracket.

Year	Interest	Depreciation
1	$8,300	$7,000
2	8,200	7,000
3	8,100	7,000

The net operating income is expected to increase by 6 percent each year beyond the first year.

    a. Calculate the net operating income (NOI) for each of the next three years.

    b. Calculate the after-tax cash flow (ATCF) for each of the next three years.

18. Bob Lanigan is contemplating selling rental property originally costing $200,000. He believes that it has appreciated in value at an annual rate of 6 percent over its four-year holding period. He will have to pay a commission equal to 5 percent of the sale price to sell the property. Currently, the property has a book value of $155,000. The mortgage balance outstanding at the time of sale (currently) is $175,000. Bob will have to pay an 18-percent tax on any capital gains.

    a. Calculate the tax payable on the proposed sale.
    b. Calculate the after-tax net proceeds associated with the proposed sale, CF_R.

19. Mary Scott has estimated the annual after-tax cash flows (ATCFs) and after-tax net proceeds from sale (CF_R) of a proposed real estate investment as noted below for the planned four-year ownership period.

Year	ATCF	CF_R
1	$6,200	
2	8,000	
3	8,300	
4	8,500	
4		$59,000

The initial required investment in the property is $55,000. Mary, at minimum, must earn 14 percent on the investment.

    a. Calculate the net present value (NPV) of the proposed investment.
    b. Calculate the approximate yield from the investment.
    c. From your findings in a and b what recommendations would you give Mary? Explain.

20. Explain why, in spite of being acceptable based on NPV or approximate yield, a real estate investment might still not be acceptable to a given investor.

CASE PROBLEMS

16.1 SAUL GOLDMAN'S APPRAISAL OF THE ROYALTY ARMS APARTMENTS

Saul Goldman wants to estimate the market value of the Royalty Arms Apartments, an 18-unit building with nine 1-bedroom units and nine 2-bedroom units. The present owner of Royalty Arms provided Saul with the following income statement. Today's date is March 1, 1984.

**OWNER'S INCOME STATEMENT,
ROYALTY ARMS APARTMENTS, 1983**

Gross income		$65,880
Less: Expenses		
Utilities	$14,260	
Property insurance	2,730	
Repairs and maintenance	1,390	
Property taxes	4,790	
Mortgage payments	18,380	
Total expenses		41,550
Net income		$24,330

Current rental rates of properties similar to Royalty Arms typically run from $300 to $315 per month for 1-bedroom units and $340 to $360 per month for 2-bedroom units. From a study of the market, Saul determined that a reasonable market capitalization rate for Royalty Arms would be 9.62 percent, and that vacancy rates for comparable apartment buildings are running around 4 percent.

Questions

1. Using Figure 16.2 as a guide, discuss how you might go about evaluating the features of this property.

2. Saul has studied economics and knows all about demand and supply; yet he doesn't understand how to apply it. Advise Saul in a practical way how he might incorporate demand and supply into an investment analysis of the Royalty Arms Apartments.

3. Should Saul accept the owner's income statement as the basis for an income appraisal of Royalty Arms? Why or why not?

4. In your opinion, what is a reasonable estimate of the market value for the Royalty Arms?

5. If Saul could buy Royalty Arms for $10,000 less than its market value, would it be a good buy for him? Explain.

16.2 ANALYZING DR. DAVIS'S PROPOSED REAL ESTATE INVESTMENT

Dr. Marilyn Davis, a 34-year-old, single heart specialist, is considering the purchase of a small office building. She wants to add some diversity to her investment portfolio, which now contains only corporate bonds and preferred stocks. In addition, because of her high tax bracket of 55 percent (federal, state, and local), Marilyn wants an investment that produces a good after-tax rate of return.

A real estate market and financial consultant has estimated that Marilyn could buy the office building for $200,000. In addition, this consultant analyzed the property's rental potential with respect to trends in demand and supply. He discussed the following items with Marilyn. (1) The office building was occupied by two tenants who each had three years remaining on their leases. (2) It was only four years old, was in excellent condition, and was located near a number of major thoroughfares. For her purposes, Marilyn decided the building should be analyzed on the basis of a three-year holding period. The gross rents in the most recent year were $32,000, and operating expenses were $15,000. The consultant pointed out that the leases had built-in 10 percent per year rent escalation clauses and that he expected operating expenses to increase by 8 percent per year. He further expected no vacancy or collection loss because both tenants were excellent credit risks.

Marilyn's accountant estimated that annual depreciation, using the most advantageous method, would be as follows for each of the next three years:

Year	Depreciation
1	$10,000
2	9,600
3	9,100

To finance the purchase of the building Marilyn has considered a variety of alternatives, one of which would involve assuming the existing $120,000 mortgage. Upon the advice of a close friend, a finance professor at the local university, Marilyn decided to arrange a $150,000, 10.5 percent, 25-year mortgage from the bank at which she maintains her business account. The annual loan payment would total $17,000. Of this, the following breakdown between interest and principal would apply in each of the first three years:

Year	Interest	Principal	Total
1	$15,750	$1,250	$17,000
2	15,620	1,380	17,000
3	15,470	1,530	17,000

The loan balance at the end of the three years would be $145,840. The consultant expects the property to appreciate by about 9 percent per year to $260,000 at the end of three years. Taxes on this gain will be approximately $14,000, and Marilyn will incur a 5 percent sales commission expense.

Questions

1. What is the expected annual after-tax cash flow (ATCF) for each of the three years?

2. At a 10 percent discount rate, will this investment produce a positive net present value?

3. What rate of return does the approximate yield formula show for this proposed investment?

4. Could Marilyn increase her returns by assuming the existing mortgage at a 9.75 percent interest rate, rather than arranging a new loan? What measure of return do you believe Marilyn should use to make this comparison?

5. Do you believe Marilyn has thought about her real estate investment objectives enough? Why or why not?

SELECTED READINGS

Carter, Malcolm N. "Getting Bargain Houses on the Auction Block." *Money,* March 1982, pp. 114–115.

"Exchanging Real Estate Can Save Taxes." *Changing Times,* September 1981, pp. 49–50.

"For Sale: Foreclosed Property." *Changing Times,* December 1982, pp. 48–51.

Hall, Craig. "Running Up Profits from Run-Down Buildings." *Money,* March 1979, pp. 49–52.

Harris, Marlys. "The Many Happy Returns on Commercial Property." *Money,* March 1979, pp. 53–55.

Hatfield, Weston. *The Weekend Real Estate Investor.* New York: McGraw-Hill, 1978.

Hedberg, Augustin. "Avoiding the Perils of Seller Financing." *Money,* July 1982, pp. 52–53.

Nossiter, Daniel D. "Building Values: REITs Adapt to Changes in the Business Climate." *Barron's,* November 1, 1982, pp. 11, 34, 35.

"REIT's Seem Ripe for a Rebound." *Changing Times,* January 1983, pp. 32–34.

Runde, Robert. "A Buyer's Guide to the New Mortgages." *Money,* July 1982, pp. 44–50.

Saporito, Bill. "Tapping Your Home Equity." *Money,* June 1983, pp. 167–172.

Sivy, Michael. "Investing in Condomania." *Money,* May 1981, pp. 59–62.

———. "Putting Money into the Boom Regions." *Money,* February 1981, pp. 74–84.

"10 Costly Mistakes Real Estate Investors Make." *Changing Times,* October 1981, pp. 60–62.

"Timely Tips for Real Estate Investors." *Changing Times,* October 1982, pp. 55–60.

Wofford, Larry E. *Real Estate,* rev. ed. New York: Wiley, 1983.

17
Tax-Sheltered Investments

The federal government is an important partner in your investment activities. Despite recent tax cuts, the federal taxes on investment income can still amount to as much as 50 percent of your pretax returns. Simply stated, the government could get an equal share of your gains—or absorb half of your losses. With a stake this high, effective tax planning is essential. Since the tax law does not treat all investment income equally, the goal of this chapter is to describe how the tax laws generally function and what specific investments bring special tax advantages. The following are key areas in the discussion:

1. What is meant by taxable income and how it is calculated.
2. The difference between tax avoidance and tax deferral and the nature of a tax shelter.
3. How investors can earn tax-favored income, with particular emphasis on income excluded from taxation, strategies that defer tax liabilities, and strategies that pay-off in long-term capital gains.
4. The characteristics of deferred annuities, their use in retirement plans, and their appeal as investment vehicles.
5. The nature of the limited partnership as an organizational form and why and how it is used to gain tax write-offs.
6. The specific types of limited partnerships available to investors—how they work, their use of leverage, their risk-return characteristics, and investment suitability.

It is often said that the necessities of life include food, clothing, and shelter. Shelter is important because it protects us from the elements—rain, wind, snow or extreme heat or cold—in the physical environment. In a similar fashion, investors need shelter from the high taxes charged on earnings. Without adequate protection, the returns earned by an investor can be greatly reduced by the ravages of the IRS. Thus, in making investment decisions we must assess not only risk and return, but also the tax effects associated with a given investment vehicle or strategy. Since the tax effects depend on one's "tax bracket" as well as the specific form of the return— ordinary income (loss) versus capital gains (loss)—it is important to choose vehicles that provide the maximum after-tax return for a given risk. A common stock paying high dividends may not be appropriate for an investor in the 50 percent federal tax bracket, just as a real estate limited partnership providing several thousand dollars of losses may be inappropriate for a person with little or no tax liability. An awareness of the various methods and vehicles available for legally reducing one's tax liability and an understanding of the role such vehicles can play in a portfolio is fundamental to obtaining the highest after-tax returns for a given level of risk. Let us begin by looking at tax fundamentals and shelters.

TAX FUNDAMENTALS AND SHELTERS

As currently structured, federal income tax law imposes increasingly higher tax burdens on higher taxable incomes. This is done through a *progressive tax rate* structure, meaning that as income (the tax base) rises, so does the tax rate. For instance, a single investor earning $16,000 in 1983 would pay additional taxes of $240 if his or her income increased by $1,000 to $17,000; but if the investor's income was $32,000 to start with, the additional tax would have been $360 on an additional $1,000 of income. In the first case, the marginal tax rate is 24 percent ($240/$1,000); in the second case, it is 36 percent ($360/$1,000). You not only pay more taxes as your taxable income increases, you pay progressively more. Table 17.1 illustrates the progressive nature of the tax rates for both single taxpayers and married taxpayers filing jointly. Notice how the marginal rates increase as taxable income increases. You might also notice that the $32,000 taxable income, while twice as much as the $16,000 taxable income, pays over three times as much tax: $7,197 versus $2,337.

The goal of *tax planning* is to seek investment income that is not included as taxable income, or is included at a reduced amount. An even more rewarding strategy is to find investments that actually save taxes by reducing other taxable income. For example, if the investor above in the 36 percent tax bracket could invest in a vehicle that reduces his or her taxable income by $1,000, it would offer an immediate return of $360 regardless of any other return potential it might have. Investment vehicles such as this are called tax shelters, and they are obviously important to investors in high tax brackets. Before examining them, though, we need to review the basic structure of the federal personal income tax, which is also summarized in Chapter 6.

Taxable Income

Taxable income, as its name implies, is the income to which tax rates are applied. From an investments perspective, it includes such items as cash dividends, interest, profits from a sole proprietorship or share in a partnership, and gains from

TABLE 17.1 TAX RATES FOR SINGLE TAXPAYERS AND MARRIED TAXPAYERS FILING JOINTLY (1983)

SINGLE TAXPAYERS

| TAXABLE INCOME | | Marginal Tax Rates | Of the Amount Over |
Over	But not Over		
$0	$2,300	—	
2,300	3,400	11%	$2,300
3,400	4,400	$121 + 13%	3,400
4,400	8,500	251 + 15%	4,400
8,400	10,800	866 + 17%	8,500
10,800	12,900	1,257 + 19%	10,800
12,900	15,000	1,656 + 21%	12,900
15,000	18,200	2,097 + 24%	15,000
18,200	23,500	2,865 + 28%	18,200
23,500	28,800	4,349 + 32%	23,500
28,000	34,100	6,045 + 36%	28,800
34,100	41,500	7,953 + 40%	34,100
41,500	55,300	10,913 + 45%	41,500
55,300	—	17,123 + 50%	55,300

Tax bracket for $16,000 taxable income; tax due = $2,097 + .24 ($16,000 − $15,000) = $2,097 + $240 = $2,337

Tax bracket for $32,000 taxable income; tax due = $6,045 + .36 ($32,000 − $28,800) = $6,045 + $1,152 = $7,197

MARRIED TAXPAYERS FILING JOINTLY

| TAXABLE INCOME | | Marginal Tax Rates | Of the Amount Over |
Over	But not Over		
$0	$3,400	—	
3,400	5,500	11%	$3,400
5,500	7,600	$231 + 13%	5,500
7,600	11,900	504 + 15%	7,600
11,900	16,000	1,149 + 17%	11,900
16,000	20,200	1,846 + 19%	16,000
20,200	24,600	2,644 + 23%	20,200
24,600	29,900	3,656 + 26%	24,600
29,900	35,200	5,034 + 30%	29,900
35,200	45,800	6,624 + 35%	35,200
45,800	60,000	10,334 + 40%	45,800
60,000	85,600	16,014 + 44%	60,000
85,600	109,400	27,278 + 48%	85,600
109,400	—	38,702 + 50%	109,400

Source: Adapted from U.S. Department of the Treasury, Internal Revenue Service, *1983 Federal Income Tax Forms.* Washington, D.C.: U.S. Government Printing Office, 1983.

the sale of securities or other assets. The tax law makes an important distinction between ordinary income and capital gains.

Ordinary income

Broadly, *ordinary income* is any compensation received for labor services provided or from invested capital. Actually, the form in which the income is received is immaterial. For example, if you owe a debt to someone and that person forgives the debt, this could wind up in taxable income to you depending on how the debt was initially created and treated for tax purposes in previous periods. Situations such as this sometimes arise in real estate tax shelters. As a general rule, *any event that increases your net worth is income, and unless it is specifically excluded from taxable income or considered a capital gain, it is ordinary income.*

Capital gains and losses

The tax law gives special treatment to gains or losses resulting from the sale of capital assets. A *capital asset* is defined as anything you own and use for personal purposes, pleasure, or investment. A house and a car are capital assets; so are stamp collections, bonds, and shares of common stock. Your *basis* in a capital asset usually means what you paid for it, including commissions and other costs related to the purchase. If an asset is sold for a price greater than its basis, a *capital gain* is the result; if the reverse is true, then you have a *capital loss*. If the asset was held for a year or longer prior to its sale, the gain or loss is *long term*; if it was held for less than a year, the gain or loss is *short term*.

The distinction between long and short term is crucial, since long-term gains and losses are treated differently from short-term gains and losses. All short-term gains are included in full as a part of ordinary income whereas only 40 percent of long-term gains are included (60 percent are therefore excluded). Moreover, only 50 percent of long-term losses can be deducted from ordinary income, whereas all short-term losses are deductible. In either case, though, the maximum deduction in any one year is $3,000; but if losses exceed this amount, they can be carried forward to future years and then deducted. (Managing the sale of securities to optimize the tax treatment of capital gains and losses is a crucial part of tax planning and is treated more thoroughly later in the chapter.)

Determining Taxable Income

Determining taxable income involves a series of steps. Since these are illustrated more clearly with an example, let us consider the 1983 income tax situation of the Edward and Martha Meyer family—a family of four. In 1983, the family had the following income items:

1. Wages and salaries—Edward $25,000
  —Martha 19,000
2. Dividends on common stock (owned jointly) 600
3. Interest on municipal bonds 400
4. Interest on savings accounts 900

    5. Capital gains on securities held—6 months   300
                            —15 months   1,500
    6. Net loss on a rental property
        (the loss includes $2,000 of depreciation expense)   (1,200)

The family also had the following deductions in 1983:

    1. Contributions to IRA accounts—Edward $ 2,000
                                —Martha   2,000
    2. Allowable itemized deductions for contributions, medical expenses,
        and other   3,000
    3. Interest on home mortgage loan and margin account with stock-
        broker   6,000
    4. Costs related to investment seminar ($250) and subscriptions to
        investment periodicals ($150)   400

The Meyers' income tax due for 1983 was $4,426, as determined in Table 17.2 and explained below.

Gross income

    Gross income begins with all includable income, but then allows certain exclusions that are provided in the tax law. Table 17.2 shows that in the Meyers' case, all income is included except interest on the municipal bonds, which is not subject to federal income tax. Notice that interest on their savings accounts is included in full (this will change in 1985), and that $200 of dividend income is excluded. Observe also that all short-term capital gains but only $600 (.4 × $1,500) of long-term capital gains are included. And although the Meyers' investment property reduced their taxable income by $1,200, the loss is not a cash loss; in fact, there is actually a positive cash flow of $800 from the property—the $1,200 loss plus $2,000 of depreciation. This treatment would be the same for other noncash items such as amortization of intangible assets, or depletion allowed on wasting assets such as oil wells or mineral deposits.

Adjustments to gross income

    These items reflect the intent of Congress to favor certain activities. Those shown for the Meyers (there are others) are contributions to their IRAs (see Chapter 7 for discussion of IRAs)—each invested the maximum $2,000—and the deduction for a married working couple. This latter item is figured at 10 percent of the spouse's lower income, up to a maximum of $3,000. Martha's income of $19,000 was the lower, so the deduction is $1,900. You should note the tax-sheltering quality of the IRAs; without them, the Meyers' would have paid taxes on an additional $4,000 of income in 1983.

Adjusted gross income

    Subtracting the total adjustments from gross income provides *adjusted gross income.* It is a necessary figure in calculating certain deductions (such as medical

TABLE 17.2 DETERMINING 1983 FEDERAL INCOME TAXES DUE FOR THE EDWARD AND MARTHA MEYER FAMILY

I. GROSS INCOME		
1. Wages and salaries ($25,000 + $19,000)		$44,000
2. Dividends	$600	
Less exclusion	200	400
3. Interest on savings account		900
4. Capital gains: short term	$300	
long term (.4 × $1,500)	600	900
5. Net loss on rental property		(1,200)
Gross income		$45,000

II. ADJUSTMENTS TO GROSS INCOME	
1. Contributions to IRAs ($2,000 + $2,000)	$ 4,000
2. Married couple deduction (.10 × $19,000)	1,900
Total adjustments to gross income	$ 5,900

III. ADJUSTED GROSS INCOME (I − II) = ($45,000 − $5,900)	$39,100

IV. ITEMIZED DEDUCTIONS	
1. Contributions, medical expenses, and others	$ 3,000
2. Interest on home mortgage loan and margin account	6,000
3. Investment seminar ($250) and periodicals costs ($150)	400
Total itemized deductions	$ 9,400
Less: Zero bracket amount	3,400
Excess itemized deductions	$ 6,000

V. EXEMPTIONS Edward, Martha, and two children (4 × $1,000)	$ 4,000

VI. TAXABLE INCOME (III − IV − V) = ($39,100 − $6,000 − $4,000)	$29,100

VII. FEDERAL INCOME TAX (per rate schedule)	$ 4,826

VIII. TAX CREDITS (investment tax credit)	$ 400

IX. TAXES DUE (VII − VIII) = ($4,826 − $400)	$ 4,426

expenses) not illustrated in our example. The Meyers' adjusted gross income is $39,100.

Itemized deductions

Many different items qualify as *itemized deductions,* but we are emphasizing those specifically related to investments. The deductibility of interest favors the use of debt to finance investment activities. All other things being equal, there is a tax advantage to home ownership, as shown by the deduction of interest on the home mortgage loan. Margin interest is also less expensive on an after-tax basis. Any expense you incur to improve your investment returns is also deductible. Along this line, Martha deducted $200 in tuition charges for an investments seminar she attended at a local university along with related travel expenses of $50; the Meyers also paid subscriptions of $150 for periodicals dealing with investments. Notice that only deductions in excess of a minimum amount—called the *zero bracket amount*—can be deducted. The zero bracket amount on a joint return in 1983 was $3,400; it was $2,300 for a single return.

Exemptions

The tax law allows a $1,000 deduction, called an *exemption,* for each qualifying dependent. There are specific rules for determining who qualifies as a dependent, and these should be reviewed if the potential dependent is not your child or an immediate member of your family residing in your home. Table 17.2 shows that the Meyers claimed four exemptions.

Taxable income

Deducting excess deductions and exemptions from adjusted gross income leaves *taxable income*; in the Meyers' case, it is $29,100. If the Meyers had not itemized, they would have calculated their tax by referring to an appropriate tax-rate table. You can use Table 17.1 to calculate the tax due for the Meyers. Since their taxable income is $29,100, this puts them in the income bracket $24,600 to $29,900. Thus, their tax is $3,656 plus 0.26 ($29,100 minus $24,600) = $3,656 plus 0.26 ($4,500) = $3,656 plus $1,170 = $4,826. The Meyers pay a 26 percent *marginal tax rate,* which means the tax rate on additional income is 26 percent. However, their income is very close to the next bracket, which is the 30 percent marginal rate. *It is the marginal tax rate that should be considered in evaluating the tax implications of an investment strategy.* By all means, do not confuse the marginal rate with the average rate. The *average tax rate* is simply their taxes divided by taxable income. The Meyers' average tax rate is 16.6 percent ($4,826/$29,100), which has absolutely no relevance to their investment decision making.

Tax credits

Many different kinds of *tax credits* are available. They are particularly attractive, since they reduce taxes on a dollar-for-dollar basis, in contrast to a deduction that only reduces taxes by an amount determined by the marginal tax rate. A credit related to investment activities is the *investment tax credit,* which applies to property purchased and used in a trade or business. There are rules to consult to determine qualifying property and allowable limits; in the Meyers' case, it is assumed that they earned a $400 investment tax credit from the purchase of assets for their rental property.

Taxes due or refund

The final amount of tax due is determined by subtracting the tax credits from the income tax. The Meyers' taxes due are $4,426. They now compare this amount to the amount of tax withheld (indicated on their year-end withholding statements) and any estimated taxes they may have paid during 1983. If these two add to more than $4,426, they are entitled to a refund of the difference; if the total is less than $4,426, they must pay the difference at the time they file their 1983 federal income tax return.

The alternative minimum tax

As a result of many taxpayers effectively using tax shelters to reduce their taxable incomes to near zero, in 1982 Congress strengthened the tax law to make every taxpayer pay at least a 20 percent rate on what is called *alternative minimum taxable income (AMTI)*. AMTI begins with adjusted gross income, as illustrated above, but then disallows certain deductions, such as the dividend exclusion and the long-term capital gain deduction. There are other deductions as well, and the procedures for determining the tax due are quite complicated. A tax expert should be consulted if you feel the alternative minimum tax might apply in your situation.

Tax Avoidance and Tax Deferral

A comprehensive tax strategy attempts to maximize the total after-tax income of an investor over his or her lifetime. This objective is accomplished by avoiding taxable income altogether, or by deferring it to another period when it may receive more favorable tax treatment, either by virtue of a lower tax rate or by converting ordinary income into long-term capital gains. Even when there is no tax reduction by deferral, it still offers the advantage of having the use of saved tax dollars over the deferral period.

Tax avoidance should not be confused with *tax evasion,* which includes illegal activities such as omitting income or overstating deductions. *Tax avoidance* is concerned with reducing or eliminating taxes in perfectly legal ways and complies with the intent of Congress, which wrote the special provisions into the tax law. We have already noted in the Meyers' example, the most popular form of tax avoidance is investing in securities offering tax-favored income. (Sources of tax-favored income will be explained in greater detail in the next section of the chapter.) Another broad approach to avoiding taxes is to distribute income-producing assets to family members (usually children) who either pay no taxes at all or pay them at much lower rates. Since this is also a highly specialized area of the tax law, we do not pursue it further in this text. You should seek professional counsel whenever a tax strategy of this type is contemplated.

Tax deferral deals with ways of delaying taxes, and can be accomplished in a number of ways. The simplest is to use those vehicles designed specifically to accomplish this end; included would be pension and retirement plans, IRAs, and annuities. The retirement vehicles were covered in Chapter 7; annuities are treated later in this chapter. Frequently taxes are deferred for only one year as part of a year-end tax strategy to shift income from one year to the next when it is known that taxable income or tax rates might be lower. This latter situation existed in 1981, 1982, and

BOX 17.1 TAXES IN THE "GOOD OLD DAYS"

Below is a copy of the original Form 1040 from 1913. Note that most Americans then—even the affluent—paid less than 2 percent taxes. Even those earning in excess of $500,000 paid only 6 percent. Can you imagine keeping over 90 percent of your earnings? Sure miss the good old days!

ORIGINAL

1913 INTERNAL REVENUE INCOME TAX RETURN

TO BE FILLED IN BY COLLECTOR	Form 1040.	TO BE FILLED IN BY INTERNAL REVENUE SERVICE
List No.	**INCOME TAX.**	File No. ....
.... District of	THE PENALTY FOR FAILURE TO HAVE THIS RETURN IN THE HANDS OF THE COLLECTOR OF INTERNAL REVENUE ON OR BEFORE MARCH 1 IS $20 TO $1,000. (SEE INSTRUCTIONS ON PAGE 4.)	Assessment List ....
Date received		Page............ Line...........................

UNITED STATES INTERNAL REVENUE.

RETURN OF ANNUAL NET INCOME OF INDIVIDUALS.
(As provided by Act of Congress, approved October 3, 1913.)

RETURN OF NET INCOME RECEIVED OR ACCRUED DURING THE YEAR ENDED DECEMBER 31, 191__
(FOR THE YEAR 1913, FROM MARCH 1, TO DECEMBER 31.)

Filed by (or for) .... of ....
(Full name of individual.)   (Street and No.)

In the City, Town, or Post Office of .... State of ....
(Fill in pages 2 and 3 before making entries below.)

1. GROSS INCOME (see page 2, line 12) .... $ ....

2. GENERAL DEDUCTIONS (see page 3, line 7) .... $ ....

3. NET INCOME .... $ ....

Deductions and exemptions allowed in computing income subject to the normal tax of 1 per cent.

4. Dividends and net earnings received or accrued, of corporations, etc., subject to like tax. (See page 2, line 11) .... $ ....

5. Amount of income on which the normal tax has been deducted and withheld at the source. (See page 2, line 9, column A) ....

6. Specific exemption of $3,000 or $4,000, as the case may be. (See Instructions 3 and 19) .... _____

   Total deductions and exemptions. (Items 4, 5, and 6) .... $ ....

7. TAXABLE INCOME on which the normal tax of 1 per cent is to be calculated. (See Instruction 3) .... $ ....

8. When the net income shown above on line 3 exceeds $20,000, the additional tax thereon must be calculated as per schedule below:

					INCOME.		TAX
1 per cent on amount over $20,000 and not exceeding			$50,000	$		$ ....
2	"	"	50,000	"	"	75,000	....
3	"	"	75,000	"	"	100,000	....
4	"	"	100,000	"	"	250,000	....
5	"	"	250,000	"	"	500,000	....
6	"	"	500,000				....

Total additional or super tax .... $ ....

Total normal tax (1 percent of amount entered on line 7) .... $ ....

Total tax liability .... $ ....

Source: Editorial, Alfred H. Kingon, editor-in-chief, *Financial World,* April 1, 1979, p. 13. Copyright © 1979 by Financial World, Inc.

1983, when tax rates were scheduled downward beginning in 1981 and ending in 1984.

Tax Shelters

A *tax shelter* refers to any investment vehicle that offers potential reductions of taxable income. Usually, this means you must be a direct—rather than indirect—owner of the vehicle. For example, if the Meyers had set up a corporation to own their investment property, rather than owning it directly, the net loss of $1,200 would have been the corporation's, and not theirs. They would have lost the tax deduction (although they could have used another tax strategy—the so called pseudo-corporation—to absorb the loss on their personal return) and the related tax saving. Similarly, when major corporations show huge losses, such as Chrysler's in the early 1980s, these are of no immediate tax benefit to the shareholders. True, the market price of the stock probably falls, which means you could sell it for a tax loss; but this is a capital loss limited to $3,000 a year. If you owned a large amount of stock, your loss might be many times that figure, but it would be of no use in reducing taxes.

Thus, there is a tax advantage in organizing certain activities as sole proprietorships or partnerships, and even more specifically, as limited partnerships. Moreover, activities that lend themselves to this tax structure are those with relatively high risks. If the investment fails, most of the cost can be written off immediately, regardless of the amount. However, not all tax shelters are tied to risky ventures. Some, perhaps the majority, are designed primarily to pass on certain tax deductions, such as depreciation, depletion, and amortization, directly to individuals. An equipment leasing venture, for example, allows individuals to purchase equipment for the tax advantage of rapid depreciation and the investment tax credit, and then lease it to a business that may not have the same tax-saving potential; it might have operating losses, or be in a lower tax bracket. The specific instances in which taxes can be saved through arrangements such as this are almost endless, and there are investment counselors who specialize in setting up tax shelters and bringing together parties who can mutually share the tax savings. The major kinds of tax shelters and the structure of the limited partnership that makes many of these legally feasible will be explained later in this chapter. Now, however, let us turn our attention to those vehicles that offer tax-favored income.

TAX-FAVORED INCOME

If one investment offers a return that is taxed at a rate less than that on other similar investments, it is said to offer *tax-favored income.* These tax "favors" have been written into the tax law to foster or promote certain activities.

Income Excluded from Taxation

Some items are simply excluded from taxation, either totally or partially; these include such items as interest earned on municipal, Treasury, and agency bonds, qualified dividends and net interest, long-term capital gains, and sale of personal residence. Naturally, the sources of such income are particularly attractive vehicles.

Municipal bond interest

Municipal bonds were described in Chapter 11. All interest received from them is free of federal income tax; in fact, it is not even reported on the return. However, any gains or losses resulting from the sale of municipal bonds are included as capital gains or losses. In addition, you cannot deduct interest paid on money borrowed to purchase municipal bonds.

Treasury and government agency issues

These were also discussed in Chapter 11. Although interest on these securities is included on the federal tax return, it is excluded for state and local income tax purposes. Since these combined income tax rates can be as high as 20 percent in some parts of the country, individuals in high tax brackets may find this exclusion worthwhile.

Dividend and net interest exclusion

As noted in the Meyers' case, $200 of dividend income is excluded for a couple filing a joint return. Beginning in 1985, a couple filing a joint return will also be able to deduct up to $900 ($450 for an individual) using the *net interest exclusion,* which is an amount equal to the excess qualified interest income over qualified interest expense. Qualified interest income is interest earned on savings deposits, corporate and Treasury debt issues, real estate investment trusts, regulated investment companies, and others. Qualified interest expense is all deductible interest expense, except for home mortgage interest expense or interest incurred on a trade or business loan. To compute the net interest exclusion, you subtract qualified interest expense (taken as an itemized deduction) from qualified interest income and multiply the difference by 15 percent. You then take either that amount or $900, whichever is less. For example, a joint return with $2,000 of qualified interest income and $400 of qualified interest expense would have a $240 (0.15 × [$2,000 − $400]) exclusion. A taxpayer who does not itemize does not have to net out interest expense. Both the dividend and net interest exclusions are particularly attractive to small investors. It makes sense to seek investment income up to the maximum limits of these shelters.

Long-term capital gains

In many respects, long-term capital gains are the ideal and most sought-after tax shelter. As explained earlier, 60 percent of such gains are excluded from taxation. Therefore, any opportunity to take a profit as a long-term capital gain is highly desirable. Before considering strategies designed to create such opportunities, you need to understand how the income tax applies to all capital gains and losses—short term as well as long term.

Figure 17.1 illustrates the steps you must take to determine capital gains or losses. First, long-term gains are netted against long-term losses to arrive at net long-term gains or losses. The same procedure is followed for short-term gains or losses. Then the net long-term gain or loss is netted against the net short-term gain or loss. Depending upon the magnitude of the total net long- and short-term losses any of four possible tax treatments, as illustrated in Figure 17.1, can result. To further

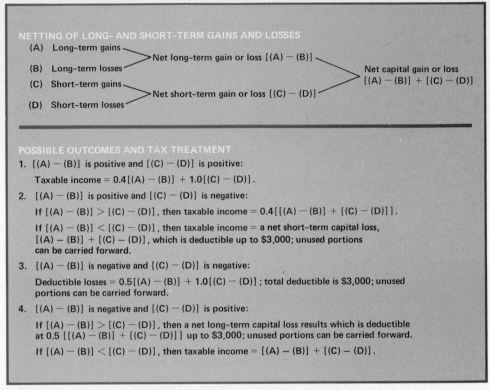

Figure 17.1 Tax Treatment of Capital Gains and Losses.
Once the amount of a net long-term gain or loss or a net short-term gain or loss has been determined, depending upon the magnitude of the total net long- and short-term losses, any of four possible tax situations—each resulting in a different computational scheme—can result. The four possible outcomes and associated tax treatments are shown here.

reinforce your understanding of these possible outcomes, let us assume Sandy Brown had the following capital gains and losses that could have been taken in 1983:

    (A) Long-term gain = $4,000
    (B) Long-term loss = ($2,000)
    (C) Short-term gain = $4,000
    (D) Short-term loss = ($2,000)

If she took all the gains and losses in 1983, her taxable income would have been $2,800, as shown below:

    (A) $4,000
    (B) ($2,000) $0.4 \times \$2,000 = \$\ \ 800$
                                  $\$2,800$
    (C) $4,000
    (D) ($2,000) $1.0 \times \$2,000 = \$2,000$

If Sandy could have timed the execution of her gains and losses, would it have made sense to do so? Yes. To illustrate, suppose she takes only the long-term gain in 1983 and defers the other three transactions to 1984. Then she would have taxable income of:

1983
$4,000 × 0.4 = $\underline{1,600}$

1984
(A) $0 ⟩ ($2,000)
(B)   ($2,000) ⟩ $0
(C) $4,000 ⟩ $2,000
(D)   ($2,000) $\underline{\underline{\$0}}$

So her taxable income for the two years is $1,600 instead of $2,800, a saving of $1,200 made just by timing the execution of her trades.

A careful review of Figure 17.1 indicates that effective capital gain and loss planning involves two simple rules: (1) Take long-term capital gains by themselves—do not offset them with long- or short-term capital losses, or you lose the 60 percent exclusion. (2) Do not take long-term capital losses by themselves, since you lose 50 percent of the possible deduction; instead, offset them against short-term capital gains, since these are taxed in full.

Sale of a personal residence

A capital gain results if you sell your personal residence for a price greater than its basis. However, provisions in the tax law soften the tax impact and actually make an investment in a home an excellent tax shelter. First, if a gain exists from the sale of your home, it can be deferred from taxation if you purchase another home at a price equal to or greater than the price of the home you sold—as long as you buy the other home within 24 months. Second, and the really important tax implication, is that you have a one-time exclusion of $125,000 from gross income from the sale of a personal residence. On a joint return, both spouses must be 55 or older and meet certain other conditions to be eligible for the exclusion. This is a major exclusion for most people and certainly enhances the investment appeal of the personal residence; it is, of course, even better than the 60 percent exclusion available on other long-term capital gains.

Strategies That Defer Tax Liabilities to the Next Year

Very often, an investor may purchase securities and enjoy sizable gains within a relatively short period of time. Suppose you bought 100 shares of NCR common stock in mid-1982; by year-end you would have almost doubled your investment, since the price of this stock increased from $45 a share to around $90. Assume you now believe the stock is fully valued in the market and would prefer to sell it and invest the $9,000 elsewhere. Since the stock has been held only, say, six months, you would be taxed on a short-term gain of $4,500 ($9,000 sale price − $4,500

BOX 17.2 HOW MUCH DO YOU KNOW ABOUT TAXES? A QUIZ

Here is a quiz to test your knowledge of the U.S. tax system. Answers appear below.

1. Why did the U.S. first enact a direct personal income tax?

(a) To raise money for the Civil War. (b) To curtail consumer spending during World War I. (c) To finance recovery from the Depression.

2. What is the top tax rate levied on personal income?

(a) 70 percent. (b) 50 percent. (c) 40 percent.

3. Which of the following could be claimed as an itemized deduction?

(a) Funeral expenses. (b) Suits you wear to work. (c) Birth-control pills.

4. Which itemized deduction saves Americans most in federal tax?

(a) Charitable contributions. (b) State and local income taxes. (c) Home-mortgage interest.

5. Who pays the most tax?

(a) A married couple with $50,000 in taxable income and filing a joint return. (b) A single person with $50,000 in taxable income. (c) Two unmarried people living together and each with $25,000 in taxable income.

6. What percentage of all individual tax returns are audited by the IRS?

(a) Almost 20 percent. (b) About 12 percent. (c) Less than 2 percent.

7. What percentage of people who are indicted for criminal violations of the tax law either plead guilty or are convicted?

(a) About 90 percent. (b) Almost 50 percent. (c) Fewer than 25 percent.

8. What is meant by the progressive-tax system in the U.S.?

(a) Lower-income people are allowed to claim bigger total deductions than upper-income people. (b) Exemptions for dependents are not allowed to families with income exceeding a certain level. (c) As taxable income gets larger, the percentage of income that is paid as tax also grows.

9. Which provision is designed to keep people from being pushed into higher tax-rate brackets by inflation?

(a) Income averaging. (b) Tax indexing. (c) The zero-bracket amount.

10. Which of the following did not go to jail for tax violations?

(a) Al Capone. (b) Spiro Agnew. (c) Bobby Baker.

11. How long must you own stock before profits from its sale qualify for a lower tax as a long-term capital gain?

(a) More than a year. (b) At least six months. (c) Until its value has increased by at least 20 percent.

12. About what share of federal receipts in 1982 was accounted for by the corporate income tax?

(a) 40 percent. (b) 8 percent. (c) 4 percent.

13. Approximately how many people does the IRS employ?

(a) Fewer than 15,000. (b) About 25,000. (c) More than 80,000.

Answers:

1(a) 2(b) 3(c) 4(c) 5(b) 6(c) 7(a) 8(c) 9(b) 10(b) 11(a) 12(b) 13(c)

Source: "How Much Do You Know About Taxes?" *U.S. News & World Report,* April 18, 1983, p. 39.

cost). Assuming a 30 percent tax bracket, this would lead to income taxes of $1,350 on the sale. But if the stock could be held for another six months and still sold at $90 a share, the long-term capital gains tax would be only $540 ($4,500 × 0.4 × 0.3), and you would save $810 ($1,350 − $540) in taxes. The major risk centers on whether or not NCR will still sell for $90 six months later. You may not wish to take this risk.

However, before you sell, there are several factors to consider. The first would be to estimate the amount by which the stock price must decline before you are worse off holding it for an additional six months; that is, the breakeven price. This can be estimated by first determining your after-tax position at the present time, which is $7,650 ($9,000 − $1,350). Then solve for the future price, FP, that leaves you in a position equivalent to your current one. The relationship is set up as follows:

$$\underbrace{\$7,650}_{\substack{\text{present} \\ \text{after-tax} \\ \text{position}}} = \underbrace{100\ FP}_{\substack{\text{what your} \\ \text{stock will} \\ \text{be worth}}} - \underbrace{100\ [(FP - \$45)\ (0.4)\ (0.3)]}_{\substack{\text{taxes you} \\ \text{will pay}}}$$

Solving for FP

$$\$7,650 = 100\ FP - 12\ FP + \$540$$
$$88\ FP = \$7,110$$
$$FP = \underline{\$80.80}$$

Thus the price of NCR must drop by about $9, to $80.80, in order to make it worthwhile to pass up the long-term capital gain. We can check the accuracy of the answer by calculating:

$$\text{proceeds from the sale} = 100 \times \$80.80 = \$8,080$$
$$\text{tax on the sale} = (\$80.80 - \$45.00)\ (100)\ (0.4)\ (0.3) = \$429.60$$
$$\text{after-tax position} = \$8,080 - \$429.60 = \$7,650.40$$

The $0.40 is due to rounding, so we confirm our conclusion that the price of NCR could fall as low as $80.80 a share before you would be worse off holding it for the long-term capital gains treatment rather than selling it now. If you think the price may drop below $80.80 by the end of the six months, then you should sell now; if you feel it will stay above $80.80, you should hold it for an additional six months.

Other techniques are available for locking in the existing $90 price without actually selling the shares and consummating the transaction. There are three common ones: (1) using a short sale against the box, (2) using a put hedge, and (3) selling a deep-in-the-money call option. These strategies either defer the payment of taxes from one year to the next, or convert short-term gains to long-term gains. Let us see how each of these works.

Mr. . . . ah . . . Brother Barnes, isn't it true that your Universal Transmission Church used to be the Barnes Auto Transmission Service?

Short sale against the box

This technique, first presented in Chapter 5, can be used to lock in a profit and defer the taxes on the profit to the next taxable year. By *shorting-against-the-box*— short selling a number of shares equal to what you already own, you lock in an existing profit, which means you eliminate any risk of a price decline. You also give up any future increases in price, but this should not be of concern, since your belief is that the current price is relatively high. For example, to lock in and defer the $4,500 short-term gain on the NCR transaction you would, prior to year-end, sell short 100 shares of NCR. No matter what happens to the price of the stock, you are guaranteed $4,500. You would then have two positions—one long and one short—but both involving an equal number (100) of NCR shares. After year-end you would use the 100 shares held long to close out the short position, thereby realizing the $4,500 short-term capital gain. One precaution should be recognized: *This tactic cannot be used to convert a short-term profit to a long-term capital gain.* Thus, if an investor held the stock for less than a year before shorting-against-the-box, that short-term profit would remain subject to ordinary income tax rates regardless of how long the short position was held; in contrast, if the investor had a long-term capital gain to begin with (held the stock for more than a year before shorting), it remains eligible for the preferential tax treatment accorded such long-term capital gains.

Put hedge

This technique was covered in Chapter 13 where its use in locking in a profit and deferring the taxes on the profit to the next taxable year was discussed. Here we emphasize its use in converting short-term capital gains into long-term capital gains.

Essentially, a *put hedge* involves buying a put option on shares currently owned. If the price of the stock falls, your losses on the shares are offset by a profit on the put option. For example, suppose when NCR was trading at $90 you could have purchased a six-month put option, with a striking price of $90, for $150. You have then locked in a price of $90, because if the price falls, say, to $80 a share, your $1,000 loss on the stock is offset exactly by a $1,000 profit on the option. However, you are still out the cost of the option—$150—but you have extended your holding period for six months, thereby converting a short-term capital gain to a long-term capital gain. At a closing price of $80, this would be your ending after-tax position.

1. Initial cost of 100 shares	$4,500
2. Profit on 100 shares [(100)($80 − $45)]	3,500
3. Profit on the put option	1,000
4. Cost of the put option	150
5. Taxable gain (ordinary income) on put option [(3) − (4)]	$ 850
6. Long-term capital gain tax on stock [($3,500)(0.4)(0.3)]	420
7. Tax on gain from put option ($850 × 0.3)	255
8. After-tax position [(1) + (2) + (5) − (6) − (7)]	$8,175

The final after-tax position here is about the same as if you had simply held the stock while its price declined to around $87 a share, but there are a few important considerations. First, the put hedge locks in this position regardless of how low the price might fall; simply holding the stock does not. Second, any price appreciation will be enjoyed with either approach (notice you do not give up this advantage as you do when shorting-against-the-box). And unlike shorting-against-the-box, you can convert a short-term capital gain to a long-term capital gain with this technique.

Deep-in-the-money call option

Selling a *deep-in-the-money call option* is a strategy similar to the put hedge, but there are important differences: In this case, you give up any potential future price increases and you lock in a price only to the extent of the amount you receive from the sale of the call option. To illustrate, suppose call options on NCR with an $80 striking price and six-month maturity were trading at $1,200 ($12 per share) when NCR was selling for $90. If six months later NCR closed at $80, it would result in this ending after-tax position:

1. Initial cost of 100 shares	$4,500
2. Profit on 100 shares [(100)($80 − $45)]	3,500
3. Profit on the sale of the option; since it closed at the striking price, profit is the total amount received	1,200
4. Long-term capital gain tax on stock [($3,500)(0.4)(0.3)]	$ 420
5. Tax on gain from sale of option ($1,200 × 0.3)	360
6. After-tax position [(1) + (2) + (3) − (4) − (5)]	$8,420

This final after-tax position is better than with the put hedge, but it closes off any price appreciation; in effect, when you sell the call option, you are agreeing to deliver

TABLE 17.3   RANKING OF STRATEGIES TO DEFER TAX LIABILITIES TO THE NEXT YEAR GIVEN DIFFERENT EXPECTATIONS ABOUT THE FUTURE PRICE OF THE STOCK*

Strategy	EXPECTATION OF FUTURE PRICE			
	Price Will Vary by a Small Amount Above or Below Current Price	Price Will Vary by a Large Amount Above or Below Current Price	Future Price Will Be Higher Than Current Price	Future Price Will Be Lower Than Current Price
Do nothing— hold for 6 months	2	4	1	4
Short sale against the box	3+	2+	4	1
Put hedge	3+	1	2	2+
Sell deep-in-the- money call option	1	2+	3	2+

*Ranking: 1, best; 4, worst.

your shares at the option's striking price. So if the price of NCR increases, say, to $100 or beyond, you do not benefit because you have agreed to sell your shares at $80. Furthermore, your downside protection extends only to the amount received for the option—$12 per share. If NCR's price went to $70 you would lose $8 a share before taxes [$90 − ($70 + $12)].

Summary of the strategies

As you can see, deferring tax liabilities to the next year is a potentially rewarding activity requiring analysis of a number of available techniques. The choice can be simplified by considering which method works best given an expectation of the future price behavior of the stock. Table 17.3 summarizes how each strategy performs under different expectations of future price behavior. To complete the analysis you would have to consider commission costs, something we have omitted. Although these can be somewhat high in absolute dollars, they are usually a minor part of the total dollars involved if the potential savings is as large as the ones we have been considering in our examples. However, if the savings is relatively small, say, under $500, then commissions may be disproportionately large in relation to the tax deferral or savings. Clearly, you need to work out the specific figures for each situation.

Strategies that Pay-off in Long-Term Capital Gains

The lower rate of taxation on long-term capital gains as opposed to ordinary income provides a strong incentive to search for ways to realize long-term gains.

From a strict tax viewpoint, whenever there are alternative ways to earn income, those that provide long-term capital gains are preferred. Some of the more common methods for realizing long-term capital gains are described below.

Growth versus income stocks

This is a simple yet basic way to earn capital gain income. Companies that pay out a low percentage of earnings as dividends usually reinvest the retained earnings to take advantage of opportunities. If you select a company that pays dividends that amount to a 10 percent current return on your investment, your after-tax return will be only 7 percent, assuming you are in a 30 percent tax bracket. In comparison, another company that pays no dividends but is expected to experience 10 percent annual growth in its share price from reinvestment of earnings will offer an after-tax rate of return of 8.8 percent $[(1.0 - (0.3 \times 0.4)) \times .10]$. Over a long period of time, the additional 1.8 percent return can significantly increase your wealth.

Public utility dividend reinvestment plans

The 1981 Tax Act gave special tax favor to stockholders of gas and electric public utilities in the form of a *dividend exclusion*. This tax provision has two attractive features. First, it allows a stockholder who chooses to receive dividends in the form of additional shares of common stock rather than cash to exclude from taxable income up to $750 ($1,500 on a joint return) in market value of such dividends received. Secondly, the basis in this new stock is zero, and as a result, a capital gain would be realized on the entire amount received from it when it is later sold. Suppose, for example, you own 1,000 shares of Cincinnati Gas & Electric common stock and the company pays a dividend of $0.50 a share, which you elect to receive in the form of additional shares. You would receive 20 shares if the price of the common was $25 a share at the time the dividend was declared (1,000 shares $\times$ $0.50 per share $=$ $500; $500/$25 per share $=$ 20 shares). You then hold the shares for more than one year and eventually sell them for $25. Your capital gain is $500, and since it is long term, the corresponding tax (assuming a 30 percent tax rate) is only $60 $[(0.3)(0.4)($500)]$ instead of $150 $[(0.3)($500)]$ had you taken the dividends in cash. With this provision, public utility stocks that qualify for the exclusion have considerable investment appeal.

Deep discount bonds

Purchasing a bond that is *selling at a price far below its par value* also offers a long-term capital gain opportunity. To illustrate, suppose you have the choice of buying ABC's bond, which has a coupon rate of 5 percent and is selling for $700 in the market. You could also buy an XYZ bond with a coupon of 10 percent selling at par. Which would you prefer if both mature at the end of 10 years? With the ABC bond, you will earn interest income of $50 a year taxed as ordinary income. At the end of 10 years, you will have a $300 long-term capital gain, but only $120 (40 percent) of it will be taxed as ordinary income. With the XYZ bond, all of your return—that is, the $100 you receive each year—is ordinary income. From a tax perspective, the ABC bond is clearly the better of the two. Remember, though, that the higher-coupon bond is giving you a higher return earlier, and that adds to its attractiveness.

To choose between the two bonds, a rate of return analysis could be performed assuming an equal number of dollars is invested in each bond. For example, an investment of $7,000 would purchase 10 ABC bonds and 7 XYZ bonds. Total annual interest on the ABC bonds would be $500, whereas on the XYZ bonds it would be $700. To an investor in a 30 percent tax bracket, the after-tax advantage of the XYZ bonds is $140 (0.7 × $200) a year. But the ABC bonds will be worth $10,000 at maturity, whereas the XYZ bonds will be worth only their current value of $7,000. On an after-tax basis, the additional $3,000 is worth $2,640 [$3,000 − [(0.4)(0.3)($3,000)]]. The choice boils down to whether you prefer $140 of additional income each year for the next 10 years, or an additional $2,640 at the end of 10 years. Using the future value techniques developed in Chapter 4, you would arrive at the conclusion that it would take about a 13 percent return to make you indifferent between the two bonds; that is, if you invest $140 a year for 10 years at 13 percent, it accumulates to around $2,640 at the end of 10 years. Interpreting this answer, if you can invest at an after-tax rate higher than 13 percent, you should select the XYZ bonds; if you feel your after-tax reinvestment rate will be lower, the ABC bonds should be selected.

Residential income property depreciation

The tax law, as noted in Chapter 16, permits the *depreciation* of residential income property such as apartment houses and similar structures. Essentially, a specified amount of annual depreciation can be deducted from ordinary pretax income. A choice of straight-line depreciation or ACRS depreciation can be made; each of these systems has certain advantages and disadvantages, discussion of which is beyond the scope of this text. Using the simpler straight-line system, if the property is sold after being held for more than one year, any amount received in excess of its book value is treated as a long-term capital gain. For example, assume you buy a duplex for $100,000, hold it for three years, and take $18,000 in depreciation during the period. Now, suppose at the end of the third year you sell it for its original $100,000 purchase price. The depreciation you took reduced ordinary income by $18,000 and was worth $5,400 if you are in a 30 percent tax bracket. Your gain on the sale is also $18,000, but it is a long-term capital gain with a corresponding tax of only $2,160 [($18,000)(0.4)(0.3)]. The net advantage under this arrangement is $3,240. The advantage is even better at higher marginal tax rates; at 50 percent, it is $5,400. This is the primary reason why real estate is often recommended as an investment for people in high tax brackets. Moreover, some deals are structured in advance in such a way that the purchaser of a property is eventually bought out at a set price after a given number of years. Much of the investment return in these deals results from the conversion of ordinary income into long-term capital gains.

To illustrate, suppose a 50 percent tax bracket investor arranged the deal described above by putting down $10,000 and borrowing the balance. Now if his or her cash flows over the three years are sufficient only to service the debt and if there are no other revenues or expenses, the investor would earn a 54 percent return ($5,400/$10,000) over the three-year holding period. Although this is not a spectacular return, remember the property was sold at the same price the investor originally paid. Price appreciation would, of course, increase the rate of return substantially.

Tax Swaps: A Strategy That Reduces or
Eliminates a Tax Liability

Thus far, we have looked at several short-term strategies that are aimed at affecting an investor's tax liability in one way or another, including: (1) ways to defer taxes from one tax year to the next, (2) procedures that convert short-term capital gains to long-term capital gains, and (3) techniques that pay-off in preferential long-term capital gains. Now we will look at a strategy that essentially reduces or eliminates a tax liability altogether. The procedure is known as a tax swap, and is extremely popular at year-end with knowledgeable stock and bond investors. Basically, a *tax swap* is nothing more than the replacement of one security with another for the purpose of partially or fully offsetting a capital gain that has been *realized* in another part of the portfolio. Of course, since we are trying to offset a gain, the security that is sold in a tax swap would be one that has performed poorly to date and, as such, has *lost* money for the investor. Thus, it involves selling one security that has experienced a capital loss and replacing it with another similar security, so that the investor's stock or bond position is essentially unchanged, though his or her tax liability has been reduced—and perhaps substantially so.

A tax swap works like this. Suppose that during the current year you realized a $1,100 long-term capital gain on the sale of bonds. Assume that in your portfolio you held 100 shares of Gulf Oil common stock, purchased 18 months earlier for $40 per share and currently selling for $30 per share. While you wish to maintain an oil stock in your portfolio, it does not matter to you whether you hold Gulf or one of the other multinational oils. To realize the $10 per share long-term capital loss on Gulf while not altering your portfolio, you sell the 100 shares of Gulf and buy 100 shares of Mobil, which is also selling for $30 per share. The result is a *realized* long-term capital loss of $1,000 [100 × ($30 − $40)], which can be used to offset all but $100 of the $1,100 long-term capital gain realized on the bonds. Clearly, the tax swap is an effective way of reducing and possibly eliminating a tax liability without altering one's portfolio.

Common stock swaps, such as illustrated above, are an important part of year-end tax planning. Even more popular are bond swaps, because it is usually far easier to find a substitute bond for the one held. Most full-service brokerage houses publish a list of recommended year-end swaps for both stocks and bonds. You might be wondering why it wouldn't make more sense just to sell the security for tax purposes and then immediately buy it back. Unfortunately, this is called a *wash sale* and is disallowed under the tax law. A sold security cannot be repurchased within 30 days without losing the tax deduction.

DEFERRED ANNUITIES

In addition to seeking tax-favored income, good tax strategy seeks to defer taxable income for extended periods of time. Although such a strategy may not reduce total taxes, the earnings on investment are not taxed when earned and are therefore available for reinvestment during the period of deferment. The additional earnings resulting from investment of pretax rather than after-tax dollars over long periods of time can be large. Put in proper perspective, a tax-deferred annuity may be worth more to an investor than any other single tax strategy. That is why it is important to understand the topic thoroughly.

Annuities: An Overview

An *annuity* is a series of payments guaranteed for a number of years or over a lifetime. The two types of annuities are classified by their purchase provisions. The *single-premium annuity* is a contract purchased with a single lump-sum payment. The purchaser pays a certain amount and receives a series of future payments that begins immediately or at some future date. The second type of contract, the *installment annuity,* is acquired by making payments over time; at a specified future date, the installment payments, plus interest earned on them, are used to purchase an annuity contract. The person to whom the future payments are directed is called the *annuitant.* Annuities are issued by hundreds of insurance companies, each offering many types of annuities.

An *immediate annuity* is a contract under which payments to the annuitant begin as soon as it is purchased. The amount of the payment is based on statistical analyses performed by the insurance company and depends on the annuitant's age and sex—the payment is a function of how long the insurance company expects the person to live. A *deferred annuity,* in contrast, is one in which the payments to the annuitant begin at some future date. The date is specified in the contract or at the annuitant's option. The amount the annuitant will periodically receive depends on his or her contributions, the interest earned on these contributions until the annuity payments commence, the annuitant's sex, and the annuitant's age when payments begin. The period of time between when payments are made to the insurance company and when the insurance company begins to pay the annuitant is the *accumulation period.* All interest earned on the accumulated payments during this period is tax deferred: It stays in the account and because it is not paid out to the purchaser, no tax liability is created.

Characteristics of Deferred Annuities

The rapid growth in popularity of deferred annuities stems from the much higher interest paid recently on these contracts. This is called the current rate; it fluctuates with interest rates in general, and it is *not* guaranteed. However, many of the new contracts also have a "bailout" provision that allows an annuity holder to withdraw the contract value—principal and all earned interest—if the company fails to pay a minimum return. In the following discussion, the contract offered and heavily promoted by the Fidelity group of mutual funds, summarized in Table 17.4, is used as a basis of discussion. It is illustrative of the contracts currently being written.

Current interest rate

An annuity contract's *current interest rate* is the yearly return the insurance company is paying now on accumulated deposits. The current interest rate fluctuates with market rates over time and is not guaranteed by the insurance company. The Fidelity policy offered a guaranteed one-year rate of 11.5 percent.

**TABLE 17.4 FEATURES OF A DEFERRED ANNUITY
OFFERED BY THE FIDELITY FUND
THROUGH CAPITAL LIFE INSURANCE**

Feature	Covered in This Contract
1. Minimum contribution	$5,000
2. Withdrawal privileges	Funds can be withdrawn at any time; there is a 5% penalty for funds withdrawn in the first year, and this penalty declines by 1% each year until it is zero in the sixth year and thereafter. However, up to 10% may be withdrawn each year without penalty.
3. Guaranteed rates	11.5% in the first year, 4% thereafter.
4. Bailout provision	Yes, whenever declared rate is one percentage point less than the initial rate (10.5% in this example).
5. Sales charges	None.
6. Payment options	Withdraw all or part in a lump sum, or choose from a variety of monthly payment plans.
7. Income tax implications	Any withdrawal of income within the first 10 years is assessed a 5% penalty unless the investor is over 59½; then penalty is also waived for death or disability. Any withdrawal of income is taxed at the investor's tax rate in the year of the withdrawal. The contract can (a tax consultant should provide an expert opinion) be rolled over to another annuity if the registration stays the same.

Source: "Fidelity Guaranteed Return Plan." Advertising brochure received February 16, 1983.

Minimum guaranteed interest rate

The deferred annuity purchase contract will specify a *minimum guaranteed interest rate* on contributions. The insurance company will guarantee this rate over the full accumulation period. The minimum rate is usually substantially less than the current interest rate. The Fidelity policy guaranteed a rate of only 4 percent, but notice that its bailout provision was tied to a minimum current rate of 10.5 percent. However, you should study a prospectus or contract and remember that *the minimum rate is all you are guaranteed.* Very often, the promotional literature provided by the company emphasizes the high current interest rate.

Special tax features

Deferred annuities, both single-premium and installment, have several advantageous tax-shelter features. First, interest earned on the purchaser's contributions is not subject to income tax until it is actually paid to the annuitant by the insurance company. Suppose that $10,000 is invested in an 11.5 percent single-premium deferred annuity. During the first year the contract is in effect, the account earns $1,150 in interest. If none of this interest is withdrawn, no income tax is due. For an investor in the 30 percent tax bracket, the first year's tax savings is $345. The tax deferral privilege permits the accumulation of substantial sums of compound interest that can be used to help provide a comfortable retirement income.

Certain employees of institutions such as schools, universities, governments, and not-for-profit organizations may qualify for the *tax-deferred annuity.* A special provision in the income tax laws allows these employees to make a *tax-free contribution* from current income to purchase a deferred annuity. The interest on these contributions is tax-deferred as well. For example, Professor Hector Gomez teaches history at Crown University in Maine. His pretax salary is $2,200 per month. Professor Gomez can contribute approximately $385 per month to a tax-deferred annuity program. This $385 is excluded from current income taxation; as a result, his taxes are based on only $1,815 per month. He does not have to pay any income tax on his contributions or his interest earnings until he actually receives annuity payments in future years. If Professor Gomez's income tax bracket is lower when he retires, he will pay a lower income tax on this deferred income. The tax-deferred annuity is attractive because it can save income taxes today as well as provide a higher level of retirement income later.

Investment payout

The investment return or *payout* provided by an annuity contract is realized when the payment stream begins. The annuitant can choose a straight annuity, which is a series of payments for the rest of his or her life. Most companies offer a variety of other payout options, including a contract specifying payments for both annuitant and spouse for the rest of both their lives, as well as a contract specifying rapid payout of accumulated payments with interest over a short period of time. The amount an annuitant receives depends on the amount accumulated in the account and the payout plan chosen. It is important to choose the program that provides the highest return for the desired payout plan. Such a plan will probably have a relatively high interest rate and a relatively low (or no) sales charge. The contract illustrated in Table 17.4 provided a number of payment options.

Withdrawal provisions and penalties

Most annuity contracts specify conditions under which accumulated contributions and interest may be withdrawn by the purchaser. These provisions should be read carefully; some insurers impose heavy penalties for premature withdrawal of funds. Fidelity's contract provided very liberal withdrawal provisions.

Sales charge

Many annuities are sold by salespersons who must be compensated for their services. Some annuities, called no load, have no sales charges paid by the purchaser; the insurance company pays the salesperson directly. This is the case with Fidelity's contract. Other annuities require the purchaser to pay commissions of up to 10 percent. Additional charges such as management fees, yearly maintenance fees, and one-time "setup charges" may also be levied. The key item for a prospective

TABLE 17.5 COMPARISON OF TWO $10,000 INVESTMENTS—A DEFERRED ANNUITY AND A NONANNUITY*

| | ANNUITY | | NONANNUITY | | |
Year	Earnings	Year-End Value	Earnings	Taxes	Year-End Value
1	$1,150	$10,000 + $1,150 = $ 11,150	$1,150	$345	$10,000 + $1,150 − $345 = $ 10,805
2	1,282	11,150 + 1,282 = 12,432	1,243	373	10,805 + 1,243 − 373 = 11,675
3	1430	12,432 + 1,430 = 13,862	1,343	403	11,675 + 1,343 − 403 = 12,615
4	1,594	13,862 + 1,594 = 15,456	1,451	435	12,615 + 1,451 − 435 = 13,631
5	1,777	15,456 + 1,777 = 17,233	1,568	470	13,631 + 1,568 − 470 = 14,729
10	—	— + — = 29,699	—	—	— + — − — = 21,689
20	—	— + — = 88,206	—	—	— + — − — = 47,043
30	—	— + — = 261,966	—	—	— + — − — = 102,033

*Assumptions: (1) Each investment earns 11.5 percent a year and (2) the investor is in the 30 percent tax bracket.

purchaser to analyze is the actual return on investment after all commissions, fees, and charges are deducted.

The Deferred Annuity: An Example

Earlier, we mentioned the attractive tax-deferral features of annuities. The following example illustrates the benefits of deferring income tax on the accumulated interest in an annuity. Assume an investor has purchased a $10,000 single-premium deferred annuity paying interest at an annual rate of 11.5 percent. As shown in Table 17.5, if the interest on the contract is allowed to accumulate, the investment will be worth $17,233 at the end of 5 years, $29,699 at the end of 10 years, and $261,966 at the end of 30 years! In this case, the interest compounds without taxes. If the $10,000 had been placed in a taxable investment at 11.5 percent interest, the accumulated amount would have been substantially less. An investor in the 30 percent bracket would have accumulated only $14,729 at the end of 5 years; $21,689 at the end of 10 years; and $102,033 at the end of 30 years. The tax-deferral feature would have allowed an additional capital buildup of almost $160,000 over the 30 years. The tax savings, coupled with more interest to compound, results in a much greater accumulation of capital. Of course, the investor will have to pay the taxes on the interest from the annuity once the payout begins. But even so, the investor has gained considerbly through the tax-deferral feature; and the benefits are even greater for someone in the 50 percent tax bracket.

Deferred Annuities and Retirement Plans

Many investors tie the purchase of deferred annuities to their overall retirement plans. You should recall from the discussion in Chapter 7 that individual retirement accounts (IRAs) and Keogh plans are partial substitutes for deferred annuities and therefore should be evaluated with them. If you are not using the full IRA exclusion each year, you may prefer adding to it as a part of your retirement plan rather than purchasing a tax-deferred annuity. Far greater benefit results from deducting from taxable income the full amount (up to the allowable limit) paid into an IRA. With an annuity, unless you're in one of the qualified professional fields denoted above, you cannot deduct its purchase price—you can only defer earned income.

On the other hand, you can begin to withdraw from an annuity without a tax penalty after it has been held only 10 years, but with an IRA you must wait until age 59½. Thus, the deferred annuity is a convenient vehicle for accumulating savings for a major expenditure, such as college education or a home. However, remember that income withdrawn from a deferred annuity will be taxed in the year it is withdrawn. Moreover, as a result of a recent Internal Revenue Service ruling, any annuity withdrawal is first viewed as income; once all income is withdrawn, subsequent withdrawals are treated as a return of principal, so any partial withdrawal will most likely be fully taxable.

Annuities as Investment Vehicles

Annuities have several potential uses in an investment program. An immediate annuity can provide a safe and predictable source of income for the balance of one's life. The deferred annuity offers tax shelter and safety features, and can provide a convenient method for accumulating funds. When considering the purchase of a deferred annuity, the investor needs to assess its investment suitability and understand the purchase procedures.

Investment suitability

The principal positive feature of deferred annuities is that they allow an investor to accumulate tax-deferred earnings in order to create a source of future income. The tax-deferred feature allows interest to accumulate more quickly than would be the case if it were taxed. For those who qualify for the tax-deferred annuity, current income tax on premium payments can be deferred as well. Annuities are also a low-risk type of investment.

On the negative side, deferred annuities can be faulted for two reasons: lack of inflation protection and high administrative and sales commission charges. Most annuities, in spite of providing a fluctuating interest rate, do not provide an annual interest rate in excess of the rate of inflation. Thus, they are not an inflation hedge. The second negative aspect of annuities is that relatively high administrative and sales commission charges are associated with them. Insurance companies have high overheads that must be met from annuity proceeds. In addition, sales commissions, whether paid by the purchaser or the insurance company, are generous and tend to lower the purchaser's return. In general, then, although annuities can play an important role in an investment portfolio, they should not be the only vehicle held. Other vehicles providing higher returns (and probably carrying higher risk) are available.

Buying annuities

Licensed insurance salespersons and many stockbrokers sell annuities. There are probably 50 or more annuity plans available through these outlets in a given community. Prior to investing in an annuity, you should obtain a prospectus and any other available literature on a number of them. These materials should be carefully compared, and the annuity chosen should be the one that offers the highest actual return on investment after all commissions, fees, and charges are deducted and contains features consistent with your investment objectives.

TAX WRITE-OFFS USING LIMITED PARTNERSHIPS

The tax write-offs from limited partnerships arise from being able to offset against other taxable income certain expenses connected with the business activity of the partnership. In essence, the cash flow, depreciation and depletion, profits, and tax benefits of the partnership are passed through directly to each of the individual partners, who then use/report them on their individual tax returns. For example, a real estate limited partnership offers the same type of depreciation deduction that we illustrated earlier in this chapter in connection with earning income in the form of long-term capital gains. As another example, if you invest in a livestock breeding limited partnership, you can deduct your share of expenses related to feeding and caring for a herd of animals until it is sold. Passing through these tax deductions to limited partners means they can offset a sizable portion of their investment in the venture within just a few years; any future return is profit—after taxes—on the investment. Ideally, this future return comes in the form of a long-term capital gain, but even if it is ordinary income, the rate of return on an after-tax investment in a limited partnership can be quite high. But so are the risks. And like any investment, limited partnership ventures should be purchased *on their investment merit*—not merely because they offer immediate tax deductions. Before we look at the investment aspects of limited partnership arrangements, we need to understand why they are used and how they work.

Pooling of Capital and Sharing of Risks

In an effort to obtain economies of scale and diversify risk, investors often pool their resources and form joint ventures. These joint ventures, frequently called *syndicates,* can take several forms: general partnerships, corporations, or limited partnerships. In a *general partnership,* all partners have management rights and all assume unlimited liability for any debts or obligations the partnership might incur. The unlimited liability feature can be disadvantageous to passive investors (those who do not wish to participate actively in the partnership's operation).

The *corporate form* of syndication provides a limited liability benefit to shareholder investors. Additionally, corporations have an indefinite life; they do not cease to exist if a stockholder dies, whereas a partnership could end if a general partner dies. However, the corporate form of syndication has a significant disadvantage in that tax losses generated by the corporation cannot be passed on to its stockholders. Only the partnership form of syndication provides for the flow-through of tax benefits. How can an investor obtain the limited liability shield of a corporation and yet obtain the tax shelter benefits possible with a partnership? The solution is ingenious—the *limited partnership.* This form of syndication combines the favorable investment features of both the general partnership and the corporation to provide an investor with a limited-liability, tax-sheltered vehicle. Let us take a closer look.

How Limited Partnerships Work

Legal structure

The limited partnership form of group investment is a legal arrangement governed principally by state law. State laws vary, of course, but typically they require that various written documents be filed with a county or state official prior to the commencement of the limited partnership's business. Additionally, the structure of the limited partnership is normally established to conform with IRS regulations; this is done to ensure that any tax shelter generated can be used by the partners. Limited partnerships can be utilized to invest in many things, and their size and scope varies widely. However, all have one common characteristic: They must have at least one general partner and at least one limited partner.

Figure 17.2 illustrates a typical limited partnership arrangement. The general partner, the active manager of the operation, runs the business. The general partner has unlimited liability. Often, to mitigate their unlimited liability, the general partners are corporations. The general partner's major contribution to the enterprise is frequently in the form of management expertise, not capital. Most of the capital is usually supplied by the limited partners, who do little else. They cannot participate in the management of the enterprise, or they will lose their limited liability protection. Normally, a limited partner's liability does not exceed his or her capital contribution, an amount specified in the partnership agreement. *Limited partners,* then, are capital suppliers whose role in the venture is passive. Usually, the only power limited partners have is to fire the general partner and/or to sell their investment.

The role of the general partner

The responsibility of managing the limited partnership rests on the *general partner,* since the limited partners cannot become involved in the management of the enterprise. An investor considering entering a limited partnership must analyze the management capabilities of the general partner. The limited partner's money is literally riding on the general partner's abilities. The general partner may find investors, assemble the partnership, and do all the negotiating. On large ventures, the services of an investment banker may be employed. Once the capital has been raised, the general partner manages the investment. For these services, the general partner is paid a fee. Compensation arrangements vary widely: For example, a general partner may receive a one-time management fee when the partnership is initially set up, plus a yearly management fee; or the general partner may receive a specified portion of the profits.

Return to investors

An investor can realize a return from a limited partnership investment in one or more ways. These include cash flow, price appreciation, and tax shelter.

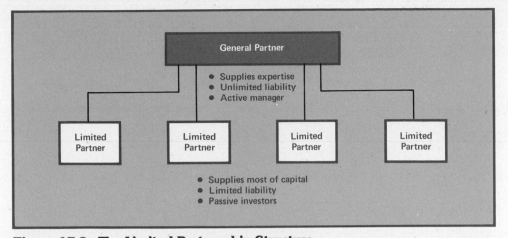

Figure 17.2 The Limited Partnership Structure.
In a limited partnership, the general partner typically provides management expertise and accepts all liability, whereas the limited partners are passive investors who supply most of the capital and accept liability limited only to the amount of their investment.

Cash flow.   Investors in a successful limited partnership operation will receive periodic cash payments as the investment generates income, often as a result of income tax savings. These periodic returns are called a project's cash flow. Limited partners receive a prorated share of the partnership's cash flow, depending on the size of their investment in the operation. Cash distributions may be made at monthly, quarterly, or yearly intervals. The general partner's management fee is normally paid prior to the distribution of cash flow. Frequently, the general partner will only take a small fee until the limited partners have had their capital investment completely repaid. Once this has occurred, the general partner's share of subsequent distributions will become larger.

Price appreciation.   Another source of investment return for limited partners is price appreciation resulting from an increase in the value of the investment. When the investment is sold, the increment in value is often taxed at favorable long-term capital gains rates. The general partner may earn a portion of the realized price appreciation as well. Investments such as real estate that increase in value due to inflation and other factors are often sources of appreciated value for limited partnership investors. Like the appreciation experienced on any investment vehicle, this form of return may be realized or unrealized (an actual return of dollars or a paper return).

Tax shelter.   By utilizing the limited partnership arrangement, high-income investors with otherwise sizable income tax liabilities can place their money in tax-sheltered investments and leave the management to the general partner. The tax shelter is generated primarily by tax deductions for depreciation and/or depletion and from investment tax credits. These tax savings are passed on to the limited

BOX 17.3 LISTED LIMITED PARTNERSHIPS: AN AFFORDABLE TAX SHELTER?

Most oil and gas drilling programs are for people with net worths of at least $250,000 and incomes of at least $50,000. Minimum investments are typically $5,000 and up. But there's a new game in town, playable with a few hundred dollars or less. It's called a listed limited partnership.

Buying a unit in a listed limited partnership is a lot like buying a share of stock. What you get is called a depositary unit. Right now [late 1982] there is one oil-and-gas listed limited partnership—Apache Petroleum Co.—on the New York Stock Exchange, and one—May Energy Partners Ltd.—on the American Stock Exchange. But listed limited partnerships may catch on. The units of Apache Petroleum began trading over-the-counter in January 1981 at about 20; recently they were at 22. Meanwhile, shares in its godparent, Apache Corp., slumped from 22 to about 11.

Apache Corp., which started Apache Petroleum and owns 13% of it, is a Minneapolis-based natural gas producer. For more than 20 years it has raised part of its drilling capital (recently about a third) through limited partnerships. But Apache Petroleum gives investors three things they have not had in traditional limited partnerships:

Greater liquidity. In most oil and gas drilling programs, you can sell your interest back to the general partner—but not for a very good price. Failing that, if you want out you must find your own buyer and suffer red tape. Depositary units, however, have a ready market on a major stock exchange, though of course the unit price can fluctuate.

Less risk. With a large pool of capital, the offering company invests in a large number of wells, mainly developmental rather than wildcat. Someone could, theoretically, start a partnership that invested in relatively few wells and emphasized exploration, but it would not be likely to get listed. In practice, most listed programs will probably have far safer mixes. Going the private route offers more chance for performance that is spectacularly good—or bad.

Longer life for the tax shelter. Many private drilling programs shower you with tax deductions (such as intangible drilling costs, depreciation and cost depletion) in the first one to three years. Then your shelter is exhausted, and your return—if you are lucky—comes in the form of a stream of income, usually taxable. Apache Petroleum estimates at least six years in the life of its tax shelter. The deductions still flow directly to the investor, but more slowly. Since it's an ongoing venture with new wells being drilled from time to time, reserves will be depleted at a gradual pace, or may even grow.

At the same time, there will be new drilling costs incurred each year, many of them deductible. (In drilling jargon, an "intangible," hence deductible, cost is one the IRS treats as a current expense. Hiring a rig at $8,000 a day is an intangible cost. A "tangible" cost is a capital expense, such as buying pumps or tanks. Tangible costs aren't deductible, but you may get depreciation and an investment tax credit.)

partners. Tax losses can be used to lower taxable income, thus lowering the income tax obligation. Tax credits can be used to offset income taxes directly.

Popular Forms of Limited Partnerships

Limited partnerships have been used to invest in many different types of assets; in fact, it is often said, "If there is an asset to be depreciated, depleted, or amortized, a limited partnership will be formed to buy it." Limited partnerships vary in risk from a conservative one formed to own a fully-rented office building with long-term leases

BOX 17.3 *Continued*

Apache Petroleum has been paying a distribution of $2 a year per unit to unit holders. This is analogous to a dividend, and since it counts as a return of capital, it's tax-free—at least for a while.

But there's a catch. In fact, two catches. First, when the sum of your distributions (which are real, cash payments) and your tax deductions (which aren't spendable, but are used to offset other income on your tax return) equals your "cost basis," then the tax benefits end.

Second catch: Your cost basis, with a public or private partnership, gradually dwindles. Say you buy in at $20 a unit. Of that sum, perhaps $16 might represent reserves; the other $4 might represent the value of undrilled inventory and other assets. In that case, your cost basis for tax purposes would be $20. Once you have received $20 a unit in return-of-capital distributions and tax deductions, the shelter ends. Any further distributions would be taxable income to you, and you get no further deductions.

Indeed, you could find yourself taxed on the venture's earnings, in addition to actual distributions to you. In our example, if Apache Petroleum earned $1.50 per unit, you would be taxed on $3.50 (the earnings plus the $2 distribution). In practice, many people would sell their units before reaching this point.

When you sell, watch it. You are taxed on the difference between your selling price and your *remaining* cost basis. Say you sold at $25 and had received $15 in distributions and deductions. Your cost basis would be down to $5, so your gain would be $20. At long-term capital gains rates, you would be taxed on 40% of the gain, or $8. If you are in the 50% bracket, your tax would be $4 a unit.

When you sell, the new buyer starts over with a fresh slate of deductions. That new buyer could even be you: You might elect to sell and buy back. For people who are shelter-minded, the time to sell is probably either the point just before you start incurring tax liability, or the point at which the available deductions no longer completely shelter your return-of-capital distribution.

Now that Apache Corp. has spawned such an attractive offspring, why should anyone invest in the original company? Why take plain vanilla when there's pistachio almond fudge? Well, some people don't care much about tax shelters. And others like to shoot for big capital gains. Gains in Apache Petroleum would probably not be spectacular. Growth could entail continued dilution through the issuance of new units. And developmental drilling doesn't have the spectacular potential of wildcatting.

But neither does it have the risks. The new listed limited partnerships, Apache's included, may be intriguing to people who want to play the drilling game with some safety and liquidity. If the little guy has to be taxed in what used to be the rich man's brackets, why shouldn't he get some of the rich man's tax breaks as well?

Source: John R. Dorfman, "Tiny Tax Shelters." *Forbes,* November 22, 1982, pp. 70–74.

to a risky one formed to own the sperm bank of a famous trotting horse that has never sired a winning offspring. Here we focus on four areas: real estate, energy resources, equipment leasing, and livestock feeding or breeding.

Real estate

Depending upon property type, a current cash flow, price appreciation, and/or tax shelter can be realized from investing in real estate. (See Chapter 16 for a detailed discussion of real estate investment analysis.) Raw land is normally purchased because of its price appreciation potential. Income property, because it can be depreciated, offers tax shelter potential. Apartment buildings, shopping centers, office buildings, and the like can provide cash flow, appreciation, and tax shelter to investors. Very often, these types of properties are syndicated and bought by limited partnerships. The typical real estate limited partnership consists of a general partner who manages the investment and the limited partners who provide most or all the capital.

There are two major types of real estate syndicates. The *blind pool syndicate* is formed by a syndicator that does not specify the properties in which it will invest; purchase and sale decisions are left to the syndicator. The *single-property syndicate* is established to purchase specific properties. Very often, the large, multiproperty limited partnership syndicates with many investors are blind pools. Single-property syndicates are generally smaller in scope, although many valuable parcels of property (the Empire State Building, for example) are owned by single-property syndicates.

Energy resources

The United States is heavily dependent on energy for its economic well-being, so the federal government has provided various tax incentives for those who invest in the search for energy. Utilizing the limited partnership investment vehicle, capital is pooled to finance exploration for oil, natural gas, coal, and geothermal steam. The most popular energy-related limited partnerships are oil and gas investments.

There are three basic types of oil and gas limited partnerships. *Exploratory programs,* also known as "wildcats," drill in areas where oil and gas is believed to exist but has not yet been discovered. *Developmental programs* finance the drilling of wells in areas of known, proved oil and gas reserves. They often drill offset wells, wells that are near already-producing oil or gas finds. *Income programs* buy existing wells with proved reserves.

The oil and gas business is risky because of the high uncertainty associated with it. Even the most knowledgeable geologists and petroleum engineers are never quite sure how much oil or gas is in a particular well or field. Oil and gas limited partnership investments therefore contain risk elements as well. The degree of risk depends on the type of program an investor buys. Exploratory programs carry the highest risk of the three types. However, these programs offer the highest potential return, and are often structured to provide the largest tax benefits of the three.

Table 17.6 illustrates a typical limited partnership engaged in drilling activities—Dyco Petroleum Corporation's 1983-1 Drilling Program. In this case, the smallest investment you can make is one unit or "interest" at $5,000. This is common among most limited partnerships. Notice that a 50 percent taxpayer is expected to recover half of his or her initial investment and subsequent assessment in the first two years. This happens because the limited partners' funds are to be used for noncapital costs. Notice also the depletion allowance, which adds to the tax offsets.

Suppose you buy an interest in this program—how well can you expect to do with your investment? Naturally, this question can't be answered until the passage of time supplies more information. However, we can ask this question: How well have prior Dyco drilling programs done? Fortunately, the prospectus helps answer that

---

TABLE 17.6 A PUBLIC LIMITED PARTNERSHIP—DYCO PETROLEUM CORPORATION'S 1983-1 DRILLING PROGRAM

The offering	12,000 units at $5,000 per unit.
Proposed activities	Conduct drilling in the Mid-Continent, Gulf Coast, and Rocky Mountain areas of the U.S. Approximately 50% of funds expended for drilling will be in the areas nearby or adjacent to productive areas (development drilling) and 50% in less explored, lower probability areas (exploratory drilling).
Analysis of offering	Dyco invests in the drilling programs by contributing at least 25% of total expenditures; participants contribute the remaining 75%. Within the exploration budget, participants pay all noncapital costs which are tax deductible. Illustration of cash investment and tax deductibility assuming two units and a 50% tax bracket:

Year 1   Cash investment—two units
       @ $5,000 $10,000
       You deduct—assuming Dyco
         spends 80% of your
         investment on noncapital costs   ($ 8,000)
       Tax savings (.50 × $8,000) $ 4,000

Year 2   Cash investment—assumes a
         15% assessment is made $ 1,500
       You deduct—assuming Dyco
         spends remainder of
         subscription funds and
         assessment amount on
         noncapital costs   ($ 3,500)
       Tax savings (.50 × $3,500) $ 1,750

Depletion allowance	The depletion allowance is another tax advantage. In 1983, 16% (declining to 15% in 1984 and thereafter) of gross income (but no more than 50% of net income) from producing wells can be received tax free, subject to certain limitations. From an investor's share of production income, you receive (as an example):

     Gross income $100
     Operating expenses (lifting costs)   (20)
     Net income $ 80
     Tax free   (16)
     Taxable income $ 64

Source: Dyco advertising brochure accompanying its prospectus for the 1983-1 and 1983-2 drilling programs.

---

question. Table 17.7 shows investor cash distributions to one unit in each of 26 other Dyco programs since 1971. To evaluate performance here, for convenience we will ignore income taxes, and assume that all cash subscribed and assessed was fully sheltered by the noncapital cost and depletion write-offs, and all cash distributed was ordinary income. (*Note:* Cost and/or percentage depletion generally will shelter about 20 percent of cash distributed.) Actually, there were some capital gain distributions in 7 of the programs, the largest being $2,540 in the 1973-1 program. The results are very interesting and certainly show that a risk is present in this type of activity. Of the programs offered through 1976—a period of time that should be long enough for evaluation purposes—6 of 13 distributed more cash than was initially subscribed and assessed. The big payoff was the 1972-1 program, as you can see. The 1976-1 program was also fairly profitable, but the other 4 were only marginally so. The investment lesson to be learned from Table 17.7 is not to put all your tax-shelter dollars into one drilling program; rather, diversify—either over time with the same general partner, such as Dyco, or among general partners in a given year. At $5,000 for a minimum investment, however, this may not be easily done.

Equipment leasing

Another popular limited partnership investment is the kind that deals with various types of leasable property—airplanes, railroad cars, machinery, computers, trucks, automobiles. In these types of investments, the limited partnership buys the equipment, such as a computer, and then leases it to someone else. The partnership is the lessor of the equipment and can depreciate the item as well as qualify for an investment tax credit when it is purchased. Normally ACRS—the fastest depreciation method—is used for tax purposes to increase the tax shelter provided the partners. Additionally, the partnership may use borrowed capital to increase potential return. The business of leasing property requires a great deal of knowledge and skill. The key to investment success in leasing is a competent general partner. Computers and various types of industrial machinery, for example, have a high obsolescence risk. For very wealthy investors, limited partnerships involving giant oil tankers are available. The tanker is leased to an oil company for a number of years, and the tanker's owners (the partners) benefit from its rental income as well as from sizable depreciation writeoffs that create attractive tax shelter.

Livestock feeding or breeding

A livestock (mostly cattle) feeding program is designed to defer taxes from one year to the next. Essentially, the program calls for purchasing young stock—feeder cattle, for example—in one tax year and deducting for tax purposes all the costs associated with fattening them for slaughter, which lasts about six to nine months. The idea is to wait until the following year to sell the cattle and recognize revenues for tax purposes. Risk is considerable in a venture such as this because of the wide fluctuation in prices of both the livestock and the grains used in their feed.

A breeding program differs from a feeding program in that the livestock is held longer—long enough to enable investors to realize a long-term capital gain on the eventual sale of the animals. Moreover, the breeder herd is also considered a productive asset, which qualifies for depreciation. And since the life of this asset is considered rather short, depreciation is rapid. A breeding program offers a similar and perhaps greater risk than a feeding program, since the holding period is somewhat longer. A particularly popular breeding program in the last several years has been one associated with developing thoroughbred horses. The tax advantage here

TABLE 17.7   DYCO PETROLEUM CORPORATION OIL AND GAS PROGRAMS INVESTOR NET CASH (ONE UNIT), AS OF JUNE 30, 1982

Drilling Program	Cash Subscribed and Assessed	Aggregate Cash Distribution	Aggregate Payout Percentage	Cash Distribution Last 12 Months Ending 6/30/82	Month and Year Commenced
1. 1971-1 program	$ 5,000	$ 6,930	139%	$ 1,600	9/72
2. 1972-1 program	5,000	42,150	843	4,400	9/73
3. 1972-2 program	5,750	5,700	99	425	3/74
4. 1973-1 program	5,500	6,751	123	901	12/74
5. 1973-2 program	5,750	5,801	101	350	9/75
6. 1973-YE program	5,750	4,066	71	600	3/77
7. 1974-1 program	5,000	3,004	60	501	3/77
8. 1974-2 program	5,750	1,867	32	212	6/77
9. 1974-YE program	5,750	3,952	69	700	12/75
10. 1975-1 program	5,750	5,302	92	1,902	3/78
11. 1975-2 program	5,750	10,007	174	3,007	3/77
12. 1976-1 program	5,750	13,236	230	4,436	3/78
13. 1976-2 program	5,750	2,561	45	911	3/79
14. 1977-1 program	5,750	2,224	39	974	12/79
15. 1977-2 program	5,750	3,707	64	1,807	6/80
16. 1977-X program	5,750	3,904	68	1,904	6/80
17. 1978-1 program	5,750	1,106	19	356	12/79
18. 1978-2 program	5,750	2,205	38	1,105	6/80
19. 1979-1 program	5,750	1,302	23	1,102	3/81
20. 1979-2 program	5,750	1,504	26	1,204	3/81
21. 1980-1 program	5,750	—	—	—	—
22. 1980-2 program	5,750	—	—	—	—
23. 1981-1 program	5,750	—	—	—	—
24. 1981-2 program	5,750	—	—	—	—
25. 1982-1 program	5,000	—	—	—	—
26. 1982-2 program	5,000	—	—	—	—
Totals	$145,500	$127,279		$28,397	

Source: Dyco Oil and Gas Program 1983-1 prospectus dated October 14, 1982, p. 53.

is the same as in any breeding program: For example, a horse is purchased as a thoroughbred yearling and later sold as a 2-year old in training; all costs related to owning and rearing the horse are taken as deductions against ordinary income, and any eventual gain on the sale becomes a long-term capital gain.

Partnership Structure: Private or Public

The size and scope of limited partnerships varies considerably. For example, three friends might establish a limited partnership to buy a six-unit apartment building. In contrast, one recently formed limited partnership had over 500 limited partners and had acquired $50 million in oil wells. There are two distinct types of limited partnerships. The *private partnership* has a limited number of investors and is not registered with a public agency; the *public partnership* is registered with the appro-

BOX 17.4 GUIDELINES FOR SELECTING A TAX SHELTER

Here are some key questions to ask your financial advisor before taking the plunge and making your initial payment. Be certain he can answer all your questions. If you encounter any hesitancy, either seek a new shelter or a new advisor.

1. What is the business you are investing in? How risky is it? Is it a true business proposition or a tax dodge?
2. Does it suit my particular needs? If you are a young doctor or other professional expecting substantially high taxable income for another 25 years, you need a shelter that will protect you for a long period of time. If you have received a large one-time sum of money, say from the sale of a book or movie script, or an inheritance, you need a shelter giving immediate write-offs.
3. Who is the sponsor? If it's an oil deal, has he been successful in the past? If it's a real estate venture, what has been the return on previous shelters?
4. What is the cash flow potential?
5. What is the capital gain potential?
6. How liquid is my investment: When can I get out any money?
7. How long will taxes be deferred?
8. What can I expect my first year deductions to be? My future deductions?
9. Are there any unusual or controversial tax factors involved?
10. Will I be asked for additional money?
11. What are the up-front fees? The brokerage fees? (Remember that the larger the number of participants the more these costs can be spread out.)
12. What portion of my investment is going to pay the general manager? To operate the business itself? Keep in mind that you are putting up the cash while the sponsor supplies the expertise and some of the equipment. Reconsider if the general partner is taking more than 50 percent.

TRAPS TO LOOK OUT FOR

The tax shelter prospectus, long, dry, and intricate, frequently manages to bury the important details in a lot of verbiage, so it's essential to seek the advice of a tax specialist. There are some specific situations, nevertheless, that you as an informed investor can avoid on your own.

priate state or federal regulators and usually has 25 or more limited partners. State and federal laws regulate offerings of limited partnership programs.

Private partnerships

Private limited partnerships are often assembled by a local real estate broker or an attorney. Often, the investors know one another personally. Potential investors in the partnership are commonly given an *offering circular,* a document describing the property to be purchased, management fees, and other financial details. It usually contains the limited partnership agreement. There are several advantages to private partnerships. First, since they do not have to be registered with a public agency, they usually have lower transaction and legal costs than public partnerships. Legal fees in connection with registration of securities are costly and are paid indirectly by the limited partners. Another advantage of a private partnership is that it may be easier to obtain first-hand knowledge about the general partner. The general partner may

BOX 17.4 *Continued*

- **Long-distance deals.** It's only logical that the farther away you are from the properties owned by a shelter, the less you will know about the operation and the greater the chance for fraud.
- **Shelters sold by mail order.** Would you purchase ruby cufflinks or a sapphire necklace through the mail?
- **Calendar panic.** The desperation factor often grips investors, turning them into shelter junkies at the end of the year. They neglect doing proper research, accepting nearly any deal that comes along.
- **Letters of credit.** An investor signs a promissory note, backed by a bank letter of credit for up to four times his original investment. The general partner then borrows against this note, providing the investor with leveraged-based deductions. Beware of this type of arrangement. If the deal is unsuccessful, the investor who is responsible for the loan may have to pay it back, out-of-pocket, if the deal brings no income
- **Poor business investments.** Any tax shelter that does not look like a solid investment should be avoided.
- **Commingling.** The investor should stay away from operations in which the asset records, cash accounts, expense sheets, and other papers of more than one operation are commingled. Check with your accountant.
- **Inadequate financing.** Although there is no set formula, be careful of real estate deals in which the net worth of the general partner is less than one-tenth the amount the shelter is trying to get through the offering. Oil and gas drilling programs require less capital to finance, therefore for these ventures this figure can be slightly less.
- **Poor previous payout performance.** The prospectus should describe prior performance. If it has taken more than a year for a conservative real estate shelter to begin cash or income payouts to its investors, decline purchasing it. For oil and gas, allow two to two and a half years.

Remember that the new tax law imposes tougher penalties for those in phony tax dodges. Now the interest that must be paid on any tax money owed will be based on the prime rate as of October of the year in which it was owed. Compare that with the old rate—at six percent. Extra penalties, up to 30 percent, can also be levied.

Source: Nancy Dunnan, "Selecting a Tax Shelter." *FACT,* July 1982, p. 57.

well be locally based and can be investigated prior to commiting any money. A good source of information on a general partner is other limited partners who have previously invested in his or her partnerships.

Public partnerships

Public limited partnership syndications must be registered with state and sometimes federal regulatory authorities. Offerings sold only within one state need comply only with that state's laws. Interstate sales of limited partnership interests must comply with federal as well as state laws. Public partnerships are sold by stockbrokers and other licensed securities dealers, and transaction costs are high. The brokerage commission on a typical oil and gas limited partnership is 8 percent. Limited partnership interests, both private and public, are relatively illiquid. Sometimes the interest cannot be sold without the approval of the state authority. A potential buyer of a public limited partnership must be given a *prospectus,* a detailed statement that contains the financial data, management information, and transaction and legal costs associated with the offering. Most public partnerships are large in scope and usually contain over $1 million in assets. An investor in a public partnership may find that his or her shares represent an investment in a diversified portfolio of real estate or energy resource properties. Geographical diversity may be easier to obtain by investing in public partnerships.

Essential Investment Considerations

Limited partnerships often provide a way to increase your after-tax income, but an earlier point should be reemphasized—buy them on the basis of their investment merit, and not solely for the tax shelter they offer. Outrageous claims of limited partnership promoters usually can be found toward the end of the year, when shady operators concoct unbelievable schemes for last-minute investors. They advertise that you can earn a sizable return on an investment *even if it fails* and you lose your initial outlay. Although this is possible it is not without risk, and generally the actual amount recovered depends on your tax bracket. For each potential investment in a limited partnership, you should review its degree of leverage, its risk and return, and its investment suitability.

Leverage

In terms of limited partnerships, the presence of leverage indicates that the business activity underlying the partnership utilizes borrowed funds—perhaps in substantial amounts. An equipment leasing venture, for example, might involve 80 to 90 percent debt financing. This means your initial investment dollar buys more tax deductions, usually in the first year, than would be the case if leverage were not used. For example, suppose a limited partnership raises $100,000, borrows $900,000 for which the partners have shared liability, and then buys computer equipment for $1,000,000 to lease to a business over a 10-year period. Suppose further that the partnership is entitled to an investment tax credit of $100,000 in the first year, along with depreciation of $200,000. If you own 5 percent of the partnership (you invested $5,000), in the first year your tax offsets are $10,000 in depreciation—worth $5,000 to you if you are in a 50 percent bracket—and $5,000 in the investment tax credit, regardless of your tax bracket. Your total first-year recovery is the sum of the two tax advantages—$10,000. This means you have recovered twice your investment in the first year. Is this possible? Yes, but you must bear in mind that you are legally liable for your share of the loan, which is $45,000 ($900,000 × .05). If the loan is with some type of captive finance company that is willing to forgive the debt in the event the partnership goes under or you do not have legal liability for your portion of the debt, the whole deal may (except in the case of real estate partnerships) be considered a sham by the Internal Revenue Service. In such a case, you not only lose your tax deductions, you will also be subject to stiff penalties and interest for back taxes. Any tax shelter that seems too good to be true probably is. For example, some year-end schemes are advertised with tax write-offs such as 4-to-1, or even as high as

12-to-1. This refers to first-year write-offs in relation to the initial investment. Our example above, which had considerable leverage, only had a 2-to-1 write-off. Remember: Leverage can increase the tax benefits, but to do so, it almost always carries more risk.

Risk and return

Evaluating the risk and return of a limited partnership investment depends on the property involved, although there are several general factors to consider. First, the general partner must be carefully studied. One should be concerned, for instance, if a general partner trying to sell an interest in an exploration project has failed to discover oil in previous projects. Read the offering circular or prospectus carefully. Find out how much the promoters (general partner and associates) are skimming off the top in commissions, legal fees, and management fees. The more they take, the less of your money is invested in the project and the less likely it is that you will receive a high return. Another factor to recognize is that most limited partnerships are not very liquid; in fact, depending on state law, you may not be able to sell them prior to their disbandment. In other words, your interest may be difficult and perhaps impossible to resell. This lack of liquidity tends to increase the risk associated with investment in limited partnerships. Finally, a risk that every investor should be aware of is receipt of an *adverse* opinion from the IRS, which could result in a loss of tax deductions as well as stiff penalties.

Investment suitability

As you have probably concluded by now, limited partnerships are not for everyone. They tend to be risky and illiquid and thus are usually not suitable for conservative investors primarily interested in the preservation of capital. An offering circular or prospectus will often contain a statement limiting purchase to investors with a net worth of at least $100,000, or a tax bracket of 50 percent or higher. This rule excluding certain types of investors is called a *suitability rule*. Its purpose is to allow only investors who can bear a high amount of risk to participate. Additionally, there is usually a statement in the prospectus that says: "The securities offered herewith are very high risk." Believe this statement; if the regulatory authorities require it, it must be a high-risk investment. Suitability rules vary, depending on applicable state and federal laws. The rules are intended to prevent the sale of high-risk projects to investors who cannot handle the loss financially. Suitability requirements are usually fairly rigid for public limited partnerships (offerings registered with securities regulators).

SUMMARY

A critical aspect of the federal income tax law is the progressive nature of the tax rates—higher incomes lead to progressively higher taxes. The tax rate is applied to taxable income, which can be either ordinary income or capital gains and losses. Taxable income is calculated through a sequence of steps: First, gross income is determined; this includes all forms of income—wages, dividends, interest, and others—except items specifically excluded, such as interest on municipal bonds, minimum amounts of interest and dividends, and 60 percent of long-term capital gains.

The second step is to make adjustments if a taxpayer is entitled to them. Important adjustments to gross income for many taxpayers are payments to IRAs and the deduction for a married working couple. Subtracting adjustments to gross income leads to adjusted gross income. The third step is to deduct itemized deductions (assuming a taxpayer elects to itemize instead of taking the zero bracket amount) and $1,000 for each qualifying exemption. After deductions and exemptions are taken, the resulting value is taxable income. The fourth step is to determine the amount of applicable income tax by referring to an appropriate tax table. The final step is to reduce income taxes by any tax credits, leaving income taxes due; this figure is then compared to the amount of tax withheld and/or paid in estimates to arrive at either a tax due the Internal Revenue Service or a refund for taxes overpaid.

Tax avoidance strategies attempt to earn tax-favored income, which is essentially income not subject to taxes. Tax deferral strategies do not necessarily reduce the amount of taxes paid, but rather attempt to defer taxes from current periods to later periods. A tax shelter is an investment vehicle that earns a portion of its return by offering potential offsets to the investor's other taxable income. The major forms of tax-favored income are municipal bond interest, Treasury and government agency issues (free of state and local income taxes), dividend and net interest exclusion, and long-term capital gains. The last item is generally the most rewarding to investors.

In determining capital gains and losses, long-term gains are netted against long-term losses and short-term gains are netted against short-term losses; the net long-term gain or loss is then netted against the net short-term gain or loss. This process of netting gains and losses can produce a variety of tax situations, but investors try to take long-term capital gains by themselves, since 60 percent of such gains are excluded from income, and to take long-term capital losses along with short-term capital gains, since only 50 percent of long-term capital losses are deductible. Provisions in the tax law, in certain cases, afford special benefits to capital gains on the sale of a personal residence.

Techniques often used to defer tax liabilities to the next year are (1) a short sale against the box, (2) a put hedge, and (3) selling a deep-in-the-money call option. Each of these has relative advantages and disadvantages, depending on the assumed future movement of the stock's price. Popular strategies that pay-off in long-term capital gains are (1) buying growth rather than income stocks, (2) using public utility dividend reinvestment plans, (3) buying deep discount bonds, and (4) investing in residential income property. Tax swaps provide a strategy that can be used to reduce or eliminate a tax liability without altering the basic portfolio.

Because they now pay relatively high market rates of interest, deferred annuities have increased considerably in popularity. Their principal advantage is that income earned on them is not taxed in the year earned, but rather as the earnings are withdrawn from the annuity. This allows the earnings to be reinvested tax-free over long periods of time and through tax-free reinvestment to produce a substantially greater value than if taxed earnings were reinvested. Tax-deferred annuities, available to employees of certain institutions, allow these employees to make a limited tax-free contribution from current income to purchase a deferred annuity. Deferred annuities are relatively low-risk vehicles that may not produce earnings on a par with inflation rates; therefore, investors should determine if they are suitable.

A limited partnership is an organizational form that allows individuals, called limited partners, to invest in a business enterprise and enjoy the tax deductibility of certain business expenses. In addition, the limited partners are not personally liable for the actions of other partners, including the general partner who actually manages the business. The return from a limited partnership comes from three potential sources: cash flow, price appreciation, and tax shelter. Limited partnerships have been formed to acquire many different kinds of assets, but the most common are real estate, energy resources, equipment for leasing purposes, and livestock feeding or breeding. They can be structured as private or public partnerships. Leverage can increase the potential tax write-offs in a limited partnership, but it also increases the risk. Investors should study the offering circular or prospectus for a limited partnership and carefully examine the risk-return characteristics to assess the investment's suitability. They should be particularly wary of any limited partnership offering substantial write-offs in relation to the amount invested. In many cases, these partnerships will not gain Internal Revenue Service approval. Often investors must meet certain suitability rules prior to investing in a limited partnership.

KEY TERMS

accumulation period
adjusted gross income
alternative minimum taxable income (AMTI)
annuitant
annuity
average tax rate
basis (in capital asset)
blind pool syndicate
capital asset
capital gain (short-term/long-term)
capital loss (short-term/long-term)
corporate form (syndication)
current interest rate (annuity)
deep discount bonds
deep-in-the-money call option
deferred annuity
depreciation
development programs (oil and gas)
dividend exclusion
equipment leasing
exemption
exploratory programs (oil and gas)
general partner
general partnership
gross income
immediate annuity
income programs (oil and gas)
installment annuity
investment tax credit
itemized deductions
limited partners

limited partnerships
marginal tax rate
minimum guaranteed interest rate
municipal bond interest
net interest exclusion
offering circular
ordinary income
payout (on an annuity)
private partnership
progressive tax rate
prospectus
public partnership
public utility dividend reinvestment plan
put hedge
shorting-against-the-box
single-premium annuity
single-property syndicate
suitability rule
syndicate
taxable income
tax avoidance
tax credit
tax deferral
tax-deferred annuity
tax evasion
tax-favored income
tax planning
tax shelter
tax swaps
wash sale
zero bracket amount

REVIEW QUESTIONS

1. Using Table 17.1, calculate Ed Robinson's income tax due on his $30,000 taxable income, assuming he files as a single taxpayer. After you make the calculation, explain to Ed what his marginal tax rate is and why it is important in making investment decisions.

2. What is a capital asset? Explain if capital asset transactions are taxed differently from ordinary income.

3. Sheila and Jim Mendez reported the following income tax items in 1983:

Salaries and wages	$50,000
Dividends (jointly owned stocks)	1,400*
Interest on bonds	1,100**
Capital gains on securities held 3 years	4,000
Itemized deductions	8,000
Payments to IRAs	2,000

*$1,100 of this total was received as additional shares of stock in qualified public utility dividend reinvestment plans.
**$400 of this total was received from municipal bonds.

If Sheila and Jim have four dependents and file a joint return for 1983, calculate their income tax due.

4. How does tax avoidance differ from tax deferral? Explain if either of these is a form of tax evasion. Is either the same thing as a tax shelter?

5. Identify and briefly discuss sources of tax-favored income.

6. Explain the netting process for capital gains and losses, and then discuss two simple rules investors should follow for recognizing long-term capital gains and losses.

7. What is the tax-shelter aspect of a personal residence with respect to capital gains? Explain.

8. Shawn Healy bought 300 shares of Apple Computer common stock at $25 a share. Ten months later, Apple was up to $40 a share and Shawn was considering selling her shares, since she believed Apple's price could drop as low as $35 within the next several months. What advice would you offer Shawn before she sells?

9. Explain conditions that favor the following strategies for deferring tax liabilities to the next year: (1) a short sale against the box, (2) a put hedge, and (3) selling a deep-in-the-money call option. When is it best simply to hold the stock and do nothing?

10. Briefly describe each of the following strategies that pay-off in long-term capital gains.

    a. Growth stocks.
    b. Public utility dividend reinvestment plans.
    c. Deep discount bonds.
    d. Residential income property depreciation.

11. Describe how a tax swap can be used to reduce or eliminate a tax liability without significantly altering the composition of the portfolio.

12. Define an annuity, explain the role it might play in an investment portfolio, and differentiate between:

    a. Single-premium and installment annuities.
    b. Immediate and deferred annuities.

13. Define the following terms as they relate to deferred annuities: (1) current interest rate, (2) minimum guaranteed interest rate, (3) payment options, and (4) withdrawal provisions and penalties.

14. Explain how a deferred annuity works as a tax shelter. How does a tax-deferred annuity work and who is eligible to purchase one? Discuss whether a deferred annuity is a better tax shelter than an IRA.

15. How does a limited partnership differ from a general partnership and a corporation? What are the functions of the general and limited partners? Why is the limited partnership necessary from a tax planning point of view?

16. In what three ways can an investor earn a return from a limited partnership? Explain.

17. What are the popular forms of limited partnerships? Explain how a livestock breeding limited partnership might produce a tax shelter for investors. What are the risks in this form of limited partnership?

18. Referring to the Dyco Petroleum example in this chapter, illustrate the tax-shelter aspects of an oil and gas limited partnership, and discuss the relative risk and return characteristics of ventures such as this one.

19. How does leverage affect a limited partnership? Explain if it can create a situation in which tax write-offs are greater than the amount invested, thereby giving you a sizable return on your investment solely through such write-offs.

20. A friend of yours wants you to invest in an equipment leasing partnership. You and the other partners will buy a computer and then lease it to a local concern. Explain the potential tax benefits and other factors you would look at in your analysis of this proposed investment.

CASE PROBLEMS

17.1 TAX PLANNING FOR THE WILSONS

Hal and Terri Wilson were fortunate enough to have most of their funds invested in common stocks in the summer of 1983, right before the big market rally that began in August. The Wilsons didn't really do very much investment planning, and they had practically no background or understanding of how income taxes might affect their investment decisions. Their holdings consisted exclusively of common stocks, selected primarily on the advice of their stockbroker, Sid Nichols. The 1983 rally, however, did produce some nice capital gains, even though several of their holdings still showed losses from their original purchase prices. A summary of their holdings on December 20, 1983 appears below:

Stock	Date Purchased	Original Cost	Current Market Value
Consolidated Power and Light	2/10/81	$10,000	$16,000
Cargon Industries	7/7/83	3,000	8,000
PYT Corporation	6/29/83	7,000	6,000
Amalgamated Iron & Steel	8/9/82	8,000	5,000
Jones Building Supplies	3/6/79	4,500	4,700

Hal feels this might be a good time to revise their portfolio, and he favors initially selling all their holdings and reinvesting the funds in several growth-oriented mutual funds and perhaps several real estate limited partnerships. Terri agrees their portfolio could use some modifications, but she is reluctant to sell everything; for one thing, she is concerned that federal income taxes might take a sizable share of their profits.

After some discussion, the Wilsons decided to consult their friend, Elaine Byer, who was a CPA for one of the big eight accounting firms. Byer indicated that she was not an expert in the investments field and couldn't therefore tell them what securities to buy or sell from that perspective, but from a tax point of view, she did not recommend selling everything in the 1983 tax year. Instead, she said that Consolidated Power and Light and Jones Building Supplies should be sold in December of 1983, but the other securities should be carried into 1984 and sold then—if that is what the Wilsons want to do.

Hal and Terri were thankful for Byer's advice, but they were a little concerned about waiting to sell the other three stocks, particularly Cargon Industries, since it showed such a sizable gain and they were afraid its price might decline sharply in a stockmarket sell-off. As a final step they contacted Nichols, who agreed with Byer's advice; he said not to worry about the Cargon situation. The stock was selling at $80 a share, and he would put in a short against the box for them; then they could deliver the shares whenever they wanted. He told them not to take similar action with PYT and Amalgamated, since they probably wouldn't experience much price change anyway.

Questions

1. Assuming the Wilsons are in a 30 percent tax bracket, calculate the resulting federal income tax: (a) If they sold all their securities in 1983 at their current market values; and (b) if they sold Consolidated Power and Light and Jones Building Supplies at their market values in 1983, and then sold the remaining securities at their current market values on January 2, 1984. What do you conclude from your calculations?

2. Nichols suggested a short sale against the box for Cargon. Explain his sentiment about the future price of this stock.

3. Suppose the Wilsons take Nichols' advice. Would you then recommend they deliver the shares immediately to close the short sale transaction, or should they wait until 7/8/1984— or perhaps even longer? Explain your answer, indicating your assumption as to whether or not they sell their other securities.

4. Suppose you thought Cargon had a good possibility for further price increases in 1984 but you were equally concerned that its price could fall sharply. Would you then agree with the strategy Nichols recommended, or would you prefer a different strategy? Explain your answer.

5. What overall strategy would you recommend to the Wilsons, given their investment objectives and tax status? Explain.

17.2 DO OIL AND FRED CRANSTON MIX?

Fred Cranston, age 36, is the West Coast marketing manager and vice-president of a major auto parts supply firm. His salary reflects his success in his job: $90,000 per year. Additionally, his firm provides him with a car, an excellent pension and profit-sharing plan, superior life and medical insurance coverage, and company stock options. Fred owns his home, which is located in the exclusive Marin County, California, area.

Fred's current financial problem is related to his tremendous success. As a single taxpayer, he needs income tax shelter. Fred's income tax burden is very heavy; his combined federal and California marginal income tax bracket is about 55 percent. In addition to Fred's house and pension and profit-sharing plans, he has a stock portfolio worth about $75,000, a municipal bond portfolio valued at $150,000, and about $100,000 in a highly liquid money market mutual fund. Fred is considering taking $50,000 out of the money market mutual fund and buying some limited partnership tax shelters. His broker, Marie Bell, has proposed that he invest $50,000, divided among five oil and gas limited partnership drilling programs. Marie's specific recommendation is to buy two exploratory programs and three developmental, each for $10,000. She explained to Fred that this $50,000 investment will enable him to reduce his taxable income by $45,000 during the year he purchases the partnership interests. The sizable tax shelter results from the high level of write-offs associated with these programs. Thus, Fred's $50,000 investment will save him nearly $25,000 in income taxes. Marie also pointed out that the programs could discover oil, in which case Fred could expect to receive additional cash returns in future years. Fred meets the suitability rules required for such investments as prescribed by the securities commission of California. Being a relatively conservative individual, he is trying to justify in his mind the reasonableness of Marie's recommendations.

Questions

1. What do you think of Marie Bell's investment recommendations for Fred? Are exploratory programs too risky? Should Fred buy five different drilling programs, or invest the entire $50,000 in one program? Explain.

2. How would you describe the legal structure of a limited partnership to Fred? What should Fred know about the general partner in each of these programs?

3. In general, do investments in oil and gas exploration make sense to you? Why or why not?

4. What other tax shelters might you suggest Fred consider? Discuss the leverage and risk-return tradeoffs involved in them.

SELECTED READINGS

Briggs, Jean A. "Should You Take Shelter?" *Forbes,* April 26, 1982, pp. 107–111.

Dreyfus, Patricia A. "Separating Good from Bad Shelters." *Money,* February 1981, pp. 58–68.

———. "Tax Shelters for the Timid." *Money,* August 1982, pp. 115–120.

Dunnan, Nancy. "In Search of Tax Shelters." *FACT,* July 1982, pp. 55–59.

Edgerton, Jerry. "Investments That Cut Your Taxes." *Money,* February 1983, pp. 60–64.

———. "Ten Terrific Tax-Saving Ideas." *Money,* June 1983, pp. 56–74.

Eisenberg, Richard. "Protecting Yourself from the Tax Bite." *Money,* February 1983, pp. 52–56.

———. "When Other Shelters Are Better." *Money,* October 1982, pp. 149–154.

Hazard, John W. "Annuities: Their Pluses, Minuses." *U.S. News and World Report,* June 21, 1982, p. 71.

The H&R Block Income Tax Workbook. New York: Macmillan, annual.

"Investing in Oil and Gas Tax Shelters." *Changing Times,* February 1981, pp. 56–58.

J.K. Lasser's Your Income Tax. New York: Simon and Schuster, annual.

Korn, Donald J. "Seeking Shelter in Real Estate." *FACT,* November 1982, pp. 47–51.

Mairken, Gene. "Plan Now—Save Later on Taxes." *Consumers Digest,* January–February 1981, pp. 14–18.

"The Perils and Payoffs in Real Estate Partnerships." *Business Week,* April 12, 1982, pp. 146–149.

Phillips, Lawrence C., and William H. Hoffman, eds. *West's Federal Taxation: Individual Income Taxes.* St. Paul, Minn.: West Publishing, annual.

"Real Estate Tax Shelters: The Risks and Rewards." *Changing Times,* November 1980, pp. 29–33.

"Shelter Your Income—But Watch Your Step." *U.S. News and World Report,* June 21, 1982, pp. 69–70.

Sloan, Allan. "Beware of Burnout." *Money,* November 1982, pp. 145–148.

Your Federal Income Tax. Internal Revenue Service Publication 17. Washington, D.C.: U.S. Department of the Treasury, annual.

18

Gold and Other Tangible Investments

During the late 1970s and in early 1980, tangible investments such as gold, silver, diamonds, and collectibles became very popular, and their prices soared. In 1981 and 1982, interest in these investments waned somewhat, and many of them experienced significant price declines. Despite these price corrections, interest in these investments remains fairly high; and they could move to the forefront again. In this chapter, we will look at:

1. The rise in popularity, key characteristics, forms, and motives for investing in tangible assets.
2. Gold, its recent price history, its investment characteristics and suitability, and ways of acquiring gold investments.
3. Silver and strategic metals, two other metal investments.
4. Diamonds, their recent price behavior, and their investment suitability.
5. Collectibles, including rare stamps, coins, artwork, and antiques.

Our objective is to cover a broad spectrum of available investments. We have examined the basic characteristics and suitability of stocks, bonds, options, commodities and financial futures, mutual funds, real estate, and tax-sheltered investments such as annuities and limited partnerships. Now we will complete our discussion by examining a variety of tangible investment vehicles, including gold, silver, strategic metals, diamonds, and collectibles. Prior to the decade of the 1970s, these investments were largely ignored by the investment community, but now they attract fairly wide investor interest.

An inflation hedge is an investment that provides an after-tax rate of return which exceeds the rate of inflation. During the decade of the 1970s, gold, silver, diamonds, and many collectibles provided inflation-beating rates of return. But these marvelous returns did not continue in 1981 and 1982. We will examine the causes of both price performances and discuss the question of timing in relation to tangible investment commitments. We begin our examination with a discussion of their general investment characteristics.

INVESTING IN TANGIBLE ASSETS

A *tangible investment* is one that can be seen and touched and that has an actual form or substance. Examples of tangible investments include real estate, precious metals and stones, stamps, coins, artwork, and antiques. A *financial asset,* in contrast, is a paper claim evidencing ownership, debt, or an option to acquire an interest in some intangible or tangible asset. Many investors own tangible investments because they can be seen and touched; others prefer tangible investments with scarcity value. During the 1970s, tangible investments became popular and generally provided inflation-beating rates of return. Their popularity appears to have peaked, but there still are many investors who prefer these vehicles. After you read this chapter, you may discover that you are one of them.

Why Were Tangibles so Popular in the 1970s?

During the decade of the 1970s, particularly in 1978 and 1979, tangible investments soared in popularity. There were several reasons for this. First, the 1970s was a period of very high inflation rates. Double-digit inflation, unknown in the United States since the late 1940s, became commonplace. These high inflation rates made investors nervous about holding financial assets such as money, bank accounts, stocks, and bonds. Their nervousness was heightened by the poor returns financial assets offered in those years. So they turned their attention to investments whose rates of return had tended to beat inflation—tangibles. The year 1979, in particular, was a period of heavy tangibles investing. During that year, inflation soared and the expectation was for even worse inflation in the future. Investors began to consider, and in many cases to buy, tangibles. Other factors that increased the popularity of tangibles included the generally unstable domestic and foreign political conditions of the 1970s. Several severe economic recessions occurred, as well as Watergate, the Arab oil boycott, the Soviet Union's invasion of Afghanistan, and the Iranian hostage crisis. The Middle East continued to be generally unstable. These conditions worried investors and lessened their faith in financial assets. So basic investor fear about the future was also an important motivation for buying tangibles.

Price Patterns

The price behavior of most tangibles follows a fairly similar pattern. During the first five years of the 1970s, tangibles tended to increase in price at rates somewhat greater than inflation. Starting in 1976, however, prices of tangibles rose at faster rates, often two to five times greater than the rate of inflation. The greatest upsurges occurred in 1979 and early 1980. Then the boom collapsed, and tangibles either

TABLE 18.1 COMPARATIVE COMPOUND ANNUAL RATES OF RETURN FOR VARIOUS INVESTMENT VEHICLES*

	10 YEARS (June 1, 1972, to June 1, 1982)		5 YEARS (June 1, 1977, to June 1, 1982)		1 YEAR (June 1, 1981, to June 1, 1982)	
	Return	Rank	Return	Rank	Return	Rank
Oil	29.9%	1	21.2%	4	6.3%	3
U.S. coins	22.5	2	21.4	3	−27.8	13
U.S. stamps	21.9	3	26.6	1	− 3.0	9
Oriental rugs	19.1	4	17.1	6	−16.2	11
Gold	18.6	5	17.3	5	−34.0	14
Chinese ceramics	15.3	6	23.7	3	− 0.5	6
Farmland	13.7	7	10.7	9	− 0.9	7
Silver	13.6	8	5.5	13	−44.5	15
Diamonds	13.3	9	13.7	7	0.0	5
Housing	9.9	10	10.0	10	3.4	4
Old Masters	9.0	11	13.7	8	−22.0	12
Consumer Price Index	8.6	12	9.6	11	6.6	2
Stocks	3.9	13	7.7	12	−10.5	10
Foreign exchange	3.6	14	1.6	14	− 1.4	8
Bonds	3.6	15	0.6	15	11.4	1

*All returns are for the period ending June 1, 1982, based on latest available data.
Source: "Battle of the Investments." *FACT,* September 1982, p. 64.

leveled off in price or experienced severe price declines. From mid-1980 through 1983, the prices of tangibles generally declined.

The dramatic change in price trends can be seen in Table 18.1, which presents compound annual rates of return for a variety of investment vehicles for the 10, 5, and 1 years ending June 1, 1982. U.S. coins, for example, increased in value at a 22.5 percent compound annual rate of return from June 1, 1972, to June 1, 1982. Most of that appreciation occurred prior to 1981, however. From June 1, 1981, to June 1, 1982, U.S. coins declined in value by 27.8 percent. As you can see, other tangibles, including Oriental rugs, gold, silver, and Old Masters (paintings) also suffered heavy price declines during the 1981–1982 period. In general, the pattern is one of rapid increases in value in the late 1970s reaching a peak in 1980, followed by price declines in 1981, 1982, and 1983.

Tangibles as Investment Vehicles

Tangible assets seem to appreciate during times of high inflation and political instability, as we have seen. Before examining specific forms of this class of investment vehicles, we need some general background information to provide a snapshot of the characteristics common to these investments.

Tangibles as a class of investments

Tangibles are real things. You can sit on a tangible chair, hide a tangible gold bar in your safe deposit box, look at a tangible work of art. Some tangibles, such as gold and diamonds, are portable; others, such as land, are not. These differences can affect the price behavior of tangibles. Land, for example, tends to appreciate fairly rapidly during periods of high inflation and relatively stable international conditions. Gold, on the other hand, is particularly preferred during periods of unstable international conditions because it is portable. Investors appear to believe that if international conditions deteriorate past the crisis point, at least they can take their gold and run. They can't take their land with them, obviously. The markets for tangibles vary widely. Diamonds and collectibles, for example, have illiquid, fragmented markets, with high transaction costs. The markets for gold and silver, in contrast, are fairly liquid, with moderate transaction costs.

Popular forms

Several basic types of tangibles will be discussed in this chapter. First, there are the precious metals, including gold and silver and the strategic metals. Gold and silver are very portable and have liquid resale markets. Strategic metals have less developed marketplaces. Precious stones include diamonds, rubies, and emeralds. We will concentrate on diamonds, a very portable investment with a relatively erratic resale market. Then we will analyze collectible investments. These are primarily of interest to the collector-investor and include rare stamps and coins, artwork, and antiques. Collectibles generally are difficult to resell, but they did experience rapid price appreciation during the 1970s.

One characteristic all these investments have in common is their relative *scarcity value.* Gold, for example, is a fairly rare metal in the earth's crust. Diamonds, particularly those of investment grade, are very rare as well. A 1933 commemorative stamp has rarity value because only a limited number of stamps were originally printed and only a fraction of those exist today. The supply of Gauguin paintings is limited because the artist died in 1903. The relative scarcity of tangibles is an investment characteristic that attracts investors.

Payoff to investors

The only source of investment return from buying most tangibles is price appreciation. Except for rental properties, as we saw in Chapter 16, tangible investments do not pay periodic interest, dividend, or rental returns. The only source of possible return is any capital gain realized upon sale. If a tangible such as gold, silver, or artwork does not appreciate in value rapidly after its purchase, an investor will incur an opportunity cost in the form of lost income that could have been earned from a stock or bond. Another factor to consider is that most tangibles have storage and/or insurance costs which require regular cash outlays. Thus, in contrast to stocks and bonds, tangible investments have periodic cash outlays for storage and/or insurance, and their only payoff is realized upon sale; there are no positive cash flows during the holding period.

When to Invest in Tangibles

As with any investment, timing is the key to a successful tangibles program. This is because prices of tangibles appear to follow a pattern correlated with several widely followed macroeconomic variables, including interest and inflation rates. Tangibles tend to appreciate most when inflation is running at historically high rates, when interest rates are not much higher than the rate of inflation, and when international tensions are high. All three of these conditions occurred in the late 1970s, particularly in 1979 and undoubtedly contributed heavily to the tangibles boom at that time. Changes in those variables can negatively affect tangibles prices as well. From mid-1980 through 1983, economic conditions changed considerably. The rate of inflation dropped, interest rates were much higher than the rate of inflation, and international tensions cooled somewhat. A severe recession occurred as well. In 1981, 1982, and 1983, for example, interest rates were 6 to 10 percent higher than the rate of inflation, and tangibles prices either tumbled or stopped rising. In general, if short-term interest rates are well above the rate of inflation and if international tensions are easing, these factors appear to motivate investors to sell non-interest-paying tangibles and switch into high-interest securities.

If you expect inflation to soar and interest rates to just barely equal or exceed the rate of inflation and/or you expect international tensions to heighten, that could signal a favorable time to consider tangibles investing. Otherwise, a tangibles investor must be prepared to wait patiently for the investment to appreciate in value. Generally, tangibles do not rise rapidly in value unless the conditions described above exist. That is not to say that tangibles cannot possibly be profitable investments under other economic conditions. They can. However, large, pronounced upward price movements are more likely to occur when inflation is rising, when interest rates are around the rate of inflation, and when international problems and tensions abound.

INVESTING IN GOLD

For thousands of years people have been fascinated with gold. Records from the age of the pharoahs in Egypt show a desire to own gold. Today, ownership of gold is still regarded as a necessity by many investors, although its price has dropped considerably since the 1980 peak of $850 per ounce. In Europe, for example, distrust of paper currencies and securities has motivated widespread gold ownership. Americans are relatively recent gold investors. This is due to the legal prohibition on gold ownership, except in jewelry form, for Americans from the mid-1930s until January 1, 1975. After that date, many Americans invested in gold. The modern-day American gold rush climaxed in early 1980. But despite a recent cooling in the desire to own gold, many Americans are still interested. Let us see why and how gold is held.

Growth in Popularity

The second half of 1970s, and in particular 1979 and early 1980, could be called the Gold Rush of the twentieth century. Just as miners and adventurers scampered to California in 1848 and to Alaska and the Yukon in 1898, modern-day

BOX 18.1 THE FORCES THAT DRIVE THE PRICE OF GOLD

Stocks and bonds have been booming, the dollar is strong. Inflation is low and going lower, leaving interest rates, although down from their peaks, historically steep in after-inflation terms. All these conditions normally are bad news for gold investors.

Yet the gold price, in fact, rallied sharply in late summer [1982]. What puzzles investors and economists is why. The answer has to lie in gold's mystifying trinity of roles. Gold is an industrial commodity, an investment medium, and the safest store of value in times of political or economic upheaval. Each role has a different, and sometimes conflicting, influence on gold's price. When gold zoomed from $330 per oz. on Aug. 11 to more than $500 on Sept. 7, the market ignored the influences on its commodity and investment roles because fears of an international banking crisis had brought its safe-haven role to the fore.

Now that the financial scare has faded from the headlines and gold has settled back to a level around $420 per oz., experts believe that the gold price again will respond to economic influences, principally a slight tightening of world supply because of higher demand by several industries that use gold as a commodity: electronics, dentistry, and jewelry. These customers are the principal users of gold, and they are in recession. As they pick up in the expected mild and halting recovery, economists suggest a gradual rise in gold prices—to an average of $450 to $500 in 1983.

"Next year will not provide the same boom conditions as 1979–80," says one gold expert. The runup to $850 per oz. at that time took place under a combination of circumstances unlikely to be duplicated. Not only was inflation raging and the dollar weak against other major currencies, but also real interest rates were low. Oil states were buying gold to diversify their reserves. A sprinkling of other nations' central banks followed suit. At the same time, international political tension was heightened by the Iranian hostage crisis, the takeover of the Grand Mosque in Mecca, the Soviet Union's invasion of Afghanistan, and the South African incursion into Namibia.

Just as gold goes in and out of fashion, so do the theories behind its price movements. During the early 1970s, before gold became a popular, and legal, investment in the U.S., it moved inversely with stock prices. That relationship no longer holds up well, as the parallel surge in gold prices and stocks this summer indicates. Since 1950, some analysts have noted, the prices of gold and oil have moved in tandem in a ratio of one oz. of gold to 18 to 22 bbl. of oil. If that held true today, gold would be at $612 to $748. That relationship, perhaps, may work only over the long term.

Actually, the closest correlation has been with inflation. The experts now say that gold will flourish again as an investment only if inflation and inflationary expectations return with a vengeance, although a financial panic that threatens confidence in all paper assets or widespread political upheaval could have a sharp impact. It is worth noting that during 1981 it required more and more intense political shocks to affect

investors raced to buy gold in the last years of the 1970s. The scramble was motivated by many factors. Two important ones were the high rates of inflation and general world instability. The rocketing price of gold also enticed investors. In 1981 and 1982, the desire to own gold cooled as inflation rates dropped and record high interest rates motivated investors to sell gold and to invest in high-yielding bonds and money market mutual funds. Beginning in late 1982 and continuing through 1983, investors also moved into stocks in order to participate in the record-breaking bull market during that period.

BOX 18.1 *Continued*

the gold market significantly. The assassination of Egypt's President Anwar Sadat and the declaration of martial law in Poland did almost nothing to the gold price.

The theory that inflation dominates is confirmed by recent history: Net investment demand for gold and the gold price peaked both in 1973–75 and in 1979–80, when the U.S. consumer price index also reached double-digit peaks.

The dollar's current strength provides another clue to gold price trends. Gold usually moves inversely to the dollar on international currency markets. The reasoning: A strong dollar implies declining U.S. inflation, and declining inflation rates weaken the gold price. Gold also is observed to move inversely to interest rates, especially real interest rates, which are defined as the gap between nominal interest rates and the rate of inflation. If inflation subsides faster than interest rates, which is what is happening now, real interest rates are high. High real interest rates strengthen the dollar abroad as foreign assets flow into U.S. investments. Where does gold fit in? Obviously, if you can make 8% a year on your money after inflation, instead of the traditional 2% or 3%, you really have to believe that gold will appreciate at least that much to justify a gold investment. So high interest rates tend to compete for investors' funds and depress the price of gold.

If you notice a certain circular quality to all this economic theory, you're right. Interest rates, inflation, currency exchange rates, and economic growth are interrelated. No one is sure whether economic stagnation and low inflation will continue, keeping gold prices down, or whether the economy will turn up, accompanied by renewed high inflation and higher gold prices. It is also possible the economy will recover in an orderly way with mild inflation, and gold's price will rise moderately. Investors, like economists, are split among the three camps.

This standoff means, in part, that gold is acting like any other commodity, with an equilibrium price set by supply and demand. That, too, points to a mild upturn in the gold price. Demand for gold by the jewelry, electronics, and dental industries depends largely on economic activity and prospects for growth. Rising gold prices during 1979 and 1980, which increased demand by investors, forced down industrial demand. The use of gold in jewelry in the noncommunist world, for example, plunged from 1,008 metric tons in 1978 to 120 metric tons in 1980. It has since recovered dramatically and should improve next year. By one account, total industrial use should be up by more than 10%. Supply, meanwhile, is not expected to increase much, if at all. Production in South Africa and other noncommunist nations is fairly constant, and supply might even decrease slightly if the Soviets continue to reduce their level of gold sales.

Source: "The Forces That Drive the Price of Gold," from "Gold Investing Comes Back to Life." *Business Week,* November 8, 1982, p. 138.

The price of gold

By any measure, the increase in the price of gold from 1968 to its 1980 peak has to be called phenomenal. During that period, gold soared from $35 to $850 per ounce. In comparison, the Dow Jones Industrial Average of stock prices declined slightly over the same time period. Investors who held gold during the entire period saw their investment grow in value by almost 25 times. The first big rise in gold prices occurred between 1972 and 1975, when gold moved up steadily from $35 to $200 per ounce. Ironically, that price peak was touched in January 1975, just when Americans were again legally allowed to buy gold. From the early 1975 high

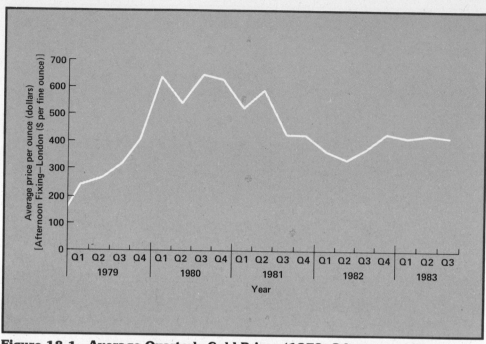

Figure 18.1   Average Quarterly Gold Prices (1979–3d quarter 1983).
The price of gold rapidly surged upward in late 1979 through early 1980, when it peaked at
$850 per ounce, and then late in 1980 began its rapid decline through 1982. At the end of
1983 it typically traded in the range of $300 to $450 per ounce. (*Source:* Data obtained from
Selected Interest and Exchange Rates, [Washington, D.C.: Board of Governors of the Federal
Reserve System, 1979–1983], weekly.)

of $200 per ounce, gold's value declined to below $150 in 1977. Then, in 1978, it
began to rise again. In 1979, gold's price skyrocketed. The $200, $300, $400, $500,
$600, and $700 price barriers were broken in rapid succession in 1979. In early
1980, the peak price of $850 per ounce was reached. Since late 1980, gold's price
has declined, as can be seen in Figure 18.1 where the average quarterly gold prices
are plotted. By 1982 and on through 1983, gold was selling in the $300 to $450
per ounce price range.

Factors affecting gold's price

Gold's price is closely related to several factors, including inflationary expectations, interest rates, and investor psychology. Usually, gold prices rise when inflation
rates are at historically high levels and when investors become nervous because of
national and international developments. In 1979, for example, the Iranian hostage
crisis and other international concerns, coupled with a very high U.S. inflation rate,
undoubtedly motivated many investors to buy gold, raising its price to record levels.
However, as inflation rates fell in the early 1980s, investors sold gold and switched
into other investments. Not only did inflation rates diminish, interest rates rose to
record levels. These factors motivated the switch out of gold and into high-yielding
securities.

In general, times of high inflation and of growing investor concern appear to be the profitable gold investing periods. If investor concerns are alleviated by a lowering of inflation rates and by a lessening of international tensions, this tends to cause a bearish reaction in gold's price. So a gold investor should closely follow the trends in inflation and in interest rates. The expectation of rising inflation would be a motivation to consider gold ownership. In contrast, if inflation appears to be diminishing, this normally bodes well for stocks and bonds, but not for gold.

Investment Forms

Gold can be purchased as coins, bullion, or jewelry and be physically held by an investor. Gold can also be purchased with gold futures, gold mining stocks, and gold certificates.

Gold coins

An easy way to own gold is nonnumismatic *gold coins.* These are coins with little or no coin collector value whose value is primarily determined by their gold content. The price of nonnumismatic gold coins is a function of gold's market price. They tend to sell for 1 to 3 percent over their underlying gold content value. The very slight price premium reflects minting costs. There are numerous issues of gold coins of this type, including U.S. Bureau of the Mint Gold Medallions, Mexican gold coins, the Canadian Maple Leaf coin, the South African Krugerrand, and the Austrian 100 Corona coin. The gold content of these coins is measured in *troy ounces* (a troy ounce contains approximately 31 grams; an avoirdupois ounce contains about 28.3 grams).

Gold coins can be purchased from banks, from gold dealers, and from the U.S. Mint (U.S. Mint Gold Medallions). Commissions vary depending on transaction size, but generally (except for U.S. Mint Gold Medallions, where there is no commission if the coins are purchased directly from the Mint) are in the 2 to 5 percent range. Gold coins are easy to transport and to store, are readily marketable, and normally do not have to be assayed upon sale.

Gold bullion

Gold bullion is the metal in ingot form. Bullion ranges in weight from 5-gram to 400-gram gold bars. A popular size is the kilogram bar, which weighs about 32.15 troy ounces. Any suitable gold bullion bar should bear the gold refiner's trademark, which certifies the bar's weight and purity. Gold bullion can be purchased through gold dealers and banks; commissions and dealer markups range from 3 to 10 percent. Usually these costs are lower on a percentage basis for larger-quantity transactions. Gold bullion may require an assay if resold by an investor. An *assay* is a metallurgical testing process to determine the gold content of a bar or other gold object.

Gold jewelry

Gold jewelry is a popular way to own gold—but it is not the best way to invest in gold. This is because gold jewelry usually sells for a premium over its underlying gold value that reflects artisan costs, retail markups, and other factors. Apparently, the beauty of gold as an ornament is more important to jewelry owners than its investment value. Most jewelry is not pure 24 carat gold; rather, it is 14 or 18 carat gold. Jewelry is usually made from a blend of gold and other nonprecious metals. For example, a gold chain that sells for $1,000 may contain only $400 worth of pure gold. The difference between its price and gold content reflects the artists' compensation and jeweler markups. If you wish to own gold as an investment solely for its metallic value, nonnumismatic coins are better vehicles because they sell for approximately their gold value.

Gold futures

Several commodities exchanges offer gold futures (see Chapter 14 for a detailed discussion of commodities and financial futures). A *gold future* is a contract to buy or to sell a specific amount of gold (usually 100 ounces) at a stated price at a specified future date. An investor is usually required to put up approximately 10 percent of the contract's value at the time of the transaction. The 10 percent earnest money is a form of margin requirement. Additional amounts may be required if gold's price changes in a manner that adversely affects the investor's position. Commissions tend to be about 1 percent of the contract's value. Gold futures are very volatile in price and are suitable only for investors who can handle very high risk of loss. It is possible to lose your entire earnest money in the contract in only a few days.

Gold mining stocks

Many investors prefer to purchase shares of gold mining companies or of mutual funds that invest in *gold stocks.* The prices of gold mining company stocks tend to move in a direct relationship to the price of gold. If gold rises in value, these stocks usually move up too. Conversely, downward movements in gold's price tend to result in a drop in the prices of gold mining stocks.

Shares of U.S. and Canadian gold mining operators are traded on the various stock exchanges and in the over-the-counter market. Homestake Mining, America's largest gold mining concern, has its common stock listed on the New York Stock Exchange. Many small gold mining companies have their stock traded in the over-the-counter market. This market is also the trading arena for the many gold mining stocks of South Africa, the world's largest gold producer. The South African gold mining companies often pay higher dividend yields than their United States or Canadian counterparts. However, the unstable political situation in South Africa adds a substantial risk element to investing in these issues.

It is also possible to purchase shares in mutual funds that invest primarily in gold mining stocks. The advantage of this method of investing is a higher measure of diversification than if only one or two stocks were purchased (see Chapter 15 for a detailed discussion of mutual funds). Most gold-oriented mutual funds own 10 or more gold mining stocks and are managed by professional managers. The shares of gold-oriented mutual funds tend to fluctuate along with the price of gold. ASA, Ltd., a closed end mutual fund, is an example of a gold-oriented fund. It holds a large portfolio of South African mining stocks, and it is listed on the New York Stock Exchange.

Figure 18.2   A Gold Certificate.
A convenient way to buy gold is to buy a gold certificate that represents ownership in a specific number of ounces of gold stored in a bank vault. (*Source:* Utica National Bank and Trust, Tulsa, Oklahoma.)

Gold certificates

A convenient and safe way to own gold is to purchase a *gold certificate* through a bank or a broker. A gold certificate represents ownership of a specific quantity of gold that is stored in a bank vault. Figure 18.2 is a facsimile of a gold certificate issued by a Tulsa, Oklahoma, bank. The advantages of gold certificates are several. First, the investor does not have the safety worry that taking physical possession of gold entails. Second, by purchasing gold certificates, state sales taxes imposed on coin or bullion purchases may be avoided. Typical sales commissions on gold certificates range from 1 to 3 percent. In addition, the bank storing the gold usually charges an annual storage fee that is approximately ½ of 1 percent.

Gold as an Investment Vehicle

Investment suitability

Gold is a fairly speculative investment vehicle whose price has fluctuated widely in recent years. Its volatile price movements are a sizable risk element to consider.

BOX 18.2 INVESTING IN STRATEGIC METALS

Had you been smart enough to pick up some cobalt in 1978 at $5 per pound, you would have seen its price skyrocket to near $50 within two years. That equals an annual compounded growth rate of over 200 percent.

But if you were foolish enough to keep your cobalt until today, or worse, bought some during the 1981 strategic metals euphoria, you would have seen its price tumble back to under $5 per pound by the end of 1982. The cobalt bubble had burst.

Cobalt is only one of about 20 so-called "strategic" minor metals whose price has escalated almost 1,000 percent within a very short time only to fall back again. Most other strategic metals, as well as base and precious metals, undergo similar price "spikes" once every few years. But the bubbles are much more pronounced with strategic metals.

In the early 1970s, antimony was a hot performer with its price increasing tenfold within a year or so. Other metals such as cadmium and selenium peaked twice during the 1970s, escalating in price within a year or two by about 300 and 700 percent, respectively.

The extreme ups and downs in prices, combined with a certain degree of predictability in when peaks would be reached, have at times proved a powerful attraction for commodity speculators and adventurous investors. Even if your timing is only half right, when prices are escalating profits can pile up quickly. But unless you are one of the professional metal traders or dealers *who know when to sell,* chances are equally good that you will see your investment melt away even faster. You may even fall victim to a fast-moving metals scam and end up with a worthless piece of paper in your safe or a useless heap of scrap metal in your backyard.

SUPPLY UNCERTAINTIES

You may already have heard the popular arguments for buying and holding strategic metals: Most of the strategics must be imported from unstable third world countries of southern Africa, and the major alternative sources are the Soviet Union or Cuba. Should East-West tensions escalate, or Marxist governments take over the rest of southern Africa as they have done in Angola, Mozambique, and Zimbabwe, then the whole NATO alliance and Japan are at risk. This could mean an embargo on supplies of strategic metals that are critical for the construction of jet engines, aircraft, missiles, nuclear weapons, tanks, ships, and stainless steel.

The U.S. Army War College even developed a vulnerability index that rates most strategic metals according to how critical they are to the U.S. defense establishment.

Cobalt is rated among the most critical, along with chromium, platinum metals, titanium, manganese, aluminum, tungsten, and vanadium. This holds true for the U.S. because we must rely on imports for most of our strategic metals. Japan and our Western European allies are in an even worse predicament. They must import almost 100 percent of many base and strategic metals. On the other hand, the Soviet Union is sitting pretty. Russia controls large resources of just about every strategic metal and is also a leading producer of chromium, cobalt, and platinum metals, which are so critical to the West.

In strategic metals, the "panic factor" plays an important role because sometimes real shortages do occur as a result of floods, droughts, earthquakes, hurricanes, terrorism, sabotage, labor strikes, and trade embargoes. During the 1970s, this was intensified by the success of the OPEC oil cartel and rampaging inflation. Increasing costs of energy and developing recession reduced the demand for many metals while their cost of production went up.

Zaire, where 70 percent of world cobalt reserves are concentrated, has been reducing

BOX 18.2 *Continued*

cobalt production since 1973. By the mid-1970s, Angola and Mozambique fell to the Marxists and civil war in neighboring Rhodesia escalated while transportation routes for copper and cobalt ores were disrupted.

As if this were not enough, in 1978 and again in 1979, Marxist rebels from Angola invaded Zaire, closing down production of copper and cobalt for a while. Another OPEC oil price hike, the Soviet invasion of Afghanistan, and the revolution in Iran further contributed to global unrest. *All those events had a cumulative effect on cobalt, gold, and other metals prices.* In the case of cobalt, panic buying by end-users rather than any actual shortage of cobalt was a major factor responsible for escalating prices. . . .

PICKING THE NEXT WINNERS

If previous price performance is an indication of things to come, several strategic metals should be peaking again during the 1984–85 period, particularly if economic recovery gets under way and new defense programs enter the production phase. Current recession, falling demand, and rock-bottom metal prices have been responsible for closing of 50 percent of North American mines already. *If economic recovery is faster than expected, current metal stockpiles and inventories could be quickly depleted.* That means a new shortage would soon set in, leading once again to price escalations in several metals.

This may look like a real opportunity shaping up for you. But as an average investor, you must still try to pick the metals that are most likely to escalate in price by several hundred percent during the next peaking period.

You could try to spread your risk by investing in 10 or 20 of the metals. But to do that you'd have to sink at least $100,000 into a metals portfolio. That's because strategic metals are traded in minimum unit sizes that range anywhere between $5,000 to $10,000 each.

As a small investor, you will always be limited to only one or two metals at a time, and your choice of the right one becomes more critical if you hope to make a killing. You will also have to pay in full for your metals when you make the purchase, and will not be able to buy on margin. Unlike the base metals, such as aluminum, copper, lead, nickel, tin, and zinc, strategic metals are not traded on any exchanges and leveraged futures or options are not available.

This brings home the fact that *strategic metals are not as liquid* an investment as various forms of gold, platinum, palladium or any of the base metals that are traded on COMEX in New York, and London Metals Exchange (LME) in England. You may find it relatively easy to buy, but when you want to sell, you must find a buyer and negotiate a price as if you were selling a piece of real estate.

There are about 1,500 metal traders around the world, but most of them do business with strategic and base metals industrial consumers and are seldom interested in transactions under $50,000. If you want to get into strategics as a small investor you must go to a metals broker who maintains his own stocks and inventories and can deal in large quantities with metal traders.

During the 1981 strategic metals euphoria, there were at least 30 strategic metals brokers in the U.S. ready to sell you any strategic metal that took your fancy. In reality, even they concentrated on those metals that are actively traded. These include antimony, cadmium, chromium, cobalt, germanium, indium, molybdenum, tantalum, tungsten, and vanadium. Several brokers also planned to set up strategic metals funds or limited partnerships with minimum investment as low as $1,000, but the recession and falling metal prices put an end to those ideas and many of the upstart brokers as well. . . .

(Continued)

BOX 18.2 *Continued*

SOME HELP IN DECIDING

If you decide that strategic metals are your bag, you must still decide which metals to buy. Recent economic trends may provide some direction. The shifting of "smokestack" industries such as steel, automobiles, and shipbuilding from industrialized countries to the third world does not augur well for strategic metals that are consumed by those industries. The ferroalloys metals such as silicon, molybdenum, manganese, chromium, and vanadium will now be consumed by the new stainless steel plants going up in developing countries, and their importance in international trade may diminish.

More promising are the "sunrise industries" materials that are used in electronics, aerospace, lasers, and telecommunications. These include iridium, gallium, germanium, magnesium, columbium, and tantalum, whose projected consumption in the future is expected to grow faster than that for other metals. But *perhaps the best opportunities will develop in gadolinium and samarium*, almost unknown rare earths metals that have unique applications in protective coatings against neutron bomb radiation, electronic "bubble memories" that use very little power and do not lose data when switched off, and provide powerful micromagnets for electronic devices of tomorrow.

Even having identified the exotic and growing markets for strategic metals of the future, you must also keep track of how fast the capacity to produce these metals has been growing in recent years. Despite the geopolitics, the import dependence, the Soviet intentions, South African instability, and your broker's assurances, it's the overall demand and supply situation that will determine the price action of your metals in the long run.

Source: Bohdan O. Szuprowicz, "Mining Profits in Strategic Metals." *FACT,* April 1983, pp. 29–33.

Additionally, gold obviously does not pay dividends. An investor's only source of potential return is possible price appreciation. Gold did provide many investors with huge capital gains during the 1970s; should inflation and international instability increase during the 1980s, gold's price could move upward again.

Basically, gold can be viewed as "insurance" against hyperinflation and/or a world economic or political disaster. Gold can be purchased in a portfolio as a hedge. Holding large quantities of gold is risky, however, as the 1980–1983 record shows. Gold should probably be purchased only by those who can bear the risk of a possible price decline.

Transaction, storage costs, and safekeeping

Transaction costs in gold vary widely, depending on the investment form chosen. At one extreme, a Hawaiian investor buying one Canadian Maple Leaf coin might pay 5 percent commission, 7 percent dealer markup, and 4 percent gross excise tax (sales tax). In contrast, a gold certificate purchase could entail only a 2 percent total commission and markup, with no sales tax. The transactions costs of buying and selling gold are generally a function of the quantity purchased. The greater the purchase or sale amount, the lower transactions costs on a percentage-of-purchase basis. Storage costs for gold vary as well. Gold coins and bars can easily be stored in a safe deposit box that costs $20 per year. Gold purchased via gold certificates usually is subject to a storage fee of less than 1 percent per year.

Gold coins, bullion, and jewelry are easy for thieves to sell, so it is imperative that these items be safely stored. A safe deposit box at a bank or other depository can alleviate this worry. Never leave gold in an unsecured place.

OTHER TANGIBLE INVESTMENTS

So far, we have considered the investment merits of gold, a tangible investment that has widespread investor interest. Other tangible investments have attracted investor attention as well, particularly during 1978, 1979, and 1980. These include other precious metals, precious gemstones, and collectibles. Most of the investments we consider next share a common trait not shared with gold or silver. That is, they lack liquidity—the ability to be sold easily for cash. Of all the investments we discuss, only silver has a fairly high degree of liquidity. Strategic metals, diamonds, and collectibles have erratic resale markets with relatively high transaction costs.

Investors dealing in strategic metals, gemstones, and collectibles encounter problems not found in the stock and bond markets. These include insurance and storage costs, as well as the lack of a good liquid resale market. Other problems include possible forgeries in the case of collectibles, and with diamonds, the fact that the market is heavily influenced by a single firm. Precious metals and gemstones and collectibles were hot investments in the late 1970s. Although their popularity has waned somewhat recently, the solid returns posted by them in earlier years merit their analysis here.

Precious Metals and Gemstones

Silver and diamond prices reached a peak in 1980. By 1983, prices had fallen substantially from the 1980 highs, although they remained above the early 1970s levels. The markets for each of these investments are markedly different, as we will see. Silver has a fairly liquid resale market, whereas diamonds do not. Our discussion concentrates on silver, strategic metals, and diamonds. Strategic metals gained popularity after silver and diamonds, but suffer from a weak resale market as well. First we will consider the investment merits of silver, then strategic metals, and finally diamonds; these are the most popular precious metal and stone investments after gold. We will not consider other related investments, such as platinum, rubies, emeralds, and sapphires, because these have very specialized markets and in general have not attracted widespread investor interest.

Silver

The price behavior of silver since 1970 is best described by one word—volatile. Silver prices skyrocketed during the 1970s, peaked then crashed in 1980, and settled, in 1981, 1982, and 1983 at levels about 80 percent below the 1980 high. From 1970 to early 1980, silver's price rose from approximately $2 per ounce to $50. Then the price dropped sharply in 1980 from the $50 peak to $10 in only a few months. This decline was related to the Hunt brothers' alleged manipulations. By

1982, silver was trading in the $5 to $11 per ounce range, well below the 1980 peak but still above early 1970s levels. At year-end 1983, silver traded at about $9 per ounce.

Many investors lost heavily during the silver debacle of 1980. At that time, the Hunt brothers of Dallas allegedly tried to corner the market for silver in an attempt to drive up its price. This alleged manipulation failed miserably, and silver prices plunged in 1980 from the peak price. The very rapid drop caused severe losses for many silver investors.

Risks in silver investment.   Potential silver investors should consider several risk factors. First, unlike gold, silver has many industrial uses, particularly in photographic products. If silver were no longer needed by the photo industry, its price could plummet. Second, enormous quantities of silver are believed to be hoarded worldwide, particularly in India. In that country, an estimated 1 billion ounces is held by investors. Any large upward price movement for silver could result in a vast outpouring of stored metal onto the market. This could keep silver's price from moving up very much. Additionally, the 1980 Hunt brothers' alleged price manipulation has turned off many investors. These investors are concerned that the metal's price could be manipulated again, and this has kept them away from the metal. All these potential risk elements should be carefully considered prior to investing in silver.

Ways to own silver.   There are several ways to own silver should you decide that you can bear the risks. These include silver bullion, coins, futures, and silver mining stocks.

The metal itself can be acquired in bullion or coin form. *Silver bullion,* in the form of bars, is available in sizes ranging from 10 to 1,000 ounces. Nonnumismatic *silver coins* offer another possible investment medium. There are many United States silver coins available because prior to 1965, the United States minted silver dimes, quarters, and half-dollars. These coins are 90 percent silver. The Kennedy half-dollars of the 1965–1970 period are 40 percent silver. Bags of both the 90-percent and 40-percent silver coins are available through dealers. Silver coins have also been minted by many other countries, including Canada, France, Holland, Mexico, and Switzerland. Transactions costs to buy silver bullion and coins vary depending on transaction size and are similar to those charged for gold bullion and coins. Silver is usually a fairly marketable metal—that is, it is fairly easy to buy and to sell, and transaction costs are not high.

Silver futures are a speculative way to invest in the metal. These high-risk, high-return-potential futures contracts are similar to gold futures contracts. Because silver's price tends to be more volatile than gold's, silver futures probably are riskier than the high-risk gold futures contracts.

Investors also can buy *silver mining stocks.* There are over 300 U.S. silver mine operators, plus additional firms in Canada. The stocks trade both on stock exchanges and in the over-the-counter market. Hecla Mining and Sunshine Mining are companies whose stock is listed on the NYSE. Many stocks of smaller silver miners trade in the OTC market. Most of these stocks are very risky investments because their price fluctuates with silver's price and because the OTC markets for them is erratic. These issues have experienced enormous price fluctuations since the mid-1970s, as has silver's price. For example, the stock of Rex-Montis Mines, a small Utah-based silver miner, rose from 25 cents to $4 per share from mid-1979 to early 1980. During the price collapse of 1980, the stock dropped from $4 to $1 per share in two months. By 1982, the stock was trading in the 10 to 25 cents per share range. You should probably avoid the shares of all silver companies except the very largest firms.

Overall, silver is a more speculative investment than gold. Its price movements have been very volatile, and there are many elements of risk to consider. Silver does not appear to be as good an inflation hedge as gold, and it should probably be considered only by risk-oriented investors.

Strategic Metals

A number of non-U.S.-mined metals are vital to the production of many U.S.-made goods. The vast American production system could be shut down fairly quickly if manufacturers could no longer import these metals, often called *strategic metals.* They include cobalt, chromium, gallium, germanium, indium, magnesium, rhodium, and titanium. Titanium, for example, is vital in the construction of fighter planes. Rhodium is used in auto catalytic converters to reduce engine emissions.

Beginning primarily in 1980 and 1981, these metals were sold to investors as hedges against a crisis-caused cutoff of supplies. Sellers argued that foreign wars, rebellions, and other related problems could leave U.S. manufacturers without these vital raw materials. Should that occur, manufacturers would pay investors almost any price to buy their stored holdings, thus providing huge profits. Although there is some logic to this line of thinking, the predictions of impending strategic metal shortages have not been realized. In fact, most strategic metal investors have not earned any profits, and many are holding large metal positions that if sold would result in a loss.

Strategic metals are a high-risk investment to avoid. High profits are possible, but there are several risk factors to consider. First, the resale markets for these metals are erratic; a position could be very difficult to sell. Commissions and dealer markups are high, and storage costs will be incurred. Plus, and most important, the cutoff of supply of these metals will probably never occur. Producer countries, such as Zaire and South Africa, generally need the export dollars these metals bring. Overall, the investment characteristics of these metals is such that they probably should be avoided by all investors except wealthy persons who can bear a high risk of loss and the possibility of holding a very illiquid vehicle.

Diamonds

During 1981 and 1982, the great diamond bust of the twentieth century occurred. After many years of continuous price rises, diamond prices plunged sharply. For example, the peak price of a one-carat (one *carat* weighs $1/142$ of an ounce) flawless stone, a favorite investment diamond, was about $60,000 in early 1980. By late 1982, this stone was worth only about $20,000—a drop of 67 percent in just over two years. The big crash in diamond prices caught most investors by surprise. They were accustomed to a long history of continued increases in diamond prices. During the 1970s, for example, diamond prices rose at a rate much higher than the rate of inflation. In fact, diamond prices had risen continually since the early 1930s. The big price drop in 1981 and in 1982 was not expected, and investors who had purchased investment diamonds during 1979 and 1980 suffered heavy losses. It should be noted, however, that diamond prices in late 1983 were still over 15 times higher than they were in 1972. Investors who bought diamonds prior to the 1979–1980 boom still find themselves in a profitable position.

Diamond fundamentals.   Diamonds interest investors for several reasons. First, they are very rare in the earth's crust and they are very expensive to find. Their rarity value attracts collector-investors as well as jewelry lovers. Second, for many years the marketing of recently mined uncut stones has been almost totally controlled by one company, DeBeers Consolidated Mines, Ltd., of South Africa. DeBeers, through its subsidiary, the Central Selling Organization, markets most of the world's raw diamond output. DeBeers sets uncut diamond prices, tries to control mine output, and controls uncut diamond sales in an attempt to control prices. For many years, the DeBeers cartel successfully kept diamond prices rising. By 1980, however, DeBeers had lost control of the investment diamond market, and the market gyrated wildly. Prior to 1980, prices had soared despite DeBeers' attempts at moderating increases. In 1981 and in 1982, prices plunged despite DeBeers' price-propping efforts. By late 1983 the market had apparently settled down, but earlier notions of DeBeers' supposed all-encompassing power were clearly under question. In the future, the DeBeers

cartel will remain a strong market force in diamonds, but not the almighty ruler it was perceived to be in the past. Also, diamond production in Zaire, Brazil, and the USSR could increase, and those stones could be marketed outside DeBeers' control.

Because each diamond is unique, its clarity, color, cut, and carat weight will strongly influence its value. Most investors, not being experienced gemologists, must rely on outside experts to evaluate a diamond. This would not normally be a problem except that experts often disagree as to a stone's value. To minimize this difficulty, the Gemological Institute of America has created a well-regarded diamond grading system. Certificates can be obtained verifying the quality and grade of a diamond. Still, two dealers, both experts, could easily offer differing opinions as to a stone's value. Investors probably should consider only top-grade diamonds that have an appropriate certificate of grade. These diamonds, although relatively difficult to resell, are more liquid than stones with lower-quality grades.

Buying investment diamonds.   Investment diamonds can be purchased through diamond dealers. Depending on quality and grade, commissions and dealer markup could range from 20 to 100 percent. Because of the difficulty in valuing diamonds, it is imperative that you select only dealers with impeccable reputations. During the 1979–1980 boom, many unethical operators moved into the investment diamond market. Avoid these dealers, because they want to sell you low-grade stones at high-grade prices. Diamonds should be purchased only by investors who can hold the stones for at least two years: High transaction costs usually prevent profitable resale after shorter holding periods. Diamonds can be difficult to resell, and sellers often wait a month or more for a stone to be sold. Diamonds also require secure storage, and there are no payoffs prior to sale. All returns are from any price appreciation realized upon sale. In general, diamonds should be purchased only by sophisticated investors who can wait patiently for any possible price appreciation.

Collectibles

Rare coins and stamps, artwork, and antiques are types of collectibles. A *collectible* has value because of its attractiveness to collectors. The many forms of collectibles include comic books, old bottles, and French Impressionist paintings. During the decade of the 1970s, many collectibles rose markedly in value. Referring back to Table 18.1, we can see that U.S. coins, U.S. stamps, Oriental rugs, and Chinese ceramics all had inflation-beating returns from 1972 to 1982. However, the large price movements of these items occurred prior to 1981, because between 1981 and 1982, most collectibles either fell in value or appreciated less than the rate of inflation.

In addition to the 1981–1982 price trend reversals, there are other factors to consider. In general, collectibles are very illiquid investments. Their resale markets are poor, and transaction costs can be very high. Artwork, for example, commonly has a 100 percent dealer markup, and sales tax is added to the retail price. An investor who wishes to sell artwork quickly may only be able to obtain 50 percent of its retail price. Works sold on consignment to a dealer may incur a 25 percent commission and may take months to sell.

BOX 18.3 ANTIQUES AS INVESTMENTS: LOVE OR MONEY?

You're in an antique shop eyeing a Pennsylvania Dutch cupboard. Perhaps it would add a touch of color to your otherwise contemporary living room or simply be the crowning touch to your rustic dining room. You're tempted, but the price seems a bit steep. The shopowner reminds you that antiques have appreciated in price 15 percent or so each year for the last decade, and he suggests that you consider the cupboard a good investment, not just a piece of furniture.

Some customers, minds aglow with visions of capital gains, might then grab the item. Should you?

If you buy the cupboard as an investment, you've probably purchased it for the wrong reason. What are the right reasons? Dealers and savvy investment specialists alike suggest that you should buy an antique because you like it, because you will feel comfortable living with it, and because its style is a statement of your taste. Investment considerations should always be secondary. Here are a few of their thoughts and caveats on purchasing antiques as investments:

- The shopowner's premise that, since prices of antiques have escalated 15 percent a year they will continue to do so, is fallacious: History is not an indicator of future prices. For example, the collectibles market, which shot up in the late 1970s, has crashed; Tiffany lamps and Ansel Adams photographs now sell for one-third to one-half what they cost two years ago; and antique furniture prices are generally down. If you purchase an extremely popular item, you run the risk of buying in at the top and then selling out at the bottom after a shift in taste.
- An investment in antiques—unlike other ventures—doesn't yield interest or dividends. That Pennsylvania Dutch cupboard you buy for $5,000 today could sell for $8,000 five years from now. But a $3,000 capital gain doesn't look quite so good when you realize that you could have made at least the same amount in a federally insured bank account.
- Appreciation in price is not equal to the profit you will realize from the sale of your antiques. The consumer buys antiques at retail prices but usually sells them at wholesale. If you buy an item for $5,000 and hear that comparable antiques are retailing for $10,000, what will an antique dealer pay you for your treasure? There's nothing immoral about a 50 percent markup—that's how dealers make a living—so your dealer may offer you $5,000, if he will take the piece at all. This means your antique must appreciate 50 to 100 percent in price before you can expect to make even a reasonable return.

Despite the disadvantages, collectibles can be a good inflation hedge during high inflation times such as the late 1970s, and they sometimes can be used to beautify a home or office. The investor can have fun collecting as well. Let's look at four types of collectible investments: stamps, coins, artwork, and antiques.

Philately (stamp collecting)

Rare stamps have appreciated substantially over long time periods. For example, an 1861 George Washington 3-cent stamp was worth about $3 in 1970. By 1982, this stamp cost $45 at retail and could be sold in the wholesale-dealer stamp market for about $20 to $30. A 1964 hunting-permit stamp bearing the likeness of a Nene Goose, Hawaii's state bird, was originally sold by the U.S. Department of the

BOX 18.3 *Continued*

- Antiques are not a liquid investment and may not be easy to sell. A dealer usually is not eager to buy an item for resale if he has something similar in stock. He might accept your antique on consignment (you own it until it's sold, and the dealer gets a commission), but it may languish in the dealer's showroom for months. This goes far to explain the popularity of auction houses like Sotheby Parke-Bernet or Christie's, where your antique will usually sell after a few minutes of bidding, and the auction house charges only a small commission.
- What's represented as an antique may not truly be antique. If you're a novice, always get at least one independent appraisal before investing big money. This is especially important when buying country furniture, which is relatively easy to counterfeit.

These cautions don't mean that you shouldn't buy antiques: They do, however, point out that only people knowledgeable about the market should make purchases with an eye towards investment. If you are not among that group, you will be happiest buying what you love and want to live with.

If you want quality and the flavor of antiques at less than premium antique cost, consider purchasing reproductions. They don't usually appreciate in price, so investment considerations should play no role in your decision. The quality of many lines is quite high: Some museums—notably the Winterthur Museum in Winterthur, Del., and the American Museum of Folk Art in New York City—are even licensing reproductions of one-of-a-kind furniture masterpieces in their collections.

It is true, though, that no copy can reproduce an antique's mellow patina or the sense of history that comes from knowing that a piece of furniture has been used for generations. If these things are all-important to you, by all means invest in antiques. Be forewarned, though; having made your purchase, you run one further risk. You may discover that an item you picked up for a song is worth a small fortune, but you may like it so much that you can't bear to part with it.

Source: "Buying Antiques as Investments: For Love or Money?" *Home,* September 1982, pp. 40–42.

Interior for $3. By 1970, this pretty stamp was worth about $5; by 1982, its value was in the $50 to $100 range.

Over long time periods, rare stamps tend to appreciate at inflation-beating rates. The key words in profitable stamp collecting are *rare* and *long*. Stamps with rarity value appreciate the most. Stamps whose numbers are limited have much greater profit potential than a large and recent Postal Service edition of commemorative stamps. The recent issue may mean hundreds of millions of stamps in existence, so there is very little rarity value. Collector-investors must also be patient and should be prepared to hold their stamps for at least several years. There are no quick profits from stamp collecting.

The market for rare stamps is not well organized, and consists of many large and small dealers. Transaction costs and dealer markups can be high. An expensive rare stamp could take months to resell, and it must be carefully stored. Stamps are an illiquid investment; no return is realized until resale. Basically, a stamp collector can enjoy the hobby and possibly reap future profits. A person who is not interested in philately as a hobby should probably avoid the investment.

Numismatics (coin collecting)

The economics of coin collecting are very similar to that of stamp collecting. Rare coins have appreciated in value over long time periods. The U.S. $20 gold piece, for example, was worth $20 in 1930, when it was legal tender. By 1970, the coin was worth about $50. During the 1970s, this coin's value, as well as that of other rare coins, soared. It sold for over $1,000 in 1980, reflecting both its gold value and its coin collector value. By 1982, the coin's value was about $600. Its price drop reflected gold's price correction after 1980 and sluggish collector demand. This example illustrates an important coin collector-investor requirement—patience. The patient, long-term investor who held the coin a long time benefited from the price rise from 1970 to 1982. A speculator, in contrast, probably bought the coin in 1980 in hope of a fast, easy profit. That person's loss position demonstrates the need for patience in stamp and coin collecting and investing.

In summary, rare coins and stamps can be interesting to collect, but they are investments that require patience. Their markets are fragmented, transactions costs are high, and they are illiquid. These investments are best suited for investor-collectors who enjoy the hobby.

Artwork

Artwork can not only provide price appreciation potential, but also a beautiful room or office. Whereas most investments provide only a monetary payoff, artwork has a dual source of return—capital gains upon sale and helping to provide a pleasant living or working environment in the meantime. During the 1970s, collector artwork tended to appreciate in value at inflation-beating rates. By *collector artwork* we mean paintings, prints, sculpture, and other works of recognized artists. A $10 painting acquired at a local motel, for example, is not collector artwork; a Picasso or Dali print is. The big artwork boom of the 1970s did not continue into 1981 and 1982. During those two years, many pieces actually declined in value. This price correction can be attributed to a prolonged recession, lower inflation rates, and interest rates well above the rate of inflation. Collector artwork prices in late 1983 were still well above 1973 levels, however, and even with the 1981–1982 correction, most quality artwork did outperform inflation during the 1972–1982 period.

There are various ways to invest in artwork. Some experts suggest that prints with rarity value may be of interest to beginning collectors. These are prints produced by known artists in limited quantities, perhaps 50 to 100. A print from an edition of 10,000, in contrast, is basically a poster with very little rarity value.

Artwork, like other collectibles, is an illiquid investment that requires patience in order to realize price appreciation. The resale market is fragmented, with high transaction costs. For those investors who enjoy artwork, the investment can make good sense. However, because of the illiquidity problem, an investor obviously would not want a substantial portion of his or her net worth tied up in artwork.

Antiques

Antiques are a form of artwork that can add a certain style to a home or an office. As an investment, they can provide potential long-term price appreciation. However, keep in mind that they are an illiquid investment, with high transaction costs.

Antique and artwork investors must be careful to avoid forgeries. A skilled furniture maker, for example, can easily reproduce a "200-year-old antique table" in his or her garage. Deal only with reputable dealers and auction houses. Be leery of great bargains; they may be forgeries. And don't forget to buy insurance on your artwork and antiques. Your standard homeowner's or renter's policy may not fully cover these items. Overall, these collectibles can appreciate over time, but they are difficult to resell.

SUMMARY

Gold, silver, diamonds, and other tangibles enjoyed a period of rising popularity and high rates of return during the decade of the 1970s. The glitter diminished, however, in the 1980–1982 period, when most of these investments suffered price declines. Silver, for example, experienced an 80 percent price decline in only several months during 1980. Diamonds dropped in value by a very significant amount as well. Basically, it appears that interest rates, if they substantially exceed the rate of inflation, negatively affect tangibles' prices. Very high interest rates (well above inflation) motivate people to sell tangibles—thereby pushing down their prices—and to buy interest-paying vehicles such as bonds and money market mutual funds.

Gold is probably the most widely held tangible asset (excluding real estate). During the 1970s, its price skyrocketed in value. From 1980 to 1982, the desire for gold cooled somewhat, and its price declined about 50 to 60 percent from the early 1980 peak of $850 per ounce. The many forms of gold investing include coins, bullion, jewelry, futures, stocks, mutual funds, and certificates.

Silver's price has declined dramatically since 1980, following a huge price rise. The decline can be attributed to the Hunt brothers' actions in 1980 and to very high interest rates in 1980 and 1981. Strategic metals are investments that could pay off if a war or other international calamity occurred, but they are not suitable investments for most people. Diamonds soared in price during the 1970s, but prices fell by about 60 to 70 percent from 1980 to 1982. Diamonds are very hard to resell, in contrast to gold and silver, which have fairly liquid markets.

Collectibles include rare stamps and coins, artwork, and antiques. These investments also soared in value during the 1970s but cooled off considerably in the early 1980s. Collectibles have illiquid resale markets and probably are best suited for collector-investors who derive psychic benefits as well as possible capital gains from investing in them.

KEY TERMS

assay
carat
collectible
collector artwork
financial asset
gold bullion
gold certificate
gold coin
gold future
gold mining stock

numismatics
philately
silver bullion
silver coin
silver future
silver mining stocks
strategic metal
tangible investment
troy ounce

REVIEW QUESTIONS

1. Compare and contrast financial assets with tangible assets as investment vehicles.

2. Explain the widespread popularity of tangible investments during the 1970s and describe the economic conditions that tend to cause tangibles to find favor with investors and rise in price.

3. Discuss the returns from tangibles in view of profits, cash flows, and capital appreciation, and compare their form of return to that available from stocks and bonds.

4. Discuss the recent price behavior of the following investment vehicles:

a. Gold.
b. Silver.
c. Diamonds.

d. Rare stamps.
e. Artwork.
f. Stocks.

5. What is the single source of investment return from a gold coin? What do you perceive the risk-return factors for such an investment to be? Explain.

6. Suppose you believe gold will soon jump in price. Would you buy numismatic coins or nonnumismatic coins? Why?

7. Describe the investment characteristics of each of these forms of gold investment:

a. Gold bullion.
b. Gold jewelry.
c. Gold futures.

d. Gold mining stocks.
e. Gold certificates.

8. Describe the mechanics of gold futures. For what type of investor would such a contract be suitable?

9. Compare and contrast the following forms of silver investment:

a. Silver bullion.
b. Silver coins.

c. Silver futures.
d. Silver mining stocks.

10. Suppose Eastman Kodak has just announced a new film that does not require silver in its manufacture or development. How will this development affect silver bullion prices? Silver mining stock prices?

11. Describe the investment characteristics of strategic metals. How do they compare and contrast with those of gold?

12. Suppose a large new field of diamonds was discovered in Brazil. How would this development affect investment diamond prices? How would this affect DeBeers stock? Explain.

13. Compare and contrast the resale markets of gold and of diamonds. Why are diamonds more difficult to resell than gold coins?

14. Discuss the investment characteristics of the following collectibles:

a. Stamps.
b. Coins.

c. Artwork.
d. Antiques.

CASE PROBLEMS

18.1 SARA STARLIGHT'S DECISION: DIAMONDS AND GOLD VERSUS STOCKS

Sara Starlight is a budding Hollywood starlet who has just signed her first major contract to costar in a TV pilot tentatively titled "The Young Musicians." In the planned TV series, Sara will play the role of a young rock star. After hundreds of auditions and a few bit parts over the past six years since Sara, now 26, moved to Hollywood, she finally feels her career is beginning to blossom. Because the studio felt Sara was the perfect person to play the role, her agent, Shady O'Brien, was able to negotiate an attractive contract that included a $50,000 signing bonus in addition to an excellent per episode salary.

Sara, while ecstatic about the wonderful opportunity, recognizes the many uncertainties of show business life. If the series takes off, she will be set financially and the door will be open for many new acting opportunites. On the other hand, if it fails, Sara will have to continue paying for acting lessons, auditioning, and working part-time as a model until she gets her next break. The insecurity of acting is clearly omnipresent in Sara's life.

Sara's current thoughts center on wisely investing the $40,000 of the signing bonus remaining after Shady deducts his agent's fee. She has talked with her brother, who is a stockbroker in her hometown of Houston, Texas. He urged Sara to invest in a high-technology growth stock with good appreciation potential. Shady, on the other hand, is prompting her to buy investment-grade diamond and gold jewelry. He points out that over the past 12 years, investment-grade diamonds and gold have appreciated at a faster rate than inflation. In addition, Shady says that Sara needs to promote an image of success in the Hollywood tradition. Flashy diamond and gold jewelry will act both as an excellent investment vehicle and a critical component in building Sara's image as a successful young starlet. In response to Sara's query about what will happen if the series doesn't take off, Shady pointed out that the high-quality jewelry in which he is proposing Sara invest can be easily sold, if necessary.

Questions

1. Assess Sara's investment objective in view of the information provided.

2. Evaluate the validity of Shady O'Brien's assessment of the historical price behavior, liquidity, and overall investment merit of the recommended diamond and gold jewelry investment.

3. Compare and contrast the two investment alternatives currently being considered by Sara, pointing out the risk-return potential of each.

4. Considering both financial and nonfinancial factors, which of the alternatives would you recommend to Sara? Explain.

18.2 THE JOHNSONS' BIG SWITCH

Having not done very well in the stock market, the Johnsons have recently decided to confine their investment activities to buying gold and silver and artwork and antiques for their home. Rick and Jan Johnson live in Fort Collins, Colorado. Both are schoolteachers, and they have no children. They are both 37 years old. They have tried investing in stocks, but found that their returns were quite erratic. In some years, such as 1982, they did quite well. In other years, their profits were not very large. So they decided to call it quits with the stock market. Rick and Jan have pension plans at their jobs that are heavily weighted toward stocks and bonds. They believe these plans more than adequately meet their securities investment needs.

In analyzing other investment vehicles, they dismissed options and commodities and financial futures as too risky. They are not interested in further real estate investments, as they do not wish to be landlords and they own their home. They are not interested in limited partnerships; Rick and Jan prefer to manage their own investments. After much deliberation and analysis, they have decided to liquidate their $70,000 stock portfolio over the next year and invest $20,000 in gold, $10,000 in silver, $20,000 in artwork, and $10,000 in antique furniture. They plan to keep a $10,000 cash reserve at Fort Collins Savings and Loan, and they believe they can contribute another $7,000 each year to this savings nestegg. Jan Johnson teaches art appreciation at Fort Collins High School, and Rick Johnson is interested in antiques. Neither is especially knowledgeable about precious metal investments.

Questions

1. What do you think of the Johnson's decision to liquidate their portfolio of stocks in order to buy gold, silver, artwork, and antiques?

2. List some problems the Johnsons could encounter with their proposed investment program. Are there nonfinancial benefits provided by these proposed investments? Explain.

3. Assume Jan bought several prints for $2,000 and held them two years. If the prints appreciated each year at a 25 percent compound annnual rate, how much would she make from her investment? Recompute her profit assuming she had to pay a 30 percent commission when the prints were sold.

4. If the Johnsons came to you for investment advice prior to taking the proposed actions, what might you advise? Explain.

SELECTED READINGS

"Adventurous Investing in Strategic Metals." *Business Week*, October 12, 1981, pp. 170–174.

Arens, Kurt W. "Gems: Sparkling Investment?" *FACT*, May 1982, pp. 35–38.

Caruana, Claudia M. "Rare Books: A Stable Collectible." *FACT*, August 1982, pp. 61–63.

Connelly, Julie. "A Guide to the Real Risks of Investing In. . . ." *Money*, January 1982, pp. 46–50.

Crumbley, Dr. Larry, and Tony L. Crumbley. "Stamps for the Beginning Investor." *National Tax Shelter Digest*, October 1982, pp. 27–29.

Dreyfus, Patricia A. "Turnaround for Tangible Assets." *Money*, January 1983, pp. 64–65.

———. "Where Is Gold Going?" *Money*, May 1983, pp. 121–126.

Genis, Robert G. "The Exotic Market in Gems." *FACT*, January 1983, pp. 16–22.

"Gold Investing Comes Back to Life." *Business Week*, November 8, 1982, pp. 136–138.

Harris, Harvey. "Taking the Mystery Out of Diamond Investments." *National Tax Shelter Digest*, October 1982, pp. 23–26.

Herzog, John E. "Old Stock Certificates Could Be Collectibles." *FACT*, May 1982, pp. 69–71.

"Investment Gems: Will They Ever Sparkle Again?" *Changing Times*, April 1982, pp. 38–39.

Kehrer, Daniel. "Old Coins Never Die." *FACT*, September 1982, pp. 17–22.

Kriss, Gary. "Baseball Cards: A Major League Investment?" *FACT*, November 1982, pp. 76–79.

"Oriental Rugs." *Changing Times*, October 1982, pp. 37–40.

Neimark, Paul, and Philip J. Neimark. "Catching the Gold Bug." *Consumers Digest*, March–April 1982, pp. 46–49.

Perrotta, Noreen. "How to Buy Silver." *FACT*, August 1982, pp. 59–60.

Rosenbaum, Lee. "Getting Smart about Art." *Money*, November 1982, pp. 201–206.

Szuprowicz, Bohdan O. "Mining Profits in Strategic Metals." *FACT*, April 1983, pp. 29–33.

Trunzo, Candace E. "Taking a Flyer on Oriental Carpets." *Money*, December 1981, pp. 124–126.

EIGHT
INVESTMENT
ADMINISTRATION

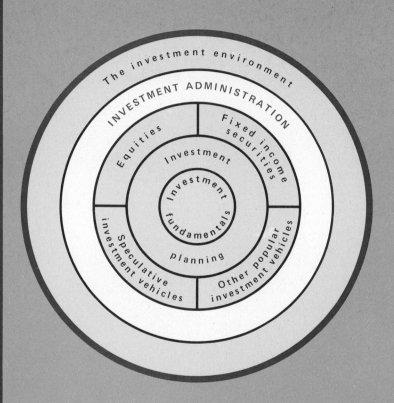

The investment environment

INVESTMENT ADMINISTRATION

Equities

Fixed income securities

Investment

Investment fundamentals

Speculative investment vehicles

Other popular investment vehicles

planning

This part of the text ties together the material presented earlier by describing the key aspects of investment administration. Chapter 19 discusses the fundamentals of portfolio management: basic principles, traditional and modern approaches to portfolio management, and the actual management process. Chapter 20 discusses the process involved in monitoring an investment portfolio and some commonly used procedures for timing portfolio transactions.

19
Portfolio Management

In order to combine various types of investment vehicles in a fashion consistent with his or her overall disposition toward risk and return, an investor needs to understand portfolio management. In this chapter, we will look at the key aspects of portfolio management and their application to investment decisions as they affect:

1. **The concept of a portfolio and the investment vehicles that are candidates for inclusion.**
2. **The two basic approaches to portfolio management—traditional management versus the modern approach.**
3. **The relationship between investor characteristics and investor objectives in portfolio decisions.**
4. **The process of formulating portfolio objectives and establishing a policy consistent with those objectives.**
5. **The relationship between investor characteristics and the risk-return profiles reflected in various types of portfolios.**

We can view the input to a portfolio as the risk-return characteristics of the individual investment vehicles and the output as the portfolio risk-return behavior. Investment vehicles can be combined to create a portfolio that has a more desirable risk-return behavior than the individual securities. Although technically there is no beneficial effect on return, the combining process can favorably affect risk. This favorable impact comes in the form of reduced risk. In other words, the combination of two investment vehicles into a portfolio can actually result in a level of risk below that exhibited by each vehicle independently.

Adding investment vehicles to a portfolio to achieve favorable results is best done by using certain analytical procedures. Although the body of knowledge relating to the creation of portfolios that provide the best risk-return tradeoffs is quite extensive, it is also based on complex mathematical concepts. So here we will emphasize only general principles and simple approaches that will allow an individual investor to develop a basic understanding of the portfolio management process. This chapter presents the basic principles and practices involved in developing and managing an investment portfolio and includes an analysis of four typical portfolios.

PRINCIPLES OF PORTFOLIO MANAGEMENT

Although we have not defined it earlier, it should be clear by now that a *portfolio* is a collection of investment vehicles assembled to meet a common investment goal. Several terms regarding portfolio objectives should be clarified at this point. A *growth-oriented portfolio's* primary orientation is long-term price appreciation. An *income-oriented portfolio* stresses current dividend and interest return.

Portfolio Objectives

The first step that must be taken by an individual investor is to establish portfolio objectives. The establishment of these objectives involves definite tradeoffs between risk and return, between potential price appreciation and current income, and between varying risk levels in the portfolio. The factors involved in the portfolio objective decisions include the investor's ability to bear risk, current income needs, and income tax bracket. The key point is that the portfolio objectives must be established before beginning to invest. Two concepts that are especially important to successful portfolio management are the effects on risk from diversification and the concept of an efficient portfolio.

Risk and diversification

Normally, a portfolio will contain two or more investments and will strive for *diversification,* the inclusion of a variety of noncomplementary investment vehicles in the portfolio for the purpose of reducing the risk. Portfolios are diversified to reduce risk of loss while meeting the investor's return objective.

Types of risk. A portfolio can become a risk-reduction vehicle because any investment vehicle possesses two types of risk. (See Chapter 4 for a detailed discussion of risk.) When a vehicle is acquired, an investor bears both diversifiable (or unsystematic) and nondiversifiable (or systematic) risk. *Diversifiable risk* is the risk unique to a particular investment vehicle—its business and financial risk. *Nondiversifiable risk* is the risk possessed by every investment vehicle; the risk that general market movements will alter a security's return is nondiversifiable risk. Thus, since the movements of the market as a whole will influence the price behavior (return performance) of most stocks, one can expect a decline in the price of a stock if the stock market in general drifts downward. As we will see, the investor can reduce only *diversifiable* risk through portfolio management.

> **BOX 19.1 PORTFOLIO SELECTION: DART FUND VERSUS THE EXPERTS**
>
> It turns out that the old saw may be true. You can select a portfolio just by throwing darts at the stock tables and do at least as well in the market as the experts—if not better. Back in May [1981], Frank Lalli, the business and financial editor of the ailing New York Daily News, conceived a "battle of the brokers" to boost circulation. Four frequently quoted Wall Street professionals—Robert Stovall of Dean Witter Reynolds, Raymond DeVoe of Bruns Norderman Rea, Michael Metz of Oppenheimer & Co. and William LeFevre of Purcell Graham & Co.—were each given an imaginary $30,000 to invest in the market for the ensuing two months. Pitted against this fearsome foursome were 10 Daily News business reporters armed with darts. By throwing one dart apiece at a stock table pinned on the wall, they selected 10 stocks in which they invested an imaginary $30,000. While the brokers were free to buy and sell the securities in their make-believe portfolio, the dart stocks were bought and held, so to speak.
>
> When the contest was over at the end of June, the Dart Fund was up by $1,045.53, or 3.4%. The paper's fickle flingers of fate had outperformed all the experts save Stovall, whose portfolio had soared 26%. He got a plaque for his efforts. As for the losers? "They received a symbol of everlasting defeat," says Lalli. "Chicago Cubs baseball caps."
>
> *Source:* "The Dart Fund." *Money,* September 1981, p. 7.

A great deal of research has been conducted on the topic of risk as it relates to security investment. The results show that, in general, *investors earn higher rates of return by buying riskier investments; to earn more return, one must bear more risk.* More startling, however, are research results that show that only with nondiversifiable risk is there a positive risk-return relationship. High levels of diversifiable risk do not result in correspondingly high levels of return. Because there is no reward for bearing diversifiable risk, an investor should minimize this form of risk in the portfolio. This can be done by diversifying the portfolio so that the only type of risk remaining is nondiversifiable risk.

Risk diversification. Diversification minimizes diversifiable risk because of a balancing effort that tends to cause the poor return of one vehicle to be balanced out by the good return on another. Minimizing diversifiable risk through careful selection of investment vehicles requires that the vehicles chosen for the portfolio come from a wide range of industries. A properly diversified portfolio contains investment vehicles from two or more unrelated industries. For example, a portfolio that contains only Ford, General Motors, and Chrysler stocks is obviously not well diversified, because these three companies have similar business and financial risks. In contrast, a portfolio consisting of International Business Machines, General Motors, and General Foods is diversified. The cyclical changes in the automobile industry will probably not affect the fortunes of IBM or General Foods. If one company in this three-stock portfolio does poorly, the other two may do well.

Given that diversification is necessary to minimize diversifiable risk, how many investment vehicles are needed in a portfolio to achieve adequate diversification?

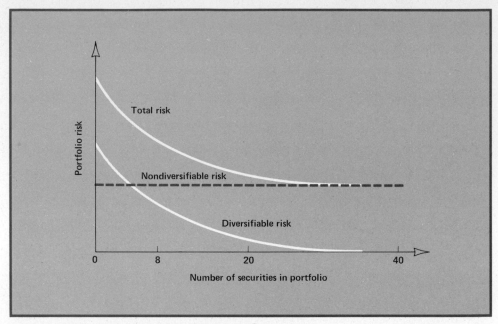

Figure 19.1   The Risk Diversification Process.
By including 8 to 20 securities in a portfolio, the diversifiable risk can be nearly eliminated so that the total, or relevant, risk of the portfolio is its nondiversifiable risk. The diversifiable risk can be eliminated even through the random selection of the 8 to 20 securities to be included in the portfolio.

Figure 19.1 depicts the two types of risk as they relate to the number of securities in the portfolio. It can be seen that the level of nondiversifiable risk remains constant in the portfolio regardless of the number of securities. Diversifiable risk declines markedly, however, as the number of securities in the portfolio rises. If 8 to 20 securities are included in the portfolio, much of the diversifiable risk is eliminated. Once the number of securities in the portfolio exceeds 20, the risk-reduction effect of increasing the number of issues in the portfolio is limited. Also plotted in Figure 19.1 is *total risk,* the sum of the diversifiable and nondiversifiable risk components. Because an investor can reduce total risk by reducing diversifiable risk, the only really *relevant risk* is that which is nondiversifiable.

In choosing the ideal number of securities for a portfolio, two factors are considered. First, somewhere between 8 and 20 issues are needed to reduce diversifiable risk substantially. Second, transactions costs must be considered if further diversification is desired. One must balance the transaction costs of a portfolio of 25 to 30 issues with the resulting risk-reduction benefits.

An efficient portfolio
The ultimate goal of an investor is the creation of an *efficient portfolio,* one that provides the highest return for a given level of risk, or has the lowest risk for a given level of return. Although it may be difficult to create such a portfolio, an investor

should at least search out reasonable investment alternatives to get the best return. When given the choice between two equally risky investments offering different returns, the investor would be expected to choose the alternative with the highest return; likewise, given two investment vehicles offering the same returns but differing in risk, the risk-averse investor would prefer the vehicle with the lower risk. In pursuing the creation of an efficient portfolio, the investor should be able to create the best portfolio possible given his or her disposition toward risk and the alternative investment vehicles available.

A Complete Investment Portfolio

Most of the discussion in this chapter centers on the management of securities' portfolios; that is, the primary focus is on stock and bond investments. But true diversification would include other investment vehicles such as options, commodities and financial futures, real estate, annuities, limited partnerships, or gold and other tangible investments. Table 19.1 presents the balance sheet of Mike and Debby Grogan, a married couple with two children. Mr. and Mrs. Grogan are 34 and 30 years old, respectively. Mr. Grogan is a vice-president of a small company located in the rural farming community of Munger, Michigan, and earns $40,000 per year. The Grogans are in a 35-percent tax bracket (federal and state combined). Looking at their balance sheet, it can be seen that the Grogans' total asset ownership mix consists of cash, money market account, stocks, bonds, a land contract—a debt owed them on property they recently sold—investment real estate, their home, and the cash value of a life insurance policy. Not included in the statement are such items as automobiles or home furnishings, which are not normally considered investment assets. Had the Grogans been antique car or furniture collectors, these items would have been added to the statement.

In the Grogan portfolio, a diversity of asset holdings is found. A life insurance policy ($100,000) on Mr. Grogan is provided for the protection of the family. The children in the family are young, and this level of life insurance protection is needed to help assure their future needs. The Grogans have wisely set aside funds in a money market account as a source of cash in case of emergency or for an attractive investment opportunity. Life insurance and a money market account provide the family with basic financial security and financial liquidity. The Grogans have two fixed income investments: two municipal bonds worth $5,000 each; and a land contract worth $25,000. The municipal bonds were issued by the Munger Unified School District and they provide the Grogans with a low-risk, tax-free investment return. This portion of their investment program, then, provides a steady source of secure income.

The Grogans own their own home, although there is a $50,000 mortgage payable on it over the next 24 years. The Grogans' investments also include a portfolio of stocks worth $40,000 and investment real estate worth $46,000. The latter has a $30,000 mortgage on it, so the Grogans' equity in that property is $16,000. The stock portfolio provides the Grogans with capital growth potential and is a relatively liquid asset. The investment property, a duplex rental unit, was acquired because of its long-term price appreciation potential and as a source of tax-sheltered income. Real estate is a less liquid asset than stocks or bonds. The Grogan portfolio seems to be a good one. First, the financial foundation of life insurance and a money

TABLE 19.1   MIKE AND DEBBY GROGAN'S BALANCE SHEET

Assets		Liabilities and Net Worth	
Cash and money market		Short-term liabilities	$ 1,000
account	$ 16,000	Home mortgage	50,000
Stocks	40,000	Investment real estate	
Municipal bonds	10,000	mortgage	30,000
Land contract	25,000	Net worth	134,000
Home	75,000	Total	$215,000
Investment real estate	46,000		
Cash value of life insurance	3,000		
Total	$215,000		

market account is included for basic protection. Second, the remaining assets consist of a diversified portfolio of stocks, fixed income securities, and real estate.

TRADITIONAL PORTFOLIO MANAGEMENT VERSUS MODERN PORTFOLIO THEORY

In this section, the two approaches currently in use by portfolio managers are compared and contrasted. The traditional approach refers to the methods money managers have been using since the evolution of the public securities markets. Modern portfolio theory (MPT) is a recent development. The theory behind this new approach has been developed only in recent years, but its popularity is rising rapidly. Some MPT concepts are indirectly used by practitioners of the traditional approach, yet there are major differences between the two.

The Traditional Approach

Traditional portfolio management emphasizes "balancing" the portfolio. The traditional portfolio manager assembles a wide variety of stocks and/or bonds within the portfolio. The typical emphasis is interindustry diversification—this means that securities of companies from a broad cross-section of American industry are represented in the portfolio. Most institutional portfolio managers utilize the security analysis techniques discussed in Chapters 9 and 10 when they select individual securities for the traditional portfolio. Figure 19.2 presents the portfolio of a typical

Figure 19.2   Portfolio of T. Rowe Price Growth Stock Fund (December 31, 1981).
The T. Rowe Price Growth Fund appears to adhere to the traditional approach to portfolio management. Its portfolio value is about $866 million in common stock, and it holds 59 different stocks from 26 industry groupings, plus about $52 million in short-term investments which include U.S. government obligations, federal agencies' issues, bankers' acceptances, certificates of deposit, and corporate notes. (*Source:* Prospectus, T. Rowe Price Growth Stock Fund, Inc., May 1, 1982.)

T. Rowe Price Growth Stock Fund, Inc.
Portfolio of Investments—December 31, 1981

Number of Shares		Average Cost	Mkt. Value ($)
COMMON STOCKS (94.2%)			
	BANK & TRUST (4.3%)		
462,000	Citicorp	$ 12,424,912	$ 11,665,500
350,000	First Interstate Bancorp	14,674,960	12,512,500
275,600	J. P. Morgan & Co. Incorporated	14,994,087	14,813,500
		42,093,959	38,991,500
	FINANCIAL SERVICES (2.1%)		
433,000	American Express Company	20,868,193	19,106,125
	INSURANCE (5.1%)		
333,646	American International Group, Inc.	9,082,852	21,603,579
354,785	Combined International Corp.	8,214,531	8,514,840
530,000	Farmers Group, Inc.	12,483,418	16,960,000
		29,780,801	47,078,419
	COSMETICS (3.1%)		
430,700	International Flavors & Fragrances, Inc. . . .	9,014,292	8,398,650
280,000	Revlon, Inc.	12,186,365	8,575,000
410,000	Richardson-Vicks, Inc.	12,127,487	11,275,000
		33,328,144	28,248,650
	BEVERAGES (4.2%)		
611,800	The Coca-Cola Company	20,062,357	21,260,050
483,600	Pepsico, Inc.	11,293,969	17,590,950
		31,356,326	38,851,000
	SPECIALIZED MERCHANDISERS (2.0%)		
495,700	Melville Corporation	18,109,694	18,712,675
	PHARMACEUTICALS (7.3%)		
370,300	Johnson & Johnson	10,601,495	13,747,388
260,000	Eli Lilly and Company	14,316,528	14,560,000
157,400	Merck & Co., Inc.	10,783,041	13,339,650
220,000	SmithKline Corporation	14,034,823	14,877,500
205,400	The Upjohn Company	9,956,598	10,937,550
		59,692,485	67,462,088
	ENTERTAINMENT & LEISURE (0.6%)		
173,700	Host International, Inc.	5,796,860	4,950,450
	MEDIA & COMMUNICATIONS (1.4%)		
273,000	The Times Mirror Company	12,178,245	12,489,750
	MISCELLANEOUS CONSUMER PRODUCTS (3.6%)		
390,200	Philip Morris Incorporated	13,264,078	19,022,250
791,000	The Stanley Works	13,660,962	13,842,500
		26,925,040	32,864,750
	AUTOMOBILES & ACCESSORIES (2.4%)		
441,200	Dana Corporation	13,506,832	13,015,400
171,800	TRW, Inc.	8,893,349	9,406,050
		22,400,181	22,421,450
	CONSUMER ELECTRONICS (3.7%)		
537,900	The Black and Decker Manufacturing Company	10,080,454	8,135,737
522,366	Milton Bradley Company	19,186,953	10,969,686
850,000	Sony Corporation	16,060,888	14,875,000
		45,328,295	33,980,423
	AEROSPACE & DEFENSE (2.7%)		
611,000	General Dynamics Corporation	18,944,469	14,969,500
400,000	The Signal Companies, Inc.	10,113,910	10,150,000
		29,058,379	25,119,500
	COMPUTER & INFORMATION PROCESSING (10.7%)		
302,500	Burroughs Corporation	21,091,501	10,322,812
261,700	Datapoint Corporation	11,489,364	13,412,125
181,000	Digital Equipment Corporation	15,973,617	15,701,750
754,368	International Business Machines Corporation	36,675,481	42,904,680
385,700	Xerox Corporation	25,925,824	15,717,275
		111,155,787	98,058,642
	CONTROL & INSTRUMENTS (3.8%)		
366,000	Hewlett-Packard Company	7,530,730	14,502,750
294,000	Honeywell Inc.	22,821,808	20,616,750
		30,352,538	35,119,500
	ELECTRICAL EQUIPMENT (2.5%)		
216,300	Emerson Electric Company	8,877,911	9,814,613
445,400	Square D Company	11,854,945	12,860,925
		20,732,856	22,675,538
	ELECTRONICS & COMPONENTS (3.7%)		
338,900	Intel Corporation	10,586,458	7,625,250
586,000	National Semiconductor Corporation	15,064,257	11,207,250
184,600	Texas Instruments Incorporated	15,176,503	14,860,300
		40,827,218	33,692,800
	MACHINERY (5.0%)		
310,000	Caterpillar Tractor Company	15,890,589	17,205,000
330,700	Deere & Company	14,728,593	11,739,850
521,300	Dresser Industries, Inc.	14,782,425	17,333,225
		45,401,607	46,278,075

Number of Shares		Average Cost	Mkt. Value ($)
	TELECOMMUNICATIONS (1.3%)		
412,000	International Telephone and Telegraph Corporation	$ 12,339,438	$ 12,257,000
	BUSINESS SERVICES (1.7%)		
297,400	Minnesota Mining and Manufacturing Company	15,175,644	16,208,300
	TRANSPORTATION SERVICES (1.9%)		
330,000	Union Pacific Corporation	21,763,639	17,160,000
	ENERGY SERVICES (7.9%)		
421,000	Baker International Corporation	18,123,883	15,998,000
452,800	Halliburton Company	13,735,256	23,602,200
592,162	Schlumberger Limited	12,385,055	33,013,031
		44,244,194	72,613,231
	EXPLORATION & PRODUCTION (3.8%)		
416,000	Apache Corporation	$ 7,042,614	$ 8,113,950
244,000	Tom Brown, Inc.	6,894,443	6,496,500
680,000	Energy Reserves Group, Inc.	11,583,139	6,800,000
350,000	Mesa Petroleum Company	6,728,935	7,131,250
245,000	Southland Royalty Company	6,910,694	6,431,250
		39,159,825	34,972,950
	INTEGRATED PETROLEUM—DOMESTIC (3.6%)		
423,000	Standard Oil Company (Indiana)	18,257,094	21,996,000
320,000	Texas Oil & Gas Corp.	11,227,067	11,200,000
		29,484,161	33,196,000
	CHEMICALS (1.0%)		
249,900	E. I. Du Pont De Nemours & Company . . .	12,227,091	9,371,250
	MISCELLANEOUS MATERIALS (1.4%)		
500,000	Diamond Shamrock Corporation	17,054,804	12,750,000
	UNDISCLOSED STOCKS BEING ACQUIRED (3.4%)	33,430,307	31,607,250
	TOTAL COMMON STOCKS (94.2%)	850,265,711	866,237,316

U. S. GOVERNMENT OBLIGATIONS, FEDERAL AGENCIES, BANKERS' ACCEPTANCES, CERTIFICATES OF DEPOSIT & CORPORATE NOTES (5.7%)

		Average Cost	Mkt. Value ($)
	U.S. GOVERNMENT OBLIGATIONS (1.1%)		
$11,000,000	U.S. Treasury Bills, 10.54% to 13.33%, 1/7/82 to 6/10/82	10,512,505	10,512,505
	FEDERAL AGENCIES (0.9%)		
9,000,000	Federal Home Loan Banks, 11.30% to 15.10%, 1/21/82 to 3/15/82 . . .	8,607,183	8,607,183
	BANKERS' ACCEPTANCES (0.2%)		
1,000,000	Pittsburg National Bank, 14.75%, 2/25/82 .	950,833	950,833
1,250,000	The Sanwa Bank, Limited, 13.60%, 4/21/82 .	1,171,611	1,171,611
		2,122,444	2,122,444
	CERTIFICATES OF DEPOSIT (3.1%)		
4,000,000	American Security Bank, N.A., 11.70% to 11.95%, 2/23/82 to 3/3/82 .	4,000,000	4,000,000
3,000,000	Bank of Montreal, 18.5%, 1/19/82 . . .	3,000,000	3,000,000
1,000,000	The Bank of Yokohama, Ltd., 14.45%, 5/5/82 .	1,000,000	1,000,000
5,000,000	Continental Illinois National Bank and Trust Company of Chicago, 12.375% to 15%, 1/13/82 to 8/16/82 .	5,000,000	5,000,000
3,000,000	First National Bank in Dallas, 11.60%, 5/26/82 .	2,990,787	2,990,787
3,000,000	First National Bank of St. Paul, 12%, 6/1/82 .	2,995,365	2,995,365
2,000,000	Hokkaido Takushoku Bank, Ltd., 16.20%, 4/19/82 .	2,000,000	2,000,000
3,000,000	The Mitsubishi Bank, Ltd., 12.75%, 5/17/82 .	2,999,231	2,999,231
3,000,000	The Royal Bank of Canada, 12.5%, 3/4/82 .	3,000,000	3,000,000
1,000,000	The Sanwa Bank, Limited, 13.30%, 5/11/82 .	1,000,000	1,000,000
		27,985,383	27,985,383
	CORPORATE NOTES (0.4%)		
350,000	American Express Credit Corporation, 11%, 1/4/82 .	350,000	350,000
3,000,000	Societe Generale North America, Inc., 12.35%, 2/1/82 .	2,938,250	2,938,250
		3,228,250	3,288,250

		Average Cost	Mkt. Value ($)
	TOTAL U.S. GOVERNMENT OBLIGATIONS, FEDERAL AGENCIES, BANKERS' ACCEPTANCES, CERTIFICATES OF DEPOSIT & CORPORATE NOTES (5.7%)	52,515,765	52,515,765
	Total Investments 99.9%	902,781,476	918,753,081
	Other Assets Less Liabilities 0.1%	673,547	673,547
	NET ASSETS 100.0%	$903,455,023	$919,426,628

NET ASSET VALUE AT DECEMBER 31, 1981
$919,426,628 ÷ 72,263,354 shares of capital stock outstanding $12.72/Share

large mutual fund. This portfolio is managed by professionals who use the traditional approach. This fund, the T. Rowe Price Growth Stock Fund, is a no-load, open-end mutual fund that has a portfolio valued at approximately $919 million as of December 31, 1981. The Growth Stock Fund is a relatively large fund. It holds shares of 59 different stocks from 26 industries. In addition, the fund holds a number of short-term money market investments including U.S. Treasury bills, agency issues, bankers' acceptances, certificates of deposit, and corporate notes.

Analyzing the stock portion of the Growth Stock Fund's portfolio, which accounts for approximately 94 percent of the fund's total assets, we can observe the traditional approach to portfolio management at work. This fund holds a variety of stocks from a diverse cross-section of the total universe of available stocks. It should be noted, however, that all the fund's stocks are those of large American corporations. The fund's largest holding is International Business Machines Corporation (IBM), a favorite of institutional investors. The fund's second largest holding is Schlumberger, Ltd., another institutional favorite. The IBM holding represents approximately 5 percent of the total portfolio and the Schlumberger position is about 4 percent of the portfolio's total market value.

Traditional portfolio managers like to invest in well-known companies for three reasons. First, these companies have been and probably will continue to be successful business enterprises. Investing in the securities of large, well-known companies is perceived as less risky than investing in lesser-known firms. A second reason professional managers prefer to invest in large companies is that the securities of these firms are more liquid and are available in large quantities. Managers of large portfolios invest substantial sums of money and need to acquire securities in large quantities to achieve an efficient order size. Traditional portfolio managers prefer well-known companies for a third reason: It is easier to convince clients to invest in portfolios of well-known corporations. "Window dressing," a Wall Street cliché, refers to the practice of many investment managers of loading up portfolios with well-known stocks to make it easier to sell their management services to their clients.

Modern Portfolio Theory (MPT)

Harry Markowitz first developed the theories that form the basis of MPT during the 1950s, and many other scholars and investment experts have contributed in developing MPT to its present advanced stage. *Modern portfolio theory* utilizes several basic statistical measures to develop portfolio strategy. One such measure is the *variance* of a security's return, which is its standard deviation squared. Another is the *correlation* of an individual security's return with the return of another security, or with the market as a whole. Portfolio construction in an MPT sense places heavy emphasis on the correlation of returns from different securities.

Figure 19.3 illustrates the relative correlation between securities' rates of returns for two portfolios (each consisting of two securities). The left graph shows the rates of return on two securities, *X* and *Y,* over time. There is obviously strong *positive correlation* between these two securities' rates of return, since they move together. The right graph of Figure 19.3 plots the returns of securities *X* and *Z.* The rates of return of these two securities exhibit strong *negative correlation,* since they move in opposite directions. Diversification, according to MPT, is achieved by combining

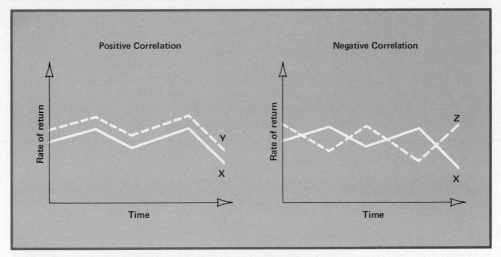

Figure 19.3   Correlation of Securities Returns.
The returns from securities X and Y are highly positively correlated and therefore do not offer an opportunity for diversification. The returns from securities X and Z are highly negatively correlated and therefore provide an opportunity to benefit from diversification. The less positive (or more negative) the correlation between security returns, the greater the benefit of diversification in terms of risk and return.

securities in a portfolio so that individual securities have negative correlations between each other's rates of return. In choosing securities for an MPT portfolio, the statistical diversification—that is, negative return correlation—is the deciding factor. For example, the portfolio consisting of securities *X* and *Y* is not well diversified because each security is a near-perfect substitute for the other. The portfolio consisting of securities *X* and *Z* is much more diversified because of the strong negative correlation between their returns.

MPT has also provided an important investment tool—beta, which was first introduced in Chapter 4 and is reviewed here.

Beta

Given that a portfolio is diversified, the primary concern is with the level of nondiversifiable risk. We can measure the nondiversifiable risk of a security or a portfolio with the beta regression equation:

$$r_{i,t} = a_i + (b_i \times r_{m,t})$$

where

$r_{i,t}$ = return on security *i* or portfolio *i* over time period *t*

a_i = regression intercept

b_i = regression coefficient—beta

$r_{m,t}$ = return on the market portfolio over time period *t*

The beta regression coefficient measures the relative volatility of a security, or a portfolio, as compared to a broadly derived measure of stock market return. In practice, the Standard & Poor's 500 stock composite index or the New York Stock Exchange composite index are utilized as measures of the return on the general market. The term *volatility* refers to the amount of fluctuation a security or portfolio has. *Beta* measures the relative fluctuation a security or a portfolio has in comparison to a market index. The coefficient indicates the relative change in the security's or portfolio's return as compared with the return on a market index. Stock betas are widely used in practice and are readily available from brokerage firms and investment advisory services like *Value Line.*

Uses of beta.   The usefulness of beta depends on how well the regression equation explains relative return fluctuations. The *coefficient of determination* (R^2) measures the explanatory power of a regression equation. That is, it indicates the percentage of the change in the dependent variable (the return from the individual security, $r_{i,t}$) explained by its relationship with the independent (market) variable, which is $r_{m,t}$ in our example. R^2 can range from .0 to 1.0. If a regression equation has an R^2 of .0, this means none (0 percent) of the variation in the security's return is explained by its relationship with the market. An R^2 of 1.0 indicates the existence of perfect correlation (100 percent) between a security and the market.

Beta is much more useful in explaining a portfolio's return fluctuations than a security's return fluctuations. A well-diversified stock portfolio will have a beta equation R^2 of around .90. This means that 90 percent of a stock portfolio's fluctuations are related to changes in the stock market as a whole. Individual security betas have a wide range of R^2s, but tend to be in the .20 to .50 range. Other factors (diversifiable risk, in particular) also cause individual security prices to fluctuate. When securities are combined into a well-diversified portfolio, most of the fluctuation in that portfolio's return is caused by the movement of the entire stock market.

Interpreting beta.   A look at the interpretation of beta may help us to understand its usefulness. If a portfolio has a beta of +1.0, the portfolio experiences changes in its rate of return equal to changes in the market's rate of return. The +1.0 beta portfolio would tend to experience a 10 percent increase in return if the stock market as a whole experienced a 10 percent increase in return. Conversely, if the market return fell by 6 percent, the return on the +1.0 beta portfolio would also fall by 6 percent. Table 19.2 lists the expected returns for three portfolio betas in two situations: The market experiences an increase in return of 10 percent and a decrease in return of 10 percent. The 2.0 beta portfolio is twice as volatile as the market. When the market returns increase by 10 percent, the portfolio return increases by 20 percent. Conversely, the portfolio's return will fall by 20 percent when the market has a decline in return of 10 percent. This portfolio would be considered a relatively high-risk, high-return portfolio. A .5 beta portfolio is considered to be a relatively low-risk, low-return portfolio. It is a conservative portfolio for investors who wish to maintain a low-risk investment posture. The .5 beta portfolio is half as volatile as the market. A beta of −1.0 indicates that the portfolio moves in a direction opposite to that of

TABLE 19.2   PORTFOLIO BETAS AND
**   ASSOCIATED CHANGES IN RETURNS**

Portfolio Beta	Change in Return on Market	Change in Expected Return on Portfolio
+2.0	+10.0%	+20.0%
	−10.0	−20.0
+ .5	+10.0	+ 5.0
	−10.0	− 5.0
−1.0	+10.0	−10.0
	−10.0	+10.0

the market. A bearish investor would probably want to own a negative beta portfolio, because this type of investment tends to rise in value when the stock market declines, and vice versa. Finding securities with negative betas is difficult, however. Most securities have positive betas, since they tend to experience return movements in the same direction as changes in the stock market.

The risk-return tradeoff:
Some closing comments

Another valuable outgrowth of modern portfolio theory is the specific delineation between nondiversifiable risk and investment return. The basic premise is that an investor must have a portfolio of relatively risky investments to earn a relatively high rate of return. That relationship is illustrated in Figure 19.4. The upward-sloping line is the *risk-return tradeoff*. The point where the risk-return line crosses the return axis (R_F) is called the *risk-free rate of return*. This is the investment return an investor can earn on a risk-free investment, such as a U.S. Treasury bill or an insured money market account. As we proceed upward along the line, portfolios of risky investments appear. For example, four investment portfolios, A through D, are depicted in Figure 19.4. Portfolios A and B are investment opportunities that provide a level of return commensurate with their respective risk levels. Portfolio C would be an excellent investment as it provides a high return at a relatively low risk level. Portfolio D is an investment situation one should avoid; this is a high-risk, low-return portfolio.

The Traditional Approach and MPT:
A Reconciliation

We have reviewed two fairly different approaches to portfolio management—the traditional approach and MPT. The question that arises now is, Which technique should be used by the individual investor? There is no definite answer; the question must be answered based on the judgment of the investor. However, a few useful ideas can be offered. The average individual investor does not have the resources, computers, and mathematical wizardry to implement an MPT portfolio strategy. Given that total MPT portfolio management is impractical for the individual investor, ideas

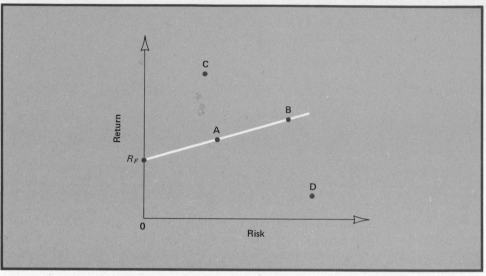

Figure 19.4   The Portfolio Risk-Return Tradeoff.
As the risk of an investment portfolio increases from zero, the return provided should increase above the risk-free rate of return, R_F. Portfolios A and B offer returns commensurate with their risk, while portfolio C provides a high return at a low-risk level and portfolio D provides a low return for high risk. Portfolio C is highly desirable; portfolio D should be avoided.

should be drawn from both MPT and the traditional approach. The traditional approach stresses security selection using fundamental and technical analysis. It also emphasizes diversification of the portfolio across industry lines. MPT stresses negative correlations between securities' rates of return for the issues within the portfolio. This approach calls for diversification to minimize diversifiable risk. So, following either strategy, diversification must be accomplished to ensure satisfactory performance.

Beta is a useful tool for determining the level of a portfolio's nondiversifiable risk and should be part of the decision-making process. We recommend the following portfolio management policy for the individual investor:

1. Determine how much risk you are willing to bear.
2. Seek diversification among different types of securities and across industry lines, and pay attention to the way the return from one security is related to another.
3. Consider how a security responds to the market and use beta when assembling a diversified portfolio as a way to keep the portfolio in line with your acceptable level of risk.
4. Evaluate alternative portfolios to make sure that the portfolio selected provides the highest return for the given level of acceptable risk.

BUILDING A PORTFOLIO

In this section, we will examine the criteria that can be used to formulate an individual portfolio strategy. We will look at investor characteristics, investor objectives, and portfolio objectives and policies. In attempting to weave the concepts of risk and diversification into a solid investment policy, we will rely on both traditional and modern approaches to investment management.

Investor Characteristics

An investor's personal financial and family situation are important inputs in determining portfolio policy. The following items are vital determinants:

1. Level and stability of income.
2. Family factors.
3. Net worth.
4. Investor experience and age.
5. Investor disposition toward risk.

The portfolio strategy of an individual investor obviously must be tailored to meet that person's needs. The types of investments in the portfolio depend upon relative income needs and ability to bear risk. The investor's income, family responsibilities, relative financial security, experience, and age all enter into the delicate equation that yields a portfolio strategy. A relatively young investor may have an aggressive investment policy: for example, if that person's family obligations are well met. A married investor with young children would not be seeking high-risk investments until some measure of financial security has been provided for the family. If the married investor has ample savings and insurance protection for the family, he or she may be ready to embark on a program with risky elements. Once financial security has been provided for, more risky ventures can be undertaken. A single investor with no family responsibilities could be better able to handle risk than an individual who has such responsibilities. Simply stated, an investor's risk exposure should not exceed that person's ability to bear risk.

The size and certainty of an investor's employment income bears on portfolio strategy. An investor with a secure job is more likely to embark on a risk-oriented investment program than an investor who has a less secure position. Income taxes bear on the investment decision as well. The higher an investor's income, the more important the tax ramifications of an investment program become. For example, municipal bonds normally yield about one-third less in annual interest than corporate bonds because the interest income on municipal bonds is tax-free. On an after-tax basis, however, municipal bonds may provide a superior return if an investor is in a tax bracket in excess of 30 percent. An individual's investment experience also influences the appropriate investment strategy. Normally, investors gradually assume levels of high investment risk over time. It is best to "get one's feet wet" in the investment market by slipping into it gradually rather than leaping in head first. Very often, investors who make risky initial investments suffer heavy losses, damaging the long-run potential of the entire investment program. A cautiously developed investment program will likely provide more favorable long-run results than an impulsive, risky one.

Finally, investors should carefully consider risk. Much of this chapter is devoted to discussions of risk and return. High-risk investments have high return potential and a high risk of loss. Remember, by going for the home run (a high-risk, high-return investment), the odds of striking out are much higher than in going for a single base hit (a more conservative investment posture). The single is less glamorous than the home run, but it is also easier to achieve.

Specifying Investor Objectives

Once an investor has developed a personal financial profile, the next question is, "What do I want from my portfolio?" This seems like an easy one to answer. We would all like to double our money every year by making low-risk investments. However, the realities of the highly competitive investment environment make this outcome unlikely. The reality of risk makes the establishment of realistic goals a basic requirement for a successful investment program. There is generally a tradeoff between earning a high current income from an investment portfolio or obtaining significant capital appreciation from it. An inverstor must choose one or the other; it is difficult to have both. The price of having high appreciation potential in the portfolio is low current income potential. One must balance the certainty of high current income and limited price appreciation with the uncertainty of high future price appreciation.

The investor's needs may determine which avenue is chosen. For instance, a retired investor whose income depends on his or her portfolio will probably choose a lower-risk, current-income-oriented approach out of the need for financial survival. In contrast, a high-income, financially secure investor (a doctor, for instance) may be much more willing to take on risky investments in the hope of improving net worth. Figure 19.5 illustrates the risk-income tradeoff as compared with an investor's age. A young investor with a secure job is less concerned about current income and is more able to bear risk. This type of investor is more appreciation-potential-oriented and may choose speculative investments. As an investor approaches age 60, the desired level of income rises as retirement approaches. The aging investor is less willing to bear risk. Such an investor wants to keep what he or she has because he or she is or will soon be utilizing these investments as a source of retirement income. The retired 75-year-old investor typically wants minimal risk in a portfolio; he or she needs a dependable source of current income. It should be clear that a portfolio must be built around the individual's needs, which depend on income, responsibilities, financial resources, age, retirement plans, and ability to bear risk.

Portfolio Objectives and Policies

Portfolio management is a very logical activity and is best implemented after careful analysis of the investor's needs and of the investment vehicles available for inclusion in the portfolio. The following objectives should be considered when structuring a portfolio:

1. Current income needs.
2. Capital preservation.
3. Capital growth.
4. Tax considerations.
5. Risk.

BOX 19.2 THREE MODEL PORTFOLIOS

Your investments should reflect your financial goals. Here are people in typical situations, and financial advisers' suggestions for their portfolios: Top, the two-income couple in their early 40s earn $54,000 and are concerned about college costs for their children, 17 and 12. Middle, the divorced mother, 30, has custody of her children, 7 and 4, and $25,000 in salary and child support; she wants the down payment on a house. Bottom, the older couple in their fifties are planning for his retirement in 10 years from his $60,000-a-year job.

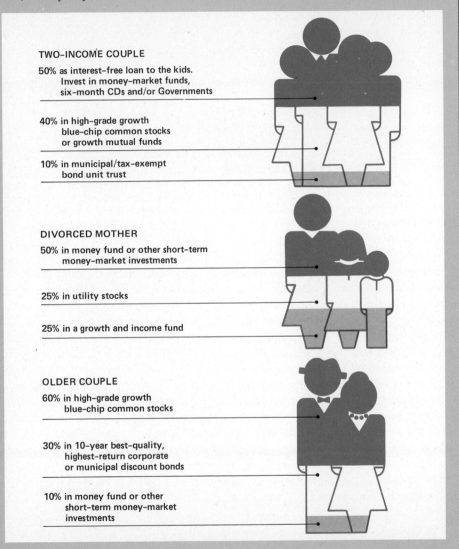

TWO-INCOME COUPLE

50% as interest-free loan to the kids. Invest in money-market funds, six-month CDs and/or Governments

40% in high-grade growth blue-chip common stocks or growth mutual funds

10% in municipal/tax-exempt bond unit trust

DIVORCED MOTHER

50% in money fund or other short-term money-market investments

25% in utility stocks

25% in a growth and income fund

OLDER COUPLE

60% in high-grade growth blue-chip common stocks

30% in 10-year best-quality, highest-return corporate or municipal discount bonds

10% in money fund or other short-term money-market investments

Source: "Model Portfolios." From Robert H. Runde, "What to Do When It's Time to Invest," *Money,* October 1982, pp. 82–86.

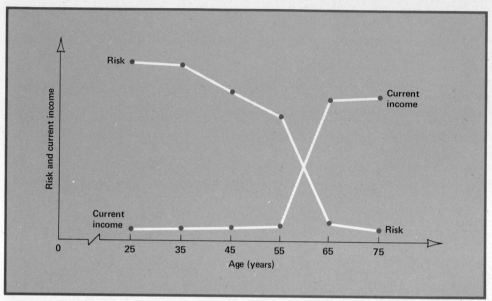

Figure 19.5   Investor Life Cycles: Risk and Current Income versus Age.
A young investor tends to be more willing to take higher risks in the expectation of earning high returns through price appreciation than the mature investor, who tends to be risk-averse and current-income-oriented. This behavior is attributable to age-related differences in financial resources and needs.

Any one or more of these factors will play an influential role in defining the type of portfolio acquired by an investor. For convenience, these factors can be tied together as follows: items 1 and 2, current income and capital preservation, are portfolio objectives synonymous with a low-risk, conservative investment strategy. Normally, a portfolio with this orientation contains low-beta (low-risk) securities. A capital growth objective (item 3) implies increased risk and a reduced level of current income. Higher-risk growth stocks, options, commodity and financial futures, real estate, gold, and other more speculative investments may be suitable for this investor. An investor's tax bracket (item 4) will influence investment strategy. A high-income investor probably wishes to earn investment returns in the form of long-term capital gains. This implies a strategy of higher-risk investments and a holding period of at least one year. Lower-bracket investors are less concerned with how they earn the income. They may wish to invest in higher current income investments. The most important item an investor must decide upon is *risk* (item 5). The risk-return tradeoff should be considered in all investment decisions.

PORTFOLIO MANAGEMENT IN ACTION

In this section four portfolios that have been developed to meet four different investment objectives will be analyzed. The principles and ideas that have been developed throughout the book will be applied to these four realistic situations.

In each of the analyses that follow, the investors' names are fictitious, but the objectives and the portfolios are real. Relevant income, age, net worth, and life-style information is provided for each investor. The specific reasons why a stock and/or bond is included in the portfolio are given (the portfolios include only stocks and bonds). As a useful exercise, the reader might want to consider each situation and develop his or her own recommendations utilizing current investment information.

The four cases have divergent risk-return profiles because the investors for whom the portfolios are designed have different incomes and life-styles. Each portfolio is constructed using the traditional approach, with the following exceptions. First, the number of securities in each portfolio is below the normal number the traditional portfolio manager would likely recommend. It is assumed that the proper interindustry diversification can be achieved with the careful selection of 8 to 12 securities in a $100,000 portfolio. A larger portfolio might have slightly more securities, but it would also probably have fewer securities than a traditionalist might recommend. Second, beta is utilized to quantify portfolio risk. Thus, these examples blend elements of modern portfolio theory (MPT) with the traditional approach to portfolio management.

Carol Nakamura: Woman Wonder

At 28 years of age, Carol Nakamura has done well for herself. She has built a $300,000 investment portfolio consisting of investment real estate in Honolulu, Hawaii, and a holding in a money market mutual fund. Ms. Nakamura is currently employed as the controller of Kamehameha Management, a real estate management firm in Honolulu. She is a CPA, and her income from salary and property rentals is $45,000 per year, putting her in a 50 percent marginal income tax bracket (federal and Hawaii state income tax combined). Ms. Nakamura is not married, and her only debts are secured by her properties.

Carol Nakamura has decided to diversify her portfolio. Most of her net worth consists of rental condominiums located in the Waikiki area of Honolulu. Clearly, diversification is needed to reduce her risk exposure and to increase her overall investment return. The Hawaii real estate market is somewhat unpredictable, and Ms. Nakamura wishes to lessen her risk exposure in that market. She asked her investment advisor, Marjorie Wong, to develop a securities portfolio for her. Carol Nakamura is currently selling one of her properties, and with the funds in her money market mutual fund she will have $75,000 to invest in stocks. Because of her relatively young age and her strong future earning capacity, Ms. Nakamura can bear the risks of a speculative investment program. Her portfolio of stocks will emphasize issues that have a strong price appreciation potential.

Ms. Nakamura's securities portfolio is presented in Table 19.3. It consists of eight stocks, all of which have above-average risk-return potential. The betas of the issues range from 1.13 to 2.31; the portfolio's beta is approximately 1.61, indicating an above-average risk exposure. (The beta for a portfolio can be calculated as a weighted average of the individual security betas within the portfolio.) The portfolio is diversified across industry lines, with a fairly diverse mix of securities. All are selected because of their above-average price appreciation potential. Aloha Airlines, an inter-island carrier in Hawaii, was chosen because of the expected increase in the

TABLE 19.3 CAROL NAKAMURA'S PORTFOLIO

OBJECTIVE: SPECULATIVE GROWTH (HIGH-RISK, HIGH-RETURN POTENTIAL)

Number of Shares	Company	Dividend per Share	Dividend Income	Price per Share	Total Cost (including commission)	Beta	Dividend Yield
1,200	Aloha Airlines	$__	$__	$ 7	$ 8,480	1.75	__%
300	Apple Computer	—	—	30	9,090	1.87	—
400	Color Tile	—	—	25	10,090	1.59	—
300	Guardian Industries	0.36	108	30	9,090	1.19	1.2
300	Heileman (G.) Brewing	0.80	240	32	9,700	1.27	2.5
300	Honda Motor ADR	0.35	105	33	10,000	1.13	1.1
500	Carl Karcher Enterprises	—	—	20	10,100	1.79	—
1,300	Pauley Petroleum	—	—	6	7,880	2.31	—
	Total		$453		$74,430		0.6%

Portfolio beta = 1.61

number of visitors to Hawaii. Apple Computer is a fast-growing personal computer manufacturer. Color Tile is a growing retailer that services the do-it-yourself home improvement market. Guardian Industries is a rapidly expanding glass manufacturer and photo processor. Heileman is a growing brewer. Honda Motor, based in Japan, provides a measure of international diversification for the portfolio. Carl Karcher Enterprises is an expanding fast food operator based in California. Pauley Petroleum is a small oil company with refining and oil production interests.

Most of the securities Ms. Wong selected for Ms. Nakamura are not "household words." Rather, they are firms with exciting growth potential at the time of purchase. The portfolio should fluctuate in value at a rate approximately 1.6 times greater than the stock market as a whole. The dividend yield on the portfolio is a relatively low 0.6 percent. Most of the return Ms. Nakamura anticipates from this portfolio is in the form of price appreciation. She anticipates holding the stocks for at least one year. By doing this, any realized profits will be taxed as long-term capital gains. Given Ms. Nakamura's marginal income tax bracket, it seems preferable for her to earn returns in the form of long-term capital gains.

Martin and Nancy Jacob: Lottery Winners

Martin Jacob, a college professor of political science at the University of West Bay City in Michigan, and his wife, Nancy, are very lucky people. After buying a $1 Michigan State Lottery Ticket at a local tavern, Professor Jacob won the $275,000 prize. After paying income taxes on the prize and after spending a small amount for personal needs, Martin and Nancy had $210,000 remaining. Because of their philosophy of saving any windfalls and not spending accumulated captial on day-to-day living expenses, they chose to invest these funds (in contrast with many lottery winners, who simply blow their winnings on fast living).

TABLE 19.4   MARTIN AND NANCY JACOB'S PORTFOLIO

OBJECTIVE: LONG-TERM GROWTH (AVERAGE RISK, MODERATE DIVIDENDS)

Number of Shares	Company	Dividend per Share	Dividend Income	Price per Share	Total Cost (including commission)	Beta	Dividend Yield
1,000	Bancorp Hawaii, Inc.	$1.20	$ 1,200	$22	$ 22,200	.86	5.4%
600	CBS	2.80	1,680	40	24,200	1.00	6.9
1,000	Florida Westcoast Banks	1.20	1,200	23	23,200	.84	5.2
1,000	Kellogg	1.60	1,600	25	25,300	.88	6.3
500	Knight-Ridder Newspapers	0.92	460	46	23,200	1.12	2.0
600	Kroger Company	1.88	1,128	37	22,400	1.07	5.0
800	Union Oil of California	1.00	800	27	21,800	1.30	3.7
600	Upjohn	2.28	1,368	40	24,200	1.04	5.7
600	Weyerhaeuser	1.30	780	36	21,800	1.32	3.6
	Total		$10,216		$208,300		4.9%

Portfolio beta = 1.05

The Jacobs have two children. Martin is 37 years of age and has a secure teaching position. His salary is approximately $30,000 per year. In addition, he earns approximately $4,000 per year from his book-publishing royalties and from several other small sources. Professor Jacob's tax bracket (federal and state) is approximately 34 percent. His life insurance protection of approximately $60,000 is provided by the university. Martin's wife Nancy is a librarian. She currently is at home with the children and is not expected to be a source of steady income for several years. The Jacob family owns (free and clear) their home in the exclusive Banks area of Bay City. In addition, they have a $16,000 money market account at a local savings and loan association. They have no outstanding debts.

Professor Jacob asked his investment advisor, Fred Craves, to develop an investment portfolio for them. Together, they decided on the following strategy. First, the professor and his wife tend to be somewhat risk-averse; that is, they do not wish to bear inordinate amounts of risk of loss. In addition, the Jacobs indicated that they would enjoy some increase in spendable income. Given these facts, Mr. Craves suggested the portfolio presented in Table 19.4. The emphasis in the portfolio is long-term growth at an average risk level, with a moderate dividend return. The portfolio consists of nine issues. There appears to be sufficient diversification. The portfolio's beta is 1.05, indicating a level of nondiversifiable risk that approximately equals that of the stock market as a whole. The portfolio's dividend yield is about 4.9 percent, which approximates the average dividend return for the entire stock market. The betas of individual securities in the portfolio vary somewhat. However, the portfolio's overall risk is moderate.

The Jacob portfolio consists of stocks from a wide range of American business. All the companies had above-average growth potential and none was engaged in high-risk businesses that could face technological obsolescence or heavy foreign competition. Two banking stocks were selected, Bancorp Hawaii, Inc., and Florida Westcoast Banks. The former is a well-managed bank holding company that owns the largest bank in Hawaii. The latter is a growing bank holding company located on the west coast of Florida. Both regions are experiencing rapid population and economic growth. CBS appears to be well positioned in the growing communications industry. Kellogg is a food processor with a solid future. Knight-Ridder is a large newspaper chain with many Sunbelt papers. Kroger is expanding as well, helped by the 1983 acquisition of Dillon Companies, a superbly managed supermarket chain. The portfolio has two natural resource stocks, Union Oil and Weyerhaeuser. These companies are well positioned in their respective industries. Upjohn is a major drug firm that should benefit from the aging demographic mix of America. All the stocks in the Jacobs' portfolio are securities of well-managed companies with growth potential. The portfolio has a moderate risk level and provides an average dividend yield. With this portfolio, the Jacobs will have potential price appreciation coupled with a steady dividend income.

Art and Helen Brandt: Retirees

Having just sold their family business and liquidated their real estate investment property, the Brandts are eager to begin their retirement. At age 60, both have worked hard for 35 years building the successful business they recently sold. In addition, they had made some successful real estate investments over the years. The sale of their business and real estate holdings netted them $600,000 after taxes. They wish to invest these funds and have asked their investment advisor, Jane Tuttle, to develop a portfolio for them. The relevant financial information about the Brandts is as follows: They own their home free and clear and have a $300,000 municipal bond portfolio that yields them tax-free yearly income of $24,000. In addition, they have $20,000 in a money market account which they do not wish to invest, but want to hold as a ready cash reserve. Mr. Brandt has a $200,000 whole life insurance policy on his life, with Mrs. Brandt the designated beneficiary.

Now that they are retired, neither of the Brandts plans to seek employment. They do have a small pension benefit that will begin paying an income of $4,000 per year in five years. However, their main source of income will be their investment portfolio. During their last few working years, their combined yearly income was approximately $80,000. Their standard of living is rather high, and they do not wish to significantly change their life-style. They do not plan to spend any of their investment capital on living expenses, since they wish to keep their estate intact for their two children. Thus, the Brandts' basic investment objective is current income with some capital appreciation potential. The Brandts do not wish to reinvest in real estate, but rather have asked Ms. Tuttle to develop a $600,000 securities portfolio for them. They already have a $300,000 municipal bond portfolio, which will be left undisturbed. Given the Brandts' tax bracket (over 50 percent federal and state), municipal bonds offer a higher after-tax rate of return than corporate bonds.

The portfolio developed for the Brandts is shown in Table 19.5. It contains nine stocks with approximately $65,000 invested in each issue. The emphasis is on quality, with low-risk, high-yield issues, and diversification. The portfolio's beta is approxi-

TABLE 19.5   ART AND HELEN BRANDT'S PORTFOLIO

OBJECTIVE: CURRENT INCOME (LOW-RISK, HIGH-YIELD)

Number of Shares	Company	Dividend per Share	Dividend Income	Price per Share	Total Cost (including commission)	Beta	Dividend Yield
3,000	Bancorp Hawaii, Inc.	$1.20	$ 3,600	$22	$ 66,600	.86	5.4%
2,000	Crocker National Corporation	2.40	4,800	30	60,600	.81	7.9
2,500	Exxon	3.00	7,500	27	68,100	1.01	11.0
2,000	Florida Power and Light	3.36	6,720	32	64,600	.63	10.4
2,000	W. R. Grace	2.80	5,600	35	70,700	1.13	7.9
2,500	Pacific Gas and Electric	3.00	7,500	28	70,700	.53	10.6
4,000	Public Service of Colorado	1.76	7,040	16	64,600	.72	10.9
2,500	Sears, Roebuck and Company	1.36	3,400	27	68,100	.92	5.0
3,000	Texas Utilities	2.04	6,120	21	63,600	.60	9.6
	Total		$52,280		$597,600		8.7%

Portfolio beta = .80

mately .80—a risk level that is below that of the general stock market. It is expected that a large portion of the portfolio's total return (dividends plus price appreciation) will be in the form of dividend income. The portfolio has a current dividend yield of approximately 8.7 percent, an above-average dividend yield. Dividend income totals over $52,000, which added to the municipal bond income and the money market account interest will provide the Brandts with a gross income of about $80,000. The Brandts' after-tax income will equal their working years' income; thus, they will not have to alter their life-style.

Analyzing the individual issues in the portfolio, we can see that four public utility stocks are included. Utility stocks are often suitable for low-risk, current-income-oriented portfolios. High-quality electric and natural gas concerns tend to have moderate growth in earnings and dividends. The four issues in the portfolio, Florida Power and Light, Pacific Gas and Electric, Public Service of Colorado, and Texas Utilities, have growing service areas and records of profit and dividend increases. The stocks of two very large American companies, Exxon and Sears, Roebuck and Company, are included in the portfolio. Exxon is the largest U.S. energy company and offers a high dividend yield. Sears is America's largest retailer, and the company is diversifying into financial services. Two bank holding company stocks were selected, Bancorp Hawaii and Crocker National. Crocker was selected for its above-average dividend yield and because the firm is well positioned in the California market. Bancorp Hawaii, also selected in the Jacobs' portfolio, offers a top-quality vehicle to participate in Hawaii's growth. Additionally, the company has raised its dividend several times in recent years, and future dividend increases are expected. W. R. Grace is a large company with chemical and other diversified operations. All the issues in the Brandt's portfolio are well-known, relatively large corporations. Stability, low risk, and a rela-

BOX 19.3 A MODEL PORTFOLIO FOR A WOMAN WHO WANTS TO BUILD CAPITAL

Allison Walzer, 30, is the news editor of the Wilkes-Barre, Pa. Times Leader, and she has more money than she knows what to do with. Her $27,000 salary more than covers her living expenses, and she has substantial savings besides. The property settlement from her divorce three years ago plus $14,000 from her father's estate and her own thrift have given her a nest egg of more than $40,000. Last year she and her boyfriend bought a house, and Allison's half of the down payment came to $16,000. Now she wants to know how to invest the $25,825 she has left so that she can both increase her assets and cut her taxes.

On the job, Allison has edited articles advising readers what to do with their money, but she's never taken any of the advice herself. Says she: "I've been keeping nearly everything in a bank certificate of deposit, reinvesting it whenever it matures—with steadily decreasing interest." Last year [1982] her taxes totaled $5,623 on $28,267 of salary and interest. "Between what I'm paying in taxes and losing on interest," she sighs, "I figure that there must be a better way."

To help put her and other young adults in similar straits on the right investing track, *Money* consulted four financial planners. They agreed that Allison's portfolio must be completely overhauled. Each month she takes home $1,416 and puts $200 to $300 into a 5½% savings account. She withdrew $1,100 to settle her bill from the IRS, and the balance is now $400. Another $5,000 is in a money-market fund paying 8.34%, and $16,350 is in an 8.7% certificate of deposit maturing June 29. Her only other assets, aside from the house, are 14 shares of Capital Cities Communications stock valued at $2,075 and a $2,000 IRA.

Says Jay Rabinowitz, who heads the financial planning department at Merrill Lynch: "At this point nearly all of her investments provide taxable income rather than appre-ciation—which is what she needs." He points out that if Allison deployed some of her capital into tax-free investments, she could immediately increase her real return by 50%. If she also put a substantial chunk of her assets into a growth-stock mutual fund, her savings would grow faster over the long term.

The experts agree that Allison's first step should be to close out her 5½% passbook account and establish a $3,500 emergency reserve, equal to 2½ months of her net salary, in a money-market fund. Douglas Hyer, president of Asset Advisory Services in Garden City, N.Y., recommends that she switch to Bull & Bear Dollar Reserves (11 Hanover Sq., New York, N.Y. 10005). Right now she's in Prudential-Bache's MoneyMart Assets. The yields are comparable, but Bull & Bear has a $250 check-writing minimum vs. Pru-Bache's $500.

As soon as Allison's CD matures, her next investment should be to put $5,000 of it in a municipal bond unit trust, Hyer says. The interest will be similar to that on the CD, but it will be exempt from federal taxes. Because trusts consist of a fixed portfolio of bonds, the yield doesn't fluctuate; that's an advantage now because rates are expected to decline a point or so by year-end.

Hyer suggests that Allison buy units in the Pennsylvania Insured Municipals Income Trust, which she can do through a local broker. The trust is insured so she doesn't have to worry about the safety of her principal or interest, and she can sell her units anytime before the trust matures if she needs to. Because she lives in Pennsylvania, the interest is free of state and local, as well as federal, taxes. The current series, No. 23, yields 8.51%, and to do as well with a taxable investment she would have to earn 12.12%.

BOX 19.3 *Continued*

Iris Taymore Schnitzer, president of the Financial Forum in Boston, thinks that Allison should put another $5,000 from the CD in a self-liquidating real estate investment trust. Such an investment will pay her income that is partially sheltered from taxes and give her assets an opportunity to grow. Both Schnitzer and Doug Hyer recommend Wespac II (111 Fashion Lane, Tustin, Calif. 92680), which buys small shoping centers and garden apartments and passes the rental income along to the shareholders. Now in the offering period, Wespac II will be sold over the counter, so Allison can bail out if she needs the money before the trust liquidates in 10 years. When Wespac's properties are eventually sold, 90% of any profits will be paid out to the shareholders as capital gains.

The planners all urge that Allison use the remaining $6,350 from her CD to buy shares in a growth-stock mutual fund. Not only is that the best way for her to accumulate capital, but if she holds her shares more than a year, they will be taxed at the favorable capital-gains rate—12% in her case. Hyer recommends the Twentieth Century Growth fund (P.O. Box 200, Kansas City, Mo. 64141). Its value has increased more than 435% over the past five years.

Some of Allison's monthly savings should go also into her growth fund. Connie S.P. Chen of Chen Financial Planning Consultants in New York City suggests that she begin a program of dollar-cost averaging, whereby she puts in a steady $200 a month whether the stock market goes up or down. "Only real technicians know exactly when to buy," says Chen. "This way Allison will pay less for her shares than their average market value."

As far as her other assets go, the planners urge Allison to continue taking advantage of the employee stock purchase plan through which she got her 14 shares of Capital Cities stock. Cap Cities owns the Wilkes-Barre Times Leader, and the stock Allison bought last year at $64 a share is now worth $148. She should add $100 to the remaining $1,900 in the Pru-Bache account and make her 1983 contribution to her IRA. Doug Hyer points out that if she waits until April 1984 she could lose almost $61,000 in compounded, tax-deferred earnings over the next 35 years.

The planners, in summary, advised Allison to apportion her assets this way for capital growth and tax savings:

Money-market fund	14%
Municipal bond unit trust	19
Real estate investment trust	19
Growth stock mutual fund	25
IRA	15
Capital cities stock	8
Total	100%

Source: Lisa Gubernick, "Model Portfolio For a Woman Who Wants to Build Capital." *Money,* June 1983, pp. 197–198.

*Ed, you're the only person I know who always makes money
in the Stock Market. What's your secret?*

tively high dividend yield with some potential for increase, characterize the stocks in this portfolio.

Elizabeth Beckett: Widow

In the preceding example, a portfolio was developed for a fairly affluent retired couple. Most retirees are less fortunate than the Brandts; they have less funds to invest. Elizabeth Beckett, age 70, was recently widowed. Between the estate of her late husband, her personal assets, and their jointly owned assets, Elizabeth has approximately $350,000 in liquid assets, all of it in savings and money market accounts. Elizabeth owns her home free and clear. Other than the interest on her savings, her income consists of $600 per month from social security. Unfortunately, her husband's employer did not have a pension plan. She has turned to her investment advisor, Barbara Puckett, to discuss strategy and to develop an investment policy.

Between social security and interest earned on her savings and money market accounts, Mrs. Beckett's current income is approximately $35,000 annually. She wishes to increase that income, if possible, while only minimally raising her risk exposure. Ms. Puckett recommended the investment portfolio presented in Table

TABLE 19.6 ELIZABETH BECKETT'S PORTFOLIO

OBJECTIVE: MAXIMIZE CURRENT INCOME (MINIMAL RISK)

Par Value	Issue	Standard & Poor's Bond Rating	Interest Income	Price	Total Cost	Yield to Maturity	Current Yield
$50,000	Burlington Northern 12 7/8% due 2005	A	$ 6,437.50	100	$ 50,000	12.875%	12.875%
50,000	Deere and Company 11 1/2% due 1989	A	5,750.00	98	49,000	11.900	11.700
50,000	Georgia-Pacific 10.70% due 1987	A	5,350.00	97	48,500	11.600	11.000
50,000	Pacific Gas and Electric 12 7/8% due 2013	AA	6,437.50	100	50,000	12.875	12.875
50,000	Pacific Telephone 12.70% due 2019	A	6,350.00	97	48,500	13.200	13.100
50,000	U.S. Life 12 1/2% due 1990	AA	6,250.00	100	50,000	12.500	12.500
	Total		$36,575.00		$296,000	12.500%	12.400%

19.6. The portfolio's objective is to maximize current income while keeping risk at a low level. Approximately $296,000 was invested in high-quality corporate bonds. The balance of $54,000 was retained in a money market account at the local savings and loan office to provide a substantial contingency reserve. By investing in the bond portfolio, Mrs. Beckett's yearly income will rise from approximately $35,000 to about $47,800 ($7,200 social security, $4,000 savings interest, $36,600 bond interest). Because social security income is currently nontaxable and because persons 65 and over receive several small tax breaks, Mrs. Beckett's marginal income tax bracket is approximately 28 percent. Taxable corporate bonds were recommended over municipal bonds because her after-tax rate of return would be greater with the former.

Turning to the portfolio, we see that there are six corporate bond issues which cost about $50,000 each. Each issuer is a high-quality company that has a very low risk of default. The portfolio is diversified in several ways. First, it contains a mix of industrial, utility, railroad, and financial issues. The two utility bond issues are Pacific Gas and Electric and Pacific Telephone. Both companies are very large and financially secure. The two industrial concerns, Deere and Georgia-Pacific, are very large as well. Burlington Northern is a financially solid railroad, and U.S. Life is a large, secure insurance company. A second added measure of diversification is attained by staggering the bonds' maturities. They mature in six different years: 1987, 1989, 1990, 2005, 2013, and 2019. The shorter-term bonds will provide ready cash when they mature, and they generally will fluctuate less in price than the longer-term bonds. The portfolio has been diversified in several ways to keep the risk of loss very low. By switching funds out of her savings and money market accounts into bonds, Mrs.

Beckett was able to increase her current income substantially while experiencing only a minimal increase in risk.

SUMMARY

An understanding of how best to combine investment vehicles to achieve a desired combination of risk and return is needed in order to manage an investment portfolio effectively. A portfolio is a collection of investment vehicles assembled to meet a common investment goal. To develop an efficient portfolio, a manager should establish a list of objectives. Portfolios may be growth-oriented or income-oriented. A portfolio may contain one investment vehicle or many. Diversification means the inclusion of various vehicles in the portfolio in order to minimize risk. Risk may be diversifiable (unsystematic) or nondiversifiable (systematic). An investor is rewarded for taking nondiversifiable risk; a positive relationship exists between its level and the level of return. The total investment portfolio should include not only securities, but options, commodities and financial futures, real estate, annuities, limited partnerships, and gold and other tangible investments as well.

The two approaches currently used by portfolio managers are the traditional approach and modern portfolio theory (MPT). Under the traditional approach, portfolios are constructed by selecting securities issued by companies from a broad cross-section of industries. Traditional portfolio managers invest in well-known companies because these companies have been and are expected to continue to be successful business enterprises. Modern portfolio theory (MPT) utilizes statistical measures such as the variance and correlation of a security's rate of return with the rate of return of another security or with the market as a whole. In choosing securities for an MPT portfolio, the statistical diversification—that is, negative return correlation—is the deciding factor. The nondiversifiable risk of a security or a portfolio can be measured with the beta regression coefficient. The beta regression coefficient measures the relative volatility or change in the security's or portfolio's return as compared to the return on a market index such as the Standard & Poor's 500 stock composite index or the New York Stock Exchange composite index. The coefficient of determination (R^2) indicates the percentage of the change in the dependent variable explained by its relationship with the independent variable. A valuable outgrowth of modern portfolio theory is the establishment of a specific relationship between nondiversifiable risk and investment return.

There is no precise technique an investor can use to develop a portfolio. It is recommended that the individual investor determine the risk he or she is willing to bear, use beta to assemble a diversified portfolio reflecting an acceptable level of risk, and evaluate alternative portfolios to make sure that the portfolio selected provides the highest return for the given level of acceptable risk.

To formulate a portfolio management strategy, the investor should consider characteristics such as level and stability of income, family factors, net worth, experience and age, and disposition toward risk. After the investor has developed a personal financial profile, he or she must specify objectives: current income, capital preservation, capital growth, tax considerations, and level of risk. Once specified, the objectives should act as a guide in structuring the portfolio.

KEY TERMS

beta	positive correlation
coefficient of determination (R^2)	relevant risk
correlation	risk
diversifiable risk	risk-free rate of return (R_F)
diversification	risk-return tradeoff
efficient portfolio	systematic risk
growth-oriented portfolio	total risk
income-oriented portfolio	traditional portfolio management
modern portfolio theory (MPT)	unsystematic risk
negative correlation	variance
nondiversifiable risk	volatility
portfolio	

REVIEW QUESTIONS

1. What is a portfolio? Explain the first step an investor should take in developing a viable portfolio.

2. Define diversification and explain the motive behind the diversification of a portfolio.

3. Identify and differentiate between the two types of risk associated with a portfolio. What is the total risk of a portfolio? Explain.

4. Graphically relate the number of securities in a portfolio to the level of (a) diversifiable, (b) nondiversifiable, and (c) total risk. Explain the significance of this graph in the portfolio management process.

5. What factors should be considered when choosing the ideal number of securities for a portfolio? Explain.

6. Define an efficient portfolio. As an investor, discuss how you would go about creating an efficient portfolio.

7. Compare and contrast traditional portfolio management with modern portfolio theory (MPT).

8. Give three reasons why traditional portfolio managers typically invest in well-established companies. Explain each reason.

9. Define beta. Explain how the nondiversifiable risk of a security or a portfolio can be measured by beta. Use examples.

10. If portfolio A has a beta of $+3.0$ and portfolio Z has a beta of -3.0, what do the two values indicate? If the return on the market portfolio rises by 20 percent what impact, if any, would this have on the return from portfolios A and Z? Explain.

11. Are there any particular techniques an investor can use as part of a portfolio strategy? Explain how traditional and modern portfolio approaches can be reconciled.

12. What role, if any, does an investor's characteristics play in establishing investment policies? Explain.

13. It is often said that a portfolio must be built around an individual's needs. Do you agree or disagree with this statement?

14. Describe the risk-income tradeoff as it relates to an investor's age. Compare and contrast the expected portfolios of: (a) a retired investor in need of income; (b) a high-income, financially secure investor; (c) a young investor with a secure job and no dependents.

15. Briefly discuss the possible investment objectives one might consider when formulating portfolio objectives and policies.

CASE PROBLEMS

19.1 TRADITIONAL VERSUS MODERN PORTFOLIO THEORY: WHO'S RIGHT?

Walt Davies and Shane O'Brien are district managers for Lee, Inc. Over the years as they moved through the firm's sales organization they became, and still remain, close friends. Walt, who is 33 years old, currently lives in Newark, New Jersey; Shane, who is 35, lives in Houston, Texas. Recently at the national sales meeting they were discussing various company matters, as well as bringing each other up to date on their families, when the subject of investments came up. Each of them had always been fascinated by the stock market and now that they had achieved some degree of financial success, they had begun actively investing. As they disccussed their investments, Walt indicated that he felt the only way an individual who did not have hundreds of thousands of dollars to invest can safely invest is to buy mutual fund shares, since they contain a large number of securities representing the stocks of the leading firms in a broad cross-section of industries. Walt emphasized that in order to be safe, a person needs to hold a broadly diversified portfolio and that only those with a lot of money and time can achieve the needed diversification that can be readily obtained by purchasing mutual fund shares.

Shane totally disagreed. He said, "Diversification! Who needs it?" He felt that what one must do is to look carefully at stocks possessing desired risk-return characteristics and then invest all one's money in that one stock. Walt told him he was crazy. He said, "There is no way to conveniently measure risk—you're just gambling." Shane disagreed. He explained how his stockbroker had acquainted him with beta, which is a measure of risk. Shane said that the higher the beta, the more risky the stock, and therefore the higher will be its return. By looking up the betas for potential stock investments in his broker's beta book, he can pick stocks having an acceptable risk level for him. Shane explained that with beta one does not need to diversify; one merely needs to be willing to accept the risk reflected by beta and then hope for the best. The conversation continued, with Walt indicating that although he knew nothing about beta, he didn't believe one could safely invest in a single stock. Shane continued to argue that his broker had explained to him that betas can be calculated not just for a single stock, but also for a portfolio of stocks such as a mutual fund. He said, "What's the difference between a stock with a beta, of say, 1.20 and a mutual fund with a beta of 1.20? They both have the same risk and should therefore provide similar returns."

As Walt and Shane continued to discuss their differing opinions relative to investment strategy, they began to get angry with each other. Neither was able to convince the other that he was right. The level of their voices now raised, they attracted the attention of the company vice-president of finance, Elmer Green, who was standing nearby. He came over to Walt and Shane and indicated he had overheard their argument about investments and thought that, given his expertise on financial matters, he might be able to resolve their disagreement. He asked them to explain the crux of their disagreement, and each reviewed his own viewpoint. After hearing their views, Elmer responded: "I have some good news and some bad news for each of you. There is some validity to what each of you says, but there also are some errors in each of your explanations. Walt tends to support the traditional approach to portfolio management; Shane's views are more supportive of modern portfolio theory." Just then, the company president interrupted them, indicating that he must talk to Elmer immediately. Elmer apologized for having to leave and made an arrangement to continue their discussion over a drink later that evening.

Questions

1. Analyze Walt's argument and explain to him why a mutual fund investment may be overdiversified and that one does not necessarily have to have hundreds of thousands of dollars in order to diversify adequately.

2. Analyze Shane's argument and explain the major error in his logic relative to the use of beta as a substitute for diversification. Explain the key assumption underlying the use of beta as a risk measure.

3. Briefly describe the traditional approach to portfolio management and relate it to the approaches supported by Walt and Shane.

4. Briefly describe modern portfolio theory (MPT) and relate it to the approaches supported by Walt and Shane. Be sure to mention diversifiable, nondiversifiable, and total risk along with the role of beta.

5. Explain how the traditional approach and modern portfolio theory can be blended into an approach to portfolio management that might prove useful to the individual investor. Relate this to reconciling Walt's and Shane's differing points of view.

19.2 MARILYN RENEAU'S INHERITED PORTFOLIO: DOES IT MEET HER NEEDS?

Marilyn Reneau is a 35-year-old divorcee currently employed as a tax attorney for a major oil and gas exploration company. She has no children and earns nearly $60,000 per year from her salary as well as through participation in the company's drilling activities. Divorced only one year, Marilyn has found being single quite exciting. An expert on oil and gas taxation, Marilyn does not concern herself with job security—she is content with her income and finds it adequate to allow her to buy and do whatever she wishes. Her current philosophy is to live each day to its fullest, not concerning herself with retirement, which is too far in the future to require her current attention.

A month ago Marilyn's only surviving parent, her father, was killed in a sailing accident. He had retired in La Jolla, California, two years earlier and had spent most of his time sailing. Prior to retirement, he owned a children's clothing manufacturing firm in South Carolina, which he sold. He invested the proceeds in a security portfolio that provided him with retirement income of over $30,000 per year. In his will, which incidentally had been drafted by Marilyn a number of years earlier, he left his entire estate to Marilyn. The estate had been structured in such a way that, in addition to a few family heirlooms, Marilyn received a security portfolio having a market value of nearly $350,000 and about $10,000 in cash. The portfolio contained 10 securities—5 bonds, 2 common stocks, and 3 mutual funds. A table listing the securities and key characteristics is given below. The two common stocks were issued by large, mature, well-known firms that had exhibited continuing patterns of dividend payment over the past five years. The stocks offered only moderate growth potential—probably no more than 2 to 3 percent appreciation per year. The three mutual funds in the portfolio were income funds invested in diversified portfolios of income-oriented stocks and bonds. They provided stable streams of dividend income with little opportunity for capital appreciation.

Now that Marilyn owns the portfolio, she wishes to determine whether or not it is suitable for her situation. She realizes that the high level of income provided by the portfolio will be taxed at a rate (federal and state) in excess of 50 percent. Since she does not currently need the income, Marilyn plans to invest the after-tax proceeds from this income in tax-sheltered oil and gas deals, real estate, and/or in common stocks offering high capital gain potential. She clearly needs to shelter taxable income; Marilyn is already paying out a sizable portion of her current income in taxes. She feels fortunate to have acquired the portfolio and wants to make certain that it provides her the maximum benefits, given her financial situation. The $10,000 cash left to her will be especially useful in paying broker's commissions associated with making portfolio adjustments.

Questions

1. Briefly assess Marilyn's financial situation and develop a portfolio objective consistent with her needs.

CASE 19.2   MARILYN RENEAU'S INHERITED SECURITIES PORTFOLIO

BONDS

Par Value	Issue	S&P Rating	Interest Income	Price	Total Cost	Current Yield
$40,000	Delta Power and Light 10⅛% due 2002	AA	$4,050	$ 98	$39,200	10.33%
30,000	Mountain Water 9¾% due 1995	A	2,925	102	30,600	9.56
50,000	California Gas 9½% due 1989	AAA	4,750	97	48,500	9.79
20,000	Trans-Pacific Gas 10% due 2000	AAA	2,000	99	19,800	10.10
20,000	Public Service 9⅞% due 1990	AA	1,975	100	20,000	9.88

COMMON STOCKS

Number of Shares	Company	Dividend per Share	Dividend Income	Price per Share	Total Cost	Dividend Yield	Beta
2,000	International Supply	$2.40	$4,800	$ 22	$44,900	10.91%	.97
3,000	Black Motor	1.50	4,500	17	52,000	8.82	.85

MUTUAL FUNDS

Number of Shares	Issue	Dividend per Share	Dividend Income	Price per Share	Total Cost	Dividend Yield	Beta
2,000	International Capital Income A Fund	$ .80	$ 1,600	$ 10	$ 20,000	8.00%	1.02
1,000	Grimner Special Income Fund	2.00	2,000	15	15,000	7.50	1.10
4,000	Ellis Diversified Income Fund	1.20	4,800	12	48,000	10.00	.90
	Total annual income		$33,400	Portfolio value	$338,000	Portfolio current yield	9.88%

2. Evaluate the portfolio left to Marilyn by her father. Assess its apparent objective and evaluate how well it may be doing in fulfilling this objective. Comment on the risk, return, and tax impact of this portfolio.

3. If Marilyn had decided to invest in a security portfolio consistent with her needs (indicated in response to question 1), describe the nature and mix, if any, of securities you would recommend she purchase. Discuss the risk, return, and tax implications of such a portfolio.

4. Compare the nature of the security portfolio inherited by Marilyn (from the response to question 2) with what you believe would be an appropriate security portfolio for her (from the response to question 3).

5. What recommendations would you give Marilyn about the inherited portfolio? Explain the steps she should take to adjust the portfolio to her needs.

SELECTED READINGS

Bettner, Jill. "New Legislation Makes It Far More Attractive to Incorporate Your Portfolio for Tax Savings." *The Wall Street Journal,* December 6, 1982, p. 48.

Bohr, Peter. "Scouting Out the Best Investments." *Money,* October 1980, pp. 80–84.

Bronson, Gail. "Model Portfolio/A Couple Facing Retirement." *Money,* April 1983, pp. 47–50.

Edgerton, Jerry. "Investing in New Industries." *Money,* March 1982, pp. 44–47.

————. "Tailoring a Portfolio to the Good Times." *Money,* May 1983, pp. 79–82.

Hagin, Robert L. *The Dow-Jones Irwin Guide to Modern Portfolio Theory.* Homewood, IL: Dow-Jones Irwin, 1979,

Runde, Robert H. "What to Do When It's Time to Invest." *Money,* October 1982, pp. 82–86.

Sharpe, William F. *Investments,* 2d ed. Englewood Cliffs, N.J.: Prentice-Hall, 1981.

Thackray, John. "Modern Portfolio Theory: Does It Really Help?" *Financial World,* January 1, 1979, pp. 25–29.

Trunzo, Candace E. "Building an Inflation-Fighting Portfolio." *Money,* October 1980, pp. 101–104.

————. "Planning Your Portfolio." *Money,* January 1983, pp. 66–70.

20
Monitoring Your Investment Portfolio

After a suitable portfolio of investment vehicles has been constructed, the individual investor's job is not done; the actual performance of the portfolio (as well as the component investment vehicles) must be assessed, and appropriately timed transactions may be required to make needed adjustments. In order to provide an understanding of the procedures for monitoring an investment portfolio, in this chapter we emphasize:

1. Sources of needed data, indexes of investment performance, and techniques for measuring the performance of investment vehicles.
2. The methods used to compare investment performance to investment goals.
3. The techniques used to measure current income, appreciation in value, and total portfolio return relative to the amount of money actually invested in the portfolio.
4. The methods used to evaluate portfolio performance relative to certain standards, the importance of portfolio revision, and the role of the personal computer.
5. The role common types of formula plans can play in timing purchase and sale decisions.
6. The use of limit and stop-loss orders in investment timing, the warehousing of liquidity, and the key factors in timing investment sales in order to achieve maximum benefits.

Imagine one of your most important personal goals is accumulating savings of $9,000 three years from now in order to have enough money to purchase your dream home. Based on your projections, the desired home will cost $75,000, and the $9,000 will be sufficient to make a 10 percent down payment and pay the associated closing costs. Your calculations indicate that this goal can be achieved by investing existing savings plus an additional $100 per month over the next three years in a vehicle earning 12 percent per year. Projections of your earnings over the three-year period indicate that you should just be able to set aside the needed $100 per month. Consultation with an investment advisor, Elbert Doofus, leads you to believe that under his management the 12 percent return can be achieved.

It seems simple: Give Elbert your existing savings and send him $100 each month over the next 36 months, and at the end of that period you will have the $9,000 needed to purchase the home. Of course, there are many uncertainties involved in this decision. For example, "What if your income proves inadequate to set aside $100 each month?" "What if Elbert fails to earn the needed 12 percent annual return?" "What if the desired house costs more than $75,000 in three years?" and so on. Clearly, one must do more than simply devise what appears to be a feasible plan for achieving a future goal. By periodically assessing progress toward the goal, one can improve the chances that the goal will be met. For example, had you found that your earnings were not adequate to permit the $100 per month investment, you might have found a new, higher-paying job; or if the required 12 percent return was not being earned on your funds, you might have found a new investment advisor. As actual outcomes occur, one must compare them to the planned outcomes and make any necessary alterations in his or her plans; if such changes do not permit goal achievement, the goal and/or its timing may have to be adjusted.

The final, and important, aspect of the personal investment process involves continuously monitoring and periodically adjusting the portfolio as needed in order to keep moving toward the achievement of financial goals. The monitoring process involves assessing actual performance, comparing it to planned performance, revising and making needed adjustments, and timing these adjustments to achieve maximum benefit. Let us see how this is done.

EVALUATING THE PERFORMANCE OF INDIVIDUAL INVESTMENTS

Investment vehicles are typically selected for inclusion in a portfolio on the basis of expected returns, associated risks, and certain tax considerations that may affect the returns. Since the actual outcomes may not necessarily coincide with those expected, we must measure and compare actual performance with anticipated performance. Here we will emphasize developing measures suitable for analyzing individual investment performance. We begin with sources of data.

Obtaining Needed Data
The first step in analyzing investment returns is gathering data that reflect the actual performance of each investment owned. As pointed out in Chapter 3, a broad range of sources of investment information is available. *The Wall Street Journal* and

Barron's, for example, contain numerous items of information useful in assessing the performance of securities. The same type of information used when making an investment decision is used to monitor the performance of investments held as part of an investment portfolio. Two areas one must keep abreast of are returns on owned investments and economic and market activity.

Return data

The basic ingredient in the analysis of investment returns is current market value information. Many publications provide daily price quotations for securities such as stocks and bonds. Investors often maintain logs that contain the cost of each investment, as well as dividends, interest, and other sources of income received. By regularly recording price and return data, an investor can create an ongoing record of price fluctuations and cumulative returns that can be used in monitoring performance. The investor should also monitor corporate earnings and dividends, since a company's earnings and dividends will affect its stock price. The two sources of investment return—current income and capital appreciation—of course must be combined to determine total return. The combination of components using the techniques presented in Chapter 4 will be illustrated for some of the more popular investment vehicles later in this chapter.

Economic and market activity

Changes in the economy and market will affect returns—both level of current income and the market value of an investment vehicle. The astute investor will keep abreast of national and local economic and market developments. By following economic and market changes, an investor should be able to assess their potential impact on individual investment returns and on the portfolio's return. For example, local real estate prices are affected by such regional indicators as home construction, local income and unemployment, and local zoning law changes. Furthermore, the prices of real estate are more commonly affected by local developments than by national policy changes. The wise real estate investor therefore should keep abreast of local as well as national developments.

Stock prices are affected by the national economy. As we pointed out in Chapter 3, national economic analyses are often available at local banks and are published by many investment services. An investor should relate macroeconomic developments to the returns on securities held in a portfolio. As economic and market conditions change, an investor must be prepared to make revisions in the portfolio to respond to new developments. In essence, a knowledgeable investor is in a much better position to profit (or avoid loss).

Indexes of Investment Performance

In measuring investment performance, it is often worthwhile to compare the investor's returns with appropriate broad-based market measures. Let us look briefly at several indexes against which an investor can compare the results of his or her investment strategies. (Detailed discussions of these averages and indexes were included in Chapter 3.) Indexes useful for the analysis of common stock include the

BOX 20.1 KNOWING WHEN TO SELL

Most investors find it harder to decide on selling than on buying. Their thinking: If our shares drop, we hate to admit we've made mistakes and think up reasons for an early recovery. Our problem is aggravated by the way brokers constantly issue studies telling us why to buy this or that stock. They rarely tell us what to sell, except perhaps a one-line notice to the effect that a company has been dropped from their recommended list.

One way out of this trap is to adopt some simple rules. Here are five that are suggested by James C. Doyle, vice president of Moseley, Hallgarten, Estabrook & Weeden:

1. When buying a stock, set a target for it. Obviously you think the firm's earnings will grow. By how much? If they do, how much do you expect the stock to rise? As time passes, if you see the company running into problems that make it less likely your goal will be achieved, you'd better sell. Chances are others will reach the same conclusion.
2. Decide at the outset how much of a loss you are willing to take if your hopes are misplaced. Doyle suggests 10 percent as a rule of thumb. If the price falls that much, sell, avoid the risk of a larger loss and put the remaining 90 percent of your money into something better.
3. Compare your stocks with some relevant index such as the Dow Jones or S&P industrials. As long as your shares are doing better than the market, consider buying more. If they do worse, sell.
4. If you are worrying about a stock, sell it. Other investors are probably worrying, too, and getting ready to sell.
5. If your broker has been touting a stock and now says it's "a hold," that means he thinks there are better places to put his customers' funds—another reason to sell.

... Rules such as these are not foolproof. Their value is in helping you discipline yourself. Above all, says Doyle, "always be prepared to sell. Don't fall in love with a stock. It's just an investment vehicle with a price and symbol on the tape."

Martin E. Zweig, an investment adviser who publishes the *Zweig Forecast*, urges an even more arbitrary system—using "stop orders." These are standing orders to your broker to sell a stock if it hits a predetermined price. Zweig suggests setting that limit 10 to 20 percent below cost when you buy a stock on the New York Stock Exchange. For shares on the American Exchange or over-the-counter market, he urges "mental stops"—telling yourself you will sell if the shares fall to a certain point. . . .

And if your stocks go up in price? Zweig says you should periodically boost the limit on the stop orders but allow somewhat greater leeway to keep from being sold out whenever an issue has a brief relapse because of profit taking.

This may cost you increased brokers' fees and added taxes if you take more short-term gains than you would otherwise. That's the price you pay for reducing risk.

Is there any advice for those who have not followed guidelines such as these and now hold stocks worth much less than they cost? Many advisers say, "Sit tight. It's too late to sell." Doyle doesn't see it that way. He figures there will always be better places to put your money than in stocks that have proven to be losers.

About the time the vast majority adopt that view and decide to sell, the bear market will be near its end.

Source: William C. Bryant, "Knowing When to Sell." *U.S. News & World Report,* March 8, 1982, p. 77.

Dow Jones industrial average (DJIA), the Standard & Poor's 500 stock composite index (S&P 500), and the New York Stock Exchange composite index (NYSE index).

Despite the widespread use of the Dow Jones industrial average by the news media, it is *not* considered the most appropriate comparative gauge of stock price movement. This is because of its narrow coverage, and because it excludes many types of stocks from its scope. For example, companies like Safeway, K-Mart, RCA, and Dow Chemical are not included in the DJIA. If an investor's portfolio is composed of a broad range of common stocks, the NYSE composite index is a more appropriate tool. This index consists of stocks that constitute approximately 55 percent of all publicly traded stocks, based upon dollar market value. The scope of coverage, as measured by market value, is three times that of the DJIA.

A number of bond market indicators are available for assessing the general behavior of these markets. These indicators consider either bond price behavior or bond yield. The Dow Jones composite bond average is a popular measure of bond price behavior based upon the closing prices of ten utility and ten industrial bonds. Like bond quotations, this average reflects the average percentage of face value at which the bonds sell. A variety of sources of bond yield data, which reflect the rate of return one would earn on a bond purchased today and held to maturity, is also available. *Barron's,* for example, quotes these yields for the Dow Jones composite bond average. Other sources are Moody's Investors Service, the *Federal Reserve Bulletins,* and the *Federal Reserve Monthly Chart Book.* Indices of bond price and bond yield performance can be obtained for specific types of bonds (industrial, utility, and municipal), as well as on a composite basis.

There are a few other indexes that cover listed options and commodities, although there are no widely publicized indexes/averages for mutual funds, tangible investments (like gold and artwork), and so on. Nor is there a broad index of real estate returns. Such returns tend to be localized—that is, they vary widely from area to area. And different types of property investments yield widely varying returns. For example, farmland moves in value in relation to farm product prices and to foreign investment in farmland. Thus, real estate investors should compare their returns with those earned by other local real estate investors. In addition, it might be wise to compare the investor's real estate returns with the Consumer Price Index and with the NYSE composite index. The former will serve as a useful comparative measure of its effectiveness as an inflation hedge. The latter is useful in comparing the relative return on a diversified stock portfolio with that from real estate investment. Similar approaches can be used in assessing other forms of property investment.

Measuring Investment Performance

Reliable techniques for consistently measuring the performance of each investment vehicle are needed to monitor an investment portfolio. In particular, the holding period return (HPR) measure first presented in Chapter 4 (and used in one form or another throughout most of this book to measure an investment's expected return), is also used to determine *actual* return performance from stocks, bonds, mutual funds, real estate, and gold and other investments. Investment holdings need to be evaluated periodically over time—at least once a year; HPR is an excellent way to assess actual return behavior, since it captures *total return* performance and is most appropriate for holding or assessment periods of one year or less. Total return in this context includes the periodic cash income from the investment, as well as price appreciation or loss, whether realized or unrealized.

Stocks and bonds

There are several measures of investment return for stocks and bonds. The dividend yield, for instance, measures the current yearly dividend return earned from a stock investment. It is calculated by dividing a stock's yearly cash dividend by its price. This measure of investment return was discussed in Chapter 8. The current yield and promised yield (yield to maturity) for bonds was analyzed in Chapter 11. These measures of investment return capture various components of an investor's return, but do not reflect actual total return. To provide a measure of total return, the holding period return method is applied. The total return on an investment in stocks or bonds consists of two components: dividend or interest income plus any capital gain or loss. *Holding period return (HPR)* measures the total return (income plus change in value) actually earned on an investment over a given investment period—we will use a holding period of approximately one year in the illustrations that follow.

Stocks.   The HPR for common and preferred stocks includes both cash dividends received as well as any price change in the security during the period of ownership. The formula for calculating HPR for stocks is:

$$\text{HPR}_{\text{stocks}} = \frac{D_t + (P_{t+1} - P_t)}{P_t}$$

where:

D_t = dividends received during time period t

P_t = stock price at the beginning of time period t

P_{t+1} = stock price at the end of time period t

Both components of an investor's return on a stock are included in the HPR measurement. Table 20.1 illustrates the actual HPR return calculation. This investor purchased 1,000 shares of Crocker National Corporation in May 1983 at a cost of $27,312 (including commissions). After holding the stock for just over one year, the stock was sold with proceeds to the investor of $32,040. The investor received $2,000 in cash dividends during the period of ownership. In addition, a $4,728 long-term capital gain was realized on the sale. The calculated HPR is 24.63 percent.

The HPR found above was calculated without consideration for income taxes paid on the dividends and the long-term capital gain. Because many investors are concerned with both pretax and after-tax rates of return, an after-tax HPR for this security is calculated in Table 20.2. The investor in this example is in the 40 percent

> ## TABLE 20.1 CALCULATION OF PRETAX HPR ON COMMON STOCK
>
> Security: Crocker National common stock
> Date of purchase: May 1, 1983
> Purchase cost: $27,312
> Date of sale: May 7, 1984
> Sale proceeds: $32,040
> Dividends received (May 1983–May 1984): $2,000
>
> $$\text{holding period return} = \frac{\$2,000 + (\$32,040 - \$27,312)}{\$27,312}$$
>
> $$= \underline{+24.63\%}$$

ordinary income tax bracket (federal and state combined). Thus, dividend income to this investor is taxed at a 40 percent rate, and long-term capital gains are taxed at a 16 percent rate (.40 × .40 = .16; only 40 percent of a long-term capital gain is taxable). Income taxes reduce the after-tax dividend income to $1,200 and the after-tax capital gain to $3,972. The after-tax HPR is 18.94 percent, a reduction of 5.69 percent. It should be clear that both the pretax and after-tax HPR are useful gauges of return.

Bonds. The HPR for a bond investment is similar to the stock formula:

$$\text{HPR}_{\text{bonds}} = \frac{I_t + (P_{t+1} - P_t)}{P_t}$$

where

I_t = interest received during time period t

P_t = bond price at the beginning of time period t

P_{t+1} = bond price at the end of time period t

The calculation holds for both straight debt and convertible issues and includes the two components of an investor's return on a bond investment: interest income and capital gain or loss realized upon sale. Calculation of the HPR on a bond investment is illustrated in Table 20.3. The investor purchased the Phoenix Brewing bonds for $10,000, held them for just over one year, and then realized $9,704 at sale. In addition, the investor earned $1,000 in interest during the period of ownership. The HPR of this investment is 7.04 percent. The HPR is lower than the bond's current yield of 10 percent ($1,000 interest ÷ $10,000 purchase price) because the bonds were sold at a capital loss.

TABLE 20.2   CALCULATION OF AFTER-TAX HPR ON COMMON STOCK*

TAX CALCULATIONS

Dividends	$2,000	Capital gain	$4,728
Income tax (tax rate = .40)	− 800	Income tax (tax rate = .16)	− 756
After-tax dividend income	$1,200	After-tax capital gain	$3,972

AFTER-TAX HPR CALCULATION

$$\text{after-tax HPR} = \frac{\$1,200 + \$3,972}{\$27,312}$$

$$= +18.94\%$$

*This table is based on use of the data presented in Table 20.1 and the assumption of a 40 percent ordinary income tax rate for the investor.

The after-tax HPR for this bond investment is calculated in Table 20.4. Assuming a tax bracket of 40 percent, the after-tax HPR is 3.51 percent—approximately half the pretax HPR. This investor would have been wise to sell the bonds (if at a loss) just prior to holding them for one year. If the bonds had been sold earlier, a short-term capital loss would have been incurred. Establishing a short-term, rather than a long-term, capital loss would have been beneficial to the investor, since only 50 percent of net long-term capital losses, up to an annual maximum of $3,000, are deductible from ordinary income, but the entire amount (up to $3,000) of net short-term capital losses is deductible from ordinary income. (See Chapter 17 for detailed discussion of taxes.) In this case, had the investor sold the bonds just four days earlier, the after-tax HPR could have been increased to 4.22 percent.

TABLE 20.3   CALCULATION OF PRETAX HPR ON A BOND

Security: Phoenix Brewing Company 10% bonds
Date of purchase: June 2, 1983
Purchase cost: $10,000
Date of sale: June 5, 1984
Sales proceeds: $9,704
Interest earned (June 1983–June 1984): $1,000

$$\text{holding period return} = \frac{\$1,000 + (\$9,704 - \$10,000)}{\$10,000}$$

$$= +7.04\%$$

TABLE 20.4 CALCULATION OF AFTER-TAX HPR ON A BOND*

TAX CALCULATION

Interest	$1,000	Capital loss	$296
Income tax (tax rate = .40)	−400	Tax savings (tax rate = .16)	−47
After-tax interest income	$ 600	After-tax capital loss	$249

AFTER-TAX CALCULATION

$$\text{after-tax HPR} = \frac{\$600 - \$249}{\$10,000}$$

$$= +3.51\%$$

*This table is based on the use of the data presented in Table 20.3 and the assumption of a 40 percent ordinary income tax rate for the investor.

Mutual funds

There are two basic components of return from a mutual fund investment: dividend income (including any capital gains distribution) plus any change in value. The basic HPR equation for mutual funds is identical to that for stocks. Table 20.5 presents a holding period return calculation for a no load mutual fund. The investor purchased 1,000 shares of the fund in July 1983 at a NAV of $10.40 per share. Because it is a no load fund, no commission is charged, so the investor's cost is $10,400. During the one-year period of ownership, the Beaver State Mutual Fund distributed investment income dividends totaling $270 and long-term capital gains dividends of $320. The investor redeemed (sold) this fund at a NAV of $10.79 per share, thereby realizing $10,790. The fund's shares were held for just over one year,

TABLE 20.5 CALCULATION OF PRETAX HPR ON A MUTUAL FUND

Security: Beaver State Mutual Fund
Date of purchase: July 1, 1983
Purchase cost: $10,400
Date of redemption: July 3, 1984
Sales proceeds: $10,790
Distributions received:
  Investment income dividends: $270
  Long-term capital gains dividends: $320

$$\text{holding period return} = \frac{(\$270 + \$320) + (\$10,790 - \$10,400)}{\$10,400}$$

$$= +9.42\%$$

TABLE 20.6 CALCULATION OF AFTER-TAX HPR ON A MUTUAL FUND*

TAX CALCULATIONS

	DIVIDENDS		
	Investment Income (tax rate = .40)	Capital Gains (tax rate = .16)	Capital Gains upon Sale (tax rate = .16)
Dividends	$270	$320	Capital gain	$390
Income tax	-108	$- 51$	Income tax	$- 62$
After-tax dividend income	$\overline{\$162}$	$\overline{\$269}$	After-tax capital gain	$\overline{\$328}$

AFTER-TAX HPR CALCULATION

$$\text{after-tax HPR} = \frac{(\$162 + \$269) + \$328}{\$10,400}$$

$$= +7.30\%$$

*This table is based upon the use of the data presented in Table 20.5 and the assumption of a 40-percent ordinary income tax rate for the investor.

qualifying any gain on sale for long-term capital gains treatment. The holding period return before income tax is seen in Table 20.5 to be 9.42 percent.

In calculating the after-tax holding period return for a mutual fund, care must be taken to distinguish between the two types of dividend distributions, because the income tax treatment of each is different. Distributions from the fund's investment income are taxable as ordinary income, just like common stock cash dividends. Dividends paid from the fund's realized long-term capital gains are called capital gains distributions and are taxed accordingly. So in analyzing the after-tax HPR for a fund, the calculations must take into account the differing tax treatment of each type of distribution. The after-tax investment return presented in Table 20.6 segregates the cash distributions according to type. The investment income dividends are taxed at the investor's ordinary income tax rate of 40 percent. The capital gains distributions are taxed as long-term capital gains at a 16 percent rate (.40 × .40). The after-tax HPR for the fund for this investor is 7.30 percent.

Real estate

The two basic components of an investor's return from real estate are the yearly after-tax cash flow and the change in property value that is likely to occur. (For a more expanded analysis of real estate investment than that given here, see Chapter 16.)

An investor who purchases raw land is interested in capital appreciation only because there is normally no positive cash flow from such an investment. Carrying costs associated with a raw land investment may include property taxes, special

> **TABLE 20.7 CALCULATION OF THE AFTER-TAX HPR ON A 40-ACRE PARCEL OF LAND IN KNOXVILLE, TENNESSEE**
>
> **REVERSION CALCULATION**
>
> | | |
> |---|---|
> | Selling price | $32,000 |
> | Selling expenses | − 1,000 |
> | Capital gains tax | − 1,000 |
> | Reversion | $30,000 |
>
> **AFTER-TAX HPR CALCULATION**
>
> $$\text{after-tax HPR} = \frac{\$30,000 - \$25,000}{\$25,000}$$
>
> $$= +20.00\%$$

assessments, and interest costs if financing is used. An investor's return from a raw land investment is normally realized on its disposition. *Reversion,* the after-tax net proceeds received upon disposition of property, is calculated by subtracting from the property's realized selling price all selling costs (commissions plus closing costs) plus any mortgage principal balances that are paid upon sale, and income taxes paid on realized capital gains from the sale. Reversion, then, is the after-tax dollars an investor puts in his or her pocket when the property is sold. An income property investment provides return in two forms: yearly after-tax cash flow and reversion. A property's yearly after-tax cash flow is basically its rental income minus operating expenses, mortgage payments, and income taxes. After-tax cash flow is the yearly net cash return an investor receives from rental properties. When calculating an investor's total return from a rental property, both yearly after-tax cash flow and reversion are included. To provide some insights into the calculation of real estate investment returns, two examples are presented below. The first illustrates the calculation of the after-tax holding period return on a raw land investment. This is followed by an apartment property return. (*Note:* Because of the more complex nature of real estate taxation, only after-tax HPR calculations are illustrated.)

Karl Jenkins, a bowling alley proprietor in Gatlinberg, Tennessee, acquired a 40-acre parcel of forest property near Knoxville, Tennessee. He bought the land for cash at $24,500 and prepaid annual property taxes of $500 at the time of purchase. He sold the property just over one year later for $32,000. The net reversion upon sale was $30,000, because he paid $1,000 in selling expenses (commission plus closing costs) and $1,000 in capital gains taxes. Thus, Mr. Jenkins's investment in the property was $25,000, and his reversion is $30,000 for the one-year holding period. No other expenses were incurred. An after-tax holding period return analysis for this transaction is given in Table 20.7. Mr. Jenkins's total cost for this investment is $25,000 and he realized ⬱30,000 after taxes upon sale of the property. Thus, the after-tax HPR on this investment is 20 percent.

The Maitland Apartments investment is more complex. This property was ac-

TABLE 20.8   CASH FLOW AND TAX STATEMENTS FOR MAITLAND APARTMENTS INVESTMENT (PAST YEAR)

REAL ESTATE CASH FLOW STATEMENT: MAITLAND APARTMENTS

Gross rents	$51,000
Vacancy and collection losses	− 1,500
Effective gross income (EGI)	$49,500
Operating expenses	− 20,000
Net operating income (NOI)	$29,500
Mortgage payments	− 20,500
Pretax cash flow	$ 9,000
Owner's income tax (from below)	− 3,000
After-tax cash flow (ATCF)	$ 6,000

OWNER'S INCOME TAX STATEMENT (FOR THIS PROPERTY)

Net operating income	$29,500
Interest	−17,000
Depreciation	− 5,000
Taxable income	$ 7,500
Owner's income tax (tax rate = .40)	$ 3,000

quired by Prudence Zwick one year ago. The holding period return analysis is presented in Tables 20.8 and 20.9. Table 20.8 presents both the proper real estate cash flow statement and owner's tax statement for the past year of ownership. These units required an initial equity investment of $100,000 and provided Ms. Zwick with an after-tax cash flow of $6,000 during the first year of ownership. Assume Ms. Zwick could sell the property at the end of the first year and, after deducting selling costs, mortgage repayments, and income taxes due to long-term capital gains, she could realize a reversion of $120,000. The after-tax holding period return analysis on these units is presented in Table 20.9. The owner's after-tax HPR on this property is 26 percent. An investor seeking to compare a securities return with real estate or other property investments' return should find the HPR calculation illustrated above a useful analytical tool.

Gold and other investment vehicles

The only source of return on gold and other investment vehicles (like options, commodities and financial futures, and tangibles such as artwork and antiques) is capital appreciation. To calculate a holding period return for an investment in gold, for instance, the basic HPR formula is used (excluding current income, of course). If an investor purchased 10 ounces of gold for $425 per ounce and sold the gold one year later for $500 per ounce, the investor's pretax holding period return would be 17.6 percent. This is simply sales proceeds ($5,000) minus cost ($4,250) divided by cost. Assuming 40 percent ordinary and 16 percent long-term capital gains tax rates, the after-tax HPR would be 14.8 percent—the after-tax gain of $630 [$750 −

TABLE 20.9   AFTER-TAX HPR ANALYSIS FOR MAITLAND APARTMENTS INVESTMENT

BASIC DATA

After-tax cash flow (from Table 20.8) = $ 6,000
Reversion = $120,000

AFTER-TAX HPR CALCULATION

$$\text{after-tax HPR} = \frac{\$6,000 + (\$120,000 - \$100,000)}{\$100,000}$$

$$= +26.00\%$$

(.16)($750)] divided by cost ($4,250). Commodities and financial futures' HPRs are calculated in a similar fashion. Because the return is in the form of capital gains only, the HPR analysis can be applied to any investment on a pretax or an after-tax basis. (The same basic procedure would be used for securities that are sold short.)

Comparing Performance to Investment Goals

After computing an HPR or yield on an investment, the investor must compare it to his or her investment goal. Keeping track of an investment's performance by periodically computing its HPR will help you decide which investments you should continue to hold and which have become possible sales candidates. Clearly, an investment holding would be a candidate for sale if: (1) it failed to perform up to expectations and no real change in performance is anticipated; or (2) it has met the original investment objective; or (3) more attractive uses of your funds are currently available (better investment outlets).

Comparing risk and return

Many times in this book, we have discussed the basic tradeoff between investment risk and return. The relationship is fundamentally as follows: To earn more return, you must take more risk. Risk is the chance that the actual investment return will be less than expected. In analyzing an investment, the key question is this: "Am I getting the proper return for the amount of investment risk that I am taking?"

Nongovernment security and property investments are by nature riskier than investing in U.S. government bonds or insured money market accounts. This fact implies that a rational investor should invest in risky situations only when the expected rate of return is well in excess of what could have been earned from a low-risk investment. Thus, when analyzing investment returns, one benchmark against which to compare them is the rate of return on low-risk investments. If one's risky investments failed to outperform low-risk investments, a careful examination of the investment strategy is in order. The fact that one's investments are outperforming low-risk investments is an indication that they are obtaining extra return for taking extra risk.

Isolating problem investments

A *problem investment* is one that has not lived up to expectations. It may be a loss situation or an investment that has provided an actual return (HPR) less than what the investor expected. Many investors try to forget about problem situations, hoping the problem will go away or the investment will turn around by itself. This is a terrible mistake. Problem investments require immediate attention, not neglect. In studying a problem investment, an investor must make the basic decision of whether or not to continue to hold it. Should I take my loss and get out, or should I hang on and hope it turns around? That is the key question. Some investors do not like to realize losses on their investments. They hold on to mediocre ones in hope that they will turn around and can eventually be sold for a profit. Such a strategy can result in a portfolio of poorly performing investments.

It is best to analyze each investment in a portfolio periodically. For each, two items should be considered. First, has it performed in a manner that could reasonably be expected? Second, if the investment were not currently in the portfolio, would you buy it for the portfolio today? If the answers to both are negative, then the investment probably should be sold. A negative answer to one of the questions qualifies the investment for the "problem list." It should be watched closely. In general, maintaining a portfolio of investments requires constant attention and analysis to ensure the best chance of satisfactory returns. Problem investments need special attention and work; they should not be neglected since they probably will not go away. Instead, problem situations should be viewed as a challenge.

A Risk-Adjusted, Market-Adjusted Return Measure (RAR)

So far, our discussion has focused on computing the rate of return on each of a variety of investment vehicles. Now we look at a risk-adjusted, market-adjusted return measure. This method of gauging investment performance is most suitable for common stocks and for portfolios of common stocks.

The risk-adjusted, market-adjusted rate of return

This measure, called RAR for short, utilizes beta and a broadly based market index. The measure provides an investor with a tool to gauge investment performance that factors out the influences of general market movements on the portfolio. For instance, if an investor has a portfolio that earned a rate of return of $+15$ percent over the past year, that return in and of itself does not provide a true comparative measure of portfolio return. An investor needs to know how the portfolio has performed in relation to other portfolios and in relation to the market in general. The raw return figure alone requires further analysis.

To develop a comparative portfolio return measurement, a risk- and market-adjusted rate of return (RAR) needs to be calculated. The formula for RAR is:

$$RAR = r_{i,t} - (b_{i,t} \times r_{m,t})$$

where

$r_{i,t}$ = return on security i or portfolio i in period t

$b_{i,t}$ = beta of security i or portfolio i in period t

$r_{m,t}$ = return on a broad market index m in period t

The return on security i or portfolio i is its holding period return over period t. The beta of security i or portfolio i is computed according to the method previously discussed. $r_{m,t}$ is the total return (dividends plus price change) an investor could have earned in period t if he or she had invested in the market portfolio, as represented by a market index. The Standard & Poor's 500 stock composite index or the New York Stock Exchange composite index are often used to represent the market portfolio.

Basically, the *risk-adjusted, market-adjusted rate of return (RAR)* is the return security i or portfolio i has earned after the effects of risk and market movements have been factored out. For example, if the portfolio that earned a 15 percent return had a beta of 1.5 and the market had earned a 10 percent return over the same time period, the RAR is zero [15% − (1.5 × 10%) = 0]. The portfolio performed exactly as it was expected to. If a stock or a portfolio has a positive RAR, it can be said that it has outperformed the market in general. Conversely, a negative RAR indicates an inferior performance relative to the market. Thus, RAR is a useful tool to gauge a security's or a portfolio's relative performance.

A stock example

Table 20.10 presents an RAR analysis for an individual stock. The stock, which had a beta of .93, was in the portfolio for one year and yielded a holding period return of 24.63 percent. In comparison, a portfolio composed of securities assembled in a manner similar to the securities in the NYSE composite index would have earned a return of 4.76 percent over the same time period. Utilizing the RAR equation, the stock's RAR for the holding period is 20.20 percent. This security outperformed the market portfolio, earning an "excess return" of approximately 20 percent during the time period of the analysis.

A portfolio example

In Chapter 19 we said that beta is more useful for portfolio investment strategy decisions than for individual stocks. This is because a smaller portion of a stock's volatility is related to nondiversifiable risk. Typically, approximately 90 percent of a diversified portfolio's volatility is due to general stock market fluctuations. Thus, the RAR analysis, while useful for individual stocks, is much more beneficial in the study of portfolio returns. Mutual funds are, of course, portfolios of stocks and bonds, so RAR analysis is particularly useful in the study of mutual fund returns. The beta and the returns on a mutual fund are easy to find and to calculate. Several publications

BOX 20.2 LIMITING PORTFOLIO LOSSES USING LOR'S APPROACH

It sounds too good to be true: a method for making money in stocks while avoiding their downside risk. Yet that's what Leland O'Brien Rubinstein Associates, a year-old California firm, is promising with a computer-based service called Protective Portfolio Management. "It does sound like a carnival act when you first hear about it," concedes Gary Brinson, chief investment officer at the First National Bank of Chicago, which recently hooked up with LOR to offer the service to the bank's pension-fund clients.

The new firm already has a couple of competitors. Kidder Peabody, the New York broker, is offering a Portfolio Insulation Package to institutions, and Santa Monica-based Wilshire Associates has come out with Portfolio Risk Control. The services are too expensive for individual investors, and so far the strategy is being used only by pension-fund managers. But the little guy should eventually be able to play: several mutual-fund organizations, including the Vanguard Group, have been studying the system.

AN ARTIFICIAL PUT

Without benefit of carnival tricks, investors have long been able to protect equities against loss by buying puts—the right to sell a stock at a given price over a given period regardless of how far it might drop. But that kind of protection is costly and not always workable since no market exists in puts for many stocks. So three years ago Hayne Leland and Mark Rubinstein, professors at the University of California at Berkeley, set about creating an artificial put that would hedge an entire portfolio. In an article in the *Financial Analysts Journal* last summer, Leland and Rubinstein demonstrated, in theory at least, that portfolio managers could control losses by varying their holdings between stocks and risk-free Treasury bills.

Simulations going back 20 years show that the synthetic puts work. And more important, so do results in the real world over the past year. The methodology doesn't involve forecasting the market or predicting a portfolio's performance; the system reacts only to what has already happened. As the market drops, the computer program cuts losses by sending instructions to shift money out of stocks into T-bills. The system, which involves a lot of trading, is a contrarian's nightmare: stocks are bought after they've moved up and sold when they've fallen. Elaborate computer programs tell clients exactly what combination of stocks and T-bills to hold as the stock market rises and falls. The formulas are secret, and although the progams can be copied, they're so costly to duplicate and master that most users would find it cheaper to buy the service.

LOR's strategy requires a user to start with part of his portfolio in T-bills; as short-term government obligations, they have little interest-rate risk. The proportion of T-bills declines as the amount of risk an investor is willing to tolerate rises. To be protected against any loss, for example, a manager must start with only half his assets in stocks and the other half in T-bills, but someone willing to risk losing 5% of his assets begins with 65% in equities.

Regardless of how much protection is specified, a move up or down of about 4% in the value of the stock portfolio triggers instructions from the computer program to "rebalance." History suggests that a portfolio having the same characteristics as the overall stock market will experience 12 changes of 4% a year. Each time the value of the equities declines, clients are told to sell a specified dollar amount of stocks and use the proceeds to buy T-bills. In a bear market the strategy eventually gets investors completely out of stocks. Conversely, if the value of the stock portfolio rises, managers are told to sell T-bills and buy more stocks; in a bull market the portfolio ends up 100% in stocks. Purveyors of the strategy leave it to clients to decide which stocks to buy or sell.

Like all hedging strategies, this one costs something. In a bull market the cost can be figured as the difference between the return from a portfolio invested entirely in stocks and the return that the protected portfolio produces—lower because the T-bill position doesn't appreciate. In a down market the cost is the amount the investor loses by having some money in stocks instead of having it all in T-bills. Figured as a percentage of the original portfolio, the costs on the upside and the downside are the same—as they are when an investor buys a put. (In that case, the cost is the price of the option.)

BOX 20.2 *Continued*

In trying to estimate in advance the annual cost of protection, volatility is a crucial variable. The cost of hedging a volatile portfolio is higher than hedging a stabler one because the system instructs the managers of volatile portfolios to trade in smaller increments. As a consequence, for example, they buy stocks more slowly when the value of their stock portfolios is rising.

T-bill rates and the dividend yield on the stocks are also important variables. If the interest on bills is way above the dividend yield on the stocks, the difference offsets some of the cost. Leland calculates that when T-bills are yielding 12%, the annual cost of protecting a portfolio with the same volatility and dividend yield as the market would be 1.6% of the portfolio's starting value, assuming the investor wants to avoid loss entirely. On a $1-million portfolio, then, the cost would be $16,000. Leland views this amount as an up-front payment, like buying a put. If the stocks take a beating, the most the investor loses is $16,000. And if the market rallies so that a portfolio fully invested in stocks would rise 20%, or $200,000, his portfolio would be up $16,000 less, or $184,000.

A decline in T-bill rates would make the strategy more expensive. If T-bills were yielding only 6%, the cost of protecting the same portfolio would increase to 3%. And even at 12% yields, the price of protecting a really risky portfolio can be high. Leland estimates the annual cost at around 4%—he figures it would have to be rebalanced 30 times during the year.

THE TRADING IS COSTLY

These expenses don't include trading costs, which can be high. Leland estimates that for a portfolio that is rebalanced 12 times a year, transaction costs knock an additional 0.4% off the annual return, raising the cost of protection from 1.6% to 2%. Volatile portfolios of thinly traded stocks are more costly to buy and sell; trading could eat up 2% or 3% of these, raising the cost from 4% to around 6% or 7%. At least some of LOR's clients think the stiff price is worth it, since some hold such risky portfolios that their assets could be halved in a bad market. To reduce the cost of protection, LOR and others are looking for ways to cut transaction costs, perhaps by using futures on stock indexes, recently introduced, or options on the indexes, . . .

Another cost of protection, of course, is the fee charged by the firm selling the strategy. LOR charges 0.2% on portfolios of $25 million or less, with a minimum of $10,000, and scales the fee down to 0.05% on amounts over $50 million. Wilshire is charging $20,000 a year plus computer time. Kidder won't say what it charges except that it prices its programs so they're cheaper for clients to buy than to copy.

The system's emphasis on trading is a big drawback, since tax-paying investors could end up with a lot of short-term capital gains that are taxed at ordinary income rates. Robert Hagin, the Kidder Peabody vice president who oversees Portfolio Insulation, argues that individuals should use the strategy—when it becomes available via mutual funds—mostly for tax-deferred investments like IRAs.

Another drawback is more fundamental. Because the strategy is based on changes in the value of the stock portfolio, the system has no built-in instructions when portfolios get pushed entirely into T-bills. In making the historical simulations that showed the system works, LOR simply kept the portfolio in T-bills until a cycle of 12 moves of 4% in the S&P 500 had been completed; then the portfolios were rebalanced by selling T-bills and restoring the stock position to its original proportion.

John Mabie, president of Mid-Continent Capital, a Chicago investment adviser, worked out his own approach when he found the portfolio entirely in T-bills early in March. He stayed out of equities but pretended to own the portfolio he had started out with last September. He fed its value to LOR's computer, and in late April he got a signal to rebalance his holdings by purchasing stocks, so he jumped back in. So far, he's happy with the result.

Source: Mary Greenebaum, "A Strategy for Limiting Portfolio Losses." *Fortune,* June 14, 1982, pp. 209–212.

TABLE 20.10   RISK-ADJUSTED, MARKET-ADJUSTED RATE OF RETURN (RAR) ANALYSIS ON COMMON STOCK

Security: Crocker National common stock
Holding period: May 1, 1983 to May 7, 1984
Holding period return: +24.63%
Stock beta (May 1, 1983):   .93
Return on the NYSE composite index (May 1, 1983 to May 7, 1984):   +4.76%

$$RAR = 24.63\% - .93\,(4.76\%)$$
$$= 24.63\% - 4.43\%$$
$$= \underline{+20.20\%}$$

periodically list both the relative fluctuations of fund NAVs as well as fund dividend distributions. Using this raw data, RAR analysis can be utilized to rank the relative performance of mutual fund investment managers. An example of mutual fund RAR analysis is presented in Table 20.11.

This fund, the no load Maize and Blue Mutual Fund, is growth-oriented, as its beta of 1.33 indicates. The fund normally has an above-average amount of nondiversifiable risk. The holding period of analysis is slightly over one year, from May 1, 1983, through May 4, 1984. During that time span, the fund paid $.40 per share in investment income dividends and $1.40 per share in long-term capital gains dividends. The fund's NAV rose from $24.12 per share to $26.41 per share. The pretax holding period return for the fund is 16.96 percent. In the RAR analysis, it is found that the fund's risk-adjusted, market-adjusted rate of return equals 10.59 percent. The RAR is less than the HPR because the fund's beta was greater than zero. However, the fund's strongly positive RAR indicates a better-than-expected return performance. A mutual fund whose management consistently earned yearly RARs of this size would be an excellent one indeed.

ASSESSING PORTFOLIO PERFORMANCE

The procedures used to assess portfolio performance are based on many of the concepts presented earlier in the chapter. Here we will look at the portfolio performance assessment process, using a hypothetical securities portfolio over a one-year holding period. The holding period return method is an important part of this assessment process.

Measuring Portfolio Return

Table 20.12 presents the investment portfolio as of January 1, 1984, of Robert K. Hathaway. Mr. Hathaway is 50 years old, a widower, and his children are married. His income is $50,000 per year. His primary investment objective is long-term growth

---

TABLE 20.11   RAR ANALYSIS ON A MUTUAL FUND PORTFOLIO

Security: Maize and Blue Mutual Fund
Holding period: May 1, 1983 to May 4, 1984
NAV, May 1, 1983: $24.12
NAV, May 4, 1984: $26.41
Fund beta (May 1, 1983) = 1.33
Distributions paid out
  Investment income dividend: $.40 per share
  Long-term capital gains dividend: $1.40 per share
Return on NYSE composite index (May 1, 1983 to May 4, 1984):   +4.79%

HOLDING PERIOD RETURN

$$\text{HPR} = \frac{(\$.40 + \$1.40) + (\$26.41 - \$24.12)}{\$24.12}$$

$$= \underline{+16.96\%}$$

RISK-ADJUSTED, MARKET-ADJUSTED RATE OF RETURN

$$\text{RAR} = 16.96\% - 1.33\,(4.79\%)$$

$$= 16.96\% - 6.37\%$$

$$= \underline{+10.59\%}$$

---

with a moderate dividend return. He selects stocks with two criteria in mind: quality and growth potential. On January 1, 1984, his portfolio consisted of 10 issues, all of good quality. Mr. Hathaway has been fortunate in his selection process in that he has approximately $74,000 in unrealized price appreciation in his portfolio. During 1984, he decided to make a change in his portfolio. On May 7, he sold 1,000 shares of Crocker National for $32,040. Mr. Hathaway's holding period return for that issue is discussed earlier in this chapter (see Tables 20.1 and 20.2). Using funds from the sale, on May 10, 1984, he acquired 1,000 additional shares of Florida Westcoast Banks, Inc. He decided to make the switch because he believed the prospects for the Florida bank holding company were better than those of Crocker National, a California-based bank holding company. Florida Westcost is based in Sarasota County, one of the fastest growing counties in terms of population and income in the United States.

Measuring the amount invested

Every investor would be wise periodically to list his or her holdings, as is done in Table 20.12. The table lists number of shares, acquisition date, cost, and current value for each issue. These data aid in continually formulating strategy decisions. The acquisition date, for example, is useful for tax purposes (the tax consequences of investment sales are discussed toward the end of the chapter). Mr. Hathaway's portfolio does not utilize the leverage of a margin account. If leverage were present,

TABLE 20.12 ROBERT K. HATHAWAY'S PORTFOLIO (JANUARY 1, 1984)

Number of Shares	Company	Date Acquired	Cost (including commissions)	Cost per Share	Current Price per Share	Current Value
1,000	Bancorp Hawaii	1/16/82	$ 21,610	$21.61	$30	$ 30,000
1,000	Crocker National	5/ 1/83	27,362	27.36	29	29,000
1,000	Dillon Companies, Inc.	4/13/78	13,704	13.70	27	27,000
500	Eastman Kodak	8/16/81	40,571	81.14	54	27,000
1,000	Florida Westcoast Banks	12/16/81	17,460	17.46	30	30,000
1,000	Georgia-Pacific	9/27/81	22,540	22.54	26	26,000
1,000	Memorex	2/27/81	19,100	19.10	47	47,000
500	Minnesota Mining and Mfg.	4/17/82	25,504	51.00	62	31,000
1,000	Phillips Petroleum	3/12/82	24,903	24.90	30	30,000
1,000	Upjohn	4/16/82	37,120	37.12	47	47,000
	Total		$249,874			$324,000

all return calculations would be based on the investor's equity in the account. Recall from Chapter 5 that an investor's equity in a margin account equals the total value of all the securities in the account minus any margin debt.

To measure Mr. Hathaway's return on his invested capital, we need to perform a one-year holding period return analysis. His invested capital as of January 1, 1984, is $324,000. No new additions of capital were made in the portfolio during 1984, although he sold one stock, Crocker National, and used the proceeds to buy another stock, Florida Westcoast Banks.

Measuring income

There are two sources of return from a portfolio of common stocks: income and capital appreciation. Current income is realized from dividends. Current income from a portfolio of bonds is earned by receiving interest. Investors must report taxable dividends and interest on federal and state income tax returns. Companies are required to furnish income reports (Form 1099-DIV for dividends and Form 1099-INT for interest) to stockholders and bondholders. Many investors maintain logs to keep track of dividend and interest income as received. Table 20.13 lists Mr. Hathaway's dividends for 1984. He received two quarterly dividends of $.45 per share before he sold the Crocker stock, and he received two $.32 per share quarterly dividends on the additional Florida Westcoast Banks shares he acquired. His total dividend income for 1984 was $10,935.

Measuring appreciation in value

An analysis of the change in price of each of the issues in the Hathaway portfolio is contained in Table 20.14. For each issue except the additional shares of Florida Westcoast Banks, the January 1, 1984, and December 31, 1984, values are listed. The amounts listed for Florida Westcoast Banks reflect the fact that 1,000 additional

TABLE 20.13 DIVIDEND INCOME ON THE HATHAWAY PORTFOLIO (CALENDAR YEAR 1984)

Number of Shares	Company	Dividends Paid per Share	Dividends Received
1,000	Bancorp Hawaii	$1.20	$ 1,200
1,000	Crocker National*	.90	900
1,000	Dillon Companies, Inc.	1.12	1,120
500	Eastman Kodak	2.00	1,000
2,000	Florida Westcoast Banks**	1.28	1,920
1,000	Georgia-Pacific	1.10	1,100
1,000	Memorex	—	—
500	Minnesota Mining and Mfg.	2.05	1,025
1,000	Phillips Petroleum	1.20	1,200
1,000	Upjohn	1.47	1,470
	Total		$10,935

*Sold May 7, 1984.
**1,000 shares acquired on May 10, 1984.

shares of the stock were acquired on May 10, 1984, at a cost of $32,040. It can be seen that Mr. Hathaway's current holdings had beginning-of-the-year values of $327,040 (including the additional Florida Westcoast Bank shares at the date of purchase) and are worth $356,000 at year-end. During 1984, the portfolio increased in value by 8.9 percent, or $28,960, in unrealized capital appreciation. In addition, Mr. Hathaway

TABLE 20.14 CHANGE IN VALUE OF HATHAWAY PORTFOLIO (JANUARY 1, 1984–DECEMBER 31, 1984)

Number of Shares	Company	Market Value (1/1/84)	Market Price (12/31/84)	Market Value (12/31/84)	Unrealized Appreciation (Loss)	Percentage Change
1,000	Bancorp Hawaii	$ 30,000	$27	$ 27,000	$(3,000)	− 10.0%
1,000	Dillon Companies, Inc.	27,000	36	36,000	9,000	+ 33.3
500	Eastman Kodak	27,000	66	33,000	6,000	+ 22.2
2,000	Florida Westcoast Banks*	62,040	35	70,000	7,960	+ 12.8
1,000	Georgia-Pacific	26,000	26	26,000	—	—
1,000	Memorex	47,000	55	55,000	8,000	+ 17.0
500	Minnesota Mining and Mfg.	31,000	60	30,000	(1,000)	− 3.2
1,000	Phillips Petroleum	30,000	36	36,000	6,000	+ 20.0
1,000	Upjohn	47,000	43	43,000	(4,000)	− 8.5
	Total	$327,040		$356,000	$28,960	+ 8.9%

*1,000 additional shares acquired on May 10, 1984, at a cost of $32,040. The value listed is the cost plus the market value of the previously owned shares as of 1/1/84.

realized a long-term capital gain in 1984 by selling his Crocker National holding. From January 1, 1984, until its sale on May 7, 1984, the Crocker holding rose in value from $29,000 to $32,040. This is the only sale in 1984; thus, total realized appreciation was $3,040. During 1984, the portfolio had both realized appreciation of $3,040 and unrealized appreciation of $28,960. The total increment in value equals the sum of the two: $32,000.

Measuring the portfolio's holding period return

To measure the total return of the Hathaway portfolio during 1984, the HPR measurement is used. The basic one-year HPR formula for portfolios is:

$$\text{HPR for a portfolio} = \frac{D + A_R + A_U}{I + \left(N \times \dfrac{n}{12}\right) - \left(W \times \dfrac{n}{12}\right)}$$

where

D = dividends plus interest received during the year
A_R = realized appreciation (loss would be negative) during the year
A_U = unrealized appreciation (loss) during the year
I = initial equity investment
N = new (additional) funds in the portfolio
W = withdrawals of funds from the portfolio
n = number of months additional funds are in the portfolio
   or number of months funds are withdrawn from the portfolio

This formula includes both the realized return (income plus appreciation) and un-realized yearly appreciation of the portfolio. Portfolio additions and deletions are time-weighted (by the $n/12$ factor) for the number of months they are in the portfolio.

A detailed change in value analysis is contained in Table 20.14, in which all the issues that are in the portfolio as of December 31, 1984, are listed. The beginning and year-end values are included for comparison purposes. The crux of the analysis is the HPR calculation for the year presented in Table 20.15. All the elements of a portfolio's return are included. Dividends total $10,935 from Table 20.13. The real-ized appreciation figure represents the increment in value of the Crocker holding from January 1, 1984, until its sale. During 1984, the portfolio had $28,960 of unrealized appreciation. There were no additions of new funds and no capital was withdrawn. Utilizing the formula for HPR, we find that the portfolio had a total return of 13.25 percent in 1984.

Comparison of Return with Overall Market Measures

The raw return figure derived from the analysis above should be utilized in a risk-adjusted, market-adjusted rate of return (RAR) analysis. This type of comparative study is useful because it can provide some idea of how your portfolio is doing in

> **TABLE 20.15** **HOLDING PERIOD RETURN CALCULATION ON HATHAWAY PORTFOLIO (JANUARY 1, 1984—DECEMBER 31, 1984 HOLDING PERIOD)**
>
> ---
>
> **DATA**
>
> ---
>
> Portfolio value (1/1/84): $324,000
> Portfolio value (12/31/84): $356,000
> Realized appreciation: $3,040 (1/1/84 to 5/7/84 when Crocker National was sold)
> Unrealized appreciation (1/1/84 to 12/31/84): $28,960
> Dividend received: $10,935
> New cash invested or withdrawn: None
>
> ---
>
> **PORTFOLIO HPR CALCULATION**
>
> $$\text{HPR} = \frac{\$10,935 + \$3,040 + \$28,960}{\$324,000}$$
>
> $$= \underline{+13.25\%}$$

comparison to the stock market as a whole. The Standard & Poor's 500 stock composite index or the New York Stock Exchange composite index are acceptable indexes for this type of analysis because they are broadly based and appear to represent the stock market as a whole. Assume that during 1984 the return on the S&P 500 index was +8.7 percent. Assume the comparable NYSE index return was +8.8 percent. These returns include both dividends and price appreciation. The return from Mr. Hathaway's portfolio was +13.25 percent. This compares very favorably with the broadly based indexes: The Hathaway portfolio performed about one and one-half times as well as these broad indicators of stock market return.

As discussed earlier in the chapter, meaningful return comparisons must consider risk; in this case, Mr. Hathaway should determine the risk-adjusted, market-adjusted return (RAR). If the RAR is positive, the portfolio performance would be superior (above-average), while a negative RAR indicates an inferior (below-average) performance. Assume that the beta of Mr. Hathaway's portfolio is 1.10, and using a market return of 8.75 percent, the RAR would be:

$$\text{RAR} = 13.25\% - 1.10 \,(8.75\%)$$
$$= 13.25\% - 9.63\%$$
$$= \underline{+3.62\%}$$

During 1984, Mr. Hathaway's portfolio earned an above-average rate of return.

Portfolio Revision

In the example presented above, one transaction occurred during the year under consideration. The reason for this transaction was that Mr. Hathaway believed the Florida Westcoast Banks stock had more return potential than the Crocker National stock. An investor should periodically analyze the portfolio with one basic question in mind: "Does this portfolio continue to meet my needs?" In other words, does the portfolio contain those issues that are best suited to the investor's risk-return needs? Investors who systematically study the issues in their portfolios will find an occasional need to sell certain issues and to purchase new securities. This process is commonly called *portfolio revision.* As the economy evolves, certain industries and stocks become more or less attractive investments. And in today's stock market, timeliness is the essence of profitability.

Given the dynamics of the investment world, periodic reallocation and rebalancing of the portfolio is a necessity. There are many circumstances when such movements or changes are required. In Chapter 19, we discussed the effect of life cycle changes on investment strategy. Basically, as an investor nears retirement, the portfolio's emphasis normally evolves from a growth/capital appreciation orientation to a more conservative preservation of capital strategy. For an investor approaching retirement, an appropriate strategy might be to switch gradually from growth issues into low-risk, high-yield securities. Changing a portfolio's emphasis normally involves an evolutionary process rather than an overnight switch. Individual issues in the portfolio often change in risk-return characteristics. As this occurs, an investor would be wise to eliminate those issues that do not meet objectives. In addition, the need for diversification is a constant one. As issues rise or fall in value, their diversification effect may be lessened. Thus, portfolio revision may be needed to maintain diversification in the portfolio.

The Role of Personal Computers

As noted in earlier chapters, many investors have personal computers (PCs). These small computers can be programmed to perform many useful functions, including portfolio management and investment performance monitoring. Software programs are available that enable an investor to do analyses such as those we have just completed. Additionally, many investors are acquiring software packages useful for fundamental and technical security analysis, bond analysis, and real estate investment analysis. By 1990, we expect many investors will find that a personal computer is a relatively inexpensive aid for use in streamlining the investment administration process, as well as providing data base access and performing numerous other investment-related functions. (See Chapter 3 for a description of some of the popular PC hardware, software, and news retrieval and data base capabilities currently available.)

TIMING TRANSACTIONS

The essence of timing is to "buy low and sell high." This is the dream of all investors. There is no tried and true way for achieving such a goal, but there are several methods you can utilize to time purchase and sale actions. These are formula plans, discussed below. Investors can also use limit and stop orders as a timing aid, follow procedures for warehousing liquidity, and take into consideration other aspects of timing when selling investments.

TABLE 20.16 DOLLAR COST AVERAGING ($500 PER MONTH, WOLVERINE MUTUAL FUND SHARES)

TRANSACTIONS

Month	Net Asset Value, Month End	Number of Shares Purchased
January	$26.00	19.23
February	27.46	18.21
March	27.02	18.50
April	24.19	20.67
May	26.99	18.53
June	25.63	19.51
July	24.70	20.24
August	24.16	20.70
September	25.27	19.79
October	26.15	19.12
November	29.60	16.89
December	30.19	16.56

ANNUAL SUMMARY

Total investment: $6,000.00
Total number of shares purchased: 227.95
Average cost per share: $26.32
Year-end portfolio value: $6,881.81

Formula Plans

Formula plans are mechanical methods of portfolio management used to try to take advantage of price changes in securities resulting from cyclical price movements. Formula plans are not set up to provide unusually high returns; rather, they are conservative strategies. Formula plans are primarily oriented toward investors who do not wish to bear a high level of risk. Four formula plans are discussed here: dollar cost averaging, the constant dollar plan, the constant ratio plan, and the variable ratio plan.

Dollar cost averaging

Dollar cost averaging is a basic type of formula plan. Following this strategy, a fixed dollar amount is invested in a security in each period. This is a passive buy and hold strategy in which periodic dollar investment is held constant. The investor must have the discipline to invest on a regular basis in order to make the plan work. The hoped-for outcome of a dollar cost averaging program is growth in the value of the security to which the funds are allocated. The price of the investment security will probably fluctuate over time. If the price declines, more shares are purchased per period; conversely, if the price rises, fewer shares are purchased per period. Table 20.16 presents an example of dollar cost averaging. The investor is investing $500 per month in the Wolverine Mutual Fund, a growth-oriented no load mutual fund.

In the illustration, during one year's time the investor has placed $6,000 in the mutual fund shares. This is a no load fund, so shares are purchased at net asset value. Purchases were made at NAVs ranging from a low of $24.16 to a high of $30.19. At year-end, the investor's holdings in the fund were valued at slightly less than $6,900. While dollar cost averaging is a passive strategy, other formula plans have a more active posture.

Constant dollar plan

A *constant dollar plan* consists of a portfolio that is divided into two parts. The speculative portion is invested in securities having high promise of capital appreciation. The conservative portion consists of very low-risk investments such as bonds or a money market account. The constant dollar plan basically skims off profits from the speculative portion of the portfolio if it rises a certain percentage or amount in value. These funds are then added to the conservative portion of the portfolio. If the speculative portion of the portfolio declines by a specific percentage or amount, funds are added to it from the conservative portion. The target dollar amount for the speculative portion is constant, and the investor establishes trigger points (upward or downward movement in the speculative portion) where funds are removed from or added to that portion.

Table 20.17 is an illustration of a constant dollar plan over time. The beginning $20,000 portfolio consists of a $10,000 portion invested in a high-beta no load mutual fund and $10,000 deposited in a money market account. The investor has decided to rebalance the portfolio every time the speculative portion is worth $2,000 more or $2,000 less than its initial value of $10,000. If the speculative portion of the portfolio equals or exceeds $12,000, sufficient shares of the fund are sold to bring its value down to $10,000. The proceeds from the sale are added to the conservative portion. If the speculative portion declines in value to $8,000 or less, funds are taken from the conservative portion and used to purchase sufficient shares to raise the value of the speculative portion to $10,000.

Two portfolio rebalancing actions are taken in the time sequence illustrated in Table 20.17. Initially, $10,000 is allocated to each portion of the portfolio. Then, when the mutual fund's NAV rises so that the speculative portion is worth $12,000, 166.67 shares valued at $2,000 are redeemed and the proceeds added to the money market account. Later, the mutual fund's NAV declines to $9.50 per share, causing the value of the speculative portion to drop below $8,000. This triggers the purchase of sufficient shares to raise the value of the speculative portion to $10,000. Over the long run, if the speculative investment of the constant dollar plan rises in value, the conservative component of the portfolio will increase in dollar value as profits are transferred into it. The next formula plan, constant ratio, relies on the ratio between the speculative and the conservative portions as a rebalancing trigger.

Constant ratio plan

The *constant ratio plan* establishes a desired fixed ratio of the speculative to the conservative portion of the portfolio. When the actual ratio of the two differs by a predetermined amount from the desired ratio, rebalancing occurs. That is, at that

TABLE 20.17 CONSTANT DOLLAR PLAN

Mutual Fund NAV	Value of Speculative Portion	Value of Conservative Portion	Total Portfolio Value	Transactions	Number of Shares in Speculative Portion
$10.00	$10,000.00	$10,000.00	$20,000.00		1,000
11.00	11,000.00	10,000.00	21,000.00		1,000
12.00	12,000.00	10,000.00	22,000.00		1,000
→12.00	10,000.00	12,000.00	22,000.00	Sold 166.67 shares	833.33
11.00	9,166.63	12,000.00	21,166.63		833.33
9.50	7,916.64	12,000.00	19,916.64		833.33
→ 9.50	10,000.00	9,916.64	19,916.64	Purchased 219.30 shares	1,052.63
10.00	10,526.30	9,916.64	20,442.94		1,052.63

point transactions are made in order to bring the actual ratio back to the desired ratio. An investor using the constant ratio plan must decide on the appropriate apportionment of the portfolio between speculative and conservative investments. Then, a decision must be made regarding the ratio trigger point at which transactions occur.

A constant ratio plan for an initial portfolio of $20,000 is illustrated in Table 20.18. The investor has decided to allocate 50 percent of the portfolio to the speculative high-beta mutual fund and 50 percent to a money market account. Rebalancing will occur when the ratio of the speculative portion to the conservative portion is greater than or equal to 1.20 or less than or equal to .80. A sequence of net asset value changes is listed in Table 20.18. Initially, $10,000 is allocated to each portion of the portfolio. When the fund NAV reaches $12, the 1.20 ratio triggers the sale of 83.33 shares. Then, the portfolio is back to its desired 1.0 ratio. Later, the fund NAV declines to $9, lowering the value of the speculative portion to $8,250. The ratio of

TABLE 20.18 CONSTANT RATIO PLAN

Mutual Fund NAV	Value of Speculative Portion	Value of Conservative Portion	Total Portfolio Value	Ratio of Speculative Portion to Conservative Portion	Transactions	Number of Shares in Speculative Portion
$10.00	$10,000.00	$10,000.00	$20,000.00	1.000		1,000
11.00	11,000.00	10,000.00	21,000.00	1.100		1,000
12.00	12,000.00	10,000.00	22,000.00	1.200		1,000
→12.00	11,000.00	11,000.00	22,000.00	1.000	Sold 83.33 shares	916.67
11.00	10,083.00	11,000.00	21,083.00	0.917		916.67
10.00	9,166.70	11,000.00	20,166.70	0.833		916.67
9.00	8,250.00	11,000.00	19,250.00	0.750		916.67
→ 9.00	9,625.00	9,625.00	19,250.00	1.000	Purchased 152.77 shares	1,069.44
10.00	10,694.40	9,625.00	20,319.40	1.110		1,069.44

BOX 20.3 INVESTING BY THE MONTH
USING DOLLAR COST AVERAGING

Putting the same amount every month into the same investment may seem about as exciting as watching grass grow, but there's a lot to be said for it if you're the type of person who gets caught up in buying frenzies, or who tends to panic and sell out just when the market is reaching a bottom. The discipline of dollar-cost averaging helps you avoid two common errors: investing all your money in the market when prices are high, and selling out at big losses when prices are deeply depressed.

The great merit of this system is that you buy more shares when the market is down and fewer when its high. Consequently, your average cost per share will be somewhat *lower* than the average price for the dates on which you're buying. For example, you invest $100 on the same day of each month, and the no-load mutual fund you've picked sells for $10 a share the first month, $8 the second, and $9 the third. The first month, your $100 buys 10 shares, the second month, 12.5, and the third, 11.1. The average price of the stock on the three purchase dates is $9, but your average cost is only $8.93 ($300 divided by 33.6 shares). If the stock returns to $10, you're well ahead. Even if the price stays depressed, you're doing much better than if you had plunked down all $300 when the stock was selling at $10.

Of course, if the market advances for several years with only minor setbacks, a lump-sum investment made at the very beginning of that rise will produce much larger profits than dollar-cost averaging. It's easy to see that with $10,000 working for you throughout a long bull market, you'll make a lot more money than by starting with $100 and adding $100 for 99 months. Buying on the installment plan is a defensive policy, well suited to periods of wild up-and-down swings, such as those of the past 20 years. And for an investor putting a small amount into an Individual Retirement Account each month, accumulating shares in a no-load common-stock fund is likely to be a rewarding long-term strategy even if the Dow fails to make its often heralded ascent to 2000.

The dangers of plunging in with a big buy at or near a market peak are apparent from the investment performance to two typical no-load mutual funds that provided *Money* with information covering the one- and 10-year periods that ended March 31. T. Rowe Price's New Horizons is an "aggressive growth" fund whose fluctuations are much sharper than those of the overall market. Scudder Stevens & Clark's Scudder Common Stock Fund has a more conservative investment policy and is considerably less volatile. But regardless of which fund he chose, an investor who put in $12,100 on March 31, 1972 would have owned fewer shares on March 31, 1982 than a person who put in $12,100 in monthly installments—that is, 121 payments of $100 each on the last day of every month for 10 years. That's astonishing, considering that $12,100 invested in 1972 would have been at work a full 10 years, whereas under the monthly installment plan the average investment over the period would have been $6,050.

More specifically, a lump-sum investment of $12,100 on March 31, 1972 would have grown 10 years later to $16,094 in the New Horizons and to $19,455 in the Scudder

---

the speculative portion to the conservative portion is then .75, which is below the .80 trigger point. A total of 152.77 shares is purchased to bring the desired ratio back up to 1.0.

The long-run expectation under a constant ratio plan is that the speculative security or securities will rise in value. When this occurs, sales of the security will be undertaken to reapportion the portfolio and increase the value of the conservative portion. The philosophy is similar to the constant dollar plan, except that a ratio is

BOX 20.3 *Continued*

fund. (This assumes you reinvested all dividends and capital gains, but it doesn't take into account the income taxes you would have had to pay on them.)

Buying shares in 121 monthly investments of $100 would have produced New Horizons shares worth $22,611 and Scudder shares worth $22,345 (also presuming you had reinvested all dividends and capital gains). These amounts are, respectively, 34% and 15% larger than the results achieved over 10 years by lump-sum investments in the two funds. They also exceed by a wide margin the $16,002 that an investor would have accumulated by putting $100 monthly into a passbook savings account.

And that's not all. The dollar-cost averaging investor could have earned interest on the uninvested portion of his $12,100 over the 10 years and picked up roughly $4,600 in a savings account. Adding in this interest, dollar-cost averaging would have produced an annually compounded return of 8.4% in New Horizons and 8.3% in Scudder. The total compounded annual return on Standard & Poor's 500-stock index over the same period was not quite 5%; on passbook savings it ranged from 5.13% to 5.65%.

But how would you have done over the past year? Again, dollar-cost averaging would have brought you out ahead. Putting a lump sum of $1,300 into New Horizons on March 31, 1981 would have given you stock worth $1,032, a year later; the same investment in Scudder would have produced $1,123. By investing $100 a month instead, you would have wound up with $1,134 of New Horizons shares and $1,259 of Scudder, plus about $40 of interest from putting uninvested cash in a savings account.

You would, of course, have done far better by dollar-cost averaging in big-winning individual stocks of the past 10 years—such as Warner Communications, Wang Laboratories or Metromedia—than by selecting a mutual fund. But picking stocks that will be among the top performers of a decade requires not only extraordinary foresight but also good luck. Moreover, brokerage costs on small transactions are prohibitively high. Many brokers—including discount brokers—charge a minimum $30 or $35 per transaction, and you can't as a rule buy fractions of shares. Merrill Lynch, however, has a plan called the Sharebuilder Account that can be used for dollar-cost averaging, and its commission rates are reasonable.

There is a way you can use dollar-cost averaging to invest in stocks without going through a broker: you buy shares in a company that has a dividend-reinvestment plan, which allows you to purchase additional shares for cash. Hundreds of companies—ranging from Aetna Life to Zurn Industries and from Abbott Laboratories to Merck and Rochester Telephone—offer such plans. Many of the companies pay all of the brokerage costs and permit you to buy up to $3,000 or $5,000 of stock per calendar quarter. A list of companies with dividend-reinvestment plans is available for $1 from Eileen Pritchard, Standard & Poor's, 25 Broadway, New York, N.Y. 10004. . . .

Source: Allan Sloan, "Investing by the Month," *Money,* June 1982, pp. 67–68.

utilized as a trigger point. The last plan presented below is a variable ratio plan. It could be said that this is the most aggressive of these fairly passive investment strategies.

Variable ratio plan

The *variable ratio plan* attempts more aggressively to capture stock market movements to the investor's advantage. It is another plan aimed at timing the market—

TABLE 20.19   VARIABLE RATIO PLAN

Mutual Fund NAV	Value of Speculative Portion	Value of Conservative Portion	Total Portfolio Value	Ratio of Speculative Portion to Total Portfolio	Transactions	Number of Shares in Speculative Portion
$10.00	$10,000.00	$10,000.00	$20,000.00	0.50		1,000
15.00	15,000.00	10,000.00	25,000.00	0.60		1,000
→15.00	11,250.00	13,750.00	25,000.00	0.45	Sold 250 shares	750
10.00	7,500.00	13,750.00	21,250.00	0.35		1,168.75
→10.00	11,687.50	9,562.50	21,250.00	0.55	Purchased 418.75 shares	1,168.75
12.00	14,025.00	9,562.50	23,587.50	0.41		

that is, it tries to "buy low and sell high." The ratio of the speculative portion to the conservative portion of the portfolio varies depending upon the movement in value of the speculative securities. When the ratio rises a certain predetermined amount, the amount committed to the speculative segment of the portfolio is reduced. Conversely, if the value of the speculative portion declines such that it drops significantly in proportion to the whole portfolio, the percentage of commitment in the speculative vehicle is increased. In implementing the variable ratio plan, an investor has several decisions to make. First, the investor must determine the initial allocation between the speculative and conservative portions of the portfolio. Next, trigger points to trigger buy or sell activity are chosen. These points are a function of the ratio between the value of the speculative portion and the value of the *total* portfolio. Finally, the adjustments in that ratio at each trigger point are set.

An example of a variable ratio plan is shown in Table 20.19. Initially, the portfolio is divided equally between the speculative and the conservative portions. The former consists of a high-beta (around 2.0) mutual fund, and the latter is a money market account. It was decided that when the speculative portion is 60 percent of the total portfolio, its proportion would be reduced to 45 percent. If the speculative portion of the portfolio dropped to 40 percent of the total portfolio, its proportion would be raised to 55 percent. The theory behind this strategy is an attempt to time the cyclical movements in the mutual fund's value. When the fund moves up in value, profits are taken and the proportion invested in the no-risk money market account is increased. When the fund declines markedly in value, the proportion of funds committed to it is increased.

A sequence of transactions is depicted in Table 20.19. When the fund NAV climbs to $15, the 60 percent ratio trigger point is reached and 250 shares of the fund are sold. The proceeds are placed in the money market account, which then represents 55 percent of the value of the portfolio. Later, the fund NAV declines to $10, causing the speculative portion of the portfolio to drop to 35 percent. This triggers a portfolio rebalancing, and 418.75 shares are purchased, moving the speculative portion to 55 percent. When the fund NAV then moves to $12, the total portfolio is worth in excess of $23,500. In comparison, if the initial investment of $20,000 had been allocated equally and no rebalancing was done between the mutual fund and the money market account, the portfolio's value at this time would be only $22,000 ($12 × 1,000 = $12,000 speculative portion plus $10,000 money market account).

Using Limit and Stop Orders

In Chapter 2, we discussed the market order, the limit order, and the stop-loss order. Here, we will see how the limit and the stop-loss orders are used to rebalance a portfolio. These types of security orders, if properly used, can increase an investor's return by lowering transaction costs.

Limit orders

In review, there are two basic types of security transaction orders. The *market order* instructs the broker to buy or sell securities at the best price available. This often means that buy orders are executed at the market maker's "ask" price and sell orders at the market maker's "bid" price. Limit orders constrain the broker as to the price and the time limit until canceled if unexecuted. A *limit order* specifies the investor's minimum sell price or the maximum price he or she will pay to buy a security. For example, if an order to sell 100 shares of Continuous Curve Contact Lens at 18 was placed with a broker, the broker would sell those shares only if a price of $18 per share or higher was obtained. Conversely, if a buy order for that security was placed, the order would be executed only if the broker could buy the stock for the customer at $18 per share or less. In addition to the price constraint, a limit order can have a time duration of one day or longer or can be *good 'til canceled (GTC)*. A GTC order, often called an "open order," remains outstanding until it is executed or canceled. In contrast, a *day order* expires at the end of the trading day it was entered if it was not executed.

There are many ways an investor can use limit orders when securities are bought or sold. For instance, if an investor has decided to add a stock to the portfolio, a limit buy order will ensure that the investor buys only at the desired purchase price or below. An investor using a limit GTC order to buy has the broker trying to buy stock until the entire order is filled. The primary risk in using limit instead of market orders is that the order may not be executed. For example, if an investor placed an order to buy 100 shares of Union Oil of California at $27 per share GTC and the stock never traded at $27 per share or less, the order would never be executed. Thus, an investor must weigh the need for immediate execution (market order) versus the possibility of a better price with a limit order. Limit orders, of course, can increase an investor's return, if they enable the investor to buy a security at a lower cost or sell at a higher price. During a typical trading day, a stock will fluctuate up and down over a trading range. For example, suppose the common shares of Honda Motor traded ten times in the following sequence: 36, 35⅞, 35¾, 35⅞, 35½, 35⅝, 35¾, 36, 36⅛, 36. A market order to sell could have been executed at somewhere between 35½ (the low) and 36⅛ (the high). A limit order to sell at 36 would have been executed at 36. Thus, a half-point per share (50 cents) might have been gained by using a limit order.

Stop-loss order

The *stop-loss order* is a specific type of a limit order that requests the broker to sell a security at the best available price only if it trades at a specific price or lower. In essence, a stop-loss order becomes a market order to sell if a stock trades at the trigger price or lower. The order can be used to limit the downside loss exposure of an investment. For example, an investor purchases 500 shares of Color Tile at 26. The investor has set a specific goal to sell the stock if it reaches 32 or drops to 23. To implement this goal, a GTC sell order is entered with a price limit of 32 and a stop-loss order is entered at a price of 23. If the issue trades at 23 or less, the stop-order becomes a market order and the stock is sold at the best price available. Conversely, if the issue trades at 32 or higher, the broker will sell the stock at 32 or higher.

The principal risk in using stop-loss orders is *whipsawing,* which refers to a situation where a stock temporarily drops in price and then bounces back upward. If Color Tile dropped to 23, then 22½, and then rallied back to 26, the investor who placed the stop-loss at 23 would have been sold out at 22½. Limit orders, including stop-loss orders, require careful analysis before they are placed. An investor must consider the stock's probable fluctuations as well as the need to purchase or sell the stock when choosing between a market, a limit, and a stop-loss order.

Warehousing Liquidity

One recommendation for an efficient portfolio is to keep a portion of it in a low-risk, highly liquid investment. Let us see why and how this works.

A buffer

Investing in risky stocks or in property offers probable returns in excess of money market accounts or bonds. However, stocks and property are risky investments. So, one reason to invest a portion of a portfolio in a low-risk asset is to protect against total loss. The low-risk asset acts as a buffer against possible investment adversity. A second reason for maintaining funds in a low-risk asset is the possibility of future opportunities. When opportunity strikes, an investor who has the extra cash available will be able to take advantage of the situation. A sudden market dip, an attractive real estate deal, or a painting available at a low price are all examples of situations where an investor with cash to invest immediately may benefit. An investor who has set aside funds in a highly liquid investment need not disturb the existing portfolio.

Choosing a liquid investment

There are two primary media for warehousing liquidity: money market accounts at financial institutions and money market mutual funds. The money market, or Super NOW, accounts at banks and savings and loan associations provide relatively easy access to funds and generally provide returns competitive with money market mutual funds. The Super NOW account began in January 1983, and is designed to compete directly with the money market mutual funds. As financial institutions become further deregulated, their products will continue to become more competitive

*I'm pleased to tell you your portfolio is outperforming the market.
For that matter, so is your grocery store.*

with those offered by mutual funds and stock brokerage firms. (See Chapter 7 for a detailed discussion of the role and vehicles available for warehousing liquidity.)

Timing Investment Sales

One of the more difficult decisions an investor must make concerns the appropriate time to sell an investment. Periodically, an investor must review the portfolio and consider possible sales and new purchases. Two items relevant to the sales decision are discussed here: tax consequences and achieving investment goals.

Tax consequences

The U.S. government has provided all investors with an incentive to hold investments for at least one year because of the favorable income tax treatment accorded long-term capital gains. An investor who sells a capital asset at a price in excess of its cost incurs a capital gain upon sale. All capital gains are subject to income taxation.

Gains on assets held for one year or less are short-term capital gains; gains on the sale of assets held for more than one year are considered long-term capital gains. Short-term capital gains are taxed as ordinary income and long-term capital gains are taxed at a much lower rate, which is equal to about 40 percent of the ordinary tax rate. Suppose an investor is in the 50 percent tax bracket. If that investor incurred a $10,000 short-term capital gain, the tax on it would be approximately $5,000. The tax to that investor for a $10,000 long-term capital gain would be much less—approximately $2,000.

When an investor sells a capital asset at a loss, this is a capital loss for tax purposes. An investor may deduct up to $3,000 per year of net capital losses from ordinary income. The distinction between long term and short term is important here as well. Short-term capital losses can be deducted dollar for dollar from ordinary income, whereas only 50 percent of the net long-term capital losses are deductible from ordinary income. For example, assume an investor has incurred a $3,000 capital loss and no capital gains. If this loss were short-term, the entire amount is deductible from ordinary income. If it is a long-term loss, only 50 percent could be deducted.

The coverage of the major tax laws and strategies in Chapter 17 makes it clear that taxes, although often complicated and affecting large investors more, affect nearly all investment actions. There are certain basics that all investors can and should understand. The one-year rule for capital gains is easy to remember; it affects a possible sale decision. If an investor has a loss position in an investment and has concluded it would be wise to sell it, the best time to sell is before it has been held for one year. Short-term capital losses provide more tax benefits than long-term capital losses. An investor who has a profitable position in an investment might wish to hold it at least one year because long-term capital gains are treated in a much more advantageous way than short-term gains.

Achieving investment goals

Every investor would enjoy selling an investment at its top price and buying it at its lowest price. At a more practical level, an investment should be sold when it no longer meets the needs of the portfolio's owner. In particular, if an investment has become more or less risky than is desired, or if it has not met its return objective or goal, it should be sold. The tax consequences mentioned above help to determine the appropriate time to sell. However, taxes are not the foremost consideration in a sale decision: the dual concepts of risk and return should be the overriding concerns.

Each investment should be examined periodically in light of its return performance and relative risk. If the investment no longer belongs in the portfolio, the investor should sell it and buy vehicles that are more suitable. And finally, an investor should not hold out for every nickel of profit. Very often, those who hold out for the top price watch the value of their holdings plummet downward. If an investment looks ripe to sell, an investor should sell it, take the profit, reinvest it in an appropriate vehicle, and enjoy his or her good fortune. An investor, in sum, should set realistic goals and criteria, and stick with them.

SUMMARY

Portfolios should contain investment vehicles selected on the basis of expected returns, associated risks, and certain tax considerations. Analyzing investment returns means gathering the necessary data reflecting the actual financial performance of each investment owned. An investor can assess the performance of an investment portfolio using comparative indexes such as the Dow Jones industrial average (DJIA), the Standard & Poor's 500 stock composite index, and the New York Stock Exchange composite index. Bond market indicators are available for assessing the general behavior of these markets. Although no broad indexes are available for assessing real estate returns, investors can compare their returns to those of other local real estate investors.

Reliable techniques often used for measuring the returns of each investment vehicle are available for monitoring an investment portfolio. Investment returns may be measured on both a pretax and an after-tax basis. Holding period return (HPR) can be used to measure the total return earned on a stock, a bond, or a mutual fund investment. An investor in real estate receives return in the form of yearly after-tax cash flows and the increment in property value that is realized upon sale. To assess real estate investment performance, an investor must calculate its after-tax holding period return. For gold and other investment vehicles, the only source of return, which can be measured using the HPR formula, comes from capital appreciation.

One benchmark against which to compare investment returns is the rate of return available on low-risk investments. If one's investments are outperforming low-risk investments, they are obtaining extra return for taking extra risk. If the opposite occurs, an investor should look closely at the portfolio. A problem investment is one that is a loss situation or that has provided an actual return below that expected by the investor.

A risk-adjusted, market-adjusted rate of return (RAR) is a method of gauging the investment performance of common stocks and portfolios of common stocks. This measure utilizes beta and a broadly based market index. If a stock, or a portfolio, has a positive RAR, it is said to have provided excess return and outperformed the market in general. A negative RAR indicates an inferior performance relative to the market as a whole. RAR analysis, while useful for individual stocks, is most beneficial in examining portfolio and mutual fund returns.

Portfolio revision is the systematic study by investors of issues in their portfolios that need to be sold and other new ones that need to be purchased. Periodic reallocation and rebalancing of one's portfolio helps eliminate issues that do not meet the portfolio's objectives.

The essence of timing in the market is to "buy low and sell high." Formula plans are methods an investor can utilize to attempt to time purchase and sales decisions. The four commonly used formula plans are the dollar cost averaging, the constant dollar plan, the constant ratio plan, and the variable ratio plan. An investor can increase return by lowering transaction costs by using certain types of security transaction orders. The limit order specifies the investor's minimum selling price or the maximum price he or she will pay to buy a security. Besides the price constraint, a limit order can have a time duration of one day or longer or can be good 'til canceled (GTC). The stop-loss order is a type of limit order that requests the broker to sell a security at the best available price only if a security trades at a specific price or lower.

Warehousing liquidity involves keeping a portion of a portfolio in a very low-risk, highly liquid investment. Two reasons for an investor to invest a portion of a portfolio in a low-risk vehicle are to protect against total loss and to be prepared to take advantage of future opportunities. The two primary media for warehousing liquidity are money market accounts (Super NOWs) and money market mutual funds. An investor who has decided to sell an investment vehicle must consider both tax consequences and investment goals. Short-term capital gains are taxed as ordinary income and long-term capital gains are taxed at a much lower rate equal to 40 percent of the ordinary tax rate. The loss on sale of a capital asset may be applied against ordinary income if it is a short-term loss; otherwise it is used to offset long-term capital gains.

KEY TERMS

constant dollar plan
constant ratio plan
day order
dollar cost averaging
formula plan
good 'til canceled (GTC)
holding period return (HPR)
limit order
market order
open order

portfolio revision
problem investment
reversion
risk-adjusted, market-adjusted rate of
  return (RAR)
stop-loss order
variable ratio plan
warehousing liquidity
whipsawing

REVIEW QUESTIONS

1. Discuss the areas with which an investor needs to be familiar before making an investment decision.

2. How do changes in economic activity affect investment returns? Explain.

3. Which indexes can an investor use to assess the results of his or her investment portfolio? Briefly explain each of these indexes.

4. What are bond market indicators and how are they different from stock market indicators? Name three sources of bond yield data.

5. Aside from comparing returns on real estate investment with those of local real estate investors, why would a real estate investor also compare returns with the Consumer Price Index and with the New York Stock Exchange composite index? Explain.

6. Briefly discuss the dividend yield measure and the holding period return (HPR) measure of investment return. Are they equivalent? Explain.

7. Mark Smith purchased 100 shares of the Tomco Corporation in December 1983, at a total cost of $1,762. He held the shares for 15 months and then sold them, netting $2,500. During the period he held the stock, the company paid him $200 in cash dividends. How much, if any, was the capital gain realized upon the sale of stock? Calculate Mark's pretax HPR for the holding period.

8. Joe Clark invested $25,000 in the bonds of Industrial Aromatics, Inc. He held them for 13 months, at the end of which he sold them for $26,746. During the period of ownership he earned $2,000 interest. Calculate the before- and after-tax HPR on Joe's investment for the holding period. Assume he is in the 40 percent tax bracket.

9. Distinguish between the types of dividend distributions mutual funds make. Explain the importance of distinguishing between them when making an after-tax HPR calculation for a mutual fund.

10. What are the two basic components of an investor's return from real estate investment? What is meant by the term *reversion,* and how is it calculated? Explain.

11. Describe the holding period return calculation for real estate. Peter Hancock bought a parcel of land in the Red Woods area one year ago for $35,000. He sold the property this year for $42,000 and his reversion from the sale was $40,000 after deducting $2,000 in closing costs and income taxes. Estimate Peter's after-tax holding period return on the investment.

12. What is a problem investment? What two items should be considered when analyzing an investment portfolio? Explain.

13. Discuss the risk-adjusted, market-adjusted rate of return (RAR) measure. How is it calculated? How can it be used to assess portfolio performance? Explain.

14. Describe the steps involved in measuring portfolio performance. Explain the role of the portfolio's HPR in this process and explain why one must differentiate between realized and unrealized appreciation.

15. Briefly define and discuss portfolio revision. Explain its role in the process of monitoring a portfolio.

16. Explain the role formula plans can play in timing security transactions. Describe the logic underlying the use of these plans.

17. Briefly describe and differentiate among each of the following formula plans.

a. Dollar cost averaging.
b. Constant dollar plan.
c. Constant ratio plan.
d. Variable ratio plan.

18. Define and differentiate among each of the following types of orders.

a. Market order.
b. Limit order.
c. Open order.
d. Day order.
e. Stop-loss order.

19. Give two reasons why an investor might be advised to maintain funds in a low-risk, highly liquid investment. Explain.

20. Describe the two items an investor should consider before reaching a decision to purchase or sell an investment vehicle. Explain.

CASE PROBLEMS

20.1 ASSESSING THE STALCHECKS' PORTFOLIO PERFORMANCE

The Stalchecks, Mary and Nick, have an investment portfolio containing four vehicles. It was developed in order to provide them with a balance between current income and capital appreciation. Rather than acquire mutual fund shares or diversify within a given class of investment vehicle, they developed their portfolio with the idea of diversifying across the various types of vehicles. The portfolio currently contains common stock, industrial bonds, mutual fund shares, and a real estate investment. They acquired each of these vehicles during the last three years, and they plan to invest in gold and other vehicles in the future.

Currently the Stalchecks are interested in measuring the return on their investment and assessing how well they have done relative to the market. They are hopeful that the return earned over the past calendar year is in excess of what they would have earned by investing in a portfolio consisting of the Standard & Poor's 500 stock composite index. Their investigation indicates that the (before-tax) return on the S&P stock portfolio during the past calendar year was 8.64 percent. With the aid of a friend, who had a sophisticated calculator, they were able to estimate the beta of their portfolio, which was 1.20. In their analysis they planned to ignore taxes, since they felt their earnings were adequately sheltered. Since they did not make any portfolio transactions during the past year, they would have to consider only unrealized capital gains, if any. In order to make the necessary calculations, the Stalchecks gathered this information on each of the four vehicles in their portfolio:

Common stock. They own 400 shares of KJ Enterprises common stock. KJ is a diversified manufacturer of metal pipe and is known for its unbroken stream of dividends.

Over the past few years it has entered new markets and as a result has offered moderate capital appreciation potential. Its share price has risen from 17¼ at the start of last calendar year to 18¾ at the end of the year. During the year, quarterly cash dividends of $.20, $.20, $.25, and $.25 were paid.

Industrial bonds.   The Stalchecks own 8 Cal Industries bonds. The bonds have a $1,000 par value, a 9¾ percent coupon, and are due in 1996. They are A-rated by Moody's. The bond was quoted at 97 at the beginning of the past calendar year and ended the calendar year at 96⅜.

Mutual fund.   They hold 500 shares in the Holt Fund, a balanced, no load mutual fund. The dividend distributions on the fund during the year consisted of $.60 in investment income and $.50 in long-term capital gains. The fund's NAV at the beginning of the calendar year was $19.45, and it ended the year at $20.02.

Real estate.   They own a parcel of raw land that had an appraised value of $26,000 at the beginning of the calendar year, and although they did not have it appraised at year-end, they were offered $30,500 for it at that time. Since the offer was made through a realtor, they would have had to pay nearly $1,500 in order to make the sale at that price.

Questions

1. Calculate the holding period return on a before-tax basis for each of the four investment vehicles described above.

2. Assuming that the Stalchecks' ordinary income is currently being taxed at a 25 percent rate, determine the after-tax HPR for each of the four investment vehicles. Assume they are eligible to receive long-term capital gain treatment on any realized or unrealized capital gains.

3. Recognizing that all gains on the Stalchecks' investments were unrealized, calculate the (before-tax) HPR for their four-vehicle portfolio during the past calendar year. Evaluate this return relative to its current income and capital gain components.

4. Perform a risk-adjusted, market-adjusted rate of return (RAR) analysis on the Stalchecks' portfolio, using your HPR findings from question 3. Assess their portfolio's performance. Also comment on the reasonableness of applying the RAR analysis to a four-vehicle portfolio.

5. Based upon your analysis in questions 1, 3, and 4, what, if any, recommendations might you offer the Stalchecks relative to the revision of their portfolio? Explain your recommendations.

20.2 EVALUATING FORMULA PLANS: CHARLES SCHULTZ'S APPROACH

Charles Schultz, a mathematician with Ansco Petroleum Company, wishes to develop a rational basis for timing his portfolio transactions. He currently holds a security portfolio with a market value of nearly $100,000, divided equally between a very conservative low-beta common stock, ConCam United, and a highly speculative high-beta common stock, Fleck Enterprises. Based upon his reading of the investments literature, Charles does not believe it is necessary to diversify one's portfolio across 8 to 20 securities. His own feeling, based on his independent mathematical analysis, is that one can achieve the same results by holding a two-security portfolio in which one security is very conservative and the other is highly speculative. Clearly, his feelings on this point will not be altered; he plans to continue to hold such a two-security portfolio until he finds that his theory does not work. During the past couple of years, he has earned a rate of return in excess of the risk-adjusted, market-adjusted rate expected on such a portfolio.

Charles's current interest centers on investigating and possibly developing his own formula plan for timing portfolio transactions. The current stage of his analysis centers on the evaluation of four commonly used formula plans in order to isolate the desirable features of each. The four plans being considered are (1) dollar cost averaging, (2) the constant dollar plan, (3) the constant ratio plan, and (4) the variable ratio plan. Charles's analysis of the plans will involve the use of two types of data. Since dollar cost averaging is a passive buy and hold strategy in which the periodic investment is held constant, while the other plans are more active in that they involve periodic purchases and sales within the portfolio, differing data are needed to evaluate each of them.

For evaluating the dollar cost averaging plan, Charles decided he would assume the investment of $500 at the end of each 45-day period. He chose to use 45-day time intervals in order to achieve certain brokerage fee savings that would be available by making larger transactions. The $500 per 45 days totaled $4,000 for the year and equaled the total amount Charles invested during the past year. In evaluating this plan, he would assume that half ($250) was invested in the conservative stock (ConCam United) and the other half in the speculative stock (Fleck Enterprises). The share prices for each of the stocks at the end of the eight 45-day periods when purchases were to be made are given below.

PRICE PER SHARE

Period	ConCam	Fleck
1	22⅛	22⅛
2	21⅞	24½
3	21⅞	25⅜
4	22	28½
5	22¼	21⅞
6	22⅛	19¼
7	22	21½
8	22¼	23⅝

In order to evaluate the other three plans, Charles planned to begin with a $4,000 portfolio evenly split between the two stocks. He chose to use $4,000, since that amount would correspond to the total amount invested in the two stocks over one year using dollar cost averaging. He planned to use the same eight points in time given earlier in order to assess and make, if required, transfers within the portfolio. For each of the three plans evaluated using these data, he established the triggering points given below.

Constant dollar plan. Each time the speculative portion of the portfolio is worth 13 percent more or less than its initial value of $2,000, the portfolio is rebalanced in order to bring the speculative portion back to its initial $2,000 value.

Constant ratio plan. Each time the ratio of the value of the speculative portion of the portfolio to the value of the conservative portion is greater than or equal to 1.15 or less than or equal to .84, the portfolio is rebalanced through sale or purchase, respectively, in order to bring the ratio back to its initial value of 1.0.

Variable ratio plan. Each time the value of the speculative portion of the portfolio rises above 54 percent of the total value of the portfolio, its proportion would be reduced to 46 percent; and each time the value of the speculative portion of the portfolio drops below 38 percent of the total value of the portfolio, its proportion would be raised to 50 percent of the portfolio value.

Questions
1. Under the dollar cost averaging plan, determine (a) the total number of shares purchased, (b) the average cost per share, and (c) the year-end portfolio value expressed both

in dollars and as a percentage of the amount invested for (1) the conservative stock, (2) the speculative stock, and (3) the total portfolio.

2. Using the constant dollar plan, determine the year-end portfolio value-expressed both in dollars and as a percentage of the amount initially invested for (1) the conservative portion, (2) the speculative portion, and (3) the total portfolio.

3. Repeat question 2 for the constant ratio plan. Be sure to answer all parts.

4. Repeat question 3 for the variable ratio plan. Be sure to answer all parts.

5. Compare and contrast your results from questions 1 through 4. You may want to summarize them in tabular form. Which plan would appear to have been most beneficial in timing Charles's portfolio activities during the past year? Explain.

SELECTED READINGS

Asinof, Lynn. "Data Retrieval Services Are Used Increasingly by Brokers and Investors for News and Prices." *The Wall Street Journal,* September 27, 1982, p. 34.

Connelly, Julie. "Taking Stock in the Future." *Money,* March 1982, pp. 50–51.

Curran, John J. "Value Line's Winning Way." *Fortune,* April 18, 1983, pp. 131–132.

Edgerton, Jerry. "How You Can Forecast the Market." *Money,* June 1982, pp. 40–42.

Managing Investment Portfolios, John L. Maginn and Donald L. Tuttle, eds. Boston: Warren, Gorham & Lamont, 1983.

Radcliffe, Robert C. *Investment: Concepts, Analysis, and Strategy.* Glenview, IL: Scott, Foresman, 1982.

Shaffer, Richard A. "Personal Computers Are Becoming More Useful to Many Investors for Managing of Portfolios." *The Wall Street Journal,* December 29, 1980, p. 24.

Sloan, Allan. "Investing by the Month." *Money,* June 1982, pp. 67–68.

———. "When to Sell a Stock." *Money,* June 1982, pp. 73–74.

"What to Do When Investments Sour." *Business Week,* July 5, 1982, pp. 106–108.

APPENDIX A
Financial Information and Computer Software

SOURCES OF FINANCIAL INFORMATION
    Economic and Current Event Information
        Financial News and Business Periodicals
        Commercial Bank Letters and Reports
    Institutional Publications
        Government Publications
        Nongovernment Publications
    Professional and Academic Publications
        Professional Journals
        Academic Journals
    Subscription Services
        Moody's Investors Services, Inc.
        Standard & Poor's Corporation
    Mutual Fund Directories
    Investment Advisories and Newsletters
    Directories and Source Finders for Financial Publications, Newsletters, and Investment Advisories
    Major Brokerage Firms
        Full-Service Brokerage
        Discount Brokers
    No-Load Mutual Funds
        Growth Funds
        Funds That Seek Maximum Capital Gains
        Income Funds
        Balanced Funds
        Municipal Bond Funds
        Money Market Funds
        Money Market Funds—U.S. Government Securities Only
        Tax-Exempt Money Market Funds
        Specialty Funds
SOURCES OF COMPUTER SOFTWARE

SOURCES OF FINANCIAL INFORMATION

ECONOMIC AND CURRENT EVENT INFORMATION

Financial News and Business Periodicals

PUBLICATION	FREQUENCY OF PUBLICATION	YEARLY SUBSCRIPTION RATE	PUBLISHER	TYPE OF INFORMATION
American Stock Exchange Weekly Bulletin	Weekly	$20.00	American Stock Exchange 86 Trinity Place New York, NY 10006	Summation of exchange activity on weekly basis.
Barron's	Weekly	$32.00	Dow Jones & Co., Inc. 22 Cortlandt St. New York, NY 10007	Newspaper. Financial and investment news; information on commodities, international trading; tables on New York Stock Exchange transactions.
Business Week	Weekly	$12.00	McGraw-Hill, Inc. 1221 Avenue of Americas New York, NY 10020	Magazine. International business and economic topics aimed at business management personnel.
Changing Times	Monthly	$12.00	Kiplinger Washington Editors, Inc. 1729 H Street, NW Washington, DC 20006	Articles of general consumer interest, tax and personal financial planning.
C.M.E. Newsletter	Quarterly	Free	Chicago Mercantile Exchange 444 West Jackson Blvd. Chicago, IL 60606	Report on activities of Chicago Mercantile Exchange.
Comex Weekly Market Report for Copper, Silver & Gold	Weekly	$25.00	Commodity Exchange, Inc. Southeast Plaza Bldg. 4 World Trade Center New York, NY 10048	Trading activity and trends in metals, futures markets; statistics.
Commodites: The Magazine of Futures Trading	Monthly	$34.00	Commodites Magazine, Inc. 250 S. Wacker Drive, Suite 250 Chicago, IL 60606 (312) 977-0999	Charts, illustrations, statistics; articles in the areas of commodities and futures trading and markets.
The Economist	Weekly	$50.00	Economist Newspaper, Ltd 25 St. James St. London, England	Covers economic and political news and trends. European perspective on U.S. business and political developments.
Everybody's Money	Quarterly	$ 2.00	Credit Union National Assn. Box 431 Madison, WI 53701 (608) 231-4000	A guide to family finance and consumer action.
FACT	11 per year	$18.00	FACT 711 Third Ave. New York, NY 10017	A money management magazine specifically aimed at the individual investor and covering all popular types of investment vehicles.

Publication	Frequency	Price	Publisher/Address	Description
Financial Planning Today	Quarterly	$40.00	Panel Publishers, 14 Plaza Road, Greenvale, NY 11548	Articles on personal financial management: estate planning, taxes, tax shelters, mutual funds, commodities, stocks and bonds.
Financial World	Semi-monthly	$33.00	Macro Communications, 919 Third Ave., New York, NY 10022	Investment analysis and forecasts for specific companies and industries as a whole.
Forbes	Fortnightly	$21.00	Forbes, Inc., 60 Fifth Avenue, New York, NY 10011	General economic and financial news; reports on various corporations, executives, stocks, and industries. August issue: Annual Performance Review of Mutual Funds.
Fortune	Biweekly	$24.00	Time, Inc., 591 N. Fairbanks Ct., Chicago, IL 60611	Business and economic developments; evaluates specific industries and corporations; banking and energy news.
Money	Monthly	$14.95	Time, Inc., 591 N. Fairbanks Ct., Chicago, IL 60611	Reports on personal finance: stock market trends, estate planning, taxes, tax shelters, and consumer affairs.
National Real Estate Investor	Monthly	$41.00	Communication Channels, Inc., 6255 Barfield Rd., Atlanta, GA 30328, (404) 256–9800	Articles, book reviews, current topics in real estate financing, marketing, partnership offerings, and taxation for professionals and serious real estate investors.
Nation's Business	Monthly	$16.75	Chamber of Commerce of the United States, 1615 H Street NW, Washington, DC 20062	Forecasts, analyzes, and interprets trends and developments in business and government.
New York Stock Exchange Fact Book	Annual	$ 3.00	New York Stock Exchange, 11 Wall St., New York, NY 10005, (212) 623–2013	Description of New York Stock Exchange activity.
New York Stock Exchange Monthly Review	Monthly	$ 4.00	New York Stock Exchange, 11 Wall St., New York, NY 10005, (212) 623–2013	Updates on New York Stock Exchange activity.
Real Estate Investment Ideas	Semi-monthly	$48.00	Institute for Business Planning, Inc., Prentice Hall, Inc., Englewood Cliffs, NJ 07632	Magazine. Articles on financing, ownership, and disposition of real estate; planning techniques and strategies.
Tax Shelter Directory	Annual	$68.00	Spectrum Finance Group, Box 1146, Menlo Park, CA 94025, (800) 227–1617, ext. 408	Two-volume resource of over 470 programs, sponsors, advisors, and brokers.
The Wall Street Journal	Daily	$68.00	Dow Jones & Company, Inc., 22 Cortlandt St., New York, NY 10007, (212) 285–5000	General business, financial, and world news with market quotations.

PUBLICATION	FREQUENCY OF PUBLICATION	YEARLY SUBSCRIPTION RATE	PUBLISHER	TYPE OF INFORMATION
Wealth Building: The Magazine of Personal Financial Planning	Monthly	$30.00	The Investor Group, Inc. 9550 Forest Lane, Suite 604 Dallas, TX 75243	Formerly the *National Tax Shelter Digest*. Articles by nationally recognized experts on current investment, tax, and legislative topics. Regular departments on investor outlook, money management, personal financial planning, Washington-wise, traditional investing, and tax-advantaged investments. Occasional "special edition" within an edition highlighting one topic or industry for tax-advantaged investing.

Commercial Bank Letters and Reports

Most large commercial banks publish regular reports, often free of charge, covering various aspects of the economy, business, and the financial markets.

A quarterly index to articles and reports found in 50 U.S. and Canadian bank publications is available as reference in most business school libraries:

An Index To Bank Letters, Bulletins, And Reviews ($45/yr)
Krause-Thompson Organization, Ltd.
Route 100
Millwood, NY 10546

Some of the major bank newsletters and reports include:

PERIODICAL	FREQUENCY OF PUBLICATION	YEARLY SUBSCRIPTION RATE	PUBLISHER	TYPE OF INFORMATION
Barometer of Business	Monthly	Free	Harris Bank 111 West Monroe St. Chicago, IL 60606	Economic conditions and current business environment.
Business Review	Bimonthly	Free	Wells Fargo Bank, Economics Dept. Box 44000 San Francisco, CA 94144	Review of general business conditions in the western United States
Chase Economic Observer	Bimonthly	Free	Chase Manhattan Bank Economics Group (Publications) One Chase Manhattan Plaza New York, NY 10015 (212) 552–2222	Report on current business and economic conditions in the United States.
Consumer Views	Monthly	$2.85 $2.99 NY	Citibank Public Affairs Dept. Publications, 18th floor 399 Park Ave. New York, NY 10022 (212) 559–0233	A monthly family financial management newsletter.

Name	Frequency	Price	Address	Description
Current Business Picture	3/yr	Free	Bankers Trust Company Economics Division Box 318 New York, NY 10015 (212) 382–4000	Review of current business trends, business statistics, and indicators.
Economic Outlook	Annual	Free	Bank of America Editorial Services Box 37000 San Francisco, CA 94137 (415) 622–3456	Three separate reports on world, U.S., and California economic growth. Evaluates future growth, inflation, capital investment, financial market trends, regional growth, and key industrial sectors.
Economic Report	Monthly	Free	Manufacturers Hanover Trust Company 350 Park Ave. New York, NY 10022 (212) 286–7359	Covers the world economy, including foreign trade.
Economic Week	Weekly	$129.00	Citibank Public Affairs Dept. Publications, 18th floor 399 Park Ave. New York, NY 10022	Weekly newsletter on U.S. economic trends, consumer prices, construction activity, exchange rates, and inventories.
Financial Talk	Monthly	Free	Harris Bank 111 West Monroe St. Chicago, IL 60606	Consumer-oriented newsletter on financial products and services.
Inside Economics	Weekly	Free	First National Bank of Chicago Business and Economic Research Div. One First National Plaza Chicago, IL 60670 (312) 732–3779	Report on current business and economic conditions in the United States.
Morgan Guaranty Survey	Monthly	Free	Morgan Guaranty Trust Company of New York Box 495, Church Street Station New York, NY 10015 (212) 483–2323	Survey of current business and economic conditions in the United States.
U.S. Economic Projections	Monthly	Free	Bank of New York Economics Department 48 Wall St. New York, NY 10015	Review of current economic conditions.
Weekly Financial Digest	Weekly	Free	Manufacturers Hanover Trust Company 350 Park Ave. New York, NY 10022 (212) 286–6000	Selected Federal Reserve data, bank loan figures, business indicators, securities market, New York and international money markets, etc.

PERIODICAL	FREQUENCY OF PUBLICATION	YEARLY SUBSCRIPTION RATE	PUBLISHER	TYPE OF INFORMATION
Wells Fargo Economic Monitor	Monthly	$200.00	Wells Fargo Bank, Economics Dept. Box 44000 San Francisco, CA 94144 (415) 396–0123	A special series of publications on business and finance. Analyzes key economic issues and developing trends. Up-to-the-minute reports on (1) the nation, providing analyses of current U.S. and international business conditions and trends along with a forecast of key economic indicators; (2) California, providing analyses similar to the national report applying to California; and (3) money and credit markets, covering Federal Reserve and administrative policies, interest rate movements, and prime rate projections. Also, subscribers may phone members of the economic department directly for answers to questions on business and finance.
World Business	Quarterly	Free	Chase Manhattan Bank One Chase Manhattan Plaza New York, NY 10015	Survey of current business conditions throughout the world.

INSTITUTIONAL PUBLICATIONS

Government Publications

Various agencies of the government publish documents that give detailed statistics on virtually all aspects of business, finance, and the economy. The major publications are available for reference in most public and college libraries. These include:

Business Conditions Digest (monthly)
Business Statistics (biennial)
Economic Indicators (monthly)
Long Term Economic Growth (book)
Statistical Abstract of U.S. (annual)
Survey of Current Business (monthly)
U.S. Industrial Outlook (annual)

Information about these publications, including prices and content description, may be obtained by writing to:

Superintendent of Documents
U.S. Government Printing Office
Washington, DC 20402

Federal Reserve Bulletin   Monthly $20.00   Federal Reserve System, Board of Governors, Division of Administrative Services, Washington, DC 20551   Covers the U.S. Federal Reserve system and its activities.

Each of the twelve district banks provides various weekly, monthly, quarterly, and yearly reports focusing on current economic issues, monetary policy, recent business activity, money and bond markets, and banking and finance. Most reports are offered free of charge. A list of publications offered may be acquired by writing to the following:

Federal Reserve Bank of Atlanta
104 Marietta St.
Atlanta, GA 30303

Federal Reserve Bank of Boston
600 Atlantic Ave.
Boston, MA 02106

Federal Reserve Bank of Cleveland
East 6th St. and Superior Ave.
Cleveland, OH 44101

Federal Reserve Bank of Chicago
Box 834
Chicago, IL 60690

Federal Reserve Bank of Dallas
Station K
Dallas, TX 75222

Federal Reserve Bank of Kansas City
Federal Reserve Station
Kansas City, MO 64198

Federal Reserve Bank of Minneapolis
250 Marquette Ave.
Minneapolis, MN 55480

Federal Reserve Bank of New York
33 Liberty St.
New York, NY 10045

Federal Reserve Bank of Philadelphia
Box 66—Public Services
Philadelphia, PA 19105

Federal Reserve Bank of Richmond
Box 27622
Richmond, VA 23261

Federal Reserve Bank of St. Louis
Box 442
St. Louis, MO 63166

Federal Reserve Bank of San Francisco
Box 7702
San Francisco, CA 94120

Nongovernment Publications

American Council of Life Insurance
1850 K Street
Washington, DC 20006
A Life Insurance Fact Book (free)
A List of Worthwhile Life and Health Insurance Books (free)

The American Economic Foundation
51 East 42 St.
New York, NY 10017
Sample packet of materials (free)

American Stock Exchange, Inc.
86 Trinity Place
New York, NY 10006
Publications catalog (free)

Chamber of Commerce of the United States
1615 H Street NW
Washington, DC 20062
Publications directory (free)

Chicago Board of Trade
Literature Services
141 W. Jackson Blvd.
Chicago, IL 60604

Chicago Mercantile Exchange
444 W. Jackson Blvd.
Chicago, IL 60606
Bibliography and information source list (free)

Dow Jones & Company, Inc.
The Educational Service Bureau
Box 300, Princeton, NJ 08540
Programs, services, and materials (free)

Dun & Bradstreet, Inc.
Public Relations Dept.
99 Church St.
New York, NY 10007
Reports and reference books (free)

New York Stock Exchange
Information Bureau
Box 252 Wall Street Station
New York, NY 10005

Tax Foundation, Inc.
Publications Catalog
50 Rockefeller Plaza
New York, NY 10020

PROFESSIONAL AND ACADEMIC PUBLICATIONS

Professional Journals

Many journals are directed primarily toward the needs of the professional broker, analyst, portfolio manager, and planner, but have many articles and features that may be of interest to investors generally. These journals are available in most public and college libraries. Those that may be of most interest to investors include the following.

PROFESSIONAL PUBLICATION	FREQUENCY OF PUBLICATION	YEARLY SUBSCRIPTION RATE	PUBLISHER	TYPE OF INFORMATION
AAII Journal	10/Year	$40.00	American Assn. of Individual Investors 612 N. Michigan Ave., Suite 317 Chicago, IL 60601 (312) 280–0170	Approaches to asset valuation, portfolio construction, and financial planning not generally covered in the popular press. Also monitors financial research and practice.
CFA Digest	Quarterly	$20.00 ($10.00 to CFAs)	Institute of Chartered Financial Analysts Box 3668 Charlottesville, VA 22903	Abstracts of articles in academic and professional journals having particular relevance to the investment community.
CLU Journal	Quarterly	$12.00	American Society of Chartered Life Underwriters Box 59 Bryn Mawr, PA 19010	Insurance education, estate and tax planning, business insurance
Commodity Journal	Bimonthly	$20.00	American Assn. of Commodity Traders 10 Park St. Concord, NH 03301 (603) 224–2376	Data on commodity market trends and analysis of raw data in detail.
Financial Analysts Journal	Bimonthly	$36.00	Financial Analysts Federation 219 E. 42 St. New York, NY 10017	Articles and transcripts of speeches of interest to securities analysts.
The Financial Planner	Monthly	$30.00	International Assn. of Financial Planners 2150 Parklake Dr. NE Suite 260 Atlanta, GA 30345	Articles for the professional financial planner related to investments, commodities, retirement planning, insurance, tax shelters, mutual funds, etc.
Institutional Investor	Monthly	$110.00	Institutional Investor Systems, Inc. 488 Madison Ave. New York, NY 10022	Articles of particular interest to managers of large institutional investment portfolios.
Journal of the Institute of Certified Financial Planners	Quarterly	$45.00	Institute of Certified Financial Planners 3443 S. Galena, Suite 190 Denver, CO 80231	A professional journal for financial planners that presents research findings as well as new tools and techniques that may prove useful. All aspects of personal financial planning, including investments, are covered.
Journal of Real Estate Taxation	Monthly	$54.00	Warren, Gorham & Lamont 210 South St. Boston, MA 02111	For professionals and sophisticated investors, articles addressing current tax issues, pending legislation, recent court cases, and tax strategies and tactics associated with

Name	Frequency	Price	Publisher / Address	Description
Journal of Taxation	Monthly	$22.00	Warren, Gorham & Lamont 210 South St. Boston, MA 02111	comments for professional tax practitioners. Tax planning ideas for individuals, small businesses, corporations.
The Journal of Taxation	Monthly	$84.00	Warren, Gorham & Lamont 210 South St. Boston, MA 02111 (800) 225–2363	A national professional journal of current news and comment for tax practitioners, with many articles and regular departments related to tax tips and planning ideas of interest to sophisticated investors.
MG Financial Weekly Market Digest	Weekly	$98.00	Media General Financial Services Box 26991 Richmond, VA 23261 (212) 541–5668	Newspaper that publishes a broad range of opinions from widely selected experts, along with factual data, to serve as informational background for investors.
The Practical Accountant	Monthly	$42.00	Institute for Continuing Professional Development, Inc. 964 Third Ave. New York, NY 10022 (212) 564–5294	Magazine with tax savings and tax planning tips as well as other accounting-related articles. Generally, articles are of interest to practicing accountants, but many articles may be of interest to sophisticated investors.
The Practical Lawyer	8/yr	$18.00	American Law Institute American Bar Assn. Committee on Continuing Education 4025 Chestnut St. Philadelphia, PA 19104 (215) 243–1600	A nontechnical magazine for practicing lawyers with many tax and legal planning ideas that would benefit sophisticated investors.
The Review of Taxation of Individuals	Quarterly	$58.00	Warren, Gorham & Lamont 210 South St. Boston, MA 02111 (800) 225–2363	Articles, essays, decisions, planning ideas, and other items of interest to practicing tax attorneys, accountants, estate planners, corporate counsel, executives, and high-income individuals.
The Tax Adviser	Monthly	$45.00	American Institute of Certified Public Accountants 666 Fifth Ave. New York, NY 10019 (212) 575–6200	Published by the American Institute of Certified Public Accountants for accountants, but with many practical and informative tips for sophisticated investors. Includes notes on relevant current cases, tax legislation, and trends in tax and tax planning.
Tax Executive	Quarterly	$15.00	Tax Executives Institute, Inc. 1300 N. 17th St., Suite 1300 Arlington, VA 22209 (703) 522–3535	A magazine with the tax adviser and highly compensated executive in mind. Review of recent tax legislation and articles on tax planning strategies and tactics for the wealthier investor.
Taxation for Accountants	Monthly	$48.00	Warren, Gorham & Lamont 210 South St. Boston, MA 02111 (800) 225–2363	A national monthly professional tax magazine for the accountant in general practice. The articles, notes, and comments often provide relevant tax planning ideas of interest to sophisticated investors.

PROFESSIONAL PUBLICATION	FREQUENCY OF PUBLICATION	YEARLY SUBSCRIPTION RATE	PUBLISHER	TYPE OF INFORMATION
Taxes—The Tax Magazine	Monthly	$60.00	Commerce Clearing House, 4025 W. Peterson Ave. Chicago, IL 60646	Published to promote sound thought in economic, legal, and accounting principles relating to all federal and state taxation. Contains articles on tax subjects of current interest and reports on recent federal and state tax matters.
Wall Street Transcript	Weekly	$780.00	Wall Street Transcript Corp. 120 Wall St. New York, NY 10005	A professional publication for the business and financial community that reproduces the text of selected brokerage house reports, speeches, and interviews by leading investment managers, and other useful items on companies, mergers, and new issues.
The Weekly Bond Buyer	Weekly	$375.00	The Bond Buyer One State Street Plaza New York, NY 10004	Newspaper that interprets international financial and economic news; covers money markets, government, and corporate bond markets and stock market.

Academic Journals

These journals will be of interest to sophisticated investors who wish to keep abreast of the most recent advances in financial and investment theory and application.

PUBLICATION	FREQUENCY OF PUBLICATION	YEARLY SUBSCRIPTION RATE	PUBLISHER	TYPE OF INFORMATION
Financial Management	Quarterly	$25.00	Financial Management Assn. College of Business Administration University of South Florida 402 Fowler Ave. Tampa, FL 33620	Reports on and refines the most advanced research and reviews developments by practitioners of financial management.
The Journal of Business	Quarterly	$18.00	University of Chicago Press Chicago, IL	Sophisticated academic articles on business and investments.
Journal of Finance	5/yr	$25.00	American Finance Assn. c/o Robert A. Kavesh, Graduate School of Business Admin. New York University 100 Trinity Pl. New York, NY 10006	Academic articles on finance, including investments.
Journal of Financial and Quantitative Analysis	5/yr	$20.00	Western Finance Assn. U. of Washington Graduate School of Business Administration	Academic articles on finance, including investments.

Title	Publisher/Address	Frequency/Price	Description
Journal of Financial Economics	Seattle, WA 98195 / North-Holland Publishing Co., Journal Division, Box 211, 1000 AE Amsterdam, The Netherlands	4/yr, $38.25	Highly technical and mathematical academic articles on investments, pricing of securities, portfolio analysis, and behavior of speculative markets.
Journal of Portfolio Management	Institutional Investor Systems, Inc. 488 Madison Ave. New York, NY 10022 (212) 832–8888	Quarterly, $95.00	Trends and developments in the management of large portfolios, both theoretical and applied.
Journal of Risk and Insurance	American Risk and Ins. Assn. c/o Dr. R. E. Johnson, Exec. Sec. Brooks Hall U. of Georgia Athens, GA 30602	Quarterly, $35.00 ($20.00 to members of ARIA)	Academic articles in insurance related areas.

SUBSCRIPTION SERVICES

Moody's Investors Services, Inc. (99 Church St., New York, NY 10007)

Title	Frequency/Price	Description
Bond Record	Monthly, $100.00	Issues, current prices, call prices, ratings, and other statistics on numerous bonds.
Bond Survey	Weekly, $850.00	Comments and recommendations on issues in various bond categories.
Dividend Record	Twice weekly (annual issue at year-end), $240.00	Dividend information on various issues.
Handbook of Common Stocks	Quarterly, $125.00	Statistics and background on common stocks.
International Manual	Biweekly, $760.00	Business and financial information on over 3,000 major corporations and multinational institutions in 95 countries.
Investors Fact Sheets	Updated daily	Single-page self-contained reports on more than 4,000 firms listed on the NYSE, ASE, and regional exchanges plus those actively traded OTC. Details on recent developments in sales, earnings, management, performance, etc.
Moody's Bank and Finance Manual	Yearly (supplemented twice weekly), $650.00	Facts and figures on financial enterprises.
Moody's Industrial Manual	Yearly (supplemented twice weekly), $650.00	Information on industrial stocks, history, management, financial data.
Moody's Municipal and Governments Manual	Yearly (supplemented twice weekly), $840.00	Information and ratings on governments, municipals, foreign bonds.
Moody's Public Utility Manual	Yearly (supplemented twice weekly), $535.00	Information on public utilities, plus special studies on market areas.
Moody's Transportation Manual	Yearly (supplemented twice weekly), $535.00	Information on transportation companies such as air, rail, bus, oil pipelines, bridge companies, trucking.
OTC Industrial Manual	Yearly (supplemented twice weekly)	Reference source for over 2,700 OTC issues.

Standard & Poor's Corporation (345 Hudson St., New York, NY 10014)

Title	Frequency	Description
Analysts Handbook	Monthly	Per share data on various industries and S&P's 425 industrials.
ASE Stock Reports	Periodically revised	Data on American Exchange issues, financial aspects, and current items.
Bond Guide	Monthly	Descriptive and statistical data on 3,000 corporate bonds. Nearly 10,000 state, municipal, general obligation and revenue bonds, over 650 convertibles and more than 200 foreign bonds.
Called Bond Record	Semi-weekly	Reports calls and tenders, sinking fund proposals, defaulted issues, forthcoming redemptions, etc.
Corporation Records	Daily revisions	Comprehensive reference library on corporations in six looseleaf binders.
Creditweek	Weekly	Comments on trends and outlook for fixed income securities, including money market instruments and corporate and government bonds. Money market rates, bond yields, federal figures, new offerings, credit analyses.
Current Market Perspectives	Monthly	Books of charts on 100 issues shows hi-lo-close for five years.
Daily Action Stock Charts	Weekly	Numerous stocks plotted on a daily basis.
Daily Stock Price Record	3 quarterly	Three sets of volumes, each set devoted to one market—NYSE, ASE, OTC. NYSE volumes cover over 2,300 issues; ASE volumes cover more than 1,000; OTC volumes cover 4,000 issues, including more than 500 mutual funds and 3,500 NASDAQ bank, insurance and industrial companies.
Dividend Record	Daily, weekly, quarterly	Authority on dividend details.
Earnings Forecaster	Weekly	Earnings estimates on about 1,600 companies prepared by S&P and over 50 leading investment organizations and brokerage firms.
Growth Stocks Handbook	Semi-annual update	Facts and figures on over 300 stocks with accelerated earnings growth over the past five years.
Industry Surveys	Yearly with 3 or 4 supplements	Surveys 65 leading industries under 32 headings, with trends and projections. Forecasts industry and economic trends; earnings supplement.
NYSE Stock Reports	Periodically revised	Data on numerous NYSE issues, including financial data and latest developments.
Oil and Gas Stocks Handbook	Semi-annual update	Over 250 stock reports on international and domestic oil companies; crude oil and gas producers; coal companies; refining companies; exploration and gathering companies; oil well service companies; offshore drilling companies; and marine construction companies. Special editorial appraising energy situation.
The Outlook	Weekly	Specific advice on individual stocks. Analyzes and projects business trends. Advice and articles on special situations, stock groups, economics, industries, options, and subjects of concern to investors.
OTC Chart Manual	Bimonthly	Charts the most active OTC stocks.
OTC Handbook	Semi-annual update	Individual stock reports on over 526 important OTC stocks; the biggest most actively traded; the fastest-growing OTC stocks; low-priced stocks, and selected banks and insurance companies.

PUBLICATION	FREQUENCY OF PUBLICATION	TYPE OF INFORMATION
OTC Stock Reports	Periodically revised	Regional and OTC stocks surveys.
Register of Corporate Directors and Executives	Yearly with 3 supplements	Directory of executive personnel.
Registered Bond Interest Record	Weekly	Weekly cumulative record of information relating to interest payment on registered bonds.
Security Dealers Directory	Semi-annual	Lists over 10,000 brokerage and investment banking houses in the United States and Canada, along with their executive rosters.
Stock Guide	Monthly	Data and reviews on over 5,100 common and preferred stocks listed and OTC. Also, special section on performance of over 380 mutual funds.
Stock Summary	Monthly	Condensed information on widely traded stocks, editorial features highlighting industries of current interest to investors and S&Ps. Rapid growth stocks feature focuses on companies with high 5-year growth rates.

MUTUAL FUND DIRECTORIES

For many investors who have limited investment capital or do not have the inclination or expertise to manage their own portfolio, mutual funds provide an attractive opportunity to invest in a diversified and professionally managed portfolio.

PUBLICATION	FREQUENCY OF PUBLICATION	YEARLY SUBSCRIPTION RATE	PUBLISHER	TYPE OF INFORMATION
Directory of No-Load Funds	Annual	$2.00	No-Load Mutual Fund Association 11 Penn Plaza, Suite 2204 New York, NY 10001 (212) 563–4540	Lists by type of fund (growth, income, balanced) the names and addresses of no-load funds that are members of the association.
Donoghue's Money Letter	Bimonthly	$87.00	Box 411 Holliston, MA 01746 (617) 429–5930	Reports exclusively on money market mutual funds: performance, portfolio composition, management, current yields.
Donoghue's Money Fund Directory	Semi-annual	$24.00	Box 411 Holliston, MA 01746 (617) 429–5930	Names, addresses, and portfolio characteristics of virtually all U.S. money funds.
Fundline	Monthly	$77.00	Fundline Box 663 Woodland Hills, CA 91365	Monthly report correlating top 38 funds and recommending those with greatest potential.
Growth Fund Guide	Monthly	$79.00	Growth Fund Research Building Box 6600 Rapid City, SD 57709	24-page publication tracking solidly proven funds. Ranks funds by the volatility of stock portfolio.
Mutual Fund Fact Book	Yearly	$1.00	Investment Company Institute 1775 K Street NW Washington, DC 20006 (202) 293–7700	Data on U.S. mutual fund industry, including trends in sales, assets, distributions, accumulations, withdrawal plans, and new types of funds.

PUBLICATION	FREQUENCY OF PUBLICATION	YEARLY SUBSCRIPTION RATE	PUBLISHER	TYPE OF INFORMATION
Mutual Fund Handbook	Annual	$28.00	No-Load Fund Investor Box 203 Hastings-on-Hudson, NY 10706 (914) 478–2381	Reports on mutual fund industry and ranks funds. Includes subscription to *Mutual Funds Almanac* which provides a directory to over 600 funds, looks at ten-year performances; statistics, tables, charts.
Mutual Fund Performance	Monthly	$225.00	Warren, Gorham & Lamont 210 South St. Boston, MA 02111	A supplement to Wiesenberger Services, Inc., *Investment Companies* providing detailed monthly data on mutual fund performance.
Mutual Fund Specialist	Monthly	$48.00	Mutual Fund Specialist Box 1025 Eau Claire, WI 54701	Tracks and ranks some 50 groups or families of funds, pinpointing top equity fund in each family. Ranks 200 money market funds as well.
Mutual Funds Forum	Bimonthly	$6.00	Investment Company Institute 1775 K Street NW Washington, DC 20006	Bimonthly newsletter contains articles of interest to the mutual fund industry.
No Load Fund Investor	Quarterly	$28.00	No-Load Fund Investor Box 203 Hastings-on-Hudson, NY 10706 (914) 478–2381	Reports on mutual fund industry and ranks funds. Includes subscription to *Mutual Funds Almanac* which provides a directory to over 600 funds, looks at ten-year performances; statistics, tables, charts.
NoLoad Fund X	Monthly	$77.00	NoLoad Fund X 235 Montgomery St. San Francisco, CA 94104	Monthly publication ranking some 280 funds. Provides switching advice among fund families.
Switch Fund Advisory	Monthly	$125.00	Switch Fund Advisory 8943 Shady Grove Ct. Gaithersburg, MD 20877	Monthly letter profiling certain funds and recommending buy or no buy decisions or switches among fund families.
Telephone Switch Newsletter	Monthly	$97.00	Telephone Switch Newsletter Box 2538 Huntington Beach, CA 92647	Monthly report providing specific market timing investment fund switching advice. Includes a telephone hot line service to inform subscribers of changes in recommendations.
United Mutual Fund Selector	Semi-monthly	$59.00	United Business Service Company 210 Newbury St. Boston, MA 02116 (617) 267–8855	Semi-monthly report evaluates mutual funds, including bond and municipal bond funds. Reports industry developments; tables and charts.
Vickers Guide to Investment Company	7/yr	$400.00	Vickers Associates 226 New York Ave. Huntington, NY 11743 (516) 432–7710	Looseleaf report supplies information on U.S. and Canadian investment companies' stock holdings and transactions.

PUBLICATION	FREQUENCY OF PUBLICATION	YEARLY SUBSCRIPTION RATE	PUBLISHER	TYPE OF INFORMATION
... Services, Inc., Investment Companies	Annual	$120.00	Warren, Gorham & Lamont 210 South St. Boston, MA 02111	The publication considered by many in the investment community to be the Bible on mutual funds and investment companies. Gives background, management policy, and financial record for all leading U.S. and Canadian investment companies. Published annually with quarterly updatings. This publication is available for reference in most public and college libraries.

INVESTMENT ADVISORIES AND NEWSLETTERS

PUBLICATION	FREQUENCY OF PUBLICATION	YEARLY SUBSCRIPTION RATE	PUBLISHER	TYPE OF INFORMATION
Alan Shawn Feinstein Insiders Report	Monthly	$60.00 ($30.00 charter subscription)	Alan Feinstein and Associates 41 Alhambra Circle Cranston, RI 02905 (401) 467–5155	Reports on special investment opportunities, inside tips, new or unusual opportunities.
Babson's Investment and Barometer Letter	Weekly	$96.00	Babson's Reports, Inc. Wellesley, MA 02181 (617) 235–0900	Weekly newsletter lists buy, hold, and sell options on promisings stocks. Reports on current market activity and reviews companies in the news.
Babson's Washington Forecast Letter	Weekly	$36.00	Babson's Reports, Inc. Wellesley, MA 02181 (617) 235–0900	Weekly newsletter interprets and forecasts the impact of federal legislation on business, stock market activity, and general Washington activities.
Better Investing	Monthly	$10.00	National Assn. of Investment Clubs 1515 E. Eleven Mile Rd. Royal Oak, MI 48067 (313) 543–0612	Guidelines and advice on investment techniques for investment clubs. Investment education: one company analyzed each month. General articles on investment topics.
Brennan Reports: on tax shelters, tax planning	Monthly	$145.00	Brennan Reports, Inc. Box 882 Valley Forge, PA 19482 (215) 783–0647	Monthly report of 4 to 8 pages discussing timely topics on tax planning, recent tax legislation, and court decisions affecting tax-advantaged investments. Reviews and summarizes the key features, risks, and rewards of 2 or 3 tax-advantaged publicly offered limited partnership offerings each month, with primary emphasis on real estate, oil and gas, equipment leasing, and agricultural programs.
Commodity Service	Weekly	$150.00	Dunn & Hargitt, Inc. 22 N. 2nd Street Lafayette, IN 47902 (317) 423–2626	Advice on commodity futures market.

PUBLICATION	FREQUENCY OF PUBLICATION	YEARLY SUBSCRIPTION RATE	PUBLISHER	TYPE OF INFORMATION
Contrary Investor	Fortnightly	$75.00	Fraser Mgmt. Assoc. Box 494 Burlington, VT 05402 (802) 658–0322	Newsletter espousing the "contrary opinion" theory of investing that reviews and comments on recommendations and trends in the traditional investment community. Broad market timing recommendations.
Daily Graphs	Weekly	$325.00: NYSE/OTC $290.00: AMEX/OTC $540.00: Both	William O'Neil & Co. Box 24933 Los Angeles, CA 90024 (213) 820–2583	Provides daily bar charts on over 2,600 NYSE, AMEX, and OTC stocks; in addition, a variety of technical, fundamental, and market information is given, including such measures as 200-day moving averages, relative price strength, short interest, and insider transactions.
Dines Letter	Biweekly	$150.00	James Dine & Company Box 22 Belvedere, CA 94920	Combines important technical, psychological, and business indicators concerning market.
Dow Theory Forecasts	Weekly	$148.00	Dow Theory Forecasts, Inc. 7412 Calument Ave. Hammond, IN 46325 (219) 931–6480	Forecasts of stock market based on Dow theory. List of blue chip stock choices.
Dow Theory Letter	Semi-monthly	$185.00	Dow Theory Letter Box 1759 La Jolla, CA 90238	Based principally on the Dow theory of technical analysis, which relies on past movements of the market averages to forecast future trends. Covers stocks, bonds, gold and T-bills for traders and investors.
Dun & Hargitt's Market Guide; Commodity Service	Weekly Weekly	$125.00 $130.00	Dunn & Hargitt, Inc. 22 N. 2nd St. Lafayette, IN 47902 (317) 423–2626	The market guide provides investment advice on stocks and options based on analyses of 1,000 leading stocks. The commodity service charts 34 of the most actively traded commodities. Includes buy and sell recommendations.
Forbes Special Situation Survey	Monthly	$395.00	Forbes Investors Advisory Inst., Inc. 60 Fifth Ave. New York, NY 10011 (212) 620–2200	Monthly looseleaf report discusses and recommends the purchase of one speculative equity security in each issue.
Granville Market Letter	46/yr	$250.00	Granville Market Letter Drawer O Holly Hill, FL 32017	Highly personal, colorful comments on political and economic developments. Relies exclusively on technical analysis for market timing and stock selection for the aggressive investor. Uses unique market indicators, which are explained in a bro-

Name	Frequency	Price	Address	Description
Growth Stock Outlook	Semi-monthly	$64.00	Growth Stock Outlook, Inc. 4405 E-W Hwy Bethesda, MD 20014 (order Box 9911, Chevy Chase, MD 20015) (301) 654–5205	calls. Those who pay an additional fee can subscribe to his telephone Early Warning Service. Reports on selected stocks with vigorous growth. The growth stock outlook gives specific buy-sell recommendations; the junior growth stock outlook does not.
Helm Investment Letter	24/yr	$150.00	Helm Investment Letter 729 SW Alder, Suite 420 Portland, OR 97205	Clearly written, with unambiguous forecasts based principally on technical analysis but also taking fundamentals into account. Recommendations include market timing, stock and bond selection, gold and silver, long and short sales. Provides separate portfolios for conservative and aggressive investors who are sufficiently sophisticated to engage in short sales.
Holt Investment Advisory	Semi-monthly	$180.00	T.J. Holt & Co., Inc. 290 Post Road West Westport, CT (203) 226–8911	Discusses the economy and stock market for investors concerned with long-term capital growth.
Investments For a Changing Economy	Monthly	Free	Merrill Lynch, Pierce, Fenner and Smith, Inc. New York, NY (offices in most major cities)	A monthly newsletter addressing one or two topics of particular current interest.
Investors Intelligence	Biweekly	$72.00	Investors Intelligence, Inc. 2 East Ave. Larchmont, NY 10538 (914) 834–5181	Evaluates stock market trends, recommends specific stocks, summarizes various investment advisory services recommendations, and notes insider transactions.
It's Your Money	Monthly	Free	Savings Banks Assn. of New York State 200 Park Ave. New York, NY 10017 (212) 598–9900	Newsletter with financial planning tips for average families.
The Johnson Survey	Monthly	$78.00	John S. Herold, Inc. 35 Mason St. Greenwich, CT 06830 (203) 869–2585	Data and comment on fast-growing OTC stocks, charts.
Junior Growth Stock Outlook	Semimonthly	$55.00	Growth Stock Outlook, Inc. 4405 E-W Hwy Bethesda, MD 20014 (order Box 9911, Chevy Chase, MD 20015) (301) 654–5205	Reports on selected stocks with vigorous growth. The growth stock outlook gives specific buy-sell recommendations; the junior growth stock outlook does not.

PUBLICATION	FREQUENCY OF PUBLICATION	YEARLY SUBSCRIPTION RATE	PUBLISHER	TYPE OF INFORMATION
The Kiplinger Washington Letter	Weekly	$42.00	Kiplinger Washington Editors, Inc. 1729 H Street, NW Washington, DC 20006	Newsletter. Briefings on business trends, pertinent government policies, and information on employment, investments, and interest rates.
Limited Partners Letter	Monthly	$197.00	Spectrum Financial Group Box 1146 Menlo Park, CA 94025 (800) 227–1617, ext. 408	Report that analyzes important tax, legal, and practical aspects of private and public partnership investments. Emphasis in the primary shelter areas of real estate, oil and gas, equipment leasing, and research and development.
MMI Memo	Semi-annual	Free	Household Finance Corporation Money Management Institute 2700 Sanders Rd. Prospect Heights, IL 60070 (312) 564–5000	Newsletter on consumer and personal finance topics.
Merrill Lynch Market Letter	24/yr	$44.00	Merrill Lynch Market Letter Box 60 Church Street Station New York, NY 10008	Draws on Merrill Lynch's research and analytical capabilities to provide comments on stock market behavior and direction and advice on individual stocks, including ML's ratings for near- and long-term performance, quality, and dividend potential.
Moody's Manuals and Financial Guides	Quarterly	Free	Moody's Investors Services, Inc. 99 Church St. New York, NY 10007	Brochure listing and describing Moody's various services and publications and providing price information.
Professionals' Financial and Tax Report	Biweekly	$125.00	J. Gary Sheets and Assoc. Box 1853 Salt Lake City, UT 84110 (801) 364–4335	Financial planning newsletter focusing on one or two investment or tax planning topics per issue. Geared toward doctors, lawyers, executives, and other highly compensated individuals.
Real Estate Investing Letter	Monthly	$79.00	Harcourt Brace Jovanovich, Inc. 757 Third Ave. New York, NY 10017 (212) 888–4444	Monthly newsletter covers real estate investments, including tax strategies, depreciation, and real estate syndication.
R.H.M. Survey of Warrants, Options & Low-Price Stocks	Weekly	$130.00	RHM Associates, Inc. 172 Forest Ave. Glen Cove, NY 11542 (516) 759–2904	Investment advice on warrants, call and put options, and low-priced stocks; tables and charts.

Name	Price	Frequency	Publisher/Address	Description
Howard Ruff's Financial Survival Report (formerly Ruff Times)	$69.00	48/yr	Howard Ruff's Financial Survival Report Box 2000 San Ramon, CA 94583	A readable, highly personal commentary on political and economic issues. Offers advice on "survival investments"—precious metals and stones, stamps and coins, gold stocks and real estate, money market funds and U.S. Treasury bonds. Ruff will not give outright buy or sell signals on stocks. Provides hot lines for updated price quotes, commentary, and personal investment advice.
Standard & Poor's Catalog of Services and Publications	Free	Quarterly	Standard & Poor's 345 Hudson St. New York, NY 10014 (212) 248–2525	Brochure listing and describing Standard & Poor's various services and publications and providing price information. Also lists addresses of S&P's branch and foreign offices.
The Stanger Report: A Guide to Tax Shelter Investing	$325.00	Monthly	Robert A. Stanger and Company 623 River Rd. Fair Haven, N.J. 07701	10-page monthly newsletter with topics of interest, tax planning ideas, news and views related to limited partnership ventures and other tax shelter investments.
Tax Angles	$60.00	Monthly	Kephart Communications 1300 N. 17th St., Suite 1660 Arlington, VA (804) 276–7100	A monthly newsletter of tax-saving ideas, strategies, and techniques and reviews of pending tax legislation of importance for personal tax and financial planning.
Tax Shelter Insider	$124.00	Monthly	Tax Reports Newsletter Associates 10076 Boca Entrada Blvd. Boca Raton, Florida 33433 (305) 483–2600	8-page monthly newsletter with 8 topic areas: Shelter Rulings—recent court cases; Shelter Strategy—tax planning strategies; Shelter News—new tax shelter ideas; Shelter Profile—key features of a current offering; Shelter Digest—topics in tax shelter financing and legislation; and Shelter Forum—answering reader queries.
Tax Shelter Investment Review	$177.00	Monthly	Leland Publishing Co. 81 Canal St. Boston, MA 02114 (617) 227–9314	Reports on currently available publicly offered tax shelter investments primarily in the major shelter industries of oil and gas, real estate, and leasing. Presents an investment outlook on these industries and provides advice on how to evaluate shelters from experts and practitioners in the shelter field.
Technical Digest	$125.00	20/yr (plus twice weekly *HOT-LINE*)	Technical Digest Woodland Rd. New Vernon, NJ 07976	A regular stock and bond market letter for investors; includes commentary, charts, statistics, recommendations, and summaries of other major market letters.

PUBLICATION	FREQUENCY OF PUBLICATION	YEARLY SUBSCRIPTION RATE	PUBLISHER	TYPE OF INFORMATION
Trendline	Weekly	$390.00	Trendline 25 Broadway New York, NY 10004 (800) 852-5200	Published by a division of Standard & Poor's, the Trendline Daily Action Stock Charts use bar charts to plot the daily price movements of NYSE, AMEX, and OTC stocks; in addition, they provide summary information on daily share volume, the 30-week moving average, and selected fundamental measures.
United Business & Investment Report	Weekly	$170.00	United Business Service Company 210 Newbury St. Boston, MA 02116 (617) 267-8855	Weekly newsletter evaluates stock market and other investment trends. Notes related federal developments; tables.
Value Line Investment Survey	Weekly	$365.00	Arnold Bernhard & Co., Inc. 5 E. 44 St. New York, NY 10017 (212) 687-3965	Weekly looseleaf booklet covers the business activities of corporations in a variety of industries; charts and graphs.
Value Line OTC Special Situations Service	Bimonthly	$300.00	Arnold Bernhard & Co., Inc. 5 E. 44 St. New York, NY 10017	Looseleaf newsletter contains information for investors on stocks traded OTC.
Weekly Insider Report	Weekly	$85.00	Stock Research Corp. 55 Liberty St. New York, NY 10005 (212) 482-8300	Information on stock transactions of 500 or more shares by corporate officers, directors, and 10% holders who buy or sell shares in their own company.
Wellington Letter	Monthly	$252.00	Wellington Letter Hawaii Bldg., Suite 1814 745 Fort St. Honolulu, HI 96813	For speculators, traders, and sophisticated investors interested in foreign currencies, interest rate futures, and metals as well as stocks and bonds. Recommendations are based on technical and fundamental analysis and consideration of economic trends.
Zweig Forecast	18/yr	$195.00	Zweig Forecast 747 Third Ave. New York, NY 10017	Tempers reliance on technical analysis for market timing, including several Zweig-developed indicators, with concern for basic economic trends. Stocks are picks derived from computer ranking based on fundamentals and market performance. Recommendations cover stocks, stock index futures, and on occa-

sion, hard money plays. Subscribers receive a telephone number to hear taped action recommendations, which are updated twice a week. Recommendations usually clear and concise.

DIRECTORIES AND SOURCE FINDERS FOR FINANCIAL PUBLICATIONS, NEWSLETTERS, AND INVESTMENT ADVISORIES

Broker-Dealer Directory	U.S. Securities and Exchange Commission Office of Registrations and Reports 500 N. Capital Street NW Washington, DC 20549	List of all broker-dealers registered with the Securities and Exchange Commission (quarterly, free).
Digest of Investment Advices	N. H. Mager, Editor Digest of Advices, Inc. 233 Broadway New York, NY 10007 (212) 233–6018	Monthly newsletter offers a digest of investment advisory services and financial and economic publications ($25).
Encyclopedia of Business Information Sources, 5th ed.	Gale Research Company Book Toner Detroit, MI 48226 (313) 961–2242	Comprehensive list and description of business and investment information sources ($148).
Investment Advisor Directory	U.S. Securities and Exchange Commission 500 N. Capital Street NW Washington, DC 20549	List of investment advisors registered with the Securities and Exchange Commission (free).
Money Market Directory	Money Market Directories, Inc. 370 Lexington Ave. New York, NY 10017 (800) 446–2810	Information on investment management including tax-exempt funds, investment services, and research departments of brokerage firms ($395).
The Performance of The Best Investment Advisory Services	R.L. Spencer Oddjohn New York, NY	Lists and evaluates the leading investment advisory services.
Sophisticated Investor	Select Information Exchange 2095 Broadway New York, NY 10023 (212) 874–6408	Irregularly issued catalog provides a directory to publications and services concerned with business and investment in the United States and abroad ($1).
Ulrich's International Periodicals Directory	R.R. Bowker Company New York, NY	Comprehensive directory of all periodicals published in the United States and abroad (annual).
Where To Find Business Information: A Worldwide Guide for Everyone Who Needs the Answers to Business Questions	David M. Brownstone and Gorton Carruth John Wiley & Sons, Inc. New York, NY 10016	Book. Names, addresses, prices, and brief description of business and financial publications cross-referenced by topic, publisher, and title.

MAJOR BROKERAGE FIRMS

Full-Service Brokerage

Brokerage houses with research departments provide much information for both individual and institutional investors. Most large brokerage houses maintain substantial research staffs. In addition to transacting clients' orders, they publish market letters or market reviews. They provide individual company analyses and recommendations and industry studies. They undertake portfolio reviews. If you tell them the approximate amount you wish to invest, they will provide a suggested portfolio in line with the investment objective you have indicated. Some of the leading full-service brokerage houses with research departments and offices in virtually every part of the country include:

Dean Witter Reynolds
Drexel Burnham Lambert
A. G. Edwards & Sons
E. F. Hutton & Company
Kidder, Peabody & Co.
Merrill Lynch, Pierce, Fenner and Smith

Paine Webber
Prudential-Bache Securities
Shearson/American Express
Smith Barney, Harris Upham & Co.
Thomson, McKinnon Securities

There are also many smaller national or regional firms that may specialize in one or more areas of investments such as commodity trading, options, stocks listed on regional exchanges, or tax-sheltered limited partnerships.

Discount Brokers

Discount brokers are brokers who simply transact their customers' orders to buy and sell as directed, offering no advice, recommendations, or research service. Commission fees are typically 30 to 70% less than commission fees for orders transacted by full-service brokerage houses. The following list provides the names and addresses of most of the major national discount brokers.

Wm. J. Aronson & Co., Inc.
39 Broadway
New York, NY 10006

Liss, Tenner & Goldberg
Securities Corp.
470 Colfax
Clifton, NJ

Rose & Company
Investment Brokers, Inc.
Board of Trade Building
141 W. Jackson, Suite 1270
Chicago, IL 60604

Source Securities Corporation
70 Pine St.
New York, NY 10005

Brown & Company Securities
7 Water St.
Boston, MA 02109

Ovest Securities, Inc.
76 Beaver St.
New York, NY 10005

Royal Investors Group, Inc.
120 Wall St.
New York, NY 10005

Stock & Trade
580 Fifth Ave.
New York, NY 10036

Discount Brokerage Corporation
67 Wall St.
New York, NY 10005

Andrew Peck Associates, Inc.
32 Broadway
New York, NY 10004

Charles Schwab & Co., Inc.
650 Fifth Ave.
New York, NY 10019

Tradex Brokerage Service, Inc.
82 Beaver St.
New York, NY 10005

Fidelity Brokerage Services, Inc.
Box 2698
161 Devonshire St.
Boston, MA 02208

Quick & Reilly, Inc.
3 Penn Center Plaza
Philadelphia, PA 19102

Muriel Siebert & Co., Inc.
77 Water St.
New York, NY 10005

York Securities, Inc.
44 Wall St.
New York, NY 10005

NO-LOAD MUTUAL FUNDS

The following is a list of no-load mutual funds. Although the list is not all-inclusive, it does contain pertinent information (addresses, phone numbers, and purchase requirements) on nearly 150 of the larger/more popular funds. The funds are listed by types, including growth funds, funds that seek maximum capital gains, income funds, balanced funds, bond funds, money funds, and specialty funds.

Growth Funds

FUND NAME / Address and Telephone	PURCHASE REQUIREMENTS Initial	Subsequent
American Investors Box 2500 Greenwich, CT 06836 (800) 243–5353/(203) 622–1600	$ 400	$ 20
Boston Company Capital Appreciation Box 2537 Boston, MA 02208 (800) 343–0573/(617) 956–9740	1,000	0
Bull and Bear Capital Growth 11 Hanover Square New York, NY 10005 (800) 847–4200/(212) 785–0900	1,000	100
Fidelity Contrafund 82 Devonshire St. Boston, MA 02109 (800) 225–6190/(617) 523–1919	1,000	250
Fidelity Trend 82 Devonshire St. Boston, MA 02109 (800) 225–6190/(617) 523–1919	1,000	250
Founders Growth 655 Broadway, Suite 700 Denver, CO 80203 (800) 525–2440/(303) 595–3863	250	25
Ivest Fund Box 2600 Valley Forge, PA 19482 (800) 523–7025/(215) 648–6000	500	50
Ivy Fund 40 Industrial Park Rd. Hingham, MA 02043 (617) 749–1416	500	100
Lehman Capital 55 Water St. New York, NY 10041 (800) 221–5350/(212) 558–3288	2,500	1,000
Lindner Fund 200 S. Bemiston Ave. St. Louis, MO 63105 (314) 727–5305	2,000	100

FUND NAME / Address and Telephone	PURCHASE REQUIREMENTS Initial	Subsequent
Mathers Fund 125 S. Wacker Dr. Chicago, IL 60606 (312) 236–8215	$ 1,000	$ 200
W. L. Morgan Growth Box 2600 Valley Forge, PA 19482 (800) 523–7025/(215) 648–6000	500	50
Mutual Shares Corporation 26 Broadway New York, NY 10004 (800) 221–7864/(212) 908–4048	1,000	0
Nicholas Fund 312 E. Wisconsin Ave. Milwaukee, WI 53202 (414) 272–6133	500	100
Partners Fund 342 Madison Ave. New York, NY 10173 (800) 225–1596/(212) 850–8300	250	0
Penn Square Mutual 101 N. Fifth St. Box 1491 Reading, PA 19603 (800) 523–8440/(215) 376–6771	250	0
T. Rowe Price Growth Stock 100 E. Pratt St. Baltimore, MD 21202 (800) 638–5660/(301) 547–2308	500	50
T. Rowe Price New Era 100 E. Pratt St. Baltimore, MD 21202 (800) 638–5660/(301) 547–2308	1,000	100
Scudder Capital Growth 175 Federal St. Boston, MA 02110 (800) 225–2470/(617) 482–3990	1,000	0

FUND NAME Address and Telephone	PURCHASE REQUIREMENTS Initial	Subsequent
Scudder Common Stock 175 Federal St. Boston, MA 02110 (800) 225–2470/(617) 482–3990	$ 1,000	$ 0
Steinroe and Farnham Capital Opportunities 150 S. Wacker Dr. Chicago, IL 60606 (800) 621–0320/(312) 368–7800	2,500	100
Steinroe and Farnham Stock 150 S. Wacker Dr. Chicago, IL 60606 (800) 621–0320/(312) 368–7800	2,500	100

FUND NAME Address and Telephone	PURCHASE REQUIREMENTS Initial	Subsequent
Steinroe Universe 150 S. Wacker Dr. Chicago, IL 60606 (800) 621–0320/(312) 368–7800	$ 5,000	$ 100
Twentieth Century Select Box 200 Kansas City, MO 64141 (816) 531–5575	0	0
USAA Mutual Growth USAA Bldg. San Antonio, TX 78288 (800) 531–8181/(512) 690–6062	1,000	25

Funds That Seek Maximum Capital Gains

FUND NAME Address and Telephone	PURCHASE REQUIREMENTS Initial	Subsequent
Acorn Fund 120 S. LaSalle St., Room 1330 Chicago, IL 60603 (312) 621–0630	$ 1,000	$ 200
Constellation Growth 331 Madison Ave. New York, NY 10017 (212) 557–8784	1,000	100
Financial Dynamics Box 2040 Denver, CO 80201 (800) 525–9831/(303) 779–1233	500	25
Explorer Box 2600 Valley Forge, PA 19482 (800) 523–7025/(215) 648–6000	3,000	50
44 Wall Street Fund 150 Broadway New York, NY 10038 (800) 221–7836/(212) 267–2820	25,000	100

FUND NAME Address and Telephone	PURCHASE REQUIREMENTS Initial	Subsequent
T. Rowe Price New Horizons 100 E. Pratt St. Baltimore, MD 21202 (800) 638–5660/(301) 547–2308	$ 1,000	$ 100
Scudder Development 175 Federal St. Boston, MA 02110 (800) 225–2470/(617) 482–3990	1,000	0
Steinroe Special Fund 150 S. Wacker Dr. Chicago, IL 60606 (800) 621–0320/(312) 368–7800	2,500	100
Tudor One New York Plaza, 30th floor New York, NY 10004 (800) 223–3332/(212) 908–9582	250	50
Twentieth Century Growth Box 200 Kansas City, MO 64141 (816) 531–5575	0	0

FUND NAME / Address and Telephone	Initial	Subsequent
655 Broadway, Suite 700 Denver, CO 80203 (800) 525-2440/(303) 595-3863		
Hartwell Leverage 515 Madison Ave. New York, NY 10022 (212) 308-3355	5,000	50
Janus 100 Fillmore St., Suite 300 Denver, CO 80206 (800) 525-3713/(303) 333-3863	1,000	100
North Star Stock 1100 Dain Tower Box 1160 Minneapolis, MN 55440 (612) 371-7780	1,000	100
Pennsylvania Mutual 1414 Avenue of the Americas New York, NY 10019 (800) 122-5585/(212) 355-7311	1,000	50
Box 200 Kansas City, MO 64141 (816) 531-5575		
USAA Sunbelt Era USAA Bldg. San Antonio, TX 78288 (800) 531-8181/(512) 690-6062	1,000	25
Value Line Leveraged Growth 711 Third Ave. New York, NY 10017 (800) 223-0818/(212) 687-3965	250	0
Value Line Special Situations 711 Third Ave. New York, NY 10017 (800) 223-0818/(212) 687-3965	250	0
Weingarten Equity 331 Madison Ave. New York, NY 10017 (212) 557-8784	1,000	100

Income Funds

FUND NAME / Address and Telephone	PURCHASE REQUIREMENTS Initial	Subsequent
Babson Income Trust 2440 Pershing Rd., G-15 Kansas City, MO 64108 (800) 821-5591/(816) 471-5200	$ 500	$ 50
Boston Co. Government Income Fund Box 2537 Boston, MA 02208 (800) 343-0573/(617) 956-9740	1,000	0
Dreyfus A Bonds Plus 600 Madison Ave. New York, NY 10022 (800) 645-6561/(212) 895-1206	2,500	100
Fidelity Corporate Bond 82 Devonshire St. Boston, MA 02109 (800) 225-6190/(617) 523-1919	2,500	250
Fidelity Equity Income 82 Devonshire St. Boston, MA 02109 (800) 225-6190/(617) 523-1919	$ 1,000	$ 250
Financial Industrial Income Box 2040 Denver, CO 80201 (800) 525-9831/(303) 779-1233	500	25
Mutual Qualified Income 26 Broadway New York, NY 10004 (800) 221-7864/(212) 908-4048	1,000	0
Northeast Investors Trust 50 Congress St. Boston, MA 02109 (800) 225-6704/(617) 523-3588	500	0

FUND NAME / Address and Telephone	PURCHASE REQUIREMENTS Initial	Subsequent
North Star Bond, 110 Dain Tower, Box 1160, Minneapolis, MN 55440, (612) 371–7780	$ 1,000	$ 100
T. Rowe Price New Income, 100 E. Pratt St., Baltimore, MD 21202, (800) 638–5660/(301) 547–2308	1,000	100
Pro Income, 1107 Bethlehem Pike, Flourtown, PA 19031, (800) 523–0864/(215) 836–1300	300	0
Qualified Dividend Portfolio l, Box 2600, Valley Forge, PA 19482, (800) 523–7025/(215) 648–6000	3,000	50
Safeco Special Bond, Safeco Plaza, T15, Seattle, WA 98185, (800) 426–6730/(206) 545–5530	200	25
Scudder Income, 175 Federal St., Boston, MA 02110, (800) 225–2470/(617) 482–3990	1,000	0

FUND NAME / Address and Telephone	PURCHASE REQUIREMENTS Initial	Subsequent
Steadman Associated, 1730 K Street NW, Washington, DC 20006, (800) 424–8570/(202) 223–1000	$ 25	$ 0
Steinroe Bond, 150 S. Wacker Dr., Chicago, IL 60606, (800) 621–0320/(312) 368–7800	2,500	100
Value Line Income, 711 Third Ave., New York, NY 10017, (800) 223–0818/(212) 687–3965	250	0
Vanguard GNMA Portfolio, Box 2600, Valley Forge, PA 19482, (800) 523–7025/(215) 648–6000	3,000	50
Vanguard High Yield Bond, Box 2600, Valley Forge, PA 19482, (800) 523–7025/(215) 648–6000	3,000	50
Wellesley Income, Box 2600, Valley Forge, PA 19482, (800) 523–7025/(215) 648–6000	500	50

Balanced Funds

FUND NAME / Address and Telephone	PURCHASE REQUIREMENTS Initial	Subsequent
Babson Investment Fund, 2440 Pershing Rd., G-15, Kansas City, MO 64108, (800) 821–5591/(816) 471–5200	$ 500	$ 50
Drexel Burnham Fund, 60 Broad St., New York, NY 10004	1,000	250

FUND NAME / Address and Telephone	PURCHASE REQUIREMENTS Initial	Subsequent
One William Street, 55 Water St., New York, NY 10041, (800) 221–5350/(212) 558–3288	$ 500	$ 50
T. Rowe Price Growth and Income, 100 E. Pratt St., Baltimore, MD 21202	1,000	100

Fund Name / Address and Telephone	Initial	Subsequent
600 Madison Ave. New York, NY 10022 (800) 645-6561/(212) 895-1206		
Fidelity Fund 82 Devonshire St. Boston, MA 02109 (800) 225-6190/(617) 523-1919	1,000	250
Financial Industrial Fund Box 2040 Denver, CO 80201 (800) 525-9831/(303) 779-1233	1,000	100
Guardian Mutual 342 Madison Ave. New York, NY 10017 (800) 225-1596/(212) 850-8300	200	50
Istel Fund 345 Park Ave. New York, NY 10154 (212) 644-2800	500	1 share
Loomis-Sayles Mutual 225 Franklin St. Boston, MA 02110 (800) 225-7670/(617) 267-6600	250	50
150 S. Wacker Dr. Chicago, IL 60606 (800) 621-0320/(312) 368-7800	250	0
Value Line Fund 711 Third Ave. New York, NY 10017 (800) 223-0818/(212) 687-3965	1,500	50
Vanguard Index Trust Box 2600 Valley Forge, PA 19482 (800) 523-7025/(215) 648-6000	500	50
Wellington Fund Box 2600 Valley Forge, PA 19482 (800) 523-7025/(215) 648-6000	500	50
Windsor Fund Box 2600 Valley Forge, PA 19482 (800) 523-7025/(215) 648-6000	500	50

Municipal Bond Funds

	PURCHASE REQUIREMENTS	
FUND NAME — Address and Telephone	Initial	Subsequent
Babson Tax-Free Income Fund—Long Term 2440 Pershing Rd., G-15 Kansas City, MO 64108 (800) 821-5591/(816) 471-5200	$ 1,000	$ 100
Calvert Tax-Free Reserve—Ltd. Term Port. 1700 Pennsylvania Ave., NW Washington, DC 20006 (800) 368-2748/(301) 951-4820	2,000	250
Composite Tax-Exempt Bond Fund Sea First Financial Center, 9th floor Spokane WA 99201 (800) 541-0830/(509) 624-4101	1,000	500
Dreyfus Tax-Exempt Bond Fund 600 Madison Ave. New York, NY 10022 (800) 645-6561/(212) 895-1206	$ 2,500	$ 100
Federated Short-Intermediate Muni Trust 421 Seventh Ave. Pittsburgh, PA 15219 (412) 288-1948	25,000	0
Fidelity High Yield Municipal 82 Devonshire St. Boston, MA 02109 (800) 225-6190/(617) 523-1919	2,500	250

FUND NAME / Address and Telephone	PURCHASE REQUIREMENTS	
	Initial	Subsequent
Fidelity Municipal Bond Fund 82 Devonshire St. Boston, MA 02109 (800) 225-6190/(617) 523-1919	$ 2,500	$ 250
Nuveen Municipal Bond Fund 208 S. LaSalle St. Chicago, IL 60604 (312) 621-3000	1,000	100
T. Rowe Price Tax-Free Income Fund 100 E. Pratt St. Baltimore, MD 21202 (800) 638-5660/(301) 547-2308	2,000	100
Safeco Municipal Bond Fund Safeco Plaza, T15 Seattle, WA 98185 (800) 426-6730/(206) 545-5530	2,500	250
Scudder Managed Municipal Bonds 175 Federal St. Boston, MA 02110 (800) 225-2470/(617) 482-3990	$ 1,000	$ 0
Steinroe Tax-Exempt Bond Fund 150 S. Wacker Dr. Chicago, IL 60606 (800) 621-0320/(312) 368-7800	2,500	100
Vanguard Municipal Bond—Intermediate Box 2600 Valley Forge, PA 19482 (800) 523-7025/(215) 648-6000	3,000	50
Vanguard Municipal Bond—Long Term Box 2600 Valley Forge, PA 19482 (800) 523-7025/(215) 648-6000	3,000	50

Money Market Funds

FUND NAME / Address and Telephone	PURCHASE REQUIREMENTS	
	Initial	Subsequent
Cash Equivalent Fund—MM Portfolio 120 S. LaSalle St. Chicago, IL 60603 (312) 781-1121	$ 1,000	$ 100
Current Investment Fund 333 Clay St., Suite 4300 Houston, TX 77002 (713) 751-2400	1,000	100
DBL Cash Fund—MM Portfolio 60 Broad St. New York, NY 10004 (212) 486-6000	1,000	100
Daily Cash Accumulation Fund 3600 S. Yosemite St. Denver, CO 80237	2,500	100
Merrill Lynch Ready Assets 165 Broadway New York, NY 10080 (212) 637-6310	$ 5,000	$1,000
Moneymart Assets 100 Gold St. New York, NY 10038 (212) 791-7123	1,000	500
National Liquid Reserves 333 W. 34 St. New York, NY 10001 (212) 613-2619	1,000	100
Paine Webber Cash Fund 140 Broadway, 27th floor New York, NY 10005 (212) 437-6817	5,000	500

FUND NAME / Address and Telephone	Initial	Subsequent
7 Penn Center Plaza, Philadelphia, PA 19103, (215) 988–1200		
Dreyfus Liquid Assets, 600 Madison Ave., New York, NY 10022, (800) 645–6561/(212) 895–1206	2,500	100
Fidelity Cash Reserves, 82 Devonshire St., Boston, MA 02109, (800) 225–6190/(617) 523–1919	1,000	250
IDS Cash Management Fund, Box 369, IDS Tower, Minneapolis, MN 55440, (800) IDS–IDEA/(612) 372–2897	2,000	100
Kemper Money Market Fund, 120 S. LaSalle St., Chicago, IL 60603, (312) 845–1810	1,000	100
Liquid Capital Income Fund, 1331 Euclid Ave., Cleveland, OH 44115, (800) 231–2322/(216) 781–4440	1,000	500
100 E. Pratt St., Baltimore, MD 21202, (800) 628–5660/(301) 547–2308		
Reserve Fund—Primary Portfolio, 810 Seventh Ave., New York, NY 10019, (212) 977–9880	1,000	1,000
Scudder Cash Investment Trust, 175 Federal St., Boston, MA 02110, (800) 225–2470/(617) 482–3990	1,000	0
Shearson Daily Dividend, Two World Trade Center, New York, NY 10048, (212) 321–6554	5,000	1,000
Vanguard Money Market Trust/Prime Portfolio, Box 2600, Valley Forge, PA 19482, (800) 523–7025/(215) 648–6000	1,000	100
Webster Cash Reserve Fund, 20 Exchange Place, New York, NY 10005, (212) 635–5081	1,500	500

Money Market Funds—U.S. Government Securities Only

FUND NAME		PURCHASE REQUIREMENTS	
Address and Telephone		Initial	Subsequent
AARP U.S. Government Money Market Trust, 421 Seventh Ave., Pittsburgh, PA 15219, (412) 392–6300		$ 500	$ 100
Capital Preservation Fund, 755 Page Mill Rd., Palo Alto, CA 94304, (800) 227–8380		1,000	100
Capital Preservation Fund II, 755 Page Mill Rd., Palo Alto, CA 94304, (800) 227–8380		5,000	100
Dreyfus Money Market Instruments—Gov't Series, 600 Madison Ave., New York, NY 10022, (800) 645–6561/(212) 895–1206		$ 2,500	$ 100
Fund for Government Investors, 1835 K Street NW, Washington, DC 20006, (202) 861–1800		2,500	500
Merrill Lynch Government Fund, 165 Broadway, New York, NY 10080, (212) 637–6310		5,000	1,000

FUND NAME / Address and Telephone	PURCHASE REQUIREMENTS Initial	Subsequent
Shearson Government and Agencies Fund Two World Trade Center New York, NY 10048 (212) 321–6554	$ 5,000	$1,000
Trust for Short-Term Fed. Securities/ Federal Funds 421 Seventh Ave. Pittsburgh, PA 15219 (412) 288–1900	1,000	0
U.S. Treasury Securities Fund—MM Box 29467 San Antonio, TX 78229 (512) 696–1234	$ 1,500	$ 50

Tax-Exempt Money Market Funds

FUND NAME / Address and Telephone	PURCHASE REQUIREMENTS Initial	Subsequent
Calvert Tax-Free Reserve—MM Portfolio 1700 Pennsylvania Ave. NW Washington, DC 20006 (800) 368–2748/(301) 951–4820	$ 2,000	$ 250
Carnegie Tax-Free Income Trust 1331 Euclid Ave. Cleveland, OH 44115 (800) 321–2322/(216) 781–4440	5,000	500
Daily Tax-Free Income Fund 100 Park Ave. New York, NY 10017 (212) 370–1110	5,000	100
Fidelity Tax-Exempt Money Market Trust 82 Devonshire St. Boston, MA 02109 (800) 225–6190/(617) 523–1919	10,000	500
Municipal Bond for Temporary Investments Webster Building, Suite 204 Concord Plaza, 3411 Silverside Rd. Wilmington, DE 19810 (800) 441–7450	1,000	0
Nuveen Tax-Free Reserves 208 S. LaSalle St. Chicago, IL 60604 (312) 621–3000	$ 1,000	$ 100
T. Rowe Price Tax-Exempt Money Fund 100 E. Pratt St. Baltimore, MD 21202 (800) 638–5660/(301) 547–2308	1,000	100
Scudder Tax-Free Money Fund 175 Federal St. Boston, MA 02110 (800) 225–2470/(617) 482–3990	1,000	0
Tax-Exempt Money Market Fund 120 S. LaSalle St. Chicago, IL 60603 (312) 845–1811	1,000	100
Tax-Free Money Fund 333 W. 34 St. New York, NY 10001 (212) 613–2619	10,000	1,000

Specialty Funds

FUND NAME / Address and Telephone	PURCHASE REQUIREMENTS Initial	Subsequent
Analytical Optioned Equity 2222 Martin St., Suite 230 Irvine, CA 92715 (714) 833–0294	$25,000	$1,000
Century Shares Trust 50 Congress St. Boston, MA 02109 (800) 225–6704/(617) 482–3060	500	25
Energy Fund 342 Madison Ave. New York, NY 10173 (800) 225–1596/(212) 850–8300	100	25
Energy and Utilities Shares Box 550 Blue Bell, PA 19422 (215) 542–8025	1,000	100
Gateway Option Income 1120 Carew Tower Cincinnati, OH 45202 (513) 621–7774	500	100
Golcanda Investors 11 Hanover Square New York, NY 10005 (800) 847–4200/(212) 785–0900	1,000	25
G. T. Pacific 601 Montgomery St., Suite 1400 San Francisco, CA 94111 (800) 824–1580/(415) 392–6181	500	100

FUND NAME / Address and Telephone	PURCHASE REQUIREMENTS Initial	Subsequent
Lexington Goldfund 580 Sylvan Ave. Englewood Cliffs, NJ 07632 (800) 526–4791	$ 1,000	$ 50
Medical Technology Fund 1107 Bethlehem Pike Flourtown, PA 19031 (800) 523–0864/(215) 836–1300	1,000	0
National Aviation and Technology Corp. 50 Broad St. New York, NY 10004 (212) 482–8100	500	0
Precious Metals Holdings One Post Office Square Boston, MA 02109 (617) 338–4420	1,000	250
T. Rowe Price International 100 E. Pratt St. Baltimore, MD 21202 (800) 638–5660/(301) 547–2308	5,000	1,000
Scudder International 175 Federal St. Boston, MA 02110 (800) 225–2470/(617) 482–3990	1,000	0
United Services Gold Shares Box 29467 San Antonio, TX 78229 (800) 531–5777/(512) 696–1234	500	50

SOURCES OF COMPUTER SOFTWARE

The following is a description of nearly 40 investment and financial planning software packages that are compatible with most of the more popular personal computers (IBM, Apple, Commodore, etc.). The list includes software that can be used with the evaluation of common stocks, bonds, stock options, commodities, financial features, convertibles, real estate, and preferred stock, as well as portfolio management, tax planning, financial planning, charting/technical analysis, and tax-sheltered investments. This list *does NOT represent an endorsement of the products*, but provides a representative sample of the types of software that are available to individual investors for use on home computers.

Aardvark Software, Inc.
783 N. Water Street
Milwaukee, WI 53202
(414) 289–9988

Estate Tax Plan: Computes complex calculations associated with estate planning. Allows "what if" assumption exploring and reviews alternatives such as the special use valuation, marital deduction options, charitable bequests, and outright gifting. Calculates the estate tax liability.

Professional Tax Plan: Problem-solving tool that determines accurate answers to various "what if" tax situations. Calculates up to five different fact situations simultaneously, facilitating comparative analysis. Calculates the federal income tax liability.

CE Software
801-73rd Street
Des Moines, IA 50312
(515) 224–1995

Bond Yielder: Provides a quick and accurate method of evaluating and comparing a variety of fixed-income securities. Provides the following calculations for any fixed-income security: yield to maturity, yield after capital gains tax, equivalent taxable return, accrued interest, and bond equivalent yield.

Chang Laboratories, Inc.
5300 Stevens Creek Blvd.
San Jose, CA 95129
(408) 246–8020

MicroPlan: Provides advanced financial planning tools with built-in formulas for cash flow analysis, capital budgeting, tax-shelter analysis, business needs, etc. Advanced financial commands include loan amortization, internal rate of return, depreciation, and tax computations.

Compu Trac
1021 9th Street
New Orleans, LA 70115
(800) 535–7990/(504) 895–1474

before- and after-tax yields, return on equity, and internal rate of return. Sensitivity analysis feature permits rapid change of assumptions and revised projections.

H & H Scientific
13507 Pendleton Street
Ft. Washington, MD 20744
(301) 292–2958

Stock Option Analyst Program (SOAP): Uses the Black/Scholes formula to calculate the fair market price of options based on the price of the underlying stock, dividends paid, volatility, current interest rates, and the time remaining on the option. Provides "what if" calculations for complicated stock options positions (straddles and spreads).

IFDS, Inc.
P.O. Box 888870
Atlanta, GA 30356
(404) 256–6447

IFDS Financial Planning Software: Integrated system that includes income tax, retirement, education and investment planning, cash management, risk management, and postmortem planning.

Independence Strategies
12077 Wilshire Blvd., Suite 755
Los Angeles, CA 90025
(213) 390–3820

Selfplan: Program facilitates the comparison of alternative investment strategies. Divides an individual's activities into four major groups: investments, lifestyle, cash management, and employment. Highlights the impact of decisions regarding these groups on an investor's cash flow and equity position.

Investech, Inc.
P.O. Box 1006
Jackson, MS 39205
(601) 355–1335

Bond Scholar: Bond system that computes, compares, and plots duration, and yield to call on mortgages, eurobonds, sinking fund preferred stock, and original issue discount bonds. Evaluates bond swaps and relative value based on reinvestment assumptions.

programs include regression analysis, on-balance volume, point and figure charts, and moving averages.

Intra-Day Analyst: Group of 14 different analytical programs with graphic representation used in conjunction with a quote machine to input tic by tic to show short-term trends for the day trader.

Crawford Data Systems
P.O. Box 705
Soomis, CA 93066
(805) 484–4159

Option X: Finds overpriced and underpriced stock options. Calculations include: intrinsic value of an option, leverage, implied volatility, dividends paid to expiration, hedge ratio, expected profit, and risk/reward ratio. Compares and analyzes the time-differentiated options on a single security to allow the investor to choose best option investment opportunity.

Dow Jones & Co.
P.O. Box 300
Princeton, NJ 08540
(800) 345–8500

Dow Jones Investment Evaluator: Interacts with Dow Jones News/Retrieval to provide a completely automated portfolio management program. System automatically updates and tracks the fundamental position and price/return performance of all the stocks held in an individual portfolio.

Dow Jones Market Analyzer: Displays and constructs moving averages, price and volume charts, support and resistance lines, and other technical analysis with information from Dow Jones News/Retrieval System.

Dow Jones Market Manager: Manages single or multiple portfolios with stock quotes from Dow Jones News/Retrieval System. Evaluates current portfolio and maintains a year-to-date record of all securities transactions. Displays gains or losses in relation to current market prices.

Dow Jones Market Microscope: Produces screening reports, price alerts, and rank matrices of financial indicators using Dow Jones News/Retrieval System. Sorts and stores extensive financial information on hundreds of companies and industries.

Good Software Corp.
12900 Preston Rd., Suite 610
Dallas, TX 75230
(214) 239–6085

Investor III: Evaluates real estate investments. Twenty-year projections can be calculated, showing ACRS (depreciation), future property values, mortgage balances, capital gains and recapture taxes.

Leonard Financial Planning Systems, Inc.
Box 30365
Raleigh, NC 27622
(919) 781–1451

The Leonard System: Sophisticated software system providing comprehensive financial planning. Addresses areas of income tax planning, vital statistics, estate planning, risk management, retirement needs, education funding, investment tracking, and leverage considerations.

Leonard Mini-Plan: Integrated software system that is less elaborate than the Leonard System. Addresses all key financial planning disciplines and is designed for brevity and flexibility.

Micro Lab
2699 Skokie Valley Road
Highland Park, IL 60035
(800) 323–9083/(312) 433–7550

Tax Manager: Complex tax management system that analyzes tax information and produces a completed 1040 form and all additional schedules.

The Wall Streeter: Collection of stock analysis and management programs. Keeps track of gains and losses on initial investments and has a data base of 1,000 records of shares owned, purchase and sale price, dates, interest and dividends. Tracks movements of security prices with use of technical analysis.

Asset Manager: Comprehensive asset management system that ensures accurate record keeping and appropriate application of current tax laws to depreciable assets. Handles 999 assets and up to 10 businesses and rental properties for an individual taxpayer.

Money Tree Software
760 SW Madison Ave.
Corvallis, OR 97333
(800) 533–3914/(503) 757–1114

MoneyCalc: Complete spreadsheet program integrating 9 different financial planning software packages. Program includes pension/profit sharing analysis, financial statements forecasting, asset analysis, income tax analysis, incorporation feasability study, investment diversification, retirement planning, buy/sell agreement, tax-sheltered investment analysis and estate planning.

Remote Computing Corp.
1076 E. Meadow Circle
Palo Alto, CA 94303
(415) 494–6111

PEAR Portfolio Management System: Organizes transaction information into two sets of files: one for securities information and one for portfolio position information. Produces a summary of capital gains and losses (realized and unrealized), investment income, and an appraisal of the portfolio.

PEAR Technical Analysis: Analyzes data using a variety of charting and graphic techniques. Retrieves and stores price, volume, and other data for publicly traded securities, financial futures, commodities, and options through Merlin's DIAL/DATA base.

Savant Corp.
P.O. Box 440278
Houston, TX 77244
(800) 231–9900/(713) 556–8363

Savant Investment Series: Three software packages which stand alone or can be integrated into one system:
Technical Investor: sophisticated technical data base and charting package
Fundamental Investor: fundamental data base and analysis package
Investor's Portfolio: complete portfolio management and analysis package

Simple Soft, Inc.
480 Eagle Drive, Suite 101
Elk Grove, IL 60007
(312) 364–0752

Real Estate Investor: Includes two systems on one disk: the Individual Residence Analysis and the Income Property Analysis. Evaluates different financing alternatives, taxes, cash flow, and the impact of inflation for investment property and individual residence. Allows investor to analyze a wide range of investment opportunities.

Loan Analyzer: Provides analysis of loans and mortgage instruments. Completely eliminates the need for payment books and is an excellent tool for borrowers and lenders.

Depreciation Analyzer: Performs a complete analysis of asset purchases, including all tax implictions. Useful for any type of asset, from small office equipment to large industrial machinery.

Sterling Wentworth Corp.
2744 Aspen Circle

Salt Lake City, UT 84109
(801) 487–2515

Planman: Financing planning computer system with "programmed intelligence." The system integrates tax planning, cash flow analysis, investment performance evaluation and asset diversification, real estate analysis, retirement and estate planning analysis, and insurance needs analysis.

Sunrise Software
36 Palm Court
Menlo Park, CA 94025
(415) 441–2351

Tax Mini-Miser: Allows investor to quickly compute and analyze effects of different tax strategies. Computes six alternative strategies in one year or one tax strategy over six years.

Technical Data
1 Post Office Square
Boston, MA 02109
(800) 343–7745/(617) 482–8799

Bond Swap Analyzer: Determines the cash flow impact of proposed bond swap. Analyzes the profitability and tax consequences of bond swaps using various market rate assumptions.

The Yield Calculator: Calculates yields and prices on a variety of bonds including the yield to maturity, yield to call, after-tax yield, and other relevant information.

Fixed Income Portfolio: Analyzes multiple fixed-income portfolios. Produces portfolio statistics, weighted averages, and distributions.

Rate of Return Analyzer: Calculates annualized rates of return for fixed-income securities based on market rate and reinvestment rate assumptions. Allows investor to choose optimum security for inclusion in a portfolio.

XQ Software, Inc.
4357 Park Drive
Norcross, GA 30093
(404) 923–2880

Investment Strategist: Determines the economic value of tax-sheltered investments. Compares expected rate of return on tax shelters with other types of investments. Analyzes tax and investment aspects of tax-sheltered investments.

Tax Strategist: Calculates the right amount of tax shelter needed to reach a desired tax reduction goal. Evaluates tax reduction strategies and capable of computing the federal income tax liability for up to ten years.

APPENDIX B
Financial Tables

Table B.1   Compound-Value Interest Factors for One Dollar
Table B.2   Compound-Value Interest Factors for a One-Dollar Annuity
Table B.3   Present-Value Interest Factors for One Dollar
Table B.4   Present-Value Interest Factors for a One-Dollar Annuity

Table B.1   Compound-Value Interest Factors for One Dollar, CVIF

INTEREST RATE

Year	1%	2%	3%	4%	5%	6%	7%	8%	9%	10%
1	1.010	1.020	1.030	1.040	1.050	1.060	1.070	1.080	1.090	1.100
2	1.020	1.040	1.061	1.082	1.102	1.124	1.145	1.166	1.188	1.210
3	1.030	1.061	1.093	1.125	1.158	1.191	1.225	1.260	1.295	1.331
4	1.041	1.082	1.126	1.170	1.216	1.262	1.311	1.360	1.412	1.464
5	1.051	1.104	1.159	1.217	1.276	1.338	1.403	1.469	1.539	1.611
6	1.062	1.126	1.194	1.265	1.340	1.419	1.501	1.587	1.677	1.772
7	1.072	1.149	1.230	1.316	1.407	1.504	1.606	1.714	1.828	1.949
8	1.083	1.172	1.267	1.369	1.477	1.594	1.718	1.851	1.993	2.144
9	1.094	1.195	1.305	1.423	1.551	1.689	1.838	1.999	2.172	2.358
10	1.105	1.219	1.344	1.480	1.629	1.791	1.967	2.159	2.367	2.594
11	1.116	1.243	1.384	1.539	1.710	1.898	2.105	2.332	2.580	2.853
12	1.127	1.268	1.426	1.601	1.796	2.012	2.252	2.518	2.813	3.138
13	1.138	1.294	1.469	1.665	1.886	2.133	2.410	2.720	3.066	3.452
14	1.149	1.319	1.513	1.732	1.980	2.261	2.579	2.937	3.342	3.797
15	1.161	1.346	1.558	1.801	2.079	2.397	2.759	3.172	3.642	4.177
16	1.173	1.373	1.605	1.873	2.183	2.540	2.952	3.426	3.970	4.595
17	1.184	1.400	1.653	1.948	2.292	2.693	3.159	3.700	4.328	5.054
18	1.196	1.428	1.702	2.026	2.407	2.854	3.380	3.996	4.717	5.560
19	1.208	1.457	1.753	2.107	2.527	3.026	3.616	4.316	5.142	6.116
20	1.220	1.486	1.806	2.191	2.653	3.207	3.870	4.661	5.604	6.727
21	1.232	1.516	1.860	2.279	2.786	3.399	4.140	5.034	6.109	7.400
22	1.245	1.546	1.916	2.370	2.925	3.603	4.430	5.436	6.658	8.140
23	1.257	1.577	1.974	2.465	3.071	3.820	4.740	5.871	7.258	8.954
24	1.270	1.608	2.033	2.563	3.225	4.049	5.072	6.341	7.911	9.850
25	1.282	1.641	2.094	2.666	3.386	4.292	5.427	6.848	8.623	10.834
30	1.348	1.811	2.427	3.243	4.322	5.743	7.612	10.062	13.267	17.449
35	1.417	2.000	2.814	3.946	5.516	7.686	10.676	14.785	20.413	28.102
40	1.489	2.208	3.262	4.801	7.040	10.285	14.974	21.724	31.408	45.258
45	1.565	2.438	3.781	5.841	8.985	13.764	21.002	31.920	48.325	72.888
50	1.645	2.691	4.384	7.106	11.467	18.419	29.456	46.900	74.354	117.386

Table B.1   Compound-Value Interest Factors for One Dollar, CVIF (Continued)

Year	INTEREST RATE									
	11%	12%	13%	14%	15%	16%	17%	18%	19%	20%
1	1.110	1.120	1.130	1.140	1.150	1.160	1.170	1.180	1.190	1.200
2	1.232	1.254	1.277	1.300	1.322	1.346	1.369	1.392	1.416	1.440
3	1.368	1.405	1.443	1.482	1.521	1.561	1.602	1.643	1.685	1.728
4	1.518	1.574	1.630	1.689	1.749	1.811	1.874	1.939	2.005	2.074
5	1.685	1.762	1.842	1.925	2.011	2.100	2.192	2.288	2.386	2.488
6	1.870	1.974	2.082	2.195	2.313	2.436	2.565	2.700	2.840	2.986
7	2.076	2.211	2.353	2.502	2.660	2.826	3.001	3.185	3.379	3.583
8	2.305	2.476	2.658	2.853	3.059	3.278	3.511	3.759	4.021	4.300
9	2.558	2.773	3.004	3.252	3.518	3.803	4.108	4.435	4.785	5.160
10	2.839	3.106	3.395	3.707	4.046	4.411	4.807	5.234	5.695	6.192
11	3.152	3.479	3.836	4.226	4.652	5.117	5.624	6.176	6.777	7.430
12	3.498	3.896	4.334	4.818	5.350	5.936	6.580	7.288	8.064	8.916
13	3.883	4.363	4.898	5.492	6.153	6.886	7.699	8.599	9.596	10.699
14	4.310	4.887	5.535	6.261	7.076	7.987	9.007	10.147	11.420	12.839
15	4.785	5.474	6.254	7.138	8.137	9.265	10.539	11.974	13.589	15.407
16	5.311	6.130	7.067	8.137	9.358	10.748	12.330	14.129	16.171	18.488
17	5.895	6.866	7.986	9.276	10.761	12.468	14.426	16.672	19.244	22.186
18	6.543	7.690	9.024	10.575	12.375	14.462	16.879	19.673	22.900	26.623
19	7.263	8.613	10.197	12.055	14.232	16.776	19.748	23.214	27.251	31.948
20	8.062	9.646	11.523	13.743	16.366	19.461	23.105	27.393	32.429	38.337
21	8.949	10.804	13.021	15.667	18.821	22.574	27.033	32.323	38.591	46.005
22	9.933	12.100	14.713	17.861	21.644	26.186	31.629	38.141	45.923	55.205
23	11.026	13.552	16.626	20.361	24.891	30.376	37.005	45.007	54.648	66.247
24	12.239	15.178	18.788	23.212	28.625	35.236	43.296	53.108	65.031	79.496
25	13.585	17.000	21.230	26.461	32.918	40.874	50.656	62.667	77.387	95.395
30	22.892	29.960	39.115	50.949	66.210	85.849	111.061	143.367	184.672	237.373
35	38.574	52.799	72.066	98.097	133.172	180.311	243.495	327.988	440.691	590.657
40	64.999	93.049	132.776	188.876	267.856	378.715	533.846	750.353	1051.642	1469.740
45	109.527	163.985	244.629	363.662	538.752	795.429	1170.425	1716.619	2509.583	3657.176
50	184.559	288.996	450.711	700.197	1083.619	1670.669	2566.080	3927.189	5988.730	9100.191

Table B.1　Compound-Value Interest Factors for One Dollar, CVIF (Continued)

INTEREST RATE

Year	21%	22%	23%	24%	25%	26%	27%	28%	29%	30%
1	1.210	1.220	1.230	1.240	1.250	1.260	1.270	1.280	1.290	1.300
2	1.464	1.488	1.513	1.538	1.562	1.588	1.613	1.638	1.664	1.690
3	1.772	1.816	1.861	1.907	1.953	2.000	2.048	2.097	2.147	2.197
4	2.144	2.215	2.289	2.364	2.441	2.520	2.601	2.684	2.769	2.856
5	2.594	2.703	2.815	2.932	3.052	3.176	3.304	3.436	3.572	3.713
6	3.138	3.297	3.463	3.635	3.815	4.001	4.196	4.398	4.608	4.827
7	3.797	4.023	4.259	4.508	4.768	5.042	5.329	5.629	5.945	6.275
8	4.595	4.908	5.239	5.589	5.960	6.353	6.767	7.206	7.669	8.157
9	5.560	5.987	6.444	6.931	7.451	8.004	8.595	9.223	9.893	10.604
10	6.727	7.305	7.926	8.594	9.313	10.086	10.915	11.806	12.761	13.786
11	8.140	8.912	9.749	10.657	11.642	12.708	13.862	15.112	16.462	17.921
12	9.850	10.872	11.991	13.215	14.552	16.012	17.605	19.343	21.236	23.298
13	11.918	13.264	14.749	16.386	18.190	20.175	22.359	24.759	27.395	30.287
14	14.421	16.182	18.141	20.319	22.737	25.420	28.395	31.691	35.339	39.373
15	17.449	19.742	22.314	25.195	28.422	32.030	36.062	40.565	45.587	51.185
16	21.113	24.085	27.446	31.242	35.527	40.357	45.799	51.923	58.808	66.541
17	25.547	29.384	33.758	38.740	44.409	50.850	58.165	66.461	75.862	86.503
18	30.912	35.848	41.523	48.038	55.511	64.071	73.869	85.070	97.862	112.454
19	37.404	43.735	51.073	59.567	69.389	80.730	93.813	108.890	126.242	146.190
20	45.258	53.357	62.820	73.863	86.736	101.720	119.143	139.379	162.852	190.047
21	54.762	65.095	77.268	91.591	108.420	128.167	151.312	178.405	210.079	247.061
22	66.262	79.416	95.040	113.572	135.525	161.490	192.165	228.358	271.002	321.178
23	80.178	96.887	116.899	140.829	169.407	203.477	244.050	292.298	349.592	417.531
24	97.015	118.203	143.786	174.628	211.758	256.381	309.943	374.141	450.974	542.791
25	117.388	144.207	176.857	216.539	264.698	323.040	393.628	478.901	581.756	705.627
30	304.471	389.748	497.904	634.810	807.793	1025.904	1300.477	1645.488	2078.208	2619.936
35	789.716	1053.370	1401.749	1861.020	2465.189	3258.053	4296.547	5653.840	7423.988	9727.598
40	2048.309	2846.941	3946.340	5455.797	7523.156	10346.879	14195.051	19426.418	26520.723	36117.754
45	5312.758	7694.418	11110.121	15994.316	22958.844	32859.457	46897.973	66748.500	94739.937	134102.187
50	13779.844	20795.680	31278.301	46889.207	70064.812	104354.562	154942.687	229345.875	338440.000	497910.125

Table B.1 Compound-Value Interest Factors for One Dollar, CVIF (Continued)

INTEREST RATE

Year	31%	32%	33%	34%	35%	36%	37%	38%	39%	40%
1	1.310	1.320	1.330	1.340	1.350	1.360	1.370	1.380	1.390	1.400
2	1.716	1.742	1.769	1.796	1.822	1.850	1.877	1.904	1.932	1.960
3	2.248	2.300	2.353	2.406	2.460	2.515	2.571	2.628	2.686	2.744
4	2.945	3.036	3.129	3.224	3.321	3.421	3.523	3.627	3.733	3.842
5	3.858	4.007	4.162	4.320	4.484	4.653	4.826	5.005	5.189	5.378
6	5.054	5.290	5.535	5.789	6.053	6.328	6.612	6.907	7.213	7.530
7	6.621	6.983	7.361	7.758	8.172	8.605	9.058	9.531	10.025	10.541
8	8.673	9.217	9.791	10.395	11.032	11.703	12.410	13.153	13.935	14.758
9	11.362	12.166	13.022	13.930	14.894	15.917	17.001	18.151	19.370	20.661
10	14.884	16.060	17.319	18.666	20.106	21.646	23.292	25.049	26.924	28.925
11	19.498	21.199	23.034	25.012	27.144	29.439	31.910	34.567	37.425	40.495
12	25.542	27.982	30.635	33.516	36.644	40.037	43.716	47.703	52.020	56.694
13	33.460	36.937	40.745	44.912	49.469	54.451	59.892	65.830	72.308	79.371
14	43.832	48.756	54.190	60.181	66.784	74.053	82.051	90.845	100.509	111.119
15	57.420	64.358	72.073	80.643	90.158	100.712	112.410	125.366	139.707	155.567
16	75.220	84.953	95.857	108.061	121.713	136.968	154.002	173.005	194.192	217.793
17	98.539	112.138	127.490	144.802	164.312	186.277	210.983	238.747	269.927	304.911
18	129.086	148.022	169.561	194.035	221.822	253.337	289.046	329.471	375.198	426.875
19	169.102	195.389	225.517	260.006	299.459	344.537	395.993	454.669	521.525	597.625
20	221.523	257.913	299.937	348.408	404.270	468.571	542.511	627.443	724.919	836.674
21	290.196	340.446	398.916	466.867	545.764	637.256	743.240	865.871	1007.637	1171.343
22	380.156	449.388	530.558	625.601	736.781	866.668	1018.238	1194.900	1400.615	1639.878
23	498.004	593.192	705.642	838.305	994.653	1178.668	1394.986	1648.961	1946.854	2295.829
24	652.385	783.013	938.504	1123.328	1342.781	1602.988	1911.129	2275.564	2706.125	3214.158
25	854.623	1033.577	1248.210	1505.258	1812.754	2180.063	2618.245	3140.275	3761.511	4499.816
30	3297.081	4142.008	5194.516	6503.285	8128.426	10142.914	12636.086	15716.703	19517.969	24201.043
35	12719.918	16598.906	21617.363	28096.695	36448.051	47190.727	60983.836	78660.188	101276.125	130158.687
40	49072.621	66519.313	89962.188	121388.437	163433.875	219558.625	294317.937	393684.687	525508.312	700022.688

Table B.2 Compound-Value Interest Factors for a One-Dollar Annuity, CVIFA

Year	1%	2%	3%	4%	5%	6%	7%	8%	9%	10%
1	1.000	1.000	1.000	1.000	1.000	1.000	1.000	1.000	1.000	1.000
2	2.010	2.020	2.030	2.040	2.050	2.060	2.070	2.080	2.090	2.100
3	3.030	3.060	3.091	3.122	3.152	3.184	3.215	3.246	3.278	3.310
4	4.060	4.122	4.184	4.246	4.310	4.375	4.440	4.506	4.573	4.641
5	5.101	5.204	5.309	5.416	5.526	5.637	5.751	5.867	5.985	6.105
6	6.152	6.308	6.468	6.633	6.802	6.975	7.153	7.336	7.523	7.716
7	7.214	7.434	7.662	7.898	8.142	8.394	8.654	8.923	9.200	9.487
8	8.286	8.583	8.892	9.214	9.549	9.897	10.260	10.637	11.028	11.436
9	9.368	9.755	10.159	10.583	11.027	11.491	11.978	12.488	13.021	13.579
10	10.462	10.950	11.464	12.006	12.578	13.181	13.816	14.487	15.193	15.937
11	11.567	12.169	12.808	13.486	14.207	14.972	15.784	16.645	17.560	18.531
12	12.682	13.412	14.192	15.026	15.917	16.870	17.888	18.977	20.141	21.384
13	13.809	14.680	15.618	16.627	17.713	18.882	20.141	21.495	22.953	24.523
14	14.947	15.974	17.086	18.292	19.598	21.015	22.550	24.215	26.019	27.975
15	16.097	17.293	18.599	20.023	21.578	23.276	25.129	27.152	29.361	31.772
16	17.258	18.639	20.157	21.824	23.657	25.672	27.888	30.324	33.003	35.949
17	18.430	20.012	21.761	23.697	25.840	28.213	30.840	33.750	36.973	40.544
18	19.614	21.412	23.414	25.645	28.132	30.905	33.999	37.450	41.301	45.599
19	20.811	22.840	25.117	27.671	30.539	33.760	37.379	41.446	46.018	51.158
20	22.019	24.297	26.870	29.778	33.066	36.785	40.995	45.762	51.159	57.274
21	23.239	25.783	28.676	31.969	35.719	39.992	44.865	50.422	56.764	64.002
22	24.471	27.299	30.536	34.248	38.505	43.392	49.005	55.456	62.872	71.402
23	25.716	28.845	32.452	36.618	41.430	46.995	53.435	60.893	69.531	79.542
24	26.973	30.421	34.426	39.082	44.501	50.815	58.176	66.764	76.789	88.496
25	28.243	32.030	36.459	41.645	47.726	54.864	63.248	73.105	84.699	98.346
30	34.784	40.567	47.575	56.084	66.438	79.057	94.459	113.282	136.305	164.491
35	41.659	49.994	60.461	73.651	90.318	111.432	138.234	172.314	215.705	271.018
40	48.885	60.401	75.400	95.024	120.797	154.758	199.630	259.052	337.872	442.580
45	56.479	71.891	92.718	121.027	159.695	212.737	285.741	386.497	525.840	718.881
50	64.461	84.577	112.794	152.664	209.341	290.325	406.516	573.756	815.051	1163.865

INTEREST RATE

Table B.2 Compound-Value Interest Factors for a One-Dollar Annuity, CVIFA (*Continued*)

INTEREST RATE

Year	11%	12%	13%	14%	15%	16%	17%	18%	19%	20%
1	1.000	1.000	1.000	1.000	1.000	1.000	1.000	1.000	1.000	1.000
2	2.110	2.120	2.130	2.140	2.150	2.160	2.170	2.180	2.190	2.200
3	3.342	3.374	3.407	3.440	3.472	3.506	3.539	3.572	3.606	3.640
4	4.710	4.779	4.850	4.921	4.993	5.066	5.141	5.215	5.291	5.368
5	6.228	6.353	6.480	6.610	6.742	6.877	7.014	7.154	7.297	7.442
6	7.913	8.115	8.323	8.535	8.754	8.977	9.207	9.442	9.683	9.930
7	9.783	10.089	10.405	10.730	11.067	11.414	11.772	12.141	12.523	12.916
8	11.859	12.300	12.757	13.233	13.727	14.240	14.773	15.327	15.902	16.499
9	14.164	14.776	15.416	16.085	16.786	17.518	18.285	19.086	19.923	20.799
10	16.722	17.549	18.420	19.337	20.304	21.321	22.393	23.521	24.709	25.959
11	19.561	20.655	21.814	23.044	24.349	25.733	27.200	28.755	30.403	32.150
12	22.713	24.133	25.650	27.271	29.001	30.850	32.824	34.931	37.180	39.580
13	26.211	28.029	29.984	32.088	34.352	36.786	39.404	42.218	45.244	48.496
14	30.095	32.392	34.882	37.581	40.504	43.672	47.102	50.818	54.841	59.196
15	34.405	37.280	40.417	43.842	47.580	51.659	56.109	60.965	66.260	72.035
16	39.190	42.753	46.671	50.980	55.717	60.925	66.648	72.938	79.850	87.442
17	44.500	48.883	53.738	59.117	65.075	71.673	78.978	87.067	96.021	105.930
18	50.396	55.749	61.724	68.393	75.836	84.140	93.404	103.739	115.265	128.116
19	56.939	63.439	70.748	78.968	88.211	98.603	110.283	123.412	138.165	154.739
20	64.202	72.052	80.946	91.024	102.443	115.379	130.031	146.626	165.417	186.687
21	72.264	81.698	92.468	104.767	118.809	134.840	153.136	174.019	197.846	225.024
22	81.213	92.502	105.489	120.434	137.630	157.414	180.169	206.342	236.436	271.028
23	91.147	104.602	120.203	138.295	159.274	183.600	211.798	244.483	282.359	326.234
24	102.173	118.154	136.829	158.656	184.166	213.976	248.803	289.490	337.007	392.480
25	114.412	133.333	155.616	181.867	212.790	249.212	292.099	342.598	402.038	471.976
30	199.018	241.330	293.192	356.778	434.738	530.306	647.423	790.932	966.698	1181.865
35	341.583	431.658	546.663	693.552	881.152	1120.699	1426.448	1816.607	2314.173	2948.294
40	581.812	767.080	1013.667	1341.979	1779.048	2360.724	3134.412	4163.094	5529.711	7343.715
45	986.613	1358.208	1874.086	2590.464	3585.031	4965.191	6879.008	9531.258	13203.105	18280.914
50	1668.723	2399.975	3459.344	4994.301	7217.488	10435.449	15088.805	21812.273	31514.492	45496.094

Table B.2 Compound-Value Interest Factors for a One-Dollar Annuity, CVIFA *(Continued)*

INTEREST RATE

Year	21%	22%	23%	24%	25%	26%	27%	28%	29%	30%
1	1.000	1.000	1.000	1.000	1.000	1.000	1.000	1.000	1.000	1.000
2	2.210	2.220	2.230	2.240	2.250	2.260	2.270	2.280	2.290	2.300
3	3.674	3.708	3.743	3.778	3.813	3.848	3.883	3.918	3.954	3.990
4	5.446	5.524	5.604	5.684	5.766	5.848	5.931	6.016	6.101	6.187
5	7.589	7.740	7.893	8.048	8.207	8.368	8.533	8.700	8.870	9.043
6	10.183	10.442	10.708	10.980	11.259	11.544	11.837	12.136	12.442	12.756
7	13.321	13.740	14.171	14.615	15.073	15.546	16.032	16.534	17.051	17.583
8	17.119	17.762	18.430	19.123	19.842	20.588	21.361	22.163	22.995	23.858
9	21.714	22.670	23.669	24.712	25.802	26.940	28.129	29.369	30.664	32.015
10	27.274	28.657	30.113	31.643	33.253	34.945	36.723	38.592	40.556	42.619
11	34.001	35.962	38.039	40.238	42.566	45.030	47.639	50.398	53.318	56.405
12	42.141	44.873	47.787	50.895	54.208	57.738	61.501	65.510	69.780	74.326
13	51.991	55.745	59.778	64.109	68.760	73.750	79.106	84.853	91.016	97.624
14	63.909	69.009	74.528	80.496	86.949	93.925	101.465	109.611	118.411	127.912
15	78.330	85.191	92.669	100.815	109.687	119.346	129.860	141.302	153.750	167.285
16	95.779	104.933	114.983	126.010	138.109	151.375	165.922	181.867	199.337	218.470
17	116.892	129.019	142.428	157.252	173.636	191.733	211.721	233.790	258.145	285.011
18	142.439	158.403	176.187	195.993	218.045	242.583	269.885	300.250	334.006	371.514
19	173.351	194.251	217.710	244.031	273.556	306.654	343.754	385.321	431.868	483.968
20	210.755	237.986	268.783	303.598	342.945	387.384	437.568	494.210	558.110	630.157
21	256.013	291.343	331.603	377.461	429.681	489.104	556.710	633.589	720.962	820.204
22	310.775	356.438	408.871	469.052	538.101	617.270	708.022	811.993	931.040	1067.265
23	377.038	435.854	503.911	582.624	673.626	778.760	900.187	1040.351	1202.042	1388.443
24	457.215	532.741	620.810	723.453	843.032	982.237	1144.237	1332.649	1551.634	1805.975
25	554.230	650.944	764.596	898.082	1054.791	1238.617	1454.180	1706.790	2002.608	2348.765
30	1445.111	1767.044	2160.459	2640.881	3227.172	3941.953	4812.891	5873.172	7162.785	8729.805
35	3755.814	4783.520	6090.227	7750.094	9856.746	12527.160	15909.480	20188.742	25596.512	32422.090
40	9749.141	12936.141	17153.691	22728.367	30088.621	39791.957	52570.707	69376.562	91447.375	120389.375
45	25294.223	34970.230	48300.660	66638.937	91831.312	126378.937	173692.875	238384.312	326686.375	447005.062

Table B.2 Compound-Value Interest Factors for a One-Dollar Annuity, CVIFA (*Continued*)

Year	31%	32%	33%	34%	35%	36%	37%	38%	39%	40%
1	1.000	1.000	1.000	1.000	1.000	1.000	1.000	1.000	1.000	1.000
2	2.310	2.320	2.330	2.340	2.350	2.360	2.370	2.380	2.390	2.400
3	4.026	4.062	4.099	4.136	4.172	4.210	4.247	4.284	4.322	4.360
4	6.274	6.362	6.452	6.542	6.633	6.725	6.818	6.912	7.008	7.104
5	9.219	9.398	9.581	9.766	9.954	10.146	10.341	10.539	10.741	10.946
6	13.077	13.406	13.742	14.086	14.438	14.799	15.167	15.544	15.930	16.324
7	18.131	18.696	19.277	19.876	20.492	21.126	21.779	22.451	23.142	23.853
8	24.752	25.678	26.638	27.633	28.664	29.732	30.837	31.982	33.167	34.395
9	33.425	34.895	36.429	38.028	39.696	41.435	43.247	45.135	47.103	49.152
10	44.786	47.062	49.451	51.958	54.590	57.351	60.248	63.287	66.473	69.813
11	59.670	63.121	66.769	70.624	74.696	78.998	83.540	88.335	93.397	98.739
12	79.167	84.320	89.803	95.636	101.840	108.437	115.450	122.903	130.822	139.234
13	104.709	112.302	120.438	129.152	138.484	148.474	159.166	170.606	182.842	195.928
14	138.169	149.239	161.183	174.063	187.953	202.925	219.058	236.435	255.151	275.299
15	182.001	197.996	215.373	234.245	254.737	276.978	301.109	327.281	355.659	386.418
16	239.421	262.354	287.446	314.888	344.895	377.690	413.520	452.647	495.366	541.985
17	314.642	347.307	383.303	422.949	466.608	514.658	567.521	625.652	689.558	759.778
18	413.180	459.445	510.792	567.751	630.920	700.935	778.504	864.399	959.485	1064.689
19	542.266	607.467	680.354	761.786	852.741	954.271	1067.551	1193.870	1334.683	1491.563
20	711.368	802.856	905.870	1021.792	1152.200	1298.809	1463.544	1648.539	1856.208	2089.188
21	932.891	1060.769	1205.807	1370.201	1556.470	1767.380	2006.055	2275.982	2581.128	2925.862
22	1223.087	1401.215	1604.724	1837.068	2102.234	2404.636	2749.294	3141.852	3588.765	4097.203
23	1603.243	1850.603	2135.282	2462.669	2839.014	3271.304	3767.532	4336.750	4989.379	5737.078
24	2101.247	2443.795	2840.924	3300.974	3833.667	4449.969	5162.516	5985.711	6936.230	8032.906
25	2753.631	3226.808	3779.428	4424.301	5176.445	6052.957	7073.645	8261.273	9642.352	11247.062
30	10632.543	12940.672	15737.945	19124.434	23221.258	28172.016	34148.906	41357.227	50043.625	60500.207

INTEREST RATE

Table B.3 Present-Value Interest Factors for One Dollar, PVIF

Year	INTEREST RATE									
	1%	2%	3%	4%	5%	6%	7%	8%	9%	10%
1	.990	.980	.971	.962	.952	.943	.935	.926	.917	.909
2	.980	.961	.943	.925	.907	.890	.873	.857	.842	.826
3	.971	.942	.915	.889	.864	.840	.816	.794	.772	.751
4	.961	.924	.888	.855	.823	.792	.763	.735	.708	.683
5	.951	.906	.863	.822	.784	.747	.713	.681	.650	.621
6	.942	.888	.837	.790	.746	.705	.666	.630	.596	.564
7	.933	.871	.813	.760	.711	.665	.623	.583	.547	.513
8	.923	.853	.789	.731	.677	.627	.582	.540	.502	.467
9	.914	.837	.766	.703	.645	.592	.544	.500	.460	.424
10	.905	.820	.744	.676	.614	.558	.508	.463	.422	.386
11	.896	.804	.722	.650	.585	.527	.475	.429	.388	.350
12	.887	.789	.701	.625	.557	.497	.444	.397	.356	.319
13	.879	.773	.681	.601	.530	.469	.415	.368	.326	.290
14	.870	.758	.661	.577	.505	.442	.388	.340	.299	.263
15	.861	.743	.642	.555	.481	.417	.362	.315	.275	.239
16	.853	.728	.623	.534	.458	.394	.339	.292	.252	.218
17	.844	.714	.605	.513	.436	.371	.317	.270	.231	.198
18	.836	.700	.587	.494	.416	.350	.296	.250	.212	.180
19	.828	.686	.570	.475	.396	.331	.277	.232	.194	.164
20	.820	.673	.554	.456	.377	.312	.258	.215	.178	.149
21	.811	.660	.538	.439	.359	.294	.242	.199	.164	.135
22	.803	.647	.522	.422	.342	.278	.226	.184	.150	.123
23	.795	.634	.507	.406	.326	.262	.211	.170	.138	.112
24	.788	.622	.492	.390	.310	.247	.197	.158	.126	.102
25	.780	.610	.478	.375	.295	.233	.184	.146	.116	.092
30	.742	.552	.412	.308	.231	.174	.131	.099	.075	.057
35	.706	.500	.355	.253	.181	.130	.094	.068	.049	.036
40	.672	.453	.307	.208	.142	.097	.067	.046	.032	.022
45	.639	.410	.264	.171	.111	.073	.048	.031	.021	.014
50	.608	.372	.228	.141	.087	.054	.034	.021	.013	.009

Table B.3   Present-Value Interest Factors for One Dollar, PVIF (Continued)

INTEREST RATE

Year	11%	12%	13%	14%	15%	16%	17%	18%	19%	20%
1	.901	.893	.885	.877	.870	.862	.855	.847	.840	.833
2	.812	.797	.783	.769	.756	.743	.731	.718	.706	.694
3	.731	.712	.693	.675	.658	.641	.624	.609	.593	.579
4	.659	.636	.613	.592	.572	.552	.534	.516	.499	.482
5	.593	.567	.543	.519	.497	.476	.456	.437	.419	.402
6	.535	.507	.480	.456	.432	.410	.390	.370	.352	.335
7	.482	.452	.425	.400	.376	.354	.333	.314	.296	.279
8	.434	.404	.376	.351	.327	.305	.285	.266	.249	.233
9	.391	.361	.333	.308	.284	.263	.243	.225	.209	.194
10	.352	.322	.295	.270	.247	.227	.208	.191	.176	.162
11	.317	.287	.261	.237	.215	.195	.178	.162	.148	.135
12	.286	.257	.231	.208	.187	.168	.152	.137	.124	.112
13	.258	.229	.204	.182	.163	.145	.130	.116	.104	.093
14	.232	.205	.181	.160	.141	.125	.111	.099	.088	.078
15	.209	.183	.160	.140	.123	.108	.095	.084	.074	.065
16	.188	.163	.141	.123	.107	.093	.081	.071	.062	.054
17	.170	.146	.125	.108	.093	.080	.069	.060	.052	.045
18	.153	.130	.111	.095	.081	.069	.059	.051	.044	.038
19	.138	.116	.098	.083	.070	.060	.051	.043	.037	.031
20	.124	.104	.087	.073	.061	.051	.043	.037	.031	.026
21	.112	.093	.077	.064	.053	.044	.037	.031	.026	.022
22	.101	.083	.068	.056	.046	.038	.032	.026	.022	.018
23	.091	.074	.060	.049	.040	.033	.027	.022	.018	.015
24	.082	.066	.053	.043	.035	.028	.023	.019	.015	.013
25	.074	.059	.047	.038	.030	.024	.020	.016	.013	.010
30	.044	.033	.026	.020	.015	.012	.009	.007	.005	.004
35	.026	.019	.014	.010	.008	.006	.004	.003	.002	.002
40	.015	.011	.008	.005	.004	.003	.002	.001	.001	.001
45	.009	.006	.004	.003	.002	.001	.001	.001	.000	.000
50	.005	.003	.002	.001	.001	.001	.000	.000	.000	.000

Table B.3   Present-Value Interest Factors for One Dollar, PVIF (Continued)

INTEREST RATE

Year	21%	22%	23%	24%	25%	26%	27%	28%	29%	30%
1	.826	.820	.813	.806	.800	.794	.787	.781	.775	.769
2	.683	.672	.661	.650	.640	.630	.620	.610	.601	.592
3	.564	.551	.537	.524	.512	.500	.488	.477	.466	.455
4	.467	.451	.437	.423	.410	.397	.384	.373	.361	.350
5	.386	.370	.355	.341	.328	.315	.303	.291	.280	.269
6	.319	.303	.289	.275	.262	.250	.238	.227	.217	.207
7	.263	.249	.235	.222	.210	.198	.188	.178	.168	.159
8	.218	.204	.191	.179	.168	.157	.148	.139	.130	.123
9	.180	.167	.155	.144	.134	.125	.116	.108	.101	.094
10	.149	.137	.126	.116	.107	.099	.092	.085	.078	.073
11	.123	.112	.103	.094	.086	.079	.072	.066	.061	.056
12	.102	.092	.083	.076	.069	.062	.057	.052	.047	.043
13	.084	.075	.068	.061	.055	.050	.045	.040	.037	.033
14	.069	.062	.055	.049	.044	.039	.035	.032	.028	.025
15	.057	.051	.045	.040	.035	.031	.028	.025	.022	.020
16	.047	.042	.036	.032	.028	.025	.022	.019	.017	.015
17	.039	.034	.030	.026	.023	.020	.017	.015	.013	.012
18	.032	.028	.024	.021	.018	.016	.014	.012	.010	.009
19	.027	.023	.020	.017	.014	.012	.011	.009	.008	.007
20	.022	.019	.016	.014	.012	.010	.008	.007	.006	.005
21	.018	.015	.013	.011	.009	.008	.007	.006	.005	.004
22	.015	.013	.011	.009	.007	.006	.005	.004	.004	.003
23	.012	.010	.009	.007	.006	.005	.004	.003	.003	.002
24	.010	.008	.007	.006	.005	.004	.003	.003	.002	.002
25	.009	.007	.006	.005	.004	.003	.003	.002	.002	.001
30	.003	.003	.002	.002	.001	.001	.001	.001	.000	.000
35	.001	.001	.001	.001	.000	.000	.000	.000	.000	.000
40	.000	.000	.000	.000	.000	.000	.000	.000	.000	.000
45	.000	.000	.000	.000	.000	.000	.000	.000	.000	.000
50	.000	.000	.000	.000	.000	.000	.000	.000	.000	.000

Table B.3 Present-Value Interest Factors for One Dollar, PVIF (Continued)

INTEREST RATE

Year	31%	32%	33%	34%	35%	36%	37%	38%	39%	40%
1	.763	.758	.752	.746	.741	.735	.730	.725	.719	.714
2	.583	.574	.565	.557	.549	.541	.533	.525	.518	.510
3	.445	.435	.425	.416	.406	.398	.389	.381	.372	.364
4	.340	.329	.320	.310	.301	.292	.284	.276	.268	.260
5	.259	.250	.240	.231	.223	.215	.207	.200	.193	.186
6	.198	.189	.181	.173	.165	.158	.151	.145	.139	.133
7	.151	.143	.136	.129	.122	.116	.110	.105	.100	.095
8	.115	.108	.102	.096	.091	.085	.081	.076	.072	.068
9	.088	.082	.077	.072	.067	.063	.059	.055	.052	.048
10	.067	.062	.058	.054	.050	.046	.043	.040	.037	.035
11	.051	.047	.043	.040	.037	.034	.031	.029	.027	.025
12	.039	.036	.033	.030	.027	.025	.023	.021	.019	.018
13	.030	.027	.025	.022	.020	.018	.017	.015	.014	.013
14	.023	.021	.018	.017	.015	.014	.012	.011	.010	.009
15	.017	.016	.014	.012	.011	.010	.009	.008	.007	.006
16	.013	.012	.010	.009	.008	.007	.006	.006	.005	.005
17	.010	.009	.008	.007	.006	.005	.005	.004	.004	.003
18	.008	.007	.006	.005	.005	.004	.003	.003	.003	.002
19	.006	.005	.004	.004	.003	.003	.003	.002	.002	.002
20	.005	.004	.003	.003	.002	.002	.002	.002	.001	.001
21	.003	.003	.003	.002	.002	.002	.001	.001	.001	.001
22	.003	.002	.002	.002	.001	.001	.001	.001	.001	.001
23	.002	.002	.001	.001	.001	.001	.001	.001	.001	.000
24	.002	.001	.001	.001	.001	.001	.001	.000	.000	.000
25	.001	.001	.001	.001	.001	.000	.000	.000	.000	.000
30	.000	.000	.000	.000	.000	.000	.000	.000	.000	.000
35	.000	.000	.000	.000	.000	.000	.000	.000	.000	.000
40	.000	.000	.000	.000	.000	.000	.000	.000	.000	.000
45	.000	.000	.000	.000	.000	.000	.000	.000	.000	.000
50	.000	.000	.000	.000	.000	.000	.000	.000	.000	.000

Table B.4 Present-Value Interest Factors for a One-Dollar Annuity, PVIFA

INTEREST RATE

Year	1%	2%	3%	4%	5%	6%	7%	8%	9%	10%
1	.990	.980	.971	.962	.952	.943	.935	.926	.917	.909
2	1.970	1.942	1.913	1.886	1.859	1.833	1.808	1.783	1.759	1.736
3	2.941	2.884	2.829	2.775	2.723	2.673	2.624	2.577	2.531	2.487
4	3.902	3.808	3.717	3.630	3.546	3.465	3.387	3.312	3.240	3.170
5	4.853	4.713	4.580	4.452	4.329	4.212	4.100	3.993	3.890	3.791
6	5.795	5.601	5.417	5.242	5.076	4.917	4.767	4.623	4.486	4.355
7	6.728	6.472	6.230	6.002	5.786	5.582	5.389	5.206	5.033	4.868
8	7.652	7.326	7.020	6.733	6.463	6.210	5.971	5.747	5.535	5.335
9	8.566	8.162	7.786	7.435	7.108	6.802	6.515	6.247	5.995	5.759
10	9.471	8.983	8.530	8.111	7.722	7.360	7.024	6.710	6.418	6.145
11	10.368	9.787	9.253	8.760	8.306	7.887	7.499	7.139	6.805	6.495
12	11.255	10.575	9.954	9.385	8.863	8.384	7.943	7.536	7.161	6.814
13	12.134	11.348	10.635	9.986	9.394	8.853	8.358	7.904	7.487	7.103
14	13.004	12.106	11.296	10.563	9.899	9.295	8.746	8.244	7.786	7.367
15	13.865	12.849	11.938	11.118	10.380	9.712	9.108	8.560	8.061	7.606
16	14.718	13.578	12.561	11.652	10.838	10.106	9.447	8.851	8.313	7.824
17	15.562	14.292	13.166	12.166	11.274	10.477	9.763	9.122	8.544	8.022
18	16.398	14.992	13.754	12.659	11.690	10.828	10.059	9.372	8.756	8.201
19	17.226	15.679	14.324	13.134	12.085	11.158	10.336	9.604	8.950	8.365
20	18.046	16.352	14.878	13.590	12.462	11.470	10.594	9.818	9.129	8.514
21	18.857	17.011	15.415	14.029	12.821	11.764	10.836	10.017	9.292	8.649
22	19.661	17.658	15.937	14.451	13.163	12.042	11.061	10.201	9.442	8.772
23	20.456	18.292	16.444	14.857	13.489	12.303	11.272	10.371	9.580	8.883
24	21.244	18.914	16.936	15.247	13.799	12.550	11.469	10.529	9.707	8.985
25	22.023	19.524	17.413	15.622	14.094	12.783	11.654	10.675	9.823	9.077
30	25.808	22.397	19.601	17.292	15.373	13.765	12.409	11.258	10.274	9.427
35	29.409	24.999	21.487	18.665	16.374	14.498	12.948	11.655	10.567	9.644
40	32.835	27.356	23.115	19.793	17.159	15.046	13.332	11.925	10.757	9.779
45	36.095	29.490	24.519	20.720	17.774	15.456	13.606	12.108	10.881	9.863
50	39.197	31.424	25.730	21.482	18.256	15.762	13.801	12.234	10.962	9.915

Table B.4 Present-Value Interest Factors for a One-Dollar Annuity, PVIFA *(Continued)*

INTEREST RATE

Year	11%	12%	13%	14%	15%	16%	17%	18%	19%	20%
1	.901	.893	.885	.877	.870	.862	.855	.847	.840	.833
2	1.713	1.690	1.668	1.647	1.626	1.605	1.585	1.566	1.547	1.528
3	2.444	2.402	2.361	2.322	2.283	2.246	2.210	2.174	2.140	2.106
4	3.102	3.037	2.974	2.914	2.855	2.798	2.743	2.690	2.639	2.589
5	3.696	3.605	3.517	3.433	3.352	3.274	3.199	3.127	3.058	2.991
6	4.231	4.111	3.998	3.889	3.784	3.685	3.589	3.498	3.410	3.326
7	4.712	4.564	4.423	4.288	4.160	4.039	3.922	3.812	3.706	3.605
8	5.146	4.968	4.799	4.639	4.487	4.344	4.207	4.078	3.954	3.837
9	5.537	5.328	5.132	4.946	4.772	4.607	4.451	4.303	4.163	4.031
10	5.889	5.650	5.426	5.216	5.019	4.833	4.659	4.494	4.339	4.192
11	6.207	5.938	5.687	5.453	5.234	5.029	4.836	4.656	4.487	4.327
12	6.492	6.194	5.918	5.660	5.421	5.197	4.988	4.793	4.611	4.439
13	6.750	6.424	6.122	5.842	5.583	5.342	5.118	4.910	4.715	4.533
14	6.982	6.628	6.303	6.002	5.724	5.468	5.229	5.008	4.802	4.611
15	7.191	6.811	6.462	6.142	5.847	5.575	5.324	5.092	4.876	4.675
16	7.379	6.974	6.604	6.265	5.954	5.669	5.405	5.162	4.938	4.730
17	7.549	7.120	6.729	6.373	6.047	5.749	5.475	5.222	4.990	4.775
18	7.702	7.250	6.840	6.467	6.128	5.818	5.534	5.273	5.033	4.812
19	7.839	7.366	6.938	6.550	6.198	5.877	5.585	5.316	5.070	4.843
20	7.963	7.469	7.025	6.623	6.259	5.929	5.628	5.353	5.101	4.870
21	8.075	7.562	7.102	6.687	6.312	5.973	5.665	5.384	5.127	4.891
22	8.176	7.645	7.170	6.743	6.359	6.011	5.696	5.410	5.149	4.909
23	8.266	7.718	7.230	6.792	6.399	6.044	5.723	5.432	5.167	4.925
24	8.348	7.784	7.283	6.835	6.434	6.073	5.747	5.451	5.182	4.937
25	8.422	7.843	7.330	6.873	6.464	6.097	5.766	5.467	5.195	4.948
30	8.694	8.055	7.496	7.003	6.566	6.177	5.829	5.517	5.235	4.979
35	8.855	8.176	7.586	7.070	6.617	6.215	5.858	5.539	5.251	4.992
40	8.951	8.244	7.634	7.105	6.642	6.233	5.871	5.548	5.258	4.997
45	9.008	8.283	7.661	7.123	6.654	6.242	5.877	5.552	5.261	4.999
50	9.042	8.305	7.675	7.133	6.661	6.246	5.880	5.554	5.262	4.999

Table B.4   Present-Value Interest Factors for a One-Dollar Annuity, PVIFA (Continued)

INTEREST RATE

Year	21%	22%	23%	24%	25%	26%	27%	28%	29%	30%
1	.826	.820	.813	.806	.800	.794	.787	.781	.775	.769
2	1.509	1.492	1.474	1.457	1.440	1.424	1.407	1.392	1.376	1.361
3	2.074	2.042	2.011	1.981	1.952	1.923	1.896	1.868	1.842	1.816
4	2.540	2.494	2.448	2.404	2.362	2.320	2.280	2.241	2.203	2.166
5	2.926	2.864	2.803	2.745	2.689	2.635	2.583	2.532	2.483	2.436
6	3.245	3.167	3.092	3.020	2.951	2.885	2.821	2.759	2.700	2.643
7	3.508	3.416	3.327	3.242	3.161	3.083	3.009	2.937	2.868	2.802
8	3.726	3.619	3.518	3.421	3.329	3.241	3.156	3.076	2.999	2.925
9	3.905	3.786	3.673	3.566	3.463	3.366	3.273	3.184	3.100	3.019
10	4.054	3.923	3.799	3.682	3.570	3.465	3.364	3.269	3.178	3.092
11	4.177	4.035	3.902	3.776	3.656	3.544	3.437	3.335	3.239	3.147
12	4.278	4.127	3.985	3.851	3.725	3.606	3.493	3.387	3.286	3.190
13	4.362	4.203	4.053	3.912	3.780	3.656	3.538	3.427	3.322	3.223
14	4.432	4.265	4.108	3.962	3.824	3.695	3.573	3.459	3.351	3.249
15	4.489	4.315	4.153	4.001	3.859	3.726	3.601	3.483	3.373	3.268
16	4.536	4.357	4.189	4.033	3.887	3.751	3.623	3.503	3.390	3.283
17	4.576	4.391	4.219	4.059	3.910	3.771	3.640	3.518	3.403	3.295
18	4.608	4.419	4.243	4.080	3.928	3.786	3.654	3.529	3.413	3.304
19	4.635	4.442	4.263	4.097	3.942	3.799	3.664	3.539	3.421	3.311
20	4.657	4.460	4.279	4.110	3.954	3.808	3.673	3.546	3.427	3.316
21	4.675	4.476	4.292	4.121	3.963	3.816	3.679	3.551	3.432	3.320
22	4.690	4.488	4.302	4.130	3.970	3.822	3.684	3.556	3.436	3.323
23	4.703	4.499	4.311	4.137	3.976	3.827	3.689	3.559	3.438	3.325
24	4.713	4.507	4.318	4.143	3.981	3.831	3.692	3.562	3.441	3.327
25	4.721	4.514	4.323	4.147	3.985	3.834	3.694	3.564	3.442	3.329
30	4.746	4.534	4.339	4.160	3.995	3.842	3.701	3.569	3.447	3.332
35	4.756	4.541	4.345	4.164	3.998	3.845	3.703	3.571	3.448	3.333
40	4.760	4.544	4.347	4.166	3.999	3.846	3.703	3.571	3.448	3.333
45	4.761	4.545	4.347	4.166	4.000	3.846	3.704	3.571	3.448	3.333
50	4.762	4.545	4.348	4.167	4.000	3.846	3.704	3.571	3.448	3.333

Table B.4   Present-Value Interest Factors for a One-Dollar Annuity, PVIFA (Continued)

INTEREST RATE

Year	31%	32%	33%	34%	35%	36%	37%	38%	39%	40%
1	.763	.758	.752	.746	.741	.735	.730	.725	.719	.714
2	1.346	1.331	1.317	1.303	1.289	1.276	1.263	1.250	1.237	1.224
3	1.791	1.766	1.742	1.719	1.696	1.673	1.652	1.630	1.609	1.589
4	2.130	2.096	2.062	2.029	1.997	1.966	1.935	1.906	1.877	1.849
5	2.390	2.345	2.302	2.260	2.220	2.181	2.143	2.106	2.070	2.035
6	2.588	2.534	2.483	2.433	2.385	2.339	2.294	2.251	2.209	2.168
7	2.739	2.677	2.619	2.562	2.508	2.455	2.404	2.355	2.308	2.263
8	2.854	2.786	2.721	2.658	2.598	2.540	2.485	2.432	2.380	2.331
9	2.942	2.868	2.798	2.730	2.665	2.603	2.544	2.487	2.432	2.379
10	3.009	2.930	2.855	2.784	2.715	2.649	2.587	2.527	2.469	2.414
11	3.060	2.978	2.899	2.824	2.752	2.683	2.618	2.555	2.496	2.438
12	3.100	3.013	2.931	2.853	2.779	2.708	2.641	2.576	2.515	2.456
13	3.129	3.040	2.956	2.876	2.799	2.727	2.658	2.592	2.529	2.469
14	3.152	3.061	2.974	2.892	2.814	2.740	2.670	2.603	2.539	2.477
15	3.170	3.076	2.988	2.905	2.825	2.750	2.679	2.611	2.546	2.484
16	3.183	3.088	2.999	2.914	2.834	2.757	2.685	2.616	2.551	2.489
17	3.193	3.097	3.007	2.921	2.840	2.763	2.690	2.621	2.555	2.492
18	3.201	3.104	3.012	2.926	2.844	2.767	2.693	2.624	2.557	2.494
19	3.207	3.109	3.017	2.930	2.848	2.770	2.696	2.626	2.559	2.496
20	3.211	3.113	3.020	2.933	2.850	2.772	2.698	2.627	2.561	2.497
21	3.215	3.116	3.023	2.935	2.852	2.773	2.699	2.629	2.562	2.498
22	3.217	3.118	3.025	2.936	2.853	2.775	2.700	2.629	2.562	2.498
23	3.219	3.120	3.026	2.938	2.854	2.775	2.701	2.630	2.563	2.499
24	3.221	3.121	3.027	2.939	2.855	2.776	2.701	2.630	2.563	2.499
25	3.222	3.122	3.028	2.939	2.856	2.776	2.702	2.631	2.563	2.499
30	3.225	3.124	3.030	2.941	2.857	2.777	2.702	2.631	2.564	2.500
35	3.226	3.125	3.030	2.941	2.857	2.778	2.703	2.632	2.564	2.500
40	3.226	3.125	3.030	2.941	2.857	2.778	2.703	2.632	2.564	2.500
45	3.226	3.125	3.030	2.941	2.857	2.778	2.703	2.632	2.564	2.500
50	3.226	3.125	3.030	2.941	2.857	2.778	2.703	2.632	2.564	2.500

GLOSSARY OF TERMS

Numbers in parentheses indicate the chapter in which the term is first discussed in detail.

A

accounts receivable turnover (9) A measure of how accounts receivable are being managed, computed as

$$\text{accounts receivable turnover} = \frac{\text{annual sales}}{\text{accounts receivable}}$$

accrual-type securities (7) Securities on which interest is paid when the security is cashed (on or before maturity), rather than periodically over the life of the security.

accumulation period (17) The time between when payments are made to the insurance company and when the insurance company begins to pay the annuitant.

activity ratio (9) A measure of the way a company utilizes its assets which compares company sales to various asset categories.

adjustable (floating) rate preferreds (12) Preferred stocks whose dividend rates are not fixed, but are adjusted quarterly in line with yields on specific Treasury issues.

adjusted gross income (17) Gross income less the total allowable adjustments for tax purposes.

aftermarket *See* secondary market.

after-tax cash flow (ATCF) (16) The yearly cash flow earned on a real estate investment after all expenses, debt service, and taxes.

agency bonds (11) Bonds issued by political subdivisions of the U.S. government, but without direct obligation of the Treasury. The two types of agency bonds are *government sponsored* and *federal agency bonds*.

alternative minimum taxable income (AMTI) (17) Amount on which every taxpayer must pay at least a 20 percent rate of tax.

annual report (3) A source of operating data on a firm published annually by most publicly held corporations. *See also* stockholder's report.

annual stockholders' meeting (8) Meeting to present major policy items for discussion or vote—annual report, future prospects, election of the board of directors, special issues.

annuitant (17) The person to whom the payments on a policy are directed.

annuity (4, 17) A series of equal-annual payments; sometimes measured in terms of a guaranteed number of years or in a life or lives, to one or more persons.

American Stock Exchange (AMEX) (3) The second largest organized securities exchange, handling roughly 9 percent of total annual organized exchange share volume.

approximate yield formula (4) Method of estimating the fully compounded yield on an investment.

ask price (2) The lowest price at which a given security is offered for sale.

assaying (18) A process that tests the gold content of a bar or other object.

assets (6, 18) The total of what is owned.

automatic reinvestment plan (15) System by which dividends or capital gains are automatically plowed back to buy additional shares in a mutual fund.

average (stock market) (3) The arithmetic average price behavior in a representative group of stocks at a given point in time.

average tax rate (17) Taxes due divided by taxable income.

B

back-end load (15) A 1 or 2 percent commission on the sale of shares in a mutual fund.

balance sheet (6, 9) A statement of an individual or company's assets, liabilities, and equity.

balanced fund (15) A mutual fund that earns both current income and capital gains. Capital growth is less than growth funds and current income is less than income funds.

bar chart (10) The simplest and probably most widely used type of chart. Market or share prices are plotted on the vertical axis, and time on the horizontal axis.

Barron's **(3)** Newspaper published weekly by Dow Jones, the same company that publishes *The Wall Street Journal.* Directed strictly to financial issues; offers lengthy articles on a variety of topics of interest to individual investors.

basis (in capital asset) (17) What the purchaser paid for the asset, including commissions and other costs related to its purchase.

bear market (2) A market characterized by falling stock prices normally associated with investor pessimism, economic slowdowns, and government restraint.

bearer bond (11) Revenue bonds whose holder is considered the owner; the issuing organization keeps no record of ownership.

bellwether stocks (10) Major stocks that are consistently accurate in reflecting the current state of the market. General Motors is considered a key bellwether stock, as are IBM, DuPont, AT&T, Exxon, and Merrill Lynch.

beneficiaries (6) The designated recipients of insurance policy proceeds.

beta (4, 19) A measure of nondiversifiable (or relevant) risk found by applying statistical techniques to data relative to the historic returns of the given security and the historic returns for the market. Measures the relative fluctuation a security or a portfolio has in comparison to a market index.

bid price (2) The highest price offered to purchase a given security.

blind pool syndicate (17) A syndicate in which purchase and sale decisions are left to the syndicator.

blue chip stock (8) Stocks that are unsurpassed in quality and have a long record of earnings and dividends; the strongest and stablest on the market.

bond (11) A debt instrument by which investors lend money to the bond issuer, who agrees to pay a stated rate of interest over a specified period of time, at the end of which the original sum will be returned.

bond fund (15) A mutual fund that deals exclusively in bonds and primarily seeks income, with capital gains as a secondary objective.

bond rating (11) Letter grade assigned to a bond issue on the basis of extensive, professionally conducted financial analyses that designate its investment quality. The two largest and best-known rating agencies are Moody's and Standard & Poor's.

bond swap (11) Bond replacement; an investor liquidates one holding and simultaneously buys another issue in its place.

bond yield (3) An annual rate of return; a measure of the return an investor would receive on a bond if it were held to maturity.

book value (8, 12, 17) The amount of stockholders' equity in a firm, derived by subtracting liabilities and preferred stocks from assets held. A measure of the amount of debt-free assets supporting each share of preferred stock, found by subtracting all liabilities from total assets and dividing the difference by the number of preferred shares outstanding. *See also* net asset value.

book value per share (9) A measure that represents the difference between total assets and total liabilities.

$$\text{book value per share} = \frac{\text{stockholders' equity}}{\text{number of common shares outstanding}}$$

breadth of the market (10) The advances and declines of stock prices in the market.

broad market (4) Markets in which demand and supply are great.

budget (6) A schedule of income and expenditure commonly broken into monthly intervals and typically covering a one-year period.

bull market (2) A market with rising stock prices normally associated with investor optimism, economic recovery, and governmental stimulus.

business cycle (9) An indication of change in total economic activity over time.

business risk (4) The degree of uncertainty associated with an investment's earnings and ability to pay interest, dividends, and other returns owed investors.

c

call (13) An option to buy a specified amount of some financial asset on or before some future date at a specified price.

call feature (11) Provision that specifies whether or not the issuer will be allowed to retire the bond prematurely.

call premium (11) A price added to a bond's par value and paid to investors along with the issue's par value at the time the bond is called.

call price (11) The sum of par value and call premium; the price the issuer must pay to retire a bond prematurely.

capital asset (6, 17) Property owned and used by a taxpayer for personal reasons, pleasure, or investment. The most common types are securities and real estate.

capital asset pricing model (CAPM) (4) Model that relates the risk measured by beta to the level of expected or required return.

capital gain (1, 4, 6, 17) A gain that results from selling a stock or other asset at a price above that originally paid; the amount by which sale proceeds exceed the original purchase price.

capital gains distribution (15) Payments made to mutual fund shareholders that come from the profits that a fund makes from the sale of its securities.

capitalization rate (16) The rate used to convert an income stream to a present value. The discount rate used to estimate the value of real estate using the *income approach*.

capital loss (4, 6, 17) A negative capital gain; results when a capital asset is sold for less than its original purchase price.

capital market (1, 2) The long-term financial market.

carat (18) Measure of weight for diamonds; 1/142 of an ounce.

cash account (2) A brokerage account in which the customer can make only cash transactions; the most common type of account.

cash dividend (8) A regular money disbursement paid by a corporation to its stockholders.

cash market (14) A transaction that takes place at a certain time and for all practical purposes is completed then and there.

cash value (insurance) (6) The amount of money set aside by the insurer to provide for the payment of the death benefit.

certificate of deposit (CD) (7) Sometimes called a savings certificate, this instrument shows the deposit of a stated sum of money in a savings institution for a specified period of time at a specified rate of interest.

chart formation (10) Data from price patterns that provide signals about the future course of the market or stock.

charting (10) Technical analysis activity of plotting the behavior of everything from the DJIA to share price movements of individual stocks by means of charts.

checkwriting privilege (15) Mutual fund feature that allows an investor to write checks against the money invested in a mutual fund.

classified common stock (8) Denotes either different voting rights and/or dividend receipts for holders.

closed-end investment company (15) A type of mutual fund in which only a limited number of shares can be sold.

coefficient of determination (R^2) (19) Measure of the explanatory power of a regression equation.

collateral value (5) The amount of money that can be borrowed to finance a margin transaction.

collectible (18) Item that has value because of its attractiveness to collectors—for example, rare coins and stamps, artwork, and antiques.

collector artwork (18) Paintings, prints, sculpture, and other works of recognized artists.

commodities (9, 14) Physical commodities like grains, metals, wood, and meat that are traded on commodities or futures markets. *See also* futures.

common stock (8) An equity investment that represents ownership in a corporate form of business.

common stock ratio (9) Portion of total profits, dividends, and equity allocated to each share of stock; used to assess the performance of a company and for stock valuation purposes.

comparative sales approach (16) Technique of estimating market value of real estate which uses the sales prices of properties similar to the subject property as the basic input variable.

compound interest (4) Interest paid on an initial deposit plus any accumulated interest from period to period.

confidence index (10) A measure that attempts to capture the sentiment of the stock market by comparing bond yields.

confirmation (10) Crucial part of the Dow theory that occurs when the secondary movements in the industrial average are confirmed by the secondary movements in the transportation average; at that point, the market has changed from bull to bear, or vice versa, and a new primary trend is established. *See also* Dow theory.

constant dollar plan (20) A formula plan for timing transactions. The portfolio is divided into two parts. The speculative portion is invested in securities having high promise of capital appreciation; the conservative portion consists of low-risk investments such as bonds or an insured savings account.

constant ratio plan (20) A formula plan for timing transactions. System that establishes a fixed desired ratio of the speculative to the conservative portions of a portfolio.

continuous compounding (4) Compounding over the smallest time interval possible; the highest effective interest rate.

contribution to savings or investment (6) The difference between total income and total expenses during a given period of time.

conventional options (13) Over-the-counter put and call options.

conversion equivalent (12) The price at which the common stock would have to sell to make the convertible security worth its present market price, found by dividing the current market price of the convertible by its conversion ratio. *See also* conversion parity.

conversion parity (12) The price at which common stock would have to sell in order to make the convertible security worth its present market price. *See also* conversion equivalent.

conversion period (12) The period during which debentures can be freely converted.

conversion premium (12) The amount above the stock value of an issue at which a convertible will usually trade. Also called *water*.

conversion price (12) The stated value per share at which common stock will be delivered to an investor when he/she converts a convertible issue.

conversion privilege (12) The conditions and specific nature of the conversion feature of an obligation.

conversion ratio (12) The number of common shares into which the bond can be converted.

conversion value (12) An indication of what a convertible issue should trade for if it were priced to sell on the basis of its stock value.

convertible security (12) A special type of fixed income obligation (a bond or preferred stock) with a conversion feature that permits an investor to convert it into a specified number of shares of common stock.

convertible term (6) Term insurance policy provision that the policy may be converted to a whole life or endowment policy at the insured's option.

corporate bonds (11) Nongovernmental bonds from corporate sources: industries, banks and financial institutions, rail/transportation, and public utilities.

cost approach to value (16) A measurement based on determining the replacement cost of a property.

coupon (11) Feature that defines the annual interest income paid by an issuer to a bondholder.

covered option (13) Option against stocks the investor (writer) already owns.

credit life insurance (6) Term insurance that will pay off the insured's installment loan balances should he or she die.

cumulative dividends (12) A protective feature on preferred stock that requires all preferred dividends in arrears to be paid before any common dividends are paid.

cumulative voting (8) The one share-one vote rule amended to allow shareholders to cast all their combined votes in any manner they choose.

currency futures (14) Trading in foreign currencies, handled much like trading in commodities.

currency options (13) Options on foreign currencies traded on the Philadelphia Exchange that give holders a claim on large amounts of the specified foreign currency.

current income (4) Cash or near-cash that is periodically received as a result of owning an investment.

current interest rate (annuity) (17) Yearly return the insurance company is currently paying on accumulated deposits under an annuity contract.

current ratio (9) A commonly cited financial ratio. It is computed as follows:

$$\text{current ratio} = \frac{\text{current assets}}{\text{current liabilities}}$$

current yield (3, 11) The amount of current income a bond provides relative to its prevailing market price.

cyclical stocks (8) Stocks issued by companies whose earnings are closely linked to the general level of business activity, such as companies in the auto, chemical, or copper industries.

D

daily price limit (14) Restriction on the interday change in the price of the underlying commodity.

data base (1, 3) Organized collections of historical as well as current information available for computer use.

date of record (8) The date of a transaction, as it is recorded.

day order (20) An order that expires at the end of the trading day it was entered if it was not executed.

day of deposit to day of withdrawal method (7) Interest method that gives depositors full credit for all funds on deposit; also called daily interest.

dealer (2) One who makes markets in certain securities by offering to buy or sell at stated prices; always the second party to a transaction.

debenture (11) An unsecured bond.

debit balance (5) The amount of money being borrowed, or the size of the margin loan.

debt (1) An intangible investment that represents funds loaned in exchange for the receipt of interest income and the promised repayment of the loan at a given future date.

debt-equity ratio (9) A measure of the relative amount of funds provided by lenders and owners.

$$\text{debt-equity ratio} = \frac{\text{long-term debt}}{\text{stockholders' equity}}$$

deep discount bond (17) A bond selling at a price far below its par value.

defensive stock (8) A stock whose price will remain stable or even prosper when economic activity is tapering off.

deferred annuity (17) Plan under which payments to the annuitant begin at some future date.

deferred call (11) Obligation that cannot be called until a stipulated length of time has passed, generally five to ten years.

deferred equity (8, 12) Securities intended to be converted eventually into shares of common stock.

deficit (budget) (6) The amount by which total expenses exceed total income.

defined benefit plan (7) Employer-sponsored retirement or pension plan that indicates exactly what the individual's benefits will be.

defined contribution plan (7) Employer-sponsored retirement or pension plan that specifies contribution amounts rather than benefit amounts.

de-listed securities (2) Securities whose firms have failed to maintain certain listing requirements.

delivery month (14) The time when a commodity or item must be delivered; defines the life of the contract.

demand (16) People's willingness and ability to buy or rent a given property; stems from a market area's economic base, the characteristics of its population, and the terms and conditions of mortgage financing.

demographics (16) Characteristics of an area's population, such as household size, age structure, occupation, sex, and marital status.

denomination (11) Standard principal amounts into which issues are broken to facilitate the marketing of bonds.

depreciation (16, 17) A tax deduction based upon the original cost of a tangible asset and creating tax shelter due to the lack of an associated *cash* outflow.

desired rate of return (10) The amount of return that should be earned by an investor.

development programs (oil and gas) (17) Limited partnerships that finance the drilling of wells in areas of known, proved reserves.

direct investment (1) An investment in which an investor directly acquires a claim on a security or property.

disability insurance (6) Insurance that provides periodic payments to replace income when the insured is unable to work due to a covered injury, illness, or disease.

discount bond (11) Issues with a market value lower than par.

discount broker (2) Brokers with low overhead operations who will make transactions at lower commissions for customers not needing the array of services offered by brokerage firms.

discounted cash flow (16) Measure of investment return calculated by subtracting the original required investment from the present value of cash flows in order to find net present value (NPV). Commonly used in real estate investment analysis.

discount rate (4) The applicable interest rate when finding present value; also called *opportunity cost.*

discount security (7) Security sold at a price less than its redemption value—for example, Treasury bills are sold at discount.

discretionary account (2) An account for which a broker purchases or sells securities on behalf of the customer at his or her discretion.

diversifiable (unsystematic) risk (4, 19) That portion of an investment's risk which can be eliminated through diversification. Also called *business and financial risk* or *unsystematic risk.*

diversification (1, 19) The inclusion of a variety of vehicles in a portfolio for the purpose of reducing risk.

dividend (1) A payment made by a firm to shareholders.

dividend arrears (12) An outstanding unfulfilled preferred dividend obligation.

dividend exclusion (6, 8, 17) Allows taxpayers to exclude $100 in dividends from taxable income on a single return ($200 on a joint return). Also, a tax favor to stockholders of gas and electric public utilities that allows a stockholder who chooses dividends in the form of additional shares to exclude from taxable income up to $750 ($1,500 on a joint return) in market value of such dividends received.

dividend model (10) Stock valuation procedure based on the assumption that the value of a share of stock is equal to the present value of all its future dividends; in pure form, the model uses an infinite holding period and assumes that dividends grow at a constant (fixed) rate forever.

dividend reinvestment plan (6, 8) Plan that enables a corporation's stockholders to reinvest in additional shares of stock by automatically paying investors in shares of common stock instead of cash dividends.

dividend yield (8) The ratio of the level of current income from dividends to the most recent share price.

$$\text{dividend yield} = \frac{\text{annual dividend income}}{\text{stock price}}$$

dividends per share (9) A method of translating total aggregate (dollar) dividends paid by the company into a per share figure.

$$\text{dividends per share} = \frac{\text{annual dividends paid}}{\text{number of common shares outstanding}}$$

dollar cost averaging plan (20) A basic formula plan for timing transactions in which a fixed dollar amount is invested in a security in each period.

Dow theory (10) An approach to market analysis based on the idea that it is the price trend in the overall market as a whole that is important; the focus is on the long-term trend in market behavior (known as the primary trend).

Dow Jones averages (3) Four stock averages prepared by Dow Jones, publisher of *The Wall Street Journal.* They are the Dow Jones Industrial Average (DJIA), and the transportation, the public utility, and the composite averages.

Dow Jones bond averages (3) These averages include a utility, an industrial, and a composite bond average. Each average reflects the simple mathematical average of the closing prices, rather than yields, for each group of bonds included.

Dow Jones industrial average (DJIA) *See* Dow Jones averages.

downtick (5) The lower price of a security since the previous transaction.

dual fund (15) A type of mutual fund in which two kinds of shares are issued: senior securities with holders entitled to all interest and dividend income, and junior securities with holders entitled to all capital gains earned by the portfolio. Offered only by closed-end investment companies.

dual listing (2) Firms whose shares are listed on more than one exchange.

E

earnings per share (EPS) (8) A measure that translates total corporate profits into profits on a per share basis; a convenient measure of the amount of earnings available to stockholders.

economic analysis (9) The study of the general state of the economy and its potential effects on security returns.

effective rate of interest (7) Annual rate of return actually earned on an investment.

efficient market (10) The idea that the market price of securities always fully reflects available information and that therefore it is difficult, if not impossible, to consistently outperform the market by picking "undervalued" stocks.

efficient portfolio (19) One that provides the highest return for a given level of risk, or has the lowest risk for a given level of return.

employer-sponsored retirement program—basic plan (7) Retirement or pension plan set up by employer; can be contributory or noncontributory.

employer-sponsored retirement program—supplemental plan *See* 401(k) deferred compensation plan.

endowment (life) insurance (6) A policy that offers life insurance protection for a specified period of time, at the end of which it may be redeemed for its face value.

equipment leasing (17) Limited partnership investment in which the partnership buys the equipment—airplanes, railroad cars, computers—and leases it to someone else; the partnership can depreciate the item as well as qualify for an investment tax credit.

equipment trust certificate (11) Senior bond securities secured by equipment; popular for railroads, airlines, and other transportation companies.

equity (1) An ownership interest in a specific business or property.

equity capital (8) Evidence of an ownership position in a firm, in the form of shares.

equity kicker (12) The tendency for the market price of convertible issues to behave much like the common stock into which they can be converted.

esthetic environment (16) Neighborhoods where buildings and landscaping are well maintained, and there is no noise, sight, or air pollution or encroaching unharmonious land uses.

excess margin (5) The presence in an account of more equity than is necessary.

ex-dividend date (8) Date four business days before the date of record which dictates whether or not the person is an official shareholder and thus eligible to receive the declared dividend.

exemption (17) A deduction of $1,000 for each qualifying dependent of the taxpayer (federal).

exercise price (13) The price of a new stock that is specifically stated in the right; always set below the prevailing market of the stock. Also called *subscription price.*

expected return (4) Return on investments projected into the future; the prospects for a return on a given investment.

expenses (6) An item of personal or business outlay chargeable against revenue for a specific period.

expiration date (13) Specification of the life of an option.

exploratory programs (oil and gas) (17) Limited partnerships formed to finance drilling in areas where gas and oil are believed to exist but have not yet been discovered.

ex-rights (13) Situations in which the company stock and its rights are trading in separate markets and distinct from one another. Also called *rights-off.*

extra dividends (8) Dividends declared whenever firm profits are above average; usually paid in the fourth quarter and clearly marked "extra" to avoid misunderstanding.

F

FIFO method (7) Withdrawals charged against the earlier or opening balances of an account in a bank or other financial institution.

financial asset (18) A paper claim evidencing ownership, debt, or an option to acquire an interest in some tangible or intangible asset.

financial future (14) Guarantee by a seller that he or she will deliver a specified commodity, foreign currency, or financial instrument at a given price by a certain date.

financial institution (1) Institutions such as banks and savings and loan associations that accept deposits and lend them out or invest them.

financial market (1) A forum in which suppliers and demanders of funds are brought together.

financial planner (3) Person who works with an individual or corporate client to (1) evaluate the present financial situation, (2) identify financial goals, and (3) present a written proposal to achieve these goals. The financial planner collects and assesses all relevant data; identifies financial problems; provides written recommendations and alternative solutions; coordinates the implementation of recommendations; and provides periodic review and update. The planner is compensated on a fee and/or a commission basis for products such as insurance, investments, and legal services provided. Today most professional financial planners possess either the CFP or the ChFC designation, or both.

financial ratios (9) Measures of the operating results and financial condition of a firm that relate one item on the balance sheet (or income statement) with another and enable an investor to assess a firm's past and present condition.

financial risk (4) The mix of debt and equity financing used for a business entity or piece of property.

financial supermarket (1) One company that services investors' total financial needs.

fiscal environment (16) Amount of property taxes and municipal assessments an owner must pay on a property and the government services to which the owner is entitled.

fiscal year (9) A twelve-month period a company has defined as its operating year, which may or may not end on December 31.

fixed charge coverage (12) An indication of how well a firm services its preferreds and lives up to its claim on income.

$$\text{fixed charge coverage} = \frac{\text{earnings before interest and taxes}}{\text{interest expense} + \dfrac{\text{preferred dividends}}{.5}}$$

fixed commission schedule (2) Charges for small transactions established by brokerage houses.

fixed income securities (11, 12) A group of investment vehicles that offers a fixed periodic return.

fixed payout ratio (8) A way of keeping payments of dividends at a constant ratio of earned money to distributable funds.

flower bond (11) Purchase of an older government bond at a discount which can be used to pay federal estate taxes at par.

flow of funds statement (9) A statement of changes in financial position that brings together items from the balance sheet and the income statement.

forced conversion (12) The calling in of bonds by the issuing firm.

formula plan (20) A mechanical method of portfolio management used to try to take advantage of price changes in securities resulting from cyclical price movements.

401(k) deferred compensation plan (7) Option for employee to divert a portion of salary to a company-sponsored, tax-sheltered savings account.

fourth market (2) Transactions directly between large institutional buyers and sellers that bypass nonmember firms or dealers.

freely callable bond (11) A bond the issuer may retire at any time.

front-end load (15) Formal contractual agreements that supposedly (though not legally) compel the investor in a long-term investment program to pay all the commissions that will be due over the life of the contract in the first several years of the contract; the investor's account is not fully credited with share purchases until after these load charges have been met.

fully taxable equivalent yield (11) The rate of return an investor must earn on a fully taxable bond issue to match the after-tax return from a municipal bond.

$$\text{fully taxable equivalent yield} = \frac{\text{yield of municipal bond}}{1 - \text{tax rate}}$$

fundamental analysis (9) In-depth analysis of the financial condition of a specific company and the underlying behavior of its common stock.

futures contract (14) A commitment to deliver a certain amount of some specified item at some specified date in the future. The seller of the contract agrees to make the specified future delivery, and the buyer agrees to accept.

futures market (14) The organized market for the trading of futures contracts.

futures options (14) The ultimate leverage vehicle: listed puts and calls on a select but growing number of standardized futures contracts.

future value (4) The amount to which a current deposite into a compound interest account will accumulate at a certain date.

G

general obligation bond (11) A bond issued by a municipality backed by the credit of the issuer as well as its taxing power.

general partner (16, 17) The managing partner who accepts all liability and makes all decisions in a partnership.

general partnership (17) An agreement in which all partners have management rights and all assume unlimited liability for any debts or obligations the partnership might incur.

go-go funds *See* performance funds.

gold bullion (18) The metal in ingot form.

gold certificate (18) Written evidence of ownership of a specific number of ounces of gold that are stored in a bank vault.

gold coin (18) Coins whose value is determined by their gold content and not by their value to coin collectors; nonnumismatic gold coins.

gold future (18) A contract to buy (or sell) a specific amount of gold at a stated price at a specified future date.

gold stock (18) Shares of a gold mining company common stock or shares of mutual funds that invest a portion or all of their portfolio in such stocks.

good 'til canceled (GTC) (2, 20) A limit order that remains outstanding until it is executed or canceled. Also called an *open order*.

government securities money funds (7) Funds that eliminate any risk of default by confining their investments to T-bills and other short-term securities of the U.S. government or its agencies.

gross income (17) All includable income for federal income tax purposes.

gross national product (GNP) (9) The market value of all goods and services produced by a country over the period of a year.

group term insurance (6) Insurance plan offered only to members of a group, such as employees, often only so long as they remain members of the group.

growth fund (15) A fund whose primary aim is capital appreciation and long-term growth.

growth-oriented portfolio (19) A portfolio whose primary orientation is long-term price appreciation.

growth stock (8) Shares that have experienced and are expected to continue to experience consistently high growth in operations and earnings and normally pay little or no dividends.

H

hardware (1, 3) The physical parts of a computer system, such as the console, key-board, processor, or printer.

health insurance (6) Insurance designed to pay the expenses associated with an illness or accident.

heart bond (11) Another name for institutional bonds, chiefly those of religious orders, hospitals, and schools.

hedge (option hedging) (13) Combining two or more securities into a single investment position to reduce risk.

hedgers (14) Producers and processors who use futures contracts as a way to protect their interest in the underlying commodity or financial instrument.

holder of record (8) An investor who is an official stockholder of the firm as of the close of business on a certain date.

holding period (4) The relevant period of time over which an investor wishes to measure the return on a specified investment vehicle.

holding period return (HPR) (4, 20) The return from the relevant period of time over which one wants to measure return on a specific investment vehicle; the total return realized on a given investment.

hybrid securities (12) Securities possessing features of both common stocks and corporate bonds.

I

immediate annuity (17) An annuity contract under which payments begin as soon as it is purchased.

improvements (16) Man-made additions to a site, such as paved parking areas, side-walks, and amenities such as swimming pools and golf courses.

income (6) Items that represent cash received during a given period; including wages, salaries, bonuses, commissions, dividends, rents received, and interest received.

income approach to value (16) An approach which employs varied analytical tech-niques. With this approach, a property's value is equal to the present value of all its future cash flows.

income bond (11) Unsecured debts which require that interest be paid only after a certain amount of income is earned; there is no legally binding requirement to meet interest payments on a timely or regular basis so long as a specified amount of income has not been earned.

income fund (15) Funds whose primary objective is current income. Portfolios usually include various combinations of high-yield common stock, attractive preferred stock, and/or an assortment of bonds.

income-oriented portfolio (19) A portfolio that stresses current dividend and interest return.

income programs (oil and gas) (17) Limited partnerships that buy existing wells with proven reserves.

income property (16) Residential, commercial, and industrial property that provides some form of rental income to its owner.

income statement (6, 9) Description of the financial activities that have taken place during a specified period of time, which is typically one year, for a given individual or firm.

income stocks (8) Issues having a long, sustained record of regularly paying higher than average dividends. Many income stocks are also blue chips.

index (stock market) (3) Measurement of the current price behavior of a representative group of stocks in relation to a base value set at an earlier point in time.

index price system (14) Technique used to price T-bill and other short-term financial futures contracts, in which yield is subtracted from an index of 100.

indirect investment (1) An investment made in a portfolio or group of securities or properties.

individual retirement account (IRA) (7) Plan that allows individuals to establish their own retirement programs. Participants are allowed to make a tax-deductible contribution up to a $2,000 annual maximum.

industrial production index (9) Measure of the activity/output in the industrial or productive segment of the economy.

industry analysis (9) Study of the industry within which a particular company operates and the outlook for that industry.

inflation (4) Period of rising price levels.

initial margin (5) The minimum money or equity to be provided by the investor at the time of purchase; the amount required to make a given investment.

installment annuity (17) An annuity acquired by making payments over time; at a specified future date, the installment payments, plus the interest earned on them, are used to purchase an annuity contract.

institutional bond (11) Bonds marketed (usually in $1,000 denominations) by a variety of private, nonprofit institutions like schools, hospitals, and churches.

insurance (6) A mechanism that allows people to reduce financial risk by sharing in the losses associated with the occurrence of uncertain events.

interest rate futures (14) Futures contracts on debt securities.

interest rate options (13) Options on fixed income (debt) securities introduced by the Chicago Board Options Exchange in 1981.

interest rate risk (4) Risk on fixed income securities—bonds, preferred stocks—offering buyers a fixed periodic return.

in-the-money (13) An option with a striking price less than the market price of the underlying common stock. A major portion of the option premium is based on (or derived from) the true value of the call.

intrinsic value (9) The worth or value of a stock, determined by fundamental analysis.

inventory turnover (9) An inventory control measure.

$$\text{inventory turnover} = \frac{\text{sales}}{\text{inventory}}$$

investment (1) The process of identifying, evaluating, selecting, and monitoring the placement of funds in some medium with the expectation of preserving value and earning a positive return.

investment advisor (3) Individuals or firms that provide investment advice—typically for a fee—to clients. Services range from recommendations on investment vehicles and strategies to complete money management.

investment analysis (16) Real estate analysis that considers not only what similar properties have sold for, but also looks at the underlying determinants of value and tries to forecast such things as economic base, population demographics and psychographics, buying power, and potential sources of competition.

investment banker (2) A firm specializing in selling new issues.

investment club (3) A legal partnership binding a group of investors (partners) to a specified organizational structure, operating procedures, and purpose.

investment goals (1) Specific statements of the timing, magnitude, form, and risks associated with a desired return.

investment letter (3) A publication that provides analyses, conclusions, and recommendations of various experts on different aspects of security investment.

investment premium (13) Difference between market price and true value; amount of excess value embedded in the quoted price of a put or call.

investment process (1) A mechanism for bringing together suppliers (those having extra funds) with demanders (those who need funds).

investment tax credit (17) A tax credit that applies to property purchased and used in a trade or business.

investment trust (15) An interest in a pool of investments (usually a portfolio of corporate or municipal bonds).

investment value (8, 12) An indication of the worth placed in a stock—what the public thinks the stock should be traded for; the price at which the bond would trade if it were nonconvertible, and if it were priced at—or near—prevailing market yields of comparable issues.

itemized deduction (17) Personal living and family expenses that can be deducted from adjusted gross income when determining taxable income in income tax computation.

J

justified price (10) Price based on present value of estimated returns to stockholders (future dividends and share price behavior).

K

Keogh Plan (7) Retirement plan that gives self-employed persons the right to certain tax advantages; allows eligible persons to contribute 25 percent of their taxable income up to a $30,000 maximum per year.

L

legal environment (16) In real estate, the restrictions on use that apply to properties surrounding or near the subject property.

leverage (13, 16) Concept which rests on the principle of reducing the level of required capital in a given investment position without affecting the payoff or capital appreciation of that investment; the substitution of debt capital for equity capital.

leverage ratio (9) The amount of indebtedness within a financial structure and the ability of a firm to service its debt. There are two widely used leverage ratios: the debt-equity ratio and the times interest earned ratio.

liabilities (6) Debts currently outstanding.

liability insurance (6) Insurance that provides protection against the risk that the insured might as the result of negligence cause property damage or bodily injury to someone else; commonly included as part of homeowner's and automobile insurance policies.

LIFO method (7) Withdrawals charged to the most recent deposits or balances in an account.

limited partner (16, 17) A passive investor who supplies most of the capital and has liability limited only to the amount of his or her investment.

limited partnership (16, 17) A business organization form under which certain partners are designated as limited partners—that is, their liability is limited to their investment.

limit order (2, 20) An order to buy at a specified price (or lower) or sell at (or above) a specified price.

liquidation value (8) What a firm would bring at auction.

liquidity (6, 7) The ability to quickly, and without loss, convert an investment into cash.

liquidity ratio (9) The ability of a firm to meet its day-to-day operating expenses and satisfy its short-term obligations as they come due.

liquidity risk (4) Risk of not being able to liquidate an investment conveniently and at a reasonable price.

listed options (13) Term used to denote put and call options traded on organized exchanges, as opposed to conventional options traded in the over-the-counter market.

load fund (15) A mutual fund that charges a commission when shares are bought.

location (16) The placement of a property; a good location rates highly on two dimensions—convenience and environment.

long position (14) Buying a security. The investor who takes a long position wants the price to rise.

long purchase (2) The most common type of transaction, in which investors buy securities in the hope that they will increase in value and can be sold at a later date at a profit.

long-term (1) Description of investment(s) with longer maturities, or no maturity at all.

long-term capital gain (6) The return in excess of cost on assets held for more than one year. Sixty percent of long-term capital gains are exempt from taxes; the remaining 40 percent is taxed as ordinary income.

M

maintenance margin (5) The minimum amount of equity investors must carry in margin accounts at all times.

majority voting (8) The most common corporate voting system: each stockholder has one vote for each share of stock owned, and he/she may cast these votes for each position on the board.

management fee (15) Fee levied annually for professional portfolio management and services; deducted off the top regardless of the gains or losses sustained.

margin account (2, 5) A special account set up with a broker to handle all margin transactions regardless of the type of security being margined. This account is opened with a minimum of $2,000 in equity, cash, or deposited securities.

marginal tax rate (17) The tax rate on additional income.

margin call (5, 14) Notification when an account becomes undermargined, which gives the investor a short time (about 72 hours) to arrange a way to bring the account up to the prevailing initial margin.

margin loan (5) Financial leverage used as a way to get increased capital gains.

margin purchase (2) A security purchase that is *not* made on a cash basis; borrowed funds may be used.

margin trading (5, 14) Buying securities with borrowed money to magnify returns; margin refers to the equity in the investment.

market order (2, 20) An order to buy or sell stock at the best price available at the time the order is placed with the broker.

market return (4) Measure usually calculated by the average return on all (or a large sample of) securities, such as Standard & Poor's 500 Stock Composite Index.

market risk (4) Risk that results independent of the given security or property investment vehicle, such as political, economic, or social events, or changes in tastes and preferences.

market value (8, 16) The prevailing market price of a security or property; an indication of how the market as a whole has assessed the security's or the property's worth.

mark-to-the-market (5, 14) Name of activity on shorted stock. When the price of shorted stock goes up, the short seller's account is reduced and funds transferred to the lender's account; if the price declines, the opposite occurs.

maturity (of debt) (1) The time at which a repayment of a debt becomes due.

maturity date (11) Date on which a debt security expires.

maximum daily price range (14) The amount the price can change during a day; usually equal to twice the daily limit restrictions.

minimum balance method (7) Method in which interest is paid on the lowest balance in the account during a quarter.

minimum guaranteed interest rate (annuity) (17) The minimum interest rate on contributions to a deferred annuity purchase contract that the insurance company will guarantee over the life of the accumulation period. The minimum rate is usually substantially less than the current interest rate.

mixed stream of returns (4) Returns that exhibit no special pattern.

modern portfolio theory (MPT) (19) A way of analyzing investments that utilizes statistical measures such as the variance and correlation of a security's rate of return with the rate of return of another security or with the market as a whole.

money market (1, 2) The short-term financial market. *See also* capital market.

money market deposit account (MMDA) (7) Bank vehicle that competes with money market mutual funds; there is a minimum balance requirement, and interest rates are competitive with money market mutual funds.

money market mutual fund (MMMF) (7, 15) A mutual fund that pools the capital of a great number of investors and uses it to invest exclusively in high-yield, short-term securities.

Moody's Investor Services (3) A subscription service that publishes a variety of useful materials. The key publications are reference manuals (*Moody's Manuals*) which are similar to S & P's *Corporation Records.*

mortgage-backed bond (11) Used in the corporate sector, these securities are issued by fiduciary institutions and are similar to Ginnie Mae pass throughs—the issue is backed by a pool of mortgages. But the mortgages are private and are not backed by government faith and credit.

mortgage bond (11) Securities secured by real estate.

mortgage life insurance (6) Term insurance that will pay the outstanding balance on the insured's home loan should he or she die.

municipal bond (11) Issues of states, counties, cities, and other political subdivisions (such as school districts, water and sewer zones) and distinguished by interest income immune to federal taxation. Also known as *tax-free bonds.*

municipal bond guarantee (11) A guarantee to the bondholder that a party other than the issuer will make principal and interest payments promptly and within a specified period of time; strengthens bond quality.

mutual fund (15) An open-end investment company that invests its shareholders' money in a diversified group of securities of other corporations.

N

naked options (13) Options that are written on stock not owned by the writer.

NASDAQ (2) National Association of Securities Dealers Automated Quotation System. A system providing up-to-date bid and ask prices on thousands of over-the-counter securities.

NASDAQ indexes (3) Indexes that reflect over-the-counter market activity; calculated like the S & P and NYSE indexes, based on a value of 100 set February 5, 1971.

natural environment (16) The physical surroundings of a particular piece of property.

negative correlation (19) The rates of return of two securities moving in opposite directions.

negotiated commission (2) Generally the rule for large institutional transactions; permits firms to compete on both services and costs.

net asset value (NAV) (12, 15) "Book value" of a preferred stock and a measure of the amount of debt-free assets supporting each share of preferred stock; also, the value of a share of stock in a particular mutual fund.

net interest exclusion (17) An amount equal to the excess qualified interest income over qualified interest expense.

net operating income (NOI) (16) Amount left after the subtraction of vacancy and collection losses and operating expenses, including property taxes and property insurance, from gross potential rental income; the property's income before debt service and owner's income taxes.

net present value (NPV) (16) The difference between the present value of the cash flows and the amount of equity required to make the investment.

net profit margin (9) The rate of profit from sales and other revenues.

$$\text{net profit margin} = \frac{\text{net profit after taxes}}{\text{total revenues}}$$

net working capital (9) An absolute measure of a company's liquidity; the dollar amount of equity in the working capital position of the firm.

net worth (6) The ownership position or amount of wealth, or equity, in the assets owned.

New York Stock Exchange (NYSE) (2) The key organized securities exchange for stock and bond transactions, accounting for about 81 percent of the total annual volume of shares traded on organized exchanges.

New York Stock Exchange (NYSE) Indexes (3) Indexes that reflect NYSE market activity; calculated like the S & P and NASDAQ indexes, based upon a value of 50 set on December 31, 1965.

no-load fund (15) A fund that does not charge a commission.

noncallable bond (11) A bond that cannot be retired before maturity.

nonconvertible security (12) A security that cannot be converted into another form.

nondiversifiable (systematic) risk (4, 19) Risk attributed to forces affecting all investments and therefore not unique to a given vehicle, such as war, inflation, international events, and political events; the risk possessed by every investment vehicle.

NOW (negotiated order of withdrawal) account (7) Checking account that pays interest at the maximum allowable rate on passbook savings; no legal minimum balance, though banks often impose one.

numismatics (18) Coin collecting as an investment medium.

O

odd lot (2) Less than 100 shares of stock.

offering circular (17) A document describing the property to be purchased, management fees, and other financial details, including the limited partnership agreement.

open-end investment company (15) A fund with no limit on the number of shares it can offer; also called *mutual fund*.

open interest (14) The amount of which indicates the number of futures contracts presently outstanding.

open order *See* good 'til canceled (GTC).

open outcry auction (14) In futures trading, auction in which actual trading is done through a series of shouts, body motions, and hand signals.

operating ratio (9) The major components of a company's cost structure; relates total operating expenses to sales.

$$\text{operating ratio} = \frac{\text{cost of goods sold} + \text{administrative and occupancy expenses}}{\text{net sales}}$$

opportunity cost (4) The annual rate of return that could be earned on a similar investment; also called *discount rate*.

option (1, 13) An agreement that provides the investor with an opportunity to purchase another security or property at a specified price over a stated period of time.

option spread (13) Combining two or more options into a single transaction.

option straddle (13) The simultaneous purchase of a put and a call on the same underlying security or financial asset. Unlike an option spread, a straddle often involves the same striking price and expiration date.

option writer (or maker) (13) The individual or institution that writes put and call options.

ordinary income (6, 17) Income from all sources such as salaries, dividends, interest, and earnings from unincorporated businesses (sole proprietorships or partnerships).

organized securities exhanges (2) Centralized institutions in which the forces of supply and demand for certain securities are brought together.

out-of-the-money (13) A call that has no real value because the striking price exceeds the market price of the stock. Since the option has no value, its price is made up solely of investment premium.

over-the-counter market (OTC) (12, 13) A mass telecommunications network through which buyers and sellers of certain securities can be brought together to make transactions.

P

paper returns (4, 5) Making money on a transaction but not yet selling the securities; returns in the form of capital gains which are not yet realized.

par value (8, 11) The stated or face value of a stock; the principal amount of a bond.

participating dividends (12) Preferred stocks on which the stockholder can enjoy additional dividends if common payouts exceed a certain amount. The amount not only specifies the annual preferred dividend, but also sets a ceiling on the common stock dividend. Beyond this maximum, additional dividends must be shared on a specified basis with preferred stockholders.

passbook savings account (7) Traditional savings vehicle; generally no minimum balance or restriction on withdrawals.

payment date (8) The actual date on which the company will mail dividend checks to the holders of record.

payout (annuity) (17) Investment return provided by an annuity contract that is realized when the payment stream begins.

payout ratio (9) An indication of the amount of earnings paid out to stockholders in the form of dividends.

$$\text{payout ratio} = \frac{\text{dividends per share}}{\text{earnings per share}}$$

performance fund (15) The so-called go-go funds of the 1960s market, highly speculative funds that seek high profits from capital gains; an extension of the growth fund concept.

personal computer (PC) (1, 3) Relatively inexpensive but powerful home computer that can perform many analysis functions for the individual investor.

personal property (16) Property that is not attached in a more or less permanent fashion to real estate.

personal residence (16) Type of real estate that includes single-family houses, condominiums, cooperatives, and townhouses.

philately (18) Stamp collecting as an investment medium.

point-and-figure charts (10) Charts used to keep track of emerging price patterns in the market or for individual stocks.

pooled diversification (15) Turning over the problems of security selection and portfolio management to professional money managers. Each shareholder owns a part of the diversified portfolio acquired with the pooled money.

portfolio (1, 19) The securities held by an investor; a collection of investment vehicles assembled to meet an investment goal.

portfolio revision (20) Selling certain issues in a portfolio in order to purchase new securities.

positive correlation (19) What happens when two securities' rates of return move together.

preemptive right (13) The right of an existing stockholder to maintain his or her proportionate ownership in a firm.

preferred (agency) ratings (12) Ratings of preferred stocks that indicate quality of the security.

preferred (Pfd) stock (12) A stock that carries a fixed, specified dividend payment, and which takes precedence over dividends to holders of common stock.

premium (13) The discrepancy between the value of a warrant (as computed by a certain formula) and its market price; the purchase price of an option.

premium bond (11) Issues with market values in excess of par. Coupons are greater than those being offered on new issues.

present value (4) The inverse of future value; measures the value of a future sum currently.

price/earnings (P/E) ratio (3, 9) The current market price divided by the previous year's per share earnings; an extension of the earnings per share ratio used to determine how the market is pricing the company's common stock.

$$P/E = \frac{\text{market price of common stock}}{\text{EPS}}$$

primary market (2) The market in which new securities are sold to the public.

principal (11) A capital amount placed at interest, due as a debt, or used as a fund.

principle of substitution (16) The principle that people do not really rent or buy real estate per se; instead, they judge properties as different sets of benefits and costs and choose those that meet their particular needs.

private limited partnership (17) Limited partnership organization with a limited number of investors and not registered with a public agency.

profitability ratio (9) A ratio used as a relative measure of success; relates the returns (profits) of a company to sales, assets, or equity.

progressive tax rate (6, 17) A tax rate structure that places an increasingly higher tax burden on higher taxable incomes.

promised yield (11) Indication of the fully compounded rate of return available to the investor, assuming the obligation is held to maturity. Also called *yield-to-maturity.*

property (1) An investment in real property or tangible personal property.

property insurance (6) Insurance to protect against certain perils which are causes of loss, such as damage from weather, riots, vandalism, fire, and so on.

prospectus (2, 3, 15, 17) A document describing in detail the key aspects of the issuer, its management and financial position, and the security to be issued; explains in detail the operatons of a fund, its investment objectives, and other key financial matters. Also called an *offering circular.*

proxy (8) A signed statement assigning the stockholders' voting rights to a designated third party, usually a member of the board of directors, who is bound to vote as directed.

psychographics (16) Characteristics that describe a population's mental disposition, such as personality, life style, and self-concept.

public limited partnership (17) A limited partnership organization registered with the appropriate state or federal regulators and usually having twenty-five or more limited partners.

publicly traded issues (8) Shares that are readily available to the general public and are bought and sold on the open market.

public offering (8) An offering to the investing public of a set number of shares of a company's stock at a set price.

public utility dividend reinvestment plan (17) Created by the 1981 Tax Act, allows stockholders of gas and electric public utilities who choose to receive dividends in additional shares of common stock to exclude from taxable income up to $750 ($1,500 on a joint return) in market values of such dividends received.

purchasing power risk (4) Possibility of price level changes in the economy.

purposive diversification (1) Selecting investment vehicles to achieve a stated portfolio purpose.

put (1, 13) An option to sell 100 shares of common stock on or before some future date at a specified price.

put hedge (17) Buying a put option on shares currently owned.

put option (2) An option to sell a given common stock.

pyramiding profits (5) The use of the margin account to build up investment holdings and to acquire additional securities.

Q

quotations (securities) (3) Price information about various types of securities, including current price data and statistics on recent price behavior.

R

random diversification (1) Selecting investment vehicles at random, such as by drawing names from a hat.

random walk hypothesis (10) The belief that price movements are unpredictable and that, as a result, security analysis will not help to predict future behavior.

ratio analysis (9) The study of the relationships among and between various financial statement accounts.

real estate (1) Investment in such things as owner-occupied homes, raw land, and a variety of forms of income property, such as apartments.

real estate investment trust (REIT) (16) A type of closed-end investment company that invests money in mortgages and various types of investment real estate.

real property (1) Land, buildings, and that which is permanently affixed to the land.

realized return (4) A return attained by the investor during a specific period of time; current income.

realized yield (11) A security's total return over time.

red herring (2) A statement indicating the tentative nature of an offer, stamped in red on the prospectus.

refunding provision (11) Bond feature exactly like a call feature except that it forbids premature retirement of an issue from the proceeds of a lower coupon refunding bond.

registered bond (11) In contrast to a bearer bond, a bond registered with the issuer, who keeps a record of the owner and regularly pays interest to the owner of record by check.

regular dividend (8) The payment of fixed dollar amount of dividends on a quarterly basis.

regular extra dividend (8) A dividend paid whenever the level of earnings is higher than normal and the firm has an extra pool of funds from which to pay dividends.

relevant risk (19) Risk that is nondiversifiable.

renewable term policy (6) Term life insurance policy that may be renewed at the option of the insured for another term of equal length.

repurchase agreement (repo) (7) High-yield investment offered by some financial institutions in which the investor buys a share in a portfolio of government securities owned by the institution, with the stipulation that the institution buys back the share within a specified period of time.

required reinvestment rate (11) What the investor must earn on each of the interim cash throwoffs (coupon receipts) to realize a return equal to or greater than the promised yield.

required return (4) The amount of return to compensate for the amount of risk.

residential properties (16) Rental units with permanent occupants.

residential property depreciation (17) Amount of depreciation that can be deducted for tax purposes from ordinary pretax income.

restricted account (5) An account that carries a margin level less than prevailing initial margin requirements.

retained earnings (8) The amount of past and current earnings not paid out as dividends, and left to accumulate in the firm to finance the operations of the company.

return (4) The expected level of profit from an investment; the reward for investing.

return on invested capital (14) Return to investors based on the amount of money actually invested in a contract.

return on investment (ROI) (9) Return to stockholders measured by relating profits to stockholders' equity.

$$\text{ROI} = \frac{\text{net profit after tax}}{\text{stockholders' equity}}$$

return on total assets (ROTA) (9) A profitability measure that looks at the amount of resources needed by the firm to support its operations.

$$\text{ROTA} = \frac{\text{net profit after tax}}{\text{total assets}}$$

revenue bond (11) An income bond and the most junior of unsecured bonds; requires that interest be paid only after a certain amount of income is earned. There is no legal, binding requirement to meet interest on timely or regular bases.

reverse stock split (8) A split that reduces shares outstanding and increases share price.

reversion (16, 20) The potential profit realized upon sale of income property (after tax profits); future interest in a property left in the control of the seller.

right (1, 13) An option to buy a fraction of a share of common stock at a stated price over a specified period of time.

rights-off (13) Situation when the company's stock and its rights are trading in separate markets and distinct from one another. Also called *ex-rights*.

rights offering (8, 13) A popular way of issuing common stock. Requires that existing stockholders be given first opportunity of buying a new issue and be permitted to purchase new shares in proportion to their prevailing ownership position in the firm.

rights-on (13) Indication that common stock is trading with the right attached to it.

risk (1, 4, 19) The chance that the value or return on an investment will differ from its expected value.

risk-adjusted, market-adjusted rate of return (RAR) (20) A method of gauging the investment performance of common stocks and portfolios of common stocks.

risk-averse (4) Investors who are shy of taking risks and require higher returns to counter risks.

risk-free rate of interest (R_F) (4) A rate of interest generally set equal to the return on a government security (zero risk).

risk-free rate of return (R_F) (19) The point where the risk-return line crosses the return axis (R_F).

risk-indifferent (4) Investors who do not require a greater-than-proportional increase in return as compensation for taking more risk.

risk-return tradeoff (4, 19) The inverse relationship between the risk associated with a given investment and its expected return.

risk-taker (4) The opposite of *risk-averse*.

round lot (2) A lot of 100 shares.

round trip commission (14) The commission costs on both ends of a transaction, buying and selling.

s

savings account (7) A deposit made to a financial institution which then pays a stated rate of interest on the funds.

savings plan (15) A systematic savings and capital accumulation program in which the investor agrees to add to a savings mutual fund regularly (monthly or quarterly); the money is used to purchase added shares.

secondary distributions (2) The sale of a large block of securities by a major shareholder, often made in the OTC market rather than on the appropriate exchange.

secondary market (2) The market in which securities are traded after they have been issued. Also called the *used security market*.

Securities Investor Protection Corporation (SIPC) (2) A federal agency established by the Securities Investor Protection Act of 1970 to protect customer accounts against the consequences of financial failure of the brokerage firm by insuring each customer's account for up to $500,000 of securities and up to $100,000 in cash balances.

securities markets (2) The mechanism that allows suppliers and demanders of funds to make transactions. *See also* capital market, money market.

security (1) An investment that represents evidence of debt, ownership of a business, or the legal right to acquire or sell an ownership interest in a business.

security analysis (9) Gathering information, organizing it into a logical format, and using the information to determine the intrinsic value of a common stock.

selling group (2) A group organized to sell a security issue made up of a large number of stock brokerage firms, each of which pledges to sell a certain portion of the issue. *See also* underwriting syndicate.

serial bond (11) A bond which has a series of different maturity dates, perhaps as many as 15 or 20, within a single issue.

settle price (14) The last price of the day or the closing price for commodities.

shorting-against-the-box (5, 17) A hedging technique to protect existing security profits, set up after the investor has generated a profit in another, earlier transaction.

short interest (10) The number of stocks sold short in the market at any given point in time; the more stocks sold short, the higher the short interest.

short position (14) The selling of borrowed securities.

short selling (2, 5) Selling borrowed securities; a transaction starting with the sale of securities, and ending with the purchase of these securities with the hope that the price is lower than when sold.

short-term (1) Describes investment(s) with a life of one year or less.

short-term capital gain (6) Capital gains on assets held for one year or less; short-term gains are taxed as ordinary income.

silver bullion (18) The metal in ingot form.

silver coin (18) Coins whose value is determined by their silver content and not by their value to collectors; nonnumismatic silver coins.

silver future (18) A contract to buy or sell a specific amount of silver at a stated price at a specified future date.

silver mining stocks (18) Shares of a silver mining company common stock or shares of mutual funds that invest in such stocks.

simple interest (4) Method of calculating interest by applying the stated interest rate to actual balances on deposit for the period of deposit; interest paid only on the actual balance for the exact deposit period. Also called the *true interest rate.*

single premium annuity (17) An annuity contract purchased with a single lump-sum payment.

single-property syndicate (17) A real estate limited partnership established to purchase specific properties.

sinking fund (11) Provision that specifies how a term bond will be paid off over time; also specifies the annual repayment schedule.

social security (7) Government income program for those who have reached a certain age and retired or are disabled and to which individuals contribute over their working lifetime. Benefits and conditions set by federal law.

socioeconomic environment (16) The demographics and life styles of the people who live or work in nearby properties.

software (1, 3) Programs designed to tell a computer what functions to perform.

specialist (2) A member of an exchange, who specializes in the trading of one or more stocks.

specialty fund (15) Concentrated holdings in one industry, or group of related industries, geographical area, or specialty. Electronics, metals, chemicals, health fields, and foreign specialties (Japanese stocks, South African gold) are all examples of specialty funds.

speculation (1, 14) The process of buying a security in which the future value and level of expected earnings are highly uncertain.

speculative property (16) Category of real estate investment that typically includes land, special purpose buildings, and time-sharing condominium units.

speculative stock (8) Shares offering little more than hope that their prices will go up. Imperfect records of success, uncertain earnings, and high instability are all qualities of speculative stock.

speculators (14) Those who trade securities and futures contracts simply to earn a profit on expected swings in the price of a security.

spinoff dividend (8) Similar to stock dividend except that the company pays in shares of stock other than its own.

split ratings (11) Different ratings given to a bond issue by the two major rating agencies.

spread (14) The difference between option premiums.

Standard & Poor's (S & P) Corporation (3) A large financial publisher that provides information on specific industries and companies on a subscription basis.

Standard & Poor's (S & P) indexes (3) Indexes prepared by Standard & Poor's Corporation. Unlike the Dow Jones averages, Standard & Poor's five common stock indexes (industrial, transportation, public utility, financial, and composite) are true indexes; they relate the current price of a group of stocks to a base established for the 1941–1943 period, which has an index value of 10.

stated interest rate (4) Interest as stated by the bank or financial institution; differs from true interest rate when compounded more often than annually.

statement of changes in stockholders' equity (9) Recap of the amount of profits reinvested in a business, the amount of dividends paid out to investors, and other changes in a firm's equity position.

stockbroker (2) One who enables investors to purchase and sell securities; also called an account executive.

stock dividend (8) Additional stock issued to shareholders instead of cash.

stockholder's report (3) A source of operating data on an individual firm published annually by publicly held corporations. It contains a wide range of information, including financial statements for the most recent period of operation, along with summarized statements for several prior years. *See also* annual report.

stock index futures (14) A new trading vehicle introduced in April 1982; futures contracts pegged to widely reported broad measures of stock market performance that allow investors to participate in the general movements in the stock market.

stock right *See* right.

stock split (8) Maneuver in which a company increases its shares outstanding by exchanging a specified number of new shares for each old share outstanding.

stock valuation (10) Obtaining a standard of performance that can be used to judge the investment merits of a share of stock.

stop-loss order (2, 20) An order to sell a stock when its market price reaches or drops below a specified level; a suspended order used primarily to protect the investor against rapid declines in prices and to limit loss.

straddle (14) The simultaneous purchase of a put and a call on the same underlying common stock.

straight term policy (6) A term insurance policy written for one year or a fixed number of years.

strategic metals (18) Metals vital to the production of many U.S.-made goods not found or mined in the United States, such as cobalt, rhodium, and titanium.

stream of returns (4) A package of single-sum returns, either a mixed stream or an annuity.

street name securities (5) Those securities held by brokers or their customers, such as stock certificates issued in the brokerage's name but held for the client's account.

striking price (13) The price contract between the buyer of an option and the writer.

subordinated debenture (11) Issues with a claim on income secondary to other debentures.

subscription price (13) The price of a new stock that is specifically stated in the right; always set below the prevailing market of the stock. Also called an *exercise price.*

subscription service (3) Service that provides information on specific industries and companies. A subscriber pays a basic fee that entitles him or her to certain information published and periodically updated by the service. The major subscription services provide both descriptive and analytical information.

suitability rule (limited partnership) (17) A rule excluding certain types of investors who cannot bear a high amount of risk from buying limited partnership interests.

supply (16) In real estate investment, the competition—potential competing properties.

Super NOW (7) Checking account on which the institution can pay any rate of interest it chooses; legal minimum balance required.

surplus (budget) (6) The amount by which total income exceeds total expenses.

sweep account (7) Account that services a wide range of activities—checking, investing, borrowing—and automatically sweeps excess funds into short-term investments.

syndicate (17) A joint venture—general partnerships, corporations, or limited partnerships—in which investors pool their resources.

systematic risk *See* nondiversifiable risk.

T

tangible investment or asset (property) (18) Asset that can be seen and touched, that has an actual form or substance. Examples include real estate, precious metals and stones, coins, stamps, artwork, and antiques.

taxable income (17) Income to which the tax rates are applied; adjusted gross income minus excess itemized deductions and exemptions.

tax avoidance (17) A comprehensive legal strategy to maximize total after-tax income over an investor's lifetime by removing or deferring income from liability to tax.

tax credit (6, 17) Provision of internal revenue regulations allowing a taxpayer to claim a credit on taxes due under certain specified conditions.

tax deferral (17) Shifting income subject to tax to a period when the rate will be lower.

tax-deferred annuity (17) A special provision in the income tax laws that allows certain employees of institutions such as schools, universities, governments, and not-for-profit organizations to make a tax-free contribution from current income to purchase a deferred annuity.

tax evasion (17) Illegal activities to evade paying taxes, such as omitting income or overstating deductions.

tax-exempt money fund (7) Fund that limits its investments to tax-exempt municipal securities with very short (30 to 90 days) maturities.

tax-favored income (17) Investment that offers a return taxed at a rate lower than that on other similar investments.

tax-free municipal bond (15) Bond whose earned interest is not subject to federal incomes taxes.

tax-free (muncipal bond) fund (15) Fund that holds only municipal bonds that generate income free from federal tax.

tax planning (17) Seeking investment income that is not included as taxable income, or is included at a reduced amount or rate.

tax shelter (1, 6, 16, 17) Certain forms of investment that can lower ordinary taxable income.

tax swap (6, 17) Replacing a security sold at a loss with a similar security issued by a similar firm in the same industry to avoid the IRS regulation prohibiting *wash sales*.

technical analysis (10) Study of the various economic forces at work in the marketplace.

term bond (11) A bond with a single, fairly lengthy maturity date; the commonest type of bond issue.

term (life) insurance (6) A policy in which the insurance company is obligated to pay a specified amount if the insured dies within the policy period.

term-to-maturity (11) The amount of time remaining for older outstanding bonds, based on the maturity date of the issue.

theory of contrary opinion (10) A theory of market behavior that uses the amount and type of odd-lot trading as an indicator of the current state of the market and pending changes.

thin market (4) A market in which demand and supply are small, and investment opportunities tend to be less.

third market (2) Name given to the OTC transactions made in securities listed on the NYSE, AMEX, or other organized exchanges. Serves the needs of large institutional investors (mutual funds, life insurance companies) by expediting large transactions at reduced cost.

ticker (3) An automated quotation device found in most brokerage offices. It is a lighted screen on which stock transactions made on the floor of the exchange are reported immediately after they occur.

times interest earned (9) Measurement of the ability of the firm to meet its fixed interest payments.

$$\text{times interest earned} = \frac{\text{earnings before interest and taxes}}{\text{interest expense}}$$

time value of money (4) The principle that it is better to have a given return sooner rather than later.

total asset turnover (9) An indication of how efficiently assets are being used to support sales.

$$\text{total asset turnover} = \frac{\text{sales}}{\text{total assets}}$$

total return (4) Current income plus capital gains return.

total risk (19) The sum of the diversifiable and nondiversifiable risk components.

trading action approach (10) An analytical approach in which daily trading activity over a long period of time is examined in detail to determine whether or not certain characteristics occur with a high degree of frequency.

traditional approach (to portfolio) (19) The approach that emphasizes "balancing" the portfolio with a wide variety of stocks and bonds.

transfer process (16) The process of obtaining information (or promoting in the event of sale) and negotiating the transfer of real estate from seller to buyer. The end result of this process is an agreed upon transaction (sale) price.

Treasury bill (T-bill) (7) Security issued by the U.S. Treasury that provides the purchaser with a known interest return over a specified period of time.

Treasury bond (11) Securities backed by the credit of the government which are highly liquid and reliable. Treasury bonds have maturity dates that extend to twenty-five years or longer; income from them is exempt from state and local taxes, but subject to federal taxes.

treasury stock (8) Stocks are acquired *back* by the issuing company and no longer outstanding; retained by the corporation and used for various purposes.

troy ounce (18) Measurement used for gold content; one troy ounce contains approximately 31 grams.

true rate of return (interest) (4) Rate of return earned on the actual balance for the actual amount of time it is on deposit.

turnaround (12) Finding preferreds with dividend arrearages and a trading value far below normal, but which is about to undergo a "turnaround."

U

undermargined account (5) Account that has dropped below the required prevailing initial margin; margin accounts are considered restricted as long as the equity remains below initial margin requirements.

underwriting (2) The name for the investment banker's selling activity.

underwriting syndicate (2) A network of underwriting firms joined as partners for a large new security sale.

unit investment trust (15) An interest in an unmanaged pool of investments; a portfolio of securities is held in safekeeping for investors under conditions set down in a trust agreement; there is no trading, so returns are fixed and predictable.

universal account (7) Comprehensive account that services a wide range of checking, investing, and borrowing activities offered by major bank and brokerage firms. *See also* sweep account.

universal life insurance (6) New form of life insurance that has such features as full disclosure of buyer-paid costs, higher yield on cash value, flexibility in coverage and premium costs, and greater policyholder flexibility.

unsystematic risk (4, 19) *See* diversifiable risk.

uptick (5) Situation when the price of a security has gone up since the last transaction.

U.S. savings bond (7) A short-term security readily available to the individual investor, issued by the U.S. Treasury.

V

valuation (1) A procedure for estimating the true worth of an investment vehicle.

Value Line Investment Survey (3) One of the most popular subscription services used by individual investors; published weekly and covering more than 1,700 companies and their stocks.

variable rate note (11) An unusual form of debt with two unique features: (1) after the first 6 to 18 months of the issue, the coupon "floats" so that every 6 months it is pegged at a certain amount (usually 1 percent) above prevailing Treasury bill or bond rates; (2) the notes are redeemable—at par and the holder's option—every 6 months, after the first year.

variable ratio plan (20) A formula plan for timing portfolio transactions in which the ratio of the speculative to the conservative portion of a portfolio varies depending on the movement in value of the speculative securities.

vested retirement plan (7) An interest in future retirement benefits carrying the legal right of present or future enjoyment.

volatility (19) The amount of fluctuation of a security or portfolio.

voting rights (8) Rights of common stockholders to vote on matters pertaining to corporate operations, usually at the annual stockholders' meeting.

W

The Wall Street Journal (3) The most popular and comprehensive source of financial news, the *WSJ* is published daily and has a circulation of over 1.9 million.

warehousing liquidity (20) Keeping a portion of a portfolio in a very low-risk, highly liquid investment such as a money market account or money market mutual fund.

warrant (1, 13) A long-lived option enabling the holder to acquire common stock. Like rights, warrants are found only in the corporate sector of the market.

wash sale (6, 17) The selling of securities on which capital losses can be realized and then immediately buying them back.

whipsawing (20) Situation in which a stock temporarily drops in price and then bounces back up.

whole life insurance (6) Insurance coverage over the entire life of an insured.

withdrawal plan (15) Investment funds that offer shareholders the opportunity to receive payments regularly on a monthly or quarterly basis.

Y

yield (4) The actual rate of return earned by an investment.

yield curve (11) Relationship between yield and maturity shown in a curve that graphically relates term to maturity to a bond's yield at a specific time.

yield spread (11) A rate differential.

This section of credits constitutes a continuation of the copyright page.

BOXES

Box 2.3: Reprinted by permission of Better Homes and Gardens Magazine. © Copyright Meridith Corporation 1982. All rights reserved.

Boxes 7.2, 15.1, 18.1: Reprinted from the November 22, 1982, August 3, 1981, and November 8, 1982, issues of *Business Week* by special permission, © 1981, 1982 by McGraw-Hill, Inc.

Boxes 3.1, 11.2, 15.2, 15.3, 16.3: Reprinted with permission from CHANGING TIMES Magazine, © 1981, 1982 Kiplinger Washington Editors, Inc. This reprint is not to be altered in any way, except with permission from CHANGING TIMES.

Box 17.4: © Nancy Dunnan. Reprinted by permission of the Author from "In Search of Tax Shelters," FACT Magazine, July 1982.

Boxes 2.2, 4.1: Reprinted by permission of FACT, The Money Management Magazine, 711 Third Avenue, New York NY 10017. © 1982, 1983, FACT.

Box 17.1: Reprinted by permission of *Financial World.*

Boxes 4.2, 10.3, 11.3, 12.1, 14.2, 17.3: Reprinted by permission of FORBES Magazine.

Boxes 5.1, 8.3, 20.2: Reprinted by permission of FORTUNE Magazine; © 1980, 1982 Time, Inc. All rights reserved.

Box 18.3: Reprinted by permission of HOME Magazine.

Boxes 1.1, 3.3, 6.2, 13.3, 16.1, 16.2, 19.1, 19.2, 19.3, 20.3: Reprinted by permission of MONEY Magazine; © 1979, 1980, 1981, 1982, 1983 Time, Inc. All rights reserved.

Box 2.1: Reprinted by permission of The New York Stock Exchange.

Box 6.3: © 1982 by The New York Times Company. Reprinted by permission.

Box 18.2: Reprinted by permission of the author, Bohdan O. Szuprowicz, president of 21st CENTURY RESEARCH, an international investment and market research firm, and publisher of SUPER-GROWTH TECHNOLOGY USA monthly report.

Boxes 1.3, 4.3, 6.1, 7.1, 7.3, 8.1, 8.2, 9.1, 9.2, 9.3, 10.1, 13.1, 13.2, 17.2, 20.1: Reprinted from "U.S. News & World Report." Copyright, 1979, 1981, 1982, 1983, U.S. News & World Report, Inc.

Boxes 1.2, 3.2, 7.4, 10.2, 11.1, 12.2, 14.1: Reprinted by permission of *The Wall Street Journal,* © Dow Jones & Company, Inc., 1980, 1981, 1982. All rights reserved.

CARTOONS

Chapters 1, 4, 5, 8, and 20: © 1984 by Sidney Harris. Reprinted by permission of Sidney Harris.

Chapters 2, 16, and 17: © 1974, 1973, 1979. Reprinted with permission from The Saturday Evening Post Co.

Chapters 3, 7, 11, and 13: From *The Wall Street Journal.* Reprinted with permission, Cartoon Features Syndicate.

Chapters 9 and 14: "Good News/Bad News." Reprinted by permission: Tribune Company Syndicate, Inc.

Chapters 15 and 19: Reprinted with permission from CHANGING TIMES Magazine, © 1974 Kiplinger Washington Editors, Inc. This reprint is not to be altered in any way, except with permission from CHANGING TIMES.

Chapter 6: Reprinted by permission of *The Wall Street Journal* and Joseph Farris.

Chapter 10: © 1980 Punch/Rothco. Reprinted by permission.

Chapter 12: Reprinted by permission of Bo Brown.

Chapter 18: Reprinted by permission of Lepper.

FIGURES

Chapter 2. Figure 2.2: Reprinted by permission of Goldman, Sachs & Co. Figure 2.3: Photos 1, 3, and 4, courtesy of Prudential-Bache, Inc.; photo 2, courtesy of The New York Stock Exchange. Figure 2.4: Reprinted by permission of Charles Schwab & Co., Inc.

Chapter 3. Figure 3.1: From Arnold Bernhard & Co., *The Value Line Investment Survey, Ratings and Reports,* edition 5, January 28, 1983, p. 759. Figure 3.2: © 1983 Mobil Corporation. Reprinted with permission of Mobil Corporation. Figures 3.3 and 3.4: Reprinted by permission of Standard & Poor's. Figure 3.5: Reprinted by permission of Hechinger Company. Figures 3.6, 3.7, 3.8, 3.9: Reprinted by permission of *The Wall Street Journal,* © Dow Jones & Company, Inc., 1983. All rights reserved. Figure 3.10: Reprinted by permission of Dow Jones News Retrieval Service, © Dow Jones & Company, Inc., 1982. All rights reserved.

Chapter 5. Figure 5.2: Courtesy of The New York Stock Exchange.

INDEX

A

Accounts receivable turnover, 330
Accrual-type securities, 239
Activity ratios, 329–332
Adjustable (floating) rate preferreds, 437
Adjusted gross income, 641–642
Agency bonds, 398
Alternative minimum taxable income (AMTI), 645
American Association of Individual Investors (AAII), 71, 90–91
American Stock Exchange (AMEX), 33, 35
    index of, 92
Analytical information, 66
Annual reports, 72, 331
Annual stockholders' meeting, 277
Annuitant, 658
Annuities, 129–131, 657–663
Antiques, 702–703, 705
Approximate yield, 133–134, 357, 620–621
Arrears, dividend, 438
Artwork, 704–705
Ask price, 37
Assay, 691
Assets, 186, 187, 322–324

Automatic reinvestment plans, 205, 288, 289, 578–579, 655
Averages, 87
    bond, 93–94, 747
    stock market, 88–92, 360–362, 747
Average tax rate, 644

B

Back-end load, 568
Back-office research reports, 77
Balanced funds, 574
Balance sheet
    corporate, 322–325
    personal, 186–187, 189–190
Bankers, 95
Bar charts, 368
Barron's, 69, 77, 92–94, 316, 363, 365, 587, 745
Basis (capital asset), 640
Basis points, 540
Bearer bonds, 395
Bear markets, 42–43
Bellwether stocks, 362
Beta, 137–140, 719–721
Bid price, 37

Blind pool syndicate, 668
Blue chip stocks, 291–292
Bond funds, 574
Bond ratings, 403–405
Bonds, 5, 17–18, 385–424, 747
   averages and indexes, 93–94
   confidence index on, 365
   convertible, 18. *See also* Convertible securities
   deep discount, 655–656
   holding period return on, 749–750
   price quotations on, 84, 411–413
   transaction costs for, 55–56, 413
   Treasury, 395–397, 496–503
   yields on, 93, 405–410, 415–418
Bond swaps, 422–423
Book value, 280–282, 442
Book value per share, 337
Breadth of the market, 137, 363
Brokerage services, 43–57
   financial planning, 15, 95
   research reports, 77
   universal and sweep accounts, 239
Budgets, 191–192
Bull markets, 42–43
Business cycle, 310–313
Business periodicals, 70–71
Business risk, 135
Business Week, 70, 313, 316, 407

C

Call feature, 388–390, 440
   deferred, 389, 397
Call options. *See* Put and call options
Call premiums, 389–390
Call price, 389–390
Canadian stock exchanges, 35–36
Capital asset pricing model (CAPM), 137–140
Capital assets, 204, 640
Capital gains (losses), 17, 115–117, 122–123, 204, 640
Capital gains distributions, 570, 578–579
Capitalization rate, 615
Capital market, 8, 30–36
Carat, 700
Cash accounts, 47
Cash dividends, 285, 287–290
Cash market, 516
Cash value (insurance), 195
Certificates of deposit (CDs), 237–238
   options on, 496–503
Changing Times, 71, 587
Chart formations, 368, 371
Charting, 366–371

Checking accounts
   with mutual funds, 234, 580–581
   NOW and Super NOW, 232–233, 774
Chicago Board of Trade (CBT), 36, 517, 520, 538
Chicago Board Options Exchange (CBOE), 36, 84–86, 482–483
Chicago Mercantile Exchange, 517, 535, 538
Classified common stock, 280
Closed end investment companies, 41, 564–565. *See also* Mutual funds
   real estate investment trusts (REITs), 599–600
Coefficient of determination (R^2), 720
Coin collecting, 704
Collateral value, 172
Collectibles, 701–705
Collector artwork, 704–705
Commercial and Financial Chronicle, 69
Commodities Exchange of New York, 517
Commodity futures, 19, 526–534
   exchanges, 36, 517–518
   price quotations, 87, 526–529
   transactions costs, 57, 522–523
Common stock, 17, 269–301
   analysis of, 307–340, 359–371
   averages and indexes, 88–92
   deferring taxes on sale of, 649–654
   dividends on. *See* Dividends
   gold mining, 692
   holding period return on, 748–749
   order types, 49–50, 773, 774
   price quotations, 79–83
   puts and calls on. *See* Put and call options
   random walk hypothesis and, 373–377
   rights for. *See* Rights
   securities convertible to. *See* Convertible securities
   silver mining, 699
   stock splits on, 273–275
   transaction costs, 53–55, 275–276
   transaction types, 50–52
   valuation of, 346–359
   warrants on. *See* Warrants
Common stock (market) ratios, 334–337
Company information, 71–77
Comparative sales approach, 613
Compound interest, 120–122
Comprehensive major medical insurance, 199
Computers. *See* Personal computers
Condominiums, 614–615
Confidence index, 365
Confirmation, 360–361

Constant dollar plan, 768
Constant ratio plan, 768–771
Continuous compounding, 121–122
Contribution to savings or investment, 188, 225
Conventional options, 482
Conversion equivalent, 453
Conversion parity, 453
Conversion period, 447–449
Conversion premium, 451–452
Conversion price, 447–449
Conversion privilege, 447–449, 579–580
Conversion ratio, 447–449
Conversion value, 453
Convertible securities, 18, 273, 446–458
Convertible term policies, 194
Corporate bonds, 402
    syndication, 663
Correlation analysis, 718
Cost approach, 613
Coupon, 387
Covered options, 494
Credit life insurance, 195
Cumulative preferred stock, 437–439
Cumulative voting, 279
Currency futures, 535–545
Currency options, 495–503
Current event information, 69–71
Current income, 115
Current interest rate (annuity), 658
Current ratio, 329
Current yield, 84, 415
Cyclical stocks, 294

D
Daily price limit, 529
Data bases, 14, 101–103
Date of record (dividend), 285
Day of deposit to day of withdrawal method, 229
Day order, 773
Dealers, 37
Debentures, 390
    convertible. See Convertible securities
    usable bonds, 439
Debit balance, 160–162
Debt, 5. See also Bonds
Debt-equity ratio, 332
Deductions, itemized, 642–644
Deep discount bonds, 655–656
Deep-in-the-money call options, 653–654
Defensive stocks, 295
Deferred annuities, 129–131, 657–663
Deferred call feature, 389, 397
Deferred compensation plans, 251–252

Deferred equity securities, 273, 446. See also Convertible securities; Warrants
Deficit (budget), 192
Defined benefit plans, 251
Defined contribution plans, 251
De-listed securities, 35
Delivery month, 520
Demand (real estate), 603–604
Demographics, 603
Denominations, 387
Depreciation, 324, 627, 656
Descriptive information, 66
Desired rate of return, 355
Developmental programs, 668
Diamonds, 700–701
Direct investment, 5
Disability insurance, 199
Discount basis securities, 225–226
Discount bonds, 387
Discount brokers, 46, 53–55
Discounted cash flow, real estate, 619–620
Discount rate, 128
Discretionary accounts, 47–49, 96
Diversifiable (unsystematic) risk, 138, 712
Diversification, 13, 560–563, 712–714
Dividend arrears, 438
Dividend exclusion feature, 205, 287–289, 655
Dividend model, 354–357
Dividend reinvestment plans (DRP), 205, 288, 289, 578–579, 655
Dividends, 17, 283–290
    preferred stock, 434–435, 437–441, 443–444
    short sales and, 167–168
    tax exemption on, 205, 287–289, 655
Dividends per share, 336
Dividend yield, 83, 287, 440–441
Dollar cost averaging, 767–768, 770–771
Dow Jones bond averages, 93, 747
Dow Jones Industrial Average (DJIA), 88–89, 92, 360–362, 747
Dow Jones Market Analyzer™, 100, 103
Dow Jones Market Manager™, 101
Dow Jones Market Microscope™, 101
Dow Jones News/Retrieval, 101–103
Downtick, 169
Dow theory, 360–361
Dual funds, 576
Dual listing, 34
Dun's Review, 70

E
Earnings per share (EPS), 284
Economic analysis, 308–317

Economic information, 69–71
Effective rate of interest, 226
Efficient markets, 373–377
    real estate and, 612
Efficient portfolio, 714–715
Employer-sponsored programs
    basic, 251
    supplemental, 251–252
Endowment (life) insurance policies,
    195–196
Energy partnerships, 668–670
Equipment leasing partnerships, 670
Equipment trust certificates, 390, 402
Equity, 5–7, 322, 325. *See also* Common
    stock; Preferred stock
    margin trading, 154–166, 170–171
Equity capital, 271–273
Equity kicker, 432, 446
Esthetic environment, 609
Excess margin, 164
Exchanges. *See* Organized securities ex-
    changes
Ex-dividend date, 285
Exemptions (tax), 644
Exercise (subscription) price, 466–467, 468,
    471
Expected return, 118–119
Expenses, 188
Expiration date, 468, 483–485
Exploratory programs, 668–670
Extendable notes, 392–395
Extra dividends, 289–290

F
FACT, 71
Federal Reserve Board, 52
    margin requirements and, 158
Federal Reserve Bulletin, 70, 747
Federal Reserve Monthly Chart Book, 747
FIFO (first-in, first-out) method, 228
Financial Analysts Journal, 71, 91
Financial asset, 684
Financial futures, 19, 534–547
    exchanges, 36, 535
    transaction costs, 57
Financial news, 69–70
Financial planning. *See* Personal financial
    planning
Financial risk, 135
Financial statements, 322–327
Financial supermarkets, 14, 15
Financial World, 71
Fiscal environment, 610
Fiscal year, 322
Fixed charge coverage, 442

Fixed commission schedules, 53
Fixed income securities, 17–18. *See also*
    Bonds; Convertible securities; Preferred
    stock
    options on, 495–503
Fixed payout ratio, 290
Floating (adjustable) rate preferreds, 437
Flower bonds, 397
Flow of funds statement, 327
Forbes, 71, 407, 587
Forced conversion, 447
Form 10-K, 72
Formula plans, 767
Fortune, 70, 313, 407
401(k) deferred compensation plans,
    251–252, 257–258
Fourth market, 39–40
Freely callable bonds, 388
Front-end load, 577
Fully taxable equivalent yield, 400
Fundamental analysis, 309, 319–339
    personal computers and, 14, 101
    random walk hypothesis and, 376
Futures. *See also* Commodity futures; Fi-
    nancial futures
    contracts on, 520
    exchanges for, 36, 517–520, 535
    gold, 692
    markets for, 516–526
    options on, 545–547
    silver, 699
Future value, 125–126

G
General obligation bonds, 398–399
General partnership, 663–664
Go-go funds, 573
Gold, 21–22, 687–697
    holding period return on, 754–755
Gold bullion, 691
Gold certificates, 693
Gold coins, 691
Gold futures, 692
Gold jewelry, 691–692
Gold mining stocks, 692
Good 'til canceled (GTC) orders, 49–50,
    773
Government, 8–9
Government securities, 647
    agency bonds, 398
    municipal bonds, 398–400, 570, 574,
    647
    mutual funds of, 237
    repurchase agreements on, 238
    Series EE savings bonds, 239–242

Treasury bills, 238–241
Treasury bonds, 395–397
Treasury Investment Growth Receipts (TIGR), 256
Treasury notes, 496–503
Government securities money funds, 237
Gross income, 641
Gross national product (GNP), 311
Group term insurance, 195
Growth funds, 573
Growth-oriented portfolio, 712
Growth stocks, 293, 655

H

Hardware, computer, 14, 98–99
Health insurance, 199
Heart bonds, 402–403
Hedging
  futures, 520–522, 532–533
  options, 490–493
  shorting-against-the-box, 176–178, 652
Holders of record (dividend), 285
Holding period, 122
Holding period return (HPR), 123–125, 354, 747–755
  portfolio, 764
Hospital insurance, 199
Hybrid securities, 430. *See also* Convertible securities; Preferred stock

I

Immediate annuity, 658
Improvements, 610–611
Income, 188
Income approach, 614–615
Income bonds, 390
Income funds, 573–574
Income-oriented portfolio, 712
Income programs, 668
Income properties, 598
Income statement
  corporate, 325–326
  personal, 187–191
Income stocks, 292, 655
Indexes, 87
  bond, 93–94
  stock market, 90–92, 747, 765
Index of industrial production, 311
Index price system, 540
Indirect investment, 5
Individual Retirement Accounts (IRAs), 253–259, 581, 641, 661–662
Industry analysis, 308–309, 317–319
Industry information, 71–77

Industry options, 503–505
Inflation, 136, 313
  common stock as hedge against, 282–283
  futures market and, 517
  level of return and, 119
Information sources, 65–87, 96
  personal computer, 101–103
Initial margin, 158–159, 523
Insider trading, 358
Installment annuity, 658
Institutional bonds, 402–403
Institutional Investor, The, 71
Insurance, 193–200
  on bank accounts, 229
  on mutual fund holdings, 581
Interest
  bonds and, 405–409
  calculation of, 120–122
  effective rate of, 226
  nominal rate of, 226
  on short-term securities and deposits, 225–230
  simple, 120, 227
Interest-free loans, 172
Interest rate futures, 535–545
Interest rate options, 495–503
Interest rate risk, 136–137
International Monetary Market (IMM), 36
In-the-money options, 488
Intrinsic value, 308
Inventory turnover, 330
Investment. *See also* specific investments
  defined, 5
  general types of, 5–8
Investment advisors, 94–97
Investment Advisors Act of 1940, 42, 94
Investment analysis, real estate, 617
Investment banking firms, 30
Investment clubs, 97
Investment Company Act of 1940, 41
Investment goals, 11–12
Investment letters, 77
Investment premium, 488
Investment process, 7
  participants in, 8–10
  personal, 10–15
  structure of, 8
  vehicles for, 12, 15–22. *See also* specific investments
Investment tax credit, 644
Investment trusts, 565–566
  real estate (REIT), 599–600
Investment value, 282, 453–454
Itemized deductions, 642–644

J

Journal of Commerce, 69
Junior bonds, 390
Justified price, 355–357

K

Kansas City Board of Trade, 517, 535
Keogh (HR10) plans, 252–253, 255–259,
    581, 661–662
Kiplinger Washington Letter, 71

L

Legal environment, 609–610
Leverage
    limited partnerships and, 674–675
    in margin trading, 154–166, 170–171
    positive or negative, 617–619
    warrants and, 469, 476–477
Leverage measures, 332–333
Liabilities, 186, 187, 322, 324–325
Liability insurance, 199–200
LIFO (last-in, first-out) method, 228–229
Limited partners, 664
Limited partnerships, 600–601, 663–675
Limit orders, 49–50, 773
Liquidation value, 282
Liquidity, 210–211
    short-term securities and, 224–243
    warehousing of, 774–775
Liquidity ratios, 329
Liquidity risk, 137
Listed options, 482–483
Livestock feeding or breeding partnerships,
    670–671
Load funds, 567–568
Location (real estate), 608
Long position, 522
Long purchase, 51
Long term, 7–8, 640
Long-term capital gains (losses), 204,
    647–649
    strategies for, 654–657
Los Angeles Times, 69

M

Magazine of Wall Street, The, 71
Maintenance margin, 159, 526
Majority voting, 278
Major medical insurance, 199
Maloney Act of 1938, 41
Management fee, 568
Margin account, 46
    for margin trading, 154–166, 170–171
    for short sales, 166–178
Marginal tax rate, 644

Margin call, 159, 526
Margin loan, 156–157
Margin purchase, 52
Margin trading, 154–166, 170–171
    defined, 153–154
    futures, 523–526
Market options, 503–505
Market order, 49, 773
Market price, 8
Market (common stock) ratios, 334–337
Market return, 138
Market risk, 137
Market value, 282
    real estate, 613–616
Market volume, 363
Mark-to-the-market, 173, 526
Maturity date, 387–388
Maximum daily price range, 529
M/G (Media General) Financial Weekly, 69
MidAmerica Commodities Exchange, 517,
    535
Minimum balance method, 228
Minimum guaranteed interest rate, 659
Minneapolis Grain Exchange, 517
Mixed stream of returns, 129–130
Modern portfolio theory (MPT), 718–722
Money Magazine, 71, 587
Money Manager, The, 71
Money market, 8, 30
Money market deposit accounts (MMDAs),
    233–234, 257
Money market mutual funds (MMMFs),
    234–237, 257, 575–576, 774
Moody's Investor Services, 72–77, 92
    bond ratings, 403–404, 747
    preferred stock ratings, 442
Mortgage-backed securities
    bonds, 402
    pass-through certificates, 398
Mortgage bonds, 390
Mortgage life insurance, 195
Municipal bond guarantees, 400
Municipal bonds, 398–400, 647
    in mutual funds, 235–236, 570, 574
Mutual funds, 5, 20, 559–593
    holding period return on, 750–752
    money market, 234–237, 257, 575–576,
    774
    price quotations, 86–87, 563–565
    transaction costs, 57, 567–568

N

Naked options, 494
National Association of Securities Dealers
    (NASD), 41

Automated Quotation system (NASDAQ), 37–38, 43, 92
Nation's Business, 70
Natural environment, 609
Negative correlation, 718–719
Negotiated commissions, 53
Net asset value (NAV), 563–564
Net interest exclusion, 647
Net long-term losses, 204
Net operating income (NOI), 619
Net present value (NPV), real estate, 619–620
Net profit margin, 333
Net short-term losses, 204
Net working capital, 329
Net worth, 186, 187
New Orleans Commodity Exchange, 518
Newsweek, 70
New York Coffee, Sugar and Cocoa Exchange, 518
New York Cotton Exchange, 518
New York Futures Exchange (NYFE), 36, 518, 535
New York Mercantile Exchange, 519
New York Stock Exchange (NYSE), 33–35, 38–39
   bond statistics, 93–94
   indexes, 92, 747, 765
   options on, 482–483
   short sales on, 168–169
New York Times, The, 69, 92
No load funds, 567–568
Nominal rate of interest, 226
Noncallable bonds, 388–389
Nondiversifiable (systematic) risk, 138, 712. *See also* Beta
NOW (negotiated order of withdrawal) accounts, 232–233, 774
Numismatics (coin collecting), 704

O

Odd lots, 35, 49, 275, 364–365
Offering circulars, 672
Open end investment companies, 41, 563–564. *See also* Mutual funds
Open interest, 529
Open orders, 49–50, 773
Open outcry auction, 520
Operating ratio, 333
Opportunity cost, 128
Options, 7, 18–19, 465–466, 482–483
   futures contracts on, 545–547
   hedging of, 490–493
   interest rate and currency, 495–503
   puts and calls. *See* Put and call options

rights. *See* Rights
   stock-index, 503–505
   warrants. *See* Warrants
Options exchanges, 36, 482, 496
Option spreading, 494–495
Option straddles, 495
Option writer (maker), 479
Order types, 49–50
Ordinary income, 202–203, 640
Organized securities exchanges, 31–36, 43
   bond, 93–94
   common stock, 33–35, 38–39, 168–169
   futures, 36, 517–520, 535
   options, 31–36, 43
Original shares, 288–289
Out-of-the-money options, 488
Over-the-counter (OTC) market, 33, 37, 43
   price quotations, 83

P

Paper profits, 164
Paper return, 122
Participating preferred stock, 439–440, 446
Partnerships, limited, 600–601, 663–675
Par value, 280
   bond, 387
Passbook savings accounts, 232
Payment date (dividend), 285
Payout (annuity), 660
Payout ratio, 336–337
Performance funds, 573
Personal computer (PC), 14–15, 97–104, 212, 766
Personal financial planner, 95, 212–213
Personal financial planning, 15, 95, 186–192
   investment program in, 208–214
   taxes in, 201–208. *See also* Taxes
Personal property, 602
Personal residences, 598, 649
Philately (stamp collecting), 702–704
Physicians' expense insurance, 199
Point-and-figure charts, 369–370
Pooled diversification, 560–561
Portfolio revision, 765–766
Portfolios, 4, 712
   assessing performance of, 760–766
   building of, 722–726
   diversification of, 13, 560–563, 712–714
   management of, 13–14, 712–722
   timing transactions in, 766–776
Positive correlation, 718
Precious metals, 21–22, 687–699
Preemptive rights, 466
Preferred (agency) ratings, 442

Preferred stock, 432–446
    convertible, 18, 445–446. *See also* Con-
        vertible securities
    holding period return on, 748–749
Premium
    call, on bonds, 389–390
    conversion, 451–452
    investment, 488
    option, 485
    warrant, 472
Premium bonds, 387
Present value, 126–132
Price/earnings (P/E) ratio, 83, 334–336
    forecasts of, 348–349
Primary market, 30
Principal, 187
    bond, 387
    safety of, 209–210, 296–299
Principle of substitution, 607–608
Private partnerships, 671–673
Problem investments, 756
Profitability measures, 333–334
Progressive tax rate, 638
Promised yield, 415–416
Property, 5
Property insurance, 199
Prospectus, 40, 77, 568–569, 674
Proxy, 277–278
Psychographic characteristics, 603
Publicly traded stock, 273
Public offerings, 273
Public partnerships, 671–674
Purchasing power risk, 136, 229
Purposive diversification, 13
Put and call options, 19, 477–505
    deep-in-the-money calls, 653–654
    price quotations, 84–86, 485–486
    transaction costs, 56–57, 485–486
Put bonds, 392
Put hedge, 652–653
Pyramiding profits, 164–166

Q
Qualifying public utilities, 205, 289, 655

R
Random diversification, 13
Random walk hypothesis, 373–377
Ratio analysis, 327–339
Real estate, 20–21, 597–631
    holding period return on, 752–754
    limited partnerships in, 600–601, 667–668
    transaction costs on, 57
Real estate investment trusts (REITs),
    599–600

Realized return, 122
Realized yield, 416–418
Real property, 5
Record date (dividend), 285
Red herring, 40
Refunding provision, 390
Regional stock exchanges, 33, 35
Registered bonds, 395
Regular dividends, 289–290
Relevant risk, 714
Renewable term policy, 194
Repurchase agreements (repos), 238
Required investment rate, 416
Residences, personal, 598, 649
Restricted accounts, 159
Retained earnings, 284–285
Retirement
    planning for, 200–201, 243–249
    programs for, 250–259, 581
Return, 209
    of capital dividends, 287
    concept of, 114–119
    on invested capital, 162–163, 175–176,
        530
    on investment (ROI), 334
    measurement of, 119–134. *See also*
        Holding period return
    realized, 122
    risk-adjusted, market-adjusted rate of
        (RAR), 756–760, 764–765
    risk and, 134, 141–142, 721, 755–756
    risk-free rate of, 134, 721
    on short-term investments, 230
    on total assets (ROTA), 333–334
Revenue bonds, 390, 399
Reverse stock splits, 275
Reversion, 753
Rights, 18, 466–467
    transaction costs on, 56
Rights-off, 467
Rights offerings, 273, 466
Rights-on, 467
Risk, 7, 134–144
    of convertible securities, 450–451
    diversification and, 712–714
    investment goals and, 209–210
    in limited partnerships, 675
    in mutual funds, 591
    in preferred stock, 435
    return and, 134, 141–142, 755–756
    of short-term securities, 229–230,
        234–235
Risk-adjusted, market-adjusted rate of return
    (RAR), 756–760, 764–765
Risk-averse, 142

Risk-free rate of return (R_F), 134, 721
Risk-indifferent, 142
Risk-return tradeoff, 721
Risk-takers, 142
Round lots, 35, 49, 275
Round trip commissions, 523

S

Safety of principal, 209–210, 296–299
Savings accounts, 232
Savings plans, 248, 577–578
Scarcity value, 686
Secondary distributions, 37
Secondary market, 31–40
Securities, 5. *See also* specific types of securities
Securities Act of 1933, 40
Securities Acts Amendments of 1975, 52–53
Securities and Exchange Commission (SEC), 40–42, 94
Securities Exchange Act of 1934, 40–41
Securities Investor Protection Corporation (SIPC), 45, 55
Securities markets, 30–43
Security analysis, 308–340
Self-directed retirement accounts, 252–259
Selling group, 30–31
Senior bonds, 390
Serial bonds, 387–388
Series EE savings bonds, 239–242
Settle price, 529
Shorting-against-the-box, 176–178, 652
Short interest, 363
Short position, 522
Short sales, 51–52, 166–178
    defined, 154
    as market indicators, 363
Short term, 7–8, 640
Short-term capital gains (losses), 204
Short-term securities, 16–17, 224–243
Silver, 697–699
Silver bullion, 699
Silver coins, 699
Silver futures, 699
Silver mining stocks, 699
Simple interest, 120, 227
Single-premium annuity, 658
Single-property syndicate, 668
Sinking funds, 390, 440
Social security, 250–251
Socioeconomic environment, 609
Software, computer, 14, 99–101
Specialists, 35, 49–50
Specialty funds, 576–577

Speculation, 7
    in futures, 522, 531–532, 541–542
    with mutual funds, 582–583
Speculative properties, 598
Speculative stocks, 294, 300
Spinoff dividends, 285–287
Split ratings, 403–404
Spreading, commodity, 532
Stamp collecting, 702–704
Standard & Poor's Corporation (S&P), 72
    bond ratings, 403–404
    common stock indexes, 90–92, 747, 765
    preferred stock ratings, 442
S & P Industry Surveys, 318
Statement of changes in financial position, 327
Statement of changes in stockholders' equity, 326
Stock, 7. *See also* Common stock; Preferred stock
Stockbrokers, 43–46, 95
Stock dividends, 285, 287
Stockholders' reports, 72, 331
Stock index futures, 538–545
Stock index options, 503–505
Stock rights. *See* Rights
Stock splits, 273–275
Stock valuation, 352–359
Stop-loss order (stop order), 50, 774
Straight term policy, 194
Strategic metals, 694–696, 699–700
Stream of returns, 129–131
Street name securities, 169–172
Striking price, 483
Subordinated debentures, 390
Subscription advisory services, 71–77, 80–81, 96
Subscription price, 466–467, 468, 471
Substitution principle, 607–608
Suitability rule, 675
Super NOW (negotiated order of withdrawal) accounts, 232–233, 774
Supply (real estate), 605–611
Surgical expense insurance, 199
Surplus (budget), 192
Survey of Current Business, 70
Sweep accounts, 239
Syndicates, 30–31, 663, 668
Systematic (nondiversifiable) risk, 138, 712.
    See also Beta
Systematic savings plans, 248

T

Tangible investments, 21–22, 684–687
Tangible personal property, 5

Taxable income, 638–640, 644
Tax avoidance, 645
Tax credits, 644
Tax deferral, 645–646, 649–654
Tax-deferred annuity, 660
Taxes, 201–208
   dividends and, 205, 287–289, 655
   fundamentals, 638–646
   investment objectives and, 210
   mutual funds and, 570–571
   on Social Security income, 250–251
   tax-favored income, 646–657
   timing investment sales and, 775–776
Tax evasion, 645
Tax-exempt money funds, 235–236, 570, 574
Tax-favored income, 646–657
Tax-free contributions, 660
Tax-free (municipal bond) funds, 235–236, 570, 574
Tax planning, 208, 638
Tax-sheltered investments, 21, 207–208, 627, 646, 657–675. *See also* Annuities
Tax swaps, 205, 422–423, 657
Technical analysis, 359–371
   personal computer, 14, 100
   random walk hypothesis and, 376
Term bonds, 387
Term (life) insurance, 194–195
Term to maturity, 387
Theory of contrary opinion, 365
Thin markets, 137
Third market, 38–39
Ticker, 78–79
Time, 70
Times interest earned, 332–333
Time value of money, 125–132
Total asset turnover, 330–332
Total return, 116–117
Total risk, 714
Trading action approach, 361–362
Traditional portfolio management, 716–718, 721–722
Transaction costs, 52–57
Transfer process, 612
Treasury investment growth receipts (TIGR), 256
Treasury stock, 275
Troy ounces, 691
True rate of return (interest), 120
Turnarounds, 444–445

U

Undermargined accounts, 159
Underwriting, 30–31

Underwriting syndicates, 30–31
U.S. News & World Report, 70
U.S. Treasury bills, 238–241
   options on, 496–503
U.S. Treasury bonds, 395–397
   options on, 496–503
U.S. Treasury notes, options on, 496–503
Unit investment trusts, 565–566
Universal accounts, 239
Universal life insurance, 196–197
Unlisted securities, 37
Unsystematic (diversifiable) risk, 138, 712
Uptick, 169
Usable bonds, 439
Utility stock, 205, 289, 655

V

Valuation process, 12
Value Line Investment Survey, 66, 77, 92
Variable-rate notes, 392
Variable ratio plan, 771–773
Variance, 718
Vesting, 251
Volatility, 720
Voluntary savings plans, 577
Voting rights, 277–280

W

Wall Street Journal, The, 69, 79, 93, 94, 234, 239, 313, 407, 744
Wall Street Transcript, The, 71
Warehousing liquidity, 774–775
Warrants, 19, 273, 468–477
   transaction costs, 56, 468
Wash sales, 204–205, 657
Whipsawing, 774
Whole life insurance, 195
Winnipeg Grain Exchange, 518
Withdrawal plans, 579

Y

Yield, 132–134
   approximate, 133–134, 357, 620–621
   bond, 93, 405–410, 415–418
   current, 84, 415
   dividend, 83, 287, 440–441
   fully taxable equivalent, 400
   promised, 415–416
Yield curves, 409
Yield spreads, 405–407
Yield to maturity, 415–416

Z

Zero-bracket amount, 644
Zero-coupon bonds, 391, 392

GENERAL SOURCES OF INVESTMENT INFORMATION
(See Chapter 3 and Appendix A for complete details.)

ECONOMIC NEWS AND CURRENT EVENTS

Financial News (Including Price Quotations)
The Wall Street Journal
Barron's
The New York Times
Commercial and Financial Chronicle
M/G Financial Weekly
Journal of Commerce
Monthly letters published by large commercial banks

Periodicals Containing Business Information
General Articles
Newsweek
Time
U.S. News & World Report
Business Week
Fortune
Dun's Review
Nation's Business
Federal Reserve Bulletin
Articles Concerning Securities and the Marketplace
Forbes
Changing Times
Money
FACT